NATHANIEL HAWTHORNE

Nathaniel Hawthorne

TALES AND SKETCHES
Including Twice-told Tales, Mosses from an Old Manse, and The Snow-Image

A WONDER BOOK FOR
GIRLS AND BOYS

TANGLEWOOD TALES FOR
GIRLS AND BOYS;
Being A Second Wonder Book

THE LIBRARY OF AMERICA

Volume arrangement, notes, and chronology Copyright © 1982 by
Literary Classics of the United States, Inc., New York, N.Y.
All rights reserved.
No part of this book may be reproduced commercially
by offset-lithographic or equivalent copying devices without
the permission of the publisher.

The texts of *Twice-told Tales, Mosses from an Old Manse, The Snow-Image,
A Wonder Book, Tanglewood Tales,* and the uncollected tales are
Copyright © 1972, 1974 by the Ohio State University Press.
All rights reserved.

Distributed to the trade in the United States
and Canada by the Viking Press.

Published outside North America by the Press Syndicate
of the University of Cambridge
The Pitt Building, Trumpington Street, Cambridge CB2IRP, England
ISBN O 521 26217 8

Library of Congress Catalog Card Number: 81–20760
For Cataloging in Publication Data, see end of *Notes* section.
ISBN 0–940450–03–8

Sixth Printing

Manufactured in the United States of America

ROY HARVEY PEARCE
WROTE THE NOTES AND CHRONOLOGY
AND SELECTED THE TEXTS
FOR THIS VOLUME

*This volume prints the texts of Hawthorne's tales from the
Centenary Edition of the Works of Nathaniel Hawthorne
edited by William Charvat, Roy Harvey Pearce, Claude M. Simpson,
Fredson Bowers, L. Neal Smith, John Manning, and J. Donald Crowley
and published by the Ohio State University Center
for Textual Studies and the Ohio State University Press,
with the permission of the publishers.*

*Grateful acknowledgement is made to the National Endowment
for the Humanities and the Ford Foundation for their
generous financial support of this series.*

Contents

TALES AND SKETCHES

Contents

The Hollow of the Three Hills

In those strange old times, when fantastic dreams and madmen's reveries were realized among the actual circumstances of life, two persons met together at an appointed hour and place. One was a lady, graceful in form and fair of feature, though pale and troubled, and smitten with an untimely blight in what should have been the fullest bloom of her years; the other was an ancient and meanly dressed woman, of ill-favored aspect, and so withered, shrunken and decrepit, that even the space since she began to decay must have exceeded the ordinary term of human existence. In the spot where they encountered, no mortal could observe them. Three little hills stood near each other, and down in the midst of them sunk a hollow basin, almost mathematically circular, two or three hundred feet in breadth, and of such depth that a stately cedar might but just be visible above the sides. Dwarf pines were numerous upon the hills, and partly fringed the outer verge of the intermediate hollow; within which there was nothing but the brown grass of October, and here and there a tree-trunk, that had fallen long ago, and lay mouldering with no green successor from its roots. One of these masses of decaying wood, formerly a majestic oak, rested close beside a pool of green and sluggish water at the bottom of the basin. Such scenes as this (so gray tradition tells) were once the resort of a Power of Evil and his plighted subjects; and here, at midnight or on the dim verge of evening, they were said to stand round the mantling pool, disturbing its putrid waters in the performance of an impious baptismal rite. The chill beauty of an autumnal sunset was now gilding the three hill-tops, whence a paler tint stole down their sides into the hollow.

"Here is our pleasant meeting come to pass," said the aged crone, "according as thou hast desired. Say quickly what thou wouldst have of me, for there is but a short hour that we may tarry here."

As the old withered woman spoke, a smile glimmered on her countenance, like lamplight on the wall of a sepulchre.

The lady trembled, and cast her eyes upward to the verge of the basin, as if meditating to return with her purpose unaccomplished. But it was not so ordained.

"I am stranger in this land, as you know," said she at length. "Whence I come it matters not;—but I have left those behind me with whom my fate was intimately bound, and from whom I am cut off forever. There is a weight in my bosom that I cannot away with, and I have come hither to inquire of their welfare."

"And who is there by this green pool, that can bring thee news from the ends of the Earth?" cried the old woman, peering into the lady's face. "Not from my lips mayst thou hear these tidings; yet, be thou bold, and the daylight shall not pass away from yonder hill-top, before thy wish be granted."

"I will do your bidding though I die," replied the lady desperately.

The old woman seated herself on the trunk of the fallen tree, threw aside the hood that shrouded her gray locks, and beckoned her companion to draw near.

"Kneel down," she said, "and lay your forehead on my knees."

She hesitated a moment, but the anxiety, that had long been kindling, burned fiercely up within her. As she knelt down, the border of her garment was dipped into the pool; she laid her forehead on the old woman's knees, and the latter drew a cloak about the lady's face, so that she was in darkness. Then she heard the muttered words of a prayer, in the midst of which she started, and would have arisen.

"Let me flee,—let me flee and hide myself, that they may not look upon me!" she cried. But, with returning recollection, she hushed herself, and was still as death.

For it seemed as if other voices—familiar in infancy, and unforgotten through many wanderings, and in all the vicissitudes of her heart and fortune—were mingling with the accents of the prayer. At first the words were faint and indistinct, not rendered so by distance, but rather resembling the dim pages of a book, which we strive to read by an imperfect and gradually brightening light. In such a manner, as the prayer proceeded, did those voices strengthen upon the ear; till at length the petition ended, and the conversation of an aged man, and of a woman broken and decayed like himself, became distinctly audible to the lady as she knelt. But those strangers appeared not to stand in the hollow depth between the three hills. Their voices were encompassed and re-echoed by the walls of a chamber, the windows of which were rattling in the breeze; the regular vibration of a clock, the crackling of a fire, and the tinkling of the embers as they fell among the ashes, rendered the scene almost as vivid as if painted to the eye. By a melancholy hearth sat these two old people, the man calmly despondent, the woman querulous and tearful, and their words were all of sorrow. They spoke of a daughter, a wanderer they knew not where, bearing dishonor along with her, and leaving shame and affliction to bring their gray heads to the grave. They alluded also to other and more recent woe, but in the midst of their talk, their voices seemed to melt into the sound of the wind sweeping mournfully among the autumn leaves; and when the lady lifted her eyes, there was she kneeling in the hollow between three hills.

"A weary and lonesome time yonder old couple have of it," remarked the old woman, smiling in the lady's face.

"And did you also hear them!" exclaimed she, a sense of intolerable humiliation triumphing over her agony and fear.

"Yea; and we have yet more to hear," replied the old woman. "Wherefore, cover thy face quickly."

Again the withered hag poured forth the monotonous words of a prayer that was not meant to be acceptable in Heaven; and soon, in the pauses of her breath, strange murmurings began to thicken, gradually increasing so as to drown and overpower the charm by which they grew. Shrieks pierced through the obscurity of sound, and were succeeded by the singing of sweet female voices, which in their turn gave way to a wild roar of laughter, broken suddenly by groanings and sobs, forming altogether a ghastly confusion of terror and mourning and mirth. Chains were rattling, fierce and stern voices uttered threats, and the scourge resounded at their command. All these noises deepened and became substantial to the listener's ear, till she could distinguish every soft and dreamy accent of the love songs, that died causelessly into funeral hymns. She shuddered at the unprovoked wrath which blazed up like the spontaneous kindling of flame, and she grew faint at the fearful merriment, raging miserably around her. In the midst of this wild scene, where unbound passions jostled each other in a drunken career, there was one solemn voice of a man, and a manly and melodious voice it might once have been. He went to-and-fro continually, and his feet sounded upon the floor. In each member of that frenzied company, whose own burning thoughts had become their exclusive world, he sought an auditor for the story of his individual wrong, and interpreted their laughter and tears as his reward of scorn or pity. He spoke of woman's perfidy, of a wife who had broken her holiest vows, of a home and heart made desolate. Even as he went on, the shout, the laugh, the shriek, the sob, rose up in unison, till they changed into the hollow, fitful, and uneven sound of the wind, as it fought among the pine-trees on those three lonely hills. The lady looked up, and there was the withered woman smiling in her face.

"Couldst thou have thought there were such merry times in a Mad House?" inquired the latter.

"True, true," said the lady to herself; "there is mirth within its walls, but misery, misery without."

"Wouldst thou hear more?" demanded the old woman.

"There is one other voice I would fain listen to again," replied the lady faintly.

"Then lay down thy head speedily upon my knees, that thou may'st get thee hence before the hour be past."

The golden skirts of day were yet lingering upon the hills, but deep shades obscured the hollow and the pool, as if sombre night were rising thence to overspread the world. Again that evil woman began to weave her spell. Long did it proceed unanswered, till the knolling of a bell stole in among the intervals of her words, like a clang that had travelled far over valley and rising ground, and was just ready to die in the air. The lady shook upon her companion's knees, as she heard that boding sound. Stronger it grew and sadder, and deepened into the tone of a death-bell, knolling dolefully from some ivy-mantled tower, and bearing tidings of mortality and woe to the cottage, to the hall, and to the solitary wayfarer, that all might weep for the doom appointed in turn to them.

Then came a measured tread, passing slowly, slowly on, as of mourners with a coffin, their garments trailing on the ground, so that the car could measure the length of their melancholy array. Before them went the priest, reading the burial-service, while the leaves of his book were rustling in the breeze. And though no voice but his was heard to speak aloud, still there were revilings and anathemas, whispered but distinct, from women and from men, breathed against the daughter who had wrung the aged hearts of her parents,—the wife who had betrayed the trusting fondness of her husband,—the mother who had sinned against natural affection, and left her child to die. The sweeping sound of the funeral train faded away like a thin vapour, and the wind, that just before had seemed to shake the coffin-pall, moaned sadly round the verge of the Hollow between three Hills. But when the old woman stirred the kneeling lady, she lifted not her head.

"Here has been a sweet hour's sport!" said the withered crone, chuckling to herself.

Sir William Phips

F EW of the personages of past times (except such as have
gained renown in fire-side legends as well as in written
history) are anything more than mere names to their successors. They seldom stand up in our Imaginations like men.
The knowledge, communicated by the historian and biographer, is analogous to that which we acquire of a country by
the map,—minute, perhaps, and accurate, and available for
all necessary purposes,—but cold and naked, and wholly destitute of the mimic charm produced by landscape painting.
These defects are partly remediable, and even without an absolute violation of literal truth, although by methods rightfully interdicted to professors of biographical exactness. A license must be assumed in brightening the materials which
time has rusted, and in tracing out the half-obliterated inscriptions on the columns of antiquity; fancy must throw her
reviving light on the faded incidents that indicate character,
whence a ray will be reflected, more or less vividly, on the
person to be described. The portrait of the ancient Governor,
whose name stands at the head of this article, will owe any
interest it may possess, not to his internal self, but to certain
peculiarities of his fortune. These must be briefly noticed.

The birth and early life of Sir William Phips were rather an
extraordinary prelude to his subsequent distinction. He was
one of the twenty six children of a gun-smith, who exercised
his trade—where hunting and war must have given it a full
encouragement—in a small frontier settlement near the
mouth of the river Keunebec. Within the boundaries of the
Puritan provinces, and wherever those governments extended
an effectual sway, no depth nor solitude of the wilderness
could exclude youth from all the common opportunities of
moral, and far more than common ones of religious education. Each settlement of the Pilgrims was a little piece of the
old world, inserted into the new,—it was like Gideon's fleece,
unwet with dew,—the desert wind, that breathed over it, left
none of its wild influences there. But the first settlers of
Maine and New-Hampshire were led thither entirely by car-

nal motives; their governments were feeble, uncertain, sometimes nominally annexed to their sister colonies, and sometimes asserting a troubled independence; their rulers might be
deemed, in more than one instance, lawless adventurers, who
found that security in the forest which they had forfeited in
Europe. Their clergy (unlike that revered band who acquired
so singular a fame elsewhere in New-England) were too often
destitute of the religious fervor which should have kept them
in the track of virtue, unaided by the restraints of human law
and the dread of worldly dishonor; and there are records of
lamentable lapses on the part of those holy men, which, if we
may argue the disorder of the sheep from the unfitness of the
shepherd, tell a sad tale as to the morality of the eastern provinces. In this state of society the future governor grew up,
and many years after, sailing with a fleet and an army to make
war upon the French, he pointed out the very hills where he
had reached the age of manhood, unskilled even to read and
write. The contrast between the commencement and close of
his life was the effect of casual circumstances. During a considerable time, he was a mariner, at a period when there was
much license on the high seas. After attaining to some rank
in the English navy, he heard of an ancient Spanish wreck off
the coast of Hispaniola, of such mighty value, that, according
to the stories of the day, the sunken gold might be seen to
glisten and the diamonds to flash, as the triumphant billows
tossed about their spoil. These treasures of the deep (by the
aid of certain noblemen, who claimed the lion's share) Sir
William Phips sought for, and recovered, and was sufficiently
enriched, even after an honest settlement with the partners of
his adventure. That the land might give him honor, as the sea
had given him wealth, he received knighthood from King
James. Returning to New-England, he professed repentance
of his sins, (of which, from the nature both of his early and
more recent life, there could scarce fail to be some slight accumulation) was baptized, and, on the accession of the Prince
of Orange to the throne, became the first governor under the
second charter. And now, having arranged these preliminaries, we shall attempt to picture forth a day of Sir William's
life, introducing no very remarkable events, because history
supplies us with none such, convertible to our purpose.

It is the forenoon of a day in summer, shortly after the governor's arrival, and he stands upon his door-steps, preparatory to a walk through the metropolis. Sir William is a stout man, an inch or two below the middle size, and rather beyond the middle point of life; his dress is of velvet, a dark purple, broadly embroidered, and his sword-hilt, and the lion's head of his cane display specimens of the gold from the Spanish wreck; on his head, in the fashion of the court of Louis XIV, is a superb full-bottomed periwig, amid whose heap of ringlets his face shows like a rough pebble in the setting that befits a diamond. Just emerging from the door are two footmen, one an African slave of shining ebony, the other an English bond-servant, the property of the governor for a term of years. As Sir William comes down the steps, he is met by three elderly gentlemen in black, grave and solemn as three tombstones on a ramble from the burying ground. These are ministers of the town, among whom we recognize Dr. Increase Mather, the late provincial agent at the English court, the author of the present governor's appointment, and the right arm of his administration. Here follow many bows and a deal of angular politeness on both sides. Sir William professes his anxiety to re-enter the house and give audience to the reverend gentlemen; they, on the other hand, cannot think of interrupting his walk; and the courteous dispute is concluded by a junction of the parties, Sir William and Dr. Mather setting forth side by side, the two other clergymen forming the centre of the column, and the black and white footmen bringing up the rear. The business in hand relates to the dealings of Satan in the town of Salem. Upon this subject the principal ministers of the province have been consulted, and these three eminent persons are their deputies, commissioned to express a doubtful opinion, implying upon the whole an exhortation to speedy and vigorous measures against the accused. To such councils, Sir William, bred in the forest and on the ocean, and tinctured with the superstitions of both, is well inclined to listen.

As the dignitaries of church and state make their way beneath the overhanging houses, the lattices are thrust ajar, and you may discern, just in the boundaries of light and shade, the prim faces of the little puritan damsels, eyeing the magnificent governor, and envious of the bolder curiosity of the men. Another object of almost equal interest, now appears in the middle of the way. It is a man clad in a hunting shirt and Indian stockings, and armed with a long gun; his feet have been wet with the waters of many an inland lake and stream, and the leaves and twigs of the tangled wilderness are intertwined with his garments; on his head he wears a trophy which we would not venture to record without good evidence of the fact, —a wig made of the long and straight black hair of his slain savage enemies. This grim old heathen stands bewildered in the midst of King-street. The governor regards him attentively, and recognizing a playmate of his youth, accosts him with a gracious smile, inquires as to the prosperity of their birth place and the life or death of their ancient neighbors, and makes appropriate remarks on the different stations allotted by fortune to two individuals, born and bred beside the same wild river. Finally, he puts into his hand, at parting, a shilling of the Massachusetts coinage, stamped with the figure of a stubbed pine tree, mistaken by King Charles for the oak which saved his royal life. Then all the people praise the humility and bountifulness of the good governor, who struts onward flourishing his gold-headed cane, while the gentleman in the straight black wig is left with a pretty accurate idea of the distance between himself and his old companion.

Meantime Sir William steers his course towards the town dock. A gallant figure is seen approaching on the opposite side of the street in a naval uniform profusely laced, and with a cutlass swinging by his side. This is Captain Short, the commander of a frigate in the service of the English King, now lying in the harbor. Sir William bristles up at sight of him, and crosses the street with a lowering front, unmindful of the hints of Dr. Mather, who is aware of an unsettled dispute between the captain and the governor, relative to the authority of the latter over a king's ship on the provincial station. Into this thorny subject Sir William plunges headlong; the captain makes answer with less deference than the dignity of the potentate requires; the affair grows hot, and the clergymen endeavor to interfere in the blessed capacity of peacemakers. The governor lifts his cane, and the captain lays his hand upon his sword, but is prevented from drawing by the zealous exertions of Doctor Mather; there is a furious stamping of feet, and a mighty uproar from every mouth, in the midst of which his Excellency inflicts several very sufficient whacks on the head of the unhappy Short. Having thus avenged himself by manual force, as befits a woodsman and a mariner, he vindicates the insulted majesty of the governor by committing his antagonist to prison. This done, Sir William removes his periwig, wipes away the sweat of the encounter, and gradually composes himself, giving vent to a few oaths, like the subsiding ebullitions of a pot that has boiled over.

It being now near twelve o'clock, the three ministers are bidden to dinner at the governor's table, where the party is completed by a few Old-Charter Senators, men reared at the feet of the pilgrims, and who remember the days when Cromwell was a nursing father to New England. Sir William presides with commendable decorum till grace is said, and the cloth removed. Then, as the grape-juice glides warm into the ventricles of his heart, it produces a change like that of a running stream upon enchanted shapes, and the rude man of the sea and wilderness appears in the very chair where the stately governor sat down. He overflows with jovial tales of the forecastle and of his father's hut, and stares to see the gravity of his guests become more and more portentous, in exact proportion as his own merriment increases. A noise of drum and fife fortunately breaks up the session.

The governor and his guests go forth, like men bound upon some grave business, to inspect the train-bands of the town. A great crowd of people is collected on the common, composed of whole families, from the hoary grandsire to the child of three years old; all ages and both sexes look with interest on the array of their defenders; and here and there stand a few dark Indians in their blankets, dull spectators of the strength that has swept away their race. The soldiers wear a proud and martial mien, conscious that beauty will reward them with her approving glances;—not to mention that there are a few less influential motives which contribute to keep up an heroic spirit, such as the dread of being made to 'ride the wooden horse,' (a very disagreeable mode of equestrian exercise,—hard riding, in the strictest sense,) or of being 'laid neck and heels,' in a position of more compendiousness than comfort. Sir William perceives some error in their tactics, and places himself with drawn sword at their head. After a variety of weary evolutions, evening begins to fall, like the veil of gray and misty years that have rolled betwixt that warlike band and us. They are drawn into a hollow square, the offi- cers in the centre, and the governor (for John Dunton's au- thority will bear us out in this particular) leans his hands upon his sword-hilt, and closes the exercises of the day with a prayer.

Mrs. Hutchinson

THE character of this female suggests a train of thought which will form as natural an introduction to her story as most of the prefaces to Gay's Fables or the tales of Prior, besides that the general soundness of the moral may excuse any want of present applicability. We will not look for a living resemblance of Mrs. Hutchinson, though the search might not be altogether fruitless.—But there are portentous indications, changes gradually taking place in the habits and feelings of the gentle sex, which seem to threaten our posterity with many of those public women, whereof one was a burthen too grievous for our fathers. The press, however, is now the medium through which feminine ambition chiefly manifests itself, and we will not anticipate the period, (trusting to be gone hence ere it arrive,) when fair orators shall be as numerous as the fair authors of our own day. The hastiest glance may show, how much of the texture and body of cis-atlantic literature is the work of those slender fingers, from which only a light and fanciful embroidery has heretofore been required, that might sparkle upon the garment without enfeebling the web. Woman's intellect should never give the tone to that of man, and even her morality is not exactly the material for masculine virtue. A false liberality which mistakes the strong division lines of Nature for arbitrary distinctions, and a courtesy, which might polish criticism but should never soften it, have done their best to add a girlish feebleness to the tottering infancy of our literature. The evil is likely to be a growing one. As yet, the great body of American women are a domestic race; but when a continuance of ill-judged incitements shall have turned their hearts away from the fireside, there are obvious circumstances which will render female pens more numerous and more prolific than those of men, though but equally encouraged; and (limited of course by the scanty support of the public, but increasing indefinitely within those limits) the ink-stained Amazons will expel their rivals by actual pressure, and petticoats wave triumphant over all the field. But, allowing that such forebodings are slightly exaggerated, is it good for woman's self that the path of fe-verish hope, of tremulous success, of bitter and ignominious disappointment, should be left wide open to her? Is the prize worth her having if she win it? Fame does not increase the peculiar respect which men pay to female excellence, and there is a delicacy, (even in rude bosoms, where few would think to find it) that perceives, or fancies, a sort of impro-priety in the display of woman's naked mind to the gaze of the world, with indications by which its inmost secrets may be searched out. In fine, criticism should examine with a stricter, instead of a more indulgent eye, the merits of females at its bar, because they are to justify themselves for an irreg-ularity which men do not commit in appearing there; and woman, when she feels the impulse of genius like a command of Heaven within her, should be aware that she is relinquish-ing a part of the loveliness of her sex, and obey the inward voice with sorrowing reluctance, like the Arabian maid who bewailed the gift of Prophecy. Hinting thus imperfectly at sentiments which may be developed on a future occasion, we proceed to consider the celebrated subject of this sketch.

Mrs. Hutchinson was a woman of extraordinary talent and strong imagination, whom the latter quality, following the general direction taken by the enthusiasm of the times, prompted to stand forth as a reformer in religion. In her na-tive country, she had shown symptoms of irregular and dar-ing thought, but, chiefly by the influence of a favorite pastor, was restrained from open indiscretion. On the removal of this clergyman, becoming dissatisfied with the ministry under which she lived, she was drawn in by the great tide of Puritan emigration, and visited Massachusetts within a few years after its first settlement. But she bore trouble in her own bosom, and could find no peace in this chosen land.—She soon be-gan to promulgate strange and dangerous opinions, tending, in the peculiar situation of the colony, and from the principles which were its basis and indispensable for its temporary sup-port, to eat into its very existence. We shall endeavor to give a more practical idea of this part of her course.

It is a summer evening. The dusk has settled heavily upon the woods, the waves, and the Trimontane peninsula, increas-ing that dismal aspect of the embryo town which was said to have drawn tears of despondency from Mrs. Hutchinson, though she believed that her mission thither was divine. The houses, straw-thatched and lowly roofed, stand irregularly along streets that are yet roughened by the roots of the trees, as if the forest, departing at the approach of man, had left its reluctant foot prints behind. Most of the dwellings are lonely and silent; from a few we may hear the reading of some sacred text, or the quiet voice of prayer; but nearly all the sombre life of the scene is collected near the extremity of the village. A crowd of hooded women, and of men in steeple-hats and close cropt hair, are assembled at the door and open windows of a house newly built. An earnest expression glows in every face, and some press inward as if the bread of life were to be dealt forth, and they feared to lose their share, while others would fain hold them back, but enter with them since they may not be restrained. We also will go in, edging through the thronged doorway to an apartment which occupies the whole breadth of the house. At the upper end, behind a table on which are placed the Scriptures and two glimmering lamps, we see a woman, plainly attired as befits her ripened years; her hair, complexion, and eyes are dark, the latter somewhat dull and heavy, but kindling up with a gradual brightness. Let us look round upon the hearers. At her right hand, his countenance suiting well with the gloomy light which discovers it, stands Vane the youthful governor, preferred by a hasty judgment of the people over all the wise and hoary heads that had preceded him to New-England. In his mysterious eyes we may read a dark enthusiasm, akin to that of the woman whose cause he has espoused, combined with a shrewd worldly foresight, which tells him that her doctrines will be productive of change and tumult, the elements of his power and delight. On her left, yet slightly drawn back so as to evince a less decided support, is Cotton, no young and hot enthusiast, but a mild, grave man in the decline of life, deep in all the learning of the age, and sanctified in heart and made venerable in feature by the long exercise of his holy profession. He also is deceived by the strange fire now laid upon the altar, and he alone among his brethren is excepted in the denunciation of the new Apostle, as sealed and set apart by Heaven to the work of the ministry. Others of the priesthood stand full in front of the woman, striving to beat her down with brows of wrinkled iron, and whispering sternly and significantly among themselves, as she unfolds her seditious doctrines and grows warm in their support. Foremost is Hugh Peters, full of holy wrath, and scarce containing himself from rushing forward to convict her of damnable heresies; there also is Ward, meditating a reply of empty puns, and quaint antitheses, and tinkling jests that puzzle us with nothing but a sound. The audience are variously affected, but none indifferent. On the foreheads of the aged, the mature, and strong-minded, you may generally read steadfast disapprobation, though here and there is one, whose faith seems shaken in those whom he had trusted for years; the females, on the other hand, are shuddering and weeping, and at times they cast a desolate look of fear around them; while the young men lean forward, fiery and impatient, fit instruments for whatever rash deed may be suggested. And what is the eloquence that gives rise to all these passions? The woman tells them, (and cites texts from the Holy Book to prove her words,) that they have put their trust in unregenerated and uncommissioned men, and have followed them into the wilderness for naught. Therefore their hearts are turning from those whom they had chosen to lead them to Heaven, and they feel like children who have been enticed far from home, and see the features of their guides change all at once, assuming a fiendish shape in some frightful solitude.

These proceedings of Mrs. Hutchinson could not long be endured by the provincial government. The present was a most remarkable case, in which religious freedom was wholly inconsistent with public safety, and where the principles of an illiberal age indicated the very course which must have been pursued by worldly policy and enlightened wisdom. Unity of faith was the star that had guided these people over the deep, and a diversity of sects would either have scattered them from the land to which they had as yet so few attachments, or perhaps have excited a diminutive civil war among those who had come so far to worship together. The opposition to what may be termed the established church had now lost its chief support, by the removal of Vane from office and his departure for England, and Mr. Cotton began to have that light in regard to his errors, which will sometimes break in upon the wisest and most pious men, when their opinions are unhappily discordant with those of the Powers that be. A Synod, the first in New England, was speedily assembled, and pronounced its condemnation of the obnoxious doctrines. Mrs. Hutchinson was next summoned before the supreme civil tribunal, at which, however, the most eminent of the clergy were present, and appear to have taken a very active part as witnesses and advisers. We shall here resume the more picturesque style of narration.

It is a place of humble aspect where the Elders of the people are met, sitting in judgment upon the disturber of Israel. The floor of the low and narrow hall is laid with planks hewn by the axe,—the beams of the roof still wear the rugged bark with which they grew up in the forest, and the hearth is formed of one broad unhammered stone, heaped with logs that roll their blaze and smoke up a chimney of wood and clay. A sleety shower beats fitfully against the windows, driven by the November blast, which comes howling onward from the northern desert, the boisterous and unwelcome herald of a New England winter. Rude benches are arranged across the apartment and along its sides, occupied by men whose piety and learning might have entitled them to seats in those high Councils of the ancient Church, whence opinions were sent forth to confirm or supersede the Gospel in the belief of the whole world and of posterity.—Here are collected all those blessed Fathers of the land, who rank in our veneration next to the Evangelists of Holy Writ, and here also are many, unpurified from the fiercest errors of the age and ready to propagate the religion of peace by violence. In the highest place sits Winthrop, a man by whom the innocent and the guilty might alike desire to be judged, the first confiding in his integrity and wisdom, the latter hoping in his mildness. Next is Endicott, who would stand with his drawn sword at the gate of Heaven, and resist to the death all pilgrims thither, except they travelled his own path. The infant eyes of one in this assembly beheld the faggots blazing round the martyrs, in bloody Mary's time; in later life he dwelt long at Leyden, with the first who went from England for conscience sake; and now, in his weary age, it matters little where

he lies down to die. There are others whose hearts were smitten in the high meridian of ambitious hope, and whose
dreams still tempt them with the pomp of the old world and
the din of its crowded cities, gleaming and echoing over the
deep. In the midst, and in the centre of all eyes, we see the
Woman. She stands loftily before her judges, with a determined brow, and, unknown to herself, there is a flash of carnal pride half hidden in her eye, as she surveys the many
learned and famous men whom her doctrines have put in fear.
They question her, and her answers are ready and acute; she
reasons with them shrewdly, and brings scripture in support
of every argument; the deepest controversialists of that scholastic day find here a woman, whom all their trained and
sharpened intellects are inadequate to foil. But by the excitement of the contest, her heart is made to rise and swell within
her, and she bursts forth into eloquence. She tells them of the
long unquietness which she had endured in England, perceiving the corruption of the church, and yearning for a purer
and more perfect light, and how, in a day of solitary prayer,
that light was given; she claims for herself the peculiar power
of distinguishing between the chosen of man and the Sealed
of Heaven, and affirms that her gifted eye can see the glory
round the foreheads of the Saints, sojourning in their mortal
state. She declares herself commissioned to separate the true
shepherds from the false, and denounces present and future
judgments on the land, if she be disturbed in her celestial
errand. Thus the accusations are proved from her own
mouth. Her judges hesitate, and some speak faintly in her
defence; but, with a few dissenting voices, sentence is pronounced, bidding her go out from among them, and trouble
the land no more.

Mrs. Hutchinson's adherents throughout the colony were
now disarmed, and she proceeded to Rhode Island, an accustomed refuge for the exiles of Massachusetts, in all seasons of
persecution. Her enemies believed that the anger of Heaven
was following her, of which Governor Winthrop does not
disdain to record a notable instance, very interesting in a scientific point of view, but fitter for his old and homely narrative than for modern repetition. In a little time, also, she lost
her husband, who is mentioned in history only as attending

her footsteps, and whom we may conclude to have been (like most husbands of celebrated women) a mere insignificant appendage of his mightier wife. She now grew uneasy among the Rhode-Island colonists, whose liberality towards her, at an era when liberality was not esteemed a christian virtue, probably arose from a comparative insolicitude on religious matters, more distasteful to Mrs. Hutchinson than even the uncompromising narrowness of the Puritans. Her final movement was to lead her family within the limits of the Dutch Jurisdiction, where, having felled the trees of a virgin soil, she became herself the virtual head, civil and ecclesiastical, of a little colony.

Perhaps here she found the repose, hitherto so vainly sought. Secluded from all whose faith she could not govern, surrounded by the dependents over whom she held an unlimited influence, agitated by none of the tumultuous billows which were left swelling behind her, we may suppose, that, in the stillness of Nature, her heart was stilled. But her impressive story was to have an awful close. Her last scene is as difficult to be portrayed as a shipwreck, where the shrieks of the victims die unheard along a desolate sea, and a shapeless mass of agony is all that can be brought home to the imagination. The savage foe was on the watch for blood. Sixteen persons assembled at the evening prayer; in the deep midnight, their cry rang through the forest; and daylight dawned upon the lifeless clay of all but one. It was a circumstance not to be unnoticed by our stern ancestors, in considering the fate of her who had so troubled their religion, that an infant daughter, the sole survivor amid the terrible destruction of her mother's household, was bred in a barbarous faith, and never learned the way to the Christian's Heaven. Yet we will hope, that there the mother and the child have met.

An Old Woman's Tale

In the house where I was born, there used to be an old woman crouching all day long over the kitchen fire, with her elbows on her knees and her feet in the ashes. Once in a while she took a turn at the spit, and she never lacked a coarse gray stocking in her lap, the foot about half finished; it tapered away with her own waning life and she knit the toe-stitch on the day of her death. She made it her serious business and sole amusement to tell me stories at any time from morning till night, in a mumbling, toothless voice, as I sat on a log of wood, grasping her check-apron in both my hands. Her personal memory included the better part of a hundred years, and she had strangely jumbled her own experience and observation with those of many old people who died in her young days; so that she might have been taken for a contemporary of Queen Elizabeth, or of John Rogers in the Primer. There are a thousand of her traditions lurking in the corners and by-places of my mind, some more marvellous than what is to follow, some less so, and a few not marvellous in the least, all which I should like to repeat, if I were as happy as she in having a listener. But I am humble enough to own, that I do not deserve a listener half so well as that old toothless woman, whose narratives possessed an excellence attributable neither to herself, nor to any single individual. Her ground-plots, seldom within the widest scope of probability, were filled up with homely and natural incidents, the gradual accretions of a long course of years, and fiction hid its grotesque extravagance in this garb of truth, like the devil (an appropriate simile, for the old woman supplies it) disguising himself, cloven-foot and all, in mortal attire. These tales generally referred to her birth-place, a village in the Valley of the Connecticut, the aspect of which she impressed with great vividness on my fancy. The houses in that tract of country, long a wild and dangerous frontier, were rendered defensible by a strength of architecture that has preserved many of them till our own times, and I cannot describe the sort of pleasure with which, two summers since, I rode through the little

town in question, while one object after another rose familiarly to my eye, like successive portions of a dream becoming
realized. Among other things equally probable, she was wont
to assert that all the inhabitants of this village (at certain intervals, but whether of twenty-five or fifty years, or a whole
century, remained a disputable point) were subject to a simultaneous slumber, continuing one hour's space. When that
mysterious time arrived, the parson snored over his half-writ-
ten sermon, though it were Saturday night and no provision
made for the morrow,—the mother's eyelids closed as she
bent over her infant, and no childish cry awakened her,—the
watcher at the bed of mortal sickness slumbered upon the
death pillow,—and the dying man anticipated his sleep of
ages by one as deep and dreamless. To speak emphatically,
there was a soporific influence throughout the village,
stronger than if every mother's son and daughter were reading a dull story; notwithstanding which, the old woman professed to hold the substance of the ensuing account from one
of those principally concerned in it.

One moonlight summer evening, a young man and a girl
sat down together in the open air. They were distant relatives,
sprung from a stock once wealthy, but of late years so poverty
stricken, that David had not a penny to pay the marriage fee,
if Esther should consent to wed. The seat they had chosen
was in an open grove of elm and walnut trees, at a right angle
of the road; a spring of diamond water just bubbled into the
moonlight beside them, and then whimpered away through
the bushes and long grass, in search of a neighboring mill-
stream. The nearest house (situate within twenty yards of
them, and the residence of their great-grandfather in his life
time) was a venerable old edifice, crowned with many high
and narrow peaks, and all overrun by innumerable creeping
plants, which hung curling about the roof like a nice young
wig on an elderly gentleman's head. Opposite to this establishment was a tavern, with a well and horse-trough before it,
and a low green bank running along the left side of the door.
Thence, the road went onward, curving scarce perceptibly,
through the village, divided in the midst by a narrow lane of
verdure, and bounded on each side by a grassy strip of twice
its own breadth. The houses had generally an odd look. Here,

the moonlight tried to get a glimpse of one, a rough old heap of ponderous timber, which, ashamed of its dilapidated aspect, was hiding behind a great thick tree; the lower story of the next had sunk almost under ground, as if the poor little house were a-weary of the world, and retiring into the seclusion of its own cellar; farther on, stood one of the few recent structures, thrusting its painted face conspicuously into the street, with an evident idea that it was the fairest thing there. About midway in the village was a grist-mill, partly concealed by the descent of the ground towards the stream which turned its wheel. At the southern extremity, just so far distant that the window-panes dazzled into each other, rose the meeting-house, a dingy old barnlike building, with an enormously disproportioned steeple sticking up straight into Heaven, as high as the Tower of Babel, and the cause of nearly as much confusion in its day. This steeple, it must be understood, was an afterthought, and its addition to the main edifice, when the latter had already begun to decay, had excited a vehement quarrel, and almost a schism in the church, some fifty years before. Here the road wound down a hill and was seen no more, the remotest object in view being the grave-yard gate, beyond the meeting-house. The youthful pair sat hand in hand beneath the trees, and for several moments they had not spoken, because the breeze was hushed, the brook scarce tinkled, the leaves had ceased their rustling, and every thing lay motionless and silent as if Nature were composing herself to slumber.

"What a beautiful night it is, Esther," remarked David, somewhat drowsily.

"Very beautiful," answered the girl, in the same tone.

"But how still!" continued David.

"Ah, too still!" said Esther, with a faint shudder, like a modest leaf when the wind kisses it.

Perhaps they fell asleep together, and, united as their spirits were by close and tender sympathies, the same strange dream might have wrapt them both in its shadowy arms. But they conceived, at the time, that they still remained wakeful by the spring of bubbling water, looking down through the village, and all along the moonlighted road, and at the queer old houses, and at the trees which thrust their great twisted branches almost into the windows. There was only a sort of mistiness over their minds, like the smoky air of an early Autumn night. At length, without any vivid astonishment, they became conscious that a great many people were either entering the village or already in the street, but whether they came from the meeting-house, or from a little beyond it, or where the devil they came from, was more than could be determined. Certainly, a crowd of people seemed to be there, men, women, and children, all of whom were yawning, rubbing their eyes, stretching their limbs and staggering from side to side of the road, as if but partially awakened from a sound slumber. Sometimes they stood stock-still, with their hands over their brows to shade their sight from the moonbeams. As they drew near, most of their countenances appeared familiar to Esther and David, possessing the peculiar features of families in the village, and that general air and aspect by which a person would recognize his own townsmen in the remotest ends of the earth. But though the whole multitude might have been taken, in the mass, for neighbors and acquaintances, there was not a single individual whose exact likeness they had ever before seen. It was a noticeable circumstance, also, that the newest fashioned garment on the backs of these people might have been worn by the great-grand parents of the existing generation. There was one figure behind all the rest, and not yet near enough to be perfectly distinguished.

"Where on earth, David, do all these odd people come from?" said Esther, with a lazy inclination to laugh.

"No where on earth, Esther," replied David, unknowing why he said so.

As they spoke, the strangers showed some symptoms of disquietude, and looked towards the fountain for an instant, but immediately appeared to resume their own trains of thought and previous purposes. They now separated to different parts of the village, with a readiness that implied intimate local knowledge, and it may be worthy of remark, that, though they were evidently loquacious among themselves, neither their footsteps nor their voices reached the ears of the beholders. Wherever there was a venerable old house, of fifty years standing and upwards, surrounded by its elm or walnut

trees, with its dark and weather-beaten barn, its well, its orchard and stone-walls, all ancient and in good repair around
it, there a little group of these people assembled. Such parties
were mostly composed of an aged man and woman, with the
younger members of a family; their faces were full of joy, so
deep that it assumed the shade of melancholy; they pointed
to each other the minutest objects about the homesteads,
things in their hearts, and were now comparing them with
the originals. But where hollow places by the way-side, grass-
grown and uneven, with unsightly chimneys rising ruinous in
the midst, gave indications of a fallen dwelling and of hearths
long cold, there did a few of the strangers sit them down on
the mouldering beams, and on the yellow moss that had overspread the door-stone. The men folded their arms sad and
speechless; the women wrung their hands with a more vivid
expression of grief; and the little children tottered to their
knees, shrinking away from the open grave of domestic love.
And wherever a recent edifice reared its white and flashy front
on the foundation of an old one, there a gray-haired man
might be seen to shake his staff in anger at it, while his aged
dame and their offspring appeared to join in their maledictions, forming a fearful picture in the ghostly moonlight.
While these scenes were passing, the one figure in the rear of
all the rest was descending the hollow towards the mill, and
the eyes of David and Esther were drawn thence to a pair
with whom they could fully sympathize. It was a youth in a
sailor's dress and a pale slender maiden, who met each other
with a sweet embrace in the middle of the street.

"How long it must be since they parted," observed David.

"Fifty years at least," said Esther.

They continued to gaze with unwondering calmness and
quiet interest, as the dream (if such it were) unrolled its
quaint and motley semblance before them, and their notice
was now attracted by several little knots of people, apparently
engaged in conversation. Of these one of the earliest collected
and most characteristic was near the tavern, the persons who
composed it being seated on the low green bank along the
left side of the door. A conspicuous figure here was a fine
corpulent old fellow in his shirt sleeves and flame-coloured
breeches, and with a stained white apron over his paunch,

beneath which he held his hands and wherewith at times he wiped his ruddy face. The stately decrepitude of one of his companions, the scar of an Indian tomahawk on his crown, and especially his worn buff-coat, were appropriate marks of a veteran belonging to an old Provincial garrison, now deaf to the roll-call. Another showed his rough face under a tarry hat and wore a pair of wide trowsers, like an ancient mariner who had tossed away his youth upon the sea, and was returned, hoary and weather beaten, to his inland home. There was also a thin young man, carelessly dressed, who ever and anon cast a sad look towards the pale maiden above mentioned. With these there sat a hunter, and one or two others, and they were soon joined by a miller, who came upward from the dusty mill, his coat as white as if besprinkled with powdered starlight. All these (by the aid of jests, which might indeed be old, but had not been recently repeated) waxed very merry, and it was rather strange, that just as their sides shook with the heartiest laughter, they appeared greatly like a group of shadows flickering in the moonshine. Four personages, very different from these, stood in front of the large house with its periwig of creeping plants. One was a little elderly figure, distinguished by the gold on his three-cornered hat and sky-blue coat, and by the seal of arms annexed to his great gold watch-chain; his air and aspect befitted a Justice of Peace and county Major, and all earth's pride and pomposity were squeezed into this small gentleman of five foot high. The next in importance was a grave person of sixty or seventy years, whose black suit and band sufficiently indicated his character, and the polished baldness of whose head was worthy of a famous preacher in the village, half a century before, who had made wigs a subject of pulpit denunciation. The two other figures, both clad in dark gray, showed the sobriety of Deacons; one was ridiculously tall and thin, like a man of ordinary bulk infinitely produced, as the mathematicians say; while the brevity and thickness of his colleague seemed a compression of the same man. These four talked with great earnestness, and their gestures intimated that they had revived the ancient dispute about the meeting-house steeple. The grave person in black spoke with composed solemnity, as if he were addressing a Synod; the short deacon grunted out

occasional sentences, as brief as himself; his tall brother drew
the long thread of his argument through the whole discussion, and (reasoning from analogy) his voice must indubitably
have been small and squeaking. But the little old man in gold-
lace was evidently scorched by his own red-hot eloquence; he
bounced from one to another, shook his cane at the steeple,
at the two deacons, and almost in the parson's face, stamping
with his foot fiercely enough to break a hole through the very
earth; though, indeed, it could not exactly be said that the
green grass bent beneath him. The figure, noticed as coming
behind all the rest, had now surmounted the ascent from the
mill, and proved to be an elderly lady with something in her
hand.

"Why does she walk so slow?" asked David.

"Don't you see she is lame?" said Esther.

This gentlewoman, whose infirmity had kept her so far in
the rear of the crowd, now came hobbling on, glided unobserved by the polemic group, and paused on the left brink of
the fountain, within a few feet of the two spectators. She was
a magnificent old dame, as ever mortal eye beheld. Her span-
gled shoes and gold-clocked stockings shone gloriously within
the spacious circle of a red hoop-petticoat, which swelled to
the very point of explosion, and was bedecked all over with
embroidery a little tarnished. Above the petticoat, and parting
in front so as to display it to the best advantage, was a figured
blue damask gown. A wide and stiff ruff encircled her neck,
a cap of the finest muslin, though rather dingy, covered her
head, and her nose was bestridden by a pair of gold-bowed
spectacles with enormous glasses. But the old lady's face was
pinched, sharp, and sallow, wearing a niggardly and avari-
cious expression, and forming an odd contrast to the splendor
of her attire, as did likewise the implement which she held in
her hand. It was a sort of iron shovel (by housewives termed
a "slice"), such as is used in clearing the oven, and with this,
selecting a spot between a walnut tree and the fountain, the
good dame made an earnest attempt to dig. The tender sods,
however, possessed a strange impenetrability. They resisted
her efforts like a quarry of living granite, and losing her
breath, she cast down the shovel and seemed to bemoan herself most piteously, gnashing her teeth (what few she had)

and wringing her thin yellow hands. Then, apparently with new hopes, she resumed her toil, which still had the same result,—a circumstance the less surprising to David and Esther, because at times they would catch the moonlight shining through the old woman, and dancing in the fountain beyond. The little man in gold-lace now happened to see her, and made his approach on tiptoe.

"How hard this elderly lady works," remarked David.

"Go and help her, David," said Esther, compassionately.

As their drowsy voices spoke, both the old woman and the pompous little figure behind her lifted their eyes, and for a moment they regarded the youth and damsel with something like kindness and affection; which, however, were dim and uncertain, and passed away almost immediately. The old woman again betook herself to the shovel, but was startled by a hand suddenly laid upon her shoulder; she turned round in great trepidation, and beheld the dignitary in the blue coat; then followed an embrace, of such closeness as would indicate no remoter connexion than matrimony between these two decorous persons. The gentleman next pointed to the shovel, appearing to enquire the purpose of his lady's occupation; while she as evidently parried his interrogatories, maintaining a demure and sanctified visage as every good woman ought, in similar cases. Howbeit, she could not forbear looking a-skew, behind her spectacles, towards the spot of stubborn turf. All the while, their figures had a strangeness in them, and it seemed as if some cunning jeweller had made their golden ornaments of the yellowest of the setting sun beams, and that the blue of their garments was brought from the dark sky near the moon, and that the gentleman's silk waist-coat was the bright side of a fiery cloud, and the lady's scarlet petticoat a remnant of the blush of morning,—and that they both were two unrealities of colored air. But now there was a sudden movement throughout the multitude. The Squire drew forth a watch as large as the dial on the famous steeple, looked at the warning hands and gat him gone, nor could his lady tarry; the party at the tavern door took to their heels, headed by the fat man in the flaming breeches; the tall deacon stalked away immediately, and the short deacon waddled after, making four steps to the yard; the mothers called their children about them and set forth, with a gentle and sad glance behind. Like cloudy fantasies that hurry by a viewless impulse from the sky, they all were fled, and the wind rose up and followed them with a strange moaning down the lonely street. Now whither these people went, is more than may be told; only David and Esther seemed to see the shadowy splendor of the ancient dame, as she lingered in the moonshine at the grave-yard gate, gazing backward to the fountain.

"Oh, Esther! I have had such a dream!" cried David, starting up and rubbing his eyes.

"And I such another!" answered Esther, gaping till her pretty red lips formed a circle.

"About an old woman with gold-bowed spectacles," continued David.

"And a scarlet hoop-petticoat," added Esther.

They now stared in each other's eyes, with great astonishment and some little fear. After a thoughtful moment or two, David drew a long breath and stood upright.

"If I live till to-morrow morning," said he, "I'll see what may be buried between that tree and the spring of water."

"And why not to-night, David?" asked Esther; for she was a sensible little girl, and bethought herself that the matter might as well be done in secrecy.

David felt the propriety of the remark and looked round for the means of following her advice. The moon shone brightly on something that rested against the side of the old house, and, on a nearer view, it proved to be an iron shovel, bearing a singular resemblance to that which they had seen in their dreams. He used it with better success than the old woman, the soil giving way so freely to his efforts, that he had soon scooped a hole as large as the basin of the spring. Suddenly, he poked his head down to the very bottom of this cavity.

"Oho!—What have we here!" cried David.

Dr. Bullivant

THIS person was not eminent enough, either by nature or circumstance, to deserve a public memorial simply for his own sake, after the lapse of a century and a half from the era in which he flourished. His character, in the view which we propose to take of it, may give a species of distinctness and point to some remarks on the tone and composition of New-England society, modified as it became by new ingredients from the eastern world, and by the attrition of sixty or seventy years over the rugged peculiarities of the original settlers. We are perhaps accustomed to employ too sombre a pencil in picturing the earlier times among the Puritans, because, at our cold distance, we form our ideas almost wholly from their severest features. It is like gazing on some scenes in the land which we inherit from them; we see the mountains, rising sternly and with frozen summits up to Heaven, and the forests, waving in massy depths where sunshine seems a profanation, and we see the gray mist, like the duskiness of years, shedding a chill obscurity over the whole; but the green and pleasant spots in the hollow of the hills, the warm places in the heart of what looks desolate, are hidden from our eyes. Still, however, a prevailing characteristic of the age was gloom, or something which cannot be more accurately expressed than by that term, and its long shadow, falling over all the intervening years, is visible, though not too distinctly, upon ourselves. Without material detriment to a deep and solid happiness, the frolic of the mind was so habitually chastened, that persons have gained a nook in history by the mere possession of animal spirits, too exuberant to be confined within the established bounds. Every vain jest and unprofitable word was deemed an item in the account of criminality, and whatever wit, or semblance thereof, came into existence, its birth place was generally the pulpit, and its parent some sour old Genevan Divine. The specimens of humour and satire, preserved in the sermons and controversial tracts of those days, are occasionally the apt expressions of pungent thoughts; but oftener they are cruel torturings and twistings of trite ideas, disgusting by the wearisome ingenuity which constitutes their only merit. Among a people where so few possessed, or were allowed to exercise, the art of extracting the mirth which lies hidden like latent caloric in almost every thing, a gay apothecary, such as Dr. Bullivant, must have been a phenomenon.

We will suppose ourselves standing in Cornhill, on a pleasant morning of the year 1670, about the hour when the shutters are unclosed and the dust swept from the doorsteps, and when Business rubs its eyes and begins to plod sleepily through the town. The street, instead of running between lofty and continuous piles of brick, is but partially lined with wooden buildings of various heights and architecture, in each of which the mercantile department is connected with the domicile, like the gingerbread and candy shops of an after date. The signs have a singular appearance to a stranger's eye. These are not a barren record of names and occupations, yellow letters on black boards, but images and hieroglyphics, sometimes typifying the principal commodity offered for sale, though generally intended to give an arbitrary designation to the establishment. Overlooking the bearded Saracens, the Indian Queens, and the wooden Bibles, let us direct our attention to the white post newly erected at the corner of the street, and surmounted by a gilded countenance which flashes in the early sunbeams like veritable gold. It is a bust of Æsculapius, evidently of the latest London manufacture, and from the door behind it steams forth a mingled smell of musk and assafœtida and other drugs of potent perfume, as if an appropriate sacrifice were just laid upon the altar of the medicinal deity. Five or six idle people are already collected, peeping curiously in at the glittering array of gallipots and phials, and decyphering the labels which tell their contents in the mysterious and imposing nomenclature of ancient physic. They are next attracted by the printed advertisement of a Panacea, promising life but one day short of eternity, and youth and health commensurate; an old man, his head as white as snow, totters in with a hasty clattering of his staff, and becomes the earliest purchaser, hoping that his wrinkles will disappear more swiftly than they gathered. The Doctor (so styled by courtesy) shows the upper half of his person behind the counter, and appears to be a slender and rather tall man; his features are difficult to describe, possessing nothing peculiar except a flexibility to assume all characters in turn, while his eye, shrewd, quick, and saucy, remains the same throughout. Whenever a customer enters the shop, if he desire a box of pills, he receives with them an equal number of hard, round, dry jokes,—or if a dose of salts, it is mingled with a potion of the salt of Attica,—or if some hot, oriental drug, it is accompanied by a racy word or two that tingle on the mental palate,—all without the least additional cost. Then there are twistings of mouths which never lost their gravity before. As each purchaser retires, the spectators see a resemblance of his visage pass over that of the apothecary, in which all the ludicrous points are made most prominent, as if a magic looking glass had caught the reflection and were making sport with it. Unwonted titterings arise and strengthen into bashful laughter, but are suddenly hushed as some minister, heavy-eyed from his last night's vigil, or magistrate, armed with the terrors of whipping post and pillory, or perhaps the governor himself, goes by like a dark cloud intercepting the sunshine.

About this period, many causes began to produce an important change, on and beneath the surface of colonial society. The early settlers were able to keep within the narrowest limits of their rigid principles, because they had adopted them in mature life, and from their own deep conviction, and were strengthened in them by that species of enthusiasm which is as sober and as enduring as reason itself. But if their immediate successors followed the same line of conduct, they were confined to it, in a great degree, by habits forced upon them, and by the severe rule under which they were educated, and in short more by the restraint, than by the free exercise, of the imagination and understanding. When therefore the old original stock, the men who looked heavenward without a wandering glance to earth, had lost a part of their domestic and public influence, yielding to infirmity or death, a relaxation naturally ensued in their theory and practice of morals and religion, and became more evident with the daily decay of its most strenuous opponents. This gradual but sure operation was assisted by the increasing commercial importance of the colonies, whither a new set of emigrants followed unworthily in the track of the pure-hearted Pilgrims. Gain being now the allurement, and almost the only one, since dissenters no longer dreaded persecution at home, the people of New-England could not remain entirely uncontaminated by an extensive intermixture with worldly men. The trade carried on by the colonists, (in the face of several inefficient acts of Parliament,) with the whole maritime world, must have had a similar tendency; nor are the desperate and dissolute visitants of the country to be forgotten among the agents of a moral revolution. Freebooters from the West Indies and the Spanish Main,—state criminals, implicated in the numerous plots and conspiracies of the period,—felons, loaded with private guilt,—numbers of these took refuge in the provinces, where the authority of the English king was obstructed by a zealous spirit of independence, and where a boundless wilderness enabled them to defy pursuit. Thus the new population, temporary and permanent, was exceedingly unlike the old, and far more apt to disseminate their own principles than to imbibe those of the Puritans. All circumstances unfavorable to virtue acquired double strength by the licentious reign of Charles II; though perhaps the example of the monarch and nobility was less likely to recommend vice to the people of New-England, than to those of any other part of the British Empire.

The clergy and the elder magistrates manifested a quick sensibility to the decline of godliness, their apprehensions being sharpened in this particular no less by a holy zeal, than because their credit and influence were intimately connected with the primitive character of the country. A Synod, convened in the year 1679, gave its opinion that the iniquity of the times had drawn down judgments from Heaven, and proposed methods to assuage the Divine wrath by a renewal of former sanctity. But neither the increased numbers nor the altered spirit of the people, nor their just sense of a freedom to do wrong, within certain limits, would now have permitted the exercise of that inquisitorial strictness, which had been wont to penetrate to men's firesides and watch their domestic life, recognizing no distinction between private ill conduct and crimes that endanger the community. Accordingly, the tide of worldly principles encroached more and more upon

the ancient landmarks, hitherto esteemed the outer boundaries of virtue. Society arranged itself into two classes, marked
by strong shades of difference, though separated by an uncertain line;—in one were included the small and feeble remnant
of the first settlers, many of their immediate descendants, the
whole body of the clergy, and all whom a gloomy temperament, or tenderness of conscience, or timidity of thought,
kept up to the strictness of their fathers; the other comprehended the new emigrants, the young and thoughtless natives, the favourers of Episcopacy, and a various mixture of
liberal and enlightened men with most of the evil-doers and
unprincipled adventurers in the country. A vivid and rather a
pleasant idea of New-England manners, when this change had
become decided, is given in the journal of John Dunton, a
cockney bookseller, who visited Boston and other towns of
Massachusetts with a cargo of pious publications, suited to
the Puritan market. Making due allowance for the flippancy
of the writer, which may have given a livelier tone to his de-
scriptions than truth precisely warrants, and also for his character, which led him chiefly among the gayest inhabitants,
there still seem to have been many who loved the wine-cup
and the song, and all sorts of delightful naughtiness. But the
degeneracy of the times had made far less progress in the interior of the country than in the seaports, and until the people
lost the elective privilege, they continued the government in
the hands of those upright old men who had só long possessed their confidence. Uncontrollable events, alone, gave a
temporary ascendancy to persons of another stamp. James II,
during the four years of his despotic reign, revoked the charters of the American colonies, arrogated the appointment of
their magistrates, and annulled all those legal and prescriptive
rights which had hitherto constituted them nearly independent states. Among the foremost advocates of the royal usur-
pations was Dr. Bullivant. Gifted with a smart and ready intellect, busy and bold, he acquired great influence in the new
government, and assisted Sir Edmund Andros, Edward Randolph, and five or six others, to browbeat the Council and
misrule the northern provinces according to their pleasure.
The strength of the popular hatred against this administration, the actual tyranny that was exercised, and the innumer-

able fears and jealousies, well grounded and fantastic, which harassed the country, may be best learned from a work of Cotton Mather, the "Remarkables" of his father. The good Divine, (though writing when a lapse of nearly forty years should have tamed the fierceness of party animosity,) speaks with most bitter and angry scorn of "Pothecary Bullevant," who probably indulged his satirical propensities, from the seat of power, in a manner which rendered him an especial object of public dislike. But the people were about to play off a piece of practical fun on the Doctor and the whole set of his coadjutors, and have the laugh all to themselves. By the first faint rumour of the attempt of the Prince of Orange on the throne, the power of James was annihilated in the colonies, and long before the abdication of the latter became known, Sir Edmund Andros, Governor General of New-England and New-York, and fifty of the most obnoxious leaders of the Court party, were tenants of a prison. We will visit our old acquaintance in his adversity.

The scene now represents a room of ten feet square, the floor of which is sunk a yard or two below the level of the ground; the walls are covered with a dirty and crumbling plaster, on which appear a crowd of ill-favoured and lugubrious faces done in charcoal, and the autographs and poetical attempts of a long succession of debtors and petty criminals. Other features of the apartment are a deep fire place, (superfluous in the sultriness of the summer's days,) a door of hardhearted oak, and a narrow window high in the wall, where the glass has long been broken, while the iron bars retain all their original strength. Through this opening come the sound of passing footsteps in the public street, and the voices of children at play. The furniture consists of a bed, or rather an old sack of barley straw, thrown down in the corner furthest from the door, and a chair and table, both aged and infirm, and leaning against the side of the room, besides lending a friendly support to each other. The atmosphere is stived and of an ill smell, as if it had been kept close prisoner for half a century, and had lost all its pure and elastic nature by feeding the tainted breath of the vicious and the sighs of the unfortunate. Such is the present abode of the man of medicine and politics, and his own appearance forms no contrast to the accompaniments. His wig is unpowdered, out of curl, and put on awry; the dust of many weeks has worked its way into the web of his coat and small-clothes, and his knees and elbows peep forth to ask why they are so ill clad; his stockings are ungartered, his shoes down at the heel, his waistcoat is without a button and discloses a shirt as dingy as the remnant of snow in a showery April day. His shoulders have become rounder and his whole person is more bent and drawn together, since we last saw him, and his face has exchanged the glow of wit and humor for a sheepish dullness. At intervals, the Doctor walks the room with an irregular and shuffling pace; anon, he throws himself flat on the sack of barley straw, muttering very reprehensible expressions between his teeth; then again he starts to his feet, and journeying from corner to corner, finally sinks into the chair, forgetful of its three-legged infirmity till it lets him down upon the floor. The grated window, his only medium of intercourse with the world, serves but to admit additional vexations. Every few moments, the steps of the passengers are heard to pause, and some well known face appears in the free sunshine behind the iron bars, brimful of mirth and drollery, the owner whereof stands on tiptoe to tickle poor Dr. Bullivant with a stinging sarcasm. Then laugh the little boys around the prison door, and the wag goes chuckling away. The apothecary would fain retaliate, but all his quips, and repartees, and sharp and facetious fancies, once so abundant, seem to have been transferred from himself to the sluggish brains of his enemies. While endeavoring to condense his whole intellect into one venomous point, in readiness for the next assailant, he is interrupted by the entrance of the turnkey with the prison fare of Indian bread and water. With these dainties we leave him.

When the turmoil of the revolution had subsided, and the authority of William and Mary was fixed on a quiet basis throughout the colonies, the deposed governor and some of his partizans were sent home to the new court, and the others released from imprisonment. The New-Englanders, as a people, are not apt to retain a revengeful sense of injury, and nowhere, perhaps, could a politician, however odious in his power, live more peacefully in his nakedness and disgrace. Dr. Bullivant returned to his former occupation, and spent rather a desirable old age. Though he sometimes hit hard with a jest, yet few thought of taking offence; for whenever a man habitually indulges his tongue at the expense of all his associates, they provide against the common annoyance by tacitly agreeing to consider his sarcasms as null and void. Thus for many years, a gray old man with a stoop in his gait, he continued to sweep out his shop at eight o'clock in summer mornings and nine in winter, and to waste whole hours in idle talk and irreverent merriment, making it his glory to raise the laughter of silly people, and his delight to sneer at them in his sleeve. At length, one pleasant day, the door and shutters of his establishment kept closed from sunrise till sunset, and his cronies marvelled a moment, and passed on;—a week after, the rector of King's Chapel said the death-rite over Dr. Bullivant;—and within the month, a new apothecary, and a new stock of drugs and medicines, made their appearance at the gilded Head of Æsculapius.

Sights from a Steeple

S o! I have climbed high, and my reward is small. Here I
stand, with wearied knees, earth, indeed, at a dizzy depth
below, but heaven far, far beyond me still. O that I could soar
up into the very zenith, where man never breathed, nor eagle
ever flew, and where the ethereal azure melts away from the
eye, and appears only a deepened shade of nothingness! And
yet I shiver at that cold and solitary thought. What clouds are
gathering in the golden west, with direful intent against the
brightness and the warmth of this summer afternoon! They
are ponderous air ships, black as death, and freighted with
the tempest; and at intervals their thunder, the signal-guns of
that unearthly squadron, rolls distant along the deep of
heaven. These nearer heaps of fleecy vapor—methinks I could
roll and toss upon them the whole day long!—seem scattered
here and there, for the repose of tired pilgrims through the
sky. Perhaps—for who can tell?—beautiful spirits are disporting themselves there, and will bless my mortal eye with
the brief appearance of their curly locks of golden light and
laughing faces, fair and faint as the people of a rosy dream.
Or, where the floating mass so imperfectly obstructs the color
of the firmament, a slender foot and fairy limb, resting too
heavily upon the frail support, may be thrust through, and
suddenly withdrawn, while longing fancy follows them in
vain. Yonder again is an airy archipelago, where the sunbeams
love to linger in their journeyings through space. Every one
of those little clouds has been dipped and steeped in radiance,
which the slightest pressure might disengage in silvery profusion, like water wrung from a sea-maid's hair. Bright they
are as young man's visions, and like them, would be realized
in chillness, obscurity and tears. I will look on them no more.

In three parts of the visible circle, whose centre is this spire,
I discern cultivated fields, villages, white country-seats, the
waving lines of rivulets, little placid lakes, and here and there
a rising ground, that would fain be termed a hill. On the
fourth side is the sea, stretching away towards a viewless
boundary, blue and calm, except where the passing anger of

42

a shadow flits across its surface, and is gone. Hitherward, a broad inlet penetrates far into the land; on the verge of the harbour, formed by its extremity, is a town; and over it am I, a watchman, all-heeding and unheeded. O that the multitude of chimneys could speak, like those of Madrid, and betray, in smoky whispers, the secrets of all who, since their first foundation, have assembled at the hearths within! O that the Limping Devil of Le Sage would perch beside me here, extend his wand over this contiguity of roofs, uncover every chamber, and make me familiar with their inhabitants! The most desirable mode of existence might be that of a spiritualized Paul Pry, hovering invisible round man and woman, witnessing their deeds, searching into their hearts, borrowing brightness from their felicity, and shade from their sorrow, and retaining no emotion peculiar to himself. But none of these things are possible; and if I would know the interior of brick walls, or the mystery of human bosoms, I can but guess.

Yonder is a fair street, extending north and south. The stately mansions are placed each on its carpet of verdant grass, and a long flight of steps descends from every door to the pavement. Ornamental trees, the broad-leafed horse-chestnut, the elm so lofty and bending, the graceful but infrequent willow, and others whereof I know not the names, grow thrivingly among brick and stone. The oblique rays of the sun are intercepted by these green citizens, and by the houses, so that one side of the street is a shaded and pleasant walk. On its whole extent there is now but a single passenger, advancing from the upper end; and he, unless distance, and the medium of a pocket spy-glass do him more than justice, is a fine young man of twenty. He saunters slowly forward; slapping his left hand with his folded gloves, bending his eyes upon the pavement, and sometimes raising them to throw a glance before him. Certainly, he has a pensive air. Is he in doubt, or in debt? Is he, if the question be allowable, in love? Does he strive to be melancholy and gentlemanlike?—Or, is he merely overcome by the heat? But I bid him farewell, for the present. The door of one of the houses, an aristocratic edifice, with curtains of purple and gold waving from the windows, is now opened, and down the steps come two ladies, swinging their parasols, and lightly arrayed for a summer ramble. Both are

young, both are pretty; but methinks the left hand lass is the
fairer of the twain; and though she be so serious at this moment, I could swear that there is a treasure of gentle fun
within her. They stand talking a little while upon the steps,
and finally proceed up the street. Meantime, as their faces are
now turned from me, I may look elsewhere.

Upon that wharf, and down the corresponding street, is a
busy contrast to the quiet scene which I have just noticed.
Business evidently has its centre there, and many a man is
wasting the summer afternoon in labor and anxiety, in losing
riches, or in gaining them, when he would be wiser to flee
away to some pleasant country village, or shaded lake in the
forest, or wild and cool sea-beach. I see vessels unlading at
the wharf, and precious merchandise strewn upon the
ground, abundantly as at the bottom of the sea, that market
whence no goods return, and where there is no captain nor
supercargo to render an account of sales. Here, the clerks are
diligent with their paper and pencils, and sailors ply the block
and tackle that hang over the hold, accompanying their toil
with cries, long-drawn and roughly melodious, till the bales
and puncheons ascend to upper air. At a little distance, a
group of gentlemen are assembled round the door of a warehouse. Grave seniors be they, and I would wager—if it were
safe, in these times, to be responsible, for any one—that the
least eminent among them, might vie with old Vincentio, that
incomparable trafficker of Pisa. I can even select the wealthiest
of the company. It is the elderly personage in somewhat rusty
black, with powdered hair, the superfluous whiteness of
which is visible upon the cape of his coat. His twenty ships
are wafted on some of their many courses by every breeze
that blows, and his name—I will venture to say, though I
know it not—is a familiar sound among the far separated
merchants of Europe and the Indies.

But I bestow too much of my attention in this quarter. On
looking again to the long and shady walk, I perceive that the
two fair girls have encountered the young man. After a sort
of shyness in the recognition, he turns back with them.
Moreover, he has sanctioned my taste in regard to his companions by placing himself on the inner side of the pave-

ment, nearest the Venus to whom I—enacting, on a steeple-top, the part of Paris on the top of Ida—adjudged the golden apple.

In two streets, converging at right angles towards my watch-tower, I distinguish three different processions. One is a proud array of voluntary soldiers in bright uniform, resembling, from the height whence I look down, the painted veterans that garrison the windows of a toy-shop. And yet, it stirs my heart; their regular advance, their nodding plumes, the sun-flash on their bayonets and musket-barrels, the roll of their drums ascending past me, and the fife ever and anon piercing through—these things have wakened a warlike fire, peaceful though I be. Close to their rear marches a battalion of school-boys, ranged in crooked and irregular platoons, shouldering sticks, thumping a harsh and unripe clatter from an instrument of tin, and ridiculously aping the intricate manœuvres of the foremost band. Nevertheless, as slight differences are scarcely perceptible from a church spire, one might be tempted to ask, 'Which are the boys?'—or rather, 'Which the men?' But, leaving these, let us turn to the third procession, which, though sadder in outward show, may excite identical reflections in the thoughtful mind. It is a funeral. A hearse, drawn by a black and bony steed, and covered by a dusty pall; two or three coaches rumbling over the stones, their drivers half asleep; a dozen couple of careless mourners in their every day attire; such was not the fashion of our fathers, when they carried a friend to his grave. There is now no doleful clang of the bell, to proclaim sorrow to the town. Was the King of Terrors more awful in those days than in our own, that wisdom and philosophy have been able to produce this change? Not so. Here is a proof that he retains his proper majesty. The military men, and the military boys, are wheeling round the corner, and meet the funeral full in the face. Immediately, the drum is silent, all but the tap that regulates each simultaneous foot-fall. The soldiers yield the path to the dusty hearse, and unpretending train, and the children quit their ranks, and cluster on the sidewalks, with timorous and instinctive curiosity. The mourners enter the church-yard at the base of the steeple, and pause by an open

grave among the burial stones; the lightning glimmers on
them as they lower down the coffin, and the thunder rattles
heavily while they throw the earth upon its lid. Verily, the
shower is near, and I tremble for the young man and the girls,
who have now disappeared from the long and shady street.

How various are the situations of the people covered by
the roofs beneath me, and how diversified are the events at
this moment befalling them! The new-born, the aged, the
dying, the strong in life, and the recent dead, are in the chambers of these many mansions. The full of hope, the happy, the
miserable, and the desperate, dwell together within the circle
of my glance. In some of the houses over which my eyes roam
so coldly, guilt is entering into hearts that are still tenanted
by a debased and trodden virtue,—guilt is on the very edge
of commission, and the impending deed might be averted;
guilt is done, and the criminal wonders if it be irrevocable.
There are broad thoughts struggling in my mind, and, were
I able to give them distinctness, they would make their way
in eloquence. Lo! the rain-drops are descending.

The clouds, within a little time, have gathered over all the
sky, hanging heavily, as if about to drop in one unbroken
mass upon the earth. At intervals, the lightning flashes from
their brooding hearts, quivers, disappears, and then comes the
thunder, travelling slowly after its twin-born flame. A strong
wind has sprung up, howls through the darkened streets, and
raises the dust in dense bodies, to rebel against the approaching storm. The disbanded soldiers fly, the funeral has already
vanished like its dead, and all people hurry homeward—all
that have a home; while a few lounge by the corners, or
trudge on desperately, at their leisure. In a narrow lane which
communicates with the shady street, I discern the rich old
merchant, putting himself to the top of his speed, lest the rain
should convert his hair-powder to a paste. Unhappy gentleman! By the slow vehemence, and painful moderation wherewith he journeys, it is but too evident that Podagra has left
its thrilling tenderness in his great toe. But yonder, at a far
more rapid pace, come three other of my acquaintance, the
two pretty girls and the young man, unseasonably interrupted
in their walk. Their footsteps are supported by the risen dust,

the wind lends them its velocity, they fly like three sea-birds driven landward by the tempestuous breeze. The ladies would not thus rival Atalanta, if they but knew that any one were at leisure to observe them. Ah! as they hasten onward, laughing in the angry face of nature, a sudden catastrophe has chanced. At the corner where the narrow lane enters into the street, they come plump against the old merchant, whose tortoise motion has just brought him to that point. He likes not the sweet encounter; the darkness of the whole air gathers speedily upon his visage, and there is a pause on both sides. Finally he thrusts aside the youth with little courtesy, seizes an arm of each of the two girls, and plods onward, like a magician with a prize of captive fairies. All this is easy to be understood. How disconsolate the poor lover stands! regardless of the rain that threatens an exceeding damage to his well-fashioned habiliments, till he catches a backward glance of mirth from a bright eye, and turns away with whatever comfort it conveys.

The old man and his daughters are safely housed, and now the storm lets loose its fury. In every dwelling I perceive the faces of the chambermaids as they shut down the windows, excluding the impetuous shower, and shrinking away from the quick fiery glare. The large drops descend with force upon the slated roofs, and rise again in smoke. There is a rush and roar, as of a river through the air, and muddy streams bubble majestically along the pavement, whirl their dusky foam into the kennel, and disappear beneath iron grates. Thus did Arethusa sink. I love not my station here aloft, in the midst of the tumult which I am powerless to direct or quell, with the blue lightning wrinkling on my brow, and the thunder muttering its first awful syllables in my ear. I will descend. Yet let me give another glance to the sea, where the foam breaks out in long white lines upon a broad expanse of blackness, or boils up in far distant points, like snowy mountain tops in the eddies of a flood; and let me look once more at the green plain, and little hills of the country, over which the giant of the storm is striding in robes of mist, and at the town, whose obscured and desolate streets might beseem a city of the dead: and turning a single moment to the sky, now gloomy as an author's prospects, I prepare to resume my station on lower earth. But stay! A little speck of azure has widened in the western heavens; the sunbeams find a passage, and go rejoicing through the tempest; and on yonder darkest cloud, born, like hallowed hopes, of the glory of another world, and the trouble and tears of this, brightens forth the Rainbow!

The Haunted Quack

A TALE OF A CANAL BOAT

IN the summer of 18—, I made an excursion to Niagara. At
Schenectady, finding the roads nearly impassable, I took
passage in a canal boat for Utica. The weather was dull and
lowering. There were but few passengers on board; and of
those few, none were sufficiently inviting in appearance, to
induce me to make any overtures to a travelling acquaintance.
A stupid answer, or a surly monosyllable, were all that I got
in return for the few simple questions I hazarded. An occasional drizzling rain, and the wet and slippery condition of
the tow path, along which the lazy beasts that dragged the
vessel travelled, rendered it impossible to vary the monotony
of the scene by walking. I had neglected to provide myself
with books, and as we crept along at the dull rate of four
miles per hour, I soon felt the foul fiend *Ennui* coming upon
me with all her horrors.

'Time and the hour,' however, 'runs through the roughest
day,' and night at length approached. By degrees the passengers, seemingly tired of each other's company, began to creep
slowly away to their berths; most of them fortifying themselves with a potation, before resigning themselves to the embrace of Morpheus. One called for a glass of hot whiskey
punch, because he felt cold; another took some brandy toddy
to prevent his taking cold; some took mint julaps; some gin-
slings, and some rum and water. One took his dram because
he felt sick; another to make him sleep well; and a third because he had nothing else to do. The last who retired from
the cabin, was an old gentleman who had been deeply engaged in a well thumbed volume all day, and whose mental
abstraction I had more than once envied. He now laid down
his book, and, pulling out a red nightcap, called for a pint of
beer, to take the vapors out of his head.

As soon as he had left the cabin, I took up the volume, and
found it to be Glanville's marvellous book, entitled the History of Witches, or the Wonders of the Invisible World Displayed. I began to peruse it, and soon got so deeply interested

in some of his wonderful narrations, that the hours slipped unconsciously away, and midnight found me poring half asleep over the pages. From this dreamy state I was suddenly aroused by a muttering, as of a suppressed voice, broken by groans and sounds of distress. Upon looking round, I saw that they proceeded from the figure of a man enveloped in a cloak, who was lying asleep upon one of the benches of the cabin, whom I had not previously noticed. I recognized him to be a young man, with whose singular appearance and behaviour during the day, I had been struck. He was tall and thin in person, rather shabbily dressed, with long, lank, black hair, and large grey eyes, which gave a visionary character to one of the most pallid, and cadaverous countenances I had ever beheld. Since he had come on board, he had appeared restless and unquiet, keeping away from the table at meal times, and seeming averse from entering into conversation with the passengers. Once or twice, on catching my eye, he had slunk away as if, conscience smitten by the remembrance of some crime, he dreaded to meet the gaze of a fellow mortal. From this behaviour I suspected that he was either a fugitive from justice, or else a little disordered in mind; and had resolved to keep my eye on him and observe what course he should take when we reached Utica.

Supposing that the poor fellow was now under the influence of nightmare, I got up with the intention of giving him a shake to rouse him, when the words, 'murder,' 'poison,' and others of extraordinary import, dropping unconnectedly from his lips, induced me to stay my hand. 'Go away, go away,' exclaimed he, as if conscious of my approach, but mistaking me for another. 'Why do you continue to torment me? If I did poison you, I didn't mean to do it, and they can't make that out more than manslaughter. Besides, what's the use of haunting me now? An't I going to give myself up, and tell all? Begone! I say, you bloody old hag, begone!' Here the bands of slumber were broken by the intensity of his feelings, and with a wild expression of countenance and a frame shaking with emotion, he started from the bench, and stood trembling before me.

Though convinced that he was a criminal, I could not help

pitying him from the forlorn appearance he now exhibited. As soon as he had collected his wandering ideas, it seemed as if he read in my countenance, the mingled sentiments of pity and abhorrence, with which I regarded him. Looking anxiously around, and seeing that we were alone, he drew the corner of the bench towards me, and sitting down, with an apparent effort to command his feelings, thus addressed me. His tone of voice was calm, and distinct; and his countenance, though deadly pale, was composed.

'I see, Sir, that from what I am conscious of having uttered in my disturbed sleep, you suspect me of some horrid crime. You are right. My conscience convicts me, and an awful nightly visitation, worse than the waking pangs of remorse, compels me to confess it. Yes, I am a murderer. I have been the unhappy cause of blotting out the life of a fellow being from the page of human existence. In these pallid features, you may read enstamped, in the same characters which the first murderer bore upon his brow, Guilt—guilt—guilt!'

Here the poor young man paused, evidently agitated by strong internal emotion. Collecting himself, however, in a few moments, he thus continued.

'Yet still, when you have heard my sad story, I think you will bestow upon me your pity. I feel that there is no peace for me, until I have disburthened my mind. Your countenance promises sympathy. Will you listen to my unhappy narrative?'

My curiosity being strongly excited by this strange exordium, I told him I was ready to hear whatever he had to communicate. Upon this, he proceeded as follows.

'My name is Hippocrates Jenkins. I was born in Nantucket, but my father emigrated to these parts when I was young. I grew up in one of the most flourishing villages on the borders of the canal. My father and mother both dying of the lake fever, I was bound apprentice to an eminent operative in the boot and shoe making line, who had lately come from New York. Would that I had remained content with this simple and useful profession. Would that I had stuck to my waxed ends and awl, and never undertaken to cobble up people's bodies. But my legs grew tired of being trussed beneath my haunches; my elbows wearied with their monotonous motion; my eyes became dim with gazing forever upon the dull brick wall which faced our shop window; and my whole heart was sick of my sedentary, and, as I foolishly deemed it, particularly mean occupation. My time was nearly expired, and I had long resolved, should any opportunity offer of getting into any other employment, I would speedily embrace it.

'I had always entertained a predilection for the study of medicine. What had given my mind this bias, I know not. Perhaps it was the perusal of an old volume of Doctor Buchan, over whose pages it was the delight of my youthful fancy to pore. Perhaps it was the oddness of my Christian cognomen, which surely was given me by my parents in a prophetic hour. Be this as it may, the summit of my earthly happiness was to be a doctor. Conceive then my delight and surprise, one Saturday evening, after having carried home a pair of new white-topped boots for Doctor Ephraim Ramshorne, who made the cure of bodies his care, in the village, to hear him ask me, how I should like to be a doctor. He then very generously offered to take me as a student. From my earliest recollections, the person and character of Doctor Ramshorne, had been regarded by me with the most profound and awful admiration. Time out of mind the successful practitioner for many miles around, I had looked upon him as the *beau idéal* of a doctor—a very Apollo in the healing art. When I speak of him, however, as the *successful* practitioner, I mean it not to be inferred that death was less busy in his doings, or funerals scarcer during his dynasty; but only that he had, by some means or other, contrived to force all those who had ventured to contest the palm with him, to quit the field. He was large and robust in person, and his ruby visage showed that if he grew fat upon drugs, it was not by swallowing them himself. It was never exactly ascertained from what college the Doctor had received his diploma; nor was he very forward to exhibit his credentials. When hard pressed, however, he would produce a musty old roll of parchment, with a red seal as broad as the palm of his hand, which looked as if it might have been the identical diploma of the great Boerhaave himself, and some cramp manuscript of a dozen pages, in an unknown tongue, said by the Doctor

to be his Greek thesis. These documents were enough to satisfy the doubts of the most sceptical. By the simple country
people, far and near, the Doctor was regarded, in point of
occult knowledge and skill, as a second Faustus. It is true the
village lawyer, a rival in popularity, used to whisper, that the
Doctor's Greek thesis was nothing but a bundle of prescriptions for the bots, wind-galls, spavins, and other veterinary
complaints, written in high Dutch by a Hessian horse doctor;
that the diploma was all a sham, and that Ephraim was no
more a doctor than his jack-ass. But these assertions were all
put down to the score of envy on the part of the lawyer. Be
this as it may, on the strength of one or two remarkable cures,
which he was said to have performed, and by dint of whee-
dling some and bullying others, it was certain that Ramshorne had worked himself into very good practice. The Doctor united in his own person, the attributes of apothecary and
physician; and as he vended, as well as prescribed his own
drugs, it was not his interest to stint his patients in their enormous boluses, or nauseous draughts. His former medical student had been worried into a consumption over the mortar
and pestle; in consequence of which, he had pitched upon me
for his successor.

'By the kindness of a few friends, I was fitted out with the
necessary requisitions for my metamorphosis. The Doctor required no fee, and, in consideration of certain little services
to be rendered him, such as taking care of his horse, cleaning
his boots, running errands, and doing little jobs about the
house, had promised to board and lodge me, besides giving
me my professional education. So with a rusty suit of black,
and an old plaid cloak, behold equipped the disciple of Esculapius.

'I cannot describe my elation of mind, when I found myself
fairly installed in the Doctor's office. Golden visions floated
before my eyes. I fancied my fortune already made, and
blessed my happy star, that had fallen under the benign influence of so munificent a patron.

'The Doctor's office, as it was called *par excellence*, was a
little nook of a room, communicating with a larger apartment
denominated the shop. The paraphernalia of this latter place
had gotten somewhat into disorder since the last student had

gone away, and I soon learnt that it was to be my task to arrange the heterogeneous mass of bottles, boxes, and galli-pots, that were strewed about in promiscuous confusion. In the office, there was a greater appearance of order. A small regiment of musty looking books, were drawn up in line upon a couple of shelves, where, to judge from the superin-cumbent strata of dust, they appeared to have peacefully re-posed for many years. A ricketty wooden clock, which the Doctor had taken in part payment from a pedlar, and the vital functions of which, to use his own expression, had long since ceased to act, stood in one corner. A mouldy plaster bust of some unknown worthy, a few bottles of pickled, and one or two dried specimens of morbid anatomy, a small chest of drawers, a table, and a couple of chairs, completed the furni-ture of this *sanctum*. The single window commanded a view of the church-yard, in which, it was said, many of the Doc-tor's former patients were quietly slumbering. With a feeling of reverence I ventured to dislodge one of the dusty tomes, and began to try to puzzle out the hard words with which it abounded; when suddenly, as if he had been conjured back, like the evil one by Cornelius Agrippa's book, the Doctor made his appearance. With a gruff air, he snatched the vol-ume from my hands, and telling me not to meddle with what I could not understand, bade me go and take care of his horse, and make haste back, as he wanted me to spread a pitch plaster, and carry the same, with a bottle of his patent catholicon, to farmer Van Pelt, who had the rheumatism. On my return, I was ordered by Mrs. Ramshorne to split some wood, and kindle a fire in the parlour, as she expected com-pany; after which Miss Euphemia Ramshorne, a sentimental young lady, who was as crooked in person and crabbed in temper as her own name, despatched me to the village circu-lating library, in quest of the Mysteries of Udolpho. I soon found out that my place was no sinecure. The greater part of my time was occupied in compounding certain quack medi-cines of Ramshorne's own invention, from which he derived great celebrity, and no inconsiderable profit. Besides his patent catholicon, and universal panacea, there was his anti-pertusso-balsamico drops, his patent calorific refrigerating anodyne, and his golden restorative of nature. Into the business of compounding these, and other articles with similar high-sounding titles, I was gradually initiated, and soon acquired so much skill in their manipulation, that my services became indispensable to my master; so much so, that he was obliged to hire a little negro to take care of his horse, and clean his boots. What chiefly reconciled me to the drudgery of the shop, was the seeing how well the Doctor got paid for his villainous compounds. A mixture of a little brick dust, rosin, and treacle, dignified with the title of the anthelminthic amalgam, he sold for half a dollar; and a bottle of vinegar and alum, with a little rose water to give it a flavor, yclept the antiscrofulous abstergent lotion, brought twice that sum. I longed for the day when I should dispense my own medicines, and in my hours of castle-building, looked forward to fortunes far beyond those of the renowned Dr. Solomon. Alas! my fond hopes have been blighted in their bud. I have drunk deeply of the nauseous draught of adversity, and been forced to swallow many bitter pills of disappointment. But I find I am beginning to smell of the shop. I must return to my sad tale. The same accident, which not unfrequently before had put a sudden stop to the Doctor's patients' taking any more of his nostrums, at length prevented him from reaping any longer their golden harvest. One afternoon, after having dined with his friend, Squire Gobbledown, he came home, and complained of not feeling very well. By his directions, I prepared for him some of his elixir sanitatis, composed of brandy and bitters, of which he took an inordinate dose. Shortly after, he was seized with a fit of apoplexy, and before bedtime, in spite of all the drugs in the shop, which I poured down with unsparing hand, he had breathed his last. In three days, Ramshorne was quietly deposited in the church-yard, in the midst of those he had sent there before him.

'Having resided with the Doctor for several years, I had become pretty well known throughout the neighbourhood, particularly among the old ladies, whose good graces I had always sedulously cultivated. I accordingly resolved to commence quacking—I mean practising—on my own account. Having obtained my late master's stock of drugs from his widow at an easy rate, and displaying my own name in golden letters as his successor, to work I went, with the internal resolve that where Ramshorne had given one dose, I would give six.

'For a time, Fortune seemed to smile upon me, and everything went on well. All the old women were loud in sounding my praises, far and near. The medicaments of my master continued to be in demand, and treacle, brick dust, and alum came to a good market. Some drawbacks, however, I occasionally met with. Having purchased the patent right of one of Thompson's steam baths, in my first experiment I came near flaying alive a rheumatic tanner, who had submitted himself to the operation. By an unfortunate mistake in regulating the steam, he was nearly parboiled; and it was supposed that the thickness of his hide alone preserved his vitals uninjured. I was myself threatened with the fate of Marsyas, by the enraged sufferer; which he was happily prevented from attempting to inflict, by a return of his malady, which has never since left him. I, however, after this gave up steaming, and confined myself to regular practice. At length, either the charm of novelty wearing off, or people beginning to discover the inefficacy of the old nostrums, I was obliged to exert my wit to invent new ones. These I generally took the precaution to try upon cats or dogs, before using them upon the human system. They were, however, mostly of an innocent nature, and I satisfied my conscience with the reflection, that if they did no good, they could at least do no harm. Happy would it have been for me, could I always have done thus. Meeting with success in my first efforts, I by degrees ventured upon more active ingredients. At length, in an evil hour, I invented a curious mixture, composed of forty-nine different articles. This I dubbed in high flowing terms, "The Antidote to Death, or the Eternal Elixir of Longevity;" knowing full well, that though

"A rose might smell as sweet by any other name,"

yet would not my drugs find as good a sale under a more humble title. This cursed compound proved the antidote to all my hopes of success. Besides forcing me to quit the village in a confounded hurry, it has embittered my life ever since, and reduced me to the ragged and miserable plight in which you see me.

'I dare say you have met with that species of old women, so frequent in all country towns, who, seeming to have outlived the common enjoyments of life, and outworn the ordinary sources of excitement, seek fresh stimulus in scenes of distress, and appear to take a morbid pleasure in beholding the varieties of human suffering, and misery. One of the most noted characters in the village was an old beldame of this description. Granny Gordon, so she was familiarly denominated, was the rib of the village Vulcan, and the din of her eternal tongue, was only equalled by the ringing of her husband's anvil. Thin and withered away in person and redolent with snuff, she bore no small resemblance to a newly exhumed mummy, and to all appearance promised to last as long as one of those ancient dames of Egypt. Not a death, a burial, a fit of sickness, a casualty, nor any of the common calamities of life ever occurred in the vicinity, but Granny Gordon made it her especial business to be present. Wrapped in an old scarlet cloak—that hideous cloak! the thought of it makes me shudder—she might be seen hovering about the dwelling of the sick. Watching her opportunity, she would make her way into the patient's chamber, and disturb his repose with long dismal stories and ill-boding predictions; and if turned from the house, which was not unfrequently the case, she would depart, muttering threats and abuse.

'As the Indians propitiate the favor of the devil, so had I, in my eagerness to acquire popularity, made a firm friend and ally, though rather a troublesome one, of this old woman. She was one of my best customers, and, provided it was something new, and had a high-sounding name to recommend it, would take my most nauseous compounds with the greatest relish. Indeed the more disgusting was the dose, the greater in her opinion was its virtue.

'I had just corked the last bottle of my antidote, when a message came to tell me, that Granny Gordon had one of her old fits, and wanted some new doctor-stuff, as the old physic didn't do her any more good. Not having yet given my new pharmaceutic preparation a trial, I felt a little doubtful about its effects; but trusting to the toughness of the old woman's system, I ventured to send a potion, with directions to take it cautiously. Not many minutes had elapsed, before the mes-

senger returned, in breathless haste, to say that Mrs. Gordon
was much worse, and that though she had taken all the stuff,
they believed she was dying. With a vague foreboding of evil,
I seized my hat, and hastened to the blacksmith's. On entering the chamber my eyes were greeted with a sad spectacle.
Granny Gordon, bolstered up in the bed, holding in her hand
the bottle I had sent her, drained of its contents, sate gasping
for breath, and occasionally agitated by strong convulsions. A
cold sweat rested on her forehead, her eyes seemed dim and
glazed, her nose, which was usually of a ruby hue, was purple
and peaked, and her whole appearance evidently betokened
approaching dissolution.

'Around the bed were collected some half dozen withered
beldames, who scowled upon me, as I entered, with ill
omened visages. Her husband, a drunken brute, who used to
beat his better half six times a week, immediately began to
load me with abuse, accusing me of having poisoned his dear,
dear wife, and threatening to be the death of me, if she died.

'My conscience smote me. I felt stupified and bewildered,
and knew not which way to turn. At this moment, the patient
perceiving me, with a hideous contortion of countenance, the
expression of which I shall carry to my dying hour, and a
voice between a scream and a groan, held up the empty bottle, and exclaimed, "This is your doing, you villainous quack
you" (here she was seized with hiccup);—"you have poisoned me, you have" (here fearful spasms shook her whole
frame);—"but I'll be revenged; day and night my ghost shall
haunt"—here her voice became inarticulate, and shaking her
withered arm at me, she fell back, and, to my extreme horror,
gave up the ghost. This was too much for my nerves. I rushed
from the house, and ran home with the dying curse ringing
in my ears, fancying that I saw her hideous physiognomy,
grinning from every bush and tree that I passed. Knowing
that as soon as the noise of this affair should get abroad, the
village would be too hot to hold me, I resolved to decamp as
silently as possible. First throwing all my recently manufactured anodyne into the canal, that it should not rise in judgment against me, I made up a little bundle of clothes, and
taking my seat in the mail stage, which was passing at the
time and fortunately empty, in a couple of days I found my-

self in the great city of New York. Having a little money with
me, I hired a mean apartment in an obscure part of the city,
in the hope that I might remain concealed till all search after
me should be over, when I might find some opportunity of
getting employment, or of resuming my old profession, under
happier auspices. By degrees the few dollars I brought with
me were expended, and after pawning my watch and some of
my clothes, I found myself reduced to the last shilling. But
not the fear of impending starvation, nor the dread of a jail,
are to be compared to the horrors I nightly suffer. Granny
Gordon has been as good as her word. Every night, at the
solemn hour of twelve' (here he looked fearfully around)—
'her ghost appears to me, wrapped in a red cloak, with her
grey hairs streaming from beneath an old nightcap of the
same color, brandishing the vial, and accusing me of having
poisoned her. These visitations have at length become so insupportable, that I have resolved to return and give myself up
to justice; for I feel that hanging itself is better than this state
of torment.'

Here the young man ceased. I plainly saw that he was a
little disordered in his intellect. To comfort him, however, I
told him, that if he had killed fifty old women, they could do
nothing to him, if he had done it professionally. And as for
the ghost, we would take means to have that put at rest, when
we reached Utica.

About the grey of the morning, we arrived at the place of
our destination. My *protégé* having unburthened his mind,
seemed more at his ease, and taking a mint julap, prepared to
accompany me on shore. As we were leaving the boat, several
persons in a wagon drove down to the wharf. As soon as my
companion observed them, he exclaimed with a start of surprise, 'Hang me, if there isn't old Graham the sheriff, with
lawyer Dickson, and Bill Gordon come to take me.' As he
spoke, his foot slipping, he lost his balance, and fell backwards into the canal. We drew him from the water, and as
soon as the persons in the wagon perceived him, they one
and all sprang out, and ran up with the greatest expressions
of joyful surprise. 'Why Hippy, my lad,' exclaimed the sheriff,
'where have you been? All our town has been in a snarl about
you. We all supposed you had been forcibly abducted. Judge

Bates offered a reward of twenty dollars for your corpse. We have dragged the canal for more than a mile, and found a mess of bottles, which made us think you had been spirited away. Betsey Wilkins made her affadavit, that she heard Bill Gordon swear that he would take your life, and here you see we have brought him down to have his trial. But come, come, jump in the wagon, we'll take you up to the tavern, to get your duds dried, and tell you all about it.'

Here a brawny fellow with a smutty face, who I found was Gordon the blacksmith, came up, and shaking Hippocrates by the hand, said, 'By goles, Doctor, I am glad to see you. If you hadn't come back, I believe it would have gone hard with me. Come, man, you must forgive the hard words I gave you. My old woman soon got well of her fit, after you went away, and says she thinks the stuff did her a mortal sight o' good.'

It is impossible to describe the singular expression the countenance of the young man now exhibited. For some time he stood in mute amazement, shaking with cold, and gazing alternately at each of his friends as they addressed him; and it required their reiterated assurances to convince him, that Granny Gordon was still in the land of the living, and that he had not been haunted by a veritable ghost.

Wishing to obtain a further explanation of this strange scene, I accompanied them to the tavern. A plain looking man in a farmer's dress, who was of the party, confirmed what the blacksmith had said, as to the supposed death of his wife, and her subsequent recovery. 'She was only in a swoond,' said he, 'but came to, soon after the Doctor had left her.' He added that it was his private opinion, that she would now last for-ever. He spoke of Hippocrates as a 'nation smart doctor, who had a power of larning, but gave severe doses.'

After discussing a good breakfast, my young friend thanked me for the sympathy and interest I had taken in his behalf. He told me he intended returning to the practice of his profession. I admonished him to be more careful in the exhi-bition of his patent medicines, telling him that all old women had not nine lives. He shook hands with me, and, gaily jump-ing into the wagon, rode off with his friends.

The Wives of the Dead

The following story, the simple and domestic incidents of which may be deemed scarcely worth relating, after such a lapse of time, awakened some degree of interest, a hundred years ago, in a principal seaport of the Bay Province. The rainy twilight of an autumn day; a parlor on the second floor of a small house, plainly furnished, as beseemed the middling circumstances of its inhabitants, yet decorated with little curiosities from beyond the sea, and a few delicate specimens of Indian manufacture,—these are the only particulars to be premised in regard to scene and season. Two young and comely women sat together by the fireside, nursing their mutual and peculiar sorrows. They were the recent brides of two brothers, a sailor and a landsman, and two successive days had brought tidings of the death of each, by the chances of Canadian warfare, and the tempestuous Atlantic. The universal sympathy excited by this bereavement, drew numerous condoling guests to the habitation of the widowed sisters. Several, among whom was the minister, had remained till the verge of evening; when one by one, whispering many comfortable passages of Scripture, that were answered by more abundant tears, they took their leave and departed to their own happier homes. The mourners, though not insensible to the kindness of their friends, had yearned to be left alone. United, as they had been, by the relationship of the living, and now more closely so by that of the dead, each felt as if whatever consolation her grief admitted, were to be found in the bosom of the other. They joined their hearts, and wept together silently. But after an hour of such indulgence, one of the sisters, all of whose emotions were influenced by her mild, quiet, yet not feeble character, began to recollect the precepts of resignation and endurance, which piety had taught her, when she did not think to need them. Her misfortune, besides, as earliest known, should earliest cease to interfere with her regular course of duties; accordingly, having placed the table before the fire, and arranged a frugal meal, she took the hand of her companion.

'Come, dearest sister; you have eaten not a morsel to-day,' she said. 'Arise, I pray you, and let us ask a blessing on that which is provided for us.'

Her sister-in-law was of a lively and irritable temperament, and the first pangs of her sorrow had been expressed by shrieks and passionate lamentation. She now shrunk from Mary's words, like a wounded sufferer from a hand that revives the throb.

'There is no blessing left for me, neither will I ask it,' cried Margaret, with a fresh burst of tears. 'Would it were His will that I might never taste food more.'

Yet she trembled at these rebellious expressions, almost as soon as they were uttered, and, by degrees, Mary succeeded in bringing her sister's mind nearer to the situation of her own. Time went on, and their usual hour of repose arrived. The brothers and their brides, entering the married state with no more than the slender means which then sanctioned such a step, had confederated themselves in one household, with equal rights to the parlor, and claiming exclusive privileges in two sleeping rooms contiguous to it. Thither the widowed ones retired, after heaping ashes upon the dying embers of their fire, and placing a lighted lamp upon the hearth. The doors of both chambers were left open, so that a part of the interior of each, and the beds with their unclosed curtains, were reciprocally visible. Sleep did not steal upon the sisters at one and the same time. Mary experienced the effect often consequent upon grief quietly borne, and soon sunk into temporary forgetfulness, while Margaret became more disturbed and feverish, in proportion as the night advanced with its deepest and stillest hours. She lay listening to the drops of rain, that came down in monotonous succession, unswayed by a breath of wind; and a nervous impulse continually caused her to lift her head from the pillow, and gaze into Mary's chamber and the intermediate apartment. The cold light of the lamp threw the shadows of the furniture up against the wall, stamping them immoveably there, except when they were shaken by a sudden flicker of the flame. Two vacant arm-chairs were in their old positions on opposite sides of the hearth, where the brothers had been wont to sit in young and laughing dignity, as heads of families; two humbler seats were near them, the true thrones of that little empire, where Mary and herself had exercised in love, a power that love had won. The cheerful radiance of the fire had shone upon the happy circle, and the dead glimmer of the lamp might have befitted their reunion now. While Margaret groaned in bitterness, she heard a knock at the street-door.

'How would my heart have leapt at that sound but yesterday!' thought she, remembering the anxiety with which she had long awaited tidings from her husband. 'I care not for it now; let them begone, for I will not arise.'

But even while a sort of childish fretfulness made her thus resolve, she was breathing hurriedly, and straining her ears to catch a repetition of the summons. It is difficult to be convinced of the death of one whom we have deemed another self. The knocking was now renewed in slow and regular strokes, apparently given with the soft end of a doubled fist, and was accompanied by words, faintly heard through several thicknesses of wall. Margaret looked to her sister's chamber, and beheld her still lying in the depths of sleep. She arose, placed her foot upon the floor, and slightly arrayed herself, trembling between fear and eagerness as she did so.

'Heaven help me!' sighed she. 'I have nothing left to fear, and methinks I am ten times more a coward than ever.'

Seizing the lamp from the hearth, she hastened to the window that overlooked the street-door. It was a lattice, turning upon hinges; and having thrown it back, she stretched her head a little way into the moist atmosphere. A lantern was reddening the front of the house, and melting its light in the neighboring puddles, while a deluge of darkness overwhelmed every other object. As the window grated on its hinges, a man in a broad brimmed hat and blanket-coat, stepped from under the shelter of the projecting story, and looked upward to discover whom his application had aroused. Margaret knew him as a friendly innkeeper of the town.

'What would you have, Goodman Parker?' cried the widow.

'Lack-a-day, is it you, Mistress Margaret?' replied the innkeeper. 'I was afraid it might be your sister Mary; for I hate to see a young woman in trouble, when I haven't a word of comfort to whisper her.'

'For Heaven's sake, what news do you bring?' screamed Margaret.

'Why, there has been an express through the town within this half hour,' said Goodman Parker, 'travelling from the eastern jurisdiction with letters from the governor and council. He tarried at my house to refresh himself with a drop and a morsel, and I asked him what tidings on the frontiers. He tells me we had the better in the skirmish you wot of, and that thirteen men reported slain are well and sound, and your husband among them. Besides, he is appointed of the escort to bring the captivated Frenchers and Indians home to the province jail. I judged you wouldn't mind being broke of your rest, and so I stept over to tell you. Good night.'

So saying, the honest man departed; and his lantern gleamed along the street, bringing to view indistinct shapes of things, and the fragments of a world, like order glimmering through chaos, or memory roaming over the past. But Margaret staid not to watch these picturesque effects. Joy flashed into her heart, and lighted it up at once, and breathless, and with winged steps, she flew to the bedside of her sister. She paused, however, at the door of the chamber, while a thought of pain broke in upon her.

'Poor Mary!' said she to herself. 'Shall I waken her, to feel her sorrow sharpened by my happiness? No; I will keep it within my own bosom till the morrow.'

She approached the bed to discover if Mary's sleep were peaceful. Her face was turned partly inward to the pillow, and had been hidden there to weep; but a look of motionless contentment was now visible upon it, as if her heart, like a deep lake, had grown calm because its dead had sunk down so far within. Happy is it, and strange, that the lighter sorrows are those from which dreams are chiefly fabricated. Margaret shrunk from disturbing her sister-in-law, and felt as if her own better fortune, had rendered her involuntarily unfaithful, and as if altered and diminished affection must be the consequence of the disclosure she had to make. With a sudden step, she turned away. But joy could not long be repressed, even by circumstances that would have excited heavy grief at another moment. Her mind was thronged with delightful thoughts, till sleep stole on and transformed them to visions, more delightful and more wild, like the breath of winter, (but what a cold comparison!) working fantastic tracery upon a window.

When the night was far advanced, Mary awoke with a sudden start. A vivid dream had latterly involved her in its unreal life, of which, however, she could only remember that it had been broken in upon at the most interesting point. For a little time, slumber hung about her like a morning mist, hindering her from perceiving the distinct outline of her situation. She listened with imperfect consciousness to two or three volleys of a rapid and eager knocking; and first she deemed the noise a matter of course, like the breath she drew; next, it appeared a thing in which she had no concern; and lastly, she became aware that it was a summons necessary to be obeyed. At the same moment, the pang of recollection darted into her mind; the pall of sleep was thrown back from the face of grief; the dim light of the chamber, and the objects therein revealed, had retained all her suspended ideas, and restored them as soon as she unclosed her eyes. Again, there was a quick peal upon the street-door. Fearing that her sister would also be disturbed, Mary wrapped herself in a cloak and hood, took the lamp from the hearth, and hastened to the window. By some accident, it had been left unhasped, and yielded easily to her hand.

'Who's there?' asked Mary, trembling as she looked forth.

The storm was over, and the moon was up; it shone upon broken clouds above, and below upon houses black with moisture, and upon little lakes of the fallen rain, curling into silver beneath the quick enchantment of a breeze. A young man in a sailor's dress, wet as if he had come out of the depths of the sea, stood alone under the window. Mary recognized him as one whose livelihood was gained by short voyages along the coast; nor did she forget, that, previous to her marriage, he had been an unsuccessful wooer of her own.

'What do you seek here, Stephen?' said she.

'Cheer up, Mary, for I seek to comfort you,' answered the rejected lover. 'You must know I got home not ten minutes ago, and the first thing my good mother told me was the news about your husband. So, without saying a word to the old woman, I clapt on my hat, and ran out of the house. I couldn't have slept a wink before speaking to you, Mary, for the sake of old times.'

'Stephen, I thought better of you!' exclaimed the widow, with gushing tears, and preparing to close the lattice; for she was no whit inclined to imitate the first wife of Zadig.

'But stop, and hear my story out,' cried the young sailor. 'I tell you we spoke a brig yesterday afternoon, bound in from Old England. And who do you think I saw standing on deck, well and hearty, only a bit thinner than he was five months ago?'

Mary leaned from the window, but could not speak.

'Why, it was your husband himself,' continued the generous seaman. 'He and three others saved themselves on a spar, when the Blessing turned bottom upwards. The brig will beat into the bay by daylight, with this wind, and you'll see him here tomorrow. There's the comfort I bring you, Mary, and so good night.'

He hurried away, while Mary watched him with a doubt of waking reality, that seemed stronger or weaker as he alternately entered the shade of the houses, or emerged into the broad streaks of moonlight. Gradually, however, a blessed flood of conviction swelled into her heart, in strength enough to overwhelm her, had its increase been more abrupt. Her first impulse was to rouse her sister-in-law, and communicate the new-born gladness. She opened the chamber-door, which had been closed in the course of the night, though not latched, advanced to the bedside, and was about to lay her hand upon the slumberer's shoulder. But then she remembered that Margaret would awake to thoughts of death and woe, rendered not the less bitter by their contrast with her own felicity. She suffered the rays of the lamp to fall upon the unconscious form of the bereaved one. Margaret lay in unquiet sleep, and the drapery was displaced around her; her young cheek was rosy-tinted, and her lips half opened in a vivid smile; an expression of joy, debarred its passage by her sealed eyelids, struggled forth like incense from the whole countenance.

'My poor sister! you will waken too soon from that happy dream,' thought Mary.

Before retiring, she set down the lamp and endeavored to arrange the bed-clothes, so that the chill air might not do harm to the feverish slumberer. But her hand trembled against Margaret's neck, a tear also fell upon her cheek, and she suddenly awoke.

My Kinsman, Major Molineux

AFTER the kings of Great Britain had assumed the right of appointing the colonial governors, the measures of the latter seldom met with the ready and general approbation, which had been paid to those of their predecessors, under the original charters. The people looked with most jealous scrutiny to the exercise of power, which did not emanate from themselves, and they usually rewarded the rulers with slender gratitude, for the compliances, by which, in softening their instructions from beyond the sea, they had incurred the reprehension of those who gave them. The annals of Massachusetts Bay will inform us, that of six governors, in the space of about forty years from the surrender of the old charter, under James II., two were imprisoned by a popular insurrection; a third, as Hutchinson inclines to believe, was driven from the province by the whizzing of a musket ball; a fourth, in the opinion of the same historian, was hastened to his grave by continual bickerings with the House of Representatives; and the remaining two, as well as their successors, till the Revolution, were favored with few and brief intervals of peaceful sway. The inferior members of the court party, in times of high political excitement, led scarcely a more desirable life. These remarks may serve as preface to the following adventures, which chanced upon a summer night, not far from a hundred years ago. The reader, in order to avoid a long and dry detail of colonial affairs, is requested to dispense with an account of the train of circumstances, that had caused much temporary inflammation of the popular mind.

It was near nine o'clock of a moonlight evening, when a boat crossed the ferry with a single passenger, who had obtained his conveyance, at that unusual hour, by the promise of an extra fare. While he stood on the landing-place, searching in either pocket for the means of fulfilling his agreement, the ferryman lifted a lantern, by the aid of which, and the newly risen moon, he took a very accurate survey of the stranger's figure. He was a youth of barely eighteen years, evidently country-bred, and now, as it should seem, upon his first visit to town. He was clad in a coarse grey coat, well worn, but in excellent repair; his under garments were durably constructed of leather, and sat tight to a pair of serviceable and well-shaped limbs; his stockings of blue yarn, were the incontrovertible handiwork of a mother or a sister; and on his head was a three-cornered hat, which in its better days had perhaps sheltered the graver brow of the lad's father. Under his left arm was a heavy cudgel, formed of an oak sapling, and retaining a part of the hardened root; and his equipment was completed by a wallet, not so abundantly stocked as to incommode the vigorous shoulders on which it hung. Brown, curly hair, well-shaped features, and bright, cheerful eyes, were nature's gifts, and worth all that art could have done for his adornment.

The youth, one of whose names was Robin, finally drew from his pocket the half of a little province-bill of five shillings, which, in the depreciation of that sort of currency, did but satisfy the ferryman's demand, with the surplus of a sexangular piece of parchment valued at three pence. He then walked forward into the town, with as light a step, as if his day's journey had not already exceeded thirty miles, and with as eager an eye, as if he were entering London city, instead of the little metropolis of a New England colony. Before Robin had proceeded far, however, it occurred to him, that he knew not whither to direct his steps; so he paused, and looked up and down the narrow street, scrutinizing the small and mean wooden buildings, that were scattered on either side.

'This low hovel cannot be my kinsman's dwelling,' thought he, 'nor yonder old house, where the moonlight enters at the broken casement; and truly I see none hereabouts that might be worthy of him. It would have been wise to inquire my way of the ferryman, and doubtless he would have gone with me, and earned a shilling from the Major for his pains. But the next man I meet will do as well.'

He resumed his walk, and was glad to perceive that the street now became wider, and the houses more respectable in their appearance. He soon discerned a figure moving on moderately in advance, and hastened his steps to overtake it. As Robin drew nigh, he saw that the passenger was a man in years, with a full periwig of grey hair, a wide-skirted coat of

dark cloth, and silk stockings rolled about his knees. He carried a long and polished cane, which he struck down perpendicularly before him, at every step; and at regular intervals he
uttered two successive hems, of a peculiarly solemn and sepulchral intonation. Having made these observations, Robin
laid hold of the skirt of the old man's coat, just when the light
from the open door and windows of a barber's shop, fell
upon both their figures.

'Good evening to you, honored Sir,' said he, making a low
bow, and still retaining his hold of the skirt. 'I pray you to
tell me whereabouts is the dwelling of my kinsman, Major
Molineux?'

The youth's question was uttered very loudly; and one of
the barbers, whose razor was descending on a well-soaped
chin, and another who was dressing a Ramillies wig, left their
occupations, and came to the door. The citizen, in the meantime, turned a long favored countenance upon Robin, and
answered him in a tone of excessive anger and annoyance. His
two sepulchral hems, however, broke into the very centre of
his rebuke, with most singular effect, like a thought of the
cold grave obtruding among wrathful passions.

'Let go my garment, fellow! I tell you, I know not the man
you speak of. What! I have authority, I have—hem, hem—
authority; and if this be the respect you show your betters,
your feet shall be brought acquainted with the stocks, by daylight, tomorrow morning!'

Robin released the old man's skirt, and hastened away, pursued by an ill-mannered roar of laughter from the barber's
shop. He was at first considerably surprised by the result of
his question, but, being a shrewd youth, soon thought himself able to account for the mystery.

'This is some country representative,' was his conclusion,
'who has never seen the inside of my kinsman's door, and
lacks the breeding to answer a stranger civilly. The man is
old, or verily—I might be tempted to turn back and smite
him on the nose. Ah, Robin, Robin! even the barber's boys
laugh at you, for choosing such a guide! You will be wiser in
time, friend Robin.'

He now became entangled in a succession of crooked and
narrow streets, which crossed each other, and meandered at

no great distance from the water-side. The smell of tar was obvious to his nostrils, the masts of vessels pierced the moonlight above the tops of the buildings, and the numerous signs, which Robin paused to read, informed him that he was near the centre of business. But the streets were empty, the shops were closed, and lights were visible only in the second stories of a few dwelling-houses. At length, on the corner of a narrow lane, through which he was passing, he beheld the broad countenance of a British hero swinging before the door of an inn, whence proceeded the voices of many guests. The casement of one of the lower windows was thrown back, and a very thin curtain permitted Robin to distinguish a party at supper, round a well-furnished table. The fragrance of the good cheer steamed forth into the outer air, and the youth could not fail to recollect, that the last remnant of his travelling stock of provision had yielded to his morning appetite, and that noon had found, and left him, dinnerless.

'Oh, that a parchment three-penny might give me a right to sit down at yonder table,' said Robin, with a sigh. 'But the Major will make me welcome to the best of his victuals; so I will even step boldly in, and inquire my way to his dwelling.'

He entered the tavern, and was guided by the murmur of voices, and fumes of tobacco, to the public room. It was a long and low apartment, with oaken walls, grown dark in the continual smoke, and a floor, which was thickly sanded, but of no immaculate purity. A number of persons, the larger part of whom appeared to be mariners, or in some way connected with the sea, occupied the wooden benches, or leather-bottomed chairs, conversing on various matters, and occasionally lending their attention to some topic of general interest. Three or four little groups were draining as many bowls of punch, which the great West India trade had long since made a familiar drink in the colony. Others, who had the aspect of men who lived by regular and laborious handicraft, preferred the insulated bliss of an unshared potation, and became more taciturn under its influence. Nearly all, in short, evinced a predilection for the Good Creature in some of its various shapes, for this is a vice, to which, as the Fast-day sermons of a hundred years ago will testify, we have a long hereditary claim. The only guests to whom Robin's sympathies inclined

him, were two or three sheepish countrymen, who were using
the inn somewhat after the fashion of a Turkish Caravansary;
they had gotten themselves into the darkest corner of the
room, and, heedless of the Nicotian atmosphere, were sup-
ping on the bread of their own ovens, and the bacon cured
in their own chimney-smoke. But though Robin felt a sort of
brotherhood with these strangers, his eyes were attracted
from them, to a person who stood near the door, holding
whispered conversation with a group of ill-dressed associates.
His features were separately striking almost to grotesqueness,
and the whole face left a deep impression in the memory. The
forehead bulged out into a double prominence, with a vale
between; the nose came boldly forth in an irregular curve,
and its bridge was of more than a finger's breadth; the eyebrows were deep and shaggy, and the eyes glowed beneath
them like fire in a cave.

While Robin deliberated of whom to inquire respecting his
kinsman's dwelling, he was accosted by the innkeeper, a little
man in a stained white apron, who had come to pay his
professional welcome to the stranger. Being in the second
generation from a French Protestant, he seemed to have inherited the courtesy of his parent nation; but no variety of
circumstance was ever known to change his voice from the
one shrill note in which he now addressed Robin.

'From the country, I presume, Sir?' said he, with a profound bow. 'Beg to congratulate you on your arrival, and
trust you intend a long stay with us. Fine town here, Sir,
beautiful buildings, and much that may interest a stranger.
May I hope for the honor of your commands in respect to
supper?'

'The man sees a family likeness! the rogue has guessed that
I am related to the Major!' thought Robin, who had hitherto
experienced little superfluous civility.

All eyes were now turned on the country lad, standing at
the door, in his worn three-cornered hat, grey coat, leather
breeches, and blue yarn stockings, leaning on an oaken cudgel, and bearing a wallet on his back.

Robin replied to the courteous innkeeper, with such an as-
sumption of consequence, as befitted the Major's relative.

'My honest friend,' he said, 'I shall make it a point to patronize your house on some occasion, when—' here he could not help lowering his voice—'I may have more than a parchment three-pence in my pocket. My present business,' continued he, speaking with lofty confidence, 'is merely to inquire the way to the dwelling of my kinsman, Major Molineux.'

There was a sudden and general movement in the room, which Robin interpreted as expressing the eagerness of each individual to become his guide. But the innkeeper turned his eyes to a written paper on the wall, which he read, or seemed to read, with occasional recurrences to the young man's figure.

'What have we here?' said he, breaking his speech into little dry fragments. ' "Left the house of the subscriber, bounden servant, Hezekiah Mudge—had on, when he went away, grey coat, leather breeches, master's third best hat. One pound currency reward to whoever shall lodge him in any jail in the province." Better trudge, boy, better trudge!'

Robin had begun to draw his hand towards the lighter end of the oak cudgel, but a strange hostility in every countenance, induced him to relinquish his purpose of breaking the courteous innkeeper's head. As he turned to leave the room, he encountered a sneering glance from the bold-featured personage whom he had before noticed; and no sooner was he beyond the door, than he heard a general laugh, in which the innkeeper's voice might be distinguished, like the dropping of small stones into a kettle.

'Now is it not strange,' thought Robin, with his usual shrewdness, 'is it not strange, that the confession of an empty pocket, should outweigh the name of my kinsman, Major Molineux? Oh, if I had one of these grinning rascals in the woods, where I and my oak sapling grew up together, I would teach him that my arm is heavy, though my purse be light!'

On turning the corner of the narrow lane, Robin found himself in a spacious street, with an unbroken line of lofty houses on each side, and a steepled building at the upper end, whence the ringing of a bell announced the hour of nine. The light of the moon, and the lamps from numerous shop windows, discovered people promenading on the pavement, and amongst them, Robin hoped to recognize his hitherto inscrutable relative. The result of his former inquiries made him unwilling to hazard another, in a scene of such publicity, and he determined to walk slowly and silently up the street, thrusting his face close to that of every elderly gentleman, in search of the Major's lineaments. In his progress, Robin encountered many gay and gallant figures. Embroidered garments, of showy colors, enormous periwigs, gold-laced hats, and silver hilted swords, glided past him and dazzled his optics. Travelled youths, imitators of the European fine gentlemen of the period, trod jauntily along, half-dancing to the fashionable tunes which they hummed, and making poor Robin ashamed of his quiet and natural gait. At length, after many pauses to examine the gorgeous display of goods in the shop windows, and after suffering some rebukes for the impertinence of his scrutiny into people's faces, the Major's kinsman found himself near the steepled building, still unsuccessful in his search. As yet, however, he had seen only one side of the thronged street; so Robin crossed, and continued the same sort of inquisition down the opposite pavement, with stronger hopes than the philosopher seeking an honest man, but with no better fortune. He had arrived about midway towards the lower end, from which his course began, when he overheard the approach of some one, who struck down a cane on the flag-stones at every step, uttering, at regular intervals, two sepulchral hems.

'Mercy on us!' quoth Robin, recognizing the sound.

Turning a corner, which chanced to be close at his right hand, he hastened to pursue his researches, in some other part of the town. His patience was now wearing low, and he seemed to feel more fatigue from his rambles since he crossed the ferry, than from his journey of several days on the other side. Hunger also pleaded loudly within him, and Robin began to balance the propriety of demanding, violently and with lifted cudgel, the necessary guidance from the first solitary passenger, whom he should meet. While a resolution to this effect was gaining strength, he entered a street of mean appearance, on either side of which, a row of ill-built houses was straggling towards the harbor. The moonlight fell upon no passenger along the whole extent, but in the third domicile which Robin passed, there was a half-opened door, and his keen glance detected a woman's garment within.

'My luck may be better here,' said he to himself.

Accordingly, he approached the door, and beheld it shut closer as he did so; yet an open space remained, sufficing for the fair occupant to observe the stranger, without a corresponding display on her part. All that Robin could discern was a strip of scarlet petticoat, and the occasional sparkle of an eye, as if the moonbeams were trembling on some bright thing.

'Pretty mistress,'—for I may call her so with a good conscience, thought the shrewd youth, since I know nothing to the contrary—'my sweet pretty mistress, will you be kind enough to tell me whereabouts I must seek the dwelling of my kinsman, Major Molineux?'

Robin's voice was plaintive and winning, and the female, seeing nothing to be shunned in the handsome country youth, thrust open the door, and came forth into the moonlight. She was a dainty little figure, with a white neck, round arms, and a slender waist, at the extremity of which her scarlet petticoat jutted out over a hoop, as if she were standing in a balloon. Moreover, her face was oval and pretty, her hair dark beneath the little cap, and her bright eyes possessed a sly freedom, which triumphed over those of Robin.

'Major Molineux dwells here,' said this fair woman.

Now her voice was the sweetest Robin had heard that night, the airy counterpart of a stream of melted silver; yet he could not help doubting whether that sweet voice spoke Gospel truth. He looked up and down the mean street, and then surveyed the house before which they stood. It was a small, dark edifice of two stories, the second of which projected over the lower floor; and the front apartment had the aspect of a shop for petty commodities.

'Now truly I am in luck,' replied Robin, cunningly, 'and so indeed is my kinsman, the Major, in having so pretty a housekeeper. But I prithee trouble him to step to the door; I will deliver him a message from his friends in the country, and then go back to my lodgings at the inn.'

'Nay, the Major has been a-bed this hour or more,' said the

lady of the scarlet petticoat; 'and it would be to little purpose
to disturb him to-night, seeing his evening draught was of
the strongest. But he is a kind-hearted man, and it would be
as much as my life's worth, to let a kinsman of his turn away
from the door. You are the good old gentleman's very picture, and I could swear that was his rainy-weather hat. Also,
he has garments very much resembling those leather—But
come in, I pray, for I bid you hearty welcome in his name.'

So saying, the fair and hospitable dame took our hero by
the hand; and though the touch was light, and the force was
gentleness, and though Robin read in her eyes what he did
not hear in her words, yet the slender waisted woman, in the
scarlet petticoat, proved stronger than the athletic country
youth. She had drawn his half-willing footsteps nearly to the
threshold, when the opening of a door in the neighborhood,
startled the Major's housekeeper, and, leaving the Major's
kinsman, she vanished speedily into her own domicile. A
heavy yawn preceded the appearance of a man, who, like the
Moonshine of Pyramus and Thisbe, carried a lantern, needlessly aiding his sister luminary in the heavens. As he walked
sleepily up the street, he turned his broad, dull face on Robin,
and displayed a long staff, spiked at the end.

'Home, vagabond, home!' said the watchman, in accents
that seemed to fall asleep as soon as they were uttered.
'Home, or we'll set you in the stocks by peep of day!'

'This is the second hint of the kind,' thought Robin. 'I
wish they would end my difficulties, by setting me there to-
night.'

Nevertheless, the youth felt an instinctive antipathy towards the guardian of midnight order, which at first prevented him from asking his usual question. But just when the
man was about to vanish behind the corner, Robin resolved
not to lose the opportunity, and shouted lustily after him—

'I say, friend! will you guide me to the house of my kinsman, Major Molineux?'

The watchman made no reply, but turned the corner and
was gone; yet Robin seemed to hear the sound of drowsy
laughter stealing along the solitary street. At that moment,
also, a pleasant titter saluted him from the open window
above his head; he looked up, and caught the sparkle of a

saucy eye; a round arm beckoned to him, and next he heard light footsteps descending the staircase within. But Robin, being of the household of a New England clergyman, was a good youth, as well as a shrewd one; so he resisted temptation, and fled away.

He now roamed desperately, and at random, through the town, almost ready to believe that a spell was on him, like that, by which a wizard of his country, had once kept three pursuers wandering, a whole winter night, within twenty paces of the cottage which they sought. The streets lay before him, strange and desolate, and the lights were extinguished in almost every house. Twice, however, little parties of men, among whom Robin distinguished individuals in outlandish attire, came hurrying along, but though on both occasions they paused to address him, such intercourse did not at all enlighten his perplexity. They did but utter a few words in some language of which Robin knew nothing, and perceiving his inability to answer, bestowed a curse upon him in plain English, and hastened away. Finally, the lad determined to knock at the door of every mansion that might appear worthy to be occupied by his kinsman, trusting that perseverance would overcome the fatality which had hitherto thwarted him. Firm in this resolve, he was passing beneath the walls of a church, which formed the corner of two streets, when, as he turned into the shade of its steeple, he encountered a bulky stranger, muffled in a cloak. The man was proceeding with the speed of earnest business, but Robin planted himself full before him, holding the oak cudgel with both hands across his body, as a bar to further passage.

'Halt, honest man, and answer me a question,' said he, very resolutely. 'Tell me, this instant, whereabouts is the dwelling of my kinsman, Major Molineux?'

'Keep your tongue between your teeth, fool, and let me pass,' said a deep, gruff voice, which Robin partly remembered. 'Let me pass, I say, or I'll strike you to the earth!'

'No, no, neighbor!' cried Robin, flourishing his cudgel, and then thrusting its larger end close to the man's muffled face. 'No, no, I'm not the fool you take me for, nor do you pass, till I have an answer to my question. Whereabouts is the dwelling of my kinsman, Major Molineux?'

The stranger, instead of attempting to force his passage, stept back into the moonlight, unmuffled his own face and stared full into that of Robin.

'Watch here an hour, and Major Molineux will pass by,' said he.

Robin gazed with dismay and astonishment, on the unprecedented physiognomy of the speaker. The forehead with its double prominence, the broad-hooked nose, the shaggy eyebrows, and fiery eyes, were those which he had noticed at the inn, but the man's complexion had undergone a singular, or, more properly, a two-fold change. One side of the face blazed of an intense red, while the other was black as midnight, the division line being in the broad bridge of the nose; and a mouth, which seemed to extend from ear to ear, was black or red, in contrast to the color of the cheek. The effect was as if two individual devils, a fiend of fire and a fiend of darkness, had united themselves to form this infernal visage. The stranger grinned in Robin's face, muffled his parti-colored features, and was out of sight in a moment.

'Strange things we travellers see!' ejaculated Robin.

He seated himself, however, upon the steps of the church-door, resolving to wait the appointed time for his kinsman's appearance. A few moments were consumed in philosophical speculations, upon the species of the *genus homo*, who had just left him, but having settled this point shrewdly, rationally, and satisfactorily, he was compelled to look elsewhere for amusement. And first he threw his eyes along the street; it was of more respectable appearance than most of those into which he had wandered, and the moon, 'creating, like the imaginative power, a beautiful strangeness in familiar objects,' gave something of romance to a scene, that might not have possessed it in the light of day. The irregular, and often quaint architecture of the houses, some of whose roofs were broken into numerous little peaks; while others ascended, steep and narrow, into a single point; and others again were square; the pure milk-white of some of their complexions, the aged darkness of others, and the thousand sparklings, reflected from bright substances in the plastered walls of many; these matters engaged Robin's attention for awhile, and then began to grow wearisome. Next he endeavored to define the forms of distant objects, starting away with almost ghostly indistinctness, just as his eye appeared to grasp them; and finally he took a minute survey of an edifice, which stood on the opposite side of the street, directly in front of the church-door, where he was stationed. It was a large square mansion, distinguished from its neighbors by a balcony, which rested on tall pillars, and by an elaborate Gothic window, communicating therewith.

'Perhaps this is the very house I have been seeking,' thought Robin.

Then he strove to speed away the time, by listening to a murmur, which swept continually along the street, yet was scarcely audible, except to an unaccustomed ear like his; it was a low, dull, dreamy sound, compounded of many noises, each of which was at too great a distance to be separately heard. Robin marvelled at this snore of a sleeping town, and marvelled more, whenever its continuity was broken, by now and then a distant shout, apparently loud where it originated. But altogether it was a sleep-inspiring sound, and to shake off its drowsy influence, Robin arose, and climbed a window-frame, that he might view the interior of the church. There the moonbeams came trembling in, and fell down upon the deserted pews, and extended along the quiet aisles. A fainter, yet more awful radiance, was hovering round the pulpit, and one solitary ray had dared to rest upon the opened page of the great Bible. Had Nature, in that deep hour, become a worshipper in the house, which man had builded? Or was that heavenly light the visible sanctity of the place, visible because no earthly and impure feet were within the walls? The scene made Robin's heart shiver with a sensation of loneliness, stronger than he had ever felt in the remotest depths of his native woods; so he turned away, and sat down again before the door. There were graves around the church, and now an uneasy thought obtruded into Robin's breast. What if the object of his search, which had been so often and so strangely thwarted, were all the time mouldering in his shroud? What if his kinsman should glide through yonder gate, and nod and smile to him in passing dimly by?

'Oh, that any breathing thing were here with me!' said Robin.

Recalling his thoughts from this uncomfortable track, he sent them over forest, hill, and stream, and attempted to imagine how that evening of ambiguity and weariness, had been spent by his father's household. He pictured them assembled at the door, beneath the tree, the great old tree, which had been spared for its huge twisted trunk, and venerable shade, when a thousand leafy brethren fell. There, at the going down of the summer sun, it was his father's custom to perform domestic worship, that the neighbors might come and join with him like brothers of the family, and that the wayfaring man might pause to drink at that fountain, and keep his heart pure by freshening the memory of home. Robin distinguished the seat of every individual of the little audience; he saw the good man in the midst, holding the Scriptures in the golden light that shone from the western clouds; he beheld him close the book, and all rise up to pray. He heard the old thanksgivings for daily mercies, the old supplications for their continuance, to which he had so often listened in weariness, but which were now among his dear remembrances. He perceived the slight inequality of his father's voice when he came to speak of the Absent One; he noted how his mother turned her face to the broad and knotted trunk; how his elder brother scorned, because the beard was rough upon his upper lip, to permit his features to be moved; how his younger sister drew down a low hanging branch before her eyes; and how the little one of all, whose sports had hitherto broken the decorum of the scene, understood the prayer for her playmate, and burst into clamorous grief. Then he saw them go in at the door; and when Robin would have entered also, the latch tinkled into its place, and he was excluded from his home.

'Am I here, or there?' cried Robin, starting; for all at once, when his thoughts had become visible and audible in a dream, the long, wide, solitary street shone out before him.

He aroused himself, and endeavored to fix his attention steadily upon the large edifice which he had surveyed before. But still his mind kept vibrating between fancy and reality; by turns, the pillars of the balcony lengthened into the tall, bare stems of pines, dwindled down to human figures, settled again in their true shape and size, and then commenced a new succession of changes. For a single moment, when he deemed himself awake, he could have sworn that a visage, one which he seemed to remember, yet could not absolutely name as his kinsman's, was looking towards him from the Gothic window. A deeper sleep wrestled with, and nearly overcame him, but fled at the sound of footsteps along the opposite pavement. Robin rubbed his eyes, discerned a man passing at the foot of the balcony, and addressed him in a loud, peevish, and lamentable cry.

'Halloo, friend! must I wait here all night for my kinsman, Major Molineux?'

The sleeping echoes awoke, and answered the voice; and the passenger, barely able to discern a figure sitting in the oblique shade of the steeple, traversed the street to obtain a nearer view. He was himself a gentleman in his prime, of open, intelligent, cheerful, and altogether prepossessing countenance. Perceiving a country youth, apparently homeless and without friends, he accosted him in a tone of real kindness, which had become strange to Robin's ears.

'Well, my good lad, why are you sitting here?' inquired he. 'Can I be of service to you in any way?'

'I am afraid not, Sir,' replied Robin, despondingly; 'yet I shall take it kindly, if you'll answer me a single question. I've been searching half the night for one Major Molineux; now, Sir, is there really such a person in these parts, or am I dreaming?'

'Major Molineux! The name is not altogether strange to me,' said the gentleman, smiling. 'Have you any objection to telling me the nature of your business with him?'

Then Robin briefly related that his father was a clergyman, settled on a small salary, at a long distance back in the country, and that he and Major Molineux were brothers' children. The Major, having inherited riches, and acquired civil and military rank, had visited his cousin in great pomp a year or two before; had manifested much interest in Robin and an elder brother, and, being childless himself, had thrown out hints respecting the future establishment of one of them in life. The elder brother was destined to succeed to the farm, which his father cultivated, in the interval of sacred duties; it was therefore determined that Robin should profit by his kinsman's generous intentions, especially as he had seemed to be rather the favorite, and was thought to possess other necessary endowments.

'For I have the name of being a shrewd youth,' observed Robin, in this part of his story.

'I doubt not you deserve it,' replied his new friend, good naturedly; 'but pray proceed.'

'Well, Sir, being nearly eighteen years old, and well-grown, as you see,' continued Robin, raising himself to his full height, 'I thought it high time to begin the world. So my mother and sister put me in handsome trim, and my father gave me half the remnant of his last year's salary, and five days ago I started for this place, to pay the Major a visit. But would you believe it, Sir? I crossed the ferry a little after dusk, and have yet found nobody that would show me the way to his dwelling; only an hour or two since, I was told to wait here, and Major Molineux would pass by.'

'Can you describe the man who told you this?' inquired the gentleman.

'Oh, he was a very ill-favored fellow, Sir,' replied Robin, 'with two great bumps on his forehead, a hook nose, fiery eyes, and, what struck me as the strangest, his face was of two different colors. Do you happen to know such a man, Sir?'

'Not intimately,' answered the stranger, 'but I chanced to meet him a little time previous to your stopping me. I believe you may trust his word, and that the Major will very shortly pass through this street. In the mean time, as I have a singular curiosity to witness your meeting, I will sit down here upon the steps, and bear you company.'

He seated himself accordingly, and soon engaged his companion in animated discourse. It was but of brief continuance, however, for a noise of shouting, which had long been remotely audible, drew so much nearer, that Robin inquired its cause.

'What may be the meaning of this uproar?' asked he. 'Truly, if your town be always as noisy, I shall find little sleep, while I am an inhabitant.'

'Why, indeed, friend Robin, there do appear to be three or four riotous fellows abroad to-night,' replied the gentleman. 'You must not expect all the stillness of your native woods, here in our streets. But the watch will shortly be at the heels of these lads, and—'

'Aye, and set them in the stocks by peep of day,' interrupted Robin, recollecting his own encounter with the drowsy lantern-bearer. 'But, dear Sir, if I may trust my ears, an army of watchmen would never make head against such a multitude of rioters. There were at least a thousand voices went to make up that one shout.'

'May not one man have several voices, Robin, as well as two complexions?' said his friend.

'Perhaps a man may; but Heaven forbid that a woman should!' responded the shrewd youth, thinking of the seductive tones of the Major's housekeeper.

The sounds of a trumpet in some neighboring street now became so evident and continual, that Robin's curiosity was strongly excited. In addition to the shouts, he heard frequent bursts from many instruments of discord, and a wild and confused laughter filled up the intervals. Robin rose from the steps, and looked wistfully towards a point, whither several people seemed to be hastening.

'Surely some prodigious merrymaking is going on,' exclaimed he. 'I have laughed very little since I left home, Sir, and should be sorry to lose an opportunity. Shall we just step round the corner by that darkish house, and take our share of the fun?'

'Sit down again, sit down, good Robin,' replied the gentleman, laying his hand on the skirt of the grey coat. 'You forget that we must wait here for your kinsman; and there is reason to believe that he will pass by, in the course of a very few moments.'

The near approach of the uproar had now disturbed the neighborhood; windows flew open on all sides; and many heads, in the attire of the pillow, and confused by sleep suddenly broken, were protruded to the gaze of whoever had leisure to observe them. Eager voices hailed each other from house to house, all demanding the explanation, which not a soul could give. Half-dressed men hurried towards the unknown commotion, stumbling as they went over the stone steps, that thrust themselves into the narrow foot-walk. The shouts, the laughter, and the tuneless bray, the antipodes of

music, came onward with increasing din, till scattered individuals, and then denser bodies, began to appear round a corner,
at the distance of a hundred yards.

'Will you recognize your kinsman, Robin, if he passes in
this crowd?' inquired the gentleman.

'Indeed, I can't warrant it, Sir; but I'll take my stand here,
and keep a bright look out,' answered Robin, descending to
the outer edge of the pavement.

A mighty stream of people now emptied into the street,
and came rolling slowly towards the church. A single horseman wheeled the corner in the midst of them, and close behind him came a band of fearful wind-instruments, sending
forth a fresher discord, now that no intervening buildings
kept it from the ear. Then a redder light disturbed the moonbeams, and a dense multitude of torches shone along the
street, concealing by their glare whatever object they illuminated. The single horseman, clad in a military dress, and bearing a drawn sword, rode onward as the leader, and, by his
fierce and variegated countenance, appeared like war personified; the red of one cheek was an emblem of fire and sword;
the blackness of the other betokened the mourning which attends them. In his train, were wild figures in the Indian dress,
and many fantastic shapes without a model, giving the whole
march a visionary air, as if a dream had broken forth from
some feverish brain, and were sweeping visibly through the
midnight streets. A mass of people, inactive, except as applauding spectators, hemmed the procession in, and several
women ran along the sidewalks, piercing the confusion of
heavier sounds, with their shrill voices of mirth or terror.

'The double-faced fellow has his eye upon me,' muttered
Robin, with an indefinite but uncomfortable idea, that he was
himself to bear a part in the pageantry.

The leader turned himself in the saddle, and fixed his glance
full upon the country youth, as the steed went slowly by.
When Robin had freed his eyes from those fiery ones, the
musicians were passing before him, and the torches were
close at hand; but the unsteady brightness of the latter
formed a veil which he could not penetrate. The rattling of
wheels over the stones sometimes found its way to his ear,
and confused traces of a human form appeared at intervals,

and then melted into the vivid light. A moment more, and
the leader thundered a command to halt; the trumpets
vomited a horrid breath, and held their peace; the shouts
and laughter of the people died away, and there remained
only a universal hum, nearly allied to silence. Right before
Robin's eyes was an uncovered cart. There the torches
blazed the brightest, there the moon shone out like day,
and there, in tar-and-feathery dignity, sate his kinsman, Major Molineux!

He was an elderly man, of large and majestic person, and
strong, square features, betokening a steady soul; but steady
as it was, his enemies had found the means to shake it. His
face was pale as death, and far more ghastly; the broad forehead was contracted in his agony, so that his eyebrows
formed one grizzled line; his eyes were red and wild, and the
foam hung white upon his quivering lip. His whole frame
was agitated by a quick, and continual tremor, which his
pride strove to quell, even in those circumstances of overwhelming humiliation. But perhaps the bitterest pang of all
was when his eyes met those of Robin; for he evidently knew
him on the instant, as the youth stood witnessing the foul
disgrace of a head that had grown grey in honor. They stared
at each other in silence, and Robin's knees shook, and his hair
bristled, with a mixture of pity and terror. Soon, however, a
bewildering excitement began to seize upon his mind; the
preceding adventures of the night, the unexpected appearance
of the crowd, the torches, the confused din, and the hush that
followed, the spectre of his kinsman reviled by that great multitude, all this, and more than all, a perception of tremendous
ridicule in the whole scene, affected him with a sort of mental
inebriety. At that moment a voice of sluggish merriment saluted Robin's ears; he turned instinctively, and just behind
the corner of the church stood the lantern-bearer, rubbing his
eyes, and drowsily enjoying the lad's amazement. Then he
heard a peal of laughter like the ringing of silvery bells; a
woman twitched his arm, a saucy eye met his, and he saw the
lady of the scarlet petticoat. A sharp, dry cachinnation appealed to his memory, and, standing on tiptoe in the crowd,
with his white apron over his head, he beheld the courteous
little innkeeper. And lastly, there sailed over the heads of the

multitude a great, broad laugh, broken in the midst by two sepulchral hems; thus—

'Haw, haw, haw—hem, hem—haw, haw, haw, haw!'

The sound proceeded from the balcony of the opposite edifice, and thither Robin turned his eyes. In front of the Gothic window stood the old citizen, wrapped in a wide gown, his grey periwig exchanged for a nightcap, which was thrust back from his forehead, and his silk stockings hanging down about his legs. He supported himself on his polished cane in a fit of convulsive merriment, which manifested itself on his solemn old features, like a funny inscription on a tomb-stone. Then Robin seemed to hear the voices of the barbers; of the guests of the inn; and of all who had made sport of him that night. The contagion was spreading among the multitude, when, all at once, it seized upon Robin, and he sent forth a shout of laughter that echoed through the street; every man shook his sides, every man emptied his lungs, but Robin's shout was the loudest there. The cloud-spirits peeped from their silvery islands, as the congregated mirth went roaring up the sky! The Man in the Moon heard the far bellow; 'Oho,' quoth he, 'the old Earth is frolicsome to-night!'

When there was a momentary calm in that tempestuous sea of sound, the leader gave the sign, the procession resumed its march. On they went, like fiends that throng in mockery round some dead potentate, mighty no more, but majestic still in his agony. On they went, in counterfeited pomp, in senseless uproar, in frenzied merriment, trampling all on an old man's heart. On swept the tumult, and left a silent street behind.

'Well, Robin, are you dreaming?' inquired the gentleman, laying his hand on the youth's shoulder.

Robin started, and withdrew his arm from the stone post, to which he had instinctively clung, while the living stream rolled by him. His cheek was somewhat pale, and his eye not quite so lively as in the earlier part of the evening.

'Will you be kind enough to show me the way to the ferry?' said he, after a moment's pause.

'You have then adopted a new subject of inquiry?' observed his companion, with a smile.

'Why, yes, Sir,' replied Robin, rather dryly. 'Thanks to you, and to my other friends, I have at last met my kinsman, and he will scarce desire to see my face again. I begin to grow weary of a town life, Sir. Will you show me the way to the ferry?'

'No, my good friend Robin, not to-night, at least,' said the gentleman. 'Some few days hence, if you continue to wish it, I will speed you on your journey. Or, if you prefer to remain with us, perhaps, as you are a shrewd youth, you may rise in the world, without the help of your kinsman, Major Molineux.'

Roger Malvin's Burial

ONE of the few incidents of Indian warfare, naturally susceptible of the moonlight of romance, was that expedition, undertaken, for the defence of the frontiers, in the year 1725, which resulted in the well-remembered 'Lovell's Fight.' Imagination, by casting certain circumstances judiciously into the shade, may see much to admire in the heroism of a little band, who gave battle to twice their number in the heart of the enemy's country. The open bravery displayed by both parties was in accordance with civilized ideas of valor, and chivalry itself might not blush to record the deeds of one or two individuals. The battle, though so fatal to those who fought, was not unfortunate in its consequences to the country; for it broke the strength of a tribe, and conduced to the peace which subsisted during several ensuing years. History and tradition are unusually minute in their memorials of this affair; and the captain of a scouting party of frontier-men has acquired as actual a military renown, as many a victorious leader of thousands. Some of the incidents contained in the following pages will be recognized, notwithstanding the substitution of fictitious names, by such as have heard, from old men's lips, the fate of the few combatants who were in a condition to retreat, after 'Lovell's Fight.'

The early sunbeams hovered cheerfully upon the tree-tops, beneath which two weary and wounded men had stretched their limbs the night before. Their bed of withered oak-leaves was strewn upon the small level space, at the foot of a rock, situated near the summit of one of the gentle swells, by which the face of the country is there diversified. The mass of granite, rearing its smooth, flat surface, fifteen or twenty feet above their heads, was not unlike a gigantic grave-stone, upon which the veins seemed to form an inscription in forgotten characters. On a tract of several acres around this rock, oaks and other hard-wood trees had supplied the place of the pines, which were the usual growth of the land; and a young and vigorous sapling stood close beside the travellers.

The severe wound of the elder man had probably deprived him of sleep; for, so soon as the first ray of sunshine rested on the top of the highest tree, he reared himself painfully from his recumbent posture, and sat erect. The deep lines of his countenance, and the scattered grey of his hair, marked him as past the middle age; but his muscular frame would, but for the effects of his wound, have been as capable of sustaining fatigue, as in the early vigor of life. Languor and exhaustion now sat upon his haggard features, and the despairing glance which he sent forward through the depths of the forest, proved his own conviction that his pilgrimage was at an end. He next turned his eyes to the companion, who reclined by his side. The youth, for he had scarcely attained the years of manhood, lay, with his head upon his arm, in the embrace of an unquiet sleep, which a thrill of pain from his wounds seemed each moment on the point of breaking. His right hand grasped a musket, and, to judge from the violent action of his features, his slumbers were bringing back a vision of the conflict, of which he was one of the few survivors. A shout,—deep and loud to his dreaming fancy,—found its way in an imperfect murmur to his lips, and, starting even at the slight sound of his own voice, he suddenly awoke. The first act of reviving recollection, was to make anxious inquiries respecting the condition of his wounded fellow traveller. The latter shook his head.

'Reuben, my boy,' said he, 'this rock, beneath which we sit, will serve for an old hunter's grave-stone. There is many and many a long mile of howling wilderness before us yet; nor would it avail me anything, if the smoke of my own chimney were but on the other side of that swell of land. The Indian bullet was deadlier than I thought.'

'You are weary with our three days' travel,' replied the youth, 'and a little longer rest will recruit you. Sit you here, while I search the woods for the herbs and roots, that must be our sustenance; and having eaten, you shall lean on me, and we will turn our faces homeward. I doubt not, that, with my help, you can attain to some one of the frontier garrisons.'

'There is not two days' life in me, Reuben,' said the other, calmly, 'and I will no longer burthen you with my useless body, when you can scarcely support your own. Your wounds are deep, and your strength is failing fast; yet, if you hasten onward alone, you may be preserved. For me there is no hope; and I will await death here.'

'If it must be so, I will remain and watch by you,' said Reuben, resolutely.

'No, my son, no,' rejoined his companion. 'Let the wish of a dying man have weight with you; give me one grasp of your hand, and get you hence. Think you that my last moments will be eased by the thought, that I leave you to die a more lingering death? I have loved you like a father, Reuben, and, at a time like this, I should have something of a father's authority. I charge you to be gone, that I may die in peace.'

'And because you have been a father to me, should I therefore leave you to perish, and to lie unburied in the wilderness?' exclaimed the youth. 'No; if your end be in truth approaching, I will watch by you, and receive your parting words. I will dig a grave here by the rock, in which, if my weakness overcome me, we will rest together; or, if Heaven gives me strength, I will seek my way home.'

'In the cities, and wherever men dwell,' replied the other, 'they bury their dead in the earth; they hide them from the sight of the living; but here, where no step may pass, perhaps for a hundred years, wherefore should I not rest beneath the open sky, covered only by the oak-leaves, when the autumn winds shall strew them? And for a monument, here is this grey rock, on which my dying hand shall carve the name of Roger Malvin; and the traveller in days to come will know, that here sleeps a hunter and a warrior. Tarry not, then, for a folly like this, but hasten away, if not for your own sake, for hers who will else be desolate.'

Malvin spoke the last few words in a faultering voice, and their effect upon his companion was strongly visible. They reminded him that there were other, and less questionable duties, than that of sharing the fate of a man whom his death could not benefit. Nor can it be affirmed that no selfish feeling strove to enter Reuben's heart, though the consciousness made him more earnestly resist his companion's entreaties.

'How terrible, to wait the slow approach of death, in this solitude!' exclaimed he. 'A brave man does not shrink in the battle, and, when friends stand round the bed, even women may die composedly; but here—'

'I shall not shrink, even here, Reuben Bourne,' interrupted Malvin. 'I am a man of no weak heart; and, if I were, there is a surer support than that of earthly friends. You are young, and life is dear to you. Your last moments will need comfort far more than mine; and when you have laid me in the earth, and are alone, and night is settling on the forest, you will feel all the bitterness of the death that may now be escaped. But I will urge no selfish motive to your generous nature. Leave me for my sake; that, having said a prayer for your safety, I may have space to settle my account, undisturbed by worldly sorrows.'

'And your daughter! How shall I dare to meet her eye?' exclaimed Reuben. 'She will ask the fate of her father, whose life I vowed to defend with my own. Must I tell her, that he travelled three days' march with me from the field of battle, and that then I left him to perish in the wilderness? Were it not better to lie down and die by your side, than to return safe, and say this to Dorcas?'

'Tell my daughter,' said Roger Malvin, 'that, though yourself sore wounded, and weak, and weary, you led my tottering footsteps many a mile, and left me only at my earnest entreaty, because I would not have your blood upon my soul. Tell her, that through pain and danger you were faithful, and that, if your life-blood could have saved me, it would have flowed to its last drop. And tell her, that you will be something dearer than a father, and that my blessing is with you both, and that my dying eyes can see a long and pleasant path, in which you will journey together.'

As Malvin spoke, he almost raised himself from the ground, and the energy of his concluding words seemed to fill the wild and lonely forest with a vision of happiness. But when he sank exhausted upon his bed of oak-leaves, the light, which had kindled in Reuben's eye, was quenched. He felt as if it were both sin and folly to think of happiness at such a moment. His companion watched his changing countenance, and sought, with generous art, to wile him to his own good.

'Perhaps I deceive myself in regard to the time I have to live,' he resumed. 'It may be, that, with speedy assistance, I might recover of my wound. The foremost fugitives must, ere this, have carried tidings of our fatal battle to the frontiers, and parties will be out to succour those in like condition with ourselves. Should you meet one of these, and guide them hither, who can tell but that I may sit by my own fireside again?'

A mournful smile strayed across the features of the dying man, as he insinuated that unfounded hope; which, however, was not without its effect on Reuben. No merely selfish motive, nor even the desolate condition of Dorcas, could have induced him to desert his companion, at such a moment. But his wishes seized upon the thought, that Malvin's life might be preserved, and his sanguine nature heightened, almost to certainty, the remote possibility of procuring human aid.

'Surely there is reason, weighty reason, to hope that friends are not far distant,' he said, half aloud. 'There fled one coward, unwounded, in the beginning of the fight, and most probably he made good speed. Every true man on the frontier would shoulder his musket, at the news; and though no party may range so far into the woods as this, I shall perhaps encounter them in one day's march. Counsel me faithfully,' he added, turning to Malvin, in distrust of his own motives. 'Were your situation mine, would you desert me while life remained?'

'It is now twenty years,' replied Roger Malvin, sighing, however, as he secretly acknowledged the wide dissimilarity between the two cases,—'it is now twenty years, since I escaped, with one dear friend, from Indian captivity, near Montreal. We journeyed many days through the woods, till at length, overcome with hunger and weariness, my friend lay down, and besought me to leave him; for he knew, that, if I remained, we both must perish. And, with but little hope of obtaining succour, I heaped a pillow of dry leaves beneath his head, and hastened on.'

'And did you return in time to save him?' asked Reuben, hanging on Malvin's words, as if they were to be prophetic of his own success.

'I did,' answered the other. 'I came upon the camp of a hunting party, before sunset of the same day. I guided them to the spot where my comrade was expecting death; and he is now a hale and hearty man, upon his own farm, far within the frontiers, while I lie wounded here, in the depths of the wilderness.'

This example, powerful in effecting Reuben's decision, was aided, unconsciously to himself, by the hidden strength of many another motive. Roger Malvin perceived that the victory was nearly won.

'Now go, my son, and Heaven prosper you!' he said. 'Turn not back with our friends, when you meet them, lest your wounds and weariness overcome you; but send hitherward two or three, that may be spared, to search for me. And believe me, Reuben, my heart will be lighter with every step you take towards home.' Yet there was perhaps a change, both in his countenance and voice, as he spoke thus; for, after all, it was a ghastly fate, to be left expiring in the wilderness.

Reuben Bourne, but half convinced that he was acting rightly, at length raised himself from the ground, and prepared himself for his departure. And first, though contrary to Malvin's wishes, he collected a stock of roots and herbs, which had been their only food during the last two days. This useless supply he placed within reach of the dying man, for whom, also, he swept together a fresh bed of dry oak-leaves. Then, climbing to the summit of the rock, which on one side was rough and broken, he bent the oak-sapling downward, and bound his handkerchief to the topmost branch. This precaution was not unnecessary, to direct any who might come in search of Malvin; for every part of the rock, except its broad, smooth front, was concealed, at a little distance, by the dense undergrowth of the forest. The handkerchief had been the bandage of a wound upon Reuben's arm; and, as he bound it to the tree, he vowed, by the blood that stained it, that he would return, either to save his companion's life, or to lay his body in the grave. He then descended, and stood, with downcast eyes, to receive Roger Malvin's parting words.

The experience of the latter suggested much and minute advice, respecting the youth's journey through the trackless forest. Upon this subject he spoke with calm earnestness, as if he were sending Reuben to the battle or the chase, while he himself remained secure at home; and not as if the human countenance, that was about to leave him, were the last he would ever behold. But his firmness was shaken, before he concluded.

'Carry my blessing to Dorcas, and say that my last prayer shall be for her and you. Bid her have no hard thoughts because you left me here'—Reuben's heart smote him—'for that your life would not have weighed with you, if its sacrifice could have done me good. She will marry you, after she has mourned a little while for her father; and Heaven grant you long and happy days! and may your children's children stand round your death-bed! And, Reuben,' added he, as the weakness of mortality made its way at last, 'return, when your wounds are healed and your weariness refreshed, return to this wild rock, and lay my bones in the grave, and say a prayer over them.'

An almost superstitious regard, arising perhaps from the customs of the Indians, whose war was with the dead, as well as the living, was paid by the frontier inhabitants to the rites of sepulture; and there are many instances of the sacrifice of life, in the attempt to bury those who had fallen by the 'sword of the wilderness.' Reuben, therefore, felt the full importance of the promise, which he most solemnly made, to return, and perform Roger Malvin's obsequies. It was remarkable, that the latter, speaking his whole heart in his parting words, no longer endeavored to persuade the youth, that even the speediest succour might avail to the preservation of his life. Reuben was internally convinced, that he should see Malvin's living face no more. His generous nature would fain have delayed him, at whatever risk, till the dying scene were past; but the desire of existence, and the hope of happiness had strengthened in his heart, and he was unable to resist them.

'It is enough,' said Roger Malvin, having listened to Reuben's promise. 'Go, and God speed you!'

The youth pressed his hand in silence, turned, and was departing. His slow and faultering steps, however, had borne him but a little way, before Malvin's voice recalled him.

'Reuben, Reuben,' said he, faintly; and Reuben returned and knelt down by the dying man.

'Raise me, and let me lean against the rock,' was his last request. 'My face will be turned towards home, and I shall see you a moment longer, as you pass among the trees.'

Reuben, having made the desired alteration in his companion's posture, again began his solitary pilgrimage. He walked more hastily at first, than was consistent with his strength; for a sort of guilty feeling, which sometimes torments men in their most justifiable acts, caused him to seek concealment from Malvin's eyes. But, after he had trodden far upon the rustling forest-leaves, he crept back, impelled by a wild and painful curiosity, and, sheltered by the earthy roots of an uptorn tree, gazed earnestly at the desolate man. The morning sun was unclouded, and the trees and shrubs imbibed the sweet air of the month of May; yet there seemed a gloom on Nature's face, as if she sympathized with mortal pain and sorrow. Roger Malvin's hands were uplifted in a fervent prayer, some of the words of which stole through the stillness of the woods, and entered Reuben's heart, torturing it with an unutterable pang. They were the broken accents of a petition for his own happiness and that of Dorcas; and, as the youth listened, conscience, or something in its similitude, pleaded strongly with him to return, and lie down again by the rock. He felt how hard was the doom of the kind and generous being whom he had deserted in his extremity. Death would come, like the slow approach of a corpse, stealing gradually towards him through the forest, and showing its ghastly and motionless features from behind a nearer, and yet a nearer tree. But such must have been Reuben's own fate, had he tarried another sunset; and who shall impute blame to him, if he shrank from so useless a sacrifice? As he gave a parting look, a breeze waved the little banner upon the sapling-oak, and reminded Reuben of his vow.

Many circumstances contributed to retard the wounded traveller, in his way to the frontiers. On the second day, the clouds, gathering densely over the sky, precluded the possibility of regulating his course by the position of the sun; and he knew not but that every effort of his almost exhausted strength, was removing him farther from the home he sought. His scanty sustenance was supplied by the berries, and other spontaneous products of the forest. Herds of deer, it is true, sometimes bounded past him, and partridges frequently whirred up before his footsteps; but his ammunition had been expended in the fight, and he had no means of slaying them. His wounds, irritated by the constant exertion in which lay the only hope of life, wore away his strength, and at intervals confused his reason. But, even in the wanderings of intellect, Reuben's young heart clung strongly to existence, and it was only through absolute incapacity of motion, that he at last sank down beneath a tree, compelled there to await death. In this situation he was discovered by a party, who, upon the first intelligence of the fight, had been despatched to the relief of the survivors. They conveyed him to the nearest settlement, which chanced to be that of his own residence.

Dorcas, in the simplicity of the olden time, watched by the bed-side of her wounded lover, and administered all those comforts, that are in the sole gift of woman's heart and hand. During several days, Reuben's recollection strayed drowsily among the perils and hardships through which he had passed, and he was incapable of returning definite answers to the inquiries, with which many were eager to harass him. No authentic particulars of the battle had yet been circulated; nor could mothers, wives, and children tell, whether their loved ones were detained by captivity, or by the stronger chain of death. Dorcas nourished her apprehensions in silence, till one afternoon, when Reuben awoke from an unquiet sleep, and seemed to recognize her more perfectly than at any previous time. She saw that his intellect had become composed, and she could no longer restrain her filial anxiety.

'My father, Reuben?' she began; but the change in her lover's countenance made her pause.

The youth shrank, as if with a bitter pain, and the blood gushed vividly into his wan and hollow cheeks. His first impulse was to cover his face; but, apparently with a desperate effort, he half raised himself, and spoke vehemently, defending himself against an imaginary accusation.

'Your father was sore wounded in the battle, Dorcas, and he bade me not burthen myself with him, but only to lead him to the lake-side, that he might quench his thirst and die. But I would not desert the old man in his extremity, and, though bleeding myself, I supported him; I gave him half my strength, and led him away with me. For three days we journeyed on together, and your father was sustained beyond my hopes; but, awaking at sunrise on the fourth day, I found him faint and exhausted,—he was unable to proceed,—his life had ebbed away fast,—and—'

'He died!' exclaimed Dorcas, faintly.

Reuben felt it impossible to acknowledge, that his selfish love of life had hurried him away, before her father's fate was decided. He spoke not; he only bowed his head; and, between shame and exhaustion, sank back and hid his face in the pillow. Dorcas wept, when her fears were thus confirmed; but the shock, as it had been long anticipated, was on that account the less violent.

'You dug a grave for my poor father, in the wilderness, Reuben?' was the question by which her filial piety manifested itself.

'My hands were weak, but I did what I could,' replied the youth in a smothered tone. 'There stands a noble tomb-stone above his head, and I would to Heaven I slept as soundly as he!'

Dorcas, perceiving the wildness of his latter words, inquired no further at the time; but her heart found ease in the thought, that Roger Malvin had not lacked such funeral rites as it was possible to bestow. The tale of Reuben's courage and fidelity lost nothing, when she communicated it to her friends; and the poor youth, tottering from his sick chamber to breathe the sunny air, experienced from every tongue the miserable and humiliating torture of unmerited praise. All acknowledged that he might worthily demand the hand of the fair maiden, to whose father he had been 'faithful unto death'; and, as my tale is not of love, it shall suffice to say, that, in the space of a few months, Reuben became the husband of Dorcas Malvin. During the marriage ceremony, the bride was covered with blushes, but the bridegroom's face was pale.

There was now in the breast of Reuben Bourne an incommunicable thought; something which he was to conceal most heedfully from her whom he most loved and trusted. He regretted, deeply and bitterly, the moral cowardice that had restrained his words, when he was about to disclose the truth to Dorcas; but pride, the fear of losing her affection, the dread of universal scorn, forbade him to rectify this falsehood. He felt, that, for leaving Roger Malvin, he deserved no censure. His presence, the gratuitous sacrifice of his own life, would have added only another, and a needless agony to the last moments of the dying man. But concealment had imparted to a justifiable act, much of the secret effect of guilt; and Reuben, while reason told him that he had done right, experienced, in no small degree, the mental horrors, which punish the perpetrator of undiscovered crime. By a certain association of ideas, he at times almost imagined himself a murderer. For years, also, a thought would occasionally recur, which, though he perceived all its folly and extravagance, he had not power to banish from his mind; it was a haunting and torturing fancy, that his father-in-law was yet sitting at the foot of the rock, on the withered forest-leaves, alive, and awaiting his pledged assistance. These mental deceptions, however, came and went, nor did he ever mistake them for realities; but in the calmest and clearest moods of his mind, he was conscious that he had a deep vow unredeemed, and that an unburied corpse was calling to him, out of the wilderness. Yet, such was the consequence of his prevarication, that he could not obey the call. It was now too late to require the assistance of Roger Malvin's friends, in performing his long-deferred sepulture; and superstitious fears, of which none were more susceptible than the people of the outward settlements, forbade Reuben to go alone. Neither did he know where, in the pathless and illimitable forest, to seek that smooth and lettered rock, at the base of which the body lay; his remembrance of every portion of his travel thence was indistinct, and the latter part had left no impression upon his mind. There was, however, a continual impulse, a voice audible only to himself, commanding him to go forth and redeem his vow; and he had a strange impression, that, were he to make the trial, he would be led straight to Malvin's bones. But, year after year, that summons, unheard but felt, was disobeyed. His one secret thought, became like a chain, binding down his spirit, and, like a serpent, gnawing into his heart; and he was transformed into a sad and downcast, yet irritable man.

In the course of a few years after their marriage, changes began to be visible in the external prosperity of Reuben and Dorcas. The only riches of the former had been his stout heart and strong arm; but the latter, her father's sole heiress, had made her husband master of a farm, under older cultivation, larger, and better stocked than most of the frontier establishments. Reuben Bourne, however, was a neglectful husbandman; and while the lands of the other settlers became annually more fruitful, his deteriorated in the same proportion. The discouragements to agriculture were greatly lessened by the cessation of Indian war, during which men held the plough in one hand, and the musket in the other; and were fortunate if the products of their dangerous labor were not destroyed, either in the field or in the barn, by the savage enemy. But Reuben did not profit by the altered condition of the country; nor can it be denied, that his intervals of industrious attention to his affairs were but scantily rewarded with success. The irritability, by which he had recently become distinguished, was another cause of his declining prosperity, as it occasioned frequent quarrels, in his unavoidable intercourse with the neighboring settlers. The results of these were innumerable law-suits; for the people of New England, in the earliest stages and wildest circumstances of the country, adopted, whenever attainable, the legal mode of deciding their differences. To be brief, the world did not go well with Reuben Bourne, and, though not till many years after his marriage, he was finally a ruined man, with but one remaining expedient against the evil fate that had pursued him. He was to throw sunlight into some deep recess of the forest, and seek subsistence from the virgin bosom of the wilderness.

The only child of Reuben and Dorcas was a son, now arrived at the age of fifteen years, beautiful in youth, and giving promise of a glorious manhood. He was peculiarly qualified for, and already began to excel in, the wild accomplishments of frontier life. His foot was fleet, his aim true, his apprehension quick, his heart glad and high; and all, who anticipated the return of Indian war, spoke of Cyrus Bourne as a future leader in the land. The boy was loved by his father, with a deep and silent strength, as if whatever was good and happy in his own nature had been transferred to his child, carrying his affections with it. Even Dorcas, though loving and beloved, was far less dear to him; for Reuben's secret thoughts and insulated emotions had gradually made him a selfish man;

and he could no longer love deeply, except where he saw, or imagined, some reflection or likeness of his own mind. In Cyrus he recognized what he had himself been in other days; and at intervals he seemed to partake of the boy's spirit, and to be revived with a fresh and happy life. Reuben was accompanied by his son in the expedition, for the purpose of selecting a tract of land, and felling and burning the timber, which necessarily preceded the removal of the household gods. Two months of autumn were thus occupied; after which Reuben Bourne and his young hunter returned, to spend their last winter in the settlements.

It was early in the month of May, that the little family snapped asunder whatever tendrils of affection had clung to inanimate objects, and bade farewell to the few, who, in the blight of fortune, called themselves their friends. The sadness of the parting moment had, to each of the pilgrims, its peculiar alleviations. Reuben, a moody man, and misanthropic because unhappy, strode onward, with his usual stern brow and downcast eye, feeling few regrets, and disdaining to acknowledge any. Dorcas, while she wept abundantly over the broken ties by which her simple and affectionate nature had bound itself to everything, felt that the inhabitants of her inmost heart moved on with her, and that all else would be supplied wherever she might go. And the boy dashed one tear-drop from his eye, and thought of the adventurous pleasures of the untrodden forest. Oh! who, in the enthusiasm of a day-dream, has not wished that he were a wanderer in a world of summer wilderness, with one fair and gentle being hanging lightly on his arm? In youth, his free and exulting step would know no barrier but the rolling ocean or the snow-topt mountains; calmer manhood would choose a home, where Nature had strewn a double wealth, in the vale of some transparent stream; and when hoary age, after long, long years of that pure life, stole on and found him there, it would find him the father of a race, the patriarch of a people, the founder of a mighty nation yet to be. When death, like the sweet sleep which we welcome after a day of happiness, came over him, his far descendants would mourn over the venerated dust. Enveloped by tradition in mysterious attributes, the men of fu-

ture generations would call him godlike; and remote posterity
would see him standing, dimly glorious, far up the valley of
a hundred centuries!

The tangled and gloomy forest, through which the personages of my tale were wandering, differed widely from the
dreamer's Land of Fantasie; yet there was something in their
way of life that Nature asserted as her own; and the gnawing
cares, which went with them from the world, were all that
now obstructed their happiness. One stout and shaggy steed,
the bearer of all their wealth, did not shrink from the added
weight of Dorcas; although her hardy breeding sustained her,
during the latter part of each day's journey, by her husband's
side. Reuben and his son, their muskets on their shoulders,
and their axes slung behind them, kept an unwearied pace,
each watching with a hunter's eye for the game that supplied
their food. When hunger bade, they halted and prepared their
meal on the bank of some unpolluted forest-brook, which, as
they knelt down with thirsty lips to drink, murmured a sweet
unwillingness, like a maiden, at love's first kiss. They slept
beneath a hut of branches, and awoke at peep of light, refreshed for the toils of another day. Dorcas and the boy went
on joyously, and even Reuben's spirit shone at intervals with
an outward gladness; but inwardly there was a cold, cold sorrow, which he compared to the snow-drifts, lying deep in the
glens and hollows of the rivulets, while the leaves were
brightly green above.

Cyrus Bourne was sufficiently skilled in the travel of the
woods, to observe, that his father did not adhere to the
course they had pursued, in their expedition of the preceding
autumn. They were now keeping farther to the north, striking
out more directly from the settlements, and into a region, of
which savage beasts and savage men were as yet the sole possessors. The boy sometimes hinted his opinions upon the subject, and Reuben listened attentively, and once or twice altered the direction of their march in accordance with his son's
counsel. But having so done, he seemed ill at ease. His quick
and wandering glances were sent forward, apparently in
search of enemies lurking behind the tree-trunks; and seeing
nothing there, he would cast his eyes backward, as if in fear
of some pursuer. Cyrus, perceiving that his father gradually

resumed the old direction, forbore to interfere; nor, though something began to weigh upon his heart, did his adventurous nature permit him to regret the increased length and the mystery of their way.

On the afternoon of the fifth day, they halted and made their simple encampment, nearly an hour before sunset. The face of the country, for the last few miles, had been diversified by swells of land, resembling huge waves of a petrified sea; and in one of the corresponding hollows, a wild and romantic spot, had the family reared their hut, and kindled their fire. There is something chilling, and yet heart-warming, in the thought of these three, united by strong bands of love, and insulated from all that breathe beside. The dark and gloomy pines looked down upon them, and, as the wind swept through their tops, a pitying sound was heard in the forest; or did those old trees groan, in fear that men were come to lay the axe to their roots at last? Reuben and his son, while Dorcas made ready their meal, proposed to wander out in search of game, of which that day's march had afforded no supply. The boy, promising not to quit the vicinity of the encampment, bounded off with a step as light and elastic as that of the deer he hoped to slay; while his father, feeling a transient happiness as he gazed after him, was about to pursue an opposite direction. Dorcas, in the meanwhile, had seated herself near their fire of fallen branches, upon the moss-grown and mouldering trunk of a tree, uprooted years before. Her employment, diversified by an occasional glance at the pot, now beginning to simmer over the blaze, was the perusal of the current year's Massachusetts Almanac, which, with the exception of an old black-letter Bible, comprised all the literary wealth of the family. None pay a greater regard to arbitrary divisions of time, than those who are excluded from society; and Dorcas mentioned, as if the information were of importance, that it was now the twelfth of May. Her husband started.

'The twelfth of May! I should remember it well,' muttered he, while many thoughts occasioned a momentary confusion in his mind. 'Where am I? Whither am I wandering? Where did I leave him?'

Dorcas, too well accustomed to her husband's wayward

moods to note any peculiarity of demeanor, now laid aside the Almanac, and addressed him in that mournful tone, which the tender-hearted appropriate to griefs long cold and dead.

'It was near this time of the month, eighteen years ago, that my poor father left this world for a better. He had a kind arm to hold his head, and a kind voice to cheer him, Reuben, in his last moments; and the thought of the faithful care you took of him, has comforted me, many a time since. Oh! death would have been awful to a solitary man, in a wild place like this!'

'Pray Heaven, Dorcas,' said Reuben, in a broken voice, 'pray Heaven, that neither of us three die solitary, and lie unburied, in this howling wilderness!' And he hastened away, leaving her to watch the fire, beneath the gloomy pines.

Reuben Bourne's rapid pace gradually slackened, as the pang, unintentionally inflicted by the words of Dorcas, became less acute. Many strange reflections, however, thronged upon him; and, straying onward, rather like a sleep-walker than a hunter, it was attributable to no care of his own, that his devious course kept him in the vicinity of the encampment. His steps were imperceptibly led almost in a circle, nor did he observe that he was on the verge of a tract of land heavily timbered, but not with pine-trees. The place of the latter was here supplied by oaks, and other of the harder woods; and around their roots clustered a dense and bushy undergrowth, leaving, however, barren spaces between the trees, thick-strewn with withered leaves. Whenever the rustling of the branches, or the creaking of the trunks made a sound, as if the forest were waking from slumber, Reuben instinctively raised the musket that rested on his arm, and cast a quick, sharp glance on every side; but, convinced by a partial observation that no animal was near, he would again give himself up to his thoughts. He was musing on the strange influence, that had led him away from his premeditated course, and so far into the depths of the wilderness. Unable to penetrate to the secret place of his soul, where his motives lay hidden, he believed that a supernatural voice had called him onward, and that a supernatural power had obstructed his retreat. He trusted that it was Heaven's intent to afford him an opportunity of expiating his sin; he hoped that he

might find the bones, so long unburied; and that, having laid
the earth over them, peace would throw its sunlight into the
sepulchre of his heart. From these thoughts he was aroused
by a rustling in the forest, at some distance from the spot to
which he had wandered. Perceiving the motion of some object behind a thick veil of undergrowth, he fired, with the
instinct of a hunter, and the aim of a practised marksman. A
low moan, which told his success, and by which even animals
can express their dying agony, was unheeded by Reuben
Bourne. What were the recollections now breaking upon
him?

The thicket, into which Reuben had fired, was near the
summit of a swell of land, and was clustered around the base
of a rock, which, in the shape and smoothness of one of its
surfaces, was not unlike a gigantic grave-stone. As if reflected
in a mirror, its likeness was in Reuben's memory. He even
recognized the veins which seemed to form an inscription in
forgotten characters; everything remained the same, except
that a thick covert of bushes shrouded the lower part of the
rock, and would have hidden Roger Malvin, had he still been
sitting there. Yet, in the next moment, Reuben's eye was
caught by another change, that time had effected, since he last
stood, where he was now standing again, behind the earthy
roots of the uptorn tree. The sapling, to which he had bound
the blood-stained symbol of his vow, had increased and
strengthened into an oak, far indeed from its maturity, but
with no mean spread of shadowy branches. There was one
singularity, observable in this tree, which made Reuben tremble. The middle and lower branches were in luxuriant life,
and an excess of vegetation had fringed the trunk, almost to
the ground; but a blight had apparently stricken the upper
part of the oak, and the very topmost bough was withered,
sapless, and utterly dead. Reuben remembered how the little
banner had fluttered on the topmost bough, when it was
green and lovely, eighteen years before. Whose guilt had
blasted it?

Dorcas, after the departure of the two hunters, continued
her preparations for their evening repast. Her sylvan table was
the moss-covered trunk of a large fallen tree, on the broadest

part of which she had spread a snow-white cloth, and arranged what were left of the bright pewter vessels, that had
been her pride in the settlements. It had a strange aspect—
that one little spot of homely comfort, in the desolate heart
of Nature. The sunshine yet lingered upon the higher
branches of the trees that grew on rising ground; but the
shades of evening had deepened into the hollow, where the
encampment was made; and the fire-light began to redden as
it gleamed up the tall trunks of the pines, or hovered on the
dense and obscure mass of foliage, that circled round the
spot. The heart of Dorcas was not sad; for she felt that it was
better to journey in the wilderness, with two whom she
loved, than to be a lonely woman in a crowd that cared not
for her. As she busied herself in arranging seats of mouldering
wood, covered with leaves, for Reuben and her son, her voice
danced through the gloomy forest, in the measure of a song
that she had learned in youth. The rude melody, the production of a bard who won no name, was descriptive of a winter
evening in a frontier-cottage, when, secured from savage in-
road by the high-piled snow-drifts, the family rejoiced by
their own fireside. The whole song possessed that nameless
charm, peculiar to unborrowed thought; but four continually-
recurring lines shone out from the rest, like the blaze of the
hearth whose joys they celebrated. Into them, working magic
with a few simple words, the poet had instilled the very essence of domestic love and household happiness, and they
were poetry and picture joined in one. As Dorcas sang, the
walls of her forsaken home seemed to encircle her; she no
longer saw the gloomy pines, nor heard the wind, which still,
as she began each verse, sent a heavy breath through the
branches, and died away in a hollow moan, from the burthen
of the song. She was aroused by the report of a gun, in the
vicinity of the encampment; and either the sudden sound, or
her loneliness by the glowing fire, caused her to tremble violently. The next moment, she laughed in the pride of a
mother's heart.

'My beautiful young hunter! my boy has slain a deer!' she
exclaimed, recollecting that, in the direction whence the shot
proceeded, Cyrus had gone to the chase.

She waited a reasonable time, to hear her son's light step

bounding over the rustling leaves, to tell of his success. But he did not immediately appear, and she sent her cheerful voice among the trees, in search of him.

'Cyrus! Cyrus!'

His coming was still delayed, and she determined, as the report had apparently been very near, to seek for him in person. Her assistance, also, might be necessary in bringing home the venison, which she flattered herself he had obtained. She therefore set forward, directing her steps by the long-past sound, and singing as she went, in order that the boy might be aware of her approach, and run to meet her. From behind the trunk of every tree, and from every hiding place in the thick foliage of the undergrowth, she hoped to discover the countenance of her son, laughing with the sportive mischief that is born of affection. The sun was now beneath the horizon, and the light that came down among the trees was sufficiently dim to create many illusions in her expecting fancy. Several times she seemed indistinctly to see his face gazing out from among the leaves; and once she imagined that he stood beckoning to her, at the base of a craggy rock. Keeping her eyes on this object, however, it proved to be no more than the trunk of an oak, fringed to the very ground with little branches, one of which, thrust out farther than the rest, was shaken by the breeze. Making her way round the foot of the rock, she suddenly found herself close to her husband, who had approached in another direction. Leaning upon the butt of his gun, the muzzle of which rested upon the withered leaves, he was apparently absorbed in the contemplation of some object at his feet.

'How is this, Reuben? Have you slain the deer, and fallen asleep over him?' exclaimed Dorcas, laughing cheerfully, on her first slight observation of his posture and appearance.

He stirred not, neither did he turn his eyes towards her; and a cold, shuddering fear, indefinite in its source and object, began to creep into her blood. She now perceived that her husband's face was ghastly pale, and his features were rigid, as if incapable of assuming any other expression than the strong despair which had hardened upon them. He gave not the slightest evidence that he was aware of her approach.

'For the love of Heaven, Reuben, speak to me!' cried Dorcas, and the strange sound of her own voice affrighted her even more than the dead silence.

Her husband started, stared into her face; drew her to the front of the rock, and pointed with his finger.

Oh! there lay the boy, asleep, but dreamless, upon the fallen forest-leaves! his cheek rested upon his arm, his curled locks were thrown back from his brow, his limbs were slightly relaxed. Had a sudden weariness overcome the youthful hunter? Would his mother's voice arouse him? She knew that it was death.

'This broad rock is the grave-stone of your near kindred, Dorcas,' said her husband. 'Your tears will fall at once over your father and your son.'

She heard him not. With one wild shriek, that seemed to force its way from the sufferer's inmost soul, she sank insensible by the side of her dead boy. At that moment, the withered topmost bough of the oak loosened itself, in the stilly air, and fell in soft, light fragments upon the rock, upon the leaves, upon Reuben, upon his wife and child, and upon Roger Malvin's bones. Then Reuben's heart was stricken, and the tears gushed out like water from a rock. The vow that the wounded youth had made, the blighted man had come to redeem. His sin was expiated, the curse was gone from him; and, in the hour, when he had shed blood dearer to him than his own, a prayer, the first for years, went up to Heaven from the lips of Reuben Bourne.

The Gentle Boy

IN the course of the year 1656, several of the people called
Quakers, led, as they professed, by the inward movement
of the spirit, made their appearance in New England. Their
reputation, as holders of mystic and pernicious principles,
having spread before them, the Puritans early endeavored to
banish, and to prevent the further intrusion of the rising sect.
But the measures by which it was intended to purge the land
of heresy, though more than sufficiently vigorous, were entirely unsuccessful. The Quakers, esteeming persecution as a
divine call to the post of danger, laid claim to a holy courage,
unknown to the Puritans themselves, who had shunned the
cross, by providing for the peaceable exercise of their religion
in a distant wilderness. Though it was the singular fact, that
every nation of the earth rejected the wandering enthusiasts
who practised peace towards all men, the place of greatest
uneasiness and peril, and therefore in their eyes the most eligible, was the province of Massachusetts Bay.

The fines, imprisonments, and stripes, liberally distributed
by our pious forefathers; the popular antipathy, so strong that
it endured nearly a hundred years after actual persecution had
ceased, were attractions as powerful for the Quakers, as peace,
honor, and reward, would have been for the worldly-minded.
Every European vessel brought new cargoes of the sect, eager
to testify against the oppression which they hoped to share;
and, when ship-masters were restrained by heavy fines from
affording them passage, they made long and circuitous journeys through the Indian country, and appeared in the province as if conveyed by a supernatural power. Their enthusiasm, heightened almost to madness by the treatment which
they received, produced actions contrary to the rules of decency, as well as of rational religion, and presented a singular
contrast to the calm and staid deportment of their sectarian
successors of the present day. The command of the spirit, inaudible except to the soul, and not to be controverted on
grounds of human wisdom, was made a plea for most indecorous exhibitions, which, abstractedly considered, well de-

served the moderate chastisement of the rod. These extravagances, and the persecution which was at once their cause and
consequence, continued to increase, till, in the year 1659, the
government of Massachusetts Bay indulged two members of
the Quaker sect with the crown of martyrdom.

An indelible stain of blood is upon the hands of all who
consented to this act, but a large share of the awful responsibility must rest upon the person then at the head of the government. He was a man of narrow mind and imperfect education, and his uncompromising bigotry was made hot and
mischievous by violent and hasty passions; he exerted his influence indecorously and unjustifiably to compass the death
of the enthusiasts; and his whole conduct, in respect to them,
was marked by brutal cruelty. The Quakers, whose revengeful
feelings were not less deep because they were inactive, remembered this man and his associates, in after times. The historian of the sect affirms that, by the wrath of Heaven, a
blight fell upon the land in the vicinity of the 'bloody town'
of Boston, so that no wheat would grow there; and he takes
his stand, as it were, among the graves of the ancient persecutors, and triumphantly recounts the judgments that overtook them, in old age or at the parting hour. He tells us that
they died suddenly, and violently, and in madness; but nothing can exceed the bitter mockery with which he records the
loathsome disease, and 'death by rottenness,' of the fierce and
cruel governor.

On the evening of the autumn day, that had witnessed the
martyrdom of two men of the Quaker persuasion, a Puritan
settler was returning from the metropolis to the neighboring
country town in which he resided. The air was cool, the sky
clear, and the lingering twilight was made brighter by the rays
of a young moon, which had now nearly reached the verge of
the horizon. The traveller, a man of middle age, wrapped in
a grey frieze cloak, quickened his pace when he had reached
the outskirts of the town, for a gloomy extent of nearly four
miles lay between him and his home. The low, straw-thatched
houses were scattered at considerable intervals along the road,
and the country having been settled but about thirty years,
the tracts of original forest still bore no small proportion to

the cultivated ground. The autumn wind wandered among
the branches, whirling away the leaves from all except the
pine-trees, and moaning as if it lamented the desolation of
which it was the instrument. The road had penetrated the
mass of woods that lay nearest to the town, and was just
emerging into an open space, when the traveller's ears were
saluted by a sound more mournful than even that of the
wind. It was like the wailing of some one in distress, and it
seemed to proceed from beneath a tall and lonely fir-tree, in
the centre of a cleared, but unenclosed and uncultivated field.
The Puritan could not but remember that this was the very
spot, which had been made accursed a few hours before, by
the execution of the Quakers, whose bodies had been thrown
together into one hasty grave, beneath the tree on which they
suffered. He struggled, however, against the superstitious
fears which belonged to the age, and compelled himself to
pause and listen.

'The voice is most likely mortal, nor have I cause to tremble
if it be otherwise,' thought he, straining his eyes through the
dim moonlight. 'Methinks it is like the wailing of a child;
some infant, it may be, which has strayed from its mother,
and chanced upon this place of death. For the ease of mine
own conscience, I must search this matter out.'

He therefore left the path, and walked somewhat fearfully
across the field. Though now so desolate, its soil was pressed
down and trampled by the thousand footsteps of those who
had witnessed the spectacle of that day, all of whom had now
retired, leaving the dead to their loneliness. The traveller at
length reached the fir-tree, which from the middle upward
was covered with living branches, although a scaffold had
been erected beneath, and other preparations made for the
work of death. Under this unhappy tree, which in after times
was believed to drop poison with its dew, sat the one solitary
mourner for innocent blood. It was a slender and light-clad
little boy, who leaned his face upon a hillock of fresh-turned
and half-frozen earth, and wailed bitterly, yet in a suppressed
tone, as if his grief might receive the punishment of crime.
The Puritan, whose approach had been unperceived, laid his
hand upon the child's shoulder, and addressed him compassionately.

'You have chosen a dreary lodging, my poor boy, and no wonder that you weep,' said he. 'But dry your eyes, and tell me where your mother dwells. I promise you, if the journey be not too far, I will leave you in her arms to-night.'

The boy had hushed his wailing at once, and turned his face upward to the stranger. It was a pale, bright-eyed countenance, certainly not more than six years old, but sorrow, fear, and want, had destroyed much of its infantile expression. The Puritan, seeing the boy's frightened gaze, and feeling that he trembled under his hand, endeavored to reassure him.

'Nay, if I intended to do you harm, little lad, the readiest way were to leave you here. What! you do not fear to sit beneath the gallows on a new-made grave, and yet you tremble at a friend's touch. Take heart, child, and tell me what is your name, and where is your home?'

'Friend,' replied the little boy, in a sweet, though faultering voice, 'they call me Ilbrahim, and my home is here.'

The pale, spiritual face, the eyes that seemed to mingle with the moonlight, the sweet, airy voice, and the outlandish name, almost made the Puritan believe, that the boy was in truth a being which had sprung up out of the grave on which he sat. But perceiving that the apparition stood the test of a short mental prayer, and remembering that the arm which he had touched was life-like, he adopted a more rational supposition. 'The poor child is stricken in his intellect,' thought he, 'but verily his words are fearful, in a place like this.' He then spoke soothingly, intending to humour the boy's fantasy.

'Your home will scarce be comfortable, Ilbrahim, this cold autumn night, and I fear you are ill provided with food. I am hastening to a warm supper and bed, and if you will go with me, you shall share them!'

'I thank thee, friend, but though I be hungry and shivering with cold, thou wilt not give me food nor lodging,' replied the boy, in the quiet tone which despair had taught him, even so young. 'My father was of the people whom all men hate. They have laid him under this heap of earth, and here is my home.'

The Puritan, who had laid hold of little Ilbrahim's hand, relinquished it as if he were touching a loathsome reptile. But he possessed a compassionate heart, which not even religious prejudice could harden into stone.

'God forbid that I should leave this child to perish, though he comes of the accursed sect,' said he to himself. 'Do we not all spring from an evil root? Are we not all in darkness till the light doth shine upon us? He shall not perish, neither in body, nor, if prayer and instruction may avail for him, in soul.' He then spoke aloud and kindly to Ilbrahim, who had again hid his face in the cold earth of the grave. 'Was every door in the land shut against you, my child, that you have wandered to this unhallowed spot?'

'They drove me forth from the prison when they took my father thence,' said the boy, 'and I stood afar off, watching the crowd of people, and when they were gone, I came hither, and found only this grave. I knew that my father was sleeping here, and I said, this shall be my home.'

'No, child, no; not while I have a roof over my head, or a morsel to share with you!' exclaimed the Puritan, whose sympathies were now fully excited. 'Rise up and come with me, and fear not any harm.'

The boy wept afresh, and clung to the heap of earth, as if the cold heart beneath it were warmer to him than any in a living breast. The traveller, however, continued to entreat him tenderly, and seeming to acquire some degree of confidence, he at length arose. But his slender limbs tottered with weakness, his little head grew dizzy, and he leaned against the tree of death for support.

'My poor boy, are you so feeble?' said the Puritan. 'When did you taste food last?'

'I ate of bread and water with my father in the prison,' replied Ilbrahim, 'but they brought him none neither yesterday nor to-day, saying that he had eaten enough to bear him to his journey's end. Trouble not thyself for my hunger, kind friend, for I have lacked food many times ere now.'

The traveller took the child in his arms and wrapped his cloak about him, while his heart stirred with shame and anger against the gratuitous cruelty of the instruments in this persecution. In the awakened warmth of his feelings, he resolved that, at whatever risk, he would not forsake the poor little defenceless being whom Heaven had confided to his care. With this determination, he left the accursed field, and re-

sumed the homeward path from which the wailing of the boy
had called him. The light and motionless burthen scarcely
impeded his progress, and he soon beheld the fire-rays from
the windows of the cottage which he, a native of a distant
clime, had built in the western wilderness. It was surrounded
by a considerable extent of cultivated ground, and the dwelling was situated in the nook of a wood-covered hill, whither
it seemed to have crept for protection.

'Look up, child,' said the Puritan to Ilbrahim, whose faint
head had sunk upon his shoulder; 'there is our home.'

At the word 'home,' a thrill passed through the child's
frame, but he continued silent. A few moments brought them
to the cottage-door, at which the owner knocked; for at that
early period, when savages were wandering everywhere
among the settlers, bolt and bar were indispensable to the
security of a dwelling. The summons was answered by a
bond-servant, a coarse-clad and dull-featured piece of humanity, who, after ascertaining that his master was the applicant,
undid the door, and held a flaring pine-knot torch to light
him in. Farther back in the passage-way, the red blaze discovered a matronly woman, but no little crowd of children came
bounding forth to greet their father's return. As the Puritan
entered, he thrust aside his cloak, and displayed Ilbrahim's
face to the female.

'Dorothy, here is a little outcast whom Providence hath put
into our hands,' observed he. 'Be kind to him, even as if he
were of those dear ones who have departed from us.'

'What pale and bright-eyed little boy is this, Tobias?' she
inquired. 'Is he one whom the wilderness folk have ravished
from some Christian mother?'

'No, Dorothy, this poor child is no captive from the wilderness,' he replied. 'The heathen savage would have given
him to eat of his scanty morsel, and to drink of his birchen
cup; but Christian men, alas! had cast him out to die.'

Then he told her how he had found him beneath the gallows, upon his father's grave; and how his heart had
prompted him, like the speaking of an inward voice, to take
the little outcast home, and be kind unto him. He acknowledged his resolution to feed and clothe him, as if he were his

own child, and to afford him the instruction which should counteract the pernicious errors hitherto instilled into his infant mind. Dorothy was gifted with even a quicker tenderness than her husband, and she approved of all his doings and intentions.

'Have you a mother, dear child?' she inquired.

The tears burst forth from his full heart, as he attempted to reply; but Dorothy at length understood that he had a mother, who, like the rest of her sect, was a persecuted wanderer. She had been taken from the prison a short time before, carried into the uninhabited wilderness, and left to perish there by hunger or wild beasts. This was no uncommon method of disposing of the Quakers, and they were accustomed to boast, that the inhabitants of the desert were more hospitable to them than civilized man.

'Fear not, little boy, you shall not need a mother, and a kind one,' said Dorothy, when she had gathered this information. 'Dry your tears, Ilbrahim, and be my child, as I will be your mother.'

The good woman prepared the little bed, from which her own children had successively been borne to another resting place. Before Ilbrahim would consent to occupy it, he knelt down, and as Dorothy listened to his simple and affecting prayer, she marvelled how the parents that had taught it to him could have been judged worthy of death. When the boy had fallen asleep, she bent over his pale and spiritual countenance, pressed a kiss upon his white brow, drew the bedclothes up about his neck, and went away with a pensive gladness in her heart.

Tobias Pearson was not among the earliest emigrants from the old country. He had remained in England during the first years of the civil war, in which he had borne some share as a cornet of dragoons, under Cromwell. But when the ambitious designs of his leader began to develop themselves, he quitted the army of the parliament, and sought a refuge from the strife, which was no longer holy, among the people of his persuasion, in the colony of Massachusetts. A more worldly consideration had perhaps an influence in drawing him thither; for New England offered advantages to men of unprosperous fortunes, as well as to dissatisfied religionists, and

Pearson had hitherto found it difficult to provide for a wife and increasing family. To this supposed impurity of motive, the more bigoted Puritans were inclined to impute the removal by death of all the children, for whose earthly good the father had been over-thoughtful. They had left their native country blooming like roses, and like roses they had perished in a foreign soil. Those expounders of the ways of Providence, who had thus judged their brother, and attributed his domestic sorrows to his sin, were not more charitable when they saw him and Dorothy endeavoring to fill up the void in their hearts, by the adoption of an infant of the accursed sect. Nor did they fail to communicate their disapprobation to Tobias; but the latter, in reply, merely pointed at the little quiet, lovely boy, whose appearance and deportment were indeed as powerful arguments as could possibly have been adduced in his own favor. Even his beauty, however, and his winning manners, sometimes produced an effect ultimately unfavorable; for the bigots, when the outer surfaces of their iron hearts had been softened and again grew hard, affirmed that no merely natural cause could have so worked upon them.

Their antipathy to the poor infant was also increased by the ill success of divers theological discussions, in which it was attempted to convince him of the errors of his sect. Ilbrahim, it is true, was not a skilful controversialist; but the feeling of his religion was strong as instinct in him, and he could neither be enticed nor driven from the faith which his father had died for. The odium of this stubbornness was shared in a great measure by the child's protectors, insomuch that Tobias and Dorothy very shortly began to experience a most bitter species of persecution, in the cold regards of many a friend whom they had valued. The common people manifested their opinions more openly. Pearson was a man of some consideration, being a Representative to the General Court, and an approved Lieutenant in the train-bands, yet, within a week after his adoption of Ilbrahim, he had been both hissed and hooted. Once, also, when walking through a solitary piece of woods, he heard a loud voice from some invisible speaker; and it cried, 'What shall be done to the backslider? Lo! the scourge is knotted for him, even the whip of nine cords, and every cord three knots!' These insults irritated Pearson's temper for the moment; they entered also into his heart, and became imperceptible but powerful workers towards an end, which his most secret thought had not yet whispered.

On the second Sabbath after Ilbrahim became a member of their family, Pearson and his wife deemed it proper that he should appear with them at public worship. They had anticipated some opposition to this measure from the boy, but he prepared himself in silence, and at the appointed hour was clad in the new mourning suit which Dorothy had wrought for him. As the parish was then, and during many subsequent years, unprovided with a bell, the signal for the commencement of religious exercises was the beat of a drum. At the first sound of that martial call to the place of holy and quiet thoughts, Tobias and Dorothy set forth, each holding a hand of little Ilbrahim, like two parents linked together by the infant of their love. On their path through the leafless woods, they were overtaken by many persons of their acquaintance, all of whom avoided them, and passed by on the other side; but a severer trial awaited their constancy when they had descended the hill, and drew near the pine-built and undecorated house of prayer. Around the door, from which the drummer still sent forth his thundering summons, was drawn up a formidable phalanx, including several of the oldest members of the congregation, many of the middle-aged, and nearly all the younger males. Pearson found it difficult to sustain their united and disapproving gaze, but Dorothy, whose mind was differently circumstanced, merely drew the boy closer to her, and faultered not in her approach. As they entered the door, they overheard the muttered sentiments of the assemblage, and when the reviling voices of the little children smote Ilbrahim's ear, he wept.

The interior aspect of the meetinghouse was rude. The low ceiling, the unplastered walls, the naked wood-work, and the undraperied pulpit, offered nothing to excite the devotion, which, without such external aids, often remains latent in the heart. The floor of the building was occupied by rows of long, cushionless benches, supplying the place of pews, and the broad-aisle formed a sexual division, impassable except by children beneath a certain age.

Pearson and Dorothy separated at the door of the meeting-house, and Ilbrahim, being within the years of infancy, was retained under the care of the latter. The wrinkled beldams involved themselves in their rusty cloaks as he passed by; even the mild-featured maidens seemed to dread contamination; and many a stern old man arose, and turned his repulsive and unheavenly countenance upon the gentle boy, as if the sanctuary were polluted by his presence. He was a sweet infant of the skies, that had strayed away from his home, and all the inhabitants of this miserable world closed up their impure hearts against him, drew back their earth-soiled garments from his touch, and said, 'We are holier than thou.'

Ilbrahim, seated by the side of his adopted mother, and retaining fast hold of her hand, assumed a grave and decorous demeanor, such as might befit a person of matured taste and understanding, who should find himself in a temple dedicated to some worship which he did not recognize, but felt himself bound to respect. The exercises had not yet commenced, however, when the boy's attention was arrested by an event, apparently of trifling interest. A woman, having her face muffled in a hood, and a cloak drawn completely about her form, advanced slowly up the broad-aisle and took place upon the foremost bench. Ilbrahim's faint color varied, his nerves fluttered, he was unable to turn his eyes from the muffled female.

When the preliminary prayer and hymn were over, the minister arose, and having turned the hour-glass which stood by the great Bible, commenced his discourse. He was now well stricken in years, a man of pale, thin countenance, and his grey hairs were closely covered by a black velvet scull-cap. In his younger days he had practically learned the meaning of persecution, from Archbishop Laud, and he was not now disposed to forget the lesson against which he had murmured then. Introducing the often discussed subject of the Quakers, he gave a history of that sect, and a description of their tenets, in which error predominated, and prejudice distorted the aspect of what was true. He adverted to the recent measures in the province, and cautioned his hearers of weaker parts against calling in question the just severity, which God-fearing magistrates had at length been compelled to exercise. He spoke of the danger of pity, in some cases a commendable and Christian virtue, but inapplicable to this pernicious sect.

He observed that such was their devilish obstinacy in error, that even the little children, the sucking babes, were hardened and desperate heretics. He affirmed that no man, without Heaven's especial warrant, should attempt their conversion, lest while he lent his hand to draw them from the slough, he should himself be precipitated into its lowest depths.

The sands of the second hour were principally in the lower half of the glass, when the sermon concluded. An approving murmur followed, and the clergyman, having given out a hymn, took his seat with much self-congratulation, and endeavored to read the effect of his eloquence in the visages of the people. But while voices from all parts of the house were tuning themselves to sing, a scene occurred, which, though not very unusual at that period in the province, happened to be without precedent in this parish.

The muffled female, who had hitherto sat motionless in the front rank of the audience, now arose, and with slow, stately, and unwavering step, ascended the pulpit stairs. The quaverings of incipient harmony were hushed, and the divine sat in speechless and almost terrified astonishment, while she undid the door, and stood up in the sacred desk from which his maledictions had just been thundered. She then divested herself of the cloak and hood, and appeared in a most singular array. A shapeless robe of sackcloth was girded about her waist with a knotted cord; her raven hair fell down upon her shoulders, and its blackness was defiled by pale streaks of ashes, which she had strewn upon her head. Her eyebrows, dark and strongly defined, added to the deathly whiteness of a countenance which, emaciated with want, and wild with enthusiasm and strange sorrows, retained no trace of earlier beauty. This figure stood gazing earnestly on the audience, and there was no sound, nor any movement, except a faint shuddering which every man observed in his neighbor, but was scarcely conscious of in himself. At length, when her fit of inspiration came, she spoke, for the first few moments, in a low voice, and not invariably distinct utterance. Her discourse gave evidence of an imagination hopelessly entangled with her reason; it was a vague and incomprehensible rhapsody, which, however, seemed to spread its own atmosphere round the hearer's soul, and to move his feelings by some influence unconnected with the words. As she proceeded, beautiful but shadowy images would sometimes be seen, like bright things moving in a turbid river; or a strong and singularly shaped idea leapt forth, and seized at once on the understanding or the heart. But the course of her unearthly eloquence soon led her to the persecutions of her sect, and from thence the step was short to her own peculiar sorrows. She was naturally a woman of mighty passions, and hatred and revenge now wrapped themselves in the garb of piety; the character of her speech was changed, her images became distinct though wild, and her denunciations had an almost hellish bitterness.

'The Governor and his mighty men,' she said, 'have gathered together, taking counsel among themselves and saying, "What shall we do unto this people—even unto the people that have come into this land to put our iniquity to the blush?" And lo! the devil entereth into the council-chamber, like a lame man of low stature and gravely appareled, with a dark and twisted countenance, and a bright, downcast eye. And he standeth up among the rulers; yea, he goeth to and fro, whispering to each; and every man lends his ear, for his word is "slay, slay!" But I say unto ye, Woe to them that slay! Woe to them that shed the blood of saints! Woe to them that have slain the husband, and cast forth the child, the tender infant, to wander homeless, and hungry, and cold, till he die; and have saved the mother alive, in the cruelty of their tender mercies! Woe to them in their life-time, cursed are they in the delight and pleasure of their hearts! Woe to them in their death hour, whether it come swiftly with blood and violence, or after long and lingering pain! Woe, in the dark house, in the rottenness of the grave, when the children's children shall revile the ashes of the fathers! Woe, woe, woe, at the judgment, when all the persecuted and all the slain in this bloody land, and the father, the mother, and the child, shall await them in a day that they cannot escape! Seed of the faith, seed of the faith, ye whose hearts are moving with a power that ye know not, arise, wash your hands of this innocent blood! Lift your voices, chosen ones, cry aloud, and call down a woe and a judgment with me!'

Having thus given vent to the flood of malignity which she

mistook for inspiration, the speaker was silent. Her voice was succeeded by the hysteric shrieks of several women, but the feelings of the audience generally had not been drawn onward in the current with her own. They remained stupefied, stranded as it were, in the midst of a torrent, which deafened them by its roaring, but might not move them by its violence. The clergyman, who could not hitherto have ejected the usurper of his pulpit otherwise than by bodily force, now addressed her in the tone of just indignation and legitimate authority.

'Get you down, woman, from the holy place which you profane,' he said. 'Is it to the Lord's house that you come to pour forth the foulness of your heart, and the inspiration of the devil? Get you down, and remember that the sentence of death is on you; yea, and shall be executed, were it but for this day's work.'

'I go, friend, I go, for the voice hath had its utterance,' replied she, in a depressed and even mild tone. 'I have done my mission unto thee and to thy people. Reward me with stripes, imprisonment, or death, as ye shall be permitted.'

The weakness of exhausted passion caused her steps to totter as she descended the pulpit stairs. The people, in the meanwhile, were stirring to and fro on the floor of the house, whispering among themselves, and glancing towards the intruder. Many of them now recognized her as the woman who had assaulted the Governor with frightful language, as he passed by the window of her prison; they knew, also, that she was adjudged to suffer death, and had been preserved only by an involuntary banishment into the wilderness. The new outrage, by which she had provoked her fate, seemed to render further lenity impossible; and a gentleman in military dress, with a stout man of inferior rank, drew towards the door of the meetinghouse, and awaited her approach. Scarcely did her feet press the floor, however, when an unexpected scene occurred. In that moment of her peril, when every eye frowned with death, a little timid boy pressed forth, and threw his arms round his mother.

'I am here, mother, it is I, and I will go with thee to prison,' he exclaimed.

She gazed at him with a doubtful and almost frightened

expression, for she knew that the boy had been cast out to perish, and she had not hoped to see his face again. She feared, perhaps, that it was but one of the happy visions, with which her excited fancy had often deceived her, in the solitude of the desert, or in prison. But when she felt his hand warm within her own, and heard his little eloquence of childish love, she began to know that she was yet a mother.

'Blessed art thou, my son,' she sobbed. 'My heart was withered; yea, dead with thee and with thy father; and now it leaps as in the first moment when I pressed thee to my bosom.'

She knelt down, and embraced him again and again, while the joy that could find no words, expressed itself in broken accents, like the bubbles gushing up to vanish at the surface of a deep fountain. The sorrows of past years, and the darker peril that was nigh, cast not a shadow on the brightness of that fleeing moment. Soon, however, the spectators saw a change upon her face, as the consciousness of her sad estate returned, and grief supplied the fount of tears which joy had opened. By the words she uttered, it would seem that the indulgence of natural love had given her mind a momentary sense of its errors, and made her know how far she had strayed from duty, in following the dictates of a wild fanaticism.

'In a doleful hour art thou returned to me, poor boy,' she said, 'for thy mother's path has gone darkening onward, till now the end is death. Son, son, I have borne thee in my arms when my limbs were tottering, and I have fed thee with the food that I was fainting for; yet I have ill performed a mother's part by thee in life, and now I leave thee no inheritance but woe and shame. Thou wilt go seeking through the world, and find all hearts closed against thee, and their sweet affections turned to bitterness for my sake. My child, my child, how many a pang awaits thy gentle spirit, and I the cause of all!'

She hid her face on Ilbrahim's head, and her long, raven hair, discolored with the ashes of her mourning, fell down about him like a veil. A low and interrupted moan was the voice of her heart's anguish, and it did not fail to move the sympathies of many who mistook their involuntary virtue for a sin. Sobs were audible in the female section of the house, and every man who was a father, drew his hand across his eyes. Tobias Pearson was agitated and uneasy, but a certain feeling like the consciousness of guilt oppressed him, so that he could not go forth and offer himself as the protector of the child. Dorothy, however, had watched her husband's eye. Her mind was free from the influence that had begun to work on his, and she drew near the Quaker woman, and addressed her in the hearing of all the congregation.

'Stranger, trust this boy to me, and I will be his mother,' she said, taking Ilbrahim's hand. 'Providence has signally marked out my husband to protect him, and he has fed at our table and lodged under our roof, now many days, till our hearts have grown very strongly unto him. Leave the tender child with us, and be at ease concerning his welfare.'

The Quaker rose from the ground, but drew the boy closer to her, while she gazed earnestly in Dorothy's face. Her mild, but saddened features, and neat, matronly attire, harmonized together, and were like a verse of fireside poetry. Her very aspect proved that she was blameless, so far as mortal could be so, in respect to God and man; while the enthusiast, in her robe of sackcloth and girdle of knotted cord, had as evidently violated the duties of the present life and the future, by fixing her attention wholly on the latter. The two females, as they held each a hand of Ilbrahim, formed a practical allegory; it was rational piety and unbridled fanaticism, contending for the empire of a young heart.

'Thou art not of our people,' said the Quaker, mournfully.

'No, we are not of your people,' replied Dorothy, with mildness, 'but we are Christians, looking upward to the same Heaven with you. Doubt not that your boy shall meet you there, if there be a blessing on our tender and prayerful guidance of him. Thither, I trust, my own children have gone before me, for I also have been a mother; I am no longer so,' she added, in a faultering tone, 'and your son will have all my care.'

'But will ye lead him in the path which his parents have trodden?' demanded the Quaker. 'Can ye teach him the enlightened faith which his father has died for, and for which I, even I, am soon to become an unworthy martyr? The boy has been baptized in blood; will ye keep the mark fresh and ruddy upon his forehead?'

'I will not deceive you,' answered Dorothy. 'If your child become our child, we must breed him up in the instruction which Heaven has imparted to us; we must pray for him the prayers of our own faith; we must do towards him according to the dictates of our own consciences, and not of yours. Were we to act otherwise, we should abuse your trust, even in complying with your wishes.'

The mother looked down upon her boy with a troubled countenance, and then turned her eyes upward to heaven. She seemed to pray internally, and the contention of her soul was evident.

'Friend,' she said at length to Dorothy. 'I doubt not that my son shall receive all earthly tenderness at thy hands. Nay, I will believe that even thy imperfect lights may guide him to a better world; for surely thou art on the path thither. But thou hast spoken of a husband. Doth he stand here among this multitude of people? Let him come forth; for I must know to whom I commit this most precious trust.'

She turned her face upon the male auditors, and after a momentary delay, Tobias Pearson came forth from among them. The Quaker saw the dress which marked his military rank, and shook her head; but then she noted the hesitating air, the eyes that struggled with her own, and were vanquished; the color that went and came, and could find no resting place. As she gazed, an unmirthful smile spread over her features, like sunshine that grows melancholy in some desolate spot. Her lips moved inaudibly, but at length she spake.

'I hear it, I hear it. The voice speaketh within me and saith, "Leave thy child, Catharine, for his place is here, and go hence, for I have other work for thee. Break the bonds of natural affection, martyr thy love, and know that in all these things eternal wisdom hath its ends." I go friends, I go. Take ye my boy, my precious jewel. I go hence, trusting that all shall be well, and that even for his infant hands there is a labor in the vineyard.'

She knelt down and whispered to Ilbrahim, who at first struggled and clung to his mother, with sobs and tears, but remained passive when she had kissed his cheek and arisen from the ground. Having held her hands over his head in mental prayer, she was ready to depart.

'Farewell, friends, in mine extremity,' she said to Pearson and his wife; 'the good deed ye have done me is a treasure laid up in heaven, to be returned a thousand fold hereafter. And farewell ye, mine enemies, to whom it is not permitted to harm so much as a hair of my head, nor to stay my footsteps even for a moment. The day is coming, when ye shall call upon me to witness for ye to this one sin uncommitted, and I will rise up and answer.'

She turned her steps towards the door, and the men, who had stationed themselves to guard it, withdrew, and suffered her to pass. A general sentiment of pity overcame the virulence of religious hatred. Sanctified by her love, and her affliction, she went forth, and all the people gazed after her till she had journeyed up the hill, and was lost behind its brow. She went, the apostle of her own unquiet heart, to renew the wanderings of past years. For her voice had been already heard in many lands of Christendom; and she had pined in the cells of a Catholic Inquisition, before she felt the lash, and lay in the dungeons of the Puritans. Her mission had extended also to the followers of the Prophet, and from them she had received the courtesy and kindness, which all the contending sects of our purer religion united to deny her. Her husband and herself had resided many months in Turkey, where even the Sultan's countenance was gracious to them; in that pagan land, too, was Ilbrahim's birthplace, and his oriental name was a mark of gratitude for the good deeds of an unbeliever.

When Pearson and his wife had thus acquired all the rights over Ilbrahim that could be delegated, their affection for him became, like the memory of their native land, or their mild sorrow for the dead, a piece of the immoveable furniture of their hearts. The boy, also, after a week or two of mental disquiet, began to gratify his protectors, by many inadvertent proofs that he considered them as parents, and their house as home. Before the winter snows were melted, the persecuted infant, the little wanderer from a remote and heathen country, seemed native in the New England cottage, and inseparable from the warmth and security of its hearth. Under the influence of kind treatment, and in the consciousness that he was loved, Ilbrahim's demeanor lost a premature manliness, which had resulted from his earlier situation; he became more child-like, and his natural character displayed itself with freedom. It was in many respects a beautiful one, yet the disordered imaginations of both his father and mother had perhaps propagated a certain unhealthiness in the mind of the boy. In his general state, Ilbrahim would derive enjoyment from the most trifling events, and from every object about him; he seemed to discover rich treasures of happiness, by a faculty analogous to that of the witch-hazle, which points to hidden gold where all is barren to the eye. His airy gaiety, coming to him from a thousand sources, communicated itself to the family, and Ilbrahim was like a domesticated sunbeam, brightening moody countenances, and chasing away the gloom from the dark corners of the cottage.

On the other hand, as the susceptibility of pleasure is also that of pain, the exuberant cheerfulness of the boy's prevailing temper sometimes yielded to moments of deep depression. His sorrows could not always be followed up to their original source, but most frequently they appeared to flow, though Ilbrahim was young to be sad for such a cause, from wounded love. The flightiness of his mirth rendered him often guilty of offences against the decorum of a Puritan household, and on these occasions he did not invariably escape rebuke. But the slightest word of real bitterness, which he was infallible in distinguishing from pretended anger, seemed to sink into his heart and poison all his enjoyments, till he became sensible that he was entirely forgiven. Of the malice, which generally accompanies a superfluity of sensitiveness, Ilbrahim was altogether destitute; when trodden upon, he would not turn; when wounded, he could but die. His mind was wanting in the stamina for self-support; it was a plant that would twine beautifully round something stronger than itself, but if repulsed, or torn away, it had no choice but to wither on the ground. Dorothy's acuteness taught her that severity would crush the spirit of the child, and she nurtured him with the gentle care of one who handles a butterfly. Her husband manifested an equal affection, although it grew daily less productive of familiar caresses.

The feelings of the neighboring people, in regard to the Quaker infant and his protectors, had not undergone a favorable change, in spite of the momentary triumph which the desolate mother had obtained over their sympathies. The scorn and bitterness, of which he was the object, were very grievous to Ilbrahim, especially when any circumstance made him sensible that the children, his equals in age, partook of the enmity of their parents. His tender and social nature had already overflowed in attachments to everything about him, and still there was a residue of unappropriated love, which he yearned to bestow upon the little ones who were taught to hate him. As the warm days of spring came on, Ilbrahim was accustomed to remain for hours, silent and inactive, within hearing of the children's voices at their play; yet, with his usual delicacy of feeling, he avoided their notice, and would flee and hide himself from the smallest individual among them. Chance, however, at length seemed to open a medium of communication between his heart and theirs; it was by means of a boy about two years older than Ilbrahim, who was injured by a fall from a tree in the vicinity of Pearson's habitation. As the sufferer's own home was at some distance, Dorothy willingly received him under her roof, and became his tender and careful nurse.

Ilbrahim was the unconscious possessor of much skill in physiognomy, and it would have deterred him, in other circumstances, from attempting to make a friend of this boy. The countenance of the latter immediately impressed a beholder disagreeably, but it required some examination to discover that the cause was a very slight distortion of the mouth, and the irregular, broken line, and near approach of the eyebrows. Analogous, perhaps, to these trifling deformities, was an almost imperceptible twist of every joint, and the uneven prominence of the breast; forming a body, regular in its general outline, but faulty in almost all its details. The disposition of the boy was sullen and reserved, and the village schoolmaster stigmatized him as obtuse in intellect; although, at a later period of life, he evinced ambition and very peculiar talents. But whatever might be his personal or moral irregularities,

Ilbrahim's heart seized upon, and clung to him, from the moment that he was brought wounded into the cottage; the child of persecution seemed to compare his own fate with that of the sufferer, and to feel that even different modes of misfortune had created a sort of relationship between them. Food, rest, and the fresh air, for which he languished, were neglected; he nestled continually by the bed-side of the little stranger, and, with a fond jealousy, endeavored to be the medium of all the cares that were bestowed upon him. As the boy became convalescent, Ilbrahim contrived games suitable to his situation, or amused him by a faculty which he had perhaps breathed in with the air of his barbaric birthplace. It was that of reciting imaginary adventures, on the spur of the moment, and apparently in inexhaustible succession. His tales were of course monstrous, disjointed, and without aim; but they were curious on account of a vein of human tenderness, which ran through them all, and was like a sweet, familiar face, encountered in the midst of wild and unearthly scenery. The auditor paid much attention to these romances, and sometimes interrupted them by brief remarks upon the incidents, displaying shrewdness above his years, mingled with a moral obliquity which grated very harshly against Ilbrahim's instinctive rectitude. Nothing, however, could arrest the progress of the latter's affection, and there were many proofs that it met with a response from the dark and stubborn nature on which it was lavished. The boy's parents at length removed him, to complete his cure under their own roof.

Ilbrahim did not visit his new friend after his departure; but he made anxious and continual inquiries respecting him, and informed himself of the day when he was to reappear among his playmates. On a pleasant summer afternoon, the children of the neighborhood had assembled in the little forest-crowned amphitheatre behind the meetinghouse, and the recovering invalid was there, leaning on a staff. The glee of a score of untainted bosoms was heard in light and airy voices, which danced among the trees like sunshine become audible; the grown men of this weary world, as they journeyed by the spot, marvelled why life, beginning in such brightness, should proceed in gloom; and their hearts, or their imaginations, answered them and said, that the bliss of childhood gushes from its innocence. But it happened that an unexpected addition was made to the heavenly little band. It was Ilbrahim, who came towards the children, with a look of sweet confidence on his fair and spiritual face, as if, having manifested his love to one of them, he had no longer to fear a repulse from their society. A hush came over their mirth, the moment they beheld him, and they stood whispering to each other while he drew nigh; but, all at once, the devil of their fathers entered into the unbreeched fanatics, and, sending up a fierce, shrill cry, they rushed upon the poor Quaker child. In an instant, he was the centre of a brood of baby-fiends, who lifted sticks against him, pelted him with stones, and displayed an instinct of destruction, far more loathsome than the blood-thirstiness of manhood.

The invalid, in the meanwhile, stood apart from the tumult, crying out with a loud voice, 'Fear not, Ilbrahim, come hither and take my hand;' and his unhappy friend endeavored to obey him. After watching the victim's struggling approach, with a calm smile and unabashed eye, the foul-hearted little villain lifted his staff, and struck Ilbrahim on the mouth, so forcibly that the blood issued in a stream. The poor child's arms had been raised to guard his head from the storm of blows; but now he dropped them at once. His persecutors beat him down, trampled upon him, dragged him by his long, fair locks, and Ilbrahim was on the point of becoming as veritable a martyr as ever entered bleeding into heaven. The uproar, however, attracted the notice of a few neighbors, who put themselves to the trouble of rescuing the little heretic, and of conveying him to Pearson's door.

Ilbrahim's bodily harm was severe, but long and careful nursing accomplished his recovery; the injury done to his sensitive spirit was more serious, though not so visible. Its signs were principally of a negative character, and to be discovered only by those who had previously known him. His gait was thenceforth slow, even, and unvaried by the sudden bursts of sprightlier motion, which had once corresponded to his over-flowing gladness; his countenance was heavier, and its former play of expression, the dance of sunshine reflected from moving water, was destroyed by the cloud over his existence; his notice was attracted in a far less degree by passing events, and he appeared to find greater difficulty in comprehending what was new to him, than at a happier period. A stranger, founding his judgment upon these circumstances, would have said that the dulness of the child's intellect widely contradicted the promise of his features; but the secret was in the direction of Ilbrahim's thoughts, which were brooding within him when they should naturally have been wandering abroad. An attempt of Dorothy to revive his former sportiveness was the single occasion, on which his quiet demeanor yielded to a violent display of grief; he burst into passionate weeping, and ran and hid himself, for his heart had become so miserably sore, that even the hand of kindness tortured it like fire. Sometimes, at night, and probably in his dreams, he was heard to cry, 'Mother! Mother!' as if her place, which a stranger had supplied while Ilbrahim was happy, admitted of no substitute in his extreme affliction. Perhaps, among the many life-weary wretches then upon the earth, there was not one who combined innocence and misery like this poor, broken-hearted infant, so soon the victim of his own heavenly nature.

While this melancholy change had taken place in Ilbrahim, one of an earlier origin and of different character had come to its perfection in his adopted father. The incident with which this tale commences found Pearson in a state of religious dulness, yet mentally disquieted, and longing for a more fervid faith than he possessed. The first effect of his kindness to Ilbrahim was to produce a softened feeling, an incipient love for the child's whole sect; but joined to this, and resulting perhaps from self-suspicion, was a proud and ostentatious contempt of their tenets and practical extravagances. In the course of much thought, however, for the subject struggled irresistibly into his mind, the foolishness of the doctrine began to be less evident, and the points which had particularly offended his reason assumed another aspect, or vanished entirely away. The work within him appeared to go on even while he slept, and that which had been a doubt, when he laid down to rest, would often hold the place of a truth, confirmed by some forgotten demonstration, when he recalled his thoughts in the morning. But while he was thus becoming assimilated to the enthusiasts, his contempt, in no-

wise decreasing towards them, grew very fierce against himself; he imagined, also, that every face of his acquaintance
wore a sneer, and that every word addressed to him was a
gibe. Such was his state of mind at the period of Ilbrahim's
misfortune; and the emotions consequent upon that event
completed the change, of which the child had been the original instrument.

In the mean time neither the fierceness of the persecutors,
nor the infatuation of their victims, had decreased. The dungeons were never empty; the streets of almost every village
echoed daily with the lash; the life of a woman, whose mild
and Christian spirit no cruelty could embitter, had been sacrificed; and more innocent blood was yet to pollute the
hands, that were so often raised in prayer. Early after the Res-
toration, the English Quakers represented to Charles II. that
a 'vein of blood was opened in his dominions;' but though
the displeasure of the voluptuous king was roused, his interference was not prompt. And now the tale must stride forward over many months, leaving Pearson to encounter ignominy and misfortune; his wife to a firm endurance of a
thousand sorrows; poor Ilbrahim to pine and droop like a
cankered rose-bud; his mother to wander on a mistaken errand, neglectful of the holiest trust which can be committed
to a woman.

A winter evening, a night of storm, had darkened over
Pearson's habitation, and there were no cheerful faces to drive
the gloom from his broad hearth. The fire, it is true, sent
forth a glowing heat and a ruddy light, and large logs, dripping with half-melted snow, lay ready to be cast upon the
embers. But the apartment was saddened in its aspect by the
absence of much of the homely wealth which had once
adorned it; for the exaction of repeated fines, and his own
neglect of temporal affairs, had greatly impoverished the
owner. And with the furniture of peace, the implements of
war had likewise disappeared; the sword was broken, the
helm and cuirass were cast away for ever; the soldier had done
with battles, and might not lift so much as his naked hand to
guard his head. But the Holy Book remained, and the table

on which it rested was drawn before the fire, while two of the persecuted sect sought comfort from its pages.

He who listened, while the other read, was the master of the house, now emaciated in form, and altered as to the expression and healthiness of his countenance; for his mind had dwelt too long among visionary thoughts, and his body had been worn by imprisonment and stripes. The hale and weather-beaten old man, who sat beside him, had sustained less injury from a far longer course of the same mode of life. In person he was tall and dignified, and, which alone would have made him hateful to the Puritans, his grey locks fell from beneath the broad-brimmed hat, and rested on his shoulders. As the old man read the sacred page, the snow drifted against the windows, or eddied in at the crevices of the door, while a blast kept laughing in the chimney, and the blaze leaped fiercely up to seek it. And sometimes, when the wind struck the hill at a certain angle, and swept down by the cottage across the wintry plain, its voice was the most doleful that can be conceived; it came as if the Past were speaking, as if the Dead had contributed each a whisper, as if the Desolation of Ages were breathed in that one lamenting sound.

The Quaker at length closed the book, retaining however his hand between the pages which he had been reading, while he looked steadfastly at Pearson. The attitude and features of the latter might have indicated the endurance of bodily pain; he leaned his forehead on his hands, his teeth were firmly closed, and his frame was tremulous at intervals with a nervous agitation.

'Friend Tobias,' inquired the old man, compassionately, 'hast thou found no comfort in these many blessed passages of Scripture?'

'Thy voice has fallen on my ear like a sound afar off and indistinct,' replied Pearson without lifting his eyes. 'Yea, and when I have harkened carefully, the words seemed cold and lifeless, and intended for another and a lesser grief than mine. Remove the book,' he added, in a tone of sullen bitterness. 'I have no part in its consolations, and they do but fret my sorrow the more.'

'Nay, feeble brother, be not as one who hath never known

the light,' said the elder Quaker, earnestly, but with mildness. 'Art thou he that wouldst be content to give all, and endure all, for conscience sake; desiring even peculiar trials, that thy faith might be purified, and thy heart weaned from worldly desires? And wilt thou sink beneath an affliction which happens alike to them that have their portion here below, and to them that lay up treasure in heaven? Faint not, for thy burthen is yet light.'

'It is heavy! It is heavier than I can bear!' exclaimed Pearson, with the impatience of a variable spirit. 'From my youth upward I have been a man marked out for wrath; and year by year, yea, day after day, I have endured sorrows such as others know not in their life-time. And now I speak not of the love that has been turned to hatred, the honor to ignominy, the ease and plentifulness of all things to danger, want, and nakedness. All this I could have borne, and counted myself blessed. But when my heart was desolate with many losses, I fixed it upon the child of a stranger, and he became dearer to me than all my buried ones; and now he too must die, as if my love were poison. Verily, I am an accursed man, and I will lay me down in the dust, and lift up my head no more.'

'Thou sinnest, brother, but it is not for me to rebuke thee; for I also have had my hours of darkness, wherein I have murmured against the cross,' said the old Quaker. He continued, perhaps in the hope of distracting his companion's thoughts from his own sorrows. 'Even of late was the light obscured within me, when the men of blood had banished me on pain of death, and the constables led me onward from village to village, towards the wilderness. A strong and cruel hand was wielding the knotted cords; they sunk deep into the flesh, and thou mightst have tracked every reel and totter of my footsteps by the blood that followed. As we went on—'

'Have I not borne all this; and have I murmured?' interrupted Pearson, impatiently.

'Nay, friend, but hear me,' continued the other. 'As we journeyed on, night darkened on our path, so that no man could see the rage of the persecutors, or the constancy of my endurance, though Heaven forbid that I should glory therein. The lights began to glimmer in the cottage windows, and I could discern the inmates as they gathered, in comfort and security, every man with his wife and children by their own evening hearth. At length we came to a tract of fertile land; in the dim light, the forest was not visible around it; and behold! there was a straw-thatched dwelling, which bore the very aspect of my home, far over the wild ocean, far in our own England. Then came bitter thoughts upon me; yea, re-membrances that were like death to my soul. The happiness of my early days was painted to me; the disquiet of my man-hood, the altered faith of my declining years. I remembered how I had been moved to go forth a wanderer, when my daughter, the youngest, the dearest of my flock, lay on her dying bed, and—'

'Couldst thou obey the command at such a moment?' ex-claimed Pearson, shuddering.

'Yea, yea,' replied the old man, hurriedly. 'I was kneeling by her bed-side when the voice spoke loud within me; but immediately I rose, and took my staff, and gat me gone. Oh! that it were permitted me to forget her woful look, when I thus withdrew my arm, and left her journeying through the dark valley alone! for her soul was faint, and she had leaned upon my prayers. Now in that night of horror I was assailed by the thought that I had been an erring Christian, and a cruel parent; yea, even my daughter, with her pale, dying fea-tures, seemed to stand by me and whisper, "Father, you are deceived; go home and shelter your grey head." Oh! Thou, to whom I have looked in my farthest wanderings,' continued the Quaker, raising his agitated eyes to heaven, 'inflict not upon the bloodiest of our persecutors the unmitigated agony of my soul, when I believed that all I had done and suffered for Thee was at the instigation of a mocking fiend! But I yielded not; I knelt down and wrestled with the tempter, while the scourge bit more fiercely into the flesh. My prayer was heard, and I went on in peace and joy towards the wilderness.'

The old man, though his fanaticism had generally all the calmness of reason, was deeply moved while reciting this tale; and his unwonted emotion seemed to rebuke and keep down that of his companion. They sat in silence, with their faces to the fire, imaging, perhaps, in its red embers, new scenes of persecution yet to be encountered. The snow still drifted hard against the windows, and sometimes, as the blaze of the logs had gradually sunk, came down the spacious chimney and hissed upon the hearth. A cautious footstep might now and then be heard in a neighboring apartment, and the sound invariably drew the eyes of both Quakers to the door which led thither. When a fierce and riotous gust of wind had led his thoughts, by a natural association, to homeless travellers on such a night, Pearson resumed the conversation.

'I have well nigh sunk under my own share of this trial,' observed he, sighing heavily; 'yet I would that it might be doubled to me, if so the child's mother could be spared. Her wounds have been deep and many, but this will be the sorest of all.'

'Fear not for Catharine,' replied the old Quaker; 'for I know that valiant woman, and have seen how she can bear the cross. A mother's heart, indeed, is strong in her, and may seem to contend mightily with her faith; but soon she will stand up and give thanks that her son has been thus early an accepted sacrifice. The boy hath done his work, and she will feel that he is taken hence in kindness both to him and her. Blessed, blessed are they, that with so little suffering can enter into peace!'

The fitful rush of the wind was now disturbed by a portentous sound; it was a quick and heavy knocking at the outer door. Pearson's wan countenance grew paler, for many a visit of persecution had taught him what to dread; the old man, on the other hand, stood up erect, and his glance was firm as that of the tried soldier who awaits his enemy.

'The men of blood have come to seek me,' he observed, with calmness. 'They have heard how I was moved to return from banishment; and now am I to be led to prison, and thence to death. It is an end I have long looked for. I will open unto them, lest they say, "Lo, he feareth!"'

'Nay, I will present myself before them,' said Pearson, with recovered fortitude. 'It may be that they seek me alone, and know not that thou abidest with me.'

'Let us go boldly, both one and the other,' rejoined his companion. 'It is not fitting that thou or I should shrink.'

They therefore proceeded through the entry to the door, which they opened, bidding the applicant 'Come in, in God's name!' A furious blast of wind drove the storm into their faces, and extinguished the lamp; they had barely time to discern a figure, so white from head to foot with the drifted snow that it seemed like Winter's self, come in human shape to seek refuge from its own desolation.

'Enter, friend, and do thy errand, be it what it may,' said Pearson. 'It must needs be pressing, since thou comest on such a bitter night.'

'Peace be with this household,' said the stranger, when they stood on the floor of the inner apartment.

Pearson started; the elder Quaker stirred the slumbering embers of the fire, till they sent up a clear and lofty blaze; it was a female voice that had spoken; it was a female form that shone out, cold and wintry, in that comfortable light.

'Catharine, blessed woman,' exclaimed the old man, 'art thou come to this darkened land again! art thou come to bear a valiant testimony as in former years? The scourge hath not prevailed against thee, and from the dungeon hast thou come forth triumphant; but strengthen, strengthen now thy heart, Catharine, for Heaven will prove thee yet this once, ere thou go to thy reward.'

'Rejoice, friends!' she replied. 'Thou who hast long been of our people, and thou whom a little child hath led to us, rejoice! Lo! I come, the messenger of glad tidings, for the day of persecution is overpast. The heart of the king, even Charles, hath been moved in gentleness towards us, and he hath sent forth his letters to stay the hands of the men of blood. A ship's company of our friends hath arrived at yonder town, and I also sailed joyfully among them.'

As Catharine spoke, her eyes were roaming about the room, in search of him for whose sake security was dear to her. Pearson made a silent appeal to the old man, nor did the latter shrink from the painful task assigned him.

'Sister,' he began, in a softened yet perfectly calm tone, 'thou tellest us of His love, manifested in temporal good; and now must we speak to thee of that self-same love, displayed in chastenings. Hitherto, Catharine, thou hast been as one journeying in a darksome and difficult path, and leading an infant by the hand; fain wouldst thou have looked heavenward continually, but still the cares of that little child have drawn thine eyes, and thy affections, to the earth. Sister! go on rejoicing, for his tottering footsteps shall impede thine own no more.'

But the unhappy mother was not thus to be consoled; she shook like a leaf, she turned white as the very snow that hung drifted into her hair. The firm old man extended his hand and held her up, keeping his eye upon hers, as if to repress any outbreak of passion.

'I am a woman, I am but a woman; will He try me above my strength?' said Catharine, very quickly, and almost in a whisper. 'I have been wounded sore; I have suffered much; many things in the body, many in the mind; crucified in myself, and in them that were dearest to me. Surely,' added she, with a long shudder, 'He hath spared me in this one thing.' She broke forth with sudden and irrepressible violence. 'Tell me, man of cold heart, what has God done to me? Hath He cast me down never to rise again? Hath He crushed my very heart in his hand? And thou, to whom I committed my child, how hast thou fulfilled thy trust? Give me back the boy, well, sound, alive, alive; or earth and heaven shall avenge me!'

The agonized shriek of Catharine was answered by the faint, the very faint voice of a child.

On this day it had become evident to Pearson, to his aged guest, and to Dorothy, that Ilbrahim's brief and troubled pilgrimage drew near its close. The two former would willingly have remained by him, to make use of the prayers and pious discourses which they deemed appropriate to the time, and which, if they be impotent as to the departing traveller's reception in the world whither he goes, may at least sustain him in bidding adieu to earth. But though Ilbrahim uttered no complaint, he was disturbed by the faces that looked upon him; so that Dorothy's entreaties, and their own conviction that the child's feet might tread heaven's pavement and not soil it, had induced the two Quakers to remove. Ilbrahim then closed his eyes and grew calm, and, except for now and then, a kind and low word to his nurse, might have been thought to slumber. As night-fall came on, however, and the storm began to rise, something seemed to trouble the repose of the boy's mind, and to render his sense of hearing active and acute. If a passing wind lingered to shake the casement, he strove to turn his head towards it; if the door jarred to

and fro upon its hinges, he looked long and anxiously thitherward; if the heavy voice of the old man, as he read the scriptures, rose but a little higher, the child almost held his dying
breath to listen; if a snow-drift swept by the cottage, with
a sound like the trailing of a garment, Ilbrahim seemed to
watch that some visitant should enter.

But, after a little time, he relinquished whatever secret hope
had agitated him, and, with one low, complaining whisper,
turned his cheek upon the pillow. He then addressed Dorothy with his usual sweetness, and besought her to draw near
him; she did so, and Ilbrahim took her hand in both of his,
grasping it with a gentle pressure, as if to assure himself that
he retained it. At intervals, and without disturbing the repose
of his countenance, a very faint trembling passed over him
from head to foot, as if a mild but somewhat cool wind had
breathed upon him, and made him shiver. As the boy thus
led her by the hand, in his quiet progress over the borders of
eternity, Dorothy almost imagined that she could discern the
near, though dim delightfulness, of the home he was about
to reach; she would not have enticed the little wanderer back,
though she bemoaned herself that she must leave him and
return. But just when Ilbrahim's feet were pressing on the
soil of Paradise, he heard a voice behind him, and it recalled
him a few, few paces of the weary path which he had travelled. As Dorothy looked upon his features, she perceived
that their placid expression was again disturbed; her own
thoughts had been so wrapt in him, that all sounds of the
storm, and of human speech, were lost to her; but when
Catharine's shriek pierced through the room, the boy strove
to raise himself.

'Friend, she is come! Open unto her!' cried he.

In a moment, his mother was kneeling by the bed-side; she
drew Ilbrahim to her bosom, and he nestled there, with no
violence of joy, but contentedly as if he were hushing himself
to sleep. He looked into her face, and reading its agony, said,
with feeble earnestness,

'Mourn not, dearest mother. I am happy now.' And with
these words, the gentle boy was dead.

The king's mandate to stay the New England persecutors

was effectual in preventing further martyrdoms; but the colonial authorities, trusting in the remoteness of their situation, and perhaps in the supposed instability of the royal government, shortly renewed their severities in all other respects. Catharine's fanaticism had become wilder by the sundering of all human ties; and wherever a scourge was lifted, there was she to receive the blow; and whenever a dungeon was unbarred, thither she came, to cast herself upon the floor. But in process of time, a more Christian spirit—a spirit of forbearance, though not of cordiality or approbation, began to pervade the land in regard to the persecuted sect. And then, when the rigid old Pilgrims eyed her rather in pity than in wrath; when the matrons fed her with the fragments of their children's food, and offered her a lodging on a hard and lowly bed; when no little crowd of school-boys left their sports to cast stones after the roving enthusiast; then did Catharine return to Pearson's dwelling, and made that her home.

As if Ilbrahim's sweetness yet lingered round his ashes; as if his gentle spirit came down from heaven to teach his parent a true religion, her fierce and vindictive nature was softened by the same griefs which had once irritated it. When the course of years had made the features of the unobtrusive mourner familiar in the settlement, she became a subject of not deep, but general interest; a being on whom the otherwise superfluous sympathies of all might be bestowed. Every one spoke of her with that degree of pity which it is pleasant to experience; every one was ready to do her the little kindnesses, which are not costly, yet manifest good will; and when at last she died, a long train of her once bitter persecutors followed her, with decent sadness and tears that were not painful, to her place by Ilbrahim's green and sunken grave.

The Seven Vagabonds

RAMBLING on foot, in the spring of my life and the summer of the year, I came one afternoon to a point which gave me the choice of three directions. Straight before me, the main road extended its dusty length to Boston; on the left a branch went towards the sea, and would have lengthened my journey a trifle, of twenty or thirty miles; while, by the right hand path, I might have gone over hills and lakes to Canada, visiting in my way, the celebrated town of Stamford. On a level spot of grass, at the foot of the guide post, appeared an object, which though locomotive on a different principle, reminded me of Gulliver's portable mansion among the Brobdingnags. It was a huge covered wagon, or, more properly, a small house on wheels, with a door on one side and a window shaded by green blinds on the other. Two horses munching provender out of the baskets which muzzled them, were fastened near the vehicle: a delectable sound of music proceeded from the interior; and I immediately conjectured that this was some itinerant show, halting at the confluence of the roads to intercept such idle travellers as myself. A shower had long been climbing up the western sky, and now hung so blackly over my onward path that it was a point of wisdom to seek shelter here.

'Halloo! Who stands guard here? Is the door keeper asleep?' cried I, approaching a ladder of two or three steps which was let down from the wagon.

The music ceased at my summons, and there appeared at the door, not the sort of figure that I had mentally assigned to the wandering show man, but a most respectable old personage, whom I was sorry to have addressed in so free a style. He wore a snuff coloured coat and small clothes, with white top boots, and exhibited the mild dignity of aspect and manner which may often be noticed in aged school masters, and sometimes in deacons, selectmen, or other potentates of that kind. A small piece of silver was my passport within his premises, where I found only one other person, hereafter to be described.

'This is a dull day for business,' said the old gentleman, as he ushered me in; 'but I merely tarry here to refresh the cattle, being bound for the camp meeting at Stamford.'

Perhaps the moveable scene of this narrative is still peregrinating New England, and may enable the reader to test the accuracy of my description. The spectacle, for I will not use the unworthy term of puppet-show, consisted of a multitude of little people assembled on a miniature stage. Among them were artisans of every kind, in the attitudes of their toil, and a group of fair ladies and gay gentlemen standing ready for the dance; a company of foot soldiers formed a line across the stage, looking stern, grim, and terrible enough, to make it a pleasant consideration that they were but three inches high; and conspicuous above the whole was seen a Merry Andrew, in the pointed cap and motley coat of his profession. All the inhabitants of this mimic world were motionless, like the figures in a picture, or like that people who one moment were alive in the midst of their business and delights, and the next were transformed to statues, preserving an eternal semblance of labour that was ended, and pleasure that could be felt no more. Anon, however, the old gentleman turned the handle of a barrel organ, the first note of which produced a most enlivening effect upon the figures, and awoke them all to their proper occupations and amusements. By the self-same impulse the tailor plied his needle, the blacksmith's hammer descended upon the anvil, and the dancers whirled away on feathery tiptoes; the company of soldiers broke into platoons, retreated from the stage, and were succeeded by a troop of horse, who came prancing onward with such a sound of trumpets and trampling of hoofs, as might have startled Don Quixote himself; while an old toper, of inveterate ill-habits, uplifted his black bottle and took off a hearty swig. Meantime the Merry Andrew began to caper and turn somersets, shaking his sides, nodding his head, and winking his eyes in as life-like a manner as if he were ridiculing the nonsense of all human affairs, and making fun of the whole multitude beneath him. At length the old magician (for I compared the show man to Prospero, entertaining his guests with a masque of shadows) paused that I might give utterance to my wonder.

'What an admirable piece of work is this!' exclaimed I, lifting up my hands in astonishment.

Indeed, I liked the spectacle, and was tickled with the old man's gravity as he presided at it, for I had none of that foolish wisdom which reproves every occupation that is not useful in this world of vanities. If there be a faculty which I possess more perfectly than most men, it is that of throwing myself mentally into situations foreign to my own, and detecting, with a cheerful eye, the desirable circumstances of each. I could have envied the life of this gray headed show man, spent as it had been in a course of safe and pleasurable adventure, in driving his huge vehicle sometimes through the sands of Cape Cod, and sometimes over the rough forest roads of the north and east, and halting now on the green before a village meeting house, and now in a paved square of the metropolis. How often must his heart have been gladdened by the delight of children, as they viewed these animated figures! or his pride indulged, by haranguing learnedly to grown men on the mechanical powers which produced such wonderful effects! or his gallantry brought into play (for this is an attribute which such grave men do not lack) by the visits of pretty maidens! And then with how fresh a feeling must he return, at intervals, to his own peculiar home!

'I would I were assured of as happy a life as his,' thought I.

Though the show man's wagon might have accommodated fifteen or twenty spectators, it now contained only himself and me, and a third person at whom I threw a glance on entering. He was a neat and trim young man of two or three and twenty; his drab hat, and green frock coat with velvet collar, were smart, though no longer new; while a pair of green spectacles, that seemed needless to his brisk little eyes, gave him something of a scholar-like and literary air. After allowing me a sufficient time to inspect the puppets, he advanced with a bow, and drew my attention to some books in a corner of the wagon. These he forthwith began to extol, with an amazing volubility of well-sounding words, and an ingenuity of praise that won him my heart, as being myself one of the most merciful of critics. Indeed his stock required some considerable powers of commendation in the salesman;

there were several ancient friends of mine, the novels of those happy days when my affections wavered between the Scottish Chiefs and Thomas Thumb; besides a few of later date, whose merits had not been acknowledged by the public. I was glad to find that dear little venerable volume, the New England Primer, looking as antique as ever, though in its thousandth new edition; a bundle of superannuated gilt picture books made such a child of me, that, partly for the glittering covers, and partly for the fairy tales within, I bought the whole; and an assortment of ballads and popular theatrical songs drew largely on my purse. To balance these expenditures, I meddled neither with sermons, nor science, nor morality, though volumes of each were there; nor with a Life of Franklin in the coarsest of paper, but so showily bound that it was emblematical of the Doctor himself, in the court dress which he refused to wear at Paris; nor with Webster's spelling book, nor some of Byron's minor poems, nor half a dozen little testaments at twenty-five cents each.

Thus far the collection might have been swept from some great book store, or picked up at an evening auction room; but there was one small blue covered pamphlet, which the pedlar handed me with so peculiar an air, that I purchased it immediately at his own price; and then, for the first time, the thought struck me, that I had spoken face to face with the veritable author of a printed book. The literary man now evinced a great kindness for me, and I ventured to inquire which way he was travelling.

'Oh,' said he, 'I keep company with this old gentleman here, and we are moving now towards the camp meeting at Stamford.'

He then explained to me, that for the present season he had rented a corner of the wagon as a book store, which, as he wittily observed, was a true Circulating Library, since there were few parts of the country where it had not gone its rounds. I approved of the plan exceedingly, and began to sum up within my mind the many uncommon felicities in the life of a book pedlar, especially when his character resembled that of the individual before me. At a high rate was to be reckoned the daily and hourly enjoyment of such interviews as the present, in which he seized upon the admiration of a passing stranger, and made him aware that a man of literary taste, and even of literary achievement, was travelling the country in a show man's wagon. A more valuable, yet not infrequent triumph, might be won in his conversations with some elderly clergyman, long vegetating in a rocky, woody, watery back settlement of New England, who, as he recruited his library from the pedlar's stock of sermons, would exhort him to seek a college education and become the first scholar in his class. Sweeter and prouder yet would be his sensations, when, talking poetry while he sold spelling books, he should charm the mind, and haply touch the heart of a fair country school mistress, herself an unhonoured poetess, a wearer of blue stockings which none but himself took pains to look at. But the scene of his completest glory would be when the wagon had halted for the night, and his stock of books was transferred to some crowded bar room. Then would he recommend to the multifarious company, whether traveller from the city, or teamster from the hills, or neighbouring squire, or the landlord himself, or his loutish hostler, works suited to each particular taste and capacity; proving, all the while, by acute criticism and profound remark, that the lore in his books was even exceeded by that in his brain.

Thus happily would he traverse the land; sometimes a herald before the march of Mind; sometimes walking arm in arm with awful Literature, and reaping every where, a harvest of real and sensible popularity, which the secluded book worms, by whose toil he lived, could never hope for.

'If ever I meddle with literature,' thought I, fixing myself in adamantine resolution, 'it shall be as a travelling book seller.'

Though it was still mid-afternoon, the air had now grown dark about us, and a few drops of rain came down upon the roof of our vehicle, pattering like the feet of birds that had flown thither to rest. A sound of pleasant voices made us listen, and there soon appeared halfway up the ladder, the pretty person of a young damsel, whose rosy face was so cheerful, that even amid the gloomy light it seemed as if the sunbeams were peeping under her bonnet. We next saw the dark and handsome features of a young man, who with easier gallantry than might have been expected in the heart of Yankee-land, was assisting her into the wagon. It became imme-

diately evident to us, when the two strangers stood within
the door, that they were of a profession kindred to those of
my companions; and I was delighted with the more than hospitable, the even paternal kindness, of the old show man's
manner, as he welcomed them; while the man of literature
hastened to lead the merry eyed girl to a seat on the long
bench.

'You are housed but just in time, my young friends,' said
the master of the wagon. 'The sky would have been down
upon you within five minutes.'

The young man's reply marked him as a foreigner, not by
any variation from the idiom and accent of good English, but
because he spoke with more caution and accuracy, than if perfectly familiar with the language.

'We knew that a shower was hanging over us,' said he, 'and
consulted whether it were best to enter the house on the top
of yonder hill, but seeing your wagon in the road—'

'We agreed to come hither,' interrupted the girl, with a
smile, 'because we should be more at home in a wandering
house like this.'

I, meanwhile, with many a wild and undetermined fantasy,
was narrowly inspecting these two doves that had flown into
our ark. The young man, tall, agile, and athletic, wore a mass
of black shining curls clustering round a dark and vivacious
countenance, which, if it had not greater expression, was at
least more active, and attracted readier notice, than the quiet
faces of our countrymen. At his first appearance, he had been
laden with a neat mahogany box, of about two feet square,
but very light in proportion to its size, which he had immediately unstrapped from his shoulders and deposited on the
floor of the wagon.

The girl had nearly as fair a complexion as our own beauties, and a brighter one than most of them; the lightness of
her figure, which seemed calculated to traverse the whole
world without weariness, suited well with the glowing cheerfulness of her face; and her gay attire combining the rainbow
hues of crimson, green, and a deep orange, was as proper to
her lightsome aspect as if she had been born in it. This gay
stranger was appropriately burthened with that mirth inspiring instrument, the fiddle, which her companion took from

her hands, and shortly began the process of tuning. Neither of us, the previous company of the wagon, needed to inquire their trade; for this could be no mystery to frequenters of brigade musters, ordinations, cattle shows, commencements, and other festal meetings in our sober land; and there is a dear friend of mine, who will smile when this page recalls to his memory a chivalrous deed performed by us, in rescuing the show box of such a couple from a mob of great double fisted countrymen.

'Come,' said I to the damsel of gay attire, 'shall we visit all the wonders of the world together?'

She understood the metaphor at once; though indeed it would not much have troubled me, if she had assented to the literal meaning of my words. The mahogany box was placed in a proper position, and I peeped in through its small round magnifying window, while the girl sat by my side, and gave short descriptive sketches, as one after another the pictures were unfolded to my view. We visited together, at least our imaginations did, full many a famous city, in the streets of which I had long yearned to tread; once, I remember, we were in the harbour of Barcelona, gazing townwards; next, she bore me through the air to Sicily, and bade me look up at blazing Ætna; then we took wing to Venice, and sat in a gondola beneath the arch of the Rialto; and anon she set me down among the thronged spectators at the coronation of Napoleon. But there was one scene, its locality she could not tell, which charmed my attention longer than all those gorgeous palaces and churches, because the fancy haunted me, that I myself, the preceding summer had beheld just such an humble meeting house, in just such a pine surrounded nook, among our own green mountains. All these pictures were tolerably executed, though far inferior to the girl's touches of description; nor was it easy to comprehend, how in so few sentences, and these, as I supposed, in a language foreign to her, she contrived to present an airy copy of each varied scene. When we had travelled through the vast extent of the mahogany box, I looked into my guide's face.

'Where are you going my pretty maid?' inquired I, in the words of an old song.

'Ah,' said the gay damsel, 'you might as well ask where the

summer wind is going. We are wanderers here, and there, and every where. Wherever there is mirth, our merry hearts are drawn to it. To-day, indeed, the people have told us of a great frolic and festival in these parts; so perhaps we may be needed at what you call the camp meeting at Stamford.'

Then in my happy youth, and while her pleasant voice yet sounded in my ears, I sighed; for none but myself, I thought, should have been her companion in a life which seemed to realize my own wild fancies, cherished all through visionary boyhood to that hour. To these two strangers, the world was in its golden age, not that indeed it was less dark and sad than ever, but because its weariness and sorrow had no community with their ethereal nature. Wherever they might appear in their pilgrimage of bliss, Youth would echo back their gladness, care stricken Maturity would rest a moment from its toil, and Age, tottering among the graves, would smile in withered joy for their sakes. The lonely cot, the narrow and gloomy street, the sombre shade, would catch a passing gleam like that now shining on ourselves, as these bright spirits wandered by. Blessed pair, whose happy home was throughout all the earth! I looked at my shoulders, and thought them broad enough to sustain those pictured towns and mountains; mine, too, was an elastic foot, as tireless as the wing of the bird of Paradise; mine was then an untroubled heart, that would have gone singing on its delightful way.

'Oh, maiden!' said I aloud, 'why did you not come hither alone?'

While the merry girl and myself were busy with the show box, the unceasing rain had driven another wayfarer into the wagon. He seemed pretty nearly of the old show man's age, but much smaller, leaner, and more withered than he, and less respectably clad in a patched suit of gray; withal, he had a thin, shrewd countenance, and a pair of diminutive gray eyes, which peeped rather too keenly out of their puckered sockets. This old fellow had been joking with the show man, in a manner which intimated previous acquaintance; but perceiving that the damsel and I had terminated our affairs, he drew forth a folded document and presented it to me. As I had anticipated, it proved to be a circular, written in a very fair and legible hand, and signed by several distinguished gentlemen whom I had never heard of, stating that the bearer had encountered every variety of misfortune, and recommending him to the notice of all charitable people. Previous disbursements had left me no more than a five dollar bill, out of which, however, I offered to make the beggar a donation, provided he would give me change for it. The object of my beneficence looked keenly in my face, and discerned that I had none of that abominable spirit, characteristic though it be of a full blooded Yankee, which takes pleasure in detecting every little harmless piece of knavery.

'Why, perhaps,' said the ragged old mendicant, 'if the bank is in good standing, I can't say but I may have enough about me to change your bill.'

'It is a bill of the Suffolk Bank,' said I, 'and better than the specie.'

As the beggar had nothing to object, he now produced a small buff leather bag, tied up carefully with a shoe string. When this was opened, there appeared a very comfortable treasure of silver coins, of all sorts and sizes, and I even fancied that I saw, gleaming among them, the golden plumage of that rare bird in our currency, the American Eagle. In this precious heap was my bank note deposited, the rate of exchange being considerably against me. His wants being thus relieved, the destitute man pulled out of his pocket an old pack of greasy cards, which had probably contributed to fill the buff leather bag, in more ways than one.

'Come,' said he, 'I spy a rare fortune in your face, and for twenty-five cents more, I'll tell you what it is.'

I never refuse to take a glimpse into futurity; so after shuffling the cards, and when the fair damsel had cut them, I dealt a portion to the prophetic beggar. Like others of his profession, before predicting the shadowy events that were moving on to meet me, he gave proof of his preternatural science, by describing scenes through which I had already passed. Here let me have credit for a sober fact. When the old man had read a page in his book of fate, he bent his keen gray eyes on mine, and proceeded to relate, in all its minute particulars, what was then the most singular event of my life. It was one which I had no purpose to disclose, till the general unfolding of all secrets; nor would it be a much stranger instance of

inscrutable knowledge, or fortunate conjecture, if the beggar
were to meet me in the street to-day, and repeat word for
word, the page which I have here written. The fortune teller,
after predicting a destiny which time seems loth to make
good, put up his cards, secreted his treasure bag, and began
to converse with the other occupants of the wagon.

'Well, old friend,' said the show man, 'you have not yet
told us which way your face is turned, this afternoon.'

'I am taking a trip northward, this warm weather,' replied
the conjurer, 'across the Connecticut first, and then up
through Vermont, and may be into Canada before the fall.
But I must stop and see the breaking up of the camp meeting
at Stamford.'

I began to think that all the vagrants in New England were
converging to the camp meeting, and had made this wagon
their rendezvous by the way. The show man now proposed,
that, when the shower was over, they should pursue the road
to Stamford together, it being sometimes the policy of these
people to form a sort of league and confederacy.

'And the young lady too,' observed the gallant bibliopolist,
bowing to her profoundly, 'and this foreign gentleman, as I
understand, are on a jaunt of pleasure to the same spot. It
would add incalculably to my own enjoyment, and I presume
to that of my colleague and his friend, if they could be prevailed upon to join our party.'

This arrangement met with approbation on all hands, nor
were any of those concerned more sensible of its advantages
than myself, who had no title to be included in it. Having
already satisfied myself as to the several modes in which the
four others attained felicity, I next set my mind at work to
discover what enjoyments were peculiar to the old "Strag-
gler," as the people of the country would have termed the
wandering mendicant and prophet. As he pretended to familiarity with the Devil, so I fancied that he was fitted to pursue
and take delight in his way of life, by possessing some of the
mental and moral characteristics, the lighter and more comic
ones, of the Devil in popular stories. Among them might be
reckoned a love of deception for its own sake, a shrewd eye
and keen relish for human weakness and ridiculous infirmity,
and the talent of petty fraud. Thus to this old man there

would be pleasure even in the consciousness so insupportable to some minds, that his whole life was a cheat upon the world, and that so far as he was concerned with the public, his little cunning had the upper hand of its united wisdom. Every day would furnish him with a succession of minute and pungent triumphs; as when, for instance, his importunity wrung a pittance out of the heart of a miser, or when my silly good nature transferred a part of my slender purse to his plump leather bag; or when some ostentatious gentleman should throw a coin to the ragged beggar who was richer than himself; or when, though he would not always be so decidedly diabolical, his pretended wants should make him a sharer in the scanty living of real indigence. And then what an inexhaustible field of enjoyment, both as enabling him to discern so much folly and achieve such quantities of minor mischief, was opened to his sneering spirit by his pretensions to prophetic knowledge.

All this was a sort of happiness which I could conceive of, though I had little sympathy with it. Perhaps had I been then inclined to admit it, I might have found that the roving life was more proper to him than to either of his companions; for Satan, to whom I had compared the poor man, has delighted, ever since the time of Job, in 'wandering up and down upon the earth;' and indeed a crafty disposition, which operates not in deep laid plans, but in disconnected tricks, could not have an adequate scope, unless naturally impelled to a continual change of scene and society. My reflections were here interrupted.

'Another visitor!' exclaimed the old show man.

The door of the wagon had been closed against the tempest, which was roaring and blustering with prodigious fury and commotion, and beating violently against our shelter, as if it claimed all those homeless people for its lawful prey, while we, caring little for the displeasure of the elements, sat comfortably talking. There was now an attempt to open the door, succeeded by a voice, uttering some strange, unintelligible gibberish, which my companions mistook for Greek, and I suspected to be thieves' Latin. However, the show man stept forward, and gave admittance to a figure which made me imagine, either that our wagon had rolled back two hundred years into past ages, or that the forest and its old inhabitants had sprung up around us by enchantment.

It was a red Indian, armed with his bow and arrow. His dress was a sort of cap, adorned with a single feather of some wild bird, and a frock of blue cotton, girded tight about him; on his breast, like orders of knighthood, hung a crescent and a circle, and other ornaments of silver; while a small crucifix betokened that our Father the Pope had interposed between the Indian and the Great Spirit, whom he had worshipped in his simplicity. This son of the wilderness, and pilgrim of the storm, took his place silently in the midst of us. When the first surprise was over, I rightly conjectured him to be one of the Penobscot tribe, parties of which I had often seen, in their summer excursions down our Eastern rivers. There they paddle their birch canoes among the coasting schooners, and build their wigwam beside some roaring mill dam, and drive a little trade in basket work where their fathers hunted deer. Our new visitor was probably wandering through the country towards Boston, subsisting on the careless charity of the people, while he turned his archery to profitable account by shooting at cents, which were to be the prize of his succesful aim.

The Indian had not long been seated, ere our merry damsel sought to draw him into conversation. She, indeed, seemed all made up of sunshine in the month of May; for there was nothing so dark and dismal that her pleasant mind could not cast a glow over it; and the wild man, like a fir-tree in his native forest, soon began to brighten into a sort of sombre cheerfulness. At length, she inquired whether his journey had any particular end or purpose.

'I go shoot at the camp meeting at Stamford,' replied the Indian.

'And here are five more,' said the girl, 'all aiming at the camp meeting too. You shall be one of us, for we travel with light hearts; and as for me, I sing merry songs, and tell merry tales, and am full of merry thoughts, and I dance merrily along the road, so that there is never any sadness among them that keep me company. But, oh, you would find it very dull indeed, to go all the way to Stamford alone!'

My ideas of the aboriginal character led me to fear that the

Indian would prefer his own solitary musings, to the gay society thus offered him; on the contrary, the girl's proposal met with immediate acceptance, and seemed to animate him with a misty expectation of enjoyment. I now gave myself up to a course of thought, which, whether it flowed naturally from this combination of events, or was drawn forth by a wayward fancy, caused my mind to thrill as if I were listening to deep music. I saw mankind, in this weary old age of the world, either enduring a sluggish existence amid the smoke and dust of cities, or, if they breathed a purer air, still lying down at night with no hope but to wear out to-morrow, and all the to-morrows which make up life, among the same dull scenes and in the same wretched toil, that had darkened the sunshine of to-day. But there were some, full of the primeval instinct, who preserved the freshness of youth to their latest years by the continual excitement of new objects, new pursuits, and new associates; and cared little, though their birth place might have been here in New England, if the grave should close over them in Central Asia. Fate was summoning a parliament of these free spirits; unconscious of the impulse which directed them to a common centre, they had come hither from far and near; and last of all, appeared the representative of those mighty vagrants, who had chased the deer during thousands of years, and were chasing it now in the Spirit Land. Wandering down through the waste of ages, the woods had vanished around his path; his arm had lost somewhat of its strength, his foot of its fleetness, his mien of its wild regality, his heart and mind of their savage virtue and uncultured force; but here, untameable to the routine of artificial life, roving now along the dusty road, as of old over the forest leaves, here was the Indian still.

'Well,' said the old show man, in the midst of my meditations, 'here is an honest company of us—one, two, three, four, five, six—all going to the camp meeting at Stamford. Now, hoping no offence, I should like to know where this young gentleman may be going?'

I started. How came I among these wanderers? The free mind, that preferred its own folly to another's wisdom; the open spirit, that found companions every where; above all, the restless impulse, that had so often made me wretched in the midst of enjoyments; these were my claims to be of their society.

'My friends!' cried I, stepping into the centre of the wagon, 'I am going with you to the camp meeting at Stamford.'

'But in what capacity?' asked the old show man, after a moment's silence. 'All of us here can get our bread in some creditable way. Every honest man should have his livelihood. You, sir, as I take it, are a mere strolling gentleman.'

I proceeded to inform the company, that, when Nature gave me a propensity to their way of life, she had not left me altogether destitute of qualifications for it; though I could not deny that my talent was less respectable, and might be less profitable, than the meanest of theirs. My design, in short, was to imitate the story tellers of whom Oriental travellers have told us, and become an itinerant novelist, reciting my own extemporaneous fictions to such audiences as I could collect.

'Either this,' said I, 'is my vocation, or I have been born in vain.'

The fortune teller, with a sly wink to the company, proposed to take me as an apprentice to one or other of his professions, either of which, undoubtedly, would have given full scope to whatever inventive talent I might possess. The bibliopolist spoke a few words in opposition to my plan, influenced partly, I suspect, by the jealousy of authorship, and partly by an apprehension that the *vivâ voce* practice would become general among novelists, to the infinite detriment of the book trade. Dreading a rejection, I solicited the interest of the merry damsel.

'Mirth,' cried I, most aptly appropriating the words of L'Allegro, 'to thee I sue! Mirth, admit me of thy crew!'

'Let us indulge the poor youth,' said Mirth, with a kindness which made me love her dearly, though I was no such coxcomb as to misinterpret her motives. 'I have espied much promise in him. True, a shadow sometimes flits across his brow, but the sunshine is sure to follow in a moment. He is never guilty of a sad thought, but a merry one is twin born with it. We will take him with us; and you shall see that he will set us all a laughing before we reach the camp meeting at Stamford.'

Her voice silenced the scruples of the rest, and gained me

admittance into the league; according to the terms of which, without a community of goods or profits, we were to lend each other all the aid, and avert all the harm, that might be in our power. This affair settled, a marvellous jollity entered into the whole tribe of us, manifesting itself characteristically in each individual. The old show man, sitting down to his barrel organ, stirred up the souls of the pigmy people with one of the quickest tunes in the music book; tailors, blacksmiths, gentlemen, and ladies, all seemed to share in the spirit of the occasion; and the Merry Andrew played his part more facetiously than ever, nodding and winking particularly at me. The young foreigner flourished his fiddle bow with a master's hand, and gave an inspiring echo to the show man's melody. The bookish man and the merry damsel started up simultaneously to dance; the former enacting the double shuffle in a style which every body must have witnessed, ere Election week was blotted out of time; while the girl, setting her arms akimbo with both hands at her slim waist, displayed such light rapidity of foot, and harmony of varying attitude and motion, that I could not conceive how she ever was to stop; imagining, at the moment, that Nature had made her, as the old show man had made his puppets, for no earthly purpose but to dance jigs. The Indian bellowed forth a succession of most hideous outcries, somewhat affrighting us, till we interpreted them as the war song, with which, in imitation of his ancestors, he was prefacing the assault on Stamford. The conjurer, meanwhile, sat demurely in a corner, extracting a sly enjoyment from the whole scene, and, like the facetious Merry Andrew, directing his queer glance particularly at me.

As for myself, with great exhilaration of fancy, I began to arrange and colour the incidents of a tale, wherewith I proposed to amuse an audience that very evening; for I saw that my associates were a little ashamed of me, and that no time was to be lost in obtaining a public acknowledgement of my abilities.

'Come, fellow labourers,' at last said the old show man, whom we had elected President; 'the shower is over, and we must be doing our duty by these poor souls at Stamford.'

'We'll come among them in procession, with music and dancing,' cried the merry damsel.

Accordingly, for it must be understood that our pilgrimage was to be performed on foot, we sallied joyously out of the wagon, each of us, even the old gentleman in his white top boots, giving a great skip as we came down the ladder. Above our heads there was such a glory of sunshine and splendour of clouds, and such brightness of verdure below, that, as I modestly remarked at the time, Nature seemed to have washed her face, and put on the best of her jewelry and a fresh green gown, in honour of our confederation. Casting our eyes northward, we beheld a horseman approaching leisurely, and splashing through the little puddles on the Stamford road. Onward he came, sticking up in his saddle with rigid perpendicularity, a tall, thin figure in rusty black, whom the show man and the conjurer shortly recognized to be, what his aspect sufficiently indicated, a travelling preacher of great fame among the Methodists. What puzzled us was the fact, that his face appeared turned from, instead of to, the camp meeting at Stamford. However, as this new votary of the wandering life drew near the little green space, where the guide post and our wagon were situated, my six fellow vagabonds and myself rushed forward and surrounded him, crying out with united voices—

'What news, what news, from the camp meeting at Stamford?'

The missionary looked down, in surprise, at as singular a knot of people as could have been selected from all his heterogeneous auditors. Indeed, considering that we might all be classified under the general head of Vagabond, there was great diversity of character among the grave old show man, the sly, prophetic beggar, the fiddling foreigner and his merry damsel, the smart bibliopolist, the sombre Indian, and myself, the itinerant novelist, a slender youth of eighteen. I even fancied, that a smile was endeavouring to disturb the iron gravity of the preacher's mouth.

'Good people,' answered he, 'the camp meeting is broke up.'

So saying, the Methodist minister switched his steed, and rode westward. Our union being thus nullified, by the removal of its object, we were sundered at once to the four winds of Heaven. The fortune teller, giving a nod to all, and a peculiar wink to me, departed on his northern tour, chuckling within himself as he took the Stamford road. The old show man and his literary coadjutor were already tackling their horses to the wagon, with a design to peregrinate south-west along the sea coast. The foreigner and the merry damsel took their laughing leave, and pursued the eastern road, which I had that day trodden; as they passed away, the young man played a lively strain, and the girl's happy spirit broke into a dance; and thus, dissolving, as it were, into sunbeams and gay music, that pleasant pair departed from my view. Finally, with a pensive shadow thrown across my mind, yet emulous of the light philosophy of my late companions, I joined myself to the Penobscot Indian, and set forth towards the distant city.

The Canterbury Pilgrims

THE summer moon, which shines in so many a tale, was beaming over a broad extent of uneven country. Some of its brightest rays were flung into a spring of water, where no traveller, toiling up the hilly road beside which it gushes, ever failed to quench his thirst. The work of neat hands and considerate art, was visible about this blessed fountain. An open cistern, hewn and hollowed out of solid stone, was placed above the waters, which filled it to the brim, but, by some invisible outlet, were conveyed away without dripping down its sides. Though the basin had not room for another drop, and the continual gush of water made a tremor on the surface, there was a secret charm that forbade it to overflow. I remember, that when I had slaked my summer thirst, and sat panting by the cistern, it was my fanciful theory, that Nature could not afford to lavish so pure a liquid, as she does the waters of all meaner fountains.

While the moon was hanging almost perpendicularly over this spot, two figures appeared on the summit of the hill, and came with noiseless footsteps down towards the spring. They were then in the first freshness of youth; nor is there a wrinkle now on either of their brows, and yet they wore a strange old fashioned garb. One, a young man with ruddy cheeks, walked beneath the canopy of a broad brimmed gray hat; he seemed to have inherited his great-grand-sire's square skirted coat, and a waistcoat that extended its immense flaps to his knees; his brown locks, also, hung down behind, in a mode unknown to our times. By his side was a sweet young damsel, her fair features sheltered by a prim little bonnet, within which appeared the vestal muslin of a cap; her close, long waisted gown, and indeed her whole attire, might have been worn by some rustic beauty who had faded half a century before. But that there was something too warm and life-like in them, I would here have compared this couple to the ghosts of two young lovers, who had died long since in the glow of passion, and now were straying out of their graves, to renew the old vows, and shadow forth the unforgotten kiss of their earthly lips, beside the moonlit spring.

'Thee and I will rest here a moment, Miriam,' said the young man, as they drew near the stone cistern, 'for there is no fear that the elders know what we have done; and this may be the last time we shall ever taste this water.'

Thus speaking, with a little sadness in his face, which was also visible in that of his companion, he made her sit down on a stone, and was about to place himself very close to her side; she, however, repelled him, though not unkindly.

'Nay, Josiah,' said she, giving him a timid push with her maiden hand, 'thee must sit farther off, on that other stone, with the spring between us. What would the sisters say, if thee were to sit so close to me?'

'But we are of the world's people now, Miriam,' answered Josiah.

The girl persisted in her prudery, nor did the youth, in fact, seem altogether free from a similar sort of shyness; so they sat apart from each other, gazing up the hill, where the moonlight discovered the tops of a group of buildings. While their attention was thus occupied, a party of travellers, who had come wearily up the long ascent, made a halt to refresh themselves at the spring. There were three men, a woman, and a little girl and boy. Their attire was mean, covered with the dust of the summer's day, and damp with the night dew; they all looked woe begone, as if the cares and sorrows of the world had made their steps heavier as they climbed the hill; even the two little children appeared older in evil days, than the young man and maiden who had first approached the spring.

'Good evening to you, young folks,' was the salutation of the travellers; and 'Good evening, friends,' replied the youth and damsel.

'Is that white building the Shaker meeting house?' asked one of the strangers. 'And are those the red roofs of the Shaker village?'

'Friend, it is the Shaker village,' answered Josiah, after some hesitation.

The travellers, who, from the first had looked suspiciously

at the garb of these young people, now taxed them with an intention, which all the circumstances, indeed, rendered too obvious to be mistaken.

'It is true, friends,' replied the young man, summoning up his courage. 'Miriam and I have a gift to love each other, and we are going among the world's people, to live after their fashion. And ye know that we do not transgress the law of the land; and neither ye, nor the elders themselves, have a right to hinder us.'

'Yet you think it expedient to depart without leave taking,' remarked one of the travellers.

'Yea, ye-a,' said Josiah, reluctantly, 'because father Job is a very awful man to speak with, and being aged himself, he has but little charity for what he calls the iniquities of the flesh.'

'Well,' said the stranger, 'we will neither use force to bring you back to the village, nor will we betray you to the elders. But sit you here awhile, and when you have heard what we shall tell you of the world which we have left, and into which you are going, perhaps you will turn back with us of your own accord. What say you?' added he, turning to his companions. 'We have travelled thus far without becoming known to each other. Shall we tell our stories, here by this pleasant spring, for our own pastime, and the benefit of these misguided young lovers?'

In accordance with this proposal, the whole party stationed themselves round the stone cistern; the two children, being very weary, fell asleep upon the damp earth, and the pretty Shaker girl, whose feelings were those of a nun or a Turkish lady, crept as close as possible to the female traveller, and as far as she well could from the unknown men. The same person who had hitherto been the chief spokesman, now stood up, waving his hat in his hand, and suffered the moonlight to fall full upon his front.

'In me,' said he, with a certain majesty of utterance, 'in me, you behold a poet.'

Though a lithographic print of this gentleman is extant, it may be well to notice that he was now nearly forty, a thin and stooping figure, in a black coat, out at elbows; notwithstanding the ill condition of his attire, there were about him several tokens of a peculiar sort of foppery, unworthy of a mature man, particularly in the arrangement of his hair, which was so disposed as to give all possible loftiness and breadth to his forehead. However, he had an intelligent eye, and on the whole a marked countenance.

'A poet!' repeated the young Shaker, a little puzzled how to understand such a designation, seldom heard in the utilitarian community where he had spent his life. 'Oh, ay, Miriam, he means a varse maker, thee must know.'

This remark jarred upon the susceptible nerves of the poet; nor could he help wondering what strange fatality had put into this young man's mouth an epithet, which ill natured people had affirmed to be more proper to his merit than the one assumed by himself.

'True, I am a verse maker,' he resumed, 'but my verse is no more than the material body into which I breathe the celestial soul of thought. Alas! how many a pang has it cost me, this same insensibility to the ethereal essence of poetry, with which you have here tortured me again, at the moment when I am to relinquish my profession forever! Oh, Fate! why hast thou warred with Nature, turning all her higher and more perfect gifts to the ruin of me, their possessor? What is the voice of song, when the world lacks the ear of taste? How can I rejoice in my strength and delicacy of feeling, when they have but made great sorrows out of little ones? Have I dreaded scorn like death, and yearned for fame as others pant for vital air, only to find myself in a middle state between obscurity and infamy? But I have my revenge! I could have given existence to a thousand bright creations. I crush them into my heart, and there let them putrify! I shake off the dust of my feet against my countrymen! But posterity, tracing my footsteps up this weary hill, will cry shame upon the unworthy age that drove one of the fathers of American song to end his days in a Shaker village!'

During this harangue, the speaker gesticulated with great energy, and, as poetry is the natural language of passion, there appeared reason to apprehend his final explosion into an ode extempore. The reader must understand, that for all these bitter words, he was a kind, gentle, harmless, poor fellow enough, whom Nature, tossing her ingredients together without looking at her recipe, had sent into the world with too much of one sort of brain and hardly any of another.

'Friend,' said the young Shaker, in some perplexity, 'thee seemest to have met with great troubles, and, doubtless, I should pity them, if—if I could but understand what they were.'

'Happy in your ignorance!' replied the poet, with an air of sublime superiority. 'To your coarser mind, perhaps, I may seem to speak of more important griefs, when I add, what I had well nigh forgotten, that I am out at elbows, and almost starved to death. At any rate, you have the advice and example of one individual to warn you back; for I am come hither, a disappointed man, flinging aside the fragments of my hopes, and seeking shelter in the calm retreat which you are so anxious to leave.'

'I thank thee, friend,' rejoined the youth, 'but I do not mean to be a poet, nor, Heaven be praised! do I think Miriam ever made a varse in her life. So we need not fear thy disappointments. But, Miriam,' he added, with real concern, 'thee knowest that the elders admit nobody that has not a gift to be useful. Now, what under the sun can they do with this poor varse maker?'

'Nay, Josiah, do not thee discourage the poor man,' said the girl, in all simplicity and kindness. 'Our hymns are very rough, and perhaps they may trust him to smooth them.'

Without noticing this hint of professional employment, the poet turned away, and gave himself up to a sort of vague reverie, which he called thought. Sometimes he watched the moon, pouring a silvery liquid on the clouds, through which it slowly melted till they became all bright; then he saw the same sweet radiance dancing on the leafy trees which rustled as if to shake it off, or sleeping on the high tops of hills, or hovering down in distant vallies, like the material of unshaped dreams; lastly, he looked into the spring, and there the light was mingling with the water. In its crystal bosom, too, beholding all heaven reflected there, he found an emblem of a pure and tranquil breast. He listened to that most ethereal of all sounds, the song of crickets, coming in full choir upon the wind, and fancied, that, if moonlight could be heard, it would sound just like that. Finally he took a draught at the Shaker spring, and, as if it were the true Castalia, was forthwith moved to compose a lyric, a Farewell to his Harp, which he swore should be its closing strain, the last verse that an ungrateful world should have from him. This effusion, with two or three other little pieces, subsequently written, he took the first opportunity to send by one of the Shaker brethren to Concord, where they were published in the New Hampshire Patriot.

Meantime, another of the Canterbury Pilgrims, one so different from the poet, that the delicate fancy of the latter could hardly have conceived of him, began to relate his sad experience. He was a small man, of quick and unquiet gestures, about fifty years old, with a narrow forehead, all wrinkled and drawn together. He held in his hand a pencil, and a card of some commission merchant in foreign parts, on the back of which, for there was light enough to read or write by, he seemed ready to figure out a calculation.

'Young man,' said he abruptly, 'what quantity of land do the Shakers own here, in Canterbury?'

'That is more than I can tell thee, friend,' answered Josiah, 'but it is a very rich establishment, and for a long way by the road-side, thee may guess the land to be ours, by the neatness of the fences.'

'And what may be the value of the whole,' continued the stranger, 'with all the buildings and improvements, pretty nearly, in round numbers?'

'Oh, a monstrous sum, more than I can reckon,' replied the young Shaker.

'Well, sir,' said the pilgrim, 'there was a day, and not very long ago, neither, when I stood at my counting room window, and watched the signal flags of three of my own ships entering the harbour, from the East Indies, from Liverpool, and from up the Straits; and I would not have given the invoice of the least of them for the title deeds of this whole Shaker settlement. You stare. Perhaps, now, you won't believe that I could have put more value on a little piece of paper, no bigger than the palm of your hand, than all these solid acres of grain, grass and pasture land, would sell for?'

'I won't dispute it, friend,' answered Josiah, 'but I know I had rather have fifty acres of this good land, than a whole sheet of thy paper.'

'You may say so now,' said the ruined merchant, bitterly, 'for my name would not be worth the paper I should write it on. Of course, you must have heard of my failure?'

And the stranger mentioned his name, which, however mighty it might have been in the commercial world, the young Shaker had never heard of among the Canterbury hills.

'Not heard of my failure!' exclaimed the merchant, considerably piqued. 'Why, it was spoken of on 'Change in London, and from Boston to New Orleans, men trembled in their shoes. At all events I did fail, and you see me here on my road to the Shaker village, where, doubtless, (for the Shakers are a shrewd sect,) they will have a due respect for my experience, and give me the management of the trading part of the concern, in which case, I think I can pledge myself to double their capital in four or five years. Turn back with me, young man, for though you will never meet with my good luck, you can hardly escape my bad.'

'I will not turn back for this,' replied Josiah, calmly, 'any more than for the advice of the varse maker, between whom and thee, friend, I see a sort of likeness, though I can't justly say where it lies. But Miriam and I can earn our daily bread among the world's people, as well as in the Shaker village. And do we want any thing more, Miriam?'

'Nothing more, Josiah,' said the girl quietly.

'Yea, Miriam, and daily bread for some other little mouths, if God send them,' observed the simple Shaker lad.

Miriam did not reply, but looked down into the spring, where she encountered the image of her own pretty face, blushing within the prim little bonnet. The third pilgrim now took up the conversation. He was a sunburnt countryman, of tall frame and bony strength, on whose rude and manly face there appeared a darker, more sullen and obstinate despondency, than on those of either the poet or the merchant.

'Well now, youngster,' he began, 'these folks have had their say, so I'll take my turn. My story will cut but a poor figure by the side of theirs; for I never supposed that I could have a right to meat and drink, and great praise besides, only for tagging rhymes together, as it seems this man does; nor ever tried to get the substance of hundreds into my own hands, like the trader there. When I was about of your years, I married me a wife, just such a neat and pretty young woman as Miriam, if that's her name, and all I asked of Providence was an ordinary blessing on the sweat of my brow, so that we might be decent and comfortable, and have daily bread for ourselves, and for some other little mouths that we soon had to feed. We had no very great prospects before us; but I never wanted to be idle, and I thought it a matter of course that the Lord would help me, because I was willing to help myself.'

'And didn't He help thee, friend?' demanded Josiah, with some eagerness.

'No,' said the yeoman, sullenly; 'for then you would not have seen me here. I have labored hard for years; and my means have been growing narrower, and my living poorer, and my heart colder and heavier, all the time; till at last I could bear it no longer. I set myself down to calculate whether I had best go on the Oregon expedition, or come here to the Shaker village; but I had not hope enough left in me to begin the world over again; and, to make my story short, here I am. And now, youngster, take my advice, and turn back; or else, some few years hence, you'll have to climb this hill, with as heavy a heart as mine.'

This simple story had a strong effect on the young fugitives. The misfortunes of the poet and merchant had won little sympathy from their plain good sense and unworldly feelings, qualities which made them such unprejudiced and inflexible judges, that few men would have chosen to take the opinion of this youth and maiden, as to the wisdom or folly of their pursuits. But here was one whose simple wishes had resembled their own, and who, after efforts which almost gave him a right to claim success from fate, had failed in accomplishing them.

'But thy wife, friend?' exclaimed the young man, 'What became of the pretty girl, like Miriam? Oh, I am afraid she is dead!'

'Yea, poor man, she must be dead, she and the children too,' sobbed Miriam.

The female pilgrim had been leaning over the spring,

wherein latterly a tear or two might have been seen to fall, and form its little circle on the surface of the water. She now looked up, disclosing features still comely, but which had acquired an expression of fretfulness, in the same long course of evil fortune that had thrown a sullen gloom over the temper of the unprosperous yeoman.

'I am his wife,' said she, a shade of irritability just perceptible in the sadness of her tone. 'These poor little things, asleep on the ground, are two of our children. We had two more, but God has provided better for them than we could, by taking them to himself.'

'And what would thee advise Josiah and me to do?' asked Miriam, this being the first question which she had put to either of the strangers.

' 'Tis a thing almost against nature, for a woman to try to part true lovers,' answered the yeoman's wife, after a pause; 'but I'll speak as truly to you as if these were my dying words. Though my husband told you some of our troubles, he didn't mention the greatest, and that which makes all the rest so hard to bear. If you and your sweetheart marry, you'll be kind and pleasant to each other for a year or two, and while that's the case, you never will repent; but by-and-by, he'll grow gloomy, rough, and hard to please, and you'll be peevish, and full of little angry fits, and apt to be complaining by the fireside, when he comes to rest himself from his troubles out of doors; so your love will wear away by little and little, and leave you miserable at last. It has been so with us; and yet my husband and I were true lovers once, if ever two young folks were.'

As she ceased, the yeoman and his wife exchanged a glance, in which there was more and warmer affection than they had supposed to have escaped the frost of a wintry fate, in either of their breasts. At that moment, when they stood on the utmost verge of married life, one word fitly spoken, or perhaps one peculiar look, had they had mutual confidence enough to reciprocate it, might have renewed all their old feelings, and sent them back, resolved to sustain each other amid the struggles of the world. But the crisis past, and never came again. Just then, also, the children, roused by their mother's voice, looked up, and added their wailing accents to the testimony borne by all the Canterbury Pilgrims against the world from which they fled.

'We are tired and hungry!' cried they. 'Is it far to the Shaker village?'

The Shaker youth and maiden looked mournfully into each other's eyes. They had but stepped across the threshold of their homes, when lo! the dark array of cares and sorrows that rose up to warn them back. The varied narratives of the strangers had arranged themselves into a parable; they seemed not merely instances of woeful fate that had befallen others, but shadowy omens of disappointed hope, and unavailing toil, domestic grief, and estranged affection, that would cloud the onward path of these poor fugitives. But after one instant's hesitation, they opened their arms, and sealed their resolve with as pure and fond an embrace as ever youthful love had hallowed.

'We will not go back,' said they. 'The world never can be dark to us, for we will always love one another.'

Then the Canterbury Pilgrims went up the hill, while the poet chanted a drear and desperate stanza of the Farewell to his Harp, fitting music for that melancholy band. They sought a home where all former ties of nature or society would be sundered, and all old distinctions levelled, and a cold and passionless security be substituted for human hope and fear, as in that other refuge of the world's weary outcasts, the grave. The lovers drank at the Shaker spring, and then, with chastened hopes, but more confiding affections, went on to mingle in an untried life.

Sir William Pepperell

THE mighty man of Kittery has a double claim to remembrance. He was a famous general, the most prominent military character in our anterevolutionary annals; and he may be taken as the representative of a class of warriors peculiar to their age and country, true citizen soldiers, who diversified a life of commerce or agriculture by the episode of a city sacked, or a battle won, and having stamped their names on the page of history went back to the routine of peaceful occupation. Sir William Pepperell's letters, written at the most critical period of his career, and his conduct then and at other times, indicate a man of plain good sense, with a large share of quiet resolution, and but little of an enterprising spirit, unless aroused by external circumstances. The Methodistic principles with which he was slightly tinctured, instead of impelling him to extravagance, assimilated themselves to his orderly habits of thought and action. Thus respectably endowed, we find him when near the age of fifty, a merchant of weight in foreign and domestic trade, a provincial counsellor, and colonel of the York county militia, filling a large space in the eyes of his generation, but likely to gain no other posthumous memorial than the letters on his tomb stone, because undistinguished from the many worshipful gentlemen who had lived prosperously and died peacefully before him. But in the year 1745, an expedition was projected against Louisbourg, a walled city of the French in the Island of Cape Breton. The idea of reducing this strong fortress was conceived by William Vaughan, a bold, energetic, and imaginative adventurer, and adopted by governor Shirley, the most bustling, though not the wisest ruler that ever presided over Massachusetts. His influence at its utmost stretch, carried the measure by a majority of only one vote in the legislature; the other New England provinces consented to lend their assistance; and the next point was to select a commander from among the gentlemen of the country, none of whom had the least particle of scientific soldiership, although some were experienced in the irregular warfare of the frontiers. In the absence of the usual qualifications for military rank, the choice was guided by other motives, and fell upon colonel Pepperell, who, as a landed proprietor in three provinces, and popular with all classes of people, might draw the greatest number of recruits to his banner. When this doubtful speculation was proposed to the prudent merchant, he sought advice from the celebrated Whitfield, then an itinerant preacher in the country, and an object of vast antipathy to many of the settled ministers. The response of the apostle of Methodism, though dark as those of the oracle at Delphos, intimating that the blood of the slain would be laid to colonel Pepperell's charge, in case of failure, and that the envy of the living would persecute him, if victorious, decided him to gird on his armor.

That the French might be taken unawares, the legislature had been laid under an oath of secrecy while their deliberations should continue; this precaution, however, was nullified by the pious perjury of a country member of the lower house, who in the performance of domestic worship at his lodgings, broke into a fervent and involuntary petition for the success of the enterprise against Louisbourg. We of the present generation, whose hearts have never been heated and amalgamated by one universal passion, and who are perhaps less excitable in the mass than our fathers, cannot easily conceive the enthusiasm with which the people seized upon the project. A desire to prove in the eyes of England the courage of her provinces, the real necessity for the destruction of this Dunkirk of America, the hope of private advantage, a remnant of the old Puritan detestation of Papist idolatry, a strong hereditary hatred of the French, who for half a hundred years, had shed the blood of the English settlers in concert with the savages, the natural proneness of the New Englanders to engage in temporary undertakings, even though doubtful and hazardous; such were some of the motives which soon drew together a host, comprehending nearly all the effective force of the country. The officers were grave deacons; justices of the peace, and other similar dignitaries, and in the ranks were many warm house holders, sons of rich farmers, mechanics in thriving business, husbands weary of their wives, and bachelors disconsolate for want of them; the disciples of Whitfield also turned their excited imaginations in this direction, and increased the resemblance borne by the Provincial army to the motley assemblages of the first crusaders. A part of the peculiarities of the affair may be grouped into one picture, by selecting the moment of general Pepperell's embarkation.

It is a bright and breezy day of March, and about twenty small white clouds are scudding seaward before the wind, airy forerunners of the fleet of privateers and transports that spread their sails to the sunshine in the harbor. The tide is at its height, and the gunwale of a barge alternately rises above the wharf and then sinks from view, as it lies rocking on the waves in readiness to convey the general and his suite on board the Shirley galley; in the back ground, the dark wooden dwellings of the town have poured forth their inhabitants, and this way rolls an earnest throng, with the great man of the day walking quietly in the midst. Before him struts a guard of honor, selected from the yeomanry of his own neighborhood, stout young rustics in their Sunday clothes; next appear six figures who demand our more minute attention. He in the centre is the general, a well proportioned man, with a slight hoar frost of age just visible upon him; he views the fleet in which he is to embark, with no stronger expression than a calm anxiety, as if he were sending a freight of his own merchandise to Europe. A scarlet British uniform, made of the best of broad cloth, because imported by himself, adorns his person, and in the left pocket of a large buff waistcoat, near the pommel of his sword, we see the square protuberance of a small Bible, which certainly may benefit his pious soul, and perchance may keep a bullet from his body. The middle aged gentleman at his right hand, to whom he pays such grave attention, in silk, gold, and velvet, and with a pair of spectacles thrust above his forehead, is governor Shirley; the quick motion of his small eyes in their puckered sockets, his grasp on one of the general's bright military buttons, the gesticulation of his fore finger, keeping time with the earnest rapidity of his words, have all something characteristic. His mind is calculated to fill up the wild conceptions of other men with its own minute ingenuities, and he seeks, as it were, to climb up to the moon by piling pebble stones one upon another. He is now impressing on the general's recollection the voluminous details of a plan for surprising

Louisbourg in the depth of midnight, and thus to finish the campaign within twelve hours after the arrival of the troops. On the left, forming a striking contrast of the unruffled deportment of Pepperell and the fidgetty vehemence of Shirley, is the martial figure of Vaughan; with one hand he has seized the general's arm, and he points the other to the sails of the vessel fluttering in the breeze, while the fire of his inward enthusiasm glows through his dark complexion and flashes in tips of flame from his eyes. Another pale and emaciated person, in neglected and scarcely decent attire, and distinguished by the abstracted fervor of his manner, presses through the crowd and attempts to lay hold of Pepperell's skirt. He has spent years in wild and shadowy studies, and has searched the crucible of the alchemist for gold, and wasted the life allotted him in a weary effort to render it immortal; the din of warlike preparation has broken in upon his solitude, and he comes forth with a fancy of his half maddened brain, the model of a flying bridge, by which the army is to be transported into the heart of the hostile fortress with the celerity of magic. But who is this, of the mild and venerable countenance shaded by locks of a hallowed whiteness, looking like Peace with its gentle thoughts in the midst of uproar and stern designs? It is the minister of an inland parish, who, after much prayer and fasting, advised by the elders of the church and the wife of his bosom, has taken his staff and journeyed townward: the benevolent old man would fain solicit the general's attention to a method of avoiding danger from the explosion of mines, and of overcoming the city without bloodshed of friend or enemy. We start as we turn from this picture of Christian love to the dark enthusiast close beside him, a preacher of the new sect; in every wrinkled line of whose visage we can read the stormy passions that have chosen religion for their outlet. Wo to the wretch that shall seek mercy there! At his back is slung an axe, wherewith he goes to hew down the carved altars and idolatrous images in the Popish Churches, and over his head he rears a banner, which, as the wind unfolds it, displays the motto given by Whitfield, C H R I S T O   D U C E, in letters red as blood. But the tide is now ebbing, and the general makes his adieus to the governor, and enters the boat; it bounds swiftly over the waves, the holy banner fluttering in the bows; a huzza from the fleet comes riotously to the shore, and the people thunder back their many voiced reply.

When the expedition sailed, the projectors could not reasonably rely on assistance from the mother country. At Canso, however, the fleet was strengthened by a squadron of British ships of the line and frigates, under commodore Warren, and this circumstance undoubtedly prevented a discomfiture, although the active business and all the dangers of the siege fell to the share of the Provincials. If we had any confidence that it could be done with half so much pleasure to the reader as to ourself, we would present a whole gallery of pictures from these rich and fresh historic scenes. Never, certainly, since man first indulged his instinctive appetite for war, did a queerer and less manageable host sit down before a hostile city; the officers, drawn from the same class of citizens with the rank and file, had neither the power to institute an awful discipline, nor enough of the trained soldier's spirit to attempt it; of headlong valor, when occasion offered, there was no lack, nor of a readiness to encounter severe fatigue; but, with few intermissions, the Provincial army made the siege one long day of frolic and disorder. Conscious that no military virtues of their own deserved the prosperous result which followed, they insisted that Heaven had fought as manifestly on their side, as ever on that of Israel in the battles of the Old Testament. We, however, if we consider the events of after years, and confine our view to a period short of the Revolution, might doubt whether the victory was granted to our fathers as a blessing or as a judgment. Most of the young men, who had left their paternal firesides, sound in constitution and pure in morals, if they returned at all, returned with ruined health, and with minds so broken up by the interval of riot, that they never after could resume the habits of good citizenship. A lust for military glory was also awakened in the country, and France and England gratified it with enough of slaughter; the former seeking to recover what she had lost, the latter to complete the conquest which the colonists had begun. There was a brief season of repose, and then a fiercer contest, raging almost from end to end of North America. Some went forth and met the red men of the wilderness, and when years had rolled, and the settler came in peace where they had come in war, there he found their unburied bones, among the fallen boughs and withered leaves of many autumns. Others were foremost in the battles of the Canadas, till, in the day that saw the downfall of the French dominion, they poured their blood with Wolfe on the heights of Abraham. Through all this troubled time, the flower of the youth were cut down by the sword, or died of physical diseases, or became unprofitable citizens by moral ones, contracted in the camp and field. Dr. Douglass, a shrewd Scotch physician of the last century, who died before war had gathered in half its harvest, computes that many thousand blooming damsels, capable and well inclined to serve the state as wives and mothers, were compelled to lead lives of barren celibacy by the consequences of the successful siege of Louisbourg. But we will not sadden ourselves with these doleful thoughts, when we are to witness the triumphal entry of the victors into the surrendered town.

The thundering of drums, irregularly beaten, grows more and more distinct, and the shattered strength of the western wall of Louisbourg stretches out before the eye, forty feet in height, and far overtopt by a rock built citadel; in yonder breach the broken timber, fractured stones, and crumbling earth, prove the effect of the Provincial cannon; the draw bridge is down over the wide moat, the gate is open, and the general and British commodore are received by the French authorities beneath the dark and lofty portal arch. Through the massive gloom of this deep avenue, there is a vista of the main street, bordered by high peaked houses, in the fashion of old France; the view is terminated by the centre square of the city, in the midst of which rises a stone cross; and shaven monks, and women with their children, are kneeling at its foot. A confused sobbing and half stifled shrieks are heard, as the tumultuous advance of the conquering army becomes audible to those within the walls. By the light which falls through the arch way, we perceive that a few months have somewhat changed the general's mien, giving it the freedom of one acquainted with peril, and accustomed to command; nor amid hopes of more solid reward, does he appear insensible to the thought that posterity will remember his name among those renowned in arms. Sir Peter Warren, who receives with him the enemy's submission, is a rough and haughty English seaman, greedy of fame, but despising those who have won it for him. Pressing forward to the portal, sword in hand, comes a comical figure in a brown suit, and blue yarn stockings, with a huge frill sticking forth from his bosom, to which the whole man seems an appendage; this is that famous worthy of Plymouth county, who went to the war with two plain shirts and a ruffled one, and is now about to solicit the post of governor in Louisbourg. In close vicinity stands Vaughan, worn down with toil and exposure, the effect of which has fallen upon him at once in the moment of accomplished hope. The group is filled up by several British officers, who fold their arms and look with scornful merriment at the Provincial army, as it stretches far behind in garments of every hue, resembling an immense strip of patch work carpeting thrown down over the uneven ground. In the nearer ranks, we may discern the variety of ingredients that compose the mass. Here advance a row of stern, unmitigable fanatics, each of whom clenches his teeth and grasps his weapon with a fist of iron at sight of the temples of the ancient faith, with the sun light glittering on their cross crowned spires; others examine the surrounding country and send scrutinizing glances through the gate way, anxious to select a spot, whither the good woman and her little ones in the Bay Province may be advantageously transported; some, who drag their diseased limbs forward in weariness and pain, have made the wretched exchange of health or life for what share of fleeting glory may fall to them among four thousand men. But these are all exceptions, and the exulting feelings of the general host combine in an expression like that of a broad laugh on an honest countenance. They roll onward riotously, flourishing their muskets above their heads, shuffling their heavy heels into an instinctive dance, and roaring out some holy verse from the New England Psalmody, or those harsh old warlike stanzas which tell the story of 'Lovell's Fight.' Thus they pour along, till the battered town and the rabble of its conquerors, and the shouts, the drums, the singing and the laughter, grow dim and die away from Fancy's eye and ear.

The arms of Great Britain were not crowned by a more

brilliant achievement during that unprosperous war, and in adjusting the terms of a subsequent peace, Louisbourg was an equivalent for many losses nearer home. The English, with very pardonable vanity, attributed the conquest chiefly to the valor of the naval force. On the continent of Europe, our fathers met with greater justice, and Voltaire has ranked this enterprise of the husbandmen of New England among the most remarkable events in the reign of Louis XV. The ostensible leaders did not fail of reward. Shirley, originally a lawyer, was commissioned in the regular army, and rose to the supreme military command in America; Warren, also, received honors and professional rank, and arrogated to himself, without scruple, the whole crop of laurels gathered at Louisbourg; Pepperell was placed at the head of a royal regiment, and first of his countrymen, was distinguished by the title of baronet. Vaughan, alone, who had been the soul of the deed, from its adventurous conception till the triumphant close, and, in every danger, and every hardship, had exhibited a rare union of ardor and perseverance—Vaughan, was entirely neglected, and died in London, whither he had gone to make known his claims. After the great era of his life, Sir William Pepperell did not distinguish himself either as a warrior or a statesman. He spent the remainder of his days in all the pomp of a colonial grandee, and laid down his aristocratic head among the humbler ashes of his fathers, just before the commencement of the earliest troubles between England and America.

Passages from a Relinquished Work

AT HOME

FROM infancy, I was under the guardianship of a village parson, who made me the subject of daily prayer and the sufferer of innumerable stripes, using no distinction, as to these marks of paternal love, between myself and his own three boys. The result, it must be owned, has been very different in their cases and mine; they being all respectable men, and well settled in life, the eldest as the successor to his father's pulpit, the second as a physician, and the third as a partner in a wholesale shoe store; while I, with better prospects than either of them, have run the course, which this volume will describe. Yet there is room for doubt, whether I should have been any better contented with such success as theirs, than with my own misfortunes; at least, till after my experience of the latter had made it too late for another trial.

My guardian had a name of considerable eminence, and fitter for the place it occupies in ecclesiastical history, than for so frivolous a page as mine. In his own vicinity, among the lighter part of his hearers, he was called Parson Thumpcushion, from the very forcible gestures with which he illustrated his doctrines. Certainly, if his powers as a preacher were to be estimated by the damage done to his pulpit furniture, none of his living brethren, and but few dead ones, would have been worthy even to pronounce a benediction after him. Such pounding and expounding, the moment he began to grow warm, such slapping with his open palm, thumping with his closed fist, and banging with the whole weight of the great Bible, convinced me that he held, in imagination, either the Old Nick or some Unitarian infidel at bay, and belabored his unhappy cushion as proxy for those abominable adversaries. Nothing but this exercise of the body, while delivering his sermons, could have supported the good parson's health under the mental toil, which they cost him in composition.

Though Parson Thumpcushion had an upright heart, and

some called it a warm one, he was invariably stern and severe, on principle, I suppose, to me. With late justice, though early enough, even now, to be tinctured with generosity, I acknowledge him to have been a good and a wise man, after his own fashion. If his management failed as to myself, it succeeded with his three sons; nor, I must frankly say, could any mode of education, with which it was possible for him to be acquainted, have made me much better than what I was, or led me to a happier fortune than the present. He could neither change the nature that God gave me, nor adapt his own inflexible mind to my peculiar character. Perhaps it was my chief misfortune that I had neither father nor mother alive; for parents have an instinctive sagacity, in regard to the welfare of their children; and the child feels a confidence both in the wisdom and affection of his parents, which he cannot transfer to any delegate of their duties, however conscientious. An orphan's fate is hard, be he rich or poor. As for Parson Thumpcushion, whenever I see the old gentleman in my dreams, he looks kindly and sorrowfully at me, holding out his hand, as if each had something to forgive. With such kindness, and such forgiveness, but without the sorrow, may our next meeting be!

I was a youth of gay and happy temperament, with an incorrigible levity of spirit, of no vicious propensities, sensible enough, but wayward and fanciful. What a character was this, to be brought in contact with the stern old Pilgrim spirit of my guardian! We were at variance on a thousand points; but our chief and final dispute arose from the pertinacity with which he insisted on my adopting a particular profession; while I, being heir to a moderate competence, had avowed my purpose of keeping aloof from the regular business of life. This would have been a dangerous resolution, any where in the world; it was fatal, in New-England. There is a grossness in the conceptions of my countrymen; they will not be convinced that any good thing may consist with what they call idleness; they can anticipate nothing but evil of a young man who neither studies physic, law, nor gospel, nor opens a store, nor takes to farming, but manifests an incomprehensible disposition to be satisfied with what his father left him. The principle is excellent, in its general influence, but most

miserable in its effect on the few that violate it. I had a quick
sensitiveness to public opinion, and felt as if it ranked me
with the tavern-haunters and town-paupers,—with the
drunken poet, who hawked his own fourth of July odes,—
and the broken soldier, who had been good for nothing since
last war. The consequence of all this, was a piece of light-
hearted desperation.

I do not over-estimate my notoriety, when I take it for
granted, that many of my readers must have heard of me, in
the wild way of life which I adopted. The idea of becoming
a wandering story teller had been suggested, a year or two
before, by an encounter with several merry vagabonds in a
showman's wagon, where they and I had sheltered ourselves
during a summer shower. The project was not more extravagant than most which a young man forms. Stranger ones are
executed every day; and not to mention my prototypes in the
East, and the wandering orators and poets whom my own
ears have heard, I had the example of one illustrious itinerant
in the other hemisphere; of Goldsmith, who planned and performed his travels through France and Italy, on a less promising scheme than mine. I took credit to myself for various
qualifications, mental and personal, suited to the undertaking.
Besides, my mind had latterly tormented me for employment,
keeping up an irregular activity even in sleep, and making me
conscious that I must toil, if it were but in catching butterflies. But my chief motives were discontent with home, and a
bitter grudge against Parson Thumpcushion, who would
rather have laid me in my father's tomb, than seen me either
a novelist or an actor; two characters which I thus hit upon
a method of uniting. After all, it was not half so foolish as if
I had written romances, instead of reciting them.

The following pages will contain a picture of my vagrant
life, intermixed with specimens, generally brief and slight, of
that great mass of fiction to which I gave existence, and which
has vanished like cloud-shapes. Besides the occasions when I
sought a pecuniary reward, I was accustomed to exercise my
narrative faculty, wherever chance had collected a little audience, idle enough to listen. These rehearsals were useful in
testing the strong points of my stories; and, indeed, the flow
of fancy soon came upon me so abundantly, that its indul-

gence was its own reward; though the hope of praise, also, became a powerful incitement. Since I shall never feel the warm gush of new thought, as I did then, let me beseech the reader to believe, that my tales were not always so cold as he may find them now. With each specimen will be given a sketch of the circumstances in which the story was told. Thus my air-drawn pictures will be set in frames, perhaps more valuable than the pictures themselves, since they will be embossed with groups of characteristic figures, amid the lake and mountain scenery, the villages and fertile fields, of our native land. But I write the book for the sake of its moral, which many a dreaming youth may profit by, though it is the experience of a wandering story teller.

A FLIGHT IN THE FOG

I set out on my rambles one morning in June, about sunrise. The day promised to be fair, though, at that early hour, a heavy mist lay along the earth, and settled, in minute globules, on the folds of my clothes, so that I looked precisely as if touched with a hoar-frost. The sky was quite obscured, and the trees and houses invisible, till they grew out of the fog as I came close upon them. There is a hill towards the west, whence the road goes abruptly down, holding a level course through the village, and ascending an eminence on the other side, behind which it disappears. The whole view comprises an extent of half a mile. Here I paused, and, while gazing through the misty veil, it partially rose and swept away, with so sudden an effect, that a gray cloud seemed to have taken the aspect of a small white town. A thin vapor being still diffused through the atmosphere, the wreaths and pillars of fog, whether hung in air or based on earth, appeared not less substantial than the edifices, and gave their own indistinctness to the whole. It was singular, that such an unromantic scene should look so visionary.

Half of the parson's dwelling was a dingy white house, and half of it was a cloud; but Squire Moody's mansion, the grandest in the village, was wholly visible, even the lattice-work of the balcony under the front window; while, in another place, only two red chimneys were seen above the mist, appertaining to my own paternal residence, then tenanted by strangers. I could not remember those with whom I had dwelt there, not even my mother. The brick edifice of the bank was in the clouds; the foundations of what was to be a great block of buildings had vanished, ominously, as it proved; the dry-good store of Mr. Nightingale seemed a doubtful concern; and Dominicus Pike's tobacco-manufactory an affair of smoke, except the splendid image of an Indian chief in front. The white spire of the meeting-house ascended out of the densest heap of vapor, as if that shadowy base were its only support; or, to give a truer interpretation, the steeple was the emblem of religion, enveloped in mystery below, yet pointing to a cloudless atmosphere, and catching the brightness of the east on its gilded vane.

As I beheld these objects, and the dewy street, with grassy intervals and a border of trees between the wheel-track and the side-walks, all so indistinct, and not to be traced without an effort, the whole seemed more like memory than reality. I would have imagined that years had already passed, and I was far away, contemplating that dim picture of my native place, which I should retain in my mind through the mist of time. No tears fell from my eyes among the dew-drops of the morning; nor does it occur to me that I heaved a sigh. In truth, I had never felt such a delicious excitement, nor known what freedom was till that moment, when I gave up my home, and took the whole world in exchange, fluttering the wings of my spirit, as if I would have flown from one star to another through the universe. I waved my hand towards the dusky village, bade it a joyous farewell, and turned away, to follow any path but that which might lead me back. Never was Childe Harold's sentiment adopted in a spirit more unlike his own.

Naturally enough, I thought of Don Quixote. Recollecting how the knight and Sancho had watched for auguries, when they took the road to Toboso, I began, between jest and earnest, to feel a similar anxiety. It was gratified, and by a more poetical phenomenon than the braying of the dappled ass, or the neigh of Rosinante. The sun, then just above the horizon, shone faintly through the fog, and formed a species of rainbow in the west, bestriding my intended road like a gigantic portal. I had never known, before, that a bow could be generated between the sunshine and the morning mist. It had no brilliancy, no perceptible hues; but was a mere unpainted frame-work, as white and ghost-like as the lunar rainbow, which is deemed ominous of evil. But, with a light heart, to which all omens were propitious, I advanced beneath the misty archway of futurity.

I had determined not to enter on my profession within a hundred miles of home, and then to cover myself with a fictitious name. The first precaution was reasonable enough, as otherwise Parson Thumpcushion might have put an untimely catastrophe to my story; but as nobody would be much affected by my disgrace, and all was to be suffered in my own person, I know not why I cared about a name. For a week or two, I travelled almost at random, seeking hardly any guidance, except the whirling of a leaf, at some turn of the road, or the green bough, that beckoned me, or the naked branch, that pointed its withered finger onward. All my care was to be farther from home each night than the preceding morning.

A FELLOW-TRAVELLER

One day at noontide, when the sun had burst suddenly out of a cloud and threatened to dissolve me, I looked round for shelter, whether of tavern, cottage, barn, or shady tree. The first which offered itself was a wood, not a forest, but a trim plantation of young oaks, growing just thick enough to keep the mass of sunshine out, while they admitted a few straggling beams, and thus produced the most cheerful gloom imaginable. A brook, so small and clear, and apparently so cool, that I wanted to drink it up, ran under the road through a little arch of stone, without once meeting the sun, in its passage from the shade on one side to the shade on the other. As there was a stepping-place over the stone-wall, and a path along the rivulet, I followed it and discovered its source,—a spring gushing out of an old barrel.

In this pleasant spot, I saw a light pack suspended from the branch of a tree, a stick leaning against the trunk, and a person seated on the grassy verge of the spring, with his back towards me. He was a slender figure, dressed in black broadcloth, which was none of the finest, nor very fashionably cut. On hearing my footsteps, he started up, rather nervously, and, turning round, showed the face of a young man about my own age, with his finger in a volume which he had been reading, till my intrusion. His book was, evidently, a pocket-Bible. Though I piqued myself, at that period, on my great penetration into people's characters and pursuits, I could not decide whether this young man in black were an unfledged divine from Andover, a college-student, or preparing for college at some academy. In either case, I would quite as willingly have found a merrier companion; such, for instance, as the comedian with whom Gil Blas shared his dinner, beside a fountain in Spain.

After a nod, which was duly returned, I made a goblet of oak-leaves, filled and emptied it two or three times, and then remarked, to hit the stranger's classical associations, that this beautiful fountain ought to flow from an urn, instead of an old barrel. He did not show that he understood the allusion, and replied, very briefly, with a shyness that was quite out of place, between persons who met in such circumstances. Had he treated my next observation in the same way, we should have parted without another word.

"It is very singular," said I, "though, doubtless, there are good reasons for it, that Nature should provide drink so abundantly, and lavish it every where by the road-side, but so seldom any thing to eat. Why should not we find a loaf of bread on this tree, as well as a barrel of good liquor at the foot of it?"

"There is a loaf of bread on the tree," replied the stranger, without even smiling at a coincidence which made me laugh. "I have something to eat in my bundle, and if you can make a dinner with me, you shall be welcome."

"I accept your offer with pleasure," said I. "A pilgrim, such as I am, must not refuse a providential meal."

The young man had risen to take his bundle from the branch of the tree, but now turned round and regarded me with great earnestness, coloring deeply at the same time. However, he said nothing, and produced part of a loaf of bread, and some cheese, the former being, evidently, home-baked, though some days out of the oven. The fare was good enough, with a real welcome, such as his appeared to be. After spreading these articles on the stump of a tree, he proceeded to ask a blessing on our food; an unexpected ceremony, and quite an impressive one at our woodland table, with the fountain gushing beside us, and the bright sky glimmering through the boughs; nor did his brief petition affect me less, because his embarrassment made his voice tremble. At the end of the meal, he returned thanks with the same tremulous fervor.

He felt a natural kindness for me, after thus relieving my necessities, and showed it by becoming less reserved. On my part, I professed never to have relished a dinner better, and, in requital of the stranger's hospitality, solicited the pleasure of his company to supper.

"Where? At your home?" asked he.

"Yes," said I, smiling.

"Perhaps our roads are not the same," observed he.

"Oh, I can take any road but one, and yet not miss my way," answered I. "This morning I breakfasted at home; I shall sup at home to-night; and a moment ago, I dined at home. To be sure, there was a certain place which I called home; but I have resolved not to see it again, till I have been quite round the globe, and enter the street on the east, as I left it on the west. In the mean time, I have a home every where or no where, just as you please to take it."

"No where, then; for this transitory world is not our home," said the young man, with solemnity. "We are all pilgrims and wanderers; but it is strange that we two should meet."

I inquired the meaning of this remark, but could obtain no satisfactory reply. But we had eaten salt together, and it was right that we should form acquaintance after that ceremony, as the Arabs of the desert do; especially as he had learned something about myself, and the courtesy of the country entitled me to as much information in return. I asked whither he was travelling.

"I do not know," said he; "but God knows."

"That is strange!" exclaimed I; "not that God should know it, but that you should not. And how is your road to be pointed out?"

"Perhaps by an inward conviction," he replied, looking sideways at me, to discover whether I smiled; "perhaps by an outward sign."

"Then believe me," said I, "the outward sign is already granted you, and the inward conviction ought to follow. We are told of pious men in old times, who committed themselves to the care of Providence, and saw the manifestation of its will in the slightest circumstances; as in the shooting of a star, the flight of a bird, or the course taken by some brute animal. Sometimes even a stupid ass was their guide. May not I be as good a one?"

"I do not know," said the pilgrim, with perfect simplicity.

We did, however, follow the same road, and were not overtaken, as I partly apprehended, by the keepers of any lunatic asylum in pursuit of a stray patient. Perhaps the stranger felt as much doubt of my sanity as I did of his, though certainly with less justice; since I was fully aware of my own extravagances, while he acted as wildly, and deemed it heavenly wisdom. We were a singular couple, strikingly contrasted, yet curiously assimilated, each of us remarkable enough by himself, and doubly so in the other's company. Without any formal compact, we kept together, day after day, till our union appeared permanent. Even had I seen nothing to love and admire in him, I could never have thought of deserting one who needed me continually; for I never knew a person, not even a woman, so unfit to roam the world in solitude, as he was—so painfully shy, so easily discouraged by slight obstacles, and so often depressed by a weight within himself.

I was now far from my native place, but had not yet stepped before the public. A slight tremor seized me, whenever I thought of relinquishing the immunities of a private character, and giving every man, and for money, too, the right, which no man yet possessed, of treating me with open scorn. But about a week after contracting the above alliance, I made my bow to an audience of nine persons, seven of whom hissed me in a very disagreeable manner, and not without good cause. Indeed, the failure was so signal, that it would have been mere swindling to retain the money which had been paid, on my implied contract to give its value of amusement; so I called in the door-keeper, bade him refund the whole receipts, a mighty sum, and was gratified with a round of applause, by way of offset to the hisses. This event would have looked most horrible in anticipation; a thing to make a man shoot himself, or run a muck, or hide himself in caverns, where he might not see his own burning blush; but the reality was not so very hard to bear. It is a fact, that I was more deeply grieved by an almost parallel misfortune, which happened to my companion on the same evening. In my own behalf, I was angry and excited, not depressed; my blood ran quick, my spirits rose buoyantly; and I had never felt such a confidence of future success, and determination to achieve it, as at that trying moment. I resolved to persevere, if it were only to wring the reluctant praise from my enemies.

Hitherto, I had immensely underrated the difficulties of my idle trade; now I recognized, that it demanded nothing short of my whole powers, cultivated to the utmost, and exerted with the same prodigality as if I were speaking for a great party, or for the nation at large, on the floor of the capitol. No talent or attainment could come amiss; every thing, indeed, was requisite; wide observation, varied knowledge, deep thoughts, and sparkling ones; pathos and levity, and a mixture of both, like sunshine in a rain-drop; lofty imagination, veiling itself in the garb of common life; and the practised art which alone could render these gifts, and more than these, available. Not that I ever hoped to be thus qualified. But my despair was no ignoble one; for, knowing the impossibility of satisfying myself, even should the world be satisfied, I did my best to overcome it, investigated the causes of every defect, and strove, with patient stubbornness, to remove them in the next attempt. It is one of my few sources of pride, that, ridiculous as the object was, I followed it up with the firmness and energy of a man.

I manufactured a great variety of plots and skeletons of tales, and kept them ready for use, leaving the filling up to the inspiration of the moment; though I cannot remember ever to have told a tale, which did not vary considerably from my pre-conceived idea, and acquire a novelty of aspect as often as I repeated it. Oddly enough, my success was generally in proportion to the difference between the conception and accomplishment. I provided two or more commencements

and catastrophes to many of the tales, a happy expedient, suggested by the double sets of sleeves and trimmings, which
diversified the suits in Sir Piercy Shafton's wardrobe. But my
best efforts had a unity, a wholeness, and a separate character,
that did not admit of this sort of mechanism.

THE VILLAGE THEATRE

About the first of September, my fellow-traveller and myself arrived at a country town, where a small company of actors, on their return from a summer's campaign in the British
Provinces, were giving a series of dramatic exhibitions. A
moderately sized hall of the tavern had been converted into a
theatre. The performances that evening were The Heir at
Law, and No Song No Supper, with the recitation of Alexander's Feast between the play and farce. The house was thin
and dull. But the next day, there appeared to be brighter
prospects, the play-bills announcing, at every corner, on the
town-pump, and, awful sacrilege! on the very door of the
meeting-house, an Unprecedented Attraction!! After setting
forth the ordinary entertainments of a theatre, the public were
informed, in the hugest type that the printing-office could
supply, that the manager had been fortunate enough to accomplish an engagement with the celebrated Story Teller. He
would make his first appearance that evening, and recite his
famous tale of "Mr. Higginbotham's Catastrophe!" which
had been received with rapturous applause, by audiences in
all the principal cities. This outrageous flourish of trumpets,
be it known, was wholly unauthorized by me, who had
merely made an engagement for a single evening, without assuming any more celebrity than the little I possessed. As for
the tale, it could hardly have been applauded by rapturous
audiences, being as yet an unfilled plot; nor, even when I
stepped upon the stage, was it decided whether Mr. Higginbotham should live or die.

In two or three places, underneath the flaming bills which
announced the Story Teller, was pasted a small slip of paper,
giving notice, in tremulous characters, of a religious meeting,
to be held at the school-house, where, with Divine permis-

sion, Eliakim Abbott would address sinners on the welfare of their immortal souls.

In the evening, after the commencement of the tragedy of Douglas, I took a ramble through the town, to quicken my ideas by active motion. My spirits were good, with a certain glow of mind, which I had already learned to depend upon as the sure prognostic of success. Passing a small and solitary school-house, where a light was burning dimly, and a few people were entering the door, I went in with them, and saw my friend Eliakim at the desk. He had collected about fifteen hearers, mostly females. Just as I entered, he was beginning to pray, in accents so low and interrupted, that he seemed to doubt the reception of his efforts, both with God and man. There was room for distrust, in regard to the latter. At the conclusion of the prayer, several of the little audience went out, leaving him to begin his discourse under such discouraging circumstances, added to his natural and agonizing diffidence. Knowing that my presence on these occasions increased his embarrassment, I had stationed myself in a dusky place near the door, and now stole softly out.

On my return to the tavern, the tragedy was already concluded, and being a feeble one in itself, and indifferently performed, it left so much the better chance for the Story Teller. The bar was thronged with customers, the toddy-stick keeping a continual tattoo, while in the hall there was a broad, deep, buzzing sound, with an occasional peal of impatient thunder, all symptoms of an overflowing house and an eager audience. I drank a glass of wine and water, and stood at the side-scene, conversing with a young person of doubtful sex. If a gentleman, how could he have performed the singing-girl, the night before, in No Song No Supper? Or if a lady, why did she enact Young Norval, and now wear a green coat and white pantaloons in the character of Little Pickle? In either case, the dress was pretty, and the wearer bewitching; so that, at the proper moment, I stepped forward, with a gay heart and a bold one; while the orchestra played a tune that had resounded at many a country ball, and the curtain, as it rose, discovered something like a country bar-room. Such a scene was well enough adapted to such a tale.

The orchestra of our little theatre consisted of two fiddles and a clarionet; but if the whole harmony of the Tremont had been there, it might have swelled in vain, beneath the tumult of applause that greeted me. The good people of the town, knowing that the world contained innumerable persons of celebrity, undreamt of by them, took it for granted that I was one, and that their roar of welcome was but a feeble echo of those which had thundered around me, in lofty theatres. Such an enthusiastic uproar was never heard; each person seemed a Briareus, clapping a hundred hands, besides keeping his feet and several cudgels in play, with stamping and thumping on the floor; while the ladies flourished their white cambric handkerchiefs, intermixed with yellow, and red bandanna, like the flags of different nations. After such a salutation, the celebrated Story Teller felt almost ashamed to produce so humble an affair as Mr. Higginbotham's Catastrophe.

This story was originally more dramatic, than as there presented, and afforded good scope for mimicry and buffoonry; neither of which, to my shame, did I spare. I never knew the "magic of a name," till I used that of Mr. Higginbotham; often as I repeated it, there were louder bursts of merriment, than those which responded to what, in my opinion, were more legitimate strokes of humor. The success of the piece was incalculably heightened by a stiff queue of horse-hair, which Little Pickle, in the spirit of that mischief-loving character, had fastened to my collar, where, unknown to me, it kept making the queerest gestures of its own, in correspondence with all mine. The audience, supposing that some enormous joke was appended to this long tail behind, were ineffably delighted, and gave way to such a tumult of approbation, that, just as the story closed, the benches broke beneath them, and left one whole row of my admirers on the floor. Even in that predicament, they continued their applause. In after times, when I had grown a bitter moralizer, I took this scene for an example, how much of fame is humbug; how much the meed of what our better nature blushes at; how much an accident; how much bestowed on mistaken principles; and how small and poor the remnant. From pit and boxes there was now a universal call for the Story Teller.

That celebrated personage came not, when they did call to

him. As I left the stage, the landlord, being also the postmaster, had given me a letter, with the postmark of my native village, and directed to my assumed name, in the stiff old hand-writing of Parson Thumpcushion. Doubtless, he had heard of the rising renown of the Story Teller, and conjectured at once, that such a nondescript luminary could be no other than his lost ward. His epistle, though I never read it, affected me most painfully. I seemed to see the puritanic figure of my guardian, standing among the fripperies of the theatre, and pointing to the players,—the fantastic and effeminate men, the painted women, the giddy girl in boy's clothes, merrier than modest,—pointing to these with solemn ridicule, and eyeing me with stern rebuke. His image was a type of the austere duty, and they of the vanities of life.

I hastened with the letter to my chamber, and held it unopened in my hand, while the applause of my buffoonry yet sounded through the theatre. Another train of thought came over me. The stern old man appeared again, but now with the gentleness of sorrow, softening his authority with love, as a father might, and even bending his venerable head, as if to say, that my errors had an apology in his own mistaken discipline. I strode twice across the chamber, then held the letter in the flame of the candle, and beheld it consume, unread. It is fixed in my mind, and was so at the time, that he had addressed me in a style of paternal wisdom, and love, and reconciliation, which I could not have resisted, had I but risked the trial. The thought still haunts me, that then I made my irrevocable choice between good and evil fate.

Meanwhile, as this occurrence had disturbed my mind, and indisposed me to the present exercise of my profession, I left the town, in spite of a laudatory critique in the newspaper, and untempted by the liberal offers of the manager. As we walked onward, following the same road, on two such different errands, Eliakim groaned in spirit, and labored, with tears, to convince me of the guilt and madness of my life.

Mr. Higginbotham's Catastrophe

A YOUNG FELLOW, a tobacco-pedler by trade, was on his way from Morristown, where he had dealt largely with the Deacon of the Shaker settlement, to the village of Parker's Falls on Salmon River. He had a neat little cart, painted green, with a box of cigars depicted on each side-pannel, and an Indian chief, holding a pipe and a golden tobacco-stalk, on the rear. The pedler drove a smart little mare, and was a young man of excellent character, keen at a bargain, but none the worse liked by the Yankees; who, as I have heard them say, would rather be shaved with a sharp razor than a dull one. Especially was he beloved by the pretty girls along the Connecticut, whose favor he used to court by presents of the best smoking-tobacco in his stock, knowing well that the country lasses of New England are generally great performers on pipes. Moreover, as will be seen in the course of my story, the pedler was inquisitive, and something of a tattler, always itching to hear the news, and anxious to tell it again.

After an early breakfast at Morristown, the tobacco-pedler, whose name was Dominicus Pike, had travelled seven miles through a solitary piece of woods, without speaking a word to any body but himself and his little gray mare. It being nearly seven o'clock, he was as eager to hold a morning gossip, as a city shopkeeper to read the morning paper. An opportunity seemed at hand, when, after lighting a cigar with a sun-glass, he looked up, and perceived a man coming over the brow of the hill, at the foot of which the pedler had stopped his green cart. Dominicus watched him as he descended, and noticed that he carried a bundle over his shoulder on the end of a stick, and travelled with a weary, yet determined pace. He did not look as if he had started in the freshness of the morning, but had footed it all night, and meant to do the same all day.

"Good morning, mister," said Dominicus, when within speaking distance. "You go a pretty good jog. What's the latest news at Parker's Falls?"

The man pulled the broad brim of a gray hat over his eyes, and answered, rather sullenly, that he did not come from Parker's Falls, which, as being the limit of his own day's journey, the pedler had naturally mentioned in his inquiry.

"Well, then," rejoined Dominicus Pike, "let's have the latest news where you did come from. I'm not particular about Parker's Falls. Any place will answer."

Being thus importuned, the traveller—who was as ill-looking a fellow as one would desire to meet, in a solitary piece of woods—appeared to hesitate a little, as if he were either searching his memory for news, or weighing the expediency of telling it. At last, mounting on the step of the cart, he whispered in the ear of Dominicus, though he might have shouted aloud, and no other mortal would have heard him.

"I do remember one little trifle of news," said he. "Old Mr. Higginbotham, of Kimballton, was murdered in his orchard, at eight o'clock last night, by an Irishman and a nigger. They strung him up to the branch of a St. Michael's pear-tree, where nobody would find him till the morning."

As soon as this horrible intelligence was communicated, the stranger betook himself to his journey again, with more speed than ever, not even turning his head when Dominicus invited him to smoke a Spanish cigar and relate all the particulars. The pedler whistled to his mare and went up the hill, pondering on the doleful fate of Mr. Higginbotham, whom he had known in the way of trade, having sold him many a bunch of long-nines, and a great deal of pig-tail, lady's twist, and fig tobacco. He was rather astonished at the rapidity, with which the news had spread. Kimballton was nearly sixty miles distant in a straight line; the murder had been perpetrated only at eight o'clock the preceding night; yet Dominicus had heard of it at seven in the morning, when, in all probability, poor Mr. Higginbotham's own family had but just discovered his corpse, hanging on the St. Michael's pear-tree. The stranger on foot must have worn seven-league boots, to travel at such a rate.

"Ill news flies fast, they say," thought Dominicus Pike; "but this beats rail-roads. The fellow ought to be hired to go express with the President's Message."

The difficulty was solved, by supposing that the narrator

had made a mistake of one day, in the date of the occurrence; so that our friend did not hesitate to introduce the story at every tavern and country-store along the road, expending a whole bunch of Spanish-wrappers among at least twenty horrified audiences. He found himself invariably the first bearer of the intelligence, and was so pestered with questions, that he could not avoid filling up the outline, till it became quite a respectable narrative. He met with one piece of corroborative evidence. Mr. Higginbotham was a trader; and a former clerk of his, to whom Dominicus related the facts, testified that the old gentleman was accustomed to return home through the orchard, about night-fall, with the money and valuable papers of the store in his pocket. The clerk manifested but little grief at Mr. Higginbotham's catastrophe, hinting, what the pedler had discovered in his own dealings with him, that he was a crusty old fellow, as close as a vice. His property would descend to a pretty niece, who was now keeping school in Kimballton.

What with telling the news for the public good, and driving bargains for his own, Dominicus was so much delayed on the road, that he chose to put up at a tavern, about five miles short of Parker's Falls. After supper, lighting one of his prime cigars, he seated himself in the bar-room, and went through the story of the murder, which had grown so fast that it took him half an hour to tell. There were as many as twenty people in the room, nineteen of whom received it all for gospel. But the twentieth was an elderly farmer, who had arrived on horseback a short time before, and was now seated in a corner, smoking his pipe. When the story was concluded, he rose up very deliberately, brought his chair right in front of Dominicus, and stared him full in the face, puffing out the vilest tobacco smoke the pedler had ever smelt.

"Will you make affidavit," demanded he, in the tone of a country justice taking an examination, "that old Squire Higginbotham of Kimballton was murdered in his orchard, the night before last, and found hanging on his great pear-tree yesterday morning?"

"I tell the story as I heard it, mister," answered Dominicus, dropping his half-burnt cigar; "I don't say that I saw the thing done. So I can't take my oath that he was murdered exactly in that way."

"But I can take mine," said the farmer, "that if Squire Higginbotham was murdered night before last, I drank a glass of bitters with his ghost this morning. Being a neighbor of mine, he called me into his store, as I was riding by, and treated me, and then asked me to do a little business for him on the road. He didn't seem to know any more about his own murder than I did."

"Why, then it can't be a fact!" exclaimed Dominicus Pike.

"I guess he'd have mentioned, if it was," said the old farmer; and he removed his chair back to the corner, leaving Dominicus quite down in the mouth.

Here was a sad resurrection of old Mr. Higginbotham! The pedler had no heart to mingle in the conversation any more, but comforted himself with a glass of gin and water, and went to bed, where, all night long, he dreamt of hanging on the St. Michael's pear-tree. To avoid the old farmer, (whom he so detested, that his suspension would have pleased him better than Mr. Higginbotham's,) Dominicus rose in the gray of the morning, put the little mare into the green cart, and trotted swiftly away towards Parker's Falls. The fresh breeze, the dewy road, and the pleasant summer dawn, revived his spirits, and might have encouraged him to repeat the old story, had there been any body awake to hear it. But he met neither ox-team, light wagon, chaise, horseman, nor foot-traveller, till, just as he crossed Salmon River, a man came trudging down to the bridge, with a bundle over his shoulder, on the end of a stick.

"Good morning, mister," said the pedler, reining in his mare. "If you come from Kimballton or that neighborhood, may be you can tell me the real fact about this affair of old Mr. Higginbotham. Was the old fellow actually murdered, two or three nights ago, by an Irishman and a nigger?"

Dominicus had spoken in too great a hurry to observe, at first, that the stranger himself had a deep tinge of negro blood. On hearing this sudden question, the Ethiopian appeared to change his skin, its yellow hue becoming a ghastly white, while, shaking and stammering, he thus replied:—

"No! no! There was no colored man! It was an Irishman that hanged him last night, at eight o'clock. I came away at seven! His folks can't have looked for him in the orchard yet."

Scarcely had the yellow man spoken, when he interrupted himself, and, though he seemed weary enough before, continued his journey at a pace, which would have kept the pedler's mare on a smart trot. Dominicus stared after him in great perplexity. If the murder had not been committed till Tuesday night, who was the prophet that had foretold it, in all its circumstances, on Tuesday morning? If Mr. Higginbotham's corpse were not yet discovered by his own family, how came the mulatto, at above thirty miles distance, to know that he was hanging in the orchard, especially as he had left Kimballton before the unfortunate man was hanged at all? These ambiguous circumstances, with the stranger's surprise and terror, made Dominicus think of raising a hue and cry after him, as an accomplice in the murder; since a murder, it seemed, had really been perpetrated.

"But let the poor devil go," thought the pedler. "I don't want his black blood on my head; and hanging the nigger wouldn't unhang Mr. Higginbotham. Unhang the old gentleman! It's a sin, I know; but I should hate to have him come to life a second time, and give me the lie!"

With these meditations, Dominicus Pike drove into the street of Parker's Falls, which, as every body knows, is as thriving a village as three cotton-factories and a slitting-mill can make it. The machinery was not in motion, and but a few of the shop-doors unbarred, when he alighted in the stable-yard of the tavern, and made it his first business to order the mare four quarts of oats. His second duty, of course, was to impart Mr. Higginbotham's catastrophe to the ostler. He deemed it advisable, however, not to be too positive as to the date of the direful fact, and also to be uncertain whether it were perpetrated by an Irishman and a mulatto, or by the son of Erin alone. Neither did he profess to relate it on his own authority, or that of any one person; but mentioned it as a report generally diffused.

The story ran through the town like fire among girdled trees, and became so much the universal talk, that nobody could tell whence it had originated. Mr. Higginbotham was as well known at Parker's Falls as any citizen of the place, being part owner of the slitting-mill, and a considerable stockholder in the cotton-factories. The inhabitants felt their own prosperity interested in his fate. Such was the excitement, that the Parker's Falls Gazette anticipated its regular day of publication, and came out with half a form of blank paper, and a column of double pica, emphasized with capitals, and headed HORRID MURDER OF MR. HIGGINBOTHAM! Among other dreadful details, the printed account described the mark of the cord round the dead man's neck, and stated the number of thousand dollars of which he had been robbed; there was much pathos, also, about the affliction of his niece, who had gone from one fainting fit to another, ever since her uncle was found hanging on the St. Michael's pear-tree, with his pockets inside out. The village poet likewise commemorated the young lady's grief, in seventeen stanzas of a ballad. The selectmen held a meeting, and, in consideration of Mr. Higginbotham's claims on the town, determined to issue handbills, offering a reward of five hundred dollars for the apprehension of his murderers, and the recovery of the stolen property.

Meanwhile, the whole population of Parker's Falls, consisting of shopkeepers, mistresses of boarding-houses, factory-girls, mill-men, and school-boys, rushed into the street, and kept up such a terrible loquacity, as more than compensated for the silence of the cotton-machines, which refrained from their usual din out of respect to the deceased. Had Mr. Higginbotham cared about posthumous renown, his untimely ghost would have exulted in this tumult. Our friend Dominicus, in his vanity of heart, forgot his intended precautions, and, mounting on the town-pump, announced himself as the bearer of the authentic intelligence, which had caused so wonderful a sensation. He immediately became the great man of the moment, and had just begun a new edition of the narrative, with a voice like a field-preacher, when the mail stage drove into the village street. It had travelled all night, and must have shifted horses in Kimballton at three in the morning.

"Now we shall hear all the particulars," shouted the crowd.

The coach rumbled up to the piazza of the tavern, followed

by a thousand people; for if any man had been minding his own business till then, he now left it at sixes and sevens, to hear the news. The pedler, foremost in the race, discovered two passengers, both of whom had been startled from a comfortable nap to find themselves in the centre of a mob. Every man assailing them with separate questions, all propounded at once, the couple were struck speechless, though one was a lawyer and the other a young lady.

"Mr. Higginbotham! Mr. Higginbotham! Tell us the particulars about old Mr. Higginbotham!" bawled the mob. "What is the coroner's verdict? Are the murderers apprehended? Is Mr. Higginbotham's niece come out of her fainting fits? Mr. Higginbotham! Mr. Higginbotham!!"

The coachman said not a word, except to swear awfully at the ostler for not bringing him a fresh team of horses. The lawyer inside had generally his wits about him, even when asleep; the first thing he did, after learning the cause of the excitement, was to produce a large red pocket-book. Meantime, Dominicus Pike, being an extremely polite young man, and also suspecting that a female tongue would tell the story as glibly as a lawyer's, had handed the lady out of the coach. She was a fine smart girl, now wide awake and bright as a button, and had such a sweet pretty mouth, that Dominicus would almost as lieves have heard a love-tale from it, as a tale of murder.

"Gentlemen and ladies," said the lawyer, to the shopkeepers, the mill-men, and the factory-girls, "I can assure you that some unaccountable mistake, or, more probably, a wilful falsehood, maliciously contrived to injure Mr. Higginbotham's credit, has excited this singular uproar. We passed through Kimballton at three o'clock this morning, and most certainly should have been informed of the murder, had any been perpetrated. But I have proof nearly as strong as Mr. Higginbotham's own oral testimony, in the negative. Here is a note, relating to a suit of his in the Connecticut courts, which was delivered me from that gentleman himself. I find it dated at ten o'clock last evening."

So saying, the lawyer exhibited the date and signature of the note, which irrefragably proved, either that this perverse Mr. Higginbotham was alive when he wrote it, or,—as some deemed the more probable case, of two doubtful ones,—that he was so absorbed in worldly business as to continue to transact it, even after his death. But unexpected evidence was forthcoming. The young lady, after listening to the pedler's explanation, merely seized a moment to smooth her gown and put her curls in order, and then appeared at the tavern-door, making a modest signal to be heard.

"Good people," said she, "I am Mr. Higginbotham's niece."

A wondering murmur passed through the crowd, on beholding her so rosy and bright; that same unhappy niece whom they had supposed, on the authority of the Parker's Falls Gazette, to be lying at death's door in a fainting fit. But some shrewd fellows had doubted, all along, whether a young lady would be quite so desperate at the hanging of a rich old uncle.

"You see," continued Miss Higginbotham, with a smile, "that this strange story is quite unfounded, as to myself; and I believe I may affirm it to be equally so, in regard to my dear uncle Higginbotham. He has the kindness to give me a home in his house, though I contribute to my own support by teaching a school. I left Kimballton this morning, to spend the vacation of commencement-week with a friend, about five miles from Parker's Falls. My generous uncle, when he heard me on the stairs, called me to his bed-side, and gave me two dollars and fifty cents to pay my stage-fare, and another dollar for my extra expenses. He then laid his pocket-book under his pillow, shook hands with me, and advised me to take some biscuits in my bag, instead of breakfasting on the road. I feel confident, therefore, that I left my beloved relative alive, and trust that I shall find him so on my return."

The young lady courtesied at the close of her speech, which was so sensible and well-worded, and delivered with such grace and propriety, that every body thought her fit to be Preceptress of the best Academy in the State. But a stranger would have supposed that Mr. Higginbotham was an object of abhorrence at Parker's Falls, and that a thanksgiving had been proclaimed for his murder; so excessive was the wrath of the inhabitants, on learning their mistake. The mill-men resolved to bestow public honors on Dominicus Pike, only hesitating whether to tar and feather him, ride him on a rail, or refresh him with an ablution at the town-pump, on the top of which he had declared himself the bearer of the news. The selectmen, by advice of the lawyer, spoke of prosecuting him for a misdemeanor, in circulating unfounded reports, to the great disturbance of the peace of the commonwealth. Nothing saved Dominicus, either from mob-law or a court of justice, but an eloquent appeal made by the young lady in his behalf. Addressing a few words of heartfelt gratitude to his benefactress, he mounted the green cart and rode out of town, under a discharge of artillery from the school-boys, who found plenty of ammunition in the neighboring clay-pits and mud-holes. As he turned his head, to exchange a farewell glance with Mr. Higginbotham's niece, a ball, of the consistence of hasty-pudding, hit him slap in the mouth, giving him a most grim aspect. His whole person was so bespattered with the like filthy missiles, that he had almost a mind to ride back, and supplicate for the threatened ablution at the town-pump; for, though not meant in kindness, it would now have been a deed of charity.

However, the sun shone bright on poor Dominicus, and the mud, an emblem of all stains of undeserved opprobrium, was easily brushed off when dry. Being a funny rogue, his heart soon cheered up; nor could he refrain from a hearty laugh at the uproar which his story had excited. The handbills of the selectmen would cause the commitment of all the vagabonds in the State; the paragraph in the Parker's Falls Gazette would be re-printed from Maine to Florida, and perhaps form an item in the London newspapers; and many a miser would tremble for his money-bags and life, on learning the catastrophe of Mr. Higginbotham. The pedler meditated with much fervor on the charms of the young school-mistress, and swore that Daniel Webster never spoke nor looked so like an angel as Miss Higginbotham, while defending him from the wrathful populace at Parker's Falls.

Dominicus was now on the Kimballton turnpike, having all along determined to visit that place, though business had drawn him out of the most direct road from Morristown. As he approached the scene of the supposed murder, he continued to revolve the circumstances in his mind, and was aston-

ished at the aspect which the whole case assumed. Had nothing occurred to corroborate the story of the first traveller, it
might now have been considered as a hoax; but the yellow
man was evidently acquainted either with the report or the
fact; and there was a mystery in his dismayed and guilty look,
on being abruptly questioned. When, to this singular combination of incidents, it was added that the rumour tallied exactly with Mr. Higginbotham's character and habits of life;
and that he had an orchard, and a St. Michael's pear-tree, near
which he always passed at night-fall; the circumstantial evidence appeared so strong, that Dominicus doubted whether
the autograph produced by the lawyer, or even the niece's
direct testimony, ought to be equivalent. Making cautious inquiries along the road, the pedler further learned that Mr.
Higginbotham had in his service an Irishman of doubtful
character, whom he had hired without a recommendation, on
the score of economy.

"May I be hanged myself," exclaimed Dominicus Pike
aloud, on reaching the top of a lonely hill, "if I'll believe old
Higginbotham is unhanged, till I see him with my own eyes,
and hear it from his own mouth! And, as he's a real shaver,
I'll have the minister, or some other responsible man, for an
endorser."

It was growing dusk when he reached the toll-house on
Kimballton turnpike, about a quarter of a mile from the village of this name. His little mare was fast bringing him up
with a man on horseback, who trotted through the gate a few
rods in advance of him, nodded to the toll-gatherer, and kept
on towards the village. Dominicus was acquainted with the
toll-man, and while making change, the usual remarks on the
weather passed between them.

"I suppose," said the pedler, throwing back his whip-lash,
to bring it down like a feather on the mare's flank, "you have
not seen any thing of old Mr. Higginbotham within a day or
two?"

"Yes," answered the toll-gatherer. "He passed the gate just
before you drove up; and yonder he rides now, if you can see
him through the dusk. He's been to Woodfield this afternoon, attending a sheriff's sale there. The old man generally
shakes hands and has a little chat with me; but to-night, he

nodded,—as if to say, 'charge my toll,'—and jogged on; for wherever he goes, he must always be at home by eight o'clock."

"So they tell me," said Dominicus.

"I never saw a man look so yellow and thin as the squire does," continued the toll-gatherer. "Says I to myself, to-night, he's more like a ghost or an old mummy than good flesh and blood."

The pedler strained his eyes through the twilight, and could just discern the horseman, now far ahead on the village-road. He seemed to recognize the rear of Mr. Higginbotham; but through the evening shadows, and amid the dust from the horse's feet, the figure appeared dim and unsubstantial; as if the shape of the mysterious old man were faintly moulded of darkness and gray light. Dominicus shivered.

"Mr. Higginbotham has come back from the other world, by way of the Kimballton turnpike," thought he.

He shook the reins and rode forward, keeping about the same distance in the rear of the gray old shadow, till the latter was concealed by a bend of the road. On reaching this point, the pedler no longer saw the man on horseback, but found himself at the head of the village street, not far from a number of stores and two taverns, clustered round the meeting-house steeple. On his left was a stone-wall and a gate, the boundary of a wood-lot, beyond which lay an orchard, further still, a mowing-field, and last of all, a house. These were the premises of Mr. Higginbotham, whose dwelling stood beside the old highway, but had been left in the back-ground by the Kimballton turnpike. Dominicus knew the place; and the little mare stopped short by instinct; for he was not conscious of tightening the reins.

"For the soul of me, I cannot get by this gate!" said he, trembling. "I never shall be my own man again, till I see whether Mr. Higginbotham is hanging on the St. Michael's pear-tree!"

He leaped from the cart, gave the rein a turn round the gate-post, and ran along the green path of the wood-lot, as if Old Nick were chasing behind. Just then the village clock tolled eight, and as each deep stroke fell, Dominicus gave a fresh bound and flew faster than before, till, dim in the solitary centre of the orchard, he saw the fated pear-tree. One great branch stretched from the old contorted trunk across the path, and threw the darkest shadow on that one spot. But something seemed to struggle beneath the branch!

The pedler had never pretended to more courage than befits a man of peaceable occupation, nor could he account for his valor on this awful emergency. Certain it is, however, that he rushed forward, prostrated a sturdy Irishman with the butt-end of his whip, and found—not, indeed, hanging on the St. Michael's pear-tree, but trembling beneath it, with a halter round his neck—the old identical Mr. Higginbotham!

"Mr. Higginbotham," said Dominicus, tremulously, "you're an honest man, and I'll take your word for it. Have you been hanged or not?"

If the riddle be not already guessed, a few words will explain the simple machinery, by which this "coming event" was made to "cast its shadow before." Three men had plotted the robbery and murder of Mr. Higginbotham; two of them, successively, lost courage and fled, each delaying the crime one night, by their disappearance; the third was in the act of perpetration, when a champion, blindly obeying the call of fate, like the heroes of old romance, appeared in the person of Dominicus Pike.

It only remains to say, that Mr. Higginbotham took the pedler into high favor, sanctioned his addresses to the pretty school-mistress, and settled his whole property on their children, allowing themselves the interest. In due time, the old gentleman capped the climax of his favors, by dying a Christian death, in bed; since which melancholy event, Dominicus Pike has removed from Kimballton, and established a large tobacco manufactory in my native village.

The Haunted Mind

WHAT a singular moment is the first one, when you have hardly begun to recollect yourself, after starting from midnight slumber! By unclosing your eyes so suddenly, you seem to have surprised the personages of your dream in full convocation round your bed, and catch one broad glance at them before they can flit into obscurity. Or, to vary the metaphor, you find yourself, for a single instant, wide awake in that realm of illusions, whither sleep has been the passport, and behold its ghostly inhabitants and wondrous scenery, with a perception of their strangeness, such as you never attain while the dream is undisturbed. The distant sound of a church clock is borne faintly on the wind. You question with yourself, half seriously, whether it has stolen to your waking ear from some gray tower, that stood within the precincts of your dream. While yet in suspense, another clock flings its heavy clang over the slumbering town, with so full and distinct a sound, and such a long murmur in the neighboring air, that you are certain it must proceed from the steeple at the nearest corner. You count the strokes—one—two—and there they cease, with a booming sound, like the gathering of a third stroke within the bell.

If you could choose an hour of wakefulness out of the whole night, it would be this. Since your sober bedtime, at eleven, you have had rest enough to take off the pressure of yesterday's fatigue; while before you, till the sun comes from 'far Cathay' to brighten your window, there is almost the space of a summer night; one hour to be spent in thought, with the mind's eye half shut, and two in pleasant dreams, and two in that strangest of enjoyments, the forgetfulness alike of joy and woe. The moment of rising belongs to another period of time, and appears so distant, that the plunge out of a warm bed into the frosty air cannot yet be anticipated with dismay. Yesterday has already vanished among the shadows of the past; to-morrow has not yet emerged from the future. You have found an intermediate space, where the business of life does not intrude; where the passing moment lingers, and becomes truly the present; a spot where Father Time, when he thinks nobody is watching him, sits down by the way side to take breath. Oh, that he would fall asleep, and let mortals live on without growing older!

Hitherto you have lain perfectly still, because the slightest motion would dissipate the fragments of your slumber. Now, being irrevocably awake, you peep through the half drawn window curtain, and observe that the glass is ornamented with fanciful devices in frost work, and that each pane presents something like a frozen dream. There will be time enough to trace out the analogy, while waiting the summons to breakfast. Seen through the clear portion of the glass, where the silvery mountain peaks of the frost scenery do not ascend, the most conspicuous object is the steeple; the white spire of which directs you to the wintry lustre of the firmament. You may almost distinguish the figures on the clock that has just told the hour. Such a frosty sky, and the snow covered roofs, and the long vista of the frozen street, all white, and the distant water hardened into rock, might make you shiver, even under four blankets and a woolen comforter. Yet look at that one glorious star! Its beams are distinguishable from all the rest, and actually cast the shadow of the casement on the bed, with a radiance of deeper hue than moonlight, though not so accurate an outline.

You sink down and muffle your head in the clothes, shivering all the while, but less from bodily chill, than the bare idea of a polar atmosphere. It is too cold even for the thoughts to venture abroad. You speculate on the luxury of wearing out a whole existence in bed, like an oyster in its shell, content with the sluggish ecstasy of inaction, and drowsily conscious of nothing but delicious warmth, such as you now feel again. Ah! that idea has brought a hideous one in its train. You think how the dead are lying in their cold shrouds and narrow coffins, through the drear winter of the grave, and cannot persuade your fancy that they neither shrink nor shiver, when the snow is drifting over their little hillocks, and the bitter blast howls against the door of the tomb. That gloomy thought will collect a gloomy multitude, and throw its complexion over your wakeful hour.

In the depths of every heart, there is a tomb and a dungeon, though the lights, the music, and revelry above may cause us to forget their existence, and the buried ones, or prisoners whom they hide. But sometimes, and oftenest at midnight, those dark receptacles are flung wide open. In an hour like this, when the mind has a passive sensibility, but no active strength; when the imagination is a mirror, imparting vividness to all ideas, without the power of selecting or controlling them; then pray that your griefs may slumber, and the brotherhood of remorse not break their chain. It is too late! A funeral train comes gliding by your bed, in which Passion and Feeling assume bodily shape, and things of the mind become dim spectres to the eye. There is your earliest Sorrow, a pale young mourner, wearing a sister's likeness to first love, sadly beautiful, with a hallowed sweetness in her melancholy features, and grace in the flow of her sable robe. Next appears a shade of ruined loveliness, with dust among her golden hair, and her bright garments all faded and defaced, stealing from your glance with drooping head, as fearful of reproach; she was your fondest Hope, but a delusive one; so call her Disappointment now. A sterner form succeeds, with a brow of wrinkles, a look and gesture of iron authority; there is no name for him unless it be Fatality, an emblem of the evil influence that rules your fortunes; a demon to whom you subjected yourself by some error at the outset of life, and were bound his slave forever, by once obeying him. See! those fiendish lineaments graven on the darkness, the writhed lip of scorn, the mockery of that living eye, the pointed finger, touching the sore place in your heart! Do you remember any act of enormous folly, at which you would blush, even in the remotest cavern of the earth? Then recognize your Shame.

Pass, wretched band! Well for the wakeful one, if, riotously miserable, a fiercer tribe do not surround him, the devils of a guilty heart, that holds its hell within itself. What if Remorse should assume the features of an injured friend? What if the fiend should come in woman's garments, with a pale beauty amid sin and desolation, and lie down by your side? What if he should stand at your bed's foot, in the likeness of a corpse, with a bloody stain upon the shroud? Sufficient without such guilt, is this nightmare of the soul; this heavy, heavy sinking of the spirits; this wintry gloom about the heart; this indis-

tinct horror of the mind, blending itself with the darkness of
the chamber.

By a desperate effort, you start upright, breaking from a
sort of conscious sleep, and gazing wildly round the bed, as
if the fiends were any where but in your haunted mind. At
the same moment, the slumbering embers on the hearth send
forth a gleam which palely illuminates the whole outer room,
and flickers through the door of the bed-chamber, but cannot
quite dispel its obscurity. Your eye searches for whatever may
remind you of the living world. With eager minuteness, you
take note of the table near the fire-place, the book with an
ivory knife between its leaves, the unfolded letter, the hat and
the fallen glove. Soon the flame vanishes, and with it the
whole scene is gone, though its image remains an instant in
your mind's eye, when darkness has swallowed the reality.
Throughout the chamber, there is the same obscurity as before, but not the same gloom within your breast. As your
head falls back upon the pillow, you think—in a whisper be
it spoken—how pleasant in these night solitudes, would be
the rise and fall of a softer breathing than your own, the
slight pressure of a tenderer bosom, the quiet throb of a purer
heart, imparting its peacefulness to your troubled one, as if
the fond sleeper were involving you in her dream.

Her influence is over you, though she have no existence
but in that momentary image. You sink down in a flowery
spot, on the borders of sleep and wakefulness, while your
thoughts rise before you in pictures, all disconnected, yet all
assimilated by a pervading gladsomeness and beauty. The
wheeling of gorgeous squadrons, that glitter in the sun, is
succeeded by the merriment of children round the door of a
school-house, beneath the glimmering shadow of old trees, at
the corner of a rustic lane. You stand in the sunny rain of a
summer shower, and wander among the sunny trees of an
autumnal wood, and look upward at the brightest of all rainbows, over-arching the unbroken sheet of snow, on the
American side of Niagara. Your mind struggles pleasantly between the dancing radiance round the hearth of a young man
and his recent bride, and the twittering flight of birds in
spring, about their new-made nest. You feel the merry
bounding of a ship before the breeze; and watch the tuneful

feet of rosy girls, as they twine their last and merriest dance, in a splendid ball room; and find yourself in the brilliant circle of a crowded theatre, as the curtain falls over a light and airy scene.

With an involuntary start, you seize hold on consciousness, and prove yourself but half awake, by running a doubtful parallel between human life and the hour which has now elapsed. In both you emerge from mystery, pass through a vicissitude that you can but imperfectly control, and are borne onward to another mystery. Now comes the peal of the distant clock, with fainter and fainter strokes as you plunge farther into the wilderness of sleep. It is the knell of a temporary death. Your spirit has departed, and strays like a free citizen, among the people of a shadowy world, beholding strange sights, yet without wonder or dismay. So calm, perhaps, will be the final change; so undisturbed, as if among familiar things, the entrance of the soul to its Eternal home!

Alice Doane's Appeal

O N a pleasant afternoon of June, it was my good fortune to be the companion of two young ladies in a walk. The direction of our course being left to me, I led them neither to Legge's Hill, nor to the Cold Spring, nor to the rude shores and old batteries of the Neck, nor yet to Paradise; though if the latter place were rightly named, my fair friends would have been at home there. We reached the outskirts of the town, and turning aside from a street of tanners and curriers, began to ascend a hill, which at a distance, by its dark slope and the even line of its summit, resembled a green rampart along the road. It was less steep than its aspect threatened. The eminence formed part of an extensive tract of pasture land, and was traversed by cow paths in various directions; but, strange to tell, though the whole slope and summit were of a peculiarly deep green, scarce a blade of grass was visible from the base upward. This deceitful verdure was occasioned by a plentiful crop of 'wood-wax,' which wears the same dark and glossy green throughout the summer, except at one short period, when it puts forth a profusion of yellow blossoms. At that season to a distant spectator, the hill appears absolutely overlaid with gold, or covered with a glory of sunshine, even beneath a clouded sky. But the curious wanderer on the hill will perceive that all the grass, and every thing that should nourish man or beast, has been destroyed by this vile and ineradicable weed: its tufted roots make the soil their own, and permit nothing else to vegetate among them; so that a physical curse may be said to have blasted the spot, where guilt and phrenzy consummated the most execrable scene, that our history blushes to record. For this was the field where superstition won her darkest triumph; the high place where our fathers set up their shame, to the mournful gaze of generations far remote. The dust of martyrs was beneath our feet. We stood on Gallows Hill.

For my own part, I have often courted the historic influence of the spot. But it is singular, how few come on pilgrimage to this famous hill; how many spend their lives almost at its base, and never once obey the summons of the shadowy past, as it beckons them to the summit. Till a year or two since, this portion of our history had been very imperfectly written, and, as we are not a people of legend or tradition, it was not every citizen of our ancient town that could tell, within half a century, so much as the date of the witchcraft delusion. Recently, indeed, an historian has treated the subject in a manner that will keep his name alive, in the only desirable connection with the errors of our ancestry, by converting the hill of their disgrace into an honorable monument of his own antiquarian lore, and of that better wisdom, which draws the moral while it tells the tale. But we are a people of the present and have no heartfelt interest in the olden time. Every fifth of November, in commemoration of they know not what, or rather without an idea beyond the momentary blaze, the young men scare the town with bonfires on this haunted height, but never dream of paying funeral honors to those who died so wrongfully, and without a coffin or a prayer, were buried here.

Though with feminine susceptibility, my companions caught all the melancholy associations of the scene, yet these could but imperfectly overcome the gayety of girlish spirits. Their emotions came and went with quick vicissitude, and sometimes combined to form a peculiar and delicious excitement, the mirth brightening the gloom into a sunny shower of feeling, and a rainbow in the mind. My own more sombre mood was tinged by theirs. With now a merry word and next a sad one, we trod among the tangled weeds, and almost hoped that our feet would sink into the hollow of a witch's grave. Such vestiges were to be found within the memory of man, but have vanished now, and with them, I believe, all traces of the precise spot of the executions. On the long and broad ridge of the eminence, there is no very decided elevation of any one point, nor other prominent marks, except the decayed stumps of two trees, standing near each other, and here and there the rocky substance of the hill, peeping just above the wood-wax.

There are few such prospects of town and village, woodland and cultivated field, steeples and country seats, as we beheld from this unhappy spot. No blight had fallen on old

Essex; all was prosperity and riches, healthfully distributed. Before us lay our native town, extending from the foot of the hill to the harbor, level as a chess board, embraced by two arms of the sea, and filling the whole peninsula with a close assemblage of wooden roofs, overtopt by many a spire, and intermixed with frequent heaps of verdure, where trees threw up their shade from unseen trunks. Beyond, was the bay and its islands, almost the only objects, in a country unmarked by strong natural features, on which time and human toil had produced no change. Retaining these portions of the scene, and also the peaceful glory and tender gloom of the declining sun, we threw, in imagination, a veil of deep forest over the land, and pictured a few scattered villages, and this old town itself a village, as when the prince of hell bore sway there. The idea thus gained, of its former aspect, its quaint edifices standing far apart, with peaked roofs and projecting stories, and its single meeting house pointing up a tall spire in the midst; the vision, in short, of the town in 1692, served to introduce a wondrous tale of those old times.

I had brought the manuscript in my pocket. It was one of a series written years ago, when my pen, now sluggish and perhaps feeble, because I have not much to hope or fear, was driven by stronger external motives, and a more passionate impulse within, than I am fated to feel again. Three or four of these tales had appeared in the Token, after a long time and various adventures, but had incumbered me with no troublesome notoriety, even in my birth place. One great heap had met a brighter destiny: they had fed the flames; thoughts meant to delight the world and endure for ages, had perished in a moment, and stirred not a single heart but mine. The story now to be introduced, and another, chanced to be in kinder custody at the time, and thus by no conspicuous merits of their own, escaped destruction.

The ladies, in consideration that I had never before intruded my performances on them, by any but the legitimate medium, through the press, consented to hear me read. I made them sit down on a moss-grown rock, close by the spot where we chose to believe that the death-tree had stood. After a little hesitation on my part, caused by a dread of renewing my acquaintance with fantasies that had lost their charm, in the ceaseless flux of mind, I began the tale, which opened darkly with the discovery of a murder.

A hundred years, and nearly half that time, have elapsed since the body of a murdered man was found, at about the distance of three miles, on the old road to Boston. He lay in a solitary spot, on the bank of a small lake, which the severe frost of December had covered with a sheet of ice. Beneath this, it seemed to have been the intention of the murderer to conceal his victim in a chill and watery grave, the ice being deeply hacked, perhaps with the weapon that had slain him, though its solidity was too stubborn for the patience of a man with blood upon his hand. The corpse therefore reclined on the earth, but was separated from the road by a thick growth of dwarf pines. There had been a slight fall of snow during the night, and as if Nature were shocked at the deed, and strove to hide it with her frozen tears, a little drifted heap had partly buried the body, and lay deepest over the pale dead face. An early traveller, whose dog had led him to the spot, ventured to uncover the features, but was affrighted by their expression. A look of evil and scornful triumph had hardened on them, and made death so life-like and so terrible, that the beholder at once took flight, as swiftly as if the stiffened corpse would rise up and follow.

I read on, and identified the body as that of a young man, a stranger in the country, but resident during several preceding months in the town which lay at our feet. The story described, at some length, the excitement caused by the murder, the unavailing quest after the perpetrator, the funeral ceremonies, and other common place matters, in the course of which, I brought forward the personages who were to move among the succeeding events. They were but three. A young man and his sister; the former characterized by a diseased imagination and morbid feelings; the latter, beautiful and virtuous, and instilling something of her own excellence into the wild heart of her brother, but not enough to cure the deep taint of his nature. The third person was a wizard; a small, gray, withered man, with fiendish ingenuity in devising evil, and superhuman power to execute it, but senseless as an idiot and feebler than a child, to all better purposes. The central scene of the story was an interview between this wretch and Leonard Doane, in the wizard's hut, situated beneath a range of rocks at some distance from the town. They sat beside a mouldering fire, while a tempest of wintry rain was beating on the roof. The young man spoke of the closeness of the tie which united him and Alice, the concentrated fervor of their affection from childhood upwards, their sense of lonely sufficiency to each other, because they only of their race had escaped death, in a night attack by the Indians. He related his discovery, or suspicion of a secret sympathy between his sister and Walter Brome, and told how a distempered jealousy had maddened him. In the following passage, I threw a glimmering light on the mystery of the tale.

'Searching,' continued Leonard, 'into the breast of Walter Brome, I at length found a cause why Alice must inevitably love him. For he was my very counterpart! I compared his mind by each individual portion, and as a whole, with mine. There was a resemblance from which I shrank with sickness, and loathing, and horror, as if my own features had come and stared upon me in a solitary place, or had met me in struggling through a crowd. Nay! the very same thoughts would often express themselves in the same words from our lips, proving a hateful sympathy in our secret souls. His education, indeed, in the cities of the old world, and mine in this rude wilderness, had wrought a superficial difference. The evil of his character, also, had been strengthened and rendered prominent by a reckless and ungoverned life, while mine had been softened and purified by the gentle and holy nature of Alice. But my soul had been conscious of the germ of all the fierce and deep passions, and of all the many varieties of wickedness, which accident had brought to their full maturity in him. Nor will I deny, that in the accursed one, I could see the withered blossom of every virtue, which by a happier culture, had been made to bring forth fruit in me. Now, here was a man, whom Alice might love with all the strength of sisterly affection, added to that impure passion which alone engrosses all the heart. The stranger would have more than the love which had been gathered to me from the many graves of our household—and I be desolate!'

Leonard Doane went on to describe the insane hatred that had kindled his heart into a volume of hellish flame. It appeared, indeed, that his jealousy had grounds, so far as that Walter Brome had actually sought the love of Alice, who also had betrayed an undefinable, but powerful interest in the unknown youth. The latter, in spite of his passion for Alice, seemed to return the loathful antipathy of her brother; the similarity of their dispositions made them like joint possessors of an individual nature, which could not become wholly the property of one, unless by the extinction of the other. At last, with the same devil in each bosom, they chanced to meet, they two on a lonely road. While Leonard spoke, the wizard had sat listening to what he already knew, yet with tokens of pleasurable interest, manifested by flashes of expression across his vacant features, by grisly smiles and by a word here and there, mysteriously filling up some void in the narrative. But when the young man told, how Walter Brome had taunted him with indubitable proofs of the shame of Alice, and before the triumphant sneer could vanish from his face, had died by her brother's hand, the wizard laughed aloud. Leonard started, but just then a gust of wind came down the chimney, forming itself into a close resemblance of the slow, unvaried laughter, by which he had been interrupted. 'I was deceived,' thought he; and thus pursued his fearful story.

'I trod out his accursed soul, and knew that he was dead; for my spirit bounded as if a chain had fallen from it and left me free. But the burst of exulting certainty soon fled, and was succeeded by a torpor over my brain and a dimness before my eyes, with the sensation of one who struggles through a dream. So I bent down over the body of Walter Brome, gazing into his face, and striving to make my soul glad with the thought, that he, in very truth, lay dead before me. I know not what space of time I had thus stood, nor how the vision came. But it seemed to me that the irrevocable years, since childhood had rolled back, and a scene, that had long been confused and broken in my memory, arrayed itself with all its first distinctness. Methought I stood a weeping infant by my father's hearth; by the cold and blood-stained hearth where he lay dead. I heard the childish wail of Alice, and my own cry arose with hers, as we beheld the features of our parent, fierce with the strife and distorted with the pain, in which his spirit had passed away. As I gazed, a cold wind whistled by, and waved my father's hair. Immediately, I stood again in the lonesome road, no more a sinless child, but a man of blood, whose tears were falling fast over the face of his dead enemy. But the delusion was not wholly gone; that face still wore a likeness of my father; and because my soul shrank from the fixed glare of the eyes, I bore the body to the lake, and would have buried it there. But before his icy sepulchre was hewn, I heard the voices of two travellers and fled.'

Such was the dreadful confession of Leonard Doane. And now tortured by the idea of his sister's guilt, yet sometimes yielding to a conviction of her purity; stung with remorse for the death of Walter Brome, and shuddering with a deeper sense of some unutterable crime, perpetrated, as he imagined, in madness or a dream; moved also by dark impulses, as if a fiend were whispering him to meditate violence against the life of Alice; he had sought this interview with the wizard, who, on certain conditions, had no power to withhold his aid in unravelling the mystery. The tale drew near its close.

The moon was bright on high; the blue firmament appeared to glow with an inherent brightness; the greater stars were burning in their spheres; the northern lights threw their mysterious glare far over the horizon; the few small clouds aloft were burthened with radiance; but the sky with all its variety of light, was scarcely so brilliant as the earth. The rain of the preceding night had frozen as it fell, and, by that simple magic, had wrought wonders. The trees were hung with diamonds and many-colored gems; the houses were overlaid with silver, and the streets paved with slippery brightness; a frigid glory was flung over all familiar things, from the cottage chimney to the steeple of the meeting house, that gleamed upward to the sky. This living world, where we sit by our firesides, or go forth to meet beings like ourselves, seemed rather the creation of wizard power, with so much of resemblance to known objects, that a man might shudder at the ghostly shape of his old beloved dwelling, and the shadow of a ghostly tree before his door. One looked to behold inhabitants suited to such a town, glittering in icy garments, with motionless features, cold, sparkling eyes, and just sensation enough in their frozen hearts to shiver at each other's presence.

By this fantastic piece of description, and more in the same style, I intended to throw a ghostly glimmer round the reader, so that his imagination might view the town through a medium that should take off its every day aspect, and make it a proper theatre for so wild a scene as the final one. Amid this unearthly show, the wretched brother and sister were represented as setting forth, at midnight, through the gleaming streets, and directing their steps to a grave yard, where all the dead had been laid, from the first corpse in that ancient town, to the murdered man who was buried three days before. As they went, they seemed to see the wizard gliding by their sides, or walking dimly on the path before them. But here I paused, and gazed into the faces of my two fair auditors, to judge whether, even on the hill where so many had been brought to death by wilder tales than this, I might venture to proceed. Their bright eyes were fixed on me; their lips apart. I took courage, and led the fated pair to a new made grave, where for a few moments, in the bright and silent midnight, they stood alone. But suddenly, there was a multitude of people among the graves.

Each family tomb had given up its inhabitants, who, one by one, through distant years, had been borne to its dark chamber, but now came forth and stood in a pale group together. There was the gray ancestor, the aged mother, and all their descendants, some withered and full of years, like themselves, and others in their prime; there, too, were the children who went prattling to the tomb, and there the maiden who yielded her early beauty to death's embrace, before passion had polluted it. Husbands and wives arose, who had lain many years side by side, and young mothers who had forgotten to kiss their first babes, though pillowed so long on their bosoms. Many had been buried in the habiliments of life, and still wore their ancient garb; some were old defenders of the infant colony, and gleamed forth in their steel caps and bright breast-plates, as if starting up at an Indian war-cry; other venerable shapes had been pastors of the church, famous among the New England clergy, and now leaned with hands clasped over their grave stones, ready to call the congregation to prayer. There stood the early settlers, those old illustrious ones, the heroes of tradition and fireside legends, the men of history whose features had been so long beneath the sod, that few alive could have remembered them. There, too, were faces of former townspeople, dimly recollected from childhood, and others, whom Leonard and Alice had wept in later years, but who now were most terrible of all, by their ghastly smile of recognition. All, in short, were there; the dead of other generations, whose moss-grown names could scarce be read upon their tomb stones, and their successors, whose graves were not yet green; all whom black funerals had followed slowly thither, now re-appeared where the mourners left them. Yet none but souls accursed were there, and fiends counterfeiting the likeness of departed saints.

The countenances of those venerable men, whose very features had been hallowed by lives of piety, were contorted now by intolerable pain or hellish passion, and now by an unearthly and derisive merriment. Had the pastors prayed, all saintlike as they seemed, it had been blasphemy. The chaste matrons, too, and the maidens with untasted lips, who had slept in their virgin graves apart from all other dust, now wore a look from which the two trembling mortals shrank, as if the unimaginable sin of twenty worlds were collected there. The faces of fond lovers, even of such as had pined into the tomb, because there their treasure was, were bent on one another with glances of hatred and smiles of bitter scorn, passions that are to devils, what love is to the blest. At times, the features of those, who had passed from a holy life to heaven, would vary to and fro, between their assumed aspect and the fiendish lineaments whence they had been transformed. The whole miserable multitude, both sinful souls and false spectres

of good men, groaned horribly and gnashed their teeth, as
they looked upward to the calm loveliness of the midnight
sky, and beheld those homes of bliss where they must never
dwell. Such was the apparition, though too shadowy for language to portray; for here would be the moonbeams on the
ice, glittering through a warrior's breast-plate, and there the
letters of a tomb stone, on the form that stood before it; and
whenever a breeze went by, it swept the old men's hoary
heads, the women's fearful beauty, and all the unreal throng,
into one indistinguishable cloud together.

I dare not give the remainder of the scene, except in a very
brief epitome. This company of devils and condemned souls
had come on a holiday, to revel in the discovery of a complicated crime; as foul a one as ever was imagined in their dreadful abode. In the course of the tale, the reader had been permitted to discover, that all the incidents were results of the
machinations of the wizard, who had cunningly devised that
Walter Brome should tempt his unknown sister to guilt and
shame, and himself perish by the hand of his twin-brother. I
described the glee of the fiends, at this hideous conception,
and their eagerness to know if it were consummated. The
story concluded with the Appeal of Alice to the spectre of
Walter Brome; his reply, absolving her from every stain; and
the trembling awe with which ghost and devil fled, as from
the sinless presence of an angel.

The sun had gone down. While I held my page of wonders
in the fading light, and read how Alice and her brother were
left alone among the graves, my voice mingled with the sigh
of a summer wind, which passed over the hill top with the
broad and hollow sound, as of the flight of unseen spirits.
Not a word was spoken, till I added, that the wizard's grave
was close beside us, and that the wood-wax had sprouted
originally from his unhallowed bones. The ladies started; perhaps their cheeks might have grown pale, had not the crimson
west been blushing on them; but after a moment they began
to laugh, while the breeze took a livelier motion, as if responsive to their mirth. I kept an awful solemnity of visage, being
indeed a little piqued, that a narrative which had good authority in our ancient superstitions, and would have brought

even a church deacon to Gallows Hill, in old witch times, should now be considered too grotesque and extravagant, for timid maids to tremble at. Though it was past supper time, I detained them a while longer on the hill, and made a trial whether truth were more powerful than fiction.

We looked again towards the town, no longer arrayed in that icy splendor of earth, tree and edifice, beneath the glow of a wintry midnight, which, shining afar through the gloom of a century, had made it appear the very home of visions in visionary streets. An indistinctness had begun to creep over the mass of buildings and blend them with the intermingled tree tops, except where the roof of a statelier mansion, and the steeples and brick towers of churches, caught the brightness of some cloud that yet floated in the sunshine. Twilight over the landscape was congenial to the obscurity of time. With such eloquence as my share of feeling and fancy could supply, I called back hoar antiquity, and bade my companions imagine an ancient multitude of people, congregated on the hill side, spreading far below, clustering on the steep old roofs, and climbing the adjacent heights, wherever a glimpse of this spot might be obtained. I strove to realize and faintly communicate, the deep, unutterable loathing and horror, the indignation, the affrighted wonder, that wrinkled on every brow, and filled the universal heart. See! the whole crowd turns pale and shrinks within itself, as the virtuous emerge from yonder street. Keeping pace with that devoted company, I described them one by one; here tottered a woman in her dotage, knowing neither the crime imputed her, nor its punishment; there another, distracted by the universal madness, till feverish dreams were remembered as realities, and she almost believed her guilt. One, a proud man once, was so broken down by the intolerable hatred heaped upon him, that he seemed to hasten his steps, eager to hide himself in the grave hastily dug, at the foot of the gallows. As they went slowly on, a mother looked behind, and beheld her peaceful dwelling; she cast her eyes elsewhere, and groaned inwardly, yet with bitterest anguish; for there was her little son among the accusers. I watched the face of an ordained pastor, who walked onward to the same death; his lips moved in prayer, no narrow petition for himself alone, but embracing all, his fellow sufferers and the frenzied multitude; he looked to heaven and trod lightly up the hill.

Behind their victims came the afflicted, a guilty and miserable band; villains who had thus avenged themselves on their enemies, and viler wretches, whose cowardice had destroyed their friends; lunatics, whose ravings had chimed in with the madness of the land; and children, who had played a game that the imps of darkness might have envied them, since it disgraced an age, and dipped a people's hands in blood. In the rear of the procession rode a figure on horseback, so darkly conspicuous, so sternly triumphant, that my hearers mistook him for the visible presence of the fiend himself; but it was only his good friend, Cotton Mather, proud of his well won dignity, as the representative of all the hateful features of his time; the one blood-thirsty man, in whom were concentrated those vices of spirit and errors of opinion, that sufficed to madden the whole surrounding multitude. And thus I marshalled them onward, the innocent who were to die, and the guilty who were to grow old in long remorse—tracing their every step, by rock, and shrub, and broken track, till their shadowy visages had circled round the hill-top, where we stood. I plunged into my imagination for a blacker horror, and a deeper woe, and pictured the scaffold——

But here my companions seized an arm on each side; their nerves were trembling; and sweeter victory still, I had reached the seldom trodden places of their hearts, and found the wellspring of their tears. And now the past had done all it could. We slowly descended, watching the lights as they twinkled gradually through the town, and listening to the distant mirth of boys at play, and to the voice of a young girl, warbling somewhere in the dusk, a pleasant sound to wanderers from old witch times. Yet ere we left the hill, we could not but regret, that there is nothing on its barren summit, no relic of old, nor lettered stone of later days, to assist the imagination in appealing to the heart. We build the memorial column on the height which our fathers made sacred with their blood, poured out in a holy cause. And here in dark, funereal stone, should rise another monument, sadly commemorative of the errors of an earlier race, and not to be cast down, while the human heart has one infirmity that may result in crime.

The Village Uncle

AN IMAGINARY RETROSPECT

COME! another log upon the hearth. True, our little parlor is comfortable, especially here, where the old man sits in his old arm chair; but on Thanksgiving night, the blaze should dance higher up the chimney, and send a shower of sparks into the outer darkness. Toss on an armful of those dry oak chips, the last relics of the Mermaid's knee timbers, the bones of your namesake, Susan. Higher yet, and clearer be the blaze, till our cottage windows glow the ruddiest in the village, and the light of our household mirth flash far across the bay to Nahant. And now, come, Susan, come, my children, draw your chairs round me, all of you. There is a dimness over your figures! You sit quivering indistinctly with each motion of the blaze, which eddies about you like a flood, so that you all have the look of visions, or people that dwell only in the firelight, and will vanish from existence, as completely as your own shadows, when the flame shall sink among the embers. Hark! let me listen for the swell of the surf; it should be audible a mile inland, on a night like this. Yes; there I catch the sound, but only an uncertain murmur, as if a good way down over the beach; though, by the almanac, it is high tide at eight o'clock, and the billows must now be dashing within thirty yards of our door. Ah! the old man's ears are failing him; and so is his eye-sight, and perhaps his mind; else you would not all be so shadowy, in the blaze of his Thanksgiving fire.

How strangely the past is peeping over the shoulders of the present! To judge by my recollections, it is but a few moments since I sat in another room; yonder model of a vessel was not there, nor the old chest of drawers, nor Susan's profile and mine, in that gilt frame; nothing, in short, except this same fire, which glimmered on books, papers, and a picture, and half discovered my solitary figure in a looking-glass. But it was paler than my rugged old self, and younger, too, by almost half a century. Speak to me, Susan; speak, my beloved ones, for the scene is glimmering on my sight again, and as it

brightens you fade away. Oh! I should be loth to lose my
treasure of past happiness, and become once more what I was
then; a hermit in the depths of my own mind; sometimes
yawning over drowsy volumes, and anon a scribbler of wea-
rier trash than what I read; a man who had wandered out of
the real world and got into its shadow, where his troubles,
joys and vicissitudes were of such slight stuff, that he hardly
knew whether he lived, or only dreamed of living. Thank
heaven, I am an old man now, and have done with all such
vanities.

Still this dimness of mine eyes! Come nearer, Susan, and
stand before the fullest blaze of the hearth. Now I behold you
illuminated from head to foot, in your clean cap and decent
gown, with the dear lock of gray hair across your forehead,
and a quiet smile about your mouth, while the eyes alone are
concealed, by the red gleam of the fire upon your spectacles.
There, you made me tremble again! When the flame quivered,
my sweet Susan, you quivered with it, and grew indistinct, as
if melting into the warm light, that my last glimpse of you
might be as visionary as the first was, full many a year since.
Do you remember it? You stood on the little bridge, over the
brook that runs across King's Beach into the sea. It was twilight; the waves rolling in, the wind sweeping by, the crimson
clouds fading in the west, and the silver moon brightening
above the hill; and on the bridge were you, fluttering in the
breeze like a sea bird that might skim away at your pleasure.
You seemed a daughter of the viewless wind, a creature of the
ocean foam and the crimson light, whose merry life was spent
in dancing on the crests of the billows, that threw up their
spray to support your footsteps. As I drew nearer, I fancied
you akin to the race of mermaids, and thought how pleasant
it would be to dwell with you among the quiet coves, in the
shadow of the cliffs, and to roam along secluded beaches of
the purest sand, and when our northern shores grew bleak, to
haunt the islands, green and lonely, far amid summer seas.
And yet it gladdened me, after all this nonsense, to find you
nothing but a pretty young girl, sadly perplexed with the rude
behaviour of the wind about your petticoats.

Thus I did with Susan as with most other things in my

earlier days, dipping her image into my mind and coloring it
of a thousand fantastic hues, before I could see her as she
really was. Now, Susan, for a sober picture of our village! It
was a small collection of dwellings that seemed to have been
cast up by the sea, with the rock weed and marine plants that
it vomits after a storm, or to have come ashore among the
pipe staves and other lumber, which had been washed from
the deck of an eastern schooner. There was just space for the
narrow and sandy street between the beach in front, and a
precipitous hill that lifted its rocky forehead in the rear,
among a waste of juniper bushes and the wild growth of a
broken pasture. The village was picturesque, in the variety of
its edifices, though all were rude. Here stood a little old
hovel, built, perhaps, of drift wood, there a row of boat
houses, and beyond them a two story dwelling, of dark and
weather-beaten aspect, the whole intermixed with one or two
snug cottages, painted white, a sufficiency of pig styes, and a
shoemaker's shop. Two grocery stores stood opposite each
other, in the centre of the village. These were the places of
resort, at their idle hours, of a hardy throng of fishermen, in
red baize shirts, oil cloth trowsers, and boots of brown leather
covering the whole leg; true seven league boots, but fitter to
wade the ocean than walk the earth. The wearers seemed amphibious, as if they did but creep out of salt water to sun
themselves; nor would it have been wonderful to see their
lower limbs covered with clusters of little shell fish, such as
cling to rocks and old ship timber over which the tide ebbs
and flows. When their fleet of boats was weather bound, the
butchers raised their price, and the spit was busier than the
frying pan; for this was a place of fish, and known as such, to
all the country round about; the very air was fishy, being perfumed with dead sculpins, hard heads and dog-fish, strewn
plentifully on the beach. You see, children, the village is but
little changed, since your mother and I were young.

How like a dream it was, when I bent over a pool of water,
one pleasant morning, and saw that the ocean had dashed its
spray over me and made me a fisherman! There was the tar-
paulin, the baize shirt, the oil cloth trowsers and seven league
boots, and there my own features, but so reddened with sun

burn and sea breezes, that methought I had another face, and
on other shoulders too. The sea gulls and the loons, and I,
had now all one trade; we skimmed the crested waves and
sought our prey beneath them, the man with as keen enjoyment as the birds. Always when the east grew purple, I
launched my dory, my little flat bottomed skiff, and rowed
cross-handed to Point Ledge, the Middle Ledge, or, perhaps,
beyond Egg Rock; often, too, did I anchor off Dread Ledge,
a spot of peril to ships unpiloted; and sometimes spread an
adventurous sail and tracked across the bay to South Shore,
casting my lines in sight of Scituate. Ere night fall, I hauled
my skiff high and dry on the beach, laden with red rock cod, or
the white bellied ones of deep water; haddock, bearing the black
marks of Saint Peter's fingers near the gills; the long bearded
hake, whose liver holds oil enough for a midnight lamp; and
now and then a mighty halibut, with a back broad as my boat. In
the autumn, I toled and caught those lovely fish, the mackerel.
When the wind was high; when the whale boats, anchored off
the Point, nodded their slender masts at each other, and the dories pitched and tossed in the surf; when Nahant Beach was
thundering three miles off, and the spray broke a hundred feet
in air, round the distant base of Egg Rock; when the brimful and
boisterous sea threatened to tumble over the street of our village; then I made a holiday on shore.

Many such a day did I sit snugly in Mr. Bartlett's store,
attentive to the yarns of uncle Parker; uncle to the whole village, by right of seniority, but of southern blood, with no
kindred in New England. His figure is before me now, en-
throned upon a mackerel barrel; a lean old man, of great
height, but bent with years, and twisted into an uncouth
shape by seven broken limbs; furrowed also, and weather
worn, as if every gale for the better part of a century, had
caught him some where on the sea. He looked like a harbinger of tempest; a shipmate of the Flying Dutchman. After
innumerable voyages aboard men-of-war and merchantmen,
fishing schooners and chebacco boats, the old salt had become
master of a hand cart, which he daily trundled about the vicinity, and sometimes blew his fish horn through the streets
of Salem. One of uncle Parker's eyes had been blown out
with gunpowder, and the other did but glimmer in its socket.

Turning it upward as he spoke, it was his delight to tell of cruises against the French, and battles with his own ship-mates, when he and an antagonist used to be seated astride of a sailor's chest, each fastened down by a spike nail through his trowsers, and there to fight it out. Sometimes he expatiated on the delicious flavor of the hagden, a greasy and goose-like fowl, which the sailors catch with hook and line on the Grand Banks. He dwelt with rapture on an interminable winter at the Isle of Sables, where he had gladdened himself, amid polar snows, with the rum and sugar saved from the wreck of a West India schooner. And wrathfully did he shake his fist, as he related how a party of Cape Cod men had robbed him and his companions of their lawful spoil, and sailed away with every keg of old Jamaica, leaving him not a drop to drown his sorrow. Villains they were, and of that wicked brotherhood who are said to tie lanterns to horses' tails, to mislead the mariner along the dangerous shores of the Cape.

Even now, I seem to see the group of fishermen, with that old salt in the midst. One fellow sits on the counter, a second bestrides an oil barrel, a third lolls at his length on a parcel of new cod lines, and another has planted the tarry seat of his trowsers on a heap of salt, which will shortly be sprinkled over a lot of fish. They are a likely set of men. Some have voyaged to the East Indies or the Pacific, and most of them have sailed in Marblehead schooners to Newfoundland; a few have been no farther than the Middle Banks, and one or two have always fished along the shore; but as uncle Parker used to say, they have all been christened in salt water, and know more than men ever learn in the bushes. A curious figure, by way of contrast, is a fish dealer from far up-country, listening with eyes wide open, to narratives that might startle Sinbad the sailor. Be it well with you, my brethren! Ye are all gone, some to your graves ashore, and others to the depths of ocean; but my faith is strong that ye are happy; for whenever I behold your forms, whether in dream or vision, each departed friend is puffing his long nine, and a mug of the right black strap goes round from lip to lip!

But where was the mermaid, in those delightful times? At a certain window near the centre of the village, appeared a pretty display of gingerbread men and horses, picture books and ballads, small fish-hooks, pins, needles, sugar-plums and brass thimbles, articles on which the young fishermen used to expend their money from pure gallantry. What a picture was Susan behind the counter! A slender maiden, though the child of rugged parents, she had the slimmest of all waists, brown hair curling on her neck, and a complexion rather pale, except when the sea breeze flushed it. A few freckles became beauty spots beneath her eyelids. How was it, Susan, that you talked and acted so carelessly, yet always for the best, doing whatever was right in your own eyes, and never once doing wrong in mine, nor shocked a taste that had been morbidly sensitive till now? And whence had you that happiest gift, of brightening every topic with an unsought gayety, quiet but irresistible, so that even gloomy spirits felt your sunshine, and did not shrink from it? Nature wrought the charm. She made you a frank, simple, kind hearted, sensible and mirthful girl. Obeying nature, you did free things without indelicacy, displayed a maiden's thoughts to every eye, and proved yourself as innocent as naked Eve.

It was beautiful to observe, how her simple and happy nature mingled itself with mine. She kindled a domestic fire within my heart, and took up her dwelling there, even in that chill and lonesome cavern, hung round with glittering icicles of fancy. She gave me warmth of feeling, while the influence of my mind made her contemplative. I taught her to love the moonlight hour, when the expanse of the encircled bay was smooth as a great mirror and slept in a transparent shadow; while beyond Nahant, the wind rippled the dim ocean into a dreamy brightness, which grew faint afar off, without becoming gloomier. I held her hand and pointed to the long surf-wave, as it rolled calmly on the beach, in an unbroken line of silver; we were silent together, till its deep and peaceful murmur had swept by us. When the Sabbath sun shone down into the recesses of the cliffs, I led the mermaid thither, and told her that those huge, gray, shattered rocks, and her native sea, that raged for ever like a storm against them, and her own slender beauty, in so stern a scene, were all combined into a strain of poetry. But on the Sabbath eve, when her mother had gone early to bed, and her gentle sister had smiled and left us, as we sat alone by the quiet hearth, with household things around, it was her turn to make me feel, that here was a deeper poetry, and that this was the dearest hour of all. Thus went on our wooing, till I had shot wild fowl enough to feather our bridal bed, and the Daughter of the Sea was mine.

I built a cottage for Susan and myself, and made a gateway in the form of a Gothic arch, by setting up a whale's jaw bones. We bought a heifer with her first calf, and had a little garden on the hill side, to supply us with potatoes and green sauce for our fish. Our parlor, small and neat, was ornamented with our two profiles in one gilt frame, and with shells and pretty pebbles on the mantle piece, selected from the sea's treasury of such things, on Nahant Beach. On the desk, beneath the looking-glass, lay the Bible, which I had begun to read aloud at the book of Genesis, and the singing book that Susan used for her evening psalm. Except the almanac, we had no other literature. All that I heard of books, was when an Indian history, or tale of shipwreck, was sold by a pedler or wandering subscription man, to some one in the village, and read through its owner's nose to a slumbrous auditory. Like my brother fishermen, I grew into the belief that all human erudition was collected in our pedagogue, whose green spectacles and solemn phiz, as he passed to his little school house, amid a waste of sand, might have gained him a diploma from any college in New England. In truth I dreaded him. When our children were old enough to claim his care, you remember, Susan, how I frowned, though you were pleased, at this learned man's encomiums on their proficiency. I feared to trust them even with the alphabet; it was the key to a fatal treasure.

But I loved to lead them by their little hands along the beach, and point to nature in the vast and the minute, the sky, the sea, the green earth, the pebbles and the shells. Then did I discourse of the mighty works and co-extensive goodness of the Deity, with the simple wisdom of a man whose mind had profited by lonely days upon the deep, and his heart by the strong and pure affections of his evening home. Sometimes my voice lost itself in a tremulous depth; for I felt His eye upon me as I spoke. Once, while my wife and all of us were gazing at ourselves, in the mirror left by the tide in a hollow of the sand, I pointed to the pictured Heaven below, and bade her observe how religion was strewn every where in our path, since even a casual pool of water recalled the idea of that home whither we were travelling, to rest for ever with our children. Suddenly, your image, Susan, and all the little faces made up of yours and mine, seemed to fade away and vanish around me, leaving a pale visage like my own of former days, within the frame of a large looking-glass. Strange illusion!

My life glided on, the past appearing to mingle with the present and absorb the future, till the whole lies before me at a glance. My manhood has long been waning with a staunch decay; my earlier contemporaries, after lives of unbroken health, are all at rest, without having known the weariness of later age; and now with a wrinkled forehead and thin white hair as badges of my dignity, I have become the patriarch, the Uncle of the village. I love that name; it widens the circle of my sympathies; it joins all the youthful to my household, in the kindred of affection.

Like uncle Parker, whose rheumatic bones were dashed against Egg Rock, full forty years ago, I am a spinner of long yarns. Seated on the gunnel of a dory, or on the sunny side of a boat house, where the warmth is grateful to my limbs, or by my own hearth, when a friend or two are there, I overflow with talk, and yet am never tedious. With a broken voice I give utterance to much wisdom. Such, heaven be praised! is the vigor of my faculties, that many a forgotten usage, and traditions ancient in my youth, and early adventures of myself or others, hitherto effaced by things more recent, acquire new distinctness in my memory. I remember the happy days when the haddock were more numerous on all the fishing grounds than sculpins in the surf; when the deep water cod swam close in shore, and the dog-fish, with his poisonous horn, had not learnt to take the hook. I can number every equinoctial storm, in which the sea has overwhelmed the street, flooded the cellars of the village, and hissed upon our kitchen hearth. I give the history of the great whale that was landed on Whale Beach, and whose jaws, being now my gateway, will last for ages after my coffin shall have passed beneath them. Thence it is an easy digression to the halibut, scarcely smaller than the whale, which ran out six cod lines, and hauled my dory to the mouth of Boston harbor, before I could touch him with the gaff.

If melancholy accidents be the theme of conversation, I tell how a friend of mine was taken out of his boat by an enormous shark; and the sad, true tale of a young man on the eve of marriage, who had been nine days missing, when his drowned body floated into the very pathway, on Marblehead neck, that had often led him to the dwelling of his bride; as if the dripping corpse would have come where the mourner was. With such awful fidelity did that lover return to fulfil his vows! Another favorite story is of a crazy maiden, who conversed with angels and had the gift of prophecy, and whom all the village loved and pitied, though she went from door to door accusing us of sin, exhorting to repentance, and foretelling our destruction by flood or earthquake. If the young men boast their knowledge of the ledges and sunken rocks, I speak of pilots who knew the wind by its scent and the wave by its taste, and could have steered blindfold to any port between Boston and Mount Desert, guided only by the rote of the shore; the peculiar sound of the surf on each island, beach, and line of rocks, along the coast. Thus do I talk, and all my auditors grow wise, while they deem it pastime.

I recollect no happier portion of my life, than this, my calm old age. It is like the sunny and sheltered slope of a valley, where, late in the autumn, the grass is greener than in August, and intermixed with golden dandelions, that had not been seen till now, since the first warmth of the year. But with me, the verdure and the flowers are not frost bitten in the midst of winter. A playfulness has revisited my mind; a sympathy with the young and gay; an unpainful interest in the business of others; a light and wandering curiosity; arising, perhaps, from the sense that my toil on earth is ended, and the brief hour till bedtime may be spent in play. Still, I have fancied that there is a depth of feeling and reflection, under this superficial levity, peculiar to one who has lived long, and is soon to die.

Show me any thing that would make an infant smile, and you shall behold a gleam of mirth over the hoary ruin of my visage. I can spend a pleasant hour in the sun, watching the sports of the village children, on the edge of the surf; now they chase the retreating wave far down over the wet sand; now it steals softly up to kiss their naked feet; now it comes onward with threatening front, and roars after the laughing crew, as they scamper beyond its reach. Why should not an old man be merry too, when the great sea is at play with those little children? I delight, also, to follow in the wake of a pleasure party of young men and girls, strolling along the beach after an early supper at the Point. Here, with handkerchiefs at nose, they bend over a heap of eel grass, entangled in which is a dead skate, so oddly accoutred with two legs and a long tail, that they mistake him for a drowned animal. A few steps further, the ladies scream, and the gentlemen make ready to protect them against a young shark of the dog-fish kind, rolling with a lifelike motion in the tide that has thrown him up. Next, they are smit with wonder at the black shells of a wagon load of live lobsters, packed in rock weed for the country market. And when they reach the fleet of dories, just hauled ashore after the day's fishing, how do I laugh in my sleeve, and sometimes roar outright, at the simplicity of these young folks and the sly humor of the fishermen! In winter, when our village is thrown into a bustle by the arrival of perhaps a score of country dealers, bargaining for frozen fish, to be transported hundreds of miles, and eaten fresh in Vermont or Canada, I am a pleased, but idle spectator in the throng. For I launch my boat no more.

When the shore was solitary, I have found a pleasure that seemed even to exalt my mind, in observing the sports or contentions of two gulls, as they wheeled and hovered about each other, with hoarse screams, one moment flapping on the foam of the wave, and then soaring aloft, till their white bosoms melted into the upper sunshine. In the calm of the summer sunset, I drag my aged limbs, with a little ostentation of activity, because I am so old, up to the rocky brow of the hill. There I see the white sails of many a vessel, outward bound or homeward from afar, and the black trail of a vapor behind the eastern steamboat; there, too, is the sun, going down, but not in gloom, and there the illimitable ocean mingling with the sky, to remind me of Eternity.

But sweetest of all is the hour of cheerful musing and pleasant talk, that comes between the dusk and the lighted candle, by my glowing fireside. And never, even on the first Thanksgiving night, when Susan and I sat alone with our hopes, nor the second, when a stranger had been sent to gladden us, and be the visible image of our affection, did I feel such joy as now. All that belong to me are here; Death has taken none, nor Disease kept them away, nor Strife divided them from their parents or each other; with neither poverty nor riches to disturb them, nor the misery of desires beyond their lot, they have kept New England's festival round the patriarch's board. For I am a patriarch! Here I sit among my descendants, in my old arm chair and immemorial corner, while the firelight throws an appropriate glory round my venerable frame. Susan! My children! Something whispers me, that this happiest hour must be the final one, and that nothing remains but to bless you all, and depart with a treasure of recollected joys to Heaven. Will you meet me there? Alas! your figures grow indistinct, fading into pictures on the air, and now to fainter outlines, while the fire is glimmering on the walls of a familiar room, and shows the book that I flung down, and the sheet that I left half written, some fifty years ago. I lift my eyes to the looking-glass, and perceive myself alone, unless those be the mermaid's features, retiring into the depths of the mirror, with a tender and melancholy smile.

Ah! One feels a chillness, not bodily, but about the heart, and, moreover, a foolish dread of looking behind him, after these pastimes. I can imagine precisely how a magician would sit down in gloom and terror, after dismissing the shadows that had personated dead or distant people, and stripping his cavern of the unreal splendor which had changed it to a palace. And now for a moral to my reverie. Shall it be, that, since fancy can create so bright a dream of happiness, it were better to dream on from youth to age, than to awake and strive doubtfully for something real? Oh! the slight tissue of a dream can no more preserve us from the stern reality of misfortune, than a robe of cobweb could repel the wintry blast. Be this the moral, then. In chaste and warm affections, humble wishes, and honest toil for some useful end, there is health for the mind, and quiet for the heart, the prospect of a happy life, and the fairest hope of Heaven.

Little Annie's Ramble

DING-DONG! Ding-dong! Ding-dong!
 The town crier has rung his bell, at a distant corner, and little Annie stands on her father's door-steps, trying to hear what the man with the loud voice is talking about. Let me listen too. Oh! he is telling the people that an elephant, and a lion, and a royal tiger, and a horse with horns, and other strange beasts from foreign countries, have come to town, and will receive all visiters who choose to wait upon them. Perhaps little Annie would like to go. Yes; and I can see that the pretty child is weary of this wide and pleasant street, with the green trees flinging their shade across the quiet sunshine, and the pavements and the side-walks all as clean as if the housemaid had just swept them with her broom. She feels that impulse to go strolling away—that longing after the mystery of the great world—which many children feel, and which I felt in my childhood. Little Annie shall take a ramble with me. See! I do but hold out my hand, and, like some bright bird in the sunny air, with her blue silk frock fluttering upwards from her white pantalettes, she comes bounding on tiptoe across the street.

Smooth back your brown curls, Annie; and let me tie on your bonnet, and we will set forth! What a strange couple to go their rambles together! One walks in black attire, with a measured step, and a heavy brow, and his thoughtful eyes bent down, while the gay little girl trips lightly along, as if she were forced to keep hold of my hand, lest her feet should dance away from the earth. Yet there is sympathy between us. If I pride myself on anything, it is because I have a smile that children love; and, on the other hand, there are few grown ladies that could entice me from the side of little Annie; for I delight to let my mind go hand in hand with the mind of a sinless child. So, come, Annie; but if I moralize as we go, do not listen to me; only look about you, and be merry!

Now we turn the corner. Here are hacks with two horses, and stage-coaches with four, thundering to meet each other, and trucks and carts moving at a slower pace, being heavily laden with barrels from the wharves, and here are rattling gigs, which perhaps will be smashed to pieces before our eyes. Hitherward, also, comes a man trundling a wheelbarrow along the pavement. Is not little Annie afraid of such a tumult? No; she does not even shrink closer to my side, but passes on with fearless confidence, a happy child amidst a great throng of grown people, who pay the same reverence to her infancy, that they would to extreme old age. Nobody jostles her; all turn aside to make way for little Annie; and what is most singular, she appears conscious of her claim to such respect. Now her eyes brighten with pleasure! A street musician has seated himself on the steps of yonder church, and pours forth his strains to the busy town, a melody that has gone astray among the tramp of footsteps, the buzz of voices, and the war of passing wheels. Who heeds the poor organ grinder? None but myself and little Annie, whose feet begin to move in unison with the lively tune, as if she were loth that music should be wasted without a dance. But where would Annie find a partner? Some have the gout in their toes, or the rheumatism in their joints; some are stiff with age; some feeble with disease; some are so lean that their bones would rattle, and others of such ponderous size that their agility would crack the flag-stones; but many, many have leaden feet, because their hearts are far heavier than lead. It is a sad thought that I have chanced upon. What a company of dancers should we be! For I, too, am a gentleman of sober footsteps, and therefore, little Annie, let us walk sedately on.

It is a question with me, whether this giddy child, or my sage self, have most pleasure in looking at the shop windows. We love the silks of sunny hue, that glow within the darkened premises of the spruce dry-goods men; we are pleasantly dazzled by the burnished silver, and the chased gold, the rings of the wedlock and the costly love-ornaments, glistening at the window of the jeweller; but Annie, more than I, seeks for a glimpse of her passing figure in the dusty looking-glasses at the hardware stores. All that is bright and gay attracts us both.

Here is a shop to which the recollections of my boyhood, as well as present partialities, give a peculiar magic. How delightful to let the fancy revel on the dainties of a confectioner;

those pies, with such white and flaky paste, their contents being a mystery, whether rich mince, with whole plums intermixed, or piquant apple, delicately rose-flavored; those cakes, heart-shaped or round, piled in a lofty pyramid; those sweet little circlets, sweetly named kisses; those dark majestic masses, fit to be bridal loaves at the wedding of an heiress, mountains in size, their summits deeply snow-covered with sugar! Then the mighty treasures of sugar plums, white, and crimson, and yellow, in large glass vases; and candy of all varieties; and those little cockles, or whatever they are called, much prized by children for their sweetness, and more for the mottoes which they enclose, by love-sick maids and bachelors! Oh! my mouth waters, little Annie, and so doth yours; but we will not be tempted, except to an imaginary feast; so let us hasten onward, devouring the vision of a plum cake.

Here are pleasures, as some people would say, of a more exalted kind, in the window of a bookseller. Is Annie a literary lady? Yes; she is deeply read in Peter Parley's tomes, and has an increasing love for fairy tales, though seldom met with now-a-days, and she will subscribe, next year, to the Juvenile Miscellany. But, truth to tell, she is apt to turn away from the printed page, and keep gazing at the pretty pictures, such as the gay-colored ones which make this shop window the continual loitering place of children. What would Annie think, if, in the book which I mean to send her, on New Year's day, she should find her sweet little self, bound up in silk or morocco with gilt edges, there to remain till she become a woman grown, with children of her own to read about their mother's childhood! That would be very queer.

Little Annie is weary of pictures, and pulls me onward by the hand, till suddenly we pause at the most wondrous shop in all the town. Oh, my stars! Is this a toy shop, or is it fairy land? For here are gilded chariots, in which the king and queen of the fairies might ride side by side, while their courtiers, on these small horses, should gallop in triumphal procession before and behind the royal pair. Here, too, are dishes of china ware, fit to be the dining set of those same princely personages, when they make a regal banquet in the stateliest hall of their palace, full five feet high, and behold their nobles feasting adown the long perspective of the table.

Betwixt the king and queen should sit my little Annie, the prettiest fairy of them all. Here stands a turbaned Turk, threatening us with his sabre, like an ugly heathen as he is. And next a Chinese mandarine, who nods his head at Annie and myself. Here we may review a whole army of horse and foot, in red and blue uniforms, with drums, fifes, trumpets and all kinds of noiseless music; they have halted on the shelf of this window, after their weary march from Lilliput. But what cares Annie for soldiers? No conquering queen is she, neither a Semiramis nor a Catharine; her whole heart is set upon that doll, who gazes at us with such a fashionable stare. This is the little girl's true plaything. Though made of wood, a doll is a visionary and ethereal personage, endowed by childish fancy with a peculiar life; the mimic lady is a heroine of romance, an actor and a sufferer in a thousand shadowy scenes, the chief inhabitant of that wild world with which children ape the real one. Little Annie does not understand what I am saying, but looks wishfully at the proud lady in the window. We will invite her home with us as we return. Meantime, good bye, Dame Doll! A toy yourself, you look forth from your window upon many ladies that are also toys, though they walk and speak, and upon a crowd in pursuit of toys, though they wear grave visages. Oh, with your never-closing eyes, had you but an intellect to moralize on all that flits before them, what a wise doll would you be! Come, little Annie, we shall find toys enough, go where we may.

Now we elbow our way among the throng again. It is curious, in the most crowded part of town, to meet with living creatures that had their birth-place in some far solitude, but have acquired a second nature in the wilderness of men. Look up, Annie, at that canary-bird, hanging out of the window in his cage. Poor little fellow! His golden feathers are all tarnished in this smoky sunshine; he would have glistened twice as brightly among the summer islands; but still he has become a citizen in all his tastes and habits, and would not sing half so well without the uproar that drowns his music. What a pity that he does not know how miserable he is! There is a parrot, too, calling out, "Pretty Poll! Pretty Poll!" as we pass by. Foolish bird, to be talking about her prettiness to strangers; especially as she is not a pretty Poll, though gaudily dressed in green and yellow. If she had said "pretty Annie," there would have been some sense in it. See that gray squirrel, at the door of the fruit-shop, whirling round and round so merrily within his wire wheel! Being condemned to the tread-mill, he makes it an amusement. Admirable philosophy!

Here comes a big, rough dog, a countryman's dog in search of his master; smelling at every body's heels, and touching little Annie's hand with his cold nose, but hurrying away, though she would fain have patted him. Success to your search, Fidelity! And there sits a great yellow cat upon a window-sill, a very corpulent and comfortable cat, gazing at this transitory world, with owl's eyes, and making pithy comments, doubtless, or what appear such, to the silly beast. Oh, sage puss, make room for me beside you, and we will be a pair of philosophers!

Here we see something to remind us of the town crier, and his ding-dong-bell! Look! look at that great cloth spread out in the air, pictured all over with wild beasts, as if they had met together to choose a king, according to their custom in the days of Æsop. But they are choosing neither a king nor a President; else we should hear a most horrible snarling! They have come from the deep woods, and the wild mountains, and the desert sands, and the polar snows, only to do homage to my little Annie. As we enter among them, the great elephant makes us a bow, in the best style of elephantic courtesy, bending lowly down his mountain bulk, with trunk abased and leg thrust out behind. Annie returns the salute, much to the gratification of the elephant, who is certainly the best bred monster in the caravan. The lion and the lioness are busy with two beef bones. The royal tiger, the beautiful, the untameable, keeps pacing his narrow cage with a haughty step, unmindful of the spectators, or recalling the fierce deeds of his former life, when he was wont to leap forth upon such inferior animals, from the jungles of Bengal.

Here we see the very same wolf—do not go near him, Annie!—the self-same wolf that devoured little Red Riding Hood and her grandmother. In the next cage, a hyena from Egypt, who has doubtless howled around the pyramids, and a black bear from our own forests, are fellow-prisoners, and most excellent friends. Are there any two living creatures, who have so few sympathies that they cannot possibly be friends? Here sits a great white bear, whom common observers would call a very stupid beast, though I perceive him to be only absorbed in contemplation; he is thinking of his voyages on an iceberg, and of his comfortable home in the vicinity of the north pole, and of the little cubs whom he left rolling in the eternal snows. In fact, he is a bear of sentiment. But, oh, those unsentimental monkeys! the ugly, grinning, aping, chattering, ill-natured, mischievous and queer little brutes. Annie does not love the monkeys. Their ugliness shocks her pure, instinctive delicacy of taste, and makes her mind unquiet, because it bears a wild and dark resemblance to humanity. But here is a little pony, just big enough for Annie to ride, and round and round he gallops in a circle, keeping time with his trampling hoofs to a band of music. And here—with a laced coat and a cocked hat, and a riding whip in his hand, here comes a little gentleman, small enough to be king of the fairies, and ugly enough to be king of the gnomes, and takes a flying leap into the saddle. Merrily, merrily, plays the music, and merrily gallops the pony, and merrily rides the little old gentleman. Come, Annie, into the street again; perchance we may see monkeys on horseback there!

Mercy on us, what a noisy world we quiet people live in! Did Annie ever read the cries of London city? With what lusty lungs doth yonder man proclaim that his wheelbarrow is full of lobsters! Here comes another mounted on a cart, and blowing a hoarse and dreadful blast from a tin horn, as much as to say "fresh fish!" And hark! a voice on high, like that of a muezzin from the summit of a mosque, announcing that some chimney sweeper has emerged from smoke and soot, and darksome caverns, into the upper air. What cares the world for that? But, well-a-day, we hear a shrill voice of affliction, the scream of a little child, rising louder with every repetition of that smart, sharp, slapping sound, produced by an open hand on tender flesh. Annie sympathizes, though without experience of such direful wo. Lo! the town crier again, with some new secret for the public ear. Will he tell us of an auction, or of a lost pocket-book, or a show of beautiful wax figures, or of some monstrous beast more horrible than any in the caravan? I guess the latter. See how he uplifts the bell in his right hand, and shakes it slowly at first, then with a hurried motion, till the clapper seems to strike both sides at once, and the sounds are scattered forth in quick succession, far and near.

Ding-dong! Ding-dong! Ding-dong!

Now he raises his clear, loud voice above all the din of the town; it drowns the buzzing talk of many tongues, and draws each man's mind from his own business; it rolls up and down the echoing street, and ascends to the hushed chamber of the sick, and penetrates downward to the cellar kitchen, where the hot cook turns from the fire to listen. Who, of all that address the public ear, whether in church, or court-house, or hall of state, has such an attentive audience as the town crier! What saith the people's orator?

"Strayed from her home, a LITTLE GIRL, of five years old, in a blue frock and white pantalettes, with brown curling hair and hazel eyes. Whoever will bring her back to her afflicted mother—"

Stop, stop, town crier! The lost is found. Oh, my pretty Annie, we forgot to tell your mother of our ramble, and she is in despair, and has sent the town crier to bellow up and down the streets, affrighting old and young, for the loss of a little girl who has not once let go my hand! Well, let us hasten homeward; and as we go, forget not to thank heaven, my Annie, that after wandering a little way into the world, you may return at the first summons, with an untainted and unwearied heart, and be a happy child again. But I have gone too far astray for the town crier to call me back!

Sweet has been the charm of childhood on my spirit, throughout my ramble with little Annie! Say not that it has been a waste of precious moments, an idle matter, a babble of childish talk, and a reverie of childish imaginations, about topics unworthy of a grown man's notice. Has it been merely this? Not so; not so. They are not truly wise who would affirm it. As the pure breath of children revives the life of aged men, so is our moral nature revived by their free and simple thoughts, their native feeling, their airy mirth, for little cause or none, their grief, soon roused and soon allayed. Their influence on us is at least reciprocal with ours on them. When our infancy is almost forgotten, and our boyhood long departed, though it seems but as yesterday; when life settles darkly down upon us, and we doubt whether to call ourselves young any more; then it is good to steal away from the society of bearded men, and even of gentler woman, and spend an hour or two with children. After drinking from those fountains of still fresh existence, we shall return into the crowd, as I do now, to struggle onward and do our part in life, perhaps as fervently as ever, but, for a time, with a kinder and purer heart, and a spirit more lightly wise. All this by thy sweet magic, dear little Annie!

The Gray Champion

THERE was once a time, when New-England groaned under the actual pressure of heavier wrongs, than those threatened ones which brought on the Revolution. James II., the bigoted successor of Charles the Voluptuous, had annulled the charters of all the colonies, and sent a harsh and unprincipled soldier to take away our liberties and endanger our religion. The administration of Sir Edmund Andros lacked scarcely a single characteristic of tyranny: a Governor and Council, holding office from the King, and wholly independent of the country; laws made and taxes levied without concurrence of the people, immediate or by their representatives; the rights of private citizens violated, and the titles of all landed property declared void; the voice of complaint stifled by restrictions on the press; and, finally, disaffection overawed by the first band of mercenary troops that ever marched on our free soil. For two years, our ancestors were kept in sullen submission, by that filial love which had invariably secured their allegiance to the mother country, whether its head chanced to be a Parliament, Protector, or popish Monarch. Till these evil times, however, such allegiance had been merely nominal, and the colonists had ruled themselves, enjoying far more freedom, than is even yet the privilege of the native subjects of Great Britain.

At length, a rumor reached our shores, that the Prince of Orange had ventured on an enterprise, the success of which would be the triumph of civil and religious rights and the salvation of New-England. It was but a doubtful whisper; it might be false, or the attempt might fail; and, in either case, the man, that stirred against King James, would lose his head. Still the intelligence produced a marked effect. The people smiled mysteriously in the streets, and threw bold glances at their oppressors; while, far and wide, there was a subdued and silent agitation, as if the slightest signal would rouse the whole land from its sluggish despondency. Aware of their danger, the rulers resolved to avert it by an imposing display of strength, and perhaps to confirm their despotism by yet

harsher measures. One afternoon in April, 1689, Sir Edmund
Andros and his favorite councillors, being warm with wine,
assembled the red-coats of the Governor's Guard, and made
their appearance in the streets of Boston. The sun was near
setting when the march commenced.

The roll of the drum, at that unquiet crisis, seemed to go
through the streets, less as the martial music of the soldiers,
than as a muster-call to the inhabitants themselves. A multitude, by various avenues, assembled in King-street, which was
destined to be the scene, nearly a century afterwards, of another encounter between the troops of Britain, and a people
struggling against her tyranny. Though more than sixty years
had elapsed, since the Pilgrims came, this crowd of their descendants still showed the strong and sombre features of their
character, perhaps more strikingly in such a stern emergency
than on happier occasions. There was the sober garb, the general severity of mien, the gloomy but undismayed expression,
the scriptural forms of speech, and the confidence in Heaven's
blessing on a righteous cause, which would have marked a
band of the original Puritans, when threatened by some peril
of the wilderness. Indeed, it was not yet time for the old spirit
to be extinct; since there were men in the street, that day,
who had worshipped there beneath the trees, before a house
was reared to the God, for whom they had become exiles.
Old soldiers of the Parliament were here too, smiling grimly
at the thought, that their aged arms might strike another
blow against the house of Stuart. Here also, were the veterans
of King Philip's war, who had burnt villages and slaughtered
young and old, with pious fierceness, while the godly souls
throughout the land were helping them with prayer. Several
ministers were scattered among the crowd, which, unlike all
other mobs, regarded them with such reverence, as if there
were sanctity in their very garments. These holy men exerted
their influence to quiet the people, but not to disperse them.
Meantime, the purpose of the Governor, in disturbing the
peace of the town, at a period when the slightest commotion
might throw the country into a ferment, was almost the universal subject of inquiry, and variously explained.

'Satan will strike his master-stroke presently,' cried some,
'because he knoweth that his time is short. All our godly pas-

tors are to be dragged to prison! We shall see them at a Smithfield fire in King-street!'

Hereupon, the people of each parish gathered closer round their minister, who looked calmly upwards and assumed a more apostolic dignity, as well befitted a candidate for the highest honor of his profession, the crown of martyrdom. It was actually fancied, at that period, that New-England might have a John Rogers of her own, to take the place of that worthy in the Primer.

'The Pope of Rome has given orders for a new St. Bartholomew!' cried others. 'We are to be massacred, man and male child!'

Neither was this rumor wholly discredited, although the wiser class believed the Governor's object somewhat less atrocious. His predecessor under the old charter, Bradstreet, a venerable companion of the first settlers, was known to be in town. There were grounds for conjecturing, that Sir Edmund Andros intended, at once, to strike terror, by a parade of military force, and to confound the opposite faction, by possessing himself of their chief.

'Stand firm for the old charter Governor!' shouted the crowd, seizing upon the idea. 'The good old Governor Bradstreet!'

While this cry was at the loudest, the people were surprised by the well known figure of Governor Bradstreet himself, a patriarch of nearly ninety, who appeared on the elevated steps of a door, and, with characteristic mildness, besought them to submit to the constituted authorities.

'My children,' concluded this venerable person, 'do nothing rashly. Cry not aloud, but pray for the welfare of New-England, and expect patiently what the Lord will do in this matter!'

The event was soon to be decided. All this time, the roll of the drum had been approaching through Cornhill, louder and deeper, till, with reverberations from house to house, and the regular tramp of martial footsteps, it burst into the street. A double rank of soldiers made their appearance, occupying the whole breadth of the passage, with shouldered matchlocks, and matches burning, so as to present a row of fires in the dusk. Their steady march was like the progress of a machine, that would roll irresistibly over every thing in its way. Next, moving slowly, with a confused clatter of hoofs on the pavement, rode a party of mounted gentlemen, the central figure being Sir Edmund Andros, elderly, but erect and soldier-like. Those around him were his favorite councillors, and the bitterest foes of New-England. At his right hand rode Edward Randolph, our arch enemy, that 'blasted wretch,' as Cotton Mather calls him, who achieved the downfall of our ancient government, and was followed with a sensible curse, through life and to his grave. On the other side was Bullivant, scattering jests and mockery as he rode along. Dudley came behind, with a downcast look, dreading, as well he might, to meet the indignant gaze of the people, who beheld him, their only countryman by birth, among the oppressors of his native land. The captain of a frigate in the harbor, and two or three civil officers under the Crown, were also there. But the figure which most attracted the public eye, and stirred up the deepest feeling, was the Episcopal clergyman of King's Chapel, riding haughtily among the magistrates in his priestly vestments, the fitting representative of prelacy and persecution, the union of church and state, and all those abominations which had driven the Puritans to the wilderness. Another guard of soldiers, in double rank, brought up the rear.

The whole scene was a picture of the condition of New-England, and its moral, the deformity of any government that does not grow out of the nature of things and the character of the people. On one side the religious multitude, with their sad visages and dark attire, and on the other, the group of despotic rulers, with the high churchman in the midst, and here and there a crucifix at their bosoms, all magnificently clad, flushed with wine, proud of unjust authority, and scoffing at the universal groan. And the mercenary soldiers, waiting but the word to deluge the street with blood, shewed the only means by which obedience could be secured.

'Oh! Lord of Hosts,' cried a voice among the crowd, 'provide a Champion for thy people!'

This ejaculation was loudly uttered, and served as a herald's cry, to introduce a remarkable personage. The crowd had rolled back, and were now huddled together nearly at the extremity of the street, while the soldiers had advanced no more than a third of its length. The intervening space was empty—a paved solitude, between lofty edifices, which threw almost a twilight shadow over it. Suddenly, there was seen the figure of an ancient man, who seemed to have emerged from among the people, and was walking by himself along the centre of the street, to confront the armed band. He wore the old Puritan dress, a dark cloak and a steeple-crowned hat, in the fashion of at least fifty years before, with a heavy sword upon his thigh, but a staff in his hand, to assist the tremulous gait of age.

When at some distance from the multitude, the old man turned slowly round, displaying a face of antique majesty, rendered doubly venerable by the hoary beard that descended on his breast. He made a gesture at once of encouragement and warning, then turned again, and resumed his way.

'Who is this gray patriarch?' asked the young men of their sires.

'Who is this venerable brother?' asked the old men among themselves.

But none could make reply. The fathers of the people, those of four-score years and upwards, were disturbed, deeming it strange that they should forget one of such evident authority, whom they must have known in their early days, the associate of Winthrop and all the old Councillors, giving laws, and making prayers, and leading them against the savage. The elderly men ought to have remembered him, too, with locks as gray in their youth, as their own were now. And the young! How could he have passed so utterly from their memories—that hoary sire, the relic of long departed times, whose awful benediction had surely been bestowed on their uncovered heads, in childhood?

'Whence did he come? What is his purpose? Who can this old man be?' whispered the wondering crowd.

Meanwhile, the venerable stranger, staff in hand, was pursuing his solitary walk along the centre of the street. As he drew near the advancing soldiers, and as the roll of their drum came full upon his ear, the old man raised himself to a loftier mien, while the decrepitude of age seemed to fall from his shoulders, leaving him in gray, but unbroken dignity. Now, he marched onward with a warrior's step, keeping time to the military music. Thus the aged form advanced on one side, and the whole parade of soldiers and magistrates on the other, till, when scarcely twenty yards remained between, the old man grasped his staff by the middle, and held it before him like a leader's truncheon.

'Stand!' cried he.

The eye, the face, and attitude of command; the solemn, yet warlike peal of that voice, fit either to rule a host in the battle-field or be raised to God in prayer, were irresistible. At the old man's word and outstretched arm, the roll of the drum was hushed at once, and the advancing line stood still. A tremulous enthusiasm seized upon the multitude. That stately form, combining the leader and the saint, so gray, so dimly seen, in such an ancient garb, could only belong to some old champion of the righteous cause, whom the oppressor's drum had summoned from his grave. They raised a shout of awe and exultation, and looked for the deliverance of New-England.

The Governor, and the gentlemen of his party, perceiving themselves brought to an unexpected stand, rode hastily forward, as if they would have pressed their snorting and affrighted horses right against the hoary apparition. He, however, blenched not a step, but glancing his severe eye round the group, which half encompassed him, at last bent it sternly on Sir Edmund Andros. One would have thought that the dark old man was chief ruler there, and that the Governor and Council, with soldiers at their back, representing the whole power and authority of the Crown, had no alternative but obedience.

'What does this old fellow here?' cried Edward Randolph, fiercely. 'On, Sir Edmund! Bid the soldiers forward, and give the dotard the same choice that you give all his countrymen—to stand aside or be trampled on!'

'Nay, nay, let us show respect to the good grandsire,' said Bullivant, laughing. 'See you not, he is some old roundheaded dignitary, who hath lain asleep these thirty years, and knows nothing of the change of times? Doubtless, he thinks to put us down with a proclamation in Old Noll's name!'

'Are you mad, old man?' demanded Sir Edmund Andros, in loud and harsh tones. 'How dare you stay the march of King James's Governor?'

'I have staid the march of a King himself, ere now,' replied the gray figure, with stern composure. 'I am here, Sir Governor, because the cry of an oppressed people hath disturbed me in my secret place; and beseeching this favor earnestly of the Lord, it was vouchsafed me to appear once again on earth, in the good old cause of his Saints. And what speak ye of James? There is no longer a popish tyrant on the throne of England, and by to-morrow noon, his name shall be a by-word in this very street, where ye would make it a word of terror. Back, thou that wast a Governor, back! With this night, thy power is ended—to-morrow, the prison!—back, lest I foretell the scaffold!'

The people had been drawing nearer and nearer, and drinking in the words of their champion, who spoke in accents long disused, like one unaccustomed to converse, except with the dead of many years ago. But his voice stirred their souls. They confronted the soldiers, not wholly without arms, and ready to convert the very stones of the street into deadly weapons. Sir Edmund Andros looked at the old man; then he cast his hard and cruel eye over the multitude, and beheld them burning with that lurid wrath, so difficult to kindle or to quench; and again he fixed his gaze on the aged form, which stood obscurely in an open space, where neither friend nor foe had thrust himself. What were his thoughts, he uttered no word which might discover. But whether the oppressor were overawed by the Gray Champion's look, or perceived his peril in the threatening attitude of the people, it is certain that he gave back, and ordered his soldiers to commence a slow and guarded retreat. Before another sunset, the Governor, and all that rode so proudly with him, were prisoners, and long ere it was known that James had abdicated, King William was proclaimed throughout New-England.

But where was the Gray Champion? Some reported, that when the troops had gone from King-street, and the people were thronging tumultuously in their rear, Bradstreet, the aged Governor, was seen to embrace a form more aged than his own. Others soberly affirmed, that while they marvelled at the venerable grandeur of his aspect, the old man had faded from their eyes, melting slowly into the hues of twilight, till, where he stood, there was an empty space. But all agreed, that the hoary shape was gone. The men of that generation watched for his re-appearance, in sunshine and in twilight, but never saw him more, nor knew when his funeral passed, nor where his grave-stone was.

And who was the Gray Champion? Perhaps his name might be found in the records of that stern Court of Justice, which passed a sentence, too mighty for the age, but glorious in all after times, for its humbling lesson to the monarch and its high example to the subject. I have heard, that, whenever the descendants of the Puritans are to show the spirit of their sires, the old man appears again. When eighty years had passed, he walked once more in King-street. Five years later, in the twilight of an April morning, he stood on the green, beside the meeting-house, at Lexington, where now the obelisk of granite, with a slab of slate inlaid, commemorates the first fallen of the Revolution. And when our fathers were toiling at the breast-work on Bunker's Hill, all through that night, the old warrior walked his rounds. Long, long may it be, ere he comes again! His hour is one of darkness, and adversity, and peril. But should domestic tyranny oppress us, or the invader's step pollute our soil, still may the Gray Champion come; for he is the type of New-England's hereditary spirit; and his shadowy march, on the eve of danger, must ever be the pledge, that New-England's sons will vindicate their ancestry.

My Visit to Niagara

NEVER did a pilgrim approach Niagara with deeper enthusiasm, than mine. I had lingered away from it, and wandered to other scenes, because my treasury of anticipated enjoyments, comprising all the wonders of the world, had nothing else so magnificent, and I was loth to exchange the pleasures of hope for those of memory so soon. At length, the day came. The stage-coach, with a Frenchman and myself on the back seat, had already left Lewiston, and in less than an hour would set us down in Manchester. I began to listen for the roar of the cataract, and trembled with a sensation like dread, as the moment drew nigh, when its voice of ages must roll, for the first time, on my ear. The French gentleman stretched himself from the window, and expressed loud admiration, while, by a sudden impulse, I threw myself back and closed my eyes. When the scene shut in, I was glad to think, that for me the whole burst of Niagara was yet in futurity. We rolled on, and entered the village of Manchester, bordering on the falls.

I am quite ashamed of myself here. Not that I ran, like a madman, to the falls, and plunged into the thickest of the spray—never stopping to breathe, till breathing was impossible; not that I committed this, or any other suitable extravagance. On the contrary, I alighted with perfect decency and composure, gave my cloak to the black waiter, pointed out my baggage, and inquired, not the nearest way to the cataract, but about the dinner-hour. The interval was spent in arranging my dress. Within the last fifteen minutes, my mind had grown strangely benumbed, and my spirits apathetic, with a slight depression, not decided enough to be termed sadness. My enthusiasm was in a deathlike slumber. Without aspiring to immortality, as he did, I could have imitated that English traveller, who turned back from the point where he first heard the thunder of Niagara, after crossing the ocean to behold it. Many a western trader, by-the-by, has performed a similar act of heroism with more heroic simplicity, deeming it no such wonderful feat to dine at the hotel and resume his route to Buffalo or Lewiston, while the cataract was roaring unseen.

Such has often been my apathy, when objects, long sought, and earnestly desired, were placed within my reach. After dinner—at which, an unwonted and perverse epicurism detained me longer than usual—I lighted a cigar and paced the piazza, minutely attentive to the aspect and business of a very ordinary village. Finally, with reluctant step, and the feeling of an intruder, I walked towards Goat Island. At the toll-house, there were further excuses for delaying the inevitable moment. My signature was required in a huge leger, containing similar records innumerable, many of which I read. The skin of a great sturgeon, and other fishes, beasts, and reptiles; a collection of minerals, such as lie in heaps near the falls; some Indian moccasins, and other trifles, made of deer-skin and embroidered with beads; several newspapers from Montreal, New-York, and Boston; all attracted me in turn. Out of a number of twisted sticks, the manufacture of a Tuscarora Indian, I selected one of curled maple, curiously convoluted, and adorned with the carved images of a snake and a fish. Using this as my pilgrim's staff, I crossed the bridge. Above and below me were the rapids, a river of impetuous snow, with here and there a dark rock amid its whiteness, resisting all the physical fury, as any cold spirit did the moral influences of the scene. On reaching Goat Island, which separates the two great segments of the falls, I chose the right-hand path, and followed it to the edge of the American cascade. There, while the falling sheet was yet invisible, I saw the vapor that never vanishes, and the Eternal Rainbow of Niagara.

It was an afternoon of glorious sunshine, without a cloud, save those of the cataracts. I gained an insulated rock, and beheld a broad sheet of brilliant and unbroken foam, not shooting in a curved line from the top of the precipice, but falling headlong down from height to depth. A narrow stream diverged from the main branch, and hurried over the crag by a channel of its own, leaving a little pine-clad island and a streak of precipice, between itself and the larger sheet. Below arose the mist, on which was painted a dazzling sunbow, with two concentric shadows—one, almost as perfect as the original brightness; and the other, drawn faintly round the broken edge of the cloud.

Still, I had not half seen Niagara. Following the verge of the island, the path led me to the Horse-shoe, where the real, broad St. Lawrence, rushing along on a level with its banks, pours its whole breadth over a concave line of precipice, and thence pursues its course between lofty crags towards Ontario. A sort of bridge, two or three feet wide, stretches out along the edge of the descending sheet, and hangs upon the rising mist, as if that were the foundation of the frail structure. Here I stationed myself, in the blast of wind, which the rushing river bore along with it. The bridge was tremulous beneath me, and marked the tremor of the solid earth. I looked along the whitening rapids, and endeavored to distinguish a mass of water far above the falls, to follow it to their verge, and go down with it, in fancy, to the abyss of clouds and storm. Casting my eyes across the river, and every side, I took in the whole scene at a glance, and tried to comprehend it in one vast idea. After an hour thus spent, I left the bridge, and, by a staircase, winding almost interminably round a post, descended to the base of the precipice. From that point, my path lay over slippery stones, and among great fragments of the cliff, to the edge of the cataract, where the wind at once enveloped me in spray, and perhaps dashed the rainbow round me. Were my long desires fulfilled? And had I seen Niagara?

Oh, that I had never heard of Niagara till I beheld it! Blessed were the wanderers of old, who heard its deep roar, sounding through the woods, as the summons to an unknown wonder, and approached its awful brink, in all the freshness of native feeling. Had its own mysterious voice been the first to warn me of its existence, then, indeed, I might have knelt down and worshipped. But I had come thither, haunted with a vision of foam and fury, and dizzy cliffs, and an ocean tumbling down out of the sky—a scene, in short, which Nature had too much good taste and calm simplicity to realize. My mind had struggled to adapt these false conceptions to the reality, and finding the effort vain, a wretched sense of disappointment weighed me down. I climbed the precipice, and threw myself on the earth—feeling that I was unworthy to look at the Great Falls, and careless about beholding them again.

All that night, as there has been and will be, for ages past and to come, a rushing sound was heard, as if a great tempest were sweeping through the air. It mingled with my dreams, and made them full of storm and whirlwind. Whenever I awoke, and heard this dread sound in the air, and the windows rattling as with a mighty blast, I could not rest again, till, looking forth, I saw how bright the stars were, and that every leaf in the garden was motionless. Never was a summer-night more calm to the eye, nor a gale of autumn louder to the ear. The rushing sound proceeds from the rapids, and the rattling of the casements is but an effect of the vibration of the whole house, shaken by the jar of the cataract. The noise of the rapids draws the attention from the true voice of Niagara, which is a dull, muffled thunder, resounding between the cliffs. I spent a wakeful hour at midnight, in distinguishing its reverberations, and rejoiced to find that my former awe and enthusiasm were reviving.

Gradually, and after much contemplation, I came to know, by my own feelings, that Niagara is indeed a wonder of the world, and not the less wonderful, because time and thought must be employed in comprehending it. Casting aside all preconceived notions, and preparation to be dire-struck or delighted, the beholder must stand beside it in the simplicity of his heart, suffering the mighty scene to work its own impression. Night after night, I dreamed of it, and was gladdened every morning by the consciousness of a growing capacity to enjoy it. Yet I will not pretend to the all-absorbing enthusiasm of some more fortunate spectators, nor deny, that very trifling causes would draw my eyes and thoughts from the cataract.

The last day that I was to spend at Niagara, before my departure for the far west, I sat upon the Table Rock. This celebrated station did not now, as of old, project fifty feet beyond the line of the precipice, but was shattered by the fall of an immense fragment, which lay distant on the shore below. Still, on the utmost verge of the rock, with my feet hanging over it, I felt as if suspended in the open air. Never before had my mind been in such perfect unison with the scene. There were intervals, when I was conscious of nothing but the great river, rolling calmly into the abyss, rather descending than precipitating itself, and acquiring tenfold majesty from its unhurried motion. It came like the march of Destiny. It was not taken by surprise, but seemed to have anticipated, in all its course through the broad lakes, that it must pour their collected waters down this height. The perfect foam of the river, after its descent, and the ever-varying shapes of mist, rising up, to become clouds in the sky, would be the very picture of confusion, were it merely transient, like the rage of a tempest. But when the beholder has stood awhile, and perceives no lull in the storm, and considers that the vapor and the foam are as everlasting as the rocks which produce them, all this turmoil assumes a sort of calmness. It soothes, while it awes the mind.

Leaning over the cliff, I saw the guide conducting two adventurers behind the falls. It was pleasant, from that high seat in the sunshine, to observe them struggling against the eternal storm of the lower regions, with heads bent down, now faltering, now pressing forward, and finally swallowed up in their victory. After their disappearance, a blast rushed out with an old hat, which it had swept from one of their heads. The rock, to which they were directing their unseen course, is marked, at a fearful distance on the exterior of the sheet, by a jet of foam. The attempt to reach it, appears both poetical and perilous, to a looker-on, but may be accomplished without much more difficulty or hazard, than in stemming a violent northeaster. In a few moments, forth came the children of the mist. Dripping and breathless, they crept along the base of the cliff, ascended to the guide's cottage, and received, I presume, a certificate of their achievement, with three verses of sublime poetry on the back.

My contemplations were often interrupted by strangers, who came down from Forsyth's to take their first view of the falls. A short, ruddy, middle-aged gentleman, fresh from old England, peeped over the rock, and evinced his approbation by a broad grin. His spouse, a very robust lady, afforded a sweet example of maternal solicitude, being so intent on the safety of her little boy that she did not even glance at Niagara.

As for the child, he gave himself wholly to the enjoyment of a stick of candy. Another traveller, a native American, and no rare character among us, produced a volume of Captain Hall's tour, and labored earnestly to adjust Niagara to the captain's description, departing, at last, without one new idea or sensation of his own. The next comer was provided, not with a printed book, but with a blank sheet of foolscap, from top to bottom of which, by means of an ever-pointed pencil, the cataract was made to thunder. In a little talk, which we had together, he awarded his approbation to the general view, but censured the position of Goat Island, observing that it should have been thrown farther to the right, so as to widen the American falls, and contract those of the Horse-shoe. Next appeared two traders of Michigan, who declared, that, upon the whole, the sight was worth looking at; there certainly was an immense water-power here; but that, after all, they would go twice as far to see the noble stone-works of Lockport, where the Grand Canal is locked down a descent of sixty feet. They were succeeded by a young fellow, in a home-spun cotton dress, with a staff in his hand, and a pack over his shoulders. He advanced close to the edge of the rock, where his attention, at first wavering among the different components of the scene, finally became fixed in the angle of the Horse-shoe falls, which is, indeed, the central point of interest. His whole soul seemed to go forth and be transported thither, till the staff slipped from his relaxed grasp, and falling down—down—down—struck upon the fragment of the Table Rock.

In this manner, I spent some hours, watching the varied impression, made by the cataract, on those who disturbed me, and returning to unwearied contemplation, when left alone. At length, my time came to depart. There is a grassy footpath, through the woods, along the summit of the bank, to a point whence a causeway, hewn in the side of the precipice, goes winding down to the ferry, about half a mile below the Table Rock. The sun was near setting, when I emerged from the shadow of the trees, and began the descent. The indirectness of my downward road continually changed the point of view, and shewed me, in rich and repeated succession—now, the whitening rapids and the majestic leap of the main river, which appeared more deeply massive as the light departed; now, the lovelier picture, yet still sublime, of Goat Island, with its rocks and grove, and the lesser falls, tumbling over the right bank of the St. Lawrence, like a tributary stream; now, the long vista of the river, as it eddied and whirled between the cliffs, to pass through Ontario towards the sea, and everywhere to be wondered at, for this one unrivalled scene. The golden sunshine tinged the sheet of the American cascade, and painted on its heaving spray the broken semicircle of a rainbow, Heaven's own beauty crowning earth's sublimity. My steps were slow, and I paused long at every turn of the descent, as one lingers and pauses, who discerns a brighter and brightening excellence in what he must soon behold no more. The solitude of the old wilderness now reigned over the whole vicinity of the falls. My enjoyment became the more rapturous, because no poet shared it—nor wretch, devoid of poetry, profaned it: but the spot, so famous through the world, was all my own!

Old News

HERE is a volume of what were once newspapers—each on a small half-sheet, yellow and time-stained, of a coarse fabric, and imprinted with a rude old type. Their aspect conveys a singular impression of antiquity, in a species of literature which we are accustomed to consider as connected only with the present moment. Ephemeral as they were intended and supposed to be, they have long outlived the printer and his whole subscription list, and have proved more durable, as to their physical existence, than most of the timber, bricks, and stone, of the town where they were issued. These are but the least of their triumphs. The government, the interests, the opinions—in short, all the moral circumstances that were contemporary with their publication, have passed away, and left no better record of what they were, than may be found in these frail leaves. Happy are the editors of newspapers! Their productions excel all others in immediate popularity, and are certain to acquire another sort of value with the lapse of time. They scatter their leaves to the wind, as the sybil did, and posterity collects them, to be treasured up among the best materials of its wisdom. With hasty pens, they write for immortality.

It is pleasant to take one of these little dingy half-sheets between the thumb and finger, and picture forth the personage, who, above ninety years ago, held it, wet from the press, and steaming, before the fire. Many of the numbers bear the name of an old colonial dignitary. There he sits, a major, a member of the council, and a weighty merchant, in his high-backed arm-chair, wearing a solemn wig and grave attire, such as befits his imposing gravity of mien, and displaying but little finery, except a huge pair of silver shoe-buckles, curiously carved. Observe the awful reverence of his visage, as he reads His Majesty's most gracious speech, and the deliberate wisdom with which he ponders over some paragraph of provincial politics, and the keener intelligence with which he glances at the ship-news and commercial advertisements. Observe, and smile! He may have been a wise man in his day; but, to us, the wisdom of the politician appears like folly, because we can compare its prognostics with actual results; and the old merchant seems to have busied himself about vanities, because we know that the expected ships have been lost at sea, or mouldered at the wharves; that his imported broadcloths were long ago worn to tatters, and his cargoes of wine quaffed to the lees; and that the most precious leaves of his leger have become waste-paper. Yet, his avocations were not so vain as our philosophic moralizing. In this world, we are the things of a moment, and are made to pursue momentary things, with here and there a thought that stretches mistily towards eternity, and perhaps may endure as long. All philosophy, that would abstract mankind from the present, is no more than words.

The first pages, of most of these old papers, are as soporific as a bed of poppies. Here we have an erudite clergyman, or perhaps a Cambridge professor, occupying several successive weeks with a criticism on Tate and Brady, as compared with the New-England version of the Psalms. Of course, the preference is given to the native article. Here are doctors disagreeing about the treatment of a putrid fever, then prevalent, and blackguarding each other with a characteristic virulence, that renders the controversy not altogether unreadable. Here are President Wigglesworth and the Rev. Dr. Colman, endeavoring to raise a fund for the support of missionaries among the Indians of Massachusetts Bay. Easy would be the duties of such a mission, now! Here—for there is nothing new under the sun—are frequent complaints of the disordered state of the currency, and the project of a bank with a capital of five hundred thousand pounds, secured on lands. Here are literary essays, from the Gentleman's Magazine; and squibs against the Pretender, from the London newspapers. And here, occasionally, are specimens of New-England humor— laboriously light and lamentably mirthful; as if some very sober person, in his zeal to be merry, were dancing a jig to the tune of a funeral-psalm. All this is wearisome, and we must turn the leaf.

There is a good deal of amusement, and some profit, in the

perusal of those little items, which characterize the manners and circumstances of the country. New-England was then in a state incomparably more picturesque than at present, or than it has been within the memory of man; there being, as yet, only a narrow strip of civilization along the edge of a vast forest, peopled with enough of its original race to contrast the savage life with the old customs of another world. The white population, also, was diversified by the influx of all sorts of expatriated vagabonds, and by the continual impor- tation of bond-servants from Ireland and elsewhere; so that there was a wild and unsettled multitude, forming a strong minority to the sober descendants of the Puritans. Then, there were the slaves, contributing their dark shade to the picture of society. The consequence of all this was, a great variety and singularity of action and incident—many in- stances of which, might be selected from these columns, where they are told with a simplicity and quaintness of style, that bring the striking points into very strong relief. It is nat- ural to suppose, too, that these circumstances affected the body of the people, and made their course of life generally less regular than that of their descendants. There is no evi- dence that the moral standard was higher then than now; or, indeed, that morality was so well defined as it has since be- come. There seem to have been quite as many frauds and rob- beries, in proportion to the number of honest deeds; there were murders, in hot blood and in malice; and bloody quar- rels, over liquor. Some of our fathers, also, appear to have been yoked to unfaithful wives—if we may trust the frequent notices of elopements from bed and board. The pillory, the whipping-post, the prison, and the gallows, each, had their use in those old times; and, in short, as often as our imagi- nation lives in the past, we find it a ruder and rougher age than our own, with hardly any perceptible advantages, and much that gave life a gloomier tinge.

In vain, we endeavor to throw a sunny and joyous air over our picture of this period; nothing passes before our fancy but a crowd of sad-visaged people, moving duskily through a dull gray atmosphere. It is certain, that winter rushed upon them with fiercer storms than now—blocking up the narrow forest-paths, and overwhelming the roads, along the sea-coast, with mountain snow-drifts; so that weeks elapsed before the newspaper could announce how many travellers had perished, or what wrecks had strewn the shore. The cold was more piercing then, and lingered farther into the spring—making the chimney-corner a comfortable seat till long past May-day. By the number of such accidents on record, we might suppose that the thunder-stone, as they termed it, fell oftener and deadlier, on steeples, dwellings, and unsheltered wretches. In fine, our fathers bore the brunt of more raging and pitiless elements than we. There were forebodings, also, of a more fearful tempest than those of the elements. At two or three dates, we have stories of drums, trumpets, and all sorts of martial music, passing athwart the midnight sky, accompanied with the roar of cannon and rattle of musketry, prophetic echoes of the sounds that were soon to shake the land. Besides these airy prognostics, there were rumors of French fleets on the coast, and of the march of French and Indians through the wilderness, along the borders of the settlements. The country was saddened, moreover, with grievous sickness. The small-pox raged in many of the towns, and seems, though so familiar a scourge, to have been regarded with as much affright as that which drove the throng from Wall-street and Broadway, at the approach of a new pestilence. There were autumnal fevers, too; and a contagious and destructive throat-distemper—diseases unwritten in medical books. The dark superstition of former days had not yet been so far dispelled, as not to heighten the gloom of the present times. There is an advertisement, indeed, by a committee of the Legislature, calling for information as to the circumstances of sufferers in the 'late calamity of 1692,' with a view to reparation for their losses and misfortunes. But the tenderness, with which, after above forty years, it was thought expedient to allude to the witchcraft delusion, indicates a good deal of lingering error, as well as the advance of more enlightened opinions. The rigid hand of Puritanism might yet be felt upon the reins of government, while some of the ordinances intimate a disorderly spirit on the part of the people. The Suffolk justices, after a preamble that great disturbances have been committed by persons entering town and leaving it in coaches, chaises, calashes, and other wheel-carriages, on the evening before the Sabbath, give notice that a watch will hereafter be set at the 'fortification-gate,' to prevent these outrages. It is amusing to see Boston assuming the aspect of a walled city—guarded, probably, by a detachment of church-members, with a deacon at their head. Governor Belcher makes proclamation against certain 'loose and dissolute people,' who have been wont to stop passengers in the streets, on the Fifth of November, 'otherwise called Pope's Day,' and levy contributions for the building of bonfires. In this instance, the populace are more puritanic than the magistrate.

The elaborate solemnities of funerals were in accordance with the sombre character of the times. In cases of ordinary death, the printer seldom fails to notice that the corpse was 'very decently interred.' But when some mightier mortal has yielded to his fate, the decease of the 'worshipful' such-a-one is announced, with all his titles of deacon, justice, councillor, and colonel; then follows an heraldic sketch of his honorable ancestors, and lastly an account of the black pomp of his funeral, and the liberal expenditure of scarfs, gloves, and mourning-rings. The burial train glides slowly before us, as we have seen it represented in the wood-cuts of that day, the coffin, and the bearers, and the lamentable friends, trailing their long black garments, while grim Death, a most misshapen skeleton, with all kinds of doleful emblems, stalks hideously in front. There was a coachmaker at this period, one John Lucas, who seems to have gained the chief of his living by letting out a sable coach to funerals.

It would not be fair, however, to leave quite so dismal an impression on the reader's mind; nor should it be forgotten that happiness may walk soberly in dark attire as well as dance lightsomely in a gala-dress. And this reminds us that there is an incidental notice of the 'dancing-school near the Orange-Tree,' whence we may infer, that the saltatory art was occasionally practised, though perhaps chastened into a characteristic gravity of movement. This pastime was probably confined to the aristocratic circle, of which the royal Governor was the centre. But we are scandalized, at the attempt of Jonathan Furness to introduce a more reprehensible amusement: he challenges the whole country to match his black gelding in a race for a hundred pounds, to be decided on Metonomy

Common or Chelsea Beach. Nothing, as to the manners of the times, can be inferred from this freak of an individual. There were no daily and continual opportunities of being merry; but sometimes the people rejoiced, in their own peculiar fashion, oftener with a calm religious smile, than with a broad laugh; as when they feasted, like one great family, at Thanksgiving time; or indulged a livelier mirth throughout the pleasant days of Election-week. This latter, was the true holyday-season of New-England. Military musters were too seriously important, in that warlike time, to be classed among amusements; but they stirred up and enlivened the public mind, and were occasions of solemn festival to the Governor and great men of the Province, at the expense of the field-officers. The Revolution blotted a feast-day out of our calendar; for the anniversary of the King's birth appears to have been celebrated with most imposing pomp, by salutes from Castle William, a military parade, a grand dinner at the town-house, and a brilliant illumination in the evening. There was nothing forced nor feigned in these testimonials of loyalty to George the Second. So long as they dreaded the re-establishment of a popish dynasty, the people were fervent for the house of Hanover; and, besides, the immediate magistracy of the country was a barrier between the monarch and the occasional discontents of the colonies; the waves of faction sometimes reached the governor's chair, but never swelled against the throne. Thus, until oppression was felt to proceed from the King's own hand, New-England rejoiced with her whole heart on His Majesty's birth-day.

But the slaves, we suspect, were the merriest part of the population—since it was their gift to be merry in the worst of circumstances; and they endured, comparatively, few hardships, under the domestic sway of our fathers. There seems to have been a great trade in these human commodities. No advertisements are more frequent than those of 'a negro fellow, fit for almost any household work;' 'a negro woman, honest, healthy, and capable;' 'a young negro wench, of many desirable qualities;' 'a negro man, very fit for a taylor.' We know not in what this natural fitness for a taylor consisted, unless it were some peculiarity of conformation that enabled him to sit cross-legged. When the slaves of a family were inconveniently prolific, it being not quite orthodox to drown the superfluous offspring, like a litter of kittens, notice was promulgated of 'a negro child to be given away.' Sometimes the slaves assumed the property of their own persons, and made their escape: among many such instances, the Governor raises a hue-and-cry after his negro Juba. But, without venturing a word in extenuation of the general system, we confess our opinion, that Cæsar, Pompey, Scipio, and all such great Roman name-sakes, would have been better advised had they staid at home, foddering the cattle, cleaning dishes—in fine, performing their moderate share of the labors of life without being harassed by its cares. The sable inmates of the mansion were not excluded from the domestic affections: in families of middling rank, they had their places at the board; and when the circle closed round the evening hearth, its blaze glowed on their dark shining faces, intermixed familiarly with their master's children. It must have contributed to reconcile them to their lot, that they saw white men and women imported from Europe, as they had been from Africa, and sold, though only for a term of years, yet as actual slaves to the highest bidder. Slave labor being but a small part of the industry of the country, it did not change the character of the people; the latter, on the contrary, modified and softened the institution, making it a patriarchal, and almost a beautiful, peculiarity of the times.

Ah! We had forgotten the good old merchant, over whose shoulder we were peeping, while he read the newspaper. Let us now suppose him putting on his three-cornered, gold-laced hat, grasping his cane, with a head inlaid of ebony and mother-of-pearl, and setting forth, through the crooked streets of Boston, on various errands, suggested by the advertisements of the day. Thus he communes with himself: I must be mindful, says he, to call at Captain Scut's, in Creek-lane, and examine his rich velvet, whether it be fit for my apparel on Election-day—that I may wear a stately aspect in presence of the Governor and my brethren of the council. I will look in, also, at the shop of Michael Cario, the jeweller; he has silver buckles of a new fashion; and mine have lasted me some half score years. My fair daughter, Miriam, shall have an apron of gold brocade, and a velvet mask—though it would

be a pity the wench should hide her comely visage; and also
a French cap, from Robert Jenkins's, on the north side of the
town-house. He hath beads, too, and ear-rings, and necklaces,
of all sorts; these are but vanities—nevertheless, they would
please the silly maiden well. My dame desireth another female
in the kitchen; wherefore, I must inspect the lot of Irish
lasses, for sale by Samuel Waldo, aboard the schooner Endeavor; as also the likely negro wench, at Captain Bulfinch's.
It were not amiss, that I took my daughter, Miriam, to see
the royal wax-work, near the town-dock, that she may learn
to honour our most gracious King and Queen, and their royal
progeny, even in their waxen images; not that I would ap-
prove of image-worship. The camel, too, that strange beast
from Africa, with two great humps, to be seen near the common; methinks I would fain go thither, and see how the old
patriarchs were wont to ride. I will tarry awhile in Queen-
street, at the book-store of my good friends, Kneeland &
Green, and purchase Doctor Colman's new sermon, and the
volume of discourses, by Mr. Henry Flynt; and look over the
controversy on baptism, between the Reverend Peter Clarke
and an unknown adversary; and see whether this George
Whitefield be as great in print as he is famed to be in the
pulpit. By that time, the auction will have commenced at the
Royal Exchange, in King-street. Moreover, I must look to the
disposal of my last cargo of West-India rum and muscovado
sugar; and also the lot of choice Cheshire cheese, lest it grow
mouldy. It were well that I ordered a cask of good English
beer, at the lower end of Milk-street. Then am I to speak with
certain dealers about the lot of stout old Vidonia, rich Canary, and Oporto wines, which I have now lying in the cellar
of the Old South meeting-house. But, a pipe or two of the
rich Canary shall be reserved, that it may grow mellow in
mine own wine-cellar, and gladden my heart when it begins
to droop with old-age.

    Provident old gentleman! But, was he mindful of his sep-
ulchre? Did he bethink him to call at the workshop of Timothy Sheaffe, in Cold-lane, and select such a grave-stone as
would best please him? There wrought the man, whose handiwork, or that of his fellow-craftsmen, was ultimately in
demand by all the busy multitude, who have left a record of

their earthly toil in these old time-stained papers. And now, as we turn over the volume, we seem to be wandering among the mossy stones of a burial-ground.

II. THE OLD FRENCH WAR

At a period about twenty years subsequent to that of our former sketch, we again attempt a delineation of some of the characteristics of life and manners in New-England. Our text-book, as before, is a file of antique newspapers. The volume, which serves us for a writing-desk, is a folio of larger dimensions than the one before described; and the papers are generally printed on a whole sheet, sometimes with a supplemental leaf of news and advertisements. They have a venerable appearance, being overspread with the duskiness of more than seventy years; and discolored, here and there, with the deeper stains of some liquid, as if the contents of a wine-glass had long since been splashed upon the page. Still, the old book conveys an impression, that, when the separate numbers were flying about town, in the first day or two of their respective existences, they might have been fit reading for very stylish people. Such newspapers could have been issued nowhere but in a metropolis, the centre, not only of public and private affairs, but of fashion and gaiety. Without any discredit to the colonial press, these might have been, and probably were, spread out on the tables of the British coffee-house, in King-street, for the perusal of the throng of officers who then drank their wine at that celebrated establishment. To interest these military gentlemen, there were bulletins of the war between Prussia and Austria; between England and France, on the old battle-plains of Flanders; and between the same antagonists, in the newer fields of the East-Indies—and in our own trackless woods, where white men never trod until they came to fight there. Or, the travelled American, the petit-maitre of the colonies—the ape of London foppery, as the newspaper was the semblance of the London journals—he, with his gray-powdered periwig, his embroidered coat, lace ruffles, and glossy silk stockings, golden-clocked—his buckles, of glittering paste, at knee-band and shoe-strap—his scented handkerchief, and chapeau beneath

his arm—even such a dainty figure need not have disdained
to glance at these old yellow pages, while they were the
mirror of passing times. For his amusement, there were essays of wit and humor, the light literature of the day, which,
for breadth and license, might have proceeded from the pen
of Fielding or Smollett; while, in other columns, he would
delight his imagination with the enumerated items of all sorts
of finery, and with the rival advertisements of half a dozen
peruke-makers. In short, newer manners and customs had almost entirely superseded those of the Puritans, even in their
own city of refuge.

It was natural that, with the lapse of time and increase of
wealth and population, the peculiarities of the early settlers
should have waxed fainter and fainter through the generations
of their descendants, who also had been alloyed by a continual accession of emigrants from many countries and of all
characters. It tended to assimilate the colonial manners to
those of the mother-country, that the commercial intercourse
was great, and that the merchants often went thither in their
own ships. Indeed, almost every man of adequate fortune felt
a yearning desire, and even judged it a filial duty, at least once
in his life, to visit the home of his ancestors. They still called
it their own home, as if New-England were to them, what
many of the old Puritans had considered it, not a permanent
abiding-place, but merely a lodge in the wilderness, until the
trouble of the times should be passed. The example of the
royal governors must have had much influence on the manners of the colonists; for these rulers assumed a degree of
state and splendor, which had never been practised by their
predecessors, who differed in nothing from republican chief-
magistrates, under the old charter. The officers of the crown,
the public characters in the interest of the administration, and
the gentlemen of wealth and good descent, generally noted
for their loyalty, would constitute a dignified circle, with the
governor in the centre, bearing a very passable resemblance
to a court. Their ideas, their habits, their code of courtesy,
and their dress, would have all the fresh glitter of fashions
immediately derived from the fountain-head, in England.
To prevent their modes of life from becoming the standard,
with all who had the ability to imitate them, there was no

longer an undue severity of religion, nor as yet any disaffection to British supremacy, nor democratic prejudices against pomp. Thus, while the colonies were attaining that strength which was soon to render them an independent republic, it might have been supposed that the wealthier classes were growing into an aristocracy, and ripening for hereditary rank, while the poor were to be stationary in their abasement, and the country, perhaps, to be a sister-monarchy with England. Such, doubtless, were the plausible conjectures, deducted from the superficial phenomena of our connexion with a monarchical government, until the prospective nobility were leveled with the mob, by the mere gathering of winds that preceded the storm of the Revolution. The portents of that storm were not yet visible in the air. A true picture of society, therefore, would have the rich effect, produced by distinctions of rank that seemed permanent, and by appropriate habits of splendor on the part of the gentry.

The people at large had been somewhat changed in character, since the period of our last sketch, by their great exploit, the conquest of Louisburg. After that event, the New-Englanders never settled into precisely the same quiet race, which all the world had imagined them to be. They had done a deed of history, and were anxious to add new ones to the record. They had proved themselves powerful enough to influence the result of a war, and were thenceforth called upon, and willingly consented, to join their strength against the enemies of England; on those fields, at least, where victory would redound to their peculiar advantage. And now, in the heat of the Old French War, they might well be termed a martial people. Every man was a soldier, or the father or brother of a soldier; and the whole land literally echoed with the roll of the drum, either beating up for recruits among the towns and villages, or striking the march towards the frontiers. Besides the provincial troops, there were twenty-three British regiments in the northern colonies. The country has never known a period of such excitement and warlike life, except during the Revolution—perhaps scarcely then; for that was a lingering war, and this a stirring and eventful one.

One would think, that no very wonderful talent was requisite for an historical novel, when the rough and hurried paragraphs of these newspapers can recall the past so magically. We seem to be waiting in the street for the arrival of the post-rider—who is seldom more than twelve hours beyond his time—with letters, by way of Albany, from the various departments of the army. Or, we may fancy ourselves in the circle of listeners, all with necks stretched out towards an old gentleman in the centre, who deliberately puts on his spectacles, unfolds the wet newspaper, and gives us the details of the broken and contradictory reports, which have been flying from mouth to mouth, ever since the courier alighted at Secretary Oliver's office. Sometimes we have an account of the Indian skirmishes near Lake George, and how a ranging party of provincials were so closely pursued, that they threw away their arms, and eke their shoes, stockings, and breeches, barely reaching the camp in their shirts, which also were terribly tattered by the bushes. Then, there is a journal of the siege of Fort Niagara, so minute, that it almost numbers the cannon-shot and bombs, and describes the effect of the latter missiles on the French commandant's stone-mansion, within the fortress. In the letters of the provincial officers, it is amusing to observe how some of them endeavor to catch the careless and jovial turn of old campaigners. One gentleman tells us, that he holds a brimming glass in his hand, intending to drink the health of his correspondent, unless a cannon ball should dash the liquor from his lips; in the midst of his letter, he hears the bells of the French churches ringing, in Quebec, and recollects that it is Sunday; whereupon, like a good Protestant, he resolves to disturb the Catholic worship by a few thirty-two pound shot. While this wicked man of war was thus making a jest of religion, his pious mother had probably put up a note, that very Sabbath-day, desiring the 'prayers of the congregation for a son gone a soldiering.' We trust, however, that there were some stout old worthies, who were not ashamed to do as their fathers did, but went to prayer, with their soldiers, before leading them to battle; and doubtless fought none the worse for that. If we had enlisted in the Old French War, it should have been under

such a captain; for we love to see a man keep the characteristics of his country.*

These letters, and other intelligence from the army, are
pleasant and lively reading, and stir up the mind like the music of a drum and fife. It is less agreeable, to meet with accounts of women slain and scalped, and infants dashed
against trees, by the Indians on the frontiers. It is a striking
circumstance, that innumerable bears, driven from the woods,
by the uproar of contending armies in their accustomed
haunts, broke into the settlements and committed great ravages, among children as well as sheep and swine. Some of
them prowled where bears had never been for a century—
penetrating within a mile or two of Boston; a fact, that gives
a strong and gloomy impression of something very terrific
going on in the forest, since these savage beasts fled townward to avoid it. But it is impossible to moralize about such
trifles, when every newspaper contains tales of military enter-
prize, and often a huzza for victory; as, for instance, the taking of Ticonderoga, long a place of awe to the provincials,
and one of the bloodiest spots in the present war. Nor is it
unpleasant, among whole pages of exultation, to find a note
of sorrow for the fall of some brave officer; it comes wailing
in, like a funeral strain amidst a peal of triumph, itself triumphant too. Such was the lamentation over Wolfe. Somewhere,
in this volume of newspapers, though we cannot now lay our
finger upon the passage, we recollect a report, that General
Wolfe was slain, not by the enemy, but by a shot from his
own soldiers.

In the advertising columns, also, we are continually reminded that the country was in a state of war. Governor
Pownall makes proclamation for the enlisting of soldiers, and
directs the militia colonels to attend to the discipline of their
regiments, and the selectmen of every town to replenish their

*The contemptuous jealousy of the British army, from the general down-
wards, was very galling to the provincial troops. In one of the newspapers,
there is an admirable letter of a New-Englandman, copied from the London
Chronicle, defending the provincials with an ability worthy of Franklin, and
somewhat in his style. The letter is remarkable, also, because it takes up the
cause of the whole range of colonies, as if the writer looked upon them all as
constituting one country, and that his own. Colonial patriotism had not hitherto been so broad a sentiment.

stocks of ammunition. The magazine, by the way, was generally kept in the upper loft of the village meeting-house. The
provincial captains are drumming up for soldiers, in every
newspaper. Sir Jeffrey Amherst advertises for batteaux-men,
to be employed on the lakes; and gives notice to the officers
of seven British regiments, dispersed on the recruiting service,
to rendezvous in Boston. Captain Hallowell, of the province
ship-of-war King George, invites able-bodied seamen to serve
his Majesty, for fifteen pounds, old tenor, per month. By the
rewards offered, there would appear to have been frequent
desertions from the New-England forces; we applaud their
wisdom, if not their valor or integrity. Cannon, of all calibres,
gunpowder and balls, firelocks, pistols, swords, and hangers,
were common articles of merchandise. Daniel Jones, at the
sign of the hat and helmet, offers to supply officers with scarlet broadcloth, gold-lace for hats and waistcoats, cockades,
and other military foppery, allowing credit until the pay-rolls
shall be made up. This advertisement gives us quite a gorgeous idea of a provincial captain in full dress.

At the commencement of the campaign of 1759, the British
general informs the farmers of New-England that a regular
market will be established at Lake George, whither they are
invited to bring provisions and refreshments of all sorts, for
the use of the army. Hence, we may form a singular picture
of petty traffic, far away from any permanent settlements,
among the hills which border that romantic lake, with the
solemn woods overshadowing the scene. Carcasses of bullocks
and fat porkers are placed upright against the huge trunks of
the trees; fowls hang from the lower branches, bobbing
against the heads of those beneath; butter-firkins, great
cheeses, and brown loaves of household bread, baked in distant ovens, are collected under temporary shelters of pine-
boughs, with gingerbread, and pumpkin-pies, perhaps, and
other toothsome dainties. Barrels of cider and spruce-beer are
running freely into the wooden canteens of the soldiers.
Imagine such a scene, beneath the dark forest canopy, with
here and there a few struggling sunbeams, to dissipate the
gloom. See the shrewd yeomen, haggling with their scarlet-
coated customers, abating somewhat in their prices, but still
dealing at monstrous profit; and then complete the picture

with circumstances that bespeak war and danger. A cannon shall be seen to belch its smoke from among the trees, against some distant canoes on the lake; the traffickers shall pause, and seem to hearken, at intervals, as if they heard the rattle of musketry or the shout of Indians; a scouting-party shall be driven in, with two or three faint and bloody men among them. And, in spite of these disturbances, business goes on briskly in the market of the wilderness.

It must not be supposed, that the martial character of the times interrupted all pursuits except those connected with war. On the contrary, there appears to have been a general vigor and vivacity diffused into the whole round of colonial life. During the winter of 1759, it was computed that about a thousand sled-loads of country produce were daily brought into Boston market. It was a symptom of an irregular and unquiet course of affairs, that innumerable lotteries were projected, ostensibly for the purpose of public improvements, such as roads and bridges. Many females seized the opportunity to engage in business; as, among others, Alice Quick, who dealt in crockery and hosiery, next door to Deacon Beautineau's; Mary Jackson, who sold butter, at the Brazen-Head, in Cornhill; Abigail Hiller, who taught ornamental-work, near the Orange-Tree, where also were to be seen the King and Queen, in wax-work; Sarah Morehead, an instructer in glass-painting, drawing, and japanning; Mary Salmon, who shod horses, at the south-end; Harriet Pain, at the Buck and Glove, and Mrs. Henrietta Maria Caine, at the Golden Fan, both fashionable milliners; Anna Adams, who advertises Quebec and Garrick bonnets, Prussian cloaks, and scarlet cardinals, opposite the old brick meeting-house; besides a lady at the head of a wine and spirit establishment. Little did these good dames expect to re-appear before the public, so long after they had made their last courtesies behind the counter. Our great-grandmothers were a stirring sisterhood, and seem not to have been utterly despised by the gentlemen at the British coffee-house; at least, some gracious bachelor, there resident, gives public notice of his willingness to take a wife, provided she be not above twenty-three, and possess brown hair, regular features, a brisk eye, and a fortune. Now, this was great condescension towards the ladies of Massachusetts-Bay, in a threadbare lieutenant of foot.

Polite literature was beginning to make its appearance. Few native works were advertised, it is true, except sermons and treatises of controversial divinity; nor were the English authors of the day much known, on this side of the Atlantic. But, catalogues were frequently offered at auction or private sale, comprising the standard English books, history, essays, and poetry, of Queen Anne's age, and the preceding century. We see nothing in the nature of a novel, unless it be 'The Two Mothers, price four coppers.' There was an American poet, however, of whom Mr. Kettell has preseved no specimen—the author of 'War, an Heroic Poem;' he publishes by subscription, and threatens to prosecute his patrons for not taking their books. We have discovered a periodical, also, and one that has a peculiar claim to be recorded here, since it bore the title of 'THE NEW-ENGLAND MAGAZINE,' a forgotten predecessor, for which we should have a filial respect, and take its excellence on trust. The fine arts, too, were budding into existence. At the 'old glass and picture shop,' in Cornhill, various maps, plates, and views, are advertised, and among them a 'Prospect of Boston,' a copper-plate engraving of Quebec, and the effigies of all the New-England ministers ever done in mezzotinto. All these must have been very saleable articles. Other ornamental wares were to be found at the same shop; such as violins, flutes, hautboys, musical books, English and Dutch toys, and London babies. About this period, Mr. Dipper gives notice of a concert of vocal and instrumental music. There had already been an attempt at theatrical exhibitions.

There are tokens, in every newspaper, of a style of luxury and magnificence, which we do not usually associate with our ideas of the times. When the property of a deceased person was to be sold, we find, among the household furniture, silk beds and hangings, damask table-cloths, Turkey carpets, pictures, pier-glasses, massive plate, and all things proper for a noble mansion. Wine was more generally drunk than now, though by no means to the neglect of ardent spirits. For the apparel of both sexes, the mercers and milliners imported good store of fine broadcloths—especially scarlet, crimson, and sky-blue, silks, satins, lawns, and velvets, gold brocade, and gold and silver lace, and silver tassels, and silver spangles, until Cornhill shone and sparkled with their merchandise. The gaudiest dress, permissible by modern taste, fades into a Quaker-like sobriety, compared with the deep, rich, glowing splendor of our ancestors. Such figures were almost too fine to go about town on foot; accordingly, carriages were so numerous as to require a tax; and it is recorded that, when Governor Bernard came to the province, he was met, between Dedham and Boston, by a multitude of gentlemen in their coaches and chariots.

Take my arm, gentle reader, and come with me into some street, perhaps trodden by your daily footsteps, but which now has such an aspect of half-familiar strangeness, that you suspect yourself to be walking abroad in a dream. True; there are some brick edifices which you remember from childhood, and which your father and grandfather remembered as well; but you are perplexed by the absence of many that were here, only an hour or two since; and still more amazing is the presence of whole rows of wooden and plastered houses, projecting over the sidewalks, and bearing iron figures on their fronts, which prove them to have stood on the same sites above a century. Where have your eyes been, that you never saw them before? Along the ghostly street—for at length, you conclude that all is unsubstantial, though it be so good a mockery of an antique town—along the ghostly street, there are ghostly people too. Every gentleman has his three-cornered hat, either on his head or under his arm, and all wear wigs, in infinite variety,—the Tie, the Brigadier, the Spencer, the Albemarle, the Major, the Ramillies, the grave Full-bottom, or the giddy Feather-top. Look at the elaborate lace-ruffles, and the square-skirted coats of gorgeous hues, bedizzened with silver and gold! Make way for the phantom-ladies, whose hoops require such breadth of passage, as they pace majestically along, in silken gowns, blue, green, or yellow, brilliantly embroidered, and with small satin hats surmounting their powdered hair. Make way; for the whole spectral show will vanish, if your earthly garments brush against their robes. Now that the scene is brightest, and the whole street glitters with imaginary sunshine—now hark to the bells of

the Old South and the Old North, ringing out with a sudden
and merry peal, while the cannon of Castle William thunder
below the town, and those of the Diana frigate repeat the
sound, and the Charlestown batteries reply with a nearer roar!
You see the crowd toss up their hats, in visionary joy. You
hear of illuminations and fire-works, and of bonfires, built on
scaffolds, raised several stories above the ground, that are to
blaze all night, in King-street, and on Beacon-hill. And here
come the trumpets and kettle-drums, and the tramping hoofs
of the Boston troop of horse-guards, escorting the governor
to King's Chapel, where he is to return solemn thanks for the
surrender of Quebec. March on, thou shadowy troop! and
vanish, ghostly crowd! and change again, old street! for those
stirring times are gone.

Opportunely for the conclusion of our sketch, a fire broke
out, on the twentieth of March, 1760, at the Brazen-Head in
Cornhill, and consumed nearly four hundred buildings. Similar disasters have always been epochs in the chronology of
Boston. That of 1711, had hitherto been termed the Great Fire,
but now resigned its baleful dignity to one which has ever
since retained it. Did we desire to move the reader's sympathies, on this subject, we would not be grandiloquent about
the sea of billowy flame, the glowing and crumbling streets,
the broad, black firmament of smoke, and the blast of wind,
that sprang up with the conflagration and roared behind it. It
would be more effective, to mark out a single family, at the
moment when the flames caught upon an angle of their
dwelling; then would ensue the removal of the bed-ridden
grandmother, the cradle with the sleeping infant, and, most
dismal of all, the dying man, just at the extremity of a lingering disease. Do but imagine the confused agony of one thus
awfully disturbed in his last hour; his fearful glance behind at
the consuming fire, raging after him, from house to house, as
its devoted victim; and finally, the almost eagerness with
which he would seize some calmer interval to die! The Great
Fire must have realized many such a scene.

Doubtless, posterity has acquired a better city by the calamity of that generation. None will be inclined to lament it, at
this late day, except the lover of antiquity, who would have
been glad to walk among those streets of venerable houses,

fancying the old inhabitants still there, that he might commune with their shadows, and paint a more vivid picture of their times.

III. THE OLD TORY

Again we take a leap, of about twenty years, and alight in the midst of the Revolution. Indeed, having just closed a volume of colonial newspapers, which represented the period when monarchical and aristocratic sentiments were at the highest; and now opening another volume, printed in the same metropolis, after such sentiments had long been deemed a sin and shame, we feel as if the leap were more than figurative. Our late course of reading has tinctured us, for the moment, with antique prejudices, and we shrink from the strangely-contrasted times, into which we emerge, like one of those immutable old Tories, who acknowledge no oppression in the Stamp-act. It may be the most effective method of going through the present file of papers, to follow out this idea, and transform ourself, perchance, from a modern Tory into such a sturdy King-man, as once wore that pliable nickname.

Well then, here we sit, an old, gray, withered, sour-visaged, threadbare sort of gentleman, erect enough, here in our solitude, but marked out by a depressed and distrustful mien abroad—as one conscious of a stigma upon his forehead, though for no crime. We were already in the decline of life, when the first tremors of the earthquake, that has convulsed the continent, were felt. Our mind had grown too rigid to change any of its opinions, when the voice of the people demanded, that all should be changed. We are an Episcopalian, and sat under the high-church doctrines of Doctor Caner; we have been a captain of the provincial forces, and love our King the better, for the blood that we shed in his cause, on the Plains of Abraham. Among all the refugees, there is not one more loyal, to the back-bone, than we. Still we lingered behind, when the British army evacuated Boston, sweeping in its train most of those with whom we held communion— the old, loyal gentlemen, the aristocracy of the colonies, the hereditary Englishman, imbued with more than native zeal

and admiration for the glorious island and its monarch, because the far intervening ocean threw a dim reverence around
them. When our brethren departed, we could not tear our
aged roots out of the soil. We have remained, therefore, enduring to be outwardly a freeman, but idolizing King
George, in secresy and silence—one true old heart, amongst
a host of enemies. We watch, with a weary hope, for the moment when all this turmoil shall subside, and the impious
novelty, that has distracted our latter years, like a wild dream,
give place to the blessed quietude of royal sway, with the
King's name in every ordinance, his prayer in the church, his
health at the board, and his love in the people's heart. Meantime, our old age finds little honor. Hustled have we been,
till driven from town-meetings; dirty water has been cast
upon our ruffles, by a Whig chambermaid; John Hancock's
coachman seizes every opportunity to bespatter us with mud;
daily are we hooted by the unbreeched rebel brats; and narrowly, once, did our gray hairs escape the ignominy of tar
and feathers. Alas! only that we cannot bear to die till the
next royal Governor comes over, we would fain be in our
quiet grave.

Such an old man among new things are we, who now hold,
at arm's length, the rebel newspaper of the day. The very
figure-head, for the thousandth time, elicits a groan of spiteful
lamentation. Where are the united heart and crown, the loyal
emblem, that used to hallow the sheet, on which it was impressed, in our younger days? In its stead, we find a continental officer, with the Declaration of Independence in one hand,
a drawn sword in the other, and, above his head, a scroll,
bearing the motto 'WE APPEAL TO HEAVEN.' Then say we,
with a prospective triumph, let Heaven judge, in its own
good time! The material of the sheet attracts our scorn. It is
a fair specimen of rebel manufacture, thick and coarse, like
wrapping-paper, all overspread with little knobs, and of such
a deep, dingy blue color, that we wipe our spectacles thrice
before we can distinguish a letter of the wretched print. Thus,
in all points, the newspaper is a type of the times, far more
fit for the rough hands of a democratic mob, than for our
own delicate, though bony fingers. Nay; we will not handle
it without our gloves!

Glancing down the page, our eyes are greeted everywhere
by the offer of lands at auction, for sale or to be leased—not
by the rightful owners, but a rebel committee; notices of the
town constable, that he is authorized to receive the taxes on
such an estate, in default of which, that also is to be knocked
down to the highest bidder; and notifications of complaints,
filed by the Attorney-general, against certain traitorous absen-
tees, and of confiscations that are to ensue. And who are these
traitors? Our own best friends—names as old, once as honored, as any in the land, where they are no longer to have a
patrimony, nor to be remembered as good men, who have
passed away. We are ashamed of not relinquishing our little
property, too; but comfort ourselves, because we still keep
our principles, without gratifying the rebels with our plunder.
Plunder, indeed, they are seizing, everywhere, by the strong
hand at sea, as well as by legal forms on shore. Here are prize-
vessels for sale—no French nor Spanish merchantmen, whose
wealth is the birthright of British subjects, but hulls of British
oak, from Liverpool, Bristol, and the Thames, laden with the
King's own stores, for his army in New-York. And what a
fleet of privateers—pirates, say we—are fitting out for new
ravages, with rebellion in their very names! The Free Yankee,
the General Green, the Saratoga, the Lafayette, and the
Grand Monarch! Yes, the Grand Monarch; so is a French
King styled, by the sons of Englishmen. And here we have an
ordinance, from the Court of Versailles, with the Bourbon's
own signature affixed, as if New-England were already a
French province. Everything is French. French soldiers,
French sailors, French surgeons—and French diseases, too, I
trow—besides, French dancing-masters and French milliners,
to debauch our daughters with French fashions! Everything
in America is French, except the Canadas—the loyal Canadas—which we helped to wrest from France. And to that old
French province, the Englishman of the colonies must go to
find his country!

Oh, the misery of seeing the whole system of things
changed in my old days, when I would be loth to change
even a pair of buckles! The British coffee-house—where oft
we sat, brimfull of wine and loyalty, with the gallant gentlemen of Amherst's army, when we wore a red-coat, too—the

British coffee-house, forsooth, must now be styled the American, with a golden eagle, instead of the royal arms, above the door. Even the street it stands in, is no longer King-street! Nothing is the King's, except this heavy heart, in my old bosom. Wherever I glance my eyes, they meet something that pricks them like a needle. This soapmaker, for instance, this Robert Hewes, has conspired against my peace, by notifying that his shop is situated near Liberty Stump. But when will their mis-named liberty have its true emblem in that Stump, hewn down by British steel!

Where shall we buy our next year's Almanac? Not this of Weatherwise's, certainly; for it contains a likeness of George Washington, the upright rebel, whom we most hate, though reverentially, as a fallen angel, with his heavenly brightness undiminished, evincing pure fame in an unhallowed cause. And here is a new book, for my evening's recreation—a History of the War till the close of the year 1779, with the heads of thirteen distinguished officers engraved on copper-plate. A plague upon their heads! We desire not to see them, till they grin at us from the balcony before the town-house, fixed on spikes, as the heads of traitors. How bloody-minded the villains make a peaceable old man! What next? An Oration, on the Horrid Massacre of 1770. When that blood was shed— the first that the British soldier ever drew from the bosoms of our countrymen—we turned sick at heart, and do so still, as often as they make it reek anew from among the stones in King-street. The pool, that we saw that night, has swelled into a lake—English blood and American—no!—all British, all blood of my brethren. And here come down tears. Shame on me, since half of them are shed for rebels! Who are not rebels now? Even the women are thrusting their white hands into the war, and come out in this very paper with proposals to form a society—the lady of George Washington at their head—for clothing the continental troops. They will strip off their stiff petticoats to cover the ragged rascals, and then enlist in the ranks themselves.

What have we here? Burgoyne's proclamation turned into Hudibrastic rhyme! And here, some verses against the King, in which the scribbler leaves a blank for the name of George, as if his doggerel might yet exalt him to the pillory. Such, after years of rebellion, is the heart's unconquerable reverence for the Lord's anointed! In the next column, we have Scripture parodied in a squib against his sacred Majesty. What would our Puritan great-grand-sires have said to that? They never laughed at God's word, though they cut off a King's head.

Yes; it was for us to prove how disloyalty goes hand in hand with irreligion, and all other vices come trooping in the train. Now-a-days, men commit robbery and sacrilege, for the mere luxury of wickedness, as this advertisement testifies. Three hundred pounds reward, for the detection of the villains who stole and destroyed the cushions and pulpit drapery of the Brattle-street and Old South churches. Was it a crime? I can scarcely think our temples hallowed, since the King ceased to be prayed for. But it is not temples only, that they rob. Here a man offers a thousand dollars—a thousand dollars, in Continental rags!—for the recovery of his stolen cloak, and other articles of clothing. Horse thieves are innumerable. Now is the day, when every beggar gets on horseback. And is not the whole land like a beggar on horse-back, riding post to the devil? Ha! Here is a murder, too. A woman slain at midnight, by an unknown ruffian, and found cold, stiff, and bloody, in her violated bed! Let the hue-and-cry follow hard after the man in the uniform of blue and buff, who last went by that way. My life on it, he is the blood-stained ravisher! These deserters, whom we see proclaimed in every column—proof, that the banditti are as false to their stars and stripes, as to the Holy Red-Cross—they bring the crimes of a rebel camp into a soil well suited to them; the bosom of a people, without the heart that kept them virtuous—their King!

Here, flaunting down a whole column, with official seal and signature, here comes a proclamation. By whose authority? Ah! the United States—those thirteen little anarchies, assembled in that one grand anarchy, their Congress. And what the import? A general Fast. By Heaven! for once, the traitorous blockheads have legislated wisely! Yea; let a misguided people kneel down in sackcloth and ashes, from end to end, from border to border, of their wasted country. Well may they fast, where there is no food—and cry aloud, for whatever remnant of God's mercy their sins may not have exhausted. We, too, will fast, even at a rebel summons. Pray others as they will, there shall be, at least, an old man kneeling for the righteous cause. Lord, put down the rebels! God save the King!

Peace to the good old Tory! One of our objects has been to exemplify, without softening a single prejudice proper to the character which we assumed, that the Americans, who clung to the losing side, in the Revolution, were men greatly to be pitied, and often worthy of our sympathy. It would be difficult to say whose lot was most lamentable—that of the active Tories, who gave up their patrimonies, for a pittance from the British pension-roll and their native land, for a cold reception in their mis-called home; or the passive ones, who remained behind to endure the coldness of former friends, and the public opprobrium, as despised citizens, under a government which they abhorred. In justice to the old gentleman, who has favored us with his discontented musings, we must remark, that the state of the country, so far as can be gathered from these papers, was of dismal augury, for the tendencies of democratic rule. It was pardonable, in the conservative of that day, to mistake the temporary evils of a change, for permanent diseases of the system which that change was to establish. A revolution, or anything, that interrupts social order, may afford opportunities for the individual display of eminent virtue; but, its effects are pernicious to general morality. Most people are so constituted, that they can be virtuous only in a certain routine; and an irregular course of public affairs demoralizes them. One great source of disorder, was the multitude of disbanded troops, who were continually returning home, after terms of service just long enough to give them a distaste to peaceable occupations; neither citizens nor soldiers, they were very liable to become ruffians. Almost all our impressions, in regard to this period are unpleasant, whether referring to the state of civil society, or to the character of the contest, which, especially where native Americans were opposed to each other, was waged with the deadly hatred of fraternal enemies. It is the beauty of war, for men to commit mutual havoc with undisturbed good humor.

The present volume of newspapers contains fewer characteristic traits than any which we have looked over. Except for the peculiarities attendant on the passing struggle, manners seem to have taken a modern cast. Whatever antique fashions lingered into the war of the Revolution, or beyond it, they were not so strongly marked as to leave their traces in the public journals. Moreover, the old newspapers had an indescribable picturesqueness, not to be found in the later ones. Whether it be something in the literary execution, or the ancient print and paper, and the idea, that those same musty pages have been handled by people—once alive and bustling amid the scenes there recorded, yet now in their graves beyond the memory of man—so it is, that in those elder volumes, we seem to find the life of a past age preserved between the leaves, like a dry specimen of foliage. It is so difficult to discover what touches are really picturesque, that we doubt whether our attempts have produced any similar effect.

Young Goodman Brown

Young Goodman Brown came forth, at sunset, into the street of Salem village, but put his head back, after crossing the threshold, to exchange a parting kiss with his young wife. And Faith, as the wife was aptly named, thrust her own pretty head into the street, letting the wind play with the pink ribbons of her cap, while she called to Goodman Brown.

'Dearest heart,' whispered she, softly and rather sadly, when her lips were close to his ear, 'pr'y thee, put off your journey until sunrise, and sleep in your own bed to-night. A lone woman is troubled with such dreams and such thoughts, that she's afeard of herself, sometimes. Pray, tarry with me this night, dear husband, of all nights in the year!'

'My love and my Faith,' replied young Goodman Brown, 'of all nights in the year, this one night must I tarry away from thee. My journey, as thou callest it, forth and back again, must needs be done 'twixt now and sunrise. What, my sweet, pretty wife, dost thou doubt me already, and we but three months married!'

'Then, God bless you!' said Faith, with the pink ribbons, 'and may you find all well, when you come back.'

'Amen!' cried Goodman Brown. 'Say thy prayers, dear Faith, and go to bed at dusk, and no harm will come to thee.'

So they parted; and the young man pursued his way, until, being about to turn the corner by the meeting-house, he looked back, and saw the head of Faith still peeping after him, with a melancholy air, in spite of her pink ribbons.

'Poor little Faith!' thought he, for his heart smote him. 'What a wretch am I, to leave her on such an errand! She talks of dreams, too. Methought, as she spoke, there was trouble in her face, as if a dream had warned her what work is to be done to-night. But, no, no! 'twould kill her to think it. Well; she's a blessed angel on earth; and after this one night, I'll cling to her skirts and follow her to Heaven.'

With this excellent resolve for the future, Goodman Brown felt himself justified in making more haste on his present evil purpose. He had taken a dreary road, darkened by all the

gloomiest trees of the forest, which barely stood aside to let
the narrow path creep through, and closed immediately behind. It was all as lonely as could be; and there is this peculiarity in such a solitude, that the traveller knows not who
may be concealed by the innumerable trunks and the thick
boughs overhead; so that, with lonely footsteps, he may yet
be passing through an unseen multitude.

'There may be a devilish Indian behind every tree,' said
Goodman Brown, to himself; and he glanced fearfully behind
him, as he added, 'What if the devil himself should be at my
very elbow!'

His head being turned back, he passed a crook of the road,
and looking forward again, beheld the figure of a man, in
grave and decent attire, seated at the foot of an old tree. He
arose, at Goodman Brown's approach, and walked onward,
side by side with him.

'You are late, Goodman Brown,' said he. 'The clock of the
Old South was striking as I came through Boston; and that
is full fifteen minutes agone.'

'Faith kept me back awhile,' replied the young man, with
a tremor in his voice, caused by the sudden appearance of his
companion, though not wholly unexpected.

It was now deep dusk in the forest, and deepest in that part
of it where these two were journeying. As nearly as could be
discerned, the second traveller was about fifty years old, apparently in the same rank of life as Goodman Brown, and
bearing a considerable resemblance to him, though perhaps
more in expression than features. Still, they might have been
taken for father and son. And yet, though the elder person
was as simply clad as the younger, and as simple in manner
too, he had an indescribable air of one who knew the world,
and would not have felt abashed at the governor's dinner-
table, or in King William's court, were it possible that his
affairs should call him thither. But the only thing about him,
that could be fixed upon as remarkable, was his staff, which
bore the likeness of a great black snake, so curiously wrought,
that it might almost be seen to twist and wriggle itself, like a
living serpent. This, of course, must have been an ocular deception, assisted by the uncertain light.

'Come, Goodman Brown!' cried his fellow-traveller, 'this is

a dull pace for the beginning of a journey. Take my staff, if you are so soon weary.'

'Friend,' said the other, exchanging his slow pace for a full stop, 'having kept covenant by meeting thee here, it is my purpose now to return whence I came. I have scruples, touching the matter thou wot'st of.'

'Sayest thou so?' replied he of the serpent, smiling apart. 'Let us walk on, nevertheless, reasoning as we go, and if I convince thee not, thou shalt turn back. We are but a little way in the forest, yet.'

'Too far, too far!' exclaimed the goodman, unconsciously resuming his walk. 'My father never went into the woods on such an errand, nor his father before him. We have been a race of honest men and good Christians, since the days of the martyrs. And shall I be the first of the name of Brown, that ever took this path, and kept—'

'Such company, thou wouldst say,' observed the elder person, interpreting his pause. 'Well said, Goodman Brown! I have been as well acquainted with your family as with ever a one among the Puritans; and that's no trifle to say. I helped your grandfather, the constable, when he lashed the Quaker woman so smartly through the streets of Salem. And it was I that brought your father a pitch-pine knot, kindled at my own hearth, to set fire to an Indian village, in King Philip's war. They were my good friends, both; and many a pleasant walk have we had along this path, and returned merrily after midnight. I would fain be friends with you, for their sake.'

'If it be as thou sayest,' replied Goodman Brown, 'I marvel they never spoke of these matters. Or, verily, I marvel not, seeing that the least rumor of the sort would have driven them from New-England. We are a people of prayer, and good works, to boot, and abide no such wickedness.'

'Wickedness or not,' said the traveller with the twisted staff, 'I have a very general acquaintance here in New-England. The deacons of many a church have drunk the communion wine with me; the selectmen, of divers towns, make me their chairman; and a majority of the Great and General Court are firm supporters of my interest. The governor and I, too—but these are state-secrets.'

'Can this be so!' cried Goodman Brown, with a stare of

amazement at his undisturbed companion. 'Howbeit, I have nothing to do with the governor and council; they have their own ways, and are no rule for a simple husbandman, like me. But, were I to go on with thee, how should I meet the eye of that good old man, our minister, at Salem village? Oh, his voice would make me tremble, both Sabbath-day and lecture-day!'

Thus far, the elder traveller had listened with due gravity, but now burst into a fit of irrepressible mirth, shaking himself so violently, that his snake-like staff actually seemed to wriggle in sympathy.

'Ha! ha! ha!' shouted he, again and again; then composing himself, 'Well, go on, Goodman Brown, go on; but pr'y thee, don't kill me with laughing!'

'Well, then, to end the matter at once,' said Goodman Brown, considerably nettled, 'there is my wife, Faith. It would break her dear little heart; and I'd rather break my own!'

'Nay, if that be the case,' answered the other, 'e'en go thy ways, Goodman Brown. I would not, for twenty old women like the one hobbling before us, that Faith should come to any harm.'

As he spoke, he pointed his staff at a female figure on the path, in whom Goodman Brown recognized a very pious and exemplary dame, who had taught him his catechism, in youth, and was still his moral and spiritual adviser, jointly with the minister and Deacon Gookin.

'A marvel, truly, that Goody Cloyse should be so far in the wilderness, at night-fall!' said he. 'But, with your leave, friend, I shall take a cut through the woods, until we have left this Christian woman behind. Being a stranger to you, she might ask whom I was consorting with, and whither I was going.'

'Be it so,' said his fellow-traveller. 'Betake you to the woods, and let me keep the path.'

Accordingly, the young man turned aside, but took care to watch his companion, who advanced softly along the road, until he had come within a staff's length of the old dame. She, meanwhile, was making the best of her way, with singular speed for so aged a woman, and mumbling some indistinct words, a prayer, doubtless, as she went. The traveller put forth his staff, and touched her withered neck with what seemed the serpent's tail.

'The devil!' screamed the pious old lady.

'Then Goody Cloyse knows her old friend?' observed the traveller, confronting her, and leaning on his writhing stick.

'Ah, forsooth, and is it your worship, indeed?' cried the good dame. 'Yea, truly is it, and in the very image of my old gossip, Goodman Brown, the grandfather of the silly fellow that now is. But—would your worship believe it?—my broomstick hath strangely disappeared, stolen, as I suspect, by that unhanged witch, Goody Cory, and that, too, when I was all anointed with the juice of smallage and cinque-foil and wolf's-bane—'

'Mingled with fine wheat and the fat of a new-born babe,' said the shape of old Goodman Brown.

'Ah, your worship knows the receipt,' cried the old lady, cackling aloud. 'So, as I was saying, being all ready for the meeting, and no horse to ride on, I made up my mind to foot it; for they tell me, there is a nice young man to be taken into communion to-night. But now your good worship will lend me your arm, and we shall be there in a twinkling.'

'That can hardly be,' answered her friend. 'I may not spare you my arm, Goody Cloyse, but here is my staff, if you will.'

So saying, he threw it down at her feet, where, perhaps, it assumed life, being one of the rods which its owner had formerly lent to the Egyptian Magi. Of this fact, however, Goodman Brown could not take cognizance. He had cast up his eyes in astonishment, and looking down again, beheld neither Goody Cloyse nor the serpentine staff, but his fellow-traveller alone, who waited for him as calmly as if nothing had happened.

'That old woman taught me my catechism!' said the young man; and there was a world of meaning in this simple comment.

They continued to walk onward, while the elder traveller exhorted his companion to make good speed and persevere in the path, discoursing so aptly, that his arguments seemed rather to spring up in the bosom of his auditor, than to be suggested by himself. As they went, he plucked a branch of maple, to serve for a walking-stick, and began to strip it of the twigs and little boughs, which were wet with evening dew. The moment his fingers touched them, they became strangely withered and dried up, as with a week's sunshine. Thus the pair proceeded, at a good free pace, until suddenly, in a gloomy hollow of the road, Goodman Brown sat himself down on the stump of a tree, and refused to go any farther.

'Friend,' said he, stubbornly, 'my mind is made up. Not another step will I budge on this errand. What if a wretched old woman do choose to go to the devil, when I thought she was going to Heaven! Is that any reason why I should quit my dear Faith, and go after her?'

'You will think better of this, by-and-by,' said his acquaintance, composedly. 'Sit here and rest yourself awhile; and when you feel like moving again, there is my staff to help you along.'

Without more words, he threw his companion the maple stick, and was as speedily out of sight, as if he had vanished into the deepening gloom. The young man sat a few moments, by the road-side, applauding himself greatly, and thinking with how clear a conscience he should meet the minister, in his morning-walk, nor shrink from the eye of good old Deacon Gookin. And what calm sleep would be his, that very night, which was to have been spent so wickedly, but purely and sweetly now, in the arms of Faith! Amidst these pleasant and praiseworthy meditations, Goodman Brown heard the tramp of horses along the road, and deemed it advisable to conceal himself within the verge of the forest, conscious of the guilty purpose that had brought him thither, though now so happily turned from it.

On came the hoof-tramps and the voices of the riders, two grave old voices, conversing soberly as they drew near. These mingled sounds appeared to pass along the road, within a few yards of the young man's hiding-place; but owing, doubtless, to the depth of the gloom, at that particular spot, neither the travellers nor their steeds were visible. Though their figures brushed the small boughs by the way-side, it could not be seen that they intercepted, even for a moment, the faint gleam from the strip of bright sky, athwart which they must have passed. Goodman Brown alternately crouched and stood on tip-toe, pulling aside the branches, and thrusting forth his head as far as he durst, without discerning so much as a shadow. It vexed him the more, because he could have sworn, were such a thing possible, that he recognized the voices of the minister and Deacon Gookin, jogging along quietly, as they were wont to do, when bound to some ordination or ecclesiastical council. While yet within hearing, one of the riders stopped to pluck a switch.

'Of the two, reverend Sir,' said the voice like the deacon's, 'I had rather miss an ordination-dinner than to-night's meeting. They tell me that some of our community are to be here from Falmouth and beyond, and others from Connecticut and Rhode-Island; besides several of the Indian powows, who, after their fashion, know almost as much deviltry as the best of us. Moreover, there is a goodly young woman to be taken into communion.'

'Mighty well, Deacon Gookin!' replied the solemn old tones of the minister. 'Spur up, or we shall be late. Nothing can be done, you know, until I get on the ground.'

The hoofs clattered again, and the voices, talking so strangely in the empty air, passed on through the forest, where no church had ever been gathered, nor solitary Christian prayed. Whither, then, could these holy men be journeying, so deep into the heathen wilderness? Young Goodman Brown caught hold of a tree, for support, being ready to sink down on the ground, faint and overburthened with the heavy sickness of his heart. He looked up to the sky, doubting whether there really was a Heaven above him. Yet, there was the blue arch, and the stars brightening in it.

'With Heaven above, and Faith below, I will yet stand firm against the devil!' cried Goodman Brown.

While he still gazed upward, into the deep arch of the firmament, and had lifted his hands to pray, a cloud, though no wind was stirring, hurried across the zenith, and hid the brightening stars. The blue sky was still visible, except directly overhead, where this black mass of cloud was sweeping swiftly northward. Aloft in the air, as if from the depths of the cloud, came a confused and doubtful sound of voices. Once, the listener fancied that he could distinguish the accents of town's-people of his own, men and women, both pious and ungodly, many of whom he had met at the communion-table, and had seen others rioting at the tavern. The next moment, so indistinct were the sounds, he doubted whether he had heard aught but the murmur of the old forest, whispering without a wind. Then came a stronger swell of those familiar tones, heard daily in the sunshine, at Salem village, but never, until now, from a cloud of night. There was one voice, of a young woman, uttering lamentations, yet with an uncertain sorrow, and entreating for some favor, which, perhaps, it would grieve her to obtain. And all the unseen multitude, both saints and sinners, seemed to encourage her onward.

'Faith!' shouted Goodman Brown, in a voice of agony and desperation; and the echoes of the forest mocked him, crying—'Faith! Faith!' as if bewildered wretches were seeking her, all through the wilderness.

The cry of grief, rage, and terror, was yet piercing the night, when the unhappy husband held his breath for a response. There was a scream, drowned immediately in a louder murmur of voices, fading into far-off laughter, as the dark cloud swept away, leaving the clear and silent sky above Goodman Brown. But something fluttered lightly down through the air, and caught on the branch of a tree. The young man seized it, and beheld a pink ribbon.

'My Faith is gone!' cried he, after one stupefied moment. 'There is no good on earth; and sin is but a name. Come, devil! for to thee is this world given.'

And maddened with despair, so that he laughed loud and long, did Goodman Brown grasp his staff and set forth again, at such a rate, that he seemed to fly along the forest-path, rather than to walk or run. The road grew wilder and drearier, and more faintly traced, and vanished at length, leaving him in the heart of the dark wilderness, still rushing onward, with the instinct that guides mortal man to evil. The whole forest was peopled with frightful sounds; the creaking of the trees, the howling of wild beasts, and the yell of Indians; while, sometimes, the wind tolled like a distant church-bell, and sometimes gave a broad roar around the traveller, as if all

Nature were laughing him to scorn. But he was himself the chief horror of the scene, and shrank not from its other horrors.

'Ha! ha! ha!' roared Goodman Brown, when the wind laughed at him. 'Let us hear which will laugh loudest! Think not to frighten me with your deviltry! Come witch, come wizard, come Indian powow, come devil himself! and here comes Goodman Brown. You may as well fear him as he fear you!'

In truth, all through the haunted forest, there could be nothing more frightful than the figure of Goodman Brown. On he flew, among the black pines, brandishing his staff with frenzied gestures, now giving vent to an inspiration of horrid blasphemy, and now shouting forth such laughter, as set all the echoes of the forest laughing like demons around him. The fiend in his own shape is less hideous, than when he rages in the breast of man. Thus sped the demoniac on his course, until, quivering among the trees, he saw a red light before him, as when the felled trunks and branches of a clearing have been set on fire, and throw up their lurid blaze against the sky, at the hour of midnight. He paused, in a lull of the tempest that had driven him onward, and heard the swell of what seemed a hymn, rolling solemnly from a distance, with the weight of many voices. He knew the tune; it was a familiar one in the choir of the village meeting-house. The verse died heavily away, and was lengthened by a chorus, not of human voices, but of all the sounds of the benighted wilderness, pealing in awful harmony together. Goodman Brown cried out; and his cry was lost to his own ear, by its unison with the cry of the desert.

In the interval of silence, he stole forward, until the light glared full upon his eyes. At one extremity of an open space, hemmed in by the dark wall of the forest, arose a rock, bearing some rude, natural resemblance either to an altar or a pulpit, and surrounded by four blazing pines, their tops aflame, their stems untouched, like candles at an evening meeting. The mass of foliage, that had overgrown the summit of the rock, was all on fire, blazing high into the night, and fitfully illuminating the whole field. Each pendent twig and leafy festoon was in a blaze. As the red light arose and fell, a numerous congregation alternately shone forth, then disappeared in shadow, and again grew, as it were, out of the darkness, peopling the heart of the solitary woods at once.

'A grave and dark-clad company!' quoth Goodman Brown.

In truth, they were such. Among them, quivering to-and-fro, between gloom and splendor, appeared faces that would be seen, next day, at the council-board of the province, and others which, Sabbath after Sabbath, looked devoutly heavenward, and benignantly over the crowded pews, from the holiest pulpits in the land. Some affirm, that the lady of the governor was there. At least, there were high dames well known to her, and wives of honored husbands, and widows, a great multitude, and ancient maidens, all of excellent repute, and fair young girls, who trembled, lest their mothers should espy them. Either the sudden gleams of light, flashing over the obscure field, bedazzled Goodman Brown, or he recognized a score of the church-members of Salem village, famous for their especial sanctity. Good old Deacon Gookin had arrived, and waited at the skirts of that venerable saint, his revered pastor. But, irreverently consorting with these grave, reputable, and pious people, these elders of the church, these chaste dames and dewy virgins, there were men of dissolute lives and women of spotted fame, wretches given over to all mean and filthy vice, and suspected even of horrid crimes. It was strange to see, that the good shrank not from the wicked, nor were the sinners abashed by the saints. Scattered, also, among their pale-faced enemies, were the Indian priests, or powows, who had often scared their native forest with more hideous incantations than any known to English witchcraft.

'But, where is Faith?' thought Goodman Brown; and, as hope came into his heart, he trembled.

Another verse of the hymn arose, a slow and mournful strain, such as the pious love, but joined to words which expressed all that our nature can conceive of sin, and darkly hinted at far more. Unfathomable to mere mortals is the lore of fiends. Verse after verse was sung, and still the chorus of the desert swelled between, like the deepest tone of a mighty organ. And, with the final peal of that dreadful anthem, there came a sound, as if the roaring wind, the rushing streams, the howling beasts, and every other voice of the unconverted wilderness, were mingling and according with the voice of guilty man, in homage to the prince of all. The four blazing pines threw up a loftier flame, and obscurely discovered shapes and visages of horror on the smoke-wreaths, above the impious assembly. At the same moment, the fire on the rock shot redly forth, and formed a glowing arch above its base, where now appeared a figure. With reverence be it spoken, the figure bore no slight similitude, both in garb and manner, to some grave divine of the New-England churches.

'Bring forth the converts!' cried a voice, that echoed through the field and rolled into the forest.

At the word, Goodman Brown stept forth from the shadow of the trees, and approached the congregation, with whom he felt a loathful brotherhood, by the sympathy of all that was wicked in his heart. He could have well nigh sworn, that the shape of his own dead father beckoned him to advance, looking downward from a smoke-wreath, while a woman, with dim features of despair, threw out her hand to warn him back. Was it his mother? But he had no power to retreat one step, nor to resist, even in thought, when the minister and good old Deacon Gookin seized his arms, and led him to the blazing rock. Thither came also the slender form of a veiled female, led between Goody Cloyse, that pious teacher of the catechism, and Martha Carrier, who had received the devil's promise to be queen of hell. A rampant hag was she! And there stood the proselytes, beneath the canopy of fire.

'Welcome, my children,' said the dark figure, 'to the communion of your race! Ye have found, thus young, your nature and your destiny. My children, look behind you!'

They turned; and flashing forth, as it were, in a sheet of flame, the fiend-worshippers were seen; the smile of welcome gleamed darkly on every visage.

'There,' resumed the sable form, 'are all whom ye have reverenced from youth. Ye deemed them holier than yourselves, and shrank from your own sin, contrasting it with their lives of righteousness, and prayerful aspirations heavenward. Yet, here are they all, in my worshipping assembly! This night it shall be granted you to know their secret deeds; how hoary-bearded elders of the church have whispered wanton words to the young maids of their households; how many a woman, eager for widow's weeds, has given her husband a drink at bed-time, and let him sleep his last sleep in her bosom; how beardless youths have made haste to inherit their fathers' wealth; and how fair damsels—blush not, sweet ones!—have dug little graves in the garden, and bidden me, the sole guest, to an infant's funeral. By the sympathy of your human hearts for sin, ye shall scent out all the places—whether in church, bed-chamber, street, field, or forest—where crime has been committed, and shall exult to behold the whole earth one stain of guilt, one mighty blood-spot. Far more than this! It shall be yours to penetrate, in every bosom, the deep mystery of sin, the fountain of all wicked arts, and which inexhaustibly supplies more evil impulses than human power—than my power, at its utmost!—can make manifest in deeds. And now, my children, look upon each other.'

They did so; and, by the blaze of the hell-kindled torches, the wretched man beheld his Faith, and the wife her husband, trembling before that unhallowed altar.

'Lo! there ye stand, my children,' said the figure, in a deep and solemn tone, almost sad, with its despairing awfulness, as if his once angelic nature could yet mourn for our miserable race. 'Depending upon one another's hearts, ye had still hoped, that virtue were not all a dream. Now are ye undeceived! Evil is the nature of mankind. Evil must be your only happiness. Welcome, again, my children, to the communion of your race!'

'Welcome!' repeated the fiend-worshippers, in one cry of despair and triumph.

And there they stood, the only pair, as it seemed, who were yet hesitating on the verge of wickedness, in this dark world. A basin was hollowed, naturally, in the rock. Did it contain water, reddened by the lurid light? or was it blood? or, perchance, a liquid flame? Herein did the Shape of Evil dip his hand, and prepare to lay the mark of baptism upon their foreheads, that they might be partakers of the mystery of sin, more conscious of the secret guilt of others, both in deed and thought, than they could now be of their own. The husband cast one look at his pale wife, and Faith at him. What polluted wretches would the next glance shew them to each other, shuddering alike at what they disclosed and what they saw!

'Faith! Faith!' cried the husband. 'Look up to Heaven, and resist the Wicked One!'

Whether Faith obeyed, he knew not. Hardly had he spoken, when he found himself amid calm night and solitude, listening to a roar of the wind, which died heavily away through the forest. He staggered against the rock and felt it chill and damp, while a hanging twig, that had been all on fire, besprinkled his cheek with the coldest dew.

The next morning, young Goodman Brown came slowly into the street of Salem village, staring around him like a bewildered man. The good old minister was taking a walk along the grave-yard, to get an appetite for breakfast and meditate his sermon, and bestowed a blessing, as he passed, on Goodman Brown. He shrank from the venerable saint, as if to avoid an anathema. Old Deacon Gookin was at domestic worship, and the holy words of his prayer were heard through the open window. 'What God doth the wizard pray to?' quoth Goodman Brown. Goody Cloyse, that excellent old Christian, stood in the early sunshine, at her own lattice, catechising a little girl, who had brought her a pint of morning's milk. Goodman Brown snatched away the child, as from the grasp of the fiend himself. Turning the corner by the meeting-house, he spied the head of Faith, with the pink ribbons, gazing anxiously forth, and bursting into such joy at sight of him, that she skipt along the street, and almost kissed her husband before the whole village. But, Goodman Brown looked sternly and sadly into her face, and passed on without a greeting.

Had Goodman Brown fallen asleep in the forest, and only dreamed a wild dream of a witch-meeting?

Be it so, if you will. But, alas! it was a dream of evil omen for young Goodman Brown. A stern, a sad, a darkly meditative, a distrustful, if not a desperate man, did he become, from the night of that fearful dream. On the Sabbath-day, when the congregation were singing a holy psalm, he could not listen, because an anthem of sin rushed loudly upon his ear, and drowned all the blessed strain. When the minister spoke from the pulpit, with power and fervid eloquence, and, with his hand on the open Bible, of the sacred truths of our religion, and of saint-like lives and triumphant deaths, and of future bliss or misery unutterable, then did Goodman Brown turn pale, dreading, lest the roof should thunder down upon the gray blasphemer and his hearers. Often, awakening suddenly at midnight, he shrank from the bosom of Faith, and at morning or eventide, when the family knelt down at prayer, he scowled, and muttered to himself, and gazed sternly at his wife, and turned away. And when he had lived long, and was borne to his grave, a hoary corpse, followed by Faith, an aged woman, and children and grand-children, a goodly procession, besides neighbors, not a few, they carved no hopeful verse upon his tomb-stone; for his dying hour was gloom.

Wakefield

IN some old magazine or newspaper, I recollect a story, told as truth, of a man—let us call him Wakefield—who absented himself for a long time, from his wife. The fact, thus abstractedly stated, is not very uncommon, nor—without a proper distinction of circumstances—to be condemned either as naughty or nonsensical. Howbeit, this, though far from the most aggravated, is perhaps the strangest instance, on record, of marital delinquency; and, moreover, as remarkable a freak as may be found in the whole list of human oddities. The wedded couple lived in London. The man, under pretence of going a journey, took lodgings in the next street to his own house, and there, unheard of by his wife or friends, and without the shadow of a reason for such self-banishment, dwelt upwards of twenty years. During that period, he beheld his home every day, and frequently the forlorn Mrs. Wakefield. And after so great a gap in his matrimonial felicity—when his death was reckoned certain, his estate settled, his name dismissed from memory, and his wife, long, long ago, resigned to her autumnal widowhood—he entered the door one evening, quietly, as from a day's absence, and became a loving spouse till death.

This outline is all that I remember. But the incident, though of the purest originality, unexampled, and probably never to be repeated, is one, I think, which appeals to the general sympathies of mankind. We know, each for himself, that none of us would perpetrate such a folly, yet feel as if some other might. To my own contemplations, at least, it has often recurred, always exciting wonder, but with a sense that the story must be true, and a conception of its hero's character. Whenever any subject so forcibly affects the mind, time is well spent in thinking of it. If the reader choose, let him do his own meditation; or if he prefer to ramble with me through the twenty years of Wakefield's vagary, I bid him welcome; trusting that there will be a pervading spirit and a moral, even should we fail to find them, done up neatly, and

condensed into the final sentence. Thought has always its efficacy, and every striking incident its moral.

What sort of a man was Wakefield? We are free to shape
out our own idea, and call it by his name. He was now in the
meridian of life; his matrimonial affections, never violent,
were sobered into a calm, habitual sentiment; of all husbands,
he was likely to be the most constant, because a certain sluggishness would keep his heart at rest, wherever it might be
placed. He was intellectual, but not actively so; his mind occupied itself in long and lazy musings, that tended to no purpose, or had not vigor to attain it; his thoughts were seldom
so energetic as to seize hold of words. Imagination, in the
proper meaning of the term, made no part of Wakefield's
gifts. With a cold, but not depraved nor wandering heart, and
a mind never feverish with riotous thoughts, nor perplexed
with originality, who could have anticipated, that our friend
would entitle himself to a foremost place among the doers of
eccentric deeds? Had his acquaintances been asked, who was
the man in London, the surest to perform nothing to-day
which should be remembered on the morrow, they would
have thought of Wakefield. Only the wife of his bosom might
have hesitated. She, without having analyzed his character,
was partly aware of a quiet selfishness, that had rusted into
his inactive mind—of a peculiar sort of vanity, the most uneasy attribute about him—of a disposition to craft, which
had seldom produced more positive effects than the keeping
of petty secrets, hardly worth revealing—and, lastly, of what
she called a little strangeness, sometimes, in the good man.
This latter quality is indefinable, and perhaps non-existent.

Let us now imagine Wakefield bidding adieu to his wife. It
is the dusk of an October evening. His equipment is a drab
great-coat, a hat covered with an oil-cloth, top-boots, an umbrella in one hand and a small portmanteau in the other. He
has informed Mrs. Wakefield that he is to take the night-
coach into the country. She would fain inquire the length of
his journey, its object, and the probable time of his return;
but, indulgent to his harmless love of mystery, interrogates
him only by a look. He tells her not to expect him positively
by the return coach, nor to be alarmed should he tarry three
or four days; but, at all events, to look for him at supper on

Friday evening. Wakefield himself, be it considered, has no suspicion of what is before him. He holds out his hand; she gives her own, and meets his parting kiss, in the matter-of-course way of a ten years' matrimony; and forth goes the middle-aged Mr. Wakefield, almost resolved to perplex his good lady by a whole week's absence. After the door has closed behind him, she perceives it thrust partly open, and a vision of her husband's face, through the aperture, smiling on her, and gone in a moment. For the time, this little incident is dismissed without a thought. But, long afterwards, when she has been more years a widow than a wife, that smile recurs, and flickers across all her reminiscences of Wakefield's visage. In her many musings, she surrounds the original smile with a multitude of fantasies, which make it strange and awful; as, for instance, if she imagines him in a coffin, that parting look is frozen on his pale features; or, if she dreams of him in Heaven, still his blessed spirit wears a quiet and crafty smile. Yet, for its sake, when all others have given him up for dead, she sometimes doubts whether she is a widow.

But, our business is with the husband. We must hurry after him, along the street, ere he lose his individuality, and melt into the great mass of London life. It would be vain searching for him there. Let us follow close at his heels, therefore, until, after several superfluous turns and doublings, we find him comfortably established by the fireside of a small apartment, previously bespoken. He is in the next street to his own, and at his journey's end. He can scarcely trust his good fortune, in having got thither unperceived—recollecting that, at one time, he was delayed by the throng, in the very focus of a lighted lantern; and, again, there were footsteps, that seemed to tread behind his own, distinct from the multitudinous tramp around him; and, anon, he heard a voice shouting afar, and fancied that it called his name. Doubtless, a dozen busybodies had been watching him, and told his wife the whole affair. Poor Wakefield! Little knowest thou thine own insignificance in this great world! No mortal eye but mine has traced thee. Go quietly to thy bed, foolish man; and, on the morrow, if thou wilt be wise, get thee home to good Mrs. Wakefield, and tell her the truth. Remove not thyself, even for a little week, from thy place in her chaste bosom. Were

she, for a single moment, to deem thee dead, or lost, or last-
ingly divided from her, thou wouldst be woefully conscious
of a change in thy true wife, forever after. It is perilous to
make a chasm in human affections; not that they gape so long
and wide—but so quickly close again!

Almost repenting of his frolic, or whatever it may be
termed, Wakefield lies down betimes, and starting from his
first nap, spreads forth his arms into the wide and solitary
waste of the unaccustomed bed. 'No'—thinks he, gathering
the bed-clothes about him—'I will not sleep alone another
night.'

In the morning, he rises earlier than usual, and sets himself
to consider what he really means to do. Such are his loose
and rambling modes of thought, that he has taken this very
singular step, with the consciousness of a purpose, indeed,
but without being able to define it sufficiently for his own
contemplation. The vagueness of the project, and the convulsive effort with which he plunges into the execution of it, are
equally characteristic of a feeble-minded man. Wakefield sifts
his ideas, however, as minutely as he may, and finds himself
curious to know the progress of matters at home—how his
exemplary wife will endure her widowhood, of a week; and,
briefly, how the little sphere of creatures and circumstances,
in which he was a central object, will be affected by his removal. A morbid vanity, therefore, lies nearest the bottom of
the affair. But, how is he to attain his ends? Not, certainly, by
keeping close in this comfortable lodging, where, though he
slept and awoke in the next street to his home, he is as effectually abroad, as if the stage-coach had been whirling him
away all night. Yet, should he reappear, the whole project is
knocked in the head. His poor brains being hopelessly puzzled with this dilemma, he at length ventures out, partly resolving to cross the head of the street, and send one hasty
glance towards his forsaken domicile. Habit—for he is a man
of habits—takes him by the hand, and guides him, wholly
unaware, to his own door, where, just at the critical moment,
he is aroused by the scraping of his foot upon the step. Wakefield! whither are you going?

At that instant, his fate was turning on the pivot. Little
dreaming of the doom to which his first backward step de-

votes him, he hurries away, breathless with agitation hitherto
unfelt, and hardly dares turn his head, at the distant corner.
Can it be, that nobody caught sight of him? Will not the
whole household—the decent Mrs. Wakefield, the smart
maid-servant, and the dirty little foot-boy—raise a hue-and-
cry, through London streets, in pursuit of their fugitive lord
and master? Wonderful escape! He gathers courage to pause
and look homeward, but is perplexed with a sense of change
about the familiar edifice, such as affects us all, when, after a
separation of months or years, we again see some hill or lake,
or work of art, with which we were friends, of old. In ordinary cases, this indescribable impression is caused by the comparison and contrast between our imperfect reminiscences and
the reality. In Wakefield, the magic of a single night has
wrought a similar transformation, because, in that brief period, a great moral change has been effected. But this is a
secret from himself. Before leaving the spot, he catches a far
and momentary glimpse of his wife, passing athwart the front
window, with her face turned towards the head of the street.
The crafty nincompoop takes to his heels, scared with the
idea, that, among a thousand such atoms of mortality, her eye
must have detected him. Right glad is his heart, though his
brain be somewhat dizzy, when he finds himself by the coal-
fire of his lodgings.

So much for the commencement of this long whim-wham.
After the initial conception, and the stirring up of the man's
sluggish temperament to put it in practice, the whole matter
evolves itself in a natural train. We may suppose him, as the
result of deep deliberation, buying a new wig, of reddish hair,
and selecting sundry garments, in a fashion unlike his customary suit of brown, from a Jew's old-clothes bag. It is accomplished. Wakefield is another man. The new system being
now established, a retrograde movement to the old would be
almost as difficult as the step that placed him in his unparal-
leled position. Furthermore, he is rendered obstinate by a
sulkiness, occasionally incident to his temper, and brought
on, at present, by the inadequate sensation which he conceives to have been produced in the bosom of Mrs. Wakefield. He will not go back until she be frightened half to
death. Well, twice or thrice has she passed before his sight,

each time with a heavier step, a paler cheek, and more anxious brow; and, in the third week of his non-appearance, he detects a portent of evil entering the house, in the guise of an apothecary. Next day, the knocker is muffled. Towards nightfall, comes the chariot of a physician, and deposits its big-wigged and solemn burthen at Wakefield's door, whence, after a quarter of an hour's visit, he emerges, perchance the herald of a funeral. Dear woman! Will she die? By this time, Wakefield is excited to something like energy of feeling, but still lingers away from his wife's bedside, pleading with his conscience, that she must not be disturbed at such a juncture. If aught else restrains him, he does not know it. In the course of a few weeks, she gradually recovers; the crisis is over; her heart is sad, perhaps, but quiet; and, let him return soon or late, it will never be feverish for him again. Such ideas glimmer through the mist of Wakefield's mind, and render him indistinctly conscious, that an almost impassable gulf divides his hired apartment from his former home. 'It is but in the next street!' he sometimes says. Fool! it is in another world. Hitherto, he has put off his return from one particular day to another; henceforward, he leaves the precise time undetermined. Not to-morrow—probably next week—pretty soon. Poor man! The dead have nearly as much chance of re-visiting their earthly homes, as the self-banished Wakefield.

Would that I had a folio to write, instead of an article of a dozen pages! Then might I exemplify how an influence, beyond our control, lays its strong hand on every deed which we do, and weaves its consequences into an iron tissue of necessity. Wakefield is spell-bound. We must leave him, for ten years or so, to haunt around his house, without once crossing the threshold, and to be faithful to his wife, with all the affection of which his heart is capable, while he is slowly fading out of hers. Long since, it must be remarked, he has lost the perception of singularity in his conduct.

Now for a scene! Amid the throng of a London street, we distinguish a man, now waxing elderly, with few characteristics to attract careless observers, yet bearing, in his whole aspect, the hand-writing of no common fate, for such as have the skill to read it. He is meagre; his low and narrow forehead is deeply wrinkled; his eyes, small and lustreless, sometimes wander apprehensively about him, but oftener seem to look inward. He bends his head, but moves with an indescribable obliquity of gait, as if unwilling to display his full front to the world. Watch him, long enough to see what we have described, and you will allow, that circumstances—which often produce remarkable men from nature's ordinary handiwork—have produced one such here. Next, leaving him to sidle along the foot-walk, cast your eyes in the opposite direction, where a portly female, considerably in the wane of life, with a prayer-book in her hand, is proceeding to yonder church. She has the placid mien of settled widowhood. Her regrets have either died away, or have become so essential to her heart, that they would be poorly exchanged for joy. Just as the lean man and well conditioned woman are passing, a slight obstruction occurs, and brings these two figures directly in contact. Their hands touch; the pressure of the crowd forces her bosom against his shoulder; they stand, face to face, staring into each other's eyes. After a ten years' separation, thus Wakefield meets his wife!

The throng eddies away, and carries them asunder. The sober widow, resuming her former pace, proceeds to church, but pauses in the portal, and throws a perplexed glance along the street. She passes in, however, opening her prayer-book as she goes. And the man? With so wild a face, that busy and selfish London stands to gaze after him, he hurries to his lodgings, bolts the door, and throws himself upon the bed. The latent feelings of years break out; his feeble mind acquires a brief energy from their strength; all the miserable strangeness of his life is revealed to him at a glance; and he cries out, passionately—'Wakefield! Wakefield! You are mad!'

Perhaps he was so. The singularity of his situation must have so moulded him to itself, that, considered in regard to his fellow-creatures and the business of life, he could not be said to possess his right mind. He had contrived, or rather he had happened, to dissever himself from the world—to vanish—to give up his place and privileges with living men, without being admitted among the dead. The life of a hermit is nowise parallel to his. He was in the bustle of the city, as of old; but the crowd swept by, and saw him not; he was, we may figuratively say, always beside his wife, and at his hearth, yet must never feel the warmth of the one, nor the affection of the other. It was Wakefield's unprecedented fate, to retain his original share of human sympathies, and to be still involved in human interests, while he had lost his reciprocal influence on them. It would be a most curious speculation, to trace out the effect of such circumstances on his heart and intellect, separately, and in unison. Yet, changed as he was, he would seldom be conscious of it, but deem himself the same man as ever; glimpses of the truth, indeed, would come, but only for the moment; and still he would keep saying—'I shall soon go back!'—nor reflect, that he had been saying so for twenty years.

I conceive, also, that these twenty years would appear, in the retrospect, scarcely longer than the week to which Wakefield had at first limited his absence. He would look on the affair as no more than an interlude in the main business of his life. When, after a little while more, he should deem it time to re-enter his parlor, his wife would clap her hands for joy, on beholding the middle-aged Mr. Wakefield. Alas, what a mistake! Would Time but await the close of our favorite follies, we should be young men, all of us, and till Doom's Day.

One evening, in the twentieth year since he vanished, Wakefield is taking his customary walk towards the dwelling which he still calls his own. It is a gusty night of autumn, with frequent showers, that patter down upon the pavement, and are gone, before a man can put up his umbrella. Pausing near the house, Wakefield discerns, through the parlor-windows of the second floor, the red glow, and the glimmer and fitful flash, of a comfortable fire. On the ceiling, appears a grotesque shadow of good Mrs. Wakefield. The cap, the nose and chin, and the broad waist, form an admirable caricature, which dances, moreover, with the up-flickering and down-sinking blaze, almost too merrily for the shade of an elderly widow. At this instant, a shower chances to fall, and is driven, by the unmannerly gust, full into Wakefield's face and bosom. He is quite penetrated with its autumnal chill. Shall he stand, wet and shivering here, when his own hearth has a good fire to warm him, and his own wife will run to fetch the gray coat and small-clothes, which, doubtless, she has kept carefully in the closet of their bed-chamber? No!

Wakefield is no such fool. He ascends the steps—heavily!—
for twenty years have stiffened his legs, since he came
down—but he knows it not. Stay, Wakefield! Would you go
to the sole home that is left you? Then step into your grave!
The door opens. As he passes in, we have a parting glimpse
of his visage, and recognize the crafty smile, which was the
precursor of the little joke, that he has ever since been playing
off at his wife's expense. How unmercifully has he quizzed
the poor woman! Well; a good night's rest to Wakefield!

This happy event—supposing it to be such—could only
have occurred at an unpremeditated moment. We will not follow our friend across the threshold. He has left us much food
for thought, a portion of which shall lend its wisdom to a
moral; and be shaped into a figure. Amid the seeming confusion of our mysterious world, individuals are so nicely adjusted to a system, and systems to one another, and to a
whole, that, by stepping aside for a moment, a man exposes
himself to a fearful risk of losing his place forever. Like Wakefield, he may become, as it were, the Outcast of the Universe.

The Ambitious Guest

ONE September night, a family had gathered round their hearth, and piled it high with the drift-wood of mountain-streams, the dry cones of the pine, and the splintered ruins of great trees, that had come crashing down the precipice. Up the chimney roared the fire, and brightened the room with its broad blaze. The faces of the father and mother had a sober gladness; the children laughed; the eldest daughter was the image of Happiness at seventeen; and the aged grandmother, who sat knitting in the warmest place, was the image of Happiness grown old. They had found the 'herb, heart's ease,' in the bleakest spot of all New-England. This family were situated in the Notch of the White Hills, where the wind was sharp throughout the year, and pitilessly cold in the winter—giving their cottage all its fresh inclemency, before it descended on the valley of the Saco. They dwelt in a cold spot and a dangerous one; for a mountain towered above their heads, so steep, that the stones would often rumble down its sides, and startle them at midnight.

The daughter had just uttered some simple jest, that filled them all with mirth, when the wind came through the Notch and seemed to pause before their cottage—rattling the door, with a sound of wailing and lamentation, before it passed into the valley. For a moment, it saddened them, though there was nothing unusual in the tones. But the family were glad again, when they perceived that the latch was lifted by some traveller, whose footsteps had been unheard amid the dreary blast, which heralded his approach, and wailed as he was entering, and went moaning away from the door.

Though they dwelt in such a solitude, these people held daily converse with the world. The romantic pass of the Notch is a great artery, through which the life-blood of internal commerce is continually throbbing, between Maine, on one side, and the Green Mountains and the shores of the St. Lawrence on the other. The stage-coach always drew up before the door of the cottage. The wayfarer, with no companion but his staff, paused here to exchange a word, that the sense of loneliness might not utterly overcome him, ere he could pass through the cleft of the mountain, or reach the first house in the valley. And here the teamster, on his way to Portland market, would put up for the night—and, if a bachelor, might sit an hour beyond the usual bed-time, and steal a kiss from the mountain-maid, at parting. It was one of those primitive taverns, where the traveller pays only for food and lodging, but meets with a homely kindness, beyond all price. When the footsteps were heard, therefore, between the outer door and the inner one, the whole family rose up, grandmother, children, and all, as if about to welcome some one who belonged to them, and whose fate was linked with theirs.

The door was opened by a young man. His face at first wore the melancholy expression, almost despondency, of one who travels a wild and bleak road, at night-fall and alone, but soon brightened up, when he saw the kindly warmth of his reception. He felt his heart spring forward to meet them all, from the old woman, who wiped a chair with her apron, to the little child that held out its arms to him. One glance and smile placed the stranger on a footing of innocent familiarity with the eldest daughter.

'Ah, this fire is the right thing!' cried he; 'especially when there is such a pleasant circle round it. I am quite benumbed; for the Notch is just like the pipe of a great pair of bellows; it has blown a terrible blast in my face, all the way from Bartlett.'

'Then you are going towards Vermont?' said the master of the house, as he helped to take a light knapsack off the young man's shoulders.

'Yes; to Burlington, and far enough beyond,' replied he. 'I meant to have been at Ethan Crawford's, to-night; but a pedestrian lingers along such a road as this. It is no matter; for, when I saw this good fire, and all your cheerful faces, I felt as if you had kindled it on purpose for me, and were waiting my arrival. So I shall sit down among you, and make myself at home.'

The frank-hearted stranger had just drawn his chair to the fire, when something like a heavy footstep was heard without, rushing down the steep side of the mountain, as with long and rapid strides, and taking such a leap, in passing the cot-

tage, as to strike the opposite precipice. The family held their
breath, because they knew the sound, and their guest held
his, by instinct.

'The old Mountain has thrown a stone at us, for fear we
should forget him,' said the landlord, recovering himself. 'He
sometimes nods his head, and threatens to come down; but
we are old neighbors, and agree together pretty well, upon
the whole. Besides, we have a sure place of refuge, hard by,
if he should be coming in good earnest.'

Let us now suppose the stranger to have finished his supper
of bear's meat; and, by his natural felicity of manner, to have
placed himself on a footing of kindness with the whole family—so that they talked as freely together, as if he belonged
to their mountain brood. He was of a proud, yet gentle
spirit—haughty and reserved among the rich and great; but
ever ready to stoop his head to the lowly cottage door, and
be like a brother or a son at the poor man's fireside. In the
household of the Notch, he found warmth and simplicity of
feeling, the pervading intelligence of New-England, and a poetry, of native growth, which they had gathered, when they
little thought of it, from the mountain-peaks and chasms, and
at the very threshold of their romantic and dangerous abode.
He had travelled far and alone; his whole life, indeed, had
been a solitary path; for, with the lofty caution of his nature,
he had kept himself apart from those who might otherwise
have been his companions. The family, too, though so kind
and hospitable, had that consciousness of unity among themselves, and separation from the world at large, which, in every
domestic circle, should still keep a holy place, where no
stranger may intrude. But, this evening, a prophetic sympathy
impelled the refined and educated youth to pour out his heart
before the simple mountaineers, and constrained them to answer him with the same free confidence. And thus it should
have been. Is not the kindred of a common fate a closer tie
than that of birth?

The secret of the young man's character was, a high and
abstracted ambition. He could have borne to live an undistinguished life, but not to be forgotten in the grave. Yearning
desire had been transformed to hope; and hope, long cherished, had become like certainty, that, obscurely as he jour-

neyed now, a glory was to beam on all his path-way—though not, perhaps, while he was treading it. But, when posterity should gaze back into the gloom of what was now the present, they would trace the brightness of his footsteps, brightening as meaner glories faded, and confess, that a gifted one had passed from his cradle to his tomb, with none to recognize him.

'As yet,' cried the stranger—his cheek glowing and his eye flashing with enthusiasm—'as yet, I have done nothing. Were I to vanish from the earth to-morrow, none would know so much of me as you; that a nameless youth came up, at night-fall, from the valley of the Saco, and opened his heart to you in the evening, and passed through the Notch, by sunrise, and was seen no more. Not a soul would ask—"Who was he?—Whither did the wanderer go?" But, I cannot die till I have achieved my destiny. Then, let Death come! I shall have built my monument!'

There was a continual flow of natural emotion, gushing forth amid abstracted reverie, which enabled the family to understand this young man's sentiments, though so foreign from their own. With quick sensibility of the ludicrous, he blushed at the ardor into which he had been betrayed.

'You laugh at me,' said he, taking the eldest daughter's hand, and laughing himself. 'You think my ambition as nonsensical as if I were to freeze myself to death on the top of Mount Washington, only that people might spy at me from the country roundabout. And truly, that would be a noble pedestal for a man's statue!'

'It is better to sit here, by this fire,' answered the girl, blushing, 'and be comfortable and contented, though nobody thinks about us.'

'I suppose,' said her father, after a fit of musing, 'there is something natural in what the young man says; and if my mind had been turned that way, I might have felt just the same. It is strange, wife, how his talk has set my head running on things, that are pretty certain never to come to pass.'

'Perhaps they may,' observed the wife. 'Is the man thinking what he will do when he is a widower?'

'No, no!' cried he, repelling the idea with reproachful kindness. 'When I think of your death, Esther, I think of mine, too. But I was wishing we had a good farm, in Bartlett, or Bethlehem, or Littleton, or some other township round the White Mountains; but not where they could tumble on our heads. I should want to stand well with my neighbors, and be called 'Squire, and sent to General Court, for a term or two; for a plain, honest man may do as much good there as a lawyer. And when I should be grown quite an old man, and you an old woman, so as not to be long apart, I might die happy enough in my bed, and leave you all crying around me. A slate grave-stone would suit me as well as a marble one—with just my name and age, and a verse of a hymn, and something to let people know, that I lived an honest man and died a Christian.'

'There now!' exclaimed the stranger; 'it is our nature to desire a monument, be it slate, or marble, or a pillar of granite, or a glorious memory in the universal heart of man.'

'We're in a strange way, to-night,' said the wife, with tears in her eyes. 'They say it's a sign of something, when folks' minds go a wandering so. Hark to the children!'

They listened accordingly. The younger children had been put to bed in another room, but with an open door between, so that they could be heard talking busily among themselves. One and all seemed to have caught the infection from the fireside circle, and were outvying each other, in wild wishes, and childish projects of what they would do, when they came to be men and women. At length, a little boy, instead of addressing his brothers and sisters, called out to his mother.

'I'll tell you what I wish, mother,' cried he. 'I want you and father and grandma'm, and all of us, and the stranger too, to start right away, and go and take a drink out of the basin of the Flume!'

Nobody could help laughing at the child's notion of leaving a warm bed, and dragging them from a cheerful fire, to visit the basin of the Flume—a brook, which tumbles over the precipice, deep within the Notch. The boy had hardly spoken, when a wagon rattled along the road, and stopped a moment before the door. It appeared to contain two or three men, who were cheering their hearts with the rough chorus of a song, which resounded, in broken notes, between the cliffs, while the singers hesitated whether to continue their journey, or put up here for the night.

'Father,' said the girl, 'they are calling you by name.'

But the good man doubted whether they had really called him, and was unwilling to show himself too solicitous of gain, by inviting people to patronize his house. He therefore did not hurry to the door; and the lash being soon applied, the travellers plunged into the Notch, still singing and laughing, though their music and mirth came back drearily from the heart of the mountain.

'There, mother!' cried the boy, again. 'They'd have given us a ride to the Flume.'

Again they laughed at the child's pertinacious fancy for a night-ramble. But it happened, that a light cloud passed over the daughter's spirit; she looked gravely into the fire, and drew a breath that was almost a sigh. It forced its way, in spite of a little struggle to repress it. Then starting and blushing, she looked quickly round the circle, as if they had caught a glimpse into her bosom. The stranger asked what she had been thinking of.

'Nothing,' answered she, with a downcast smile. 'Only I felt lonesome just then.'

'Oh, I have always had a gift of feeling what is in other people's hearts,' said he, half seriously. 'Shall I tell the secrets of yours? For I know what to think, when a young girl shivers by a warm hearth, and complains of lonesomeness at her mother's side. Shall I put these feelings into words?'

'They would not be a girl's feelings any longer, if they could be put into words,' replied the mountain-nymph, laughing, but avoiding his eye.

All this was said apart. Perhaps a germ of love was springing in their hearts, so pure that it might blossom in Paradise, since it could not be matured on earth; for women worship such gentle dignity as his; and the proud, contemplative, yet kindly soul is oftenest captivated by simplicity like hers. But, while they spoke softly, and he was watching the happy sadness, the lightsome shadows, the shy yearnings of a maiden's nature, the wind, through the Notch, took a deeper and drearier sound. It seemed, as the fanciful stranger said, like the choral strain of the spirits of the blast, who, in old Indian times, had their dwelling among these mountains, and made their heights and recesses a sacred region. There was a wail, along the road, as if a funeral were passing. To chase away the gloom, the family threw pine branches on their fire, till the dry leaves crackled and the flame arose, discovering once again a scene of peace and humble happiness. The light hovered about them fondly, and caressed them all. There were the little faces of the children, peeping from their bed apart, and here the father's frame of strength, the mother's subdued and careful mien, the high-browed youth, the budding girl, and the good old grandam, still knitting in the warmest place. The aged woman looked up from her task, and, with fingers ever busy, was the next to speak.

'Old folks have their notions,' said she, 'as well as young ones. You've been wishing and planning; and letting your heads run on one thing and another, till you've set my mind a wandering too. Now what should an old woman wish for, when she can go but a step or two before she comes to her grave? Children, it will haunt me night and day, till I tell you.'

'What is it, mother?' cried the husband and wife, at once.

Then the old woman, with an air of mystery, which drew the circle closer round the fire, informed them that she had provided her grave-clothes some years before—a nice linen shroud, a cap with a muslin ruff, and everything of a finer sort than she had worn since her wedding-day. But, this evening, an old superstition had strangely recurred to her. It used to be said, in her younger days, that, if anything were amiss with a corpse, if only the ruff were not smooth, or the cap did not set right, the corpse, in the coffin and beneath the clods, would strive to put up its cold hands and arrange it. The bare thought made her nervous.

'Don't talk so, grandmother!' said the girl, shuddering.

'Now,'—continued the old woman, with singular earnestness, yet smiling strangely at her own folly,—'I want one of you, my children—when your mother is drest, and in the coffin—I want one of you to hold a looking-glass over my face. Who knows but I may take a glimpse at myself, and see whether all's right?'

'Old and young, we dream of graves and monuments,' murmured the stranger-youth. 'I wonder how mariners feel, when the ship is sinking, and they, unknown and undistinguished, are to be buried together in the ocean—that wide and nameless sepulchre!'

For a moment, the old woman's ghastly conception so engrossed the minds of her hearers, that a sound, abroad in the night, rising like the roar of a blast, had grown broad, deep, and terrible, before the fated group were conscious of it. The house, and all within it, trembled; the foundations of the earth seemed to be shaken, as if this awful sound were the peal of the last trump. Young and old exchanged one wild glance, and remained an instant, pale, affrighted, without utterance, or power to move. Then the same shriek burst simultaneously from all their lips.

'The Slide! The Slide!'

The simplest words must intimate, but not portray, the unutterable horror of the catastrophe. The victims rushed from their cottage, and sought refuge in what they deemed a safer spot—where, in contemplation of such an emergency, a sort of barrier had been reared. Alas! they had quitted their security, and fled right into the pathway of destruction. Down came the whole side of the mountain, in a cataract of ruin. Just before it reached the house, the stream broke into two branches—shivered not a window there, but overwhelmed the whole vicinity, blocked up the road, and annihilated everything in its dreadful course. Long ere the thunder of that great Slide had ceased to roar among the mountains, the mortal agony had been endured, and the victims were at peace. Their bodies were never found.

The next morning, the light smoke was seen stealing from the cottage-chimney, up the mountain-side. Within, the fire was yet smouldering on the hearth, and the chairs in a circle round it, as if the inhabitants had but gone forth to view the devastation of the Slide, and would shortly return, to thank Heaven for their miraculous escape. All had left separate tokens, by which those, who had known the family, were made to shed a tear for each. Who has not heard their name? The story had been told far and wide, and will forever be a legend of these mountains. Poets have sung their fate.

There were circumstances, which led some to suppose that a stranger had been received into the cottage on this awful night, and had shared the catastrophe of all its inmates. Others denied that there were sufficient grounds for such a conjecture. Wo, for the high-souled youth, with his dream of Earthly Immortality! His name and person utterly unknown; his history, his way of life, his plans, a mystery never to be solved; his death and his existence, equally a doubt! Whose was the agony of that death-moment?

A Rill from the Town-Pump

(SCENE—*the corner of two principal streets.* *
The TOWN-PUMP *talking through its nose.*)

NOON, by the north clock! Noon, by the east! High
noon, too, by these hot sunbeams, which fall, scarcely
aslope, upon my head, and almost make the water bubble and
smoke, in the trough under my nose. Truly, we public characters have a tough time of it! And, among all the town-offi-
cers, chosen at March meeting, where is he that sustains, for
a single year, the burthen of such manifold duties as are imposed, in perpetuity, upon the Town-Pump? The title of
'town-treasurer' is rightfully mine, as guardian of the best
treasure, that the town has. The overseers of the poor ought
to make me their chairman, since I provide bountifully for
the pauper, without expense to him that pays taxes. I am at
the head of the fire-department, and one of the physicians to
the board of health. As a keeper of the peace, all water-drinkers will confess me equal to the constable. I perform some of
the duties of the town clerk, by promulgating public notices,
when they are posted on my front. To speak within bounds,
I am the chief person of the municipality, and exhibit, moreover, an admirable pattern to my brother officers, by the cool,
steady, upright, downright, and impartial discharge of my
business, and the constancy with which I stand to my post.
Summer or winter, nobody seeks me in vain; for, all day long,
I am seen at the busiest corner, just above the market, stretching out my arms, to rich and poor alike; and at night, I hold
a lantern over my head, both to show where I am, and keep
people out of the gutters.

At this sultry noontide, I am cup-bearer to the parched
populace, for whose benefit an iron goblet is chained to my
waist. Like a dram-seller on the mall, at muster-day, I cry
aloud to all and sundry, in my plainest accents, and at the
very tip-top of my voice. Here it is, gentlemen! Here is
the good liquor! Walk up, walk up, gentlemen, walk up, walk
up! Here is the superior stuff! Here is the unadulterated ale

*Essex and Washington Streets, Salem.

of father Adam—better than Cognac, Hollands, Jamaica, strong-beer, or wine of any price; here it is, by the hogshead or the single glass, and not a cent to pay! Walk up, gentlemen, walk up, and help yourselves!

It were a pity, if all this outcry should draw no customers. Here they come. A hot day, gentlemen! Quaff, and away again, so as to keep yourselves in a nice cool sweat. You, my friend, will need another cup-full, to wash the dust out of your throat, if it be as thick there as it is on your cowhide shoes. I see that you have trudged half a score of miles, to-day; and, like a wise man, have passed by the taverns, and stopped at the running-brooks and well-curbs. Otherwise, betwixt heat without and fire within, you would have been burnt to a cinder, or melted down to nothing at all, in the fashion of a jelly-fish. Drink, and make room for that other fellow, who seeks my aid to quench the fiery fever of last night's potations, which he drained from no cup of mine. Welcome, most rubicund Sir! You and I have been great strangers, hitherto; nor, to confess the truth, will my nose be anxious for a closer intimacy, till the fumes of your breath be a little less potent. Mercy on you, man! The water absolutely hisses down your red-hot gullet, and is converted quite to steam, in the miniature tophet, which you mistake for a stomach. Fill again, and tell me, on the word of an honest toper, did you ever, in cellar, tavern, or any kind of a dram-shop, spend the price of your children's food, for a swig half so delicious? Now, for the first time these ten years, you know the flavor of cold water. Good b'ye; and, whenever you are thirsty, remember that I keep a constant supply, at the old stand. Who next? Oh, my little friend, you are let loose from school, and come hither to scrub your blooming face, and drown the memory of certain taps of the ferule, and other school-boy troubles, in a draught from the Town-Pump. Take it, pure as the current of your young life. Take it, and may your heart and tongue never be scorched with a fiercer thirst than now! There, my dear child, put down the cup, and yield your place to this elderly gentleman, who treads so tenderly over the paving-stones, that I suspect he is afraid of breaking them. What! He limps by, without so much as thanking me, as if my hospitable offers were meant only for people, who have no wine-cellars. Well, well, sir—no harm done, I hope! Go draw the cork, tip the decanter; but, when your great-toe shall set you a-roaring, it will be no affair of mine. If gentlemen love the pleasant titillation of the gout, it is all one to the Town-Pump. This thirsty dog, with his red tongue lolling out, does not scorn my hospitality, but stands on his hind-legs, and laps eagerly out of the trough. See how lightly he capers away again! Jowler, did your worship ever have the gout?

Are you all satisfied? Then wipe your mouths, my good friends; and, while my spout has a moment's leisure, I will delight the town with a few historical reminiscences. In far antiquity, beneath a darksome shadow of venerable boughs, a spring bubbled out of the leaf-strewn earth, in the very spot where you now behold me, on the sunny pavement. The water was as bright and clear, and deemed as precious, as liquid diamonds. The Indian sagamores drank of it, from time immemorial, till the fatal deluge of the fire-water burst upon the red men, and swept their whole race away from the cold fountains. Endicott, and his followers, came next, and often knelt down to drink, dipping their long beards in the spring. The richest goblet, then, was of birch-bark. Governor Winthrop, after a journey afoot from Boston, drank here, out of the hollow of his hand. The elder Higginson here wet his palm, and laid it on the brow of the first town-born child. For many years, it was the watering-place, and, as it were, the wash-bowl of the vicinity—whither all decent folks resorted, to purify their visages, and gaze at them afterwards—at least, the pretty maidens did—in the mirror which it made. On Sabbath-days, whenever a babe was to be baptized, the sexton filled his basin here, and placed it on the communion-table of the humble meeting-house, which partly covered the site of yonder stately brick one. Thus, one generation after another was consecrated to Heaven by its waters, and cast their waxing and waning shadows into its glassy bosom, and vanished from the earth, as if mortal life were but a flitting image in a fountain. Finally, the fountain vanished also. Cellars were dug on all sides; and cart-loads of gravel flung upon its source, whence oozed a turbid stream, forming a mud-puddle, at the corner of two streets. In the hot months, when its refresh-

ment was most needed, the dust flew in clouds over the forgotten birthplace of the waters, now their grave. But, in the
course of time, a Town-Pump was sunk into the source of the
ancient spring; and when the first decayed, another took its
place—and then another, and still another—till here stand I,
gentlemen and ladies, to serve you with my iron goblet.
Drink, and be refreshed! The water is as pure and cold as that
which slaked the thirst of the red sagamore, beneath the aged
boughs, though now the gem of the wilderness is treasured
under these hot stones, where no shadow falls, but from the
brick buildings. And be it the moral of my story, that, as this
wasted and long-lost fountain is now known and prized
again, so shall the virtues of cold water, too little valued since
your fathers' days, be recognized by all.

Your pardon, good people! I must interrupt my stream of
eloquence, and spout forth a stream of water, to replenish the
trough for this teamster and his two yoke of oxen, who have
come from Topsfield, or somewhere along that way. No part
of my business is pleasanter than the watering of cattle. Look!
how rapidly they lower the water-mark on the sides of the
trough, till their capacious stomachs are moistened with a gal-
lon or two apiece, and they can afford time to breathe it in,
with sighs of calm enjoyment. Now they roll their quiet eyes
around the brim of their monstrous drinking-vessel. An ox is
your true toper.

But I perceive, my dear auditors, that you are impatient for
the remainder of my discourse. Impute it, I beseech you, to
no defect of modesty, if I insist a little longer on so fruitful a
topic as my own multifarious merits. It is altogether for your
good. The better you think of me, the better men and women
will you find yourselves. I shall say nothing of my all-important aid on washing-days; though, on that account alone, I
might call myself the household-god of a hundred families.
Far be it from me, also, to hint, my respectable friends, at the
show of dirty faces, which you would present, without my
pains to keep you clean. Nor will I remind you how often,
when the midnight-bells make you tremble for your combustible town, you have fled to the Town-Pump, and found me
always at my post, firm, amid the confusion, and ready to
drain my vital current in your behalf. Neither is it worth

while to lay much stress on my claims to a medical diploma, as the physician, whose simple rule of practice is preferable to all the nauseous lore, which has found men sick or left them so, since the days of Hippocrates. Let us take a broader view of my beneficial influence on mankind.

No; these are trifles, compared with the merits which wise men concede to me—if not in my single self, yet as the representative of a class—of being the grand reformer of the age. From my spout, and such spouts as mine, must flow the stream, that shall cleanse our earth of the vast portion of its crime and anguish, which has gushed from the fiery fountains of the still. In this mighty enterprise, the cow shall be my great confederate. Milk and water! The TOWN-PUMP and the COW! Such is the glorious copartnership, that shall tear down the distilleries and brew-houses, uproot the vineyards, shatter the cider-presses, ruin the tea and coffee trade, and, finally monopolize the whole business of quenching thirst. Blessed consummation! Then, Poverty shall pass away from the land, finding no hovel so wretched, where her squalid form may shelter itself. Then Disease, for lack of other victims, shall gnaw its own heart, and die. Then Sin, if she do not die, shall lose half her strength. Until now, the phrensy of hereditary fever has raged in the human blood, transmitted from sire to son, and re-kindled, in every generation, by fresh draughts of liquid flame. When that inward fire shall be extinguished, the heat of passion cannot but grow cool, and war—the drunkenness of nations—perhaps will cease. At least, there will be no war of households. The husband and wife, drinking deep of peaceful joy—a calm bliss of temperate affections—shall pass hand in hand through life, and lie down, not reluctantly, at its protracted close. To them, the past will be no turmoil of mad dreams, nor the future an eternity of such moments as follow the delirium of the drunkard. Their dead faces shall express what their spirits were, and are to be, by a lingering smile of memory and hope.

Ahem! Dry work, this speechifying; especially to an unpractised orator. I never conceived, till now, what toil the temperance-lecturers undergo for my sake. Hereafter, they shall have the business to themselves. Do, some kind Christian, pump a stroke or two, just to wet my whistle. Thank you, sir! My dear hearers, when the world shall have been regenerated, by my instrumentality, you will collect your useless vats and liquor-casks, into one great pile, and make a bonfire, in honor of the Town-Pump. And, when I shall have decayed, like my predecessors, then, if you revere my memory, let a marble fountain, richly sculptured, take my place upon this spot. Such monuments should be erected everywhere, and inscribed with the names of the distinguished champions of my cause. Now listen; for something very important is to come next.

There are two or three honest friends of mine—and true friends, I know, they are—who, nevertheless, by their fiery pugnacity in my behalf, do put me in fearful hazard of a broken nose, or even of a total overthrow upon the pavement, and the loss of the treasure which I guard. I pray you, gentlemen, let this fault be amended. Is it decent, think you, to get tipsy with zeal for temperance, and take up the honorable cause of the Town-Pump, in the style of a toper fighting for his brandy-bottle? Or, can the excellent qualities of cold water be no otherwise exemplified, than by plunging, slap-dash, into hot-water, and wofully scalding yourselves and other people? Trust me, they may. In the moral warfare, which you are to wage—and, indeed, in the whole conduct of your lives—you cannot choose a better example than myself, who have never permitted the dust, and sultry atmosphere, the turbulence and manifold disquietudes of the world around me, to reach that deep, calm well of purity, which may be called my soul. And whenever I pour out that soul, it is to cool earth's fever, or cleanse its stains.

One o'clock! Nay, then, if the dinner-bell begins to speak, I may as well hold my peace. Here comes a pretty young girl of my acquaintance, with a large stone-pitcher for me to fill. May she draw a husband, while drawing her water, as Rachel did of old. Hold out your vessel, my dear! There it is, full to the brim; so now run home, peeping at your sweet image in the pitcher, as you go; and forget not, in a glass of my own liquor, to drink—'SUCCESS TO THE TOWN-PUMP!'

The White Old Maid

THE moonbeams came through two deep and narrow windows, and showed a spacious chamber, richly furnished in an antique fashion. From one lattice, the shadow of the diamond panes was thrown upon the floor; the ghostly light, through the other, slept upon a bed, falling between the heavy silken curtains, and illuminating the face of a young man. But, how quietly the slumberer lay! how pale his features! and how like a shroud the sheet was wound about his frame! Yes; it was a corpse, in its burial-clothes.

Suddenly, the fixed features seemed to move, with dark emotion. Strange fantasy! It was but the shadow of the fringed curtain, waving betwixt the dead face and the moonlight, as the door of the chamber opened, and a girl stole softly to the bedside. Was there delusion in the moonbeams, or did her gesture and her eye betray a gleam of triumph, as she bent over the pale corpse—pale as itself—and pressed her living lips to the cold ones of the dead? As she drew back from that long kiss, her features writhed, as if a proud heart were fighting with its anguish. Again it seemed that the features of the corpse had moved, responsive to her own. Still an illusion! The silken curtain had waved, a second time, betwixt the dead face and the moonlight, as another fair young girl unclosed the door, and glided, ghostlike, to the bedside. There the two maidens stood, both beautiful, with the pale beauty of the dead between them. But she, who had first entered, was proud and stately; and the other, a soft and fragile thing.

'Away!' cried the lofty one. 'Thou hadst him living! The dead is mine!'

'Thine!' returned the other, shuddering, 'Well hast thou spoken! The dead is thine!'

The proud girl started, and stared into her face, with a ghastly look. But a wild and mournful expression passed across the features of the gentle one; and, weak and helpless, she sank down on the bed, her head pillowed beside that of the corpse, and her hair mingling with his dark locks. A creature of hope and joy, the first draught of sorrow had bewildered her.

'Edith!' cried her rival.

Edith groaned, as with a sudden compression of the heart; and removing her cheek from the dead youth's pillow, she stood upright, fearfully encountering the eyes of the lofty girl.

'Wilt thou betray me?' said the latter, calmly.

'Till the dead bid me speak, I will be silent,' answered Edith. 'Leave us alone together! Go, and live many years, and then return, and tell me of thy life. He, too, will be here! Then, if thou tellest of sufferings more than death, we will both forgive thee.'

'And what shall be the token?' asked the proud girl, as if her heart acknowledged a meaning in these wild words.

'This lock of hair,' said Edith, lifting one of the dark, clustering curls, that lay heavily on the dead man's brow.

The two maidens joined their hands over the bosom of the corpse, and appointed a day and hour, far, far in time to come, for their next meeting in that chamber. The statelier girl gave one deep look at the motionless countenance, and departed—yet turned again and trembled, ere she closed the door, almost believing that her dead lover frowned upon her. And Edith, too! Was not her white form fading into the moonlight? Scorning her own weakness, she went forth, and perceived that a negro slave was waiting in the passage, with a wax-light, which he held between her face and his own, and regarded her, as she thought, with an ugly expression of merriment. Lifting his torch on high, the slave lighted her down the staircase, and undid the portal of the mansion. The young clergyman of the town had just ascended the steps, and bowing to the lady, passed in without a word.

Years, many years rolled on; the world seemed new again, so much older was it grown, since the night when those pale girls had clasped their hands across the bosom of the corpse. In the interval, a lonely woman had passed from youth to extreme age, and was known by all the town, as the 'Old Maid in the Winding-Sheet.' A taint of insanity had affected her whole life, but so quiet, sad, and gentle, so utterly free from violence, that she was suffered to pursue her harmless fantasies, unmolested by the world, with whose business or pleasures she had nought to do. She dwelt alone, and never came into the daylight, except to follow funerals. Whenever a corpse was borne along the street, in sunshine, rain, or snow, whether a pompous train, of the rich and proud, thronged after it, or few and humble were the mourners, behind them came the lonely woman, in a long, white garment, which the people called her shroud. She took no place among the kindred or the friends, but stood at the door to hear the funeral prayer, and walked in the rear of the procession, as one whose earthly charge it was to haunt the house of mourning, and be the shadow of affliction, and see that the dead were duly buried. So long had this been her custom, that the inhabitants of the town deemed her a part of every funeral, as much as the coffin-pall, or the very corpse itself, and augured ill of the sinner's destiny, unless the 'Old Maid in the Winding-Sheet' came gliding, like a ghost, behind. Once, it is said, she affrighted a bridal party, with her pale presence, appearing suddenly in the illuminated hall, just as the priest was uniting a false maid to a wealthy man, before her lover had been dead a year. Evil was the omen to that marriage! Sometimes she stole forth by moonlight, and visited the graves of venerable Integrity, and wedded Love, and virgin Innocence, and every spot where the ashes of a kind and faithful heart were mouldering. Over the hillocks of those favored dead, would she stretch out her arms, with a gesture, as if she were scattering seeds; and many believed that she brought them from the garden of Paradise; for the graves, which she had visited, were green beneath the snow, and covered with sweet flowers from April to November. Her blessing was better than a holy verse upon the tomb-stone. Thus wore away her long, sad, peaceful, and fantastic life, till few were so old as she, and the people of later generations wondered how the dead had ever been buried, or mourners had endured their grief, without the 'Old Maid in the Winding-Sheet.'

Still, years went on, and still she followed funerals, and was not yet summoned to her own festival of death. One afternoon, the great street of the town was all alive with business and bustle, though the sun now gilded only the upper half of the church-spire, having left the house-tops and loftiest trees in shadow. The scene was cheerful and animated, in spite of the sombre shade between the high brick buildings. Here were pompous merchants, in white wigs and laced velvet; the bronzed faces of sea-captains; the foreign garb and air of Spanish creoles; and the disdainful port of natives of Old England; all contrasted with the rough aspect of one or two back-settlers, negociating sales of timber, from forests where axe had never sounded. Sometimes a lady passed, swelling roundly forth in an embroidered petticoat, balancing her steps in high-heeled shoes, and courtesying, with lofty grace, to the punctilious obeisances of the gentlemen. The life of the town seemed to have its very centre not far from an old mansion, that stood somewhat back from the pavement, surrounded by neglected grass, with a strange air of loneliness, rather deepened than dispelled by the throng so near it. Its site would have been suitably occupied by a magnificent Exchange, or a brick-block, lettered all over with various signs; or the large house itself might have made a noble tavern, with the 'King's Arms' swinging before it, and guests in every chamber, instead of the present solitude. But, owing to some dispute about the right of inheritance, the mansion had been long without a tenant, decaying from year to year, and throwing the stately gloom of its shadow over the busiest part of the town. Such was the scene, and such the time, when a figure, unlike any that have been described, was observed at a distance down the street.

'I espy a strange sail, yonder,' remarked a Liverpool captain; 'that woman, in the long white garment!'

The sailor seemed much struck by the object, as were several others, who, at the same moment, caught a glimpse of the figure, that had attracted his notice. Almost immediately, the various topics of conversation gave place to speculations, in an under tone, on this unwonted occurrence.

'Can there be a funeral, so late this afternoon?' inquired some.

They looked for the signs of death at every door—the sexton, the hearse, the assemblage of black-clad relatives—all that makes up the woeful pomp of funerals. They raised their eyes, also, to the sun-gilt spire of the church, and wondered that no clang proceeded from its bell, which had always tolled till now, when this figure appeared in the light of day. But none had heard, that a corpse was to be borne to its home that afternoon, nor was there any token of a funeral, except the apparition of the 'Old Maid in the Winding-Sheet.'

'What may this portend?' asked each man of his neighbor.

All smiled as they put the question, yet with a certain trouble in their eyes, as if pestilence, or some other wide calamity, were prognosticated by the untimely intrusion, among the living, of one whose presence had always been associated with death and woe. What a comet is to the earth, was that sad woman to the town. Still she moved on, while the hum of surprise was hushed at her approach, and the proud and the humble stood aside, that her white garment might not wave against them. It was a long, loose robe, of spotless purity. Its wearer appeared very old, pale, emaciated, and feeble, yet glided onward, without the unsteady pace of extreme age. At one point of her course, a little rosy boy burst forth from a door, and ran, with open arms, towards the ghostly woman, seeming to expect a kiss from her bloodless lips. She made a slight pause, fixing her eye upon him with an expression of no earthly sweetness, so that the child shivered and stood awe-struck, rather than affrighted, while the Old Maid passed on. Perhaps her garment might have been polluted, even by an infant's touch; perhaps her kiss would have been death to the sweet boy, within the year.

'She is but a shadow!' whispered the superstitious. 'The child put forth his arms, and could not grasp her robe!'

The wonder was increased, when the Old Maid passed beneath the porch of the deserted mansion, ascended the moss-covered steps, lifted the iron knocker, and gave three raps. The people could only conjecture, that some old remembrance, troubling her bewildered brain, had impelled the poor woman hither to visit the friends of her youth; all gone from their home, long since and forever, unless their ghosts still haunted it—fit company for the 'Old Maid in the Winding-Sheet.' An elderly man approached the steps, and reverently uncovering his gray locks, essayed to explain the matter.

'None, Madam,' said he, 'have dwelt in this house these fifteen years agone—no, not since the death of old Colonel Fenwicke, whose funeral you may remember to have followed. His heirs, being ill-agreed among themselves, have let the mansion-house go to ruin.'

The Old Maid looked slowly round, with a slight gesture of one hand, and a finger of the other upon her lip, appearing more shadow-like than ever, in the obscurity of the porch. But, again she lifted the hammer, and gave, this time, a single rap. Could it be, that a footstep was now heard, coming down the staircase of the old mansion, which all conceived to have been so long untenanted? Slowly, feebly, yet heavily, like the pace of an aged and infirm person, the step approached, more distinct on every downward stair, till it reached the portal. The bar fell on the inside; the door was opened. One upward glance, towards the church-spire, whence the sunshine had just faded, was the last that the people saw of the 'Old Maid in the Winding-Sheet.'

'Who undid the door?' asked many.

This question, owing to the depth of shadow beneath the porch, no one could satisfactorily answer. Two or three aged men, while protesting against an inference, which might be drawn, affirmed that the person within was a negro, and bore a singular resemblance to old Cæsar, formerly a slave in the house, but freed by death some thirty years before.

'Her summons has waked up a servant of the old family,' said one, half seriously.

'Let us wait here,' replied another. 'More guests will knock at the door, anon. But, the gate of the grave-yard should be thrown open!'

Twilight had overspread the town, before the crowd began to separate, or the comments on this incident were exhausted. One after another was wending his way homeward, when a coach—no common spectacle in those days—drove slowly into the street. It was an old-fashioned equipage, hanging close to the ground, with arms on the pannels, a footman behind, and a grave, corpulent coachman seated high in front—the whole giving an idea of solemn state and dignity. There was something awful, in the heavy rumbling of the wheels. The coach rolled down the street, till, coming to the gateway of the deserted mansion, it drew up, and the footman sprang to the ground.

'Whose grand coach is this?' asked a very inquisitive body.

The footman made no reply, but ascended the steps of the old house, gave three raps, with the iron hammer, and returned to open the coach-door. An old man, possessed of the heraldic lore so common in that day, examined the shield of arms on the pannel.

'Azure, a lion's head erased, between three flower de luces,' said he; then whispered the name of the family to whom these bearings belonged. The last inheritor of its honors was recently dead, after a long residence amid the splendor of the British court, where his birth and wealth had given him no mean station. 'He left no child,' continued the herald, 'and these arms, being in a lozenge, betoken that the coach appertains to his widow.'

Further disclosures, perhaps, might have been made, had not the speaker suddenly been struck dumb, by the stern eye of an ancient lady, who thrust forth her head from the coach, preparing to descend. As she emerged, the people saw that her dress was magnificent, and her figure dignified, in spite of age and infirmity—a stately ruin, but with a look, at once, of pride and wretchedness. Her strong and rigid features had an awe about them, unlike that of the white Old Maid, but as of something evil. She passed up the steps, leaning on a gold-headed cane; the door swung open, as she ascended—and the light of a torch glittered on the embroidery of her dress, and gleamed on the pillars of the porch. After a momentary pause—a glance backwards—and then a desperate effort—she went in. The decypherer of the coat of arms had ventured up the lowest step, and shrinking back immediately, pale and tremulous, affirmed that the torch was held by the very image of old Cæsar.

'But, such a hideous grin,' added he, 'was never seen on the face of mortal man, black or white! It will haunt me till my dying day.'

Meantime, the coach had wheeled round, with a prodigious clatter on the pavement, and rumbled up the street, disappearing in the twilight, while the ear still tracked its course. Scarcely was it gone, when the people began to question, whether the coach and attendants, the ancient lady, the spectre of old Cæsar, and the Old Maid herself, were not all

a strangely combined delusion, with some dark purport in its
mystery. The whole town was astir, so that, instead of dispersing, the crowd continually increased, and stood gazing up
at the windows of the mansion, now silvered by the brightening moon. The elders, glad to indulge the narrative propensity of age, told of the long faded splendor of the family,
the entertainments they had given, and the guests, the greatest of the land, and even titled and noble ones from abroad,
who had passed beneath that portal. These graphic reminiscences seemed to call up the ghosts of those to whom they
referred. So strong was the impression, on some of the more
imaginative hearers, that two or three were seized with trembling fits, at one and the same moment, protesting that they
had distinctly heard three other raps of the iron knocker.

'Impossible!' exclaimed others. 'See! The moon shines beneath the porch, and shows every part of it, except in the
narrow shade of that pillar. There is no one there!'

'Did not the door open?' whispered one of these fanciful
persons.

'Didst thou see it, too?' said his companion, in a startled
tone.

But the general sentiment was opposed to the idea, that a
third visitant had made application at the door of the deserted
house. A few, however, adhered to this new marvel, and even
declared that a red gleam, like that of a torch, had shone
through the great front window, as if the negro were lighting
a guest up the staircase. This, too, was pronounced a mere
fantasy. But, at once, the whole multitude started, and each
man beheld his own terror painted in the faces of all the rest.

'What an awful thing is this!' cried they.

A shriek, too fearfully distinct for doubt, had been heard
within the mansion, breaking forth suddenly, and succeeded
by a deep stillness, as if a heart had burst in giving it utterance. The people knew not whether to fly from the very sight
of the house, or to rush trembling in, and search out the
strange mystery. Amid their confusion and affright, they were
somewhat reassured by the appearance of their clergyman, a
venerable patriarch, and equally a saint, who had taught them
and their fathers the way to Heaven, for more than the space
of an ordinary life-time. He was a reverend figure, with long,

white hair upon his shoulders, a white beard upon his breast, and a back so bent over his staff, that he seemed to be looking downward, continually, as if to choose a proper grave for his weary frame. It was some time, before the good old man, being deaf, and of impaired intellect, could be made to comprehend such portions of the affair, as were comprehensible at all. But, when possessed of the facts, his energies assumed unexpected vigor.

'Verily,' said the old gentleman, 'it will be fitting that I enter the mansion-house of the worthy Colonel Fenwicke, lest any harm should have befallen that true Christian woman, whom ye call the "Old Maid in the Winding-Sheet." '

Behold, then, the venerable clergyman ascending the steps of the mansion, with a torch-bearer behind him. It was the elderly man, who had spoken to the Old Maid, and the same who had afterwards explained the shield of arms, and recognized the features of the negro. Like their predecessors, they gave three raps, with the iron hammer.

'Old Cæsar cometh not,' observed the priest. 'Well I wot, he no longer doth service in this mansion.'

'Assuredly, then, it was something worse, in old Cæsar's likeness!' said the other adventurer.

'Be it as God wills,' answered the clergyman. 'See! my strength, though it be much decayed, hath sufficed to open this heavy door. Let us enter, and pass up the staircase.'

Here occurred a singular exemplification of the dreamy state of a very old man's mind. As they ascended the wide flight of stairs, the aged clergyman appeared to move with caution, occasionally standing aside, and oftener bending his head, as it were in salutation, thus practicing all the gestures of one who makes his way through a throng. Reaching the head of the staircase, he looked around, with sad and solemn benignity, laid aside his staff, bared his hoary locks, and was evidently on the point of commencing a prayer.

'Reverend Sir,' said his attendant, who conceived this a very suitable prelude to their further search, 'would it not be well, that the people join with us in prayer?'

'Well-a-day!' cried the old clergyman, staring strangely around him. 'Art thou here with me, and none other? Verily, past times were present to me, and I deemed that I was to make a funeral prayer, as many a time heretofore, from the head of this staircase. Of a truth, I saw the shades of many that are gone. Yea, I have prayed at their burials, one after another, and the "Old Maid in the Winding-Sheet" hath seen them to their graves!'

Being now more thoroughly awake to their present purpose, he took his staff, and struck forcibly on the floor, till there came an echo from each deserted chamber, but no menial, to answer their summons. They therefore walked along the passage, and again paused, opposite to the great front window, through which was seen the crowd, in the shadow and partial moonlight of the street beneath. On their right hand, was the open door of a chamber, and a closed one on their left. The clergyman pointed his cane to the carved oak pannel of the latter.

'Within that chamber,' observed he, 'a whole life-time since, did I sit by the death-bed of a goodly young man, who, being now at the last gasp—'

Apparently, there was some powerful excitement in the ideas which had now flashed across his mind. He snatched the torch from his companion's hand, and threw open the door with such sudden violence, that the flame was extinguished, leaving them no other light than the moonbeams, which fell through two windows into the spacious chamber. It was sufficient to discover all that could be known. In a high-backed, oaken arm-chair, upright, with her hands clasped across her breast, and her head thrown back, sat the 'Old Maid in the Winding-Sheet.' The stately dame had fallen on her knees, with her forehead on the holy knees of the Old Maid, one hand upon the floor, and the other pressed convulsively against her heart. It clutched a lock of hair, once sable, now discolored with a greenish mould. As the priest and layman advanced into the chamber, the Old Maid's features assumed such a semblance of shifting expression, that they trusted to hear the whole mystery explained, by a single word. But it was only the shadow of a tattered curtain, waving betwixt the dead face and the moonlight.

'Both dead!' said the venerable man. 'Then who shall divulge the secret? Methinks it glimmers to-and-fro in my mind, like the light and shadow across the Old Maid's face. And now, 'tis gone!'

The Vision of the Fountain

AT fifteen, I became a resident in a country village, more than a hundred miles from home. The morning after my arrival—a September morning, but warm and bright as any in July—I rambled into a wood of oaks, with a few walnut-trees intermixed, forming the closest shade above my head. The ground was rocky, uneven, overgrown with bushes and clumps of young saplings, and traversed only by cattle-paths. The track, which I chanced to follow, led me to a crystal spring, with a border of grass, as freshly green as on May morning, and overshadowed by the limb of a great oak. One solitary sunbeam found its way down, and played like a goldfish in the water.

From my childhood, I have loved to gaze into a spring. The water filled a circular basin, small, but deep, and set round with stones, some of which were covered with slimy moss, the others naked, and of variegated hue, reddish, white, and brown. The bottom was covered with coarse sand, which sparkled in the lonely sunbeam, and seemed to illuminate the spring with an unborrowed light. In one spot, the gush of the water violently agitated the sand, but without obscuring the fountain, or breaking the glassiness of its surface. It appeared as if some living creature were about to emerge, the Naiad of the spring, perhaps, in the shape of a beautiful young woman, with a gown of filmy water-moss, a belt of rainbow drops, and a cold, pure, passionless countenance. How would the beholder shiver, pleasantly, yet fearfully, to see her sitting on one of the stones, paddling her white feet in the ripples, and throwing up water, to sparkle in the sun! Wherever she laid her hands on grass and flowers, they would immediately be moist, as with morning dew. Then would she set about her labors, like a careful housewife, to clear the fountain of withered leaves, and bits of slimy wood, and old acorns from the oaks above, and grains of corn left by cattle in drinking, till the bright sand, in the bright water, were like a treasury of diamonds. But, should the intruder approach too near, he would find only the drops of a summer shower, glistening about the spot where he had seen her.

Reclining on the border of grass, where the dewy goddess should have been, I bent forward, and a pair of eyes met mine within the watery mirror. They were the reflection of my own. I looked again, and lo! another face, deeper in the fountain than my own image, more distinct in all the features, yet faint as thought. The vision had the aspect of a fair young girl, with locks of paly gold. A mirthful expression laughed in the eyes and dimpled over the whole shadowy countenance, till it seemed just what a fountain would be, if, while dancing merrily into the sunshine, it should assume the shape of woman. Through the dim rosiness of the cheeks, I could see the brown leaves, the slimy twigs, the acorns, and the sparkling sand. The solitary sunbeam was diffused among the golden hair, which melted into its faint brightness, and became a glory round that head so beautiful!

My description can give no idea how suddenly the fountain was thus tenanted, and how soon it was left desolate. I breathed; and there was the face! I held my breath; and it was gone! Had it passed away, or faded into nothing? I doubted whether it had ever been.

My sweet readers, what a dreamy and delicious hour did I spend, where that vision found and left me! For a long time, I sat perfectly still, waiting till it should reappear, and fearful that the slightest motion, or even the flutter of my breath, might frighten it away. Thus have I often started from a pleasant dream, and then kept quiet, in hopes to wile it back. Deep were my musings, as to the race and attributes of that ethereal being. Had I created her? Was she the daughter of my fancy, akin to those strange shapes which peep under the lids of children's eyes? And did her beauty gladden me, for that one moment, and then die? Or was she a water-nymph within the fountain, or fairy, or woodland goddess peeping over my shoulder, or the ghost of some forsaken maiden, who had drowned herself for love? Or, in good truth, had a lovely girl, with a warm heart, and lips that would bear pressure, stolen softly behind me, and thrown her image into the spring?

I watched and waited, but no vision came again. I departed, but with a spell upon me, which drew me back, that same afternoon, to the haunted spring. There was the water gushing, the sand sparkling, and the sunbeam glimmering. There the vision was not, but only a great frog, the hermit of that solitude, who immediately withdrew his speckled snout and made himself invisible, all except a pair of long legs, beneath a stone. Methought he had a devilish look! I could have slain him as an enchanter, who kept the mysterious beauty imprisoned in the fountain.

Sad and heavy, I was returning to the village. Between me and the church-spire, rose a little hill, and on its summit a group of trees, insulated from all the rest of the wood, with their own share of radiance hovering on them from the west, and their own solitary shadow falling to the east. The afternoon being far declined, the sunshine was almost pensive, and the shade almost cheerful; glory and gloom were mingled in the placid light; as if the spirits of the Day and Evening had met in friendship under those trees, and found themselves akin. I was admiring the picture, when the shape of a young girl emerged from behind the clump of oaks. My heart knew her; it was the Vision; but, so distant and ethereal did she seem, so unmixed with earth, so imbued with the pensive glory of the spot where she was standing, that my spirit sunk within me, sadder than before. How could I ever reach her!

While I gazed, a sudden shower came pattering down upon the leaves. In a moment the air was full of brightness, each rain-drop catching a portion of sunlight as it fell, and the whole gentle shower appearing like a mist, just substantial enough to bear the burthen of radiance. A rainbow, vivid as Niagara's, was painted in the air. Its southern limb came down before the group of trees, and enveloped the fair Vision, as if the hues of Heaven were the only garment for her beauty. When the rainbow vanished, she, who had seemed a part of it, was no longer there. Was her existence absorbed in nature's loveliest phenomenon, and did her pure frame dissolve away in the varied light? Yet, I would not despair of her return; for, robed in the rainbow, she was the emblem of Hope.

Thus did the Vision leave me; and many a doleful day succeeded to the parting moment. By the spring, and in the wood, and on the hill, and through the village; at dewy sunrise, burning noon, and at that magic hour of sunset, when she had vanished from my sight, I sought her, but in vain. Weeks came and went, months rolled away, and she appeared not in them. I imparted my mystery to none, but wandered to-and-fro, or sat in solitude, like one that had caught a glimpse of Heaven, and could take no more joy on earth. I withdrew into an inner world, where my thoughts lived and breathed, and the Vision in the midst of them. Without intending it, I became at once the author and hero of a romance, conjuring up rivals, imagining events, the actions of others and my own, and experiencing every change of passion, till jealousy and despair had their end in bliss. Oh, had I the burning fancy of my early youth, with manhood's colder gift, the power of expression, your hearts, sweet ladies, should flutter at my tale!

In the middle of January, I was summoned home. The day before my departure, visiting the spots which had been hallowed by the Vision, I found that the spring had a frozen bosom, and nothing but the snow and a glare of winter sunshine on the hill of the rainbow. 'Let me hope,' thought I, 'or my heart will be as icy as the fountain, and the whole world as desolate as this snowy hill.' Most of the day was spent in preparing for the journey, which was to commence at four o'clock the next morning. About an hour after supper, when all was in readiness, I descended from my chamber to the sitting-room, to take leave of the old clergyman and his family, with whom I had been an inmate. A gust of wind blew out my lamp as I passed through the entry.

According to their invariable custom, so pleasant a one when the fire blazes cheerfully, the family were sitting in the parlor, with no other light than what came from the hearth. As the good clergyman's scanty stipend compelled him to use all sorts of economy, the foundation of his fires was always a large heap of tan, or ground bark, which would smoulder away, from morning till night, with a dull warmth and no flame. This evening, the heap of tan was newly put on, and surmounted with three sticks of red oak, full of moisture, and a few pieces of dry pine, that had not yet kindled. There was no light, except the little that came sullenly from two half-burnt brands, without even glimmering on the andirons. But

I knew the position of the old minister's arm-chair, and also where his wife sat, with her knitting-work, and how to avoid his two daughters, one a stout country lass, and the other a consumptive girl. Groping through the gloom, I found my own place next to that of the son, a learned collegian, who had come home to keep school in the village during the winter vacation. I noticed that there was less room than usual, to-night, between the collegian's chair and mine.

As people are always taciturn in the dark, not a word was said for some time after my entrance. Nothing broke the stillness but the regular click of the matron's knitting-needles. At times, the fire threw out a brief and dusky gleam, which twinkled on the old man's glasses, and hovered doubtfully round our circle, but was far too faint to portray the individuals who composed it. Were we not like ghosts? Dreamy as the scene was, might it not be a type of the mode in which departed people, who had known and loved each other here, would hold communion in eternity? We were aware of each other's presence, not by sight, nor sound, nor touch, but by an inward consciousness. Would it not be so among the dead?

The silence was interrupted by the consumptive daughter, addressing a remark to some one in the circle, whom she called Rachel. Her tremulous and decayed accents were answered by a single word, but in a voice that made me start, and bend towards the spot whence it had proceeded. Had I ever heard that sweet, low tone? If not, why did it rouse up so many old recollections, or mockeries of such, the shadows of things familiar, yet unknown, and fill my mind with confused images of her features who had spoken, though buried in the gloom of the parlor? Whom had my heart recognized, that it throbbed so? I listened, to catch her gentle breathing, and strove, by the intensity of my gaze, to picture forth a shape where none was visible.

Suddenly, the dry pine caught; the fire blazed up with a ruddy glow; and where the darkness had been, there was she—the Vision of the Fountain! A spirit of radiance only, she had vanished with the rainbow, and appeared again in the fire-light, perhaps to flicker with the blaze, and be gone. Yet, her cheek was rosy and life-like, and her features, in the bright warmth of the room, were even sweeter and tenderer than my recollection of them. She knew me! The mirthful expression, that had laughed in her eyes and dimpled over her countenance, when I beheld her faint beauty in the fountain, was laughing and dimpling there now. One moment, our glance mingled—the next, down rolled the heap of tan upon the kindled wood—and darkness snatched away that Daughter of the Light, and gave her back to me no more!

Fair ladies, there is nothing more to tell. Must the simple mystery be revealed, then, that Rachel was the daughter of the village 'Squire, and had left home for a boarding-school, the morning after I arrived, and returned the day before my departure? If I transformed her to an angel, it is what every youthful lover does for his mistress. Therein consists the essence of my story. But, slight the change, sweet maids, to make angels of yourselves!

The Devil in Manuscript

O N a bitter evening of December, I arrived by mail in a large town, which was then the residence of an intimate friend, one of those gifted youths who cultivate poetry and the belles lettres, and call themselves students at law. My first business, after supper, was to visit him at the office of his distinguished instructer. As I have said, it was a bitter night, clear starlight, but cold as Nova Zembla—the shop-windows along the street being frosted, so as almost to hide the lights, while the wheels of coaches thundered equally loud over frozen earth and pavements of stone. There was no snow, either on the ground or the roofs of the houses. The wind blew so violently, that I had but to spread my cloak like a mainsail, and scud along the street at the rate of ten knots, greatly envied by other navigators who were beating slowly up, with the gale right in their teeth. One of these I capsized, but was gone on the wings of the wind before he could even vociferate an oath.

After this picture of an inclement night, behold us seated by a great blazing fire, which looked so comfortable and delicious that I felt inclined to lie down and roll among the hot coals. The usual furniture of a lawyer's office was around us—rows of volumes in sheepskin, and a multitude of writs, summonses, and other legal papers, scattered over the desks and tables. But there were certain objects which seemed to intimate that we had little dread of the intrusion of clients, or of the learned counsellor himself, who, indeed, was attending court in a distant town. A tall, decanter-shaped bottle stood on the table, between two tumblers, and beside a pile of blotted manuscripts, altogether dissimilar to any law documents recognized in our courts. My friend, whom I shall call Oberon—it was a name of fancy and friendship between him and me—my friend Oberon looked at these papers with a peculiar expression of disquietude.

'I do believe,' said he, soberly, 'or, at least, I would believe, if I chose, that there is a devil in this pile of blotted papers. You have read them, and know what I mean—that conception, in which I endeavored to embody the character of a fiend, as represented in our traditions and the written records of witchcraft. Oh! I have a horror of what was created in my own brain, and shudder at the manuscripts in which I gave that dark idea a sort of material existence. Would they were out of my sight!'

'And of mine too,' thought I.

'You remember,' continued Oberon, 'how the hellish thing used to suck away the happiness of those who, by a simple concession that seemed almost innocent, subjected themselves to his power. Just so my peace is gone, and all by these accursed manuscripts. Have you felt nothing of the same influence?'

'Nothing,' replied I, 'unless the spell be hid in a desire to turn novelist, after reading your delightful tales.'

'Novelist!' exclaimed Oberon, half seriously. 'Then, indeed, my devil has his claw on you! You are gone! You cannot even pray for deliverance! But we will be the last and only victims; for this night I mean to burn the manuscripts, and commit the fiend to his retribution in the flames.'

'Burn your tales!' repeated I, startled at the desperation of the idea.

'Even so,' said the author, despondingly. 'You cannot conceive what an effect the composition of these tales has had on me. I have become ambitious of a bubble, and careless of solid reputation. I am surrounding myself with shadows, which bewilder me, by aping the realities of life. They have drawn me aside from the beaten path of the world, and led me into a strange sort of solitude—a solitude in the midst of men—where nobody wishes for what I do, nor thinks nor feels as I do. The tales have done all this. When they are ashes, perhaps I shall be as I was before they had existence. Moreover, the sacrifice is less than you may suppose; since nobody will publish them.'

'That does make a difference, indeed,' said I.

'They have been offered, by letter,' continued Oberon, reddening with vexation, 'to some seventeen booksellers. It would make you stare to read their answers; and read them you should, only that I burnt them as fast as they arrived. One man publishes nothing but school-books; another has five novels already under examination—'

'What a voluminous mass the unpublished literature of America must be!' cried I.

'Oh! the Alexandrian manuscripts were nothing to it,' said my friend. 'Well; another gentleman is just giving up business, on purpose, I verily believe, to escape publishing my book. Several, however, would not absolutely decline the agency, on my advancing half the cost of an edition, and giving bonds for the remainder, besides a high percentage to themselves, whether the book sells or not. Another advises a subscription.'

'The villain!' exclaimed I.

'A fact!' said Oberon. 'In short, of all the seventeen booksellers, only one has vouchsafed even to read my tales; and he—a literary dabbler himself, I should judge—has the impertinence to criticize them, proposing what he calls vast improvements, and concluding, after a general sentence of condemnation, with the definitive assurance that he will not be concerned on any terms.'

'It might not be amiss to pull that fellow's nose,' remarked I.

'If the whole "trade" had one common nose, there would be some satisfaction in pulling it,' answered the author. 'But, there does seem to be one honest man among these seventeen unrighteous ones, and he tells me fairly, that no American publisher will meddle with an American work, seldom if by a known writer, and never if by a new one, unless at the writer's risk.'

'The paltry rogues!' cried I. 'Will they live by literature, and yet risk nothing for its sake? But, after all, you might publish on your own account.'

'And so I might,' replied Oberon. 'But the devil of the business is this. These people have put me so out of conceit with the tales, that I loathe the very thought of them, and actually experience a physical sickness of the stomach, whenever I glance at them on the table. I tell you there is a demon in them! I anticipate a wild enjoyment in seeing them in the blaze; such as I should feel in taking vengeance on an enemy, or destroying something noxious.'

I did not very strenuously oppose this determination, being privately of opinion, in spite of my partiality for the author, that his tales would make a more brilliant appearance in the

fire than anywhere else. Before proceeding to execution, we
broached the bottle of champagne, which Oberon had provided for keeping up his spirits in this doleful business. We
swallowed each a tumblerfull, in sparkling commotion; it
went bubbling down our throats, and brightened my eyes at
once, but left my friend sad and heavy as before. He drew the
tales towards him, with a mixture of natural affection and natural disgust, like a father taking a deformed infant into his
arms.

'Pooh! Pish! Pshaw!' exclaimed he, holding them at arm's
length. 'It was Gray's idea of Heaven, to lounge on a sofa
and read new novels. Now, what more appropriate torture
would Dante himself have contrived, for the sinner who per-
petrates a bad book, than to be continually turning over the
manuscript?'

'It would fail of effect,' said I, 'because a bad author is always his own great admirer.'

'I lack that one characteristic of my tribe, the only desirable
one,' observed Oberon. 'But how many recollections throng
upon me, as I turn over these leaves! This scene came into my
fancy as I walked along a hilly road, on a starlight October
evening; in the pure and bracing air, I became all soul, and
felt as if I could climb the sky and run a race along the Milky
Way. Here is another tale, in which I wrapt myself during a
dark and dreary night-ride in the month of March, till the
rattling of the wheels and the voices of my companions
seemed like faint sounds of a dream, and my visions a bright
reality. That scribbled page describes shadows which I summoned to my bedside at midnight; they would not depart
when I bade them; the gray dawn came, and found me wide
awake and feverish, the victim of my own enchantments!'

'There must have been a sort of happiness in all this,' said
I, smitten with a strange longing to make proof of it.

'There may be happiness in a fever fit,' replied the author.
'And then the various moods in which I wrote! Sometimes
my ideas were like precious stones under the earth, requiring
toil to dig them up, and care to polish and brighten them;
but often, a delicious stream of thought would gush out upon
the page at once, like water sparkling up suddenly in the desert; and when it had passed, I gnawed my pen hopelessly, or

blundered on with cold and miserable toil, as if there were a wall of ice between me and my subject.'

'Do you now perceive a corresponding difference,' inquired I, 'between the passages which you wrote so coldly, and those fervid flashes of the mind?'

'No,' said Oberon, tossing the manuscripts on the table. 'I find no traces of the golden pen, with which I wrote in characters of fire. My treasure of fairy coin is changed to worthless dross. My picture, painted in what seemed the loveliest hues, presents nothing but a faded and indistinguishable surface. I have been eloquent and poetical and humorous in a dream— and behold! it is all nonsense, now that I am awake.'

My friend now threw sticks of wood and dry chips upon the fire, and seeing it blaze like Nebuchadnezzar's furnace, seized the champagne bottle, and drank two or three brimming bumpers, successively. The heady liquor combined with his agitation to throw him into a species of rage. He laid violent hands on the tales. In one instant more, their faults and beauties would alike have vanished in a glowing purgatory. But, all at once, I remembered passages of high imagination, deep pathos, original thoughts, and points of such varied excellence, that the vastness of the sacrifice struck me most forcibly. I caught his arm.

'Surely, you do not mean to burn them!' I exclaimed.

'Let me alone!' cried Oberon, his eyes flashing fire. 'I will burn them! Not a scorched syllable shall escape! Would you have me a damned author?—To undergo sneers, taunts, abuse, and cold neglect, and faint praise, bestowed, for pity's sake, against the giver's conscience! A hissing and a laughing-stock to my own traitorous thoughts! An outlaw from the protection of the grave—one whose ashes every careless foot might spurn, unhonored in life, and remembered scornfully in death! Am I to bear all this, when yonder fire will ensure me from the whole? No! There go the tales! May my hand wither when it would write another!'

The deed was done. He had thrown the manuscripts into the hottest of the fire, which at first seemed to shrink away, but soon curled around them, and made them a part of its own fervent brightness. Oberon stood gazing at the conflagration, and shortly began to soliloquize, in the wildest strain, as if Fancy resisted and became riotous, at the moment when he would have compelled her to ascend that funeral pile. His words described objects which he appeared to discern in the fire, fed by his own precious thoughts; perhaps the thousand visions, which the writer's magic had incorporated with those pages, became visible to him in the dissolving heat, brightening forth ere they vanished forever; while the smoke, the vivid sheets of flame, the ruddy and whitening coals, caught the aspect of a varied scenery.

'They blaze,' said he, 'as if I had steeped them in the intensest spirit of genius. There I see my lovers clasped in each other's arms. How pure the flame that bursts from their glowing hearts! And yonder the features of a villain, writhing in the fire that shall torment him to eternity. My holy men, my pious and angelic women, stand like martyrs amid the flames, their mild eyes lifted heavenward. Ring out the bells! A city is on fire. See!—destruction roars through my dark forests, while the lakes boil up in steaming billows, and the mountains are volcanoes, and the sky kindles with a lurid brightness! All elements are but one pervading flame! Ha! The fiend!'

I was somewhat startled by this latter exclamation. The tales were almost consumed, but just then threw forth a broad sheet of fire, which flickered as with laughter, making the whole room dance in its brightness, and then roared portentously up the chimney.

'You saw him? You must have seen him!' cried Oberon. 'How he glared at me and laughed, in that last sheet of flame, with just the features that I imagined for him! Well! The tales are gone.'

The papers were indeed reduced to a heap of black cinders, with a multitude of sparks hurrying confusedly among them, the traces of the pen being now represented by white lines, and the whole mass fluttering to and fro, in the draughts of air. The destroyer knelt down to look at them.

'What is more potent than fire!' said he, in his gloomiest tone. 'Even thought, invisible and incorporeal as it is, cannot escape it. In this little time, it has annihilated the creations of long nights and days, which I could no more reproduce, in their first glow and freshness, than cause ashes and whitened bones to rise up and live. There, too, I sacrificed the unborn children of my mind. All that I had accomplished—all that I planned for future years—has perished by one common ruin, and left only this heap of embers. The deed has been my fate. And what remains? A weary and aimless life—a long repentance of this hour—and at last an obscure grave, where they will bury and forget me.'

As the author concluded his dolorous moan, the extinguished embers arose and settled down and arose again, and finally flew up the chimney, like a demon with sable wings. Just as they disappeared, there was a loud and solitary cry in the street below us. 'Fire! Fire!' Other voices caught up that terrible word, and it speedily became the shout of a multitude. Oberon started to his feet, in fresh excitement.

'A fire on such a night!' cried he. 'The wind blows a gale, and wherever it whirls the flames, the roofs will flash up like gunpowder. Every pump is frozen up, and boiling water would turn to ice the moment it was flung from the engine. In an hour, this wooden town will be one great bonfire! What a glorious scene for my next——Pshaw!'

The street was now all alive with footsteps, and the air full of voices. We heard one engine thundering round a corner, and another rattling from a distance over the pavements. The bells of three steeples clanged out at once, spreading the alarm to many a neighboring town, and expressing hurry, confusion and terror, so inimitably that I could almost distinguish in their peal the burthen of the universal cry—'Fire! Fire! Fire!'

'What is so eloquent as their iron tongues!' exclaimed Oberon. 'My heart leaps and trembles, but not with fear. And that other sound, too—deep and awful as a mighty organ—the roar and thunder of the multitude on the pavement below! Come! We are losing time. I will cry out in the loudest of the uproar, and mingle my spirit with the wildest of the confusion, and be a bubble on the top of the ferment!'

From the first outcry, my forebodings had warned me of the true object and centre of alarm. There was nothing now but uproar—above, beneath, and around us; footsteps stumbling pell-mell up the public stair-case, eager shouts and heavy thumps at the door, the whiz and dash of water from the engines, and the crash of furniture thrown upon the pavement. At once, the truth flashed upon my friend. His frenzy took the hue of joy, and, with a wild gesture of exultation, he leaped almost to the ceiling of the chamber.

'My tales!' cried Oberon. 'The chimney! The roof! The Fiend has gone forth by night, and startled thousands in fear and wonder from their beds! Here I stand—a triumphant author! Huzza! Huzza! My brain has set the town on fire! Huzza!'

Sketches from Memory

THE NOTCH OF THE WHITE MOUNTAINS

It was now the middle of September. We had come since sunrise from Bartlett, passing up through the valley of the Saco, which extends between mountainous walls, sometimes with a steep ascent, but often as level as a church-aisle. All that day and two preceding ones, we had been loitering towards the heart of the White Mountains—those old crystal hills, whose mysterious brilliancy had gleamed upon our distant wanderings before we thought of visiting them. Height after height had risen and towered one above another, till the clouds began to hang below the peaks. Down their slopes, were the red path-ways of the Slides, those avalanches of earth, stones and trees, which descend into the hollows, leaving vestiges of their track, hardly to be effaced by the vegetation of ages. We had mountains behind us and mountains on each side, and a group of mightier ones ahead. Still our road went up along the Saco, right towards the centre of that group, as if to climb above the clouds, in its passage to the farther region.

In old times, the settlers used to be astounded by the inroads of the northern Indians, coming down upon them from this mountain rampart, through some defile known only to themselves. It is indeed a wondrous path. A demon, it might be fancied, or one of the Titans, was travelling up the valley, elbowing the heights carelessly aside as he passed, till at length a great mountain took its stand directly across his intended road. He tarries not for such an obstacle, but rending it asunder, a thousand feet from peak to base, discloses its treasures of hidden minerals, its sunless waters, all the secrets of the mountain's inmost heart, with a mighty fracture of rugged precipices on each side. This is the Notch of the White Hills. Shame on me, that I have attempted to describe it by so mean an image—feeling, as I do, that it is one of those symbolic scenes, which lead the mind to the sentiment, though not to the conception, of Omnipotence.

338

We had now reached a narrow passage, which showed almost the appearance of having been cut by human strength and artifice in the solid rock. There was a wall of granite on each side, high and precipitous, especially on our right, and so smooth that a few evergreens could hardly find foothold enough to grow there. This is the entrance, or, in the direction we were going, the extremity of the romantic defile of the Notch. Before emerging from it, the rattling of wheels approached behind us, and a stage-coach rumbled out of the mountain, with seats on top and trunks behind, and a smart driver, in a drab great-coat, touching the wheel horses with the whip-stock, and reining in the leaders. To my mind, there was a sort of poetry in such an incident, hardly inferior to what would have accompanied the painted array of an Indian war-party, gliding forth from the same wild chasm. All the passengers, except a very fat lady on the back seat, had alighted. One was a mineralogist, a scientific, green-spectacled figure in black, bearing a heavy hammer, with which he did great damage to the precipices, and put the fragments in his pocket. Another was a well-dressed young man, who carried an opera-glass set in gold, and seemed to be making a quotation from some of Byron's rhapsodies on mountain scenery. There was also a trader, returning from Portland to the upper part of Vermont; and a fair young girl, with a very faint bloom, like one of those pale and delicate flowers, which sometimes occur among Alpine cliffs.

They disappeared, and we followed them, passing through a deep pine forest, which, for some miles, allowed us to see nothing but its own dismal shade. Towards night-fall, we reached a level amphitheatre, surrounded by a great rampart of hills, which shut out the sunshine long before it left the external world. It was here that we obtained our first view, except at a distance, of the principal group of mountains. They are majestic, and even awful, when contemplated in a proper mood; yet, by their breadth of base, and the long ridges which support them, give the idea of immense bulk, rather than of towering height. Mount Washington, indeed, looked near to Heaven; he was white with snow a mile downward, and had caught the only cloud that was sailing through the atmosphere, to veil his head. Let us forget the other

names of American statesmen, that have been stamped upon
these hills, but still call the loftiest—WASHINGTON. Mountains are Earth's undecaying monuments. They must stand
while she endures, and never should be consecrated to the
mere great men of their own age and country, but to the
mighty ones alone, whose glory is universal, and whom all
time will render illustrious.

The air, not often sultry in this elevated region, nearly two
thousand feet above the sea, was now sharp and cold, like
that of a clear November evening in the low-lands. By morning, probably, there would be a frost, if not a snow-fall, on
the grass and rye, and an icy surface over the standing water.
I was glad to perceive a prospect of comfortable quarters, in
a house which we were approaching, and of pleasant company in the guests who were assembled at the door.

OUR EVENING PARTY AMONG THE MOUNTAINS

We stood in front of a good substantial farm-house, of old
date in that wild country. A sign over the door denoted it to
be the White Mountain Post-Office, an establishment which
distributes letters and newspapers to perhaps a score of persons, comprising the population of two or three townships
among the hills. The broad and weighty antlers of a deer, 'a
stag of ten,' were fastened at a corner of the house; a fox's
bushy tail was nailed beneath them; and a huge black paw lay
on the ground, newly severed and still bleeding—the trophy
of a bear-hunt. Among several persons collected about the
door-steps, the most remarkable was a sturdy mountaineer, of
six feet two and corresponding bulk, with a heavy set of features, such as might be moulded on his own blacksmith's anvil, but yet indicative of mother-wit and rough humor. As we
appeared, he uplifted a tin trumpet, four or five feet long, and
blew a tremendous blast, either in honor of our arrival, or to
awaken an echo from the opposite hill.

Ethan Crawford's guests were of such a motley description
as to form quite a picturesque group, seldom seen together,
except at some place like this, at once the pleasure-house of
fashionable tourists, and the homely inn of country travellers.
Among the company at the door, were the mineralogist and

the owner of the gold opera-glass, whom we had encountered in the Notch; two Georgian gentlemen, who had chilled their southern blood, that morning, on the top of Mount Washington; a physician and his wife, from Conway; a trader, of Burlington, and an old 'Squire, of the Green Mountains; and two young married couples, all the way from Massachusetts, on the matrimonial jaunt. Besides these strangers, the rugged county of Coos, in which we were, was represented by half a dozen wood-cutters, who had slain a bear in the forest and smitten off his paw.

I had joined the party, and had a moment's leisure to examine them, before the echo of Ethan's blast returned from the hill. Not one, but many echoes had caught up the harsh and tuneless sound, untwisted its complicated threads, and found a thousand aerial harmonies in one stern trumpet-tone. It was a distinct, yet distant and dreamlike symphony of melodious instruments, as if an airy band had been hidden on the hill-side, and made faint music at the summons. No subsequent trial produced so clear, delicate, and spiritual a concert as the first. A field-piece was then discharged from the top of a neighboring hill, and gave birth to one long reverberation, which ran round the circle of mountains in an unbroken chain of sound, and rolled away without a separate echo. After these experiments, the cold atmosphere drove us all into the house, with the keenest appetites for supper.

It did one's heart good to see the great fires that were kindled in the parlor and bar-room, especially the latter, where the fire-place was built of rough stone, and might have contained the trunk of an old tree for a back-log. A man keeps a comfortable hearth when his own forest is at his very door. In the parlor, when the evening was fairly set in, we held our hands before our eyes, to shield them from the ruddy glow, and began a pleasant variety of conversation. The mineralogist and the physician talked about the invigorating qualities of the mountain air, and its excellent effect on Ethan Crawford's father, an old man of seventy-five, with the unbroken frame of middle life. The two brides and the doctor's wife held a whispered discussion, which, by their frequent titterings and a blush or two, seemed to have reference to the trials or enjoyments of the matrimonial state. The bridegrooms sat together in a corner, rigidly silent, like Quakers whom the spirit moveth not, being still in the odd predicament of bashfulness towards their own young wives. The Green Mountain 'Squire chose me for his companion, and described the difficulties he had met with, half a century ago, in travelling from the Connecticut river through the Notch to Conway, now a single day's journey, though it had cost him eighteen. The Georgians held the album between them, and favored us with the few specimens of its contents, which they considered ridiculous enough to be worth hearing. One extract met with deserved applause. It was a 'Sonnet to the Snow on Mount Washington,' and had been contributed that very afternoon, bearing a signature of great distinction in magazines and annuals. The lines were elegant and full of fancy, but too remote from familiar sentiment, and cold as their subject, resembling those curious specimens of crystallized vapor, which I observed next day on the mountain-top. The poet was understood to be the young gentleman of the gold opera-glass, who heard our laudatory remarks with the composure of a veteran.

Such was our party, and such their ways of amusement. But, on a winter evening, another set of guests assembled at the hearth, where these summer travellers were now sitting. I once had it in contemplation to spend a month hereabouts, in sleighing-time, for the sake of studying the yeomen of New-England, who then elbow each other through the Notch by hundreds, on their way to Portland. There could be no better school for such a purpose than Ethan Crawford's inn. Let the student go thither in December, sit down with the teamsters at their meals, share their evening merriment, and repose with them at night, when every bed has its three occupants, and parlor, bar-room and kitchen are strewn with slumberers around the fire. Then let him rise before daylight, button his great-coat, muffle up his ears, and stride with the departing caravan a mile or two, to see how sturdily they make head against the blast. A treasure of characteristic traits will repay all inconveniences, even should a frozen nose be of the number.

The conversation of our party soon became more animated and sincere, and we recounted some traditions of the Indians,

who believed that the father and mother of their race were
saved from a deluge by ascending the peak of Mount Washington. The children of that pair have been overwhelmed, and
found no such refuge. In the mythology of the savage, these
mountains were afterwards considered sacred and inaccessible, full of unearthly wonders, illuminated at lofty heights by
the blaze of precious stones, and inhabited by deities, who
sometimes shrouded themselves in the snowstorm, and came
down on the lower world. There are few legends more poetical than that of the 'Great Carbuncle' of the White Mountains. The belief was communicated to the English settlers,
and is hardly yet extinct, that a gem, of such immense size as
to be seen shining miles away, hangs from a rock over a clear,
deep lake, high up among the hills. They who had once beheld its splendor, were enthralled with an unutterable yearning to possess it. But a spirit guarded that inestimable jewel,
and bewildered the adventurer with a dark mist from the enchanted lake. Thus, life was worn away in the vain search for
an unearthly treasure, till at length the deluded one went up
the mountain, still sanguine as in youth, but returned no
more. On this theme, methinks I could frame a tale with a
deep moral.

The hearts of the pale-faces would not thrill to these superstitions of the red men, though we spoke of them in the
centre of their haunted region. The habits and sentiments of
that departed people were too distinct from those of their
successors to find much real sympathy. It has often been a
matter of regret to me, that I was shut out from the most
peculiar field of American fiction, by an inability to see any
romance, or poetry, or grandeur, or beauty in the Indian
character, at least, till such traits were pointed out by others.
I do abhor an Indian story. Yet no writer can be more secure
of a permanent place in our literature, than the biographer of
the Indian chiefs. His subject, as referring to tribes which
have mostly vanished from the earth, gives him a right to be
placed on a classic shelf, apart from the merits which will sustain him there.

I made inquiries whether, in his researches about these
parts, our mineralogist had found the three 'Silver Hills,'
which an Indian sachem sold to an Englishman, nearly two

hundred years ago, and the treasure of which the posterity of the purchaser have been looking for ever since. But the man of science had ransacked every hill along the Saco, and knew nothing of these prodigious piles of wealth. By this time, as usual with men on the eve of great adventure, we had prolonged our session deep into the night, considering how early we were to set out on our six miles' ride to the foot of Mount Washington. There was now a general breaking-up. I scrutinized the faces of the two bridegrooms, and saw but little probability of their leaving the bosom of earthly bliss, in the first week of the honey-moon, and at the frosty hour of three, to climb above the clouds. Nor, when I felt how sharp the wind was, as it rushed through a broken pane, and eddied between the chinks of my unplastered chamber, did I anticipate much alacrity on my own part, though we were to seek for the 'Great Carbuncle.'

THE CANAL-BOAT

I was inclined to be poetical about the Grand Canal. In my imagination, De Witt Clinton was an enchanter, who had waved his magic wand from the Hudson to Lake Erie, and united them by a watery highway, crowded with the commerce of two worlds, till then inaccessible to each other. This simple and mighty conception had conferred inestimable value on spots which Nature seemed to have thrown carelessly into the great body of the earth, without foreseeing that they could ever attain importance. I pictured the surprise of the sleepy Dutchmen when the new river first glittered by their doors, bringing them hard cash or foreign commodities, in exchange for their hitherto unmarketable produce. Surely, the water of this canal must be the most fertilizing of all fluids; for it causes towns—with their masses of brick and stone, their churches and theatres, their business and hubbub, their luxury and refinement, their gay dames and polished citizens—to spring up, till, in time, the wondrous stream may flow between two continuous lines of buildings, through one thronged street, from Buffalo to Albany. I embarked about thirty miles below Utica, determining to voyage along the whole extent of the canal, at least twice in the course of the summer.

Behold us, then, fairly afloat, with three horses harnessed to our vessel, like the steeds of Neptune to a huge scallop-shell, in mythological pictures. Bound to a distant port, we had neither chart nor compass, nor cared about the wind, nor felt the heaving of a billow, nor dreaded shipwreck, however fierce the tempest, in our adventurous navigation of an interminable mud-puddle—for a mud-puddle it seemed, and as dark and turbid as if every kennel in the land paid contribution to it. With an imperceptible current, it holds its drowsy way through all the dismal swamps and unimpressive scenery, that could be found between the great lakes and the sea-coast. Yet there is variety enough, both on the surface of the canal and along its banks, to amuse the traveller, if an overpowering tedium did not deaden his perceptions.

Sometimes we met a black and rusty-looking vessel, laden with lumber, salt from Syracuse, or Genesee flour, and shaped at both ends like a square-toed boot; as if it had two sterns, and were fated always to advance backward. On its deck would be a square hut, and a woman seen through the window at her household work, with a little tribe of children, who perhaps had been born in this strange dwelling and knew no other home. Thus, while the husband smoked his pipe at the helm, and the eldest son rode one of the horses, on went the family, travelling hundreds of miles in their own house, and carrying their fireside with them. The most frequent species of craft were the 'line boats,' which had a cabin at each end, and a great bulk of barrels, bales, and boxes in the midst; or light packets, like our own, decked all over, with a row of curtained windows from stem to stern, and a drowsy face at every one. Once, we encountered a boat, of rude construction, painted all in gloomy black, and manned by three Indians, who gazed at us in silence and with a singular fixedness of eye. Perhaps these three alone, among the ancient possessors of the land, had attempted to derive benefit from the white man's mighty projects, and float along the current of his enterprise. Not long after, in the midst of a swamp and beneath a clouded sky, we overtook a vessel that seemed full of mirth and sunshine. It contained a little colony of Swiss, on their way to Michigan, clad in garments of strange fashion and gay colors, scarlet, yellow and bright blue, singing, laughing, and making merry, in odd tones and a babble of outlandish words. One pretty damsel, with a beautiful pair of naked white arms, addressed a mirthful remark to me; she spoke in her native tongue, and I retorted in good English, both of us laughing heartily at each other's unintelligible wit. I cannot describe how pleasantly this incident affected me. These honest Swiss were an itinerant community of jest and fun, journeying through a gloomy land and among a dull race of money-getting drudges, meeting none to understand their mirth and only one to sympathize with it, yet still retaining the happy lightness of their own spirit.

Had I been on my feet at the time, instead of sailing slowly along in a dirty canal-boat, I should often have paused to contemplate the diversified panorama along the banks of the canal. Sometimes the scene was a forest, dark, dense, and impervious, breaking away occasionally and receding from a lonely tract, covered with dismal black stumps, where, on the verge of the canal, might be seen a log-cottage, and a sallow-faced woman at the window. Lean and aguish, she looked like Poverty personified, half clothed, half fed, and dwelling in a desert, while a tide of wealth was sweeping by her door. Two or three miles further would bring us to a lock, where the slight impediment to navigation had created a little mart of trade. Here would be found commodities of all sorts, enumerated in yellow letters on the window-shutters of a small grocery-store, the owner of which had set his soul to the gathering of coppers and small change, buying and selling through the week, and counting his gains on the blessed Sabbath. The next scene might be the dwelling-houses and stores of a thriving village, built of wood or small gray stones, a church-spire rising in the midst, and generally two taverns, bearing over their piazzas the pompous titles of 'hotel,' 'exchange,' 'tontine,' or 'coffee-house.' Passing on, we glide now into the unquiet heart of an inland city—of Utica, for instance—and find ourselves amid piles of brick, crowded docks and quays, rich warehouses and a busy population. We feel the eager and hurrying spirit of the place, like a stream and eddy whirling us along with it. Through the thickest of the tumult goes the canal, flowing between lofty rows of buildings and arched bridges of hewn stone. Onward, also, go we, till the hum and bustle of struggling enterprise die away behind us, and we are threading an avenue of the ancient woods again.

This sounds not amiss in description, but was so tiresome in reality, that we were driven to the most childish expedients for amusement. An English traveller paraded the deck with a rifle in his walking-stick, and waged war on squirrels and woodpeckers, sometimes sending an unsuccessful bullet among flocks of tame ducks and geese, which abound in the dirty water of the canal. I, also, pelted these foolish birds with apples, and smiled at the ridiculous earnestness of their scrambles for the prize, while the apple bobbed about like a thing of life. Several little accidents afforded us good-natured diversion. At the moment of changing horses, the tow-rope caught a Massachusetts farmer by the leg, and threw him down in a very indescribable posture, leaving a purple mark around his sturdy limb. A new passenger fell flat on his back, in attempting to step on deck, as the boat emerged from under a bridge. Another, in his Sunday clothes, as good luck would have it, being told to leap aboard from the bank, forthwith plunged up to his third waistcoat button in the canal, and was fished out in a very pitiable plight, not at all amended by our three rounds of applause. Anon, a Virginia schoolmaster, too intent on a pocket Virgil to heed the helmsman's warning—'Bridge! bridge!'—was saluted by the said bridge on his knowledge-box. I had prostrated myself, like a pagan before his idol, but heard the dull leaden sound of the contact, and fully expected to see the treasures of the poor man's cranium scattered about the deck. However, as there was no harm done, except a large bump on the head, and probably a corresponding dent in the bridge, the rest of us exchanged glances and laughed quietly. Oh, how pitiless are idle people!

The table being now lengthened through the cabin, and spread for supper, the next twenty minutes were the pleasantest I had spent on the canal—the same space at dinner excepted. At the close of the meal, it had become dusky enough for lamplight. The rain pattered unceasingly on the deck, and sometimes came with a sullen rush against the windows, driven by the wind, as it stirred through an opening of the forest. The intolerable dullness of the scene engendered an evil spirit in me. Perceiving that the Englishman was taking notes in a memorandum-book, with occasional glances round the cabin, I presumed that we were all to figure in a future volume of travels, and amused my ill-humor by falling into the probable vein of his remarks. He would hold up an imaginary mirror, wherein our reflected faces would appear ugly and ridiculous, yet still retain an undeniable likeness to the originals. Then, with more sweeping malice, he would make these caricatures the representatives of great classes of my countrymen.

He glanced at the Virginia schoolmaster, a Yankee by birth, who, to recreate himself, was examining a freshman from Schenectady college, in the conjugation of a Greek verb. Him, the Englishman would portray as the scholar of America, and compare his erudition to a schoolboy's Latin theme, made up of scraps, ill-selected and worse put together. Next, the tourist looked at the Massachusetts farmer, who was delivering a dogmatic harangue on the iniquity of Sunday mails. Here was the far-famed yeoman of New-England; his religion, writes the Englishman, is gloom on the Sabbath, long prayers every morning and eventide, and illiberality at all times; his boasted information is merely an abstract and compound of newspaper paragraphs, Congress debates, caucus harangues, and the argument and judge's charge in his own lawsuits. The bookmonger cast his eye at a Detroit merchant, and began scribbling faster than ever. In this sharp-eyed man, this lean man, of wrinkled brow, we see daring enterprise and close-fisted avarice combined; here is the worshipper of Mammon at noonday; here is the three-times bankrupt, richer after every ruin; here, in one word, (Oh, wicked Englishman to say it!) here is the American! He lifted his eye-glass to inspect a western lady, who at once became aware of the glance, reddened, and retired deeper into the female part of the cabin. Here was the pure, modest, sensitive, and shrinking woman of America; shrinking when no evil is intended; and sensitive like diseased flesh, that thrills if you but point at it; and strangely modest, without confidence in the modesty of other people; and admirably pure, with such a quick apprehension of all impurity.

In this manner, I went all through the cabin, hitting everybody as hard a lash as I could, and laying the whole blame on the infernal Englishman. At length, I caught the eyes of my own image in the looking-glass, where a number of the party were likewise reflected, and among them the Englishman, who, at that moment, was intently observing myself.

The crimson curtain being let down between the ladies and gentlemen, the cabin became a bed-chamber for twenty persons, who were laid on shelves, one above another. For a long time, our various incommodities kept us all awake, except five or six, who were accustomed to sleep nightly amid the uproar of their own snoring, and had little to dread from any other species of disturbance. It is a curious fact, that these snorers had been the most quiet people in the boat, while awake, and became peace-breakers only when others ceased to be so, breathing tumult out of their repose. Would it were possible to affix a wind instrument to the nose, and thus make melody of a snore, so that a sleeping lover might serenade his mistress, or a congregation snore a psalm-tune! Other, though fainter sounds than these, contributed to my restlessness. My head was close to the crimson curtain—the sexual division of the boat—behind which I continually heard whispers and stealthy footsteps; the noise of a comb laid on the table, or a slipper dropt on the floor; the twang, like a broken harp-string, caused by loosening a tight belt; the rustling of a gown in its descent; and the unlacing of a pair of stays. My ear seemed to have the properties of an eye; a visible image pestered my fancy in the darkness; the curtain was withdrawn between me and the western lady, who yet disrobed herself without a blush.

Finally, all was hushed in that quarter. Still, I was more broad awake than through the whole preceding day, and felt a feverish impulse to toss my limbs miles apart, and appease the unquietness of mind by that of matter. Forgetting that my berth was hardly so wide as a coffin, I turned suddenly over, and fell like an avalanche on the floor, to the disturbance of the whole community of sleepers. As there were no bones broken, I blessed the accident, and went on deck. A lantern was burning at each end of the boat, and one of the crew was stationed at the bows, keeping watch, as mariners do on the ocean. Though the rain had ceased, the sky was all one cloud, and the darkness so intense, that there seemed to be no world, except the little space on which our lanterns glimmered. Yet, it was an impressive scene.

We were traversing the 'long level,' a dead flat between Utica and Syracuse, where the canal has not rise or fall enough to require a lock for nearly seventy miles. There can hardly be a more dismal tract of country. The forest which covers it, consisting chiefly of white cedar, black ash, and other trees that live in excessive moisture, is now decayed and death-struck, by the partial draining of the swamp into the great ditch of the canal. Sometimes, indeed, our lights were reflected from pools of stagnant water, which stretched far in among the trunks of the trees, beneath dense masses of dark foliage. But generally, the tall stems and intermingled branches were naked, and brought into strong relief, amid the surrounding gloom, by the whiteness of their decay. Often, we beheld the prostrate form of some old sylvan giant, which had fallen, and crushed down smaller trees under its immense ruin. In spots, where destruction had been riotous, the lanterns showed perhaps a hundred trunks, erect, half overthrown, extended along the ground, resting on their shattered limbs, or tossing them desperately into the darkness, but all of one ashy-white, all naked together, in desolate confusion. Thus growing out of the night as we drew nigh, and vanishing as we glided on, based on obscurity, and overhung and bounded by it, the scene was ghost-like—the very land of unsubstantial things, whither dreams might betake themselves, when they quit the slumberer's brain.

My fancy found another emblem. The wild Nature of America had been driven to this desert-place by the encroachments of civilized man. And even here, where the savage queen was throned on the ruins of her empire, did we penetrate, a vulgar and worldly throng, intruding on her latest solitude. In other lands, Decay sits among fallen palaces; but here, her home is in the forests.

Looking ahead, I discerned a distant light, announcing the approach of another boat, which soon passed us, and proved to be a rusty old scow—just such a craft as the 'Flying

Dutchman' would navigate on the canal. Perhaps it was that celebrated personage himself, whom I imperfectly distinguished at the helm, in a glazed hat and rough great-coat, with a pipe in his mouth, leaving the fumes of tobacco a hundred yards behind. Shortly after, our boatman blew a horn, sending a long and melancholy note through the forest-avenue, as a signal for some watcher in the wilderness to be ready with a change of horses. We had proceeded a mile or two with our fresh team, when the tow-rope got entangled in a fallen branch on the edge of the canal, and caused a momentary delay, during which I went to examine the phosphoric light of an old tree, a little within the forest. It was not the first delusive radiance that I had followed.

The tree lay along the ground, and was wholly converted into a mass of diseased splendor, which threw a ghastliness around. Being full of conceits that night, I called it a frigid fire; a funeral light, illumining decay and death; an emblem of fame, that gleams around the dead man without warming him; or of genius, when it owes its brilliancy to moral rottenness; and was thinking that such ghost-like torches were just fit to light up this dead forest, or to blaze coldly in tombs, when, starting from my abstraction, I looked up the canal. I recollected myself, and discovered the lanterns glimmering far away.

'Boat ahoy!' shouted I, making a trumpet of my closed fists.

Though the cry must have rung for miles along that hollow passage of the woods, it produced no effect. These packet-boats make up for their snail-like pace by never loitering day nor night, especially for those who have paid their fare. Indeed, the captain had an interest in getting rid of me, for I was his creditor for a breakfast.

'They are gone! Heaven be praised!' ejaculated I; 'for I cannot possibly overtake them! Here am I, on the "long level," at midnight, with the comfortable prospect of a walk to Syracuse, where my baggage will be left; and now to find a house or shed, wherein to pass the night.' So thinking aloud, I took a flambeau from the old tree, burning, but consuming not, to light my steps withal, and, like a Jack-o'-the-lantern, set out on my midnight tour.

The Wedding-Knell

T HERE is a certain church in the city of New-York, which
I have always regarded with peculiar interest, on account
of a marriage there solemnized, under very singular circumstances, in my grandmother's girlhood. That venerable lady
chanced to be a spectator of the scene, and ever after made it
her favorite narrative. Whether the edifice, now standing on
the same site, be the identical one to which she referred, I am
not antiquarian enough to know; nor would it be worth
while to correct myself, perhaps, of an agreeable error, by
reading the date of its erection on the tablet over the door. It
is a stately church, surrounded by an inclosure of the loveliest
green, within which appear urns, pillars, obelisks, and other
forms of monumental marble, the tributes of private affection,
or more splendid memorials of historic dust. With such a
place, though the tumult of the city rolls beneath its tower,
one would be willing to connect some legendary interest.

The marriage might be considered as the result of an early
engagement, though there had been two intermediate weddings on the lady's part, and forty years of celibacy on that of
the gentleman. At sixty-five, Mr. Ellenwood was a shy, but
not quite a secluded man; selfish, like all men who brood over
their own hearts, yet manifesting, on rare occasions, a vein of
generous sentiment; a scholar, throughout life, though always
an indolent one, because his studies had no definite object
either of public advantage or personal ambition; a gentleman,
high-bred and fastidiously delicate, yet sometimes requiring
a considerable relaxation, in his behalf, of the common rules
of society. In truth, there were so many anomalies in his
character, and, though shrinking with diseased sensibility
from public notice, it had been his fatality so often to become
the topic of the day, by some wild eccentricity of conduct,
that people searched his lineage for an hereditary taint of
insanity. But there was no need of this. His caprices had their
origin in a mind that lacked the support of an engrossing
purpose, and in feelings that preyed upon themselves, for want
of other food. If he were mad, it was the consequence, and

not the cause, of an aimless and abortive life.

The widow was as complete a contrast to her third bride-groom, in every thing but age, as can well be conceived. Compelled to relinquish her first engagement, she had been united to a man of twice her own years, to whom she became an exemplary wife, and by whose death she was left in pos-session of a splendid fortune. A Southern gentleman, consid-erably younger than herself, succeeded to her hand, and car-ried her to Charleston, where, after many uncomfortable years, she found herself again a widow. It would have been singular, if any uncommon delicacy of feeling had survived through such a life as Mrs. Dabney's; it could not but be crushed and killed by her early disappointment, the cold duty of her first marriage, the dislocation of the heart's principles, consequent on a second union, and the unkindness of her Southern husband, which had inevitably driven her to con-nect the idea of his death with that of her comfort. To be brief, she was that wisest, but unloveliest variety of woman, a philosopher, bearing troubles of the heart with equanimity, dispensing with all that should have been her happiness, and making the best of what remained. Sage in most matters, the widow was perhaps the more amiable, for the one frailty that made her ridiculous. Being childless, she could not remain beautiful by proxy, in the person of a daughter; she therefore refused to grow old and ugly, on any consideration; she struggled with Time and held fast her roses in spite of him, till the venerable thief appeared to have relinquished the spoil, as not worth the trouble of acquiring it.

The approaching marriage of this woman of the world, with such an unworldly man as Mr. Ellenwood, was an-nounced soon after Mrs. Dabney's return to her native city. Superficial observers, and deeper ones, seemed to concur, in supposing that the lady must have borne no inactive part, in arranging the affair; there were considerations of expediency, which she would be far more likely to appreciate than Mr. Ellenwood; and there was just the specious phantom of sen-timent and romance, in this late union of two early lovers, which sometimes makes a fool of a woman, who has lost her true feelings among the accidents of life. All the wonder was, how the gentleman, with his lack of worldly wisdom, and agonizing consciousness of ridicule, could have been induced to take a measure, at once so prudent and so laughable. But while people talked, the wedding-day arrived. The ceremony was to be solemnized according to the Episcopalian forms, and in open church, with a degree of publicity that attracted many spectators, who occupied the front seats of the galleries, and the pews near the altar and along the broad-aisle. It had been arranged, or possibly it was the custom of the day, that the parties should proceed separately to church. By some accident, the bridegroom was a little less punctual than the widow and her bridal attendants; with whose arrival, after this tedious but necessary preface, the action of our tale may be said to commence.

The clumsy wheels of several old-fashioned coaches were heard, and the gentlemen and ladies, composing the bridal party, came through the church-door, with the sudden and gladsome effect of a burst of sunshine. The whole group except the principal figure, was made up of youth and gaiety. As they streamed up the broad-aisle, while the pews and pillars seemed to brighten on either side, their steps were as buoyant as if they mistook the church for a ball-room, and were ready to dance hand in hand to the altar. So brilliant was the spectacle, that few took notice of a singular phenomenon that had marked its entrance. At the moment when the bride's foot touched the threshold, the bell swung heavily in the tower above her, and sent forth its deepest knell. The vibrations died away and returned, with prolonged solemnity, as she entered the body of the church.

'Good Heavens! what an omen,' whispered a young lady to her lover.

'On my honor,' replied the gentleman, 'I believe the bell has the good taste to toll of its own accord. What has she to do with weddings? If you, dearest Julia, were approaching the altar, the bell would ring out its merriest peal. It has only a funeral knell for her.'

The bride, and most of her company, had been too much occupied with the bustle of entrance, to hear the first boding stroke of the bell, or at least to reflect on the singularity of such a welcome to the altar. They therefore continued to advance, with undiminished gaiety. The gorgeous dresses of the time, the crimson velvet coats, the gold-laced hats, the hoop-petticoats, the silk, satin, brocade and embroidery, the buckles, canes, and swords, all displayed to the best advantage on persons suited to such finery, made the group appear more like a bright-colored picture, than any thing real. But by what perversity of taste, had the artist represented his principal figure as so wrinkled and decayed, while yet he had decked her out in the brightest splendor of attire, as if the loveliest maiden had suddenly withered into age, and become a moral to the beautiful around her! On they went, however, and had glittered along about a third of the aisle, when another stroke of the bell seemed to fill the church with a visible gloom, dimming and obscuring the bright pageant, till it shone forth again as from a mist.

This time, the party wavered, stopt, and huddled closer together, while a slight scream was heard from some of the ladies and a confused whispering among the gentlemen. Thus tossing to and fro, they might have been fancifully compared to a splendid bunch of flowers, suddenly shaken by a puff of wind, which threatened to scatter the leaves of an old, brown, withered rose, on the same stalk with two dewy buds; such being the emblem of the widow between her fair young bridemaids. But her heroism was admirable. She had started, with an irrepressible shudder, as if the stroke of the bell had fallen directly on her heart; then recovering herself, while her attendants were yet in dismay, she took the lead, and paced calmly up the aisle. The bell continued to swing, strike, and vibrate, with the same doleful regularity as when a corpse is on its way to the tomb.

'My young friends here have their nerves a little shaken,' said the widow with a smile, to the clergyman at the altar. 'But so many weddings have been ushered in with the merriest peal of the bells, and yet turned out unhappily, that I shall hope for better fortune under such different auspices.'

'Madam,' answered the rector, in great perplexity, 'this strange occurrence brings to my mind a marriage sermon of the famous Bishop Taylor, wherein he mingles so many thoughts of mortality and future woe, that, to speak somewhat after his own rich style, he seems to hang the bridal-chamber in black, and cut the wedding garment out of a coffin-pall. And it has been the custom of divers nations to infuse something of sadness into their marriage ceremonies; so to keep death in mind, while contracting that engagement which is life's chiefest business. Thus we may draw a sad, but profitable moral from this funeral knell.'

But, though the clergyman might have given his moral even a keener point, he did not fail to dispatch an attendant to inquire into the mystery, and stop those sounds, so dismally appropriate to such a marriage. A brief space elapsed, during which the silence was broken only by whispers, and a few suppressed titterings, among the wedding party and the spectators, who, after the first shock, were disposed to draw an ill-natured merriment from the affair. The young have less charity for aged follies, than the old for those of youth. The widow's glance was observed to wander, for an instant, towards a window of the church, as if searching for the time-worn marble that she had dedicated to her first husband; then her eyelids dropt over their faded orbs, and her thoughts were drawn irresistibly to another grave. Two buried men, with a voice at her ear and a cry afar off, were calling her to lie down beside them. Perhaps, with momentary truth of feeling, she thought how much happier had been her fate, if, after years of bliss, the bell were now tolling for her funeral, and she were followed to the grave by the old affection of her earliest lover, long her husband. But why had she returned to him, when their cold hearts shrank from each other's touch!

Still the death-bell tolled so mournfully, that the sunshine seemed to fade in the air. A whisper, communicated from those who stood nearest the windows, now spread through the church; a hearse, with a train of several coaches, was creeping along the street, conveying some dead man to the church yard, while the bride awaited a living one at the altar. Immediately after, the footsteps of the bridegroom and his friends were heard at the door. The widow looked down the aisle, and clenched the arm of one of her bridemaids in her bony hand, with such unconscious violence that the fair girl trembled.

'You frighten me, my dear madam!' cried she. 'For heaven's sake, what is the matter?'

'Nothing, my dear, nothing,' said the widow; then whispering close to her ear,—'There is a foolish fancy that I cannot get rid of. I am expecting my bridegroom to come into the church, with my two first husbands for groomsmen!'

'Look, look!' screamed the bridemaid. 'What is here? The funeral!'

As she spoke, a dark procession paced into the church. First came an old man and woman, like chief mourners at a funeral, attired from head to foot in the deepest black, all but their pale features and hoary hair; he leaning on a staff, and supporting her decrepit form with his nerveless arm. Behind, appeared another, and another pair, as aged, as black, and mournful as the first. As they drew near, the widow recognized in every face some trait of former friends, long forgotten, but now returning, as if from their old graves, to warn her to prepare a shroud, or, with purpose almost as unwelcome, to exhibit their wrinkles and infirmity, and claim her as their companion by the tokens of her own decay. Many a merry night had she danced with them, in youth. And now, in joyless age, she felt that some withered partner should request her hand, and all unite in a dance of death, to the music of the funeral bell.

While these aged mourners were passing up the aisle, it was observed, that, from pew to pew, the spectators shuddered with irrepressible awe, as some object, hitherto concealed by the intervening figures, came full in sight. Many turned away their faces; others kept a fixed and rigid stare; and a young girl giggled hysterically, and fainted with the laughter on her lips. When the spectral procession approached the altar, each couple separated and slowly diverged, till, in the centre, appeared a form that had been worthily ushered in with all this gloomy pomp, the death-knell, and the funeral. It was the bridegroom in his shroud!

No garb but that of the grave could have befitted such a death-like aspect; the eyes, indeed, had the wild gleam of a sepulchral lamp; all else was fixed in the stern calmness which old men wear in the coffin. The corpse stood motionless, but addressed the widow in accents that seemed to melt into the clang of the bell, which fell heavily on the air while he spoke.

'Come, my bride!' said those pale lips. 'The hearse is ready. The sexton stands waiting for us at the door of the tomb. Let us be married; and then to our coffins!'

How shall the widow's horror be represented! It gave her the ghastliness of a dead man's bride. Her youthful friends stood apart, shuddering at the mourners, the shrouded bridegroom, and herself; the whole scene expressed, by the strongest imagery, the vain struggle of the gilded vanities of this world, when opposed to age, infirmity, sorrow, and death. The awe-struck silence was first broken by the clergyman.

'Mr. Ellenwood,' said he, soothingly, yet with somewhat of authority, 'you are not well. Your mind has been agitated by the unusual circumstances in which you are placed. The ceremony must be deferred. As an old friend, let me intreat you to return home.'

'Home! yes; but not without my bride,' answered he, in the same hollow accents. 'You deem this mockery; perhaps madness. Had I bedizened my aged and broken frame with scarlet and embroidery—had I forced my withered lips to smile at my dead heart—that might have been mockery, or madness. But now, let young and old declare, which of us has come hither without a wedding garment,—the bridegroom, or the bride!'

He stept forward, at a ghostly pace, and stood beside the widow, contrasting the awful simplicity of his shroud with the glare and glitter in which she had arrayed herself for this unhappy scene. None, that beheld them, could deny the terrible strength of the moral which his disordered intellect had contrived to draw.

'Cruel! cruel!' groaned the heart-stricken bride.

'Cruel!' repeated he; then losing his death-like composure in a wild bitterness,—'Heaven judge, which of us has been cruel to the other! In youth, you deprived me of my happiness, my hopes, my aims; you took away all the substance of my life, and made it a dream, without reality enough even to grieve at—with only a pervading gloom, through which I walked wearily, and cared not whither. But after forty years, when I have built my tomb, and would not give up the thought of resting there—no, not for such a life as we once pictured—you call me to the altar. At your summons, I am here. But other husbands have enjoyed your youth, your beauty, your warmth of heart, and all that could be termed your life. What is there for me but your decay and death?

And therefore I have bidden these funeral friends, and be-spoken the sexton's deepest knell, and am come, in my shroud, to wed you, as with a burial service, that we may join our hands at the door of the sepulchre, and enter it together.'

It was not frenzy; it was not merely the drunkenness of strong emotion, in a heart unused to it, that now wrought upon the bride. The stern lesson of the day had done its work; her worldliness was gone. She seized the bridegroom's hand.

'Yes!' cried she. 'Let us wed, even at the door of the sep-ulchre!—My life is gone, in vanity and emptiness. But at its close, there is one true feeling. It has made me what I was in youth; it makes me worthy of you. Time is no more, for both of us. Let us wed for Eternity!'

With a long and deep regard, the bridegroom looked into her eyes, while a tear was gathering in his own. How strange that gush of human feeling from the frozen bosom of a corpse! He wiped away the tear, even with his shroud.

'Beloved of my youth,' said he, 'I have been wild. The de-spair of my whole lifetime had returned at once, and mad-dened me. Forgive; and be forgiven. Yes; it is evening with us now; and we have realized none of our morning dreams of happiness. But let us join our hands before the altar, as lovers, whom adverse circumstances have separated through life, yet who meet again as they are leaving it, and find their earthly affection changed into something holy as religion. And what is Time, to the married of Eternity?'

Amid the tears of many, and a swell of exalted sentiment, in those who felt aright, was solemnized the union of two immortal souls. The train of withered mourners, the hoary bridegroom in his shroud, the pale features of the aged bride, and the death-bell tolling through the whole, till its deep voice overpowered the marriage words, all marked the funeral of earthly hopes. But as the ceremony proceeded, the organ, as if stirred by the sympathies of this impressive scene, poured forth an anthem, first mingling with the dismal knell, then rising to a loftier strain, till the soul looked down upon its woe. And when the awful rite was finished, and, with cold hand in cold hand, the Married of Eternity withdrew, the or-gan's peal of solemn triumph drowned the Wedding-Knell.

The May-Pole of Merry Mount

There is an admirable foundation for a philosophic romance, in the curious history of the early settlement of Mount Wollaston, or Merry Mount. In the slight sketch here attempted, the facts, recorded on the grave pages of our New England annalists, have wrought themselves, almost spontaneously, into a sort of allegory. The masques, mummeries, and festive customs, described in the text, are in accordance with the manners of the age. Authority on these points may be found in Strutt's Book of English Sports and Pastimes.

BRIGHT were the days at Merry Mount, when the May-Pole was the banner-staff of that gay colony! They who reared it, should their banner be triumphant, were to pour sunshine over New England's rugged hills, and scatter flower-seeds throughout the soil. Jollity and gloom were contending for an empire. Midsummer eve had come, bringing deep verdure to the forest, and roses in her lap, of a more vivid hue than the tender buds of Spring. But May, or her mirthful spirit, dwelt all the year round at Merry Mount, sporting with the Summer months, and revelling with Autumn, and basking in the glow of Winter's fireside. Through a world of toil and care, she flitted with a dreamlike smile, and came hither to find a home among the lightsome hearts of Merry Mount.

Never had the May-Pole been so gaily decked as at sunset on midsummer eve. This venerated emblem was a pine tree, which had preserved the slender grace of youth, while it equalled the loftiest height of the old wood monarchs. From its top streamed a silken banner, colored like the rainbow. Down nearly to the ground, the pole was dressed with birchen boughs, and others of the liveliest green, and some with silvery leaves, fastened by ribbons that fluttered in fantastic knots of twenty different colors, but no sad ones. Garden flowers, and blossoms of the wilderness, laughed gladly forth amid the verdure, so fresh and dewy, that they must have grown by magic on that happy pine tree. Where this green and flowery splendor terminated, the shaft of the May-

Pole was stained with the seven brilliant hues of the banner
at its top. On the lowest green bough hung an abundant
wreath of roses, some that had been gathered in the sunniest
spots of the forest, and others, of still richer blush, which
the colonists had reared from English seed. Oh, people of
the Golden Age, the chief of your husbandry, was to raise
flowers!

But what was the wild throng that stood hand in hand
about the May-Pole? It could not be, that the Fauns and
Nymphs, when driven from their classic groves and homes of
ancient fable, had sought refuge, as all the persecuted did, in
the fresh woods of the West. These were Gothic monsters,
though perhaps of Grecian ancestry. On the shoulders of a
comely youth, uprose the head and branching antlers of a
stag; a second, human in all other points, had the grim visage
of a wolf; a third, still with the trunk and limbs of a mortal
man, showed the beard and horns of a venerable he-goat.
There was the likeness of a bear erect, brute in all but his hind
legs, which were adorned with pink silk stockings. And here
again, almost as wondrous, stood a real bear of the dark forest, lending each of his fore paws to the grasp of a human
hand, and as ready for the dance as any in that circle. His
inferior nature rose half-way, to meet his companions as they
stooped. Other faces wore the similitude of man or woman,
but distorted or extravagant, with red noses pendulous before
their mouths, which seemed of awful depth, and stretched
from ear to ear in an eternal fit of laughter. Here might be
seen the Salvage Man, well known in heraldry, hairy as a ba-
boon, and girdled with green leaves. By his side, a nobler
figure, but still a counterfeit, appeared an Indian hunter, with
feathery crest and wampum belt. Many of this strange company wore fools-caps, and had little bells appended to their
garments, tinkling with a silvery sound, responsive to the inaudible music of their gleesome spirits. Some youths and
maidens were of soberer garb, yet well maintained their places
in the irregular throng, by the expression of wild revelry upon
their features. Such were the colonists of Merry Mount, as
they stood in the broad smile of sunset, round their venerated
May-Pole.

Had a wanderer, bewildered in the melancholy forest,

heard their mirth, and stolen a half-affrighted glance, he might have fancied them the crew of Comus, some already transformed to brutes, some midway between man and beast, and the others rioting in the flow of tipsey jollity that foreran the change. But a band of Puritans, who watched the scene, invisible themselves, compared the masques to those devils and ruined souls, with whom their supersitition peopled the black wilderness.

Within the ring of monsters, appeared the two airiest forms, that had ever trodden on any more solid footing than a purple and golden cloud. One was a youth, in glistening apparel, with a scarf of the rainbow pattern crosswise on his breast. His right hand held a gilded staff, the ensign of high dignity among the revellers, and his left grasped the slender fingers of a fair maiden, not less gaily decorated than himself. Bright roses glowed in contrast with the dark and glossy curls of each, and were scattered round their feet, or had sprung up spontaneously there. Behind this lightsome couple, so close to the May-Pole that its boughs shaded his jovial face, stood the figure of an English priest, canonically dressed, yet decked with flowers, in heathen fashion, and wearing a chaplet of the native vine leaves. By the riot of his rolling eye, and the pagan decorations of his holy garb, he seemed the wildest monster there, and the very Comus of the crew.

'Votaries of the May-Pole,' cried the flower-decked priest, 'merrily, all day long, have the woods echoed to your mirth. But be this your merriest hour, my hearts! Lo, here stand the Lord and Lady of the May, whom I, a clerk of Oxford, and high priest of Merry Mount, am presently to join in holy matrimony. Up with your nimble spirits, ye morrice-dancers, green-men, and glee-maidens, bears and wolves, and horned gentlemen! Come; a chorus now, rich with the old mirth of Merry England, and the wilder glee of this fresh forest; and then a dance, to show the youthful pair what life is made of, and how airily they should go through it! All ye that love the May-Pole, lend your voices to the nuptial song of the Lord and Lady of the May!'

This wedlock was more serious than most affairs of Merry Mount, where jest and delusion, trick and fantasy, kept up a continued carnival. The Lord and Lady of the May, though their titles must be laid down at sunset, were really and truly to be partners for the dance of life, beginning the measure that same bright eve. The wreath of roses, that hung from the lowest green bough of the May-Pole, had been twined for them, and would be thrown over both their heads, in symbol of their flowery union. When the priest had spoken, therefore, a riotous uproar burst from the rout of monstrous figures.

'Begin you the stave, reverend Sir,' cried they all; 'and never did the woods ring to such a merry peal, as we of the May-Pole shall send up!'

Immediately a prelude of pipe, cittern, and viol, touched with practised minstrelsy, began to play from a neighboring thicket, in such a mirthful cadence, that the boughs of the May-Pole quivered to the sound. But the May Lord, he of the gilded staff, chancing to look into his Lady's eyes, was wonderstruck at the almost pensive glance that met his own.

'Edith, sweet Lady of the May,' whispered he, reproachfully, 'is yon wreath of roses a garland to hang above our graves, that you look so sad? Oh, Edith, this is our golden time! Tarnish it not by any pensive shadow of the mind; for it may be, that nothing of futurity will be brighter than the mere remembrance of what is now passing.'

'That was the very thought that saddened me! How came it in your mind too?' said Edith, in a still lower tone than he; for it was high treason to be sad at Merry Mount. 'Therefore do I sigh amid this festive music. And besides, dear Edgar, I struggle as with a dream, and fancy that these shapes of our jovial friends are visionary, and their mirth unreal, and that we are no true Lord and Lady of the May. What is the mystery in my heart?'

Just then, as if a spell had loosened them, down came a little shower of withering rose leaves from the May-Pole. Alas, for the young lovers! No sooner had their hearts glowed with real passion, than they were sensible of something vague and unsubstantial in their former pleasures, and felt a dreary presentiment of inevitable change. From the moment that they truly loved, they had subjected themselves to earth's doom of care, and sorrow, and troubled joy, and had no more a home at Merry Mount. That was Edith's mystery. Now leave we the priest to marry them, and the masquers to sport round the May-Pole, till the last sunbeam be withdrawn from its summit, and the shadows of the forest mingle gloomily in the dance. Meanwhile, we may discover who these gay people were.

Two hundred years ago, and more, the old world and its inhabitants became mutually weary of each other. Men voyaged by thousands to the West; some to barter glass beads, and such like jewels, for the furs of the Indian hunter; some to conquer virgin empires; and one stern band to pray. But none of these motives had much weight with the colonists of Merry Mount. Their leaders were men who had sported so long with life, that when Thought and Wisdom came, even these unwelcome guests were led astray, by the crowd of vanities which they should have put to flight. Erring Thought and perverted Wisdom were made to put on masques, and play the fool. The men of whom we speak, after losing the heart's fresh gaiety, imagined a wild philosophy of pleasure, and came hither to act out their latest day-dream. They gathered followers from all that giddy tribe, whose whole life is like the festal days of soberer men. In their train were minstrels, not unknown in London streets; wandering players, whose theatres had been the halls of noblemen; mummers, rope-dancers, and mountebanks, who would long be missed at wakes, church-ales, and fairs; in a word, mirth-makers of every sort, such as abounded in that age, but now began to be discountenanced by the rapid growth of Puritanism. Light had their footsteps been on land, and as lightly they came across the sea. Many had been maddened by their previous troubles into a gay despair; others were as madly gay in the flush of youth, like the May Lord and his Lady; but whatever might be the quality of their mirth, old and young were gay at Merry Mount. The young deemed themselves happy. The elder spirits, if they knew that mirth was but the counterfeit of happiness, yet followed the false shadow wilfully, because at least her garments glittered brightest. Sworn triflers of a lifetime, they would not venture among the sober truths of life, not even to be truly blest.

All the hereditary pastimes of Old England were transplanted hither. The King of Christmas was duly crowned, and the Lord of Misrule bore potent sway. On the eve of Saint John, they felled whole acres of the forest to make bonfires, and danced by the blaze all night, crowned with garlands, and throwing flowers into the flame. At harvest time, though their crop was of the smallest, they made an image with the sheaves of Indian corn, and wreathed it with autumnal garlands, and bore it home triumphantly. But what chiefly characterized the colonists of Merry Mount, was their veneration for the May-Pole. It has made their true history a poet's tale. Spring decked the hallowed emblem with young blossoms and fresh green boughs; Summer brought roses of the deepest blush, and the perfected foliage of the forest; Autumn enriched it with that red and yellow gorgeousness, which converts each wild-wood leaf into a painted flower; and Winter silvered it with sleet, and hung it round with icicles, till it flashed in the cold sunshine, itself a frozen sunbeam. Thus each alternate season did homage to the May-Pole, and paid it a tribute of its own richest splendor. Its votaries danced round it, once, at least, in every month; sometimes they called it their religion, or their altar; but always, it was the banner-staff of Merry Mount.

Unfortunately, there were men in the new world, of a sterner faith than these May-Pole worshippers. Not far from Merry Mount was a settlement of Puritans, most dismal wretches, who said their prayers before daylight, and then wrought in the forest or the cornfield, till evening made it prayer time again. Their weapons were always at hand, to shoot down the straggling savage. When they met in conclave, it was never to keep up the old English mirth, but to hear sermons three hours long, or to proclaim bounties on the heads of wolves and the scalps of Indians. Their festivals were fast-days, and their chief pastime the singing of psalms. Woe to the youth or maiden, who did but dream of a dance! The selectman nodded to the constable; and there sat the light-heeled reprobate in the stocks; or if he danced, it was round the whipping-post, which might be termed the Puritan May-Pole.

A party of these grim Puritans, toiling through the difficult woods, each with a horse-load of iron armor to burthen his footsteps, would sometimes draw near the sunny precincts of

Merry Mount. There were the silken colonists, sporting round their May-Pole; perhaps teaching a bear to dance, or striving to communicate their mirth to the grave Indian; or masquerading in the skins of deer and wolves, which they had hunted for that especial purpose. Often, the whole colony were playing at blindman's buff, magistrates and all with their eyes bandaged, except a single scape-goat, whom the blinded sinners pursued by the tinkling of the bells at his garments. Once, it is said, they were seen following a flower-decked corpse, with merriment and festive music, to his grave. But did the dead man laugh? In their quietest times, they sang ballads and told tales, for the edification of their pious visiters; or perplexed them with juggling tricks; or grinned at them through horse-collars; and when sport itself grew wearisome, they made game of their own stupidity, and began a yawning match. At the very least of these enormities, the men of iron shook their heads and frowned so darkly, that the revellers looked up, imagining that a momentary cloud had overcast the sunshine, which was to be perpetual there. On the other hand, the Puritans affirmed, that, when a psalm was pealing from their place of worship, the echo, which the forest sent them back, seemed often like the chorus of a jolly catch, closing with a roar of laughter. Who but the fiend, and his bond-slaves, the crew of Merry Mount, had thus disturbed them! In due time, a feud arose, stern and bitter on one side, and as serious on the other as any thing could be, among such light spirits as had sworn allegiance to the May-Pole. The future complexion of New England was involved in this important quarrel. Should the grisly saints establish their jurisdiction over the gay sinners, then would their spirits darken all the clime, and make it a land of clouded visages, of hard toil, of sermon and psalm, forever. But should the banner-staff of Merry Mount be fortunate, sunshine would break upon the hills, and flowers would beautify the forest, and late posterity do homage to the May-Pole!

After these authentic passages from history, we return to the nuptials of the Lord and Lady of the May. Alas! we have delayed too long, and must darken our tale too suddenly. As we glance again at the May-Pole, a solitary sunbeam is fading from the summit, and leaves only a faint golden tinge,

blended with the hues of the rainbow banner. Even that dim
light is now withdrawn, relinquishing the whole domain of
Merry Mount to the evening gloom, which has rushed so instantaneously from the black surrounding woods. But some
of these black shadows have rushed forth in human shape.

Yes: with the setting sun, the last day of mirth had passed
from Merry Mount. The ring of gay masquers was disordered
and broken; the stag lowered his antlers in dismay; the wolf
grew weaker than a lamb; the bells of the morrice-dancers
tinkled with tremulous affright. The Puritans had played a
characteristic part in the May-Pole mummeries. Their darksome figures were intermixed with the wild shapes of their
foes, and made the scene a picture of the moment, when waking thoughts start up amid the scattered fantasies of a dream.
The leader of the hostile party stood in the centre of the circle, while the rout of monsters cowered around him, like evil
spirits in the presence of a dread magician. No fantastic foolery could look him in the face. So stern was the energy of his
aspect, that the whole man, visage, frame, and soul, seemed
wrought of iron, gifted with life and thought, yet all of one
substance with his head-piece and breast-plate. It was the Puritan of Puritans; it was Endicott himself!

'Stand off, priest of Baal!' said he, with a grim frown, and
laying no reverent hand upon the surplice. 'I know thee,
Blackstone!* Thou art the man, who couldst not abide the
rule even of thine own corrupted church, and hast come
hither to preach iniquity, and to give example of it in thy life.
But now shall it be seen that the Lord hath sanctified this
wilderness for his peculiar people. Woe unto them that would
defile it! And first for this flower-decked abomination, the
altar of thy worship!'

And with his keen sword, Endicott assaulted the hallowed
May-Pole. Nor long did it resist his arm. It groaned with a
dismal sound; it showered leaves and rose-buds upon the remorseless enthusiast; and finally, with all its green boughs,
and ribbons, and flowers, symbolic of departed pleasures,

*Did Governor Endicott speak less positively, we should suspect a mistake
here. The Rev. Mr. Blackstone, though an eccentric, is not known to have
been an immoral man. We rather doubt his identity with the priest of Merry
Mount.

down fell the banner-staff of Merry Mount. As it sank, tradition says, the evening sky grew darker, and the woods threw forth a more sombre shadow.

'There,' cried Endicott, looking triumphantly on his work, 'there lies the only May-Pole in New England! The thought is strong within me, that, by its fall, is shadowed forth the fate of light and idle mirth-makers, amongst us and our posterity. Amen, saith John Endicott!'

'Amen!' echoed his followers.

But the votaries of the May-Pole gave one groan for their idol. At the sound, the Puritan leader glanced at the crew of Comus, each a figure of broad mirth, yet, at this moment, strangely expressive of sorrow and dismay.

'Valiant captain,' quoth Peter Palfrey, the Ancient of the band, 'what order shall be taken with the prisoners?'

'I thought not to repent me of cutting down a May-Pole,' replied Endicott, 'yet now I could find in my heart to plant it again, and give each of these bestial pagans one other dance round their idol. It would have served rarely for a whipping-post!'

'But there are pine trees enow,' suggested the lieutenant.

'True, good Ancient,' said the leader. 'Wherefore, bind the heathen crew, and bestow on them a small matter of stripes apiece, as earnest of our future justice. Set some of the rogues in the stocks to rest themselves, so soon as Providence shall bring us to one of our own well-ordered settlements, where such accommodations may be found. Further penalties, such as branding and cropping of ears, shall be thought of hereafter.'

'How many stripes for the priest?' inquired Ancient Palfrey.

'None as yet,' answered Endicott, bending his iron frown upon the culprit. 'It must be for the Great and General Court to determine, whether stripes and long imprisonment, and other grievous penalty, may atone for his transgressions. Let him look to himself! For such as violate our civil order, it may be permitted us to show mercy. But woe to the wretch that troubleth our religion!'

'And this dancing bear,' resumed the officer. 'Must he share the stripes of his fellows?'

'Shoot him through the head!' said the energetic Puritan. 'I suspect witchcraft in the beast.'

'Here be a couple of shining ones,' continued Peter Palfrey, pointing his weapon at the Lord and Lady of the May. 'They seem to be of high station among these mis-doers. Methinks their dignity will not be fitted with less than a double share of stripes.'

Endicott rested on his sword, and closely surveyed the dress and aspect of the hapless pair. There they stood, pale, downcast, and apprehensive. Yet there was an air of mutual support, and of pure affection, seeking aid and giving it, that showed them to be man and wife, with the sanction of a priest upon their love. The youth, in the peril of the moment, had dropped his gilded staff, and thrown his arm about the Lady of the May, who leaned against his breast, too lightly to burthen him, but with weight enough to express that their destinies were linked together, for good or evil. They looked first at each other, and then into the grim captain's face. There they stood, in the first hour of wedlock, while the idle pleasures, of which their companions were the emblems, had given place to the sternest cares of life, personified by the dark Puritans. But never had their youthful beauty seemed so pure and high, as when its glow was chastened by adversity.

'Youth,' said Endicott, 'ye stand in an evil case, thou and thy maiden wife. Make ready presently; for I am minded that ye shall both have a token to remember your wedding-day!'

'Stern man,' cried the May Lord, 'how can I move thee? Were the means at hand, I would resist to the death. Being powerless, I entreat! Do with me as thou wilt; but let Edith go untouched!'

'Not so,' replied the immitigable zealot. 'We are not wont to show an idle courtesy to that sex, which requireth the stricter discipline. What sayest thou, maid? Shall thy silken bridegroom suffer thy share of the penalty, besides his own?'

'Be it death,' said Edith, 'and lay it all on me!'

Truly, as Endicott had said, the poor lovers stood in a woeful case. Their foes were triumphant, their friends captive and abased, their home desolate, the benighted wilderness around them, and a rigorous destiny, in the shape of the Puritan leader, their only guide. Yet the deepening twilight could not altogether conceal, that the iron man was softened; he smiled, at the fair spectacle of early love; he almost sighed, for the inevitable blight of early hopes.

'The troubles of life have come hastily on this young couple,' observed Endicott. 'We will see how they comport themselves under their present trials, ere we burthen them with greater. If, among the spoil, there be any garments of a more decent fashion, let them be put upon this May Lord and his Lady, instead of their glistening vanities. Look to it, some of you.'

'And shall not the youth's hair be cut?' asked Peter Palfrey, looking with abhorrence at the love-lock and long glossy curls of the young man.

'Crop it forthwith, and that in the true pumpkin-shell fashion,' answered the captain. 'Then bring them along with us, but more gently than their fellows. There be qualities in the youth, which may make him valiant to fight, and sober to toil, and pious to pray; and in the maiden, that may fit her to become a mother in our Israel, bringing up babes in better nurture than her own hath been. Nor think ye, young ones, that they are the happiest, even in our lifetime of a moment, who misspend it in dancing round a May-Pole!'

And Endicott, the severest Puritan of all who laid the rock-foundation of New England, lifted the wreath of roses from the ruin of the May-Pole, and threw it, with his own gauntleted hand, over the heads of the Lord and Lady of the May. It was a deed of prophecy. As the moral gloom of the world overpowers all systematic gaiety, even so was their home of wild mirth made desolate amid the sad forest. They returned to it no more. But, as their flowery garland was wreathed of the brightest roses that had grown there, so, in the tie that united them, were intertwined all the purest and best of their early joys. They went heavenward, supporting each other along the difficult path which it was their lot to tread, and never wasted one regretful thought on the vanities of Merry Mount.

The Minister's Black Veil

A PARABLE*

THE sexton stood in the porch of Milford meeting-house, pulling lustily at the bell-rope. The old people of the village came stooping along the street. Children, with bright faces, tript merrily beside their parents, or mimicked a graver gait, in the conscious dignity of their Sunday clothes. Spruce bachelors looked sidelong at the pretty maidens, and fancied that the Sabbath sunshine made them prettier than on weekdays. When the throng had mostly streamed into the porch, the sexton began to toll the bell, keeping his eye on the Reverend Mr. Hooper's door. The first glimpse of the clergyman's figure was the signal for the bell to cease its summons.

'But what has good Parson Hooper got upon his face?' cried the sexton in astonishment.

All within hearing immediately turned about, and beheld the semblance of Mr. Hooper, pacing slowly his meditative way towards the meeting-house. With one accord they started, expressing more wonder than if some strange minister were coming to dust the cushions of Mr. Hooper's pulpit.

'Are you sure it is our parson?' inquired Goodman Gray of the sexton.

'Of a certainty it is good Mr. Hooper,' replied the sexton. 'He was to have exchanged pulpits with Parson Shute of Westbury; but Parson Shute sent to excuse himself yesterday, being to preach a funeral sermon.'

The cause of so much amazement may appear sufficiently slight. Mr. Hooper, a gentlemanly person of about thirty, though still a bachelor, was dressed with due clerical neatness,

*Another clergyman in New England, Mr. Joseph Moody, of York, Maine, who died about eighty years since, made himself remarkable by the same eccentricity that is here related of the Reverend Mr. Hooper. In his case, however, the symbol had a different import. In early life he had accidentally killed a beloved friend; and from that day till the hour of his own death, he hid his face from men.

as if a careful wife had starched his band, and brushed the weekly dust from his Sunday's garb. There was but one thing remarkable in his appearance. Swathed about his forehead, and hanging down over his face, so low as to be shaken by his breath, Mr. Hooper had on a black veil. On a nearer view, it seemed to consist of two folds of crape, which entirely concealed his features, except the mouth and chin, but probably did not intercept his sight, farther than to give a darkened aspect to all living and inanimate things. With this gloomy shade before him, good Mr. Hooper walked onward, at a slow and quiet pace, stooping somewhat and looking on the ground, as is customary with abstracted men, yet nodding kindly to those of his parishioners who still waited on the meeting-house steps. But so wonder-struck were they, that his greeting hardly met with a return.

'I can't really feel as if good Mr. Hooper's face was behind that piece of crape,' said the sexton.

'I don't like it,' muttered an old woman, as she hobbled into the meeting-house. 'He has changed himself into something awful, only by hiding his face.'

'Our parson has gone mad!' cried Goodman Gray, following him across the threshold.

A rumor of some unaccountable phenomenon had preceded Mr. Hooper into the meeting-house, and set all the congregation astir. Few could refrain from twisting their heads towards the door; many stood upright, and turned directly about; while several little boys clambered upon the seats, and came down again with a terrible racket. There was a general bustle, a rustling of the women's gowns and shuffling of the men's feet, greatly at variance with that hushed repose which should attend the entrance of the minister. But Mr. Hooper appeared not to notice the perturbation of his people. He entered with an almost noiseless step, bent his head mildly to the pews on each side, and bowed as he passed his oldest parishioner, a white-haired great-grandsire, who occupied an arm-chair in the centre of the aisle. It was strange to observe, how slowly this venerable man became conscious of something singular in the appearance of his pastor. He seemed not fully to partake of the prevailing wonder, till Mr. Hooper had ascended the stairs, and showed himself in the pulpit, face to face with his congregation, except for the black veil. That mysterious emblem was never once withdrawn. It shook with his measured breath as he gave out the psalm; it threw its obscurity between him and the holy page, as he read the Scriptures; and while he prayed, the veil lay heavily on his uplifted countenance. Did he seek to hide it from the dread Being whom he was addressing?

Such was the effect of this simple piece of crape, that more than one woman of delicate nerves was forced to leave the meeting-house. Yet perhaps the pale-faced congregation was almost as fearful a sight to the minister, as his black veil to them.

Mr. Hooper had the reputation of a good preacher, but not an energetic one: he strove to win his people heavenward, by mild persuasive influences, rather than to drive them thither, by the thunders of the Word. The sermon which he now delivered, was marked by the same characteristics of style and manner, as the general series of his pulpit oratory. But there was something, either in the sentiment of the discourse itself, or in the imagination of the auditors, which made it greatly the most powerful effort that they had ever heard from their pastor's lips. It was tinged, rather more darkly than usual, with the gentle gloom of Mr. Hooper's temperament. The subject had reference to secret sin, and those sad mysteries which we hide from our nearest and dearest, and would fain conceal from our own consciousness, even forgetting that the Omniscient can detect them. A subtle power was breathed into his words. Each member of the congregation, the most innocent girl, and the man of hardened breast, felt as if the preacher had crept upon them, behind his awful veil, and discovered their hoarded iniquity of deed or thought. Many spread their clasped hands on their bosoms. There was nothing terrible in what Mr. Hooper said; at least, no violence; and yet, with every tremor of his melancholy voice, the hearers quaked. An unsought pathos came hand in hand with awe. So sensible were the audience of some unwonted attribute in their minister, that they longed for a breath of wind to blow aside the veil, almost believing that a stranger's visage would be discovered, though the form, gesture, and voice were those of Mr. Hooper.

At the close of the services, the people hurried out with indecorous confusion, eager to communicate their pent-up amazement, and conscious of lighter spirits, the moment they lost sight of the black veil. Some gathered in little circles, huddled closely together, with their mouths all whispering in the centre; some went homeward alone, wrapt in silent meditation; some talked loudly, and profaned the Sabbath-day with ostentatious laughter. A few shook their sagacious heads, intimating that they could penetrate the mystery; while one or two affirmed that there was no mystery at all, but only that Mr. Hooper's eyes were so weakened by the midnight lamp, as to require a shade. After a brief interval, forth came good Mr. Hooper also, in the rear of his flock. Turning his veiled face from one group to another, he paid due reverence to the hoary heads, saluted the middle-aged with kind dignity, as their friend and spiritual guide, greeted the young with mingled authority and love, and laid his hands on the little children's heads to bless them. Such was always his custom on the Sabbath-day. Strange and bewildered looks repaid him for his courtesy. None, as on former occasions, aspired to the honor of walking by their pastor's side. Old Squire Saunders, doubtless by an accidental lapse of memory, neglected to invite Mr. Hooper to his table, where the good clergyman had been wont to bless the food, almost every Sunday since his settlement. He returned, therefore, to the parsonage, and, at the moment of closing the door, was observed to look back upon the people, all of whom had their eyes fixed upon the minister. A sad smile gleamed faintly from beneath the black veil, and flickered about his mouth, glimmering as he disappeared.

'How strange,' said a lady, 'that a simple black veil, such as any woman might wear on her bonnet, should become such a terrible thing on Mr. Hooper's face!'

'Something must surely be amiss with Mr. Hooper's intellects,' observed her husband, the physician of the village. 'But the strangest part of the affair is the effect of this vagary, even on a sober-minded man like myself. The black veil, though it covers only our pastor's face, throws its influence over his whole person, and makes him ghost-like from head to foot. Do you not feel it so?'

'Truly do I,' replied the lady; 'and I would not be alone with him for the world. I wonder he is not afraid to be alone with himself!'

'Men sometimes are so,' said her husband.

The afternoon service was attended with similar circumstances. At its conclusion, the bell tolled for the funeral of a young lady. The relatives and friends were assembled in the house, and the more distant acquaintances stood about the door, speaking of the good qualities of the deceased, when their talk was interrupted by the appearance of Mr. Hooper, still covered with his black veil. It was now an appropriate emblem. The clergyman stepped into the room where the corpse was laid, and bent over the coffin, to take a last farewell of his deceased parishioner. As he stooped, the veil hung straight down from his forehead, so that, if her eye-lids had not been closed for ever, the dead maiden might have seen his face. Could Mr. Hooper be fearful of her glance, that he so hastily caught back the black veil? A person, who watched the interview between the dead and living, scrupled not to affirm, that, at the instant when the clergyman's features were disclosed, the corpse had slightly shuddered, rustling the shroud and muslin cap, though the countenance retained the composure of death. A superstitious old woman was the only witness of this prodigy. From the coffin, Mr. Hooper passed into the chamber of the mourners, and thence to the head of the staircase, to make the funeral prayer. It was a tender and heart-dissolving prayer, full of sorrow, yet so imbued with celestial hopes, that the music of a heavenly harp, swept by the fingers of the dead, seemed faintly to be heard among the saddest accents of the minister. The people trembled, though they but darkly understood him, when he prayed that they, and himself, and all of mortal race, might be ready, as he trusted this young maiden had been, for the dreadful hour that should snatch the veil from their faces. The bearers went heavily forth, and the mourners followed, saddening all the street, with the dead before them, and Mr. Hooper in his black veil behind.

'Why do you look back?' said one in the procession to his partner.

'I had a fancy,' replied she, 'that the minister and the maiden's spirit were walking hand in hand.'

'And so had I, at the same moment,' said the other.

That night, the handsomest couple in Milford village were to be joined in wedlock. Though reckoned a melancholy man, Mr. Hooper had a placid cheerfulness for such occasions, which often excited a sympathetic smile, where livelier merriment would have been thrown away. There was no quality of his disposition which made him more beloved than this. The company at the wedding awaited his arrival with impatience, trusting that the strange awe, which had gathered over him throughout the day, would now be dispelled. But such was not the result. When Mr. Hooper came, the first thing that their eyes rested on was the same horrible black veil, which had added deeper gloom to the funeral, and could portend nothing but evil to the wedding. Such was its immediate effect on the guests, that a cloud seemed to have rolled duskily from beneath the black crape, and dimmed the light of the candles. The bridal pair stood up before the minister. But the bride's cold fingers quivered in the tremulous hand of the bridegroom, and her death-like paleness caused a whisper, that the maiden who had been buried a few hours before, was come from her grave to be married. If ever another wedding were so dismal, it was that famous one, where they tolled the wedding-knell. After performing the ceremony, Mr. Hooper raised a glass of wine to his lips, wishing happiness to the new-married couple, in a strain of mild pleasantry that ought to have brightened the features of the guests, like a cheerful gleam from the hearth. At that instant, catching a glimpse of his figure in the looking-glass, the black veil involved his own spirit in the horror with which it overwhelmed all others. His frame shuddered—his lips grew white—he spilt the untasted wine upon the carpet—and rushed forth into the darkness. For the Earth, too, had on her Black Veil.

The next day, the whole village of Milford talked of little else than Parson Hooper's black veil. That, and the mystery concealed behind it, supplied a topic for discussion between acquaintances meeting in the street, and good women gossiping at their open windows. It was the first item of news that the tavern-keeper told to his guests. The children babbled of it on their way to school. One imitative little imp covered his face with an old black handkerchief, thereby so affrighting his playmates, that the panic seized himself, and he well nigh lost his wits by his own waggery.

It was remarkable, that, of all the busy-bodies and impertinent people in the parish, not one ventured to put the plain question to Mr. Hooper, wherefore he did this thing. Hitherto, whenever there appeared the slightest call for such interference, he had never lacked advisers, nor shown himself averse to be guided by their judgment. If he erred at all, it was by so painful a degree of self-distrust, that even the mildest censure would lead him to consider an indifferent action as a crime. Yet, though so well acquainted with this amiable weakness, no individual among his parishioners chose to make the black veil a subject of friendly remonstrance. There was a feeling of dread, neither plainly confessed nor carefully concealed, which caused each to shift the responsibility upon another, till at length it was found expedient to send a deputation of the church, in order to deal with Mr. Hooper about the mystery, before it should grow into a scandal. Never did an embassy so ill discharge its duties. The minister received them with friendly courtesy, but became silent, after they were seated, leaving to his visiters the whole burthen of introducing their important business. The topic, it might be supposed, was obvious enough. There was the black veil, swathed round Mr. Hooper's forehead, and concealing every feature above his placid mouth, on which, at times, they could perceive the glimmering of a melancholy smile. But that piece of crape, to their imagination, seemed to hang down before his heart, the symbol of a fearful secret between him and them. Were the veil but cast aside, they might speak freely of it, but not till then. Thus they sat a considerable time, speechless, confused, and shrinking uneasily from Mr. Hooper's eye, which they felt to be fixed upon them with an invisible glance. Finally, the deputies returned abashed to their constituents, pronouncing the matter too weighty to be handled, except by a council of the churches, if, indeed, it might not require a general synod.

But there was one person in the village, unappalled by the awe with which the black veil had impressed all beside herself. When the deputies returned without an explanation, or even venturing to demand one, she, with the calm energy of her character, determined to chase away the strange cloud that appeared to be settling round Mr. Hooper, every moment more darkly than before. As his plighted wife, it should be her privilege to know what the black veil concealed. At the minister's first visit, therefore, she entered upon the subject, with a direct simplicity, which made the task easier both for him and her. After he had seated himself, she fixed her eyes steadfastly upon the veil, but could discern nothing of the dreadful gloom that had so overawed the multitude: it was but a double fold of crape, hanging down from his forehead to his mouth, and slightly stirring with his breath.

'No,' said she aloud, and smiling, 'there is nothing terrible in this piece of crape, except that it hides a face which I am always glad to look upon. Come, good sir, let the sun shine from behind the cloud. First lay aside your black veil: then tell me why you put it on.'

Mr. Hooper's smile glimmered faintly.

'There is an hour to come,' said he, 'when all of us shall cast aside our veils. Take it not amiss, beloved friend, if I wear this piece of crape till then.'

'Your words are a mystery too,' returned the young lady. 'Take away the veil from them, at least.'

'Elizabeth, I will,' said he, 'so far as my vow may suffer me. Know, then, this veil is a type and a symbol, and I am bound to wear it ever, both in light and darkness, in solitude and before the gaze of multitudes, and as with strangers, so with my familiar friends. No mortal eye will see it withdrawn. This dismal shade must separate me from the world: even you, Elizabeth, can never come behind it!'

'What grievous affliction hath befallen you,' she earnestly inquired, 'that you should thus darken your eyes for ever?'

'If it be a sign of mourning,' replied Mr. Hooper, 'I, perhaps, like most other mortals, have sorrows dark enough to be typified by a black veil.'

'But what if the world will not believe that it is the type of an innocent sorrow?' urged Elizabeth. 'Beloved and respected as you are, there may be whispers, that you hide your face under the consciousness of secret sin. For the sake of your holy office, do away this scandal!'

The color rose into her cheeks, as she intimated the nature of the rumors that were already abroad in the village. But Mr. Hooper's mildness did not forsake him. He even smiled again—that same sad smile, which always appeared like a faint glimmering of light, proceeding from the obscurity beneath the veil.

'If I hide my face for sorrow, there is cause enough,' he merely replied; 'and if I cover it for secret sin, what mortal might not do the same?'

And with this gentle, but unconquerable obstinacy, did he resist all her entreaties. At length Elizabeth sat silent. For a few moments she appeared lost in thought, considering, probably, what new methods might be tried, to withdraw her lover from so dark a fantasy, which, if it had no other meaning, was perhaps a symptom of mental disease. Though of a firmer character than his own, the tears rolled down her cheeks. But, in an instant, as it were, a new feeling took the place of sorrow: her eyes were fixed insensibly on the black veil, when, like a sudden twilight in the air, its terrors fell around her. She arose, and stood trembling before him.

'And do you feel it then at last?' said he mournfully.

She made no reply, but covered her eyes with her hand, and turned to leave the room. He rushed forward and caught her arm.

'Have patience with me, Elizabeth!' cried he passionately. 'Do not desert me, though this veil must be between us here on earth. Be mine, and hereafter there shall be no veil over my face, no darkness between our souls! It is but a mortal veil—it is not for eternity! Oh! you know not how lonely I am, and how frightened to be alone behind my black veil. Do not leave me in this miserable obscurity for ever!'

'Lift the veil but once, and look me in the face,' said she.

'Never! It cannot be!' replied Mr. Hooper.

'Then, farewell!' said Elizabeth.

She withdrew her arm from his grasp, and slowly departed, pausing at the door, to give one long, shuddering gaze, that seemed almost to penetrate the mystery of the black veil. But, even amid his grief, Mr. Hooper smiled to think that only a

material emblem had separated him from happiness, though
the horrors which it shadowed forth, must be drawn darkly
between the fondest of lovers.

From that time no attempts were made to remove Mr.
Hooper's black veil, or, by a direct appeal, to discover the
secret which it was supposed to hide. By persons who claimed
a superiority to popular prejudice, it was reckoned merely an
eccentric whim, such as often mingles with the sober actions
of men otherwise rational, and tinges them all with its own
semblance of insanity. But with the multitude, good Mr.
Hooper was irreparably a bugbear. He could not walk the
streets with any peace of mind, so conscious was he that the
gentle and timid would turn aside to avoid him, and that others would make it a point of hardihood to throw themselves
in his way. The impertinence of the latter class compelled him
to give up his customary walk, at sunset, to the burial ground,
for when he leaned pensively over the gate, there would always be faces behind the grave-stones, peeping at his black
veil. A fable went the rounds, that the stare of the dead people drove him thence. It grieved him, to the very depth of his
kind heart, to observe how the children fled from his approach, breaking up their merriest sports, while his melancholy figure was yet afar off. Their instinctive dread caused
him to feel, more strongly than aught else, that a preternatural horror was interwoven with the threads of the black
crape. In truth, his own antipathy to the veil was known to
be so great, that he never willingly passed before a mirror,
nor stooped to drink at a still fountain, lest, in its peaceful
bosom, he should be affrighted by himself. This was what
gave plausibility to the whispers, that Mr. Hooper's conscience tortured him for some great crime, too horrible to be
entirely concealed, or otherwise than so obscurely intimated.
Thus, from beneath the black veil, there rolled a cloud into
the sunshine, an ambiguity of sin or sorrow, which enveloped
the poor minister, so that love or sympathy could never reach
him. It was said, that ghost and fiend consorted with him
there. With self-shudderings and outward terrors, he walked
continually in its shadow, groping darkly within his own soul,
or gazing through a medium that saddened the whole world.
Even the lawless wind, it was believed, respected his dreadful

secret, and never blew aside the veil. But still good Mr. Hooper sadly smiled, at the pale visages of the worldly throng as he passed by.

Among all its bad influences, the black veil had the one desirable effect, of making its wearer a very efficient clergyman. By the aid of his mysterious emblem—for there was no other apparent cause—he became a man of awful power, over souls that were in agony for sin. His converts always regarded him with a dread peculiar to themselves, affirming, though but figuratively, that, before he brought them to celestial light, they had been with him behind the black veil. Its gloom, indeed, enabled him to sympathize with all dark affections. Dying sinners cried aloud for Mr. Hooper, and would not yield their breath till he appeared; though ever, as he stooped to whisper consolation, they shuddered at the veiled face so near their own. Such were the terrors of the black veil, even when Death had bared his visage! Strangers came long distances to attend service at his church, with the mere idle purpose of gazing at his figure, because it was forbidden them to behold his face. But many were made to quake ere they departed! Once, during Governor Belcher's administration, Mr. Hooper was appointed to preach the election sermon. Covered with his black veil, he stood before the chief magistrate, the council, and the representatives, and wrought so deep an impression, that the legislative measures of that year, were characterized by all the gloom and piety of our earliest ancestral sway.

In this manner Mr. Hooper spent a long life, irreproachable in outward act, yet shrouded in dismal suspicions; kind and loving, though unloved, and dimly feared; a man apart from men, shunned in their health and joy, but ever summoned to their aid in mortal anguish. As years wore on, shedding their snows above his sable veil, he acquired a name throughout the New-England churches, and they called him Father Hooper. Nearly all his parishioners, who were of mature age when he was settled, had been borne away by many a funeral: he had one congregation in the church, and a more crowded one in the church-yard; and having wrought so late into the evening, and done his work so well, it was now good Father Hooper's turn to rest.

Several persons were visible by the shaded candlelight, in the death-chamber of the old clergyman. Natural connections he had none. But there was the decorously grave, though unmoved physician, seeking only to mitigate the last pangs of the patient whom he could not save. There were the deacons, and other eminently pious members of his church. There, also, was the Reverend Mr. Clark, of Westbury, a young and zealous divine, who had ridden in haste to pray by the bedside of the expiring minister. There was the nurse, no hired handmaiden of death, but one whose calm affection had endured thus long, in secresy, in solitude, amid the chill of age, and would not perish, even at the dying hour. Who, but Elizabeth! And there lay the hoary head of good Father Hooper upon the death-pillow, with the black veil still swathed about his brow and reaching down over his face, so that each more difficult gasp of his faint breath caused it to stir. All through life that piece of crape had hung between him and the world: it had separated him from cheerful brotherhood and woman's love, and kept him in that saddest of all prisons, his own heart; and still it lay upon his face, as if to deepen the gloom of his darksome chamber, and shade him from the sunshine of eternity.

For some time previous, his mind had been confused, wavering doubtfully between the past and the present, and hovering forward, as it were, at intervals, into the indistinctness of the world to come. There had been feverish turns, which tossed him from side to side, and wore away what little strength he had. But in his most convulsive struggles, and in the wildest vagaries of his intellect, when no other thought retained its sober influence, he still showed an awful solicitude lest the black veil should slip aside. Even if his bewildered soul could have forgotten, there was a faithful woman at his pillow, who, with averted eyes, would have covered that aged face, which she had last beheld in the comeliness of manhood. At length the death-stricken old man lay quietly in the torpor of mental and bodily exhaustion, with an imperceptible pulse, and breath that grew fainter and fainter, except when a long, deep, and irregular inspiration seemed to prelude the flight of his spirit.

The minister of Westbury approached the bedside.

'Venerable Father Hooper,' said he, 'the moment of your release is at hand. Are you ready for the lifting of the veil, that shuts in time from eternity?'

Father Hooper at first replied merely by a feeble motion of his head; then, apprehensive, perhaps, that his meaning might be doubtful, he exerted himself to speak.

'Yea,' said he, in faint accents, 'my soul hath a patient weariness until that veil be lifted.'

'And is it fitting,' resumed the Reverend Mr. Clark, 'that a man so given to prayer, of such a blameless example, holy in deed and thought, so far as mortal judgment may pronounce; is it fitting that a father in the church should leave a shadow on his memory, that may seem to blacken a life so pure? I pray you, my venerable brother, let not this thing be! Suffer us to be gladdened by your triumphant aspect, as you go to your reward. Before the veil of eternity be lifted, let me cast aside this black veil from your face!'

And thus speaking, the Reverend Mr. Clark bent forward to reveal the mystery of so many years. But, exerting a sudden energy, that made all the beholders stand aghast, Father Hooper snatched both his hands from beneath the bedclothes, and pressed them strongly on the black veil, resolute to struggle, if the minister of Westbury would contend with a dying man.

'Never!' cried the veiled clergyman. 'On earth, never!'

'Dark old man!' exclaimed the affrighted minister, 'with what horrible crime upon your soul are you now passing to the judgment?'

Father Hooper's breath heaved; it rattled in his throat; but, with a mighty effort, grasping forward with his hands, he caught hold of life, and held it back till he should speak. He even raised himself in bed; and there he sat, shivering with the arms of death around him, while the black veil hung down, awful, at that last moment, in the gathered terrors of a life-time. And yet the faint, sad smile, so often there, now seemed to glimmer from its obscurity, and linger on Father Hooper's lips.

'Why do you tremble at me alone?' cried he, turning his veiled face round the circle of pale spectators. 'Tremble also at each other! Have men avoided me, and women shown no pity, and children screamed and fled, only for my black veil? What, but the mystery which it obscurely typifies, has made this piece of crape so awful? When the friend shows his inmost heart to his friend; the lover to his best-beloved; when man does not vainly shrink from the eye of his Creator, loathsomely treasuring up the secret of his sin; then deem me a monster, for the symbol beneath which I have lived, and die! I look around me, and, lo! on every visage a Black Veil!'

While his auditors shrank from one another, in mutual affright, Father Hooper fell back upon his pillow, a veiled corpse, with a faint smile lingering on the lips. Still veiled, they laid him in his coffin, and a veiled corpse they bore him to the grave. The grass of many years has sprung up and withered on that grave, the burial-stone is moss-grown, and good Mr. Hooper's face is dust; but awful is still the thought, that it mouldered beneath the Black Veil!

Old Ticonderoga

THE greatest attraction, in this vicinity, is the famous old fortress of Ticonderoga; the remains of which are visible from the piazza of the tavern, on a swell of land that shuts in the prospect of the lake. Those celebrated heights, Mount Defiance and Mount Independence, familiar to all Americans in history, stand too prominent not to be recognized, though neither of them precisely correspond to the images excited by their names. In truth, the whole scene, except the interior of the fortress, disappointed me. Mount Defiance, which one pictures as a steep, lofty, and rugged hill, of most formidable aspect, frowning down with the grim visage of a precipice on old Ticonderoga, is merely a long and wooded ridge; and bore, at some former period, the gentle name of Sugar Hill. The brow is certainly difficult to climb, and high enough to look into every corner of the fortress. St. Clair's most probable reason, however, for neglecting to occupy it, was the deficiency of troops to man the works already constructed, rather than the supposed inaccessibility of Mount Defiance. It is singular that the French never fortified this height, standing, as it does, in the quarter whence they must have looked for the advance of a British army.

In my first view of the ruins I was favored with the scientific guidance of a young lieutenant of engineers, recently from West Point, where he had gained credit for great military genius. I saw nothing but confusion in what chiefly interested him; straight lines and zigzags, defence within defence, wall opposed to wall, and ditch intersecting ditch; oblong squares of masonry below the surface of the earth, and huge mounds, or turf-covered hills of stone, above it. On one of these artificial hillocks, a pine-tree has rooted itself, and grown tall and strong, since the banner-staff was levelled. But where my unmilitary glance could trace no regularity, the young lieutenant was perfectly at home. He fathomed the meaning of every ditch, and formed an entire plan of the fortress from its half-obliterated lines. His description of Ticonderoga would be as accurate as a geometrical theorem, and as barren of the poetry that has clustered round its decay. I viewed Ticonderoga as a place of ancient strength, in ruins for half a century; where the flags of three nations had successively waved, and none waved now; where armies had struggled, so long ago that the bones of the slain were mouldered; where Peace had found a heritage in the forsaken haunts of War. Now the young West Pointer, with his lectures on ravelins, counterscarps, angles, and covered ways, made it an affair of brick and mortar and hewn stone, arranged on certain regular principles, having a good deal to do with mathematics but nothing at all with poetry.

I should have been glad of a hoary veteran to totter by my side, and tell me, perhaps, of the French garrisons and their Indian allies—of Abercrombie, Lord Howe, and Amherst— of Ethan Allen's triumph and St. Clair's surrender. The old soldier and the old fortress would be emblems of each other. His reminiscences, though vivid as the image of Ticonderoga in the lake, would harmonize with the gray influence of the scene. A survivor of the long-disbanded garrisons, though but a private soldier, might have mustered his dead chiefs and comrades—some from Westminster Abbey, and English church-yards, and battle-fields in Europe—others from their graves here in America—others, not a few, who lie sleeping round the fortress; he might have mustered them all, and bid them march through the ruined gateway, turning their old historic faces on me as they passed. Next to such a companion, the best is one's own fancy.

At another visit I was alone, and, after rambling all over the ramparts, sat down to rest myself in one of the roofless barracks. These are old French structures, and appear to have occupied three sides of a large area, now overgrown with grass, nettles, and thistles. The one, in which I sat, was long and narrow, as all the rest had been, with peaked gables. The exterior walls were nearly entire, constructed of gray, flat, unpicked stones, the aged strength of which promised long to resist the elements, if no other violence should precipitate their fall. The roof, floors, partitions, and the rest of the wood-work, had probably been burnt, except some bars of stanch old oak, which were blackened with fire but still re-

mained embedded into the window-sills and over the doors.
There were a few particles of plastering near the chimney,
scratched with rude figures, perhaps by a soldier's hand. A
most luxuriant crop of weeds had sprung up within the edifice and hid the scattered fragments of the wall. Grass and
weeds grew in the windows, and in all the crevices of the
stone, climbing, step by step, till a tuft of yellow flowers was
waving on the highest peak of the gable. Some spicy herb
diffused a pleasant odor through the ruin. A verdant heap of
vegetation had covered the hearth of the second floor, clustering on the very spot where the huge logs had mouldered
to glowing coals, and flourished beneath the broad flue,
which had so often puffed the smoke over a circle of French
or English soldiers. I felt that there was no other token of
decay so impressive as that bed of weeds in the place of the
back-log.

Here I sat, with those roofless walls about me, the clear sky
over my head, and the afternoon sunshine falling gently
bright through the window-frames and doorway. I heard the
tinkling of a cow-bell, the twittering of birds, and the pleasant
hum of insects. Once a gay butterfly, with four gold-speckled
wings, came and fluttered about my head, then flew up and
lighted on the highest tuft of yellow flowers, and at last took
wing across the lake. Next a bee buzzed through the sunshine, and found much sweetness among the weeds. After
watching him till he went off to his distant hive, I closed my
eyes on Ticonderoga in ruins, and cast a dream-like glance
over pictures of the past, and scenes of which this spot had
been the theatre.

At first, my fancy saw only the stern hills, lonely lakes, and
venerable woods. Not a tree, since their seeds were first scattered over the infant soil, had felt the axe, but had grown up
and flourished through its long generation, had fallen beneath
the weight of years, been buried in green moss, and nourished the roots of others as gigantic. Hark! A light paddle
dips into the lake, a birch canoe glides round the point, and
an Indian chief has passed, painted and feather-crested, armed
with a bow of hickory, a stone tomahawk, and flint-headed
arrows. But the ripple had hardly vanished from the water,
when a white flag caught the breeze, over a castle in the wil-

derness with frowning ramparts and a hundred cannon. There stood a French chevalier, commandant of the fortress, paying court to a copper-colored lady, the princess of the land, and winning her wild love by the arts which had been successful with Parisian dames. A war-party of French and Indians were issuing from the gate to lay waste some village of New England. Near the fortress there was a group of dancers. The merry soldiers footing it with the swart savage maids; deeper in the wood, some red men were growing frantic around a keg of the fire-water; and elsewhere a Jesuit preached the faith of high cathedrals beneath a canopy of forest boughs, and distributed crucifixes to be worn beside English scalps.

I tried to make a series of pictures from the old French war, when fleets were on the lake and armies in the woods, and especially of Abercrombie's disastrous repulse, where thousands of lives were utterly thrown away; but being at a loss how to order the battle, I chose an evening scene in the barracks after the fortress had surrendered to Sir Jeffrey Amherst. What an immense fire blazes on that hearth, gleaming on swords, bayonets, and musket barrels, and blending with the hue of the scarlet coats till the whole barrack-room is quivering with ruddy light! One soldier has thrown himself down to rest, after a deer-hunt, or perhaps a long run through the woods, with Indians on his trail. Two stand up to wrestle, and are on the point of coming to blows. A fifer plays a shrill accompaniment to a drummer's song—a strain of light love and bloody war, with a chorus thundered forth by twenty voices. Meantime, a veteran in the corner is prosing about Dettingen and Fontenoye, and relates camp-traditions of Marlborough's battles; till his pipe, having been roguishly charged with gunpowder, makes a terrible explosion under his nose. And now they all vanish in a puff of smoke from the chimney.

I merely glanced at the ensuing twenty years, which glided peacefully over the frontier fortress, till Ethan Allen's shout was heard, summoning it to surrender "in the name of the great Jehovah and of the Continental Congress." Strange allies! thought the British captain. Next came the hurried muster of the soldiers of liberty, when the cannon of Burgoyne, pointing down upon their strong-hold from the brow of

Mount Defiance, announced a new conqueror of Ticonderoga. No virgin fortress, this! Forth rushed the motley throng from the barracks, one man wearing the blue and buff of the Union, another the red coat of Britain, a third a dragoon's jacket, and a fourth a cotton frock; here was a pair of leather breeches, and striped trowsers there; a grenadier's cap on one head, and a broad-brimmed hat, with a tall feather, on the next; this fellow shouldering a king's arm, that might throw a bullet to Crown Point, and his comrade a long fowling-piece, admirable to shoot ducks on the lake. In the midst of the bustle, when the fortress was all alive with its last warlike scene, the ringing of a bell on the lake made me suddenly unclose my eyes, and behold only the gray and weed-grown ruins. They were as peaceful in the sun as a warrior's grave.

Hastening to the rampart, I perceived that the signal had been given by the steam-boat Franklin, which landed a passenger from Whitehall at the tavern, and resumed its progress northward, to reach Canada the next morning. A sloop was pursuing the same track; a little skiff had just crossed the ferry; while a scow, laden with lumber, spread its huge square sail and went up the lake. The whole country was a cultivated farm. Within musket shot of the ramparts lay the neat villa of Mr. Pell, who, since the Revolution, has become proprietor of a spot for which France, England, and America have so often struggled. How forcibly the lapse of time and change of circumstances came home to my apprehension! Banner would never wave again, nor cannon roar, nor blood be shed, nor trumpet stir up a soldier's heart, in this old fort of Ticonderoga. Tall trees had grown upon its ramparts, since the last garrison marched out, to return no more, or only at some dreamer's summons, gliding from the twilight past to vanish among realities.

A Visit to the Clerk of the Weather

"I DON'T KNOW—I have not yet spoken to the clerk of the weather,"—said I, in common parlance to my friend and kinsman, who had asked me the wise question—"Do you think we shall have an early spring?" We stood on the steps of the M—— hotel. The night was not very dark, but sundry flakes of snow, that came wavering to the ground, served to render the vision indistinct. Nevertheless I could plainly perceive that a little old woman in a gray cloak, who was passing at the moment, had caught my words; and her small black eyes rayed up through the mist as I spoke, with an expression of intelligence rather uncomfortable to a sober citizen like myself. My friend, at the same moment, turned on his heel with a slight shudder, and sought a warmer climate within. The little old woman stood at my side in a twinkling, and when I would have withdrawn myself, I felt her bony hand encircling my arm as if I had been in the grasp of a skeleton.

"Unhand me, madam, or by Heaven——"

"You have taken *his* name in vain," said she, in a hoarse whisper, "often enough, and it is evident that you believe not in his existence. Come with me. Nay, do not hesitate, or I will weigh your manhood against the courage of an old woman."

"On, fool!" exclaimed I.

Away scampered the old woman, and I followed—drawn by an impulse which I could not resist. Streets, houses, woods, fences, seemed running back as we progressed, so rapid was our motion. At length I was lifted from my feet, and whirled through the air at such a rate that I nearly lost my breath. The gray cloak of the old woman could be discerned at some distance before me—clouds sprang apart, and rolled themselves in ridges on either hand of her as she passed, making a clear path for herself and follower. How far we travelled thus I am unable to say. But suddenly we struck the land, and I stood upon the green turf. The sun flamed full upon my head, and I now, for the first time, felt travel-worn and faint.

"I can assist you no farther," said the old woman; and in a moment she had disappeared.

At a little distance from the spot where I stood, was a pile of rocks of a singular form. About a dozen tall, slate-colored rocks—each one of which was several acres in height—had been thrown together in a circle in the form of a pyramid, the points meeting at the top. As I stood gazing at this singular structure, I observed a light smoke rising up through a small aperture on the very apex of this gigantic cone. I determined to obtain ingress to this strange dwelling, for that it was inhabited I no longer doubted. I walked around the natural fabric several times before I discovered an entrance; several rugged rocks had hidden it from my view. But the opening was large enough to admit a dozen horsemen abreast. Slowly and cautiously I entered the lofty chamber. It was about five hundred yards in circumference. Several singular objects immediately drew my attention; of course the animated forms were honored with my first notice. There were three gigantic beings lounging about in different parts of the room, while a venerable, stately old man, with long gray locks, sat at the farther side of the apartment busily engaged in writing. Before advancing to speak to any of my new acquaintances, I glanced around the rocky cavern. In one corner was piled a heap of red-hot thunderbolts. Against the wall hung several second-hand rainbows, covered with dust and much faded. Several hundred cart loads of hail-stones, two large sacks of wind, and a portable tempest, firmly secured with iron bands, next engaged my attention. But I saw that the venerable personage mentioned above had become sensible of my presence, and as he had half risen from his seat, I hastened to present myself. As I drew near to him, I was struck by the size of his massive frame and the fierce expression of his eyes. He had stuck his pen behind his ear—which pen was neither more nor less than the top of a poplar tree, which some storm had rudely disengaged from its trunk, and the butt of which he had hewed down to a proper size for dipping into his inkhorn. He took my hand into his broad palm, and squeezed it too cordially for my bodily comfort, but greatly to the satisfaction of my mind, which had experienced some painful misgivings from my first entrance. I saluted him in the fashion of my country, and he replied,

"I am tolerably well, I thank you, for an old man of three-score centuries—from whence come you?"

"I am last from Boston, sir."

"I do not recollect any planet of that name," said he.

"I beg pardon—from the earth, I should have said."

He thought a moment. "Yes, yes, I do recollect a little mud-ball somewhere in this direction;"—he pointed with his arm—"but, truly, I had almost forgotten it. Hum! we have neglected you of late. It must be looked to. Our ally, Mr. John Frost, has had some claims on us, which we have liquidated by giving him permission to erect sundry ice-palaces, and throw up a few fortifications on your soil; but I fear the rogue has made too much of his privilege. He must be checked!"

"Really, sir, not only my gratitude, but the gratitude of all the world would be yours, if you would attend to us a little more vigilantly than you have done."

He looked grave a moment—shook his head, and rejoined—"But, sir, I have, myself, some complaints to make with regard to you. I have been somewhat slandered by your fellows, and, in truth, that was one inducement that led me to yield so readily to the request of my kinsman, Mr. Frost. You probably know there are some persons on your little planet who pretend to be of my council, and who send out little printed missiles, pretending to great ingenuity, wherein it is set forth that on such and such a day there shall be a snow-storm—a tempest—thunder and lightning—or fervent heat. Nay, some of them have carried it so far as to publish caricatures and grotesque drawings—have prophesied that there should be snow in August, and——"

Here we were interrupted by a loud hissing noise, which caused me to start and turn round.

"You must have a care. You have scorched your garments, I fear," cried my host to a squat figure, who came trudging towards us, wrapped in sheets of ice and wearing a huge wig powdered with snow.

"It is nothing, your Honor," answered the other, in a hollow voice which chilled my blood—"I only trod upon that cursed coil of chain lightning which your servant has placed so near the door to be my bane as often as I visit you!"

I was too much taken up with this uncouth visiter to notice the entrance of another guest, who had placed herself directly between me and the clerk of the weather before I beheld her. She was a lovely young damsel, dressed in a variegated gown, of the most beautiful colors, her head surmounted by a green turban, and her feet shod with moccasins of the same hue, bespangled with dew-drops. The icy dwarf shrunk aside as she approached, and lowered at her from under his thick brows. She cast a glance at him, and pouted like a spoiled child. She then turned to me, and said in a tone of ineffable sweetness,

"You are the stranger from the Earth, I conclude?"

"At your service, fair lady."

"I heard of your arrival," continued she; "and hastened to meet you. I wish to inquire after my good friends, the inhabitants of your globe. My name is Spring."

"My dear lady," said I, "your countenance would gladden the hearts of us all; I assure you that your presence has been desired and earnestly prayed for by all classes of my fellow-sufferers."

"It is too provoking!" cried she, dashing her green turban upon the ground, and stamping with her little foot until I was besprinkled with the dew-drops that it shed. "I suppose that I am blamed—nay, execrated, for my tardiness by my children of the earth—while heaven knows that I long to bound over your valleys and hills, and linger by the side of your running brooks as of yore. But that wretch—that mis-shapen wretch—" and she pointed at Jack Frost, for he it was, "that soulless, withering demon, holds me in his power. I brought an action against him last year; but, unfortunately, I was advised to put the case in Chancery, and summer arrived before it was decided. But assure your fellows that I will not neglect them in future. I shall be amongst them early. Mr. Frost is obliged to take a journey to the north to procure a polar bear for his wife, who has lingered amongst you, with her husband, so long, that she affects some of your customs, and must needs have a substitute for a lap-dog." She then turned away and held communion with the clerk of the weather, while I sauntered about the cavern to examine its singular contents. A gigantic fellow was sweating over the fire and cooking his master's breakfast. In a moment, I saw him ascend by a sort of rope ladder, and pick a small white cloud out of the heavens wherewith to settle the coffee. I sauntered on until I came to a heap of granite, behind which sat a dozen little black fellows, cross-legged, who were laboring with all their might to weave a thunder gust. The part of the business which seemed to puzzle them most was, the working in of the bolts, which they were obliged to handle with long pincers. Another important point was sewing on the fringe, which was made of chain lightning. While I stood surveying these apprentices, a strapping fellow came reeling towards me, and inquired whether I had visited the forge. I told him that I had not. He said that it was not now in operation, as there was a sufficient quantity of thunderbolts manufactured for present use, although there might soon be a trifle of an earthquake to patch up. I observed that his wrist was swathed with a crimson bandage, and inquired if he was injured in that part. He said that he had received a trifling scratch there, for that last year he had been commissioned to discharge several thunderbolts upon our earth, which he did to his satisfaction until he came to the last, which, having been hurled like a rocket against our globe, unfortunately alighted on the head of a certain member of Congress, where it met with so much resistance that it bounded back to the skies and grazed his wrist.

At this moment somebody seized my arm from behind; I turned my head and saw the little old woman in the gray cloak. I was hurried from the massive hall, and conveyed, with as much speed as before, back to the world from which I had set out on this strange and wonderful adventure.

Monsieur du Miroir

THAN the gentleman above-named, there is nobody, in the whole circle of my acquaintance, whom I have more attentively studied, yet of whom I have less real knowledge, beneath the surface which it pleases him to present. Being anxious to discover who and what he really is, and how connected with me, and what are to be the results, to him and to myself, of the joint interest, which, without any choice on my part, seems to be permanently established between us—and incited, furthermore, by the propensities of a student of human nature, though doubtful whether M. du Miroir have aught of humanity but the figure—I have determined to place a few of his remarkable points before the public, hoping to be favored with some clew to the explanation of his character.—Nor let the reader condemn any part of the narrative as frivolous, since a subject of such grave reflection diffuses its importance through the minutest particulars, and there is no judging, beforehand, what odd little circumstance may do the office of a blind man's dog, among the perplexities of this dark investigation. And however extraordinary, marvellous, preternatural, and utterly incredible, some of the meditated disclosures may appear, I pledge my honor to maintain as sacred a regard to fact, as if my testimony were given on oath, and involved the dearest interests of the personage in question. Not that there is matter for a criminal accusation against M. du Miroir; nor am I the man to bring it forward, if there were. The chief that I complain of is his impenetrable mystery, which is no better than nonsense, if it conceal anything good, and much worse, in the contrary case.

But, if undue partialities could be supposed to influence me, M. du Miroir might hope to profit, rather than to suffer by them; for, in the whole of our long intercourse, we have seldom had the slightest disagreement; and, moreover, there are reasons for supposing him a near relative of mine, and consequently entitled to the best word that I can give him. He bears, indisputably, a strong personal resemblance to myself, and generally puts on mourning at the funerals of the family. On the other hand, his name would indicate a French descent; in which case, infinitely preferring that my blood should flow from a bold British and pure Puritan source, I beg leave to disclaim all kindred with M. du Miroir. Some genealogists trace his origin to Spain, and dub him a knight of the order of the CABALLEROS DE LOS ESPEJOS, one of whom was overthrown by Don Quixote. But what says M. du Miroir, himself, of his paternity and his father-land? Not a word did he ever say about the matter; and herein, perhaps, lies one of his most especial reasons for maintaining such a vexatious mystery—that he lacks the faculty of speech to expound it. His lips are sometimes seen to move; his eyes and countenance are alive with shifting expression, as if corresponding by visible hieroglyphics to his modulated breath; and anon, he will seem to pause, with as satisfied an air, as if he had been talking excellent sense. Good sense or bad, M. du Miroir is the sole judge of his own conversational powers, never having whispered so much as a syllable, that reached the ears of any other auditor. Is he really dumb?—or is all the world deaf?—or is it merely a piece of my friend's waggery, meant for nothing but to make fools of us? If so, he has the joke all to himself.

This dumb devil, which possesses M. du Miroir, is, I am persuaded, the sole reason that he does not make me the most flattering protestations of friendship. In many particulars— indeed, as to all his cognizable and not preternatural points, except that, once in a great while, I speak a word or two— there exists the greatest apparent sympathy between us. Such is his confidence in my taste, that he goes astray from the general fashion, and copies all his dresses after mine. I never try on a new garment, without expecting to meet M. du Miroir in one of the same pattern. He has duplicates of all my waistcoats and cravats, shirt-bosoms of precisely a similar plait, and an old coat for private wear, manufactured, I suspect, by a Chinese tailor, in exact imitation of a beloved old coat of mine, with a facsimile, stitch by stitch, of a patch upon the elbow. In truth, the singular and minute coincidences that occur, both in the accidents of the passing day and the serious events of our lives, remind me of those doubtful legends of lovers, or twin-children, twins of fate, who have

lived, enjoyed, suffered, and died, in unison, each faithfully
repeating the least tremor of the other's breath, though separated by vast tracts of sea and land. Strange to say, my incommodities belong equally to my companion, though the
burthen is nowise alleviated by his participation. The other
morning, after a night of torment from the toothache, I met
M. du Miroir with such a swollen anguish in his cheek, that
my own pangs were redoubled, as were also his, if I might
judge by a fresh contortion of his visage. All the inequalities
of my spirits are communicated to him, causing the unfortunate M. du Miroir to mope and scowl through a whole summer's day, or to laugh as long, for no better reason than the
gay or gloomy crotchets of my brain. Once we were joint
sufferers of a three months' sickness, and met like mutual
ghosts in the first days of convalescence. Whenever I have
been in love, M. du Miroir has looked passionate and tender,
and never did my mistress discard me, but this too susceptible
gentleman grew lack-a-daisical. His temper, also, rises to
blood-heat, fever-heat, or boiling-water heat, according to the
measure of any wrong which might seem to have fallen entirely on myself. I have sometimes been calmed down, by the
sight of my own inordinate wrath, depicted on his frowning
brow. Yet, however prompt in taking up my quarrels, I cannot call to mind that he ever struck a downright blow in my
behalf; nor, in fact, do I perceive that any real and tangible
good has resulted from his constant interference in my affairs;
so that, in my distrustful moods, I am apt to suspect M. du
Miroir's sympathy to be mere outward show, not a whit better nor worse than other people's sympathy. Nevertheless, as
mortal man must have something in the guise of sympathy,
and whether the true metal, or merely copper-washed, is of
less moment, I choose rather to content myself with M. du
Miroir's, such as it is, than to seek the sterling coin, and perhaps miss even the counterfeit.

In my age of vanities, I have often seen him in the ball-
room, and might again, were I to seek him there. We have
encountered each other at the Tremont theatre, where, however, he took his seat neither in the dress-circle, pit, nor upper
regions, nor threw a single glance at the stage, though the
brightest star, even Fanny Kemble herself, might be culminat-

ing there. No; this whimsical friend of mine chose to linger in the saloon, near one of the large looking-glasses which throw back their pictures of the illuminated room. He is so full of these unaccountable eccentricities, that I never like to notice M. du Miroir, nor to acknowledge the slightest connection with him, in places of public resort. He, however, has no scruple about claiming my acquaintance, even when his common sense, if he had any, might teach him that I would as willingly exchange a nod with the Old Nick. It was but the other day, that he got into a large brass kettle, at the entrance of a hardware store, and thrust his head, the moment afterwards, into a bright new warming-pan, whence he gave me a most merciless look of recognition. He smiled, and so did I; but these childish tricks make decent people rather shy of M. du Miroir, and subject him to more dead cuts than any other gentleman in town.

One of this singular person's most remarkable peculiarities is his fondness for water, wherein he excels any temperance-man whatever. His pleasure, it must be owned, is not so much to drink it, (in which respect, a very moderate quantity will answer his occasions,) as to souse himself over head and ears, wherever he may meet with it. Perhaps he is a merman, or born of a mermaid's marriage with a mortal, and thus amphibious by hereditary right, like the children which the old river deities, or nymphs of fountains, gave to earthly love. When no cleaner bathing-place happened to be at hand, I have seen the foolish fellow in a horse-pond. Sometimes he refreshes himself in the trough of a town-pump, without caring what the people think about him. Often, while carefully picking my way along the street, after a heavy shower, I have been scandalized to see M. du Miroir, in full dress, paddling from one mud-puddle to another, and plunging into the filthy depths of each. Seldom have I peeped into a well, without discerning this ridiculous gentleman at the bottom, whence he gazes up, as through a long telescopic tube, and probably makes discoveries among the stars by daylight. Wandering along lonesome paths, or in pathless forests, when I have come to virgin-fountains, of which it would have been pleasant to deem myself the first discoverer, I have started to find M. du Miroir there before me. The solitude seemed lonelier for his presence. I have leaned from a precipice that frowns over Lake George—which the French called Nature's font of sacramental water, and used it in their log-churches here, and their cathedrals beyond the sea—and seen him far below, in that pure element. At Niagara, too, where I would gladly have forgotten both myself and him, I could not help observing my companion, in the smooth water, on the very verge of the cataract, just above the Table Rock. Were I to reach the sources of the Nile, I should expect to meet him there. Unless he be another Ladurlad, whose garments the depths of ocean could not moisten, it is difficult to conceive how he keeps himself in any decent pickle; though I am bound to confess, that his clothes seem always as dry and comfortable as my own. But, as a friend, I could wish that he would not so often expose himself in liquor.

All that I have hitherto related may be classed among those little personal oddities which agreeably diversify the surface of society; and, though they may sometimes annoy us, yet keep our daily intercourse fresher and livelier than if they were done away. By an occasional hint, however, I have endeavored to pave the way for stranger things to come, which, had they been disclosed at once, M. du Miroir might have been deemed a shadow, and myself a person of no veracity, and this truthful history a fabulous legend. But, now that the reader knows me worthy of his confidence, I will begin to make him stare.

To speak frankly, then, I could bring the most astounding proofs that M. du Miroir is at least a conjuror, if not one of that unearthly tribe with whom conjurors deal. He has inscrutable methods of conveying himself from place to place, with the rapidity of the swiftest steam-boat, or rail-car. Brick walls, and oaken doors, and iron bolts, are no impediment to his passage. Here in my chamber, for instance, as the evening deepens into night, I sit alone—the key turned and withdrawn from the lock—the key-hole stuffed with paper, to keep out a peevish little blast of wind. Yet, lonely as I seem, were I to lift one of the lamps and step five paces eastward, M. du Miroir would be sure to meet me, with a lamp also in his hand. And, were I to take the stage coach to-morrow, without giving him the least hint of my design, and post on-

ward till the week's end, at whatever hotel I might find myself, I should expect to share my private apartment with this
inevitable M. du Miroir. Or, out of a mere wayward fantasy,
were I to go, by moonlight, and stand beside the stone font
of the Shaker Spring at Canterbury, M. du Miroir would set
forth on the same fool's errand, and would not fail to meet
me there. Shall I heighten the reader's wonder? While writing
these latter sentences, I happened to glance towards the large
round globe of one of the brass andirons; and lo!—a miniature apparition of M. du Miroir, with his face widened and
grotesquely contorted, as if he were making fun of my amazement. But he has played so many of these jokes, that they
begin to lose their effect. Once, presumptuous that he was,
he stole into the heaven of a young lady's eyes, so that while
I gazed, and was dreaming only of herself, I found him also
in my dream. Years have so changed him since, that he need
never hope to enter those heavenly orbs again.

From these veritable statements, it will be readily concluded, that, had M. du Miroir played such pranks in old
witch times, matters might have gone hard with him; at least,
if the constable and posse comitatus could have executed a
warrant, or the jailor had been cunning enough to keep him.
But it has often occurred to me as a very singular circumstance, and as betokening either a temperament morbidly suspicious, or some weighty cause of apprehension, that he never
trusts himself within the grasp even of his most intimate
friend. If you step forward to meet him, he readily advances;
if you offer him your hand, he extends his own, with an air
of the utmost frankness; but though you calculate upon a
hearty shake, you do not get hold of his little finger. Ah, this
M. du Miroir is a slippery fellow!

These, truly, are matters of special admiration. After vainly
endeavoring, by the strenuous exertion of my own wits, to
gain a satisfactory insight into the character of M. du Miroir,
I had recourse to certain wise men, and also to books of ab-
struse philosophy, seeking who it was that haunted me, and
why. I heard long lectures, and read huge volumes, with little
profit beyond the knowledge that many former instances are
recorded, in successive ages, of similar connections between
ordinary mortals and beings possessing the attributes of M.

du Miroir. Some now alive, perhaps, besides myself, have such attendants. Would that M. du Miroir could be persuaded to transfer his attachment to one of those, and allow some other of his race to assume the situation that he now holds in regard to me! If I must needs have so intrusive an intimate, who stares me in the face in my closest privacy, and follows me even to my bed-chamber, I should prefer—scandal apart—the laughing bloom of a young girl, to the dark and bearded gravity of my present companion. But such desires are never to be gratified. Though the members of M. du Miroir's family have been accused, perhaps justly, of visiting their friends often in splendid halls and seldom in darksome dungeons, yet they exhibit a rare constancy to the objects of their first attachment, however unlovely in person or unamiable in disposition, however unfortunate, or even infamous, and deserted by all the world besides. So will it be with my associate. Our fates appear inseparably blended. It is my belief, as I find him mingling with my earliest recollections, that we came into existence together, as my shadow follows me into the sunshine, and that, hereafter, as heretofore, the brightness or gloom of my fortunes will shine upon, or darken, the face of M. du Miroir. As we have been young together, and as it is now near the summer noon with both of us, so, if long life be granted, shall each count his own wrinkles on the other's brow, and his white hairs on the other's head. And when the coffin lid shall have closed over me, and that face and form, which, more truly than the lover swears it to his beloved, are the sole light of his existence, when they shall be laid in that dark chamber, whither his swift and secret footsteps cannot bring him,—then what is to become of poor M. du Miroir! Will he have the fortitude, with my other friends, to take a last look at my pale countenance? Will he walk foremost in the funeral train? Will he come often and haunt around my grave, and weed away the nettles, and plant flowers amid the verdure, and scrape the moss out of the letters of my burial-stone? Will he linger where I have lived, to remind the neglectful world of one who staked much to win a name, but will not then care whether he lost or won?

Not thus will he prove his deep fidelity. Oh, what terror, if this friend of mine, after our last farewell, should step into the crowded street, or roam along our old frequented path, by the still waters, or sit down in the domestic circle, where our faces are most familiar and beloved! No; but when the ray of Heaven shall bless me no more, nor the thoughtful lamp-light gleam upon my studies, nor the cheerful fireside gladden the meditative man, then, his task fulfilled, shall this mysterious being vanish from the earth forever. He will pass to the dark realm of Nothingness, but will not find me there.

There is something fearful in bearing such a relation to a creature so imperfectly known, and in the idea that, to a certain extent, all which concerns myself will be reflected in its consequences upon him. When we feel that another is to share the self-same fortune with ourselves, we judge more severely of our prospects, and withhold our confidence from that delusive magic which appears to shed an infallibility of happiness over our own pathway. Of late years, indeed, there has been much to sadden my intercourse with M. du Miroir. Had not our union been a necessary condition of our life, we must have been estranged ere now. In early youth, when my affections were warm and free, I loved him well, and could always spend a pleasant hour in his society, chiefly because it gave me an excellent opinion of myself. Speechless as he was, M. du Miroir had then a most agreeable way of calling me a handsome fellow; and I, of course, returned the compliment; so that, the more we kept each other's company, the greater coxcombs we mutually grew. But neither of us need apprehend any such misfortune now. When we chance to meet— for it is chance oftener than design—each glances sadly at the other's forehead, dreading wrinkles there, and at our temples, whence the hair is thinning away too early, and at the sunken eyes, which no longer shed a gladsome light over the whole face. I involuntarily peruse him as a record of my heavy youth, which has been wasted in sluggishness, for lack of hope and impulse, or equally thrown away in toil, that had no wise motive, and has accomplished no good end. I perceive that the tranquil gloom of a disappointed soul has darkened through his countenance, where the blackness of the future seems to mingle with the shadows of the past, giving him the aspect of a fated man. Is it too wild a thought, that my fate may have assumed this image of myself, and therefore haunts me with such inevitable pertinacity, originating every act which it appears to imitate, while it deludes me by pretending to share the events, of which it is merely the emblem and the prophecy? I must banish this idea, or it will throw too deep an awe round my companion. At our next meeting, especially if it be at midnight or in solitude, I fear that I shall glance aside and shudder; in which case, as M. du Miroir is extremely sensitive to ill-treatment, he also will avert his eyes, and express horror or disgust.

But no! This is unworthy of me. As, of old, I sought his society for the bewitching dreams of woman's love which he inspired, and because I fancied a bright fortune in his aspect, so now will I hold daily and long communion with him, for the sake of the stern lessons that he will teach my manhood. With folded arms, we will sit face to face, and lengthen out our silent converse, till a wiser cheerfulness shall have been wrought from the very texture of despondency. He will say, perhaps indignantly, that it befits only him to mourn for the decay of outward grace, which, while he possessed it, was his all. But have not you, he will ask, a treasure in reserve, to which every year may add far more value than age, or death itself, can snatch from that miserable clay? He will tell me, that, though the bloom of life has been nipt with a frost, yet the soul must not sit shivering in its cell, but bestir itself manfully, and kindle a genial warmth from its own exercise, against the autumnal and the wintry atmosphere. And I, in return, will bid him be of good cheer, nor take it amiss that I must blanch his locks and wrinkle him up like a wilted apple, since it shall be my endeavor so to beautify his face with intellect and mild benevolence, that he shall profit immensely by the change. But here a smile will glimmer somewhat sadly over M. du Miroir's visage.

When this subject shall have been sufficiently discussed, we may take up others as important. Reflecting upon his power of following me to the remotest regions and into the deepest privacy, I will compare the attempt to escape him to the hopeless race that men sometimes run with memory, or their own hearts, or their moral selves, which, though burthened with cares enough to crush an elephant, will never be one step behind. I will be self-contemplative, as nature bids me, and make him the picture or visible type of what I muse upon, that my mind may not wander so vaguely as heretofore, chasing its own shadow through a chaos, and catching only the monsters that abide there. Then will we turn our thoughts to the spiritual world, of the reality of which, my companion shall furnish me an illustration, if not an argument. For, as we have only the testimony of the eye to M. du Miroir's existence, while all the other senses would fail to inform us that such a figure stands within arm's length, wherefore should there not be beings innumerable, close beside us, and filling heaven and earth with their multitude, yet of whom no corporeal perception can take cognizance? A blind man might as reasonably deny that M. du Miroir exists, as we, because the Creator has hitherto withheld the spiritual perception, can therefore contend that there are no spirits. Oh, there are! And, at this moment, when the subject of which I write has grown strong within me, and surrounded itself with those solemn and awful associations which might have seemed most alien to it, I could fancy that M. du Miroir is himself a wanderer from the spiritual world, with nothing human, except his illusive garment of visibility. Methinks I should tremble now, were his wizard power, of gliding through all impediments in search of me, to place him suddenly before my eyes.

Ha! What is yonder? Shape of mystery, did the tremor of my heart-strings vibrate to thine own, and call thee from thy home, among the dancers of the Northern Lights, and shadows flung from departed sunshine, and giant spectres that appear on clouds at daybreak, and affright the climber of the Alps? In truth, it startled me, as I threw a wary glance eastward across the chamber, to discern an unbidden guest, with his eyes bent on mine. The identical MONSIEUR DU MIROIR! Still, there he sits, and returns my gaze with as much of awe and curiosity, as if he, too, had spent a solitary evening in fantastic musings, and made me his theme. So inimitably does he counterfeit, that I could almost doubt which of us is the visionary form, or whether each be not the other's mystery, and both twin brethren of one fate, in mutually reflected spheres. Oh, friend, canst thou not hear and answer me?

Break down the barrier between us! Grasp my hand! Speak! Listen! A few words, perhaps, might satisfy the feverish yearning of my soul for some master-thought, that should guide me through this labyrinth of life, teaching wherefore I was born, and how to do my task on earth, and what is death. Alas! Even that unreal image should forget to ape me, and smile at these vain questions.—Thus do mortals deify, as it were, a mere shadow of themselves, a spectre of human reason, and ask of that to unveil the mysteries, which Divine Intelligence has revealed so far as needful to our guidance, and hid the rest.

Farewell, Monsieur du Miroir! Of you, perhaps, as of many men, it may be doubted whether you are the wiser, though your whole business is REFLECTION.

Mrs. Bullfrog

IT makes me melancholy to see how like fools some very sensible people act, in the matter of choosing wives. They perplex their judgments by a most undue attention to little niceties of personal appearance, habits, disposition, and other trifles, which concern nobody but the lady herself. An unhappy gentleman, resolving to wed nothing short of perfection, keeps his heart and hand till both get so old and withered, that no tolerable woman will accept them.—Now, this is the very height of absurdity. A kind Providence has so skilfully adapted sex to sex, and the mass of individuals to each other, that, with certain obvious exceptions, any male and female may be moderately happy in the married state. The true rule is, to ascertain that the match is fundamentally a good one, and then to take it for granted that all minor objections, should there be such, will vanish, if you let them alone. Only put yourself beyond hazard, as to the real basis of matrimonial bliss, and it is scarcely to be imagined what miracles, in the way of reconciling smaller incongruities, connubial love will effect.

For my own part, I freely confess, that, in my bachelorship, I was precisely such an over-curious simpleton, as I now advise the reader not to be. My early habits had gifted me with a feminine sensibility, and too exquisite refinement.—I was the accomplished graduate of a dry-goods store, where, by dint of ministering to the whims of fine ladies, and suiting silken hose to delicate limbs, and handling satins, ribbons, chintzes, calicoes, tapes, gauze, and cambric needles, I grew up a very lady-like sort of a gentleman. It is not assuming too much, to affirm that the ladies themselves were hardly so lady-like as Thomas Bullfrog. So painfully acute was my sense of female imperfection, and such varied excellence did I require in the woman whom I could love, that there was an awful risk of my getting no wife at all, or of being driven to perpetrate matrimony with my own image in the looking-glass. Besides the fundamental principle, already hinted at, I demanded the fresh bloom of youth, pearly teeth, glossy ring-

lets, and the whole list of lovely items, with the utmost delicacy of habits and sentiments, a silken texture of mind, and,
above all, a virgin heart. In a word, if a young angel, just
from Paradise, yet dressed in earthly fashion, had come and
offered me her hand, it is by no means certain that I should
have taken it. There was every chance of my becoming a most
miserable old bachelor, when, by the best luck in the world,
I made a journey into another state, and was smitten by, and
smote again, and wooed, won, and married the present Mrs.
Bullfrog, all in the space of a fortnight. Owing to these extempore measures, I not only gave my bride credit for certain
perfections, which have not as yet come to light, but also
overlooked a few trifling defects, which, however, glimmered
on my perception, long before the close of the honey-moon.
Yet, as there was no mistake about the fundamental principle
aforesaid, I soon learned, as will be seen, to estimate Mrs.
Bullfrog's deficiencies and superfluities at exactly their proper
value.

The same morning that Mrs. Bullfrog and I came together
as a unit, we took two seats in the stage-coach, and began
our journey towards my place of business. There being no
other passengers, we were as much alone, and as free to give
vent to our raptures, as if I had hired a hack for the matrimonial jaunt. My bride looked charmingly, in a green silk
calash, and riding-habit of pelisse cloth, and whenever her red
lips parted with a smile, each tooth appeared like an inestimable pearl. Such was my passionate warmth, that—we had
rattled out of the village, gentle reader, and were lonely as
Adam and Eve in Paradise—I plead guilty to no less freedom
than a kiss!—The gentle eye of Mrs. Bullfrog scarcely re-
buked me for the profanation. Emboldened by her indulgence, I threw back the calash from her polished brow, and
suffered my fingers, white and delicate as her own, to stray
among those dark and glossy curls, which realized my day-
dreams of rich hair.

'My love,' said Mrs. Bullfrog, tenderly, 'you will disarrange
my curls.'

'Oh, no, my sweet Laura!' replied I, still playing with the
glossy ringlet. 'Even your fair hand could not manage a curl
more delicately than mine.—I propose myself the pleasure of

doing up your hair in papers, every evening, at the same time with my own.'

'Mr. Bullfrog,' repeated she, 'you must not disarrange my curls.'

This was spoken in a more decided tone than I had happened to hear, until then, from my gentlest of all gentle brides. At the same time, she put up her hand and took mine prisoner, but merely drew it away from the forbidden ringlet, and then immediately released it. Now, I am a fidgetty little man, and always love to have something in my fingers; so that, being debarred from my wife's curls, I looked about me for any other plaything. On the front seat of the coach, there was one of those small baskets in which travelling ladies, who are too delicate to appear at a public table, generally carry a supply of gingerbread, biscuits and cheese, cold ham, and other light refreshments, merely to sustain nature to the journey's end. Such airy diet will sometimes keep them in pretty good flesh, for a week together. Laying hold of this same little basket, I thrust my hand under the newspaper, with which it was carefully covered.

'What's this, my dear?' cried I; for the black neck of a bottle had popped out of the basket.

'A bottle of Kalydor, Mr. Bullfrog,' said my wife, coolly taking the basket from my hands, and replacing it on the front seat.

There was no possibility of doubting my wife's word; but I never knew genuine Kalydor, such as I use for my own complexion, to smell so much like cherry-brandy. I was about to express my fears that the lotion would injure her skin, when an accident occurred, which threatened more than a skin-deep injury. Our Jehu had carelessly driven over a heap of gravel, and fairly capsized the coach, with the wheels in the air, and our heels where our heads should have been. What became of my wits, I cannot imagine; they have always had a perverse trick of deserting me, just when they were most needed; but so it chanced, that, in the confusion of our overthrow, I quite forgot that there was a Mrs. Bullfrog in the world. Like many men's wives, the good lady served her husband as a stepping-stone. I had scrambled out of the coach, and was instinctively settling my cravat, when somebody brushed roughly by me, and I heard a smart thwack upon the coachman's ear.

'Take that, you villain!' cried a strange, hoarse voice. 'You have ruined me, you blackguard! I shall never be the woman I have been!'

And then came a second thwack, aimed at the driver's other ear, but which missed it, and hit him on the nose, causing a terrible effusion of blood. Now, who, or what fearful apparition, was inflicting this punishment on the poor fellow, remained an impenetrable mystery to me. The blows were given by a person of grisly aspect, with a head almost bald, and sunken cheeks, apparently of the feminine gender, though hardly to be classed in the gentler sex. There being no teeth to modulate the voice, it had a mumbled fierceness, not passionate, but stern, which absolutely made me quiver like a calves foot jelly. Who could the phantom be? The most awful circumstance of the affair is yet to be told; for this ogre, or whatever it was, had a riding-habit like Mrs. Bullfrog's, and also a green silk calash, dangling down her back by the strings. In my terror and turmoil of mind, I could imagine nothing less, than that the Old Nick, at the moment of our overturn, had annihilated my wife and jumped into her petticoats. This idea seemed the more probable, since I could nowhere perceive Mrs. Bullfrog alive, nor, though I looked very sharp about the coach, could I detect any traces of that beloved woman's dead body. There would have been a comfort in giving her Christian burial!

'Come, sir, bestir yourself! Help this rascal to set up the coach,' said the hobgoblin to me; then, with a terrific screech to three countrymen, at a distance—'Here, you fellows, an't you ashamed to stand off, when a poor woman is in distress?'

The countrymen, instead of fleeing for their lives, came running at full speed, and laid hold of the topsy-turvy coach. I, also, though a small-sized man, went to work like a son of Anak. The coachman, too, with the blood still streaming from his nose, tugged and toiled most manfully, dreading, doubtless, that the next blow might break his head. And yet, bemauled as the poor fellow had been, he seemed to glance at me with an eye of pity, as if my case were more deplorable than his. But I cherished a hope that all would turn out a dream, and seized the opportunity, as we raised the coach, to jam two of my fingers under the wheel, trusting that the pain would awaken me.

'Why, here we are all to rights again!' exclaimed a sweet voice, behind. 'Thank you for your assistance, gentlemen. My dear Mr. Bullfrog, how you perspire! Do let me wipe your face. Don't take this little accident too much to heart, good driver. We ought to be thankful that none of our necks are broke!'

'We might have spared one neck out of the three,' muttered the driver, rubbing his ear and pulling his nose, to ascertain whether he had been cuffed or not.—'Why, the woman's a witch!'

I fear that the reader will not believe, yet it is positively a fact, that there stood Mrs. Bullfrog, with her glossy ringlets curling on her brow, and two rows of orient pearls gleaming between her parted lips, which wore a most angelic smile. She had regained her riding-habit and calash from the grisly phantom, and was, in all respects, the lovely woman who had been sitting by my side, at the instant of our overturn. How she had happened to disappear, and who had supplied her place, and whence did she now return, were problems too knotty for me to solve. There stood my wife. That was the one thing certain among a heap of mysteries. Nothing remained, but to help her into the coach, and plod on, through the journey of the day and the journey of life, as comfortably as we could. As the driver closed the door upon us, I heard him whisper to the three countrymen—

'How do you suppose a fellow feels, shut up in a cage with a she-tiger?'

Of course, this query could have no reference to my situation. Yet, unreasonable as it may appear, I confess that my feelings were not altogether so ecstatic as when I first called Mrs. Bullfrog mine. True, she was a sweet woman, and an angel of a wife; but what if a gorgon should return, amid the transports of our connubial bliss, and take the angel's place! I recollected the tale of a fairy, who half the time was a beautiful woman, and half the time a hideous monster. Had I taken that very fairy to be the wife of my bosom? While such whims and chimeras were flitting across my fancy, I began to look askance at Mrs. Bullfrog, almost expecting that the transformation would be wrought before my eyes.

To divert my mind, I took up the newspaper which had covered the little basket of refreshments, and which now lay at the bottom of the coach, blushing with a deep-red stain, and emitting a potent spirituous fume, from the contents of the broken bottle of Kalydor. The paper was two or three years old, but contained an article of several columns, in which I soon grew wonderfully interested. It was the report of a trial for breach of promise of marriage, giving the testimony in full, with fervid extracts from both the gentleman's and lady's amatory correspondence. The deserted damsel had personally appeared in court, and had borne energetic evidence to her lover's perfidy, and the strength of her blighted affections.—On the defendant's part, there had been an attempt, though insufficiently sustained, to blast the plaintiff's character, and a plea in mitigation of damages, on account of her unamiable temper. A horrible idea was suggested by the lady's name.

'Madam,' said I, holding the newspaper before Mrs. Bullfrog's eyes—and, though a small, delicate, and thin-visaged man, I feel assured that I looked very terrific—'Madam,' repeated I, through my shut teeth, 'were you the plaintiff in this cause?'

'Oh, my dear Mr. Bullfrog,' replied my wife, sweetly, 'I thought all the world knew that.'

'Horror! horror!' exclaimed I, sinking back on the seat.

Covering my face with both hands, I emitted a deep and deathlike groan, as if my tormented soul were rending me asunder. I, the most exquisitely fastidious of men, and whose wife was to have been the most delicate and refined of women, with all the fresh dew-drops glittering on her virgin rosebud of a heart! I thought of the glossy ringlets and pearly teeth—I thought of the Kalydor—I thought of the coachman's bruised ear and bloody nose—I thought of the tender love-secrets, which she had whispered to the judge and jury, and a thousand tittering auditors—and gave another groan!

'Mr. Bullfrog,' said my wife.

As I made no reply, she gently took my hands within her own, removed them from my face, and fixed her eyes steadfastly on mine.

'Mr. Bullfrog,' said she, not unkindly, yet with all the decision of her strong character, 'let me advise you to overcome this foolish weakness, and prove yourself, to the best of your ability, as good a husband as I will be a wife. You have discovered, perhaps, some little imperfections in your bride. Well—what did you expect? Women are not angels. If they were, they would go to Heaven for husbands—or, at least, be more difficult in their choice on earth.'

'But why conceal those imperfections?' interposed I, tremulously.

'Now, my love, are not you a most unreasonable little man?' said Mrs. Bullfrog, patting me on the cheek. 'Ought a woman to disclose her frailties earlier than the wedding-day? Few husbands, I assure you, make the discovery in such good season, and still fewer complain that these trifles are concealed too long. Well, what a strange man you are! Poh! you are joking.'

'But the suit for breach of promise!' groaned I.

'Ah! and is that the rub?' exclaimed my wife. 'Is it possible that you view that affair in an objectionable light? Mr. Bullfrog, I never could have dreamt it! Is it an objection, that I have triumphantly defended myself against slander, and vindicated my purity in a court of justice? Or, do you complain, because your wife has shown the proper spirit of a woman, and punished the villain who trifled with her affections?'

'But,' persisted I—shrinking into a corner of the coach, however; for I did not know precisely how much contradiction the proper spirit of a woman would endure—'but, my love, would it not have been more dignified to treat the villain with the silent contempt he merited?'

'That is all very well, Mr. Bullfrog,' said my wife, slily; 'but, in that case, where would have been the five thousand dollars, which are to stock your dry-goods store?'

'Mrs. Bullfrog, upon your honor,' demanded I, as if my life hung upon her words, 'is there no mistake about those five thousand dollars?'

'Upon my word and honor, there is none,' replied she. 'The

jury gave me every cent the rascal had—and I have kept it all for my dear Bullfrog!'

'Then, thou dear woman,' cried I, with an overwhelming gush of tenderness, 'let me fold thee to my heart! The basis of matrimonial bliss is secure, and all thy little defects and frailties are forgiven. Nay, since the result has been so fortunate, I rejoice at the wrongs which drove thee to this blessed law-suit. Happy Bullfrog that I am!'

Sunday at Home

EVERY Sabbath morning, in the summer time, I thrust back the curtain, to watch the sunrise stealing down a steeple, which stands opposite my chamber window. First, the weathercock begins to flash; then, a fainter lustre gives the spire an airy aspect; next it encroaches on the tower, and causes the index of the dial to glisten like gold, as it points to the gilded figure of the hour. Now, the loftiest window gleams, and now the lower. The carved frame-work of the portal is marked strongly out. At length, the morning glory, in its descent from Heaven, comes down the stone steps, one by one; and there stands the steeple, glowing with fresh radiance, while the shades of twilight still hide themselves among the nooks of the adjacent buildings. Methinks, though the same sun brightens it, every fair morning, yet the steeple has a peculiar robe of brightness for the Sabbath.

By dwelling near a church, a person soon contracts an attachment for the edifice. We naturally personify it, and conceive its massy walls, and its dim emptiness, to be instinct with a calm, and meditative, and somewhat melancholy spirit. But the steeple stands foremost, in our thoughts, as well as locally. It impresses us as a giant, with a mind comprehensive and discriminating enough to care for the great and small concerns of all the town. Hourly, while it speaks a moral to the few that think, it reminds thousands of busy individuals of their separate and most secret affairs. It is the steeple, too, that flings abroad the hurried and irregular accents of general alarm; neither have gladness and festivity found a better utterance, than by its tongue; and when the dead are slowly passing to their home, the steeple has a melancholy voice to bid them welcome. Yet, in spite of this connection with human interests, what a moral loneliness, on week-days, broods round about its stately height! It has no kindred with the houses above which it towers; it looks down into the narrow thoroughfare, the lonelier, because the crowd are elbowing their passage at its base. A glance at the body of the church deepens this impression. Within, by the light of distant windows, amid refracted shadows, we discern the vacant pews and empty galleries, the silent organ, the voiceless pulpit, and the clock, which tells to solitude how time is passing. Time— where man lives not—what is it but eternity? And in the church, we might suppose, are garnered up, throughout the week, all thoughts and feelings that have reference to eternity, until the holy day comes round again, to let them forth. Might not, then, its more appropriate site be in the outskirts of the town, with space for old trees to wave around it, and throw their solemn shadows over a quiet green? We will say more of this, hereafter.

But, on the Sabbath, I watch the earliest sunshine, and fancy that a holier brightness marks the day, when there shall be no buzz of voices on the Exchange, nor traffic in the shops, nor crowd, nor business, anywhere but at church. Many have fancied so. For my own part, whether I see it scattered down among tangled woods, or beaming broad across the fields, or hemmed in between brick buildings, or tracing out the figure of the casement on my chamber floor, still I recognize the Sabbath sunshine.—And ever let me recognize it! Some illusions, and this among them, are the shadows of great truths. Doubts may flit around me, or seem to close their evil wings, and settle down; but, so long as I imagine that the earth is hallowed, and the light of heaven retains its sanctity, on the Sabbath—while that blessed sunshine lives within me—never can my soul have lost the instinct of its faith. If it have gone astray, it will return again.

I love to spend such pleasant Sabbaths, from morning till night, behind the curtain of my open window. Are they spent amiss? Every spot, so near the church as to be visited by the circling shadow of the steeple, should be deemed consecrated ground, to-day. With stronger truth be it said, that a devout heart may consecrate a den of thieves, as an evil one may convert a temple to the same. My heart, perhaps, has not such holy, nor, I would fain trust, such impious potency. It must suffice, that, though my form be absent, my inner man goes constantly to church, while many, whose bodily presence fills the accustomed seats, have left their souls at home. But I am there, even before my friend, the sexton. At length, he comes—a man of kindly, but sombre aspect, in dark gray clothes, and hair of the same mixture—he comes, and applies his key to the wide portal. Now, my thoughts may go in among the dusty pews, or ascend the pulpit without sacrilege, but soon come forth again, to enjoy the music of the bell. How glad, yet solemn too! All the steeples in town are talking together, aloft in the sunny air, and rejoicing among themselves, while their spires point heavenward. Meantime, here are the children assembling to the Sabbath-school, which is kept somewhere within the church. Often, while looking at the arched portal, I have been gladdened by the sight of a score of these little girls and boys, in pink, blue, yellow, and crimson frocks, bursting suddenly forth into the sunshine, like a swarm of gay butterflies that had been shut up in the solemn gloom. Or I might compare them to cherubs, haunting that holy place.

About a quarter of an hour before the second ringing of the bell, individuals of the congregation begin to appear. The earliest is invariably an old woman in black, whose bent frame and rounded shoulders are evidently laden with some heavy affliction, which she is eager to rest upon the altar. Would that the Sabbath came twice as often, for the sake of that sorrowful old soul! There is an elderly man, also, who arrives in good season, and leans against the corner of the tower, just within the line of its shadow, looking downward with a darksome brow. I sometimes fancy that the old woman is the happier of the two. After these, others drop in singly, and by twos and threes, either disappearing through the door-way, or taking their stand in its vicinity. At last, and always with an unexpected sensation, the bell turns in the steeple overhead, and throws out an irregular clangor, jarring the tower to its foundation. As if there were magic in the sound, the sidewalks of the street, both up and down along, are immediately thronged with two long lines of people, all converging hitherward, and streaming into the church. Perhaps the far-off roar of a coach draws nearer—a deeper thunder by its contrast with the surrounding stillness—until it sets down the wealthy worshippers at the portal, among their humblest brethren. Beyond that entrance, in theory at least, there are no distinctions of earthly rank; nor, indeed, by the goodly apparel which is flaunting in the sun, would there seem to be such, on the hither side. Those pretty girls! Why will they disturb my pious meditations! Of all days in the week, they should strive to look least fascinating on the Sabbath, instead of heightening their mortal loveliness, as if to rival the blessed angels, and keep our thoughts from heaven. Were I the minister himself, I must needs look. One girl is white muslin from the waist upward, and black silk downward to her slippers; a second blushes from top-knot to shoe-tie, one universal scarlet; another shines of a pervading yellow, as if she had made a garment of the sunshine. The greater part, however, have adopted a milder cheerfulness of hue. Their veils, especially when the wind raises them, give a lightness to the general effect, and make them appear like airy phantoms, as they flit up the steps, and vanish into the sombre door-way. Nearly all—though it is very strange that I should know it—wear white stockings, white as snow, and neat slippers, laced crosswise with black ribbon, pretty high above the ankles. A white stocking is infinitely more effective than a black one.

Here comes the clergyman, slow and solemn, in severe simplicity, needing no black silk gown to denote his office. His aspect claims my reverence, but cannot win my love. Were I to picture Saint Peter, keeping fast the gate of Heaven, and frowning, more stern than pitiful, on the wretched applicants, that face should be my study. By middle age, or sooner, the creed has generally wrought upon the heart, or been attempered by it. As the minister passes into the church, the bell holds its iron tongue, and all the low murmur of the congregation dies away. The gray sexton looks up and down the street, and then at my window curtain, where, through the small peep-hole, I half fancy that he has caught my eye. Now, every loiterer has gone in, and the street lies asleep in the quiet sun, while a feeling of loneliness comes over me, and brings also an uneasy sense of neglected privileges and duties. Oh, I ought to have gone to church! The bustle of the rising congregation reaches my ears. They are standing up to pray. Could I bring my heart into unison with those who are praying in yonder church, and lift it heavenward, with a fervor of supplication, but no distinct request, would not that be the safest kind of prayer? 'Lord, look down upon me in mercy!' With that sentiment gushing from my soul, might I not leave all the rest to Him?

Hark! the hymn. This, at least, is a portion of the service which I can enjoy better than if I sat within the walls, where the full choir, and the massive melody of the organ, would fall with a weight upon me. At this distance, it thrills through my frame, and plays upon my heart-strings, with a pleasure both of the sense and spirit. Heaven be praised, I know nothing of music, as a science; and the most elaborate harmonies, if they please me, please as simply as a nurse's lullaby. The strain has ceased, but prolongs itself in my mind, with fanciful echoes, till I start from my reverie, and find that the sermon has commenced. It is my misfortune seldom to fructify, in a regular way, by any but printed sermons. The first strong idea, which the preacher utters, gives birth to a train of thought, and leads me onward, step by step, quite out of hearing of the good man's voice, unless he be indeed a son of thunder. At my open window, catching now and then a sentence of the 'parson's saw,' I am as well situated as at the foot of the pulpit stairs. The broken and scattered fragments of this one discourse will be the texts of many sermons, preached by those colleague pastors—colleagues, but often disputants—my Mind and Heart. The former pretends to be a scholar, and perplexes me with doctrinal points; the latter takes me on the score of feeling; and both, like several other preachers, spend their strength to very little purpose. I, their sole auditor, cannot always understand them.

Suppose that a few hours have passed, and behold me still behind my curtain, just before the close of the afternoon service. The hour hand on the dial has passed beyond four o'clock. The declining sun is hidden behind the steeple, and throws its shadow straight across the street, so that my chamber is darkened, as with a cloud. Around the church door, all is solitude, and an impenetrable obscurity, beyond the threshold. A commotion is heard. The seats are slammed down, and the pew doors thrown back—a multitude of feet are trampling along the unseen aisles—and the congregation bursts suddenly through the portal. Foremost, scampers a rabble of boys, behind whom moves a dense and dark phalanx of

grown men, and lastly, a crowd of females, with young children, and a few scattered husbands. This instantaneous outbreak of life into loneliness is one of the pleasantest scenes of
the day. Some of the good people are rubbing their eyes,
thereby intimating that they have been wrapt, as it were, in a
sort of holy trance, by the fervor of their devotion. There is
a young man, a third-rate coxcomb, whose first care is always
to flourish a white handkerchief, and brush the seat of a tight
pair of black silk pantaloons, which shine as if varnished.
They must have been made of the stuff called 'everlasting,' or
perhaps of the same piece as Christian's garments, in the Pilgrim's Progress, for he put them on two summers ago, and
has not yet worn the gloss off. I have taken a great liking to
those black silk pantaloons. But, now, with nods and greetings among friends, each matron takes her husband's arm,
and paces gravely homeward, while the girls also flutter away,
after arranging sunset walks with their favored bachelors. The
Sabbath eve is the eve of love. At length, the whole congregation is dispersed. No; here, with faces as glossy as black
satin, come two sable ladies and a sable gentleman, and close
in their rear, the minister, who softens his severe visage, and
bestows a kind word on each. Poor souls! To them, the most
captivating picture of bliss in Heaven, is—'There we shall be
white!'

All is solitude again. But, hark!—a broken warbling of
voices, and now, attuning its grandeur to their sweetness, a
stately peal of the organ. Who are the choristers? Let me
dream, that the angels, who came down from Heaven, this
blessed morn, to blend themselves with the worship of the
truly good, are playing and singing their farewell to the
earth.—On the wings of that rich melody, they were borne
upward.

This, gentle reader, is merely a flight of poetry. A few of
the singing men and singing women had lingered behind
their fellows, and raised their voices fitfully, and blew a careless note upon the organ. Yet, it lifted my soul higher than all
their former strains. They are gone—the sons and daughters
of music—and the gray sexton is just closing the portal. For
six days more, there will be no face of man in the pews, and
aisles, and galleries, nor a voice in the pulpit, nor music in the

choir. Was it worth while to rear this massive edifice, to be a desert in the heart of the town, and populous only for a few hours of each seventh day? Oh! but the church is a symbol of religion. May its site, which was consecrated on the day when the first tree was felled, be kept holy forever, a spot of solitude and peace, amid the trouble and vanity of our week-day world! There is a moral, and a religion too, even in the silent walls. And, may the steeple still point heavenward, and be decked with the hallowed sunshine of the Sabbath morn!

The Man of Adamant

An Apologue

In the old times of religious gloom and intolerance, lived Richard Digby, the gloomiest and most intolerant of a stern brotherhood. His plan of salvation was so narrow, that, like a plank in a tempestuous sea, it could avail no sinner but himself, who bestrode it triumphantly, and hurled anathemas against the wretches whom he saw struggling with the billows of eternal death. In his view of the matter, it was a most abominable crime—as, indeed, it is a great folly—for men to trust to their own strength, or even to grapple to any other fragment of the wreck, save this narrow plank, which, moreover, he took special care to keep out of their reach. In other words, as his creed was like no man's else, and being well pleased that Providence had entrusted him, alone of mortals, with the treasure of a true faith, Richard Digby determined to seclude himself to the sole and constant enjoyment of his happy fortune.

'And verily,' thought he, 'I deem it a chief condition of Heaven's mercy to myself, that I hold no communion with those abominable myriads which it hath cast off to perish. Peradventure, were I to tarry longer in the tents of Kedar, the gracious boon would be revoked, and I also be swallowed up in the deluge of wrath, or consumed in the storm of fire and brimstone, or involved in whatever new kind of ruin is ordained for the horrible perversity of this generation.'

So Richard Digby took an axe, to hew space enough for a tabernacle in the wilderness, and some few other necessaries, especially a sword and gun, to smite and slay any intruder upon his hallowed seclusion; and plunged into the dreariest depths of the forest. On its verge, however, he paused a moment, to shake off the dust of his feet against the village where he had dwelt, and to invoke a curse on the meeting-house, which he regarded as a temple of heathen idolatry. He felt a curiosity, also, to see whether the fire and brimstone would not rush down from Heaven at once, now that the one righteous man had provided for his own safety. But, as the sunshine continued to fall peacefully on the cottages and fields, and the husbandmen labored and children played, and as there were many tokens of present happiness, and nothing ominous of a speedy judgment, he turned away, somewhat disappointed. The further he went, however, and the lonelier he felt himself, and the thicker the trees stood along his path, and the darker the shadow overhead, so much the more did Richard Digby exult. He talked to himself, as he strode onward; he read his Bible to himself, as he sat beneath the trees; and, as the gloom of the forest hid the blessed sky, I had almost added, that, at morning, noon, and eventide, he prayed to himself. So congenial was this mode of life to his disposition, that he often laughed to himself, but was displeased when an echo tossed him back the long, loud roar.

In this manner, he journeyed onward three days and two nights, and came, on the third evening, to the mouth of a cave, which, at first sight, reminded him of Elijah's cave at Horeb, though perhaps it more resembled Abraham's sepulchral cave, at Machpelah. It entered into the heart of a rocky hill. There was so dense a veil of tangled foliage about it, that none but a sworn lover of gloomy recesses would have discovered the low arch of its entrance, or have dared to step within its vaulted chamber, where the burning eyes of a panther might encounter him. If Nature meant this remote and dismal cavern for the use of man, it could only be, to bury in its gloom the victims of a pestilence, and then to block up its mouth with stones, and avoid the spot forever after. There was nothing bright nor cheerful near it, except a bubbling fountain, some twenty paces off, at which Richard Digby hardly threw away a glance. But he thrust his head into the cave, shivered, and congratulated himself.

'The finger of Providence hath pointed my way!' cried he, aloud, while the tomb-like den returned a strange echo, as if some one within were mocking him. 'Here my soul will be at peace; for the wicked will not find me. Here I can read the Scriptures, and be no more provoked with lying interpretations. Here I can offer up acceptable prayers, because my voice will not be mingled with the sinful supplications of the multitude. Of a truth, the only way to Heaven leadeth through the narrow entrance of this cave—and I alone have found it!'

In regard to this cave, it was observable that the roof, so far as the imperfect light permitted it to be seen, was hung with substances resembling opaque icicles; for the damps of unknown centuries, dripping down continually, had become as hard as adamant; and wherever that moisture fell, it seemed to possess the power of converting what it bathed to stone. The fallen leaves and sprigs of foliage, which the wind had swept into the cave, and the little feathery shrubs, rooted near the threshold, were not wet with a natural dew, but had been embalmed by this wondrous process. And here I am put in mind, that Richard Digby, before he withdrew himself from the world, was supposed by skilful physicians to have contracted a disease, for which no remedy was written in their medical books. It was a deposition of calculous particles within his heart, caused by an obstructed circulation of the blood, and unless a miracle should be wrought for him, there was danger that the malady might act on the entire substance of the organ, and change his fleshly heart to stone. Many, indeed, affirmed that the process was already near its consummation. Richard Digby, however, could never be convinced that any such direful work was going on within him; nor when he saw the sprigs of marble foliage, did his heart even throb the quicker, at the similitude suggested by these once tender herbs. It may be, that this same insensibility was a symptom of the disease.

Be that as it might, Richard Digby was well contented with his sepulchral cave. So dearly did he love this congenial spot, that, instead of going a few paces to the bubbling spring for water, he allayed his thirst with now and then a drop of moisture from the roof, which, had it fallen any where but on his tongue, would have been congealed into a pebble. For a man predisposed to stoniness of the heart, this surely was unwholesome liquor. But there he dwelt, for three days more, eating herbs and roots, drinking his own destruction, sleeping, as it were, in a tomb, and awaking to the solitude of death, yet esteeming this horrible mode of life as hardly inferior to celestial bliss. Perhaps superior; for, above the sky, there would be angels to disturb him. At the close of the third day, he sat in the portal of his mansion, reading the Bible aloud, because no other ear could profit by it, and reading it amiss, because the rays of the setting sun did not penetrate the dismal depth of shadow roundabout him, nor fall upon the sacred page. Suddenly, however, a faint gleam of light was thrown over the volume, and raising his eyes, Richard Digby saw that a young woman stood before the mouth of the cave, and that the sunbeams bathed her white garment, which thus seemed to possess a radiance of its own.

'Good evening, Richard,' said the girl, 'I have come from afar to find thee.'

The slender grace and gentle loveliness of this young woman were at once recognized by Richard Digby. Her name was Mary Goffe. She had been a convert to his preaching of the word in England, before he yielded himself to that exclusive bigotry, which now enfolded him with such an iron grasp, that no other sentiment could reach his bosom. When he came a pilgrim to America, she had remained in her father's hall, but now, as it appeared, had crossed the ocean after him, impelled by the same faith that led other exiles hither, and perhaps by love almost as holy. What else but faith and love united could have sustained so delicate a creature, wandering thus far into the forest, with her golden hair dishevelled by the boughs, and her feet wounded by the thorns! Yet, weary and faint though she must have been, and affrighted at the dreariness of the cave, she looked on the lonely man with a mild and pitying expression, such as might beam from an angel's eyes, towards an afflicted mortal. But the recluse, frowning sternly upon her, and keeping his finger between the leaves of his half closed Bible, motioned her away with his hand.

'Off!' cried he. 'I am sanctified, and thou art sinful. Away!'

'Oh, Richard,' said she, earnestly, 'I have come this weary way, because I heard that a grievous distemper had seized upon thy heart; and a great Physician hath given me the skill to cure it. There is no other remedy than this which I have brought thee. Turn me not away, therefore, nor refuse my medicine; for then must this dismal cave be thy sepulchre.'

'Away!' replied Richard Digby, still with a dark frown. 'My

heart is in better condition than thine own. Leave me, earthly one; for the sun is almost set; and when no light reaches the door of the cave, then is my prayer time!'

Now, great as was her need, Mary Goffe did not plead with this stony hearted man for shelter and protection, nor ask any thing whatever for her own sake. All her zeal was for his welfare.

'Come back with me!' she exclaimed, clasping her hands — 'Come back to thy fellow men; for they need thee, Richard; and thou hast tenfold need of them. Stay not in this evil den; for the air is chill, and the damps are fatal; nor will any, that perish within it, ever find the path to Heaven. Hasten hence, I entreat thee, for thine own soul's sake; for either the roof will fall upon thy head, or some other speedy destruction is at hand.'

'Perverse woman!' answered Richard Digby, laughing aloud; for he was moved to bitter mirth by her foolish vehemence. 'I tell thee that the path to Heaven leadeth straight through this narrow portal, where I sit. And, moreover, the destruction thou speakest of, is ordained, not for this blessed cave, but for all other habitations of mankind, throughout the earth. Get thee hence speedily, that thou may'st have thy share!'

So saying, he opened his Bible again, and fixed his eyes intently on the page, being resolved to withdraw his thoughts from this child of sin and wrath, and to waste no more of his holy breath upon her. The shadow had now grown so deep, where he was sitting, that he made continual mistakes in what he read, converting all that was gracious and merciful, to denunciations of vengeance and unutterable woe, on every created being but himself. Mary Goffe, meanwhile, was leaning against a tree, beside the sepulchral cave, very sad, yet with something heavenly and ethereal in her unselfish sorrow. The light from the setting sun still glorified her form, and was reflected a little way within the darksome den, discovering so terrible a gloom, that the maiden shuddered for its self-doomed inhabitant. Espying the bright fountain near at hand, she hastened thither, and scooped up a portion of its water, in a cup of birchen bark. A few tears mingled with the draught, and perhaps gave it all its efficacy. She then returned to the mouth of the cave, and knelt down at Richard Digby's feet.

'Richard,' she said, with passionate fervor, yet a gentleness in all her passion, 'I pray thee, by thy hope of Heaven, and as thou wouldst not dwell in this tomb forever, drink of this hallowed water, be it but a single drop! Then, make room for me by thy side, and let us read together one page of that blessed volume—and, lastly, kneel down with me and pray! Do this; and thy stony heart shall become softer than a babe's, and all be well.'

But Richard Digby, in utter abhorrence of the proposal, cast the Bible at his feet, and eyed her with such a fixed and evil frown, that he looked less like a living man than a marble statue, wrought by some dark imagined sculptor to express the most repulsive mood that human features could assume. And, as his look grew even devilish, so, with an equal change, did Mary Goffe become more sad, more mild, more pitiful, more like a sorrowing angel. But, the more heavenly she was, the more hateful did she seem to Richard Digby, who at length raised his hand, and smote down the cup of hallowed water upon the threshold of the cave, thus rejecting the only medicine that could have cured his stony heart. A sweet perfume lingered in the air for a moment, and then was gone.

'Tempt me no more, accursed woman,' exclaimed he, still with his marble frown, 'lest I smite thee down also! What hast thou to do with my Bible?—what with my prayers?—what with my Heaven?'

No sooner had he spoken these dreadful words, than Richard Digby's heart ceased to beat; while—so the legend says—the form of Mary Goffe melted into the last sunbeams, and returned from the sepulchral cave to Heaven. For Mary Goffe had been buried in an English churchyard, months before; and either it was her ghost that haunted the wild forest, or else a dreamlike spirit, typifying pure Religion.

Above a century afterwards, when the trackless forest of Richard Digby's day had long been interspersed with settlements, the children of a neighbouring farmer were playing at the foot of a hill. The trees, on account of the rude and broken surface of this acclivity, had never been felled, and were crowded so densely together, as to hide all but a few rocky prominences, wherever their roots could grapple with the soil. A little boy and girl, to conceal themselves from their playmates, had crept into the deepest shade, where not only the darksome pines, but a thick veil of creeping plants suspended from an overhanging rock, combined to make a twilight at noonday, and almost a midnight at all other seasons. There the children hid themselves, and shouted, repeating the cry at intervals, till the whole party of pursuers were drawn thither, and pulling aside the matted foliage, let in a doubtful glimpse of daylight. But scarcely was this accomplished, when the little group uttered a simultaneous shriek and tumbled headlong down the hill, making the best of their way homeward, without a second glance into the gloomy recess. Their father, unable to comprehend what had so startled them, took his axe, and by felling one or two trees, and tearing away the creeping plants, laid the mystery open to the day. He had discovered the entrance of a cave, closely resembling the mouth of a sepulchre, within which sat the figure of a man, whose gesture and attitude warned the father and children to stand back, while his visage wore a most forbidding frown. This repulsive personage seemed to have been carved in the same gray stone that formed the walls and portal of the cave. On minuter inspection, indeed, such blemishes were observed, as made it doubtful whether the figure were really a statue, chiselled by human art, and somewhat worn and defaced by the lapse of ages, or a freak of Nature, who might have chosen to imitate, in stone, her usual handiwork of flesh. Perhaps it was the least unreasonable idea, suggested by this strange spectacle, that the moisture of the cave possessed a petrifying quality, which had thus awfully embalmed a human corpse.

There was something so frightful in the aspect of this Man of Adamant, that the farmer, the moment that he recovered from the fascination of his first gaze, began to heap stones into the mouth of the cavern. His wife, who had followed him to the hill, assisted her husband's efforts. The children, also, approached as near as they durst, with their little hands full of pebbles, and cast them on the pile. Earth was then thrown into the crevices, and the whole fabric overlaid with

sods. Thus all traces of the discovery were obliterated, leaving
only a marvellous legend, which grew wilder from one generation to another, as the children told it to their grandchildren, and they to their posterity, till few believed that there
had ever been a cavern or a statue, where now they saw but
a grassy patch on the shadowy hill-side. Yet, grown people
avoid the spot, nor do children play there. Friendship, and
Love, and Piety, all human and celestial sympathies, should
keep aloof from that hidden cave; for there still sits, and, unless an earthquake crumble down the roof upon his head,
shall sit forever, the shape of Richard Digby, in the attitude
of repelling the whole race of mortals—not from Heaven—
but from the horrible loneliness of his dark, cold sepulchre.

David Swan

A Fantasy

WE can be but partially acquainted even with events which actually influence our course through life, and our final destiny. There are innumerable other events, if such they may be called, which come close upon us, yet pass away without actual results, or even betraying their near approach, by the reflection of any light or shadow across our minds. Could we know all the vicissitudes of our fortunes, life would be too full of hope and fear, exultation or disappointment, to afford us a single hour of true serenity. This idea may be illustrated by a page from the secret history of David Swan.

We have nothing to do with David, until we find him, at the age of twenty, on the high road from his native place to the city of Boston, where his uncle, a small dealer in the grocery line, was to take him behind the counter. Be it enough to say, that he was a native of New Hampshire, born of respectable parents, and had received an ordinary school education, with a classic finish by a year at Gilmanton academy. After journeying on foot, from sunrise till nearly noon of a summer's day, his weariness and the increasing heat determined him to sit down in the first convenient shade, and await the coming up of the stage coach. As if planted on purpose for him, there soon appeared a little tuft of maples, with a delightful recess in the midst, and such a fresh bubbling spring, that it seemed never to have sparkled for any wayfarer but David Swan. Virgin or not, he kissed it with his thirsty lips, and then flung himself along the brink, pillowing his head upon some shirts and a pair of pantaloons, tied up in a striped cotton handkerchief. The sunbeams could not reach him; the dust did not yet rise from the road, after the heavy rain of yesterday; and his grassy lair suited the young man better than a bed of down. The spring murmured drowsily beside him; the branches waved dreamily across the blue sky, overhead; and a deep sleep, perchance hiding dreams within its depths, fell upon David Swan. But we are to relate events which he did not dream of.

While he lay sound asleep in the shade, other people were wide awake, and passed to and fro, a-foot, on horseback, and in all sorts of vehicles, along the sunny road by his bed-chamber. Some looked neither to the right hand nor to the left, and knew not that he was there; some merely glanced that way, without admitting the slumberer among their busy thoughts; some laughed to see how soundly he slept; and several, whose hearts were brimming full of scorn, ejected their venomous superfluity on David Swan. A middle aged widow, when nobody else was near, thrust her head a little way into the recess, and vowed that the young fellow looked charming in his sleep. A temperance lecturer saw him, and wrought poor David into the texture of his evening's discourse, as an awful instance of dead drunkenness by the road-side. But, censure, praise, merriment, scorn, and indifference, were all one, or rather all nothing, to David Swan.

He had slept only a few moments, when a brown carriage, drawn by a handsome pair of horses, bowled easily along, and was brought to a stand-still, nearly in front of David's resting place. A linch pin had fallen out, and permitted one of the wheels to slide off. The damage was slight, and occasioned merely a momentary alarm to an elderly merchant and his wife, who were returning to Boston in the carriage. While the coachman and a servant were replacing the wheel, the lady and gentleman sheltered themselves beneath the maple trees, and there espied the bubbling fountain, and David Swan asleep beside it. Impressed with the awe which the humblest sleeper usually sheds around him, the merchant trod as lightly as the gout would allow; and his spouse took good heed not to rustle her silk gown, lest David should start up, all of a sudden.

'How soundly he sleeps!' whispered the old gentleman. 'From what a depth he draws that easy breath! Such sleep as that, brought on without an opiate, would be worth more to me than half my income; for it would suppose health, and an untroubled mind.'

'And youth, besides,' said the lady. 'Healthy and quiet age does not sleep thus. Our slumber is no more like his, than our wakefulness.'

The longer they looked, the more did this elderly couple feel interested in the unknown youth, to whom the way side and the maple shade were as a secret chamber, with the rich gloom of damask curtains brooding over him. Perceiving that a stray sunbeam glimmered down upon his face, the lady contrived to twist a branch aside, so as to intercept it. And having done this little act of kindness, she began to feel like a mother to him.

'Providence seems to have laid him here,' whispered she to her husband, 'and to have brought us hither to find him, after our disappointment in our cousin's son. Methinks I can see a likeness to our departed Henry. Shall we waken him?'

'To what purpose?' said the merchant, hesitating. 'We know nothing of the youth's character.'

'That open countenance!' replied his wife, in the same hushed voice, yet earnestly. 'This innocent sleep!'

While these whispers were passing, the sleeper's heart did not throb, nor his breath become agitated, nor his features betray the least token of interest.—Yet Fortune was bending over him, just ready to let fall a burthen of gold. The old merchant had lost his only son, and had no heir to his wealth, except a distant relative, with whose conduct he was dissatisfied. In such cases, people sometimes do stranger things than to act the magician, and awaken a young man to splendor, who fell asleep in poverty.

'Shall we not waken him?' repeated the lady, persuasively.

'The coach is ready, Sir,' said the servant, behind.

The old couple started, reddened, and hurried away, mutually wondering, that they should ever have dreamed of doing any thing so very ridiculous. The merchant threw himself back in the carriage, and occupied his mind with the plan of a magnificent asylum for unfortunate men of business. Meanwhile, David Swan enjoyed his nap.

The carriage could not have gone above a mile or two, when a pretty young girl came along, with a tripping pace, which shewed precisely how her little heart was dancing in her bosom. Perhaps it was this merry kind of motion that caused—is there any harm in saying it?—her garter to slip its knot. Conscious that the silken girth, if silk it were, was relax-

ing its hold, she turned aside into the shelter of the maple
trees, and there found a young man asleep by the spring!
Blushing, as red as any rose, that she should have intruded
into a gentleman's bed-chamber, and for such a purpose too,
she was about to make her escape on tiptoe. But, there was
peril near the sleeper. A monster of a bee had been wandering
overhead—buzz, buzz, buzz—now among the leaves, now
flashing through the strips of sunshine, and now lost in the
dark shade, till finally he appeared to be settling on the eyelid
of David Swan. The sting of a bee is sometimes deadly. As
freehearted as she was innocent, the girl attacked the intruder
with her handkerchief, brushed him soundly, and drove him
from beneath the maple shade. How sweet a picture! This
good deed accomplished, with quickened breath, and a
deeper blush, she stole a glance at the youthful stranger, for
whom she had been battling with a dragon in the air.

'He is handsome!' thought she, and blushed redder yet.

How could it be that no dream of bliss grew so strong
within him, that, shattered by its very strength, it should part
asunder, and allow him to perceive the girl among its phantoms? Why, at least, did no smile of welcome brighten upon
his face? She was come, the maid whose soul, according to
the old and beautiful idea, had been severed from his own,
and whom, in all his vague but passionate desires, he yearned
to meet. Her, only, could he love with a perfect love—him,
only, could she receive into the depths of her heart—and
now her image was faintly blushing in the fountain, by his
side; should it pass away, its happy lustre would never gleam
upon his life again.

'How sound he sleeps!' murmured the girl.

She departed, but did not trip along the road so lightly as
when she came.

Now, this girl's father was a thriving country merchant in
the neighbourhood, and happened, at that identical time, to
be looking out for just such a young man as David Swan.
Had David formed a way side acquaintance with the daughter, he would have become the father's clerk, and all else in
natural succession. So here, again, had good fortune—the
best of fortunes—stolen so near, that her garments brushed
against him; and he knew nothing of the matter.

The girl was hardly out of sight, when two men turned aside beneath the maple shade. Both had dark faces, set off by cloth caps, which were drawn down aslant over their brows. Their dresses were shabby, yet had a certain smartness. These were a couple of rascals, who got their living by whatever the devil sent them, and now, in the interim of other business, had staked the joint profits of their next piece of villany on a game of cards, which was to have been decided here under the trees. But, finding David asleep by the spring, one of the rogues whispered to his fellow,

'Hist!—Do you see that bundle under his head?'

The other villain nodded, winked, and leered.

'I'll bet you a horn of brandy,' said the first, 'that the chap has either a pocket book, or a snug little hoard of small change, stowed away amongst his shirts. And if not there, we shall find it in his pantaloons' pocket.'

'But how if he wakes?' said the other.

His companion thrust aside his waistcoat, pointed to the handle of a dirk, and nodded.

'So be it!' muttered the second villain.

They approached the unconscious David, and, while one pointed the dagger towards his heart, the other began to search the bundle beneath his head. Their two faces, grim, wrinkled, and ghastly with guilt and fear, bent over their victim, looking horrible enough to be mistaken for fiends, should he suddenly awake. Nay, had the villains glanced aside into the spring, even they would hardly have known themselves, as reflected there. But David Swan had never worn a more tranquil aspect, even when asleep on his mother's breast.

'I must take away the bundle,' whispered one.

'If he stirs, I'll strike,' muttered the other.

But, at this moment, a dog, scenting along the ground, came in beneath the maple trees, and gazed alternately at each of these wicked men, and then at the quiet sleeper. He then lapped out of the fountain.

'Pshaw!' said one villain. 'We can do nothing now. The dog's master must be close behind.'

'Let's take a drink, and be off,' said the other.

The man, with the dagger, thrust back the weapon into his

bosom, and drew forth a pocket pistol, but not of that kind which kills by a single discharge. It was a flask of liquor, with a block tin tumbler screwed upon the mouth. Each drank a comfortable dram, and left the spot, with so many jests, and such laughter at their unaccomplished wickedness, that they might be said to have gone on their way rejoicing. In a few hours, they had forgotten the whole affair, nor once imagined that the recording angel had written down the crime of murder against their souls, in letters as durable as eternity. As for David Swan, he still slept quietly, neither conscious of the shadow of death when it hung over him, nor of the glow of renewed life, when that shadow was withdrawn.

He slept, but no longer so quietly as at first. An hour's repose had snatched, from his elastic frame, the weariness with which many hours of toil had burthened it. Now, he stirred—now, moved his lips, without a sound—now, talked, in an inward tone, to the noon-day spectres of his dream. But a noise of wheels came rattling louder and louder along the road, until it dashed through the dispersing mist of David's slumber—and there was the stage coach. He started up, with all his ideas about him.

'Halloo, driver!—Take a passenger?' shouted he.

'Room on top!' answered the driver.

Up mounted David, and bowled away merrily towards Boston, without so much as a parting glance at that fountain of dreamlike vicissitude. He knew not that a phantom of Wealth had thrown a golden hue upon its waters—nor that one of Love had sighed softly to their murmur—nor that one of Death had threatened to crimson them with his blood— all, in the brief hour since he lay down to sleep. Sleeping or waking, we hear not the airy footsteps of the strange things that almost happen. Does it not argue a superintending Providence, that, while viewless and unexpected events thrust themselves continually athwart our path, there should still be regularity enough, in mortal life, to render foresight even partially available?

The Great Carbuncle*

A MYSTERY OF THE WHITE MOUNTAINS

AT nightfall, once, in the olden time, on the rugged side of one of the Crystal Hills, a party of adventurers were refreshing themselves, after a toilsome and fruitless quest for the Great Carbuncle. They had come thither, not as friends, nor partners in the enterprise, but each, save one youthful pair, impelled by his own selfish and solitary longing for this wondrous gem. Their feeling of brotherhood, however, was strong enough to induce them to contribute a mutual aid in building a rude hut of branches, and kindling a great fire of shattered pines, that had drifted down the headlong current of the Amonoosuck, on the lower bank of which they were to pass the night. There was but one of their number, perhaps, who had become so estranged from natural sympathies, by the absorbing spell of the pursuit, as to acknowledge no satisfaction at the sight of human faces, in the remote and solitary region whither they had ascended. A vast extent of wilderness lay between them and the nearest settlement, while scant a mile above their heads, was that bleak verge, where the hills throw off their shaggy mantle of forest trees, and either robe themselves in clouds, or tower naked into the sky. The roar of the Amonoosuck would have been too awful for endurance, if only a solitary man had listened, while the mountain stream talked with the wind.

The adventurers, therefore, exchanged hospitable greetings, and welcomed one another to the hut, where each man was the host, and all were the guests of the whole company. They spread their individual supplies of food on the flat surface of a rock, and partook of a general repast; at the close of which, a sentiment of good-fellowship was perceptible among the

---

*The Indian tradition, on which this somewhat extravagant tale is founded, is both too wild and too beautiful, to be adequately wrought up, in prose. Sullivan, in his history of Maine, written since the Revolution, remarks, that even then, the existence of the Great Carbuncle was not entirely discredited.

party, though repressed by the idea, that the renewed search
for the Great Carbuncle must make them strangers again, in
the morning. Seven men and one young woman, they
warmed themselves together at the fire, which extended its
bright wall along the whole front of their wigwam. As they
observed the various and contrasted figures that made up the
assemblage, each man looking like a caricature of himself, in
the unsteady light that flickered over him, they came mutually
to the conclusion, that an odder society had never met, in city
or wilderness—on mountain or plain.

The eldest of the group, a tall, lean, weather-beaten man,
some sixty years of age, was clad in the skins of wild animals,
whose fashion of dress he did well to imitate, since the deer,
the wolf, and the bear, had long been his most intimate companions. He was one of those ill-fated mortals, such as the
Indians told of, whom in their early youth, the Great Carbuncle smote with a peculiar madness, and became the passionate
dream of their existence. All, who visited that region, knew
him as the Seeker, and by no other name. As none could
remember when he first took up the search, there went a fable
in the valley of the Saco, that for his inordinate lust after the
Great Carbuncle, he had been condemned to wander among
the mountains till the end of time, still with the same feverish
hopes at sunrise—the same despair at eve. Near this miserable Seeker sat a little elderly personage, wearing a high
crowned hat, shaped somewhat like a crucible. He was from
beyond the sea, a Doctor Cacaphodel, who had wilted and
dried himself into a mummy, by continually stooping over
charcoal furnaces, and inhaling unwholesome fumes, during
his researches in chemistry and alchymy. It was told of him,
whether truly or not, that, at the commencement of his studies, he had drained his body of all its richest blood, and
wasted it, with other inestimable ingredients, in an unsuccessful experiment—and had never been a well man since. Another of the adventurers was Master Ichabod Pigsnort, a
weighty merchant and selectman of Boston, and an elder of
the famous Mr. Norton's church. His enemies had a ridiculous story, that Master Pigsnort was accustomed to spend a
whole hour, after prayer time, every morning and evening, in
wallowing naked among an immense quantity of pine-tree

shillings, which were the earliest silver coinage of Massachusetts. The fourth, whom we shall notice, had no name, that his companions knew of, and was chiefly distinguished by a sneer that always contorted his thin visage, and by a prodigious pair of spectacles, which were supposed to deform and discolor the whole face of nature, to this gentleman's perception. The fifth adventurer likewise lacked a name, which was the greater pity, as he appeared to be a poet. He was a bright-eyed man, but wofully pined away, which was no more than natural, if, as some people affirmed, his ordinary diet was fog, morning mist, and a slice of the densest cloud within his reach, sauced with moonshine, whenever he could get it. Certain it is, that the poetry, which flowed from him, had a smack of all these dainties. The sixth of the party was a young man of haughty mien, and sat somewhat apart from the rest, wearing his plumed hat loftily among his elders, while the fire glittered on the rich embroidery of his dress, and gleamed intensely on the jewelled pommel of his sword. This was the Lord de Vere, who, when at home, was said to spend much of his time in the burial vault of his dead progenitors, rummaging their mouldy coffins in search of all the earthly pride and vain glory, that was hidden among bones and dust; so that, besides his own share, he had the collected haughtiness of his whole line of ancestry.

Lastly, there was a handsome youth in rustic garb, and by his side, a blooming little person, in whom a delicate shade of maiden reserve was just melting into the rich glow of a young wife's affection. Her name was Hannah, and her husband's Matthew; two homely names, yet well enough adapted to the simple pair, who seemed strangely out of place among the whimsical fraternity whose wits had been set agog by the Great Carbuncle.

Beneath the shelter of one hut, in the bright blaze of the same fire, sat this varied group of adventurers, all so intent upon a single object, that, of whatever else they began to speak, their closing words were sure to be illuminated with the Great Carbuncle. Several related the circumstances that brought them thither. One had listened to a traveller's tale of this marvellous stone, in his own distant country, and had immediately been seized with such a thirst for beholding it,

as could only be quenched in its intensest lustre. Another, so
long ago as when the famous Captain Smith visited these
coasts, had seen it blazing far at sea, and had felt no rest in
all the intervening years, till now that he took up the search.
A third, being encamped on a hunting expedition, full forty
miles south of the White Mountains, awoke at midnight, and
beheld the Great Carbuncle gleaming like a meteor, so that
the shadows of the trees fell backward from it. They spoke of
the innumerable attempts, which had been made to reach the
spot, and of the singular fatality which had hitherto withheld
success from all adventurers, though it might seem so easy to
follow to its source a light that overpowered the moon, and
almost matched the sun. It was observable that each smiled
scornfully at the madness of every other, in anticipating better
fortune than the past, yet nourished a scarcely hidden conviction, that he would himself be the favoured one. As if to allay
their too sanguine hopes, they recurred to the Indian traditions, that a spirit kept watch about the gem, and bewildered
those who sought it, either by removing it from peak to peak
of the higher hills, or by calling up a mist from the enchanted
lake over which it hung. But these tales were deemed unworthy of credit; all professing to believe, that the search had
been baffled by want of sagacity or perseverance in the adventurers, or such other causes as might naturally obstruct the
passage to any given point, among the intricacies of forest,
valley, and mountain.

In a pause of the conversation, the wearer of the prodigious
spectacles looked round upon the party, making each individual, in turn, the object of the sneer which invariably dwelt
upon his countenance.

'So, fellow-pilgrims,' said he, 'here we are, seven wise men
and one fair damsel—who, doubtless, is as wise as any gray
beard of the company: here we are, I say, all bound on the
same goodly enterprise. Methinks now, it were not amiss,
that each of us declare what he proposes to do with the Great
Carbuncle, provided he have the good hap to clutch it. What
says our friend in the bear-skin? How mean you, good Sir, to
enjoy the prize which you have been seeking, the Lord knows
how long, among the Crystal Hills?'

'How enjoy it!' exclaimed the aged Seeker, bitterly. 'I hope for no enjoyment from it—that folly has past, long ago! I keep up the search for this accursed stone, because the vain ambition of my youth has become a fate upon me, in old age. The pursuit alone is my strength—the energy of my soul— the warmth of my blood, and the pith and marrow of my bones! Were I to turn my back upon it, I should fall down dead, on the hither side of the Notch, which is the gate-way of this mountain region. Yet, not to have my wasted life time back again, would I give up my hopes of the Great Carbuncle! Having found it, I shall bear it to a certain cavern that I wot of, and there, grasping it in my arms, lie down and die, and keep it buried with me for ever.'

'Oh, wretch, regardless of the interests of science!' cried Doctor Cacaphodel, with philosophic indignation. 'Thou art not worthy to behold, even from afar off, the lustre of this most precious gem that ever was concocted in the laboratory of Nature. Mine is the sole purpose for which a wise man may desire the possession of the Great Carbuncle. Immediately on obtaining it—for I have a presentiment, good people, that the prize is reserved to crown my scientific reputation—I shall return to Europe, and employ my remaining years in reducing it to its first elements. A portion of the stone will I grind to impalpable powder; other parts shall be dissolved in acids, or whatever solvents will act upon so admirable a composition; and the remainder I design to melt in the crucible, or set on fire with the blow-pipe. By these various methods, I shall gain an accurate analysis, and finally bestow the result of my labours upon the world, in a folio volume.'

'Excellent!' quoth the man with the spectacles. 'Nor need you hesitate, learned Sir, on account of the necessary destruction of the gem; since the perusal of your folio may teach every mother's son of us to concoct a Great Carbuncle of his own.'

'But, verily,' said Master Ichabod Pigsnort, 'for mine own part, I object to the making of these counterfeits, as being calculated to reduce the marketable value of the true gem. I tell ye frankly, Sirs, I have an interest in keeping up the price. Here have I quitted my regular traffic, leaving my warehouse in the care of my clerks, and putting my credit to great hazard, and furthermore, have put myself to peril of death or captivity by the accursed heathen savages—and all this without daring to ask the prayers of the congregation, because the quest for the Great Carbuncle is deemed little better than a traffic with the evil one. Now think ye that I would have done this grievous wrong to my soul, body, reputation and estate, without a reasonable chance of profit?'

'Not I, pious Master Pigsnort,' said the man with the spectacles.—'I never laid such a great folly to thy charge.'

'Truly, I hope not,' said the merchant. 'Now, as touching this Great Carbuncle, I am free to own that I have never had a glimpse of it; but be it only the hundredth part so bright as people tell, it will surely outvalue the Great Mogul's best diamond, which he holds at an incalculable sum. Wherefore, I am minded to put the Great Carbuncle on ship board, and voyage with it to England, France, Spain, Italy, or into Heathendom, if Providence should send me thither, and, in a word, dispose of the gem to the best bidder among the potentates of the earth, that he may place it among his crown jewels. If any of ye have a wiser plan, let him expound it.'

'That have I, thou sordid man!' exclaimed the poet. 'Dost thou desire nothing brighter than gold, that thou wouldst transmute all this ethereal lustre into such dross, as thou wallowest in already? For myself, hiding the jewel under my cloak, I shall hie me back to my attic chamber, in one of the darksome alleys of London. There, night and day, will I gaze upon it—my soul shall drink its radiance—it shall be diffused throughout my intellectual powers, and gleam brightly in every line of poesy that I indite. Thus, long ages after I am gone, the splendor of the Great Carbuncle will blaze around my name!'

'Well said, Master Poet!' cried he of the spectacles. 'Hide it under thy cloak, say'st thou? Why, it will gleam through the holes, and make thee look like a Jack o'lanthern!'

'To think!'—ejaculated the Lord de Vere, rather to himself, than his companions, the best of whom he held utterly unworthy of his intercourse,—'to think that a fellow in a tattered cloak should talk of conveying the Great Carbuncle to a garret in Grub street! Have not I resolved within myself, that the whole earth contains no fitter ornament for the great hall of my ancestral castle? There shall it flame for ages, making a noonday of midnight, glittering on the suits of armour, the banners, and escutcheons, that hang around the wall, and keeping bright the memory of heroes. Wherefore have all other adventurers sought the prize in vain, but that I might win it, and make it a symbol of the glories of our lofty line? And never, on the diadem of the White Mountains, did the Great Carbuncle hold a place half so honored, as is reserved for it in the hall of the de Veres!'

'It is a noble thought,' said the Cynic, with an obsequious sneer. 'Yet, might I presume to say so, the gem would make a rare sepulchral lamp, and would display the glories of your lordship's progenitors more truly in the ancestral vault, than in the castle hall.'

'Nay forsooth,' observed Matthew, the young rustic, who sat hand in hand with his bride, 'the gentleman has bethought himself of a profitable use for this bright stone. Hannah here and I are seeking it for a like purpose.'

'How, fellow!' exclaimed his lordship, in surprise. 'What castle hall hast thou to hang it in?'

'No castle,' replied Matthew, 'but as neat a cottage as any within sight of the Crystal Hills. Ye must know, friends, that Hannah and I, being wedded the last week, have taken up the search of the Great Carbuncle, because we shall need its light in the long winter evenings; and it will be such a pretty thing to show the neighbors, when they visit us. It will shine through the house, so that we may pick up a pin in any corner, and will set all the windows a-glowing, as if there were a great fire of pine knots in the chimney. And then how pleasant, when we awake in the night, to be able to see one another's faces!'

There was a general smile among the adventurers, at the simplicity of the young couple's project, in regard to this wondrous and invaluable stone, with which the greatest monarch on earth might have been proud to adorn his palace. Especially the man with spectacles, who had sneered at all the company in turn, now twisted his visage into such an expression of ill-natured mirth, that Matthew asked him, rather peevishly, what he himself meant to do with the Great Carbuncle.

'The Great Carbuncle!' answered the Cynic, with ineffable scorn. 'Why, you blockhead, there is no such thing, in rerum naturâ. I have come three thousand miles, and am resolved to set my foot on every peak of these mountains, and poke my head into every chasm, for the sole purpose of demonstrating to the satisfaction of any man, one whit less an ass than thyself, that the Great Carbuncle is all a humbug!'

Vain and foolish were the motives that had brought most of the adventurers to the Crystal Hills, but none so vain, so foolish, and so impious too, as that of the scoffer with the prodigious spectacles. He was one of those wretched and evil men, whose yearnings are downward to the darkness, instead of Heavenward, and who, could they but extinguish the lights which God hath kindled for us, would count the midnight gloom their chiefest glory. As the Cynic spoke, several of the party were startled by a gleam of red splendor, that showed the huge shapes of the surrounding mountains, and the rock-bestrewn bed of the turbulent river, with an illumination unlike that of their fire, on the trunks and black boughs of the forest trees. They listened for the roll of thunder, but heard nothing, and were glad that the tempest came not near them. The stars, those dial-points of Heaven, now warned the adventurers to close their eyes on the blazing logs, and open them, in dreams, to the glow of the Great Carbuncle.

The young married couple had taken their lodgings in the furthest corner of the wigwam, and were separated from the rest of the party by a curtain of curiously woven twigs, such as might have hung, in deep festoons around the bridal bower of Eve. The modest little wife had wrought this piece of tapestry, while the other guests were talking. She and her husband fell asleep with hands tenderly clasped, and awoke, from visions of unearthly radiance, to meet the more blessed light of one another's eyes. They awoke at the same instant, and with one happy smile beaming over their two faces, which grew brighter, with their consciousness of the reality of life and love. But no sooner did she recollect where they were, than the bride peeped through the interstices of the leafy curtain, and saw that the outer room of the hut was deserted.

'Up, dear Matthew!' cried she, in haste. 'The strange folk

are all gone! Up, this very minute, or we shall lose the Great Carbuncle!'

In truth, so little did these poor young people deserve the mighty prize which had lured them thither, that they had slept peacefully all night, and till the summits of the hills were glittering with sunshine; while the other adventurers had tossed their limbs in feverish wakefulness, or dreamed of climbing precipices, and set off to realize their dreams with the earliest peep of dawn. But Matthew and Hannah, after their calm rest, were as light as two young deer, and merely stopt to say their prayers, and wash themselves in a cold pool of the Amonoosuck, and then to taste a morsel of food, ere they turned their faces to the mountain-side. It was a sweet emblem of conjugal affection, as they toiled up the difficult ascent, gathering strength from the mutual aid which they afforded. After several little accidents, such as a torn robe, a lost shoe, and the entanglement of Hannah's hair in a bough, they reached the upper verge of the forest, and were now to pursue a more adventurous course. The innumerable trunks and heavy foliage of the trees had hitherto shut in their thoughts, which now shrank affrighted from the region of wind, and cloud, and naked rocks, and desolate sunshine, that rose immeasurably above them. They gazed back at the obscure wilderness which they had traversed, and longed to be buried again in its depths, rather than trust themselves to so vast and visible a solitude.

'Shall we go on?' said Matthew, throwing his arm round Hannah's waist, both to protect her, and to comfort his heart by drawing her close to it.

But the little bride, simple as she was, had a woman's love of jewels, and could not forego the hope of possessing the very brightest in the world, in spite of the perils with which it must be won.

'Let us climb a little higher,' whispered she, yet tremulously, as she turned her face upward to the lonely sky.

'Come then,' said Matthew, mustering his manly courage, and drawing her along with him; for she became timid again, the moment that he grew bold.

And upward, accordingly, went the pilgrims of the Great

Carbuncle, now treading upon the tops and thickly interwoven branches of dwarf pines, which, by the growth of centuries, though mossy with age, had barely reached three feet
in altitude. Next, they came to masses and fragments of naked
rock, heaped confusedly together, like a cairn reared by
giants, in memory of a giant chief. In this bleak realm of upper air, nothing breathed, nothing grew; there was no life but
what was concentred in their two hearts; they had climbed so
high, that Nature herself seemed no longer to keep them
company. She lingered beneath them, within the verge of the
forest trees, and sent a farewell glance after her children, as
they strayed where her own green footprints had never been.
But soon they were to be hidden from her eye. Densely and
dark, the mists began to gather below, casting black spots of
shadow on the vast landscape, and sailing heavily to one
centre, as if the loftiest mountain peak had summoned a
council of its kindred clouds. Finally, the vapors welded
themselves, as it were, into a mass, presenting the appearance
of a pavement over which the wanderers might have trodden,
but where they would vainly have sought an avenue to the
blessed earth which they had lost. And the lovers yearned to
behold that green earth again, more intensely, alas! than, beneath a clouded sky, they had ever desired a glimpse of
Heaven. They even felt it a relief to their desolation, when
the mists, creeping gradually up the mountain, concealed its
lonely peak, and thus annihilated, at least for them, the whole
region of visible space. But they drew closer together, with a
fond and melancholy gaze, dreading lest the universal cloud
should snatch them from each other's sight.

Still, perhaps, they would have been resolute to climb as far
and as high, between earth and heaven, as they could find
foothold, if Hannah's strength had not begun to fail, and
with that, her courage also. Her breath grew short. She refused to burthen her husband with her weight, but often tottered against his side, and recovered herself each time by a
feebler effort. At last, she sank down on one of the rocky
steps of the acclivity.

'We are lost, dear Matthew,' said she, mournfully. 'We
shall never find our way to the earth again. And, Oh, how
happy we might have been in our cottage!'

'Dear heart!—we will yet be happy there,' answered Matthew. 'Look! In this direction, the sunshine penetrates the dismal mist. By its aid, I can direct our course to the passage of the Notch. Let us go back, love, and dream no more of the Great Carbuncle!'

'The sun cannot be yonder,' said Hannah, with despondence. 'By this time, it must be noon. If there could ever be any sunshine here, it would come from above our heads.'

'But, look!' repeated Matthew, in a somewhat altered tone. 'It is brightening every moment. If not sunshine, what can it be?'

Nor could the young bride any longer deny, that a radiance was breaking through the mist, and changing its dim hue to a dusky red, which continually grew more vivid, as if brilliant particles were interfused with the gloom. Now, also, the cloud began to roll away from the mountain, while, as it heavily withdrew, one object after another started out of its impenetrable obscurity into sight, with precisely the effect of a new creation, before the indistinctness of the old chaos had been completely swallowed up. As the process went on, they saw the gleaming of water close at their feet, and found themselves on the very border of a mountain lake, deep, bright, clear, and calmly beautiful, spreading from brim to brim of a basin that had been scooped out of the solid rock. A ray of glory flashed across its surface. The pilgrims looked whence it should proceed, but closed their eyes with a thrill of awful admiration, to exclude the fervid splendor that glowed from the brow of a cliff, impending over the enchanted lake. For the simple pair had reached that lake of mystery, and found the long sought shrine of the Great Carbuncle!

They threw their arms around each other, and trembled at their own success; for, as the legends of this wondrous gem rushed thick upon their memory, they felt themselves marked out by fate—and the consciousness was fearful. Often, from childhood upward, they had seen it shining like a distant star. And now that star was throwing its intensest lustre on their hearts. They seemed changed to one another's eyes, in the red brilliancy that flamed upon their cheeks, while it lent the same fire to the lake, the rocks, and sky, and to the mists which had rolled back before its power. But, with their next glance, they beheld an object that drew their attention even from the mighty stone. At the base of the cliff, directly beneath the Great Carbuncle, appeared the figure of a man, with his arms extended in the act of climbing, and his face turned upward, as if to drink the full gush of splendor. But he stirred not, no more than if changed to marble.

'It is the Seeker,' whispered Hannah, convulsively grasping her husband's arm. 'Matthew, he is dead!'

'The joy of success has killed him,' replied Matthew, trembling violently.—'Or perhaps the very light of the Great Carbuncle was death!'

'The Great Carbuncle,' cried a peevish voice behind them. 'The Great Humbug! If you have found it, prithee point it out to me.'

They turned their heads, and there was the Cynic, with his prodigious spectacles set carefully on his nose, staring now at the lake, now at the rocks, now at the distant masses of vapor, now right at the Great Carbuncle itself, yet seemingly as unconscious of its light, as if all the scattered clouds were condensed about his person. Though its radiance actually threw the shadow of the unbeliever at his own feet, as he turned his back upon the glorious jewel, he would not be convinced that there was the least glimmer there.

'Where is your Great Humbug?' he repeated. 'I challenge you to make me see it!'

'There,' said Matthew, incensed at such perverse blindness, and turning the Cynic round towards the illuminated cliff. 'Take off those abominable spectacles, and you cannot help seeing it!'

Now these colored spectacles probably darkened the Cynic's sight, in at least as great a degree as the smoked glasses through which people gaze at an eclipse. With resolute bravado, however, he snatched them from his nose, and fixed a bold stare full upon the ruddy blaze of the Great Carbuncle. But, scarcely had he encountered it, when, with a deep, shuddering groan, he dropt his head, and pressed both hands across his miserable eyes. Thenceforth there was, in very truth, no light of the Great Carbuncle, nor any other light on earth, nor light of Heaven itself, for the poor Cynic. So long accustomed to view all objects through a medium that deprived them of every glimpse of brightness, a single flash of so glorious a phenomenon, striking upon his naked vision, had blinded him forever.

'Matthew,' said Hannah, clinging to him, 'let us go hence!'

Matthew saw that she was faint, and kneeling down, supported her in his arms, while he threw some of the thrillingly cold water of the enchanted lake upon her face and bosom. It revived her, but could not renovate her courage.

'Yes, dearest!' cried Matthew, pressing her tremulous form to his breast,—'we will go hence, and return to our humble cottage. The blessed sunshine, and the quiet moonlight, shall come through our window. We will kindle the cheerful glow of our hearth, at eventide, and be happy in its light. But never again will we desire more light than all the world may share with us.'

'No,' said his bride, 'for how could we live by day, or sleep by night, in this awful blaze of the Great Carbuncle!'

Out of the hollow of their hands, they drank each a draught from the lake, which presented them its waters uncontaminated by an earthly lip. Then, lending their guidance to the blinded Cynic, who uttered not a word, and even stifled his groans in his own most wretched heart, they began to descend the mountain. Yet, as they left the shore, till then untrodden, of the Spirit's lake, they threw a farewell glance towards the cliff, and beheld the vapors gathering in dense volumes, through which the gem burned duskily.

As touching the other pilgrims of the Great Carbuncle, the legend goes on to tell, that the worshipful Master Ichabod Pigsnort soon gave up the quest, as a desperate speculation, and wisely resolved to betake himself again to his warehouse, near the town-dock, in Boston. But, as he passed through the Notch of the mountains, a war party of Indians captured our unlucky merchant, and carried him to Montreal, there holding him in bondage, till, by the payment of a heavy ransom, he had wofully subtracted from his hoard of pine-tree shillings. By his long absence, moreover, his affairs had become so disordered, that, for the rest of his life, instead of wallowing in silver, he had seldom a sixpence worth of copper. Doctor Cacaphodel, the alchymist, returned to his laboratory with a prodigious fragment of granite, which he ground to powder, dissolved in acids, melted in the crucible, and burnt with the blow-pipe, and published the result of his experiments in one of the heaviest folios of the day. And, for all these purposes, the gem itself could not have answered better than the granite. The poet, by a somewhat similar mistake, made prize of a great piece of ice, which he found in a sunless chasm of the mountains, and swore that it corresponded, in all points, with his idea of the Great Carbuncle. The critics say, that, if his poetry lacked the splendor of the gem, it retained all the coldness of the ice. The Lord de Vere went back to his ancestral hall, where he contented himself with a wax-lighted chandelier, and filled, in due course of time, another coffin in the ancestral vault. As the funeral torches gleamed within that dark receptacle, there was no need of the Great Carbuncle to shew the vanity of earthly pomp.

The Cynic, having cast aside his spectacles, wandered about the world, a miserable object, and was punished with an agonizing desire of light, for the wilful blindness of his former life. The whole night long, he would lift his splendor-blasted orbs to the moon and stars; he turned his face eastward, at sunrise, as duly as a Persian idolater; he made a pilgrimage to Rome, to witness the magnificent illumination of Saint Peter's church; and finally perished in the great fire of London, into the midst of which he had thrust himself, with the desperate idea of catching one feeble ray from the blaze, that was kindling earth and heaven.

Matthew and his bride spent many peaceful years, and were fond of telling the legend of the Great Carbuncle. The tale, however, towards the close of their lengthened lives, did not meet with the full credence that had been accorded to it by those, who remembered the ancient lustre of the gem. For it is affirmed, that, from the hour when two mortals had shown themselves so simply wise, as to reject a jewel which would have dimmed all earthly things, its splendor waned. When other pilgrims reached the cliff, they found only an opaque stone, with particles of mica glittering on its surface. There is also a tradition that, as the youthful pair departed, the gem was loosened from the forehead of the cliff, and fell into the enchanted lake, and that, at noontide, the Seeker's form may still be seen to bend over its quenchless-gleam.

Some few believe that this inestimable stone is blazing, as of old, and say that they have caught its radiance, like a flash of summer lightning, far down the valley of the Saco. And be it owned, that, many a mile from the Crystal Hills, I saw a wondrous light around their summits, and was lured, by the faith of poesy, to be the latest pilgrim of the GREAT CAR- BUNCLE.

Fancy's Show Box

A Morality

WHAT is Guilt? A stain upon the soul. And it is a point of vast interest, whether the soul may contract such stains, in all their depth and flagrancy, from deeds which may have been plotted and resolved upon, but which, physically, have never had existence. Must the fleshly hand, and visible frame of man, set its seal to the evil designs of the soul, in order to give them their entire validity against the sinner? Or, while none but crimes perpetrated are cognizable before an earthly tribunal, will guilty thoughts—of which guilty deeds are no more than shadows—will these draw down the full weight of a condemning sentence, in the supreme court of eternity? In the solitude of a midnight chamber, or in a desert, afar from men, or in a church, while the body is kneeling, the soul may pollute itself even with those crimes, which we are accustomed to deem altogether carnal. If this be true, it is a fearful truth.

Let us illustrate the subject by an imaginary example. A venerable gentleman, one Mr. Smith, who had long been regarded as a pattern of moral excellence, was warming his aged blood with a glass or two of generous wine. His children being gone forth about their worldly business, and his grandchildren at school, he sat alone, in a deep, luxurious armchair, with his feet beneath a richly carved mahogany table. Some old people have a dread of solitude, and when better company may not be had, rejoice even to hear the quiet breathing of a babe, asleep upon the carpet. But Mr. Smith, whose silver hair was the bright symbol of a life unstained, except by such spots as are inseparable from human nature, he had no need of a babe to protect him by its purity, nor of a grown person, to stand between him and his own soul. Nevertheless, either Manhood must converse with Age, or Womanhood must soothe him with gentle cares, or Infancy must sport around his chair, or his thoughts will stray into the misty region of the past, and the old man be chill and sad. Wine will not always cheer him. Such might have been the case with Mr. Smith, when, through the brilliant medium of his glass of old Madeira, he beheld three figures entering the room. These were Fancy, who had assumed the garb and aspect of an itinerant showman, with a box of pictures on her back; and Memory, in the likeness of a clerk, with a pen behind her ear, an ink-horn at her button-hole, and a huge manuscript volume beneath her arm; and lastly, behind the other two, a person shrouded in a dusky mantle, which concealed both face and form. But Mr. Smith had a shrewd idea that it was Conscience.

How kind of Fancy, Memory, and Conscience, to visit the old gentleman, just as he was beginning to imagine that the wine had neither so bright a sparkle, nor so excellent a flavor, as when himself and the liquor were less aged! Through the dim length of the apartment, where crimson curtains muffled the glare of sunshine, and created a rich obscurity, the three guests drew near the silver-haired old man. Memory, with a finger between the leaves of her huge volume, placed herself at his right hand. Conscience, with her face still hidden in the dusky mantle, took her station on the left, so as to be next his heart; while Fancy set down her picture-box upon the table, with the magnifying glass convenient to his eye. We can sketch merely the outlines of two or three, out of the many pictures, which, at the pulling of a string, successively peopled the box with the semblances of living scenes.

One was a moonlight picture; in the back-ground, a lowly dwelling; and in front, partly shadowed by a tree, yet besprinkled with flakes of radiance, two youthful figures, male and female. The young man stood with folded arms, a haughty smile upon his lip, and a gleam of triumph in his eye, as he glanced downward at the kneeling girl. She was almost prostrate at his feet, evidently sinking under a weight of shame and anguish, which hardly allowed her to lift her clasped hands in supplication. Her eyes she could not lift. But neither her agony, nor the lovely features on which it was depicted, nor the slender grace of the form which it convulsed, appeared to soften the obduracy of the young man. He was the personification of triumphant scorn. Now, strange to say, as old Mr. Smith peeped through the magnifying glass, which made the objects start out from the canvass with magical deception, he began to recognize the farm-house, the tree, and both the figures of the picture. The young man, in times long past, had often met his gaze within the looking-glass; the girl was the very image of his first love—his cottage-love—his Martha Burroughs! Mr. Smith was scandalized. 'Oh, vile and slanderous picture!' he exclaims. 'When have I triumphed over ruined innocence? Was not Martha wedded, in her teens, to David Tomkins, who won her girlish love, and long enjoyed her affection as a wife? And ever since his death, she has lived a reputable widow!' Meantime, Memory was turning over the leaves of her volume, rustling them to and fro with uncertain fingers, until, among the earlier pages, she found one which had reference to this picture. She reads it, close to the old gentleman's ear; it is a record merely of sinful thought, which never was embodied in an act; but, while Memory is reading, Conscience unveils her face, and strikes a dagger to the heart of Mr. Smith. Though not a death-blow, the torture was extreme.

The exhibition proceeded. One after another, Fancy displayed her pictures, all of which appeared to have been painted by some malicious artist, on purpose to vex Mr. Smith. Not a shadow of proof could have been adduced, in any earthly court, that he was guilty of the slightest of those sins which were thus made to stare him in the face. In one scene, there was a table set out, with several bottles, and glasses half filled with wine, which threw back the dull ray of an expiring lamp. There had been mirth and revelry, until the hand of the clock stood just at midnight, when Murder stept between the boon-companions. A young man had fallen on the floor, and lay stone dead, with a ghastly wound crushed into his temple, while over him, with a delirium of mingled rage and horror in his countenance, stood the youthful likeness of Mr. Smith. The murdered youth wore the features of Edward Spencer! 'What does this rascal of a painter mean?' cries Mr. Smith, provoked beyond all patience. 'Edward Spencer was my earliest and dearest friend, true to me as I to him, through more than half a century. Neither I, nor any other, ever murdered him. Was he not alive within five years, and did he not, in token of our long friendship, bequeath me

his gold-headed cane, and a mourning ring?' Again had Memory been turning over her volume, and fixed at length upon
so confused a page, that she surely must have scribbled it
when she was tipsy. The purport was, however, that, while
Mr. Smith and Edward Spencer were heating their young
blood with wine, a quarrel had flashed up between them, and
Mr. Smith, in deadly wrath, had flung a bottle at Spencer's
head. True, it missed its aim, and merely smashed a looking-
glass; and the next morning, when the incident was imperfectly remembered, they had shaken hands with a hearty
laugh. Yet, again, while Memory was reading, Conscience unveiled her face, struck a dagger to the heart of Mr. Smith, and
quelled his remonstrance with her iron frown. The pain was
quite excruciating.

Some of the pictures had been painted with so doubtful a
touch, and in colors so faint and pale, that the subjects could
barely be conjectured. A dull, semi-transparent mist had been
thrown over the surface of the canvass, into which the figures
seemed to vanish, while the eye sought most earnestly to fix
them. But, in every scene, however dubiously portrayed, Mr.
Smith was invariably haunted by his own lineaments, at various ages, as in a dusty mirror. After poring several minutes
over one of these blurred and almost indistinguishable pictures, he began to see, that the painter had intended to represent him, now in the decline of life, as stripping the clothes
from the backs of three half-starved children. 'Really, this
puzzles me!' quoth Mr. Smith, with the irony of conscious
rectitude. 'Asking pardon of the painter, I pronounce him a
fool, as well as a scandalous knave. A man of my standing in
the world, to be robbing little children of their clothes! Ridiculous!'—But while he spoke, Memory had searched her
fatal volume, and found a page, which, with her sad, calm
voice, she poured into his ear. It was not altogether inapplicable to the misty scene. It told how Mr. Smith had been
grievously tempted, by many devilish sophistries, on the
ground of a legal quibble, to commence a law-suit against
three orphan children, joint heirs to a considerable estate.
Fortunately, before he was quite decided, his claims had
turned out nearly as devoid of law, as justice. As Memory
ceased to read, Conscience again thrust aside her mantle, and

would have struck her victim with the envenomed dagger, only that he struggled, and clasped his hands before his heart. Even then, however, he sustained an ugly gash.

Why should we follow Fancy through the whole series of those awful pictures? Painted by an artist of wondrous power, and terrible acquaintance with the secret soul, they embodied the ghosts of all the never perpetrated sins, that had glided through the life-time of Mr. Smith. And could such beings of cloudy fantasy, so near akin to nothingness, give valid evidence against him, at the day of judgment? Be that the case or not, there is reason to believe, that one truly penitential tear would have washed away each hateful picture, and left the canvass white as snow. But Mr. Smith, at a prick of Conscience too keen to be endured, bellowed aloud, with impatient agony, and suddenly discovered that his three guests were gone. There he sat alone, a silver-haired and highly venerated old man, in the rich gloom of the crimson-curtained room, with no box of pictures on the table, but only a decanter of most excellent Madeira. Yet his heart still seemed to fester with the venom of the dagger.

Nevertheless, the unfortunate old gentleman might have argued the matter with Conscience, and alleged many reasons wherefore she should not smite him so pitilessly. Were we to take up his cause, it should be somewhat in the following fashion. A scheme of guilt, till it be put in execution, greatly resembles a train of incidents in a projected tale. The latter, in order to produce a sense of reality in the reader's mind, must be conceived with such proportionate strength by the author as to seem, in the glow of fancy, more like truth, past, present, or to come, than purely fiction. The prospective sinner, on the other hand, weaves his plot of crime, but seldom or never feels a perfect certainty that it will be executed. There is a dreaminess diffused about his thoughts; in a dream, as it were, he strikes the death-blow into his victim's heart, and starts to find an indelible blood-stain on his hand. Thus a novel-writer, or a dramatist, in creating a villain of romance, and fitting him with evil deeds, and the villain of actual life, in projecting crimes that will be perpetrated, may almost meet each other, half-way between reality and fancy. It is not until the crime is accomplished, that guilt clenches its gripe upon the guilty heart and claims it for its own. Then, and not before, sin is actually felt and acknowledged, and, if unaccompanied by repentance, grows a thousand fold more virulent by its self-consciousness. Be it considered, also, that men often over-estimate their capacity for evil. At a distance, while its attendant circumstances do not press upon their notice, and its results are dimly seen, they can bear to contemplate it. They may take the steps which lead to crime, impelled by the same sort of mental action as in working out a mathematical problem, yet be powerless with compunction, at the final moment. They knew not what deed it was, that they deemed themselves resolved to do. In truth, there is no such thing in man's nature, as a settled and full resolve, either for good or evil, except at the very moment of execution. Let us hope, therefore, that all the dreadful consequences of sin will not be incurred, unless the act have set its seal upon the thought.

Yet, with the slight fancy-work which we have framed, some sad and awful truths are interwoven. Man must not disclaim his brotherhood, even with the guiltiest, since, though his hand be clean, his heart has surely been polluted by the flitting phantoms of iniquity. He must feel, that, when he shall knock at the gate of Heaven, no semblance of an unspotted life can entitle him to entrance there. Penitence must kneel, and Mercy come from the footstool of the throne, or that golden gate will never open!

The Prophetic Pictures*

'**B**UT this painter!' cried Walter Ludlow, with animation. 'He not only excels in his peculiar art, but possesses vast acquirements in all other learning and science. He talks Hebrew with Doctor Mather, and gives lectures in anatomy to Doctor Boylston. In a word, he will meet the best instructed man among us, on his own ground. Moreover, he is a polished gentleman—a citizen of the world—yes, a true cosmopolite; for he will speak like a native of each clime and country on the globe, except our own forests, whither he is now going. Nor is all this what I most admire in him.'

'Indeed!' said Elinor, who had listened with a woman's interest to the description of such a man. 'Yet this is admirable enough.'

'Surely it is,' replied her lover, 'but far less so than his natural gift of adapting himself to every variety of character, insomuch that all men—and all women too, Elinor—shall find a mirror of themselves in this wonderful painter. But the greatest wonder is yet to be told.'

'Nay, if he have more wonderful attributes than these,' said Elinor, laughing, 'Boston is a perilous abode for the poor gentleman. Are you telling me of a painter, or a wizard?'

'In truth,' answered he, 'that question might be asked much more seriously than you suppose. They say that he paints not merely a man's features, but his mind and heart. He catches the secret sentiments and passions, and throws them upon the canvass, like sunshine—or perhaps, in the portraits of dark-souled men, like a gleam of infernal fire. It is an awful gift,' added Walter, lowering his voice from its tone of enthusiasm. 'I shall be almost afraid to sit to him.'

'Walter, are you in earnest?' exclaimed Elinor.

'For Heaven's sake, dearest Elinor, do not let him paint the look which you now wear,' said her lover, smiling, though rather perplexed. 'There: it is passing away now, but when

*This story was suggested by an anecdote of Stuart, related in Dunlap's History of the Arts of Design—a most entertaining book to the general reader, and a deeply interesting one, we should think, to the artist.

you spoke, you seemed frightened to death, and very sad besides. What were you thinking of?'

'Nothing; nothing,' answered Elinor, hastily. 'You paint my face with your own fantasies. Well, come for me tomorrow, and we will visit this wonderful artist.'

But when the young man had departed, it cannot be denied that a remarkable expression was again visible on the fair and youthful face of his mistress. It was a sad and anxious look, little in accordance with what should have been the feelings of a maiden on the eve of wedlock. Yet Walter Ludlow was the chosen of her heart.

'A look!' said Elinor to herself. 'No wonder that it startled him, if it expressed what I sometimes feel. I know, by my own experience, how frightful a look may be. But it was all fancy. I thought nothing of it at the time—I have seen nothing of it since—I did but dream it.'

And she busied herself about the embroidery of a ruff, in which she meant that her portrait should be taken.

The painter, of whom they had been speaking, was not one of those native artists, who at a later period than this, borrowed their colors from the Indians, and manufactured their pencils of the furs of wild beasts. Perhaps, if he could have revoked his life and pre-arranged his destiny, he might have chosen to belong to that school without a master, in the hope of being at least original, since there were no works of art to imitate, nor rules to follow. But he had been born and educated in Europe. People said, that he had studied the grandeur or beauty of conception, and every touch of the master-hand, in all the most famous pictures, in cabinets and galleries, and on the walls of churches, till there was nothing more for his powerful mind to learn. Art could add nothing to its lessons, but Nature might. He had therefore visited a world, whither none of his professional brethren had preceded him, to feast his eyes on visible images, that were noble and picturesque, yet had never been transferred to canvass. America was too poor to afford other temptations to an artist of eminence, though many of the colonial gentry, on the painter's arrival, had expressed a wish to transmit their lineaments to posterity, by means of his skill. Whenever such proposals were made, he fixed his piercing eyes on the applicant, and seemed to look him through and through. If he beheld only a sleek and comfortable visage, though there were a gold-laced coat to adorn the picture, and golden guineas to pay for it, he civilly rejected the task and the reward. But if the face were the index of anything uncommon, in thought, sentiment, or experience; or if he met a beggar in the street, with a white beard and a furrowed brow; or if sometimes, a child happened to look up and smile: he would exhaust all the art on them, that he denied to wealth.

Pictorial skill being so rare in the colonies, the painter became an object of general curiosity. If few or none could appreciate the technical merit of his productions, yet there were points, in regard to which the opinion of the crowd was as valuable as the refined judgment of the amateur. He watched the effect that each picture produced on such untutored beholders, and derived profit from their remarks, while they would as soon have thought of instructing Nature herself, as him who seemed to rival her. Their admiration, it must be owned, was tinctured with the prejudices of the age and country. Some deemed it an offence against the Mosaic law, and even a presumptuous mockery of the Creator, to bring into existence such lively images of his creatures. Others, frightened at the art which could raise phantoms at will, and keep the form of the dead among the living, were inclined to consider the painter as a magician, or perhaps the famous Black Man of old witch-times, plotting mischief in a new guise. These foolish fancies were more than half believed, among the mob. Even in superior circles, his character was invested with a vague awe, partly rising like smoke-wreaths from the popular superstitions, but chiefly caused by the varied knowledge and talents which he made subservient to his profession.

Being on the eve of marriage, Walter Ludlow and Elinor were eager to obtain their portraits, as the first of what, they doubtless hoped, would be a long series of family pictures. The day after the conversation above recorded, they visited the painter's rooms. A servant ushered them into an apartment, where, though the artist himself was not visible, there were personages, whom they could hardly forbear greeting with reverence. They knew, indeed, that the whole assembly were but pictures, yet felt it impossible to separate the idea of life and intellect from such striking counterfeits. Several of the portraits were known to them, either as distinguished characters of the day, or their private acquaintances. There was Governor Burnet, looking as if he had just received an undutiful communication from the House of Representatives, and were inditing a most sharp response. Mr. Cooke hung beside the ruler whom he opposed, sturdy, and somewhat puritanical, as befitted a popular leader. The ancient lady of Sir William Phips eyed them from the wall, in ruff and farthingale, an imperious old dame, not unsuspected of witchcraft. John Winslow, then a very young man, wore the expression of warlike enterprise, which long afterwards made him a distinguished general. Their personal friends were recognized at a glance. In most of the pictures, the whole mind and character were brought out on the countenance, and concentrated into a single look, so that, to speak paradoxically, the originals hardly resembled themselves so strikingly as the portraits did.

Among these modern worthies, there were two old bearded Saints, who had almost vanished into the darkening canvass. There was also a pale, but unfaded Madonna, who had perhaps been worshipped in Rome, and now regarded the lovers with such a mild and holy look, that they longed to worship too.

'How singular a thought,' observed Walter Ludlow, 'that this beautiful face has been beautiful for above two hundred years! Oh, if all beauty would endure so well! Do you not envy her, Elinor?'

'If Earth were Heaven, I might,' she replied. 'But where all things fade, how miserable to be the one that could not fade!'

'This dark old St. Peter has a fierce and ugly scowl, saint though he be,' continued Walter. 'He troubles me. But the Virgin looks kindly at us.'

'Yes; but very sorrowfully, methinks,' said Elinor.

The easel stood beneath these three old pictures, sustaining one that had been recently commenced. After a little inspection, they began to recognize the features of their own minister, the Rev. Dr. Colman, growing into shape and life, as it were, out of a cloud.

'Kind old man!' exclaimed Elinor. 'He gazes at me, as if he were about to utter a word of paternal advice.'

'And at me,' said Walter, 'as if he were about to shake his head and rebuke me, for some suspected iniquity. But so does the original. I shall never feel quite comfortable under his eye, till we stand before him to be married.'

They now heard a footstep on the floor, and turning, beheld the painter, who had been some moments in the room, and had listened to a few of their remarks. He was a middle-aged man, with a countenance well worthy of his own pencil. Indeed, by the picturesque, though careless arrangement of his rich dress, and, perhaps, because his soul dwelt always among painted shapes, he looked somewhat like a portrait himself. His visiters were sensible of a kindred between the artist and his works, and felt as if one of the pictures had stept from the canvass to salute them.

Walter Ludlow, who was slightly known to the painter, explained the object of their visit. While he spoke, a sunbeam was falling athwart his figure and Elinor's, with so happy an effect, that they also seemed living pictures of youth and beauty, gladdened by bright fortune. The artist was evidently struck.

'My easel is occupied for several ensuing days, and my stay in Boston must be brief,' said he, thoughtfully; then after an observant glance, he added: 'but your wishes shall be gratified, though I disappoint the chief Justice and Madam Oliver. I must not lose this opportunity, for the sake of painting a few ells of broadcloth and brocade.'

The painter expressed a desire to introduce both their portraits into one picture, and represent them engaged in some appropriate action. This plan would have delighted the lovers, but was necessarily rejected, because so large a space of canvass would have been unfit for the room which it was intended to decorate. Two half length portraits were therefore fixed upon. After they had taken leave, Walter Ludlow asked Elinor, with a smile, whether she knew what an influence over their fates the painter was about to acquire.

'The old women of Boston affirm,' continued he, 'that after he has once got possession of a person's face and figure, he may paint him in any act or situation whatever—and the picture will be prophetic. Do you believe it?'

'Not quite,' said Elinor, smiling. 'Yet if he has such magic, there is something so gentle in his manner, that I am sure he will use it well.'

It was the painter's choice to proceed with both the portraits at the same time, assigning as a reason, in the mystical language which he sometimes used, that the faces threw light upon each other. Accordingly, he gave now a touch to Walter, and now to Elinor, and the features of one and the other began to start forth so vividly, that it appeared as if his triumphant art would actually disengage them from the canvass. Amid the rich light and deep shade, they beheld their phantom selves. But, though the likeness promised to be perfect, they were not quite satisfied with the expression; it seemed more vague than in most of the painter's works. He, however, was satisfied with the prospect of success, and being much interested in the lovers, employed his leisure moments unknown to them, in making a crayon sketch of their two figures. During their sittings, he engaged them in conversation, and kindled up their faces with characteristic traits, which, though continually varying, it was his purpose to combine and fix. At length he announced, that, at their next visit, both the portraits would be ready for delivery.

'If my pencil will but be true to my conception, in the few last touches which I meditate,' observed he, 'these two pictures will be my very best performances. Seldom, indeed, has an artist such subjects.'

While speaking, he still bent his penetrative eye upon them, nor withdrew it till they had reached the bottom of the stairs.

Nothing, in the whole circle of human vanities, takes stronger hold of the imagination, than this affair of having a portrait painted. Yet why should it be so? The looking-glass, the polished globes of the andirons, the mirror-like water, and all other reflecting surfaces, continually present us with portraits, or rather ghosts of ourselves, which we glance at, and straightway forget them. But we forget them, only because they vanish. It is the idea of duration—of earthly immortality—that gives such a mysterious interest to our own portraits. Walter and Elinor were not insensible to this feeling, and hastened to the painter's rooms, punctually at the appointed hour, to meet those pictured shapes, which were to be their representatives with posterity. The sunshine flashed after them into the apartment, but left it somewhat gloomy, as they closed the door.

Their eyes were immediately attracted to their portraits, which rested against the farthest wall of the room. At the first glance, through the dim light and the distance, seeing themselves in precisely their natural attitudes, and with all the air that they recognized so well, they uttered a simultaneous exclamation of delight.

'There we stand,' cried Walter, enthusiastically, 'fixed in sunshine forever! No dark passions can gather on our faces!'

'No,' said Elinor, more calmly; 'no dreary change can sadden us.'

This was said while they were approaching, and had yet gained only an imperfect view of the pictures. The painter, after saluting them, busied himself at a table in completing a crayon sketch, leaving his visiters to form their own judgment as to his perfected labors. At intervals, he sent a glance from beneath his deep eyebrows, watching their countenances in profile, with his pencil suspended over the sketch. They had now stood some moments, each in front of the other's picture, contemplating it with entranced attention, but without uttering a word. At length, Walter stepped forward—then back—viewing Elinor's portrait in various lights, and finally spoke.

'Is there not a change?' said he, in a doubtful and meditative tone. 'Yes; the perception of it grows more vivid, the longer I look. It is certainly the same picture that I saw yesterday; the dress—the features—all are the same; and yet something is altered.'

'Is then the picture less like than it was yesterday?' inquired the painter, now drawing near, with irrepressible interest.

'The features are perfect Elinor,' answered Walter; 'and, at the first glance, the expression seemed also hers. But, I could fancy that the portrait has changed countenance, while I have been looking at it. The eyes are fixed on mine with a strangely sad and anxious expression. Nay, it is grief and terror! Is this like Elinor?'

'Compare the living face with the pictured one,' said the painter.

Walter glanced sidelong at his mistress, and started. Mo-

tionless and absorbed—fascinated, as it were—in contemplation of Walter's portrait, Elinor's face had assumed precisely
the expression of which he had just been complaining. Had
she practised for whole hours before a mirror, she could not
have caught the look so successfully. Had the picture itself
been a mirror, it could not have thrown back her present aspect, with stronger and more melancholy truth. She appeared
quite unconscious of the dialogue between the artist and her
lover.

'Elinor,' exclaimed Walter, in amazement, 'what change has
come over you?'

She did not hear him, nor desist from her fixed gaze, till he
seized her hand, and thus attracted her notice; then, with a
sudden tremor, she looked from the picture to the face of the
original.

'Do you see no change in your portrait?' asked she.

'In mine?—None!' replied Walter, examining it. 'But let
me see! Yes; there is a slight change—an improvement, I
think, in the picture, though none in the likeness. It has a
livelier expression than yesterday, as if some bright thought
were flashing from the eyes, and about to be uttered from the
lips. Now that I have caught the look, it becomes very decided.'

While he was intent on these observations, Elinor turned
to the painter. She regarded him with grief and awe, and felt
that he repaid her with sympathy and commiseration, though
wherefore, she could but vaguely guess.

'That look!' whispered she, and shuddered. 'How came it
there?'

'Madam,' said the painter, sadly, taking her hand, and leading her apart, 'in both these pictures, I have painted what I
saw. The artist—the true artist—must look beneath the exterior. It is his gift—his proudest, but often a melancholy
one—to see the inmost soul, and, by a power indefinable
even to himself, to make it glow or darken upon the canvass,
in glances that express the thought and sentiment of years.
Would that I might convince myself of error in the present
instance!'

They had now approached the table, on which were heads
in chalk, hands almost as expressive as ordinary faces, ivied

church-towers, thatched cottages, old thunder stricken trees, oriented and antique costume, and all such picturesque vagaries of an artist's idle moments. Turning them over, with seeming carelessness, a crayon sketch of two figures was disclosed.

'If I have failed,' continued he; — 'if your heart does not see itself reflected in your own portrait—if you have no secret cause to trust my delineation of the other—it is not yet too late to alter them. I might change the action of these figures too. But would it influence the event?'

He directed her notice to the sketch. A thrill ran through Elinor's frame; a shriek was upon her lips; but she stifled it, with the self-command that becomes habitual to all, who hide thoughts of fear and anguish within their bosoms. Turning from the table, she perceived that Walter had advanced near enough to have seen the sketch, though she could not determine whether it had caught his eye.

'We will not have the pictures altered,' said she, hastily. 'If mine is sad, I shall but look the gayer for the contrast.'

'Be it so,' answered the painter, bowing. 'May your griefs be such fanciful ones, that only your picture may mourn for them! For your joys—may they be true and deep, and paint themselves upon this lovely face, till it quite belie my art!'

After the marriage of Walter and Elinor, the pictures formed the two most splendid ornaments of their abode. They hung side by side, separated by a narrow panel, appearing to eye each other constantly, yet always returning the gaze of the spectator. Travelled gentlemen, who professed a knowledge of such subjects, reckoned these among the most admirable specimens of modern portraiture; while common observers compared them with the originals, feature by feature, and were rapturous in praise of the likeness. But, it was on a third class—neither travelled connoisseurs nor common observers, but people of natural sensibility—that the pictures wrought their strongest effect. Such persons might gaze carelessly at first, but, becoming interested, would return day after day, and study these painted faces like the pages of a mystic volume. Walter Ludlow's portrait attracted their earliest notice. In the absence of himself and his bride, they sometimes disputed as to the expression which the painter had intended to throw upon the features; all agreeing that there was a look of earnest import, though no two explained it alike. There was less diversity of opinion in regard to Elinor's picture. They differed, indeed, in their attempts to estimate the nature and depth of the gloom that dwelt upon her face, but agreed that it was gloom, and alien from the natural temperament of their youthful friend. A certain fanciful person announced, as the result of much scrutiny, that both these pictures were parts of one design, and that the melancholy strength of feeling, in Elinor's countenance, bore reference to the more vivid emotion, or, as he termed it, the wild passion, in that of Walter. Though unskilled in the art, he even began a sketch, in which the action of the two figures was to correspond with their mutual expression.

It was whispered among friends, that, day by day, Elinor's face was assuming a deeper shade of pensiveness, which threatened soon to render her too true a counterpart of her melancholy picture. Walter, on the other hand, instead of acquiring the vivid look which the painter had given him on the canvass, became reserved and downcast, with no outward flashes of emotion, however it might be smouldering within. In course of time, Elinor hung a gorgeous curtain of purple silk, wrought with flowers, and fringed with heavy golden tassels, before the pictures, under pretence that the dust would tarnish their hues, or the light dim them. It was enough. Her visiters felt, that the massive folds of the silk must never be withdrawn, nor the portraits mentioned in her presence.

Time wore on; and the painter came again. He had been far enough to the north to see the silver cascade of the Crystal Hills, and to look over the vast round of cloud and forest, from the summit of New-England's loftiest mountain. But he did not profane that scene by the mockery of his art. He had also lain in a canoe on the bosom of Lake George, making his soul the mirror of its loveliness and grandeur, till not a picture in the Vatican was more vivid than his recollection. He had gone with the Indian hunters to Niagara, and there, again, had flung his hopeless pencil down the precipice, feeling that he could as soon paint the roar, as aught else that goes to make up the wondrous cataract. In truth, it was sel-

dom his impulse to copy natural scenery, except as a frame
work for the delineations of the human form and face, instinct with thought, passion, or suffering. With store of such,
his adventurous ramble had enriched him; the stern dignity
of Indian chiefs; the dusky loveliness of Indian girls; the domestic life of wigwams; the stealthy march; the battle beneath
gloomy pine-trees; the frontier fortress with its garrison; the
anomaly of the old French partizan, bred in courts, but
grown gray in shaggy deserts; such were the scenes and portraits that he had sketched. The glow of perilous moments;
flashes of wild feeling; struggles of fierce power—love, hate,
grief, frenzy—in a word, all the worn-out heart of the old
earth, had been revealed to him under a new form. His portfolio was filled with graphic illustrations of the volume of his
memory, which genius would transmute into its own substance, and imbue with immortality. He felt that the deep
wisdom in his art, which he had sought so far, was found.

But, amid stern or lovely nature, in the perils of the forest,
or its overwhelming peacefulness, still there had been two
phantoms, the companions of his way. Like all other men
around whom an engrossing purpose wreathes itself, he was
insulated from the mass of human kind. He had no aim—no
pleasure—no sympathies—but what were ultimately connected with his art. Though gentle in manner, and upright in
intent and action, he did not possess kindly feelings; his heart
was cold; no living creature could be brought near enough to
keep him warm. For these two beings, however, he had felt,
in its greatest intensity, the sort of interest which always allied
him to the subjects of his pencil. He had pryed into their
souls with his keenest insight, and pictured the result upon
their features, with his utmost skill, so as barely to fall short
of that standard which no genius ever reached, his own severe
conception. He had caught from the duskiness of the
future—at least, so he fancied—a fearful secret, and had obscurely revealed it on the portraits. So much of himself—of
his imagination and all other powers—had been lavished on
the study of Walter and Elinor, that he almost regarded them
as creations of his own, like the thousands with which he had
peopled the realms of Picture. Therefore did they flit through
the twilight of the woods, hover on the mist of waterfalls,

look forth from the mirror of the lake, nor melt away in the noon-tide sun. They haunted his pictorial fancy, not as mockeries of life, nor pale goblins of the dead, but in the guise of portraits, each with the unalterable expression which his magic had evoked from the caverns of the soul. He could not recross the Atlantic, till he had again beheld the originals of those airy pictures.

'Oh, glorious Art!' thus mused the enthusiastic painter, as he trod the street. 'Thou art the image of the Creator's own. The innumerable forms, that wander in nothingness, start into being at thy beck. The dead live again. Thou recallest them to their old scenes, and givest their gray shadows the lustre of a better life, at once earthly and immortal. Thou snatchest back the fleeing moments of History. With thee, there is no Past; for, at thy touch, all that is great becomes forever present; and illustrious men live through long ages, in the visible performance of the very deeds, which made them what they are. Oh, potent Art! as thou bringest the faintly revealed Past to stand in that narrow strip of sunlight, which we call Now, canst thou summon the shrouded Future to meet her there? Have I not achieved it! Am I not thy Prophet?'

Thus, with a proud, yet melancholy fervor, did he almost cry aloud, as he passed through the toilsome street, among people that knew not of his reveries, nor could understand nor care for them. It is not good for man to cherish a solitary ambition. Unless there be those around him, by whose example he may regulate himself, his thoughts, desires, and hopes will become extravagant, and he the semblance, perhaps the reality, of a madman. Reading other bosoms, with an acuteness almost preternatural, the painter failed to see the disorder of his own.

'And this should be the house,' said he, looking up and down the front, before he knocked. 'Heaven help my brains! That picture! Methinks it will never vanish. Whether I look at the windows or the door, there it is framed within them, painted strongly, and glowing in the richest tints—the faces of the portraits—the figures and action of the sketch!'

He knocked.

'The Portraits! Are they within?' enquired he, of the domestic; then recollecting himself—'your master and mistress! Are they at home?'

'They are, Sir,' said the servant, adding, as he noticed that picturesque aspect of which the painter could never divest himself,—'and the Portraits too!'

The guest was admitted into a parlor, communicating by a central door, with an interior room of the same size. As the first apartment was empty, he passed to the entrance of the second, within which, his eyes were greeted by those living personages, as well as their pictured representatives, who had long been the objects of so singular an interest. He involuntarily paused on the threshold.

They had not perceived his approach. Walter and Elinor were standing before the portraits, whence the former had just flung back the rich and voluminous folds of the silken curtain, holding its golden tassel with one hand, while the other grasped that of his bride. The pictures, concealed for months, gleamed forth again in undiminished splendor, appearing to throw a sombre light across the room, rather than to be disclosed by a borrowed radiance. That of Elinor had been almost prophetic. A pensiveness, and next a gentle sorrow, had successively dwelt upon her countenance, deepening, with the lapse of time, into a quiet anguish. A mixture of affright would now have made it the very expression of the portrait. Walter's face was moody and dull, or animated only by fitful flashes, which left a heavier darkness for their momentary illumination. He looked from Elinor to her portrait, and thence to his own, in the contemplation of which he finally stood absorbed.

The painter seemed to hear the step of Destiny approaching behind him, on its progress towards its victims. A strange thought darted into his mind. Was not his own the form in which that Destiny had embodied itself, and he a chief agent of the coming evil which he had foreshadowed?

Still, Walter remained silent before the picture, communing with it, as with his own heart, and abandoning himself to the spell of evil influence, that the painter had cast upon the features. Gradually his eyes kindled; while as Elinor watched the increasing wildness of his face, her own assumed a look of terror; and when at last, he turned upon her, the resemblance of both to their portraits was complete.

'Our fate is upon us!' howled Walter. 'Die!'

Drawing a knife, he sustained her, as she was sinking to the ground, and aimed it at her bosom. In the action, and in the look and attitude of each, the painter beheld the figures of his sketch. The picture, with all its tremendous coloring, was finished.

'Hold, madman!' cried he sternly.

He had advanced from the door, and interposed himself between the wretched beings, with the same sense of power to regulate their destiny, as to alter a scene upon the canvass. He stood like a magician, controlling the phantoms which he had evoked.

'What!' muttered Walter Ludlow, as he relapsed from fierce excitement into sullen gloom. 'Does Fate impede its own decree?'

'Wretched lady!' said the painter. 'Did I not warn you?'

'You did,' replied Elinor calmly, as her terror gave place to the quiet grief which it had disturbed. 'But—I loved him!'

Is there not a deep moral in the tale? Could the result of one, or all our deeds, be shadowed forth and set before us—some would call it Fate, and hurry onward—others be swept along by their passionate desires—and none be turned aside by the PROPHETIC PICTURES.

Dr. Heidegger's Experiment

THAT very singular man, old Dr. Heidegger, once invited four venerable friends to meet him in his study. There were three white-bearded gentlemen, Mr. Medbourne, Colonel Killigrew, and Mr. Gascoigne, and a withered gentlewoman, whose name was the Widow Wycherly. They were all melancholy old creatures, who had been unfortunate in life, and whose greatest misfortune it was, that they were not long ago in their graves. Mr. Medbourne, in the vigor of his age, had been a prosperous merchant, but had lost his all by a frantic speculation, and was now little better than a mendicant. Colonel Killigrew had wasted his best years, and his health and substance, in the pursuit of sinful pleasures, which had given birth to a brood of pains, such as the gout, and divers other torments of soul and body. Mr. Gascoigne was a ruined politician, a man of evil fame, or at least had been so, till time had buried him from the knowledge of the present generation, and made him obscure instead of infamous. As for the Widow Wycherly, tradition tells us that she was a great beauty in her day; but, for a long while past, she had lived in deep seclusion, on account of certain scandalous stories, which had prejudiced the gentry of the town against her. It is a circumstance worth mentioning, that each of these three old gentlemen, Mr. Medbourne, Colonel Killigrew, and Mr. Gascoigne, were early lovers of the Widow Wycherly, and had once been on the point of cutting each other's throats for her sake. And, before proceeding farther, I will merely hint, that Dr. Heidegger and all his four guests were

NOTE—In an English Review, not long since, I have been accused of plagiarizing the idea of this story from a chapter in one of the novels of Alexandre Dumas. There has undoubtedly been a plagiarism, on one side or the other; but as my story was written a good deal more than twenty years ago, and as the novel is of considerably more recent date, I take pleasure in thinking that M. Dumas has done me the honour to appropriate one of the fanciful conceptions of my earlier days. He is heartily welcome to it; nor is it the only instance, by many, in which the great French Romancer has exercised the privilege of commanding genius by confiscating the intellectual property of less famous people to his own use and behoof.

September, 1860.

sometimes thought to be a little beside themselves; as is not unfrequently the case with old people, when worried either by present troubles or woful recollections.

'My dear old friends,' said Dr. Heidegger, motioning them to be seated, 'I am desirous of your assistance in one of those little experiments with which I amuse myself here in my study.'

If all stories were true, Dr. Heidegger's study must have been a very curious place. It was a dim, old-fashioned chamber, festooned with cobwebs, and besprinkled with antique dust. Around the walls stood several oaken book-cases, the lower shelves of which were filled with rows of gigantic folios, and black-letter quartos, and the upper with little parchment covered duodecimos. Over the central book-case was a bronze bust of Hippocrates, with which, according to some authorities, Dr. Heidegger was accustomed to hold consultations, in all difficult cases of his practice. In the obscurest corner of the room stood a tall and narrow oaken closet, with its door ajar, within which doubtfully appeared a skeleton. Between two of the book-cases hung a looking-glass, presenting its high and dusty plate within a tarnished gilt frame. Among many wonderful stories related of this mirror, it was fabled that the spirits of all the doctor's deceased patients dwelt within its verge, and would stare him in the face whenever he looked thitherward. The opposite side of the chamber was ornamented with the full length portrait of a young lady, arrayed in the faded magnificence of silk, satin, and brocade, and with a visage as faded as her dress. Above half a century ago, Dr. Heidegger had been on the point of marriage with this young lady; but, being affected with some slight disorder, she had swallowed one of her lover's prescriptions, and died on the bridal evening. The greatest curiosity of the study remains to be mentioned: it was a ponderous folio volume, bound in black leather, with massive silver clasps. There were no letters on the back, and nobody could tell the title of the book. But it was well known to be a book of magic; and once, when a chambermaid had lifted it, merely to brush away the dust, the skeleton had rattled in its closet, the picture of the young lady had stepped one foot upon the floor, and several ghastly faces had peeped forth from the mirror;

while the brazen head of Hippocrates frowned, and said—
'Forbear!'

Such was Dr. Heidegger's study. On the summer afternoon of our tale, a small round table, as black as ebony, stood
in the centre of the room, sustaining a cut-glass vase, of beautiful form and elaborate workmanship. The sunshine came
through the window, between the heavy festoons of two
faded damask curtains, and fell directly across this vase; so
that a mild splendor was reflected from it on the ashen visages
of the five old people who sat around. Four champaigne
glasses were also on the table.

'My dear old friends,' repeated Dr. Heidegger, 'may I reckon on your aid in performing an exceedingly curious experiment?'

Now Dr. Heidegger was a very strange old gentleman,
whose eccentricity had become the nucleus for a thousand
fantastic stories. Some of these fables, to my shame be it spoken, might possibly be traced back to mine own veracious
self; and if any passages of the present tale should startle the
reader's faith, I must be content to bear the stigma of a fiction-monger.

When the doctor's four guests heard him talk of his proposed experiment, they anticipated nothing more wonderful
than the murder of a mouse in an air-pump, or the examination of a cobweb by the microscope, or some similar nonsense, with which he was constantly in the habit of pestering
his intimates. But without waiting for a reply, Dr. Heidegger
hobbled across the chamber, and returned with the same ponderous folio, bound in black leather, which common report
affirmed to be a book of magic. Undoing the silver clasps, he
opened the volume, and took from among its black-letter
pages a rose, or what was once a rose, though now the green
leaves and crimson petals had assumed one brownish hue, and
the ancient flower seemed ready to crumble to dust in the
doctor's hands.

'This rose,' said Dr. Heidegger, with a sigh, 'this same
withered and crumbling flower, blossomed five-and-fifty years
ago. It was given me by Sylvia Ward, whose portrait hangs
yonder; and I meant to wear it in my bosom at our wedding.
Five-and-fifty years it has been treasured between the leaves

of this old volume. Now, would you deem it possible that this rose of half a century could ever bloom again?'

'Nonsense!' said the Widow Wycherly, with a peevish toss of her head. 'You might as well ask whether an old woman's wrinkled face could ever bloom again.'

'See!' answered Dr. Heidegger.

He uncovered the vase, and threw the faded rose into the water which it contained. At first, it lay lightly on the surface of the fluid, appearing to imbibe none of its moisture. Soon, however, a singular change began to be visible. The crushed and dried petals stirred, and assumed a deepening tinge of crimson, as if the flower were reviving from a death-like slumber; the slender stalk and twigs of foliage became green; and there was the rose of half a century, looking as fresh as when Sylvia Ward had first given it to her lover. It was scarcely full-blown; for some of its delicate red leaves curled modestly around its moist bosom, within which two or three dewdrops were sparkling.

'That is certainly a very pretty deception,' said the doctor's friends; carelessly, however, for they had witnessed greater miracles at a conjurer's show: 'pray how was it effected?'

'Did you never hear of the "Fountain of Youth,"' asked Dr. Heidegger, 'which Ponce De Leon, the Spanish adventurer, went in search of, two or three centuries ago?'

'But did Ponce De Leon ever find it?' said the Widow Wycherly.

'No,' answered Dr. Heidegger, 'for he never sought it in the right place. The famous Fountain of Youth, if I am rightly informed, is situated in the southern part of the Floridian peninsula, not far from Lake Macaco. Its source is overshadowed by several gigantic magnolias, which, though numberless centuries old, have been kept as fresh as violets, by the virtues of this wonderful water. An acquaintance of mine, knowing my curiosity in such matters, has sent me what you see in the vase.'

'Ahem!' said Colonel Killigrew, who believed not a word of the doctor's story: 'and what may be the effect of this fluid on the human frame?'

'You shall judge for yourself, my dear colonel,' replied Dr. Heidegger; 'and all of you, my respected friends, are welcome to so much of this admirable fluid, as may restore to you the bloom of youth. For my own part, having had much trouble in growing old, I am in no hurry to grow young again. With your permission, therefore, I will merely watch the progress of the experiment.'

While he spoke, Dr. Heidegger had been filling the four champaigne glasses with the water of the Fountain of Youth. It was apparently impregnated with an effervescent gas, for little bubbles were continually ascending from the depths of the glasses, and bursting in silvery spray at the surface. As the liquor diffused a pleasant perfume, the old people doubted not that it possessed cordial and comfortable properties; and, though utter skeptics as to its rejuvenescent power, they were inclined to swallow it at once. But Dr. Heidegger besought them to stay a moment.

'Before you drink, my respectable old friends,' said he, 'it would be well that, with the experience of a life-time to direct you, you should draw up a few general rules for your guidance, in passing a second time through the perils of youth. Think what a sin and shame it would be, if, with your peculiar advantages, you should not become patterns of virtue and wisdom to all the young people of the age!'

The doctor's four venerable friends made him no answer, except by a feeble and tremulous laugh; so very ridiculous was the idea, that, knowing how closely repentance treads behind the steps of error, they should ever go astray again.

'Drink, then,' said the doctor, bowing: 'I rejoice that I have so well selected the subjects of my experiment.'

With palsied hands, they raised the glasses to their lips. The liquor, if it really possessed such virtues as Dr. Heidegger imputed to it, could not have been bestowed on four human beings who needed it more wofully. They looked as if they had never known what youth or pleasure was, but had been the offspring of Nature's dotage, and always the gray, decrepit, sapless, miserable creatures, who now sat stooping round the doctor's table, without life enough in their souls or bodies to be animated even by the prospect of growing young again. They drank off the water, and replaced their glasses on the table.

Assuredly there was an almost immediate improvement in

the aspect of the party, not unlike what might have been produced by a glass of generous wine, together with a sudden glow of cheerful sunshine, brightening over all their visages at once. There was a healthful suffusion on their cheeks, instead of the ashen hue that had made them look so corpselike. They gazed at one another, and fancied that some magic power had really begun to smooth away the deep and sad inscriptions which Father Time had been so long engraving on their brows. The Widow Wycherly adjusted her cap, for she felt almost like a woman again.

'Give us more of this wondrous water!' cried they, eagerly. 'We are younger—but we are still too old! Quick!—give us more!'

'Patience, patience!' quoth Dr. Heidegger, who sat watching the experiment, with philosophic coolness. 'You have been a long time growing old. Surely, you might be content to grow young in half an hour! But the water is at your service.'

Again he filled their glasses with the liquor of youth, enough of which still remained in the vase to turn half the old people in the city to the age of their own grand-children. While the bubbles were yet sparkling on the brim, the doctor's four guests snatched their glasses from the table, and swallowed the contents at a single gulp. Was it delusion! Even while the draught was passing down their throats, it seemed to have wrought a change on their whole systems. Their eyes grew clear and bright; a dark shade deepened among their silvery locks; they sat around the table, three gentlemen of middle age, and a woman, hardly beyond her buxom prime.

'My dear widow, you are charming!' cried Colonel Killigrew, whose eyes had been fixed upon her face, while the shadows of age were flitting from it like darkness from the crimson day-break.

The fair widow knew, of old, that Colonel Killigrew's compliments were not always measured by sober truth; so she started up and ran to the mirror, still dreading that the ugly visage of an old woman would meet her gaze. Meanwhile, the three gentlemen behaved in such a manner, as proved that the water of the Fountain of Youth possessed some intoxicating qualities; unless, indeed, their exhilaration of spirits were merely a lightsome dizziness, caused by the sudden removal of the weight of years. Mr. Gascoigne's mind seemed to run on political topics, but whether relating to the past, present, or future, could not easily be determined, since the same ideas and phrases have been in vogue these fifty years. Now he rattled forth full-throated sentences about patriotism, national glory, and the people's right; now he muttered some perilous stuff or other, in a sly and doubtful whisper, so cautiously that even his own conscience could scarcely catch the secret; and now, again, he spoke in measured accents, and a deeply deferential tone, as if a royal ear were listening to his well-turned periods. Colonel Killigrew all this time had been trolling forth a jolly bottle-song, and ringing his glass in symphony with the chorus, while his eyes wandered towards the buxom figure of the Widow Wycherly. On the other side of the table, Mr. Medbourne was involved in a calculation of dollars and cents, with which was strangely intermingled a project for supplying the East Indies with ice, by harnessing a team of whales to the polar icebergs.

As for the Widow Wycherly, she stood before the mirror, curtseying and simpering to her own image, and greeting it as the friend whom she loved better than all the world beside. She thrust her face close to the glass, to see whether some long-remembered wrinkle or crow's-foot had indeed vanished. She examined whether the snow had so entirely melted from her hair, that the venerable cap could be safely thrown aside. At last, turning briskly away, she came with a sort of dancing step to the table.

'My dear old doctor,' cried she, 'pray favor me with another glass!'

'Certainly, my dear madam, certainly!' replied the complaisant doctor; 'see! I have already filled the glasses.'

There, in fact, stood the four glasses, brim full of this wonderful water, the delicate spray of which, as it effervesced from the surface, resembled the tremulous glitter of diamonds. It was now so nearly sunset, that the chamber had grown duskier than ever; but a mild and moon-like splendor gleamed from within the vase, and rested alike on the four guests, and on the doctor's venerable figure. He sat in a high-backed, elaborately-carved, oaken arm-chair, with a gray dignity of aspect that might have well befitted that very Father Time, whose power had never been disputed, save by this fortunate company. Even while quaffing the third draught of the Fountain of Youth, they were almost awed by the expression of his mysterious visage.

But, the next moment, the exhilarating gush of young life shot through their veins. They were now in the happy prime of youth. Age, with its miserable train of cares, and sorrows, and diseases, was remembered only as the trouble of a dream, from which they had joyously awoke. The fresh gloss of the soul, so early lost, and without which the world's successive scenes had been but a gallery of faded pictures, again threw its enchantment over all their prospects. They felt like new-created beings, in a new-created universe.

'We are young! We are young!' they cried, exultingly.

Youth, like the extremity of age, had effaced the strongly marked characteristics of middle life, and mutually assimilated them all. They were a group of merry youngsters, almost maddened with the exuberant frolicksomeness of their years. The most singular effect of their gayety was an impulse to mock the infirmity and decrepitude of which they had so lately been the victims. They laughed loudly at their old-fashioned attire, the wide-skirted coats and flapped waistcoats of the young men, and the ancient cap and gown of the blooming girl. One limped across the floor, like a gouty grandfather; one set a pair of spectacles astride of his nose, and pretended to pore over the black-letter pages of the book of magic; a third seated himself in an arm-chair, and strove to imitate the venerable dignity of Dr. Heidegger. Then all shouted mirthfully, and leaped about the room. The Widow Wycherly—if so fresh a damsel could be called a widow— tripped up to the doctor's chair, with a mischievous merriment in her rosy face.

'Doctor, you dear old soul,' cried she, 'get up and dance with me!' And then the four young people laughed louder than ever, to think what a queer figure the poor old doctor would cut.

'Pray excuse me,' answered the doctor, quietly. 'I am old and rheumatic, and my dancing days were over long ago. But either of these gay young gentlemen will be glad of so pretty a partner.'

'Dance with me, Clara!' cried Colonel Killigrew.

'No, no, I will be her partner!' shouted Mr. Gascoigne.

'She promised me her hand, fifty years ago!' exclaimed Mr. Medbourne.

They all gathered round her. One caught both her hands in his passionate grasp—another threw his arm about her waist—the third buried his hand among the glossy curls that clustered beneath the widow's cap. Blushing, panting, struggling, chiding, laughing, her warm breath fanning each of their faces by turns, she strove to disengage herself, yet still remained in their triple embrace. Never was there a livelier picture of youthful rivalship, with bewitching beauty for the prize. Yet, by a strange deception, owing to the duskiness of the chamber, and the antique dresses which they still wore, the tall mirror is said to have reflected the figures of the three old, gray, withered grand-sires, ridiculously contending for the skinny ugliness of a shrivelled grand-dam.

But they were young: their burning passions proved them so. Inflamed to madness by the coquetry of the girl-widow, who neither granted nor quite withheld her favors, the three rivals began to interchange threatening glances. Still keeping hold of the fair prize, they grappled fiercely at one another's throats. As they struggled to and fro, the table was over-turned, and the vase dashed into a thousand fragments. The precious Water of Youth flowed in a bright stream across the floor, moistening the wings of a butterfly, which, grown old in the decline of summer, had alighted there to die. The insect fluttered lightly through the chamber, and settled on the snowy head of Dr. Heidegger.

'Come, come, gentlemen!—come, Madam Wycherly,' exclaimed the doctor, 'I really must protest against this riot.'

They stood still, and shivered; for it seemed as if gray Time were calling them back from their sunny youth, far down into the chill and darksome vale of years. They looked at old Dr. Heidegger, who sat in his carved arm-chair, holding the rose of half a century, which he had rescued from among the fragments of the shattered vase. At the motion of his hand, the four rioters resumed their seats; the more readily, because their violent exertions had wearied them, youthful though they were.

'My poor Sylvia's rose!' ejaculated Dr. Heidegger, holding it in the light of the sunset clouds: 'it appears to be fading again.'

And so it was. Even while the party were looking at it, the flower continued to shrivel up, till it became as dry and fragile as when the doctor had first thrown it into the vase. He shook off the few drops of moisture which clung to its petals.

'I love it as well thus, as in its dewy freshness,' observed he, pressing the withered rose to his withered lips. While he spoke, the butterfly fluttered down from the doctor's snowy head, and fell upon the floor.

His guests shivered again. A strange chillness, whether of the body or spirit they could not tell, was creeping gradually over them all. They gazed at one another, and fancied that each fleeting moment snatched away a charm, and left a deepening furrow where none had been before. Was it an illusion? Had the changes of a life-time been crowded into so brief a space, and were they now four aged people, sitting with their old friend, Dr. Heidegger?

'Are we grown old again, so soon!' cried they, dolefully.

In truth, they had. The Water of Youth possessed merely a virtue more transient than that of wine. The delirium which it created had effervesced away. Yes! they were old again. With a shuddering impulse, that showed her a woman still, the widow clasped her skinny hands before her face, and wished that the coffin-lid were over it, since it could be no longer beautiful.

'Yes, friends, ye are old again,' said Dr. Heidegger; 'and lo! the Water of Youth is all lavished on the ground. Well—I bemoan it not; for if the fountain gushed at my very doorstep, I would not stoop to bathe my lips in it—no, though its delirium were for years instead of moments. Such is the lesson ye have taught me!'

But the doctor's four friends had taught no such lesson to themselves. They resolved forthwith to make a pilgrimage to Florida, and quaff at morning, noon, and night, from the Fountain of Youth.

A Bell's Biography

HEARKEN to our neighbor with the iron tongue! While I sit musing over my sheet of foolscap, he emphatically tells the hour, in tones loud enough for all the town to hear, though doubtless intended only as a gentle hint to myself, that I may begin his biography before the evening shall be farther wasted. Unquestionably, a personage in such an elevated position, and making so great a noise in the world, has a fair claim to the services of a biographer. He is the representative and most illustrious member of that innumerable class, whose characteristic feature is the tongue, and whose sole business, to clamor for the public good. If any of his noisy brethren, in our tongue-governed democracy, be envious of the superiority which I have assigned him, they have my free consent to hang themselves as high as he. And for his history, let not the reader apprehend an empty repetition of ding-dong-bell. He has been the passive hero of wonderful vicissitudes, with which I have chanced to become acquainted, possibly from his own mouth; while the careless multitude supposed him to be talking merely of the time of day, or calling them to dinner or to church, or bidding drowsy people go bedward, or the dead to their graves. Many a revolution has it been his fate to go through, and invariably with a prodigious uproar. And whether or no he have told me his reminiscences, this at least is true, that the more I study his deep-toned language, the more sense, and sentiment, and soul, do I discover in it.

This bell—for we may as well drop our quaint personification—is of antique French manufacture, and the symbol of the cross betokens that it was meant to be suspended in the belfry of a Romish place of worship. The old people hereabout have a tradition, that a considerable part of the metal was supplied by a brass cannon, captured in one of the victories of Louis the Fourteenth over the Spaniards, and that a Bourbon princess threw her golden crucifix into the molten mass. It is said, likewise, that a bishop baptized and blessed the bell, and prayed that a heavenly influence might mingle with its tones. When all due ceremonies had been performed, the Grand Monarque bestowed the gift—than which none could resound his beneficence more loudly—on the Jesuits, who were then converting the American Indians to the spiritual dominion of the Pope. So the bell—our self-same bell, whose familiar voice we may hear at all hours, in the streets—this very bell sent forth its first-born accents from the tower of a log-built chapel, westward of Lake Champlain, and near the mighty stream of the Saint Lawrence. It was called Our Lady's Chapel of the Forest. The peal went forth as if to redeem and consecrate the heathen wilderness. The wolf growled at the sound, as he prowled stealthily through the underbrush—the grim bear turned his back, and stalked sullenly away—the startled doe leaped up, and led her fawn into a deeper solitude. The red men wondered what awful voice was speaking amid the wind that roared through the tree-tops; and following reverentially its summons, the dark-robed fathers blessed them, as they drew near the cross-crowned chapel. In a little time, there was a crucifix on every dusky bosom. The Indians knelt beneath the lowly roof, worshipping in the same forms that were observed under the vast dome of Saint Peter's, when the Pope performed high mass in the presence of kneeling princes. All the religious festivals, that awoke the chiming bells of lofty cathedrals, called forth a peal from Our Lady's Chapel of the Forest. Loudly rang the bell of the wilderness, while the streets of Paris echoed with rejoicings for the birthday of the Bourbon, or whenever France had triumphed on some European battle-field. And the solemn woods were saddened with a melancholy knell, as often as the thick-strewn leaves were swept away from the virgin soil, for the burial of an Indian chief.

Meantime, the bells of a hostile people and a hostile faith were ringing on Sabbaths and lecture-days, at Boston and other Puritan towns. Their echoes died away hundreds of miles south-eastward of Our Lady's Chapel. But scouts had threaded the pathless desert that lay between, and, from behind the huge tree-trunks, perceived the Indians assembling at the summons of the bell. Some bore flaxen-haired scalps at their girdles, as if to lay those bloody trophies on Our Lady's altar. It was reported, and believed, all through New-En-

gland, that the Pope of Rome, and the King of France, had
established this little chapel in the forest, for the purpose of
stirring up the red men to a crusade against the English settlers. The latter took energetic measures to secure their religion and their lives. On the eve of an especial fast of the
Romish church, while the bell tolled dismally, and the priests
were chanting a doleful stave, a band of New-England rangers rushed from the surrounding woods. Fierce shouts, and
the report of musketry, pealed suddenly within the chapel.
The ministering priests threw themselves before the altar, and
were slain even on its steps. If, as antique traditions tell us,
no grass will grow where the blood of martyrs has been shed,
there should be a barren spot, to this very day, on the site of
that desecrated altar.

While the blood was still plashing from step to step, the
leader of the rangers seized a torch, and applied it to the drapery of the shrine. The flame and smoke arose, as from a burnt-
sacrifice, at once illuminating and obscuring the whole interior of the chapel, now hiding the dead priests in a sable
shroud, now revealing them and their slayers in one terrific
glare. Some already wished that the altar-smoke could cover
the deed from the sight of Heaven. But one of the rangers—
a man of sanctified aspect, though his hands were bloody—
approached the captain.

'Sir,' said he, 'our village meeting-house lacks a bell, and
hitherto we have been fain to summon the good people to
worship, by beat of drum. Give me, I pray you, the bell of
this popish chapel, for the sake of the godly Mr. Rogers, who
doubtless hath remembered us in the prayers of the congregation, ever since we began our march. Who can tell what
share of this night's good success we owe to that holy man's
wrestling with the Lord?'

'Nay, then,' answered the captain, 'if good Mr. Rogers hath
holpen our enterprise, it is right that he should share the
spoil. Take the bell and welcome, Deacon Lawson, if you will
be at the trouble of carrying it home. Hitherto it hath spoken
nothing but papistry, and that too in the French or Indian
gibberish; but I warrant me, if Mr. Rogers consecrate it
anew, it will talk like a good English and Protestant bell.'

So Deacon Lawson and half a score of his townsmen took

down the bell, suspended it on a pole, and bore it away on their sturdy shoulders, meaning to carry it to the shore of Lake Champlain, and thence homeward by water. Far through the woods gleamed the flames of Our Lady's Chapel, flinging fantastic shadows from the clustered foliage, and glancing on brooks that had never caught the sunlight. As the rangers traversed the midnight forest, staggering under their heavy burden, the tongue of the bell gave many a tremendous stroke—clang, clang, clang!—a most doleful sound, as if it were tolling for the slaughter of the priests and the ruin of the chapel. Little dreamed Deacon Lawson and his townsmen that it was their own funeral knell. A war-party of Indians had heard the report of musketry, and seen the blaze of the chapel, and now were on the track of the rangers, summoned to vengeance by the bell's dismal murmurs. In the midst of a deep swamp, they made a sudden onset on the retreating foe. Good Deacon Lawson battled stoutly, but had his skull cloven by a tomahawk, and sank into the depths of the morass, with the ponderous bell above him. And, for many a year thereafter, our hero's voice was heard no more on earth, neither at the hour of worship, nor at festivals nor funerals.

And is he still buried in that unknown grave? Scarcely so, dear reader. Hark! How plainly we hear him at this moment, the spokesman of Time, proclaiming that it is nine o'clock at night! We may therefore safely conclude, that some happy chance has restored him to upper air.

But there lay the bell, for many silent years; and the wonder is, that he did not lie silent there a century, or perhaps a dozen centuries, till the world should have forgotten not only his voice, but the voices of the whole brotherhood of bells. How would the first accent of his iron tongue have startled his resurrectionists! But he was not fated to be a subject of discussion among the antiquaries of far posterity. Near the close of the Old French War, a party of New-England axe-men, who preceded the march of Colonel Bradstreet towards Lake Ontario, were building a bridge of logs through a swamp. Plunging down a stake, one of these pioneers felt it graze against some hard, smooth substance. He called his comrades, and by their united efforts, the top of the bell was raised to the surface, a rope made fast to it, and thence passed over the horizontal limb of a tree. Heave-oh! up they hoisted their prize, dripping with moisture, and festooned with verdant water-moss. As the base of the bell emerged from the swamp, the pioneers perceived that a skeleton was clinging with its bony fingers to the clapper, but immediately relaxing its nerveless grasp, sank back into the stagnant water. The bell then gave forth a sullen clang. No wonder that he was in haste to speak, after holding his tongue for such a length of time! The pioneers shoved the bell to-and-fro, thus ringing a loud and heavy peal, which echoed widely through the forest, and reached the ears of Colonel Bradstreet, and his three thousand men. The soldiers paused on their march; a feeling of religion, mingled with home-tenderness, overpowered their rude hearts; each seemed to hear the clangor of the old church-bell, which had been familiar to him from infancy, and had tolled at the funerals of all his forefathers. By what magic had that holy sound strayed over the wide-murmuring ocean, and become audible amid the clash of arms, the loud crashing of the artillery over the rough wilderness-path, and the melancholy roar of the wind among the boughs!

The New-Englanders hid their prize in a shadowy nook, betwixt a large gray stone and the earthy roots of an overthrown tree; and when the campaign was ended, they conveyed our friend to Boston, and put him up at auction on the side-walk of King-street. He was suspended, for the nonce, by a block and tackle, and being swung backward and forward, gave such loud and clear testimony to his own merits, that the auctioneer had no need to say a word. The highest bidder was a rich old representative from our town, who piously bestowed the bell on the meeting-house where he had been a worshipper for half a century. The good man had his reward. By a strange coincidence, the very first duty of the sexton, after the bell had been hoisted into the belfry, was to toll the funeral knell of the donor. Soon, however, those doleful echoes were drowned by a triumphant peal for the surrender of Quebec.

Ever since that period, our hero has occupied the same elevated station, and has put in his word on all matters of public importance, civil, military, or religious. On the day when Independence was first proclaimed in the street beneath, he uttered a peal which many deemed ominous and fearful, rather than triumphant. But he has told the same story these sixty years, and none mistake his meaning now. When Washington, in the fullness of his glory, rode through our flower-strewn streets, this was the tongue that bade the Father of his Country welcome! Again the same voice was heard when La Fayette came to gather in his half-century's harvest of gratitude. Meantime, vast changes have been going on below. His voice, which once floated over a little provincial sea-port, is now reverberated between brick edifices, and strikes the ear amid the buzz and tumult of a city. On the Sabbaths of olden time, the summons of the bell was obeyed by a picturesque and varied throng; stately gentlemen in purple velvet coats, embroidered waistcoats, white wigs, and gold-laced hats, stepping with grave courtesy beside ladies in flowered satin gowns, and hoop-petticoats of majestic circumference; while behind followed a liveried slave or bondsman, bearing the psalm-book and a stove for his mistress's feet. The commonalty, clad in homely garb, gave precedence to their betters at the door of the meeting-house, as if admitting that there were distinctions between them, even in the sight of God. Yet, as their coffins were borne one after another through the street, the bell has tolled a requiem for all alike. What mattered it, whether or no there were a silver scutcheon on the coffin-lid? 'Open thy bosom, Mother Earth!' Thus spake the bell. 'Another of thy children is coming to his long rest. Take him to thy bosom, and let him slumber in peace.' Thus spake the bell, and Mother Earth received her child. With the self-same tones will the present generation be ushered to the embraces of their mother; and Mother Earth will still receive her children. Is not thy tongue a-weary, mournful talker of two centuries? Oh, funeral bell! wilt thou never be shattered with thine own melancholy strokes? Yea; and a trumpet-call shall arouse the sleepers, whom thy heavy clang could awake no more!

Again—again, thy voice, reminding me that I am wasting the 'midnight oil.' In my lonely fantasy, I can scarce believe that other mortals have caught the sound, or that it vibrates elsewhere than in my secret soul. But to many hast thou spoken. Anxious men have heard thee on their sleepless pillows, and bethought themselves anew of to-morrow's care. In a brief interval of wakefulness, the sons of toil have heard thee, and say, 'Is so much of our quiet slumber spent?—is the morning so near at hand?' Crime has heard thee, and mutters, 'Now is the very hour!' Despair answers thee, 'Thus much of this weary life is gone!' The young mother, on her bed of pain and ecstasy, has counted thy echoing strokes, and dates from them her first-born's share of life and immortality. The bride-groom and the bride have listened, and feel that their night of rapture flits like a dream away. Thine accents have fallen faintly on the ear of the dying man, and warned him that, ere thou speakest again, his spirit shall have passed whither no voice of time can ever reach. Alas for the departing traveller, if thy voice—the voice of fleeting time—have taught him no lessons for Eternity!

Fragments from the Journal of a Solitary Man

MY poor friend "Oberon"—for let me be allowed to distinguish him by so quaint a name—sleeps with the silent of ages. He died calmly. Though his disease was pulmonary, his life did not flicker out like a wasted lamp, sometimes shooting up into a strange temporary brightness; but the tide of being ebbed away, and the moon of his existence waned till, in the simple phraseology of Scripture, "he was not." The last words he said to me were, "Burn my papers—all that you can find in yonder escritoire; for I fear there are some there which you may be betrayed into publishing. I have published enough; as for the old disconnected journal in your possession———" But here my poor friend was checked in his utterance by that same hollow cough which would never let him alone. So he coughed himself tired, and sunk to slumber. I watched from that midnight hour till high noon on the morrow for his waking. The chamber was dark; till, longing for light, I opened the window-shutter, and the broad day looked in on the marble features of the dead!

I religiously obeyed his instructions with regard to the papers in the escritoire, and burned them in a heap without looking into one, though sorely tempted. But the old journal I kept. Perhaps in strict conscience I ought also to have burned that; but, casting my eye over some half-torn leaves the other day, I could not resist an impulse to give some fragments of it to the public. To do this satisfactorily, I am obliged to twist this thread, so as to string together into a semblance of order my Oberon's "random pearls."

If any body that holds any commerce with his fellow-men can be called solitary, Oberon was a "solitary man." He lived in a small village at some distance from the metropolis, and never came up to the city except once in three months for the purpose of looking into a book-store, and of spending two hours and a half with me. In that space of time I would tell him all that I could remember of interest which had occurred in the interim of his visits. He would join very heartily in the conversation; but as soon as the time of his usual tarrying had elapsed, he would take up his hat and depart. He was un-equivocally the most original person I ever knew. His style of composition was very charming. No tales that have ever appeared in our popular journals have been so generally admired as his. But a sadness was on his spirit; and this, added to the shrinking sensitiveness of his nature, rendered him not misanthropic, but singularly averse to social intercourse. Of the disease, which was slowly sapping the springs of his life, he first became fully conscious after one of those long abstractions in which he was so wont to indulge. It is remarkable, however, that his first idea of this sort, instead of deepening his spirit with a more melancholy hue, restored him to a more natural state of mind.

He had evidently cherished a secret hope that some impulse would at length be given him, or that he would muster sufficient energy of will to return into the world, and act a wiser and happier part than his former one. But life never called the dreamer forth; it was Death that whispered him. It is to be regretted that this portion of his old journal contains so few passages relative to this interesting period; since the little which he has recorded, though melancholy enough, breathes the gentleness of a spirit newly restored to communion with its kind. If there be any thing bitter in the following reflections, its source is in human sympathy, and its sole object is himself.

"It is hard to die without one's happiness; to none more so than myself, whose early resolution it had been to partake largely of the joys of life, but never to be burthened with its cares. Vain philosophy! The very hardships of the poorest laborer, whose whole existence seems one long toil, has something preferable to my best pleasures.

Merely skimming the surface of life, I know nothing, by my own experience, of its deep and warm realities. I have achieved none of those objects which the instinct of mankind especially prompts them to pursue, and the accomplishment of which must therefore beget a native satisfaction. The truly wise, after all their speculations, will be led into the common path, and, in homage to the human nature that pervades them, will gather gold, and till the earth, and set out trees, and build a house. But I have scorned such wisdom. I have rejected, also, the settled, sober, careful gladness of a man by his own fireside, with those around him whose welfare is committed to his trust and their guidance to his fond authority. Without influence among serious affairs, my footsteps were not imprinted on the earth, but lost in air; and I shall leave no son to inherit my share of life, with a better sense of its privileges and duties, when his father should vanish like a bubble; so that few mortals, even the humblest and the weakest, have been such ineffectual shadows in the world, or die so utterly as I must. Even a young man's bliss has not been mine. With a thousand vagrant fantasies, I have never truly loved, and perhaps shall be doomed to loneliness throughout the eternal future, because, here on earth, my soul has never married itself to the soul of woman.

Such are the repinings of one who feels, too late, that the sympathies of his nature have avenged themselves upon him. They have frustrated, with a joyless life and the prospect of a reluctant death, my selfish purpose to keep aloof from mortal disquietudes, and be a pleasant idler among care-stricken and laborious men. I have other regrets, too, savoring more of my old spirit. The time has been when I meant to visit every region of the earth, except the Poles and central Africa. I had a strange longing to see the Pyramids. To Persia and Arabia, and all the gorgeous East, I owed a pilgrimage for the sake of their magic tales. And England, the land of my ancestors! Once I had fancied that my sleep would not be quiet in the grave unless I should return, as it were, to my home of past ages, and see the very cities, and castles, and battle-fields of history, and stand within the holy gloom of its cathedrals, and kneel at the shrines of its immortal poets, there asserting myself their hereditary countryman. This feeling lay among the deepest in my heart. Yet, with this home-sickness for the father-land, and all these plans of remote travel,—which I yet believe that my peculiar instinct impelled me to form, and upbraided me for not accomplishing—the utmost limit of my wanderings has been little more than six hundred miles from my native village. Thus, in whatever way I consider my life, or what must be termed such, I cannot feel as if I have lived at all.

I am possessed, also, with the thought that I have never yet discovered the real secret of my powers; that there has been a mighty treasure within my reach, a mine of gold beneath my feet, worthless because I have never known how to seek for it; and for want of perhaps one fortunate idea, I am to die

'Unwept, unhonored, and unsung.'

Once, amid the troubled and tumultuous enjoyment of my life, there was one dreary thought that haunted me,—the terrible necessity imposed on mortals to grow old or die. I could not bear the idea of losing one youthful grace. True: I saw other men, who had once been young and now were old, enduring their age with equanimity, because each year reconciled them to its own added weight. But for myself, I felt that age would be not less miserable, creeping upon me slowly, than if it fell at once. I sometimes looked in the glass, and endeavored to fancy my cheeks yellow and interlaced with furrows, my forehead wrinkled deeply across, the top of my head bald and polished, my eye-brows and side-locks iron-gray, and a grisly beard sprouting on my chin. Shuddering at the picture, I changed it for the dead face of a young man, with dark locks clustering heavily round its pale beauty, which would decay, indeed, but not with years, nor in the sight of men. The latter visage shocked me least.

Such a repugnance to the hard conditions of long life is common to all sensitive and thoughtful men, who minister to the luxury, the refinements, the gaiety and lightsomeness, to any thing, in short, but the real necessities of their fellow-creatures. He who has a part in the serious business of life, though it be only as a shoemaker, feels himself equally respectable in youth and age, and therefore is content to live, and look forward to wrinkles and decrepitude in their due season. It is far otherwise with the busy idlers of the world. I was particularly liable to this torment, being a meditative person in spite of my levity. The truth could not be concealed, nor the contemplation of it avoided. With deep inquietude I became aware that what was graceful now, and seemed appropriate enough to my age of flowers, would be ridiculous in middle life; and that the world, so indulgent to the fantastic youth, would scorn the bearded man, still telling love-tales, loftily ambitious of a maiden's tear, and squeezing out, as it were, with his brawny strength, the essence of roses. And in his old age the sweet lyrics of Anacreon made the girls laugh at his white hairs the more. With such sentiments, conscious that my part in the drama of life was fit only for a youthful performer, I nourished a regretful desire to be summoned early from the scene. I set a limit to myself, the age of twenty-five, few years indeed, but too many to be thrown away. Scarcely had I thus fixed the term of my mortal pilgrimage, than the thought grew into a presentiment that, when the space should be completed, the world would have one butterfly the less, by my far flight.

Oh, how fond I was of life, even while allotting, as my proper destiny, an early death! I loved the world, its cities, its villages, its grassy roadsides, its wild forests, its quiet scenes, its gay, warm, enlivening bustle; in every aspect, I loved the world so long as I could behold it with young eyes and dance through it with a young heart. The earth had been made so beautiful, that I longed for no brighter sphere, but only an ever youthful eternity in this. I clung to earth as if my beginning and ending were to be there, unable to imagine any but an earthly happiness, and choosing such, with all its imperfections, rather than perfect bliss which might be alien from it. Alas! I had not yet known that weariness by which the soul proves itself ethereal."

Turning over the old journal, I open, by chance, upon a passage which affords a signal instance of the morbid fancies to which Oberon frequently yielded himself. Dreams like the following were probably engendered by the deep gloom sometimes thrown over his mind by his reflections on death.

"I dreamed that one bright forenoon I was walking through Broadway, and seeking to cheer myself with the warm and busy life of that far-famed promenade. Here a coach thundered over the pavement, and there an unwieldy omnibus, with spruce gigs rattling past, and horsemen prancing through all the bustle. On the side-walk people were looking at the rich display of goods, the plate and jewelry, or

the latest caricature in the booksellers' windows; while fair
ladies and whiskered gentlemen tripped gaily along, nodding
mutual recognitions, or shrinking from some rough countryman or sturdy laborer whose contact might have ruffled their
finery. I found myself in this animated scene, with a dim and
misty idea that it was not my proper place, or that I had
ventured into the crowd with some singularity of dress or
aspect which made me ridiculous. Walking in the sunshine, I
was yet cold as death. By degrees, too, I perceived myself the
object of universal attention, and, as it seemed, of horror and
affright. Every face grew pale; the laugh was hushed, and the
voices died away in broken syllables; the people in the shops
crowded to the doors with a ghastly stare, and the passengers
on all sides fled as from an embodied pestilence. The horses
reared and snorted. An old beggar woman sat before St.
Paul's church, with her withered palm stretched out to all,
but drew it back from me, and pointed to the graves and
monuments in that populous church-yard. Three lovely girls,
whom I had formerly known, ran shrieking across the street.
A personage in black, whom I was about to overtake, suddenly turned his head, and showed the features of a long-lost
friend. He gave me a look of horror and was gone.

I passed not one step further, but threw my eyes on a looking-glass which stood deep within the nearest shop. At the
first glimpse of my own figure I awoke, with a horrible sensation of self-terror and self-loathing. No wonder that the affrighted city fled! I had been promenading Broadway in my
shroud!"

I should be doing injustice to my friend's memory, were I
to publish other extracts even nearer to insanity than this,
from the scarcely legible papers before me. I gather from
them,—for I do not remember that he ever related to me the
circumstances,—that he once made a journey, chiefly on foot,
to Niagara. Some conduct of the friends among whom he
resided in his native village was construed by him into
oppression. These were the friends to whose care he had been
committed by his parents, who died when Oberon was about
twelve years of age. Though he had always been treated by
them with the most uniform kindness, and though a favourite

among the people of the village rather on account of the sympathy which they felt in his situation than from any merit of his own, such was the waywardness of his temper, that on a slight provocation he ran away from the home that sheltered him, expressing openly his determination to die sooner than return to the detested spot. A severe illness overtook him after he had been absent about four months. While ill, he felt how unsoothing were the kindest looks and tones of strangers. He rose from his sick bed a better man, and determined upon a speedy self-atonement by returning to his native town. There he lived, solitary and sad, but forgiven and cherished by his friends till the day he died. That part of the journal which contained a description of this journey is mostly destroyed. Here and there is a fragment. I cannot select, for the pages are very scanty; but I do not withhold the following fragments, because they indicate a better and more cheerful frame of mind than the foregoing.

"On reaching the ferry-house, a rude structure of boards at the foot of the cliff, I found several of these wretches devoid of poetry, and lost some of my own poetry by contact with them. The hut was crowded by a party of provincials—a simple and merry set, who had spent the afternoon fishing near the Falls, and were bartering black and white bass and eels for the ferryman's whiskey. A greyhound and three spaniels, brutes of much more grace and decorous demeanor than their masters, sat at the door. A few yards off, yet wholly unnoticed by the dogs, was a beautiful fox, whose countenance betokened all the sagacity attributed to him in ancient fable. He had a comfortable bed of straw in an old barrel, whither he retreated, flourishing his bushy tail as I made a step towards him, but soon came forth and surveyed me with a keen and intelligent eye. The Canadians bartered their fish and drank their whiskey, and were loquacious on trifling subjects, and merry at simple jests, with as little regard to the scenery as they could have shown to the flattest part of the Grand Canal. Nor was I entitled to despise them; for I amused myself with all those foolish matters of fishermen, and dogs, and fox, just as if Sublimity and Beauty were not married at that place and moment; as if their nuptial band were not the brightest of all rainbows on the opposite shore; as if the gray precipice were not frowning above my head and Niagara thundering around me.

The grim ferryman, a black-whiskered giant, half drunk withal, now thrust the Canadians by main force out of his door, launched a boat, and bade me sit down in the stern-sheets. Where we crossed, the river was white with foam, yet did not offer much resistance to a straight passage, which brought us close to the outer edge of the American falls. The rainbow vanished as we neared its misty base, and when I leaped ashore, the sun had left all Niagara in shadow."

"A sound of merriment, sweet voices and girlish laughter, came dancing through the solemn roar of waters. In old times, when the French and afterwards the English, held garrisons near Niagara, it used to be deemed a feat worthy of a soldier, a frontier man, or an Indian, to cross the rapids to Goat Island. As the country became less rude and warlike, a long space intervened, in which it was but half believed, by a faint and doubtful tradition, that mortal foot had ever trod this wild spot of precipice and forest clinging between two cataracts. The island is no longer a tangled forest, but a grove of stately trees, with grassy intervals about their roots and woodland paths among their trunks. There was neither soldier nor Indian here now, but a vision of three lovely girls, running brief races through the broken sunshine of the grove, hiding behind the trees, and pelting each other with the cones of the pine. When their sport had brought them near me, it so happened that one of the party ran up and shook me by the hand—a greeting which I heartily returned, and would have done the same had it been tenderer. I had known this wild little black-eyed lass in my youth and her childhood, before I had commenced my rambles.

We met on terms of freedom and kindness, which elder ladies might have thought unsuitable with a gentleman of my description. When I alluded to the two fair strangers, she shouted after them by their Christian names, at which summons, with grave dignity, they drew near, and honored me with a distant curtsey. They were from the upper part of Vermont. Whether sisters, or cousins, or at all related to each other, I cannot tell; but they are planted in my memory like 'two twin roses on one stem,' with the fresh dew in both their bosoms; and when I would have pure and pleasant thoughts, I think of them. Neither of them could have seen seventeen years. They both were of a height, and that a moderate one. The rose-bloom of their cheeks could hardly be called bright in her who was the rosiest, nor faint, though a shade less deep, in her companion. Both had delicate eye-brows, not strongly defined, yet somewhat darker than their hair; both had small sweet mouths, maiden mouths, of not so warm and deep a tint as ruby, but only red as the reddest rose; each had those gems, the rarest, the most precious, a pair of clear, soft, bright blue eyes. Their style of dress was similar; one had on a black silk gown, with a stomacher of velvet, and scalloped cuffs of the same from the wrist to the elbow; the other wore cuffs and stomacher of the like pattern and material, over a gown of crimson silk. The dress was rather heavy for their slight figures, but suited to September. They and the darker beauty all carried their straw bonnets in their hands."

I cannot better conclude these fragments than with poor Oberon's description of his return to his native village after his slow recovery from his illness. How beautifully does he express his penitential emotions! A beautiful moral may be indeed drawn from the early death of a sensitive recluse, who had shunned the ordinary avenues to distinction, and with splendid abilities sank into an early grave, almost unknown to mankind, and without any record save what my pen hastily leaves upon these tear-blotted pages.

MY HOME RETURN

"When the stage-coach had gained the summit of the hill, I alighted to perform the small remainder of my journey on foot. There had not been a more delicious afternoon than this, in all the train of summer—the air being a sunny perfume, made up of balm, and warmth, and gentle brightness. The oak and walnut-trees, over my head, retained their deep masses of foliage, and the grass, though for months the pasturage of stray cattle, had been revived with the freshness of early June, by the autumnal rains of the preceding week. The garb of Autumn, indeed, resembled that of Spring. Dandelions and buttercups were sprinkled along the road-side, like drops of brightest gold in greenest grass, and a star-shaped little flower of blue, with a golden centre. In a rocky spot, and rooted under the stone-wall, there was one wild rose-bush, bearing three roses, very faintly tinted, but blessed with a spicy fragrance. The same tokens would have announced that the year was brightening into the glow of summer. There were violets, too, though few and pale ones. But the breath of September was diffused through the mild air, and became perceptible, too thrillingly for my enfeebled frame, whenever a little breeze shook out the latent coolness.

I was standing on the hill at the entrance of my native village, whence I had looked back to bid farewell, and forward to the pale mist-bow that over-arched my path, and was the omen of my fortunes. How had I misinterpreted that augury, the ghost of hope, with none of hope's bright hues! Nor could I deem that all its portents were yet accomplished, though from the same western sky the declining sun shone brightly in my face. But I was calm and not depressed. Turning to the village, so dim and dream-like at my last view, I saw the white houses and brick stores, the intermingled trees, the foot-paths with their wide borders of grass, and the dusty road between; all a picture of peaceful gladness in the sunshine.

'Why have I never loved my home before?' thought I, as my spirit reposed itself on the quiet beauty of the scene.

On the side of the opposite hill was the grave-yard, sloping towards the farther extremity of the village. The sun shone as cheerfully there as on the abodes of the living, and showed all the little hillocks and the burial stones, white marble or slate, and here and there a tomb, with the pleasant grass about them all. A single tree was tinged with glory from the west, and threw a pensive shade behind. Not far from where it fell, was the tomb of my parents, whom I had hardly thought of in bidding adieu to the village, but had remembered them more faithfully among the feelings that drew me homeward. At my departure their tomb had been hidden in the morning mist. Beholding it in the sunshine now, I felt a sensation through my frame as if a breeze had thrown the coolness of September over me, though not a leaf was stirred, nor did the thistle down take flight. Was I to roam no more through this beautiful world, but only to the other end of the village? Then let me lie down near my parents, but not with them, because I love a green grave better than a tomb.

Moving slowly forward, I heard shouts and laughter, and perceived a considerable throng of people, who came from behind the meeting-house and made a stand in front of it. Thither all the idlers of the village were congregated to witness the exercises of the engine company, this being the afternoon of their monthly practice. They deluged the roof of the meeting-house, till the water fell from the eaves in a broad cascade; then the stream beat against the dusty windows like a thunder storm; and sometimes they flung it up beside the steeple, sparkling in an ascending shower about the weathercock. For variety's sake, the engineer made it undulate horizontally, like a great serpent flying over the earth. As his last effort, being roguishly inclined, he seemed to take aim at the sky, falling rather short of which, down came the fluid, transformed to drops of silver, on the thickest crowd of the spectators. Then ensued a prodigious rout and mirthful uproar, with no little wrath of the surly ones, whom this is an infallible method of distinguishing. The joke afforded infinite amusement to the ladies at the windows and some old people under the hay scales. I also laughed at a distance, and was glad to find myself susceptible, as of old, to the simple mirth of such a scene.

But the thoughts that it excited were not all mirthful. I had witnessed hundreds of such spectacles in my youth, and one precisely similar only a few days before my departure. And now, the aspect of the village being the same, and the crowd composed of my old acquaintances, I could hardly realize that years had past, or even months, or that the very drops of water were not falling at this moment which had been flung up then. But I pressed the conviction home, that, brief as the time appeared, it had been long enough for me to wander away and return again, with my fate accomplished, and little more hope in this world. The last throb of an adventurous and wayward spirit kept me from repining. I felt as if it were better, or not worse, to have compressed my enjoyments and sufferings into a few wild years, and then to rest myself in an early grave, than to have chosen the untroubled and ungladdened course of the crowd before me, whose days were all alike, and a long lifetime like each day. But the sentiment startled me. For a moment I doubted whether my dearbought wisdom were any thing but the incapacity to pursue fresh follies, and whether, if health and strength could be restored that night, I should be found in the village after tomorrow's dawn.

Among other novelties, I noticed that the tavern was now designated as a Temperance House, in letters extending across the whole front, with a smaller sign promising Hot Coffee at all hours, and Spruce Beer to lodgers gratis. There were few new buildings, except a Methodist chapel and a printing office, with a book store in the lower story. The golden mortar still ornamented the apothecary's door, nor had the Indian Chief, with his gilded tobacco stalk, been relieved from doing centinel's duty before Dominicus Pike's grocery. The gorgeous silks, though of later patterns, were still flaunting like a banner in front of Mr. Nightingale's dry goods store. Some of the signs introduced me to strangers, whose predecessors had failed, or emigrated to the West, or removed merely to the other end of the village, transferring their names from the sign-boards to slabs of marble or slate. But, on the whole, Death and Vicissitude had done very little. There were old men, scattered about the street, who had been old in my earliest reminiscences; and, as if their venerable forms were permanent parts of the creation, they appeared to be hale and hearty old men yet. The less elderly were more altered, having generally contracted a stoop, with hair woefully thinned and whitened. Some I could hardly recognize; at my last glance they had been boys and girls, but were young men and women when I looked again; and there were happy little things too, rolling about on the grass, whom God had made since my departure.

But now, in my lingering course I had descended the hill, and began to consider, painfully enough, how I should meet my townspeople, and what reception they would give me. Of many an evil prophecy, doubtless, had I been the subject. And would they salute me with a roar of triumph or a low hiss of scorn, on beholding their worst anticipations more than accomplished?

'No,' said I, 'they will not triumph over me. And should they ask the cause of my return, I will tell them that a man may go far and tarry long away, if his health be good and his hopes high; but that when flesh and spirit begin to fail, he remembers his birthplace and the old burial-ground, and hears a voice calling him to come home to his father and mother. They will know, by my wasted frame and feeble step, that I have heard the summons and obeyed. And, the first greetings over, they will let me walk among them unnoticed, and linger in the sunshine while I may, and steal into my grave in peace.'

With these reflections I looked kindly at the crowd, and drew off my glove, ready to give my hand to the first that should put forth his. It occurred to me, also, that some youth among them, now at the crisis of his fate, might have felt his bosom thrill at my example, and be emulous of my wild life and worthless fame. But I would save him.

'He shall be taught,' said I, 'by my life, and by my death, that the world is a sad one for him who shrinks from its sober duties. My experience shall warn him to adopt some great and serious aim, such as manhood will cling to, that he may not feel himself, too late, a cumberer of this overladen earth, but a man among men. I will beseech him not to follow an eccentric path, nor, by stepping aside from the highway of human affairs, to relinquish his claim upon human sympathy. And often, as a text of deep and varied meaning, I will remind him that he is an American.'

By this time I had drawn near the meeting-house, and perceived that the crowd were beginning to recognize me."

These are the last words traced by his hand. Has not so chastened a spirit found true communion with the pure in Heaven?

"Until of late, I never could believe that I was seriously ill: the past, I thought, could not extend its misery beyond itself; life was restored to me, and should not be misused again. I had day-dreams even of wedded happiness. Still, as the days wear on, a faintness creeps through my frame and spirit, recalling the consciousness that a very old man might as well nourish hope and young desire as I at twenty-four. Yet the consciousness of my situation does not always make me sad. Sometimes I look upon the world with a quiet interest, because it cannot concern me personally, and a loving one for the same reason, because nothing selfish can interfere with the sense of brotherhood. Soon to be all spirit, I have already a spiritual sense of human nature, and see deeply into the hearts of mankind, discovering what is hidden from the wisest. The loves of young men and virgins are known to me, before the first kiss, before the whispered word, with the birth of the first sigh. My glance comprehends the crowd, and penetrates the breast of the solitary man. I think better of the world than formerly, more generously of its virtues, more mercifully of its faults, with a higher estimate of its present happiness, and brighter hopes of its destiny. My mind has put forth a second crop of blossoms, as the trees do in the Indian summer. No winter will destroy their beauty, for they are fanned by the breeze and freshened by the shower that breathes and falls in the gardens of Paradise!"

Edward Fane's Rosebud

THERE is hardly a more difficult exercise of fancy, than, while gazing at a figure of melancholy age, to re-create its youth, and, without entirely obliterating the identity of form and features, to restore those graces which time has snatched away. Some old people, especially women, so age-worn and woful are they, seem never to have been young and gay. It is easier to conceive that such gloomy phantoms were sent into the world as withered and decrepit as we behold them now, with sympathies only for pain and grief, to watch at death-beds, and weep at funerals. Even the sable garments of their widowhood appear essential to their existence; all their attributes combine to render them darksome shadows, creeping strangely amid the sunshine of human life. Yet it is no unprofitable task, to take one of these doleful creatures, and set fancy resolutely at work to brighten the dim eye, and darken the silvery locks, and paint the ashen-cheek with rose-color, and repair the shrunken and crazy form, till a dewy maiden shall be seen in the old matron's elbow-chair. The miracle being wrought, then let the years roll back again, each sadder than the last, and the whole weight of age and sorrow settle down upon the youthful figure. Wrinkles and furrows, the hand-writing of Time, may thus be deciphered, and found to contain deep lessons of thought and feeling. Such profit might be derived, by a skilful observer, from my much-respected friend, the Widow Toothaker, a nurse of great repute, who has breathed the atmosphere of sick-chambers and dying-breaths, these forty years.

See! she sits cowering over her lonesome hearth, with her gown and upper petticoat drawn upward, gathering thriftily into her person the whole warmth of the fire, which, now at nightfall, begins to dissipate the autumnal chill of her chamber. The blaze quivers capriciously in front, alternately glimmering into the deepest chasms of her wrinkled visage, and then permitting a ghostly dimness to mar the outlines of her venerable figure. And Nurse Toothaker holds a tea-spoon in her right hand, with which to stir up the contents of a tumbler in her left, whence steams a vapory fragrance, abhorred of temperance societies. Now she sips—now stirs—now sips again. Her sad old heart has need to be revived by the rich infusion of Geneva, which is mixed half-and-half with hot water, in the tumbler. All day long she has been sitting by a death-pillow, and quitted it for her home, only when the spirit of her patient left the clay, and went homeward too. But now are her melancholy meditations cheered, and her torpid blood warmed, and her shoulders lightened of at least twenty ponderous years, by a draught from the true Fountain of Youth, in a case-bottle. It is strange that men should deem that fount a fable, when its liquor fills more bottles than the congress-water! Sip it again, good nurse, and see whether a second draught will not take off another score of years, and perhaps ten more, and show us, in your high-backed chair, the blooming damsel who plighted troths with Edward Fane. Get you gone, Age and Widowhood! Come back, unwedded Youth! But, alas! the charm will not work. In spite of fancy's most potent spell, I can see only an old dame cowering over the fire, a picture of decay and desolation, while the November blast roars at her in the chimney, and fitful showers rush suddenly against the window.

Yet there was a time when Rose Grafton—such was the pretty maiden-name of Nurse Toothaker—possessed beauty that would have gladdened this dim and dismal chamber, as with sunshine. It won for her the heart of Edward Fane, who has since made so great a figure in the world, and is now a grand old gentleman, with powdered hair, and as gouty as a lord. These early lovers thought to have walked hand in hand through life. They had wept together for Edward's little sister Mary, whom Rose tended in her sickness, partly because she was the sweetest child that ever lived or died, but more for love of him. She was but three years old. Being such an infant, Death could not embody his terrors in her little corpse; nor did Rose fear to touch the dead child's brow, though chill, as she curled the silken hair around it, nor to take her tiny hand, and clasp a flower within its fingers. Afterward, when she looked through the pane of glass in the coffin-lid, and beheld Mary's face, it seemed not so much like death, or life, as like a wax-work, wrought into the perfect image of a child asleep, and dreaming of its mother's smile. Rose thought her too fair a thing to be hidden in the grave, and wondered that an angel did not snatch up little Mary's coffin, and bear the slumbering babe to heaven, and bid her wake immortal. But when the sods were laid on little Mary, the heart of Rose was troubled. She shuddered at the fantasy, that, in grasping the child's cold fingers, her virgin hand had exchanged a first greeting with mortality, and could never lose the earthly taint. How many a greeting since! But as yet, she was a fair young girl, with the dew-drops of fresh feeling in her bosom; and instead of Rose, which seemed too mature a name for her half-opened beauty, her lover called her Rosebud.

The rosebud was destined never to bloom for Edward Fane. His mother was a rich and haughty dame, with all the aristocratic prejudices of colonial times. She scorned Rose Grafton's humble parentage, and caused her son to break his faith, though, had she let him choose, he would have prized his Rosebud above the richest diamond. The lovers parted, and have seldom met again. Both may have visited the same mansions, but not at the same time; for one was bidden to the festal hall, and the other to the sick-chamber; he was the guest of Pleasure and Prosperity, and she of Anguish. Rose, after their separation, was long secluded within the dwelling of Mr. Toothaker, whom she married with the revengeful hope of breaking her false lover's heart. She went to her bridegroom's arms with bitterer tears, they say, than young girls ought to shed, at the threshold of the bridal chamber. Yet, though her husband's head was getting gray, and his heart had been chilled with an autumnal frost, Rose soon began to love him, and wondered at her own conjugal affection. He was all she had to love; there were no children.

In a year or two, poor Mr. Toothaker was visited with a wearisome infirmity, which settled in his joints, and made him weaker than a child. He crept forth about his business, and came home at dinner-time and eventide, not with the manly tread that gladdens a wife's heart, but slowly— feebly—jotting down each dull footstep with a melancholy dub of his staff. We must pardon his pretty wife, if she sometimes blushed to own him. Her visiters, when they heard him coming, looked for the appearance of some old, old man; but he dragged his nerveless limbs into the parlor—and there was Mr. Toothaker! The disease increasing, he never went into the sunshine, save with a staff in his right hand, and his left on his wife's shoulder, bearing heavily downward, like a dead man's hand. Thus, a slender woman, still looking maiden-like, she supported his tall, broad-chested frame along the pathway of their little garden, and plucked the roses for her gray-haired husband, and spoke soothingly, as to an infant. His mind was palsied with his body; its utmost energy was pee-vishness. In a few months more, she helped him up the stair-case, with a pause at every step, and a longer one upon the landing-place, and a heavy glance behind, as he crossed the threshold of his chamber. He knew, poor man, that the pre-cincts of those four walls would thenceforth be his world— his world, his home, his tomb—at once a dwelling and a burial-place, till he were borne to a darker and a narrower one. But Rose was with him in the tomb. He leaned upon her, in his daily passage from the bed to the chair by the fireside, and back again from the weary chair to the joyless bed—his bed and hers—their marriage-bed; till even this short journey ceased, and his head lay all day upon the pillow, and hers all night beside it. How long poor Mr. Toothaker was kept in misery! Death seemed to draw near the door, and often to lift the latch, and sometimes to thrust his ugly skull into the chamber, nodding to Rose, and pointing at her hus-band, but still delayed to enter. 'This bed-ridden wretch can-not escape me!' quoth Death. 'I will go forth, and run a race with the swift, and fight a battle with the strong, and come back for Toothaker at my leisure!' Oh, when the deliverer came so near, in the dull anguish of her worn-out sympathies, did she never long to cry, 'Death, come in!'

But, no! We have no right to ascribe such a wish to our friend Rose. She never failed in a wife's duty to her poor sick husband. She murmured not, though a glimpse of the sunny sky was as strange to her as him, nor answered peevishly, though his complaining accents roused her from her sweetest dream, only to share his wretchedness. He knew her faith, yet nourished a cankered jealousy; and when the slow disease had chilled all his heart, save one lukewarm spot, which Death's frozen fingers were searching for, his last words were: 'What would my Rose have done for her first love, if she has been so true and kind to a sick old man like me!' And then his poor soul crept away, and left the body lifeless, though hardly more so than for years before, and Rose a widow, though in truth it was the wedding night that widowed her. She felt glad, it must be owned, when Mr. Toothaker was buried, because his corpse had retained such a likeness to the man half alive, that she hearkened for the sad murmur of his voice, bidding her shift his pillow. But all through the next winter, though the grave had held him many a month, she fancied him calling from that cold bed, 'Rose! Rose! come put a blanket on my feet!'

So now the Rosebud was the Widow Toothaker. Her troubles had come early, and, tedious as they seemed, had passed before all her bloom was fled. She was still fair enough to captivate a bachelor, or, with a widow's cheerful gravity, she might have won a widower, stealing into his heart in the very guise of his dead wife. But the Widow Toothaker had no such projects. By her watchings and continual cares, her heart had become knit to her first husband with a constancy which changed its very nature, and made her love him for his infirmities, and infirmity for his sake. When the palsied old man was gone, even her early lover could not have supplied his place. She had dwelt in a sick-chamber, and been the companion of a half-dead wretch, till she should scarcely breathe in a free air, and felt ill at ease with the healthy and the happy. She missed the fragrance of the doctor's stuff. She walked the chamber with a noiseless foot-fall. If visiters came in, she spoke in soft and soothing accents, and was startled and shocked by their loud voices. Often, in the lonesome evening, she looked timorously from the fireside to the bed, with almost a hope of recognizing a ghastly face upon the pillow. Then went her thoughts sadly to her husband's grave. If one impatient throb had wronged him in his lifetime—if she had secretly repined, because her buoyant youth was imprisoned with his torpid age—if ever, while slumbering beside him, a treacherous dream had admitted another into her heart—yet the sick man had been preparing a revenge, which the dead now claimed. On his painful pillow, he had cast a spell around her; his groans and misery had proved more captivating charms than gayety and youthful grace; in his semblance, Disease itself had won the Rosebud for a bride; nor could his death dissolve the nuptials. By that indissoluble bond she had gained a home in every sick-chamber, and nowhere else; there were her brethren and sisters; thither her husband summoned her, with that voice which had seemed to issue from the grave of Toothaker. At length she recognized her destiny.

We have beheld her as the maid, the wife, the widow; now we see her in a separate and insulated character: she was, in all her attributes, Nurse Toothaker. And Nurse Toothaker alone, with her own shrivelled lips, could make known her experience in that capacity. What a history might she record of the great sicknesses, in which she has gone hand in hand with the exterminating angel! She remembers when the small-pox hoisted a red-banner on almost every house along the street. She has witnessed when the typhus fever swept off a whole household, young and old, all but a lonely mother, who vainly shrieked to follow her last loved one. Where would be Death's triumph, if none lived to weep! She can speak of strange maladies that have broken out, as if spontaneously, but were found to have been imported from foreign lands, with rich silks and other merchandise, the costliest portion of the cargo. And once, she recollects, the people died of what was considered a new pestilence, till the doctors traced it to the ancient grave of a young girl, who thus caused many deaths a hundred years after her own burial. Strange that such black mischief should lurk in a maiden's grave! She loves to tell how strong men fight with fiery fevers, utterly refusing to give up their breath; and how consumptive virgins fade out of the world, scarcely reluctant, as if their lovers were wooing them to a far country. Tell us, thou fearful woman! tell us the death-secrets! Fain would I search out the meaning of words, faintly gasped with intermingled sobs, and broken sentences, half-audibly spoken between earth and the judgment-seat!

An awful woman! She is the patron-saint of young physicians, and the bosom friend of old ones. In the mansions where she enters, the inmates provide themselves black garments; the coffin-maker follows her; and the bell tolls as she comes away from the threshold. Death himself has met her at so many a bed-side, that he puts forth his bony hand to greet Nurse Toothaker. She is an awful woman! And, oh! is it conceivable, that this handmaid of human infirmity and affliction—so darkly stained, so thoroughly imbued with all that is saddest in the doom of mortals—can ever again be bright and gladsome, even though bathed in the sunshine of eternity? By her long communion with wo, has she not forfeited her inheritance of immortal joy? Does any germ of bliss survive within her?

Hark! an eager knocking at Nurse Toothaker's door. She starts from her drowsy reverie, sets aside the empty tumbler and tea-spoon, and lights a lamp at the dim embers of the fire. Rap, rap, rap! again; and she hurries adown the staircase, wondering which of her friends can be at death's door now, since there is such an earnest messenger at Nurse Toothaker's. Again the peal resounds, just as her hand is on the lock. 'Be quick, Nurse Toothaker!' cries a man on the doorstep; 'old General Fane is taken with the gout in his stomach, and has sent for you to watch by his death-bed. Make haste, for there is no time to lose!' 'Fane! Edward Fane! And has he sent for me at last? I am ready! I will get on my cloak and begone. So,' adds the sable-gowned, ashen-visaged, funereal old figure, 'Edward Fane remembers his Rosebud!'

Our question is answered. There is a germ of bliss within her. Her long-hoarded constancy—her memory of the bliss that was—remaining amid the gloom of her after life, like a sweet-smelling flower in a coffin, is a symbol that all may be renewed. In some happier clime, the Rosebud may revive again with all the dew-drops in its bosom.

The Toll-Gatherer's Day

A SKETCH OF TRANSITORY LIFE

METHINKS, for a person whose instinct bids him rather to pore over the current of life, than to plunge into its tumultuous waves, no undesirable retreat were a toll-house beside some thronged thoroughfare of the land. In youth, perhaps, it is good for the observer to run about the earth—to leave the track of his footsteps far and wide—to mingle himself with the action of numberless vicissitudes—and finally, in some calm solitude, to feed a musing spirit on all that he has seen and felt. But there are natures too indolent, or too sensitive, to endure the dust, the sunshine, or the rain, the turmoil of moral and physical elements, to which all the wayfarers of the world expose themselves. For such a man, how pleasant a miracle, could life be made to roll its variegated length by the threshold of his own hermitage, and the great globe, as it were, perform its revolutions and shift its thousand scenes before his eyes without whirling him onward in its course. If any mortal be favored with a lot analogous to this, it is the toll-gatherer. So, at least, have I often fancied, while lounging on a bench at the door of a small square edifice which stands between shore and shore in the midst of a long bridge. Beneath the timbers ebbs and flows an arm of the sea; while above, like the life-blood through a great artery, the travel of the north and east is continually throbbing. Sitting on the aforesaid bench, I amuse myself with a conception, illustrated by numerous pencil-sketches in the air, of the toll-gatherer's day.

In the morning—dim, gray, dewy summer's morn—the distant roll of ponderous wheels begins to mingle with my old friend's slumbers, creaking more and more harshly through the midst of his dream, and gradually replacing it with realities. Hardly conscious of the change from sleep to wakefulness, he finds himself partly clad and throwing wide the toll-gates for the passage of a fragrant load of hay. The timbers groan beneath the slow-revolving wheels; one sturdy

yeoman stalks beside the oxen, and peering from the summit
of the hay, by the glimmer of the half-extinguished lantern
over the toll-house, is seen the drowsy visage of his comrade,
who has enjoyed a nap some ten miles long. The toll is
paid—creak, creak, again go the wheels, and the huge hay-
mow vanishes into the morning mist. As yet, nature is but
half awake, and familiar objects appear visionary. But yonder,
dashing from the shore with a rattling thunder of the wheels
and a confused clatter of hoofs, comes the never-tiring mail,
which has hurried onward at the same headlong, restless rate,
all through the quiet night. The bridge resounds in one continued peal as the coach rolls on without a pause, merely affording the toll-gatherer a glimpse at the sleepy passengers,
who now bestir their torpid limbs, and snuff a cordial in the
briny air. The morn breathes upon them and blushes, and
they forget how wearily the darkness toiled away. And behold
now the fervid day, in his bright chariot, glittering aslant over
the waves, nor scorning to throw a tribute of his golden
beams on the toll-gatherer's little hermitage. The old man
looks eastward, and (for he is a moralizer) frames a simile of
the stage-coach and the sun.

While the world is rousing itself we may glance slightly at
the scene of our sketch. It sits above the bosom of the broad
flood, a spot not of earth, but in the midst of waters, which
rush with a murmuring sound among the massive beams beneath. Over the door is a weather-beaten board inscribed
with the rates of toll, in letters so nearly effaced that the gilding of the sunshine can hardly make them legible. Beneath
the window is a wooden bench, on which a long succession
of weary wayfarers have reposed themselves. Peeping within
doors, we perceive the whitewashed walls bedecked with sundry lithographic prints and advertisements of various import,
and the immense show-bill of a wandering caravan. And there
sits our good old toll-gatherer, glorified by the early sunbeams. He is a man, as his aspect may announce, of quiet
soul, and thoughtful, shrewd, yet simple mind, who, of the
wisdom which the passing world scatters along the wayside,
has gathered a reasonable store.

Now the sun smiles upon the landscape, and earth smiles
back again upon the sky. Frequent, now, are the travellers.

The toll-gatherer's practised ear can distinguish the weight of every vehicle, the number of its wheels, and how many horses beat the resounding timbers with their iron tramp. Here, in a substantial family chaise, setting forth betimes to take advantage of the dewy road, come a gentleman and his wife, with their rosy-cheeked little girl sitting gladsomely between them. The bottom of the chaise is heaped with multifarious band-boxes and carpet bags, and beneath the axle swings a leathern trunk, dusty with yesterday's journey. Next appears a four-wheeled carryall, peopled with a round half dozen of pretty girls, all drawn by a single horse, and driven by a single gentleman. Luckless wight, doomed, through a whole summer day, to be the butt of mirth and mischief among the frolicksome maidens! Bolt upright in a sulkey rides a thin, sour-visaged man, who, as he pays his toll, hands the toll-gatherer a printed card to stick upon the wall. The vinegar-faced traveller proves to be a manufacturer of pickles. Now paces slowly from timber to timber a horseman clad in black, with a meditative brow, as of one who, whithersoever his steed might bear him, would still journey through a mist of brooding thought. He is a country preacher, going to labor at a protracted meeting. The next object passing townward is a butcher's cart, canopied with its arch of snow-white cotton. Behind comes a 'sauceman,' driving a wagon full of new potatoes, green ears of corn, beets, carrots, turnips, and summer squashes; and next, two wrinkled, withered, witch-looking old gossips, in an antediluvian chaise drawn by a horse of former generations, and going to peddle out a lot of huckleberries. See there, a man trundling a wheelbarrow load of lobsters. And now a milk cart rattles briskly onward, covered with green canvass, and conveying the contributions of a whole herd of cows, in large tin canisters. But let all these pay their toll and pass. Here comes a spectacle that causes the old toll-gatherer to smile benignantly, as if the travellers brought sunshine with them and lavished its gladsome influence all along the road.

It is a barouche of the newest style, the varnished panels of which reflect the whole moving panorama of the landscape, and show a picture, likewise, of our friend, with his visage broadened; so that his meditative smile is transformed to grotesque merriment. Within sits a youth, fresh as the summer morn, and beside him a young lady in white, with white gloves upon her slender hands, and a white veil flowing down over her face. But methinks her blushing cheek burns through the snowy veil. Another white-robed virgin sits in front. And who are these, on whom, and on all that appertains to them, the dust of earth seems never to have settled? Two lovers, whom the priest has blessed this blessed morn, and sent them forth, with one of the bridemaids, on the matrimonial tour. Take my blessing too, ye happy ones! May the sky not frown upon you, nor clouds bedew you with their chill and sullen rain! May the hot sun kindle no fever in your hearts! May your whole life's pilgrimage be as blissful as this first day's journey, and its close be gladdened with even brighter anticipation than those which hallow your bridal night!

They pass; and ere the reflection of their joy has faded from his face, another spectacle throws a melancholy shadow over the spirit of the observing man. In a close carriage sits a fragile figure, muffled carefully, and shrinking even from the mild breath of summer. She leans against a manly form, and his arm enfolds her, as if to guard his treasure from some enemy. Let but a few weeks pass, and when he shall strive to embrace that loved one, he will press only desolation to his heart.

And now has morning gathered up her dewy pearls, and fled away. The sun rolls blazing through the sky, and cannot find a cloud to cool his face with. The horses toil sluggishly along the bridge, and heave their glistening sides in short quick pantings, when the reins are tightened at the toll-house. Glisten, too, the faces of the travellers. Their garments are thickly bestrewn with dust; their whiskers and hair look hoary; their throats are choked with the dusty atmosphere which they have left behind them. No air is stirring on the road. Nature dares draw no breath, lest she should inhale a stifling cloud of dust. 'A hot and dusty day!' cry the poor pilgrims, as they wipe their begrimed foreheads, and woo the doubtful breeze which the river bears along with it. 'Awful hot! Dreadful dusty!' answers the sympathetic toll-gatherer. They start again, to pass through the fiery furnace, while he re-enters his cool hermitage, and besprinkles it with a pail of briny water from the stream beneath. He thinks within himself, that the sun is not so fierce here as elsewhere, and that the gentle air doth not forget him in these sultry days. Yes, old friend; and a quiet heart will make a dog-day temperate. He hears a weary footstep, and perceives a traveller with pack and staff, who sits down upon the hospitable bench, and removes the hat from his wet brow. The toll-gatherer administers a cup of cold water, and discovering his guest to be a man of homely sense, he engages him in profitable talk, uttering the maxims of a philosophy which he has found in his own soul, but knows not how it came there. And as the wayfarer makes ready to resume his journey, he tells him a sovereign remedy for blistered feet.

Now comes the noon-tide hour—of all the hours, nearest akin to midnight; for each has its own calmness and repose. Soon, however, the world begins to turn again upon its axis, and it seems the busiest epoch of the day; when an accident impedes the march of sublunary things. The draw being lifted to permit the passage of a schooner, laden with wood from the eastern forests, she sticks immoveably, right athwart the bridge! Meanwhile, on both sides of the chasm, a throng of impatient travellers fret and fume. Here are two sailors in a gig, with the top thrown back, both puffing cigars, and swearing all sorts of for'c'stle oaths; there, in a smart chaise, a dashingly dressed gentleman and lady, he from a tailor's shop-board, and she from a milliner's back room—the aristocrats of a summer afternoon. And what are the haughtiest of us, but the ephemeral aristocrats of a summer's day? Here is a tin-pedler, whose glittering ware bedazzles all beholders, like a travelling meteor, or opposition sun; and on the other side, a seller of spruce beer, which brisk liquor is confined in several dozen of stone bottles. Here come a party of ladies on horseback, in green riding-habits, and gentlemen attendant; and there a flock of sheep for the market, pattering over the bridge with a multitudinous clatter of their little hoofs. Here a Frenchman, with a hand-organ on his shoulder; and there an itinerant Swiss jeweller. On this side, heralded by a blast of clarions and bugles, appears a train of wagons, conveying all the wild beasts of a caravan; and on that, a company of summer soldiers, marching from village to village on a festival campaign, attended by the 'brass band.' Now look at the scene, and it presents an emblem of the mysterious confusion, the apparently insolvable riddle, in which individuals, or the great world itself, seem often to be involved. What miracle shall set all things right again?

But see! the schooner has thrust her bulky carcass through the chasm; the draw descends; horse and foot pass onward, and leave the bridge vacant from end to end. 'And thus,' muses the toll-gatherer, 'have I found it with all stoppages, even though the universe seemed to be at a stand.' The sage old man!

Far westward now, the reddening sun throws a broad sheet of splendor across the flood, and to the eyes of distant boatmen gleams brightly among the timbers of the bridge. Strollers come from the town to quaff the freshening breeze. One or two let down long lines, and haul up flapping flounders, or cunners, or small cod, or perhaps an eel. Others, and fair girls among them, with the flush of the hot day still on their cheeks, bend over the railing and watch the heaps of sea-weed floating upward with the flowing tide. The horses now tramp heavily along the bridge, and wistfully bethink them of their stables. Rest, rest, thou weary world! for to-morrow's round of toil and pleasure will be as wearisome as to-day's has been; yet both shall bear thee onward a day's march of eternity. Now the old toll-gatherer looks seaward, and discerns the light-house kindling on a far island, and the stars, too, kindling in the sky, as if but a little way beyond; and mingling reveries of Heaven with remembrances of Earth, the whole procession of mortal travellers, all the dusty pilgrimage which he has witnessed, seems like a flitting show of phantoms for his thoughtful soul to muse upon.

Sylph Etherege

O N a bright summer evening, two persons stood among the shrubbery of a garden, stealthily watching a young girl, who sat in the window-seat of a neighbouring mansion. One of these unseen observers, a gentleman, was youthful, and had an air of high breeding and refinement, and a face marked with intellect, though otherwise of unprepossessing aspect. His features wore even an ominous, though somewhat mirthful expression, while he pointed his long forefinger at the girl, and seemed to regard her as a creature completely within the scope of his influence.

"The charm works!" said he, in a low, but emphatic whisper.

"Do you know, Edward Hamilton,—since so you choose to be named,—do you know," said the lady beside him, "that I have almost a mind to break the spell at once? What if the lesson should prove too severe! True; if my ward could be thus laughed out of her fantastic nonsense, she might be the better for it through life. But then she is such a delicate creature! And besides, are you not ruining your own chance, by putting forward this shadow of a rival?"

"But will he not vanish into thin air, at my bidding?" rejoined Edward Hamilton. "Let the charm work!"

The girl's slender and sylph-like figure, tinged with radiance from the sunset clouds, and overhung with the rich drapery of the silken curtains, and set within the deep frame of the window, was a perfect picture; or rather, it was like the original loveliness in a painter's fancy, from which the most finished picture is but an imperfect copy. Though her occupation excited so much interest in the two spectators, she was merely gazing at a miniature which she held in her hand, encased in white satin and red morocco; nor did there appear to be any other cause for the smile of mockery and malice with which Hamilton regarded her.

"The charm works!" muttered he, again. "Our pretty Sylvia's scorn will have a dear retribution!"

At this moment the girl raised her eyes, and, instead of a

lifelike semblance of the miniature, beheld the ill-omened shape of Edward Hamilton, who now stepped forth from his concealment in the shrubbery.

Sylvia Etherege was an orphan girl, who had spent her life, till within a few months past, under the guardianship, and in the secluded dwelling, of an old bachelor uncle. While yet in her cradle, she had been the destined bride of a cousin, who was no less passive in the betrothal than herself. Their future union had been projected, as the means of uniting two rich estates, and was rendered highly expedient, if not indispensable, by the testamentary dispositions of the parents on both sides. Edgar Vaughan, the promised bridegroom, had been bred from infancy in Europe, and had never seen the beautiful girl, whose heart he was to claim as his inheritance. But already, for several years, a correspondence had been kept up between the cousins, and had produced an intellectual intimacy, though it could but imperfectly acquaint them with each other's character.

Sylvia was shy, sensitive, and fanciful; and her guardian's secluded habits had shut her out from even so much of the world as is generally open to maidens of her age. She had been left to seek associates and friends for herself, in the haunts of imagination, and to converse with them, sometimes in the language of dead poets, oftener in the poetry of her own mind. The companion whom she chiefly summoned up, was the cousin, with whose idea her earliest thoughts had been connected. She made a vision of Edgar Vaughan, and tinted it with stronger hues than a mere fancy-picture, yet graced it with so many bright and delicate perfections, that her cousin could nowhere have encountered so dangerous a rival. To this shadow she cherished a romantic fidelity. With its airy presence sitting by her side, or gliding along her favorite paths, the loneliness of her young life was blissful; her heart was satisfied with love, while yet its virgin purity was untainted by the earthliness that the touch of a real lover would have left there. Edgar Vaughan seemed to be conscious of her character; for, in his letters, he gave her a name that was happily appropriate to the sensitiveness of her disposition, the delicate peculiarity of her manners, and the ethereal beauty both of her

mind and person. Instead of Sylvia, he called her Sylph,—
with the prerogative of a cousin and a lover,—his dear Sylph
Etherege.

When Sylvia was seventeen her guardian died, and she
passed under the care of Mrs. Grosvenor, a lady of wealth
and fashion, and Sylvia's nearest relative, though a distant
one. While an inmate of Mrs. Grosvenor's family, she still
preserved somewhat of her life-long habits of seclusion, and
shrank from a too familiar intercourse with those around her.
Still, too, she was faithful to her cousin, or to the shadow
which bore his name.

The time now drew near, when Edgar Vaughan, whose education had been completed by an extensive range of travel,
was to revisit the soil of his nativity. Edward Hamilton, a
young gentleman, who had been Vaughan's companion, both
in his studies and rambles, had already recrossed the Atlantic,
bringing letters to Mrs. Grosvenor and Sylvia Etherege.
These credentials insured him an earnest welcome, which,
however, on Sylvia's part, was not followed by personal partiality, or even the regard that seemed due to her cousin's
most intimate friend. As she herself could have assigned no
cause for her repugnance, it might be termed instinctive.
Hamilton's person, it is true, was the reverse of attractive,
especially when beheld for the first time. Yet, in the eyes of
the most fastidious judges, the defect of natural grace was
compensated by the polish of his manners, and by the intellect which so often gleamed through his dark features. Mrs.
Grosvenor, with whom he immediately became a prodigious
favorite, exerted herself to overcome Sylvia's dislike. But, in
this matter, her ward could neither be reasoned with, nor persuaded. The presence of Edward Hamilton was sure to render
her cold, shy, and distant, abstracting all the vivacity from her
deportment, as if a cloud had come betwixt her and the sunshine.

The simplicity of Sylvia's demeanor rendered it easy for so
keen an observer as Hamilton to detect her feelings. Whenever any slight circumstance made him sensible of them, a
smile might be seen to flit over the young man's sallow visage. None, that had once beheld this smile, were in any danger of forgetting it; whenever they recalled to memory the

features of Edward Hamilton, they were always duskily illuminated by this expression of mockery and malice.

In a few weeks after Hamilton's arrival, he presented to
Sylvia Etherege a miniature of her cousin, which, as he informed her, would have been delivered sooner, but was detained with a portion of his baggage. This was the miniature,
in the contemplation of which we beheld Sylvia so absorbed,
at the commencement of our story. Such, in truth, was too
often the habit of the shy and musing girl. The beauty of the
pictured countenance was almost too perfect to represent a
human creature, that had been born of a fallen and world-
worn race, and had lived to manhood amid ordinary troubles
and enjoyments, and must become wrinkled with age and
care. It seemed too bright for a thing formed of dust, and
doomed to crumble into dust again. Sylvia feared that such a
being would be too refined and delicate to love a simple girl
like her. Yet, even while her spirit drooped with that apprehension, the picture was but the masculine counterpart of
Sylph Etherege's sylph-like beauty. There was that resemblance between her own face and the miniature, which is said
often to exist between lovers whom Heaven has destined for
each other, and which, in this instance, might be owing to
the kindred blood of the two parties. Sylvia felt, indeed, that
there was something familiar in the countenance, so like a
friend did the eyes smile upon her, and seem to imply a
knowledge of her thoughts. She could account for this
impression only by supposing, that, in some of her day-
dreams, imagination had conjured up the true similitude of
her distant and unseen lover.

But now could Sylvia give a brighter semblance of reality
to those day-dreams. Clasping the miniature to her heart, she
could summon forth, from that haunted cell of pure and blissful fantasies, the life-like shadow, to roam with her in the
moonlight garden. Even at noontide it sat with her in the
arbour, when the sunshine threw its broken flakes of gold
into the clustering shade. The effect upon her mind was
hardly less powerful, than if she had actually listened to, and
reciprocated, the vows of Edgar Vaughan; for, though the
illusion never quite deceived her, yet the remembrance was as
distinct as of a remembered interview. Those heavenly eyes

gazed for ever into her soul, which drank at them as at a
fountain, and was disquieted if reality threw a momentary
cloud between. She heard the melody of a voice breathing
sentiments with which her own chimed in like music. Oh,
happy, yet hapless girl! Thus to create the being whom she
loves, to endow him with all the attributes that were most
fascinating to her heart, and then to flit with the airy creature
into the realm of fantasy and moonlight, where dwelt his
dreamy kindred! For her lover wiled Sylvia away from earth,
which seemed strange, and dull, and darksome, and lured her
to a country where her spirit roamed in peaceful rapture,
deeming that it had found its home. Many, in their youth,
have visited that land of dreams, and wandered so long in its
enchanted groves, that, when banished thence, they feel like
exiles everywhere.

The dark-browed Edward Hamilton, like the villain of a
tale, would often glide through the romance wherein poor
Sylvia walked. Sometimes, at the most blissful moment of her
ecstasy, when the features of the miniature were pictured
brightest in the air, they would suddenly change, and darken,
and be transformed into his visage. And always, when such
change occurred, the intrusive visage wore that peculiar smile,
with which Hamilton had glanced at Sylvia.

Before the close of summer, it was told Sylvia Etherege,
that Vaughan had arrived from France, and that she would
meet him,—would meet, for the first time, the loved of
years,—that very evening. We will not tell how often and
how earnestly she gazed upon the miniature, thus endeavouring to prepare herself for the approaching interview, lest the
throbbing of her timorous heart should stifle the words of
welcome. While the twilight grew deeper and duskier, she sat
with Mrs. Grosvenor in an inner apartment, lighted only by
the softened gleam from an alabaster lamp, which was burning at a distance, on the centre-table of the drawing-room.
Never before had Sylph Etherege looked so sylph-like. She
had communed with a creature of imagination, till her own
loveliness seemed but the creation of a delicate and dreamy
fancy. Every vibration of her spirit was visible in her frame,
as she listened to the rattling of wheels and the tramp upon
the pavement, and deemed that even the breeze bore the

sound of her lover's footsteps, as if he trode upon the view-less air. Mrs. Grosvenor, too, while she watched the tremulous flow of Sylvia's feelings, was deeply moved; she looked uneasily at the agitated girl, and was about to speak, when the opening of the street door arrested the words upon her lips.

Footsteps ascended the staircase, with a confident and familiar tread, and some one entered the drawing-room. From the sofa where they sat, in the inner apartment, Mrs. Grosvenor and Sylvia could not discern the visiter.

"Sylph!" cried a voice. "Dearest Sylph! Where are you, sweet Sylph Etherege? Here is your Edgar Vaughan!"

But instead of answering, or rising to meet her lover,— who had greeted her by the sweet and fanciful name, which, appropriate as it was to her character, was known only to him,— Sylvia grasped Mrs. Grosvenor's arm, while her whole frame shook with the throbbing of her heart.

"Who is it?" gasped she. "Who calls me Sylph?"

Before Mrs. Grosvenor could reply, the stranger entered the room, bearing the lamp in his hand. Approaching the sofa, he displayed to Sylvia the features of Edward Hamilton, illuminated by that evil smile, from which his face derived so marked an individuality.

"Is not the miniature an admirable likeness?" inquired he.

Sylvia shuddered, but had not power to turn away her white face from his gaze. The miniature, which she had been holding in her hand, fell down upon the floor, where Hamilton, or Vaughan, set his foot upon it, and crushed the ivory counterfeit to fragments.

"There, my sweet Sylph!" he exclaimed. "It was I that created your phantom-lover, and now I annihilate him! Your dream is rudely broken. Awake, Sylph Etherege, awake to truth! I am the only Edgar Vaughan."

"We have gone too far, Edgar Vaughan," said Mrs. Grosvenor, catching Sylvia in her arms. The revengeful freak, which Vaughan's wounded vanity had suggested, had been countenanced by this lady, in the hope of curing Sylvia of her romantic notions, and reconciling her to the truths and realities of life. "Look at the poor child!" she continued. "I protest I tremble for the consequences!"

"Indeed, Madam!" replied Vaughan, sneeringly, as he threw the light of the lamp on Sylvia's closed eyes and marble features. "Well, my conscience is clear. I did but look into this delicate creature's heart; and with the pure fantasies that I found there, I made what seemed a man,—and the delusive shadow has wiled her away to Shadowland, and vanished there! It is no new tale. Many a sweet maid has shared the lot of poor Sylph Etherege!"

"And now, Edgar Vaughan," said Mrs. Grosvenor, as Sylvia's heart began faintly to throb again, "now try, in good earnest, to win back her love from the phantom which you conjured up. If you succeed, she will be the better her whole life long, for the lesson we have given her."

Whether the result of the lesson corresponded with Mrs. Grosvenor's hopes, may be gathered from the closing scene of our story. It had been made known to the fashionable world, that Edgar Vaughan had returned from France, and, under the assumed name of Edward Hamilton, had won the affections of the lovely girl, to whom he had been affianced in his boyhood. The nuptials were to take place at an early date. One evening, before the day of anticipated bliss arrived, Edgar Vaughan entered Mrs. Grosvenor's drawing-room, where he found that lady and Sylph Etherege.

"Only that Sylvia makes no complaint," remarked Mrs. Grosvenor, "I should apprehend that the town air is ill suited to her constitution. She was always, indeed, a delicate creature; but now she is a mere gossamer. Do but look at her! Did you ever imagine any thing so fragile?"

Vaughan was already attentively observing his mistress, who sat in a shadowy and moonlighted recess of the room, with her dreamy eyes fixed steadfastly upon his own. The bough of a tree was waving before the window, and sometimes enveloped her in the gloom of its shadow, into which she seemed to vanish.

"Yes," he said, to Mrs. Grosvenor. "I can scarcely deem her 'of the earth, earthy.' No wonder that I call her Sylph! Methinks she will fade into the moonlight, which falls upon her through the window. Or, in the open air, she might flit away upon the breeze, like a wreath of mist!"

Sylvia's eyes grew yet brighter. She waved her hand to Edgar Vaughan, with a gesture of ethereal triumph.

"Farewell!" she said. "I will neither fade into the moonlight, nor flit away upon the breeze. Yet you cannot keep me here!"

There was something in Sylvia's look and tones, that startled Mrs. Grosvenor with a terrible apprehension. But, as she was rushing towards the girl, Vaughan held her back.

"Stay!" cried he, with a strange smile of mockery and anguish. "Can our sweet Sylph be going to Heaven, to seek the original of the miniature?"

Peter Goldthwaite's Treasure

"And so, Peter, you won't even consider of the business?" said Mr. John Brown, buttoning his surtout over the snug rotundity of his person, and drawing on his gloves. "You positively refuse to let me have this crazy old house, and the land under and adjoining, at the price named?"

"Neither at that, nor treble the sum," responded the gaunt, grizzled, and threadbare Peter Goldthwaite. "The fact is, Mr. Brown, you must find another site for your brick block, and be content to leave my estate with the present owner. Next summer, I intend to put a splendid new mansion over the cellar of the old house."

"Pho, Peter!" cried Mr. Brown, as he opened the kitchen door; "content yourself with building castles in the air, where house-lots are cheaper than on earth, to say nothing of the cost of bricks and mortar. Such foundations are solid enough for your edifices; while this underneath us is just the thing for mine; and so we may both be suited. What say you, again?"

"Precisely what I said before, Mr. Brown," answered Peter Goldthwaite. "And, as for castles in the air, mine may not be as magnificent as that sort of architecture, but perhaps as substantial, Mr. Brown, as the very respectable brick block with dry-goods stores, tailors' shops, and banking-rooms on the lower floor, and lawyers' offices in the second story, which you are so anxious to substitute."

"And the cost, Peter, eh?" said Mr. Brown, as he withdrew, in something of a pet. "That, I suppose, will be provided for, off-hand, by drawing a check on Bubble Bank!"

John Brown and Peter Goldthwaite had been jointly known to the commercial world between twenty and thirty years before, under the firm of Goldthwaite and Brown; which copartnership, however, was speedily dissolved, by the natural incongruity of its constituent parts. Since that event, John Brown, with exactly the qualities of a thousand other John Browns, and by just such plodding methods as they used, had prospered wonderfully, and become one of the wealthiest John Browns on earth. Peter Goldthwaite, on the contrary, after innumerable schemes, which ought to have collected all the coin and paper currency of the country into his coffers, was as needy a gentleman as ever wore a patch upon his elbow. The contrast between him and his former partner may be briefly marked: for Brown never reckoned upon luck, yet always had it; while Peter made luck the main condition of his projects, and always missed it. While the means held out, his speculations had been magnificent, but were chiefly confined, of late years, to such small business as adventures in the lottery. Once, he had gone on a gold-gathering expedition, somewhere to the South, and ingeniously contrived to empty his pockets more thoroughly than ever; while others, doubtless, were filling theirs with native bullion by the handfull. More recently, he had expended a legacy of a thousand or two of dollars in purchasing Mexican scrip, and thereby became the proprietor of a province; which, however, so far as Peter could find out, was situated where he might have had an empire for the same money,—in the clouds. From a search after this valuable real estate, Peter returned so gaunt and threadbare, that, on reaching New England, the scarecrows in the corn-fields beckoned to him, as he passed by. "They did but flutter in the wind," quoth Peter Goldthwaite. No, Peter, they beckoned; for the scarecrows knew their brother!

At the period of our story, his whole visible income would not have paid the tax of the old mansion in which we find him. It was one of those rusty, moss-grown, many-peaked, wooden houses, which are scattered about the streets of our elder towns, with a beetle-browed second story projecting over the foundation, as if it frowned at the novelty around it. This old paternal edifice, needy as he was, and though, being centrally situated on the principal street of the town, it would have brought him a handsome sum, the sagacious Peter had his own reasons for never parting with, either by auction or private sale. There seemed, indeed, to be a fatality that connected him with his birth-place; for, often as he had stood on the verge of ruin, and standing there even now, he had not yet taken the step beyond it, which would have compelled him to surrender the house to his creditors. So here he dwelt with bad luck, till good should come.

Here, then, in his kitchen, the only room where a spark of fire took off the chill of a November evening, poor Peter Goldthwaite had just been visited by his rich old partner. At the close of their interview, Peter, with rather a mortified look, glanced downwards at his dress, parts of which appeared as ancient as the days of Goldthwaite and Brown. His upper garment was a mixed surtout, wofully faded, and patched with newer stuff on each elbow; beneath this, he wore a threadbare black coat, some of the silk buttons of which had been replaced with others of a different pattern; and, lastly, though he lacked not a pair of gray pantaloons, they were very shabby ones, and had been partially turned brown, by the frequent toasting of Peter's shins before a scanty fire. Peter's person was in keeping with his goodly apparel. Gray-headed, hollow-eyed, pale-cheeked, and lean-bodied, he was the perfect picture of a man who had fed on windy schemes and empty hopes, till he could neither live on such unwholesome trash, nor stomach more substantial food. But, withal, this Peter Goldthwaite, crack-brained simpleton as, perhaps, he was, might have cut a very brilliant figure in the world, had he employed his imagination in the airy business of poetry, instead of making it a demon of mischief in mercantile pursuits. After all, he was no bad fellow, but as harmless as a child, and as honest and honorable, and as much of the gentleman which nature meant him for, as an irregular life and depressed circumstances will permit any man to be.

As Peter stood on the uneven bricks of his hearth, looking round at the disconsolate old kitchen, his eyes began to kindle with the illumination of an enthusiasm that never long deserted him. He raised his hand, clenched it, and smote it energetically against the smoky panel over the fireplace.

"The time is come!" said he. "With such a treasure at command, it were folly to be a poor man any longer. To-morrow morning I will begin with the garret, nor desist till I have torn the house down!"

Deep in the chimney-corner, like a witch in a dark cavern, sat a little old woman, mending one of the two pairs of stockings wherewith Peter Goldthwaite kept his toes from being frost-bitten. As the feet were ragged past all darning, she had cut pieces out of a cast-off flannel petticoat, to make new soles. Tabitha Porter was an old maid, upwards of sixty years of age, fifty-five of which she had sat in that same chimney-corner, such being the length of time since Peter's grand-father had taken her from the almshouse. She had no friend but Peter, nor Peter any friend but Tabitha; so long as Peter might have a shelter for his own head, Tabitha would know where to shelter hers; or, being homeless elsewhere, she would take her master by the hand, and bring him to her native home, the almshouse. Should it ever be necessary, she loved him well enough to feed him with her last morsel, and clothe him with her under-petticoat. But Tabitha was a queer old woman, and, though never infected with Peter's flighti-ness, had become so accustomed to his freaks and follies, that she viewed them all as matters of course. Hearing him threaten to tear the house down, she looked quietly up from her work.

"Best leave the kitchen till the last, Mr. Peter," said she.

"The sooner we have it all down the better," said Peter Goldthwaite. "I am tired to death of living in this cold, dark, windy, smoky, creaking, groaning, dismal old house. I shall feel like a younger man, when we get into my splendid brick mansion, as, please Heaven, we shall, by this time next au-tumn. You shall have a room on the sunny side, old Tabby, finished and furnished as best may suit your own notions."

"I should like it pretty much such a room as this kitchen," answered Tabitha. "It will never be like home to me, till the chimney-corner gets as black with smoke as this; and that won't be these hundred years. How much do you mean to lay out on the house, Mr. Peter?"

"What is that to the purpose?" exclaimed Peter, loftily. "Did not my great-grand-uncle, Peter Goldthwaite, who died seventy years ago, and whose namesake I am, leave treasure enough to build twenty such?"

"I can't say but he did, Mr. Peter," said Tabitha, threading her needle.

Tabitha well understood, that Peter had reference to an im-mense hoard of the precious metals, which was said to exist somewhere in the cellar or walls, or under the floors, or in some concealed closet, or other out-of-the-way nook, of the old house. This wealth, according to tradition, had been ac-

cumulated by a former Peter Goldthwaite, whose character
seems to have borne a remarkable similitude to that of the
Peter of our story. Like him, he was a wild projector, seeking
to heap up gold by the bushel and the cart-load, instead of
scraping it together, coin by coin. Like Peter the second, too,
his projects had almost invariably failed, and, but for the magnificent success of the final one, would have left him with
hardly a coat and pair of breeches to his gaunt and grizzled
person. Reports were various, as to the nature of his fortunate
speculation; one intimating, that the ancient Peter had made
the gold by alchymy; another, that he had conjured it out of
people's pockets by the black art; and a third, still more unaccountable, that the devil had given him free access to the
old provincial treasury. It was affirmed, however, that some
secret impediment had debarred him from the enjoyment of
his riches, and that he had a motive for concealing them from
his heir, or, at any rate, had died without disclosing the place
of deposit. The present Peter's father had faith enough in the
story to cause the cellar to be dug over. Peter himself chose
to consider the legend as an indisputable truth, and, amid his
many troubles, had this one consolation, that, should all other
resources fail, he might build up his fortunes by tearing his
house down. Yet, unless he felt a lurking distrust of the
golden tale, it is difficult to account for his permitting the
paternal roof to stand so long, since he had never yet seen the
moment, when his predecessor's treasure would not have
found plenty of room in his own strong-box. But, now was
the crisis. Should he delay the search a little longer, the house
would pass from the lineal heir, and with it the vast heap of
gold, to remain in its burial-place, till the ruin of the aged
walls should discover it to strangers of a future generation.

"Yes!" cried Peter Goldthwaite, again; "to-morrow I will
set about it."

The deeper he looked at the matter, the more certain of
success grew Peter. His spirits were naturally so elastic, that,
even now, in the blasted autumn of his age, he could often
compete with the spring-time gayety of other people. Enlivened by his brightening prospects, he began to caper about
the kitchen like a hobgoblin, with the queerest antics of his
lean limbs, and gesticulations of his starved features. Nay, in

the exuberance of his feelings, he seized both of Tabitha's hands, and danced the old lady across the floor, till the oddity of her rheumatic motions set him into a roar of laughter, which was echoed back from the rooms and chambers, as if Peter Goldthwaite were laughing in every one. Finally, he bounded upward, almost out of sight, into the smoke that clouded the roof of the kitchen, and, alighting safely on the floor again, endeavoured to resume his customary gravity.

"To-morrow, at sunrise," he repeated, taking his lamp, to retire to bed, "I'll see whether this treasure be hid in the wall of the garret."

"And, as we're out of wood, Mr. Peter," said Tabitha, puffing and panting with her late gymnastics, "as fast as you tear the house down, I'll make a fire with the pieces."

Gorgeous, that night, were the dreams of Peter Goldthwaite! At one time, he was turning a ponderous key in an iron door, not unlike the door of a sepulchre, but which, being opened, disclosed a vault, heaped up with gold coin, as plentifully as golden corn in a granary. There were chased goblets, also, and tureens, salvers, dinner-dishes, and dish-covers, of gold, or silver-gilt, besides chains and other jewels, incalculably rich, though tarnished with the damps of the vault; for, of all the wealth that was irrevocably lost to man, whether buried in the earth, or sunken in the sea, Peter Goldthwaite had found it in this one treasure-place. Anon, he had returned to the old house, as poor as ever, and was received at the door, by the gaunt and grizzled figure of a man, whom he might have mistaken for himself, only that his garments were of a much elder fashion. But the house, without losing its former aspect, had been changed into a palace of the precious metals. The floors, walls, and ceilings, were of burnished silver; the doors, the window-frames, the cornices, the balustrades, and the steps of the staircase, of pure gold; and silver, with gold bottoms, were the chairs, and gold, standing on silver legs, the high chests of drawers, and silver the bedsteads, with blankets of woven gold, and sheets of silver tissue. The house had evidently been transmuted by a single touch; for it retained all the marks that Peter remembered, but in gold or silver, instead of wood; and the initials of his name, which, when a boy, he had cut in the wooden door-

post, remained as deep in the pillar of gold. A happy man
would have been Peter Goldthwaite, except for a certain ocular deception, which, whenever he glanced backward, caused
the house to darken from its glittering magnificence into the
sordid gloom of yesterday.

Up, betimes, rose Peter, seized an axe, hammer, and saw,
which he had placed by his bedside, and hied him to the garret. It was but scantily lighted up, as yet, by the frosty fragments of a sunbeam, which began to glimmer through the
almost opaque bull's eyes of the window. A moralizer might
find abundant themes for his speculative and impracticable
wisdom, in a garret. There is the limbo of departed fashions,
aged trifles of a day, and whatever was valuable only to one
generation of men, and which passed to the garret when that
generation passed to the grave, not for safe keeping, but to
be out of the way. Peter saw piles of yellow and musty ac-
count-books, in parchment covers, wherein creditors, long
dead and buried, had written the names of dead and buried
debtors, in ink now so faded, that their moss-grown tomb-
stones were more legible. He found old, moth-eaten garments, all in rags and tatters, or Peter would have put them
on. Here was a naked and rusty sword, not a sword of service, but a gentleman's small French rapier, which had never
left its scabbard till it lost it. Here were canes of twenty different sorts, but no gold-headed ones, and shoe-buckles of
various pattern and material, but not silver, nor set with precious stones. Here was a large box full of shoes, with high
heels and peaked toes. Here, on a shelf, were a multitude of
phials, half filled with old apothecary's stuff, which, when the
other half had done its business on Peter's ancestors, had
been brought hither from the death-chamber. Here,—not to
give a longer inventory of articles that will never be put up at
auction,—was the fragment of a full-length looking-glass,
which, by the dust and dimness of its surface, made the picture of these old things look older than the reality. When
Peter, not knowing that there was a mirror there, caught the
faint traces of his own figure, he partly imagined that the former Peter Goldthwaite had come back, either to assist or
impede his search for the hidden wealth. And at that moment
a strange notion glimmered through his brain, that he was

the identical Peter who had concealed the gold, and ought to know whereabout it lay. This, however, he had unaccountably forgotten.

"Well, Mr. Peter!" cried Tabitha, on the garret stairs. "Have you torn the house down enough to heat the tea-kettle?"

"Not yet, old Tabby," answered Peter; "but that's soon done,—as you shall see."

With the word in his mouth, he uplifted the axe, and laid about him so vigorously, that the dust flew, the boards crashed, and, in a twinkling, the old woman had an apron full of broken rubbish.

"We shall get our winter's wood cheap," quoth Tabitha.

The good work being thus commenced, Peter beat down all before him, smiting and hewing at the joists and timbers, unclenching spike-nails, ripping and tearing away boards, with a tremendous racket, from morning till night. He took care, however, to leave the outside shell of the house untouched, so that the neighbours might not suspect what was going on.

Never, in any of his vagaries, though each had made him happy while it lasted, had Peter been happier than now. Perhaps, after all, there was something in Peter Goldthwaite's turn of mind, which brought him an inward recompense for all the external evil that it caused. If he were poor, ill clad, even hungry, and exposed, as it were, to be utterly annihilated by a precipice of impending ruin, yet only his body remained in these miserable circumstances, while his aspiring soul enjoyed the sunshine of a bright futurity. It was his nature to be always young, and the tendency of his mode of life to keep him so. Gray hairs were nothing, no, nor wrinkles, nor infirmity; he might look old, indeed, and be somewhat disagreeably connected with a gaunt old figure, much the worse for wear; but the true, the essential Peter, was a young man of high hopes, just entering on the world. At the kindling of each new fire, his burnt-out youth rose afresh from the old embers and ashes. It rose exulting now. Having lived thus long,—not too long, but just to the right age,—a susceptible bachelor, with warm and tender dreams, he resolved, so soon as the hidden gold should flash to light, to go a wooing, and win the love of the fairest maid in town. What heart could resist him? Happy Peter Goldthwaite!

Every evening,—as Peter had long absented himself from his former lounging-places, at insurance offices, news-rooms, and bookstores, and as the honor of his company was seldom requested in private circles,—he and Tabitha used to sit down sociably by the kitchen hearth. This was always heaped plentifully with the rubbish of his day's labor. As the foundation of the fire, there would be a goodly sized backlog of red oak, which, after being sheltered from rain or damp above a century, still hissed with the heat, and distilled streams of water from each end, as if the tree had been cut down within a week or two. Next, there were large sticks, sound, black and heavy, which had lost the principle of decay, and were indestructible except by fire, wherein they glowed like red-hot bars of iron. On this solid basis, Tabitha would rear a lighter structure, composed of the splinters of door-panels, ornamented mouldings, and such quick combustibles, which caught like straw, and threw a brilliant blaze high up the spacious flue, making its sooty sides visible almost to the chimney-top. Meantime, the gloom of the old kitchen would be chased out of the cob-webbed corners, and away from the dusky cross-beams overhead, and driven nobody could tell whither, while Peter smiled like a gladsome man, and Tabitha seemed a picture of comfortable age. All this, of course, was but an emblem of the bright fortune, which the destruction of the house would shed upon its occupants.

While the dry pine was flaming and crackling, like an irregular discharge of fairy musketry, Peter sat looking and listening, in a pleasant state of excitement. But, when the brief blaze and uproar were succeeded by the dark red glow, the substantial heat, and the deep singing sound, which were to last throughout the evening, his humor became talkative. One night, for the hundredth time, he teased Tabitha to tell him something new about his great-grand-uncle.

"You have been sitting in that chimney-corner fifty-five years, old Tabby, and must have heard many a tradition about him," said Peter. "Did not you tell me, that, when you first came to the house, there was an old woman sitting where you sit now, who had been housekeeper to the famous Peter Goldthwaite?"

"So there was, Mr. Peter," answered Tabitha; "and she was near about a hundred years old. She used to say, that she and old Peter Goldthwaite had often spent a sociable evening by the kitchen fire,—pretty much as you and I are doing now, Mr. Peter."

"The old fellow must have resembled me in more points than one," said Peter, complacently, "or he never would have grown so rich. But, methinks, he might have invested the money better than he did,—no interest!—nothing but good security!—and the house to be torn down to come at it! What made him hide it so snug, Tabby?"

"Because he could not spend it," said Tabitha; "for, as often as he went to unlock the chest, the Old Scratch came behind and caught his arm. The money, they say, was paid Peter out of his purse; and he wanted Peter to give him a deed of this house and land, which Peter swore he would not do."

"Just as I swore to John Brown, my old partner," remarked Peter. "But this is all nonsense, Tabby! I don't believe the story."

"Well; it may not be just the truth," said Tabitha; "for some folks say, that Peter did make over the house to the Old Scratch; and that's the reason it has always been so unlucky to them that lived in it. And as soon as Peter had given him the deed, the chest flew open, and Peter caught up a handfull of the gold. But, lo and behold!—there was nothing in his fist, but a parcel of old rags."

"Hold your tongue, you silly old Tabby!" cried Peter, in great wrath. "They were as good golden guineas as ever bore the effigies of the king of England. It seems as if I could recollect the whole circumstance, and how I, or old Peter, or whoever it was, thrust in my hand, or his hand, and drew it out, all of a blaze with gold. Old rags, indeed!"

But it was not an old woman's legend that would discourage Peter Goldthwaite. All night long, he slept among pleasant dreams, and awoke at daylight with a joyous throb of the heart, which few are fortunate enough to feel, beyond their boyhood. Day after day, he labored hard, without wasting a moment, except at meal-times, when Tabitha summoned him to the pork and cabbage, or such other sustenance as she had picked up, or Providence had sent them. Being a truly pious man, Peter never failed to ask a blessing; if the food were none of the best, then so much the more earnestly, as it was more needed;—nor to return thanks, if the dinner had been scanty, yet for the good appetite, which was better than a sick stomach at a feast. Then did he hurry back to his toil, and, in a moment, was lost to sight in a cloud of dust from the old walls, though sufficiently perceptible to the ear, by the clatter which he raised in the midst of it. How enviable is the consciousness of being usefully employed! Nothing troubled Peter; or nothing but those phantoms of the mind, which seem like vague recollections, yet have also the aspect of presentiments. He often paused, with his axe uplifted in the air, and said to himself,—"Peter Goldthwaite, did you never strike this blow before?"—or,—"Peter, what need of tearing the whole house down? Think, a little while, and you will remember where the gold is hidden." Days and weeks passed on, however, without any remarkable discovery. Sometimes, indeed, a lean, gray rat peeped forth at the lean, gray man, wondering what devil had got into the old house, which had always been so peaceable till now. And, occasionally, Peter sympathized with the sorrows of a female mouse, who had brought five or six pretty, little, soft, and delicate young ones into the world, just in time to see them crushed by its ruin. But, as yet, no treasure!

By this time, Peter, being as determined as Fate, and as diligent as Time, had made an end with the uppermost regions, and got down to the second story, where he was busy in one of the front chambers. It had formerly been the state bedchamber, and was honored by tradition as the sleeping apartment of Governor Dudley, and many other eminent guests. The furniture was gone. There were remnants of faded and tattered paper-hangings, but larger spaces of bare wall, ornamented with charcoal sketches, chiefly of people's heads in profile. These being specimens of Peter's youthful genius, it went more to his heart to obliterate them, than if they had been pictures on a church wall by Michael Angelo. One sketch, however, and that the best one, affected him differently. It represented a ragged man, partly supporting himself on a spade, and bending his lean body over a hole in the earth, with one hand extended to grasp something that he had found. But, close behind him, with a fiendish laugh on his features, appeared a figure with horns, a tufted tail, and a cloven hoof.

"Avaunt, Satan!" cried Peter. "The man shall have his gold!"

Uplifting his axe, he hit the horned gentleman such a blow on the head, as not only demolished him, but the treasure-seeker also, and caused the whole scene to vanish like magic. Moreover, his axe broke quite through the plaster and laths, and discovered a cavity.

"Mercy on us, Mr. Peter, are you quarrelling with the Old Scratch?" said Tabitha, who was seeking some fuel to put under the dinner-pot.

Without answering the old woman, Peter broke down a further space of the wall, and laid open a small closet or cupboard, on one side of the fireplace, about breast-high from the ground. It contained nothing but a brass lamp, covered with verdigris, and a dusty piece of parchment. While Peter inspected the latter, Tabitha seized the lamp, and began to rub it with her apron.

"There is no use in rubbing it, Tabitha," said Peter. "It is not Aladdin's lamp, though I take it to be a token of as much luck. Look here, Tabby!"

Tabitha took the parchment, and held it close to her nose, which was saddled with a pair of iron-bound spectacles. But no sooner had she begun to puzzle over it, than she burst into a chuckling laugh, holding both her hands against her sides.

"You can't make a fool of the old woman!" cried she. "This is your own handwriting, Mr. Peter! the same as in the letter you sent me from Mexico."

"There is certainly a considerable resemblance," said Peter, again examining the parchment. "But you know yourself, Tabby, that this closet must have been plastered up before you came to the house, or I came into the world. No; this is old Peter Goldthwaite's writing; these columns of pounds, shillings, and pence, are his figures, denoting the amount of the treasure; and this, at the bottom, is, doubtless, a reference to the place of concealment. But the ink has either faded or peeled off, so that it is absolutely illegible. What a pity!"

"Well; this lamp is as good as new. That's some comfort," said Tabitha.

"A lamp!" thought Peter. "That indicates light on my researches."

For the present, Peter felt more inclined to ponder on this discovery, than to resume his labors. After Tabitha had gone down stairs, he stood poring over the parchment, at one of the front windows, which was so obscured with dust, that the sun could barely throw an uncertain shadow of the casement across the floor. Peter forced it open, and looked out upon the great street of the town, while the sun looked in at his old house. The air, though mild, and even warm, thrilled Peter, as with a dash of water.

It was the first day of the January thaw. The snow lay deep upon the house-tops, but was rapidly dissolving into millions of water-drops, which sparkled downwards through the sunshine, with the noise of a summer shower beneath the eaves. Along the street, the trodden snow was as hard and solid as a pavement of white marble, and had not yet grown moist, in the spring-like temperature. But, when Peter thrust forth his head, he saw that the inhabitants, if not the town, were already thawed out by this warm day, after two or three weeks of winter weather. It gladdened him,—a gladness with a sigh breathing through it,—to see the stream of ladies, gliding along the slippery side-walks, with their red cheeks set off by quilted hoods, boas, and sable capes, like roses amidst a new kind of foliage. The sleigh-bells jingled to and fro continually, sometimes announcing the arrival of a sleigh from Vermont, laden with the frozen bodies of porkers, or sheep, and perhaps a deer or two; sometimes, of a regular market-man, with chickens, geese, and turkeys, comprising the whole colony of a barn-yard; and sometimes, of a farmer and his dame, who had come to town partly for the ride, partly to go a shopping, and partly for the sale of some eggs and butter. This couple rode in an old-fashioned square sleigh, which had served them twenty winters, and stood twenty summers in the sun, beside their door. Now, a gentleman and lady skimmed the snow, in an elegant car, shaped somewhat like a cockle-shell. Now, a stage-sleigh, with its cloth curtains thrust aside to admit the sun, dashed rapidly down the street, whirling in and out among the vehicles that obstructed its passage. Now came, round a corner, the similitude of Noah's ark, on runners, being an immense open sleigh, with seats for fifty people, and drawn by a dozen horses. This spacious receptacle was populous with merry maids and merry bachelors, merry girls and boys, and merry old folks, all alive with fun, and grinning to the full width of their mouths. They kept up a buzz of babbling voices and low laughter, and sometimes burst into a deep, joyous shout, which the spectators answered with three cheers, while a gang of roguish boys let drive their snowballs right among the pleasure-party. The sleigh passed on, and, when concealed by a bend of the street, was still audible by a distant cry of merriment.

Never had Peter beheld a livelier scene than was constituted by all these accessories: the bright sun; the flashing water-drops; the gleaming snow; the cheerful multitude; the variety of rapid vehicles; and the jingle-jangle of merry bells, which made the heart dance to their music. Nothing dismal was to be seen, except that peaked piece of antiquity, Peter Goldthwaite's house, which might well look sad externally, since such a terrible consumption was preying on its insides. And Peter's gaunt figure, half visible in the projecting second story, was worthy of his house.

"Peter! How goes it, friend Peter?" cried a voice across the street, as Peter was drawing in his head. "Look out here, Peter!"

Peter looked, and saw his old partner, Mr. John Brown, on the opposite side-walk, portly and comfortable, with his furred cloak thrown open, disclosing a handsome surtout beneath. His voice had directed the attention of the whole town to Peter Goldthwaite's window, and to the dusty scarecrow which appeared at it.

"I say, Peter," cried Mr. Brown, again, "what the devil are you about there, that I hear such a racket, whenever I pass by? You are repairing the old house, I suppose,—making a new one of it,—eh?"

"Too late for that, I am afraid, Mr. Brown," replied Peter.

"If I make it new, it will be new inside and out, from the cellar upwards."

"Had not you better let me take the job?" said Mr. Brown, significantly.

"Not yet!" answered Peter, hastily shutting the window; for, ever since he had been in search of the treasure, he hated to have people stare at him.

As he drew back, ashamed of his outward poverty, yet proud of the secret wealth within his grasp, a haughty smile shone out on Peter's visage, with precisely the effect of the dim sunbeams in the squalid chamber. He endeavoured to assume such a mien as his ancestor had probably worn, when he gloried in the building of a strong house for a home to many generations of his posterity. But the chamber was very dark to his snow-dazzled eyes, and very dismal too, in contrast with the living scene that he had just looked upon. His brief glimpse into the street had given him a forcible impression of the manner in which the world kept itself cheerful and prosperous, by social pleasures and an intercourse of business, while he, in seclusion, was pursuing an object that might possibly be a phantasm, by a method which most people would call madness. It is one great advantage of a gregarious mode of life, that each person rectifies his mind by other minds, and squares his conduct to that of his neighbours, so as seldom to be lost in eccentricity. Peter Goldthwaite had exposed himself to this influence, by merely looking out of the window. For a while, he doubted whether there were any hidden chest of gold, and, in that case, whether it was so exceedingly wise to tear the house down, only to be convinced of its non-existence.

But this was momentary. Peter, the Destroyer, resumed the task which fate had assigned him, nor faltered again, till it was accomplished. In the course of his search, he met with many things that are usually found in the ruins of an old house, and also with some that are not. What seemed most to the purpose, was a rusty key, which had been thrust into a chink of the wall, with a wooden label appended to the handle, bearing the initials, P. G. Another singular discovery was that of a bottle of wine, walled up in an old oven. A tradition ran in the family, that Peter's grandfather, a jovial officer in

the old French war, had set aside many dozens of the precious
liquor, for the benefit of topers then unborn. Peter needed no
cordial to sustain his hopes, and therefore kept the wine to
gladden his success. Many halfpence did he pick up, that had
been lost through the cracks of the floor, and some few Spanish coins, and the half of a broken sixpence, which had doubtless been a love-token. There was likewise a silver coronation
medal of George the Third. But, old Peter Goldthwaite's
strong-box fled from one dark corner to another, or otherwise
eluded the second Peter's clutches, till, should he seek much
further, he must burrow into the earth.

We will not follow him in his triumphant progress, step by
step. Suffice it, that Peter worked like a steam engine, and
finished, in that one winter, the job, which all the former inhabitants of the house, with time and the elements to aid
them, had only half done in a century. Except the kitchen,
every room and chamber was now gutted. The house was
nothing but a shell,—the apparition of a house,—as unreal
as the painted edifices of a theatre. It was like the perfect rind
of a great cheese, in which a mouse had dwelt and nibbled,
till it was a cheese no more. And Peter was the mouse.

What Peter had torn down, Tabitha had burnt up: for she
wisely considered, that, without a house, they should need no
wood to warm it; and therefore economy was nonsense. Thus
the whole house might be said to have dissolved in smoke,
and flown up among the clouds, through the great black flue
of the kitchen chimney. It was an admirable parallel to the
feat of the man who jumped down his own throat.

On the night between the last day of winter and the first of
spring, every chink and cranny had been ransacked, except
within the precincts of the kitchen. This fated evening was an
ugly one. A snow-storm had set in some hours before, and
was still driven and tossed about the atmosphere by a real
hurricane, which fought against the house, as if the prince of
the air, in person, were putting the final stroke to Peter's labors. The framework being so much weakened, and the inward props removed, it would have been no marvel, if, in
some stronger wrestle of the blast, the rotten walls of the edifice, and all the peaked roofs, had come crashing down upon
the owner's head. He, however, was careless of the peril, but

as wild and restless as the night itself, or as the flame that quivered up the chimney, at each roar of the tempestuous wind.

"The wine, Tabitha!" he cried. "My grandfather's rich old wine! We will drink it now!"

Tabitha arose from her smoke-blackened bench in the chimney-corner, and placed the bottle before Peter, close beside the old brass lamp, which had likewise been the prize of his researches. Peter held it before his eyes, and looking through the liquid medium, beheld the kitchen illuminated with a golden glory, which also enveloped Tabitha, and gilded her silver hair, and converted her mean garments into robes of queenly splendor. It reminded him of his golden dream.

"Mr. Peter," remarked Tabitha, "must the wine be drunk before the money is found?"

"The money *is* found!" exclaimed Peter, with a sort of fierceness. "The chest is within my reach. I will not sleep, till I have turned this key in the rusty lock. But, first of all, let us drink!"

There being no corkscrew in the house, he smote the neck of the bottle with old Peter Goldthwaite's rusty key, and decapitated the sealed cork at a single blow. He then filled two little china teacups, which Tabitha had brought from the cupboard. So clear and brilliant was this aged wine, that it shone within the cups, and rendered the sprig of scarlet flowers, at the bottom of each, more distinctly visible, than when there had been no wine there. Its rich and delicate perfume wasted itself round the kitchen.

"Drink, Tabitha!" cried Peter. "Blessings on the honest old fellow, who set aside this good liquor for you and me! And here's to Peter Goldthwaite's memory!"

"And good cause have we to remember him," quoth Tabitha, as she drank.

How many years, and through what changes of fortune, and various calamity, had that bottle hoarded up its effervescent joy, to be quaffed at last by two such boon companions! A portion of the happiness of a former age had been kept for them, and was now set free, in a crowd of rejoicing visions, to sport amid the storm and desolation of the present time.

Until they have finished the bottle, we must turn our eyes elsewhere.

It so chanced, that, on this stormy night, Mr. John Brown found himself ill at ease, in his wire-cushioned arm-chair, by the glowing grate of anthracite, which heated his handsome parlour. He was naturally a good sort of man, and kind and pitiful, whenever the misfortunes of others happened to reach his heart through the padded vest of his own prosperity. This evening, he had thought much about his old partner, Peter Goldthwaite, his strange vagaries, and continual ill luck, the poverty of his dwelling, at Mr. Brown's last visit, and Peter's crazed and haggard aspect, when he had talked with him at the window.

"Poor fellow!" thought Mr. John Brown. "Poor, crackbrained Peter Goldthwaite! For old acquaintance' sake, I ought to have taken care that he was comfortable, this rough winter."

These feelings grew so powerful, that, in spite of the inclement weather, he resolved to visit Peter Goldthwaite immediately. The strength of the impulse was really singular. Every shriek of the blast seemed a summons, or would have seemed so, had Mr. Brown been accustomed to hear the echoes of his own fancy in the wind. Much amazed at such active benevolence, he huddled himself in his cloak, muffled his throat and ears in comforters and handkerchiefs, and, thus fortified, bade defiance to the tempest. But, the powers of the air had rather the best of the battle. Mr. Brown was just weathering the corner, by Peter Goldthwaite's house, when the hurricane caught him off his feet, tossed him face downward into a snow-bank, and proceeded to bury his protuberant part beneath fresh drifts. There seemed little hope of his re-appearance, earlier than the next thaw. At the same moment, his hat was snatched away, and whirled aloft into some far distant region, whence no tidings have as yet returned.

Nevertheless Mr. Brown contrived to burrow a passage through the snow-drift, and, with his bare head bent against the storm, floundered onward to Peter's door. There was such a creaking, and groaning, and rattling, and such an ominous shaking throughout the crazy edifice, that the loudest rap would have been inaudible to those within. He therefore entered, without ceremony, and groped his way to the kitchen.

His intrusion, even there, was unnoticed. Peter and Tabitha stood with their backs to the door, stooping over a large chest, which, apparently, they had just dragged from a cavity, or concealed closet, on the left side of the chimney. By the lamp in the old woman's hand, Mr. Brown saw that the chest was barred and clamped with iron, strengthened with iron plates, and studded with iron nails, so as to be a fit receptacle in which the wealth of one century might be hoarded up for the wants of another. Peter Goldthwaite was inserting a key into the lock.

"Oh, Tabitha!" cried he, with tremulous rapture, "how shall I endure the effulgence? The gold!—the bright, bright gold! Methinks I can remember my last glance at it, just as the iron-plated lid fell down. And ever since, being seventy years, it has been blazing in secret, and gathering its splendor against this glorious moment! It will flash upon us like the noon-day sun!"

"Then shade your eyes, Mr. Peter!" said Tabitha, with somewhat less patience than usual. "But, for mercy's sake, do turn the key!"

And, with a strong effort of both hands, Peter did force the rusty key through the intricacies of the rusty lock. Mr. Brown, in the mean time, had drawn near, and thrust his eager visage between those of the other two, at the instant that Peter threw up the lid. No sudden blaze illuminated the kitchen.

"What's here?" exclaimed Tabitha, adjusting her spectacles, and holding the lamp over the open chest. "Old Peter Goldthwaite's hoard of old rags!"

"Pretty much so, Tabby," said Mr. Brown, lifting a handfull of the treasure.

Oh, what a ghost of dead and buried wealth had Peter Goldthwaite raised, to scare himself out of his scanty wits withal! Here was the semblance of an incalculable sum, enough to purchase the whole town, and build every street anew, but which, vast as it was, no sane man would have given a solid sixpence for. What then, in sober earnest, were the delusive treasures of the chest? Why, here were old provincial bills of credit, and treasury notes, and bills of land-banks, and all other bubbles of the sort, from the first issue, above a century and a half ago, down nearly to the Revolution. Bills of a thousand pounds were intermixed with parchment pennies, and worth no more than they.

"And this, then, is old Peter Goldthwaite's treasure!" said John Brown. "Your namesake, Peter, was something like yourself; and, when the provincial currency had depreciated fifty or seventy-five per cent., he bought it up, in expectation of a rise. I have heard my grandfather say, that old Peter gave his father a mortgage of this very house and land, to raise cash for his silly project. But the currency kept sinking, till nobody would take it as a gift; and there was old Peter Goldthwaite, like Peter the second, with thousands in his strong-box, and hardly a coat to his back. He went mad upon the strength of it. But, never mind, Peter! It is just the sort of capital for building castles in the air."

"The house will be down about our ears!" cried Tabitha, as the wind shook it with increasing violence.

"Let it fall!" said Peter, folding his arms, as he seated himself upon the chest.

"No, no, my old friend Peter," said John Brown. "I have house-room for you and Tabby, and a safe vault for the chest of treasure. To-morrow we will try to come to an agreement about the sale of this old house. Real estate is well up, and I could afford you a pretty handsome price."

"And I," observed Peter Goldthwaite, with reviving spirits, "have a plan for laying out the cash to great advantage."

"Why, as to that," muttered John Brown to himself, "we must apply to the next court for a guardian to take care of the solid cash; and if Peter insists upon speculating, he may do it, to his heart's content, with old PETER GOLDTHWAITE'S TREASURE."

Endicott and the Red Cross

A T noon of an autumnal day, more than two centuries ago, the English colors were displayed by the standard-bearer of the Salem trainband, which had mustered for martial exercise under the orders of John Endicott. It was a period, when the religious exiles were accustomed often to buckle on their armour, and practise the handling of their weapons of war. Since the first settlement of New England, its prospects had never been so dismal. The dissensions between Charles the First and his subjects were then, and for several years afterwards, confined to the floor of Parliament. The measures of the King and ministry were rendered more tyrannically violent by an opposition, which had not yet acquired sufficient confidence in its own strength, to resist royal injustice with the sword. The bigoted and haughty primate, Laud, Archbishop of Canterbury, controlled the religious affairs of the realm, and was consequently invested with powers which might have wrought the utter ruin of the two Puritan colonies, Plymouth and Massachusetts. There is evidence on record, that our forefathers perceived their danger, but were resolved that their infant country should not fall without a struggle, even beneath the giant strength of the King's right arm.

Such was the aspect of the times, when the folds of the English banner, with the Red Cross in its field, were flung out over a company of Puritans. Their leader, the famous Endicott, was a man of stern and resolute countenance, the effect of which was heightened by a grizzled beard that swept the upper portion of his breastplate. This piece of armour was so highly polished, that the whole surrounding scene had its image in the glittering steel. The central object, in the mirrored picture, was an edifice of humble architecture, with neither steeple nor bell to proclaim it,—what nevertheless it was,—the house of prayer. A token of the perils of the wilderness was seen in the grim head of a wolf, which had just been slain within the precincts of the town, and, according to the regular mode of claiming the bounty, was nailed on the

porch of the meetinghouse. The blood was still plashing on
the door-step. There happened to be visible, at the same
noontide hour, so many other characteristics of the times and
manners of the Puritans, that we must endeavour to represent
them in a sketch, though far less vividly than they were reflected in the polished breastplate of John Endicott.

In close vicinity to the sacred edifice appeared that important engine of Puritanic authority, the whipping-post,—with
the soil around it well trodden by the feet of evil-doers, who
had there been disciplined. At one corner of the meeting-
house was the pillory, and at the other the stocks; and, by a
singular good fortune for our sketch, the head of an Episcopalian and suspected Catholic was grotesquely encased in the
former machine; while a fellow-criminal, who had boisterously quaffed a health to the King, was confined by the legs
in the latter. Side by side, on the meetinghouse steps, stood
a male and a female figure. The man was a tall, lean, haggard
personification of fanaticism, bearing on his breast this
label,—A WANTON GOSPELLER,—which betokened that he
had dared to give interpretations of Holy Writ, unsanctioned
by the infallible judgment of the civil and religious rulers. His
aspect showed no lack of zeal to maintain his heterodoxies,
even at the stake. The woman wore a cleft stick on her
tongue, in appropriate retribution for having wagged that unruly member against the elders of the church; and her countenance and gestures gave much cause to apprehend, that, the
moment the stick should be removed, a repetition of the offence would demand new ingenuity in chastising it.

The abovementioned individuals had been sentenced to undergo their various modes of ignominy, for the space of one
hour at noonday. But among the crowd were several, whose
punishment would be life-long; some, whose ears had been
cropt, like those of puppy-dogs; others, whose cheeks had
been branded with the initials of their misdemeanors; one,
with his nostrils slit and seared; and another, with a halter
about his neck, which he was forbidden ever to take off, or
to conceal beneath his garments. Methinks he must have been
grievously tempted to affix the other end of the rope to some
convenient beam or bough. There was likewise a young
woman, with no mean share of beauty, whose doom it was

to wear the letter A on the breast of her gown, in the eyes of all the world and her own children. And even her own children knew what that initial signified. Sporting with her infamy, the lost and desperate creature had embroidered the fatal token in scarlet cloth, with golden thread, and the nicest art of needle-work; so that the capital A might have been thought to mean Admirable, or any thing rather than Adulteress.

Let not the reader argue, from any of these evidences of iniquity, that the times of the Puritans were more vicious than our own, when, as we pass along the very street of this sketch, we discern no badge of infamy on man or woman. It was the policy of our ancestors to search out even the most secret sins, and expose them to shame, without fear or favor, in the broadest light of the noonday sun. Were such the custom now, perchance we might find materials for a no less piquant sketch than the above.

Except the malefactors whom we have described, and the diseased or infirm persons, the whole male population of the town, between sixteen years and sixty, were seen in the ranks of the trainband. A few stately savages, in all the pomp and dignity of the primeval Indian, stood gazing at the spectacle. Their flint-headed arrows were but childish weapons, compared with the matchlocks of the Puritans, and would have rattled harmlessly against the steel caps and hammered iron breastplates, which enclosed each soldier in an individual fortress. The valiant John Endicott glanced with an eye of pride at his sturdy followers, and prepared to renew the martial toils of the day.

"Come, my stout hearts!" quoth he, drawing his sword. "Let us show these poor heathen that we can handle our weapons like men of might. Well for them, if they put us not to prove it in earnest!"

The iron-breasted company straightened their line, and each man drew the heavy butt of his matchlock close to his left foot, thus awaiting the orders of the captain. But, as Endicott glanced right and left along the front, he discovered a personage at some little distance, with whom it behoved him to hold a parley. It was an elderly gentleman, wearing a black cloak and band, and a high-crowned hat, beneath which was a velvet skull-cap, the whole being the garb of a Puritan minister. This reverend person bore a staff, which seemed to have been recently cut in the forest, and his shoes were bemired, as if he had been travelling on foot through the swamps of the wilderness. His aspect was perfectly that of a pilgrim, heightened also by an apostolic dignity. Just as Endicott perceived him, he laid aside his staff, and stooped to drink at a bubbling fountain, which gushed into the sunshine about a score of yards from the corner of the meetinghouse. But, ere the good man drank, he turned his face heavenward in thankfulness, and then, holding back his gray beard with one hand, he scooped up his simple draught in the hollow of the other.

"What, ho! good Mr. Williams," shouted Endicott. "You are welcome back again to our town of peace. How does our worthy Governor Winthrop? And what news from Boston?"

"The Governor hath his health, worshipful Sir," answered Roger Williams, now resuming his staff, and drawing near. "And, for the news, here is a letter, which, knowing I was to travel hitherward to-day, his Excellency committed to my charge. Belike it contains tidings of much import; for a ship arrived yesterday from England."

Mr. Williams, the minister of Salem, and of course known to all the spectators, had now reached the spot where Endicott was standing under the banner of his company, and put the Governor's epistle into his hand. The broad seal was impressed with Winthrop's coat of arms. Endicott hastily unclosed the letter, and began to read; while, as his eye passed down the page, a wrathful change came over his manly countenance. The blood glowed through it, till it seemed to be kindling with an internal heat; nor was it unnatural to suppose that his breastplate would likewise become red-hot, with the angry fire of the bosom which it covered. Arriving at the conclusion, he shook the letter fiercely in his hand, so that it rustled as loud as the flag above his head.

"Black tidings these, Mr. Williams," said he; "blacker never came to New England. Doubtless you know their purport?"

"Yea, truly," replied Roger Williams; "for the Governor consulted, respecting this matter, with my brethren in the ministry at Boston; and my opinion was likewise asked. And his Excellency entreats you by me, that the news be not suddenly noised abroad, lest the people be stirred up unto some outbreak, and thereby give the King and the Archbishop a handle against us."

"The Governor is a wise man,—a wise man, and a meek and moderate," said Endicott, setting his teeth grimly. "Nevertheless, I must do according to my own best judgment. There is neither man, woman, nor child in New England, but has a concern as dear as life in these tidings; and, if John Endicott's voice be loud enough, man, woman, and child shall hear them. Soldiers, wheel into a hollow square! Ho, good people! Here are news for one and all of you."

The soldiers closed in around their captain; and he and Roger Williams stood together under the banner of the Red Cross; while the women and the aged men pressed forward, and the mothers held up their children to look Endicott in the face. A few taps of the drum gave signal for silence and attention.

"Fellow-soldiers,—fellow-exiles," began Endicott, speaking under strong excitement, yet powerfully restraining it, "wherefore did ye leave your native country? Wherefore, I say, have we left the green and fertile fields, the cottages, or, perchance, the old gray halls, where we were born and bred, the church-yards where our forefathers lie buried? Wherefore have we come hither to set up our own tombstones in a wilderness? A howling wilderness it is! The wolf and the bear meet us within halloo of our dwellings. The savage lieth in wait for us in the dismal shadow of the woods. The stubborn roots of the trees break our ploughshares, when we would till the earth. Our children cry for bread, and we must dig in the sands of the sea-shore to satisfy them. Wherefore, I say again, have we sought this country of a rugged soil and wintry sky? Was it not for the enjoyment of our civil rights? Was it not for liberty to worship God according to our conscience?"

"Call you this liberty of conscience?" interrupted a voice on the steps of the meetinghouse.

It was the Wanton Gospeller. A sad and quiet smile flitted across the mild visage of Roger Williams. But Endicott, in the excitement of the moment, shook his sword wrathfully at the culprit,—an ominous gesture from a man like him.

"What hast thou to do with conscience, thou knave?" cried

he. "I said, liberty to worship God, not license to profane and ridicule him. Break not in upon my speech; or I will lay thee neck and heels till this time to-morrow! Hearken to me, friends, nor heed that accursed rhapsodist. As I was saying, we have sacrificed all things, and have come to a land whereof the old world hath scarcely heard, that we might make a new world unto ourselves, and painfully seek a path from hence to Heaven. But what think ye now? This son of a Scotch tyrant,—this grandson of a papistical and adulterous Scotch woman, whose death proved that a golden crown doth not always save an anointed head from the block—"

"Nay, brother, nay," interposed Mr. Williams; "thy words are not meet for a secret chamber, far less for a public street."

"Hold thy peace, Roger Williams!" answered Endicott, imperiously. "My spirit is wiser than thine, for the business now in hand. I tell ye, fellow-exiles, that Charles of England, and Laud, our bitterest persecutor, arch-priest of Canterbury, are resolute to pursue us even hither. They are taking counsel, saith this letter, to send over a governor-general, in whose breast shall be deposited all the law and equity of the land. They are minded, also, to establish the idolatrous forms of English Episcopacy; so that, when Laud shall kiss the Pope's toe, as cardinal of Rome, he may deliver New England, bound hand and foot, into the power of his master!"

A deep groan from the auditors,—a sound of wrath, as well as fear and sorrow,—responded to this intelligence.

"Look ye to it, brethren," resumed Endicott, with increasing energy. "If this king and this arch-prelate have their will, we shall briefly behold a cross on the spire of this tabernacle which we have builded, and a high altar within its walls, with wax tapers burning round it at noonday. We shall hear the sacring-bell, and the voices of the Romish priests saying the mass. But think ye, Christian men, that these abominations may be suffered without a sword drawn? without a shot fired? without blood spilt, yea, on the very stairs of the pulpit? No,—be ye strong of hand, and stout of heart! Here we stand on our own soil, which we have bought with our goods, which we have won with our swords, which we have cleared with our axes, which we have tilled with the sweat of our brows, which we have sanctified with our prayers to the

God that brought us hither! Who shall enslave us here? What have we to do with this mitred prelate,—with this crowned king? What have we to do with England?"

Endicott gazed round at the excited countenances of the people, now full of his own spirit, and then turned suddenly to the standard-bearer, who stood close behind him.

"Officer, lower your banner!" said he.

The officer obeyed; and, brandishing his sword, Endicott thrust it through the cloth, and, with his left hand, rent the Red Cross completely out of the banner. He then waved the tattered ensign above his head.

"Sacrilegious wretch!" cried the high-churchman in the pillory, unable longer to restrain himself; "thou hast rejected the symbol of our holy religion!"

"Treason, treason!" roared the royalist in the stocks. "He hath defaced the King's banner!"

"Before God and man, I will avouch the deed," answered Endicott. "Beat a flourish, drummer!—shout, soldiers and people!—in honor of the ensign of New England. Neither Pope nor Tyrant hath part in it now!"

With a cry of triumph, the people gave their sanction to one of the boldest exploits which our history records. And, for ever honored be the name of Endicott! We look back through the mist of ages, and recognize, in the rending of the Red Cross from New England's banner, the first omen of that deliverance which our fathers consummated, after the bones of the stern Puritan had lain more than a century in the dust.

Night Sketches

BENEATH AN UMBRELLA

PLEASANT is a rainy winter's day, within doors! The best study for such a day, or the best amusement,—call it which you will,—is a book of travels, describing scenes the most unlike that sombre one, which is mistily presented through the windows. I have experienced, that fancy is then most successful in imparting distinct shapes and vivid colors to the objects which the author has spread upon his page, and that his words become magic spells to summon up a thousand varied pictures. Strange landscapes glimmer through the familiar walls of the room, and outlandish figures thrust themselves almost within the sacred precincts of the hearth. Small as my chamber is, it has space enough to contain the ocean-like circumference of an Arabian desert, its parched sands tracked by the long line of a caravan, with the camels patiently journeying through the heavy sunshine. Though my ceiling be not lofty, yet I can pile up the mountains of Central Asia beneath it, till their summits shine far above the clouds of the middle atmosphere. And, with my humble means, a wealth that is not taxable, I can transport hither the magnificent merchandise of an Oriental bazaar, and call a crowd of purchasers from distant countries, to pay a fair profit for the precious articles which are displayed on all sides. True it is, however, that, amid the bustle of traffic, or whatever else may seem to be going on around me, the rain-drops will occasionally be heard to patter against my window-panes, which look forth upon one of the quietest streets in a New England town. After a time, too, the visions vanish, and will not appear again at my bidding. Then, it being nightfall, a gloomy sense of unreality depresses my spirits, and impels me to venture out, before the clock shall strike bedtime, to satisfy myself that the world is not entirely made up of such shadowy materials, as have busied me throughout the day. A dreamer may dwell so long among fantasies, that the things without him will seem as unreal as those within.

When eve has fairly set in, therefore, I sally forth, tightly buttoning my shaggy over-coat, and hoisting my umbrella, the silken dome of which immediately resounds with the heavy drumming of the invisible rain-drops. Pausing on the lowest door-step, I contrast the warmth and cheerfulness of my deserted fireside, with the drear obscurity and chill discomfort, into which I am about to plunge. Now come fearful auguries, innumerable as the drops of rain. Did not my manhood cry shame upon me, I should turn back within doors, resume my elbow-chair, my slippers, and my book, pass such an evening of sluggish enjoyment as the day has been, and go to bed inglorious. The same shivering reluctance, no doubt, has quelled, for a moment, the adventurous spirit of many a traveller, when his feet, which were destined to measure the earth around, were leaving their last tracks in the home-paths.

In my own case, poor human nature may be allowed a few misgivings. I look upward, and discern no sky, not even an unfathomable void, but only a black, impenetrable nothingness, as though heaven and all its lights were blotted from the system of the universe. It is as if Nature were dead, and the world had put on black, and the clouds were weeping for her. With their tears upon my cheek, I turn my eyes earthward, but find little consolation here below. A lamp is burning dimly at the distant corner, and throws just enough of light along the street, to show, and exaggerate by so faintly showing, the perils and difficulties which beset my path. Yonder dingily white remnant of a huge snowbank,—which will yet cumber the sidewalk till the latter days of March,—over or through that wintry waste must I stride onward. Beyond, lies a certain Slough of Despond, a concoction of mud and liquid filth, ankle-deep, leg-deep, neck-deep,—in a word, of unknown bottom,—on which the lamp-light does not even glimmer, but which I have occasionally watched, in the gradual growth of its horrors, from morn till nightfall. Should I flounder into its depths, farewell to upper earth! And hark! how roughly resounds the roaring of a stream, the turbulent career of which is partially reddened by the gleam of the lamp, but elsewhere brawls noisily through the densest gloom. Oh, should I be swept away in fording that impetuous and unclean torrent, the coroner will have a job with an

unfortunate gentleman, who would fain end his troubles anywhere but in a mud-puddle!

Pshaw! I will linger not another instant at arm's length
from these dim terrors, which grow more obscurely formidable, the longer I delay to grapple with them. Now for the
onset! And lo! with little damage, save a dash of rain in the
face and breast, a splash of mud high up the pantaloons, and
the left boot full of ice-cold water, behold me at the corner of
the street. The lamp throws down a circle of red light around
me; and, twinkling onward from corner to corner, I discern
other beacons, marshalling my way to a brighter scene. But
this is a lonesome and dreary spot. The tall edifices bid
gloomy defiance to the storm, with their blinds all closed,
even as a man winks when he faces a spattering gust. How
loudly tinkles the collected rain down the tin spouts! The
puffs of wind are boisterous, and seem to assail me from various quarters at once. I have often observed that this corner
is a haunt and loitering-place for those winds which have no
work to do upon the deep, dashing ships against our iron-
bound shores; nor in the forest, tearing up the sylvan giants
with half a rood of soil at their vast roots. Here they amuse
themselves with lesser freaks of mischief. See, at this moment,
how they assail yonder poor woman, who is passing just
within the verge of the lamp-light! One blast struggles for her
umbrella, and turns it wrong side outward; another whisks
the cape of her cloak across her eyes; while a third takes most
unwarrantable liberties with the lower part of her attire. Happily, the good dame is no gossamer, but a figure of rotundity
and fleshly substance; else would these aërial tormentors whirl
her aloft, like a witch upon a broomstick, and set her down,
doubtless, in the filthiest kennel hereabout.

From hence I tread upon firm pavements into the centre of
the town. Here there is almost as brilliant an illumination as
when some great victory has been won, either on the battle-
field or at the polls. Two rows of shops, with windows down
nearly to the ground, cast a glow from side to side, while the
black night hangs overhead like a canopy, and thus keeps the
splendor from diffusing itself away. The wet sidewalks gleam
with a broad sheet of red light. The rain-drops glitter, as if
the sky were pouring down rubies. The spouts gush with fire.

Methinks the scene is an emblem of the deceptive glare, which mortals throw around their footsteps in the moral world, thus bedazzling themselves, till they forget the impenetrable obscurity that hems them in, and that can be dispelled only by radiance from above. And, after all, it is a cheerless scene, and cheerless are the wanderers in it. Here comes one who has so long been familiar with tempestuous weather, that he takes the bluster of the storm for a friendly greeting, as if it should say, "How fare ye, brother?" He is a retired sea-captain, wrapped in some nameless garment of the pea-jacket order, and is now laying his course towards the Marine Insurance Office, there to spin yarns of gale and ship-wreck, with a crew of old sea-dogs like himself. The blast will put in its word among their hoarse voices, and be understood by all of them. Next I meet an unhappy slip-shod gentleman, with a cloak flung hastily over his shoulders, running a race with boisterous winds, and striving to glide between the drops of rain. Some domestic emergency or other has blown this miserable man from his warm fireside, in quest of a doctor! See that little vagabond,—how carelessly he has taken his stand right underneath a spout, while staring at some object of curiosity in a shop-window! Surely the rain is his native element; he must have fallen with it from the clouds, as frogs are supposed to do.

Here is a picture, and a pretty one. A young man and a girl, both enveloped in cloaks, and huddled beneath the scanty protection of a cotton umbrella. She wears rubber over-shoes; but he is in his dancing-pumps; and they are on their way, no doubt, to some cotillon-party, or subscription-ball at a dollar a head, refreshments included. Thus they struggle against the gloomy tempest, lured onward by a vision of festal splendor. But, ah! a most lamentable disaster. Bewildered by the red, blue, and yellow meteors in an apothecary's window, they have stepped upon a slippery remnant of ice, and are precipitated into a confluence of swollen floods, at the corner of two streets. Luckless lovers! Were it my nature to be other than a looker-on in life, I would attempt your rescue. Since that may not be, I vow, should you be drowned, to weave such a pathetic story of your fate, as shall call forth tears enough to drown you both anew. Do ye touch bottom, my young friends? Yes; they emerge like a water-nymph and a river-deity, and paddle hand-in-hand out of the depths of the dark pool. They hurry homeward, dripping, disconsolate, abashed, but with love too warm to be chilled by the cold water. They have stood a test which proves too strong for many. Faithful, though over head and ears in trouble!

Onward I go, deriving a sympathetic joy or sorrow from the varied aspect of mortal affairs, even as my figure catches a gleam from the lighted windows, or is blackened by an interval of darkness. Not that mine is altogether a chameleon spirit, with no hue of its own. Now I pass into a more retired street, where the dwellings of wealth and poverty are intermingled, presenting a range of strongly contrasted pictures. Here, too, may be found the golden mean. Through yonder casement I discern a family circle,—the grandmother, the parents, and the children,—all flickering, shadow-like, in the glow of a wood-fire. Bluster, fierce blast, and beat, thou wintry rain, against the window-panes! Ye cannot damp the enjoyment of that fireside. Surely my fate is hard, that I should be wandering homeless here, taking to my bosom night, and storm, and solitude, instead of wife and children. Peace, murmurer! Doubt not that darker guests are sitting round the hearth, though the warm blaze hides all but blissful images. Well; here is still a brighter scene. A stately mansion, illuminated for a ball, with cut-glass chandeliers and alabaster lamps in every room, and sunny landscapes hanging round the walls. See! a coach has stopped, whence emerges a slender beauty, who, canopied by two umbrellas, glides within the portal, and vanishes amid lightsome thrills of music. Will she ever feel the night-wind and the rain? Perhaps,—perhaps! And will Death and Sorrow ever enter that proud mansion? As surely as the dancers will be gay within its halls to-night. Such thoughts sadden, yet satisfy my heart; for they teach me that the poor man, in this mean, weather-beaten hovel, without a fire to cheer him, may call the rich his brother,—brethren by Sorrow, who must be an inmate of both their households,—brethren by Death, who will lead them both to other homes.

Onward, still onward, I plunge into the night. Now have

I reached the utmost limits of the town, where the last lamp struggles feebly with the darkness, like the farthest star that stands sentinel on the borders of uncreated space. It is strange what sensations of sublimity may spring from a very humble source. Such are suggested by this hollow roar of a subterranean cataract, where the mighty stream of a kennel precipitates itself beneath an iron grate, and is seen no more on earth. Listen awhile to its voice of mystery; and fancy will magnify it, till you start, and smile at the illusion. And now another sound,—the rumbling of wheels,—as the mailcoach, outward bound, rolls heavily off the pavements, and splashes through the mud and water of the road. All night long, the poor passengers will be tossed to and fro between drowsy watch and troubled sleep, and will dream of their own quiet beds, and awake to find themselves still jolting onward. Happier my lot, who will straightway hie me to my familiar room, and toast myself comfortably before the fire, musing, and fitfully dozing, and fancying a strangeness in such sights as all may see. But first let me gaze at this solitary figure, who comes hitherward with a tin lantern, which throws the circular pattern of its punched holes on the ground about him. He passes fearlessly into the unknown gloom, whither I will not follow him.

This figure shall supply me with a moral, wherewith, for lack of a more appropriate one, I may wind up my sketch. He fears not to tread the dreary path before him, because his lantern, which was kindled at the fireside of his home, will light him back to that same fireside again. And thus we, night-wanderers through a stormy and dismal world, if we bear the lamp of Faith, enkindled at a celestial fire, it will surely lead us home to that Heaven whence its radiance was borrowed.

The Shaker Bridal

ONE DAY, in the sick chamber of Father Ephraim, who had been forty years the presiding elder over the Shaker settlement at Goshen, there was an assemblage of several of the chief men of the sect. Individuals had come from the rich establishment at Lebanon, from Canterbury, Harvard, and Alfred, and from all the other localities, where this strange people have fertilized the rugged hills of New England by their systematic industry. An elder was likewise there, who had made a pilgrimage of a thousand miles from a village of the faithful in Kentucky, to visit his spiritual kindred, the children of the sainted Mother Ann. He had partaken of the homely abundance of their tables, had quaffed the far-famed Shaker cider, and had joined in the sacred dance, every step of which is believed to alienate the enthusiast from earth, and bear him onward to heavenly purity and bliss. His brethren of the north had now courteously invited him to be present on an occasion when the concurrence of every eminent member of their community was peculiarly desirable.

The venerable Father Ephraim sat in his easy-chair, not only hoary-headed and infirm with age, but worn down by a lingering disease, which, it was evident, would very soon transfer his patriarchal staff to other hands. At his footstool stood a man and woman, both clad in the Shaker garb.

"My brethren," said Father Ephraim to the surrounding elders, feebly exerting himself to utter these few words, "here are the son and daughter to whom I would commit the trust, of which Providence is about to lighten my weary shoulders. Read their faces, I pray you, and say whether the inward movement of the spirit hath guided my choice aright."

Accordingly, each elder looked at the two candidates with a most scrutinizing gaze. The man, whose name was Adam Colburn, had a face sunburnt with labor in the fields, yet intelligent, thoughtful, and traced with cares enough for a whole lifetime, though he had barely reached middle age. There was something severe in his aspect, and a rigidity throughout his person, characteristics that caused him generally to be taken for a schoolmaster; which vocation, in fact, he had formerly exercised for several years. The woman, Martha Pierson, was somewhat above thirty, thin and pale, as a Shaker sister almost invariably is, and not entirely free from that corpse-like appearance, which the garb of the sisterhood is so well calculated to impart.

"This pair are still in the summer of their years," observed the elder from Harvard, a shrewd old man. "I would like better to see the hoar frost of autumn on their heads. Methinks, also, they will be exposed to peculiar temptations, on account of the carnal desires which have heretofore subsisted between them."

"Nay, brother," said the elder from Canterbury, "the hoar frost, and the black frost, hath done its work on Brother Adam and Sister Martha, even as we sometimes discern its traces in our cornfields, while they are yet green. And why should we question the wisdom of our venerable Father's purpose, although this pair, in their early youth, have loved one another as the world's people love? Are there not many brethren and sisters among us, who have lived long together in wedlock, yet, adopting our faith, find their hearts purified from all but spiritual affection?"

Whether or no the early loves of Adam and Martha had rendered it inexpedient that they should now preside together over a Shaker village, it was certainly most singular that such should be the final result of many warm and tender hopes. Children of neighbouring families, their affection was older even than their school-days; it seemed an innate principle, interfused among all their sentiments and feelings, and not so much a distinct remembrance, as connected with their whole volume of remembrances. But, just as they reached a proper age for their union, misfortunes had fallen heavily on both, and made it necessary that they should resort to personal labor for a bare subsistence. Even under these circumstances, Martha Pierson would probably have consented to unite her fate with Adam Colburn's, and, secure of the bliss of mutual love, would patiently have awaited the less important gifts of fortune. But Adam, being of a calm and cautious character, was loath to relinquish the advantages which a single man possesses for raising himself in the world. Year after year,

therefore, their marriage had been deferred. Adam Colburn
had followed many vocations, had travelled far, and seen
much of the world and of life. Martha had earned her bread
sometimes as a sempstress, sometimes as help to a farmer's
wife, sometimes as schoolmistress of the village children,
sometimes as a nurse or watcher of the sick, thus acquiring a
varied experience, the ultimate use of which she little anticipated. But nothing had gone prosperously with either of the
lovers; at no subsequent moment would matrimony have
been so prudent a measure, as when they had first parted, in
the opening bloom of life, to seek a better fortune. Still they
had held fast their mutual faith. Martha might have been the
wife of a man, who sat among the senators of his native state,
and Adam could have won the hand, as he had unintentionally won the heart, of a rich and comely widow. But neither
of them desired good fortune, save to share it with the other.

At length that calm despair, which occurs only in a strong
and somewhat stubborn character, and yields to no second
spring of hope, settled down on the spirit of Adam Colburn.
He sought an interview with Martha, and proposed that they
should join the Society of Shakers. The converts of this sect
are oftener driven within its hospitable gates by worldly misfortune, than drawn thither by fanaticism, and are received
without inquisition as to their motives. Martha, faithful still,
had placed her hand in that of her lover, and accompanied
him to the Shaker village. Here the natural capacity of each,
cultivated and strengthened by the difficulties of their previous lives, had soon gained them an important rank in the
Society, whose members are generally below the ordinary
standard of intelligence. Their faith and feelings had, in some
degree, become assimilated to those of their fellow-worship-
pers. Adam Colburn gradually acquired reputation, not only
in the management of the temporal affairs of the Society, but
as a clear and efficient preacher of their doctrines. Martha was
not less distinguished in the duties proper to her sex. Finally,
when the infirmities of Father Ephraim had admonished him
to seek a successor in his patriarchal office, he thought of
Adam and Martha, and proposed to renew, in their persons,
the primitive form of Shaker government, as established by
Mother Ann. They were to be the Father and Mother of the

village. The simple ceremony, which would constitute them such, was now to be performed.

"Son Adam, and daughter Martha," said the venerable Father Ephraim, fixing his aged eyes piercingly upon them, "if ye can conscientiously undertake this charge, speak, that the brethren may not doubt of your fitness."

"Father," replied Adam, speaking with the calmness of his character, "I came to your village a disappointed man, weary of the world, worn out with continual trouble, seeking only a security against evil fortune, as I had no hope of good. Even my wishes of worldly success were almost dead within me. I came hither as a man might come to a tomb, willing to lie down in its gloom and coldness, for the sake of its peace and quiet. There was but one earthly affection in my breast, and it had grown calmer since my youth; so that I was satisfied to bring Martha to be my sister, in our new abode. We are brother and sister; nor would I have it otherwise. And in this peaceful village I have found all that I hope for,—all that I desire. I will strive, with my best strength, for the spiritual and temporal good of our community. My conscience is not doubtful in this matter. I am ready to receive the trust."

"Thou hast spoken well, son Adam," said the Father. "God will bless thee in the office which I am about to resign."

"But our sister!" observed the elder from Harvard; "hath she not likewise a gift to declare her sentiments?"

Martha started, and moved her lips, as if she would have made a formal reply to this appeal. But, had she attempted it, perhaps the old recollections, the long-repressed feelings of childhood, youth, and womanhood, might have gushed from her heart, in words that it would have been profanation to utter there.

"Adam has spoken," said she, hurriedly; "his sentiments are likewise mine."

But, while speaking these few words, Martha grew so pale, that she looked fitter to be laid in her coffin, than to stand in the presence of Father Ephraim and the elders; she shuddered, also, as if there were something awful or horrible in her situation and destiny. It required, indeed, a more than feminine strength of nerve, to sustain the fixed observance of men so exalted and famous throughout the sect, as these were. They had overcome their natural sympathy with human frailties and affections. One, when he joined the Society, had brought with him his wife and children, but never, from that hour, had spoken a fond word to the former, or taken his best-loved child upon his knee. Another, whose family refused to follow him, had been enabled,—such was his gift of holy fortitude,—to leave them to the mercy of the world. The youngest of the elders, a man of about fifty, had been bred from infancy in a Shaker village, and was said never to have clasped a woman's hand in his own, and to have no conception of a closer tie than the cold fraternal one of the sect. Old Father Ephraim was the most awful character of all. In his youth, he had been a dissolute libertine, but was converted by Mother Ann herself, and had partaken of the wild fanaticism of the early Shakers. Tradition whispered, at the firesides of the village, that Mother Ann had been compelled to sear his heart of flesh with a red-hot iron, before it could be purified from earthly passions.

However that might be, poor Martha had a woman's heart, and a tender one, and it quailed within her as she looked round at those strange old men, and from them to the calm features of Adam Colburn. But, perceiving that the elders eyed her doubtfully, she gasped for breath, and again spoke.

"With what strength is left me by my many troubles," said she, "I am ready to undertake this charge, and to do my best in it."

"My children, join your hands," said Father Ephraim.

They did so. The elders stood up around, and the Father feebly raised himself to a more erect position, but continued sitting in his great chair.

"I have bidden you to join your hands," said he, "not in earthly affection, for ye have cast off its chains for ever; but as brother and sister in spiritual love, and helpers of one another in your allotted task. Teach unto others the faith which ye have received. Open wide your gates,—I deliver you the keys thereof,—open them wide to all who will give up the iniquities of the world, and come hither to lead lives of purity and peace. Receive the weary ones, who have known the vanity of earth,—receive the little children, that they may never learn that miserable lesson. And a blessing be upon your la-

bors; so that the time may hasten on, when the mission of
Mother Ann shall have wrought its full effect,—when children shall no more be born and die, and the last survivor of
mortal race, some old and weary man like me, shall see the
sun go down, never more to rise on a world of sin and sorrow!"

The aged Father sank back exhausted, and the surrounding
elders deemed, with good reason, that the hour was come,
when the new heads of the village must enter on their patriarchal duties. In their attention to Father Ephraim, their eyes
were turned from Martha Pierson, who grew paler and paler,
unnoticed even by Adam Colburn. He, indeed, had withdrawn his hand from hers, and folded his arms with a sense
of satisfied ambition. But paler and paler grew Martha by his
side, till, like a corpse in its burial clothes, she sank down at
the feet of her early lover; for, after many trials firmly borne,
her heart could endure the weight of its desolate agony no
longer.

Foot-prints on the Sea-shore

I*T* must be a spirit much unlike my own, which can keep itself in health and vigor without sometimes stealing from the sultry sunshine of the world, to plunge into the cool bath of solitude. At intervals, and not infrequent ones, the forest and the ocean summon me—one with the roar of its waves, the other with the murmur of its boughs—forth from the haunts of men. But I must wander many a mile, ere I could stand beneath the shadow of even one primeval tree, much less be lost among the multitude of hoary trunks, and hidden from earth and sky by the mystery of darksome foliage. Nothing is within my daily reach more like a forest than the acre or two of woodland near some suburban farm-house. When, therefore, the yearning for seclusion becomes a necessity within me, I am drawn to the sea-shore, which extends its line of rude rocks and seldom-trodden sands, for leagues around our bay. Setting forth, at my last ramble, on a September morning, I bound myself with a hermit's vow, to interchange no thoughts with man or woman, to share no social pleasure, but to derive all that day's enjoyment from shore, and sea, and sky,—from my soul's communion with these, and from fantasies, and recollections, or anticipated realities. Surely here is enough to feed a human spirit for a single day. Farewell, then, busy world! Till your evening lights shall shine along the street—till they gleam upon my sea-flushed face, as I tread homeward—free me from your ties, and let me be a peaceful outlaw.

Highways and cross-paths are hastily traversed; and, clambering down a crag, I find myself at the extremity of a long beach. How gladly does the spirit leap forth, and suddenly enlarge its sense of being to the full extent of the broad, blue, sunny deep! A greeting and a homage to the Sea! I descend over its margin, and dip my hand into the wave that meets me, and bathe my brow. That far-resounding roar is Ocean's voice of welcome. His salt breath brings a blessing along with it. Now let us pace together—the reader's fancy arm in arm with mine—this noble beach, which extends a mile or more from that craggy promontory to yonder rampart of broken rocks. In front, the sea; in the rear, a precipitous bank, the grassy verge of which is breaking away, year after year, and flings down its tufts of verdure upon the barrenness below. The beach itself is a broad space of sand, brown and spar-kling, with hardly any pebbles intermixed. Near the water's edge there is a wet margin, which glistens brightly in the sun-shine, and reflects objects like a mirror; and as we tread along the glistening border, a dry spot flashes around each footstep, but grows moist again, as we lift our feet. In some spots, the sand receives a complete impression of the sole—square toe and all; elsewhere, it is of such marble firmness, that we must stamp heavily to leave a print even of the iron-shod heel. Along the whole of this extensive beach gambols the surf-wave; now it makes a feint of dashing onward in a fury, yet dies away with a meek murmur, and does but kiss the strand; now, after many such abortive efforts, it rears itself up in an unbroken line, heightening as it advances, without a speck of foam on its green crest. With how fierce a roar it flings itself forward, and rushes far up the beach!

As I threw my eyes along the edge of the surf, I remember that I was startled, as Robinson Crusoe might have been, by the sense that human life was within the magic circle of my solitude. Afar off in the remote distance of the beach, appear-ing like sea-nymphs, or some airier things, such as might tread upon the feathery spray, was a group of girls. Hardly had I beheld them, when they passed into the shadow of the rocks and vanished. To comfort myself—for truly I would fain have gazed a while longer—I made acquaintance with a flock of beach-birds. These little citizens of the sea and air preceded me by about a stone's-throw along the strand, seek-ing, I suppose, for food upon its margin. Yet, with a philos-ophy which mankind would do well to imitate, they drew a continual pleasure from their toil for a subsistence. The sea was each little bird's great playmate. They chased it down-ward as it swept back, and again ran up swiftly before the impending wave, which sometimes overtook them and bore them off their feet. But they floated as lightly as one of their own feathers on the breaking crest. In their airy flutterings, they seemed to rest on the evanescent spray. Their images,—

long-legged little figures, with grey backs and snowy bosoms,—were seen as distinctly as the realities in the mirror of
the glistening strand. As I advanced, they flew a score or two
of yards, and, again alighting, recommenced their dalliance
with the surf-wave; and thus they bore me company along
the beach, the types of pleasant fantasies, till, at its extremity,
they took wing over the ocean, and were gone. After forming
a friendship with these small surf-spirits, it is really worth a
sigh, to find no memorial of them save their multitudinous
little tracks in the sand.

When we have paced the length of the beach, it is pleasant,
and not unprofitable, to retrace our steps, and recall the
whole mood and occupation of the mind during the former
passage. Our tracks, being all discernible, will guide us with
an observing consciousness through every unconscious wandering of thought and fancy. Here we followed the surf in its
reflux, to pick up a shell which the sea seemed loth to relinquish. Here we found a sea-weed, with an immense brown
leaf, and trailed it behind us by its long snake-like stalk. Here
we seized a live horse-shoe by the tail, and counted the many
claws of that queer monster. Here we dug into the sand for
pebbles, and skipped them upon the surface of the water.
Here we wet our feet while examining a jelly-fish, which the
waves, having just tossed it up, now sought to snatch away
again. Here we trod along the brink of a fresh-water brooklet,
which flows across the beach, becoming shallower and more
shallow, till at last it sinks into the sand, and perishes in the
effort to bear its little tribute to the main. Here some vagary
appears to have bewildered us; for our tracks go round and
round, and are confusedly intermingled, as if we had found a
labyrinth upon the level beach. And here, amid our idle pastime, we sat down upon almost the only stone that breaks the
surface of the sand, and were lost in an unlooked-for and
overpowering conception of the majesty and awfulness of the
great deep. Thus, by tracking our foot-prints in the sand, we
track our own nature in its wayward course, and steal a glance
upon it, when it never dreams of being so observed. Such
glances always make us wiser.

This extensive beach affords room for another pleasant pastime. With your staff, you may write verses—love-verses, if

they please you best—and consecrate them with a woman's name. Here, too, may be inscribed thoughts, feelings, desires, warm outgushings from the heart's secret places, which you would not pour upon the sand without the certainty that, almost ere the sky has looked upon them, the sea will wash them out. Stir not hence, till the record be effaced. Now—for there is room enough on your canvass—draw huge faces—huge as that of the Sphynx on Egyptian sands—and fit them with bodies of corresponding immensity, and legs which might stride half-way to yonder island. Child's play becomes magnificent on so grand a scale. But, after all, the most fascinating employment is simply to write your name in the sand. Draw the letters gigantic, so that two strides may barely measure them, and three for the long strokes! Cut deep, that the record may be permanent! Statesmen, and warriors, and poets, have spent their strength in no better cause than this. Is it accomplished? Return, then, in an hour or two, and seek for this mighty record of a name. The sea will have swept over it, even as time rolls its effacing waves over the names of statesmen, and warriors, and poets. Hark, the surf-wave laughs at you!

Passing from the beach, I begin to clamber over the crags, making my difficult way among the ruins of a rampart, shattered and broken by the assaults of a fierce enemy. The rocks rise in every variety of attitude; some of them have their feet in the foam, and are shagged half-way upward with sea-weed; some have been hollowed almost into caverns by the unwearied toil of the sea, which can afford to spend centuries in wearing away a rock, or even polishing a pebble. One huge rock ascends in monumental shape, with a face like a giant's tombstone, on which the veins resemble inscriptions, but in an unknown tongue. We will fancy them the forgotten characters of an antediluvian race; or else that nature's own hand has here recorded a mystery, which, could I read her language, would make mankind the wiser and the happier. How many a thing has troubled me with that same idea! Pass on, and leave it unexplained. Here is a narrow avenue, which might seem to have been hewn through the very heart of an enormous crag, affording passage for the rising sea to thunder back and forth, filling it with tumultuous foam, and then leaving its floor of black pebbles bare and glistening. In this chasm there was once an intersecting vein of softer stone, which the waves have gnawed away piecemeal, while the granite walls remain entire on either side. How sharply, and with what harsh clamor, does the sea rake back the pebbles, as it momentarily withdraws into its own depths! At intervals, the floor of the chasm is left nearly dry; but anon, at the outlet, two or three great waves are seen struggling to get in at once; two hit the walls athwart, while one rushes straight through, and all three thunder, as if with rage and triumph. They heap the chasm with a snow-drift of foam and spray. While watching this scene, I can never rid myself of the idea, that a monster, endowed with life and fierce energy, is striving to burst his way through the narrow pass. And what a contrast, to look through the stormy chasm, and catch a glimpse of the calm bright sea beyond!

Many interesting discoveries may be made among these broken cliffs. Once, for example, I found a dead seal, which a recent tempest had tossed into a nook of the rocks, where his shaggy carcass lay rolled in a heap of eel-grass, as if the sea-monster sought to hide himself from my eye. Another time, a shark seemed on the point of leaping from the surf to swallow me; nor did I, wholly without dread, approach near enough to ascertain that the man-eater had already met his own death from some fisherman in the bay. In the same ramble, I encountered a bird—a large grey bird—but whether a loon, or a wild goose, or the identical albatross of the Ancient Mariner, was beyond my ornithology to decide. It reposed so naturally on a bed of dry sea-weed, with its head beside its wing, that I almost fancied it alive, and trod softly lest it should suddenly spread its wings skyward. But the sea-bird would soar among the clouds no more, nor ride upon its native waves; so I drew near, and pulled out one of its mottled tail-feathers for a remembrance. Another day, I discovered an immense bone, wedged into a chasm of the rocks; it was at least ten feet long, curved like a scimetar, bejewelled with barnacles and small shell-fish, and partly covered with a growth of sea-weed. Some leviathan of former ages had used this ponderous mass as a jaw-bone. Curiosities of a minuter order may be observed in a deep reservoir, which is replenished with water at every tide, but becomes a lake among the crags, save when the sea is at its height. At the bottom of this rocky basin grow marine plants, some of which tower high beneath the water, and cast a shadow in the sunshine. Small fishes dart to and fro, and hide themselves among the sea-weed; there is also a solitary crab, who appears to lead the life of a hermit, communing with none of the other denizens of the place; and likewise several five-fingers—for I know no other name than that which children give them. If your imagination be at all accustomed to such freaks, you may look down into the depths of this pool, and fancy it the mysterious depth of ocean. But where are the hulks and scattered timbers of sunken ships?—where the treasures that old Ocean hoards?—where the corroded cannon?—where the corpses and skeletons of seamen, who went down in storm and battle?

On the day of my last ramble, (it was a September day, yet as warm as summer,) what should I behold as I approached the above described basin but three girls sitting on its margin, and—yes, it is veritably so—laving their snowy feet in the sunny water! These, these are the warm realities of those three visionary shapes that flitted from me on the beach. Hark! their merry voices, as they toss up the water with their feet! They have not seen me. I must shrink behind this rock, and steal away again.

In honest truth, vowed to solitude as I am, there is something in the encounter that makes the heart flutter with a strangely pleasant sensation. I know these girls to be realities of flesh and blood, yet, glancing at them so briefly, they mingle like kindred creatures with the ideal beings of my mind. It is pleasant, likewise, to gaze down from some high crag, and watch a group of children, gathering pebbles and pearly shells, and playing with the surf, as with old Ocean's hoary beard. Nor does it infringe upon my seclusion, to see yonder boat at anchor off the shore, swinging dreamily to and fro, and rising and sinking with the alternate swell; while the crew—four gentlemen in round-about jackets—are busy with their fishing-lines. But, with an inward antipathy and a headlong flight, do I eschew the presence of any meditative stroller like myself, known by his pilgrim staff, his sauntering step, his shy demeanour, his observant yet abstracted eye.

From such a man, as if another self had scared me, I scramble hastily over the rocks and take refuge in a nook which many a secret hour has given me a right to call my own. I would do battle for it even with the churl that should produce the title-deeds. Have not my musings melted into its rocky walls and sandy floor, and made them a portion of myself?

It is a recess in the line of cliffs, walled round by a rough, high precipice, which almost encircles and shuts in a little space of sand. In front, the sea appears as between the pillars of a portal. In the rear, the precipice is broken and intermixed with earth, which gives nourishment not only to clinging and twining shrubs, but to trees, that gripe the rock with their naked roots, and seem to struggle hard for footing and for soil enough to live upon. These are fir trees; but oaks hang their heavy branches from above, and throw down acorns on the beach, and shed their withering foliage upon the waves. At this autumnal season, the precipice is decked with variegated splendor; trailing wreaths of scarlet flaunt from the summit downward; tufts of yellow-flowering shrubs, and rose bushes, with their reddened leaves and glossy seed-berries, sprout from each crevice; at every glance, I detect some new light or shade of beauty, all contrasting with the stern, grey rock. A rill of water trickles down the cliff and fills a little cistern near the base. I drain it at a draught, and find it fresh and pure. This recess shall be my dining-hall. And what the feast? A few biscuits, made savory by soaking them in sea-water, a tuft of samphire gathered from the beach, and an apple for the dessert. By this time, the little rill has filled its reservoir again; and, as I quaff it, I thank God more heartily than for a civic banquet, that He gives me the healthful appetite to make a feast of bread and water.

Dinner being over, I throw myself at length upon the sand, and basking in the sunshine, let my mind disport itself at will. The walls of this my hermitage have no tongue to tell my follies, though I sometimes fancy that they have ears to hear them, and a soul to sympathize. There is a magic in this spot. Dreams haunt its precincts, and flit around me in broad sunlight, nor require that sleep shall blindfold me to real objects, ere these be visible. Here can I frame a story of two lovers, and make their shadows live before me, and be mirrored in the tranquil water, as they tread along the sand, leaving no foot-prints. Here, should I will it, I can summon up a single shade, and be myself her lover. Yes, dreamer,—but your lonely heart will be the colder for such fancies. Sometimes, too, the Past comes back, and finds me here, and in her train come faces which were gladsome, when I knew them, yet seem not gladsome now. Would that my hiding place were lonelier, so that the Past might not find me! Get ye all gone, old friends, and let me listen to the murmur of the sea,—a melancholy voice, but less sad than yours. Of what mysteries is it telling? Of sunken ships, and whereabouts they lie? Of islands afar and undiscovered, whose tawny children are unconscious of other islands and of continents, and deem the stars of heaven their nearest neighbours? Nothing of all this. What then? Has it talked for so many ages, and meant nothing all the while? No; for those ages find utterance in the sea's unchanging voice, and warn the listener to withdraw his interest from mortal vicissitudes, and let the infinite idea of eternity pervade his soul. This is wisdom; and, therefore, will I spend the next half-hour in shaping little boats of drift-wood, and launching them on voyages across the cove, with the feather of a sea-gull for a sail. If the voice of ages tell me true, this is as wise an occupation as to build ships of five hundred tons, and launch them forth upon the main, bound to 'far Cathay.' Yet, how would the merchant sneer at me!

And, after all, can such philosophy be true? Methinks I could find a thousand arguments against it. Well, then, let yonder shaggy rock, mid-deep in the surf—see! he is somewhat wrathful,—he rages and roars and foams—let that tall rock be my antagonist, and let me exercise my oratory like him of Athens, who bandied words with an angry sea and got the victory. My maiden speech is a triumphant one; for the gentleman in sea-weed has nothing to offer in reply, save an immitigable roaring. His voice, indeed, will be heard a long while after mine is hushed. Once more I shout, and the cliffs reverberate the sound. Oh, what joy for a shy man to feel himself so solitary, that he may lift his voice to its highest pitch without hazard of a listener! But, hush!—be silent, my good friend!—whence comes that stifled laughter? It was musical,—but how should there be such music in my solitude? Looking upwards, I catch a glimpse of three faces, peeping from the summit of the cliff, like angels between me and their native sky. Ah, fair girls, you may make yourselves merry at my eloquence,—but it was my turn to smile when I saw your white feet in the pool! Let us keep each other's secrets.

The sunshine has now passed from my hermitage, except a gleam upon the sand just where it meets the sea. A crowd of gloomy fantasies will come and haunt me, if I tarry longer here, in the darkening twilight of these grey rocks. This is a dismal place in some moods of the mind. Climb we, therefore, the precipice, and pause a moment on the brink, gazing down into that hollow chamber by the deep, where we have been, what few can be, sufficient to our own pastime—yes, say the word outright!—self-sufficient to our own happiness. How lonesome looks the recess now, and dreary too,—like all other spots where happiness has been! There lies my shadow in the departing sunshine with its head upon the sea. I will pelt it with pebbles. A hit! a hit! I clap my hands in triumph, and see my shadow clapping its unreal hands, and claiming the triumph for itself. What a simpleton must I have been all day, since my own shadow makes a mock of my fooleries!

Homeward! homeward! It is time to hasten home. It is time; it is time; for as the sun sinks over the western wave, the sea grows melancholy, and the surf has a saddened tone. The distant sails appear astray, and not of earth, in their remoteness amid the desolate waste. My spirit wanders forth afar, but finds no resting place, and comes shivering back. It is time that I were hence. But grudge me not the day that has been spent in seclusion, which yet was not solitude, since the great sea has been my companion, and the little sea-birds my friends, and the wind has told me his secrets, and airy shapes have flitted around me in my hermitage. Such companionship works an effect upon a man's character, as if he had been admitted to the society of creatures that are not mortal. And when, at noontide, I tread the crowded streets, the influence of this day will still be felt; so that I shall walk among men kindly and as a brother, with affection and sympathy, but yet shall not melt into the indistinguishable mass of human kind.

I shall think my own thoughts, and feel my own emotions, and possess my individuality unviolated.

But it is good, at the eve of such a day, to feel and know that there are men and women in the world. That feeling and that knowledge are mine, at this moment; for, on the shore, far below me, the fishing-party have landed from their skiff, and are cooking their scaly prey by a fire of drift-wood, kindled in the angle of two rude rocks. The three visionary girls are likewise there. In the deepening twilight, while the surf is dashing near their hearth, the ruddy gleam of the fire throws a strange air of comfort over the wild cove, bestrewn as it is with pebbles and sea-weed, and exposed to the 'melancholy main.' Moreover, as the smoke climbs up the precipice, it brings with it a savory smell from a pan of fried fish, and a black kettle of chowder, and reminds me that my dinner was nothing but bread and water, and a tuft of samphire, and an apple. Methinks the party might find room for another guest, at that flat rock which serves them for a table; and if spoons be scarce, I could pick up a clam-shell on the beach. They see me now; and—the blessing of a hungry man upon him!— one of them sends up a hospitable shout—halloo, Sir Solitary! come down and sup with us! The ladies wave their handkerchiefs. Can I decline? No; and be it owned, after all my solitary joys, that this is the sweetest moment of a Day by the Sea-Shore.

Thomas Green Fessenden

T HOMAS GREEN FESSENDEN was the eldest of nine children of the Rev. Thomas Fessenden. He was born on the 22d of April, 1771, at Walpole, in New Hampshire, where his father, a man of learning and talent, was long settled in the ministry. On the maternal side, likewise, he was of clerical extraction; his mother, whose piety and amiable qualities are remembered by her descendants, being the daughter of the Rev. Samuel Kendal, of New Salem. The early education of Thomas Green was chiefly acquired at the common school of his native place, under the tuition of students from the college at Hanover; and such was his progress, that he became himself the instructor of a school in New Salem at the age of sixteen. He spent most of his youthful days, however, in bodily labor upon the farm, thus contributing to the support of a numerous family; and the practical knowledge of agriculture, which he then obtained, was long afterwards applied to the service of the public. Opportunities for cultivating his mind were afforded him, not only in his father's library, but by the more miscellaneous contents of a large book-store. He had passed the age of twenty-one, when his inclination for mental pursuits determined him to become a student at Dartmouth College. His father being able to give him but little assistance, his chief resources at college consisted in his wages as teacher of a village school during the vacations. At times, also, he gave instruction to an evening class in Psalmody.

From his childhood, upward, Mr. Fessenden had shown symptoms of that humorous turn which afterwards so strongly marked his writings; but, his first effort in verse, as he himself told me, was made during his residence at college. The themes, or exercises of his fellow-students in English composition, whether prose or rhyme, were characterized by the lack of native thought and feeling, the cold pedantry, the mimicry of classic models, common to all such productions. Mr. Fessenden had the good taste to disapprove of these vapid and spiritless performances, and resolved to strike out a new course for himself. On one occasion, when his class-

mates had gone through with their customary round of ver-
biage and threadbare sentiment, he electrified them and their
instructor, President Wheelock, by reading "JONATHAN'S
COURTSHIP." There has never, to this day, been produced,
by any of our countrymen, a more original and truly Yankee
effusion. He had caught the rare art of sketching familiar
manners, and of throwing into verse the very spirit of society
as it existed around him; and he had imbued each line with a
peculiar, yet perfectly natural and homely humor. This excellent ballad compels me to regret that, instead of becoming a
satirist in politics and science, and wasting his strength on
temporary and evangelical topics, he had not continued to be
a rural poet. A volume of such sketches as "Jonathan's Courtship," describing various aspects of life among the yeomanry
of New England, could not have failed to gain a permanent
place in American literature. The effort in question met with
unexampled success; it ran through the newspapers of the
day, re-appeared on the other side of the Atlantic, and was
warmly applauded by the English critics; nor has it yet lost
its popularity. New editions may be found, every year, at the
ballad-stalls; and I saw, last summer, on the veteran author's
table, a broadside copy of his maiden poem, which he had
himself bought in the street.

Mr. Fessenden passed through college with a fair reputation for scholarship, and took his degree in 1796. It had been
his father's wish that he should imitate the example of some
of his ancestors on both sides, by devoting himself to the
ministry. He, however, preferred the law, and commenced
the study of that profession at Rutland, in Vermont, with
Nathaniel Chipman, then the most eminent practitioner in
the State. After his admission to the bar, Mr. Chipman received him into partnership. But Mr. Fessenden was ill-qual-
ified to succeed in the profession of law, by his simplicity of
character, and his utter inability to acquire an ordinary share
of shrewdness and worldly wisdom. Moreover, the success of
"Jonathan's Courtship," and other poetical effusions, had
turned his thoughts from law to literature, and had procured
him the acquaintance of several literary luminaries of those
days; none of whose names, probably, have survived to our
own generation, save that of Joseph Dennie, once esteemed

the finest writer in America. His intercourse with these people tempted Mr. Fessenden to spend much time in writing for newspapers and periodicals. A taste for scientific pursuits still further diverted him from his legal studies, and soon engaged him in an affair which influenced the complexion of all his after-life.

A Mr. Langdon had brought forward a newly-invented hydraulic machine, which was supposed to possess the power of raising water to a greater height than had hitherto been considered possible. A company of mechanics and others became interested in this machine, and appointed Mr. Fessenden their agent for the purpose of obtaining a patent in London. He was likewise a member of the company. Mr. Fessenden was urged to hasten his departure, in consequence of a report that certain persons had acquired the secret of the invention, and were determined to anticipate the proprietors in securing a patent. Scarcely time was allowed for testing the efficacy of the machine by a few hasty experiments, which, however, appeared satisfactory. Taking passage immediately, Mr. Fessenden arrived in London on the 4th of July, 1801, and waited on Mr. King, then our Minister, by whom he was introduced to Mr. Nicholson, a gentleman of eminent scientific reputation. After thoroughly examining the invention, Mr. Nicholson gave an opinion unfavorable to its merits; and the question was soon settled by a letter from one of the Vermont proprietors to Mr. Fessenden, informing him that the apparent advantages of the machine had been found altogether deceptive. In short, Mr. Fessenden had been lured from his profession and country by as empty a bubble as that of the perpetual motion. Yet it is creditable both to his ability and energy, that, laying hold of what was really valuable in Langdon's contrivance, he constructed the model of a machine for raising water from coal mines, and other great depths, by means of what he termed the "renovated pressure of the atmosphere." On communicating this invention to Mr. Nicholson and other eminent mechanicians, they acknowledged its originality and ingenuity, and thought that, in some situations, it might be useful. But the expenses of a patent in England, the difficulty of obtaining patronage for such a project, and the uncertainty of the result, were obstacles too weighty to be overcome. Mr. Fessenden threw aside the scheme, and, after a two months' residence in London, was preparing to return home; when a new and characteristic adventure arrested him.

He received a visit, at his lodgings in the Strand, from a person whom he had never before seen, but who introduced himself to his good-will as being likewise an American. His business was of a nature well calculated to excite Mr. Fessenden's interest. He produced the model of an ingenious contrivance for grinding corn. A patent had already been obtained, and a company, with the Lord Mayor of London at its head, was associated for the construction of mills upon this new principle. The inventor, according to his own story, had disposed of one fourth part of his patent for £500, and was willing to accommodate his countryman with another fourth. After some inquiry into the stranger's character, and the accuracy of his statements, Mr. Fessenden became a purchaser of the share that was offered him; on what terms, is not stated; but probably such as to involve his whole property in the adventure. The result was disastrous. The Lord Mayor soon withdrew his countenance from the project. It ultimately appeared that Mr. Fessenden was the only real purchaser of any part of the patent; and as the original patentee shortly afterwards quitted the concern, the former was left to manage the business as he best could. With a perseverance not less characteristic than his credulity, he associated himself with four partners, and undertook to superintend the construction of one of these patent mills upon the Thames. But his associates, who were men of no respectability, thwarted his plans; and after much toil of body, as well as distress of mind, he found himself utterly ruined,—friendless and penniless in the midst of London. No other event could have been anticipated, when a man so devoid of guile was thrown among a set of crafty adventurers.

Being now in the situation in which many a literary man before him had been, he remembered the success of his fugitive poems, and betook himself to the pen as his most natural resource. A subject was offered him, in which no other poet would have found a theme for the muse. It seemed to be his fatality to form connexions with schemers of all sorts; and he had become acquainted with Benjamin Douglas Perkins, the patentee of the famous Metallic Tractors. These implements were then in great vogue for the cure of inflammatory diseases, by removing the superfluous electricity. Perkinism, as the doctrine of Metallic Tractors was styled, had some converts among scientific men, and many among the people; but was violently opposed by the regular corps of physicians and surgeons. Mr. Fessenden, as might be expected, was a believer in the efficacy of the Tractors, and, at the request of Perkins, consented to make them the subject of a poem in Hudibrastic verse, the satire of which was to be levelled against their opponents. "TERRIBLE TRACTORATION" was the result. It professes to be a poetical petition from Doctor Christopher Caustic, a medical gentleman who has been ruined by the success of the Metallic Tractors, and who applies to the Royal College of Physicians for relief and redress. The wits of the poor Doctor have been somewhat shattered by his misfortunes; and with crazy ingenuity he contrives to heap ridicule on his medical brethren, under pretence of railing against Perkinism. The poem is in four cantos, the first of which is the best, and the most characteristic of the author. It is occupied with Doctor Caustic's description of his mechanical and scientific contrivances, embracing all sorts of possible and impossible projects; every one of which, however, has a ridiculous plausibility. The inexhaustible variety in which they flow forth, proves the author's invention unrivalled in its way. It shows what had been the nature of Mr. Fessenden's mental toil during his residence in London, continually brooding over the miracles of mechanism and science, his enthusiasm for which had cost him so dear. Long afterwards, speaking of the first conception of this poem, the author told me that he had shaped it out during a solitary day's ramble in the outskirts of London; and the character of Doctor Caustic so strongly impressed itself on his mind, that, as he walked homeward through the crowded streets, he burst into frequent fits of laughter. The truth is, that, in the sketch of this wild projector, Mr. Fessenden had caricatured some of his own features; and when he laughed so heartily, it was at the perception of the resemblance.

"Terrible Tractoration," is a work of strange and grotesque

ideas, aptly expressed; its rhymes are of a most singular character, yet fitting each to each as accurately as echoes. As in all
Mr. Fessenden's productions, there is great exactness in the
language; the author's thoughts being thrown off as distinctly
as impressions from a type. In regard to the pleasure to be
derived from reading this poem, there is room for diversity of
taste; but that it is an original and remarkable work, no person competent to pass judgment on a literary question, will
deny. It was first published early in the year 1803, in an octavo
pamphlet of about fifty pages. Being highly applauded by the
principal reviews, and eagerly purchased by the public, a new
edition appeared at the end of two months, in a volume of
nearly two hundred pages, illustrated with engravings. It received the praise of Gifford, the severest of English critics. Its
continued success encouraged the author to publish a volume
of "ORIGINAL POEMS," consisting chiefly of his fugitive
pieces from the American newspapers. This, also, was favorably received. He was now, what so few of his countrymen
have ever been, a popular author in London; and, in the
midst of his triumphs, he bethought himself of his native
land.

    Mr. Fessenden returned to America in 1804. He came back
poorer than he went, but with an honorable reputation, and
with unstained integrity, although his evil fortune had connected him with men far unlike himself. His fame had preceded him across the Atlantic. Shortly before his arrival, an
edition of "Terrible Tractoration" had been published at Philadelphia, with a prefatory memoir of the author, the tone of
which proves that the American people felt themselves honored in the literary success of their countryman. Another edition appeared in New-York in 1806, considerably enlarged,
with a new satire on the topics of the day. It is symptomatic
of the course which the author had now adopted, that much
of this new satire was directed against democratic principles
and the prominent upholders of them. This was soon followed by "DEMOCRACY UNVEILED," a more elaborate attack
on the same political party.

    In "Democracy Unveiled," our friend, Dr. Caustic, appears
as a citizen of the United States, and pours out six cantos of
vituperative verse, with copious notes of the same tenor, on

the heads of President Jefferson and his supporters. Much of the satire is unpardonably coarse: the literary merits of the work are inferior to those of "Terrible Tractoration," but it is no less original and peculiar. Even where the matter is a mere versification of newspaper slander, Dr. Caustic's manner gives it an individuality not to be mistaken. The book passed through three editions in the course of a few months. Its most pungent portions were copied into all the opposition prints; its strange, jog-trot stanzas, were familiar to every ear; and Mr. Fessenden may fairly be allowed the credit of having given expression to the feelings of the great Federal party.

On the 30th of August, 1806, Mr. Fessenden commenced the publication, at New-York, of the "WEEKLY INSPECTOR," a paper at first of eight, and afterwards of sixteen octavo pages. It appeared every Saturday. The character of this Journal was mainly political; but there are also a few flowers and sweet-scented twigs of literature, intermixed among the nettles and burrs, which alone flourish in the arena of party strife. Its columns are profusely enriched with scraps of satirical verse, in which Dr. Caustic, in his capacity of ballad-maker to the Federal faction, spared not to celebrate every man or measure of government that was anywise susceptible of ridicule. Many of his prose articles are carefully and ably written, attacking not men so much as principles and measures; and his deeply-felt anxiety for the welfare of his country sometimes gives an impressive dignity to his thoughts and style. The dread of French domination seems to have haunted him like a night-mare. But, in spite of the editor's satirical reputation, the "Weekly Inspector" was too conscientious a paper, too sparingly spiced with the red pepper of personal abuse, to succeed in those outrageous times. The publication continued but for a single year, at the end of which we find Mr. Fessenden's valedictory to his readers. Its tone is despondent, both as to the prospects of the country and his own private fortunes. The next token of his labors, that has come under my notice, is a small volume of verse, published at Philadelphia in 1809, and alliteratively entitled, "PILLS, POETICAL, POLITICAL, and PHILOSOPHICAL; prescribed for the Purpose of Purging the Public of Piddling Philosophers, of Penny Poetasters, of Paltry Politicians, and Petty Partizans. By PE-

TER PEPPER-BOX, Poet and Physician." This satire had been
written during the Embargo, but not making its appearance
till after the repeal of that measure, met with less success than
"Democracy Unveiled."

Every body who has known Mr. Fessenden, must have
wondered how the kindest-hearted man in all the world could
have likewise been the most noted satirist of his day. For my
part, I have tried in vain to form a conception of my venerable and peaceful friend, as a champion in the stormy strife of
party, flinging mud full in the faces of his foes, and shouting
forth the bitter laughter that rang from border to border of
the land. And I can hardly believe—though well assured of
it—that his antagonists should ever have meditated personal
violence against the gentlest of human creatures. I am sure, at
least, that nature never meant him for a satirist. On careful
examination of his works, I do not find, in any of them, the
ferocity of the true blood-hound of literature—such as Swift,
or Churchill, or Cobbett—which fastens upon the throat of
its victim, and would fain drink his life-blood. In my opinion
Mr. Fessenden never felt the slightest personal ill-will against
the objects of his satire, except, indeed, they had endeavored
to detract from his literary reputation; an offence which he
resented with a poet's sensibility, and seldom failed to punish.
With such exceptions, his works are not properly satirical, but
the offspring of a mind inexhaustibly fertile in ludicrous ideas,
which it appended to any topic in hand. At times, doubtless,
the all-pervading frenzy of the times inspired him with a bitterness not his own. But, in the least defensible of his writings, he was influenced by an honest zeal for the public good.
There was nothing mercenary in his connexion with politics.
To an antagonist who had taunted him with being poor, he
calmly replied, that he "need not have been accused of the
crime of poverty, could he have prostituted his principles to
party purposes, and become the hireling assassin of the dom-
inant faction." Nor can there be a doubt that the administration would gladly have purchased the pen of so popular a
writer.

I have gained hardly any information of Mr. Fessenden's
life between the years 1807 and 1812; at which latter period,
and probably some time previous, he was settled at the village

of Bellows' Falls, on Connecticut River, in the practice of the law. In May of that year he had the good fortune to become acquainted with Miss Lydia Tuttle, daughter of Mr. John Tuttle, an independent and intelligent farmer at Littleton, Massachusetts. She was then on a visit in Vermont. After her return home, a correspondence ensued between this lady and Mr. Fessenden, and was continued till their marriage in September, 1813. She was considerably younger than himself, but endowed with the qualities most desirable in the wife of such a man; and it would not be easy to over-estimate how much his prosperity and happiness were increased by this union. Mrs. Fessenden could appreciate what was excellent in her husband and supply what was deficient. In her affectionate good sense, he found a substitute for the worldly sagacity which he did not possess, and could not learn. To her he entrusted the pecuniary cares, always so burthensome to a literary man. Her influence restrained him from such imprudent enterprises as had caused the misfortunes of his earlier years. She smoothed his path of life, and made it pleasant to him, and lengthened it; for, as he once told me—(I believe it was while advising me to take, betimes, a similar treasure to myself)—he would have been in his grave long ago, but for her care.

Mr. Fessenden continued to practise law at Bellows' Falls till 1815, when he removed to Brattleboro, and assumed the editorship of the Brattleboro Reporter, a political newspaper. The following year, in compliance with a pressing invitation from the inhabitants, he returned to Bellows' Falls, and edited, with much success, a literary and political paper called the Intelligencer. He held this employment till the year 1822, at the same time practising law, and composing a volume of poetry—"THE LADIES' MONITOR;" besides compiling several works in Law, the Arts, and Agriculture. During this part of his life he usually spent sixteen hours of the twenty-four in study. In 1822 he came to Boston as editor of the "NEW-ENGLAND FARMER," a weekly journal, then first established, and devoted principally to the diffusion of agricultural knowledge.

His management of the Farmer met with unreserved approbation. Having been bred upon a farm, and passed much of his later life in the country, and being thoroughly conversant with the writers on rural economy, he was admirably qualified to conduct such a journal. It was extensively circulated throughout New England, and may be said to have fertilized the soil like rain from heaven. Numerous papers on the same plan sprung up in various parts of the country, but none attained the standard of their prototype. Besides his editorial labors, Mr. Fessenden published, from time to time, various compilations on agricultural subjects, or adaptations of English treatises to the use of the American husbandman. Verse he no longer wrote, except now and then an ode or song for some Agricultural festivity. His poems, being connected with topics of temporary interest, ceased to be read, now that the Metallic Tractors were thrown aside, and that the blending and merging of parties had created an entire change of political aspects, since the days of "Democracy Unveiled." The poetic laurel withered among his gray hairs, and dropt away, leaf by leaf. His name—once the most familiar—was forgotten in the list of American bards. I know not that this oblivion was to be regretted. Mr. Fessenden, if my observation of his temperament be correct, was peculiarly sensitive and nervous in regard to the trials of authorship; a little censure did him more harm than much praise could do him good; and methinks the repose of total neglect was better for him than a feverish notoriety. Were it worth while to imagine any other course for the latter part of his life, which he made so useful and so honorable, it might be wished that he could have devoted himself entirely to scientific research. He had a strong taste for studies of that kind, and sometimes used to lament that his daily drudgery afforded him no leisure to compose a work on Caloric—which subject he had thoroughly investigated.

In January, 1836, I became, and continued for a few months, an inmate of Mr. Fessenden's family. It was my first acquaintance with him. His image is before my mind's eye at this moment; slowly approaching me with a lamp in his hand, his hair grey, his face solemn and pale, his tall and portly figure bent with heavier infirmity than befitted his years. His dress—though he had improved in this particular since middle life—was marked by a truly scholastic negligence. He greeted me kindly, and with a plain, old-fashioned courtesy;

though I fancied that he somewhat regretted the interruption of his evening studies. After a few moments' talk, he invited me to accompany him to his study, and give my opinion on some passages of satirical verse, which were to be inserted in a new edition of "Terrible Tractoration." Years before I had lighted on an illustrated copy of this poem, bestrewn with venerable dust, in a corner of a college library; and it seemed strange and whimsical that I should find it still in progress of composition, and be consulted about it by Doctor Caustic himself. While Mr. Fessenden read, I had leisure to glance around at his study, which was very characteristic of the man and his occupations. The table, and great part of the floor, was covered with books and pamphlets on agricultural subjects, newspapers from all quarters, manuscript articles for the New England Farmer, and manuscript stanzas for "Terrible Tractoration." There was such a litter as always gathers round a literary man. It bespoke, at once, Mr. Fessenden's amiable temper and his abstracted habits, that several members of the family, old and young, were sitting in the room, and engaged in conversation, apparently without giving him the least disturbance. A specimen of Doctor Caustic's inventive genius was seen in the "Patent Steam and Hot-water Stove," which heated the apartment, and kept up a pleasant singing sound, like that of a tea kettle,—thereby making the fireside more cheerful. It appears to me, that, having no children of flesh and blood, Mr. Fessenden had contracted a fatherly fondness for this stove, as being his mental progeny; and it must be owned that the stove well deserved his affection, and repaid it with much warmth.

The new edition of "Tractoration" came out not long afterwards. It was noticed with great kindness by the press, but was not warmly received by the public. Mr. Fessenden imputed the failure, in part, to the illiberality of the 'Trade,' and avenged himself by a little poem, in his best style, entitled "WOODEN BOOKSELLERS;" so that the last blow of his satirical scourge was given in the good old cause of Authors against Publishers.

Notwithstanding a wide difference of age, and many more points of dissimilarity than of resemblance, Mr. Fessenden and myself soon became friends. His partiality seemed not to be the result of any nice discrimination of my good and evil qualities—(for he had no acuteness in that way)—but to be given instinctively, like the affection of a child. On my part, I loved the old man, because his heart was as transparent as a fountain; and I could see nothing in it but integrity and purity, and simple faith in his fellow-man and good-will towards all the world. His character was so open, that I did not need to correct my original conception of it; he never seemed to me like a new acquaintance, but as one with whom I had been familiar from my infancy. Yet he was a rare man, such as few meet with in the course of a lifetime.

It is remarkable, that, with such kindly affections, Mr. Fessenden was so deeply absorbed in thought and study as scarcely to allow himself time for domestic and social enjoyment. During the winter when I first knew him, his mental drudgery was almost continual. Besides the New-England Farmer, he had the editorial charge of two other journals,—the "HORTICULTURAL REGISTER" and the "SILK MANUAL;" in addition to which employment, he was a member of the State legislature, and took some share in its debates. The new matter of "Terrible Tractoration" likewise cost him intense thought. Sometimes I used to meet him in the street, making his way onward apparently by a sort of instinct; while his eyes took note of nothing, and would perhaps pass over my face without sign of recognition. He confessed to me that he was apt to go astray when intent on rhyme. With so much to abstract him from outward life, he could hardly be said to live in the world that was bustling around him. Almost the only relaxation that he allowed himself, was an occasional performance on a bass-viol which stood in the corner of his study, and from which he loved to elicit some old-fashioned tune of soothing potency. At meal-times, however, dragged down and harassed as his spirits were, he brightened up, and generally gladdened the whole table with a flash of Doctor Caustic's humor.

Had I anticipated being Mr. Fessenden's biographer, I might have drawn from him many details that would have been well worth remembering. But he had not the tendency of most men in advanced life, to be copious in personal reminiscences; nor did he often speak of the noted writers and

politicians, with whom the chances of earlier years had associated him. Indeed, lacking a turn for observation of character, his former companions had passed before him like images
in a mirror, giving him little knowledge of their inner nature.
Moreover, till his latest day, he was more inclined to form
prospects for the future than to dwell upon the past. I remember—the last time, save one, that we ever met—I found
him on the bed, suffering with a dizziness of the brain. He
roused himself, however, and grew very cheerful; talking,
with a youthful glow of fancy, about emigrating to Illinois,
where he possessed a farm, and picturing a new life for both
of us in that Western region. It has since come to my memory, that while he spoke there was a purple flush across his
brow—the harbinger of death.

I saw him but once more, alive. On the 13th day of November last, while on my way to Boston, expecting shortly to take
him by the hand, a letter met me with an invitation to his
funeral. He had been struck with apoplexy on Friday evening,
three days before, and had lain insensible till Saturday night,
when he expired. The burial took place at Mount Auburn on
the ensuing Tuesday. It was a gloomy day; for the first snow-
storm of the season had been drifting through the air since
morning; and the "garden of graves" looked the dreariest spot
on earth. The snow came down so fast, that it covered the
coffin in its passage from the hearse to the sepulchre. The few
male friends, who had followed to the cemetery, descended
into the tomb; and it was there that I took my last glance at
the features of a man, who will hold a place in my remembrance apart from other men. He was like no other. In his
long pathway through life, from his cradle to the place we
had now laid him, he had come—a man, indeed, in intellect
and achievement—but in guileless simplicity, a child. Dark
would have been the hour, if, when we closed the door of the
tomb upon his perishing mortality, we had believed that our
friend was there!

It is contemplated to erect a monument, by subscription,
to Mr. Fessenden's memory. It is right that he should be thus
honored. Mount Auburn will long remain a desert, barren of
consecrated marbles, if worth like his be yielded to oblivion.
Let his grave be marked out, that the yeomen of New En-

gland may know where he sleeps; for he was their familiar friend, and has visited them at all their firesides. He has toiled for them at seed-time and harvest; he has scattered the good grain in every field; and they have garnered the increase. Mark out his grave, as that of one worthy to be remembered both in the literary and political annals of our country; and let the laurel be carved on his memorial-stone—for it will cover the ashes of a man of genius.

Time's Portraiture

BEING THE CARRIER'S ADDRESS TO THE PATRONS
OF THE SALEM GAZETTE, FOR THE FIRST
OF JANUARY, 1838

KIND PATRONS.

We newspaper-carriers are Time's errand-boys; and all the year round, the old gentleman sends us from one of your doors to another, to let you know what he is talking about and what he is doing. We are a strange set of urchins; for, punctually on New-Year's morning, one and all of us are seized with a fit of rhyme, and break forth in such hideous strains, that it would be no wonder if the infant Year, with her step upon the threshold, were frightened away by the discord with which we strive to welcome her. On these occasions, most generous Patrons, you never fail to give us a taste of your bounty; but whether as a reward for our verses, or to purchase a respite from further infliction of them, is best known to your worshipful selves. Moreover, we, Time's errand-boys as aforesaid, feel it incumbent upon us, on the first day of every year, to present a sort of summary of our master's dealings with the world, throughout the whole of the preceding twelvemonth. Now it has so chanced, by a misfortune heretofore unheard-of, that I, your present petitioner, have been altogether forgotten by the Muse. Instead of being able (as I naturally expected) to measure my ideas into six-foot lines and tack a rhyme at each of their tails, I find myself, this blessed morning, the same simple proser that I was yesterday, and shall probably be to-morrow. And to my further mortification, being a humble-minded little sinner, I feel nowise capable of talking to your Worships with the customary wisdom of my brethren, and giving sage opinions as to what Time has done right, and what he has done wrong, and what of right or wrong he means to do hereafter. Such being my unhappy predicament, it is with no small confusion of face, that I make bold to present myself at your doors. Yet it were surely a pity, that my non-appearance should defeat your

bountiful designs for the replenishing of my pockets. Wherefore I have bethought me, that it might not displease your
Worships to hear a few particulars about the person and
habits of Father Time; with whom, as being one of his errand-boys, I have more acquaintance than most lads of my
years.

For a great many years past, there has been a wood-cut on
the cover of the Farmer's Almanac, pretending to be a portrait of Father Time. It represents that respectable personage
as almost in a state of nudity, with a single lock of hair on his
forehead, wings on his shoulders, and accoutred with a scythe
and an hour glass. These two latter symbols appear to betoken, that the old fellow works in haying time by the hour.
But, within my recollection, Time has never carried a scythe
and an hour glass, nor worn a pair of wings, nor shown himself in the half naked condition that the Almanac would make
us believe. Now-a-days, he is the most fashionably dressed
figure about town; and I take it to be his natural disposition,
old as he is, to adopt every fashion of the day and of the
hour. Just at the present period, you may meet him in a
furred surtout, with pantaloons strapped under his narrow-
toed boots; on his head, instead of a single forelock, he wears
a smart auburn wig, with bushy whiskers of the same hue,
the whole surmounted by a German-lustre hat. He has exchanged his hour glass for a gold patent lever watch, which
he carries in his vest pocket; and as for his scythe, he has
either thrown it aside altogether, or converted its handle into
a cane, not much stouter than a riding-switch. If you stare
him full in the face, you will perhaps detect a few wrinkles;
but, on a hasty glance, you might suppose him to be in the
very hey-day of life, as fresh as he was in the garden of Eden.
So much for the present aspect of Time; but I by no means
insure that the description shall suit him a month hence, or
even at this hour to-morrow.

It is another very common mistake, to suppose that Time
wanders among old ruins and sits on mouldering walls and
moss-grown stones, meditating about matters which every
body else has forgotten. Some people, perhaps, would expect
to find him at the burial-ground in Broad-street, poring over
the half-illegible inscriptions on the tombs of the Higginsons,

the Hathornes,* the Holyokes, the Brownes, the Olivers, the Pickmans, the Pickerings, and other worthies, with whom he kept company of old. Some would look for him on the ridge of Gallows-Hill, where, in one of his darkest moods, he and Cotton Mather hung the witches. But they need not seek him there. Time is invariably the first to forget his own deeds, his own history, and his own former associates. His place is in the busiest bustle of the world. If you would meet Time face to face, you have only to promenade in Essex-street, between the hours of twelve and one; and there, among beaus and belles, you will see old Father Time, apparently the gayest of the gay. He walks arm in arm with the young men, talking about balls and theatres, and afternoon rides, and midnight merry makings; he recommends such and such a fashionable tailor, and sneers at every garment of six months' antiquity; and generally, before parting, he invites his friends to drink champagne—a wine in which Time delights, on account of its rapid effervescence. And Time treads lightly beside the fair girls, whispering to them (the Old Deceiver!) that they are the sweetest angels he ever was acquainted with. He tells them that they have nothing to do but dance and sing, and twine roses in their hair, and gather a train of lovers, and that the world will always be like an illuminated ball room. And Time goes to the Commercial News-Room, and visits the Insurance Offices, and stands at the corner of Essex and St. Peter's street, talking with the merchants about the arrival of ships, the rise and fall of stocks, the price of cotton and bread stuffs, the prospects of the Whaling-business and the cod-fishery and all other news of the day. And the young gentlemen, and the pretty girls, and the merchants, and all others with whom he makes acquaintance, are apt to think that there is nobody like Time, and that Time is all in all.

But Time is not near so good a fellow as they take him for. He is continually on the watch for mischief, and often seizes a sly opportunity to lay his cane over the shoulders of some middle-aged gentleman; and lo and behold! the poor man's

*Not '*Haw*thorne,'—as one of the present representatives of the family, has seen fit to transmogrify a good old name. However, Time seldom has occasion to mention the gentleman's name, so that it is no great matter how he spells or pronounces it.

back is bent, his hair turns gray, and his face looks like a shrivelled apple. This is what is meant by being 'time-stricken.' It is the worst feature in Time's character, that he always inflicts the greatest injuries on his oldest friends. Yet, shamefully as he treats them, they evince no desire to cut his acquaintance, and can seldom bear to think of a final separation.

Again, there is a very prevalent idea, that Time loves to sit by the fire-side, telling stories of the Puritans, the Witch persecutors, and the heroes of the Old French War and the Revolution; and that he has no memory of anything more recent than the days of the first President Adams. This is another great mistake. Time is so eager to talk of novelties, that he never fails to give circulation to the most incredible rumours of the day, though at the hazard of being compelled to eat his own words to-morrow. He shows numberless instances of this propensity, while the national elections are in progress. A month ago, his mouth was full of the wonderful Whig victories; and to do him justice, he really seems to have told the truth for once. Whether the same story will hold good another year, we must leave Time himself to show. He has a good deal to say, at the present juncture, concerning the revolutionary movements in Canada; he blusters a little, about the north-eastern boundary question; he expresses great impatience at the sluggishness of our commanders in the Florida war; he gets considerably excited, whenever the subject of abolition is brought forward, and so much the more, as he appears hardly to have made up his mind on one side or the other. Whenever this happens to be the case—as it often does—Time works himself into such a rage, that you would think he were going to tear the universe to pieces; but I never yet knew him to proceed, in good earnest, to such terrible extremities. During the last six or seven months, he has been seized with intolerable sulkiness at the slightest mention of the currency; for nothing vexes Time so much as to be refused cash upon the nail. The above are the chief topics of general interest, which Time is just now in the habit of discussing. For his more private gossip, he has rumours of new matches, or of old ones broken off, with now and then a whisper of good-natured scandal; sometimes, too, he condescends to criticise a sermon, or a Lyceum lecture, or a performance of the Glee-Club; and, to be brief, catch the volatile essence of present talk and transitory opinions, and you will have Time's gossip, word for word. I may as well add, that he expresses great approbation of Mr. Russell's vocal abilities, and means to be present from beginning to end of his next concert. It is not every singer that could *keep Time* with his voice and instrument, for a whole evening.

Perhaps you will inquire, 'What are Time's literary tastes?' And here, again, there is a general mistake. It is conceived by many, that Time spends his leisure hours at the Athenaeum, turning over the musty leaves of those huge worm-eaten folios, which nobody else has disturbed since the death of the venerable Doctor Oliver. So far from this being the case, Time's profoundest studies are the new novels from Messrs. Ives and Jewett's Circulating Library. He skims over the lighter articles in the periodicals of the day, glances at the newspapers, and then throws them aside forever; all except the Salem Gazette, of which he preserves a file, for his amusement a century or two hence.

We will now consider Time as a man of business. In this capacity, our citizens are in the habit of complaining, not wholly without reason, that Time is sluggish and dull. You may see him occasionally at the end of Derby-Wharf, leaning against a post or sitting on the breech of an iron cannon, staring listlessly at an unrigged East-Indiaman. Or if you look through the windows of the Union Marine Insurance Office, you may get a glimpse of him there, nodding over a newspaper, among the old weather-beaten sea-captains who recollect when Time was quite a different sort of fellow. If you enter any of the dry good stores along Essex-street, you will be likely to find him with his elbows on the counter, bargaining for a yard of tape or a paper of pins. To catch him in his idlest mood, you must visit the office of some young lawyer. Still, however, Time does contrive to do a little business among us, and should not be denied the credit of it. During the past season he has worked pretty diligently upon the Railroad, and promises to start the cars by the middle of next summer. Then we may fly from Essex-street to State-street, and be back again before Time misses us. In conjunction with our worthy Mayor (with whose ancestor, the Lord Mayor of London, Time was well acquainted, more than two hundred years ago) he has laid the corner stone of a new City Hall, the granite front of which is already an ornament to Court-street. But, besides these public affairs, Time busies himself a good deal in private. Just at this season of the year, he is engaged in collecting bills, and may be seen at almost any hour peregrinating from street to street, and knocking at half the doors in town, with a great bundle of these infernal documents. On such errands, he appears in the likeness of an under-sized, portly old gentleman, with gray hair, a bluff red face, and a loud tone of voice; and many people mistake him for the penny-post.

Never does a marriage take place, but Time is present among the wedding-guests; for marriage is an affair in which Time takes more interest than in almost any other. He generally gives away the bride, and leads the bridegroom by the hand, to the threshold of the bridal chamber. Although Time pretends to be very merry on these occasions, yet if you watch him well, you may often detect a sigh. Whenever a babe is born into this weary world, Time is in attendance and receives the wailing infant in his arms. And the poor babe shudders instinctively at his embrace, and sets up a feeble cry. Then again, from the birth chamber, he must hurry to the bedside of some old acquaintance, whose business with Time is ended forever, though their accounts remain to be settled at a future day. It is terrible, sometimes, to perceive the lingering reluctance, the shivering agony, with which the poor souls bid Time farewell, if they have gained no other friend to supply the gray deceiver's place. How do they cling to Time, and steal another and yet another glance at his familiar aspect! But Time, the hard hearted old fellow! goes through such scenes with infinite composure, and dismisses his best friends from memory, the moment they are out of sight. Others, who have not been too intimate with Time, as knowing him to be a dangerous character, and apt to ruin his associates—these take leave of him with joy, and pass away with a look of triumph on their features. They know, that in spite of all his flattering promises, he could not make them happy, but that now they shall be so, long after Time is dead and buried.

For Time is not immortal. Time must die, and be buried in the deep grave of eternity. And let him die! From the hour when he passed forth through the gate of Eden, till this very moment, he has gone to and fro about the earth staining his hands with blood, committing crimes innumerable, and bringing misery on himself and all mankind. Sometimes he has been a pagan; sometimes a persecutor. Sometimes he has spent centuries in darkness, where he could neither read nor write. These were called the Dark Ages. There has hardly been a single year, when he has not stirred up strife among the nations. Sometimes—as in France, less than fifty years ago—he has been seized with fits of frenzy, and murdered thousands of innocent people, at noon day. He pretends indeed that he has grown wiser and better now. Trust him who will, for my part, I rejoice that Time shall not live forever. He hath an appointed office to perform. Let him do his task, and die. Fresh and young as he would make himself appear, he is already hoary with age, and the very garments that he wears about the town, were put on thousands of years ago, and have been patched and pieced, to suit the present fashion. There is nothing new in him nor about him. Were he to die, while I am speaking, we could not pronounce it an untimely death. Methinks, with his heavy heart and weary brain, Time should himself be glad to die!

Meanwhile, gentle Patrons, as Time has brought round another New Year, pray remember your poor petitioner! For so small a lad, you will agree that I talk pretty passably well, and have fairly earned whatever spare specie Time has left in your pockets. Be kind to me; and I have good hope that Time will be kind to you.—After all the hard things which I have said about him, he is really—that is, if you take him for neither more nor less than he is worth, and use him as not abusing him—Time is really a very tolerable old fellow, and may be endured for the little while that we are to keep him company. Be generous kind Patrons, to Time's errand boy. So may he bring to the Merchant his ship safe from the Indies,—to the Lawyer, a goodly number of new suits,—to the Doctor, a crowd of patients with the dyspepsia and fat purses,—to the Farmer, a golden crop and a ready market,—to the Mechanic, steady employment and good wages,—to the idle Gentleman, some honest business,—to the Rich, kind hearts and liberal hands,—to the Poor, warm fire-sides and food enough, patient spirits and the hope of better days,—to our Country, a return of specie payments,—and to you, sweet Maid, the youth who stole into your dream, last night! And next New Year's day, (if I find nothing better to do in the meanwhile,) may Time again bring to your doors your loving little friend,

THE CARRIER.

Snow-Flakes

THERE is snow in yonder cold gray sky of the morning!—and through the partially frosted window-panes, I love to watch the gradual beginning of the storm. A few feathery flakes are scattered widely through the air, and hover downward with uncertain flight, now almost alighting on the earth, now whirled again aloft into remote regions of the atmosphere. These are not the big flakes, heavy with moisture, which melt as they touch the ground, and are portentous of a soaking rain. It is to be, in good earnest, a wintry storm. The two or three people visible on the side-walks, have an aspect of endurance, a blue-nosed, frosty fortitude, which is evidently assumed in anticipation of a comfortless and blustering day. By nightfall, or at least before the sun sheds another glimmering smile upon us, the street and our little garden will be heaped with mountain snow-drifts. The soil, already frozen for weeks past, is prepared to sustain whatever burthen may be laid upon it; and, to a northern eye, the landscape will lose its melancholy bleakness and acquire a beauty of its own, when Mother Earth, like her children, shall have put on the fleecy garb of her winter's wear. The cloud-spirits are slowly weaving her white mantle. As yet, indeed, there is barely a rime like hoar frost over the brown surface of the street; the withered green of the grass-plat is still discernible; and the slated roofs of the houses do but begin to look gray, instead of black. All the snow that has yet fallen within the circumference of my view, were it heaped up together, would hardly equal the hillock of a grave. Thus gradually, by silent and stealthy influences, are great changes wrought. These little snow-particles, which the storm-spirit flings by handfulls through the air, will bury the great earth under their accumulated mass, nor permit her to behold her sister sky again for dreary months. We, likewise, shall lose sight of our mother's familiar visage, and must content ourselves with looking heavenward the oftener.

Now, leaving the storm to do his appointed office, let us sit down, pen in hand, by our fireside. Gloomy as it may

seem, there is an influence productive of cheerfulness and favorable to imaginative thought, in the atmosphere of a snowy
day. The native of a southern clime may woo the muse beneath the heavy shade of summer foliage, reclining on banks
of turf, while the sound of singing birds and warbling rivulets
chimes in with the music of his soul. In our brief summer, I
do not think, but only exist in the vague enjoyment of a
dream. My hour of inspiration—if that hour ever comes—is
when the green log hisses upon the hearth, and the bright
flame, brighter for the gloom of the chamber, rustles high up
the chimney, and the coals drop tinkling down among the
growing heaps of ashes. When the casement rattles in the
gust, and the snow-flakes or the sleety rain-drops pelt hard
against the window-panes, then I spread out my sheet of paper, with the certainty that thoughts and fancies will gleam
forth upon it, like stars at twilight, or like violets in May—
perhaps to fade as soon. However transitory their glow, they
at least shine amid the darksome shadow which the clouds of
the outward sky fling through the room. Blessed, therefore,
and reverently welcomed by me, her true-born son, be New-
England's winter, which makes us, one and all, the nurslings
of the storm, and sings a familiar lullaby even in the wildest
shriek of the December blast. Now look we forth again, and
see how much of his task the storm-spirit has done.

    Slow and sure! He has the day, perchance the week, before
him, and may take his own time to accomplish Nature's burial
in snow. A smooth mantle is scarcely yet thrown over the
withered grass-plat, and the dry stalks of annuals still thrust
themselves through the white surface in all parts of the garden. The leafless rose bushes stand shivering in a shallow
snow-drift, looking, poor things! as disconsolate as if they
possessed a human consciousness of the dreary scene. This is
a sad time for the shrubs that do not perish with the summer;
they neither live nor die; what they retain of life seems but
the chilling sense of death. Very sad are the flower-shrubs in
mid-winter! The roofs of the houses are now all white, save
where the eddying wind has kept them bare at the bleak corners. To discern the real intensity of the storm, we must fix
upon some distant object,—as yonder spire,—and observe
how the riotous gust fights with the descending snow

throughout the intervening space. Sometimes the entire prospect is obscured; then, again, we have a distinct, but transient glimpse of the tall steeple, like a giant's ghost; and now the dense wreaths sweep between, as if demons were flinging snow-drifts at each other, in mid-air. Look next into the street, where we have an amusing parallel to the combat of those fancied demons in the upper regions. It is a snow-battle of school-boys. What a pretty satire on war and military glory might be written, in the form of a child's story, by describing the snow-ball fights of two rival schools, the alternate defeats and victories of each, and the final triumph of one party, or perhaps of neither! What pitched battles, worthy to be chanted in Homeric strains! What storming of fortresses, built all of massive snow-blocks! What feats of individual prowess, and embodied onsets of martial enthusiasm! And when some well contested and decisive victory had put a period to the war, both armies should unite to build a lofty monument of snow upon the battle-field, and crown it with the victor's statue, hewn of the same frozen marble. In a few days or weeks thereafter, the passer-by would observe a shapeless mound upon the level common; and, unmindful of the famous victory, would ask—'How came it there? Who reared it? And what means it?' The shattered pedestal of many a battle-monument has provoked these questions, when none could answer.

Turn we again to the fireside, and sit musing there, lending our ears to the wind, till perhaps it shall seem like an articulate voice, and dictate wild and airy matter for the pen. Would it might inspire me to sketch out the personification of a New-England winter! And that idea, if I can seize the snow-wreathed figures that flit before my fancy, shall be the theme of the next page.

How does Winter herald his approach? By the shrieking blast of latter autumn, which is Nature's cry of lamentation, as the destroyer rushes among the shivering groves where she has lingered, and scatters the sear leaves upon the tempest. When that cry is heard the people wrap themselves in cloaks, and shake their heads disconsolately, saying—'Winter is at hand!' Then the axe of the wood-cutter echoes sharp and diligently in the forest,—then the coal-merchants rejoice, be-

cause each shriek of Nature in her agony adds something to
the price of coal per ton—then the peat-smoke spreads its
aromatic fragrance through the atmosphere. A few days
more; and at eventide, the children look out of the window,
and dimly perceive the flaunting of a snowy mantle in the air.
It is stern Winter's vesture. They crowd around the hearth,
and cling to their mother's gown, or press between their father's knees, affrighted by the hollow roaring voice, that bellows adown the wide flue of the chimney. It is the voice of
Winter; and when parents and children hear it, they shudder
and exclaim—'Winter is come! Cold Winter has begun his
reign already!' Now, throughout New-England, each hearth
becomes an altar, sending up the smoke of a continued sacrifice to the immitigable deity who tyrannizes over forest, coun-
try-side, and town. Wrapt in his white mantle, his staff a huge
icicle, his beard and hair a wind-tossed snow-drift, he travels
over the land, in the midst of the northern blast; and wo to
the homeless wanderer whom he finds upon his path! There
he lies stark and stiff, a human shape of ice, on the spot where
Winter overtook him. On strides the tyrant over the rushing
rivers and broad lakes, which turn to rock beneath his footsteps. His dreary empire is established; all around stretches
the desolation of the Pole. Yet not ungrateful be his New-
England children—(for Winter is our sire, though a stern and
rough one)—not ungrateful even for the severities, which
have nourished our unyielding strength of character. And let
us thank him, too, for the sleigh-rides, cheered by the music
of merry bells—for the crackling and rustling hearth, when
the ruddy fire-light gleams on hardy Manhood and the
blooming cheek of Woman—for all the home-enjoyments,
and the kindred virtues, which flourish in a frozen soil. Not
that we grieve, when, after some seven months of storm and
bitter frost, Spring, in the guise of a flower-crowned virgin,
is seen driving away the hoary despot, pelting him with violets by the handful, and strewing green grass on the path
behind him. Often, ere he will give up his empire, old Winter
rushes fiercely back, and hurls a snow-drift at the shrinking
form of Spring; yet, step by step, he is compelled to retreat
northward, and spends the summer months within the Arctic
circle.

Such fantasies, intermixed among graver toils of mind, have made the winter's day pass pleasantly. Meanwhile, the storm has raged without abatement, and now, as the brief afternoon declines, is tossing denser volumes to and fro about the atmosphere. On the window-sill, there is a layer of snow, reaching half way up the lowest pane of glass. The garden is one unbroken bed. Along the street are two or three spots of uncovered earth, where the gust has whirled away the snow, heaping it elsewhere to the fence-tops, or piling huge banks against the doors of houses. A solitary passenger is seen, now striding mid-leg deep across a drift, now scudding over the bare ground, while his cloak is swollen with the wind. And now the gingling of bells, a sluggish sound, responsive to the horse's toilsome progress through the unbroken drifts, announces the passage of a sleigh, with a boy clinging behind, and ducking his head to escape detection by the driver. Next comes a sledge, laden with wood for some unthrifty housekeeper, whom winter has surprised at a cold hearth. But what dismal equipage now struggles along the uneven street? A sable hearse, bestrewn with snow, is bearing a dead man through the storm to his frozen bed. Oh, how dreary is a burial in winter, when the bosom of Mother Earth has no warmth for her poor child!

Evening—the early eve of December—begins to spread its deepening veil over the comfortless scene; the fire-light gradually brightens, and throws my flickering shadow upon the walls and ceiling of the chamber; but still the storm rages and rattles against the windows. Alas! I shiver, and think it time to be disconsolate. But, taking a farewell glance at dead Nature in her shroud, I perceive a flock of snow-birds, skimming lightsomely through the tempest, and flitting from drift to drift, as sportively as swallows in the delightful prime of summer. Whence come they? Where do they build their nests, and seek their food? Why, having airy wings, do they not follow summer around the earth, instead of making themselves the playmates of the storm, and fluttering on the dreary verge of the winter's eve? I know not whence they come, nor why; yet my spirit has been cheered by that wandering flock of snow-birds.

The Threefold Destiny

A FAËRY LEGEND

I HAVE sometimes produced a singular and not unpleasing effect, so far as my own mind was concerned, by imagining a train of incidents, in which the spirit and mechanism of the faëry legend should be combined with the characters and manners of familiar life. In the little tale which follows, a subdued tinge of the wild and wonderful is thrown over a sketch of New-England personages and scenery, yet, it is hoped, without entirely obliterating the sober hues of nature. Rather than a story of events claiming to be real, it may be considered as an allegory, such as the writers of the last century would have expressed in the shape of an eastern tale, but to which I have endeavored to give a more life-like warmth than could be infused into those fanciful productions.

In the twilight of a summer eve, a tall, dark figure, over which long and remote travel had thrown an outlandish aspect, was entering a village, not in "Faëry Londe," but within our own familiar boundaries. The staff, on which this traveller leaned, had been his companion from the spot where it grew, in the jungles of Hindostan; the hat, that overshadowed his sombre brow, had shielded him from the suns of Spain; but his cheek had been blackened by the red-hot wind of an Arabian desert, and had felt the frozen breath of an Arctic region. Long sojourning amid wild and dangerous men, he still wore beneath his vest the ataghan which he had once struck into the throat of a Turkish robber. In every foreign clime he had lost something of his New-England characteristics; and, perhaps, from every people he had unconsciously borrowed a new peculiarity; so that when the world-wanderer again trod the street of his native village, it is no wonder that he passed unrecognized, though exciting the gaze and curiosity of all. Yet, as his arm casually touched that of a young woman, who was wending her way to an evening lecture, she started, and almost uttered a cry.

"Ralph Cranfield!" was the name that she half articulated.

"Can that be my old playmate, Faith Egerton?" thought the traveller, looking round at her figure, but without pausing.

Ralph Cranfield, from his youth upward, had felt himself marked out for a high destiny. He had imbibed the idea—we say not whether it were revealed to him by witchcraft, or in a dream of prophecy, or that his brooding fancy had palmed its own dictates upon him as the oracles of a Sybil—but he had imbibed the idea, and held it firmest among his articles of faith, that three marvellous events of his life were to be confirmed to him by three signs.

The first of these three fatalities, and perhaps the one on which his youthful imagination had dwelt most fondly, was the discovery of the maid, who alone, of all the maids on earth, could make him happy by her love. He was to roam around the world till he should meet a beautiful woman, wearing on her bosom a jewel in the shape of a heart; whether of pearl, or ruby, or emerald, or carbuncle, or a changeful opal, or perhaps a priceless diamond, Ralph Cranfield little cared, so long as it were a heart of one peculiar shape. On encountering this lovely stranger, he was bound to address her thus:—"Maiden, I have brought you a heavy heart. May I rest its weight on you?" And if she were his fated bride—if their kindred souls were destined to form a union here below, which all eternity should only bind more closely—she would reply, with her finger on the heart-shaped jewel:—"This token, which I have worn so long, is the assurance that you may!"

And secondly, Ralph Cranfield had a firm belief that there was a mighty treasure hidden somewhere in the earth, of which the burial-place would be revealed to none but him. When his feet should press upon the mysterious spot, there would be a hand before him, pointing downward—whether carved of marble, or hewn in gigantic dimensions on the side of a rocky precipice, or perchance a hand of flame in empty air, he could not tell; but, at least, he would discern a hand, the fore-finger pointing downward, and beneath it the Latin word EFFODE—Dig! And digging thereabouts, the gold in coin or ingots, the precious stones, or of whatever else the treasure might consist, would be certain to reward his toil.

The third and last of the miraculous events in the life of
this high-destined man, was to be the attainment of extensive
influence and sway over his fellow-creatures. Whether he were
to be a king, and founder of an hereditary throne, or the victorious leader of a people contending for their freedom, or
the apostle of a purified and regenerated faith, was left for
futurity to show. As messengers of the sign, by which Ralph
Cranfield might recognize the summons, three venerable men
were to claim audience of him. The chief among them, a dignified and majestic person, arrayed, it may be supposed, in
the flowing garments of an ancient sage, would be the bearer
of a wand, or prophet's rod. With this wand, or rod, or staff,
the venerable sage would trace a certain figure in the air, and
then proceed to make known his heaven-instructed message;
which, if obeyed, must lead to glorious results.

With this proud fate before him, in the flush of his imaginative youth, Ralph Cranfield had set forth to seek the maid,
the treasure, and the venerable sage, with his gift of extended
empire. And had he found them? Alas! it was not with the
aspect of a triumphant man, who had achieved a nobler destiny than all his fellows, but rather with the gloom of one
struggling against peculiar and continual adversity, that he
now passed homeward to his mother's cottage. He had come
back, but only for a time, to lay aside the pilgrim's staff, trusting that his weary manhood would regain somewhat of the
elasticity of youth in the spot where his threefold fate had
been foreshown him. There had been few changes in the village; for it was not one of those thriving places where a year's
prosperity makes more than the havoc of a century's decay;
but, like a gray hair in a young man's head, an antiquated
little town, full of old maids, and aged elms, and moss-grown
dwellings. Few seemed to be the changes here. The drooping
elms, indeed, had a more majestic spread; the weather-black-
ened houses were adorned with a denser thatch of verdant
moss; and doubtless there were a few more grave-stones in
the burial-ground, inscribed with names that had once been
familiar in the village street. Yet, summing up all the mischief
that ten years had wrought, it seemed scarcely more than if
Ralph Cranfield had gone forth that very morning, and
dreamed a day-dream till the twilight, and then turned back

again. But his heart grew cold, because the village did not remember him as he remembered the village.

"Here is the change!" sighed he, striking his hand upon his breast. "Who is this man of thought and care, weary with world-wandering, and heavy with disappointed hopes? The youth returns not, who went forth so joyously!"

And now Ralph Cranfield was at his mother's gate, in front of the small house where the old lady, with slender but sufficient means, had kept herself comfortable during her son's long absence. Admitting himself within the inclosure, he leaned against a great, old tree, trifling with his own impatience, as people often do in those intervals when years are summed into a moment. He took a minute survey of the dwelling—its windows, brightened with the sky gleam, its door-way, with the half of a mill-stone for a step, and the faintly-traced path waving thence to the gate. He made friends again with his childhood's friend, the old tree against which he leaned; and glancing his eye adown its trunk, beheld something that excited a melancholy smile. It was a half-obliterated inscription—the Latin word EFFODE—which he remembered to have carved in the bark of the tree, with a whole day's toil, when he had first begun to muse about his exalted destiny. It might be accounted a rather singular coincidence, that the bark, just above the inscription, had put forth an excrescence, shaped not unlike a hand, with the fore-finger pointing obliquely at the word of fate. Such, at least, was its appearance in the dusky light.

"Now a credulous man," said Ralph Cranfield carelessly to himself, "might suppose that the treasure which I have sought round the world, lies buried, after all, at the very door of my mother's dwelling. That would be a jest indeed!"

More he thought not about the matter; for now the door was opened, and an elderly woman appeared on the threshold, peering into the dusk to discover who it might be that had intruded on her premises, and was standing in the shadow of her tree. It was Ralph Cranfield's mother. Pass we over their greeting, and leave the one to her joy and the other to his rest—if quiet rest he found.

But when morning broke, he arose with a troubled brow; for his sleep and his wakefulness had alike been full of dreams.

All the fervor was rekindled with which he had burned of yore to unravel the threefold mystery of his fate. The crowd of his early visions seemed to have awaited him beneath his mother's roof, and thronged riotously around to welcome his return. In the well-remembered chamber—on the pillow where his infancy had slumbered—he had passed a wilder night than ever in an Arab tent, or when he had reposed his head in the ghastly shades of a haunted forest. A shadowy maid had stolen to his bedside, and laid her finger on the scintillating heart; a hand of flame had glowed amid the darkness, pointing downward to a mystery within the earth; a hoary sage had waved his prophetic wand, and beckoned the dreamer onward to a chair of state. The same phantoms, though fainter in the daylight, still flitted about the cottage, and mingled among the crowd of familiar faces that were drawn thither by the news of Ralph Cranfield's return, to bid him welcome for his mother's sake. There they found him, a tall, dark, stately man, of foreign aspect, courteous in demeanor and mild of speech, yet with an abstracted eye, which seemed often to snatch a glance at the invisible.

Meantime the widow Cranfield went bustling about the house, full of joy that she again had somebody to love, and be careful of, and for whom she might vex and teaze herself with the petty troubles of daily life. It was nearly noon, when she looked forth from the door, and descried three personages of note coming along the street, through the hot sunshine and the masses of elm-tree shade. At length they reached her gate, and undid the latch.

"See, Ralph!" exclaimed she, with maternal pride, "here is Squire Hawkwood and the two other selectmen, coming on purpose to see you! Now do tell them a good long story about what you have seen in foreign parts."

The foremost of the three visiters, Squire Hawkwood, was a very pompous, but excellent old gentleman, the head and prime mover in all the affairs of the village, and universally acknowledged to be one of the sagest men on earth. He wore, according to a fashion even then becoming antiquated, a three-cornered hat, and carried a silver-headed cane, the use of which seemed to be rather for flourishing in the air than for assisting the progress of his legs. His two companions were elderly and respectable yeomen, who, retaining an ante-revolutionary reverence for rank and hereditary wealth, kept a little in the Squire's rear. As they approached along the pathway, Ralph Cranfield sat in an oaken elbow-chair, half unconsciously gazing at the three visiters, and enveloping their homely figures in the misty romance that pervaded his mental world.

"Here," thought he, smiling at the conceit, "here come three elderly personages, and the first of the three is a venerable sage with a staff. What if this embassy should bring me the message of my fate!"

While Squire Hawkwood and his colleagues entered, Ralph rose from his seat, and advanced a few steps to receive them; and his stately figure and dark countenance, as he bent courteously towards his guests, had a natural dignity; contrasting well with the bustling importance of the Squire. The old gentleman, according to invariable custom, gave an elaborate preliminary flourish with his cane in the air, then removed his three-cornered hat in order to wipe his brow, and finally proceeded to make known his errand.

"My colleagues and myself," began the Squire, "are burthened with momentous duties, being jointly selectmen of this village. Our minds, for the space of three days past, have been laboriously bent on the selection of a suitable person to fill a most important office, and take upon himself a charge and rule, which, wisely considered, may be ranked no lower than those of kings and potentates. And whereas you, our native townsman, are of good natural intellect, and well cultivated by foreign travel, and that certain vagaries and fantasies of your youth are doubtless long ago corrected; taking all these matters, I say, into due consideration, we are of opinion that Providence hath sent you hither, at this juncture, for our very purpose."

During this harangue, Cranfield gazed fixedly at the speaker, as if he beheld something mysterious and unearthly in his pompous little figure, and as if the Squire had worn the flowing robes of an ancient sage, instead of a square-skirted coat, flapped waistcoat, velvet breeches and silk stockings. Nor was his wonder without sufficient cause; for the flourish of the Squire's staff, marvellous to relate, had described pre-

cisely the signal in the air which was to ratify the message of
the prophetic Sage, whom Cranfield had sought around the
world.

"And what," inquired Ralph Cranfield, with a tremor in his
voice, "what may this office be, which is to equal me with
kings and potentates?"

"No less than instructor of our village school," answered
Squire Hawkwood; "the office being now vacant by the death
of the venerable Master Whitaker, after a fifty years' incum-
bency."

"I will consider of your proposal," replied Ralph Cranfield
hurriedly, "and will make known my decision within three
days."

After a few more words, the village dignitary and his companions took their leave. But to Cranfield's fancy their images
were still present, and became more and more invested with
the dim awfulness of figures which had first appeared to him
in a dream, and afterwards had shown themselves in his waking moments, assuming homely aspects among familiar
things. His mind dwelt upon the features of the Squire, till
they grew confused with those of the visionary Sage, and one
appeared but the shadow of the other. The same visage, he
now thought, had looked forth upon him from the Pyramid
of Cheops; the same form had beckoned to him among the
colonnades of the Alhambra; the same figure had mistily revealed itself through the ascending steam of the Great Geyser.
At every effort of his memory he recognized some trait of the
dreamy Messenger of Destiny, in this pompous, bustling, self-
important, little great man of the village. Amid such musings,
Ralph Cranfield sat all day in the cottage, scarcely hearing and
vaguely answering his mother's thousand questions about his
travels and adventures. At sunset, he roused himself to take a
stroll, and, passing the aged elm-tree, his eye was again
caught by the semblance of a hand, pointing downward at
the half-obliterated inscription.

As Cranfield walked down the street of the village, the level
sunbeams threw his shadow far before him; and he fancied
that, as his shadow walked among distant objects, so had
there been a presentiment stalking in advance of him

throughout his life. And when he drew near each object, over which his tall shadow had preceded him, still it proved to be one of the familiar recollections of his infancy and youth. Every crook in the pathway was remembered. Even the more transitory characteristics of the scene were the same as in bygone days. A company of cows were grazing on the grassy road-side, and refreshed him with their fragrant breath. "It is sweeter," thought he, "than the perfume which was wafted to our ship from the Spice Islands." The round little figure of a child rolled from a door-way, and lay laughing, almost beneath Cranfield's feet. The dark and stately man stooped down, and lifting the infant, restored him to his mother's arms. "The children," said he to himself—and sighed, and smiled—"the children are to be my charge!" And while a flow of natural feeling gushed like a well-spring in his heart, he came to a dwelling which he could nowise forbear to enter. A sweet voice, which seemed to come from a deep and tender soul, was warbling a plaintive little air, within.

He bent his head, and passed through the lowly door. As his foot sounded upon the threshold, a young woman advanced from the dusky interior of the house, at first hastily, and then with a more uncertain step, till they met face to face. There was a singular contrast in their two figures; he dark and picturesque—one who had battled with the world— whom all suns had shone upon, and whom all winds had blown on a varied course; she neat, comely, and quiet—quiet even in her agitation—as if all her emotions had been subdued to the peaceful tenor of her life. Yet their faces, all unlike as they were, had an expression that seemed not so alien —a glow of kindred feeling, flashing upward anew from half-extinguished embers.

"You are welcome home!" said Faith Egerton.

But Cranfield did not immediately answer; for his eye had been caught by an ornament in the shape of a Heart, which Faith wore as a brooch upon her bosom. The material was the ordinary white quartz; and he recollected having himself shaped it out of one of those Indian arrow-heads, which are so often found in the ancient haunts of the red men. It was precisely on the pattern of that worn by the visionary Maid.

When Cranfield departed on his shadowy search he had bestowed this brooch, in a gold setting, as a parting gift to Faith Egerton.

"So, Faith, you have kept the Heart!" said he, at length.

"Yes," said she, blushing deeply—then more gaily, "and what else have you brought me from beyond the sea?"

"Faith!" replied Ralph Cranfield, uttering the fated words by an uncontrollable impulse, "I have brought you nothing but a heavy heart! May I rest its weight on you?"

"This token, which I have worn so long," said Faith, laying her tremulous finger on the Heart, "is the assurance that you may!"

"Faith! Faith!" cried Cranfield, clasping her in his arms, "you have interpreted my wild and weary dream!"

Yes; the wild dreamer was awake at last. To find the mysterious treasure, he was to till the earth around his mother's dwelling, and reap its products! Instead of warlike command, or regal or religious sway, he was to rule over the village children! And now the visionary Maid had faded from his fancy, and in her place he saw the playmate of his childhood! Would all, who cherish such wild wishes, but look around them, they would oftenest find their sphere of duty, of prosperity, and happiness, within those precincts, and in that station where Providence itself has cast their lot. Happy they who read the riddle without a weary world-search, or a lifetime spent in vain!

Jonathan Cilley

THE subject of this brief memorial had barely begun to be an actor in the great scenes, where his part could not have failed to be a prominent one. The nation did not have time to recognize him. His death, aside from the shock with which the manner of it has thrilled every bosom, is looked upon merely as causing a vacancy in the delegation of his State, which a new member may fill as creditably as the departed. It will perhaps be deemed praise enough to say of Cilley, that he would have proved himself an active and efficient partizan. But those who knew him longest and most intimately, conscious of his high talents and rare qualities—his energy of mind and force of character—must claim much more than such a meed, for their lost friend. They feel that not merely a party nor a section, but our collective Country has lost a man, who had the heart and the ability to serve her well. It would be doing injustice to the hopes which lie withered upon his untimely grave, if, in paying a farewell tribute to his memory, we were to ask a narrower sympathy than that of the people at large. May no bitterness of party prejudices influence him who writes, nor those, of whatever political opinions, who may read!

Jonathan Cilley was born at Nottingham, New-Hampshire, on the second of July, 1802. His grandfather, Colonel Joseph Cilley, commanded a New-Hampshire regiment during the Revolutionary war, and established a character for energy and intrepidity, of which more than one of his descendants have proved themselves the inheritors. Greenleaf Cilley, son of the preceding, died in 1808, leaving a family of four sons and three daughters. The aged mother of this family, and the three daughters, are still living. Of the sons the only survivor is Joseph Cilley, who was an officer in the late war, and served with great distinction on the Canadian frontier. Jonathan, being desirous of a liberal education, commenced his studies at Atkinson Academy, at about the age of seventeen, and became a member of the freshman-class of Bowdoin College, Brunswick, Maine, in 1821. Inheriting but little property from his father, he adopted the usual expedient of a young New-Englander in similar circumstances, and gained a small income by teaching a country school during the winter months, both before and after his entrance at college.

Cilley's character and standing at college afforded high promise of usefulness and distinction in after life. Though not the foremost scholar of his class, he stood in the front rank; and probably derived all the real benefit from the prescribed course of study, that it could bestow on so practical a mind. His true education consisted in the exercise of those faculties which fitted him to be a popular leader. His influence among his fellow-students was probably greater than that of any other individual; and he had already made himself powerful, in that limited sphere, by a free and natural eloquence—a flow of pertinent ideas, in language of unstudied appropriateness, which seemed always to accomplish precisely the result on which he had calculated. This gift was sometimes displayed in class-meetings, when measures, important to those concerned, were under discussion; sometimes in mock trials at law, when judge, jury, lawyers, prisoner, and witnesses, were personated by the students, and Cilley played the part of a fervid and successful advocate; and besides these exhibitions of power, he regularly trained himself in the forensic debates of a literary society, of which he afterwards became president. Nothing could be less artificial than his style of oratory. After filling his mind with the necessary information, he trusted everything else to his mental warmth and the inspiration of the moment, and poured himself out with an earnest and irresistible simplicity. There was a singular contrast between the flow of thought from his lips, and the coldness and constraint with which he wrote; and though, in maturer life, he acquired a considerable facility in exercising the pen, he always felt the tongue to be his peculiar instrument.

In private intercourse, Cilley possessed a remarkable fascination. It was impossible not to regard him with the kindliest feelings, because his companions were intuitively certain of a like kindliness on his part. He had a power of sympathy which enabled him to understand every character, and hold communion with human nature in all its varieties. He never shrank from the intercourse of man with man; and it was to his freedom in this particular that he owed much of his subsequent popularity, among a people who are accustomed to take a personal interest in the men whom they elevate to office. In few words, let us characterize him at the outset of life as a young man of quick and powerful intellect; endowed with sagacity and tact, yet frank and free in his mode of action; ambitious of good influence, earnest, active, and persevering; with an elasticity and cheerful strength of mind which made difficulties easy, and the struggle with them a pleasure. Mingled with the amiable qualities that were like sunshine to his friends, there were harsher and sterner traits, which fitted him to make head against an adverse world; but it was only at the moment of need, that the iron frame-work of his character became perceptible.

Immediately on quitting college, Mr. Cilley took up his residence in Thomaston, and began the study of law in the office of John Ruggles, Esq., now a Senator in Congress. Mr. Ruggles being then a prominent member of the Democratic party, it was natural that the pupil should lend his aid to promote the political views of his instructor; especially as he would thus uphold the principles which he had cherished from boyhood. From year to year, the election of Mr. Ruggles to the State legislature was strongly opposed. Cilley's services in overcoming this opposition were too valuable to be dispensed with; and thus, at a period when most young men still stand aloof from the world, he had already taken his post as a leading politician. He afterwards found cause to regret that so much time had been abstracted from his professional studies; nor did the absorbing and exciting nature of his political career afford him any subsequent opportunity to supply the defects of his legal education. He was admitted an Attorney at Law in 1829, and, in April of the same year, was married to Miss Deborah Prince, daughter of Hon. Hezekiah Prince of Thomaston where Mr. Cilley continued to reside, and entered upon the practice of his profession.

In 1831, Mr. Ruggles having been appointed a Judge of the Court of Common Pleas, it became necessary to send a new representative from Thomaston to the legislature of the State. Mr. Cilley was brought forward as the Democratic candidate—obtained his election, and took his seat in January,

1832. But, in the course of this year, the friendly relations between Judge Ruggles and Mr. Cilley were broken off. The
former gentleman, it appears, had imbibed the idea that his
political aspirations (which were then directed towards a seat
in the Senate of the United-States) did not receive all the aid
which he was disposed to claim from the influence of his late
pupil. When, therefore, Mr. Cilley was held up as a candidate
for re-election to the legislature, the whole strength of Judge
Ruggles and his adherents was exerted against him. This was
the first act and declaration of a political hostility, which was
too warm and earnest not to become in some degree personal, and which rendered Mr. Cilley's subsequent career a
continual struggle with those, to whom he might naturally
have looked for friendship and support. It sets his abilities
and force of character in the strongest light, to view him, at
the very outset of public life, without the aid of powerful
connections, an isolated young man, forced into a position of
hostility not merely with the enemies of his party, but likewise with a large body of its adherents, even accused of
treachery to its principles, yet gaining triumph after triumph,
and making his way steadily onward. Surely his was a mental
and moral energy which death alone could have laid prostrate!

We have the testimony of those who knew Mr. Cilley well,
that his own feelings were never so embittered by these con-
flicts, as to prevent him from interchanging the courtesies of
society with his most violent opponents. While their resent-
ments rendered his very presence intolerable to them, he
could address them with as much ease and composure, as if
their mutual relations had been those of perfect harmony.
There was no affectation in this; it was the good-natured consciousness of his own strength that enabled him to keep his
temper; it was the same chivalrous sentiment which impels
hostile warriors to shake hands, in the intervals of battle. Mr.
Cilley was slow to withdraw his confidence from any man
whom he deemed a friend; and it has been mentioned as almost his only weak point, that he was too apt to suffer himself to be betrayed, before he would condescend to suspect.
His prejudices, however, when once adopted, partook of the
depth and strength of his character, and could not be readily

overcome; he loved to subdue his foes; but no man could use a triumph more generously than he.

Let us resume our narrative. In spite of the opposition of Judge Ruggles and his friends, combined with that to the Whigs, Mr. Cilley was re-elected to the legislature of 1833, and was equally successful in each of the succeeding years, until his election to Congress. He was five successive years the representative of Thomaston. In 1834, when Mr. Dunlap was nominated as the Democratic candidate for governor, Mr. Cilley gave his support to Governor Smith, in the belief that the substitution of a new candidate had been unfairly effected. He considered it a strategem, intended to promote the election of Judge Ruggles to the Senate of the United States. Early in the legislative session of the same year, the Ruggles party obtained a temporary triumph over Mr. Cilley, effected his expulsion from the Democratic caucuses, and attempted to stigmatize him as a traitor to his political friends. But Mr. Cilley's high and honorable course was ere long understood and appreciated by his party and the people. He told them, openly and boldly, that they might undertake to expel him from their caucuses, but they could not expel him from the Democratic party; they might stigmatize him with any appellation they might choose, but they could not reach the height on which he stood, nor shake his position with the people. But a few weeks had elapsed, and Mr. Cilley was the acknowledged head and leader of that party in the Legislature. During the same session, Mr. Speaker Clifford (one of the friends of Judge Ruggles) being appointed Attorney-General, the Ruggles party were desirous of securing the election of another of their adherents to the chair; but as it was obvious that Mr. Cilley's popularity would gain him the place, the incumbent was induced to delay his resignation till the end of the term. At the session of 1835, Messrs. Cilley, Davee, and McCrate, being candidates for the chair, Mr. Cilley withdrew in favor of Mr. Davee. That gentleman was accordingly elected, but being soon afterwards appointed Sheriff of Somerset county, Mr. Cilley succeeded him as Speaker, and filled the same office during the session of 1836. All parties awarded him the praise of being the best presiding officer that the house ever had.

In 1836, he was nominated by a large portion of the Democratic electors of the Lincoln Congressional District, as their candidate for Congress. That District has recently shown itself to possess a decided Whig majority; and this would have been equally the case in 1836, had any other man than Mr. Cilley appeared on the Democratic side. He had likewise to contend, as in all the former scenes of his political life, with that portion of his own party which adhered to Mr. Ruggles. There was still another formidable obstacle, in the high character of Judge Bailey, who then represented the District, and was a candidate for re-election. All these difficulties, however, served only to protract the contest, but could not snatch the victory from Mr. Cilley, who obtained a majority of votes at the third trial. It was a fatal triumph!

In the summer of 1837, a few months after his election to Congress, I met Mr. Cilley for the first time since early youth, when he had been to me almost as an elder brother. The two or three days, which I spent in his neighborhood, enabled us to renew our former intimacy. In his person there was very little change, and that little was for the better; he had an impending brow, deep-set eyes, and a thin and thoughtful countenance, which, in his abstracted moments, seemed almost stern; but, in the intercourse of society, it was brightened with a kindly smile, that will live in the recollection of all who knew him. His manners had not a fastidious polish, but were characterized by the simplicity of one who had dwelt remote from cities, holding free companionship with the yeomen of the land. I thought him as true a representative of the people as ever theory could portray; his earlier and later habits of life, his feelings, partialities, and prejudices, were those of the people; the strong and shrewd sense, which constituted so marked a feature of his mind, was but a higher degree of the popular intellect. He loved the people, and respected them, and was prouder of nothing than of his brotherhood with those who had intrusted their public interests to his care. His continual struggles in the political arena had strengthened his bones and sinews; opposition had kept him ardent; while success had cherished the generous warmth of his nature, and assisted the growth both of his powers and sympathies. Disappointment might have soured and contracted him; but it appeared to me that his triumphant warfare had been no less beneficial to his heart than to his mind. I was aware, indeed, that his harsher traits had grown apace with his milder ones—that he possessed iron resolution, indomitable perseverance, and an almost terrible energy—but these features had imparted no hardness to his character, in private intercourse. In the hour of public need these strong qualities would have shown themselves the most prominent ones, and would have encouraged his countrymen to rally round him as one of their natural leaders.

In his private and domestic relations, Mr. Cilley was most exemplary; and he enjoyed no less happiness than he conferred. He had been the father of four children, two of whom were in the grave,—leaving, I thought, a more abiding impression of tenderness and regret, than the death of infants usually makes in the masculine mind. Two boys, the elder seven or eight years of age, and the younger two, still remained to him; and the fondness of these children for their father—their evident enjoyment of his society—was proof enough of his gentle and amiable character within the precincts of his family. In that bereaved household there is now another child, whose face the father never saw. Mr. Cilley's domestic habits were simple and primitive to a degree unusual in most parts of our country, among men of so eminent a station as he had attained. It made me smile, though with anything but scorn, in contrast to the aristocratic stateliness which I have witnessed elsewhere, to see him driving home his own cow, after a long search for her through the village. That trait alone would have marked him as a man whose greatness lay within himself. He appeared to take much interest in the cultivation of his garden, and was very fond of flowers. He kept bees, and told me that he loved to sit for whole hours by the hives, watching the labors of the insects, and soothed by the hum with which they filled the air. I glance at these minute particulars of his daily life, because they form so strange a contrast with the circumstances of his death. Who could have believed, that, with his thoroughly New-England character, in so short a time after I had seen him in that peaceful and happy home, among those simple occupations and pure enjoyments, he would be stretched in his own blood—slain for an almost impalpable punctilio!

It is not my purpose to dwell upon Mr. Cilley's brief career in Congress. Brief as it was, his character and talents had more than begun to be felt, and would soon have linked his name with the history of every important measure, and have borne it onward with the progress of the principles which he supported. He was not eager to seize opportunities of thrusting himself into notice; but when time and occasion summoned him, he came forward, and poured forth his ready and natural eloquence with as much effect in the councils of the nation, as he had done in those of his own State. With every effort that he made, the hopes of his party rested more decidedly upon him, as one who would hereafter be found in the vanguard of many a Democratic victory. Let me spare myself the details of the awful catastrophe by which all those proud hopes perished; for I write with a blunted pen and a hand benumbed, and am the less able to express my feelings as they lie deep at heart and inexhaustible.

On the 23d of February last, Mr. Cilley received a challenge from Mr. Graves of Kentucky, through the hands of Mr. Wise of Virginia. This measure, as is declared in the challenge itself, was grounded on Mr. Cilley's refusal to receive a message, of which Mr. Graves had been the bearer, from a person of disputed respectability; although no exception to that person's character had been expressed by Mr. Cilley; nor need such an inference have been drawn, unless Mr. Graves were conscious that public opinion held his friend in a doubtful light. The challenge was accepted, and the parties met on the following day. They exchanged two shots with rifles. After each shot, a conference was held between the friends of both parties, and the most generous avowals of respect and kindly feeling were made, on the part of Mr. Cilley, towards his antagonist, but without avail. A third shot was exchanged, and Mr. Cilley fell dead into the arms of one of his friends. While I write, a Committee of Investigation is sitting upon this affair; but the public has not waited for its award; and the writer, in accordance with the public, has formed his opinion on the official statement of Messrs. Wise and Jones. A challenge was never given on a more shadowy pretext; a duel was never pressed to a fatal close, in the face of such open kindness as was expressed by Mr. Cilley; and the conclusion is inevitable, that Mr. Graves, and his principal second, Mr. Wise, have gone farther than their own dreadful Code will warrant them, and overstepped the imaginary distinction which, on their own principles, separates Manslaughter from Murder.

Alas, that, over the grave of a dear friend, my sorrow for the bereavement must be mingled with another grief—that he threw away his life in so miserable a cause! Why, as he was true to the Northern character in all things else, did he swerve from his Northern principles in this final scene! But his error was a generous one; since he fought for what he deemed the honor of New-England; and now that death has paid the forfeit, the most rigid may forgive him. If that dark pitfall—that bloody grave—had not lain in the midst of his path, whither, whither might it not have led him! It has ended there; yet, so strong was my conception of his energies—so like Destiny did it appear, that he should achieve everything at which he aimed—that, even now, my fancy will not dwell upon his grave, but pictures him still amid the struggles and triumphs of the present and the future.

Chippings with a Chisel

PASSING a summer, several years since, at Edgartown, on the island of Martha's Vineyard, I became acquainted with a certain carver of tomb-stones, who had travelled and voyaged thither from the interior of Massachusetts, in search of professional employment. The speculation had turned out so successful that my friend expected to transmute slate and marble into silver and gold to the amount of at least a thousand dollars, during the few months of his sojourn at Nantucket and the Vineyard. The secluded life, and the simple and primitive spirit which still characterizes the inhabitants of those islands, especially of Martha's Vineyard, insure their dead friends a longer and dearer remembrance than the daily novelty, and revolving bustle of the world, can elsewhere afford to beings of the past. Yet while every family is anxious to erect a memorial to its departed members, the untainted breath of ocean bestows such health and length of days upon the people of the isles as would cause a melancholy dearth of business to a resident artist in that line. His own monument, recording his decease by starvation, would probably be an early specimen of his skill. Grave-stones, therefore, have generally been an article of imported merchandise.

In my walks through the burial-ground of Edgartown—where the dead have lain so long that the soil, once enriched by their decay, has returned to its original barrenness—in that ancient burial-ground I noticed much variety of monumental sculpture. The elder stones, dated a century back, or more, have borders elaborately carved with flowers, and are adorned with a multiplicity of death's-heads, cross-bones, scythes, hour-glasses, and other lugubrious emblems of mortality, with here and there a winged cherub to direct the mourner's spirit upward. These productions of Gothic taste must have been quite beyond the colonial skill of the day, and were probably carved in London, and brought across the ocean to commemorate the defunct worthies of this lonely isle. The more recent monuments are mere slabs of slate, in the ordinary style, without any superfluous flourishes to set off the bald inscriptions. But others—and those far the most impressive, both to my taste and feelings—were roughly hewn from the gray rocks of the island, evidently by the unskilled hands of surviving friends and relatives. On some there were merely the initials of a name; some were inscribed with misspelt prose or rhyme, in deep letters, which the moss and wintry rain of many years had not been able to obliterate. These, these were graves where loved ones slept! It is an old theme of satire, the falsehood and vanity of monumental eulogies; but when affection and sorrow grave the letters with their own painful labor, then we may be sure that they copy from the record on their hearts.

My acquaintance, the sculptor—he may share that title with Greenough, since the dauber of signs is a painter as well as Raphael—had found a ready market for all his blank slabs of marble, and full occupation in lettering and ornamenting them. He was an elderly man, a descendant of the old Puritan family of Wigglesworth, with a certain simplicity and singleness, both of heart and mind, which, methinks, is more rarely found among us Yankees than in any other community of people. In spite of his gray head and wrinkled brow, he was quite like a child in all matters save what had some reference to his own business; he seemed, unless my fancy misled me, to view mankind in no other relation than as people in want of tomb-stones; and his literary attainments evidently comprehended very little, either of prose or poetry, which had not, at one time or other, been inscribed on slate or marble. His sole task and office among the immortal pilgrims of the tomb—the duty for which Providence had sent the old man into the world, as it were with a chisel in his hand—was to label the dead bodies, lest their names should be forgotten at the resurrection. Yet he had not failed, within a narrow scope, to gather a few sprigs of earthly, and more than earthly, wisdom,—the harvest of many a grave.

And lugubrious as his calling might appear, he was as cheerful an old soul as health, and integrity, and lack of care, could make him, and used to set to work upon one sorrowful inscription or another with that sort of spirit which impels a man to sing at his labor. On the whole, I found Mr. Wigglesworth an entertaining, and often instructive, if not an interesting character; and partly for the charm of his society, and still more because his work has an invariable attraction for 'man that is born of woman,' I was accustomed to spend some hours a day at his work-shop. The quaintness of his remarks, and their not infrequent truth—a truth condensed and pointed by the limited sphere of his view—gave a raciness to his talk, which mere worldliness and general cultivation would at once have destroyed.

Sometimes we would discuss the respective merits of the various qualities of marble, numerous slabs of which were resting against the walls of the shop; or sometimes an hour or two would pass quietly, without a word on either side, while I watched how neatly his chisel struck out letter after letter of the names of the Nortons, the Mayhews, the Luces, the Daggets, and other immemorial families of the Vineyard. Often, with an artist's pride, the good old sculptor would speak of favorite productions of his skill, which were scattered throughout the village grave-yards of New England. But my chief and most instructive amusement was to witness his interviews with his customers, who held interminable consultations about the form and fashion of the desired monuments, the buried excellence to be commemorated, the anguish to be expressed, and finally, the lowest price in dollars and cents for which a marble transcript of their feelings might be obtained. Really, my mind received many fresh ideas, which, perhaps, may remain in it even longer than Mr. Wigglesworth's hardest marble will retain the deepest strokes of his chisel.

An elderly lady came to bespeak a monument for her first-love, who had been killed by a whale in the Pacific Ocean no less than forty years before. It was singular that so strong an impression of early feeling should have survived through the changes of her subsequent life, in the course of which she had been a wife and mother, and, so far as I could judge, a comfortable and happy woman. Reflecting within myself, it appeared to me that this life-long sorrow—as, in all good faith, she deemed it—was one of the most fortunate circumstances of her history. It had given an ideality to her mind; it had kept her purer and less earthly than she would otherwise have been, by drawing a portion of her sympathies apart from earth. Amid the throng of enjoyments, and the pressure of worldly care, and all the warm materialism of this life, she had communed with a vision, and had been the better for such intercourse. Faithful to the husband of her maturity, and loving him with a far more real affection than she ever could have felt for this dream of her girlhood, there had still been an imaginative faith to the ocean-buried, so that an ordinary character had thus been elevated and refined. Her sighs had been the breath of Heaven to her soul. The good lady earnestly desired that the proposed monument should be ornamented with a carved border of marine plants, intertwined with twisted sea-shells, such as were probably waving over her lover's skeleton, or strewn around it in the far depths of the Pacific. But Mr. Wigglesworth's chisel being inadequate to the task, she was forced to content herself with a rose, hanging its head from a broken stem. After her departure I remarked that the symbol was none of the most apt.

"And yet," said my friend the sculptor, embodying in this image the thoughts that had been passing through my own mind, "that broken rose has shed its sweet smell through forty years of the good woman's life."

It was seldom that I could find such pleasant food for contemplation as in the above instance. None of the applicants, I think, affected me more disagreeably than an old man who came, with his fourth wife hanging on his arm, to bespeak grave-stones for the three former occupants of his marriage-bed. I watched with some anxiety to see whether his remembrance of either were more affectionate than of the other two, but could discover no symptom of the kind. The three monuments were all to be of the same material and form, and each decorated, in bas-relief, with two weeping willows, one of these sympathetic trees bending over its fellow, which was to be broken in the midst and rest upon a sepulchral urn. This, indeed, was Mr. Wigglesworth's standing emblem of conjugal bereavement. I shuddered at the gray polygamist, who had so utterly lost the holy sense of individuality in wedlock, that methought he was fain to reckon upon his fingers how many women who had once slept by his side were now sleeping in their graves. There was even—if I wrong him it is no great matter—a glance side-long at his living spouse, as if he were inclined to drive a thriftier bargain by bespeaking

four grave-stones in a lot. I was better pleased with a rough
old whaling captain, who gave directions for a broad marble
slab, divided into two compartments, one of which was to
contain an epitaph on his deceased wife, and the other to be
left vacant, till death should engrave his own name there. As
is frequently the case among the whalers of Martha's Vineyard, so much of this storm-beaten widower's life had been
tossed away on distant seas, that out of twenty years of matrimony he had spent scarce three, and those at scattered intervals, beneath his own roof. Thus the wife of his youth,
though she died in his and her declining age, retained the
bridal dew-drops fresh around her memory.

My observations gave me the idea, and Mr. Wigglesworth
confirmed it, that husbands were more faithful in setting up
memorials to their dead wives than widows to their dead husbands. I was not ill-natured enough to fancy that women, less
than men, feel so sure of their own constancy as to be willing
to give a pledge of it in marble. It is more probably the fact,
that while men are able to reflect upon their lost companions
as remembrances apart from themselves, women, on the other
hand, are conscious that a portion of their being has gone
with the departed whithersoever he has gone. Soul clings to
soul; the living dust has a sympathy with the dust of the
grave; and, by the very strength of that sympathy, the wife of
the dead shrinks the more sensitively from reminding the
world of its existence. The link is already strong enough; it
needs no visible symbol. And, though a shadow walks ever by
her side, and the touch of a chill hand is on her bosom, yet
life, and perchance its natural yearnings, may still be warm
within her, and inspire her with new hopes of happiness.
Then would she mark out the grave, the scent of which
would be perceptible on the pillow of the second bridal?
No—but rather level its green mound with the surrounding
earth, as if, when she dug up again her buried heart, the spot
had ceased to be a grave. Yet, in spite of these sentimentali-
ties, I was prodigiously amused by an incident of which I had
not the good fortune to be a witness, but which Mr. Wigglesworth related with considerable humor. A gentlewoman
of the town, receiving news of her husband's loss at sea, had
bespoken a handsome slab of marble, and came daily to watch

the progress of my friend's chisel. One afternoon, when the good lady and the sculptor were in the very midst of the epitaph, which the departed spirit might have been greatly comforted to read, who should walk into the work-shop but the deceased himself, in substance as well as spirit! He had been picked up at sea, and stood in no present need of tomb-stone or epitaph.

"And how," inquired I, "did his wife bear the shock of joyful surprise?"

"Why," said the old man, deepening the grin of a death's-head, on which his chisel was just then employed, "I really felt for the poor woman; it was one of my best pieces of marble—and to be thrown away on a living man!"

A comely woman, with a pretty rose-bud of a daughter, came to select a grave-stone for a twin-daughter, who had died a month before. I was impressed with the different nature of their feelings for the dead; the mother was calm and woefully resigned, fully conscious of her loss, as of a treasure which she had not always possessed, and therefore had been aware that it might be taken from her; but the daughter evidently had no real knowledge of what death's doings were. Her thoughts knew, but not her heart. It seemed to me, that by the print and pressure which the dead sister had left upon the survivor's spirit, her feelings were almost the same as if she still stood side by side, and arm in arm, with the departed, looking at the slabs of marble; and once or twice she glanced around with a sunny smile, which, as its sister-smile had faded forever, soon grew confusedly overshadowed. Perchance her consciousness was truer than her reflection—perchance her dead sister was a closer companion than in life. The mother and daughter talked a long while with Mr. Wigglesworth about a suitable epitaph, and finally chose an ordinary verse of ill-matched rhymes, which had already been inscribed upon innumerable tomb-stones. But, when we ridicule the triteness of monumental verses, we forget that Sorrow reads far deeper in them than we can, and finds a profound and individual purport in what seems so vague and inexpressive, unless interpreted by her. She makes the epitaph anew, though the self-same words may have served for a thousand graves.

"And yet," said I afterwards to Mr. Wigglesworth, "they

might have made a better choice than this. While you were discussing the subject, I was struck by at least a dozen simple and natural expressions from the lips of both mother and daughter. One of these would have formed an inscription equally original and appropriate."

"No, no," replied the sculptor, shaking his head, "there is a good deal of comfort to be gathered from these little old scraps of poetry; and so I always recommend them in preference to any new-fangled ones. And somehow, they seem to stretch to suit a great grief, and shrink to fit a small one."

It was not seldom that ludicrous images were excited by what took place between Mr. Wigglesworth and his customers. A shrewd gentlewoman, who kept a tavern in the town, was anxious to obtain two or three grave-stones for the deceased members of her family, and to pay for these solemn commodities by taking the sculptor to board. Hereupon a fantasy arose in my mind, of good Mr. Wigglesworth sitting down to dinner at a broad, flat tomb-stone, carving one of his own plump little marble cherubs, gnawing a pair of crossbones, and drinking out of a hollow death's-head, or perhaps a lacrymatory vase, or sepulchral urn; while his hostess's dead children waited on him at the ghastly banquet. On communicating this nonsensical picture to the old man, he laughed heartily, and pronounced my humor to be of the right sort.

"I have lived at such a table all my days," said he, "and eaten no small quantity of slate and marble."

"Hard fare!" rejoined I, smiling; "but you seemed to have found it excellent of digestion, too."

A man of fifty, or thereabouts, with a harsh, unpleasant countenance, ordered a stone for the grave of his bitter enemy, with whom he had waged warfare half a lifetime, to their mutual misery and ruin. The secret of this phenomenon was, that hatred had become the sustenance and enjoyment of the poor wretch's soul; it had supplied the place of all kindly affections; it had been really a bond of sympathy between himself and the man who shared the passion; and when its object died, the unappeasable foe was the only mourner for the dead. He expressed a purpose of being buried side by side with his enemy.

"I doubt whether their dust will mingle," remarked the old

sculptor to me; for often there was an earthliness in his conceptions.

"Oh yes," replied I, who had mused long upon the incident; "and when they rise again, these bitter foes may find themselves dear friends. Methinks what they mistook for hatred was but love under a mask."

A gentleman of antiquarian propensities provided a memorial for an Indian of Chabbiquidick, one of the few of untainted blood remaining in that region, and said to be an hereditary chieftain, descended from the sachem who welcomed Governor Mayhew to the Vineyard. Mr. Wigglesworth exerted his best skill to carve a broken bow and scattered sheaf of arrows, in memory of the hunters and warriors whose race was ended here; but he likewise sculptured a cherub, to denote that the poor Indian had shared the Christian's hope of immortality.

"Why," observed I, taking a perverse view of the winged boy and the bow and arrows, "it looks more like Cupid's tomb than an Indian chief's!"

"You talk nonsense," said the sculptor, with the offended pride of art; he then added with his usual good-nature, "how can Cupid die when there are such pretty maidens in the Vineyard?"

"Very true," answered I,—and for the rest of the day I thought of other matters than tomb-stones.

At our next meeting I found him chiselling an open book upon a marble head-stone, and concluded that it was meant to express the erudition of some black-letter clergyman of the Cotton Mather school. It turned out, however, to be emblematical of the scriptural knowledge of an old woman who had never read any thing but her Bible; and the monument was a tribute to her piety and good works, from the Orthodox church, of which she had been a member. In strange contrast with this Christian woman's memorial was that of an infidel, whose grave-stone, by his own direction, bore an avowal of his belief that the spirit within him would be extinguished like a flame, and that the nothingness whence he sprang would receive him again. Mr. Wigglesworth consulted me as to the propriety of enabling a dead man's dust to utter this dreadful creed.

"If I thought," said he, "that a single mortal would read the inscription without a shudder, my chisel should never cut a letter of it. But when the grave speaks such falsehoods, the soul of man will know the truth by its own horror."

"So it will," said I, struck by the idea; "the poor infidel may strive to preach blasphemies from his grave; but it will be only another method of impressing the soul with a consciousness of immortality."

There was an old man by the name of Norton, noted throughout the island for his great wealth, which he had accumulated by the exercise of strong and shrewd faculties, combined with a most penurious disposition. This wretched miser, conscious that he had not a friend to be mindful of him in his grave, had himself taken the needful precautions for posthumous remembrance, by bespeaking an immense slab of white marble, with a long epitaph in raised letters, the whole to be as magnificent as Mr. Wigglesworth's skill could make it. There was something very characteristic in this contrivance to have his money's worth even from his own tombstone, which, indeed, afforded him more enjoyment in the few months that he lived thereafter, than it probably will in a whole century, now that it is laid over his bones. This incident reminds me of a young girl, a pale, slender, feeble creature, most unlike the other rosy and healthful damsels of the Vineyard, amid whose brightness she was fading away. Day after day did the poor maiden come to the sculptor's shop, and pass from one piece of marble to another, till at last she pencilled her name upon a slender slab, which, I think, was of a more spotless white than all the rest. I saw her no more, but soon afterwards found Mr. Wigglesworth cutting her virgin name into the stone which she had chosen.

"She is dead—poor girl," said he, interrupting the tune which he was whistling, "and she chose a good piece of stuff for her head-stone. Now which of these slabs would you like best to see your own name upon?"

"Why, to tell you the truth, my good Mr. Wigglesworth," replied I, after a moment's pause,—for the abruptness of the question had somewhat startled me,—"to be quite sincere with you, I care little or nothing about a stone for my own grave, and am somewhat inclined to scepticism as to the propriety of erecting monuments at all, over the dust that once was human. The weight of these heavy marbles, though unfelt by the dead corpse or the enfranchised soul, presses drearily upon the spirit of the survivor, and causes him to connect the idea of death with the dungeon-like imprisonment of the tomb, instead of with the freedom of the skies. Every gravestone that you ever made is the visible symbol of a mistaken system. Our thoughts should soar upward with the butterfly—not linger with the exuviæ that confined him. In truth and reason, neither those whom we call the living, and still less the departed, have any thing to do with the grave."

"I never heard any thing so heathenish!" said Mr. Wigglesworth, perplexed and displeased at sentiments which controverted all his notions and feelings, and implied the utter waste, and worse, of his whole life's labor,—"would you forget your dead friends, the moment they are under the sod!"

"They are not under the sod," I rejoined; "then why should I mark the spot where there is no treasure hidden! Forget them? No! But to remember them aright, I would forget what they have cast off. And to gain the truer conception of DEATH, I would forget the GRAVE!"

But still the good old sculptor murmured, and stumbled, as it were, over the grave-stones amid which he had walked through life. Whether he were right or wrong, I had grown the wiser from our companionship, and from my observations of nature and character, as displayed by those who came, with their old griefs or their new ones, to get them recorded upon his slabs of marble. And yet, with my gain of wisdom, I had likewise gained perplexity; for there was a strange doubt in my mind, whether the dark shadowing of this life, the sorrows and regrets, have not as much real comfort in them—leaving religious influences out of the question—as what we term life's joys.

Legends of the Province-House

I. HOWE'S MASQUERADE

ONE afternoon, last summer, while walking along Washington street, my eye was attracted by a sign-board protruding over a narrow arch-way, nearly opposite the Old South Church. The sign represented the front of a stately edifice, which was designated as the "OLD PROVINCE-HOUSE, kept by Thomas Waite." I was glad to be thus reminded of a purpose, long entertained, of visiting and rambling over the mansion of the old royal governors of Massachusetts; and entering the arched passage, which penetrated through the middle of a brick row of shops, a few steps transported me from the busy heart of modern Boston, into a small and secluded court-yard. One side of this space was occupied by the square front of the Province-House, three stories high, and surmounted by a cupola, on the top of which a gilded Indian was discernible, with his bow bent and his arrow on the string, as if aiming at the weathercock on the spire of the Old South. The figure has kept this attitude for seventy years or more, ever since good Deacon Drowne, a cunning carver of wood, first stationed him on his long sentinel's watch over the city.

The Province-House is constructed of brick, which seems recently to have been overlaid with a coat of light colored paint. A flight of red free-stone steps, fenced in by a balustrade of curiously wrought iron, ascends from the court-yard to the spacious porch, over which is a balcony, with an iron balustrade of similar pattern and workmanship to that beneath. These letters and figures—16 P.S. 79—are wrought into the iron-work of the balcony, and probably express the date of the edifice, with the initials of its founder's name. A wide door with double leaves admitted me into the hall or entry, on the right of which is the entrance to the bar-room.

It was in this apartment, I presume, that the ancient governors held their levees, with vice-regal pomp, surrounded by the military men, the councillors, the judges, and other offi-

cers of the crown, while all the loyalty of the province
thronged to do them honor. But the room, in its present condition, cannot boast even of faded magnificence. The panelled
wainscot is covered with dingy paint, and acquires a duskier
hue from the deep shadow into which the Province-House is
thrown by the brick block that shuts it in from Washington
street. A ray of sunshine never visits this apartment any more
than the glare of the festal torches, which have been extinguished from the era of the revolution. The most venerable
and ornamental object, is a chimney-piece set round with
Dutch tiles of blue-figured China, representing scenes from
Scripture; and, for aught I know, the lady of Pownall or Bernard, may have sate beside this fire-place, and told her children the story of each blue tile. A bar in modern style, well
replenished with decanters, bottles, cigar-boxes, and net-work
bags of lemons, and provided with a beer-pump and a soda-
fount, extends along one side of the room. At my entrance,
an elderly person was smacking his lips, with a zest which
satisfied me that the cellars of the Province-House still hold
good liquor, though doubtless of other vintages than were
quaffed by the old governors. After sipping a glass of port-
sangaree, prepared by the skilful hands of Mr. Thomas Waite,
I besought that worthy successor and representative of so
many historic personages to conduct me over their time-honored mansion.

He readily complied; but, to confess the truth, I was forced
to draw strenuously upon my imagination, in order to find
aught that was interesting in a house which, without its historic associations would have seemed merely such a tavern as
is usually favored by the custom of decent city-boarders, and
old fashioned country gentlemen. The chambers, which were
probably spacious in former times, are now cut up by partitions and subdivided into little nooks, each affording scanty
room for the narrow bed, and chair, and dressing-table, of a
single lodger. The great staircase, however, may be termed,
without much hyperbole, a feature of grandeur and magnificence. It winds through the midst of the house by flights of
broad steps, each flight terminating in a square landing-place,
whence the ascent is continued towards the cupola. A carved
balustrade, freshly painted in the lower stories, but growing

dingier as we ascend, borders the staircase with its quaintly twisted and intertwined pillars, from top to bottom. Up these stairs the military boots, or perchance the gouty shoes of many a governor have trodden, as the wearers mounted to the cupola, which afforded them so wide a view over their metropolis and the surrounding country. The cupola is an octagon, with several windows, and a door opening upon the roof. From this station, as I pleased myself with imagining, Gage may have beheld his disastrous victory on Bunker-Hill, (unless one of the tri-mountains intervened,) and Howe have marked the approaches of Washington's besieging army; although the buildings, since erected in the vicinity, have shut out almost every object, save the steeple of the Old South, which seems almost within arm's length. Descending from the cupola, I paused in the garret to observe the ponderous white-oak frame-work, so much more massive than the frames of modern houses, and thereby resembling an antique skeleton. The brick walls, the materials of which were imported from Holland, and the timbers of the mansion, are still as sound as ever; but the floors and other interior parts being greatly decayed, it is contemplated to gut the whole, and build a new house within the ancient frame and brick-work. Among other inconveniences of the present edifice, mine host mentioned that any jar or motion was apt to shake down the dust of ages out of the ceiling of one chamber upon the floor of that beneath it.

We stepped forth from the great front window into the balcony, where, in old times, it was doubtless the custom of the King's representative to show himself to a loyal populace, requiting their huzzas and tossed-up hats with stately bendings of his dignified person. In those days, the front of the Province-House looked upon the street; and the whole site now occupied by the brick range of stores, as well as the present court-yard, was laid out in grass plats, overshadowed by trees and bordered by a wrought iron fence. Now, the old aristocratic edifice hides its time-worn visage behind an upstart modern building; at one of the back windows I observed some pretty tailoresses, sewing, and chatting, and laughing, with now and then a careless glance towards the balcony. Descending thence, we again entered the bar-room, where the

elderly gentleman above mentioned, the smack of whose lips
had spoken so favorably for Mr. Waite's good liquor, was still
lounging in his chair. He seemed to be, if not a lodger, at
least a familiar visiter of the house, who might be supposed
to have his regular score at the bar, his summer seat at the
open window, and his prescriptive corner at the winter's fireside. Being of a sociable aspect, I ventured to address him
with a remark, calculated to draw forth his historical reminiscences, if any such were in his mind; and it gratified me to
discover, that, between memory and tradition, the old gentleman was really possessed of some very pleasant gossip about
the Province-House. The portion of his talk which chiefly interested me, was the outline of the following legend. He professed to have received it, at one or two removes, from an
eye-witness; but this derivation, together with the lapse of
time, must have afforded opportunities for many variations of
the narrative; so that, despairing of literal and absolute truth,
I have not scrupled to make such further changes as seemed
conducive to the reader's profit and delight.

At one of the entertainments given at the Province-House,
during the latter part of the siege of Boston, there passed a
scene which has never yet been satisfactorily explained. The
officers of the British army, and the loyal gentry of the province, most of whom were collected within the beleaguered
town, had been invited to a masqued ball; for it was the policy of Sir William Howe to hide the distress and danger of
the period, and the desperate aspect of the siege, under an
ostentation of festivity. The spectacle of this evening, if the
oldest members of the provincial court-circle might be believed, was the most gay and gorgeous affair that had occurred in the annals of the government. The brilliantly lighted
apartments were thronged with figures that seemed to have
stepped from the dark canvass of historic portraits, or to have
flitted forth from the magic pages of romance, or at least to
have flown hither from one of the London theatres, without
a change of garments. Steeled knights of the Conquest,
bearded statesmen of Queen Elizabeth, and high-ruffed ladies
of her court, were mingled with characters of comedy, such
as a parti-colored Merry Andrew, gingling his cap and bells;

a Falstaffe, almost as provocative of laughter as his prototype; and a Don Quixote, with a bean-pole for a lance, and a pot-lid for a shield.

But the broadest merriment was excited by a group of figures ridiculously dressed in old regimentals, which seemed to have been purchased at a military rag-fair, or pilfered from some receptacle of the cast-off clothes of both the French and British armies. Portions of their attire had probably been worn at the siege of Louisburg, and the coats of most recent cut might have been rent and tattered by sword, ball, or bayonet, as long ago as Wolfe's victory. One of these worthies— a tall, lank figure, brandishing a rusty sword of immense longitude—purported to be no less a personage than General George Washington; and the other principal officers of the American army, such as Gates, Lee, Putnam, Schuyler, Ward and Heath, were represented by similar scare-crows. An interview, in the mock-heroic style, between the rebel warriors and the British commander-in-chief, was received with immense applause, which came loudest of all from the loyalists of the colony. There was one of the guests, however, who stood apart, eyeing these antics sternly and scornfully, at once with a frown and a bitter smile.

It was an old man, formerly of high station and great repute in the province, and who had been a very famous soldier in his day. Some surprise had been expressed, that a person of Colonel Joliffe's known whig principles, though now too old to take an active part in the contest, should have remained in Boston during the siege, and especially that he should consent to show himself in the mansion of Sir William Howe. But thither he had come, with a fair grand-daughter under his arm; and there, amid all the mirth and buffoonery, stood this stern old figure, the best sustained character in the masquerade, because so well representing the antique spirit of his native land. The other guests affirmed that Colonel Joliffe's black puritanical scowl threw a shadow round about him; although, in spite of his sombre influence, their gaiety continued to blaze higher, like—(an ominous comparison)—the flickering brilliancy of a lamp which has but a little while to burn. Eleven strokes, full half an hour ago, had pealed from the clock of the Old South, when a rumor was circulated among the company, that some new spectacle or pageant was about to be exhibited, which should put a fitting close to the splendid festivities of the night.

"What new jest has your Excellency in hand?" asked the Reverend Mather Byles, whose Presbyterian scruples had not kept him from the entertainment. "Trust me, sir, I have already laughed more than beseems my cloth, at your Homeric confabulation with yonder ragamuffin General of the rebels. One other such fit of merriment, and I must throw off my clerical wig and band."

"Not so, good Doctor Byles," answered Sir William Howe; "if mirth were a crime, you had never gained your doctorate in divinity. As to this new foolery, I know no more about it than yourself; perhaps not so much. Honestly now, Doctor, have you not stirred up the sober brains of some of your countrymen to enact a scene in our masquerade?"

"Perhaps," slily remarked the grand-daughter of Colonel Joliffe, whose high spirit had been stung by many taunts against New England,—"perhaps we are to have a masque of allegorical figures. Victory, with trophies from Lexington and Bunker-Hill. Plenty, with her overflowing horn, to typify the present abundance in this good town—and Glory, with a wreath for his Excellency's brow."

Sir William Howe smiled at words which he would have answered with one of his darkest frowns, had they been uttered by lips that wore a beard. He was spared the necessity of a retort, by a singular interruption. A sound of music was heard without the house, as if proceeding from a full band of military instruments stationed in the street, playing not such a festal strain as was suited to the occasion; but a slow, funeral march. The drums appeared to be muffled, and the trumpets poured forth a wailing breath, which at once hushed the merriment of the auditors, filling all with wonder, and some with apprehension. The idea occurred to many, that either the funeral procession of some great personage had halted in front of the Province-House, or that a corpse, in a velvet-covered and gorgeously decorated coffin, was about to be borne from the portal. After listening a moment, Sir William Howe called in a stern voice to the leader of the musicians, who had hitherto enlivened the entertainment with gay and lightsome melodies. The man was drum-major to one of the British regiments.

"Dighton," demanded the General, "what means this foolery? Bid your band silence that dead march—or, by my word, they shall have sufficient cause for their lugubrious strains! Silence it, sirrah!"

"Please your honor," answered the drum-major, whose rubicund visage had lost all its color, "the fault is none of mine. I and my band are all here together; and I question whether there be a man of us that could play that march without book. I never heard it but once before, and that was at the funeral of his late Majesty, King George the Second."

"Well, well!" said Sir William Howe, recovering his composure—"It is the prelude to some masquerading antic. Let it pass."

A figure now presented itself, but among the many fantastic masks that were dispersed through the apartments, none could tell precisely from whence it came. It was a man in an old fashioned dress of black serge, and having the aspect of a steward, or principal domestic in the household of a nobleman, or great English landholder. This figure advanced to the outer door of the mansion, and throwing both its leaves wide open, withdrew a little to one side and looked back towards the grand staircase, as if expecting some person to descend. At the same time, the music in the street sounded a loud and doleful summons. The eyes of Sir William Howe and his guests being directed to the staircase, there appeared, on the uppermost landing-place that was discernible from the bottom, several personages descending towards the door. The foremost was a man of stern visage, wearing a steeple-crowned hat and a scull-cap beneath it; a dark cloak, and huge wrinkled boots that came half way up his legs. Under his arm was a rolled-up banner, which seemed to be the banner of England, but strangely rent and torn; he had a sword in his right hand, and grasped a Bible in his left. The next figure was of milder aspect, yet full of dignity, wearing a broad ruff, over which descended a beard, a gown of wrought velvet, and a doublet and hose of black satin. He carried a roll of manuscript in his hand. Close behind these two, came a young man of very striking countenance and demeanor, with deep thought and contemplation on his brow, and perhaps a flash of enthusiasm in his eye. His garb, like that of his predecessors, was of an antique fashion, and there was a stain of blood upon his ruff. In the same group with these, were three or four others, all men of dignity and evident command, and bearing themselves like personages who were accustomed to the gaze of the multitude. It was the idea of the beholders, that these figures went to join the mysterious funeral that had halted in front of the Province-House; yet that supposition seemed to be contradicted by the air of triumph with which they waved their hands, as they crossed the threshold and vanished through the portal.

"In the devil's name, what is this?" muttered Sir William Howe to a gentleman beside him; "a procession of the regicide judges of King Charles, the martyr?"

"These," said Colonel Joliffe, breaking silence almost for the first time that evening—"these, if I interpret them aright, are the Puritan governors—the rulers of the old, original Democracy of Massachusetts. Endicott, with the banner from which he had torn the symbol of subjection, and Winthrop, and Sir Henry Vane, and Dudley, Haynes, Bellingham, and Leverett."

"Why had that young man a stain of blood upon his ruff?" asked Miss Joliffe.

"Because, in after years," answered her grandfather, "he laid down the wisest head in England upon the block, for the principles of liberty."

"Will not your Excellency order out the guard?" whispered Lord Percy, who, with other British officers, had now assembled round the General. "There may be a plot under this mummery."

"Tush! We have nothing to fear," carelessly replied Sir William Howe. "There can be no worse treason in the matter than a jest, and that somewhat of the dullest. Even were it a sharp and bitter one, our best policy would be to laugh it off. See—here come more of these gentry."

Another group of characters had now partly descended the staircase. The first was a venerable and white-bearded patriarch, who cautiously felt his way downward with a staff. Treading hastily behind him, and stretching forth his gauntleted hand as if to grasp the old man's shoulder, came a tall, soldier-like figure, equipped with a plumed cap of steel, a bright breast-plate, and a long sword which rattled against the stairs. Next was seen a stout man, dressed in rich and courtly attire, but not of courtly demeanor; his gait had the swinging motion of a seaman's walk; and chancing to stumble on the staircase, he suddenly grew wrathful and was heard to mutter an oath. He was followed by a noble-looking personage in a curled wig, such as are represented in the portraits of Queen Anne's time and earlier; and the breast of his coat was decorated with an embroidered star. While advancing to the door, he bowed to the right hand and to the left, in a very gracious and insinuating style; but as he crossed the threshold, unlike the early Puritan governors, he seemed to wring his hands with sorrow.

"Prithee, play the part of a chorus, good Doctor Byles," said Sir William Howe. "What worthies are these?"

"If it please your Excellency, they lived somewhat before my day," answered the doctor; "but doubtless our friend, the Colonel, has been hand and glove with them."

"Their living faces I never looked upon," said Colonel Joliffe, gravely; "although I have spoken face to face with many rulers of this land, and shall greet yet another with an old man's blessing, ere I die. But we talk of these figures. I take the venerable patriarch to be Bradstreet, the last of the Puritans, who was governor at ninety, or thereabouts. The next is Sir Edmund Andros, a tyrant, as any New England schoolboy will tell you; and therefore the people cast him down from his high seat into a dungeon. Then comes Sir William Phips, shepherd, cooper, sea-captain, and governor—may many of his countrymen rise as high, from as low an origin! Lastly, you saw the gracious Earl of Bellamont, who ruled us under King William."

"But what is the meaning of it all?" asked Lord Percy.

"Now, were I a rebel," said Miss Joliffe, half aloud, "I might fancy that the ghosts of these ancient governors had been summoned to form the funeral procession of royal authority in New England."

Several other figures were now seen at the turn of the staircase. The one in advance had a thoughtful, anxious, and

somewhat crafty expression of face; and in spite of his loftiness of manner, which was evidently the result both of an
ambitious spirit and of long continuance in high stations, he
seemed not incapable of cringing to a greater than himself. A
few steps behind came an officer in a scarlet and embroidered
uniform, cut in a fashion old enough to have been worn by
the Duke of Marlborough. His nose had a rubicund tinge,
which, together with the twinkle of his eye, might have
marked him as a lover of the wine-cup and good-fellowship;
notwithstanding which tokens, he appeared ill at ease, and
often glanced around him, as if apprehensive of some secret
mischief. Next came a portly gentleman, wearing a coat of
shaggy cloth, lined with silken velvet; he had sense, shrewdness, and humor in his face, and a folio volume under his
arm; but his aspect was that of a man vexed and tormented
beyond all patience, and harassed almost to death. He went
hastily down, and was followed by a dignified person, dressed
in a purple velvet suit, with very rich embroidery; his demeanor would have possessed much stateliness, only that a
grievous fit of the gout compelled him to hobble from stair
to stair, with contortions of face and body. When Doctor
Byles beheld this figure on the staircase, he shivered as with
an ague, but continued to watch him steadfastly, until the
gouty gentleman had reached the threshold, made a gesture
of anguish and despair, and vanished into the outer gloom,
whither the funeral music summoned him.

"Governor Belcher!—my old patron!—in his very shape
and dress!" gasped Doctor Byles. "This is an awful mockery!"

"A tedious foolery, rather," said Sir William Howe, with
an air of indifference. "But who were the three that preceded
him?"

"Governor Dudley, a cunning politician—yet his craft once
brought him to a prison," replied Colonel Joliffe. "Governor
Shute, formerly a Colonel under Marlborough, and whom
the people frightened out of the province; and learned Governor Burnet, whom the legislature tormented into a mortal
fever."

"Methinks they were miserable men, these royal governors
of Massachusetts," observed Miss Joliffe. "Heavens, how dim
the light grows!"

It was certainly a fact that the large lamp, which illuminated the staircase, now burned dim and duskily; so that several figures, which passed hastily down the stairs and went forth from the porch, appeared rather like shadows than persons of fleshly substance. Sir William Howe and his guests stood at the doors of the contiguous apartments, watching the progress of this singular pageant, with various emotions of anger, contempt, or half-acknowledged fear, but still with an anxious curiosity. The shapes, which now seemed hastening to join the mysterious procession, were recognized rather by striking peculiarities of dress, or broad characteristics of manner, than by any perceptible resemblance of features to their prototypes. Their faces, indeed, were invariably kept in deep shadow. But Doctor Byles, and other gentlemen who had long been familiar with the successive rulers of the province, were heard to whisper the names of Shirley, of Pownall, of Sir Francis Bernard, and of the well-remembered Hutchinson; thereby confessing that the actors, whoever they might be, in this spectral march of governors, had succeeded in putting on some distant portraiture of real personages. As they vanished from the door, still did these shadows toss their arms into the gloom of night, with a dread expression of wo. Following the mimic representative of Hutchinson, came a military figure, holding before his face the cocked hat which he had taken from his powdered head; but his epaulettes and other insignia of rank were those of a general officer; and something in his mien reminded the beholders of one who had recently been master of the Province-House, and chief of all the land.

"The shape of Gage, as true as in a looking-glass," exclaimed Lord Percy, turning pale.

"No, surely," cried Miss Joliffe, laughing hysterically; "it could not be Gage, or Sir William would have greeted his old comrade in arms! Perhaps he will not suffer the next to pass unchallenged."

"Of that be assured, young lady," answered Sir William Howe, fixing his eyes, with a very marked expression, upon the immoveable visage of her grandfather. "I have long enough delayed to pay the ceremonies of a host to these departing guests. The next that takes his leave shall receive due courtesy."

A wild and dreary burst of music came through the open door. It seemed as if the procession, which had been gradually filling up its ranks, were now about to move, and that this loud peal of the wailing trumpets, and roll of the muffled drums, were a call to some loiterer to make haste. Many eyes, by an irresistible impulse, were turned upon Sir William Howe, as if it were he whom the dreary music summoned to the funeral of departed power.

"See!—here comes the last!" whispered Miss Joliffe, pointing her tremulous finger to the staircase.

A figure had come into view as if descending the stairs; although, so dusky was the region whence it emerged, some of the spectators fancied that they had seen this human shape suddenly moulding itself amid the gloom. Downward the figure came, with a stately and martial tread, and reaching the lowest stair was observed to be a tall man, booted and wrapped in a military cloak, which was drawn up around the face so as to meet the flapped brim of a laced hat. The features, therefore, were completely hidden. But the British officers deemed that they had seen that military cloak before, and even recognized the frayed embroidery on the collar, as well as the gilded scabbard of a sword which protruded from the folds of the cloak and glittered in a vivid gleam of light. Apart from these trifling particulars there were characteristics of gait and bearing which impelled the wondering guests to glance from the shrouded figure to Sir William Howe, as if to satisfy themselves that their host had not suddenly vanished from the midst of them.

With a dark flush of wrath upon his brow, they saw the General draw his sword and advance to meet the figure in the cloak before the latter had stepped one pace upon the floor.

"Villain, unmuffle yourself!" cried he. "You pass no further!"

The figure, without blenching a hair's-breadth from the sword which was pointed at his breast, made a solemn pause and lowered the cape of the cloak from about his face, yet not sufficiently for the spectators to catch a glimpse of it. But Sir William Howe had evidently seen enough. The sternness of his countenance gave place to a look of wild amazement, if not horror, while he recoiled several steps from the figure and let fall his sword upon the floor. The martial shape again drew the cloak about his features and passed on; but reaching the threshold, with his back towards the spectators, he was seen to stamp his foot and shake his clenched hands in the air. It was afterwards affirmed that Sir William Howe had repeated that self-same gesture of rage and sorrow, when, for the last time, and as the last royal governor, he passed through the portal of the Province-House.

"Hark!—the procession moves," said Miss Joliffe.

The music was dying away along the street, and its dismal strains were mingled with the knell of midnight from the steeple of the Old South, and with the roar of artillery, which announced that the beleaguering army of Washington had intrenched itself upon a nearer height than before. As the deep boom of the cannon smote upon his ear, Colonel Joliffe raised himself to the full height of his aged form and smiled sternly on the British General.

"Would your Excellency inquire further into the mystery of the pageant?" said he.

"Take care of your gray head!" cried Sir William Howe, fiercely, though with a quivering lip. "It has stood too long on a traitor's shoulders!"

"You must make haste to chop it off, then," calmly replied the Colonel, "for, a few hours longer, and not all the power of Sir William Howe, nor of his master, shall cause one of these gray hairs to fall. The empire of Britain, in this ancient province, is at its last gasp to-night;—almost while I speak, it is a dead corpse;—and, methinks the shadows of the old governors are fit mourners at its funeral!"

With these words Colonel Joliffe threw on his cloak, and drawing his grand-daughter's arm within his own, retired from the last festival that a British ruler ever held in the old province of Massachusetts Bay. It was supposed that the Colonel and the young lady possessed some secret intelligence in regard to the mysterious pageant of that night. However this might be, such knowledge has never become general. The actors in the scene have vanished into deeper obscurity than even that wild Indian band who scattered the cargoes of the tea ships on the waves, and gained a place in history, yet left no names. But superstition, among other legends of this mansion, repeats the wondrous tale that, on the anniversary night of Britain's discomfiture, the ghosts of the ancient governors of Massachusetts still glide through the portal of the Province-House. And, last of all, comes a figure shrouded in a military cloak, tossing his clenched hands into the air, and stamping his iron-shod boots upon the broad free-stone steps with a semblance of feverish despair, but without the sound of a foot-tramp.

When the truth-telling accents of the elderly gentleman were hushed, I drew a long breath and looked round the room, striving, with the best energy of my imagination, to throw a tinge of romance and historic grandeur over the realities of the scene. But my nostrils snuffed up a scent of cigar smoke, clouds of which the narrator had emitted by way of visible emblem, I suppose, of the nebulous obscurity of his tale. Moreover, my gorgeous fantasies were wofully disturbed by the rattling of the spoon in a tumbler of whiskey-punch, which Mr. Thomas Waite was mingling for a customer. Nor did it add to the picturesque appearance of the panelled walls, that the slate of the Brookline stage was suspended against them, instead of the armorial escutcheon of some far-descended governor. A stage-driver sat at one of the windows, reading a penny paper of the day,—the Boston Times,—and presenting a figure which could nowise be brought into any picture of 'Times in Boston,' seventy or a hundred years ago. On the window-seat lay a bundle, neatly done up in brown paper, the direction of which I had the idle curiosity to read. "Miss SUSAN HUGGINS, at the PROVINCE-HOUSE." A pretty chamber-maid, no doubt. In truth, it is desperately hard work, when we attempt to throw the spell of hoar antiquity over localities with which the living world, and the day that is passing over us, have aught to do. Yet, as I glanced at the stately staircase, down which the procession of the old governors had descended, and as I emerged through the venerable portal, whence their figures had preceded me, it gladdened me to be conscious of a thrill of awe. Then diving through the narrow arch-way, a few strides transported me into the densest throng of Washington street.

Legends of the Province-House

II. EDWARD RANDOLPH'S PORTRAIT

THE old legendary guest of the Province-House abode in my remembrance from mid-summer till January. One idle evening, last winter, confident that he would be found in the snuggest corner of the bar-room, I resolved to pay him another visit, hoping to deserve well of my country by snatching from oblivion some else unheard-of fact of history. The night was chill and raw, and rendered boisterous by almost a gale of wind, which whistled along Washington street, causing the gas-lights to flare and flicker within the lamps. As I hurried onward, my fancy was busy with a comparison between the present aspect of the street, and that which it probably wore when the British Governors inhabited the mansion whither I was now going. Brick edifices in those times were few, till a succession of destructive fires had swept, and swept again, the wooden dwellings and ware-houses from the most populous quarters of the town. The buildings stood insulated and independent, not, as now, merging their separate existences into connected ranges, with a front of tiresome identity,—but each possessing features of its own, as if the owner's individual taste had shaped it,—and the whole presenting a picturesque irregularity, the absence of which is hardly compensated by any beauties of our modern architecture. Such a scene, dimly vanishing from the eye by the ray of here and there a tallow candle, glimmering through the small panes of scattered windows, would form a sombre contrast to the street, as I beheld it, with the gas-lights blazing from corner to corner, flaming within the shops, and throwing a noon-day brightness through the huge plates of glass.

But the black, lowering sky, as I turned my eyes upward, wore, doubtless, the same visage as when it frowned upon the ante-revolutionary New Englanders. The wintry blast had the same shriek that was familiar to their ears. The Old South Church, too, still pointed its antique spire into the darkness, and was lost between earth and heaven; and as I passed, its clock, which had warned so many generations how transitory was their life-time, spoke heavily and slow the same unregarded moral to myself. "Only seven o'clock," thought I. "My old friend's legends will scarcely kill the hours 'twixt this and bed-time."

Passing through the narrow arch, I crossed the court-yard, the confined precincts of which were made visible by a lantern over the portal of the Province-House. On entering the bar-room, I found, as I expected, the old tradition-monger seated by a special good fire of anthracite, compelling clouds of smoke from a corpulent cigar. He recognized me with evident pleasure; for my rare properties as a patient listener invariably make me a favorite with elderly gentlemen and ladies, of narrative propensities. Drawing a chair to the fire, I desired mine host to favor us with a glass a-piece of whiskey punch, which was speedily prepared, steaming hot, with a slice of lemon at the bottom, a dark-red stratum of port wine upon the surface, and a sprinkling of nutmeg strewn over all. As we touched our glasses together, my legendary friend made himself known to me as Mr. Bela Tiffany; and I rejoiced at the oddity of the name, because it gave his image and character a sort of individuality in my conception. The old gentleman's draught acted as a solvent upon his memory, so that it overflowed with tales, traditions, anecdotes of famous dead people, and traits of ancient manners, some of which were childish as a nurse's lullaby, while others might have been worth the notice of the grave historian. Nothing impressed me more than a story of a black, mysterious picture, which used to hang in one of the chambers of the Province-House, directly above the room where we were now sitting. The following is as correct a version of the fact as the reader would be likely to obtain from any other source; although, assuredly, it has a tinge of romance approaching to the marvellous:

In one of the apartments of the Province-House there was long preserved an ancient picture, the frame of which was as black as ebony, and the canvass itself so dark with age, damp, and smoke, that not a touch of the painter's art could be discerned. Time had thrown an impenetrable veil over it, and left to tradition, and fable, and conjecture, to say what had

once been there portrayed. During the rule of many successive governors, it had hung, by prescriptive and undisputed
right, over the mantel-piece of the same chamber; and it still
kept its place when Lieutenant-Governor Hutchinson assumed the administration of the province, on the departure
of Sir Francis Bernard.

The Lieutenant-Governor sat, one afternoon, resting his
head against the carved back of his stately arm chair, and gazing up thoughtfully at the void blackness of the picture. It
was scarcely a time for such inactive musing, when affairs of
the deepest moment required the ruler's decision; for, within
that very hour, Hutchinson had received intelligence of the
arrival of a British fleet, bringing three regiments from Halifax to overawe the insubordination of the people. These
troops awaited his permission to occupy the fortress of Castle
William, and the town itself. Yet, instead of affixing his signature to an official order, there sat the Lieutenant-Governor,
so carefully scrutinizing the black waste of canvass, that his
demeanour attracted the notice of two young persons who
attended him. One, wearing a military dress of buff, was his
kinsman, Francis Lincoln, the Provincial Captain of Castle
William; the other, who sat on a low stool beside his chair,
was Alice Vane, his favorite niece.

She was clad entirely in white, a pale, ethereal creature,
who, though a native of New England, had been educated
abroad, and seemed not merely a stranger from another clime,
but almost a being from another world. For several years,
until left an orphan, she had dwelt with her father in sunny
Italy, and there had acquired a taste and enthusiasm for sculpture and painting, which she found few opportunities of gratifying in the undecorated dwellings of the colonial gentry. It
was said that the early productions of her own pencil exhibited no inferior genius, though, perhaps, the rude atmosphere
of New England had cramped her hand, and dimmed the
glowing colors of her fancy. But observing her uncle's steadfast gaze, which appeared to search through the mist of years
to discover the subject of the picture, her curiosity was excited.

"Is it known, my dear uncle," inquired she, "what this old
picture once represented? Possibly, could it be made visible,

it might prove a masterpiece of some great artist—else why has it so long held such a conspicuous place?"

As her uncle, contrary to his usual custom, (for he was as attentive to all the humors and caprices of Alice as if she had been his own best beloved child,) did not immediately reply, the young Captain of Castle William took that office upon himself.

"This dark old square of canvass, my fair cousin," said he, "has been an heir-loom in the Province-House from time immemorial. As to the painter, I can tell you nothing; but, if half the stories told of it be true, not one of the great Italian masters has ever produced so marvellous a piece of work, as that before you."

Captain Lincoln proceeded to relate some of the strange fables and fantasies, which, as it was impossible to refute them by ocular demonstration, had grown to be articles of popular belief, in reference to this old picture. One of the wildest, and at the same time the best accredited accounts, stated it to be an original and authentic portrait of the Evil One, taken at a witch meeting near Salem; and that its strong and terrible resemblance had been confirmed by several of the confessing wizards and witches, at their trial, in open court. It was likewise affirmed that a familiar spirit, or demon, abode behind the blackness of the picture, and had shown himself, at seasons of public calamity, to more than one of the royal governors. Shirley, for instance, had beheld this ominous apparition, on the even of General Abercrombie's shameful and bloody defeat under the walls of Ticonderoga. Many of the servants of the Province-House had caught glimpses of a visage frowning down upon them, at morning or evening twilight,—or in the depths of night, while raking up the fire that glimmered on the hearth beneath; although, if any were bold enough to hold a torch before the picture, it would appear as black and undistinguishable as ever. The oldest inhabitant of Boston recollected that his father, in whose days the portrait had not wholly faded out of sight, had once looked upon it, but would never suffer himself to be questioned as to the face which was there represented. In connection with such stories, it was remarkable that over the top of the frame there were some ragged remnants of black silk, indicating that a veil had formerly hung down before the picture, until the duskiness of time had so effectually concealed it. But, after all, it was the most singular part of the affair, that so many of the pompous governors of Massachusetts had allowed the obliterated picture to remain in the state-chamber of the Province-House.

"Some of these fables are really awful," observed Alice Vane, who had occasionally shuddered, as well as smiled, while her cousin spoke. "It would be almost worth while to wipe away the black surface of the canvass, since the original picture can hardly be so formidable as those which fancy paints instead of it."

"But would it be possible," inquired her cousin, "to restore this dark picture to its pristine hues?"

"Such arts are known in Italy," said Alice.

The Lieutenant-Governor had roused himself from his abstracted mood, and listened with a smile to the conversation of his young relatives. Yet his voice had something peculiar in its tones, when he undertook the explanation of the mystery.

"I am sorry, Alice, to destroy your faith in the legends of which you are so fond," remarked he; "but my antiquarian researches have long since made me acquainted with the subject of this picture—if picture it can be called—which is no more visible, nor ever will be, than the face of the long buried man whom it once represented. It was the portrait of Edward Randolph, the founder of this house, a person famous in the history of New England."

"Of that Edward Randolph," exclaimed Captain Lincoln, "who obtained the repeal of the first provincial charter, under which our forefathers had enjoyed almost democratic privileges! He that was styled the arch enemy of New England, and whose memory is still held in detestation, as the destroyer of our liberties!"

"It was the same Randolph," answered Hutchinson, moving uneasily in his chair. "It was his lot to taste the bitterness of popular odium."

"Our annals tell us," continued the Captain of Castle William, "that the curse of the people followed this Randolph wherever he went, and wrought evil in all the subsequent events of his life, and that its effect was seen likewise in the manner of his death. They say, too, that the inward misery of that curse worked itself outward, and was visible on the wretched man's countenance, making it too horrible to be looked upon. If so, and if this picture truly represented his aspect, it was in mercy that the cloud of blackness has gathered over it."

"These traditions are folly, to one who has proved, as I have, how little of historic truth lies at the bottom," said the Lieutenant-Governor. "As regards the life and character of Edward Randolph, too implicit credence has been given to Dr. Cotton Mather, who—I must say it, though some of his blood runs in my veins—has filled our early history with old women's tales, as fanciful and extravagant as those of Greece or Rome."

"And yet," whispered Alice Vane, "may not such fables have a moral? And methinks, if the visage of this portrait be so dreadful, it is not without a cause that it has hung so long in a chamber of the Province-House. When the rulers feel themselves irresponsible, it were well that they should be reminded of the awful weight of a People's curse."

The Lieutenant-Governor started, and gazed for a moment at his niece, as if her girlish fantasies had struck upon some feeling in his own breast, which all his policy or principles could not entirely subdue. He knew, indeed, that Alice, in spite of her foreign education, retained the native sympathies of a New England girl.

"Peace, silly child," cried he, at last, more harshly than he had ever before addressed the gentle Alice. "The rebuke of a king is more to be dreaded than the clamor of a wild, misguided multitude. Captain Lincoln, it is decided. The fortress of Castle William must be occupied by the Royal troops. The two remaining regiments shall be billeted in the town, or encamped upon the Common. It is time, after years of tumult, and almost rebellion, that his majesty's government should have a wall of strength about it."

"Trust, sir—trust yet awhile to the loyalty of the people," said Captain Lincoln; "nor teach them that they can ever be on other terms with British soldiers than those of brotherhood, as when they fought side by side through the French

war. Do not convert the streets of your native town into a
camp. Think twice before you give up old Castle William, the
key of the province, into other keeping than that of true born
New Englanders." .

"Young man, it is decided," repeated Hutchinson, rising
from his chair. "A British officer will be in attendance this
evening, to receive the necessary instructions for the disposal
of the troops. Your presence also will be required. Till then,
farewell."

With these words the Lieutenant-Governor hastily left the
room, while Alice and her cousin more slowly followed, whispering together, and once pausing to glance back at the mysterious picture. The Captain of Castle William fancied that
the girl's air and mien were such as might have belonged to
one of those spirits of fable—fairies, or creatures of a more
antique mythology, who sometimes mingled their agency
with mortal affairs, half in caprice, yet with a sensibility to
human weal or wo. As he held the door for her to pass, Alice
beckoned to the picture and smiled.

"Come forth, dark and evil Shape!" cried she. "It is thine
hour!"

In the evening, Lieutenant-Governor Hutchinson sat in the
same chamber where the foregoing scene had occurred, surrounded by several persons whose various interests had summoned them together. There were the Selectmen of Boston,
plain, patriarchal fathers of the people, excellent representatives of the old puritanical founders, whose sombre
strength had stamped so deep an impress upon the New
England character. Contrasting with these were one or two
members of the Council, richly dressed in the white wigs,
the embroidered waistcoats and other magnificence of the
time, and making a somewhat ostentatious display of court-
ier-like ceremonial. In attendance, likewise, was a major of
the British army, awaiting the Lieutenant-Governor's orders
for the landing of the troops, which still remained on
board the transports. The Captain of Castle William stood
beside Hutchinson's chair, with folded arms, glancing
rather haughtily at the British officer, by whom he was
soon to be superseded in his command. On a table, in the
centre of the chamber, stood a branched silver candlestick,

throwing down the glow of half a dozen wax lights upon a paper apparently ready for the Lieutenant-Governor's signature.

Partly shrouded in the voluminous folds of one of the window-curtains, which fell from the ceiling to the floor, was seen the white drapery of a lady's robe. It may appear strange that Alice Vane should have been there, at such a time; but there was something so child-like, so wayward, in her singular character, so apart from ordinary rules, that her presence did not surprise the few who noticed it. Meantime, the chairman of the Selectmen was addressing to the Lieutenant-Governor a long and solemn protest against the reception of the British troops into the town.

"And if your Honor," concluded this excellent, but somewhat prosy old gentleman, "shall see fit to persist in bringing these mercenary sworders and musketeers into our quiet streets, not on our heads be the responsibility. Think, sir, while there is yet time, that if one drop of blood be shed, that blood shall be an eternal stain upon your Honor's memory. You, sir, have written, with an able pen, the deeds of our forefathers. The more to be desired is it, therefore, that yourself should deserve honorable mention, as a true patriot and upright ruler, when your own doings shall be written down in history."

"I am not insensible, my good sir, to the natural desire to stand well in the annals of my country," replied Hutchinson, controlling his impatience into courtesy, "nor know I any better method of attaining that end than by withstanding the merely temporary spirit of mischief, which, with your pardon, seems to have infected elder men than myself. Would you have me wait till the mob shall sack the Province-House, as they did my private mansion? Trust me, sir, the time may come when you will be glad to flee for protection to the King's banner, the raising of which is now so distasteful to you."

"Yes," said the British major, who was impatiently expecting the Lieutenant-Governor's orders. "The demagogues of this Province have raised the devil, and cannot lay him again. We will exorcise him, in God's name and the King's."

"If you meddle with the devil, take care of his claws!" answered the Captain of Castle William, stirred by the taunt against his countrymen.

"Craving your pardon, young sir," said the venerable Selectman, "let not an evil spirit enter into your words. We will strive against the oppressor with prayer and fasting, as our forefathers would have done. Like them, moreover, we will submit to whatever lot a wise Providence may send us,—always, after our own best exertions to amend it."

"And there peep forth the devil's claws!" muttered Hutchinson, who well understood the nature of Puritan submission. "This matter shall be expedited forthwith. When there shall be a sentinel at every corner, and a court of guard before the town-house, a loyal gentleman may venture to walk abroad. What to me is the outcry of a mob, in this remote province of the realm? The King is my master, and England is my country! Upheld by their armed strength, I set my foot upon the rabble, and defy them!"

He snatched a pen, and was about to affix his signature to the paper that lay on the table, when the Captain of Castle William placed his hand upon his shoulder. The freedom of the action, so contrary to the ceremonious respect which was then considered due to rank and dignity, awakened general surprise, and in none more than in the Lieutenant-Governor himself. Looking angrily up, he perceived that his young relative was pointing his finger to the opposite wall. Hutchinson's eye followed the signal; and he saw, what had hitherto been unobserved, that a black silk curtain was suspended before the mysterious picture, so as completely to conceal it. His thoughts immediately recurred to the scene of the preceding afternoon; and, in his surprise, confused by indistinct emotions, yet sensible that his niece must have had an agency in this phenomenon, he called loudly upon her.

"Alice!—Come hither, Alice!"

No sooner had he spoken than Alice Vane glided from her station, and pressing one hand across her eyes, with the other snatched away the sable curtain that concealed the portrait. An exclamation of surprise burst from every beholder; but the Lieutenant-Governor's voice had a tone of horror.

"By Heaven," said he, in a low, inward murmur, speaking rather to himself than to those around him, "if the spirit of

Edward Randolph were to appear among us from the place of torment, he could not wear more of the terrors of hell upon his face!"

"For some wise end," said the aged Selectman, solemnly, "hath Providence scattered away the mist of years that had so long hid this dreadful effigy. Until this hour no living man hath seen what we behold!"

Within the antique frame, which so recently had enclosed a sable waste of canvass, now appeared a visible picture, still dark, indeed, in its hues and shadings, but thrown forward in strong relief. It was a half-length figure of a gentleman in a rich, but very old-fashioned dress of embroidered velvet, with a broad ruff and a beard, and wearing a hat, the brim of which overshadowed his forehead. Beneath this cloud the eyes had a peculiar glare, which was almost life-like. The whole portrait started so distinctly out of the back-ground, that it had the effect of a person looking down from the wall at the astonished and awe-stricken spectators. The expression of the face, if any words can convey an idea of it, was that of a wretch detected in some hideous guilt, and exposed to the bitter hatred, and laughter, and withering scorn, of a vast surrounding multitude. There was the struggle of defiance, beaten down and overwhelmed by the crushing weight of ignominy. The torture of the soul had come forth upon the countenance. It seemed as if the picture, while hidden behind the cloud of immemorial years, had been all the time acquiring an intenser depth and darkness of expression, till now it gloomed forth again, and threw its evil omen over the present hour. Such, if the wild legend may be credited, was the portrait of Edward Randolph, as he appeared when a people's curse had wrought its influence upon his nature.

" 'Twould drive me mad—that awful face!" said Hutchinson, who seemed fascinated by the contemplation of it.

"Be warned, then!" whispered Alice. "He trampled on a people's rights. Behold his punishment—and avoid a crime like his!"

The Lieutenant-Governor actually trembled for an instant; but, exerting his energy—which was not, however, his most characteristic feature—he strove to shake off the spell of Randolph's countenance.

"Girl!" cried he, laughing bitterly, as he turned to Alice, "have you brought hither your painter's art—your Italian spirit of intrigue—your tricks of stage-effect—and think to influence the councils of rulers and the affairs of nations, by such shallow contrivances? See here!"

"Stay yet awhile," said the Selectman, as Hutchinson again snatched the pen; "for if ever mortal man received a warning from a tormented soul, your Honor is that man!"

"Away!" answered Hutchinson fiercely. "Though yonder senseless picture cried 'Forbear!'—it should not move me!"

Casting a scowl of defiance at the pictured face, (which seemed, at that moment, to intensify the horror of its miserable and wicked look,) he scrawled on the paper, in characters that betokened it a deed of desperation, the name of Thomas Hutchinson. Then, it is said, he shuddered, as if that signature had granted away his salvation.

"It is done," said he; and placed his hand upon his brow.

"May Heaven forgive the deed," said the soft, sad accents of Alice Vane, like the voice of a good spirit flitting away.

When morning came there was a stifled whisper through the household, and spreading thence about the town, that the dark, mysterious picture had started from the wall, and spoken face to face with Lieutenant-Governor Hutchinson. If such a miracle had been wrought, however, no traces of it remained behind; for within the antique frame, nothing could be discerned, save the impenetrable cloud, which had covered the canvass since the memory of man. If the figure had, indeed, stepped forth, it had fled back, spirit-like, at the day-dawn, and hidden itself behind a century's obscurity. The truth probably was, that Alice Vane's secret for restoring the hues of the picture had merely effected a temporary renovation. But those who, in that brief interval, had beheld the awful visage of Edward Randolph, desired no second glance, and ever afterwards trembled at the recollection of the scene, as if an evil spirit had appeared visibly among them. And as for Hutchinson, when, far over the ocean, his dying hour drew on, he gasped for breath, and complained that he was choking with the blood of the Boston Massacre; and Francis Lincoln, the former Captain of Castle William, who was standing at his bedside, perceived a likeness in his frenzied look to that of Edward Randolph. Did his broken spirit feel, at that dread hour, the tremendous burthen of a People's curse?

At the conclusion of this miraculous legend I inquired of mine host whether the picture still remained in the chamber over our heads, but Mr. Tiffany informed me that it had long since been removed, and was supposed to be hidden in some out-of-the-way corner of the New England Museum. Perchance some curious antiquary may light upon it there, and, with the assistance of Mr. Howorth, the picture-cleaner, may supply a not unnecessary proof of the authenticity of the facts here set down. During the progress of the story a storm had been gathering abroad, and raging and rattling so loudly in the upper regions of the Province-House, that it seemed as if all the old Governors and great men were running riot above stairs, while Mr. Bela Tiffany babbled of them below. In the course of generations, when many people have lived and died in an ancient house, the whistling of the wind through its crannies, and the creaking of its beams and rafters, become strangely like the tones of the human voice, or thundering laughter, or heavy footsteps treading the deserted chambers. It is as if the echoes of half a century were revived. Such were the ghostly sounds that roared and murmured in our ears, when I took leave of the circle round the fireside of the Province-House, and plunging down the door-steps, fought my way homeward against a drifting snow-storm.

Legends of the Province-House

III. Lady Eleanore's Mantle

MINE excellent friend, the landlord of the Province-House, was pleased, the other evening, to invite Mr. Tiffany and myself to an oyster supper. This slight mark of respect and gratitude, as he handsomely observed, was far less than the ingenious tale-teller, and I, the humble note-taker of his narratives, had fairly earned, by the public notice which our joint lucubrations had attracted to his establishment. Many a segar had been smoked within his premises—many a glass of wine, or more potent aqua vitæ, had been quaffed—many a dinner had been eaten by curious strangers, who, save for the fortunate conjunction of Mr. Tiffany and me, would never have ventured through that darksome avenue, which gives access to the historic precincts of the Province-House. In short, if any credit be due to the courteous assurances of Mr. Thomas Waite, we had brought his forgotten mansion almost as effectually into public view as if we had thrown down the vulgar range of shoe-shops and dry-good stores, which hides its aristocratic front from Washington street. It may be unadvisable, however, to speak too loudly of the increased custom of the house, lest Mr. Waite should find it difficult to renew the lease on so favorable terms as heretofore.

Being thus welcomed as benefactors, neither Mr. Tiffany nor myself felt any scruple in doing full justice to the good things that were set before us. If the feast were less magnificent than those same panelled walls had witnessed, in a by-gone century—if mine host presided with somewhat less of state, than might have befitted a successor of the royal Governors—if the guests made a less imposing show than the bewigged, and powdered, and embroidered dignitaries, who erst banquetted at the gubernatorial table, and now sleep within their armorial tombs on Copp's Hill, or round King's Chapel—yet never, I may boldly say, did a more comfortable little party assemble in the Province-House, from Queen

Anne's days to the Revolution. The occasion was rendered more interesting by the presence of a venerable personage, whose own actual reminiscences went back to the epoch of Gage and Howe, and even supplied him with a doubtful anecdote or two of Hutchinson. He was one of that small, and now all but extinguished class, whose attachment to royalty, and to the colonial institutions and customs that were connected with it, had never yielded to the democratic heresies of aftertimes. The young queen of Britain has not a more loyal subject in her realm—perhaps not one who would kneel before her throne with such reverential love—as this old grandsire whose head has whitened beneath the mild sway of the Republic, which still, in his mellower moments, he terms a usurpation. Yet prejudices so obstinate have not made him an ungentle or impracticable companion. If the truth must be told, the life of the aged loyalist has been of such a scrambling and unsettled character—he has had so little choice of friends, and been so often destitute of any—that I doubt whether he would refuse a cup of kindness with either Oliver Cromwell or John Hancock; to say nothing of any democrat now upon the stage. In another paper of this series, I may perhaps give the reader a closer glimpse of his portrait.

Our host, in due season, uncorked a bottle of Madeira, of such exquisite perfume and admirable flavor, that he surely must have discovered it in an ancient bin, down deep beneath the deepest cellar, where some jolly old butler stored away the Governor's choicest wine, and forgot to reveal the secret on his death-bed. Peace to his red-nosed ghost, and a libation to his memory! This precious liquor was imbibed by Mr. Tiffany with peculiar zest; and after sipping the third glass, it was his pleasure to give us one of the oddest legends which he had yet raked from the store-house, where he keeps such matters. With some suitable adornments from my own fancy, it ran pretty much as follows:

Not long after Colonel Shute had assumed the government of Massachusetts Bay, now nearly a hundred and twenty years ago, a young lady of rank and fortune arrived from England, to claim his protection as her guardian. He was her distant relative, but the nearest who had survived the gradual extinction of her family; so that no more eligible shelter could be found for the rich and high-born Lady Eleanore Rochcliffe, than within the Province-House of a trans-atlantic colony. The consort of Governor Shute, moreover, had been as a mother to her childhood, and was now anxious to receive her in the hope that a beautiful young woman would be exposed to infinitely less peril from the primitive society of New England, than amid the artifices and corruptions of a court. If either the Governor or his lady had especially consulted their own comfort, they would probably have sought to devolve the responsibility on other hands; since with some noble and splendid traits of character, Lady Eleanore was remarkable for a harsh unyielding pride, a haughty consciousness of her hereditary and personal advantages, which made her almost incapable of control. Judging from many traditionary anecdotes, this peculiar temper was hardly less than a monomania; or, if the acts which it inspired were those of a sane person, it seemed due from Providence that pride so sinful should be followed by as severe a retribution. That tinge of the marvellous which is thrown over so many of these half-forgotten legends, has probably imparted an additional wildness to the strange story of Lady Eleanore Rochcliffe.

The ship in which she came passenger had arrived at Newport, whence Lady Eleanore was conveyed to Boston in the Governor's coach, attended by a small escort of gentlemen on horseback. The ponderous equipage with its four black horses attracted much notice as it rumbled through Cornhill, surrounded by the prancing steeds of half a dozen cavaliers, with swords dangling to their stirrups and pistols at their holsters. Through the large glass windows of the coach, as it rolled along, the people could discern the figure of Lady Eleanore, strangely combining an almost queenly stateliness with the grace and beauty of a maiden in her teens. A singular tale had gone abroad among the ladies of the province, that their fair rival was indebted for much of the irresistible charm of her appearance to a certain article of dress—an embroidered mantle—which had been wrought by the most skilful artist in London, and possessed even magical properties of adornment. On the present occasion, however, she owed nothing to the witchery of dress, being clad in a riding-habit of velvet, which would have appeared stiff and ungraceful on any other form.

The coachman reined in his four black steeds, and the whole cavalcade came to a pause in front of the contorted iron balustrade that fenced the Province-House from the public street. It was an awkward coincidence, that the bell of the Old South was just then tolling for a funeral; so that, instead of a gladsome peal with which it was customary to announce the arrival of distinguished strangers, Lady Eleanore Rochcliffe was ushered by a doleful clang, as if calamity had come embodied in her beautiful person.

"A very great disrespect!" exclaimed Captain Langford, an English officer, who had recently brought despatches to Governor Shute. "The funeral should have been deferred, lest Lady Eleanore's spirits be affected by such a dismal welcome."

"With your pardon, sir," replied Doctor Clarke, a physician, and a famous champion of the popular party, "whatever the heralds may pretend, a dead beggar must have precedence of a living queen. King Death confers high privileges."

These remarks were interchanged while the speakers waited a passage through the crowd, which had gathered on each side of the gateway, leaving an open avenue to the portal of the Province-House. A black slave in livery now leaped from behind the coach, and threw open the door; while at the same moment Governor Shute descended the flight of steps from his mansion, to assist Lady Eleanore in alighting. But the Governor's stately approach was anticipated in a manner that excited general astonishment. A pale young man, with his black hair all in disorder, rushed from the throng, and prostrated himself beside the coach, thus offering his person as a footstool for Lady Eleanore Rochcliffe to tread upon. She held back an instant; yet with an expression as if doubting whether the young man were worthy to bear the weight of her footstep, rather than dissatisfied to receive such awful reverence from a fellow-mortal.

"Up, sir," said the Governor sternly, at the same time lifting his cane over the intruder. "What means the Bedlamite by this freak?"

"Nay," answered Lady Eleanore playfully, but with more scorn than pity in her tone, "your Excellency shall not strike him. When men seek only to be trampled upon, it were a pity to deny them a favor so easily granted—and so well deserved!"

Then, though as lightly as a sunbeam on a cloud, she placed her foot upon the cowering form, and extended her hand to meet that of the Governor. There was a brief interval, during which Lady Eleanore retained this attitude; and never, surely, was there an apter emblem of aristocracy and hereditary pride, trampling on human sympathies and the kindred of nature, than these two figures presented at that moment. Yet the spectators were so smitten with her beauty, and so essential did pride seem to the existence of such a creature, that they gave a simultaneous acclamation of applause.

"Who is this insolent young fellow?" inquired Captain Langford, who still remained beside Doctor Clarke. "If he be in his senses, his impertinence demands the bastinado. If mad, Lady Eleanore should be secured from further inconvenience, by his confinement."

"His name is Jervase Helwyse," answered the Doctor—"a youth of no birth or fortune, or other advantages, save the mind and soul that nature gave him; and being secretary to our colonial agent in London, it was his misfortune to meet this Lady Eleanore Rochcliffe. He loved her—and her scorn has driven him mad."

"He was mad so to aspire," observed the English officer.

"It may be so," said Doctor Clarke, frowning as he spoke. "But I tell you, sir, I could well nigh doubt the justice of the Heaven above us, if no signal humiliation overtake this lady, who now treads so haughtily into yonder mansion. She seeks to place herself above the sympathies of our common nature, which envelopes all human souls. See, if that nature do not assert its claim over her in some mode that shall bring her level with the lowest!"

"Never!" cried Captain Langford indignantly—"neither in life nor when they lay her with her ancestors."

Not many days afterwards the Governor gave a ball in honor of Lady Eleanore Rochcliffe. The principal gentry of the colony received invitations, which were distributed to their residences, far and near, by messengers on horseback, bearing missives sealed with all the formality of official despatches. In obedience to the summons, there was a general gathering of rank, wealth, and beauty; and the wide door of the Province-House had seldom given admittance to more numerous and honorable guests than on the evening of Lady Eleanore's ball. Without much extravagance of eulogy, the spectacle might even be termed splendid; for, according to the fashion of the times, the ladies shone in rich silks and satins, outspread over wide-projecting hoops; and the gentlemen glittered in gold embroidery, laid unsparingly upon the purple, or scarlet, or sky-blue velvet, which was the material of their coats and waistcoats. The latter article of dress was of great importance, since it enveloped the wearer's body nearly to the knees, and was perhaps bedizened with the amount of his whole year's income, in golden flowers and foliage. The altered taste of the present day—a taste symbolic of a deep change in the whole system of society—would look upon almost any of those gorgeous figures as ridiculous; although that evening the guests sought their reflections in the pierglasses, and rejoiced to catch their own glitter amid the glittering crowd. What a pity that one of the stately mirrors has not preserved a picture of the scene, which, by the very traits that were so transitory, might have taught us much that would be worth knowing and remembering!

Would, at least, that either painter or mirror could convey to us some faint idea of a garment, already noticed in this legend—the Lady Eleanore's embroidered mantle—which the gossips whispered was invested with magic properties, so as to lend a new and untried grace to her figure each time that she put it on! Idle fancy as it is, this mysterious mantle has thrown an awe around my image of her, partly from its fabled virtues, and partly because it was the handiwork of a dying woman, and, perchance, owed the fantastic grace of its conception to the delirium of approaching death.

After the ceremonial greetings had been paid, Lady Eleanore Rochcliffe stood apart from the mob of guests, insulating herself within a small and distinguished circle, to whom she accorded a more cordial favor than to the general throng. The waxen torches threw their radiance vividly over the scene, bringing out its brilliant points in strong relief; but she gazed carelessly, and with now and then an expression of weariness or scorn, tempered with such feminine grace, that her audi-

tors scarcely perceived the moral deformity of which it was
the utterance. She beheld the spectacle not with vulgar ridicule, as disdaining to be pleased with the provincial mockery
of a court festival, but with the deeper scorn of one whose
spirit held itself too high to participate in the enjoyment of
other human souls. Whether or no the recollections of those
who saw her that evening were influenced by the strange
events with which she was subsequently connected, so it was,
that her figure ever after recurred to them as marked by something wild and unnatural; although, at the time, the general
whisper was of her exceeding beauty, and of the indescribable
charm which her mantle threw around her. Some close observers, indeed, detected a feverish flush and alternate paleness
of countenance, with a corresponding flow and revulsion of
spirits, and once or twice a painful and helpless betrayal of
lassitude, as if she were on the point of sinking to the ground.
Then, with a nervous shudder, she seemed to arouse her energies, and threw some bright and playful, yet half-wicked sarcasm into the conversation. There was so strange a characteristic in her manners and sentiments, that it astonished every
right-minded listener; till looking in her face, a lurking and
incomprehensible glance and smile perplexed them with
doubts both as to her seriousness and sanity. Gradually, Lady
Eleanore Rochcliffe's circle grew smaller, till only four gentlemen remained in it. These were Captain Langford, the English officer before mentioned; a Virginian planter, who had
come to Massachusetts on some political errand; a young
Episcopal clergyman, the grandson of a British Earl; and
lastly, the private secretary of Governor Shute, whose obse-
quiousness had won a sort of tolerance from Lady Eleanore.

   At different periods of the evening the liveried servants of
the Province-House passed among the guests, bearing huge
trays of refreshments, and French and Spanish wines. Lady
Eleanore Rochcliffe, who refused to wet her beautiful lips
even with a bubble of Champaigne, had sunk back into a
large damask chair, apparently overwearied either with the excitement of the scene or its tedium; and while, for an instant,
she was unconscious of voices, laughter, and music, a young
man stole forward, and knelt down at her feet. He bore a
salver in his hand, on which was a chased silver goblet, filled

to the brim with wine, which he offered as reverentially as to a crowned queen, or rather with the awful devotion of a priest doing sacrifice to his idol. Conscious that some one touched her robe, Lady Eleanore started, and unclosed her eyes upon the pale, wild features and dishevelled hair of Jervase Helwyse.

"Why do you haunt me thus?" said she, in a languid tone, but with a kindlier feeling than she ordinarily permitted herself to express. "They tell me that I have done you harm."

"Heaven knows if that be so," replied the young man solemnly. "But, Lady Eleanore, in requital of that harm, if such there be, and for your own earthly and heavenly welfare, I pray you to take one sip of this holy wine, and then to pass the goblet round among the guests. And this shall be a symbol that you have not sought to withdraw yourself from the chain of human sympathies—which whoso would shake off must keep company with fallen angels."

"Where has this mad fellow stolen that sacramental vessel?" exclaimed the Episcopal clergyman.

This question drew the notice of the guests to the silver cup, which was recognized as appertaining to the communion plate of the Old South Church; and, for aught that could be known, it was brimming over with the consecrated wine.

"Perhaps it is poisoned," half whispered the Governor's secretary.

"Pour it down the villain's throat!" cried the Virginian, fiercely.

"Turn him out of the house!" cried Captain Langford, seizing Jervase Helwyse so roughly by the shoulder that the sacramental cup was overturned, and its contents sprinkled upon Lady Eleanore's mantle. "Whether knave, fool, or Bedlamite, it is intolerable that the fellow should go at large."

"Pray, gentlemen, do my poor admirer no harm," said Lady Eleanore, with a faint and weary smile. "Take him out of my sight if such be your pleasure; for I can find in my heart to do nothing but laugh at him—whereas, in all decency and conscience, it would become me to weep for the mischief I have wrought!"

But while the bystanders were attempting to lead away the unfortunate young man, he broke from them, and with a wild, impassioned earnestness, offered a new and equally strange petition to Lady Eleanore. It was no other than that she should throw off the mantle, which, while he pressed the silver cup of wine upon her, she had drawn more closely around her form, so as almost to shroud herself within it.

"Cast it from you!" exclaimed Jervase Helwyse, clasping his hands in an agony of entreaty. "It may not yet be too late! Give the accursed garment to the flames!"

But Lady Eleanore, with a laugh of scorn, drew the rich folds of the embroidered mantle over her head, in such a fashion as to give a completely new aspect to her beautiful face, which—half-hidden, half-revealed—seemed to belong to some being of mysterious character and purposes.

"Farewell, Jervase Helwyse!" said she. "Keep my image in your remembrance, as you behold it now."

"Alas, lady!" he replied, in a tone no longer wild, but sad as a funeral bell. "We must meet shortly, when your face may wear another aspect—and that shall be the image that must abide within me."

He made no more resistance to the violent efforts of the gentlemen and servants, who almost dragged him out of the apartment, and dismissed him roughly from the iron gate of the Province-House. Captain Langford, who had been very active in this affair, was returning to the presence of Lady Eleanore Rochcliffe, when he encountered the physician, Doctor Clarke, with whom he had held some casual talk on the day of her arrival. The Doctor stood apart, separated from Lady Eleanore by the width of the room, but eyeing her with such keen sagacity, that Captain Langford involuntarily gave him credit for the discovery of some deep secret.

"You appear to be smitten, after all, with the charms of this queenly maiden," said he, hoping thus to draw forth the physician's hidden knowledge.

"God forbid!" answered Doctor Clarke, with a grave smile; "and if you be wise you will put up the same prayer for yourself. Wo to those who shall be smitten by this beautiful Lady Eleanore! But yonder stands the Governor—and I have a word or two for his private ear. Good night!"

He accordingly advanced to Governor Shute, and addressed him in so low a tone that none of the bystanders

could catch a word of what he said; although the sudden
change of his Excellency's hitherto cheerful visage betokened
that the communication could be of no agreeable import. A
very few moments afterwards, it was announced to the guests
that an unforeseen circumstance rendered it necessary to put
a premature close to the festival.

The ball at the Province-House supplied a topic of conversation for the colonial metropolis, for some days after its occurrence, and might still longer have been the general theme,
only that a subject of all engrossing interest thrust it, for a
time, from the public recollection. This was the appearance of
a dreadful epidemic, which, in that age, and long before and
afterwards, was wont to slay its hundreds and thousands, on
both sides of the Atlantic. On the occasion of which we
speak, it was distinguished by a peculiar virulence, insomuch
that it has left its traces—its pitmarks, to use an appropriate
figure—on the history of the country, the affairs of which
were thrown into confusion by its ravages. At first, unlike its
ordinary course, the disease seemed to confine itself to the
higher circles of society, selecting its victims from among the
proud, the well-born and the wealthy, entering unabashed
into stately chambers, and lying down with the slumberers in
silken beds. Some of the most distinguished guests of the
Province-House—even those whom the haughty Lady Eleanore Rochcliffe had deemed not unworthy of her favor—
were stricken by this fatal scourge. It was noticed, with an
ungenerous bitterness of feeling, that the four gentlemen—
the Virginian, the British officer, the young clergyman, and
the Governor's secretary—who had been her most devoted
attendants on the evening of the ball, were the foremost on
whom the plague-stroke fell. But the disease, pursuing its onward progress, soon ceased to be exclusively a prerogative of
aristocracy. Its red brand was no longer conferred like a noble's star, or an order of knighthood. It threaded its way
through the narrow and crooked streets, and entered the low,
mean, darksome dwellings, and laid its hand of death upon
the artisans and laboring classes of the town. It compelled
rich and poor to feel themselves brethren, then; and stalking
to and fro across the Three Hills, with a fierceness which
made it almost a new pestilence, there was that mighty con-

queror—that scourge and horror of our forefathers—the Small-Pox!

We cannot estimate the affright which this plague inspired of yore, by contemplating it as the fangless monster of the present day. We must remember, rather, with what awe we watched the gigantic footsteps of the Asiatic cholera, striding from shore to shore of the Atlantic, and marching like destiny upon cities far remote, which flight had already half depopulated. There is no other fear so horrible and unhumanizing, as that which makes man dread to breathe Heaven's vital air, lest it be poison, or to grasp the hand of a brother or friend, lest the gripe of the pestilence should clutch him. Such was the dismay that now followed in the track of the disease, or ran before it throughout the town. Graves were hastily dug, and the pestilential relics, as hastily covered, because the dead were enemies of the living, and strove to draw them headlong, as it were, into their own dismal pit. The public councils were suspended, as if mortal wisdom might relinquish its devices, now that an unearthly usurper had found his way into the ruler's mansion. Had an enemy's fleet been hovering on the coast, or his armies trampling on our soil, the people would probably have committed their defence to that same direful conqueror, who had wrought their own calamity, and would permit no interference with his sway. This conqueror had a symbol of his triumphs. It was a blood-red flag, that fluttered in the tainted air, over the door of every dwelling into which the Small-Pox had entered.

Such a banner was long since waving over the portal of the Province-House; for thence, as was proved by tracking its footsteps back, had all this dreadful mischief issued. It had been traced back to a lady's luxurious chamber—to the proudest of the proud—to her that was so delicate, and hardly owned herself of earthly mould—to the haughty one, who took her stand above human sympathies—to Lady Eleanore! There remained no room for doubt, that the contagion had lurked in that gorgeous mantle, which threw so strange a grace around her at the festival. Its fantastic splendor had been conceived in the delirious brain of a woman on her death-bed and was the last toil of her stiffening fingers, which had interwoven fate and misery with its golden threads. This dark tale, whispered at first, was now bruited far and wide. The people raved against the Lady Eleanore, and cried out that her pride and scorn had evoked a fiend, and that, between them both, this monstrous evil had been born. At times, their rage and despair took the semblance of grinning mirth; and whenever the red flag of the pestilence was hoisted over another, and yet another door, they clapt their hands and shouted through the streets, in bitter mockery, "Behold a new triumph for the Lady Eleanore!"

One day in the midst of these dismal times, a wild figure approached the portal of the Province-House, and folding his arms, stood contemplating the scarlet banner, which a passing breeze shook fitfully, as if to fling abroad the contagion that it typified. At length, climbing one of the pillars by means of the iron balustrade, he took down the flag, and entered the mansion, waving it above his head. At the foot of the staircase he met the Governor, booted and spurred, with his cloak drawn around him, evidently on the point of setting forth upon a journey.

"Wretched lunatic, what do you seek here?" exclaimed Shute, extending his cane to guard himself from contact. "There is nothing here but Death. Back—or you will meet him!"

"Death will not touch me, the banner-bearer of the pestilence!" cried Jervase Helwyse, shaking the red flag aloft. "Death and the Pestilence, who wears the aspect of the Lady Eleanore, will walk through the streets to-night, and I must march before them with this banner!"

"Why do I waste words on the fellow?" muttered the Governor, drawing his cloak across his mouth. "What matters his miserable life, when none of us are sure of twelve hours' breath? On, fool, to your own destruction!"

He made way for Jervase Helwyse, who immediately ascended the staircase, but, on the first landing-place, was arrested by the firm grasp of a hand upon his shoulder. Looking fiercely up, with a madman's impulse to struggle with, and rend asunder his opponent, he found himself powerless beneath a calm, stern eye, which possessed the mysterious property of quelling frenzy at its height. The person whom he had now encountered was the physician, Doctor Clarke, the duties of whose sad profession had led him to the Province-House, where he was an infrequent guest in more prosperous times.

"Young man, what is your purpose?" demanded he.

"I seek the Lady Eleanore," answered Jervase Helwyse, submissively.

"All have fled from her," said the physician. "Why do you seek her now? I tell you, youth, her nurse fell death-stricken on the threshhold of that fatal chamber. Know ye not, that never came such a curse to our shores as this lovely Lady Eleanore? that her breath has filled the air with poison?—that she has shaken pestilence and death upon the land, from the folds of her accursed mantle?"

"Let me look upon her!" rejoined the mad youth, more wildly. "Let me behold her, in her awful beauty, clad in the regal garments of the pestilence! She and Death sit on a throne together. Let me kneel down before them!"

"Poor youth!" said Doctor Clarke; and, moved by a deep sense of human weakness, a smile of caustic humor curled his lip even then. "Wilt thou still worship the destroyer, and surround her image with fantasies the more magnificent, the more evil she has wrought? Thus man doth ever to his tyrants! Approach, then! Madness, as I have noted, has that good efficacy, that it will guard you from contagion—and perchance its own cure may be found in yonder chamber."

Ascending another flight of stairs, he threw open a door, and signed to Jervase Helwyse that he should enter. The poor lunatic, it seems probable, had cherished a delusion that his haughty mistress sat in state, unharmed herself by the pestilential influence, which, as by enchantment, she scattered round about her. He dreamed, no doubt, that her beauty was not dimmed, but brightened into superhuman splendor. With such anticipations, he stole reverentially to the door at which the physician stood, but paused upon the threshold, gazing fearfully into the gloom of the darkened chamber.

"Where is the Lady Eleanore?" whispered he.

"Call her," replied the physician.

"Lady Eleanore!—Princess!—Queen of Death!" cried Jervase Helwyse, advancing three steps into the chamber. "She is not here! There on yonder table, I behold the sparkle of a

diamond, which once she wore upon her bosom. There"—
and he shuddered—"there hangs her mantle, on which a dead
woman embroidered a spell of dreadful potency. But where is
the Lady Eleanore!"

Something stirred within the silken curtains of a canopied
bed; and a low moan was uttered, which, listening intently,
Jervase Helwyse began to distinguish as a woman's voice,
complaining dolefully of thirst. He fancied, even, that he recognized its tones.

"My throat!—my throat is scorched," murmured the voice.
"A drop of water!"

"What thing art thou?" said the brain-stricken youth, drawing near the bed and tearing asunder its curtains. "Whose
voice hast thou stolen for thy murmurs and miserable peti-
tions, as if Lady Eleanore could be conscious of mortal infirmity? Fie! Heap of diseased mortality, why lurkest thou in
my lady's chamber?"

"Oh, Jervase Helwyse," said the voice—and as it spoke, the
figure contorted itself, struggling to hide its blasted face—
"look not now on the woman you once loved! The curse of
Heaven hath stricken me, because I would not call man my
brother, nor woman sister. I wrapt myself in PRIDE as in a
MANTLE, and scorned the sympathies of nature; and therefore
has nature made this wretched body the medium of a dreadful
sympathy. You are avenged—they are all avenged—Nature
is avenged—for I am Eleanore Rochcliffe!"

The malice of his mental disease, the bitterness lurking at
the bottom of his heart, mad as he was, for a blighted and
ruined life, and love that had been paid with cruel scorn,
awoke within the breast of Jervase Helwyse. He shook his
finger at the wretched girl, and the chamber echoed, the curtains of the bed were shaken, with his outburst of insane merriment.

"Another triumph for the Lady Eleanore!" he cried. "All
have been her victims! Who so worthy to be the final victim
as herself?"

Impelled by some new fantasy of his crazed intellect, he
snatched the fatal mantle, and rushed from the chamber and
the house. That night, a procession passed, by torch light,
through the streets, bearing in the midst, the figure of a

woman, enveloped with a richly embroidered mantle; while in advance stalked Jervase Helwyse, waving the red flag of the pestilence. Arriving opposite the Province-House, the mob burned the effigy, and a strong wind came and swept away the ashes. It was said, that, from that very hour, the pestilence abated, as if its sway had some mysterious connection, from the first plague-stroke to the last, with Lady Eleanore's Mantle. A remarkable uncertainty broods over that unhappy lady's fate. There is a belief, however, that, in a certain chamber of this mansion, a female form may sometimes be duskily discerned, shrinking into the darkest corner, and muffling her face within an embroidered mantle. Supposing the legend true, can this be other than the once proud Lady Eleanore?

Mine host, and the old loyalist, and I, bestowed no little warmth of applause upon this narrative, in which we had all been deeply interested; for the reader can scarcely conceive how unspeakably the effect of such a tale is heightened, when, as in the present case, we may repose perfect confidence in the veracity of him who tells it. For my own part, knowing how scrupulous is Mr. Tiffany to settle the foundation of his facts, I could not have believed him one whit the more faithfully, had he professed himself an eye-witness of the doings and sufferings of poor Lady Eleanore. Some sceptics, it is true, might demand documentary evidence, or even require him to produce the embroidered mantle, forgetting that— Heaven be praised—it was consumed to ashes. But now the old loyalist, whose blood was warmed by the good cheer, began to talk, in his turn, about the traditions of the Province-House, and hinted that he, if it were agreeable, might add a few reminiscences to our legendary stock. Mr. Tiffany, having no cause to dread a rival, immediately besought him to favor us with a specimen; my own entreaties, of course, were urged to the same effect; and our venerable guest, well pleased to find willing auditors, awaited only the return of Mr. Thomas Waite, who had been summoned forth to provide accommodations for several new arrivals. Perchance the public—but be this as its own caprice and ours shall settle the matter—may read the result in another Legend of the Province-House.

Legends of the Province-House

IV. OLD ESTHER DUDLEY

OUR host having resumed the chair, he, as well as Mr. Tiffany and myself, expressed much eagerness to be made acquainted with the story to which the loyalist had alluded. That venerable man first of all saw fit to moisten his throat with another glass of wine, and then, turning his face towards our coal-fire, looked steadfastly for a few moments into the depths of its cheerful glow. Finally, he poured forth a great fluency of speech. The generous liquid that he had imbibed, while it warmed his age-chilled blood, likewise took off the chill from his heart and mind, and gave him an energy to think and feel, which we could hardly have expected to find beneath the snows of fourscore winters. His feelings, indeed, appeared to me more excitable than those of a younger man; or, at least, the same degree of feeling manifested itself by more visible effects, than if his judgment and will had possessed the potency of meridian life. At the pathetic passages of his narrative, he readily melted into tears. When a breath of indignation swept across his spirit, the blood flushed his withered visage even to the roots of his white hair; and he shook his clenched fist at the trio of peaceful auditors, seeming to fancy enemies in those who felt very kindly towards the desolate old soul. But ever and anon, sometimes in the midst of his most earnest talk, this ancient person's intellect would wander vaguely, losing its hold of the matter in hand, and groping for it amid misty shadows. Then would he cackle forth a feeble laugh, and express a doubt whether his wits— for by that phrase it pleased our ancient friend to signify his mental powers—were not getting a little the worse for wear.

Under these disadvantages, the old loyalist's story required more revision to render it fit for the public eye, than those of the series which have preceded it; nor should it be concealed, that the sentiment and tone of the affair may have undergone some slight, or perchance more than slight metamorphosis, in its transmission to the reader through the medium of a thorough-going democrat. The tale itself is a mere sketch, with no involution of plot, nor any great interest of events, yet possessing, if I have rehearsed it aright, that pensive influence over the mind, which the shadow of the old Province-House flings upon the loiterer in its court-yard.

The hour had come—the hour of defeat and humiliation— when Sir William Howe was to pass over the threshold of the Province-House, and embark, with no such triumphal cere- monies as he once promised himself, on board the British fleet. He bade his servants and military attendants go before him, and lingered a moment in the loneliness of the mansion, to quell the fierce emotions that struggled in his bosom as with a death-throb. Preferable, then, would he have deemed his fate, had a warrior's death left him a claim to the narrow territory of a grave, within the soil which the King had given him to defend. With an ominous perception that, as his de- parting footsteps echoed adown the staircase, the sway of Britain was passing forever from New England, he smote his clenched hand on his brow, and cursed the destiny that had flung the shame of a dismembered empire upon him.

"Would to God," cried he, hardly repressing his tears of rage, "that the rebels were even now at the door-step! A blood-stain upon the floor should then bear testimony that the last British ruler was faithful to his trust."

The tremulous voice of a woman replied to his exclama- tion.

"Heaven's cause and the King's are one," it said. "Go forth, Sir William Howe, and trust in Heaven to bring back a Royal Governor in triumph."

Subduing at once the passion to which he had yielded only in the faith that it was unwitnessed, Sir William Howe be- came conscious that an aged woman, leaning on a gold- headed staff, was standing betwixt him and the door. It was old Esther Dudley, who had dwelt almost immemorial years in this mansion, until her presence seemed as inseparable from it as the recollections of its history. She was the daugh- ter of an ancient and once eminent family, which had fallen into poverty and decay, and left its last descendant no re- source save the bounty of the King, nor any shelter except within the walls of the Province-House. An office in the household, with merely nominal duties, had been assigned to her as a pretext for the payment of a small pension, the greater part of which she expended in adorning herself with an antique magnificence of attire. The claims of Esther Dudley's gentle blood were acknowledged by all the successive Governors; and they treated her with the punctilious courtesy which it was her foible to demand, not always with success, from a neglectful world. The only actual share which she assumed in the business of the mansion, was to glide through its passages and public chambers, late at night, to see that the servants had dropped no fire from their flaring torches, nor left embers crackling and blazing on the hearths. Perhaps it was this invariable custom of walking her rounds in the hush of midnight, that caused the superstition of the times to invest the old woman with attributes of awe and mystery; fabling that she had entered the portal of the Province-House, none knew whence, in the train of the first Royal Governor, and that it was her fate to dwell there till the last should have departed. But Sir William Howe, if he ever heard this legend, had forgotten it.

"Mistress Dudley, why are you loitering here?" asked he, with some severity of tone. "It is my pleasure to be the last in this mansion of the King."

"Not so, if it please your Excellency," answered the time-stricken woman. "This roof has sheltered me long. I will not pass from it until they bear me to the tomb of my forefathers. What other shelter is there for old Esther Dudley, save the Province-House or the grave?"

"Now Heaven forgive me!" said Sir William Howe to himself. "I was about to leave this wretched old creature to starve or beg. Take this, good Mistress Dudley," he added, putting a purse into her hands. "King George's head on these golden guineas is sterling yet, and will continue so, I warrant you, even should the rebels crown John Hancock their king. That purse will buy a better shelter than the Province-House can now afford."

"While the burthen of life remains upon me, I will have no other shelter than this roof," persisted Esther Dudley, striking her staff upon the floor, with a gesture that expressed immovable resolve. "And when your Excellency returns in triumph, I will totter into the porch to welcome you."

"My poor old friend!" answered the British General,—and all his manly and martial pride could no longer restrain a gush of bitter tears. "This is an evil hour for you and me. The province which the King entrusted to my charge is lost. I go hence in misfortune—perchance in disgrace—to return no more. And you, whose present being is incorporated with the past—who have seen Governor after Governor, in stately pageantry, ascend these steps—whose whole life has been an observance of majestic ceremonies, and a worship of the King— how will you endure the change? Come with us! Bid farewell to a land that has shaken off its allegiance, and live still under a Royal government, at Halifax."

"Never, never!" said the pertinacious old dame. "Here will I abide; and King George shall still have one true subject in his disloyal province."

"Beshrew the old fool!" muttered Sir William Howe, growing impatient of her obstinacy, and ashamed of the emotion into which he had been betrayed. "She is the very moral of old-fashioned prejudice, and could exist nowhere but in this musty edifice. Well, then, Mistress Dudley, since you will needs tarry, I give the Province-House in charge to you. Take this key, and keep it safe until myself, or some other Royal Governor, shall demand it of you."

Smiling bitterly at himself and her, he took the heavy key of the Province-House, and delivering it into the old lady's hands, drew his cloak around him for departure. As the General glanced back at Esther Dudley's antique figure, he deemed her well-fitted for such a charge, as being so perfect a representative of the decayed past—of an age gone by, with its manners, opinions, faith, and feelings, all fallen into oblivion or scorn—of what had once been a reality, but was now merely a vision of faded magnificence. Then Sir William Howe strode forth, smiting his clenched hands together, in the fierce anguish of his spirit; and old Esther Dudley was left to keep watch in the lonely Province-House, dwelling there with memory;—and if Hope ever seemed to flit around her, still it was Memory in disguise.

The total change of affairs that ensued on the departure of

the British troops did not drive the venerable lady from her strong-hold. There was not, for many years afterwards, a Governor of Massachusetts; and the magistrates, who had charge of such matters, saw no objection to Esther Dudley's residence in the Province-House, especially as they must otherwise have paid a hireling for taking care of the premises, which with her was a labor of love. And so they left her the undisturbed mistress of the old historic edifice. Many and strange were the fables which the gossips whispered about her, in all the chimney-corners of the town. Among the time-worn articles of furniture that had been left in the mansion, there was a tall, antique mirror, which was well worthy of a tale by itself, and perhaps may hereafter be the theme of one. The gold of its heavily-wrought frame was tarnished, and its surface so blurred, that the old woman's figure, whenever she paused before it, looked indistinct and ghostlike. But it was the general belief that Esther could cause the Governors of the overthrown dynasty, with the beautiful ladies who had once adorned their festivals, the Indian chiefs who had come up to the Province-House to hold council or swear allegiance, the grim Provincial warriors, the severe clergymen—in short, all the pageantry of gone days—all the figures that ever swept across the broad plate of glass in former times—she could cause the whole to re-appear, and people the inner world of the mirror with shadows of old life. Such legends as these, together with the singularity of her isolated existence, her age, and the infirmity that each added winter flung upon her, made Mistress Dudley the object both of fear and pity; and it was partly the result of either sentiment, that, amid all the angry license of the times, neither wrong nor insult ever fell upon her unprotected head. Indeed, there was so much haughtiness in her demeanour towards intruders, among whom she reckoned all persons acting under the new authorities, that it was really an affair of no small nerve to look her in the face. And to do the people justice, stern republicans as they had now become, they were well content that the old gentlewoman, in her hoop-petticoat and faded embroidery, should still haunt the palace of ruined pride and overthrown power, the symbol of a departed system embodying a history in her person. So Esther Dudley dwelt, year after year, in the

Province-House, still reverencing all that others had flung aside, still faithful to her King, who, so long as the venerable dame yet held her post, might be said to retain one true subject in New England, and one spot of the empire that had been wrested from him.

And did she dwell there in utter loneliness? Rumor said, not so. Whenever her chill and withered heart desired warmth, she was wont to summon a black slave of Governor Shirley's from the blurred mirror, and send him in search of guests who had long ago been familiar in those deserted chambers. Forth went the sable messenger, with the starlight or the moonshine gleaming through him, and did his errand in the burial-grounds, knocking at the iron doors of tombs, or upon the marble slabs that covered them, and whispering to those within: "My mistress, old Esther Dudley, bids you to the Province-House at midnight." And, punctually as the clock of the Old South told twelve, came the shadows of the Olivers, the Hutchinsons, the Dudleys, all the grandees of a by-gone generation, gliding beneath the portal into the well-known mansion, where Esther mingled with them as if she likewise were a shade. Without vouching for the truth of such traditions, it is certain that Mistress Dudley sometimes assembled a few of the staunch, though crest-fallen old tories, who had lingered in the rebel town during those days of wrath and tribulation. Out of a cobwebbed bottle, containing liquor that a Royal Governor might have smacked his lips over, they quaffed healths to the King, and babbled treason to the Republic, feeling as if the protecting shadow of the throne were still flung around them. But, draining the last drops of their liquor, they stole timorously homeward, and answered not again, if the rude mob reviled them in the street.

Yet Esther Dudley's most frequent and favored guests were the children of the town. Towards them she was never stern. A kindly and loving nature, hindered elsewhere from its free course by a thousand rocky prejudices, lavished itself upon these little ones. By bribes of gingerbread of her own making, stamped with a royal crown, she tempted their sunny sportiveness beneath the gloomy portal of the Province-House, and would often beguile them to spend a whole play-day there, sitting in a circle round the verge of her hoop-petticoat, greedily attentive to her stories of a dead world. And when these little boys and girls stole forth again from the dark mysterious mansion, they went bewildered, full of old feelings that graver people had long ago forgotten, rubbing their eyes at the world around them as if they had gone astray into ancient times, and become children of the past. At home, when their parents asked where they had loitered such a weary while, and with whom they had been at play, the children would talk of all the departed worthies of the Province, as far back as Governor Belcher, and the haughty dame of Sir William Phips. It would seem as though they had been sitting on the knees of these famous personages, whom the grave had hidden for half a century, and had toyed with the embroidery of their rich waistcoats, or roguishly pulled the long curls of their flowing wigs. "But Governor Belcher has been dead this many a year," would the mother say to her little boy. "And did you really see him at the Province-House?" "Oh, yes, dear mother! yes!" the half dreaming child would answer. "But when old Esther had done speaking about him he faded away out of his chair." Thus, without affrighting her little guests, she led them by the hand into the chambers of her own desolate heart, and made childhood's fancy discern the ghosts that haunted there.

Living so continually in her own circle of ideas, and never regulating her mind by a proper reference to present things, Esther Dudley appears to have grown partially crazed. It was found that she had no right sense of the progress and true state of the Revolutionary war, but held a constant faith that the armies of Britain were victorious on every field, and destined to be ultimately triumphant. Whenever the town rejoiced for a battle won by Washington, or Gates, or Morgan, or Greene, the news, in passing through the door of the Province-House, as through the ivory gate of dreams, became metamorphosed into a strange tale of the prowess of Howe, Clinton, or Cornwallis. Sooner or later, it was her invincible belief, the colonies would be prostrate at the footstool of the King. Sometimes she seemed to take for granted that such was already the case. On one occasion, she startled the town's people by a brilliant illumination of the Province-House, with candles at every pane of glass, and a transparency of the

King's initials and a crown of light, in the great balcony window. The figure of the aged woman, in the most gorgeous of her mildewed velvets and brocades, was seen passing from casement to casement, until she paused before the balcony, and flourished a huge key above her head. Her wrinkled visage actually gleamed with triumph, as if the soul within her were a festal lamp.

"What means this blaze of light? What does old Esther's joy portend?" whispered a spectator. "It is frightful to see her gliding about the chambers, and rejoicing there without a soul to bear her company."

"It is as if she were making merry in a tomb," said another.

"Pshaw! It is no such mystery," observed an old man, after some brief exercise of memory. "Mistress Dudley is keeping jubilee for the King of England's birth-day."

Then the people laughed aloud, and would have thrown mud against the blazing transparency of the King's crown and initials, only that they pitied the poor old dame, who was so dismally triumphant amid the wreck and ruin of the system to which she appertained.

Oftentimes it was her custom to climb the weary staircase that wound upward to the cupola, and thence strain her dimmed eyesight seaward and countryward, watching for a British fleet, or for the march of a grand procession, with the King's banner floating over it. The passengers in the street below would discern her anxious visage, and send up a shout—"When the golden Indian on the Province-House shall shoot his arrow, and when the cock on the Old South spire shall crow, then look for a Royal Governor again!"— for this had grown a by-word through the town. And at last, after long, long years, old Esther Dudley knew, or perchance she only dreamed, that a Royal Governor was on the eve of returning to the Province-House, to receive the heavy key which Sir William Howe had committed to her charge. Now it was the fact, that intelligence bearing some faint analogy to Esther's version of it, was current among the town's people. She set the mansion in the best order that her means allowed, and arraying herself in silks and tarnished gold, stood long before the blurred mirror to admire her own magnificence. As she gazed, the gray and withered lady moved her ashen lips, murmuring half aloud, talking to shapes that she saw within the mirror, to shadows of her own fantasies, to the household friends of memory, and bidding them rejoice with her, and come forth to meet the Governor. And while absorbed in this communion, Mistress Dudley heard the tramp of many footsteps in the street, and looking out at the window, beheld what she construed as the Royal Governor's arrival.

"Oh, happy day! oh, blessed, blessed hour!" she exclaimed. "Let me but bid him welcome within the portal, and my task in the Province-House, and on earth, is done!"

Then with tottering feet, which age and tremulous joy caused to tread amiss, she hurried down the grand staircase, her silks sweeping and rustling as she went, so that the sound was as if a train of spectral courtiers were thronging from the dim mirror. And Esther Dudley fancied, that as soon as the wide door should be flung open, all the pomp and splendor of by-gone times would pace majestically into the Province-House, and the gilded tapestry of the past would be brightened by the sunshine of the present. She turned the key—withdrew it from the lock—unclosed the door—and stept across the threshold. Advancing up the court-yard, appeared a person of most dignified mien, with tokens, as Esther interpreted them, of gentle blood, high rank, and long accustomed authority, even in his walk and every gesture. He was richly dressed, but wore a gouty shoe, which, however, did not lessen the stateliness of his gait. Around and behind him were people in plain civic dresses, and two or three war-worn veterans, evidently officers of rank, arrayed in a uniform of blue and buff. But Esther Dudley, firm in the belief that had fastened its roots about her heart, beheld only the principal personage, and never doubted that this was the long-looked-for Governor, to whom she was to surrender up her charge. As he approached, she involuntarily sank down on her knees, and tremblingly held forth the heavy key.

"Receive my trust! take it quickly!" cried she; "for methinks Death is striving to snatch away my triumph. But he comes too late. Thank Heaven for this blessed hour! God save King George!"

"That, Madam, is a strange prayer to be offered up at such

a moment," replied the unknown guest of the Province-House, and courteously removing his hat, he offered his arm to raise the aged woman. "Yet, in reverence for your gray hairs and long-kept faith, Heaven forbid that any here should say you nay. Over the realms which still acknowledge his sceptre, God save King George!"

Esther Dudley started to her feet, and hastily clutching back the key, gazed with fearful earnestness at the stranger; and dimly and doubtfully, as if suddenly awakened from a dream, her bewildered eyes half recognized his face. Years ago, she had known him among the gentry of the Province. But the ban of the King had fallen upon him! How, then, came the doomed victim here? Proscribed, excluded from mercy, the monarch's most dreaded and hated foe, this New England merchant had stood triumphantly against a kingdom's strength; and his foot now trod upon humbled Royalty, as he ascended the steps of the Province-House, the people's chosen Governor of Massachusetts.

"Wretch, wretch that I am!" muttered the old woman, with such a heart-broken expression, that the tears gushed from the stranger's eyes. "Have I bidden a traitor welcome! Come, Death! come quickly!"

"Alas, venerable lady!" said Governor Hancock, lending her his support with all the reverence that a courtier would have shown to a queen. "Your life has been prolonged until the world has changed around you. You have treasured up all that time has rendered worthless—the principles, feelings, manners, modes of being and acting, which another generation has flung aside—and you are a symbol of the past. And I, and these around me—we represent a new race of men, living no longer in the past, scarcely in the present—but projecting our lives forward into the future. Ceasing to model ourselves on ancestral superstitions, it is our faith and principle to press onward, onward! Yet," continued he, turning to his attendants, "let us reverence, for the last time, the stately and gorgeous prejudices of the tottering Past!"

While the Republican Governor spoke, he had continued to support the helpless form of Esther Dudley; her weight grew heavier against his arm; but at last, with a sudden effort to free herself, the ancient woman sank down beside one of the pillars of the portal. The key of the Province-House fell from her grasp, and clanked against the stone.

"I have been faithful unto death," murmured she. "God save the King!"

"She hath done her office!" said Hancock solemnly. "We will follow her reverently to the tomb of her ancestors; and then, my fellow-citizens, onward—onward! We are no longer children of the Past!"

As the old loyalist concluded his narrative, the enthusiasm which had been fitfully flashing within his sunken eyes, and quivering across his wrinkled visage, faded away, as if all the lingering fire of his soul were extinguished. Just then, too, a lamp upon the mantle-piece threw out a dying gleam, which vanished as speedily, as it shot upward, compelling our eyes to grope for one another's features by the dim glow of the hearth. With such a lingering fire, methought, with such a dying gleam, had the glory of the ancient system vanished from the Province-House, when the spirit of old Esther Dudley took its flight. And now, again, the clock of the Old South threw its voice of ages on the breeze, knolling the hourly knell of the Past, crying out far and wide through the multitudinous city, and filling our ears, as we sat in the dusky chamber, with its reverberating depth of tone. In that same mansion—in that very chamber—what a volume of history had been told off into hours, by the same voice that was now trembling in the air. Many a Governor had heard those midnight accents, and longed to exchange his stately cares for slumber. And as for mine host, and Mr. Bela Tiffany, and the old loyalist, and me, we had babbled about dreams of the past, until we almost fancied that the clock was still striking in a by-gone century. Neither of us would have wondered, had a hoop-petticoated phantom of Esther Dudley tottered into the chamber, walking her rounds in the hush of midnight, as of yore, and motioned us to quench the fading embers of the fire, and leave the historic precincts to herself and her kindred shades. But as no such vision was vouchsafed, I retired unbidden, and would advise Mr. Tiffany to lay hold of another auditor, being resolved not to show my face in the Province-House for a good while hence—if ever.

The Sister Years

L AST NIGHT, between eleven and twelve o'clock, when the Old Year was leaving her final foot-prints on the borders of Time's empire, she found herself in possession of a few spare moments, and sat down—of all places in the world—on the steps of our new City Hall. The wintry moonlight showed that she looked weary of body, and sad of heart, like many another wayfarer of earth. Her garments having been exposed to much foul weather and rough usage, were in very ill condition; and as the hurry of her journey had never before allowed her to take an instant's rest, her shoes were so worn as to be scarcely worth the mending. But, after trudging only a little distance further, this poor Old Year was destined to enjoy a long, long sleep. I forgot to mention, that when she seated herself on the steps, she deposited by her side a very capacious band-box, in which, as is the custom among travellers of her sex, she carried a great deal of valuable property. Besides this luggage, there was a folio book under her arm, very much resembling the annual volume of a newspaper. Placing this volume across her knees, and resting her elbows upon it, with her forehead in her hands, the weary, bedraggled, world-worn Old Year heaved a heavy sigh, and appeared to be taking no very pleasant retrospect of her past existence.

While she thus awaited the midnight knell, that was to summon her to the innumerable sisterhood of departed Years, there came a young maiden treading lightsomely on tip-toe along the street, from the direction of the Railroad Depôt. She was evidently a stranger, and perhaps had come to town by the evening train of cars. There was a smiling cheerfulness in this fair maiden's face, which bespoke her fully confident of a kind reception from the multitude of people, with whom she was soon to form acquaintance. Her dress was rather too airy for the season, and was bedizened with fluttering ribbons and other vanities, which were likely soon to be rent away by the fierce storms, or to fade in the hot sunshine, amid which she was to pursue her changeful course. But still she was a wonderfully pleasant looking figure, and had so much promise and such an indescribable hopefulness in her aspect, that hardly anybody could meet her without anticipating some very desirable thing—the consummation of some long sought good—from her kind offices. A few dismal characters there may be, here and there about the world, who have so often been trifled with by young maidens as promising as she, that they have now ceased to pin any faith upon the skirts of the New Year. But, for my own part, I have great faith in her; and should I live to see fifty more such, still, from each of those successive sisters, I shall reckon upon receiving something that will be worth living for.

The New Year—for this young maiden was no less a personage—carried all her goods and chattels in a basket of no great size or weight, which hung upon her arm. She greeted the disconsolate Old Year with great affection, and sat down beside her on the steps of the City Hall, waiting for the signal to begin her rambles through the world. The two were own sisters, being both grand daughters of Time; and though one looked so much older than the other, it was rather owing to hardships and trouble than to age, since there was but a twelvemonth's difference between them.

'Well, my dear sister,' said the New Year, after the first salutations, 'you look almost tired to death. What have you been about during your sojourn in this part of Infinite Space?'

'Oh, I have it all recorded here in my Book of Chronicles,' answered the Old Year, in a heavy tone. 'There is nothing that would amuse you; and you will soon get sufficient knowledge of such matters from your own personal experience. It is but tiresome reading.'

Nevertheless, she turned over the leaves of the folio, and glanced at them by the light of the moon, feeling an irresistible spell of interest in her own biography, although its incidents were remembered without pleasure. The volume, though she termed it her Book of Chronicles, seemed to be neither more nor less than the Salem Gazette for 1838; in the accuracy of which journal this sagacious Old Year had so much confidence, that she deemed it needless to record her history with her own pen.

'What have you been doing in the political way?' asked the New Year.

'Why, my course here in the United States,' said the Old
Year—'though perhaps I ought to blush at the confession—
my political course, I must acknowledge, has been rather vac-
illatory, sometimes inclining towards the Whigs—then causing the Administration party to shout for triumph—and now
again uplifting what seemed the almost prostrate banner of
the Opposition; so that historians will hardly know what to
make of me, in this respect. But the Loco Focos—'

'I do not like these party nicknames,' interrupted her sister,
who seemed remarkably touchy about some points. 'Perhaps
we shall part in better humor, if we avoid any political discussion.'

'With all my heart,' replied the Old Year, who had already
been tormented half to death with squabbles of this kind. 'I
care not if the names of Whig or Tory, with their interminable brawls about Banks and the Sub Treasury, Abolition,
Texas, the Florida War, and a million of other topics—which
you will learn soon enough for your own comfort—I care
not, I say, if no whisper of these matters ever reaches my ears
again. Yet they have occupied so large a share of my attention, that I scarcely know what else to tell you. There has
indeed been a curious sort of war on the Canada border,
where blood has streamed in the names of Liberty and Patriotism; but it must remain for some future, perhaps far distant, Year, to tell whether or no those holy names have been
rightfully invoked. Nothing so much depresses me, in my
view of mortal affairs, as to see high energies wasted, and
human life and happiness thrown away, for ends that appear
oftentimes unwise; and still oftener remain unaccomplished.
But the wisest people and the best keep a steadfast faith that
the progress of Mankind is onward and upward, and that the
toil and anguish of the path serve to wear away the imperfections of the Immortal Pilgrim, and will be felt no more, when
they have done their office.'

'Perhaps,' cried the hopeful New Year—'perhaps I shall see
that happy day!'

'I doubt whether it be so close at hand,' answered the Old
Year, gravely smiling. 'You will soon grow weary of looking
for that blessed consummation, and will turn for amusement
(as has frequently been my own practice) to the affairs of

some sober little city, like this of Salem. Here we sit, on the steps of the new City Hall, which has been completed under my administration; and it would make you laugh to see how the game of politics, of which the Capitol at Washington is the great chess-board, is here played in miniature. Burning Ambition finds its fuel here; here Patriotism speaks boldly in the people's behalf, and virtuous Economy demands retrenchment in the emoluments of a lamplighter; here the Aldermen range their senatorial dignity around the Mayor's chair of state, and the Common Council feel that they have liberty in charge. In short, human weakness and strength, passion and policy, Man's tendencies, his aims and modes of pursuing them, his individual character, and his character in the mass, may be studied almost as well here as on the theatre of nations; and with this great advantage, that, be the lesson ever so disastrous, its Lilliputian scope still makes the beholder smile.'

'Have you done much for the improvement of the City?' asked the New Year. 'Judging from what little I have seen, it appears to be ancient and time-worn.'

'I have opened the Rail-Road,' said the elder Year, 'and half a dozen times a day, you will hear the bell (which once summoned the Monks of a Spanish Convent to their devotions) announcing the arrival or departure of the cars. Old Salem now wears a much livelier expression than when I first beheld her. Strangers rumble down from Boston by hundreds at a time. New faces throng in Essex street. Rail-road hacks and omnibusses rattle over the pavements. There is a perceptible increase of oyster-shops, and other establishments for the accommodation of a transitory diurnal multitude. But a more important change awaits the venerable town. An immense accumulation of musty prejudices will be carried off by the free circulation of society. A peculiarity of character, of which the inhabitants themselves are hardly sensible, will be rubbed down and worn away by the attrition of foreign substances. Much of the result will be good; there will likewise be a few things not so good. Whether for better or worse, there will be a probable diminution of the moral influence of wealth, and the sway of an aristocratic class, which, from an era far beyond my memory, has held firmer dominion here than in any other New England town.'

The Old Year, having talked away nearly all of her little remaining breath, now closed her Book of Chronicles, and was about to take her departure. But her sister detained her a while longer, by inquiring the contents of the huge bandbox, which she was so painfully lugging along with her.

'These are merely a few trifles,' replied the Old Year, 'which I have picked up in my rambles, and am going to deposit, in the receptacle of things past and forgotten. We sisterhood of Years never carry anything really valuable out of the world with us. Here are patterns of most of the fashions which I brought into vogue, and which have already lived out their allotted term. You will supply their place, with others equally ephemeral. Here, put up in little China pots, like rouge, is a considerable lot of beautiful women's bloom, which the disconsolate fair ones owe me a bitter grudge for stealing. I have likewise a quantity of men's dark hair, instead of which, I have left grey locks, or none at all. The tears of widows and other afflicted mortals, who have received comfort during the last twelve months, are preserved in some dozens of essence bottles, well corked and sealed. I have several bundles of love-letters, eloquently breathing an eternity of burning passion, which grew cold and perished, almost before the ink was dry. Moreover, here is an assortment of many thousand broken promises, and other broken ware, all very light and packed into little space. The heaviest articles in my possession are a large parcel of disappointed hopes, which, a little while ago, were buoyant enough to have inflated Mr. Lauriat's balloon.'

'I have a fine lot of hopes here in my basket,' remarked the New Year. 'They are a sweet-smelling flower—a species of rose.'

'They soon lose their perfume,' replied the sombre Old Year. 'What else have you brought to insure a welcome from the discontented race of mortals?'

'Why, to say the truth, little or nothing else,' said her sister, with a smile—'save a few new Annuals and Almanacks, and some New Year's gifts for the children. But I heartily wish well to poor mortals, and mean to do all I can for their improvement and happiness.'

'It is a good resolution,' rejoined the Old Year; 'and, by the way, I have a plentiful assortment of good resolutions, which have now grown so stale and musty, that I am ashamed to carry them any further. Only for fear that the City authorities would send constable Mansfield, with a warrant after me, I should toss them into the street at once. Many other matters go to make up the contents of my band-box; but the whole lot would not fetch a single bid, even at an auction of worn out furniture; and as they are worth nothing either to you or any body else, I need not trouble you with a longer catalogue.'

'And must I also pick up such worthless luggage in my travels?' asked the New Year.

'Most certainly—and well if you have no heavier load to bear,' replied the other. 'And now, my dear sister, I must bid you farewell, earnestly advising and exhorting you to expect no gratitude nor good will from this peevish, unreasonable, inconsiderate, ill-intending and worse-behaving world. However warmly its inhabitants may seem to welcome you, yet, do what you may, and lavish on them what means of happiness you please, they will still be complaining,—still craving what it is not in your power to give,—still looking forward to some other Year for the accomplishment of projects which ought never to have been formed, and which, if successful, would only provide new occasions of discontent. If these ridiculous people ever see any thing tolerable in you, it will be after you are gone forever.'

'But I,' cried the fresh-hearted New Year, 'I shall try to leave men wiser than I find them. I will offer them freely whatever good gifts Providence permits me to distribute, and will tell them to be thankful for what they have, and humbly hopeful for more; and surely, if they are not absolute fools, they will condescend to be happy, and will allow me to be a happy Year. For my happiness must depend on them.'

'Alas for you, then, my poor sister!' said the Old Year, sighing, as she uplifted her burthen. 'We grand children of Time are born to trouble. Happiness, they say, dwells in the mansions of Eternity; but we can only lead mortals thither, step by step, with reluctant murmurings, and ourselves must perish on the threshold. But hark! My task is done.'

The clock in the tall steeple of Dr. Emerson's church struck

twelve; there was a response from Dr. Flint's, in the opposite
quarter of the City; and while the strokes were yet dropping
into the air, the Old Year either flitted or faded away—and
not the wisdom and might of Angels, to say nothing of the
remorseful yearnings of the millions who had used her ill,
could have prevailed with that departed Year to return one
step. But she, in the company of Time and all her kindred,
must hereafter hold a reckoning with Mankind. So shall it be,
likewise, with the maidenly New Year, who, as the clock
ceased to strike, arose from the steps of the City Hall, and set
out rather timorously on her earthly course.

'A happy New Year!' cried a watchman, eyeing her figure
very questionably, but without the least suspicion that he was
addressing the New Year in person.

'Thank you kindly!' said the New Year; and she gave the
watchman one of the roses of hope from her basket. 'May this
flower keep a sweet smell, long after I have bidden you good
bye.'

Then she stept on more briskly through the silent streets;
and such as were awake at the moment, heard her foot-fall,
and said—'The New Year is come!' Wherever there was a
knot of midnight roisterers, they quaffed her health. She
sighed, however, to perceive that the air was tainted—as the
atmosphere of this world must continually be—with the
dying breaths of mortals who had lingered just long enough
for her to bury them. But there were millions left alive, to
rejoice at her coming; and so she pursued her way with confidence, strewing emblematic flowers on the door-step of almost every dwelling, which some persons will gather up and
wear in their bosoms, and others will trample under foot. The
Carrier Boy can only say further, that, early this morning, she
filled his basket with New Year's Addresses, assuring him that
the whole City, with our new Mayor, and the Aldermen and
Common Council at its head, would make a general rush to
secure copies. Kind Patrons, will not you redeem the pledge
of the NEW YEAR?

The Lily's Quest

AN APOLOGUE

Two lovers, once upon a time, had planned a little summer-house, in the form of an antique Temple, which it was their purpose to consecrate to all manner of refined and innocent enjoyments. There they would hold pleasant intercourse with one another, and the circle of their familiar friends; there they would give festivals of delicious fruit; there they would hear lightsome music, intermingled with the strains of pathos which make joy more sweet; there they would read poetry and fiction, and permit their own minds to flit away in day-dreams and romance; there, in short—for why should we shape out the vague sunshine of their hopes?—there all pure delights were to cluster like roses among the pillars of the edifice, and blossom ever new and spontaneously. So, one breezy and cloudless afternoon, Adam Forrester and Lilias Fay set out upon a ramble over the wide estate which they were to possess together, seeking a proper site for their Temple of Happiness. They were themselves a fair and happy spectacle, fit priest and priestess for such a shrine; although, making poetry of the pretty name of Lilias, Adam Forrester was wont to call her LILY, because her form was as fragile and her cheek almost as pale.

As they passed hand in hand down the avenue of drooping elms, that led from the portal of Lilias Fay's paternal mansion, they seemed to glance like winged creatures through the strips of sunshine, and to scatter brightness where the deep shadows fell. But, setting forth at the same time with this youthful pair, there was a dismal figure, wrapt in a black velvet cloak that might have been made of a coffin-pall, and with a sombre hat, such as mourners wear, drooping its broad brim over his heavy brows. Glancing behind them, the lovers well knew who it was that followed, but wished from their hearts that he had been elsewhere, as being a companion so strangely unsuited to their joyous errand. It was a near relative of Lilias Fay, an old man by the name of Walter Gascoigne, who had long labored under the burthen of a melancholy spirit, which was sometimes maddened into absolute insanity, and always had a tinge of it. What a contrast between the young pilgrims of bliss, and their unbidden associate! They looked as if moulded of Heaven's sunshine, and he of Earth's gloomiest shade; they flitted along like Hope and Joy, roaming hand in hand through life; while his darksome figure stalked behind, a type of all the woeful influences which life could fling upon them. But the Three had not gone far, when they reached a spot that pleased the gentle Lily; and she paused.

"What sweeter place shall we find than this?" said she. "Why should we seek further for the site of our Temple?"

It was indeed a delightful spot of earth, though undistinguished by any very prominent beauties, being merely a nook in the shelter of a hill, with the prospect of a distant lake in one direction, and of a church-spire in another. There were vistas and pathways, leading onward and onward into the green woodlands, and vanishing away in the glimmering shade. The Temple, if erected here, would look towards the West; so that the lovers could shape all sorts of magnificent dreams out of the purple, violet, and gold of the sunset sky; and few of their anticipated pleasures were dearer than this sport of fantasy.

"Yes," said Adam Forrester, "we might seek all day, and find no lovelier spot. We will build our Temple here."

But their sad old companion, who had taken his stand on the very site which they proposed to cover with a marble floor, shook his head and frowned; and the young man and the Lily deemed it almost enough to blight the spot, and desecrate it for their airy Temple, that his dismal figure had thrown its shadow there. He pointed to some scattered stones, the remnants of a former structure, and to flowers such as young girls delight to nurse in their gardens, but which had now relapsed into the wild simplicity of nature.

"Not here!" cried old Walter Gascoigne. "Here, long ago, other mortals built their Temple of Happiness. Seek another site for yours!"

"What!" exclaimed Lilias Fay. "Have any ever planned such a Temple, save ourselves?"

"Poor child!" said her gloomy kinsman. "In one shape or other, every mortal has dreamed your dream."

Then he told the lovers, how—not, indeed, an antique Temple—but a dwelling had once stood there, and that a dark-clad guest had dwelt among its inmates, sitting forever at the fireside, and poisoning all their household mirth. Under this type, Adam Forrester and Lilias saw that the old man spake of Sorrow. He told of nothing that might not be recorded in the history of almost every household; and yet his hearers felt as if no sunshine ought to fall upon a spot, where human grief had left so deep a stain; or, at least, that no joyous Temple should be built there.

"This is very sad," said the Lily, sighing.

"Well; there are lovelier spots than this," said Adam Forrester, soothingly—"spots which Sorrow has not blighted."

So they hastened away, and the melancholy Gascoigne followed them, looking as if he had gathered up all the gloom of the deserted spot, and were bearing it as a burthen of inestimable treasure. But still they rambled on, and soon found themselves in a rocky dell, through the midst of which ran a streamlet, with ripple, and foam, and a continual voice of inarticulate joy. It was a wild retreat, walled on either side with gray precipices, which would have frowned somewhat too sternly, had not a profusion of green shrubbery rooted itself into their crevices, and wreathed gladsome foliage around their solemn brows. But the chief joy of the dell was in the little stream, which seemed like the presence of a blissful child, with nothing earthly to do, save to babble merrily and disport itself, and make every living soul its playfellow, and throw the sunny gleams of its spirit upon all.

"Here! Here is the spot!" cried the two lovers with one voice, as they reached a level space on the brink of a small cascade. "This glen was made on purpose for our Temple!"

"And the glad song of the brook will be always in our ears," said Lilias Fay.

"And its long melody shall sing the bliss of our life-time," said Adam Forrester.

"Ye must build no Temple here!" murmured their dismal companion.

And there again was the old lunatic, standing just on the

spot where they meant to rear their lightsome dome, and looking like the embodied symbol of some great woe, that, in forgotten days, had happened there. And, alas! there had been woe, nor that alone. A young man, more than a hundred years before, had lured hither a girl that loved him, and on this spot had murdered her, and washed his bloody hands in the stream which sang so merrily. And ever since, the victim's death-shrieks were often heard to echo between the cliffs.

"And see!" cried old Gascoigne. "Is the stream yet pure from the stain of the murderer's hands?"

"Methinks it has a tinge of blood," faintly answered the Lily; and being as slight as the gossamer, she trembled and clung to her lover's arm, whispering, "Let us flee from this dreadful vale!"

"Come then," said Adam Forrester, as cheerily as he could. "We shall soon find a happier spot."

They set forth again, young Pilgrims on that quest which millions—which every child of Earth—has tried in turn. And were the Lily and her lover to be more fortunate than all those millions? For a long time, it seemed not so. The dismal shape of the old lunatic still glided behind them; and for every spot that looked lovely in their eyes, he had some legend of human wrong or suffering, so miserably sad, that his auditors could never afterwards connect the idea of joy with the place where it had happened. Here, a heart-broken woman, kneeling to her own child, had been spurned from his feet; here, a desolate old creature had prayed to the Evil One, and had received a fiendish malignity of soul, in answer to her prayer; here, a new-born infant, sweet blossom of life, had been found dead, with the impress of its mother's fingers round its throat; and here, under a shattered oak, two lovers had been stricken by lightning, and fell blackened corpses in each other's arms. The dreary Gascoigne had a gift to know whatever evil and lamentable thing had stained the bosom of Mother Earth; and when his funereal voice had told the tale, it appeared like a prophecy of future woe, as well as a tradition of the past. And now, by their sad demeanor, you would have fancied that the pilgrim lovers were seeking, not a Temple of earthly joy, but a tomb for themselves and their posterity.

"Where, in this world," exclaimed Adam Forrester, despondingly, "shall we build our Temple of Happiness!"

"Where in this world, indeed!" repeated Lilias Fay; and being faint and weary, the more so by the heaviness of her heart, the Lily drooped her head, and sat down on the summit of a knoll, repeating, "Where, in this world, shall we build our Temple!"

"Ah! Have you already asked yourselves that question?" said their companion, his shaded features growing even gloomier with the smile that dwelt on them. "Yet there is a place, even in this world, where ye may build it."

While the old man spoke, Adam Forrester and Lilias had carelessly thrown their eyes around, and perceived that the spot, where they had chanced to pause, possessed a quiet charm, which was well enough adapted to their present mood of mind. It was a small rise of ground, with a certain regularity of shape, that had perhaps been bestowed by art; and a group of trees, which almost surrounded it, threw their pensive shadows across and far beyond, although some softened glory of the sunshine found its way there. The ancestral mansion, wherein the lovers would dwell together, appeared on one side, and the ivied church, where they were to worship, on another. Happening to cast their eyes on the ground, they smiled, yet with a sense of wonder, to see that a pale lily was growing at their feet.

"We will build our Temple here!" said they simultaneously, and with an indescribable conviction that they had at last found the very spot.

Yet, while they uttered this exclamation, the young man and the Lily turned an apprehensive glance at their dreary associate, deeming it hardly possible that some tale of earthly affliction should not make those precincts loathsome, as in every former case. The old man stood just behind them, so as to form the chief figure in the group, with his sable cloak muffling the lower part of his visage, and his sombre hat overshadowing his brows. But he gave no word of dissent from their purpose; and an inscrutable smile was accepted by the lovers as a token, that here had been no foot-print of guilt or sorrow, to desecrate the site of their Temple of Happiness.

In a little time longer, while summer was still in its prime, the fairy structure of the Temple arose on the summit of the knoll, amid the solemn shadows of the trees, yet often gladdened with bright sunshine. It was built of white marble, with slender and graceful pillars, supporting a vaulted dome; and beneath the centre of this dome, upon a pedestal, was a slab of dark-veined marble, on which books and music might be strewn. But there was a fantasy among the people of the neighborhood, that the edifice was planned after an ancient mausoleum, and was intended for a tomb, and that the central slab of dark-veined marble was to be inscribed with the names of buried ones. They doubted, too, whether the form of Lilias Fay could appertain to a creature of this earth, being so very delicate, and growing every day more fragile, so that she looked as if the summer breeze should snatch her up, and waft her heavenward. But still she watched the daily growth of the Temple; and so did old Walter Gascoigne, who now made that spot his continual haunt, leaning whole hours together on his staff, and giving as deep attention to the work as though it had been indeed a tomb. In due time it was finished, and a day appointed for a simple rite of dedication.

On the preceding evening, after Adam Forrester had taken leave of his mistress, he looked back towards the portal of her dwelling, and felt a strange thrill of fear; for he imagined that, as the setting sunbeams faded from her figure, she was exhaling away, and that something of her ethereal substance was withdrawn, with each lessening gleam of light. With his farewell glance, a shadow had fallen over the portal, and Lilias was invisible. His foreboding spirit deemed it an omen, at the time; and so it proved; for the sweet earthly form, by which the Lily had been manifested to the world, was found lifeless, the next morning, in the Temple, with her head resting on her arms, which were folded upon the slab of dark-veined marble. The chill winds of the Earth had long since breathed a blight into this beautiful flower, so that a loving hand had now transplanted it, to blossom brightly in the garden of Paradise.

But alas, for the Temple of Happiness! In his unutterable grief, Adam Forrester had no purpose more at heart, than to convert this Temple of many delightful hopes into a tomb, and bury his dead mistress there. And lo! a wonder. Digging a grave beneath the Temple's marble floor, the sexton found no virgin earth, such as was meet to receive the maiden's dust, but an ancient sepulchre, in which were treasured up the bones of generations that had died long ago. Among those forgotten ancestors was the Lily to be laid. And when the funeral procession brought Lilias thither in her coffin, they beheld old Walter Gascoigne standing beneath the dome of the Temple, with his cloak of pall and face of darkest gloom; and wherever that figure might take its stand, the spot would seem a sepulchre. He watched the mourners, as they lowered the coffin down.

"And so," said he to Adam Forrester, with the strange smile in which his insanity was wont to gleam forth, "you have found no better foundation for your happiness, than on a Grave!"

But, as the Shadow of Affliction spoke, a vision of Hope and Joy had its birth in Adam's mind, even from the old man's taunting words; for then he knew what was betokened by the parable in which the Lily and himself had acted; and the mystery of Life and Death was opened to him.

"Joy! Joy!" he cried, throwing his arms towards Heaven. "On a Grave be the site of our Temple; and now our happiness is for Eternity!"

With those words, a ray of sunshine broke through the dismal sky, and glimmered down into the sepulchre; while, at the same moment, the shape of old Walter Gascoigne stalked drearily away, because his gloom, symbolic of all earthly sorrow, might no longer abide there now that the darkest riddle of humanity was read.

John Inglefield's Thanksgiving

O N the evening of Thanksgiving day, John Inglefield, the blacksmith, sat in his elbow-chair, among those who had been keeping festival at his board. Being the central figure of the domestic circle, the fire threw its strongest light on his massive and sturdy frame, reddening his rough visage, so that it looked like the head of an iron statue, all a-glow from his own forge, and with its features rudely fashioned on his own anvil. At John Inglefield's right hand was an empty chair. The other places round the hearth were filled by the members of the family, who all sat quietly, while, with a semblance of fantastic merriment, their shadows danced on the wall behind them. One of the group was John Inglefield's son, who had been bred at college, and was now a student of theology at Andover. There was also a daughter of sixteen, whom nobody could look at without thinking of a rose-bud almost blossomed. The only other person at the fireside was Robert Moore, formerly an apprentice of the blacksmith, but now his journeyman, and who seemed more like an own son of John Inglefield than did the pale and slender student.

Only these four had kept New England's festival beneath that roof. The vacant chair at John Inglefield's right hand, was in memory of his wife, whom death had snatched from him since the previous Thanksgiving. With a feeling that few would have looked for in his rough nature, the bereaved husband had himself set the chair in its place next his own; and often did his eye glance thitherward, as if he deemed it possible that the cold grave might send back its tenant to the cheerful fireside, at least for that one evening. Thus did he cherish the grief that was dear to him. But there was another grief which he would fain have torn from his heart; or, since that could never be, have buried it too deep for others to behold, or for his own remembrance. Within the past year another member of his household had gone from him—but not to the grave. Yet they kept no vacant chair for her.

While John Inglefield and his family were sitting round the hearth, with the shadows dancing behind them on the wall, the outer door was opened, and a light footstep came along the passage. The latch of the inner door was lifted by some familiar hand, and a young girl came in, wearing a cloak and hood, which she took off, and laid on the table beneath the looking-glass. Then, after gazing a moment at the fireside circle, she approached, and took the seat at John Inglefield's right hand, as if it had been reserved on purpose for her.

"Here I am at last, father," said she. "You ate your Thanksgiving dinner without me; but I have come back to spend the evening with you."

Yes—it was Prudence Inglefield. She wore the same neat and maidenly attire, which she had been accustomed to put on when the household work was over for the day, and her hair was parted from her brow, in the simple and modest fashion that became her best of all. If her cheek might otherwise have been pale, yet the glow of the fire suffused it with a healthful bloom. If she had spent the many months of her absence in guilt and infamy, yet they seemed to have left no traces on her gentle aspect. She could not have looked less altered, had she merely stept away from her father's fireside for half an hour, and returned while the blaze was quivering upwards from the same brands that were burning at her departure. And to John Inglefield she was the very image of his buried wife, such as he remembered her on the first Thanksgiving which they had passed under their own roof. Therefore, though naturally a stern and rugged man, he could not speak unkindly to his sinful child, nor yet could he take her to his bosom.

"You are welcome home, Prudence," said he, glancing sideways at her, and his voice faltered. "Your mother would have rejoiced to see you, but she has been gone from us these four months."

"I know it, father, I know it," replied Prudence quickly. "And yet when I first came in, my eyes were so dazzled by the fire-light, that she seemed to be sitting in this very chair!"

By this time the other members of the family had begun to recover from their surprise, and became sensible that it was no ghost from the grave, nor vision of their vivid recollections, but Prudence her own self. Her brother was the next that greeted her. He advanced and held out his hand affectionately, as a brother should; yet not entirely like a brother, for, with all his kindness, he was still a clergyman, and speaking to a child of sin.

"Sister Prudence," said he earnestly, "I rejoice that a merciful Providence has turned your steps homeward, in time for me to bid you a last farewell. In a few weeks, sister, I am to sail as a missionary to the far islands of the Pacific. There is not one of these beloved faces, that I shall ever hope to behold again on this earth. Oh, may I see all of them—yours and all—beyond the grave!"

A shadow flitted across the girl's countenance.

"The grave is very dark, brother," answered she, withdrawing her hand somewhat hastily from his grasp. "You must look your last at me by the light of this fire."

While this was passing, the twin-girl—the rose-bud that had grown on the same stem with the cast-away—stood gazing at her sister, longing to fling herself upon her bosom, so that the tendrils of their hearts might intertwine again. At first she was restrained by mingled grief and shame, and by a dread that Prudence was too much changed to respond to her affection, or that her own purity would be felt as a reproach by the lost one. But as she listened to the familiar voice, while the face grew more and more familiar, she forgot everything, save that Prudence had come back. Springing forward, she would have clasped her in a close embrace. At that very instant, however, Prudence started from her chair, and held out both her hands, with a warning gesture.

"No, Mary—no, my sister," cried she, "do not you touch me. Your bosom must not be pressed to mine!"

Mary shuddered, and stood still, for she felt that something darker than the grave was between Prudence and herself, though they seemed so near each other in the light of their father's hearth, where they had grown up together. Meanwhile Prudence threw her eyes around the room, in search of one who had not yet bidden her welcome. He had withdrawn from his seat by the fireside, and was standing near the door, with his face averted, so that his features could be discerned only by the flickering shadow of the profile upon the wall. But Prudence called to him, in a cheerful and kindly tone:

"Come, Robert," said she, "won't you shake hands with your old friend?"

Robert Moore held back for a moment; but affection struggled powerfully, and overcame his pride and resentment; he rushed towards Prudence, seized her hand, and pressed it to his bosom.

"There, there, Robert!" said she, smiling sadly as she withdrew her hand, "you must not give me too warm a welcome."

And now, having exchanged greetings with each member of the family, Prudence again seated herself in the chair at John Inglefield's right hand. She was naturally a girl of quick and tender sensibilities, gladsome in her general mood, but with a bewitching pathos interfused among her merriest words and deeds. It was remarked of her, too, that she had a faculty, even from childhood, of throwing her own feelings like a spell over her companions. Such as she had been in her days of innocence, so did she appear this evening. Her friends, in the surprise and bewilderment of her return, almost forgot that she had ever left them, or that she had forfeited any of her claims to their affection. In the morning, perhaps, they might have looked at her with altered eyes, but by the Thanksgiving fireside they felt only that their own Prudence had come back to them, and were thankful. John Inglefield's rough visage brightened with the glow of his heart, as it grew warm and merry within him; once or twice, even, he laughed till the room rang again, yet seemed startled by the echo of his own mirth. The grave young minister became as frolicsome as a school-boy. Mary, too, the rose-bud, forgot that her twin blossom had ever been torn from the stem, and trampled in the dust. And as for Robert Moore, he gazed at Prudence with the bashful earnestness of love new-born, while she, with sweet maiden coquetry, half smiled upon, and half discouraged him.

In short, it was one of those intervals when sorrow vanishes in its own depth of shadow, and joy starts forth in transitory brightness. When the clock struck eight, Prudence poured out her father's customary draught of herb tea, which had been steeping by the fireside ever since twilight.

"God bless you, child," said John Inglefield, as he took the cup from her hand; "you have made your old father happy again. But we miss your mother sadly, Prudence—sadly. It seems as if she ought to be here now."

"Now, father, or never," replied Prudence.

It was now the hour for domestic worship. But while the family were making preparations for this duty, they suddenly perceived that Prudence had put on her cloak and hood, and was lifting the latch of the door.

"Prudence, Prudence! where are you going?" cried they all with one voice.

As Prudence passed out of the door, she turned towards them, and flung back her hand with a gesture of farewell. But her face was so changed that they hardly recognized it. Sin and evil passions glowed through its comeliness, and wrought a horrible deformity; a smile gleamed in her eyes, as of triumphant mockery at their surprise and grief.

"Daughter," cried John Inglefield, between wrath and sorrow, "stay and be your father's blessing—or take his curse with you!"

For an instant Prudence lingered and looked back into the fire-lighted room, while her countenance wore almost the expression as if she were struggling with a fiend, who had power to seize his victim even within the hallowed precincts of her father's hearth. The fiend prevailed; and Prudence vanished into the outer darkness. When the family rushed to the door, they could see nothing, but heard the sound of wheels rattling over the frozen ground.

That same night, among the painted beauties at the theatre of a neighboring city, there was one whose dissolute mirth seemed inconsistent with any sympathy for pure affections, and for the joys and griefs which are hallowed by them. Yet this was Prudence Inglefield. Her visit to the Thanksgiving fireside was the realization of one of those waking dreams in which the guilty soul will sometimes stray back to its innocence. But Sin, alas! is careful of her bond-slaves; they hear her voice, perhaps at the holiest moment, and are constrained to go whither she summons them. The same dark power that drew Prudence Inglefield from her father's hearth—the same in its nature, though heightened then to a dread necessity—would snatch a guilty soul from the gate of Heaven, and make its sin and its punishment alike eternal.

A Virtuoso's Collection

THE other day, having a leisure hour at my disposal, I stept into a new museum, to which my notice was casually drawn by a small and unobtrusive sign: "To be seen here, a Virtuoso's Collection." Such was the simple, yet not altogether unpromising announcement, that turned my steps aside, for a little while, from the sunny sidewalk of our principal thoroughfare. Mounting a sombre staircase, I pushed open a door at its summit, and found myself in the presence of a person, who mentioned the moderate sum that would entitle me to admittance:

"Three shillings, Massachusetts tenor," said he; "no, I mean half a dollar, as you reckon in these days."

While searching my pocket for the coin, I glanced at the door-keeper, the marked character and individuality of whose aspect encouraged me to expect something not quite in the ordinary way. He wore an old-fashioned great-coat, much faded, within which his meagre person was so completely enveloped that the rest of his attire was undistinguishable. But his visage was remarkably wind-flushed, sun-burnt, and weather-worn, and had a most unquiet, nervous, and apprehensive expression. It seemed as if this man had some all-important object in view, some point of deepest interest to be decided, some momentous question to ask, might he but hope for a reply. As it was evident, however, that I could have nothing to do with his private affairs, I passed through an open door-way, which admitted me into the extensive hall of the Museum.

Directly in front of the portal was the bronze statue of a youth with winged feet. He was represented in the act of flitting away from earth, yet wore such a look of earnest invitation that it impressed me like a summons to enter the hall.

"It is the original statue of Opportunity, by the ancient sculptor Lysippus," said a gentleman who now approached me; "I place it at the entrance of my Museum, because it is not at all times that one can gain admittance to such a collection."

The speaker was a middle-aged person, of whom it was not easy to determine whether he had spent his life as a scholar, or as a man of action; in truth, all outward and obvious peculiarities had been worn away by an extensive and promiscuous intercourse with the world. There was no mark about him of profession, individual habits, or scarcely of country; although his dark complexion and high features made me conjecture that he was a native of some southern clime of Europe. At all events, he was evidently the Virtuoso in person.

"With your permission," said he, "as we have no descriptive catalogue, I will accompany you through the Museum, and point out whatever may be most worthy of attention. In the first place, here is a choice collection of stuffed animals."

Nearest the door stood the outward semblance of a wolf, exquisitely prepared, it is true, and showing a very wolfish fierceness in the large glass eyes, which were inserted into its wild and crafty head. Still it was merely the skin of a wolf, with nothing to distinguish it from other individuals of that unlovely breed.

"How does this animal deserve a place in your collection?" inquired I.

"It is the wolf that devoured Little Red Riding-Hood," answered the Virtuoso; "and by his side,—with a milder and more matronly look, as you perceive,—stands the she-wolf that suckled Romulus and Remus."

"Ah, indeed!" exclaimed I. "And what lovely lamb is this, with the snow-white fleece, which seems to be of as delicate a texture as innocence itself?"

"Methinks you have but carelessly read Spenser," replied my guide, "or you would at once recognize the 'milk-white lamb' which Una led. But I set no great value upon the lamb. The next specimen is better worth our notice."

"What!" cried I, "this strange animal, with the black head of an ox upon the body of a white horse? Were it possible to suppose it, I should say that this was Alexander's steed Bucephalus."

"The same," said the Virtuoso. "And can you likewise give a name to the famous charger that stands beside him?"

Next to the renowned Bucephalus stood the mere skeleton

of a horse, with the white bones peeping through its ill-con-
ditioned hide. But, if my heart had not warmed towards that
pitiful anatomy, I might as well have quitted the Museum at
once. Its rarities had not been collected with pain and toil
from the four quarters of the earth, and from the depths of
the sea, and from the palaces and sepulchres of ages, for those
who could mistake this illustrious steed.

"It is Rosinante!" exclaimed I, with enthusiasm.

And so it proved! My admiration for the noble and gallant
horse caused me to glance with less interest at the other animals, although many of them might have deserved the notice
of Cuvier himself. There was the donkey which Peter Bell
cudgelled so soundly; and a brother of the same species, who
had suffered a similar infliction from the ancient prophet Ba-
laam. Some doubts were entertained, however, as to the authenticity of the latter beast. My guide pointed out the venerable Argus, that faithful dog of Ulysses, and also another
dog, (for so the skin bespoke it,) which, though imperfectly
preserved, seemed once to have had three heads. It was Cerberus. I was considerably amused at detecting, in an obscure
corner, the fox that became so famous by the loss of his tail.
There were several stuffed cats, which, as a dear lover of that
comfortable beast, attracted my affectionate regards. One was
Dr. Johnson's cat Hodge; and in the same row stood the favorite cats of Mahomet, Gray, and Walter Scott, together
with Puss in Boots, and a cat of very noble aspect who had
once been a deity of ancient Egypt. Byron's tame bear came
next. I must not forget to mention the Erymanthean boar,
the skin of St. George's Dragon, and that of the serpent Py-
thon; and another skin, with beautifully variegated hues, supposed to have been the garment of the "spirited sly snake,"
which tempted Eve. Against the wall were suspended the
horns of the stag that Shakspeare shot; and on the floor lay
the ponderous shell of the tortoise which fell upon the head
of Æschylus. In one row, as natural as life, stood the sacred
bull Apis, the "cow with the crumpled horn," and a very wild
looking young heifer, which I guessed to be the cow that
jumped over the moon. She was probably killed by the rapidity of her descent. As I turned away, my eyes fell upon an
indescribable monster, which proved to be a griffin.

"I look in vain," observed I, "for the skin of an animal which might well deserve the closest study of a naturalist,—the winged horse Pegasus."

"He is not yet dead," replied the Virtuoso, "but he is so hard ridden by many young gentlemen of the day, that I hope soon to add his skin and skeleton to my collection."

We now passed to the next alcove of the hall, in which was a multitude of stuffed birds. They were very prettily arranged, some upon the branches of trees, others brooding upon nests, and others suspended by wires so artificially that they seemed in the very act of flight. Among them was a white dove, with a withered branch of olive leaves in her mouth.

"Can this be the very dove," inquired I, "that brought the message of peace and hope to the tempest-beaten passengers of the ark?"

"Even so," said my companion.

"And this raven, I suppose," continued I, "is the same that fed Elijah in the wilderness."

"The raven?—no," said the Virtuoso, "it is a bird of modern date. He belonged to one Barnaby Rudge; and many people fancied that the devil himself was disguised under his sable plumage. But poor Grip has drawn his last cork, and has been forced to 'say die' at last. This other raven, hardly less curious, is that in which the soul of King George the First revisited his lady love, the Duchess of Kendall."

My guide next pointed out Minerva's owl, and the vulture that preyed upon the liver of Prometheus. There was likewise the sacred Ibis of Egypt, and one of the Stymphalides, which Hercules shot in his sixth labor. Shelley's sky-lark, Bryant's water-fowl, and a pigeon from the belfry of the Old South Church, preserved by N. P. Willis, were placed on the same perch. I could not but shudder on beholding Coleridge's albatross, transfixed with the Ancient Mariner's crossbow shaft. Beside this bird of awful poesy stood a gray goose of very ordinary aspect.

"Stuffed goose is no such rarity," observed I. "Why do you preserve such a specimen in your Museum?"

"It is one of the flock whose cackling saved the Roman Capitol," answered the Virtuoso. "Many geese have cackled and hissed, both before and since; but none, like those, have clamored themselves into immortality."

There seemed to be little else that demanded notice in this department of the Museum, unless we except Robinson Crusoe's parrot, a live phœnix, a footless bird of Paradise, and a splendid peacock, supposed to be the same that once contained the soul of Pythagoras. I therefore passed to the next alcove, the shelves of which were covered with a miscellaneous collection of curiosities, such as are usually found in similar establishments. One of the first things that took my eye was a strange looking cap, woven of some substance that appeared to be neither woollen, cotton, nor linen.

"Is this a magician's cap?" I asked.

"No," replied the Virtuoso, "it is merely Dr. Franklin's cap of asbestos. But here is one which, perhaps, may suit you better. It is the wishing-cap of Fortunatus. Will you try it on?"

"By no means," answered I, putting it aside with my hand. "The day of wild wishes is past with me. I desire nothing that may not come in the ordinary course of Providence."

"Then, probably," returned the Virtuoso, "you will not be tempted to rub this lamp?"

While speaking, he took from the shelf an antique brass lamp, curiously wrought with embossed figures, but so covered with verdigris that the sculpture was almost eaten away.

"It is a thousand years," said he, "since the genius of this lamp constructed Aladdin's palace in a single night. But he still retains his power; and the man who rubs Aladdin's lamp, has but to desire either a palace or a cottage."

"I might desire a cottage," replied I, "but I would have it founded on sure and stable truth, not on dreams and fantasies. I have learned to look for the real and the true."

My guide next showed me Prospero's magic wand, broken into three fragments by the hand of its mighty master. On the same shelf lay the gold ring of ancient Gyges, which enabled the wearer to walk invisible. On the other side of the alcove was a tall looking-glass in a frame of ebony, but veiled with a curtain of purple silk, through the rents of which the gleam of the mirror was perceptible.

"This is Cornelius Agrippa's magic glass," observed the

Virtuoso. "Draw aside the curtain, and picture any human form within your mind, and it will be reflected in the mirror."

"It is enough if I can picture it within my mind," answered I. "Why should I wish it to be repeated in the mirror? But, indeed, these works of magic have grown wearisome to me. There are so many greater wonders in the world, to those who keep their eyes open, and their sight undimmed by custom, that all the delusions of the old sorcerers seem flat and stale. Unless you can show me something really curious, I care not to look further into your Museum."

"Ah, well, then," said the Virtuoso, composedly, "perhaps you may deem some of my antiquarian rarities deserving of a glance."

He pointed out the Iron Mask, now corroded with rust; and my heart grew sick at the sight of this dreadful relic, which had shut out a human being from sympathy with his race. There was nothing half so terrible in the axe that beheaded King Charles, nor in the dagger that slew Henry of Navarre, nor in the arrow that pierced the heart of William Rufus,—all of which were shown to me. Many of the articles derived their interest, such as it was, from having been formerly in the possession of royalty. For instance, here was Charlemagne's sheepskin cloak, the flowing wig of Louis Quatorze, the spinning-wheel of Sardanapalus, and King Stephen's famous breeches, which cost him but a crown. The heart of the Bloody Mary, with the word "Calais" worn into its diseased substance, was preserved in a bottle of spirits; and near it lay the golden case in which the queen of Gustavus Adolphus treasured up that hero's heart. Among these relics and heirlooms of kings, I must not forget the long, hairy ears of Midas, and a piece of bread, which had been changed to gold by the touch of that unlucky monarch. And as Grecian Helen was a queen, it may here be mentioned, that I was permitted to take into my hand a lock of her golden hair, and the bowl which a sculptor modelled from the curve of her perfect breast. Here, likewise, was the robe that smothered Agamemnon, Nero's fiddle, the Czar Peter's brandy-bottle, the crown of Semiramis, and Canute's sceptre, which he extended over the sea. That my own land may not deem itself neglected, let me add, that I was favored with a sight of the skull of King Philip, the famous Indian chief, whose head the Puritans smote off and exhibited upon a pole.

"Show me something else," said I to the Virtuoso. "Kings are in such an artificial position, that people in the ordinary walks of life cannot feel an interest in their relics. If you could show me the straw hat of sweet little Nell, I would far rather see it than a king's golden crown."

"There it is," said my guide, pointing carelessly with his staff to the straw hat in question. "But, indeed, you are hard to please. Here are the seven-league boots. Will you try them on?"

"Our modern railroads have superseded their use," answered I; "and as to these cow-hide boots, I could show you quite as curious a pair at the transcendental community in Roxbury."

We next examined a collection of swords and other weapons, belonging to different epochs, but thrown together without much attempt at arrangement. Here was Arthur's sword Excalibar, and that of the Cid Campeador, and the sword of Brutus rusted with Cæsar's blood and his own, and the sword of Joan of Arc, and that of Horatius, and that with which Virginius slew his daughter, and the one which Dionysius suspended over the head of Damocles. Here, also, was Arria's sword, which she plunged into her own breast, in order to taste of death before her husband. The crooked blade of Saladin's scimetar next attracted my notice. I know not by what chance, but so it happened that the sword of one of our own militia generals was suspended between Don Quixote's lance and the brown blade of Hudibras. My heart throbbed high at the sight of the helmet of Miltiades, and the spear that was broken in the breast of Epaminondas. I recognized the shield of Achilles, by its resemblance to the admirable cast in the possession of Professor Felton. Nothing in this department interested me more than Major Pitcairn's pistol, the discharge of which, at Lexington, began the war of the revolution, and was reverberated in thunder around the land for seven long years. The bow of Ulysses, though unstrung for ages, was placed against the wall, together with a sheaf of Robin Hood's arrows, and the rifle of Daniel Boone.

"Enough of weapons," said I, at length; "although I would

gladly have seen the sacred shield which fell from Heaven in the time of Numa. And surely you should obtain the sword which Washington unsheathed at Cambridge. But the collection does you much credit. Let us pass on."

In the next alcove we saw the golden thigh of Pythagoras, which had so divine a meaning; and, by one of the queer analogies to which the Virtuoso seemed to be addicted, this ancient emblem lay on the same shelf with Peter Stuyvesant's wooden leg, that was fabled to be of silver. Here was a remnant of the Golden Fleece; and a sprig of yellow leaves that resembled the foliage of a frost-bitten elm, but was duly authenticated as a portion of the golden branch by which Æneas gained admittance to the realm of Pluto. Atalanta's golden apple, and one of the apples of discord, were wrapt in the napkin of gold which Rampsinitus brought from Hades; and the whole were deposited in the golden vase of Bias, with its inscription: "To THE WISEST."

"And how did you obtain this vase?" said I to the Virtuoso.

"It was given me long ago," replied he, with a scornful expression in his eye, "because I had learned to despise all things."

It had not escaped me that, though the Virtuoso was evidently a man of high cultivation, yet he seemed to lack sympathy with the spiritual, the sublime, and the tender. Apart from the whim that had led him to devote so much time, pains, and expense to the collection of this Museum, he impressed me as one of the hardest and coldest men of the world whom I had ever met.

"To despise all things!" repeated I. "This, at best, is the wisdom of the understanding. It is the creed of a man whose soul,—whose better and diviner part,—has never been awakened, or has died out of him."

"I did not think that you were still so young," said the Virtuoso. "Should you live to my years, you will acknowledge that the vase of Bias was not ill bestowed."

Without farther discussion of the point, he directed my attention to other curiosities. I examined Cinderella's little glass slipper, and compared it with one of Diana's sandals, and with Fanny Elssler's shoe, which bore testimony to the muscular character of her illustrious foot. On the same shelf were

Thomas the Rhymer's green velvet shoes, and the brazen shoe of Empedocles, which was thrown out of Mount Ætna. Anacreon's drinking-cup was placed in apt juxtaposition with one of Tom Moore's wine-glasses and Circe's magic bowl. These were symbols of luxury and riot; but near them stood the cup whence Socrates drank his hemlock; and that which Sir Philip Sydney put from his death-parched lips to bestow the draught upon a dying soldier. Next appeared a cluster of tobacco pipes, consisting of Sir Walter Raleigh's, the earliest on record, Dr. Parr's, Charles Lamb's, and the first calumet of peace which was ever smoked between a European and an Indian. Among other musical instruments, I noticed the lyre of Orpheus, and those of Homer and Sappho, Dr. Franklin's famous whistle, the trumpet of Anthony Van Corlear, and the flute which Goldsmith played upon in his rambles through the French provinces. The staff of Peter the Hermit stood in a corner, with that of good old Bishop Jewel, and one of ivory, which had belonged to Papirius, the Roman Senator. The ponderous club of Hercules was close at hand. The Virtuoso showed me the chisel of Phidias, Claude's palette, and the brush of Apelles, observing that he intended to bestow the former either on Greenough, Crawford, or Powers, and the two latter upon Washington Allston. There was a small vase of oracular gas from Delphos, which, I trust, will be submitted to the scientific analysis of Professor Silliman. I was deeply moved on beholding a phial of the tears into which Niobe was dissolved; nor less so, on learning that a shapeless fragment of salt was a relic of that victim of despondency and sinful regrets, Lot's wife. My companion appeared to set great value upon some Egyptian darkness in a blacking jug. Several of the shelves were covered by a collection of coins; among which, however, I remember none but the Splendid Shilling, celebrated by Phillips, and a dollar's worth of the iron money of Lycurgus, weighing about fifty pounds.

Walking carelessly onward, I had nearly fallen over a huge bundle, like a pedlar's pack, done up in sackcloth and very securely strapped and corded.

"It is Christian's burthen of sin," said the Virtuoso.

"Oh, pray let us open it!" cried I. "For many a year I have longed to know its contents."

"Look into your own consciousness and memory," replied the Virtuoso. "You will there find a list of whatever it contains."

As this was an undeniable truth, I threw a melancholy look at the burthen, and passed on. A collection of old garments, hanging on pegs, was worthy of some attention, especially the shirt of Nessus, Cæsar's mantle, Joseph's coat of many colors, the Vicar of Bray's cassock, Goldsmith's peach-bloom suit, a pair of President Jefferson's scarlet breeches, John Randolph's red baize hunting-shirt, the drab small clothes of the Stout Gentleman, and the rags of the "man all tattered and torn." George Fox's hat impressed me with deep reverence, as a relic of perhaps the truest apostle that has appeared on earth for these eighteen hundred years. My eye was next attracted by an old pair of shears, which I should have taken for a memorial of some famous tailor, only that the Virtuoso pledged his veracity that they were the identical scissors of Atropos. He also showed me a broken hour-glass, which had been thrown aside by Father Time, together with the old gentleman's gray forelock, tastefully braided into a brooch. In the hour-glass was the handful of sand, the grains of which had numbered the years of the Cumæan Sibyl. I think it was in this alcove that I saw the inkstand which Luther threw at the Devil, and the ring which Essex, while under sentence of death, sent to Queen Elizabeth. And here was the blood-encrusted pen of steel with which Faust signed away his salvation.

The Virtuoso now opened the door of a closet, and showed me a lamp burning, while three others stood unlighted by its side. One of the three was the lamp of Diogenes, another that of Guy Faux, and the third that which Hero set forth to the midnight breeze in the high tower of Abydos.

"See!" said the Virtuoso, blowing with all his force at the lighted lamp.

The flame quivered and shrank away from his breath, but clung to the wick, and resumed its brilliancy as soon as the blast was exhausted.

"It is an undying lamp from the tomb of Charlemagne," observed my guide. "That flame was kindled a thousand years ago."

"How ridiculous, to kindle an unnatural light in tombs!" exclaimed I. "We should seek to behold the dead in the light of Heaven. But what is the meaning of this chafing-dish of glowing coals?"

"That," answered the Virtuoso, "is the original fire which Prometheus stole from Heaven. Look steadfastly into it, and you will discern another curiosity."

I gazed into that fire,—which, symbolically, was the origin of all that was bright and glorious in the soul of man,—and in the midst of it, behold! a little reptile, sporting with evident enjoyment of the fervid heat. It was a salamander.

"What a sacrilege!" cried I, with inexpressible disgust. "Can you find no better use for this ethereal fire than to cherish a loathsome reptile in it? Yet there are men who abuse the sacred fire of their own souls to as foul and guilty a purpose."

The Virtuoso made no answer, except by a dry laugh, and an assurance that the salamander was the very same which Benvenuto Cellini had seen in his father's household fire. He then proceeded to show me other rarities; for this closet appeared to be the receptacle of what he considered most valuable in his collection.

"There," said he, "is the Great Carbuncle of the White Mountains."

I gazed with no little interest at this mighty gem, which it had been one of the wild projects of my youth to discover. Possibly it might have looked brighter to me in those days than now; at all events, it had not such brilliancy as to detain me long from the other articles of the Museum. The Virtuoso pointed out to me a crystalline stone, which hung by a gold chain against the wall.

"That is the Philosopher's Stone," said he.

"And have you the Elixir Vitæ, which generally accompanies it?" inquired I.

"Even so,—this urn is filled with it," he replied. "A draught would refresh you. Here is Hebe's cup,—will you quaff a health from it?"

My heart thrilled within me at the idea of such a reviving draught; for methought I had great need of it, after travelling so far on the dusty road of life. But I know not whether it were a peculiar glance in the Virtuoso's eye, or the circumstance that this most precious liquid was contained in an antique sepulchral urn, that made me pause. Then came many a thought, with which, in the calmer and better hours of life, I had strengthened myself to feel that Death is the very friend whom, in his due season, even the happiest mortal should be willing to embrace.

"No, I desire not an earthly immortality," said I. "Were man to live longer on the earth, the spiritual would die out of him. The spark of ethereal fire would be choked by the material, the sensual. There is a celestial something within us that requires, after a certain time, the atmosphere of Heaven to preserve it from decay and ruin. I will have none of this liquid. You do well to keep it in a sepulchral urn; for it would produce death, while bestowing the shadow of life."

"All this is unintelligible to me," responded my guide, with indifference. "Life,—earthly life,—is the only good. But you refuse the draught? Well, it is not likely to be offered twice within one man's experience. Probably you have griefs which you seek to forget in death. I can enable you to forget them in life. Will you take a draught of Lethe?"

As he spoke, the Virtuoso took from the shelf a crystal vase containing a sable liquor, which caught no reflected image from the objects around.

"Not for the world!" exclaimed I, shrinking back. "I can spare none of my recollections,—not even those of error or sorrow. They are all alike the food of my spirit. As well never to have lived, as to lose them now."

Without further parley we passed to the next alcove, the shelves of which were burthened with ancient volumes, and with those rolls of papyrus, in which was treasured up the eldest wisdom of the earth. Perhaps the most valuable work in the collection, to a bibliomaniac, was the Book of Hermes. For my part, however, I would have given a higher price for those six of the Sibyl's books which Tarquin refused to purchase, and which the Virtuoso informed me he had himself found in the cave of Trophonius. Doubtless these old volumes contain prophecies of the fate of Rome, both as respects the decline and fall of her temporal empire, and the rise of her spiritual one. Not without value, likewise, was the work of Anaxagoras on Nature, hitherto supposed to be irrecover-

ably lost; and the missing treatises of Longinus, by which
modern criticism might profit; and those books of Livy, for
which the classic student has so long sorrowed without hope.
Among these precious tomes I observed the original manuscript of the Koran, and also that of the Mormon Bible, in
Joe Smith's authentic autograph. Alexander's copy of the
Iliad was also there, enclosed in the jewelled casket of Da-
rius, still fragrant of the perfumes which the Persian kept in it.

Opening an iron-clasped volume, bound in black leather, I
discovered it to be Cornelius Agrippa's book of magic; and it
was rendered still more interesting by the fact that many flow-
ers, ancient and modern, were pressed between its leaves.
Here was a rose from Eve's bridal bower, and all those red
and white roses which were plucked in the garden of the
Temple, by the partizans of York and Lancaster. Here was
Halleck's Wild Rose of Alloway. Cowper had contributed a
Sensitive Plant, and Wordsworth an Eglantine, and Burns a
Mountain Daisy, and Kirke White a Star of Bethlehem, and
Longfellow a Sprig of Fennel, with its yellow flowers. James
Russell Lowell had given a Pressed Flower, but fragrant still,
which had been shadowed in the Rhine. There was also a
sprig from Southey's Holly-Tree. One of the most beautiful
specimens was a Fringed Gentian, which had been plucked
and preserved for immortality by Bryant. From Jones Very,—
a poet whose voice is scarcely heard among us, by reason of
its depth,—there was a Wind Flower and a Columbine.

As I closed Cornelius Agrippa's magic volume, an old, mildewed letter fell upon the floor; it proved to be an autograph
from the Flying Dutchman to his wife. I could linger no
longer among books, for the afternoon was waning, and there
was yet much to see. The bare mention of a few more curiosities must suffice. The immense skull of Polyphemus was
recognizable by the cavernous hollow in the centre of the
forehead, where once had blazed the giant's single eye. The
tub of Diogenes, Medea's cauldron, and Psyche's vase of
beauty, were placed one within another. Pandora's box, without the lid, stood next, containing nothing but the girdle of
Venus, which had been carelessly flung into it. A bundle of
birch rods, which had been used by Shenstone's schoolmistress, were tied up with the Countess of Salisbury's garter. I

knew not which to value most, a Roc's egg, as big as an ordinary hogshead, or the shell of the egg which Columbus set
upon its end. Perhaps the most delicate article in the whole
Museum was Queen Mab's chariot, which, to guard it from
the touch of meddlesome fingers, was placed under a glass
tumbler.

Several of the shelves were occupied by specimens of ento-
mology. Feeling but little interest in the science, I noticed
only Anacreon's Grasshopper and a Humble-Bee, which had
been presented to the Virtuoso by Ralph Waldo Emerson.

In the part of the hall which we had now reached, I observed a curtain that descended from the ceiling to the floor
in voluminous folds, of a depth, richness, and magnificence
which I had never seen equalled. It was not to be doubted
that this splendid, though dark and solemn veil, concealed a
portion of the Museum even richer in wonders than that
through which I had already passed. But, on my attempting
to grasp the edge of the curtain and draw it aside, it proved
to be an illusive picture.

"You need not blush," remarked the Virtuoso, "for that
same curtain deceived Zeuxis. It is the celebrated painting of
Parrhasius."

In a range with the curtain, there were a number of other
choice pictures, by artists of ancient days. Here was the famous Cluster of Grapes by Zeuxis, so admirably depicted that
it seemed as if the ripe juice were bursting forth. As to the
picture of the Old Woman, by the same illustrious painter,
and which was so ludicrous that he himself died with laughing at it, I cannot say that it particularly moved my risibility.
Ancient humor seems to have little power over modern mus-
cles. Here, also, was the Horse, painted by Apelles, which
living horses neighed at; his first portrait of Alexander the
Great, and his last unfinished picture of Venus Asleep. Each
of these works of art, together with others by Parrhasius, Ti-
manthes, Polygnotus, Apollodorus, Pausias, and Pamphilus,
required more time and study than I could bestow, for the
adequate perception of their merits. I shall therefore leave
them undescribed and uncriticised, nor attempt to settle the
question of superiority between ancient and modern art.

For the same reason I shall pass lightly over the specimens

of antique sculpture, which this indefatigable and fortunate Virtuoso had dug out of the dust of fallen empires. Here was Ætion's cedar statue of Æsculapius, much decayed, and Alcon's iron statue of Hercules, lamentably rusted. Here was the statue of Victory, six feet high, which the Jupiter Olympus of Phidias had held in his hand. Here was a fore-finger of the Colossus of Rhodes, seven feet in length. Here was the Venus Urania of Phidias, and other images of male and female beauty or grandeur, wrought by sculptors who appear never to have debased their souls by the sight of any meaner forms than those of gods, or godlike mortals. But the deep simplicity of these great works was not to be comprehended by a mind excited and disturbed as mine was by the various objects that had recently been presented to it. I therefore turned away, with merely a passing glance, resolving, on some future occasion, to brood over each individual statue and picture, until my inmost spirit should feel their excellence. In this department, again, I noticed the tendency to whimsical combinations and ludicrous analogies, which seemed to influence many of the arrangements of the Museum. The wooden statue, so well known as the Palladium of Troy, was placed in close apposition with the wooden head of General Jackson, which was stolen, a few years since, from the bows of the frigate Constitution.

We had now completed the circuit of the spacious hall, and found ourselves again near the door. Feeling somewhat wearied with the survey of so many novelties and antiquities, I sat down upon Cowper's sofa, while the Virtuoso threw himself carelessly into Rabelais's easy-chair. Casting my eyes upon the opposite wall, I was surprised to perceive the shadow of a man, flickering unsteadily across the wainscot, and looking as if it were stirred by some breath of air that found its way through the door or windows. No substantial figure was visible, from which this shadow might be thrown; nor, had there been such, was there any sunshine that would have caused it to darken upon the wall.

"It is Peter Schlemihl's Shadow," observed the Virtuoso, "and one of the most valuable articles in my collection."

"Methinks a shadow would have made a fitting door-keeper

to such a Museum," said I, "although, indeed, yonder figure
has something strange and fantastic about him, which suits
well enough with many of the impressions which I have received here. Pray, who is he?"

While speaking, I gazed more scrutinizingly than before at
the antiquated presence of the person who had admitted me,
and who still sat on his bench, with the same restless aspect,
and dim, confused, questioning anxiety, that I had noticed on
my first entrance. At this moment he looked eagerly towards
us, and half-starting from his seat, addressed me.

"I beseech you, kind sir," said he, in a cracked, melancholy
tone, "have pity on the most unfortunate man in the world!
For heaven's sake answer me a single question! Is this the
town of Boston?"

"You have recognized him now," said the Virtuoso. "It is
Peter Rugg, the Missing Man. I chanced to meet him, the
other day, still in search of Boston, and conducted him
hither; and, as he could not succeed in finding his friends, I
have taken him into my service as door-keeper. He is somewhat too apt to ramble, but otherwise a man of trust and
integrity."

"And—might I venture to ask," continued I, "to whom am
I indebted for this afternoon's gratification?"

The Virtuoso, before replying, laid his hand upon an antique dart or javelin, the rusty steel head of which seemed to
have been blunted, as if it had encountered the resistance of
a tempered shield or breast-plate.

"My name has not been without its distinction in the
world, for a longer period than that of any other man alive,"
answered he. "Yet many doubt of my existence,—perhaps
you will do so, to-morrow. This dart, which I hold in my
hand, was once grim Death's own weapon. It served him well
for the space of four thousand years. But it fell blunted, as
you see, when he directed it against my breast."

These words were spoken with the calm and cold courtesy
of manner that had characterized this singular personage
throughout our interview. I fancied, it is true, that there was
a bitterness indefinably mingled with his tone, as of one cut
off from natural sympathies, and blasted with a doom that
had been inflicted on no other human being, and by the re-

sults of which he had ceased to be human. Yet, withal, it seemed one of the most terrible consequences of that doom, that the victim no longer regarded it as a calamity, but had finally accepted it as the greatest good that could have befallen him.

"You are the Wandering Jew!" exclaimed I.

The Virtuoso bowed, without emotion of any kind; for, by centuries of custom, he had almost lost the sense of strangeness in his fate, and was but imperfectly conscious of the astonishment and awe with which it affected such as are capable of death.

"Your doom is indeed a fearful one!" said I, with irrepressible feeling, and a frankness that afterwards startled me; "yet perhaps the ethereal spirit is not entirely extinct, under all this corrupted or frozen mass of earthly life. Perhaps the immortal spark may yet be rekindled by a breath of Heaven. Perhaps you may yet be permitted to die, before it is too late to live eternally. You have my prayers for such a consummation. Farewell."

"Your prayers will be in vain," replied he, with a smile of cold triumph. "My destiny is linked with the realities of earth. You are welcome to your visions and shadows of a future state; but give me what I can see, and touch, and understand, and I ask no more."

"It is indeed too late," thought I. "The soul is dead within him!"

Struggling between pity and horror, I extended my hand, to which the Virtuoso gave his own, still with the habitual courtesy of a man of the world, but without a single heart-throb of human brotherhood. The touch seemed like ice, yet I know not whether morally or physically. As I departed, he bade me observe that the inner door of the hall was constructed with the ivory leaves of the gateway through which Æneas and the Sibyl had been dismissed from Hades.

The Old Apple-Dealer

THE lover of the moral picturesque may sometimes find what he seeks in a character, which is, nevertheless, of too negative a description to be seized upon, and represented to the imaginative vision by word-painting. As an instance, I remember an old man who carries on a little trade of ginger-bread and apples, at the depôt of one of our rail-roads. While awaiting the departure of the cars, my observation, flitting to and fro among the livelier characteristics of the scene, has often settled insensibly upon this almost hueless object. Thus, unconsciously to myself, and unsuspected by him, I have studied the old apple-dealer, until he has become a naturalized citizen of my inner world. How little would he imagine—poor, neglected, friendless, unappreciated, and with little that demands appreciation—that the mental eye of an utter stranger has so often reverted to his figure! Many a noble form—many a beautiful face—has flitted before me, and vanished like a shadow. It is a strange witchcraft, whereby this faded and featureless old apple-dealer has gained a settlement in my memory!

He is a small man with gray hair and gray stubble beard, and is invariably clad in a shabby surtout of snuff-color, closely buttoned, and half-concealing a pair of gray pantaloons; the whole dress, though clean and entire, being evidently flimsy with much wear. His face, thin, withered, furrowed, and with features which even age has failed to render impressive, has a frost-bitten aspect. It is a moral frost, which no physical warmth or comfortableness could counteract. The summer sunshine may fling its white heat upon him, or the good fire of the depôt-room may make him the focus of its blaze, on a winter's day; but all in vain; for still the old man looks as if he were in a frosty atmosphere, with scarcely warmth enough to keep life in the region about his heart. It is a patient, long-suffering, quiet, hopeless, shivering aspect. He is not desperate—that, though its etymology implies no more, would be too positive an expression—but merely devoid of hope. As all his past life, probably, offers no spots of brightness to his memory, so he takes his present poverty and discomfort as entirely a matter of course; he thinks it the definition of existence, so far as himself is concerned, to be poor, cold, and uncomfortable. It may be added, that time has not thrown dignity, as a mantle, over the old man's figure; there is nothing venerable about him; you pity him without a scruple.

He sits on a bench in the depôt-room; and before him, on the floor, are deposited two baskets, of a capacity to contain his whole stock in trade. Across, from one basket to the other, extends a board, on which is displayed a plate of cakes and gingerbread, some russet and red cheeked apples, and a box containing variegated sticks of candy; together with that delectable condiment, known by children as Gibraltar rock, neatly done up in white paper. There is likewise a half-peck measure of cracked walnuts, and two or three tin half-pints or gills, filled with the nut kernels, ready for purchasers. Such are the small commodities with which our old friend comes daily before the world, ministering to its petty needs and little freaks of appetite, and seeking thence the solid subsistence— so far as he may subsist—of his life.

A slight observer would speak of the old man's quietude. But, on closer scrutiny, you discover that there is a continual unrest within him, which somewhat resembles the fluttering action of the nerves, in a corpse from which life has recently departed. Though he never exhibits any violent action, and, indeed, might appear to be sitting quite still, yet you perceive, when his minuter peculiarities begin to be detected, that he is always making some little movement or other. He looks anxiously at his plate of cakes, or pyramid of apples, and slightly alters their arrangement, with an evident idea that a great deal depends on their being disposed exactly thus and so. Then, for a moment, he gazes out of the window; then he shivers, quietly, and folds his arms across his breast, as if to draw himself closer within himself, and thus keep a flicker of warmth in his lonesome heart. Now he turns again to his merchandise of cakes, apples, and candy, and discovers that this cake or that apple, or yonder stick of red and white candy, has, somehow, got out of its proper position. And is there not a walnut-kernel too many, or too few, in one of those small tin measures? Again, the whole arrangement appears to be settled to his mind; but, in the course of a minute or two, there will assuredly be something to set right. At times, by an indescribable shadow upon his features—too quiet, however, to be noticed, until you are familiar with his ordinary aspect—the expression of frost-bitten, patient despondency becomes very touching. It seems as if, just at that instant, the suspicion occurred to him, that, in his chill decline of life, earning scanty bread by selling cakes, apples, and candy, he is a very miserable old fellow.

But, if he think so, it is a mistake. He can never suffer the extreme of misery, because the tone of his whole being is too much subdued for him to feel any thing acutely.

Occasionally, one of the passengers, to while away a tedious interval, approaches the old man, inspects the articles upon his board, and even peeps curiously into the two baskets. Another, striding to and fro along the room, throws a look at the apples and gingerbread, at every turn. A third, it may be, of a more sensitive and delicate texture of being, glances shyly thitherward, cautious not to excite expectations of a purchaser, while yet undetermined whether to buy. But there appears to be no need of such a scrupulous regard to our old friend's feelings. True, he is conscious of the remote possibility of selling a cake or an apple, but innumerable disappointments have rendered him so far a philosopher, that, even if the purchased article should be returned, he will consider it altogether in the ordinary train of events. He speaks to none, and makes no sign of offering his wares to the public; not that he is deterred by pride, but by the certain conviction that such demonstrations would not increase his custom. Besides, this activity in business would require an energy that never could have been a characteristic of his almost passive disposition, even in youth. Whenever an actual customer appears, the old man looks up with a patient eye; if the price and the article are approved, he is ready to make change; otherwise, his eyelids droop again, sadly enough, but with no heavier despondency than before. He shivers, perhaps, folds his lean arms around his lean body, and resumes the life-long, frozen patience, in which consists his strength. Once in a while, a schoolboy comes hastily up, places a cent or two upon the board, and takes up a cake or a stick of candy, or a measure of walnuts, or an apple as red cheeked as himself. There are no words as to the price, that being as well known to the buyer as to the seller. The old apple-dealer never speaks an unnecessary word; not that he is sullen and morose; but there is none of the cheeriness and briskness in him, that stirs up people to talk.

Not seldom, he is greeted by some old neighbor, a man well-to-do in the world, who makes a civil, patronizing observation about the weather; and then, by way of performing a charitable deed, begins to chaffer for an apple. Our friend presumes not on any past acquaintance; he makes the briefest possible response to all general remarks, and shrinks quietly into himself again. After every diminution of his stock, he takes care to produce from the basket another cake, another stick of candy, another apple, or another measure of walnuts, to supply the place of the article sold. Two or three attempts—or, perchance, half a dozen—are requisite, before the board can be re-arranged to his satisfaction. If he have received a silver coin, he waits till the purchaser is out of sight, then examines it closely, and tries to bend it with his finger and thumb; finally, he puts it into his waistcoat pocket, with seemingly a gentle sigh. This sigh, so faint as to be hardly perceptible, and not expressive of any definite emotion, is the accompaniment and conclusion of all his actions. It is the symbol of the chillness and torpid melancholy of his old age, which only make themselves felt sensibly, when his repose is slightly disturbed.

Our man of gingerbread and apples is not a specimen of the 'needy man who has seen better days.' Doubtless, there have been better and brighter days in the far-off time of his youth; but none with so much sunshine of prosperity in them, that the chill, the depression, the narrowness of means, in his declining years, can have come upon him by surprise. His life has all been of a piece. His subdued and nerveless boyhood prefigured his abortive prime, which, likewise, contained within itself the prophecy and image of his lean and torpid age. He was perhaps a mechanic, who never came to be a master in his craft, or a petty tradesman, rubbing onward between passably-to-do and poverty. Possibly, he may look back to some brilliant epoch of his career, when there were a hundred or two of dollars to his credit, in the Savings Bank. Such must have been the extent of his better fortune—his little measure of this world's triumphs—all that he has known of success. A meek, downcast, humble, uncomplaining creature, he probably has never felt himself entitled to more than so much of the gifts of Providence. Is it not still something, that he has never held out his hand for charity, nor has yet been driven to that sad home and household of Earth's forlorn and broken-spirited children, the alms-house? He cherishes no quarrel, therefore, with his destiny, nor with the Author of it. All is as it should be.

If, indeed, he have been bereaved of a son—a bold, energetic, vigorous young man, on whom the father's feeble nature leaned, as on a staff of strength—in that case, he may have felt a bitterness that could not otherwise have been generated in his heart. But, methinks, the joy of possessing such a son, and the agony of losing him, would have developed the old man's moral and intellectual nature to a much greater degree than we now find it. Intense grief appears to be as much out of keeping with his life, as fervid happiness.

To confess the truth, it is not the easiest matter in the world, to define and individualize a character like this which we are now handling. The portrait must be so generally negative, that the most delicate pencil is likely to spoil it by introducing some too positive tint. Every touch must be kept down or else you destroy the subdued tone, which is absolutely essential to the whole effect. Perhaps more may be done by contrast, than by direct description. For this purpose, I make use of another cake-and-candy merchant, who likewise infests the rail-road depôt. This latter worthy is a very smart and well-dressed boy, of ten years old or thereabouts, who skips briskly hither and thither, addressing the passengers in a pert voice, yet with somewhat of good breeding in his tone and pronunciation. Now he has caught my eye, and skips across the room with a pretty pertness, which I should like to correct with a box on the ear. "Any cake, sir?—any candy?"

No; none for me, my lad. I did but glance at your brisk figure, in order to catch a reflected light, and throw it upon your old rival yonder.

Again, in order to invest my conception of the old man with a more decided sense of reality, I look at him in the very moment of intensest bustle, on the arrival of the cars. The shriek of the engine, as it rushes into the car-house, is the utterance of the steam-fiend, whom man has subdued by magic spells, and compels to serve as a beast of burden. He has skimmed rivers in his headlong rush, dashed through forests, plunged into the hearts of mountains, and glanced from the city to the desert-place, and again to a far-off city, with a meteoric progress, seen, and out of sight, while his reverberating roar still fills the ear. The travellers swarm forth from the cars. All are full of the momentum which they have caught from their mode of conveyance. It seems as if the whole world, both morally and physically, were detached from its old standfasts, and set in rapid motion. And, in the midst of this terrible activity, there sits the old man of gingerbread, so subdued, so hopeless, so without a stake in life, and yet not positively miserable—there he sits, the forlorn old creature, one chill and sombre day after another, gathering scanty coppers for his cakes, apples and candy—there sits the old apple-dealer, in his threadbare suit of snuff-color and gray, and his grisly stubble-beard. See! he folds his lean arms around his lean figure, with that quiet sigh, and that scarcely perceptible shiver, which are the tokens of his inward state. I have him now. He and the steam-fiend are each other's antipodes; the latter is the type of all that go ahead—and the old man, the representative of that melancholy class who, by some sad witchcraft, are doomed never to share in the world's exulting progress. Thus the contrast between mankind and this desolate brother becomes picturesque, and even sublime.

And now farewell, old friend! Little do you suspect, that a student of human life has made your character the theme of more than one solitary and thoughtful hour. Many would say, that you have hardly individuality enough to be the object of your own self-love. How, then, can a stranger's eye detect any thing in your mind and heart, to study and to wonder at? Yet could I read but a tithe of what is written there, it would be a volume of deeper and more comprehensive import than all that the wisest mortals have given to the world; for the soundless depths of the human soul, and of eternity, have an opening through your breast. God be praised, were it only for your sake, that the present shapes of human existence are not cast in iron, nor hewn in everlasting adamant, but moulded of the vapors that vanish away while the essence flits upward to the infinite. There is a spiritual essence in this gray and lean old shape that shall flit upward too. Yes; doubtless there is a region, where the life-long shiver will pass away from his being, and that quiet sigh, which it has taken him so many years to breathe, will be brought to a close for good and all.

The Antique Ring

"Yes, indeed; the gem is as bright as a star, and curiously set," said Clara Pemberton, examining an antique ring, which her betrothed lover had just presented to her, with a very pretty speech. "It needs only one thing to make it perfect."

"And what is that?" asked Mr. Edward Caryl, secretly anxious for the credit of his gift. "A modern setting, perhaps?"

"Oh, no! That would destroy the charm at once," replied Clara. "It needs nothing but a story. I long to know how many times it has been the pledge of faith between two lovers, and whether the vows, of which it was the symbol, were always kept or often broken. Not that I should be too scrupulous about facts. If you happen to be unacquainted with its authentic history, so much the better. May it not have sparkled upon a queen's finger? Or who knows, but it is the very ring which Posthumus received from Imogen? In short, you must kindle your imagination at the lustre of this diamond, and make a legend for it."

Now such a task—and doubtless Clara knew it—was the most acceptable that could have been imposed on Edward Caryl. He was one of that multitude of young gentlemen—limbs, or rather twigs, of the law—whose names appear in gilt letters on the front of Tudor's Buildings, and other places in the vicinity of the Court-House, which seem to be the haunt of the gentler, as well as the severer muses. Edward, in the dearth of clients, was accustomed to employ his much leisure in assisting the growth of American literature; to which good cause he had contributed not a few quires of the finest letter paper, containing some thought, some fancy, some depth of feeling, together with a young writer's abundance of conceits. Sonnets, stanzas of Tennysonian sweetness, tales imbued with German mysticism, versions from Jean Paul, criticisms of the old English poets, and essays smacking of Dialistic philosophy, were among his multifarious productions. The editors of the fashionable periodicals were familiar with his autography, and inscribed his name in those brilliant

bead-rolls of ink-stained celebrity, which illustrate the first
page of their covers. Nor did fame withhold her laurel. Hillard had included him among the lights of the New-England
metropolis, in his Boston Book; Bryant had found room for
some of his stanzas, in the Selections from American Poetry;
and Mr. Griswold, in his recent assemblage of the sons and
daughters of song, had introduced Edward Caryl into the inner court of the temple, among his fourscore choicest bards.
There was a prospect, indeed, of his assuming a still higher
and more independent position. Interviews had been held
with Ticknor, and a correspondence with the Harpers, respecting a proposed volume, chiefly to consist of Mr. Caryl's
fugitive pieces in the Magazines, but to be accompanied with
a poem of some length, never before published. Not improbably, the public may yet be gratified with this collection.

Meanwhile, we sum up our sketch of Edward Caryl, by
pronouncing him, though somewhat of a carpet knight in literature, yet no unfavorable specimen of a generation of rising
writers, whose spirit is such that we may reasonably expect
creditable attempts from all, and good and beautiful results
from some. And, it will be observed, Edward was the very
man to write pretty legends, at a lady's instance, for an old-
fashioned diamond ring. He took the jewel in his hand, and
turned it so as to catch its scintillating radiance, as if hoping,
in accordance with Clara's suggestion, to light up his fancy
with that star-like gleam.

"Shall it be a ballad?—a tale in verse?" he inquired. "Enchanted rings often glisten in old English poetry. I think
something may be done with the subject; but it is fitter for
rhyme than prose."

"No, no," said Miss Pemberton.—"We will have no more
rhyme than just enough for a posy to the ring. You must tell
the legend in simple prose; and when it is finished, I will
make a little party to hear it read."

The young gentleman promised obedience; and going
to his pillow, with his head full of the familiar spirits that
used to be worn in rings, watches, and sword-hilts, he had
the good fortune to possess himself of an available idea
in a dream. Connecting this with what he himself chanced
to know of the ring's real history, his task was done. Clara

Pemberton invited a select few of her friends, all holding the stanchest faith in Edward's genius, and therefore the most genial auditors, if not altogether the fairest critics, that a writer could possibly desire. Blessed be woman for her faculty of admiration, and especially for her tendency to admire with her heart, when man, at most, grants merely a cold approval with his mind!

Drawing his chair beneath the blaze of a solar lamp, Edward Caryl untied a roll of glossy paper, and began as follows:

THE LEGEND

After the death-warrant had been read to the Earl of Essex, and on the evening before his appointed execution, the Countess of Shrewsbury paid his lordship a visit, and found him, as it appeared, toying childishly with a ring. The diamond, that enriched it, glittered like a little star, but with a singular tinge of red. The gloomy prison-chamber in the Tower, with its deep and narrow windows piercing the walls of stone, was now all that the earl possessed of worldly prospect; so that there was the less wonder that he should look stedfastly into the gem, and moralize upon earth's deceitful splendor, as men in darkness and ruin seldom fail to do. But the shrewd observations of the countess,—an artful and unprincipled woman,—the pretended friend of Essex, but who had come to glut her revenge for a deed of scorn, which he himself had forgotten;—her keen eye detected a deeper interest attached to this jewel. Even while expressing his gratitude for her remembrance of a ruined favorite, and condemned criminal, the earl's glance reverted to the ring, as if all that remained of time and its affairs were collected within that small golden circlet.

"My dear lord," observed the countess, "there is surely some matter of great moment wherewith this ring is connected, since it so absorbs your mind. A token, it may be, of some fair lady's love,—alas, poor lady, once richest in possessing such a heart! Would you that the jewel be returned to her?"

"The queen! the queen! It was her majesty's own gift," replied the earl, still gazing into the depths of the gem. "She took it from her finger, and told me, with a smile, that it was an heir-loom from her Tudor ancestors, and had once been the property of Merlin, the British wizard, who gave it to the lady of his love. His art had made this diamond the abiding-place of a spirit, which, though of fiendish nature, was bound to work only good, so long as the ring was an unviolated pledge of love and faith, both with the giver and receiver. But should love prove false, and faith be broken, then the evil spirit would work his own devilish will, until the ring were purified by becoming the medium of some good and holy act, and again the pledge of faithful love. The gem soon lost its virtue; for the wizard was murdered by the very lady to whom he gave it."

"An idle legend!" said the countess.

"It is so," answered Essex, with a melancholy smile. "Yet the queen's favor, of which this ring was the symbol, has proved my ruin. When death is nigh, men converse with dreams and shadows. I have been gazing into the diamond, and fancying—but you will laugh at me,—that I might catch a glimpse of the evil spirit there. Do you observe this red glow—dusky, too, amid all the brightness? It is the token of his presence; and even now, methinks, it grows redder and duskier, like an angry sunset."

Nevertheless, the earl's manner testified how slight was his credence in the enchanted properties of the ring. But there is a kind of playfulness that comes in moments of despair, when the reality of misfortune, if entirely felt, would crush the soul at once. He now, for a brief space, was lost in thought, while the countess contemplated him with malignant satisfaction.

"This ring," he resumed, in another tone, "alone remains, of all that my royal mistress's favor lavished upon her servant. My fortunes once shone as brightly as the gem. And now, such a darkness has fallen around me, methinks it would be no marvel if its gleam,—the sole light of my prison-house, were to be forthwith extinguished; inasmuch as my last earthly hope depends upon it."

"How say you, my lord?" asked the Countess of Shrewsbury. "The stone is bright; but there should be strange magic in it, if it can keep your hopes alive, at this sad hour. Alas!

these iron bars and ramparts of the Tower, are unlike to yield to such a spell."

Essex raised his head, involuntarily; for there was something in the countess's tone that disturbed him, although he could not suspect that an enemy had intruded upon the sacred privacy of a prisoner's dungeon, to exult over so dark a ruin of such once brilliant fortunes. He looked her in the face, but saw nothing to awaken his distrust. It would have required a keener eye than even Cecil's to read the secret of a countenance, which had been worn so long in the false light of a court, that it was now little better than a masque, telling any story save the true one. The condemned nobleman again bent over the ring, and proceeded:

"It once had power in it—this bright gem—the magic that appertains to the talisman of a great queen's favor. She bade me, if hereafter I should fall into her disgrace—how deep soever, and whatever might be my crime—to convey this jewel to her sight, and it should plead for me. Doubtless, with her piercing judgment, she had even then detected the rashness of my nature, and foreboded some such deed as has now brought destruction upon my head. And knowing, too, her own hereditary rigor, she designed, it may be, that the memory of gentler and kindlier hours should soften her heart in my behalf, when my need should be the greatest. I have doubted—I have distrusted—yet who can tell, even now, what happy influence this ring might have?"

"You have delayed full long to show the ring, and plead her majesty's gracious promise," remarked the countess— "your state being what it is."

"True," replied the earl; "but for my honor's sake, I was loth to entreat the queen's mercy, while I might hope for life, at least, from the justice of the laws. If, on a trial by my peers, I had been acquitted of meditating violence against her sacred life, then would I have fallen at her feet, and presenting the jewel, have prayed no other favor than that my love and zeal should be put to the severest test. But now, it were confessing too much—it were cringing too low—to beg the miserable gift of life, on no other score than the tenderness which her majesty deems me to have forfeited!"

"Yet it is your only hope," said the countess.

"And besides," continued Essex, pursuing his own reflections, "of what avail will be this token of womanly feeling, when, on the other hand are arrayed the all-prevailing motives of state policy, and the artifices and intrigues of courtiers, to consummate my downfall? Will Cecil or Raleigh suffer her heart to act for itself, even if the spirit of her father were not in her? It is in vain to hope it."

But still Essex gazed at the ring with an absorbed attention, that proved how much hope his sanguine temperament had concentrated here, when there was none else for him in the wide world, save what lay in the compass of that hoop of gold. The spark of brightness within the diamond, which gleamed like an intenser than earthly fire, was the memorial of his dazzling career. It had not paled with the waning sunshine of his mistress's favor; on the contrary, in spite of its remarkable tinge of dusky red, he fancied that it had never shone so brightly. The glow of festal torches—the blaze of perfumed lamps—the bonfires that had been kindled for him, when he was the darling of the people—the splendor of the royal court, where he had been the peculiar star—all seemed to have collected their moral or material glory into the gem, and to burn with a radiance caught from the future, as well as gathered from the past. That radiance might break forth again. Bursting from the diamond, into which it was now narrowed, it might beam first upon the gloomy walls of the Tower—then wider, wider, wider—till all England, and the seas around her cliffs, should be gladdened with the light. It was such an ecstasy as often ensues after long depression, and has been supposed to precede the circumstances of darkest fate that may befall mortal man. The earl pressed the ring to his heart as if it were indeed a talisman, the habitation of a spirit, as the queen had playfully assured him—but a spirit of happier influences than her legend spake of.

"Oh, could I but make my way to her footstool!" cried he, waving his hand aloft, while he paced the stone pavement of his prison-chamber with an impetuous step.—"I might kneel down, indeed, a ruined man, condemned to the block—but how should I rise again? Once more the favorite of Elizabeth!—England's proudest noble!—with such prospects as ambition never aimed at! Why have I tarried so long in this weary dungeon? The ring has power to set me free! The palace wants me! Ho, jailer, unbar the door!"

But then occurred the recollection of the impossibility of obtaining an interview with his fatally estranged mistress, and testing the influence over her affections, which he still flattered himself with possessing.—Could he step beyond the limits of his prison, the world would be all sunshine; but here was only gloom and death.

"Alas!" said he, slowly and sadly, letting his head fall upon his hands.—"I die for lack of one blessed word."

The Countess of Shrewsbury, herself forgotten amid the earl's gorgeous visions, had watched him with an aspect that could have betrayed nothing to the most suspicious observer; unless that it was too calm for humanity, while witnessing the flutterings, as it were, of a generous heart in the death-agony. She now approached him.

"My good lord," she said, "what mean you to do?"

"Nothing—my deeds are done!" replied he, despondingly. —"Yet, had a fallen favorite any friends, I would entreat one of them to lay this ring at her majesty's feet; albeit with little hope, save that, hereafter, it might remind her that poor Essex, once far too highly favored, was at last too severely dealt with."

"I will be that friend," said the countess. "There is no time to be lost. Trust this precious ring with me. This very night, the queen's eye shall rest upon it; nor shall the efficacy of my poor words be wanting, to strengthen the impression which it will doubtless make."

The earl's first impulse was to hold out the ring. But looking at the countess, as she bent forward to receive it, he fancied that the red glow of the gem tinged all her face, and gave it an ominous expression. Many passages of past times recurred to his memory. A preternatural insight, perchance caught from approaching death, threw its momentary gleam, as from a meteor, all round his position.

"Countess," he said, "I know not wherefore I hesitate, being in a plight so desperate, and having so little choice of friends. But have you looked into your own heart? Can you perform this office with the truth—the earnestness—the zeal, even to tears, and agony of spirit—wherewith the holy gift of human life should be pleaded for? Wo be unto you, should you undertake this task, and deal towards me otherwise than with utmost faith! For your own soul's sake, and as you would have peace at your death-hour, consider well in what spirit you receive this ring!"

The countess did not shrink.

"My lord!—my good lord!" she exclaimed, "wrong not a woman's heart by these suspicions. You might choose another messenger; but who, save a lady of her bed-chamber, can obtain access to the queen at this untimely hour? It is for your life—for your life—else I would not renew my offer."

"Take the ring," said the earl.

"Believe that it shall be in the queen's hands before the lapse of another hour," replied the countess, as she received this sacred trust of life and death.—"To-morrow morning, look for the result of my intercession."

She departed. Again the earl's hopes rose high. Dreams visited his slumber, not of the sable-decked scaffold in the Tower-yard, but of canopies of state, obsequious courtiers, pomp, splendor, the smile of the once more gracious queen, and a light beaming from the magic gem, which illuminated his whole future.

History records, how foully the Countess of Shrewsbury betrayed the trust, which Essex, in his utmost need, confided to her. She kept the ring, and stood in the presence of Elizabeth, that night, without one attempt to soften her stern hereditary temper, in behalf of the former favorite. The next day, the earl's noble head rolled upon the scaffold. On her death-bed, tortured, at last, with a sense of the dreadful guilt which she had taken upon her soul, the wicked countess sent for Elizabeth, revealed the story of the ring, and besought forgiveness for her treachery. But the queen, still obdurate, even while remorse for past obduracy was tugging at her heart-strings, shook the dying woman in her bed, as if struggling with death for the privilege of wreaking her revenge and spite. The spirit of the countess passed away, to undergo the justice, or receive the mercy, of a higher tribunal; and tradition says, that the fatal ring was found upon her breast, where it had imprinted a dark red circle, resembling the effect of the intensest heat. The attendants, who prepared the body for burial, shuddered, whispering one to another, that the ring must have derived its heat from the glow of infernal fire. They left it on her breast, in the coffin, and it went with that guilty woman to the tomb.

Many years afterwards, when the church that contained the monuments of the Shrewsbury family, was desecrated by Cromwell's soldiers, they broke open the ancestral vaults, and stole whatever was valuable from the noble personages who reposed there. Merlin's antique ring passed into the possession of a stout serjeant of the Ironsides, who thus became subject to the influences of the evil spirit that still kept his abode within the gem's enchanted depths. The serjeant was soon slain in battle, thus transmitting the ring, though without any legal form of testament, to a gay cavalier, who forthwith pawned it, and expended the money in liquor, which speedily brought him to the grave. We next catch the sparkle of the magic diamond at various epochs of the merry reign of Charles the Second. But its sinister fortune still attended it. From whatever hand this ring of portent came, and whatever finger it encircled, ever it was the pledge of deceit between man and man, or man and woman, of faithless vows, and unhallowed passion; and whether to lords and ladies, or to village-maids—for sometimes it found its way so low,—still it brought nothing but sorrow and disgrace. No purifying deed was done, to drive the fiend from his bright home in this little star. Again, we hear of it at a later period, when Sir Robert Walpole bestowed the ring, among far richer jewels, on the lady of a British legislator, whose political honor he wished to undermine. Many a dismal and unhappy tale might be wrought out of its other adventures. All this while, its ominous tinge of dusky red had been deepening and darkening, until, if laid upon white paper, it cast the mingled hue of night and blood, strangely illuminated with scintillating light, in a circle round about. But this peculiarity only made it the more valuable.

Alas, the fatal ring! When shall its dark secret be discovered, and the doom of ill, inherited from one possessor to another, be finally revoked?

The legend now crosses the Atlantic, and comes down to our own immediate time. In a certain church of our city, not

many evenings ago, there was a contribution for a charitable
object. A fervid preacher had poured out his whole soul in a
rich and tender discourse, which had at least excited the tears,
and perhaps the more effectual sympathy, of a numerous audience. While the choristers sang sweetly, and the organ
poured forth its melodious thunder, the deacons passed up
and down the aisles, and along the galleries, presenting their
mahogany boxes, in which each person deposited whatever
sum he deemed it safe to lend to the Lord, in aid of human
wretchedness. Charity became audible—chink, chink, chink,
—as it fell, drop by drop, into the common receptacle. There
was a hum—a stir,—the subdued bustle of people putting
their hands into their pockets; while, ever and anon, a vagrant
coin fell upon the floor, and rolled away, with long reverberation, into some inscrutable corner.

At length, all having been favored with an opportunity to
be generous, the two deacons placed their boxes on the communion-table, and thence, at the conclusion of the services,
removed them into the vestry. Here these good old gentlemen sat down together, to reckon the accumulated treasure.

"Fie, fie, brother Tilton," said Deacon Trott, peeping into
Deacon Tilton's box, "what a heap of copper you have picked
up! Really, for an old man, you must have had a heavy job to
lug it along. Copper! copper! copper! Do people expect to
get admittance into Heaven at the price of a few coppers?"

"Don't wrong them, brother," answered Deacon Tilton, a
simple and kindly old man. "Copper may do more for one
person, than gold will for another. In the galleries, where I
present my box, we must not expect such a harvest as you
gather among the gentry in the broad-aisle, and all over the
floor of the church. My people are chiefly poor mechanics
and laborers, sailors, seamstresses, and servant-maids, with a
most uncomfortable intermixture of roguish school-boys."

"Well, well," said Deacon Trott;—"but there is a great
deal, brother Tilton, in the method of presenting a contribution-box. It is a knack that comes by nature, or not at all."

They now proceeded to sum up the avails of the evening,
beginning with the receipts of Deacon Trott. In good sooth,
that worthy personage had reaped an abundant harvest, in
which he prided himself no less, apparently, than if every dol-

lar had been contributed from his own individual pocket. Had the good deacon been meditating a jaunt to Texas, the treasures of the mahogany-box might have sent him on his way rejoicing. There were bank-notes, mostly, it is true, of the smallest denominations in the giver's pocket-book, yet making a goodly average upon the whole. The most splendid contribution was a check for a hundred dollars, bearing the name of a distinguished merchant, whose liberality was duly celebrated in the newspapers of the next day. No less than seven half eagles, together with an English sovereign, glittered amidst an indiscriminate heap of silver; the box being polluted with nothing of the copper kind; except a single bright new cent, wherewith a little boy had performed his first charitable act.

"Very well! very well indeed!" said Deacon Trott, self-approvingly. "A handsome evening's work! And now, brother Tilton, let's see whether you can match it."

Here was a sad contrast! They poured forth Deacon Tilton's treasure upon the table, and it really seemed as if the whole copper coinage of the country, together with an amazing quantity of shopkeepers' tokens, and English and Irish half-pence, mostly of base metal, had been congregated into the box. There was a very substantial pencil-case, and the semblance of a shilling; but the latter proved to be made of tin, and the former of German silver. A gilded brass button was doing duty as a gold coin, and a folded shop-bill had assumed the character of a bank-note. But Deacon Tilton's feelings were much revived, by the aspect of another bank-note, new and crisp, adorned with beautiful engravings, and stamped with the indubitable word, TWENTY, in large black letters. Alas! it was a counterfeit. In short, the poor old Deacon was no less unfortunate than those who trade with fairies, and whose gains are sure to be transformed into dried leaves, pebbles, and other valuables of that kind.

"I believe the Evil One is in the box," said he, with some vexation.

"Well done, Deacon Tilton!" cried his brother Trott, with a hearty laugh.—"You ought to have a statue in copper."

"Never mind, brother," replied the good Deacon, recovering his temper. "I'll bestow ten dollars from my own pocket,

and may Heaven's blessing go along with it! But look! what
do you call this?"

Under the copper mountain, which it had cost them so
much toil to remove, lay an antique ring! It was enriched
with a diamond, which, so soon as it caught the light, began
to twinkle and glimmer, emitting the whitest and purest
lustre that could possibly be conceived. It was as brilliant as
if some magician had condensed the brightest star in heaven
into a compass fit to be set in a ring, for a lady's delicate
finger.

"How is this?" said Deacon Trott, examining it carefully,
in the expectation of finding it as worthless as the rest of his
colleague's treasure. "Why, upon my word, this seems to be
a real diamond, and of the purest water. Whence could it
have come?"

"Really, I cannot tell," quoth Deacon Tilton, "for my spectacles were so misty that all faces looked alike. But now I
remember, there was a flash of light came from the box, at
one moment; but it seemed a dusky red, instead of a pure
white, like the sparkle of this gem. Well; the ring will make
up for the copper; but I wish the giver had thrown its history
into the box along with it."

It has been our good luck to recover a portion of that history. After transmitting misfortune from one possessor to another, ever since the days of British Merlin, the identical ring
which Queen Elizabeth gave to the Earl of Essex was finally
thrown into the contribution-box of a New-England church.
The two deacons deposited it in the glass-case of a fashionable jeweller, of whom it was purchased by the humble re-
hearser of this legend, in the hope that it may be allowed to
sparkle on a fair lady's finger. Purified from the foul fiend, so
long its inhabitant, by a deed of unostentatious charity, and
now made the symbol of faithful and devoted love, the gentle
bosom of its new possessor need fear no sorrow from its
influence.

"Very pretty!—Beautiful!—How original!—How sweetly
written!—What nature!—What imagination!—What power!
—What pathos!—What exquisite humor!"—were the excla-

mations of Edward Caryl's kind and generous auditors, at the conclusion of the legend.

"It is a pretty tale," said Miss Pemberton, who, conscious that her praise was to that of all others as a diamond to a pebble, was therefore the less liberal in awarding it. "It is really a pretty tale, and very proper for any of the Annuals. But, Edward, your moral does not satisfy me. What thought did you embody in the ring?"

"Oh, Clara, this is too bad!" replied Edward, with a half-reproachful smile.—"You know that I can never separate the idea from the symbol in which it manifests itself. However, we may suppose the Gem to be the human heart, and the Evil Spirit to be Falsehood, which, in one guise or another, is the fiend that causes all the sorrow and trouble in the world. I beseech you, to let this suffice."

"It shall," said Clara, kindly. "And believe me, whatever the world may say of the story, I prize it far above the diamond which enkindled your imagination."

The Hall of Fantasy

IT has happened to me, on various occasions, to find myself in a certain edifice, which would appear to have some of the characteristics of a public Exchange. Its interior is a spacious hall, with a pavement of white marble. Overhead is a lofty dome, supported by long rows of pillars, of fantastic architecture, the idea of which was probably taken from the Moorish ruins of the Alhambra, or perhaps from some enchanted edifice in the Arabian Tales. The windows of this hall have a breadth and grandeur of design, and an elaborateness of workmanship, that have nowhere been equalled, except in the Gothic cathedrals of the old world. Like their prototypes, too, they admit the light of heaven only through stained and pictured glass, thus filling the hall with many-colored radiance, and painting its marble floor with beautiful or grotesque designs; so that its inmates breathe, as it were, a visionary atmosphere, and tread upon the fantasies of poetic minds. These peculiarities, combining a wilder mixture of styles than even an American architect usually recognizes as allowable—Grecian, Gothic, Oriental, and nondescript—cause the whole edifice to give the impression of a dream, which might be dissipated and shattered to fragments, by merely stamping the foot upon the pavement. Yet, with such modifications and repairs as successive ages demand, the Hall of Fantasy is likely to endure longer than the most substantial structure that ever cumbered the earth.

It is not at all times that one can gain admittance into this edifice; although most persons enter it at some period or other of their lives—if not in their waking moments, then by the universal passport of a dream. At my last visit, I wandered thither unawares, while my mind was busy with an idle tale, and was startled by the throng of people who seemed suddenly to rise up around me.

"Bless me! Where am I?" cried I, with but a dim recognition of the place.

"You are in a spot," said a friend, who chanced to be near at hand, "which occupies, in the world of fancy, the same

734

position which the Bourse, the Rialto, and the Exchange, do in the commercial world. All who have affairs in that mystic region, which lies above, below, or beyond the Actual, may here meet, and talk over the business of their dreams."

"It is a noble hall," observed I.

"Yes," he replied. "Yet we see but a small portion of the edifice. In its upper stories are said to be apartments, where the inhabitants of earth may hold converse with those of the moon. And beneath our feet are gloomy cells, which communicate with the infernal regions, and where monsters and chimeras are kept in confinement, and fed with all unwholesomeness."

In niches and on pedestals, around about the hall, stood the statues or busts of men, who, in every age, have been rulers and demi-gods in the realms of imagination, and its kindred regions. The grand old countenance of Homer; the shrunken and decrepit form, but vivid face of Æsop; the dark presence of Dante; the wild Ariosto; Rabelais's smile of deep-wrought mirth; the profound, pathetic humor of Cervantes; the all-glorious Shakespeare; Spenser, meet guest for an allegoric structure; the severe divinity of Milton; and Bunyan, moulded of homeliest clay, but instinct with celestial fire— were those that chiefly attracted my eye. Fielding, Richardson, and Scott, occupied conspicuous pedestals. In an obscure and shadowy niche was reposited the bust of our countryman, the author of Arthur Mervyn.

"Besides these indestructible memorials of real genius," remarked my companion, "each century has erected statues of its own ephemeral favorites, in wood."

"I observe a few crumbling relics of such," said I. "But ever and anon, I suppose, Oblivion comes with her huge broom, and sweeps them all from the marble floor. But such will never be the fate of this fine statue of Goethe."

"Nor of that next to it—Emanuel Swedenborg," said he. "Were ever two men of transcendent imagination more unlike?"

In the centre of the hall springs an ornamental fountain, the water of which continually throws itself into new shapes, and snatches the most diversified hues from the stained atmosphere around. It is impossible to conceive what a strange vivacity is imparted to the scene by the magic dance of this fountain, with its endless transformations, in which the imaginative beholder may discern what form he will. The water is supposed by some to flow from the same source as the Castalian spring, and is extolled by others as uniting the virtues of the Fountain of Youth with those of many other enchanted wells, long celebrated in tale and song. Having never tasted it, I can bear no testimony to its quality.

"Did you ever drink this water?" I inquired of my friend.

"A few sips, now and then," answered he. "But there are men here who make it their constant beverage—or, at least, have the credit of doing so. In some instances, it is known to have intoxicating qualities."

"Pray let us look at these water-drinkers," said I.

So we passed among the fantastic pillars, till we came to a spot where a number of persons were clustered together, in the light of one of the great stained windows, which seemed to glorify the whole group, as well as the marble that they trod on. Most of them were men of broad foreheads, meditative countenances, and thoughtful, inward eyes; yet it required but a trifle to summon up mirth, peeping out from the very midst of grave and lofty musings. Some strode about, or leaned against the pillars of the hall, alone and in silence; their faces wore a rapt expression, as if sweet music were in the air around them, or as if their inmost souls were about to float away in song. One or two, perhaps, stole a glance at the bystanders, to watch if their poetic absorption were observed. Others stood talking in groups, with a liveliness of expression, a ready smile, and a light, intellectual laughter, which showed how rapidly the shafts of wit were glancing to-and-fro among them.

A few held higher converse, which caused their calm and melancholy souls to beam moonlight from their eyes. As I lingered near them—for I felt an inward attraction towards these men, as if the sympathy of feeling, if not of genius, had united me to their order—my friend mentioned several of their names. The world has likewise heard those names; with some it has been familiar for years; and others are daily making their way deeper into the universal heart.

"Thank heaven," observed I to my companion, as we

passed to another part of the hall, "we have done with this techy, wayward, shy, proud, unreasonable set of laurel-gatherers. I love them in their works, but have little desire to meet them elsewhere."

"You have adopted an old prejudice, I see," replied my friend, who was familiar with most of these worthies, being himself a student of poetry, and not without the poetic flame. "But so far as my experience goes, men of genius are fairly gifted with the social qualities; and in this age, there appears to be a fellow-feeling among them, which had not heretofore been developed. As men, they ask nothing better than to be on equal terms with their fellow-men; and as authors, they have thrown aside their proverbial jealousy, and acknowledge a generous brotherhood."

"The world does not think so," answered I. "An author is received in general society pretty much as we honest citizens are in the Hall of Fantasy. We gaze at him as if he had no business among us, and question whether he is fit for any of our pursuits."

"Then it is a very foolish question," said he. "Now, here are a class of men, whom we may daily meet on 'Change. Yet what poet in the hall is more a fool of fancy than the sagest of them?"

He pointed to a number of persons, who, manifest as the fact was, would have deemed it an insult to be told that they stood in the Hall of Fantasy. Their visages were traced into wrinkles and furrows, each of which seemed the record of some actual experience in life. Their eyes had the shrewd, calculating glance, which detects so quickly and so surely all that it concerns a man of business to know, about the characters and purposes of his fellow-men. Judging them as they stood, they might be honored and trusted members of the Chamber of Commerce, who had found the genuine secret of wealth, and whose sagacity gave them the command of fortune. There was a character of detail and matter-of-fact in their talk, which concealed the extravagance of its purport, insomuch that the wildest schemes had the aspect of every-day realities. Thus the listener was not startled at the idea of cities to be built, as if by magic, in the heart of pathless forests; and of streets to be laid out, where now the sea was tossing; and of mighty rivers to be staid in their courses, in order to turn the machinery of a cotton-mill. It was only by an effort—and scarcely then—that the mind convinced itself that such spec-ulations were as much matter of fantasy as the old dream of Eldorado, or as Mammon's Cave, or any other vision of gold, ever conjured up by the imagination of needy poet or roman-tic adventurer.

"Upon my word," said I, "it is dangerous to listen to such dreamers as these! Their madness is contagious."

"Yes," said my friend, "because they mistake the Hall of Fantasy for actual brick and mortar, and its purple atmo-sphere for unsophisticated sunshine. But the poet knows his whereabout, and therefore is less likely to make a fool of him-self in real life."

"Here again," observed I, as we advanced a little further, "we see another order of dreamers—peculiarly characteristic, too, of the genius of our country."

These were the inventors of fantastic machines. Models of their contrivances were placed against some of the pillars of the hall, and afforded good emblems of the result generally to be anticipated from an attempt to reduce day-dreams to prac-tice. The analogy may hold in morals, as well as physics. For instance, here was the model of a railroad through the air, and a tunnel under the sea. Here was a machine—stolen, I believe—for the distillation of heat from moonshine; and an-other for the condensation of morning-mist into square blocks of granite, wherewith it was proposed to rebuild the entire Hall of Fantasy. One man exhibited a sort of lens, whereby he had succeeded in making sunshine out of a lady's smile; and it was his purpose wholly to irradiate the earth, by means of this wonderful invention.

"It is nothing new," said I, "for most of our sunshine comes from woman's smile already."

"True," answered the inventor; "but my machine will se-cure a constant supply for domestic use—whereas, hitherto, it has been very precarious."

Another person had a scheme for fixing the reflections of objects in a pool of water, and thus taking the most life-like portraits imaginable; and the same gentleman demonstrated the practicability of giving a permanent dye to ladies' dresses, in the gorgeous clouds of sunset. There were at least fifty kinds of perpetual motion, one of which was applicable to the wits of newspaper editors and writers of every description. Professor Espy was here, with a tremendous storm in a gum-elastic bag. I could enumerate many more of these Utopian inventions; but, after all, a more imaginative collection is to be found in the Patent Office at Washington.

Turning from the inventors, we took a more general survey of the inmates of the hall. Many persons were present, whose right of entrance appeared to consist in some crochet of the brain, which, so long as it might operate, produced a change in their relation to the actual world. It is singular how very few there are, who do not occasionally gain admittance on such a score, either in abstracted musings, or momentary thoughts, or bright anticipations, or vivid remembrances; for even the actual becomes ideal, whether in hope or memory, and beguiles the dreamer into the Hall of Fantasy. Some unfortunates make their whole abode and business here, and contract habits which unfit them for all the real employments of life. Others—but these are few—possess the faculty, in their occasional visits, of discovering a purer truth than the world can impart, among the lights and shadows of these pictured windows.

And with all its dangerous influences, we have reason to thank God, that there is such a place of refuge from the gloom and chillness of actual life. Hither may come the prisoner, escaping from his dark and narrow cell, and cankerous chain, to breathe free air in this enchanted atmosphere. The sick man leaves his weary pillow, and finds strength to wander hither, though his wasted limbs might not support him even to the threshold of his chamber. The exile passes through the Hall of Fantasy, to revisit his native soil. The burthen of years rolls down from the old man's shoulders, the moment that the door uncloses. Mourners leave their heavy sorrows at the entrance, and here rejoin the lost ones, whose faces would else be seen no more, until thought shall have become the only fact. It may be said, in truth, that there is but half a life—the meaner and earthlier half—for those who never find their way into the hall. Nor must I fail to mention, that, in the observatory of the edifice, is kept that wonderful perspective glass, through which the shepherds of the Delectable Mountains showed Christian the far-off gleam of the Celestial City. The eye of Faith still loves to gaze through it.

"I observe some men here," said I to my friend, "who might set up a strong claim to be reckoned among the most real personages of the day."

"Certainly," he replied. "If a man be in advance of his age, he must be content to make his abode in this hall, until the lingering generations of his fellow-men come up with him. He can find no other shelter in the universe. But the fantasies of one day are the deepest realities of a future one."

"It is difficult to distinguish them apart, amid the gorgeous and bewildering light of this hall," rejoined I. "The white sunshine of actual life is necessary in order to test them. I am rather apt to doubt both men and their reasonings, till I meet them in that truthful medium."

"Perhaps your faith in the ideal is deeper than you are aware," said my friend. "You are at least a Democrat; and methinks no scanty share of such faith is essential to the adoption of that creed."

Among the characters who had elicited these remarks, were most of the noted reformers of the day, whether in physics, politics, morals, or religion. There is no surer method of arriving at the Hall of Fantasy, than to throw oneself into the current of a theory; for, whatever landmarks of fact may be set up along the stream, there is a law of nature that impels it thither. And let it be so; for here the wise head and capacious heart may do their work; and what is good and true becomes gradually hardened into fact, while error melts away and vanishes among the shadows of the hall. Therefore may none, who believe and rejoice in the progress of mankind, be angry with me because I recognized their apostles and leaders, amid the fantastic radiance of those pictured windows. I love and honor such men, as well as they.

It would be endless to describe the herd of real or self-styled reformers, that peopled this place of refuge. They were the representatives of an unquiet period, when mankind is seeking to cast off the whole tissue of ancient custom, like a tattered garment. Many of them had got possession of some crystal fragment of truth, the brightness of which so dazzled them, that they could see nothing else in the wide universe. Here were men, whose faith had embodied itself in the form of a potatoe; and others whose long beards had a deep spiritual significance. Here was the abolitionist, brandishing his one idea like an iron flail. In a word, there were a thousand shapes of good and evil, faith and infidelity, wisdom and nonsense,—a most incongruous throng.

Yet, withal, the heart of the stanchest conservative, unless he abjured his fellowship with man, could hardly have helped throbbing in sympathy with the spirit that pervaded these innumerable theorists. It was good for the man of unquickened heart to listen even to their folly. Far down, beyond the fathom of the intellect, the soul acknowledged that all these varying and conflicting developments of humanity were united in one sentiment. Be the individual theory as wild as fancy could make it, still the wiser spirit would recognize the struggle of the race after a better and purer life, than had yet been realized on earth. My faith revived, even while I rejected all their schemes. It could not be, that the world should continue forever what it has been; a soil where Happiness is so rare a flower, and Virtue so often a blighted fruit; a battlefield where the good principle, with its shield flung above its head, can hardly save itself amid the rush of adverse influences. In the enthusiasm of such thoughts, I gazed through one of the pictured windows; and, behold! the whole external world was tinged with the dimly glorious aspect that is peculiar to the Hall of Fantasy; insomuch that it seemed practicable, at that very instant, to realize some plan for the perfection of mankind. But, alas! if reformers would understand the sphere in which their lot is cast, they must cease to look through pictured windows. Yet they not only use this medium, but mistake it for the whitest sunshine.

"Come," said I to my friend, starting from a deep reverie,—"let us hasten hence, or I shall be tempted to make a theory—after which, there is little hope of any man."

"Come hither, then," answered he. "Here is one theory, that swallows up and annihilates all others."

He led me to a distant part of the hall, where a crowd of deeply attentive auditors were assembled round an elderly man, of plain, honest, trustworthy aspect. With an earnestness that betokened the sincerest faith in his own doctrine, he announced that the destruction of the world was close at hand.

"It is Father Miller himself!" exclaimed I.

"No less a man," said my friend, "and observe how picturesque a contrast between his dogma, and those of the reformers whom we have just glanced at. They look for the earthly perfection of mankind, and are forming schemes, which imply that the immortal spirit will be connected with a physical nature, for innumerable ages of futurity. On the other hand, here comes good Father Miller, and, with one puff of his relentless theory, scatters all their dreams like so many withered leaves upon the blast."

"It is, perhaps, the only method of getting mankind out of the various perplexities, into which they have fallen," I replied. "Yet I could wish that the world might be permitted to endure, until some great moral shall have been evolved. A riddle is propounded. Where is the solution? The sphinx did not slay herself, until her riddle had been guessed. Will it not be so with the world? Now, if it should be burnt to-morrow morning, I am at a loss to know what purpose will have been accomplished, or how the universe will be wiser or better for our existence and destruction."

"We cannot tell what mighty truths may have been embodied in act, through the existence of the globe and its inhabitants," rejoined my companion. "Perhaps it may be revealed to us, after the fall of the curtain over our catastrophe; or not impossibly, the whole drama, in which we are involuntary actors, may have been performed for the instruction of another set of spectators. I cannot perceive that our own comprehension of it is at all essential to the matter. At any rate, while our view is so ridiculously narrow and superficial, it would be absurd to argue the continuance of the world from the fact, that it seems to have existed hitherto in vain."

"The poor old Earth," murmured I. "She has faults enough, in all conscience; but I cannot bear to have her perish."

"It is no great matter," said my friend. "The happiest of us has been weary of her, many a time and oft."

"I doubt it," answered I, pertinaciously; "the root of human nature strikes down deep into this earthly soil; and it is but reluctantly that we submit to be transplanted, even for a higher cultivation in Heaven. I query whether the destruction of the earth would gratify any one individual; except, perhaps, some embarrassed man of business, whose notes fall due a day after the day of doom."

Then, methought, I heard the expostulating cry of a multitude against the consummation, prophesied by Father Miller. The lover wrestled with Providence for his fore-shadowed bliss. Parents entreated that the earth's span of endurance might be prolonged by some seventy years, so that their new-born infant should not be defrauded of his life-time. A youthful poet murmured, because there would be no posterity to recognize the inspiration of his song. The reformers, one and all, demanded a few thousand years, to test their theories, after which the universe might go to wreck. A mechanician, who was busied with an improvement of the steam-engine, asked merely time to perfect his model. A miser insisted that the world's destruction would be a personal wrong to himself, unless he should first be permitted to add a specified sum to his enormous heap of gold. A little boy made dolorous inquiry whether the last day would come before Christmas, and thus deprive him of his anticipated dainties. In short, nobody seemed satisfied that this mortal scene of things should have its close just now. Yet, it must be confessed, the motives of the crowd for desiring its continuance were mostly so absurd, that, unless Infinite Wisdom had been aware of much better reasons, the solid Earth must have melted away at once.

For my own part, not to speak of a few private and personal ends, I really desired our old Mother's prolonged existence, for her own dear sake.

"The poor old Earth!" I repeated. "What I should chiefly regret in her destruction would be that very earthliness, which no other sphere or state of existence can renew or compensate. The fragrance of flowers, and of new-mown hay; the genial warmth of sunshine, and the beauty of a sunset among clouds; the comfort and cheerful glow of the fireside; the deliciousness of fruits, and of all good cheer; the magnificence of mountains, and seas, and cataracts, and the softer charm of rural scenery; even the fast-falling snow, and the gray atmosphere through which it descends—all these, and innumerable other enjoyable things of earth, must perish with her. Then the country frolics; the homely humor; the broad, open-mouthed roar of laughter, in which body and soul conjoin so heartily! I fear that no other world can show us anything just like this. As for purely moral enjoyments, the good will find them in every state of being. But where the material and the moral exist together, what is to happen then? And then our mute four-footed friends, and the winged songsters of our woods! Might it not be lawful to regret them, even in the hallowed groves of Paradise?"

"You speak like the very spirit of earth, imbued with a scent of freshly-turned soil!" exclaimed my friend.

"It is not that I so much object to giving up these enjoyments, on my own account," continued I; "but I hate to think that they will have been eternally annihilated from the list of joys."

"Nor need they be," he replied. "I see no real force in what you say. Standing in this Hall of Fantasy, we perceive what even the earth-clogged intellect of man can do, in creating circumstances, which, though we call them shadowy and visionary, are scarcely more so than those that surround us in actual life. Doubt not, then, that man's disembodied spirit may recreate Time and the World for itself, with all their peculiar enjoyments, should there still be human yearnings amid life eternal and infinite. But I doubt whether we shall be inclined to play such a poor scene over again."

"Oh, you are ungrateful to our Mother Earth!" rejoined I. "Come what may, I never will forget her! Neither will it satisfy me to have her exist merely in idea. I want her great, round, solid self to endure interminably, and still to be peopled with the kindly race of man, whom I uphold to be much better than he thinks himself. Nevertheless, I confide the whole matter to Providence, and shall endeavor so to live, that the world may come to an end at any moment, without leaving me at a loss to find foothold somewhere else."

"It is an excellent resolve," said my companion, looking at his watch. "But come; it is the dinner hour. Will you partake of my vegetable diet?"

A thing so matter-of-fact as an invitation to dinner, even when the fare was to be nothing more substantial than vegetables and fruit, compelled us forthwith to remove from the Hall of Fantasy. As we passed out of the portal, we met the spirits of several persons, who had been sent thither in magnetic sleep. I looked back among the sculptured pillars, and at the transformations of the gleaming fountain, and almost desired that the whole of life might be spent in that visionary scene, where the actual world, with its hard angles, should never rub against me, and only be viewed through the medium of pictured windows. But, for those who waste all their days in the Hall of Fantasy, good Father Miller's prophecy is already accomplished, and the solid earth has come to an untimely end. Let us be content, therefore, with merely an occasional visit, for the sake of spiritualizing the grossness of this actual life, and prefiguring to ourselves a state, in which the Idea shall be all in all.

The New Adam and Eve

WE, who are born into the world's artificial system, can never adequately know how little in our present state and circumstances is natural, and how much is merely the interpolation of the perverted mind and heart of man. Art has become a second and stronger Nature; she is a step-mother, whose crafty tenderness has taught us to despise the bountiful and wholesome ministrations of our true parent. It is only through the medium of the imagination that we can loosen those iron fetters, which we call truth and reality, and make ourselves even partially sensible what prisoners we are. For instance, let us conceive good Father Miller's interpretation of the prophecies to have proved true. The Day of Doom has burst upon the globe, and swept away the whole race of men. From cities and fields, sea-shore and mid-land mountain region, vast continents, and even the remotest islands of the ocean—each living thing is gone. No breath of a created being disturbs this earthly atmosphere. But the abodes of man, and all that he has accomplished, the foot-prints of his wanderings, and the results of his toil, the visible symbols of his intellectual cultivation and moral progress—in short, everything physical that can give evidence of his present position—shall remain untouched by the hand of destiny. Then, to inherit and repeople this waste and deserted earth, we will suppose a new Adam and a new Eve to have been created, in the full development of mind and heart, but with no knowledge of their predecessors, nor of the diseased circumstances that had become encrusted around them. Such a pair would at once distinguish between art and nature. Their instincts and intuitions would immediately recognize the wisdom and simplicity of the latter; while the former, with its elaborate perversities, would offer them a continual succession of puzzles.

Let us attempt, in a mood half-sportive and half-thoughtful, to track these imaginary heirs of our mortality through their first day's experience. No longer ago than yesterday, the flame of human life was extinguished; there has been a breathless night; and now another morn approaches, expecting to find the earth no less desolate than at eventide.

It is dawn. The east puts on its immemorial blush, although no human eye is gazing at it; for all the phenomena of the natural world renew themselves, in spite of the solitude that now broods around the globe. There is still beauty of earth, sea, and sky, for beauty's sake. But soon there are to be spectators. Just when the earliest sunshine gilds earth's mountain tops, two beings have come into life, not in such an Eden as bloomed to welcome our first parents, but in the heart of a modern city. They find themselves in existence, and gazing into one another's eyes. Their emotion is not astonishment; nor do they perplex themselves with efforts to discover what, and whence, and why they are. Each is satisfied to be, because the other exists likewise; and their first consciousness is of calm and mutual enjoyment, which seems not to have been the birth of that very moment, but prolonged from a past eternity. Thus content with an inner sphere which they inhabit together, it is not immediately that the outward world can obtrude itself upon their notice.

Soon, however, they feel the invincible necessity of this earthly life, and begin to make acquaintance with the objects and circumstances that surround them. Perhaps no other stride so vast remains to be taken, as when they first turn from the reality of their mutual glance, to the dreams and shadows that perplex them everywhere else.

"Sweetest Eve, where are we?" exclaims the new Adam,— for speech, or some equivalent mode of expression, is born with them, and comes just as natural as breath;—"Methinks I do not recognize this place."

"Nor I, dear Adam," replies the new Eve. "And what a strange place too! Let me come closer to thy side, and behold thee only; for all other sights trouble and perplex my spirit."

"Nay, Eve," replies Adam, who appears to have the stronger tendency towards the material world; "it were well that we gain some insight into these matters. We are in an odd situation here! Let us look about us."

Assuredly, there are sights enough to throw the new inheritors of earth into a state of hopeless perplexity. The long lines of edifices, their windows glittering in the yellow sunrise, and the narrow street between, with its barren pavement, tracked and battered by wheels that have now rattled into an irrevocable past! The signs, with their unintelligible hieroglyphics! The squareness and ugliness, and regular or irregular deformity, of everything that meets the eye! The marks of wear and tear, and unrenewed decay, which distinguish the works of man from the growth of nature! What is there in all this, capable of the slightest significance to minds that know nothing of the artificial system which is implied in every lamp-post and each brick of the houses? Moreover, the utter loneliness and silence, in a scene that originally grew out of noise and bustle, must needs impress a feeling of desolation even upon Adam and Eve, unsuspicious as they are of the recent extinction of human existence. In a forest, solitude would be life; in the city, it is death.

The new Eve looks round with a sensation of doubt and distrust, such as a city dame, the daughter of numberless generations of citizens, might experience, if suddenly transported to the garden of Eden. At length, her downcast eye discovers a small tuft of grass, just beginning to sprout among the stones of the pavement; she eagerly grasps it, and is sensible that this little herb awakens some response within her heart. Nature finds nothing else to offer her. Adam, after staring up and down the street, without detecting a single object that his comprehension can lay hold of, finally turns his forehead to the sky. There, indeed, is something which the soul within him recognizes.

"Look up yonder, mine own Eve!" he cries; "surely we ought to dwell among those gold-tinged clouds, or in the blue depths beyond them. I know not how nor when, but evidently we have strayed away from our home; for I see nothing hereabouts that seems to belong to us."

"Can we not ascend thither?" inquires Eve.

"Why not?" answers Adam, hopefully. "But no! Something drags us down in spite of our best efforts. Perchance we may find a path hereafter."

In the energy of new life, it appears no such impracticable feat to climb into the sky! But they have already received a woful lesson, which may finally go far towards reducing them to the level of the departed race, when they acknowledge the necessity of keeping the beaten track of earth. They now set forth on a ramble through the city, in the hope of making their escape from this uncongenial sphere. Already, in the fresh elasticity of their spirits they have found the idea of weariness. We will watch them as they enter some of the shops, and public or private edifices; for every door, whether of alderman or beggar, church or hall of state, has been flung wide open by the same agency that swept away the inmates.

It so happens—and not unluckily for an Adam and Eve who are still in the costume that might better have befitted Eden—it so happens, that their first visit is to a fashionable dry-good store. No courteous and importunate attendants hasten to receive their orders; no throng of ladies are tossing over the rich Parisian fabrics. All is deserted; trade is at a stand-still; and not even an echo of the national watchword—"Go ahead!"—disturbs the quiet of the new customers. But specimens of the latest earthly fashions, silks of every shade, and whatever is most delicate or splendid for the decoration of the human form, lie scattered around, profusely as bright autumnal leaves in a forest. Adam looks at a few of the articles, but throws them carelessly aside, with whatever exclamation may correspond to "Pish!" or "Pshaw!" in the new vocabulary of nature. Eve, however,—be it said without offence to her native modesty,—examines these treasures of her sex with somewhat livelier interest. A pair of corsets chance to lie upon the counter; she inspects them curiously, but knows not what to make of them. Then she handles a fashionable silk with dim yearnings—thoughts that wander hither and thither—instincts groping in the dark.

"On the whole, I do not like it," she observes, laying the glossy fabric upon the counter. "But, Adam, it is very strange! What can these things mean? Surely I ought to know—yet they put me in a perfect maze!"

"Poh! my dear Eve, why trouble thy little head about such nonsense?" cries Adam, in a fit of impatience. "Let us go somewhere else. But stay! How very beautiful! My loveliest Eve, what a charm you have imparted to that robe, by merely throwing it over your shoulders!"

For Eve, with the taste that nature moulded into her composition, has taken a remnant of exquisite silver gauze and drawn it around her form, with an effect that gives Adam his first idea of the witchery of dress. He beholds his spouse in a new light and with renewed admiration, yet is hardly reconciled to any other attire than her own golden locks. However, emulating Eve's example, he makes free with a mantle of blue velvet, and puts it on so picturesquely, that it might seem to have fallen from Heaven upon his stately figure. Thus garbed, they go in search of new discoveries.

They next wander into a Church, not to make a display of their fine clothes, but attracted by its spire, pointing upward to the sky, whither they have already yearned to climb. As they enter the portal, a clock, which it was the last earthly act of the sexton to wind up, repeats the hour in deep reverberating tones; for Time has survived his former progeny, and, with the iron tongue that man gave him, is now speaking to his two grandchildren. They listen, but understand him not. Nature would measure time by the succession of thoughts and acts which constitute real life, and not by hours of emptiness. They pass up the church aisle, and raise their eyes to the ceiling. Had our Adam and Eve become mortal in some European city, and strayed into the vastness and sublimity of an old cathedral, they might have recognized the purpose for which the deep-souled founders reared it. Like the dim awfulness of an ancient forest, its very atmosphere would have incited them to prayer. Within the snug walls of a metropolitan church there can be no such influence.

Yet some odor of religion is still lingering here, the bequest of pious souls, who had grace to enjoy a foretaste of immortal life. Perchance, they breathe a prophecy of a better world to their successors, who have become obnoxious to all their own cares and calamities in the present one.

"Eve, something impels me to look upward," says Adam. "But it troubles me to see this roof between us and the sky. Let us go forth, and perhaps we shall discern a Great Face looking down upon us."

"Yes; a Great Face, with a beam of love brightening over it, like sunshine," responds Eve. "Surely, we have seen such a countenance somewhere!"

They go out of the church, and kneeling at its threshold give way to the spirit's natural instinct of adoration towards a beneficent Father. But, in truth, their life thus far has been a continual prayer. Purity and simplicity hold converse, at every moment, with their Creator.

We now observe them entering a Court of Justice. But what remotest conception can they attain of the purposes of such an edifice? How should the idea occur to them, that human brethren, of like nature with themselves, and originally included in the same law of love which is their only rule of life, should ever need an outward enforcement of the true voice within their souls? And what, save a woful experience, the dark result of many centuries, could teach them the sad mysteries of crime? Oh, Judgment Seat, not by the pure in heart wast thou established, nor in the simplicity of nature; but by hard and wrinkled men, and upon the accumulated heap of earthly wrong! Thou art the very symbol of man's perverted state.

On as fruitless an errand our wanderers next visit a Hall of Legislature, where Adam places Eve in the Speaker's chair, unconscious of the moral which he thus exemplifies. Man's intellect, moderated by Woman's tenderness and moral sense! Were such the legislation of the world, there would be no need of State Houses, Capitols, Halls of Parliament, nor even of those little assemblages of patriarchs beneath the shadowy trees, by whom freedom was first interpreted to mankind on our native shores.

Whither go they next? A perverse destiny seems to perplex them with one after another of the riddles which mankind put forth to the wandering universe, and left unsolved in their own destruction. They enter an edifice of stern grey stone, standing insulated in the midst of others, and gloomy even in the sunshine, which it barely suffers to penetrate through its iron-grated windows. It is a Prison. The jailer has left his post at the summons of a stronger authority than the sheriff's. But the prisoners? Did the messenger of fate, when he shook open all the doors, respect the magistrate's warrant and the judge's sentence, and leave the inmates of the dungeons to be delivered by due course of earthly law? No; a new trial has been granted, in a higher court, which may set judge, jury, and prisoner at its bar all in a row, and perhaps find one no less guilty than another. The jail, like the whole earth, is now a

solitude, and has thereby lost something of its dismal gloom.
But here are the narrow cells, like tombs, only drearier and
deadlier because in these the immortal spirit was buried with
the body. Inscriptions appear on the walls, scribbled with a
pencil, or scratched with a rusty nail; brief words of agony,
perhaps, or guilt's desperate defiance to the world, or merely
a record of a date, by which the writer strove to keep up with
the march of life. There is not a living eye that could now
decipher these memorials.

Nor is it while so fresh from their Creator's hand, that the
new denizens of earth—no, nor their descendants for a thousand years—could discover that this edifice was a hospital for
the direst disease which could afflict their predecessors. Its
patients bore the outward marks of that leprosy with which
all were more or less infected. They were sick—and so were
the purest of their brethren—with the plague of sin. A deadly
sickness, indeed! Feeling its symptoms within the breast, men
concealed it with fear and shame, and were only the more
cruel to those unfortunates whose pestiferous sores were fla-
grant to the common eye. Nothing, save a rich garment,
could ever hide the plague-spot. In the course of the world's
lifetime, every remedy was tried for its cure and extirpation,
except the single one, the flower that grew in Heaven, and
was sovereign for all the miseries of earth. Man never had
attempted to cure sin by LOVE! Had he but once made the
effort, it might well have happened, that there would have
been no more need of the dark lazar-house into which Adam
and Eve have wandered. Hasten forth, with your native innocence, lest the damps of these still conscious walls infect
you likewise, and thus another fallen race be propagated!

Passing from the interior of the prison into the space
within its outward wall, Adam pauses beneath a structure of
the simplest contrivance, yet altogether unaccountable to him.
It consists merely of two upright posts, supporting a trans-
verse beam, from which dangles a cord.

"Eve, Eve!" cries Adam, shuddering with a nameless horror. "What can this thing be?"

"I know not," answers Eve; "but, Adam, my heart is sick!
There seems to be no more sky!—no more sunshine!"

Well might Adam shudder, and poor Eve be sick at heart;

for this mysterious object was the type of mankind's whole system, in regard to the great difficulties which God had given to be solved—a system of fear and vengeance, never successful, yet followed to the last. Here, on the morning when the final summons came, a criminal—one criminal, where none were guiltless—had died upon the gallows. Had the world heard the foot-fall of its own approaching doom, it would have been no inappropriate act, thus to close the record of its deeds by one so characteristic.

The two pilgrims now hurry from the prison. Had they known how the former inhabitants of earth were shut up in artificial error, and cramped and chained by their perversions, they might have compared the whole moral world to a prison-house, and have deemed the removal of the race a general jail-delivery.

They next enter, unannounced—but they might have rung at the door in vain—a private mansion, one of the stateliest in Beacon street. A wild and plaintive strain of music is quivering through the house, now rising like a solemn organ peal, and now dying into the faintest murmur; as if some spirit, that had felt an interest in the departed family, were bemoaning itself in the solitude of hall and chamber. Perhaps, a virgin, the purest of mortal race, has been left behind, to perform a requiem for the whole kindred of humanity? Not so! These are the tones of an Æolian harp, through which Nature pours the harmony that lies concealed in her every breath, whether of summer breeze or tempest. Adam and Eve are lost in rapture, unmingled with surprise. The passing wind, that stirred the harp-strings, has been hushed, before they can think of examining the splendid furniture, the gorgeous carpets, and the architecture of the rooms. These things amuse their unpractised eyes, but appeal to nothing within their hearts. Even the pictures upon the walls scarcely excite a deeper interest; for there is something radically artificial and deceptive in painting, with which minds in the primal simplicity cannot sympathize. The unbidden guests examine a row of family portraits, but are too dull to recognize them as men and women, beneath the disguise of a preposterous garb, and with features and expression debased, because inherited through ages of moral and physical decay.

Chance, however, presents them with pictures of human beauty, fresh from the hand of Nature. As they enter a magnificent apartment, they are astonished, but not affrighted, to perceive two figures advancing to meet them. Is it not awful to imagine that any life, save their own, should remain in the wide world?

"How is this?" exclaims Adam. "My beautiful Eve, are you in two places at once?"

"And you, Adam!" answers Eve, doubtful, yet delighted. "Surely that noble and lovely form is yours. Yet here you are by my side! I am content with one—methinks there should not be two!"

This miracle is wrought by a tall looking-glass, the mystery of which they soon fathom, because Nature creates a mirror for the human face in every pool of water, and for her own great features in waveless lakes. Pleased and satisfied with gazing at themselves, they now discover the marble statue of a child in a corner of the room, so exquisitely idealized, that it is almost worthy to be the prophetic likeness of their first-born. Sculpture, in its highest excellence, is more genuine than painting, and might seem to be evolved from a natural germ, by the same law as a leaf or flower. The statue of the child impresses the solitary pair as if it were a companion; it likewise hints at secrets both of the past and future.

"My husband!" whispers Eve.

"What would you say, dearest Eve?" inquires Adam.

"I wonder if we are alone in the world," she continues, with a sense of something like fear at the thought of other inhabitants. "This lovely little form! Did it ever breathe? Or is it only the shadow of something real, like our pictures in the mirror?"

"It is strange!" replies Adam, pressing his hand to his brow. "There are mysteries all around us. An idea flits continually before me—would that I could seize it! Eve, Eve, are we treading in the footsteps of beings that bore a likeness to ourselves? If so, whither are they gone?—and why is their world so unfit for our dwelling-place?"

"Our great Father only knows," answers Eve. "But something tells me that we shall not always be alone. And how sweet if other beings were to visit us in the shape of this fair image!"

Then they wander through the house, and everywhere find tokens of human life, which now, with the idea recently suggested, excite a deeper curiosity in their bosoms. Woman has here left traces of her delicacy and refinement, and of her gentle labors. Eve ransacks a work-basket, and instinctively thrusts the rosy tip of her finger into a thimble. She takes up a piece of embroidery, glowing with mimic flowers, in one of which a fair damsel of the departed race has left her needle. Pity that the Day of Doom should have anticipated the completion of such a useful task! Eve feels almost conscious of the skill to finish it. A piano-forte has been left open. She flings her hand carelessly over the keys, and strikes out a sudden melody, no less natural than the strains of the Æolian harp, but joyous with the dance of her yet unburthened life. Passing through a dark entry, they find a broom behind the door; and Eve, who comprises the whole nature of womanhood, has a dim idea that it is an instrument proper for her hand. In another apartment they behold a canopied bed, and all the appliances of luxurious repose. A heap of forest-leaves would be more to the purpose. They enter the nursery, and are perplexed with the sight of little gowns and caps, tiny shoes, and a cradle; amid the drapery of which is still to be seen the impress of a baby's form. Adam slightly notices these trifles; but Eve becomes involved in a fit of mute reflection, from which it is hardly possible to rouse her.

By a most unlucky arrangement, there was to have been a grand dinner-party in this mansion on the very day when the whole human family, including the invited guests, were summoned to the unknown regions of illimitable space. At the moment of fate, the table was actually spread, and the company on the point of sitting down. Adam and Eve come unbidden to the banquet; it has now been some time cold, but otherwise furnishes them with highly favorable specimens of the gastronomy of their predecessors. But it is difficult to imagine the perplexity of the unperverted couple, in endeavoring to find proper food for their first meal, at a table where the cultivated appetites of a fashionable party were to have been gratified. Will Nature teach them the mystery of a plate of turtle soup? Will she embolden them to attack a haunch of venison? Will she initiate them into the merits of a Parisian pasty, imported by the last steamer that ever crossed the Atlantic? Will she not, rather, bid them turn with disgust from fish, fowl, and flesh, which, to their pure nostrils, steam with a loathsome odor of death and corruption? — Food? The bill of fare contains nothing which they recognize as such.

Fortunately, however, the dessert is ready upon a neighboring table. Adam, whose appetite and animal instincts are quicker than those of Eve, discovers this fitting banquet.

"Here, dearest Eve," he exclaims, "here is food."

"Well," answers she, with the germ of a housewife stirring within her, "we have been so busy to-day, that a picked-up dinner must serve."

So Eve comes to the table, and receives a red-cheeked apple from her husband's hand, in requital of her predecessor's fatal gift to our common grandfather. She eats it without sin, and, let us hope, with no disastrous consequences to her future progeny. They make a plentiful, yet temperate meal of fruit, which, though not gathered in Paradise, is legitimately derived from the seeds that were planted there. Their primal appetite is satisfied.

"What shall we drink, Eve?" inquires Adam.

Eve peeps among some bottles and decanters, which, as they contain fluids, she naturally conceives must be proper to quench thirst. But never before did claret, hock, and madeira, of rich and rare perfume, excite such disgust as now.

"Pah!" she exclaims, after smelling at various wines. "What stuff is here? The beings who have gone before us could not have possessed the same nature that we do; for neither their hunger nor thirst were like our own!"

"Pray hand me yonder bottle," says Adam. "If it be drinkable by any manner of mortal, I must moisten my throat with it."

After some remonstrances, she takes up a champagne bottle, but is frightened by the sudden explosion of the cork, and drops it upon the floor. There the untasted liquor effervesces. Had they quaffed it, they would have experienced that brief delirium, whereby, whether excited by moral or physical causes, man sought to recompense himself for the calm, life-long joys which he had lost by his revolt from Nature. At length, in a refrigerator, Eve finds a glass pitcher of water, pure, cold, and bright, as ever gushed from a fountain among the hills. Both drink; and such refreshment does it bestow, that they question one another if this precious liquid be not identical with the stream of life within them.

"And now," observes Adam, "we must again try to discover what sort of a world this is, and why we have been sent hither."

"Why?—To love one another!" cries Eve. "Is not that employment enough?"

"Truly is it," answers Adam, kissing her; "but still—I know not—something tells us there is labor to be done. Perhaps our allotted task is no other than to climb into the sky, which is so much more beautiful than earth."

"Then would we were there now," murmurs Eve, "that no task or duty might come between us!"

They leave the hospitable mansion; and we next see them passing down State street. The clock on the old State House points to high noon, when the Exchange should be in its glory, and present the liveliest emblem of what was the sole business of life, as regarded a multitude of the fore-gone worldlings. It is over now. The Sabbath of eternity has shed its stillness along the street. Not even a news-boy assails the two solitary passers-by, with an extra penny-paper from the office of the Times or Mail, containing a full account of yesterday's terrible catastrophe. Of all the dull times that merchants and speculators have known, this is the very worst; for, so far as they were concerned, creation itself has taken the benefit of the bankrupt-act. After all, it is a pity. Those mighty capitalists, who had just attained the wished-for wealth! Those shrewd men of traffic, who had devoted so many years to the most intricate and artificial of sciences, and had barely mastered it, when the universal bankruptcy was announced by peal of trumpet! Can they have been so incautious as to provide no currency of the country whither they have gone, nor any bills of exchange, or letters of credit, from the needy on earth to the cash-keepers of Heaven?

Adam and Eve enter a Bank. Start not, ye whose funds are treasured there! You will never need them now. Call not for the police! The stones of the street and the coin of the vaults are of equal value to this simple pair. Strange sight! They take up the bright gold in handfuls, and throw it sportively into the air, for the sake of seeing the glittering worthlessness descend again in a shower. They know not that each of those small yellow circles was once a magic spell, potent to sway men's hearts, and mystify their moral sense. Here let them pause in the investigation of the past. They have discovered the main-spring, the life, the very essence, of the system that had wrought itself into the vitals of mankind, and choked their original nature in its deadly gripe. Yet how powerless over these young inheritors of earth's hoarded wealth! And here, too, are huge packages of bank-notes, those talismanic slips of paper, which once had the efficacy to build up enchanted palaces, like exhalations, and work all kinds of perilous wonders, yet were themselves but the ghosts of money, the shadows of a shade. How like is this vault to a magician's cave, when the all-powerful wand is broken, and the visionary splendor vanished, and the floor strewn with fragments of shattered spells, and lifeless shapes once animated by demons!

"Everywhere, my dear Eve," observes Adam, "we find heaps of rubbish of one kind or another. Somebody, I am convinced, has taken pains to collect them—but for what purpose? Perhaps, hereafter, we shall be moved to do the like. Can that be our business in the world?"

"Oh, no, no, Adam!" answers Eve. "It would be better to sit down quietly and look upward to the sky."

They leave the Bank, and in good time; for had they tarried later, they would probably have encountered some gouty old goblin of a capitalist, whose soul could not long be anywhere, save in the vault with his treasure.

Next, they drop into a jeweller's shop. They are pleased with the glow of gems; and Adam twines a string of beautiful pearls around the head of Eve, and fastens his own mantle with a magnificent diamond brooch. Eve thanks him, and views herself with delight in the nearest looking-glass. Shortly afterward, observing a boquet of roses and other brilliant flowers in a vase of water, she flings away the inestimable pearls, and adorns herself with these lovelier gems of nature. They charm her with sentiment as well as beauty.

"Surely they are living beings," she remarks to Adam.

"I think so," replies Adam, "and they seem to be as little at home in the world as ourselves."

We must not attempt to follow every footstep of these investigators whom their Creator has commissioned to pass unconscious judgment upon the works and ways of the vanished race. By this time, being endowed with quick and accurate perceptions, they begin to understand the purpose of the many things around them. They conjecture, for instance, that the edifices of the city were erected, not by the immediate hand that made the world, but by beings somewhat similar to themselves, for shelter and convenience. But how will they explain the magnificence of one habitation, as compared with the squalid misery of another? Through what medium can the idea of servitude enter their minds? When will they comprehend the great and miserable fact,—the evidences of which appeal to their senses everywhere,—that one portion of earth's lost inhabitants was rolling in luxury, while the multitude was toiling for scanty food? A wretched change, indeed, must be wrought in their own hearts, ere they can conceive the primal decree of Love to have been so completely abrogated, that a brother should ever want what his brother had. When their intelligence shall have reached so far, Earth's new progeny will have little reason to exult over her old rejected one!

Their wanderings have now brought them into the suburbs of the city. They stand on a grassy brow of a hill, at the foot of a granite obelisk, which points its great finger upward, as if the human family had agreed, by a visible symbol of age-long endurance, to offer some high sacrifice of thanksgiving or supplication. The solemn height of the monument, its deep simplicity, and the absence of any vulgar and practical use, all strengthen its effect upon Adam and Eve, and lead them to interpret it by a purer sentiment than the builders thought of expressing.

"Eve, it is a visible prayer," observes Adam.

"And we will pray too," she replies.

Let us pardon these poor children of neither father nor mother, for so absurdly mistaking the purport of the memorial, which man founded and woman finished, on far-famed

Bunker Hill. The idea of war is not native to their souls. Nor have they sympathies for the brave defenders of liberty, since oppression is one of their unconjectured mysteries. Could they guess that the green sward on which they stand so peacefully, was once strewn with human corpses and purple with their blood, it would equally amaze them, that one generation of men should perpetrate such carnage, and that a subsequent generation should triumphantly commemorate it.

With a sense of delight, they now stroll across green fields and along the margin of a quiet river. Not to track them too closely, we next find the wanderers entering a Gothic edifice of grey stone, where the by-gone world has left whatever it deemed worthy of record, in the rich library of Harvard University.

No student ever yet enjoyed such solitude and silence as now broods within its deep alcoves. Little do the present visitors understand what opportunities are thrown away upon them. Yet Adam looks anxiously at the long rows of volumes, those storied heights of human lore, ascending one above another from floor to ceiling. He takes up a bulky folio. It opens in his hands, as if spontaneously to impart the spirit of its author to the yet unworn and untainted intellect of the fresh-created mortal. He stands poring over the regular columns of mystic characters, seemingly in studious mood; for the unintelligible thought upon the page has a mysterious relation to his mind, and makes itself felt, as if it were a burthen flung upon him. He is even painfully perplexed, and grasps vainly at he knows not what. Oh, Adam, it is too soon, too soon by at least five thousand years, to put on spectacles, and busy yourself in the alcoves of a library!

"What can this be?" he murmurs at last. "Eve, methinks nothing is so desirable as to find out the mystery of this big and heavy object with its thousand thin divisions. See! it stares me in the face, as if it were about to speak!"

Eve, by a feminine instinct, is dipping into a volume of fashionable poetry, the production of certainly the most fortunate of earthly bards, since his lay continues in vogue when all the great masters of the lyre have passed into oblivion. But let not his ghost be too exultant! The world's one lady tosses the book upon the floor, and laughs merrily at her husband's abstracted mien.

"My dear Adam," cries she, "you look pensive and dismal! Do fling down that stupid thing; for even if it should speak, it would not be worth attending to. Let us talk with one another, and with the sky, and the green earth, and its trees and flowers. They will teach us better knowledge than we can find here."

"Well, Eve, perhaps you are right," replies Adam, with a sort of sigh. "Still, I cannot help thinking that the interpretation of the riddles amid which we have been wandering all day long might here be discovered."

"It may be better not to seek the interpretation," persists Eve. "For my part, the air of this place does not suit me. If you love me, come away!"

She prevails, and rescues him from the mysterious perils of the library. Happy influence of woman! Had he lingered there long enough to obtain a clue to its treasures,—as was not impossible, his intellect being of human structure, indeed, but with an untransmitted vigor and acuteness,—had he then and there become a student, the annalist of our poor world would soon have recorded the downfall of a second Adam. The fatal apple of another Tree of Knowledge would have been eaten. All the perversions and sophistries, and false wisdom so aptly mimicking the true; all the narrow truth, so partial that it becomes more deceptive than falsehood; all the wrong principles and worse practice, the pernicious examples and mistaken rules of life; all the specious theories, which turn earth into cloud-land, and men into shadows; all the sad experience, which it took mankind so many ages to accumulate, and from which they never drew a moral for their future guidance—the whole heap of this disastrous lore would have tumbled at once upon Adam's head. There would have been nothing left for him, but to take up the already abortive experiment of life, where we had dropped it, and toil onward with it a little further.

But, blessed in his ignorance, he may still enjoy a new world in our worn-out one. Should he fall short of good, even as far as we did, he has at least the freedom—no worthless one—to make errors for himself. And his literature, when the progress of centuries shall create it, will be no interminably repeated echo of our own poetry, and reproduction of the images that were moulded by our great fathers of song and fiction, but a melody never yet heard on earth, and intellectual forms unbreathed upon by our conceptions. Therefore let the dust of ages gather upon the volumes of the library, and, in due season, the roof of the edifice crumble down upon the whole. When the second Adam's descendants shall have collected as much rubbish of their own, it will be time enough to dig into our ruins, and compare the literary advancement of two independent races.

But we are looking forward too far. It seems to be the vice of those who have a long past behind them. We will return to the new Adam and Eve, who, having no reminiscences, save dim and fleeting visions of a pre-existence, are content to live and be happy in the present.

The day is near its close, when these pilgrims, who derive their being from no dead progenitors, reach the cemetery of Mount Auburn. With light hearts—for earth and sky now gladden each other with beauty—they tread along the winding paths, among marble pillars, mimic temples, urns, obelisks, and sarcophagi, sometimes pausing to contemplate these fantasies of human growth, and sometimes to admire the flowers wherewith Nature converts decay to loveliness. Can Death, in the midst of his old triumphs, make them sensible that they have taken up the heavy burthen of mortality, which a whole species had thrown down? Dust kindred to their own has never lain in the grave. Will they then recognize, and so soon, that Time and the elements have an indefeasible claim upon their bodies? Not improbably, they may. There must have been shadows enough, even amid the primal sunshine of their existence, to suggest the thought of the soul's incongruity with its circumstances. They have already learned that something is to be thrown aside. The idea of Death is in them, or not far off. But were they to choose a symbol for him, it would be the Butterfly soaring upward, or the bright Angel beckoning them aloft, or the Child asleep, with soft dreams visible through her transparent purity.

Such a Child, in whitest marble, they have found among the monuments of Mount Auburn.

"Sweetest Eve," observes Adam, while hand in hand they contemplate this beautiful object, "yonder sun has left us, and the whole world is fading from our sight. Let us sleep, as this lovely little figure is sleeping. Our Father only knows, whether what outward things we have possessed to-day are to be snatched from us for ever. But should our earthly life be leaving us with the departing light, we need not doubt that another morn will find us somewhere beneath the smile of God. I feel that He has imparted the boon of existence, never to be resumed."

"And no matter where we exist," replies Eve, "for we shall always be together."

The Birth-mark

IN the latter part of the last century, there lived a man of science—an eminent proficient in every branch of natural philosophy—who, not long before our story opens, had made experience of a spiritual affinity, more attractive than any chemical one. He had left his laboratory to the care of an assistant, cleared his fine countenance from the furnace-smoke, washed the stain of acids from his fingers, and persuaded a beautiful woman to become his wife. In those days, when the comparatively recent discovery of electricity, and other kindred mysteries of nature, seemed to open paths into the region of miracle, it was not unusual for the love of science to rival the love of woman, in its depth and absorbing energy. The higher intellect, the imagination, the spirit, and even the heart, might all find their congenial aliment in pursuits which, as some of their ardent votaries believed, would ascend from one step of powerful intelligence to another, until the philosopher should lay his hand on the secret of creative force, and perhaps make new worlds for himself. We know not whether Aylmer possessed this degree of faith in man's ultimate control over nature. He had devoted himself, however, too unreservedly to scientific studies, ever to be weaned from them by any second passion. His love for his young wife might prove the stronger of the two; but it could only be by intertwining itself with his love of science, and uniting the strength of the latter to its own.

Such a union accordingly took place, and was attended with truly remarkable consequences, and a deeply impressive moral. One day, very soon after their marriage, Aylmer sat gazing at his wife, with a trouble in his countenance that grew stronger, until he spoke.

"Georgiana," said he, "has it never occurred to you that the mark upon your cheek might be removed?"

"No, indeed," said she, smiling; but perceiving the seriousness of his manner, she blushed deeply. "To tell you the truth, it has been so often called a charm, that I was simple enough to imagine it might be so."

"Ah, upon another face, perhaps it might," replied her husband. "But never on yours! No, dearest Georgiana, you came so nearly perfect from the hand of Nature, that this slightest possible defect—which we hesitate whether to term a defect or a beauty—shocks me, as being the visible mark of earthly imperfection."

"Shocks you, my husband!" cried Georgiana, deeply hurt; at first reddening with momentary anger, but then bursting into tears. "Then why did you take me from my mother's side? You cannot love what shocks you!"

To explain this conversation, it must be mentioned, that, in the centre of Georgiana's left cheek, there was a singular mark, deeply interwoven, as it were, with the texture and substance of her face. In the usual state of her complexion,—a healthy, though delicate bloom,—the mark wore a tint of deeper crimson, which imperfectly defined its shape amid the surrounding rosiness. When she blushed, it gradually became more indistinct, and finally vanished amid the triumphant rush of blood, that bathed the whole cheek with its brilliant glow. But, if any shifting emotion caused her to turn pale, there was the mark again, a crimson stain upon the snow, in what Aylmer sometimes deemed an almost fearful distinctness. Its shape bore not a little similarity to the human hand, though of the smallest pigmy size. Georgiana's lovers were wont to say, that some fairy, at her birth-hour, had laid her tiny hand upon the infant's cheek, and left this impress there, in token of the magic endowments that were to give her such sway over all hearts. Many a desperate swain would have risked life for the privilege of pressing his lips to the mysterious hand. It must not be concealed, however, that the impression wrought by this fairy sign-manual varied exceedingly, according to the difference of temperament in the beholders. Some fastidious persons—but they were exclusively of her own sex—affirmed that the Bloody Hand, as they chose to call it, quite destroyed the effect of Georgiana's beauty, and rendered her countenance even hideous. But it would be as reasonable to say, that one of those small blue stains, which sometimes occur in the purest statuary marble, would convert the Eve of Powers to a monster. Masculine observers, if the birth-mark did not heighten their admiration, contented themselves with wishing it away, that the world might possess one living specimen of ideal loveliness, without the semblance of a flaw. After his marriage—for he thought little or nothing of the matter before—Aylmer discovered that this was the case with himself.

Had she been less beautiful—if Envy's self could have found aught else to sneer at—he might have felt his affection heightened by the prettiness of this mimic hand, now vaguely portrayed, now lost, now stealing forth again, and glimmering to-and-fro with every pulse of emotion that throbbed within her heart. But, seeing her otherwise so perfect, he found this one defect grow more and more intolerable, with every moment of their united lives. It was the fatal flaw of humanity, which Nature, in one shape or another, stamps ineffaceably on all her productions, either to imply that they are temporary and finite, or that their perfection must be wrought by toil and pain. The Crimson Hand expressed the ineludible gripe, in which mortality clutches the highest and purest of earthly mould, degrading them into kindred with the lowest, and even with the very brutes, like whom their visible frames return to dust. In this manner, selecting it as the symbol of his wife's liability to sin, sorrow, decay, and death, Alymer's sombre imagination was not long in rendering the birth-mark a frightful object, causing him more trouble and horror than ever Georgiana's beauty, whether of soul or sense, had given him delight.

At all the seasons which should have been their happiest, he invariably, and without intending it—nay, in spite of a purpose to the contrary—reverted to this one disastrous topic. Trifling as it at first appeared, it so connected itself with innumerable trains of thought, and modes of feeling, that it became the central point of all. With the morning twilight, Aylmer opened his eyes upon his wife's face, and recognized the symbol of imperfection; and when they sat together at the evening hearth, his eyes wandered stealthily to her cheek, and beheld, flickering with the blaze of the wood fire, the spectral Hand that wrote mortality, where he would fain have worshipped. Georgiana soon learned to shudder at his gaze. It needed but a glance, with the peculiar expression that his face often wore, to change the roses of her cheek into a deathlike paleness, amid which the Crimson Hand was brought strongly out, like a bas-relief of ruby on the whitest marble.

Late, one night, when the lights were growing dim, so as hardly to betray the stain on the poor wife's cheek, she herself, for the first time, voluntarily took up the subject.

"Do you remember, my dear Aylmer," said she, with a feeble attempt at a smile—"have you any recollection of a dream, last night, about this odious Hand?"

"None!—none whatever!" replied Aylmer, starting; but then he added in a dry, cold tone, affected for the sake of concealing the real depth of his emotion:—"I might well dream of it; for before I fell asleep, it had taken a pretty firm hold of my fancy."

"And you did dream of it," continued Georgiana, hastily; for she dreaded lest a gush of tears should interrupt what she had to say—"A terrible dream! I wonder that you can forget it. Is it possible to forget this one expression?—'It is in her heart now—we must have it out!'—Reflect, my husband; for by all means I would have you recall that dream."

The mind is in a sad note, when Sleep, the all-involving, cannot confine her spectres within the dim region of her sway, but suffers them to break forth, affrighting this actual life with secrets that perchance belong to a deeper one. Aylmer now remembered his dream. He had fancied himself, with his servant Aminadab, attempting an operation for the removal of the birth-mark. But the deeper went the knife, the deeper sank the Hand, until at length its tiny grasp appeared to have caught hold of Georgiana's heart; whence, however, her husband was inexorably resolved to cut or wrench it away.

When the dream had shaped itself perfectly in his memory, Aylmer sat in his wife's presence with a guilty feeling. Truth often finds its way to the mind close-muffled in robes of sleep, and then speaks with uncompromising directness of matters in regard to which we practise an unconscious self-deception, during our waking moments. Until now, he had not been aware of the tyrannizing influence acquired by one idea over his mind, and of the lengths which he might find in his heart to go, for the sake of giving himself peace.

"Aylmer," resumed Georgiana, solemnly, "I know not what

may be the cost to both of us, to rid me of this fatal birth-mark. Perhaps its removal may cause cureless deformity. Or, it may be, the stain goes as deep as life itself. Again, do we know that there is a possibility, on any terms, of unclasping the firm gripe of this little Hand, which was laid upon me before I came into the world?"

"Dearest Georgiana, I have spent much thought upon the subject," hastily interrupted Aylmer—"I am convinced of the perfect practicability of its removal."

"If there be the remotest possibility of it," continued Georgiana, "let the attempt be made, at whatever risk. Danger is nothing to me; for life—while this hateful mark makes me the object of your horror and disgust—life is a burthen which I would fling down with joy. Either remove this dreadful Hand, or take my wretched life! You have deep science! All the world bears witness of it. You have achieved great wonders! Cannot you remove this little, little mark, which I cover with the tips of two small fingers? Is this beyond your power, for the sake of your own peace, and to save your poor wife from madness?"

"Noblest—dearest—tenderest wife!" cried Aylmer, raptur-ously. "Doubt not my power. I have already given this mat-ter the deepest thought—thought which might almost have enlightened me to create a being less perfect than yourself. Georgiana, you have led me deeper than ever into the heart of science. I feel myself fully competent to render this dear cheek as faultless as its fellow; and then, most beloved, what will be my triumph, when I shall have corrected what Nature left imperfect, in her fairest work! Even Pygmalion, when his sculptured woman assumed life, felt not greater ecstasy than mine will be."

"It is resolved, then," said Georgiana, faintly smiling,— "And, Aylmer, spare me not, though you should find the birth-mark take refuge in my heart at last."

Her husband tenderly kissed her cheek—her right cheek— not that which bore the impress of the Crimson Hand.

The next day, Aylmer apprized his wife of a plan that he had formed, whereby he might have opportunity for the in-tense thought and constant watchfulness, which the proposed operation would require; while Georgiana, likewise, would enjoy the perfect repose essential to its success. They were to seclude themselves in the extensive apartments occupied by Aylmer as a laboratory, and where, during his toilsome youth, he had made discoveries in the elemental powers of nature, that had roused the admiration of all the learned societies in Europe. Seated calmly in this laboratory, the pale philosopher had investigated the secrets of the highest cloud-region, and of the profoundest mines; he had satisfied himself of the causes that kindled and kept alive the fires of the volcano; and had explained the mystery of fountains, and how it is that they gush forth, some so bright and pure, and others with such rich medicinal virtues, from the dark bosom of the earth. Here, too, at an earlier period, he had studied the wonders of the human frame, and attempted to fathom the very process by which Nature assimilates all her precious influences from earth and air, and from the spiritual world, to create and foster Man, her masterpiece. The latter pursuit, however, Aylmer had long laid aside, in unwilling recognition of the truth, against which all seekers sooner or later stumble, that our great creative Mother, while she amuses us with apparently working in the broadest sunshine, is yet severely careful to keep her own secrets, and, in spite of her pretended openness, shows us nothing but results. She permits us indeed, to mar, but seldom to mend, and, like a jealous patentee, on no account to make. Now, however, Aylmer resumed these half-forgotten investigations; not, of course, with such hopes or wishes as first suggested them; but because they involved much physiological truth, and lay in the path of his proposed scheme for the treatment of Georgiana.

As he led her over the threshold of the laboratory, Georgiana was cold and tremulous. Aylmer looked cheerfully into her face, with intent to reassure her, but was so startled with the intense glow of the birth-mark upon the whiteness of her cheek, that he could not restrain a strong convulsive shudder. His wife fainted.

"Aminadab! Aminadab!" shouted Aylmer, stamping violently on the floor.

Forthwith, there issued from an inner apartment a man of low stature, but bulky frame, with shaggy hair hanging about his visage, which was grimed with the vapors of the furnace.

This personage had been Aylmer's under-worker during his whole scientific career, and was admirably fitted for that office by his great mechanical readiness, and the skill with which, while incapable of comprehending a single principle, he executed all the practical details of his master's experiments. With his vast strength, his shaggy hair, his smoky aspect, and the indescribable earthiness that incrusted him, he seemed to represent man's physical nature; while Aylmer's slender figure, and pale, intellectual face, were no less apt a type of the spiritual element.

"Throw open the door of the boudoir, Aminadab," said Aylmer, "and burn a pastille."

"Yes, master," answered Aminadab, looking intently at the lifeless form of Georgiana; and then he muttered to himself:—"If she were my wife, I'd never part with that birth-mark."

When Georgiana recovered consciousness, she found herself breathing an atmosphere of penetrating fragrance, the gentle potency of which had recalled her from her deathlike faintness. The scene around her looked like enchantment. Aylmer had converted those smoky, dingy, sombre rooms, where he had spent his brightest years in recondite pursuits, into a series of beautiful apartments, not unfit to be the secluded abode of a lovely woman. The walls were hung with gorgeous curtains, which imparted the combination of grandeur and grace, that no other species of adornment can achieve; and as they fell from the ceiling to the floor, their rich and ponderous folds, concealing all angles and straight lines, appeared to shut in the scene from infinite space. For aught Georgiana knew, it might be a pavilion among the clouds. And Aylmer, excluding the sunshine, which would have interfered with his chemical processes, had supplied its place with perfumed lamps, emitting flames of various hue, but all uniting in a soft, empurpled radiance. He now knelt by his wife's side, watching her earnestly, but without alarm; for he was confident in his science, and felt that he could draw a magic circle round her, within which no evil might intrude.

"Where am I?—Ah, I remember!" said Georgiana, faintly; and she placed her hand over her cheek, to hide the terrible mark from her husband's eyes.

"Fear not, dearest!" exclaimed he. "Do not shrink from me! Believe me, Georgiana, I even rejoice in this single imperfection, since it will be such rapture to remove it."

"Oh, spare me!" sadly replied his wife—"Pray do not look at it again. I never can forget that convulsive shudder."

In order to soothe Georgiana, and, as it were, to release her mind from the burthen of actual things, Aylmer now put in practice some of the light and playful secrets, which science had taught him among its profounder lore. Airy figures, absolutely bodiless ideas, and forms of unsubstantial beauty, came and danced before her, imprinting their momentary footsteps on beams of light. Though she had some indistinct idea of the method of these optical phenomena, still the illusion was almost perfect enough to warrant the belief, that her husband possessed sway over the spiritual world. Then again, when she felt a wish to look forth from her seclusion, immediately, as if her thoughts were answered, the procession of external existence flitted across a screen. The scenery and the figures of actual life were perfectly represented, but with that bewitching, yet indescribable difference, which always makes a picture, an image, or a shadow, so much more attractive than the original. When wearied of this, Aylmer bade her cast her eyes upon a vessel, containing a quantity of earth. She did so, with little interest at first, but was soon startled, to perceive the germ of a plant, shooting upward from the soil. Then came the slender stalk—the leaves gradually unfolded themselves—and amid them was a perfect and lovely flower.

"It is magical!" cried Georgiana, "I dare not touch it."

"Nay, pluck it," answered Aylmer, "pluck it, and inhale its brief perfume while you may. The flower will wither in a few moments, and leave nothing save its brown seed-vessels—but thence may be perpetuated a race as ephemeral as itself."

But Georgiana had no sooner touched the flower than the whole plant suffered a blight, its leaves turning coal-black, as if by the agency of fire.

"There was too powerful a stimulus," said Aylmer thoughtfully.

To make up for this abortive experiment, he proposed to take her portrait by a scientific process of his own invention. It was to be effected by rays of light striking upon a polished plate of metal. Georgiana assented—but, on looking at the result, was affrighted to find the features of the portrait blurred and indefinable; while the minute figure of a hand appeared where the cheek should have been. Aylmer snatched the metallic plate, and threw it into a jar of corrosive acid.

Soon, however, he forgot these mortifying failures. In the intervals of study and chemical experiment, he came to her, flushed and exhausted, but seemed invigorated by her presence, and spoke in glowing language of the resources of his art. He gave a history of the long dynasty of the Alchemists, who spent so many ages in quest of the universal solvent, by which the Golden Principle might be elicted from all things vile and base. Aylmer appeared to believe, that, by the plainest scientific logic, it was altogether within the limits of possibility to discover this long-sought medium; but, he added, a philosopher who should go deep enough to acquire the power, would attain too lofty a wisdom to stoop to the exercise of it. Not less singular were his opinions in regard to the Elixir Vitæ. He more than intimated, that it was his option to concoct a liquid that should prolong life for years—perhaps interminably—but that it would produce a discord in nature, which all the world, and chiefly the quaffer of the immortal nostrum, would find cause to curse.

"Aylmer, are you in earnest?" asked Georgiana, looking at him with amazement and fear; "it is terrible to possess such power, or even to dream of possessing it!"

"Oh, do not tremble, my love!" said her husband, "I would not wrong either you or myself by working such inharmonious effects upon our lives. But I would have you consider how trifling, in comparison, is the skill requisite to remove this little Hand."

At the mention of the birth-mark, Georgiana, as usual, shrank, as if a red-hot iron had touched her cheek.

Again Aylmer applied himself to his labors. She could hear his voice in the distant furnace-room, giving directions to Aminadab, whose harsh, uncouth, misshapen tones were audible in response, more like the grunt or growl of a brute than human speech. After hours of absence, Aylmer reappeared, and proposed that she should now examine his cabinet of chemical products, and natural treasures of the earth. Among the former he showed her a small vial, in which, he remarked, was contained a gentle yet most powerful fragrance, capable of impregnating all the breezes that blow across a kingdom. They were of inestimable value, the contents of that little vial; and, as he said so, he threw some of the perfume into the air, and filled the room with piercing and invigorating delight.

"And what is this?" asked Georgiana, pointing to a small crystal globe, containing a gold-colored liquid. "It is so beautiful to the eye, that I could imagine it the Elixir of Life."

"In one sense it is," replied Aylmer, "or rather the Elixir of Immortality. It is the most precious poison that ever was concocted in this world. By its aid, I could apportion the lifetime of any mortal at whom you might point your finger. The strength of the dose would determine whether he were to linger out years, or drop dead in the midst of a breath. No king, on his guarded throne, could keep his life, if I, in my private station, should deem that the welfare of millions justified me in depriving him of it."

"Why do you keep such a terrific drug?" inquired Georgiana in horror.

"Do not mistrust me, dearest!" said her husband, smiling; "its virtuous potency is yet greater than its harmful one. But, see! here is a powerful cosmetic. With a few drops of this, in a vase of water, freckles may be washed away as easily as the hands are cleansed. A stronger infusion would take the blood out of the cheek, and leave the rosiest beauty a pale ghost."

"Is it with this lotion that you intend to bathe my cheek?" asked Georgiana anxiously.

"Oh, no!" hastily replied her husband—"this is merely superficial. Your case demands a remedy that shall go deeper."

In his interviews with Georgiana, Aylmer generally made minute inquiries as to her sensations, and whether the confinement of the rooms, and the temperature of the atmosphere, agreed with her. These questions had such a particular drift, that Georgiana began to conjecture that she was already subjected to certain physical influences, either breathed in with the fragrant air, or taken with her food. She fancied, likewise—but it might be altogether fancy—that there was a stirring up of her system,—a strange indefinite sensation creeping through her veins, and tingling, half painfully, half pleasurably, at her heart. Still, whenever she dared to look into the mirror, there she beheld herself, pale as a white rose, and with the crimson birth-mark stamped upon her cheek. Not even Aylmer now hated it so much as she.

To dispel the tedium of the hours which her husband found it necessary to devote to the processes of combination and analysis, Georgiana turned over the volumes of his scientific library. In many dark old tomes, she met with chapters full of romance and poetry. They were the works of the philosophers of the middle ages, such as Albertus Magnus, Cornelius Agrippa, Paracelsus, and the famous friar who created the prophetic Brazen Head. All these antique naturalists stood in advance of their centuries, yet were imbued with some of their credulity, and therefore were believed, and perhaps imagined themselves, to have acquired from the investigation of nature a power above nature, and from physics a sway over the spiritual world. Hardly less curious and imaginative were the early volumes of the Transactions of the Royal Society, in which the members, knowing little of the limits of natural possibility, were continually recording wonders, or proposing methods whereby wonders might be wrought.

But, to Georgiana, the most engrossing volume was a large folio from her husband's own hand, in which he had recorded every experiment of his scientific career, with its original aim, the methods adopted for its development, and its final success or failure, with the circumstances to which either event was attributable. The book, in truth, was both the history and emblem of his ardent, ambitious, imaginative, yet practical and laborious, life. He handled physical details, as if there were nothing beyond them; yet spiritualized them all, and redeemed himself from materialism, by his strong and eager aspiration towards the infinite. In his grasp, the veriest clod of earth assumed a soul. Georgiana, as she read, reverenced Aylmer, and loved him more profoundly than ever, but with a less entire dependence on his judgment than heretofore. Much as he had accomplished, she could not but observe that his most splendid successes were almost invariably failures, if compared with the ideal at which he aimed. His brightest diamonds were the merest pebbles, and felt to be so by himself, in comparison with the inestimable gems which lay hidden beyond his reach. The volume, rich with achievements that had won renown for its author, was yet as melancholy a record as ever mortal hand had penned. It was the sad confession, and continual exemplification, of the short-comings of the composite man—the spirit burthened with clay and working in matter—and of the despair that assails the higher nature, at finding itself so miserably thwarted by the earthly part. Perhaps every man of genius, in whatever sphere, might recognize the image of his own experience in Aylmer's journal.

So deeply did these reflections affect Georgiana, that she laid her face upon the open volume, and burst into tears. In this situation she was found by her husband.

"It is dangerous to read in a sorcerer's books," said he, with a smile, though his countenance was uneasy and displeased. "Georgiana, there are pages in that volume, which I can scarcely glance over and keep my senses. Take heed lest it prove as detrimental to you!"

"It has made me worship you more than ever," said she.

"Ah! wait for this one success," rejoined he, "then worship me if you will. I shall deem myself hardly unworthy of it. But, come! I have sought you for the luxury of your voice. Sing to me, dearest!"

So she poured out the liquid music of her voice to quench the thirst of his spirit. He then took his leave, with a boyish exuberance of gaiety, assuring her that her seclusion would endure but a little longer, and that the result was already certain. Scarcely had he departed, when Georgiana felt irresistibly impelled to follow him. She had forgotten to inform Aylmer of a symptom, which, for two or three hours past, had begun to excite her attention. It was a sensation in the fatal birth-mark, not painful, but which induced a restlessness throughout her system. Hastening after her husband, she intruded, for the first time, into the laboratory.

The first thing that struck her eye was the furnace, that hot and feverish worker, with the intense glow of its fire, which, by the quantities of soot clustered above it, seemed to have been burning for ages. There was a distilling apparatus in full operation. Around the room were retorts, tubes, cylinders, crucibles, and other apparatus of chemical research. An electrical machine stood ready for immediate use. The atmosphere felt oppressively close, and was tainted with gaseous odors, which had been tormented forth by the processes of science. The severe and homely simplicity of the apartment, with its naked walls and brick pavement, looked strange, accustomed as Georgiana had become to the fantastic elegance of her boudoir. But what chiefly, indeed almost solely, drew her attention, was the aspect of Aylmer himself.

He was pale as death, anxious, and absorbed, and hung over the furnace as if it depended upon his utmost watchfulness whether the liquid, which it was distilling, should be the draught of immortal happiness or misery. How different from the sanguine and joyous mien that he had assumed for Georgiana's encouragement!

"Carefully now, Aminadab! Carefully, thou human machine! Carefully, thou man of clay!" muttered Aylmer, more to himself than his assistant. "Now, if there be a thought too much or too little, it is all over!"

"Hoh! hoh!" mumbled Aminadab—"look, master, look!"

Aylmer raised his eyes hastily, and at first reddened, then grew paler than ever, on beholding Georgiana. He rushed towards her, and seized her arm with a gripe that left the print of his fingers upon it.

"Why do you come hither? Have you no trust in your husband?" cried he impetuously. "Would you throw the blight of that fatal birth-mark over my labors? It is not well done. Go, prying woman, go!"

"Nay, Aylmer," said Georgiana, with the firmness of which she possessed no stinted endowment, "it is not you that have a right to complain. You mistrust your wife! You have concealed the anxiety with which you watch the development of this experiment. Think not so unworthily of me, my husband! Tell me all the risk we run; and fear not that I shall shrink, for my share in it is far less than your own!"

"No, no, Georgiana!" said Aylmer impatiently, "it must not be."

"I submit," replied she calmly. "And, Aylmer, I shall quaff whatever draught you bring me; but it will be on the same principle that would induce me to take a dose of poison, if offered by your hand."

"My noble wife," said Aylmer, deeply moved, "I knew not the height and depth of your nature, until now. Nothing shall be concealed. Know, then, that this Crimson Hand, superficial as it seems, has clutched its grasp into your being, with a strength of which I had no previous conception. I have already administered agents powerful enough to do aught except to change your entire physical system. Only one thing remains to be tried. If that fail us, we are ruined!"

"Why did you hesitate to tell me this?" asked she.

"Because, Georgiana," said Aylmer, in a low voice, "there is danger!"

"Danger? There is but one danger—that this horrible stigma shall be left upon my cheek!" cried Georgiana. "Remove it! remove it!—whatever be the cost—or we shall both go mad!"

"Heaven knows, your words are too true," said Aylmer, sadly. "And now, dearest, return to your boudoir. In a little while, all will be tested."

He conducted her back, and took leave of her with a solemn tenderness, which spoke far more than his words how much was now at stake. After his departure, Georgiana became wrapt in musings. She considered the character of Aylmer, and did it completer justice than at any previous moment. Her heart exulted, while it trembled, at his honorable love, so pure and lofty that it would accept nothing less than perfection, nor miserably make itself contented with an earthlier nature than he had dreamed of. She felt how much more precious was such a sentiment, than that meaner kind which would have borne with the imperfection for her sake, and have been guilty of treason to holy love, by degrading its perfect idea to the level of the actual. And, with her whole spirit, she prayed, that, for a single moment, she might satisfy his highest and deepest conception. Longer than one moment, she well knew, it could not be; for his spirit was ever on the march—ever ascending—and each instant required something that was beyond the scope of the instant before.

The sound of her husband's footsteps aroused her. He bore a crystal goblet, containing a liquor colorless as water, but bright enough to be the draught of immortality. Aylmer was pale; but it seemed rather the consequence of a highly wrought state of mind, and tension of spirit, than of fear or doubt.

"The concoction of the draught has been perfect," said he, in answer to Georgiana's look. "Unless all my science have deceived me, it cannot fail."

"Save on your account, my dearest Aylmer," observed his wife, "I might wish to put off this birth-mark of mortality by relinquishing mortality itself, in preference to any other mode. Life is but a sad possession to those who have attained precisely the degree of moral advancement at which I stand. Were I weaker and blinder, it might be happiness. Were I stronger, it might be endured hopefully. But, being what I find myself, methinks I am of all mortals the most fit to die."

"You are fit for heaven without tasting death!" replied her husband. "But why do we speak of dying? The draught cannot fail. Behold its effect upon this plant!"

On the window-seat there stood a geranium, diseased with yellow blotches, which had overspread all its leaves. Aylmer poured a small quantity of the liquid upon the soil in which it grew. In a little time, when the roots of the plant had taken up the moisture, the unsightly blotches began to be extinguished in a living verdure.

"There needed no proof," said Georgiana, quietly. "Give me the goblet. I joyfully stake all upon your word."

"Drink, then, thou lofty creature!" exclaimed Aylmer, with fervid admiration. "There is no taint of imperfection on thy spirit. Thy sensible frame, too, shall soon be all perfect!"

She quaffed the liquid, and returned the goblet to his hand.

"It is grateful," said she, with a placid smile. "Methinks it is like water from a heavenly fountain; for it contains I know not what of unobtrusive fragrance and deliciousness. It allays a feverish thirst, that had parched me for many days. Now, dearest, let me sleep. My earthly senses are closing over my spirit, like the leaves round the heart of a rose, at sunset."

She spoke the last words with a gentle reluctance, as if it required almost more energy than she could command to pronounce the faint and lingering syllables. Scarcely had they loitered through her lips, ere she was lost in slumber. Aylmer sat by her side, watching her aspect with the emotions proper to a man, the whole value of whose existence was involved in the process now to be tested. Mingled with this mood, however, was the philosophic investigation, characteristic of the man of science. Not the minutest symptom escaped him. A heightened flush of the cheek—a slight irregularity of breath—a quiver of the eyelid—a hardly perceptible tremor through the frame—such were the details which, as the moments passed, he wrote down in his folio volume. Intense thought had set its stamp upon every previous page of that volume; but the thoughts of years were all concentrated upon the last.

While thus employed, he failed not to gaze often at the fatal Hand, and not without a shudder. Yet once, by a strange and unaccountable impulse, he pressed it with his lips. His spirit recoiled, however, in the very act, and Georgiana, out of the midst of her deep sleep, moved uneasily and murmured, as if in remonstrance. Again, Aylmer resumed his watch. Nor was it without avail. The Crimson Hand, which at first had been strongly visible upon the marble paleness of Georgiana's cheek now grew more faintly outlined. She remained not less pale than ever; but the birth-mark, with every breath that came and went, lost somewhat of its former distinctness. Its presence had been awful; its departure was more awful still. Watch the stain of the rainbow fading out of the sky; and you will know how that mysterious symbol passed away.

"By Heaven, it is well nigh gone!" said Aylmer to himself, in almost irrepressible ecstasy. "I can scarcely trace it now. Success! Success! And now it is like the faintest rose-color. The slightest flush of blood across her cheek would overcome it. But she is so pale!"

He drew aside the window-curtain, and suffered the light of natural day to fall into the room, and rest upon her cheek. At the same time, he heard a gross, hoarse chuckle, which he had long known as his servant Aminadab's expression of delight.

"Ah, clod! Ah, earthly mass!" cried Aylmer, laughing in a

sort of frenzy. "You have served me well! Matter and Spirit—Earth and Heaven—have both done their part in this! Laugh, thing of senses! You have earned the right to laugh."

These exclamations broke Georgiana's sleep. She slowly unclosed her eyes, and gazed into the mirror, which her husband had arranged for that purpose. A faint smile flitted over her lips, when she recognized how barely perceptible was now that Crimson Hand, which had once blazed forth with such disastrous brilliancy as to scare away all their happiness. But then her eyes sought Aylmer's face, with a trouble and anxiety that he could by no means account for.

"My poor Aylmer!" murmured she.

"Poor? Nay, richest! Happiest! Most favored!" exclaimed he. "My peerless bride, it is successful! You are perfect!"

"My poor Aylmer!" she repeated, with a more than human tenderness. "You have aimed loftily!—you have done nobly! Do not repent, that, with so high and pure a feeling, you have rejected the best that earth could offer. Aylmer—dearest Aylmer—I am dying!"

Alas, it was too true! The fatal Hand had grappled with the mystery of life, and was the bond by which an angelic spirit kept itself in union with a mortal frame. As the last crimson tint of the birth-mark—that sole token of human imperfection—faded from her cheek, the parting breath of the now perfect woman passed into the atmosphere, and her soul, lingering a moment near her husband, took its heavenward flight. Then a hoarse, chuckling laugh was heard again! Thus ever does the gross Fatality of Earth exult in its invariable triumph over the immortal essence, which, in this dim sphere of half-development, demands the completeness of a higher state. Yet, had Aylmer reached a profounder wisdom, he need not thus have flung away the happiness, which would have woven his mortal life of the self-same texture with the celestial. The momentary circumstance was too strong for him; he failed to look beyond the shadowy scope of Time, and living once for all in Eternity, to find the perfect Future in the present.

Egotism;* or, The Bosom-Serpent

FROM THE UNPUBLISHED "ALLEGORIES OF THE HEART"

"HERE HE COMES!" shouted the boys along the street.— "Here comes the man with a snake in his bosom!"

This outcry, saluting Herkimer's ears, as he was about to enter the iron gate of the Elliston mansion, made him pause. It was not without a shudder that he found himself on the point of meeting his former acquaintance, whom he had known in the glory of youth, and whom now, after an interval of five years, he was to find the victim either of a diseased fancy, or a horrible physical misfortune.

"A snake in his bosom!" repeated the young sculptor to himself. "It must be he. No second man on earth has such a bosom-friend! And now, my poor Rosina, Heaven grant me wisdom to discharge my errand aright! Woman's faith must be strong indeed, since thine has not yet failed."

Thus musing, he took his stand at the entrance of the gate, and waited until the personage, so singularly announced, should make his appearance. After an instant or two, he beheld the figure of a lean man, of unwholesome look, with glittering eyes and long black hair, who seemed to imitate the motion of a snake; for, instead of walking straight forward with open front, he undulated along the pavement in a curved line. It may be too fanciful to say, that something, either in his moral or material aspect, suggested the idea that a miracle had been wrought, by transforming a serpent into a man; but so imperfectly, that the snaky nature was yet hidden, and scarcely hidden, under the mere outward guise of humanity. Herkimer remarked that his complexion had a greenish tinge over its sickly white, reminding him of a species of marble out of which he had once wrought a head of Envy, with her snaky locks.

The wretched being approached the gate, but, instead of

*The physical fact, to which it is here attempted to give a moral significa- tion, has been known to occur in more than one instance.

entering, stopt short, and fixed the glitter of his eye full upon the compassionate, yet steady countenance of the sculptor.

"It gnaws me! It gnaws me!" he exclaimed.

And then there was an audible hiss, but whether it came from the apparent lunatic's own lips, or was the real hiss of a serpent, might admit of discussion. At all events, it made Herkimer shudder to his heart's core.

"Do you know me, George Herkimer?" asked the snake-possessed.

Herkimer did know him. But it demanded all the intimate and practical acquaintance with the human face, acquired by modelling actual likenesses in clay, to recognize the features of Roderick Elliston in the visage that now met the sculptor's gaze. Yet it was he. It added nothing to the wonder, to reflect that the once brilliant young man had undergone this odious and fearful change, during the no more than five brief years of Herkimer's abode at Florence. The possibility of such a transformation being granted, it was as easy to conceive it effected in a moment as in an age. Inexpressibly shocked and startled, it was still the keenest pang, when Herkimer remembered that the fate of his cousin Rosina, the ideal of gentle womanhood, was indissolubly interwoven with that of a being whom Providence seemed to have unhumanized.

"Elliston! Roderick!" cried he, "I had heard of this; but my conception came far short of the truth. What has befallen you? Why do I find you thus?"

"Oh, 'tis a mere nothing! A snake! A snake! The commonest thing in the world. A snake in the bosom—that's all," answered Roderick Elliston. "But how is your own breast?" continued he, looking the sculptor in the eye, with the most acute and penetrating glance that it had ever been his fortune to encounter. "All pure and wholesome? No reptile there? By my faith and conscience, and by the devil within me, here is a wonder! A man without a serpent in his bosom!"

"Be calm, Elliston," whispered George Herkimer, laying his hand upon the shoulder of the snake-possessed. "I have crossed the ocean to meet you. Listen!—let us be private—I bring a message from Rosina!—from your wife!"

"It gnaws me! It gnaws me!" muttered Roderick.

With this exclamation, the most frequent in his mouth, the

unfortunate man clutched both hands upon his breast, as if an intolerable sting or torture impelled him to rend it open, and let out the living mischief, even were it intertwined with his own life. He then freed himself from Herkimer's grasp, by a subtle motion, and gliding through the gate, took refuge in his antiquated family residence. The sculptor did not pursue him. He saw that no available intercourse could be expected at such a moment, and was desirous, before another meeting, to inquire closely into the nature of Roderick's disease, and the circumstances that had reduced him to so lamentable a condition. He succeeded in obtaining the necessary information from an eminent medical gentleman.

Shortly after Elliston's separation from his wife—now nearly four years ago—his associates had observed a singular gloom spreading over his daily life, like those chill, grey mists that sometimes steal away the sunshine from a summer's morning. The symptoms caused them endless perplexity. They knew not whether ill health were robbing his spirits of elasticity; or whether a canker of the mind was gradually eating, as such cankers do, from his moral system into the physical frame, which is but the shadow of the former. They looked for the root of this trouble in his shattered schemes of domestic bliss—wilfully shattered by himself—but could not be satisfied of its existence there. Some thought that their once brilliant friend was in an incipient stage of insanity, of which his passionate impulses had perhaps been the forerunners; others prognosticated a general blight and gradual decline. From Roderick's own lips, they could learn nothing. More than once, it is true, he had been heard to say, clutching his hands convulsively upon his breast—"It gnaws me! It gnaws me!"—but, by different auditors, a great diversity of explanation was assigned to this ominous expression. What could it be, that gnawed the breast of Roderick Elliston? Was it sorrow? Was it merely the tooth of physical disease? Or, in his reckless course, often verging upon profligacy, if not plunging into its depths, had he been guilty of some deed, which made his bosom a prey to the deadlier fangs of remorse? There was plausible ground for each of these conjectures; but it must not be concealed that more than one elderly gentleman, the victim of good cheer and slothful habits, magisterially pronounced the secret of the whole matter to be Dyspepsia!

Meanwhile, Roderick seemed aware how generally he had become the subject of curiosity and conjecture, and, with a morbid repugnance to such notice, or to any notice whatsoever, estranged himself from all companionship. Not merely the eye of man was a horror to him; not merely the light of a friend's countenance; but even the blessed sunshine, likewise, which, in its universal beneficence, typifies the radiance of the Creator's face, expressing his love for all the creatures of his hand. The dusky twilight was now too transparent for Roderick Elliston; the blackest midnight was his chosen hour to steal abroad; and if ever he were seen, it was when the watchman's lantern gleamed upon his figure, gliding along the street, with his hands clutched upon his bosom, still muttering:—"It gnaws me! It gnaws me!" What could it be that gnawed him?

After a time, it became known that Elliston was in the habit of resorting to all the noted quacks that infested the city, or whom money would tempt to journey thither from a distance. By one of these persons, in the exultation of a supposed cure, it was proclaimed far and wide, by dint of handbills and little pamphlets on dingy paper, that a distinguished gentleman, Roderick Elliston, Esq., had been relieved of a SNAKE in his stomach! So here was the monstrous secret, ejected from its lurking-place into public view, in all its horrible deformity. The mystery was out; but not so the bosom-serpent. He, if it were anything but a delusion, still lay coiled in his living den. The empiric's cure had been a sham, the effect, it was supposed, of some stupefying drug, which more nearly caused the death of the patient than of the odious reptile that possessed him. When Roderick Elliston regained entire sensibility, it was to find his misfortune the town talk—the more than nine days' wonder and horror—while, at his bosom, he felt the sickening motion of a thing alive, and the gnawing of that restless fang, which seemed to gratify at once a physical appetite and a fiendish spite.

He summoned the old black servant, who had been bred up in his father's house, and was a middle-aged man while Roderick lay in his cradle.

"Scipio!" he began; and then paused, with his arms folded over his heart—"What do people say of me, Scipio?"

"Sir! my poor master! that you had a serpent in your bosom," answered the servant, with hesitation.

"And what else?" asked Roderick, with a ghastly look at the man.

"Nothing else, dear master," replied Scipio;—"only that the Doctor gave you a powder, and that the snake leapt out upon the floor."

"No, no!" muttered Roderick to himself, as he shook his head, and pressed his hands with a more convulsive force upon his breast,—"I feel him still. It gnaws me! It gnaws me!"

From this time, the miserable sufferer ceased to shun the world, but rather solicited and forced himself upon the notice of acquaintances and strangers. It was partly the result of desperation, on finding that the cavern of his own bosom had not proved deep and dark enough to hide the secret, even while it was so secure a fortress for the loathsome fiend that had crept into it. But still more, this craving for notoriety was a symptom of the intense morbidness which now pervaded his nature. All persons, chronically diseased, are egotists, whether the disease be of the mind or body; whether it be sin, sorrow, or merely the more tolerable calamity of some endless pain, or mischief among the cords of mortal life. Such individuals are made acutely conscious of a self, by the torture in which it dwells. Self, therefore, grows to be so prominent an object with them, that they cannot but present it to the face of every casual passer-by. There is a pleasure—perhaps the greatest of which the sufferer is susceptible—in displaying the wasted or ulcerated limb, or the cancer in the breast; and the fouler the crime, with so much the more difficulty does the perpetrator prevent it from thrusting up its snake-like head, to frighten the world; for it is that cancer, or that crime, which constitutes their respective individuality. Roderick Elliston, who, a little while before, had held himself so scornfully above the common lot of men, now paid full allegiance to this humiliating law. The snake in his bosom seemed the symbol of a monstrous egotism, to which everything was referred, and which he pampered, night and day, with a continual and exclusive sacrifice of devil-worship.

He soon exhibited what most people considered indubitable tokens of insanity. In some of his moods, strange to say, he prided and gloried himself on being marked out from the ordinary experience of mankind, by the possession of a double nature, and a life within a life. He appeared to imagine that the snake was a divinity—not celestial, it is true, but darkly infernal—and that he thence derived an eminence and a sanctity, horrid, indeed, yet more desirable than whatever ambition aims at. Thus he drew his misery around him like a regal mantle, and looked down triumphantly upon those whose vitals nourished no deadly monster. Oftener, however, his human nature asserted its empire over him, in the shape of a yearning for fellowship. It grew to be his custom to spend the whole day in wandering about the streets, aimlessly, unless it might be called an aim, to establish a species of brotherhood between himself and the world. With cankered ingenuity, he sought out his own disease in every breast. Whether insane or not, he showed so keen a perception of frailty, error, and vice, that many persons gave him credit for being possessed not merely with a serpent, but with an actual fiend, who imparted this evil faculty of recognizing whatever was ugliest in man's heart.

For instance, he met an individual, who, for thirty years, had cherished a hatred against his own brother. Roderick, amidst the throng of the street, laid his hand on this man's chest, and looking full into his forbidding face,

"How is the snake to-day?"—he inquired, with a mock expression of sympathy.

"The snake!" exclaimed the brother-hater—"What do you mean?"

"The snake! The snake! Does he gnaw you?" persisted Roderick. "Did you take counsel with him, this morning, when you should have been saying your prayers? Did he sting, when you thought of your brother's health, wealth, and good repute? Did he caper for joy, when you remembered the profligacy of his only son? And whether he stung, or whether he frolicked, did you feel his poison throughout your body and soul, converting everything to sourness and bitterness? That is the way of such serpents. I have learned the whole nature of them from my own!"

"Where is the police?" roared the object of Roderick's persecution, at the same time giving an instinctive clutch to his breast. "Why is this lunatic allowed to go at large?"

"Ha, ha!" chuckled Roderick, releasing his grasp of the man. — "His bosom-serpent has stung him then!"

Often, it pleased the unfortunate young man to vex people with a lighter satire, yet still characterized by somewhat of snake-like virulence. One day, he encountered an ambitious statesman, and gravely inquired after the welfare of his boa constrictor; for of that species, Roderick affirmed, this gentleman's serpent must needs be, since its appetite was enormous enough to devour the whole country and constitution. At another time, he stopped a close-fisted old fellow, of great wealth, but who skulked about the city, in the guise of a scare-crow, with a patched blue surtout, brown hat, and mouldy boots, scraping pence together, and picking up rusty nails. Pretending to look earnestly at this respectable person's stomach, Roderick assured him that his snake was a copperhead, and had been generated by the immense quantities of that base metal, with which he daily defiled his fingers. Again, he assaulted a man of rubicund visage, and told him that few bosom-serpents had more of the devil in them, than those that breed in the vats of a distillery. The next whom Roderick honored with his attention was a distinguished clergyman, who happened just then to be engaged in a theological controversy, where human wrath was more perceptible than divine inspiration.

"You have swallowed a snake, in a cup of sacramental wine," quoth he.

"Profane wretch!" exclaimed the divine; but nevertheless, his hand stole to his breast.

He met a person of sickly sensibility, who, on some early disappointment, had retired from the world, and thereafter held no intercourse with his fellow-men, but brooded sullenly or passionately over the irrevocable past. This man's very heart, if Roderick might be believed, had been changed into a serpent, which would finally torment both him and itself to death. Observing a married couple, whose domestic troubles were matter of notoriety, he condoled with both on having mutually taken a house-adder to their bosoms. To an envious author, who depreciated works which he could never equal, he said, that his snake was the slimiest and filthiest of all the reptile tribe, but was fortunately without a sting. A man of impure life, and a brazen face, asking Roderick if there were any serpent in his breast, he told him that there was, and of the same species that once tortured Don Rodrigo, the Goth. He took a fair young girl by the hand, and gazing sadly into her eyes, warned her that she cherished a serpent of the deadliest kind within her gentle breast; and the world found the truth of those ominous words, when, a few months afterwards, the poor girl died of love and shame. Two ladies, rivals in fashionable life, who tormented one another with a thousand little stings of womanish spite, were given to understand, that each of their hearts was a nest of diminutive snakes, which did quite as much mischief as one great one.

But nothing seemed to please Roderick better, than to lay hold of a person infected with jealousy, which he represented as an enormous green reptile, with an ice-cold length of body, and the sharpest sting of any snake save one.

"And what one is that?" asked a bystander, overhearing him.

It was a dark-browed man, who put the question; he had an evasive eye, which, in the course of a dozen years, had looked no mortal directly in the face. There was an ambiguity about this person's character—a stain upon his reputation— yet none could tell precisely of what nature; although the city-gossips, male and female, whispered the most atrocious surmises. Until a recent period, he had followed the sea, and was, in fact, the very ship-master whom George Herkimer had encountered, under such singular circumstances, in the Grecian Archipelago.

"What bosom-serpent has the sharpest sting?" repeated this man; but he put the question as if by a reluctant necessity, and grew pale while he was uttering it.

"Why need you ask?" replied Roderick, with a look of dark intelligence. "Look into your own breast! Hark, my serpent bestirs himself! He acknowledges the presence of a master-fiend!"

And then, as the bystanders afterwards affirmed, a hissing sound was heard, apparently in Roderick Elliston's breast. It was said, too, that an answering hiss came from the vitals of the shipmaster, as if a snake were actually lurking there, and had been aroused by the call of its brother-reptile. If there were in fact any such sound, it might have been caused by a malicious exercise of ventriloquism, on the part of Roderick.

Thus, making his own actual serpent—if a serpent there actually was in his bosom—the type of each man's fatal error, or hoarded sin, or unquiet conscience, and striking his sting so unremorsefully into the sorest spot, we may well imagine that Roderick became the pest of the city. Nobody could elude him; none could withstand him. He grappled with the ugliest truth that he could lay his hand on, and compelled his adversary to do the same. Strange spectacle in human life, where it is the instinctive effort of one and all to hide those sad realities, and leave them undisturbed beneath a heap of superficial topics, which constitute the materials of inter- course between man and man! It was not to be tolerated that Roderick Elliston should break through the tacit compact, by which the world has done its best to secure repose, without relinquishing evil. The victims of his malicious remarks, it is true, had brothers enough to keep them in countenance; for, by Roderick's theory, every mortal bosom harbored either a brood of small serpents, or one overgrown monster, that had devoured all the rest. Still, the city could not bear this new apostle. It was demanded by nearly all, and particularly by the most respectable inhabitants, that Roderick should no longer be permitted to violate the received rules of decorum, by ob- truding his own bosom-serpent to the public gaze, and drag- ging those of decent people from their lurking-places.

Accordingly, his relatives interfered, and placed him in a private asylum for the insane. When the news was noised abroad, it was observed that many persons walked the streets with freer countenances, and covered their breasts less care- fully with their hands.

His confinement, however, although it contributed not a little to the peace of the town, operated unfavorably upon Roderick himself. In solitude, his melancholy grew more black and sullen. He spent whole days—indeed, it was his sole occupation—in communing with the serpent. A conversation was sustained, in which as it seemed, the hidden monster bore a part, though unintelligibly to the listeners, and inaudible, except in a hiss. Singular as it may appear, the sufferer had now contracted a sort of affection for his tormentor; mingled, however, with the intensest loathing and horror. Nor were such discordant emotions incompatible; each, on the contrary, imparted strength and poignancy to its opposite. Horrible love—horrible antipathy—embracing one another in his bosom, and both concentrating themselves upon a being that had crept into his vitals, or been engendered there, and which was nourished with his food, and lived upon his life, and was as intimate with him as his own heart, and yet was the foulest of all created things! But not the less was it the true type of a morbid nature.

Sometimes, in his moments of rage and bitter hatred against the snake and himself, Roderick determined to be the death of him, even at the expense of his own life. Once he attempted it by starvation. But, while the wretched man was on the point of famishing, the monster seemed to feed upon his heart, and to thrive and wax gamesome, as if it were his sweetest and most congenial diet. Then he privily took a dose of active poison, imagining that it would not fail to kill either himself, or the devil that possessed him, or both together. Another mistake; for if Roderick had not yet been destroyed by his own poisoned heart, nor the snake by gnawing it, they had little to fear from arsenic or corrosive sublimate. Indeed, the venomous pest appeared to operate as an antidote against all other poisons. The physicians tried to suffocate the fiend with tobacco-smoke. He breathed it as freely as if it were his native atmosphere. Again, they drugged their patient with opium, and drenched him with intoxicating liquors, hoping that the snake might thus be reduced to stupor, and perhaps be ejected from the stomach. They succeeded in rendering Roderick insensible; but, placing their hands upon his breast, they were inexpressibly horror-stricken to feel the monster wriggling, twining, and darting to and fro, within his narrow limits, evidently enlivened by the opium or alcohol, and incited to unusual feats of activity. Thenceforth, they gave up all attempts at cure or palliation. The doomed sufferer submitted to his fate, resumed his former loathsome affection for the bosom-fiend, and spent whole miserable days before a looking glass, with his mouth wide open, watching, in hope and horror, to catch a glimpse of the snake's head, far down within his throat. It is supposed that he succeeded; for the attendants once heard a frenzied shout, and rushing into the room, found Roderick lifeless upon the floor.

He was kept but little longer under restraint. After minute investigation, the medical directors of the asylum decided that his mental disease did not amount to insanity, nor would warrant his confinement; especially as its influence upon his spirits was unfavorable, and might produce the evil which it was meant to remedy. His eccentricities were doubtless great—he had habitually violated many of the customs and prejudices of society; but the world was not, without surer ground, entitled to treat him as a madman. On this decision of such competent authority, Roderick was released, and had returned to his native city, the very day before his encounter with George Herkimer.

As soon as possible after learning these particulars, the sculptor, together with a sad and tremulous companion, sought Elliston at his own house. It was a large, sombre edifice of wood with pilasters and a balcony, and was divided from one of the principal streets by a terrace of three elevations, which was ascended by successive flights of stone steps. Some immense old elms almost concealed the front of the mansion. This spacious and once magnificent family-residence was built by a grandee of the race, early in the past century; at which epoch, land being of small comparative value, the garden and other grounds had formed quite an extensive domain. Although a portion of the ancestral heritage had been alienated, there was still a shadowy enclosure in the rear of the mansion, where a student, or a dreamer, or a man of stricken heart, might lie all day upon the grass, amid the solitude of murmuring boughs, and forget that a city had grown up around him.

Into this retirement, the sculptor and his companion were ushered by Scipio, the old black servant, whose wrinkled visage grew almost sunny with intelligence and joy, as he paid his humble greetings to one of the two visitors.

"Remain in the arbor," whispered the sculptor to the figure that leaned upon his arm, "you will know whether, and when, to make your appearance."

"God will teach me," was the reply. "May he support me too!"

Roderick was reclining on the margin of a fountain, which gushed into the fleckered sunshine with the same clear sparkle, and the same voice of airy quietude, as when trees of primeval growth flung their shadows across its bosom. How strange is the life of a fountain, born at every moment, yet of an age coeval with the rocks, and far surpassing the venerable antiquity of a forest!

"You are come! I have expected you," said Elliston, when he became aware of the sculptor's presence.

His manner was very different from that of the preceding day—quiet, courteous, and, as Herkimer thought, watchful both over his guest and himself. This unnatural restraint was almost the only trait that betokened anything amiss. He had just thrown a book upon the grass, where it lay half-opened, thus disclosing itself to be a natural history of the serpent-tribe, illustrated by life-like plates. Near it lay that bulky volume, the Ductor Dubitantium of Jeremy Taylor, full of cases of conscience, and in which most men, possessed of a conscience, may find something applicable to their purpose.

"You see," observed Elliston, pointing to the book of serpents, while a smile gleamed upon his lips, "I am making an effort to become better acquainted with my bosom-friend. But I find nothing satisfactory in this volume. If I mistake not, he will prove to be *sui generis,* and akin to no other reptile in creation."

"Whence came this strange calamity?" inquired the sculptor.

"My sable friend, Scipio, has a story," replied Roderick, "of a snake that had lurked in this fountain—pure and innocent as it looks—ever since it was known to the first settlers. This insinuating personage once crept into the vitals of my great-grandfather, and dwelt there many years, tormenting the old gentleman beyond mortal endurance. In short, it is a family peculiarity. But, to tell you the truth, I have no faith in this idea of the snake's being an heir-loom. He is my own snake, and no man's else."

"But what was his origin?" demanded Herkimer.

"Oh! there is poisonous stuff in any man's heart, sufficient to generate a brood of serpents," said Elliston, with a hollow laugh. "You should have heard my homilies to the good townspeople. Positively, I deem myself fortunate in having bred but a single serpent. You, however, have none in your bosom, and therefore, cannot sympathize with the rest of the world. It gnaws me! It gnaws me!"

With this exclamation, Roderick lost his self-control and threw himself upon the grass, testifying his agony by intricate writhings, in which Herkimer could not but fancy a resemblance to the motions of a snake. Then, likewise, was heard that frightful hiss, which often ran through the sufferer's speech, and crept between the words and syllables, without interrupting their succession.

"This is awful indeed!" exclaimed the sculptor—"an awful infliction, whether it be actual or imaginary! Tell me, Roderick Elliston, is there any remedy for this loathsome evil?"

"Yes, but an impossible one," muttered Roderick, as he lay wallowing with his face in the grass. "Could I, for one instant, forget myself, the serpent might not abide within me. It is my diseased self-contemplation that has engendered and nourished him!"

"Then forget yourself, my husband," said a gentle voice above him—"forget yourself in the idea of another!"

Rosina had emerged from the arbor, and was bending over him, with the shadow of his anguish reflected in her countenance, yet so mingled with hope and unselfish love, that all anguish seemed but an earthly shadow and a dream. She touched Roderick with her hand. A tremor shivered through his frame. At that moment, if report be trustworthy, the sculptor beheld a waving motion through the grass, and heard a tinkling sound, as if something had plunged into the fountain. Be the truth as it might, it is certain that Roderick Elliston sat up, like a man renewed, restored to his right mind, and rescued from the fiend, which had so miserably overcome him in the battle-field of his own breast.

"Rosina!" cried he, in broken and passionate tones, but with nothing of the wild wail that had haunted his voice so long. "Forgive! Forgive!"

Her happy tears bedewed his face.

"The punishment has been severe," observed the sculptor. "Even Justice might now forgive—how much more a woman's tenderness! Roderick Elliston, whether the serpent was a physical reptile, or whether the morbidness of your nature suggested that symbol to your fancy, the moral of the story is not the less true and strong. A tremendous Egotism—manifesting itself, in your case, in the form of jealousy—is as fearful a fiend as ever stole into the human heart. Can a breast, where it has dwelt so long, be purified?"

"Oh, yes!" said Rosina, with a heavenly smile. "The serpent was but a dark fantasy, and what it typified was as shadowy as itself. The past, dismal as it seems, shall fling no gloom upon the future. To give it its due importance, we must think of it but as an anecdote in our Eternity!"

The Procession of Life

LIFE figures itself to me as a festal or funereal procession. All of us have our places, and are to move onward under the direction of a Chief-Marshal. The grand difficulty results from the invariably mistaken principles on which the deputy-marshals seek to arrange this immense concourse of people, so much more numerous than those that train their interminable length through streets and highways in times of political excitement. Their scheme is ancient, far beyond the memory of man, or even the record of history, and has hitherto been very little modified by the innate sense of something wrong, and the dim perception of better methods, that have disquieted all the ages through which the procession has taken its march. Its members are classified by the merest external circumstances, and thus are more certain to be thrown out of their true positions, than if no principle of arrangement were attempted. In one part of the procession we see men of landed estate or moneyed capital, gravely keeping each other company, for the preposterous reason that they chance to have a similar standing in the tax-gatherer's book. Trades and professions march together with scarcely a more real bond of union. In this manner, it cannot be denied, people are disentangled from the mass, and separated into various classes according to certain apparent relations; all have some artificial badge, which the world, and themselves among the first, learn to consider as a genuine characteristic. Fixing our attention on such outside shows of similarity or difference, we lose sight of those realities by which nature, fortune, fate, or Providence, has constituted for every man a brotherhood, wherein it is one great office of human wisdom to classify him. When the mind has once accustomed itself to a proper arrangement of the Procession of Life, or a true classification of society, even though merely speculative, there is thenceforth a satisfaction which pretty well suffices for itself, without the aid of any actual reformation in the order of march.

For instance, assuming to myself the power of marshalling the aforesaid procession, I direct a trumpeter to send forth a

blast loud enough to be heard from hence to China; and a
herald, with world-pervading voice, to make proclamation for
a certain class of mortals to take their places. What shall be
their principle of union? After all, an external one, in comparison with many that might be found, yet far more real than
those which the world has selected for a similar purpose. Let
all who are afflicted with like physical diseases form themselves into ranks!

Our first attempt at classification is not very successful. It
may gratify the pride of aristocracy to reflect, that Disease,
more than any other circumstance of human life, pays due
observance to the distinctions which rank and wealth, and
poverty and lowliness, have established among mankind.
Some maladies are rich and precious, and only to be acquired
by the right of inheritance, or purchased with gold. Of this
kind is the gout, which serves as a bond of brotherhood to
the purple-visaged gentry, who obey the herald's voice, and
painfully hobble from all civilized regions of the globe to take
their post in the grand procession. In mercy to their toes, let
us hope that the march may not be long! The Dyspeptics,
too, are people of good standing in the world. For them the
earliest salmon is caught in our eastern rivers, and the shy
woodcock stains the dry leaves with his blood, in his remotest
haunts; and the turtle comes from the far Pacific islands to be
gobbled up in soup. They can afford to flavor all their dishes
with indolence, which, in spite of the general opinion, is a
sauce more exquisitely piquant than appetite won by exercise.
Apoplexy is another highly respectable disease. We will rank
together all who have the symptom of dizziness in the brain,
and, as fast as any drop by the way, supply their places with
new members of the board of aldermen.

On the other hand, here come whole tribes of people,
whose physical lives are but a deteriorated variety of life, and
themselves a meaner species of mankind; so sad an effect has
been wrought by the tainted breath of cities, scanty and unwholesome food, destructive modes of labor, and the lack of
those moral supports that might partially have counteracted
such bad influences. Behold here a train of house-painters, all
afflicted with a peculiar sort of colic. Next in place we will
marshal those workmen in cutlery, who have breathed a fatal

disorder into their lungs, with the impalpable dust of steel. Tailors and shoemakers, being sedentary men, will chiefly congregate into one part of the procession, and march under similar banners of disease; but among them we may observe here and there a sickly student, who has left his health between the leaves of classic volumes; and clerks, likewise, who have caught their deaths on high official stools; and men of genius, too, who have written sheet after sheet, with pens dipped in their heart's blood. These are a wretched, quaking, short-breathed set. But what is this crowd of pale-cheeked, slender girls, who disturb the ear with the multiplicity of their short, dry coughs? They are seamstresses, who have plied the daily and nightly needle in the service of master-tailors and close-fisted contractors, until now it is almost time for each to hem the borders of her own shroud. Consumption points their place in the procession. With their sad sisterhood are intermingled many youthful maidens, who have sickened in aristocratic mansions, and for whose aid science has unavailingly searched its volumes, and whom breathless love has watched. In our ranks the rich maiden and the poor seamstress may walk arm in arm. We might find innumerable other instances, where the bond of mutual disease—not to speak of nation-sweeping pestilences—embraces high and low, and makes the king a brother of the clown. But it is not hard to own that Disease is the natural aristocrat. Let him keep his state, and have his established orders of rank, and wear his royal mantle of the color of a fever-flush; and let the noble and wealthy boast their own physical infirmities, and display their symptoms as the badges of high station! All things considered, these are as proper subjects of human pride as any relations of human rank that men can fix upon.

Sound again, thou deep-breathed trumpeter! and herald, with thy voice of might, shout forth another summons, that shall reach the old baronial castles of Europe, and the rudest cabin of our western wilderness! What class is next to take its place in the procession of mortal life? Let it be those whom the gifts of intellect have united in a noble brotherhood!

Aye, this is a reality, before which the conventional distinctions of society melt away, like a vapor when we would grasp it with the hand. Were Byron now alive, and Burns, the first would come from his ancestral Abbey, flinging aside, although unwillingly, the inherited honors of a thousand years, to take the arm of the mighty peasant, who grew immortal while he stooped behind his plough. These are gone; but the hall, the farmer's fireside, the hut, perhaps the palace, the counting-room, the workshop, the village, the city, life's high places and low ones, may all produce their poets, whom a common temperament pervades like an electric sympathy. Peer or ploughman, we will muster them, pair by pair, and shoulder to shoulder. Even society, in its most artificial state, consents to this arrangement. These factory girls from Lowell shall mate themselves with the pride of drawing-rooms and literary circles—the bluebells in fashion's nose-gay, the Sapphos, and Montagues, and Nortons, of the age. Other modes of intellect bring together as strange companies. Silk-gowned professor of languages, give your arm to this sturdy blacksmith, and deem yourself honored by the conjunction, though you behold him grimy from the anvil. All varieties of human speech are like his mother tongue to this rare man. Indiscriminately, let those take their places, of whatever rank they come, who possess the kingly gifts to lead armies, or to sway a people,—Nature's generals, her lawgivers, her kings, —and with them, also, the deep philosophers, who think the thought in one generation that is to revolutionize society in the next. With the hereditary legislator, in whom eloquence is a far-descended attainment—a rich echo repeated by powerful voices, from Cicero downward—we will match some wondrous backwoodsman, who has caught a wild power of language from the breeze among his native forest boughs. But we may safely leave brethren and sisterhood to settle their own congenialities. Our ordinary distinctions become so trifling, so impalpable, so ridiculously visionary, in comparison with a classification founded on truth, that all talk about the matter is immediately a common-place.

Yet, the longer I reflect, the less am I satisfied with the idea of forming a separate class of mankind on the basis of high intellectual power. At best, it is but a higher development of innate gifts common to all. Perhaps, moreover, he, whose genius appears deepest and truest, excels his fellows in nothing save the knack of expression; he throws out, occasionally, a lucky hint at truths of which every human soul is profoundly, though unutterably, conscious. Therefore, though we suffer the brotherhood of intellect to march onward together, it may be doubted whether their peculiar relation will not begin to vanish, as soon as the procession shall have passed beyond the circle of this present world. But we do not classify for eternity.

And next, let the trumpet pour forth a funereal wail, and the herald's voice give breath, in one vast cry, to all the groans and grievous utterances that are audible throughout the earth. We appeal now to the sacred bond of sorrow, and summon the great multitude who labor under similar afflictions, to take their places in the march.

How many a heart, that would have been insensible to any other call, has responded to the doleful accents of that voice! It has gone far and wide, and high and low, and left scarcely a mortal roof unvisited. Indeed, the principle is only too universal for our purpose, and, unless we limit it, will quite break up our classification of mankind, and convert the whole procession into a funeral train. We will therefore be at some pains to discriminate. Here comes a lonely rich man; he has built a noble fabric for his dwelling-house, with a front of stately architecture, and marble floors, and doors of precious woods; the whole structure is as beautiful as a dream, and as substantial as the native rock. But the visionary shapes of a long posterity, for whose home this mansion was intended, have faded into nothingness, since the death of the founder's only son. The rich man gives a glance at his sable garb in one of the splendid mirrors of his drawing-room, and, descending a flight of lofty steps, instinctively offers his arm to yonder poverty-stricken widow, in the rusty black bonnet, and with a check-apron over her patched gown. The sailor-boy, who was her sole earthly stay, was washed overboard in a late tempest. This couple, from the palace and the alms-house, are but the types of thousands more, who represent the dark tragedy of life, and seldom quarrel for the upper parts. Grief is such a leveller, with its own dignity and its own humility, that the noble and the peasant, the beggar and the monarch, will waive their pretensions to external rank, without the officiousness of interference on our part. If pride—the influence of the world's false distinctions—remain in the heart, then sorrow lacks the earnestness which makes it holy and reverend. It loses its reality, and becomes a miserable shadow. On this ground, we have an opportunity to assign over multitudes who would willingly claim places here, to other parts of the procession. If the mourner have anything dearer than his grief, he must seek his true position elsewhere. There are so many unsubstantial sorrows, which the necessity of our mortal state begets on idleness, that an observer, casting aside sentiment, is sometimes led to question whether there be any real woe, except absolute physical suffering, and the loss of closest friends. A crowd, who exhibit what they deem to be broken hearts—and among them many love-lorn maids and bachelors, and men of disappointed ambition in arts, or politics, and the poor who were once rich, or who have sought to be rich in vain—the great majority of these may ask admittance into some other fraternity. There is no room here. Perhaps we may institute a separate class, where such unfortunates will naturally fall into the procession. Meanwhile let them stand aside, and patiently await their time.

If our trumpeter can borrow a note from the doomsday trumpet-blast, let him sound it now! The dread alarum should make the earth quake to its centre, for the herald is about to address mankind with a summons, to which even the purest mortal may be sensible of some faint responding echo in his breast. In many bosoms it will awaken a still, small voice, more terrible than its own reverberating uproar.

The hideous appeal has swept around the globe. Come, all ye guilty ones, and rank yourselves in accordance with the brotherhood of crime! This, indeed, is an awful summons. I almost tremble to look at the strange partnerships that begin to be formed, reluctantly, but by the invincible necessity of like to like, in this part of the procession. A forger from the state prison seizes the arm of a distinguished financier. How indignantly does the latter plead his fair reputation upon 'Change, and insist that his operations, by their magnificence of scope, were removed into quite another sphere of morality than those of his pitiful companion! But, let him cut the connection if he can. Here comes a murderer, with his clanking chains, and pairs himself—horrible to tell!—with as pure and

upright a man, in all observable respects, as ever partook of
the consecrated bread and wine. He is one of those, perchance the most hopeless of all sinners, who practise such an
exemplary system of outward duties, that even a deadly crime
may be hidden from their own sight and remembrance, under
this unreal frost-work. Yet he now finds his place. Why do
that pair of flaunting girls, with the pert, affected laugh, and
the sly leer at the bystanders, intrude themselves into the same
rank with yonder decorous matron, and that somewhat prud-
ish maiden? Surely, these poor creatures, born to vice, as their
sole and natural inheritance, can be no fit associates for
women who have been guarded round about by all the pro-
prieties of domestic life, and who could not err, unless they
first created the opportunity! Oh, no; it must be merely the
impertinence of those unblushing hussies; and we can only
wonder how such respectable ladies should have responded
to a summons that was not meant for them.

We shall make short work of this miserable class, each
member of which is entitled to grasp any other member's
hand, by that vile degradation wherein guilty error has buried
all alike. The foul fiend, to whom it properly belongs, must
relieve us of our loathsome task. Let the bond-servants of sin
pass on. But neither man nor woman, in whom good pre-
dominates, will smile or sneer, nor bid the Rogues' March be
played, in derision of their array. Feeling within their breasts
a shuddering sympathy, which at least gives token of the sin
that might have been, they will thank God for any place in
the grand procession of human existence, save among those
most wretched ones. Many, however, will be astonished at
the fatal impulse that drags them thitherward. Nothing is
more remarkable than the various deceptions by which guilt
conceals itself from the perpetrator's conscience, and oftenest,
perhaps, by the splendor of its garments. Statesmen, rulers,
generals, and all men who act over an extensive sphere, are
most liable to be deluded in this way; they commit wrong,
devastation, and murder, on so grand a scale, that it impresses
them as speculative rather than actual; but, in our procession,
we find them linked in detestable conjunction with the meanest criminals, whose deeds have the vulgarity of petty details.
Here, the effect of circumstance and accident is done away,

and a man finds his rank according to the spirit of his crime, in whatever shape it may have been developed.

We have called the Evil; now let us call the Good. The trumpet's brazen throat should pour heavenly music over the earth, and the herald's voice go forth with the sweetness of an angel's accents, as if to summon each upright man to his reward. But, how is this? Do none answer to the call? Not one: for the just, the pure, the true, and all who might most worthily obey it, shrink sadly back, as most conscious of error and imperfection. Then let the summons be to those whose pervading principle is Love. This classification will embrace all the truly good, and none in whose souls there exists not something that may expand itself into a heaven, both of well-doing and felicity.

The first that presents himself is a man of wealth, who has bequeathed the bulk of his property to a hospital; his ghost, methinks, would have a better right here than his living body. But here they come, the genuine benefactors of their race. Some have wandered about the earth, with pictures of bliss in their imagination, and with hearts that shrank sensitively from the idea of pain and woe, yet have studied all varieties of misery that human nature can endure. The prison, the insane asylum, the squalid chambers of the alms-house, the manufactory where the demon of machinery annihilates the human soul, and the cotton-field where God's image becomes a beast of burthen; to these, and every other scene where man wrongs or neglects his brother, the apostles of humanity have penetrated. This missionary, black with India's burning sunshine, shall give his arm to a pale-faced brother who has made himself familiar with the infected alleys and loathsome haunts of vice, in one of our own cities. The generous founder of a college shall be the partner of a maiden lady, of narrow substance, one of whose good deeds it has been, to gather a little school of orphan children. If the mighty merchant whose benefactions are reckoned by thousands of dollars, deem himself worthy, let him join the procession with her whose love has proved itself by watchings at the sick-bed, and all those lowly offices which bring her into actual contact with disease and wretchedness. And with those whose impulses have guided them to benevolent actions, we will rank others, to whom Providence has assigned a different tendency and different powers. Men who have spent their lives in generous and holy contemplation for the human race; those who, by a certain heavenliness of spirit, have purified the atmosphere around them, and thus supplied a medium in which good and high things may be projected and performed,—give to these a lofty place among the benefactors of mankind, although no deed, such as the world calls deeds, may be recorded of them. There are some individuals, of whom we cannot conceive it proper that they should apply their hands to any earthly instrument, or work out any definite act; and others, perhaps not less high, to whom it is an essential attribute to labor, in body as well as spirit, for the welfare of their brethren. Thus, if we find a spiritual sage, whose unseen, inestimable influence has exalted the moral standard of mankind, we will choose for his companion some poor laborer, who has wrought for love in the potatoe-field of a neighbor poorer than himself.

We have summoned this various multitude—and, to the credit of our nature, it is a large one—on the principle of Love. It is singular, nevertheless, to remark the shyness that exists among many members of the present class, all of whom we might expect to recognize one another by the free-masonry of mutual goodness, and to embrace like brethren, giving God thanks for such various specimens of human excellence. But it is far otherwise. Each sect surrounds its own righteousness with a hedge of thorns. It is difficult for the good Christian to acknowledge the good Pagan; almost impossible for the good Orthodox to grasp the hand of the good Unitarian, leaving to their Creator to settle the matters in dispute, and giving their mutual efforts strongly and trustingly to whatever right thing is too evident to be mistaken. Then again, though the heart be large, yet the mind is often of such moderate dimensions as to be exclusively filled up with one idea. When a good man has long devoted himself to a particular kind of beneficence—to one species of reform— he is apt to become narrowed into the limits of the path wherein he treads, and to fancy that there is no other good to be done on earth but that self-same good to which he has put his hand, and in the very mode that best suits his own conceptions. All else is worthless; his scheme must be wrought out by the united strength of the whole world's stock of love, or the world is no longer worthy of a position in the universe. Moreover, powerful Truth, being the rich grape-juice expressed from the vineyard of the ages, has an intoxicating quality, when imbibed by any save a powerful intellect, and often, as it were, impels the quaffer to quarrel in his cups. For such reasons, strange to say, it is harder to contrive a friendly arrangement of these brethren of love and righteousness, in the procession of life, than to unite even the wicked, who, indeed, are chained together by their crimes. The fact is too preposterous for tears, too lugubrious for laughter.

But, let good men push and elbow one another as they may, during their earthly march, all will be peace among them when the honorable array of their procession shall tread on heavenly ground. There they will doubtless find, that they have been working each for the other's cause, and that every well-delivered stroke, which, with an honest purpose, any mortal struck, even for a narrow object, was indeed stricken for the universal cause of good. Their own view may be bounded by country, creed, profession, the diversities of in-dividual character—but above them all is the breadth of Providence. How many, who have deemed themselves antag-onists, will smile hereafter, when they look back upon the world's wide harvest field, and perceive that, in unconscious brotherhood, they were helping to bind the self-same sheaf!

But, come! The sun is hastening westward, while the march of human life, that never paused before, is delayed by our attempt to re-arrange its order. It is desirable to find some comprehensive principle, that shall render our task easier by bringing thousands into the ranks, where hitherto we have brought one. Therefore let the trumpet, if possible, split its brazen throat with a louder note than ever, and the herald summon all mortals who, from whatever cause, have lost, or never found, their proper places in the world.

Obedient to this call, a great multitude come together, most of them with a listless gait, betokening weariness of soul, yet with a gleam of satisfaction in their faces, at the prospect of at length reaching those positions which, hitherto, they have vainly sought. But here will be another disappointment; for we can attempt no more than merely to associate, in one fraternity, all who are afflicted with the same vague trouble. Some great mistake in life is the chief condition of admittance into this class. Here are members of the learned professions, whom Providence endowed with special gifts for the plough, the forge, and the wheel-barrow, or for the routine of unintellectual business. We will assign to them, as partners in the march, those lowly laborers and handicraftsmen, who have pined, as with a dying thirst, after the unattainable fountains of knowledge. The latter have lost less than their companions; yet more, because they deem it infinite. Perchance the two species of unfortunates may comfort one another. Here are Quakers with the instinct of battle in them; and men of war who should have worn the broad-brim. Authors shall be ranked here, whom some freak of Nature, making game of her poor children, has imbued with the confidence of genius, and strong desire of fame, but has favored with no corresponding power; and others, whose lofty gifts were unaccompanied with the faculty of expression, or any of that earthly machinery, by which ethereal endowments must be manifested to mankind. All these, therefore, are melancholy laughing-stocks. Next, here are honest and well-intentioned persons, who, by a want of tact—by inaccurate perceptions—by a distorting imagination—have been kept continually at cross-purposes with the world, and bewildered upon the path of life. Let us see, if they can confine themselves within the line of our procession. In this class, likewise, we must assign places to those who have encountered that worst of ill-success, a higher fortune than their abilities could vindicate; writers, actors, painters, the pets of a day, but whose laurels wither unrenewed amid their hoary hair; politicians, whom some malicious contingency of affairs has thrust into conspicuous station, where, while the world stands gazing at them, the dreary consciousness of imbecility makes them curse their birth-hour. To such men, we give for a companion him whose rare talents, which perhaps require a revolution for their exercise, are buried in the tomb of sluggish circumstances.

Not far from these, we must find room for one whose suc-

cess has been of the wrong kind; the man who should have
lingered in the cloisters of a university, digging new treasures
out of the Herculaneum of antique lore, diffusing depth and
accuracy of literature throughout his country, and thus making for himself a great and quiet fame. But the outward tendencies around him have proved too powerful for his inward
nature, and have drawn him into the arena of political tumult,
there to contend at disadvantage, whether front to front, or
side by side, with the brawny giants of actual life. He becomes, it may be, a name for brawling parties to bandy to
and fro, a legislator of the Union; a governor of his native
State; an ambassador to the courts of kings or queens; and
the world may deem him a man of happy stars. But not so
the wise; and not so himself, when he looks through his experience, and sighs to miss that fitness, the one invaluable
touch, which makes all things true and real. So much
achieved, yet how abortive is his life! Whom shall we choose
for his companion? Some weak-framed blacksmith, perhaps,
whose delicacy of muscle might have suited a tailor's shop-
board better than the anvil.

Shall we bid the trumpet sound again? It is hardly worth
the while. There remain a few idle men of fortune, tavern and
grog-shop loungers, lazzaroni, old bachelors, decaying maidens, and people of crooked intellect or temper, all of whom
may find their like, or some tolerable approach to it, in the
plentiful diversity of our latter class. There, too, as his ultimate destiny, must we rank the dreamer, who, all his life
long, has cherished the idea that he was peculiarly apt for
something, but never could determine what it was; and there
the most unfortunate of men, whose purpose it has been to
enjoy life's pleasures, but to avoid a manful struggle with its
toil and sorrow. The remainder, if any, may connect themselves with whatever rank of the procession they shall find
best adapted to their tastes and consciences. The worst possible fate would be, to remain behind, shivering in the solitude of time, while all the world is on the move towards eternity. Our attempt to classify society is now complete. The
result may be anything but perfect; yet better—to give it the
very lowest praise—than the antique rule of the herald's office, or the modern one of the tax-gatherer, whereby the ac-

cidents and superficial attributes, with which the real nature of individuals has least to do, are acted upon as the deepest characteristics of mankind. Our task is done. Now let the grand procession move!

Yet pause awhile! We had forgotten the Chief-Marshal.

Hark! That world-wide swell of solemn music, with the clang of a mighty bell breaking forth through its regulated uproar, announces his approach. He comes; a severe, sedate, immovable, dark rider, waving his truncheon of universal sway, as he passes along the lengthened line, on the pale horse of the Revelations. It is Death! Who else could assume the guidance of a procession that comprehends all humanity? And if some, among these many millions, should deem themselves classed amiss, yet let them take to their hearts the comfortable truth, that Death levels us all into one great brotherhood, and that another state of being will surely rectify the wrong of this. Then breathe thy wail upon the earth's wailing wind, thou band of melancholy music, made up of every sigh that the human heart, unsatisfied, has uttered! There is yet triumph in thy tones. And now we move! Beggars in their rags, and Kings trailing the regal purple in the dust; the Warrior's gleaming helmet; the Priest in his sable robe; the hoary Grandsire, who has run life's circle and come back to childhood; the ruddy School-boy with his golden curls, frisking along the march; the Artisan's stuff-jacket; the Noble's star-decorated coat;—the whole presenting a motley spectacle, yet with a dusky grandeur brooding over it. Onward, onward, into that dimness where the lights of Time, which have blazed along the procession, are flickering in their sockets! And whither? We know not; and Death, hitherto our leader, deserts us by the wayside, as the tramp of our innumerable footsteps echoes beyond his sphere. He knows not, more than we, our destined goal. But God, who made us, knows, and will not leave us on our toilsome and doubtful march, either to wander in infinite uncertainty, or perish by the way!

The Celestial Rail-road

Not a great while ago, passing through the gate of dreams, I visited that region of the earth in which lies the famous city of Destruction. It interested me much to learn, that, by the public spirit of some of the inhabitants, a rail-road has recently been established between this populous and flourishing town, and the Celestial City. Having a little time upon my hands, I resolved to gratify a liberal curiosity by making a trip thither. Accordingly, one fine morning, after paying my bill at the hotel, and directing the porter to stow my luggage behind a coach, I took my seat in the vehicle, and set out for the Station House. It was my good fortune to enjoy the company of a gentleman—one Mr. Smooth-it-away—who, though he had never actually visited the Celestial City, yet seemed as well acquainted with its laws, customs, policy, and statistics, as with those of the city of Destruction, of which he was a native townsman. Being, moreover, a director of the rail-road corporation, and one of its largest stockholders, he had it in his power to give me all desirable information respecting that praiseworthy enterprise.

Our coach rattled out of the city, and, at a short distance from its outskirts, passed over a bridge, of elegant construction, but somewhat too slight, as I imagined, to sustain any considerable weight. On both sides lay an extensive quagmire, which could not have been more disagreeable either to sight or smell, had all the kennels of the earth emptied their pollution there.

"This," remarked Mr. Smooth-it-away, "is the famous Slough of Despond—a disgrace to all the neighborhood; and the greater, that it might so easily be converted into firm ground."

"I have understood," said I, "that efforts have been made for that purpose, from time immemorial. Bunyan mentions that above twenty thousand cart-loads of wholesome instructions had been thrown in here, without effect."

"Very probably!—and what effect could be anticipated from such unsubstantial stuff?" cried Mr. Smooth-it-away.

"You observe this convenient bridge. We obtained a sufficient foundation for it by throwing into the slough some editions of books of morality, volumes of French philosophy and German rationalism, tracts, sermons, and essays of modern clergymen, extracts from Plato, Confucius, and various Hindoo sages, together with a few ingenious commentaries upon texts of Scripture—all of which, by some scientific process, have been converted into a mass like granite. The whole bog might be filled up with similar matter."

It really seemed to me, however, that the bridge vibrated and heaved up and down, in a very formidable manner; and, spite of Mr. Smooth-it-away's testimony to the solidity of its foundation, I should be loth to cross it in a crowded omnibus; especially if each passenger were encumbered with as heavy luggage as that gentleman and myself. Nevertheless, we got over without accident, and soon found ourselves at the Station House. This very neat and spacious edifice is erected on the site of the little Wicket-Gate, which formerly, as all old pilgrims will recollect, stood directly across the highway, and, by its inconvenient narrowness, was a great obstruction to the traveller of liberal mind and expansive stomach. The reader of John Bunyan will be glad to know, that Christian's old friend Evangelist, who was accustomed to supply each pilgrim with a mystic roll, now presides at the ticket-office. Some malicious persons, it is true, deny the identity of this reputable character with the Evangelist of old times, and even pretend to bring competent evidence of an imposture. Without involving myself in the dispute, I shall merely observe, that, so far as my experience goes, the square pieces of pasteboard, now delivered to passengers, are much more convenient and useful along the road, than the antique roll of parchment. Whether they will be as readily received at the gate of the Celestial City, I decline giving an opinion.

A large number of passengers were already at the Station House, awaiting the departure of the cars. By the aspect and demeanor of these persons, it was easy to judge that the feelings of the community had undergone a very favorable change, in reference to the Celestial pilgrimage. It would have done Bunyan's heart good to see it. Instead of a lonely and ragged man, with a huge burthen on his back, plodding along sorrowfully on foot, while the whole city hooted after him, here were parties of the first gentry and most respectable people in the neighborhood, setting forth towards the Celestial City, as cheerfully as if the pilgrimage were merely a summer tour. Among the gentlemen were characters of deserved eminence, magistrates, politicians, and men of wealth, by whose example religion could not but be greatly recommended to their meaner brethren. In the ladies' apartment, too, I rejoiced to distinguish some of those flowers of fashionable society, who are so well fitted to adorn the most elevated circles of the Celestial City. There was much pleasant conversation about the news of the day, topics of business, politics, or the lighter matters of amusement; while religion, though indubitably the main thing at heart, was thrown tastefully into the back-ground. Even an infidel would have heard little or nothing to shock his sensibility.

One great convenience of the new method of going on pilgrimage, I must not forget to mention. Our enormous burthens, instead of being carried on our shoulders, as had been the custom of old, were all snugly deposited in the baggage-car, and, as I was assured, would be delivered to their respective owners, at the journey's end. Another thing, likewise, the benevolent reader will be delighted to understand. It may be remembered that there was an ancient feud between Prince Beelzebub and the keeper of the Wicket-Gate, and that the adherents of the former distinguished personage were accustomed to shoot deadly arrows at honest pilgrims, while knocking at the door. This dispute, much to the credit as well of the illustrious potentate above-mentioned as of the worthy and enlightened Directors of the rail-road, has been pacifically arranged, on the principle of mutual compromise. The prince's subjects are now pretty numerously employed about the Station House, some in taking care of the baggage, others in collecting fuel, feeding the engines, and such congenial occupations; and I can conscientiously affirm, that persons more attentive to their business, more willing to accommodate, or more generally agreeable to the passengers, are not to be found on any rail-road. Every good heart must surely exult at so satisfactory an arrangement of an immemorial difficulty.

"Where is Mr. Greatheart?" inquired I. "Beyond a doubt,

the Directors have engaged that famous old champion to be chief engineer on the rail-road?"

"Why, no," said Mr. Smooth-it-away, with a dry cough. "He was offered the situation of brake-man; but, to tell you the truth, our friend Greatheart has grown preposterously stiff and narrow, in his old age. He has so often guided pilgrims over the road, on foot, that he considers it a sin to travel in any other fashion. Besides, the old fellow had entered so heartily into the ancient feud with Prince Beelzebub, that he would have been perpetually at blows or ill language with some of the prince's subjects, and thus have embroiled us anew. So, on the whole, we were not sorry when honest Greatheart went off to the Celestial City in a huff, and left us at liberty to choose a more suitable and accommodating man. Yonder comes the engineer of the train. You will probably recognize him at once."

The engine at this moment took its station in advance of the cars, looking, I must confess, much more like a sort of mechanical demon, that would hurry us to the infernal regions, than a laudable contrivance for smoothing our way to the Celestial City. On its top sat a personage almost enveloped in smoke and flame, which—not to startle the reader—appeared to gush from his own mouth and stomach, as well as from the engine's brazen abdomen.

"Do my eyes deceive me?" cried I. "What on earth is this! A living creature?—if so, he is own brother to the engine that he rides upon!"

"Poh, poh; you are obtuse!" said Mr. Smooth-it-away, with a hearty laugh. "Don't you know Apollyon, Christian's old enemy, with whom he fought so fierce a battle in the Valley of Humiliation? He was the very fellow to manage the engine; and so we have reconciled him to the custom of going on pilgrimage, and engaged him as chief engineer."

"Bravo, bravo!" exclaimed I, with irrepressible enthusiasm. "This shows the liberality of the age; this proves, if anything can, that all musty prejudices are in a fair way to be obliterated. And how will Christian rejoice to hear of this happy transformation of his old antagonist! I promise myself great pleasure in informing him of it, when we reach the Celestial City."

The passengers being all comfortably seated, we now rattled away merrily, accomplishing a greater distance in ten minutes, than Christian probably trudged over, in a day. It was laughable, while we glanced along, as it were, at the tail of a thunder-bolt, to observe two dusty foot-travellers, in the old pilgrim-guise, with cockle-shell and staff, their mystic rolls of parchment in their hands, and their intolerable burthens on their backs. The preposterous obstinacy of these honest people, in persisting to groan and stumble along the difficult pathway, rather than take advantage of modern improvements, excited great mirth among our wiser brotherhood. We greeted the two pilgrims with many pleasant gibes and a roar of laughter; whereupon, they gazed at us with such woeful and absurdly compassionate visages, that our merriment grew tenfold more obstreperous. Apollyon, also, entered heartily into the fun, and contrived to flirt the smoke and flame of the engine, or of his own breath, into their faces, and enveloped them in an atmosphere of scalding steam. These little practical jokes amused us mightily, and doubtless afforded the pilgrims the gratification of considering themselves martyrs.

At some distance from the rail-road, Mr. Smooth-it-away pointed to a large, antique edifice, which, he observed, was a tavern of long standing, and had formerly been a noted stopping-place for pilgrims. In Bunyan's road-book, it is mentioned as the Interpreter's House.

"I have long had a curiosity to visit that old mansion," remarked I.

"It is not one of our stations, as you perceive," said my companion. "The keeper was violently opposed to the railroad; and well he might be, as the track left his house of entertainment on one side, and thus was pretty certain to deprive him of all his reputable customers. But the foot-path still passes his door; and the old gentleman now and then receives a call from some simple traveller, and entertains him with fare as old-fashioned as himself."

Before our talk on this subject came to a conclusion, we were rushing by the place where Christian's burthen fell from his shoulders, at the sight of the cross. This served as a theme for Mr. Smooth-it-away, Mr. Live-for-the-world, Mr. Hide-sin-in-the-heart, Mr. Scaly Conscience, and a knot of gentlemen from the town of Shun Repentance, to descant upon the inestimable advantages resulting from the safety of our baggage. Myself, and all the passengers indeed, joined with great unanimity in this view of the matter; for our burthens were rich in many things, esteemed precious throughout the world; and, especially, we each of us possessed a great variety of favorite Habits, which we trusted would not be out of fashion, even in the polite circles of the Celestial City. It would have been a sad spectacle, to see such an assortment of valuable articles tumbling into the sepulchre. Thus pleasantly conversing on the favorable circumstances of our position, as compared with those of past pilgrims, and of narrow-minded ones at the present day, we soon found ourselves at the foot of the Hill Difficulty. Through the very heart of this rocky mountain a tunnel has been constructed, of most admirable architecture, with a lofty arch and a spacious double-track; so that, unless the earth and rocks should chance to crumble down, it will remain an eternal monument of the builder's skill and enterprise. It is a great, though incidental advantage, that the materials from the heart of the Hill Difficulty have been employed in filling up the Valley of Humiliation; thus obviating the necessity of descending into that disagreeable and unwholesome hollow.

"This is a wonderful improvement, indeed," said I. "Yet I should have been glad of an opportunity to visit the Palace Beautiful, and be introduced to the charming young ladies— Miss Prudence, Miss Piety, Miss Charity, and the rest—who have the kindness to entertain pilgrims there."

"Young ladies!" cried Mr. Smooth-it-away, as soon as he could speak for laughing. "And charming young ladies! Why, my dear fellow, they are old maids, every soul of them— prim, starched, dry, and angular—and not one of them, I will venture to say, has altered so much as the fashion of her gown, since the days of Christian's pilgrimage."

"Ah, well," said I, much comforted. "Then I can very readily dispense with their acquaintance."

The respectable Apollyon was now putting on the steam at a prodigious rate, anxious, perhaps, to get rid of the unpleasant reminiscences, connected with the spot where he had so disastrously encountered Christian. Consulting Mr. Bunyan's road-book, I perceived that we must now be within a few miles of the Valley of the Shadow of Death; into which doleful region, at our present speed, we should plunge much sooner than seemed at all desirable. In truth, I expected nothing better than to find myself in the ditch on one side, or the quag on the other. But, on communicating my apprehensions to Mr. Smooth-it-away, he assured me that the difficulties of this passage, even in its worst condition, had been vastly exaggerated, and that, in its present state of improvement, I might consider myself as safe as on any rail-road in Christendom.

Even while we were speaking, the train shot into the entrance of this dreaded Valley. Though I plead guilty to some foolish palpitations of the heart, during our headlong rush over the causeway here constructed, yet it were unjust to withhold the highest encomiums on the boldness of its original conception, and the ingenuity of those who executed it. It was gratifying, likewise, to observe how much care had been taken to dispel the everlasting gloom, and supply the defect of cheerful sunshine; not a ray of which has ever penetrated among these awful shadows. For this purpose, the inflammable gas, which exudes plentifully from the soil, is collected by means of pipes, and thence communicated to a quadruple row of lamps, along the whole extent of the passage. Thus a radiance has been created, even out of the fiery and sulphurous curse that rests forever upon the Valley; a radiance hurtful, however, to the eyes, and somewhat bewildering, as I discovered by the changes which it wrought in the visages of my companions. In this respect, as compared with natural daylight, there is the same difference as between truth and falsehood; but, if the reader have ever travelled through the Dark Valley, he will have learned to be thankful for any light that he could get; if not from the sky above, then from the blasted soil beneath. Such was the red brilliancy of these lamps, that they appeared to build walls of fire on both sides of the track, between which we held our course at lightning-speed, while a reverberating thunder filled the Valley with its echoes. Had the engine run off the track—a catastrophe, it is whispered, by no means unprecedented—the bottomless pit, if there be any such place, would undoubtedly have received us. Just as some dismal fooleries of this nature had made my heart quake, there came a tremendous shriek, careering along the Valley as if a thousand devils had burst their lungs to utter it, but which proved to be merely the whistle of the engine, on arriving at a stopping-place.

The spot, where we had now paused, is the same that our friend Bunyan—a truthful man, but infected with many fantastic notions—has designated, in terms plainer than I like to repeat, as the mouth of the infernal region. This, however, must be a mistake; inasmuch as Mr. Smooth-it-away, while we remained in the smoky and lurid cavern, took occasion to prove that Tophet has not even a metaphorical existence. The place, he assured us, is no other than the crater of a half-extinct volcano, in which the Directors had caused forges to be set up, for the manufacture of rail-road iron. Hence, also, is obtained a plentiful supply of fuel for the use of the engines. Whoever had gazed into the dismal obscurity of the broad cavern-mouth, whence, ever and anon, darted huge tongues of dusky flame,—and had seen the strange, half-shaped monsters, and visions of faces horribly grotesque, into which the smoke seemed to wreathe itself,—and had heard the awful murmurs, and shrieks, and deep shuddering whispers of the blast, sometimes forming itself into words almost articulate,—he would have seized upon Mr. Smooth-it-away's comfortable explanation, as greedily as we did. The inhabitants of the cavern, moreover, were unlovely personages, dark, smoke-begrimed, generally deformed, with mis-shapen feet, and a glow of dusky redness in their eyes; as if their hearts had caught fire, and were blazing out of the upper windows. It struck me as a peculiarity, that the laborers at the forge, and those who brought fuel to the engine, when they began to draw short breath, positively emitted smoke from their mouth and nostrils.

Among the idlers about the train, most of whom were puffing cigars which they had lighted at the flame of the crater, I was perplexed to notice several, who, to my certain knowledge, had heretofore set forth by rail-road for the Celestial City. They looked dark, wild, and smoky, with a singular resemblance, indeed, to the native inhabitants; like whom, also, they had a disagreeable propensity to ill-natured gibes and sneers; the habit of which had wrought a settled contortion of their visages. Having been on speaking terms with one of these persons—an indolent, good-for-nothing fellow, who went by the name of Take-it-easy—I called to him, and inquired what was his business there.

"Did you not start," said I, "for the Celestial City?"

"That's a fact," said Mr. Take-it-easy, carelessly puffing some smoke into my eyes. "But I heard such bad accounts, that I never took pains to climb the hill, on which the city stands. No business doing—no fun going on—nothing to drink, and no smoking allowed—and a thrumming of church-music from morning till night! I would not stay in such a place, if they offered me house-room and living free."

"But, my good Mr. Take-it-easy," cried I, "why take up your residence here, of all places in the world?"

"Oh," said the loafer, with a grin, "it is very warm hereabouts, and I meet with plenty of old acquaintances, and altogether the place suits me. I hope to see you back again, some day soon. A pleasant journey to you!"

While he was speaking, the bell of the engine rang, and we dashed away, after dropping a few passengers, but receiving no new ones. Rattling onward through the Valley, we were dazzled with the fiercely gleaming gas-lamps, as before. But sometimes, in the dark of intense brightness, grim faces, that bore the aspect and expression of individual sins, or evil passions, seemed to thrust themselves through the veil of light, glaring upon us, and stretching forth a great dusky hand, as if to impede our progress. I almost thought, that they were my own sins that appalled me there. These were freaks of imagination—nothing more, certainly,—mere delusions, which I ought to be heartily ashamed of—but, all through the Dark Valley, I was tormented, and pestered, and dolefully bewildered, with the same kind of waking dreams. The mephitic gasses of that region intoxicate the brain. As the light of natural day, however, began to struggle with the glow of the lanterns, these vain imaginations lost their vividness, and finally vanished with the first ray of sunshine that greeted our escape from the Valley of the Shadow of Death. Ere we had gone a mile beyond it, I could well nigh have taken my oath that this whole gloomy passage was a dream.

At the end of the Valley, as John Bunyan mentions, is a

cavern, where, in his days, dwelt two cruel giants, Pope and Pagan, who had strewn the ground about their residence with the bones of slaughtered pilgrims. These vile old troglodytes are no longer there; but into their deserted cave another terrible giant has thrust himself, and makes it his business to seize upon honest travellers, and fat them for his table with plentiful meals of smoke, mist, moonshine, raw potatoes, and saw-dust. He is a German by birth, and is called Giant Transcendentalist; but as to his form, his features, his substance, and his nature generally, it is the chief peculiarity of this huge miscreant, that neither he for himself, nor anybody for him, has ever been able to describe them. As we rushed by the cavern's mouth, we caught a hasty glimpse of him, looking somewhat like an ill-proportioned figure, but considerably more like a heap of fog and duskiness. He shouted after us, but in so strange a phraseology that we knew not what he meant, nor whether to be encouraged or affrighted.

It was late in the day, when the train thundered into the ancient city of Vanity, where Vanity Fair is still at the height of prosperity, and exhibits an epitome of whatever is brilliant, gay, and fascinating, beneath the sun. As I purposed to make a considerable stay here, it gratified me to learn that there is no longer the want of harmony between the townspeople and pilgrims, which impelled the former to such lamentably mistaken measures as the persecution of Christian, and the fiery martyrdom of Faithful. On the contrary, as the new rail-road brings with it great trade and a constant influx of strangers, the lord of Vanity Fair is its chief patron, and the capitalists of the city are among the largest stockholders. Many passengers stop to take their pleasure or make their profit in the Fair, instead of going onward to the Celestial City. Indeed, such are the charms of the place, that people often affirm it to be the true and only heaven; stoutly contending that there is no other, that those who seek further are mere dreamers, and that, if the fabled brightness of the Celestial City lay but a bare mile beyond the gates of Vanity, they would not be fools enough to go thither. Without subscribing to these, perhaps, exaggerated encomiums, I can truly say, that my abode in the city was mainly agreeable, and my intercourse with the inhabitants productive of much amusement and instruction.

Being naturally of a serious turn, my attention was directed to the solid advantages derivable from a residence here, rather than to the effervescent pleasures, which are the grand object with too many visitants. The Christian reader, if he have had no accounts of the city later than Bunyan's time, will be surprised to hear that almost every street has its church, and that the reverend clergy are nowhere held in higher respect than at Vanity Fair. And well do they deserve such honorable estimation; for the maxims of wisdom and virtue, which fall from their lips, come from as deep a spiritual source, and tend to us as lofty a religious aim, as those of the sagest philosophers of old. In justification of this high praise, I need only mention the names of the Rev. Mr. Shallow-deep; the Rev. Mr. Stumble-at-truth; that fine old clerical character, the Rev. Mr. This-to-day, who expects shortly to resign his pulpit to the Rev. Mr. That-to-morrow; together with the Rev. Mr. Bewilderment; the Rev. Mr. Clog-the-spirit; and, last and greatest, the Rev. Dr. Wind-of-doctrine. The labors of these eminent divines are aided by those of innumerable lecturers, who diffuse such a various profundity, in all subjects of human or celestial science, that any man may acquire an omnigenous erudition, without the trouble of even learning to read. Thus literature is etherealized by assuming for its medium the human voice; and knowledge, depositing all its heavier particles—except, doubtless, its gold—becomes exhaled into a sound, which forthwith steals into the ever-open ear of the community. These ingenious methods constitute a sort of machinery, by which thought and study are done to every person's hand, without his putting himself to the slightest inconvenience in the matter. There is another species of machine for the wholesale manufacture of individual morality. This excellent result is effected by societies for all manner of virtuous purposes; with which a man has merely to connect himself, throwing, as it were, his quota of virtue into the common stock; and the president and directors will take care that the aggregate amount be well applied. All these, and other wonderful improvements in ethics, religion, and literature, being made plain to my comprehension by the ingenious Mr. Smooth-it-away, inspired me with a vast admiration of Vanity Fair.

It would fill a volume, in an age of pamphlets, were I to record all my observations in this great capital of human business and pleasure. There was an unlimited range of society— the powerful, the wise, the witty, and the famous in every walk of life—princes, presidents, poets, generals, artists, actors, and philanthropists, all making their own market at the Fair, and deeming no price too exorbitant for such commodities as hit their fancy. It was well worth one's while, even if he had no idea of buying or selling, to loiter through the bazaars, and observe the various sorts of traffic that were going forward.

Some of the purchasers, I thought, made very foolish bargains. For instance, a young man, having inherited a splendid fortune, laid out a considerable portion of it in the purchase of diseases, and finally spent all the rest for a heavy lot of repentance and a suit of rags. A very pretty girl bartered a heart as clear as crystal, and which seemed her most valuable possession, for another jewel of the same kind, but so worn and defaced as to be utterly worthless. In one shop, there were a great many crowns of laurel and myrtle, which soldiers, authors, statesmen, and various other people, pressed eagerly to buy; some purchased these paltry wreaths with their lives; others by a toilsome servitude of years; and many sacrificed whatever was most valuable, yet finally slunk away without the crown. There was a sort of stock or scrip, called Conscience, which seemed to be in great demand, and would purchase almost anything. Indeed, few rich commodities were to be obtained without paying a heavy sum in this particular stock; and a man's business was seldom very lucrative, unless he knew precisely when and how to throw his hoard of Conscience into the market. Yet, as this stock was the only thing of permanent value, whoever parted with it was sure to find himself a loser, in the long run. Several of the speculations were of a questionable character. Occasionally, a member of congress recruited his pocket by the sale of his constituents; and I was assured that public officers have often sold their country, at very moderate prices. Thousands sold their happiness for a whim. Gilded chains were in great demand, and purchased with almost any sacrifice. In truth, those who desired, according to the old adage, to sell anything valuable for a song, might find customers all over the Fair; and there were innumerable messes of pottage, piping hot, for such as chose to buy them with their birth-rights. A few articles, however, could not be found genuine, at Vanity Fair. If a customer wished to renew his stock of youth, the dealers offered him a set of false teeth and an auburn wig; if he demanded peace of mind, they recommended opium or a brandy-bottle.

Tracts of land and golden mansions, situate in the Celestial City, were often exchanged, at very disadvantageous rates, for a few years lease of small, dismal, inconvenient tenements in Vanity Fair. Prince Beelzebub himself took great interest in this sort of traffic, and sometimes condescended to meddle with smaller matters. I once had the pleasure to see him bargaining with a miser for his soul, which, after much ingenious skirmishing on both sides, his Highness succeeded in obtaining at about the value of sixpence. The prince remarked, with a smile, that he was a loser by the transaction.

Day after day, as I walked the streets of Vanity, my manners and deportment became more and more like those of the inhabitants. The place began to seem like home; the idea of pursuing my travels to the Celestial City was almost obliterated from my mind. I was reminded of it, however, by the sight of the same pair of simple pilgrims at whom we had laughed so heartily, when Apollyon puffed smoke and steam into their faces, at the commencement of our journey. There they stood amid the densest bustle of Vanity—the dealers offering them their purple, and fine linen, and jewels; the men of wit and humor gibing at them; a pair of buxom ladies ogling them askance; while the benevolent Mr. Smooth-it-away whispered some of his wisdom at their elbows, and pointed to a newly erected temple—but there were these worthy simpletons, making the scene look wild and monstrous, merely by their sturdy repudiation of all part in its business or pleasures.

One of them—his name was Stick-to-the-right—perceived in my face, I suppose, a species of sympathy and almost admiration, which, to my own great surprise, I could not help feeling for this pragmatic couple. It prompted him to address me.

"Sir," inquired he, with a sad, yet mild and kindly voice, "do you call yourself a pilgrim?"

"Yes," I replied. "My right to that appellation is indubitable. I am merely a sojourner here in Vanity Fair, being bound for the Celestial City, by the new rail-road."

"Alas, friend," rejoined Mr. Stick-to-the-right, "I do assure you, and beseech you to receive the truth of my words, that that whole concern is a bubble. You may travel on it all your life-time, were you to live thousands of years, and yet never get beyond the limits of Vanity Fair! Yea; though you should deem yourself entering the gates of the Blessed City, it will be nothing but a miserable delusion."

"The Lord of the Celestial City," began the other pilgrim, whose name was Mr. Foot-it-to-Heaven, "has refused, and will ever refuse, to grant an act of incorporation for this rail-road; and unless that be obtained, no passenger can ever hope to enter his dominions. Wherefore, every man, who buys a ticket, must lay his account with losing the purchase-money—which is the value of his own soul."

"Poh, nonsense!" said Mr. Smooth-it-away, taking my arm and leading me off. "These fellows ought to be indicted for a libel. If the law stood as it once did in Vanity Fair, we should see them grinning through the iron-bars of the prison-window."

This incident made a considerable impression on my mind, and contributed with other circumstances to indispose me to a permanent residence in the city of Vanity; although, of course, I was not simple enough to give up my original plan of gliding along easily and commodiously by rail-road. Still, I grew anxious to be gone. There was one strange thing that troubled me; amid the occupations or amusements of the Fair, nothing was more common than for a person—whether at a feast, theatre, or church, or trafficking for wealth and honors, or whatever he might be doing, and however unseasonable the interruption—suddenly to vanish like a soap-bubble, and be never more seen of his fellows; and so accustomed were the latter to such little accidents, that they went on with their business, as quietly as if nothing had happened. But it was otherwise with me.

Finally, after a pretty long residence at the Fair, I resumed my journey towards the Celestial City, still with Mr. Smooth-it-away at my side. At a short distance beyond the suburbs of

Vanity, we passed the ancient silver-mine, of which Demas was the first discoverer, and which is now wrought to great advantage, supplying nearly all the coined currency of the world. A little further onward was the spot where Lot's wife had stood for ages, under the semblance of a pillar of salt. Curious travellers have long since carried it away piece-meal. Had all regrets been punished as rigorously as this poor dame's were, my yearning for the relinquished delights of Vanity Fair might have produced a similar change in my own corporeal substance, and left me a warning to future pilgrims.

The next remarkable object was a large edifice, constructed of moss-grown stone, but in a modern and airy style of architecture. The engine came to a pause in its vicinity, with the usual tremendous shriek.

"This was formerly the castle of the redoubted giant Despair," observed Mr. Smooth-it-away; "but, since his death, Mr. Flimsy-faith has repaired it, and now keeps an excellent house of entertainment here. It is one of our stopping-places."

"It seems but slightly put together," remarked I, looking at the frail, yet ponderous walls. "I do not envy Mr. Flimsy-faith his habitation. Some day, it will thunder down upon the heads of the occupants."

"We shall escape, at all events," said Mr. Smooth-it-away; "for Apollyon is putting on the steam again."

The road now plunged into a gorge of the Delectable Mountains, and traversed the field where, in former ages, the blind men wandered and stumbled among the tombs. One of these ancient tomb-stones had been thrust across the track, by some malicious person, and gave the train of cars a terrible jolt. Far up the rugged side of a mountain, I perceived a rusty iron-door, half-overgrown with bushes and creeping-plants, but with smoke issuing from its crevices.

"Is that," inquired I, "the very door in the hill-side, which the shepherds assured Christian was a by-way to hell?"

"That was a joke on the part of the shepherds," said Mr. Smooth-it-away, with a smile. "It is neither more nor less than the door of a cavern, which they use as a smoke-house for the preparation of mutton-hams."

My recollections of the journey are now, for a little space, dim and confused; inasmuch as a singular drowsiness here overcame me, owing to the fact that we were passing over the Enchanted Ground, the air of which encourages a disposition to sleep. I awoke, however, as soon as we crossed the borders of the pleasant land of Beulah. All the passengers were rubbing their eyes, comparing watches, and congratulating one another on the prospect of arriving so seasonably at the journey's end. The sweet breezes of this happy clime came refreshingly to our nostrils; we beheld the glimmering gush of silver fountains, overhung by trees of beautiful foliage and delicious fruit, which were propagated by grafts from the Celestial gardens. Once, as we dashed onward like a hurricane, there was a flutter of wings, and the bright appearance of an angel in the air, speeding forth on some heavenly mission. The engine now announced the close vicinity of the final Station House, by one last and horrible scream, in which there seemed to be distinguishable every kind of wailing and woe, and bitter fierceness of wrath, all mixed up with the wild laughter of a devil or a madman. Throughout our journey, at every stopping-place, Apollyon had exercised his ingenuity in screwing the most abominable sounds out of the whistle of the steam-engine; but, in this closing effort, he outdid himself, and created an infernal uproar, which, besides disturbing the peaceful inhabitants of Beulah, must have sent its discord even through the Celestial gates.

While the horrid clamor was still ringing in our ears, we heard an exulting strain, as if a thousand instruments of music, with height, and depth, and sweetness in their tones, at once tender and triumphant, were struck in unison, to greet the approach of some illustrious hero, who had fought the good fight, and won a glorious victory, and was come to lay aside his battered arms forever. Looking to ascertain what might be the occasion of this glad harmony, I perceived, on alighting from the cars, that a multitude of Shining Ones had assembled on the other side of the river, to welcome two poor pilgrims, who were just emerging from its depths. They were the same whom Apollyon and ourselves had persecuted with taunts and gibes, and scalding steam, at the commencement of our journey; the same whose unworldly aspect and impressive words had stirred my conscience, amid the wild revellers of Vanity Fair.

"How amazingly well those men have got on!" cried I to Mr. Smooth-it-away. "I wish we were secure of as good a reception."

"Never fear—never fear!" answered my friend. "Come!—make haste!—the ferry-boat will be off directly; and in three minutes you will be on the other side of the river. No doubt you will find coaches to carry you up to the city-gates."

A steam ferry-boat, the last improvement on this important route, lay at the river-side, puffing, snorting, and emitting all those other disagreeable utterances, which betoken the departure to be immediate. I hurried on board, with the rest of the passengers, most of whom were in great perturbation; some bawling out for their baggage; some tearing their hair, and exclaiming that the boat would explode or sink; some already pale with the heaving of the stream; some gazing affrighted at the ugly aspect of the steersman; and some still dizzy with the slumberous influences of the Enchanted Ground. Looking back to the shore, I was amazed to discern Mr. Smooth-it-away, waving his hand in token of farewell!

"Don't you go over to the Celestial City?" exclaimed I.

"Oh, no!" answered he with a queer smile, and that same disagreeable contortion of visage, which I had remarked in the inhabitants of the Dark Valley. "Oh, no! I have come thus far only for the sake of your pleasant company. Good bye! We shall meet again."

And then did my excellent friend, Mr. Smooth-it-away, laugh outright; in the midst of which cachinnation, a smoke-wreath issued from his mouth and nostrils; while a twinkle of lurid flame darted out of either eye, proving indubitably that his heart was all of a red blaze. The impudent Fiend! To deny the existence of Tophet, when he felt its fiery tortures raging within his breast! I rushed to the side of the boat, intending to fling myself on shore. But the wheels, as they began their revolutions, threw a dash of spray over me, so cold—so deadly cold, with the chill that will never leave those waters, until Death be drowned in his own river—that, with a shiver and a heart-quake, I awoke. Thank Heaven, it was a Dream!

Buds and Bird-Voices

BALMY SPRING—weeks later than we expected, and months later than we longed for her—comes at last, to revive the moss on the roof and walls of our old mansion. She peeps brightly into my study-window, inviting me to throw it open, and create a summer atmosphere by the inter-mixture of her genial breath with the black and cheerless comfort of the stove. As the casement ascends, forth into infinite space fly the innumerable forms of thought or fancy, that have kept me company in the retirement of this little chamber, during the sluggish lapse of wintry weather;—visions, gay, grotesque, and sad; pictures of real life, tinted with nature's homely gray and russet; scenes in dream-land, bedizened with rainbow-hues, which faded before they were well laid on;—all these may vanish now, and leave me to mould a fresh existence out of sunshine. Brooding meditation may flap her dusky wings, and take her owl-like flight, blinking amid the cheerfulness of noontide. Such companions befit the season of frosted window-panes and crackling fires, when the blast howls through the black ash-trees of our avenue, and the drifting snow-storm chokes up the wood-paths, and fills the highway from stone-wall to stone-wall. In the spring and summer time, all sombre thoughts should follow the winter northward, with the sombre and thoughtful crows. The old, paradisiacal economy of life is again in force; we live, not to think, nor to labor, but for the simple end of being happy; nothing, for the present hour, is worthy of man's infinite capacity, save to imbibe the warm smile of heaven, and sympathize with the reviving earth.

The present Spring comes onward with fleeter footsteps, because winter lingered so unconscionably long, that, with her best diligence, she can hardly retrieve half the allotted period of her reign. It is but a fortnight, since I stood on the brink of our swollen river, and beheld the accumulated ice of four frozen months go down the stream. Except in streaks here and there upon the hill-sides, the whole visible universe was then covered with deep snow, the nethermost layer of which had been deposited by an early December storm. It was a sight to make the beholder torpid, in the impossibility of imagining how this vast white napkin was to be removed from the face of the corpselike world, in less time than had been required to spread it there. But who can estimate the power of gentle influences, whether amid material desolation, or the moral winter of man's heart! There have been no tempestuous rains,—even, no sultry days,—but a constant breath of southern winds, with now a day of kindly sunshine, and now a no less kindly mist, or a soft descent of showers, in which a smile and a blessing seemed to have been steeped. The snow has vanished as if by magic; whatever heaps may be hidden in the woods and deep gorges of the hills, only two solitary specks remain in the landscape; and those I shall almost regret to miss, when, to-morrow, I look for them in vain. Never before, methinks, has spring pressed so closely on the footsteps of retreating winter. Along the road-side, the green blades of grass have sprouted on the very edge of the snowdrifts. The pastures and mowing fields have not yet assumed a general aspect of verdure; but neither have they the cheerless brown tint which they wear in latter autumn, when vegetation has entirely ceased; there is now a faint shadow of life, gradually brightening into the warm reality. Some tracts, in a happy exposure—as, for instance, yonder south-western slope of an orchard, in front of that old red farm-house, beyond the river—such patches of land already wear a beautiful and tender green, to which no future luxuriance can add a charm. It looks unreal—a prophecy—a hope—a transitory effect of some peculiar light, which will vanish with the slightest motion of the eye. But beauty is never a delusion; not these verdant tracts, but the dark and barren landscape, all around them, is a shadow and a dream. Each moment wins some portion of the earth from death to life; a sudden gleam of verdure brightens along the sunny slope of a bank, which, an instant ago, was brown and bare. You look again, and behold an apparition of green grass!

The trees, in our orchard and elsewhere, are as yet naked, but already appear full of life and vegetable blood. It seems as if, by one magic touch, they might instantaneously burst into full foliage, and that the wind, which now sighs through their naked branches, might make sudden music amid innumerable leaves. The moss-grown willow-tree, which, for forty years past, has overshadowed these western windows, will be among the first to put on its green attire. There are some objections to the willow; it is not a dry and cleanly tree, and impresses the beholder with an association of sliminess. No trees, I think, are perfectly agreeable as companions, unless they have glossy leaves, dry bark, and a firm and hard texture of trunk and branches. But the willow is almost the earliest to gladden us with the promise and reality of beauty, in its graceful and delicate foliage, and the last to scatter its yellow, yet scarcely withered leaves, upon the ground. All through the winter, too, its yellow twigs give it a sunny aspect, which is not without a cheering influence, even in the grayest and gloomiest day. Beneath a clouded sky, it faithfully remembers the sunshine. Our old house would lose a charm, were the willow to be cut down, with its golden crown over the snow-covered roof, and its heap of summer verdure.

The lilac-shrubs, under my study-window, are likewise al-most in leaf; in two or three days more, I may put forth my hand, and pluck the topmost bough in its freshest green. These lilacs are very aged, and have lost the luxuriant foliage of their prime. The heart, or the judgment, or the moral sense, or the taste, is dissatisfied with their present aspect. Old age is not venerable, when it embodies itself in lilacs, rose-bushes, or any other ornamental shrubs; it seems as if such plants, as they grow only for beauty, ought to flourish in im-mortal youth, or, at least, to die before their sad decrepitude. Trees of beauty are trees of Paradise, and therefore not sub-ject to decay, by their original nature, though they have lost that precious birth-right by being transplanted to an earthly soil. There is a kind of ludicrous unfitness in the idea of a time-stricken and grandfatherly lilac-bush. The analogy holds good in human life. Persons who can only be graceful and ornamental—who can give the world nothing but flowers—should die young, and never be seen with gray hair and wrin-kles, any more than the flower-shrubs with mossy bark and blighted foliage, like the lilacs under my window. Not that beauty is worthy of less than immortality—no; the beautiful should live forever—and thence, perhaps, the sense of impro-priety, when we see it triumphed over by time. Apple-trees, on the other hand, grow old without reproach. Let them live as long as they may, and contort themselves into whatever perversity of shape they please, and deck their withered limbs with a springtime gaudiness of pink-blossoms, still they are respectable, even if they afford us only an apple or two in a season. Those few apples—or, at all events, the remembrance of apples in by-gone years—are the atonement which utilitarianism inexorably demands, for the privilege of lengthened life. Human flower-shrubs, if they will grow old on earth, should, beside their lovely blossoms, bear some kind of fruit that will satisfy earthly appetites; else neither man, nor the decorum of nature, will deem it fit that the moss should gather on them.

One of the first things that strike the attention, when the white sheet of winter is withdrawn, is the neglect and disarray that lay hidden beneath it. Nature is not cleanly, according to our prejudices. The beauty of preceding years, now transformed to brown and blighted deformity, obstructs the brightening loveliness of the present hour. Our avenue is strewn with the whole crop of Autumn's withered leaves. There are quantities of decayed branches, which one tempest after another has flung down, black and rotten; and one or two with the ruin of a bird's nest clinging to them. In the garden are the dried bean-vines, the brown stalks of the asparagus-bed, and melancholy old cabbages, which were frozen into the soil before their unthrifty cultivator could find time to gather them. How invariably, throughout all the forms of life, do we find these intermingled memorials of death! On the soil of thought, and in the garden of the heart, as well as in the sensual world, lie withered leaves; the ideas and feelings that we have done with. There is no wind strong enough to sweep them away; infinite space will not garner them from our sight. What mean they? Why may we not be permitted to live and enjoy, as if this were the first life, and our own the primal enjoyment, instead of treading always on these dry bones and mouldering relics, from the aged accumulation of which springs all that now appears so young and new? Sweet must have been the springtime of Eden, when no earlier year had strewn its decay upon the virgin turf, and no former experience had ripened into summer, and faded into autumn, in the hearts of its inhabitants! That was a world worth living in! Oh, thou murmurer, it is out of the very wantonness of such a life, that thou feignest these idle lamentations! There is no decay. Each human soul is the first created inhabitant of its own Eden. We dwell in an old moss-covered mansion, and tread in the worn footprints of the past, and have a gray clergyman's ghost for our daily and nightly inmate; yet all these outward circumstances are made less than visionary, by the renewing power of the spirit. Should the spirit ever lose this power—should the withered leaves, and the rotten branches, and the moss-covered house, and the ghost of the gray past, ever become its realities, and the verdure and the freshness merely its faint dream—then let it pray to be released from earth. It will need the air of heaven, to revive its pristine energies!

What an unlooked-for flight was this, from our shadowy avenue of black ash and Balm of Gilead trees, into the infinite! Now we have our feet again upon the turf. Nowhere does the grass spring up so industriously as in this homely yard, along the base of the stone-wall, and in the sheltered nooks of the buildings, and especially around the southern door-step; a locality which seems particularly favorable to its growth; for it is already tall enough to bend over, and wave in the wind. I observe that several weeds—and, most frequently, a plant that stains the fingers with its yellow juice—have survived, and retained their freshness and sap throughout the winter. One knows not how they have deserved such an exception from the common lot of their race. They are now the patriarchs of the departed year, and may preach mortality to the present generation of flowers and weeds.

Among the delights of spring, how is it possible to forget the birds! Even the crows were welcome, as the sable harbingers of a brighter and livelier race. They visited us before the snow was off, but seem mostly to have departed now, or else to have betaken themselves to remote depths of the woods, which they haunt all summer long. Many a time shall I disturb them there, and feel as if I had intruded among a company of silent worshippers, as they sit in sabbath-stillness among the tree-tops. Their voices, when they speak, are in admirable accordance with the tranquil solitude of a summer afternoon; and, resounding so far above the head, their loud clamor increases the religious quiet of the scene, instead of breaking it. A crow, however, has no real pretensions to religion, in spite of his gravity of mien and black attire; he is certainly a thief, and probably an infidel. The gulls are far more respectable, in a moral point of view. These denizens of sea-beaten rocks, and haunters of the lonely beach, come up our inland river, at this season, and soar high overhead, flapping their broad wings in the upper sunshine. They are among the most picturesque of birds, because they so float and rest upon the air as to become almost stationary parts of the landscape. The imagination has time to grow acquainted with them; they have not flitted away in a moment. You go up among the clouds, and greet these lofty-flighted gulls, and repose confidently with them upon the sustaining atmosphere. Ducks have their haunts along the solitary places of the river, and alight in flocks upon the broad bosom of the overflowed meadows. Their flight is too rapid and determined for the eye to catch enjoyment from it, although it never fails to stir up the heart with the sportsman's ineradicable instinct. They have now gone farther northward, but will visit us again in autumn.

The smaller birds—the little songsters of the woods, and those that haunt man's dwellings, and claim human friendship by building their nests under the sheltering eaves, or among the orchard-trees—these require a touch more delicate and a gentler heart than mine, to do them justice. Their outburst of melody is like a brook let loose from wintry chains. We need not deem it a too high and solemn word, to call it a hymn of praise to the Creator; since Nature, who pictures the reviving year in so many sights of beauty, has expressed the sentiment of renewed life in no other sound, save the notes of these blessed birds. Their musick, however, just now, seems to be incidental, and not the result of a set purpose. They are discussing the economy of life and love, and the site and architecture of their summer residences, and have no time to sit on a twig, and pour forth solemn hymns, or overtures, operas, symphonies, and waltzes. Anxious questions are asked; grave subjects are settled in quick and animated debate; and

only by occasional accident, as from pure ecstasy, does a rich
warble roll its tiny waves of golden sound through the atmosphere. Their little bodies are as busy as their voices; they
are in a constant flutter and restlessness. Even when two or
three retreat to a tree-top, to hold council, they wag their tails
and heads all the time, with the irrepressible activity of their
nature, which perhaps renders their brief span of life in reality
as long as the patriarchal age of sluggish man. The blackbirds, three species of which consort together, are the noisiest
of all our feathered citizens. Great companies of them—more
than the famous 'four-and-twenty,' whom Mother Goose has
immortalized—congregate in contiguous tree-tops, and vociferate with all the clamor and confusion of a turbulent political meeting. Politics, certainly, must be the occasion of such
tumultuous debates; but still—unlike all other politicians—
they instil melody into their individual utterances, and produce harmony as a general effect. Of all bird-voices, none are
more sweet and cheerful to my ear than those of swallows, in
the dim, sun-streaked interior of a lofty barn; they address the
heart with even a closer sympathy than Robin Redbreast.
But, indeed, all these winged people, that dwell in the vicinity
of homesteads, seem to partake of human nature, and possess
the germ, if not the developement, of immortal souls. We
hear them saying their melodious prayers, at morning's blush
and eventide. A little while ago, in the deep of night, there
came the lively thrill of a bird's note from a neighboring tree;
a real song, such as greets the purple dawn, or mingles with
the yellow sunshine. What could the little bird mean, by
pouring it forth at midnight? Probably the music gushed out
of the midst of a dream, in which he fancied himself in Paradise with his mate, but suddenly awoke on a cold, leafless
bough, with a New-England mist penetrating through his
feathers. That was a sad exchange of imagination for reality!

Insects are among the earliest births of spring. Multitudes,
of I know not what species, appeared long ago, on the surface
of the snow. Clouds of them, almost too minute for sight,
hover in a beam of sunshine, and vanish, as if annihilated,
when they pass into the shade. A musquitoe has already been
heard to sound the small horror of his bugle-horn. Wasps
infest the sunny windows of the house. A bee entered one of

the chambers, with a prophecy of flowers. Rare butterflies came before the snow was off, flaunting in the chill breeze, and looking forlorn and all astray, in spite of the magnificence of their dark velvet cloaks, with golden borders.

The fields and wood-paths have as yet few charms to entice the wanderer. In a walk, the other day, I found no violets nor anemones, nor anything in the likeness of a flower. It was worth while, however, to ascend our opposite hill, for the sake of gaining a general idea of the advance of spring, which I had hitherto been studying in its minute developements. The river lay around me in a semi-circle, overflowing all the meadows which give it its Indian name, and offering a noble breadth to sparkle in the sunbeams. Along the hither shore, a row of trees stood up to their knees in water; and afar off, on the surface of the stream, tufts of bushes thrust up their heads, as it were, to breathe. The most striking objects were great solitary trees, here and there, with a mile-wide waste of water all around them. The curtailment of the trunk, by its immersion in the river, quite destroys the fair proportions of the tree, and thus makes us sensible of a regularity and pro-priety in the usual forms of nature. The flood of the present season—though it never amounts to a freshet, on our quiet stream—has encroached farther upon the land than any pre-vious one, for at least a score of years. It has overflowed stone-fences, and even rendered a portion of the highway navigable for boats. The waters, however, are now gradually subsiding; islands become annexed to the mainland; and other islands emerge, like new creations, from the watery waste. The scene supplies an admirable image of the receding of the Nile—except that there is no deposit of black slime;— or of Noah's flood—only that there is a freshness and novelty in these recovered portions of the continent, which give the impression of a world just made, rather than of one so pol-luted that a deluge had been requisite to purify it. These up-springing islands are the greenest spots in the landscape; the first gleam of sunlight suffices to cover them with verdure.

Thank Providence for Spring! The earth—and man him-self, by sympathy with his birth-place—would be far other than we find them, if life toiled wearily onward, without this periodical infusion of the primal spirit. Will the world ever be so decayed, that spring may not renew its greenness? Can man be so dismally age-stricken, that no faintest sunshine of his youth may revisit him once a year? It is impossible. The moss on our time-worn mansion brightens into beauty; the good old pastor, who once dwelt here, renewed his prime, regained his boyhood, in the genial breezes of his ninetieth spring. Alas for the worn and heavy soul, if, whether in youth or age, it have outlived its privilege of springtime sprightliness! From such a soul, the world must hope no reformation of its evil—no sympathy with the lofty faith and gallant struggles of those who contend in its behalf. Summer works in the present, and thinks not of the future; Autumn is a rich conservative; Winter has utterly lost its faith, and clings tremulously to the remembrance of what has been; but Spring, with its outgushing life, is the true type of the Movement!

Little Daffydowndilly

DAFFYDOWNDILLY was so called, because in his nature he resembled a flower, and loved to do only what was beautiful and agreeable, and took no delight in labor of any kind. But, while Daffydowndilly was yet a little boy, his mother sent him away from his pleasant home, and put him under the care of a very strict schoolmaster, who went by the name of Mr. Toil. Those who knew him best, affirmed that this Mr. Toil was a very worthy character; and that he had done more good, both to children and grown people, than anybody else in the world. Certainly, he had lived long enough to do a great deal of good; for, if all stories be true, he had dwelt upon earth ever since Adam was driven from the garden of Eden.

Nevertheless, Mr. Toil had a severe and ugly countenance, especially for such little boys or big men as were inclined to be idle; his voice, too, was harsh; and all his ways and customs seemed very disagreeable to our friend Daffydowndilly. The whole day long, this terrible old schoolmaster sat at his desk overlooking the scholars, or stalked about the schoolroom, with a certain awful birch rod in his hand. Now came a rap over the shoulders of a boy, whom Mr. Toil had caught at play; now he punished a whole class, who were behindhand with their lessons; and, in short, unless a lad chose to attend quietly and constantly to his book, he had no chance of enjoying a quiet moment in the schoolroom of Mr. Toil.

"This will never do for me," thought Daffydowndilly.

Now the whole of Daffydowndilly's life had hitherto been passed with his dear mother, who had a much sweeter face than old Mr. Toil, and who had always been very indulgent to her little boy. No wonder, therefore, that poor Daffydowndilly found it a woful change, to be sent away from the good lady's side, and put under the care of this ugly-visaged schoolmaster, who never gave him any apples or cakes, and seemed to think that little boys were created only to get lessons.

"I can't bear it any longer," said Daffydowndilly to himself, when he had been at school about a week. "I'll run away, and try to find my dear mother; and, at any rate, I shall never find anybody half so disagreeable as this old Mr. Toil!"

So the very next morning, off started poor Daffydowndilly, and began his rambles about the world, with only some bread and cheese for his breakfast, and very little pocket-money to pay his expenses. But he had gone only a short distance, when he overtook a man of grave and sedate appearance, who was trudging at a moderate pace along the road.

"Good morning, my fine lad," said the stranger; and his voice seemed hard and severe, but yet had a sort of kindness in it; "whence do you come so early, and whither are you going?"

Little Daffydowndilly was a boy of very ingenuous disposition, and had never been known to tell a lie in all his life. Nor did he tell one now. He hesitated a moment or two, but finally confessed that he had run away from school, on account of his great dislike to Mr. Toil, and that he was resolved to find some place in the world, where he should never see or hear of the old schoolmaster again.

"Oh, very well, my little friend!" answered the stranger. "Then we will go together; for I, likewise, have had a good deal to do with Mr. Toil, and should be glad to find some place where he was never heard of."

Our friend Daffydowndilly would have been better pleased with a companion of his own age, with whom he might have gathered flowers along the road-side, or have chased butterflies, or have done many other things to make the journey pleasant. But he had wisdom enough to understand, that he should get along through the world much easier, by having a man of experience to show him the way. So he accepted the stranger's proposal, and they walked on very sociably together.

They had not gone far, when the road passed by a field where some haymakers were at work, mowing down the tall grass and spreading it out in the sun to dry. Daffydowndilly was delighted with the sweet smell of the new-mown grass, and thought how much pleasanter it must be to make hay in the sunshine, under the blue sky, and with the birds singing sweetly in the neighboring trees and bushes, than to be shut up in a dismal schoolroom, learning lessons all day long, and continually scolded by old Mr. Toil. But, in the midst of these thoughts, while he was stopping to peep over the stone-wall, he started back and caught hold of his companion's hand.

"Quick, quick!" cried he. "Let us run away, or he will catch us!"

"Who will catch us?" asked the stranger.

"Mr. Toil, the old schoolmaster!" answered Daffydowndilly. "Don't you see him amongst the haymakers?"

And Daffydowndilly pointed to an elderly man, who seemed to be the owner of the field and the employer of the men at work there. He had stripped off his coat and waistcoat, and was busily at work in his shirt-sleeves. The drops of sweat stood upon his brow; but he gave himself not a moment's rest, and kept crying out to the haymakers to make haste while the sun shone. Now, strange to say, the figure and features of this old farmer were precisely the same as those of old Mr. Toil, who, at that very moment, must have been just entering his schoolroom.

"Don't be afraid," said the stranger. "This is not Mr. Toil the schoolmaster, but a brother of his, who was bred a farmer; and people say he is the most disagreeable man of the two. However, he won't trouble you, unless you become a laborer on the farm."

Little Daffydowndilly believed what his companion said, but was very glad, nevertheless, when they were out of sight of the old farmer, who bore such a singular resemblance to Mr. Toil. The two travellers had gone but a little farther, when they came to a spot where some carpenters were erecting a house. Daffydowndilly begged his companion to stop a moment; for it was a very pretty sight to see how neatly the carpenters did their work, with their broad-axes, and saws, and planes, and hammers, shaping out the doors, and putting in the window-sashes, and nailing on the clapboards; and he could not help thinking that he should like to take a broad-axe, a saw, a plane, and a hammer, and build a little house for himself. And then, when he should have a house of his own, old Mr. Toil would never dare to molest him.

But, just while he was delighting himself with this idea,

little Daffydowndilly beheld something that made him catch hold of his companion's hand, all in a fright.

"Make haste! Quick, quick!" cried he. "There he is again!"

"Who?" asked the stranger, very quietly.

"Old Mr. Toil," said Daffydowndilly, trembling. "There! he that is overseeing the carpenters. 'Tis my old schoolmaster, as sure as I'm alive!"

The stranger cast his eyes where Daffydowndilly pointed his finger; and he saw an elderly man, with a carpenter's rule and compasses in his hand. This person went to and fro about the unfinished house, measuring pieces of timber, and marking out the work that was to be done, and continually exhorting the other carpenters to be diligent. And wherever he turned his hard and wrinkled visage the men seemed to feel that they had a taskmaster over them, and sawed, and hammered, and planed, as if for dear life.

"Oh, no! this is not Mr. Toil, the schoolmaster," said the stranger. "It is another brother of his, who follows the trade of carpenter!"

"I am very glad to hear it," quoth Daffydowndilly; "but, if you please, sir, I should like to get out of his way as soon as possible."

Then they went on a little farther, and soon heard the sound of a drum and fife. Daffydowndilly pricked up his ears at this, and besought his companion to hurry forward, that they might not miss seeing the soldiers. Accordingly, they made what haste they could, and soon met a company of soldiers, gaily dressed, with beautiful feathers in their caps, and bright muskets on their shoulders. In front, marched two drummers and two fifers, beating on their drums and playing on their fifes with might and main, and making such lively music, that little Daffydowndilly would gladly have followed them to the end of the world. And if he was only a soldier, then, he said to himself, old Mr. Toil would never venture to look him in the face.

"Quick step! Forward march!" shouted a gruff voice.

Little Daffydowndilly started, in great dismay; for this voice, which had spoken to the soldiers, sounded precisely the same as that which he had heard every day in Mr. Toil's schoolroom, out of Mr. Toil's own mouth. And, turning his eyes to the captain of the company, what should he see but the very image of old Mr. Toil himself, with a smart cap and feather on his head, a pair of gold epaulets on his shoulders, a laced coat on his back, a purple sash round his waist, and a long sword instead of a birch rod in his hand! And though he held his head so high, and strutted like a turkey-cock, still he looked quite as ugly and disagreeable as when he was hearing lessons in the schoolroom.

"This is certainly old Mr. Toil," said Daffydowndilly in a trembling voice. "Let us run away, for fear he should make us enlist in his company!"

"You are mistaken again, my little friend," replied the stranger, very composedly. "This is not Mr. Toil, the schoolmaster, but a brother of his, who has served in the army all his life. People say he's a terribly severe fellow; but you and I need not be afraid of him."

"Well, well," said little Daffydowndilly, "but, if you please, sir, I don't want to see the soldiers any more."

So the child and the stranger resumed their journey; and, by-and-by, they came to a house by the road-side, where a number of people were making merry. Young men and rosy-cheeked girls, with smiles on their faces, were dancing to the sound of a fiddle. It was the pleasantest sight that Daffydowndilly had yet met with, and it comforted him for all his disappointments.

"Oh, let us stop here," cried he to his companion; "for Mr. Toil will never dare to show his face where there is a fiddler, and where people are dancing and making merry. We shall be quite safe here!"

But these last words died away upon Daffydowndilly's tongue; for, happening to cast his eyes on the fiddler, whom should he behold again, but the likeness of Mr. Toil, holding a fiddle-bow instead of a birch rod, and flourishing it with as much ease and dexterity as if he had been a fiddler all his life! He had somewhat the air of a Frenchman, but still looked exactly like the old schoolmaster; and Daffydowndilly even fancied that he nodded and winked at him, and made signs for him to join in the dance.

"Oh, dear me!" whispered he, turning pale. "It seems as if

there was nobody but Mr. Toil in the world. Who could have thought of his playing on a fiddle!"

"This is not your old schoolmaster," observed the stranger, "but another brother of his, who was bred in France, where he learned the profession of a fiddler. He is ashamed of his family, and generally calls himself Monsieur le Plaisir; but his real name is Toil, and those who have known him best, think him still more disagreeable than his brothers."

"Pray let us go a little farther," said Daffydowndilly, "I don't like the looks of this fiddler at all."

Well; thus the stranger and little Daffydowndilly went wandering along the highway, and in shady lanes, and through pleasant villages; and whithersoever they went, behold! there was the image of old Mr. Toil. He stood like a scarecrow in the cornfields. If they entered a house, he sat in the parlor; if they peeped into the kitchen, he was there! He made himself at home in every cottage, and stole, under one disguise or another, into the most splendid mansions. Everywhere there was sure to be somebody wearing the likeness of Mr. Toil, and who, as the stranger affirmed, was one of the old schoolmaster's innumerable brethren.

Little Daffydowndilly was almost tired to death, when he perceived some people reclining lazily in a shady place, by the side of the road. The poor child entreated his companion that they might sit down there, and take some repose.

"Old Mr. Toil will never come here," said he; "for he hates to see people taking their ease."

But, even while he spoke, Daffydowndilly's eyes fell upon a person who seemed the laziest, and heaviest, and most torpid, of all those lazy, and heavy, and torpid people, who had lain down to sleep in the shade. Who should it be, again, but the very image of Mr. Toil!

"There is a large family of these Toils," remarked the stranger. "This is another of the old schoolmaster's brothers, who was bred in Italy, where he acquired very idle habits, and goes by the name of Signor Far Niente. He pretends to lead an easy life, but is really the most miserable fellow in the family."

"Oh, take me back!—take me back!" cried poor little Daffydowndilly, bursting into tears. "If there is nothing but Toil all the world over, I may just as well go back to the school-house!"

"Yonder it is—there is the schoolhouse!" said the stranger; for though he and little Daffydowndilly had taken a great many steps, they had travelled in a circle, instead of a straight line. "Come; we will go back to school together."

There was something in his companion's voice that little Daffydowndilly now remembered; and it is strange that he had not remembered it sooner. Looking up into his face, be-hold! there again was the likeness of old Mr. Toil; so that the poor child had been in company with Toil all day, even while he was doing his best to run away from him. Some people to whom I have told little Daffydowndilly's story, are of opinion that old Mr. Toil was a magician, and possessed the power of multiplying himself into as many shapes as he saw fit.

Be this as it may, little Daffydowndilly had learned a good lesson, and from that time forward was diligent at his task, because he knew that diligence is not a whit more toilsome than sport or idleness. And when he became better ac-quainted with Mr. Toil, he began to think that his ways were not so very disagreeable, and that the old schoolmaster's smile of approbation made his face almost as pleasant as even that of Daffydowndilly's mother.

Fire-Worship

IT is a great revolution in social and domestic life—and no less so in the life of the secluded student—this almost universal exchange of the open fire-place for the cheerless and ungenial stove. On such a morning as now lowers around our old grey parsonage, I miss the bright face of my ancient friend, who was wont to dance upon the hearth, and play the part of a more familiar sunshine. It is sad to turn from the clouded sky and sombre landscape—from yonder hill, with its crown of rusty, black pines, the foliage of which is so dismal in the absence of the sun; that bleak pasture-land, and the broken surface of the potato field, with the brown clods partly concealed by the snow-fall of last night; the swollen and sluggish river, with ice-encrusted borders, dragging its blueish grey stream along the verge of our orchard, like a snake half torpid with the cold—it is sad to turn from an outward scene of so little comfort, and find the same sullen influences brooding within the precincts of my study. Where is that brilliant guest—that quick and subtle spirit whom Prometheus lured from Heaven to civilize mankind, and cheer them in their wintry desolation—that comfortable inmate, whose smile, during eight months of the year, was our sufficient consolation for summer's lingering advance and early flight? Alas! blindly inhospitable, grudging the food that kept him cheery and mercurial, we have thrust him into an iron prison, and compel him to smoulder away his life on a daily pittance which once would have been too scanty for his breakfast! Without a metaphor, we now make our fire in an air-tight stove, and supply it with some half-a-dozen sticks of wood between dawn and nightfall.

I never shall be reconciled to this enormity. Truly may it be said, that the world looks darker for it. In one way or another, here and there, and all around us, the inventions of mankind are fast blotting the picturesque, the poetic, and the beautiful out of human life. The domestic fire was a type of all these attributes, and seemed to bring might and majesty, and wild Nature, and a spiritual essence, into our inmost home, and yet to dwell with us in such friendliness, that its mysteries and marvels excited no dismay. The same mild companion, that smiled so placidly in our faces, was he that comes roaring out of Ætna, and rushes madly up the sky, like a fiend breaking loose from torment, and fighting for a place among the upper angels. He it is, too, that leaps from cloud to cloud amid the crashing thunder-storm. It was he whom the Gheber worshipped, with no unnatural idolatry; and it was he who devoured London and Moscow, and many another famous city, and who loves to riot through our own dark forests, and sweep across our prairies, and to whose ravenous maw, it is said, the universe shall one day be given as a final feast. Meanwhile he is the great artizan and laborer by whose aid men are enabled to build a world within a world, or, at least, to smoothe down the rough creation which Nature flung to us. He forges the mighty anchor, and every lesser instrument. He drives the steamboat and drags the rail-car. And it was he—this creature of terrible might, and so many-sided utility, and all-comprehensive destructiveness—that used to be the cheerful, homely friend of our wintry days, and whom we have made the prisoner of this iron cage!

How kindly he was, and, though the tremendous agent of change, yet bearing himself with such gentleness, so rendering himself a part of all life-long and age-coeval associations, that it seemed as if he were the great conservative of Nature! While a man was true to the fireside, so long would he be true to country and law—to the God whom his fathers worshipped—to the wife of his youth—and to all things else which instinct or religion have taught us to consider sacred. With how sweet humility did this elemental spirit perform all needful offices for the household in which he was domesticated! He was equal to the concoction of a grand dinner, yet scorned not to roast a potato, or toast a bit of cheese. How humanely did he cherish the schoolboy's icy fingers, and thaw the old man's joints with a genial warmth, which almost equalled the glow of youth! And how carefully did he dry the cow-hide boots that had trudged through mud and snow, and the shaggy outside garment, stiff with frozen sleet; taking heed, likewise, to the comfort of the faithful dog who had followed his master through the storm! When did he refuse a coal to light a pipe, or even a part of his own substance to kindle a neighbor's fire? And then, at twilight, when laborer or scholar, or mortal of whatever age, sex, or degree, drew a chair beside him, and looked into his glowing face, how acute, how profound, how comprehensive was his sympathy with the mood of each and all! He pictured forth their very thoughts. To the youthful, he showed the scenes of the adventurous life before them; to the aged, the shadows of departed love and hope; and, if all earthly things had grown distasteful, he could gladden the fireside muser with golden glimpses of a better world. And, amid this varied communion with the human soul, how busily would the sympathizer, the deep moralist, the painter of magic pictures, be causing the tea-kettle to boil!

Nor did it lessen the charm of his soft, familiar courtesy and helpfulness, that the mighty spirit, were opportunity offered him, would run riot through the peaceful house, wrap its inmates in his terrible embrace, and leave nothing of them save their whitened bones. This possibility of mad destruction only made his domestic kindness the more beautiful and touching. It was so sweet of him, being endowed with such power, to dwell, day after day, and one long, lonesome night after another, on the dusky hearth, only now and then betraying his wild nature, by thrusting his red tongue out of the chimney-top! True, he had done much mischief in the world, and was pretty certain to do more; but his warm heart atoned for all. He was kindly to the race of man; and they pardoned his characteristic imperfections.

The good old clergyman, my predecessor in this mansion, was well acquainted with the comforts of the fireside. His yearly allowance of wood, according to the terms of his settlement, was no less than sixty cords. Almost an annual forest was converted from oak logs into ashes, in the kitchen, the parlor, and this little study, where now an unworthy successor—not in the pastoral office, but merely in his earthly abode—sits scribbling beside an air-tight stove. I love to fancy one of those fireside days, while the good man, a contemporary of the Revolution, was in his early prime, some five-and-sixty years ago. Before sunrise, doubtless, the blaze hovered upon the grey skirts of night, and dissolved the frost-work that had gathered like a curtain over the small window-panes. There is something peculiar in the aspect of the morning fireside; a fresher, brisker glare; the absence of that mellowness, which can be produced only by half-consumed logs, and shapeless brands with the white ashes on them, and mighty coals, the remnant of tree-trunks that the hungry element has gnawed for hours. The morning hearth, too, is newly swept, and the brazen andirons well brightened, so that the cheerful fire may see its face in them. Surely it was happiness, when the pastor, fortified with a substantial breakfast, sat down in his arm-chair and slippers, and opened the Whole Body of Divinity, or the Commentary on Job, or whichever of his old folios or quartos might fall within the range of his weekly sermons. It must have been his own fault, if the warmth and glow of this abundant hearth did not permeate the discourse, and keep his audience comfortable, in spite of the bitterest northern blast that ever wrestled with the church-steeple. He reads, while the heat warps the stiff covers of the volume; he writes, without numbness either in his heart or fingers; and, with unstinted hand, he throws fresh sticks of wood upon the fire.

A parishioner comes in. With what warmth of benevolence—how should he be otherwise than warm, in any of his attributes?—does the minister bid him welcome, and set a chair for him in so close proximity to the hearth, that soon the guest finds it needful to rub his scorched shins with his great red hands. The melted snow drips from his steaming boots, and bubbles upon the hearth. His puckered forehead unravels its entanglement of crisscross wrinkles. We lose much of the enjoyment of fireside heat, without such an opportunity of marking its genial effect upon those who have been looking the inclement weather in the face. In the course of the day our clergyman himself strides forth, perchance to pay a round of pastoral visits, or, it may be, to visit his mountain of a wood-pile, and cleave the monstrous logs into billets suitable for the fire. He returns with fresher life to his beloved hearth. During the short afternoon, the western sunshine comes into the study, and strives to stare the ruddy blaze out of countenance, but with only a brief triumph, soon to be succeeded by brighter glories of its rival. Beautiful it is to see the strengthening gleam—the deepening light—that gradually casts distinct shadows of the human figure, the table, and the high-backed chairs, upon the opposite wall, and at length, as twilight comes on, replenishes the room with living radiance, and makes life all rose-color. Afar, the wayfarer discerns the flickering flame, as it dances upon the windows, and hails it as a beacon-light of humanity, reminding him, in his cold and lonely path, that the world is not all snow, and solitude, and desolation. At eventide, probably, the study was peopled with the clergyman's wife and family; and children tumbled themselves upon the hearth-rug, and grave Puss sat with her back to the fire, or gazed, with a semblance of human meditation, into its fervid depths. Seasonably, the plenteous ashes of the day were raked over the mouldering brands, and from the heap came jets of flame, and an incense of night-long smoke, creeping quietly up the chimney.

Heaven forgive the old clergyman! In his latter life, when, for almost ninety winters, he had been gladdened by the firelight—when it had gleamed upon him from infancy to extreme age, and never without brightening his spirits as well as his visage, and perhaps keeping him alive so long—he had the heart to brick up his chimney-place, and bid farewell to the face of his old friend for ever! Why did not he take an eternal leave of the sunshine too? His sixty cords of wood had probably dwindled to a far less ample supply, in modern times; and it is certain that the parsonage had grown crazy with time and tempest, and pervious to the cold; but still, it was one of the saddest tokens of the decline and fall of open fire-places, that the grey patriarch should have deigned to warm himself at an air-tight stove.

And I, likewise—who have found a home in this ancient owl's nest, since its former occupant took his heavenward flight—I, to my shame, have put up stoves in kitchen, and parlor, and chamber. Wander where you will about the house, not a glimpse of the earth-born, heaven-aspiring fiend of Ætna—him that sports in the thunder-storm—the idol of the Ghebers—the devourer of cities, the forest rioter, and prairie sweeper—the future destroyer of our earth—the old chimney-corner companion, who mingled himself so sociably with household joys and sorrows—not a glimpse of this mighty and kindly one will greet your eyes. He is now an invisible presence. There is his iron cage. Touch it, and he scorches your fingers. He delights to singe a garment, or perpetrate any other little unworthy mischief; for his temper is ruined by the ingratitude of mankind, for whom he cherished such warmth of feeling, and to whom he taught all their arts, even that of making his own prison-house. In his fits of rage, he puffs volumes of smoke and noisome gas through the crevices of the door, and shakes the iron walls of his dungeon, so as to overthrow the ornamental urn upon its summit. We tremble, lest he should break forth amongst us. Much of his time is spent in sighs, burthened with unutterable grief, and long-drawn through the funnel. He amuses himself, too, with repeating all the whispers, the moans, and the louder utterances or tempestuous howls of the wind; so that the stove becomes a microcosm of the aërial world. Occasionally, there are strange combinations of sounds—voices, talking almost articulately within the hollow chest of iron—insomuch that fancy beguiles me with the idea, that my fire wood must have grown in that infernal forest of lamentable trees, which breathed their complaints to Dante. When the listener is half-asleep, he may readily take these voices for the conversation of spirits, and assign them an intelligible meaning. Anon, there is a pattering noise—drip, drip, drip—as if a summer shower were falling within the narrow circumference of the stove.

These barren and tedious eccentricities are all that the air-tight stove can bestow, in exchange for the invaluable moral influences which we have lost by our desertion of the open fire-place. Alas! is this world so very bright, that we can afford to choke up such a domestic fountain of gladsomeness, and sit down by its darkened source, without being conscious of a gloom?

It is my belief, that social intercourse cannot long continue what it has been, now that we have subtracted from it so important and vivifying an element as fire-light. The effects will be more perceptible on our children, and the generations that shall succeed them, than on ourselves, the mechanism of whose life may remain unchanged, though its spirit be far other than it was. The sacred trust of the household-fire has been transmitted in unbroken succession from the earliest ages, and faithfully cherished, in spite of every discouragement, such as the Curfew law of the Norman conquerors; until, in these evil days, physical science has nearly succeeded in extinguishing it. But we at least have our youthful recollections tinged with the glow of the hearth, and our life-long habits and associations arranged on the principle of a mutual bond in the domestic fire. Therefore, though the sociable friend be for ever departed, yet in a degree he will be spiritually present to us; and still more will the empty forms, which were once full of his rejoicing presence, continue to rule our manners. We shall draw our chairs together, as we and our forefathers have been wont, for thousands of years back, and sit around some blank and empty corner of the room, babbling, with unreal cheerfulness, of topics suitable to the homely fireside. A warmth from the past—from the ashes of by-gone years, and the raked-up embers of long ago—will sometimes thaw the ice about our hearts. But it must be otherwise with our successors. On the most favorable supposition, they will be acquainted with the fireside in no better shape than that of the sullen stove; and more probably, they will have grown up amid furnace-heat, in houses which might be fancied to have their foundation over the infernal pit, whence sulphurous steams and unbreathable exhalations ascend through the apertures of the floor. There will be nothing to attract these poor children to one centre. They will never behold one another through that peculiar medium of vision—the ruddy gleam of blazing wood or bituminous coal—which gives the human spirit so deep an insight into its fellows, and melts all humanity into one cordial heart of hearts. Domestic life—if it may still be termed domestic—will seek its separate corners, and never gather itself into groups. The easy gossip—the merry, yet unambitious jest—the life-long, practical discussion of real matters in a casual way—the soul of truth, which is so often incarnated in a simple fireside word—will disappear from earth. Conversation will contract the air of a debate, and all moral intercourse be chilled with a fatal frost.

In classic times, the exhortation to fight "pro aris et focis"—for the altars and the hearths—was considered the strongest appeal that could be made to patriotism. And it seemed an immortal utterance; for all subsequent ages and people have acknowledged its force, and responded to it with the full portion of manhood that Nature had assigned to each. Wisely were the Altar and the Hearth conjoined in one mighty sentence! For the hearth, too, had its kindred sanctity. Religion sat down beside it, not in the priestly robes which decorated, and perhaps disguised, her at the altar, but arrayed in a simple matron's garb, and uttering her lessons with the tenderness of a mother's voice and heart. The holy Hearth! If any earthly and material thing—or rather, a divine idea, embodied in brick and mortar—might be supposed to possess the permanence of mortal truth, it was this. All revered it. The man, who did not put off his shoes upon this holy ground, would have deemed it pastime to trample upon the altar. It has been our task to uproot the hearth. What further reform is left for our children to achieve, unless they overthrow the altar too? And by what appeal, hereafter, when the breath of hostile armies may mingle with the pure, cold breezes of our country, shall we attempt to rouse up native valor? Fight for your hearths? There will be none throughout the land. FIGHT FOR YOUR STOVES! Not I, in faith. If, in such a cause, I strike a blow, it shall be on the invader's part; and Heaven grant that it may shatter the abomination all to pieces!

The Christmas Banquet

FROM THE UNPUBLISHED
"ALLEGORIES OF THE HEART"

"I HAVE here attempted," said Roderick, unfolding a few sheets of manuscript, as he sat with Rosina and the sculptor in the summer-house—"I have attempted to seize hold of a personage who glides past me, occasionally, in my walk through life. My former sad experience, as you know, has gifted me with some degree of insight into the gloomy mysteries of the human heart, through which I have wandered like one astray in a dark cavern, with his torch fast flickering to extinction. But this man—this class of men—is a hopeless puzzle."

"Well, but propound him," said the sculptor. "Let us have an idea of him, to begin with."

"Why, indeed," replied Roderick, "he is such a being as I could conceive you to carve out of marble, and some yet unrealized perfection of human science to endow with an exquisite mockery of intellect; but still there lacks the last inestimable touch of a divine Creator. He looks like a man, and, perchance, like a better specimen of man than you ordinarily meet. You might esteem him wise—he is capable of cultivation and refinement, and has at least an external conscience—but the demands that spirit makes upon spirit, are precisely those to which he cannot respond. When, at last, you come close to him, you find him chill and unsubstantial—a mere vapor."

"I believe," said Rosina, "I have a glimmering idea of what you mean."

"Then be thankful," answered her husband, smiling; "but do not anticipate any further illumination from what I am about to read. I have here imagined such a man to be—what, probably, he never is—conscious of the deficiency in his spiritual organization. Methinks the result would be a sense of cold unreality, wherewith he would go shivering through the world, longing to exchange his load of ice for any burthen of real grief that fate could fling upon a human being."

Contenting himself with this preface, Roderick began to read.

In a certain old gentleman's last will and testament, there appeared a bequest, which, as his final thought and deed, was singularly in keeping with a long life of melancholy eccentricity. He devised a considerable sum for establishing a fund, the interest of which was to be expended, annually forever, in preparing a Christmas Banquet for ten of the most miserable persons that could be found. It seemed not to be the testator's purpose to make these half-a-score of sad hearts merry, but to provide that the stern or fierce expression of human discontent should not be drowned, even for that one holy and joyful day, amid the acclamations of festal gratitude which all Christendom sends up. And he desired, likewise, to perpetuate his own remonstrance against the earthly course of Providence, and his sad and sour dissent from those systems of religion or philosophy which either find sunshine in the world, or draw it down from heaven.

The task of inviting the guests, or of selecting among such as might advance their claims to partake of this dismal hospitality, was confided to the two trustees or stewards of the fund. These gentlemen, like their deceased friend, were sombre humorists, who made it their principal occupation to number the sable threads in the web of human life, and drop all the golden ones out of the reckoning. They performed their present office with integrity and judgment. The aspect of the assembled company, on the day of the first festival, might not, it is true, have satisfied every beholder that these were especially the individuals, chosen forth from all the world, whose griefs were worthy to stand as indicators of the mass of human suffering. Yet, after due consideration, it could not be disputed that here was a variety of hopeless discomfort, which, if it sometimes arose from causes apparently inadequate, was thereby only the shrewder imputation against the nature and mechanism of life.

The arrangements and decorations of the banquet were probably intended to signify that death-in-life which had been the testator's definition of existence. The hall, illuminated by torches, was hung round with curtains of deep and dusky purple, and adorned with branches of cypress and wreaths of artificial flowers, imitative of such as used to be strewn over the dead. A sprig of parsley was laid by every plate. The main reservoir of wine was a sepulchral urn of silver, whence the liquor was distributed around the table in small vases, accurately copied from those that held the tears of ancient mourners. Neither had the stewards—if it were their taste that arranged these details—forgotten the fantasy of the old Egyptians, who seated a skeleton at every festive board, and mocked their own merriment with the imperturbable grin of a death's-head. Such a fearful guest, shrouded in a black mantle, sat now at the head of the table. It was whispered, I know not with what truth, that the testator himself had once walked the visible world with the machinery of that same skeleton, and that it was one of the stipulations of his will, that he should thus be permitted to sit, from year to year, at the banquet which he had instituted. If so, it was perhaps covertly implied that he had cherished no hopes of bliss beyond the grave to compensate for the evils which he felt or imagined here. And if, in their bewildered conjectures as to the purpose of earthly existence, the banqueters should throw aside the veil, and cast an inquiring glance at this figure of death, as seeking thence the solution otherwise unattainable, the only reply would be a stare of the vacant eye-caverns, and a grin of the skeleton-jaws. Such was the response that the dead man had fancied himself to receive, when he asked of Death to solve the riddle of his life; and it was his desire to repeat it when the guests of his dismal hospitality should find themselves perplexed with the same question.

"What means that wreath?" asked several of the company, while viewing the decorations of the table.

They alluded to a wreath of cypress, which was held on high by a skeleton-arm, protruding from within the black mantle.

"It is a crown," said one of the stewards, "not for the worthiest, but for the wofullest, when he shall prove his claim to it."

The guest earliest bidden to the festival, was a man of soft and gentle character, who had not energy to struggle against the heavy despondency to which his temperament rendered him liable; and therefore, with nothing outwardly to excuse him from happiness, he had spent a life of quiet misery, that made his blood torpid, and weighed upon his breath, and sat like a ponderous night-fiend upon every throb of his unresisting heart. His wretchedness seemed as deep as his original nature, if not identical with it. It was the misfortune of a second guest to cherish within his bosom a diseased heart, which had become so wretchedly sore, that the continual and unavoidable rubs of the world, the blow of an enemy, the careless jostle of a stranger, and even the faithful and loving touch of a friend, alike made ulcers in it. As is the habit of people thus afflicted, he found his chief employment in exhibiting these miserable sores to any who would give themselves the pain of viewing them. A third guest was a hypochondriac, whose imagination wrought necromancy in his outward and inward world, and caused him to see monstrous faces in the household fire, and dragons in the clouds of sunset, and fiends in the guise of beautiful women, and something ugly or wicked beneath all the pleasant surfaces of nature. His neighbor at table was one who, in his early youth, had trusted mankind too much, and hoped too highly in their behalf, and, in meeting with many disappointments, had become desperately soured. For several years back, this misanthrope had employed himself in accumulating motives for hating and despising his race—such as murder, lust, treachery, ingratitude, faithlessness of trusted friends, instinctive vices of children, impurity of women, hidden guilt in men of saint-like aspect—and, in short, all manner of black realities that sought to decorate themselves with outward grace or glory. But, at every atrocious fact that was added to his catalogue— at every increase of the sad knowledge which he spent his life to collect—the native impulses of the poor man's loving and confiding heart made him groan with anguish. Next, with his heavy brow bent downward, there stole into the hall a man naturally earnest and impassioned, who, from his immemorial infancy, had felt the consciousness of a high message to the world, but, essaying to deliver it, had found either no voice or form of speech, or else no ears to listen. Therefore his whole life was a bitter questioning of himself—"Why have not men acknowledged my mission? Am I not a self-deluding

fool? What business have I on earth? Where is my grave?"
Throughout the festival, he quaffed frequent draughts from
the sepulchral urn of wine, hoping thus to quench the celestial fire that tortured his own breast, and could not benefit his
race.

Then there entered—having flung away a ticket for a
ball—a gay gallant of yesterday, who had found four or five
wrinkles in his brow, and more grey hairs than he could well
number, on his head. Endowed with sense and feeling, he
had nevertheless spent his youth in folly, but had reached at
last that dreary point in life, where Folly quits us of her own
accord, leaving us to make friends with Wisdom if we can.
Thus, cold and desolate, he had come to seek Wisdom at the
banquet, and wondered if the skeleton were she. To eke out
the company, the stewards had invited a distressed poet from
his home in the alms-house, and a melancholy idiot from the
street corner. The latter had just the glimmering of sense that
was sufficient to make him conscious of a vacancy, which the
poor fellow, all his life long, had mistily sought to fill up with
intelligence, wandering up and down the streets, and groaning miserably, because his attempts were ineffectual. The only
lady in the hall was one who had fallen short of absolute and
perfect beauty, merely by the trifling defect of a slight cast in
her left eye. But this blemish, minute as it was, so shocked
the pure ideal of her soul, rather than her vanity, that she
passed her life in solitude, and veiled her countenance even
from her own gaze. So the skeleton sat shrouded at one end
of the table, and this poor lady at the other.

One other guest remains to be described. He was a young
man of smooth brow, fair cheek, and fashionable mien. So far
as his exterior developed him, he might much more suitably
have found a place at some merry Christmas table, than have
been numbered among the blighted, fate-stricken, fancy-tor-
tured set of ill-starred banqueters. Murmurs arose among the
guests, as they noted the glance of general scrutiny which the
intruder threw over his companions. What had he to do
among them? Why did not the skeleton of the dead founder
of the feast unbend its rattling joints, arise, and motion the
unwelcome stranger from the board?

"Shameful!" said the morbid man, while a new ulcer broke

out in his heart. "He comes to mock us!—we shall be the jest
of his tavern friends!—he will make a farce of our miseries,
and bring it out upon the stage!"

"Oh, never mind him!" said the hypochondriac, smiling
sourly. "He shall feast from yonder tureen of viper soup, and
if there is a fricassee of scorpions on the table, pray let him
have his share of it. For the dessert, he shall taste the apples
of Sodom. Then, if he like our Christmas fare, let him return
again next year!"

"Trouble him not," murmured the melancholy man, with
gentleness. "What matters it whether the consciousness of
misery come a few years sooner or later? If this youth deem
himself happy now, yet let him sit with us, for the sake of the
wretchedness to come."

The poor idiot approached the young man, with that
mournful aspect of vacant inquiry which his face continually
wore, and which caused people to say that he was always in
search of his missing wits. After no little examination, he
touched the stranger's hand, but immediately drew back his
own, shaking his head and shivering.

"Cold, cold, cold!" muttered the idiot.

The young man shivered too—and smiled.

"Gentlemen—and you, madam,"—said one of the stewards of the festival, "do not conceive so ill, either of our caution or judgment, as to imagine that we have admitted this
young stranger—Gervayse Hastings by name—without a full
investigation and thoughtful balance of his claims. Trust me,
not a guest at the table is better entitled to his seat."

The steward's guarantee was perforce satisfactory. The
company, therefore, took their places, and addressed themselves to the serious business of the feast, but were soon disturbed by the hypochondriac, who thrust back his chair, complaining that a dish of stewed toads and vipers was set before
him, and that there was green ditch-water in his cup of wine.
This mistake being amended, he quietly resumed his seat. The
wine, as it flowed freely from the sepulchral urn, seemed to
come imbued with all gloomy inspirations; so that its influence was not to cheer, but either to sink the revellers into a
deeper melancholy, or elevate their spirits to an enthusiasm of
wretchedness. The conversation was various. They told sad

stories about people who might have been worthy guests at such a festival as the present. They talked of grisly incidents in human history; of strange crimes, which, if truly considered, were but convulsions of agony; of some lives that had been altogether wretched, and of others, which, wearing a general semblance of happiness, had yet been deformed, sooner or later, by misfortune, as by the intrusion of a grim face at a banquet; of death-bed scenes, and what dark intimations might be gathered from the words of dying men; of suicide, and whether the more eligible mode were by halter, knife, poison, drowning, gradual starvation, or the fumes of charcoal. The majority of the guests, as is the custom with people thoroughly and profoundly sick at heart, were anxious to make their own woes the theme of discussion, and prove themselves most excellent in anguish. The misanthropist went deep into the philosophy of evil, and wandered about in the darkness, with now and then a gleam of discolored light hovering on ghastly shapes and horrid scenery. Many a miserable thought, such as men have stumbled upon from age to age, did he now rake up again, and gloat over it as an inestimable gem, a diamond, a treasure far preferable to those bright, spiritual revelations of a better world, which are like precious stones from heaven's pavement. And then, amid his lore of wretchedness, he hid his face and wept.

It was a festival at which the woful man of Uz might suitably have been a guest, together with all, in each succeeding age, who have tasted deepest of the bitterness of life. And be it said, too, that every son or daughter of woman, however favored with happy fortune, might, at one sad moment or another, have claimed the privilege of a stricken heart, to sit down at this table. But, throughout the feast, it was remarked that the young stranger, Gervayse Hastings, was unsuccessful in his attempts to catch its pervading spirit. At any deep, strong thought that found utterance, and which was torn out, as it were, from the saddest recesses of human consciousness, he looked mystified and bewildered; even more than the poor idiot, who seemed to grasp at such things with his earnest heart, and thus occasionally to comprehend them. The young man's conversation was of a colder and lighter kind, often brilliant, but lacking the powerful characteristics of a nature that had been developed by suffering.

"Sir," said the misanthropist, bluntly, in reply to some observation by Gervayse Hastings, "pray do not address me again. We have no right to talk together. Our minds have nothing in common. By what claim you appear at this banquet, I cannot guess; but methinks, to a man who could say what you have just now said, my companions and myself must seem no more than shadows, flickering on the wall. And precisely such a shadow are you to us!"

The young man smiled and bowed, but drawing himself back in his chair, he buttoned his coat over his breast, as if the banqueting-hall were growing chill. Again the idiot fixed his melancholy stare upon the youth, and murmured— "Cold! cold! cold!"

The banquet drew to its conclusion, and the guests departed. Scarcely had they stepped across the threshold of the hall, when the scene that had there passed seemed like the vision of a sick fancy, or an exhalation from a stagnant heart. Now and then, however, during the year that ensued, these melancholy people caught glimpses of one another, transient, indeed, but enough to prove that they walked the earth with the ordinary allotment of reality. Sometimes, a pair of them came face to face, while stealing through the evening twilight, enveloped in their sable cloaks. Sometimes, they casually met in church-yards. Once, also, it happened, that two of the dismal banqueters mutually started, at recognizing each other in the noon-day sunshine of a crowded street, stalking there like ghosts astray. Doubtless, they wondered why the skeleton did not come abroad at noonday, too!

But, whenever the necessity of their affairs compelled these Christmas guests into the bustling world, they were sure to encounter the young man, who had so unaccountably been admitted to the festival. They saw him among the gay and fortunate; they caught the sunny sparkle of his eye; they heard the light and careless tones of his voice—and muttered to themselves, with such indignation as only the aristocracy of wretchedness could kindle:—"The traitor! The vile impostor! Providence, in its own good time, may give him a right to feast among us!" But the young man's unabashed eye dwelt upon their gloomy figures, as they passed him, seeming to say, perchance with somewhat of a sneer—"First, know my secret!—then, measure your claims with mine!"

The step of Time stole onward, and soon brought merry Christmas round again, with glad and solemn worship in the churches, and sports, games, festivals, and everywhere the bright face of Joy beside the household fire. Again, likewise, the hall, with its curtains of dusky purple, was illuminated by the death-torches, gleaming on the sepulchral decorations of the banquet. The veiled skeleton sat in state, lifting the cypress wreath above its head, as the guerdon of some guest, illustrious in the qualifications which there claimed precedence. As the stewards deemed the world inexhaustible in misery, and were desirous of recognizing it in all its forms, they had not seen fit to re-assemble the company of the former year. New faces now threw their gloom across the table.

There was a man of nice conscience, who bore a bloodstain in his heart—the death of a fellow-creature—which, for his more exquisite torture, had chanced with such a peculiarity of circumstances, that he could not absolutely determine whether his will had entered into the deed, or not. Therefore, his whole life was spent in the agony of an inward trial for murder, with a continual sifting of the details of his terrible calamity, until his mind had no longer any thought, nor his soul any emotion, disconnected with it. There was a mother, too—a mother once, but a desolation now—who, many years before, had gone out on a pleasure-party, and, returning, found her infant smothered in its little bed. And ever since she had been tortured with the fantasy, that her buried baby lay smothering in its coffin. Then there was an aged lady, who had lived from time immemorial with a constant tremor quivering through her frame. It was terrible to discern her dark shadow tremulous upon the wall; her lips, likewise, were tremulous; and the expression of her eyes seemed to indicate that her soul was trembling too. Owing to the bewilderment and confusion which made almost a chaos of her intellect, it was impossible to discover what dire misfortune had thus shaken her nature to its depths; so that the stewards had admitted her to the table, not from any acquaintance with her history, but on the safe testimony of her miserable aspect. Some surprise was expressed at the presence of a bluff, red-faced gentleman, a certain Mr. Smith, who had evidently the fat of many a rich feast within him, and the habitual twinkle of whose eye betrayed a disposition to break forth into uproarious laughter, for little cause or none. It turned out, however, that, with the best possible flow of spirits, our poor friend was afflicted with a physical disease of the heart, which threatened instant death on the slightest cachinnatory indulgence, or even that titillation of the bodily frame, produced by merry thoughts. In this dilemma, he had sought admittance to the banquet, on the ostensible plea of his irksome and miserable state, but, in reality, with the hope of imbibing a life-preserving melancholy.

A married couple had been invited, from a motive of bitter humor; it being well understood, that they rendered each other unutterably miserable whenever they chanced to meet, and therefore must necessarily be fit associates at the festival. In contrast with these, was another couple, still unmarried, who had interchanged their hearts in early life, but had been divided by circumstances as impalpable as morning mist, and kept apart so long, that their spirits now found it impossible to meet. Therefore, yearning for communion, yet shrinking from one another, and choosing none beside, they felt themselves companionless in life, and looked upon eternity as a boundless desert. Next to the skeleton sat a mere son of earth—a haunter of the Exchange—a gatherer of shining dust—a man whose life's record was in his leger, and whose soul's prison-house, the vaults of the bank where he kept his deposits. This person had been greatly perplexed at his invitation, deeming himself one of the most fortunate men in the city; but the stewards persisted in demanding his presence, assuring him that he had no conception how miserable he was.

And now appeared a figure, which we must acknowledge as our acquaintance of the former festival. It was Gervayse Hastings, whose presence had then caused so much question and criticism, and who now took his place with the composure of one whose claims were satisfactory to himself, and must needs be allowed by others. Yet his easy and unruffled face betrayed no sorrow. The well-skilled beholders gazed a moment into his eyes, and shook their heads, to miss the un-uttered sympathy—the countersign, never to be falsified—of those whose hearts are cavern-mouths, through which they descend into a region of illimitable wo, and recognize other wanderers there.

"Who is this youth?" asked the man with a blood-stain on his conscience. "Surely he has never gone down into the depths! I know all the aspects of those who have passed through the dark valley. By what right is he among us?"

"Ah, it is a sinful thing to come hither without a sorrow," murmured the aged lady, in accents that partook of the eternal tremor which pervaded her whole being. "Depart, young man! Your soul has never been shaken; and therefore I tremble so much the more to look at you."

"His soul shaken! No; I'll answer for it," said bluff Mr. Smith, pressing his hand upon his heart, and making himself as melancholy as he could, for fear of a fatal explosion of laughter. "I know the lad well; he has as fair prospects as any young man about town, and has no more right among us, miserable creatures, than the child unborn. He never was miserable, and probably never will be!"

"Our honored guests," interposed the stewards, "pray have patience with us, and believe, at least, that our deep veneration for the sacredness of this solemnity would preclude any wilful violation of it. Receive this young man to your table. It may not be too much to say, that no guest here would exchange his own heart for the one that beats within that youthful bosom!"

"I'd call it a bargain, and gladly too," muttered Mr. Smith, with a perplexing mixture of sadness and mirthful conceit. "A plague upon their nonsense! My own heart is the only really miserable one in the company—it will certainly be the death of me at last!"

Nevertheless, as on the former occasion, the judgment of the stewards being without appeal, the company sat down. The obnoxious guest made no more attempt to obtrude his conversation on those about him, but appeared to listen to the table-talk with peculiar assiduity, as if some inestimable secret, otherwise beyond his reach, might be conveyed in a casual word. And, in truth, to those who could understand

and value it, there was rich matter in the upgushings and out-
pourings of these initiated souls, to whom sorrow had been
a talisman, admitting them into spiritual depths which no
other spell can open. Sometimes, out of the midst of densest
gloom, there flashed a momentary radiance, pure as crystal,
bright as the flame of stars, and shedding such a glow upon
the mystery of life, that the guests were ready to exclaim,
"Surely the riddle is on the point of being solved!" At such
illuminated intervals, the saddest mourners felt it to be revealed, that mortal griefs are but shadowy and external; no
more than the sable robes, voluminously shrouding a certain
divine reality, and thus indicating what might otherwise be
altogether invisible to mortal eye.

"Just now," remarked the trembling old woman, "I seemed
to see beyond the outside. And then my everlasting tremor
passed away!"

"Would that I could dwell always in these momentary
gleams of light!" said the man of stricken conscience. "Then
the blood-stain in my heart would be washed clean away."

This strain of conversation appeared so unintelligibly absurd to good Mr. Smith, that he burst into precisely the fit of
laughter which his physicians had warned him against, as
likely to prove instantaneously fatal. In effect, he fell back
in his chair, a corpse with a broad grin upon his face; while
his ghost, perchance, remained beside it, bewildered at its
unpremeditated exit. This catastrophe, of course, broke up
the festival.

"How is this? You do not tremble?" observed the tremulous old woman to Gervayse Hastings, who was gazing at the
dead man with singular intentness. "Is it not awful to see him
so suddenly vanish out of the midst of life—this man of flesh
and blood, whose earthly nature was so warm and strong?
There is a never-ending tremor in my soul; but it trembles
afresh at this! And you are calm!"

"Would that he could teach me somewhat!" said Gervayse
Hastings, drawing a long breath. "Men pass before me like
shadows on the wall—their actions, passions, feelings, are
flickerings of the light—and then they vanish! Neither the
corpse, nor yonder skeleton, nor this old woman's everlasting
tremor, can give me what I seek."

And then the company departed.

We cannot linger to narrate, in such detail, more circumstances of these singular festivals, which, in accordance with the founder's will, continued to be kept with the regularity of an established institution. In process of time, the stewards adopted the custom of inviting, from far and near, those individuals whose misfortunes were prominent above other men's, and whose mental and moral development might, therefore, be supposed to possess a corresponding interest. The exiled noble of the French Revolution, and the broken soldier of the Empire, were alike represented at the table. Fallen monarchs, wandering about the earth, have found places at that forlorn and miserable feast. The statesman, when his party flung him off, might, if he chose it, be once more a great man for the space of a single banquet. Aaron Burr's name appears on the record, at a period when his ruin—the profoundest and most striking, with more of moral circumstance in it than that of almost any other man—was complete, in his lonely age. Stephen Girard, when his wealth weighed upon him like a mountain, once sought admittance of his own accord. It is not probable, however, that these men had any lessons to teach in the lore of discontent and misery, which might not equally well have been studied in the common walks of life. Illustrious unfortunates attract a wider sympathy, not because their griefs are more intense, but because, being set on lofty pedestals, they the better serve mankind as instances and by-words of calamity.

It concerns our present purpose to say that, at each successive festival, Gervayse Hastings showed his face, gradually changing from the smooth beauty of his youth to the thoughtful comeliness of manhood, and thence to the bald, impressive dignity of age. He was the only individual invariably present. Yet, on every occasion, there were murmurs, both from those who knew his character and position, and from them whose hearts shrank back, as denying his companionship in their mystic fraternity.

"Who is this impassive man?" had been asked a hundred times. "Has he suffered? Has he sinned? There are no traces of either. Then wherefore is he here?"

"You must inquire of the stewards, or of himself," was the

constant reply. "We seem to know him well, here in our city, and know nothing of him but what is creditable and fortunate. Yet hither he comes, year after year, to this gloomy banquet, and sits among the guests like a marble statue. Ask yonder skeleton—perhaps that may solve the riddle!"

It was, in truth, a wonder. The life of Gervayse Hastings was not merely a prosperous, but a brilliant one. Everything had gone well with him. He was wealthy, far beyond the expenditure that was required by habits of magnificence, a taste of rare purity and cultivation, a love of travel, a scholar's instinct to collect a splendid library, and, moreover, what seemed a munificent liberality to the distressed. He had sought domestic happiness, and not vainly, if a lovely and tender wife, and children of fair promise, could insure it. He had, besides, ascended above the limit which separates the obscure from the distinguished, and had won a stainless reputation in affairs of the widest public importance. Not that he was a popular character, or had within him the mysterious attributes which are essential to that species of success. To the public, he was a cold abstraction, wholly destitute of those rich hues of personality, that living warmth, and the peculiar faculty of stamping his own heart's impression on a multitude of hearts, by which the people recognize their favorites. And it must be owned that, after his most intimate associates had done their best to know him thoroughly, and love him warmly, they were startled to find how little hold he had upon their affections. They approved—they admired—but still, in those moments when the human spirit most craves reality, they shrank back from Gervayse Hastings, as powerless to give them what they sought. It was the feeling of distrustful regret, with which we should draw back the hand, after extending it, in an illusive twilight, to grasp the hand of a shadow upon the wall.

As the superficial fervency of youth decayed, this peculiar effect of Gervayse Hastings' character grew more perceptible. His children, when he extended his arms, came coldly to his knees, but never climbed them of their own accord. His wife wept secretly, and almost adjudged herself a criminal, because she shivered in the chill of his bosom. He, too, occasionally appeared not unconscious of the chillness of his moral atmosphere, and willing, if it might be so, to warm himself at a kindly fire. But age stole onward, and benumbed him more and more. As the hoar-frost began to gather on him, his wife went to her grave, and was doubtless warmer there; his children either died, or were scattered to different homes of their own; and old Gervayse Hastings, unscathed by grief—alone, but needing no companionship—continued his steady walk through life, and still, on every Christmas-day, attended at the dismal banquet. His privilege as a guest had become prescriptive now. Had he claimed the head of the table, even the skeleton would have been ejected from its seat.

Finally, at the merry Christmas-tide, when he had numbered four-score years complete, this pale, high-browed, marble-featured old man once more entered the long-frequented hall, with the same impassive aspect that had called forth so much dissatisfied remark at his first attendance. Time, except in matters merely external, had done nothing for him, either of good or evil. As he took his place, he threw a calm, inquiring glance around the table, as if to ascertain whether any guest had yet appeared, after so many unsuccessful banquets, who might impart to him the mystery—the deep, warm secret—the life within the life—which, whether manifested in joy or sorrow, is what gives substance to a world of shadows.

"My friends," said Gervayse Hastings, assuming a position which his long conversance with the festival caused to appear natural, "you are welcome! I drink to you all in this cup of sepulchral wine."

The guests replied courteously, but still in a manner that proved them unable to receive the old man as a member of their sad fraternity. It may be well to give the reader an idea of the present company at the banquet.

One was formerly a clergyman, enthusiastic in his profession, and apparently of the genuine dynasty of those old Puritan divines whose faith in their calling, and stern exercise of it, had placed them among the mighty of the earth. But, yielding to the speculative tendency of the age, he had gone astray from the firm foundation of an ancient faith, and wandered into a cloud region, where everything was misty and deceptive, ever mocking him with a semblance of reality, but still dissolving when he flung himself upon it for support and rest. His instinct and early training demanded something steadfast; but, looking forward, he beheld vapors piled on vapors, and, behind him, an impassable gulf between the man of yesterday and to-day; on the borders of which he paced to and fro, sometimes wringing his hands in agony, and often making his own wo a theme of scornful merriment. This, surely, was a miserable man. Next, there was a theorist—one of a numerous tribe, although he deemed himself unique since the creation—a theorist, who had conceived a plan by which all the wretchedness of earth, moral and physical, might be done away, and the bliss of the millennium at once accomplished. But, the incredulity of mankind debarring him from action, he was smitten with as much grief as if the whole mass of wo which he was denied the opportunity to remedy, were crowded into his own bosom. A plain old man in black attracted much of the company's notice, on the supposition that he was no other than Father Miller, who, it seemed, had given himself up to despair at the tedious delay of the final conflagration. Then there was a man distinguished for native pride and obstinacy, who, a little while before, had possessed immense wealth, and held the control of a vast moneyed interest, which he had wielded in the same spirit as a despotic monarch would wield the power of his empire, carrying on a tremendous moral warfare, the roar and tremor of which was felt at every fireside in the land. At length came a crushing ruin—a total overthrow of fortune, power, and character— the effect of which on his imperious, and, in many respects, noble and lofty nature, might have entitled him to a place, not merely at our festival, but among the peers of Pandemonium.

There was a modern philanthropist, who had become so deeply sensible of the calamities of thousands and millions of his fellow creatures, and of the impracticableness of any general measures for their relief, that he had no heart to do what little good lay immediately within his power, but contented himself with being miserable for sympathy. Near him sat a gentleman in a predicament hitherto unprecedented, but of which the present epoch, probably, affords numerous examples. Ever since he was of capacity to read a newspaper, this person had prided himself on his consistent adherence to one political party, but, in the confusion of these latter days, had got bewildered, and knew not whereabouts his party was. This wretched condition, so morally desolate and disheartening to a man who has long accustomed himself to merge his individuality in the mass of a great body, can only be conceived by such as have experienced it. His next companion was a popular orator who had lost his voice, and—as it was pretty much all that he had to lose—had fallen into a state of hopeless melancholy. The table was likewise graced by two of the gentler sex—one, a half-starved, consumptive seamstress, the representative of thousands just as wretched; the other, a woman of unemployed energy, who found herself in the world with nothing to achieve, nothing to enjoy, and nothing even to suffer. She had, therefore, driven herself to the verge of madness by dark broodings over the wrongs of her sex, and its exclusion from a proper field of action. The roll of guests being thus complete, a side-table had been set for three or four disappointed office-seekers, with hearts as sick as death, whom the stewards had admitted, partly because their calamities really entitled them to entrance here, and partly that they were in especial need of a good dinner. There was likewise a homeless dog, with his tail between his legs, licking up the crumbs and gnawing the fragments of the feast—such a melancholy cur as one sometimes sees about the streets, without a master, and willing to follow the first that will accept his service.

In their own way, these were as wretched a set of people as ever had assembled at the festival. There they sat, with the veiled skeleton of the founder, holding aloft the cypress wreath, at one end of the table; and at the other, wrapt in furs, the withered figure of Gervayse Hastings, stately, calm, and cold, impressing the company with awe, yet so little interesting their sympathy, that he might have vanished into thin air, without their once exclaiming—"Whither is he gone?"

"Sir," said the philanthropist, addressing the old man, "you have been so long a guest at this annual festival, and have thus been conversant with so many varieties of human affliction, that, not improbably, you have thence derived some great and important lessons. How blessed were your lot,

could you reveal a secret by which all this mass of wo might
be removed!"

"I know of but one misfortune," answered Gervayse Hastings, quietly, "and that is my own."

"Your own!" rejoined the philanthropist. "And, looking
back on your serene and prosperous life, how can you claim
to be the sole unfortunate of the human race?"

"You will not understand it," replied Gervayse Hastings,
feebly, and with a singular inefficiency of pronunciation, and
sometimes putting one word for another. "None have understood it—not even those who experience the like. It is a chillness—a want of earnestness—a feeling as if what should be
my heart were a thing of vapor—a haunting perception of
unreality! Thus, seeming to possess all that other men have—
all that men aim at—I have really possessed nothing, neither
joys nor griefs. All things—all persons—as was truly said to
me at this table long and long ago—have been like shadows
flickering on the wall. It was so with my wife and children—
with those who seemed my friends: it is so with yourselves,
whom I see now before me. Neither have I myself any real
existence, but am a shadow like the rest!"

"And how is it with your views of a future life?" inquired
the speculative clergyman.

"Worse than with you," said the old man, in a hollow and
feeble tone; "for I cannot conceive it earnestly enough to feel
either hope or fear. Mine—mine is the wretchedness! This
cold heart—this unreal life! Ah! it grows colder still."

It so chanced, that at this juncture the decayed ligaments of
the skeleton gave way, and the dry bones fell together in a
heap, thus causing the dusty wreath of cypress to drop upon
the table. The attention of the company being thus diverted,
for a single instant, from Gervayse Hastings, they perceived,
on turning again towards him, that the old man had undergone a change. His shadow had ceased to flicker on the wall.

"Well, Rosina, what is your criticism?" asked Roderick, as
he rolled up the manuscript.

"Frankly, your success is by no means complete," replied
she. "It is true, I have an idea of the character you endeavor

to describe; but it is rather by dint of my own thought than your expression."

"That is unavoidable," observed the sculptor, "because the characteristics are all negative. If Gervayse Hastings could have imbibed one human grief at the gloomy banquet, the task of describing him would have been infinitely easier. Of such persons—and we do meet with these moral monsters now and then—it is difficult to conceive how they came to exist here, or what there is in them capable of existence hereafter. They seem to be on the outside of everything; and nothing wearies the soul more than an attempt to comprehend them within its grasp."

A Good Man's Miracle

In every good action there is a divine quality, which does not end with the completion of that particular deed, but goes on to bring forth good works in an infinite series. It is seldom possible, indeed, for human eyes to trace out the chain of blessed consequences, that extends from a benevolent man's simple and conscientious act, here on earth, and connects it with those labors of love which the angels make it their joy to perform, in Heaven above. Sometimes, however, we meet with an instance in which this wonderful and glorious connection may clearly be perceived. It has always appeared to me, that a well-known incident in the life of Mr. Robert Raikes offers us one of the most hopeful and inspiring arguments, never to neglect even the humblest opportunities of doing good, as not knowing what vast purposes of Providence we may thereby subserve. This little story has been often told, but may here be related anew, because it so strikingly illustrates the remark with which we began.

Mr. Raikes, being in London, happened one day to pass through a certain street, which was inhabited chiefly by poor and ignorant people. In great cities, it is unfortunately the case, that the poor are compelled to be the neighbors and fellow-lodgers of the vicious; and that the ignorant seeing so much temptation around them, and having no kind advisers to direct them aright, almost inevitably go astray and increase the number of the bad. Thus, though doubtless there are many virtuous poor people, amidst all the vice that hides itself in the obscure streets of a great city, like London, still it seems as if they were kept virtuous only by the special providence of God. If He should turn away His eyes for a single instant, they would be lost in the flood of evil that continually surrounds them. Now, Mr. Raikes, as he passed along, saw much to make him sad, for there were so many tokens of sin and wretchedness on all sides, that most persons, hopeless of doing any good, would have endeavored to forget the whole scene as soon as possible.

There is hardly a gloomier spectacle in the world than one of those obscure streets of London. The houses, which were old and ruinous, stood so close together as almost to shut out the sky, and even the sunshine, where a glimpse of it could be seen, was made dusky and dim by the smoke of the city. A kennel of muddy water flowed through the street. The general untidiness about the houses proved that the inhabitants felt no affection for their homes, nor took pride in making them decent and respectable. In these houses, it is to be feared that there were many people sick, suffering for food, and shivering with cold, and many, alas! who had fallen into the sore disease of sin, and sought to render their lives easier by dishonest practices. In short, the street seemed a place seldom visited by angels of mercy, or trodden by the footsteps of good men. Yet it were well that good men should often go thither, and be saddened by such reflections as now occurred to Mr. Raikes, in order that their hearts might be stirred up to attempt a reformation.

"Alas, what a spectacle is here!" thought this good man to himself. "How can any Christian remain idle, when there is so much evil to be remedied within a morning's walk of his own home?"

But we have not yet mentioned what it was that chiefly moved the heart of Mr. Raikes with sorrow and compassion. There were children at play in the street. Some were dabbling in the kennel, and splashing its dirty water over their companions, out of the mere love of mischief. Others, who had already been taught to gamble, were playing at pitch-and-toss for half-pence. Others, perhaps, were quarrelling and fighting. In a word—for we will not describe what it was so sad to witness—these poor children were growing up in idleness, with none but bad examples before their eyes, and without the opportunity of learning anything but evil. Their little, unclean faces looked already old in naughtiness; it seemed as if the vice and misery of the world had been born with them, and would cling to them as long as they existed. How sad a spectacle was this for a man like Mr. Raikes, who had always delighted in little children, and felt as if the world was made more beautiful, and his own heart the better, by their bright and happy faces! But, as he gazed at these poor little creatures, he thought that the world had never looked so dark, ugly, and sorrowful, as it did then.

"Oh, that I could save them!" thought he. "It were better for them to have been born among the wildest savages, than to grow up thus in a Christian country."

Now, at the door of one of the houses, there stood a woman, who, though she looked poor and needy, yet seemed neater and more respectable than the other inhabitants of this wretched street. She, like Mr. Raikes, was gazing at the children; and perhaps her mind was occupied with reflections similar to his. It might be, that she had children of her own, and was ready to shed tears at the thought, that they must grow up in the midst of such bad examples. At all events, when Mr. Raikes beheld this woman, he felt as if he had found somebody that could sympathize with him in his grief and anxiety.

"My good woman," said he, pointing to the children, "this is a dismal sight—so many of God's creatures growing up in idleness and ignorance, with no instruction but to do evil."

"Alas, good Sir," answered the woman, "it is bad enough on week-days, as you see;—but if you were to come into the street on a Sunday, you would find it a thousand times worse. On other days some of the children find employment, good or bad; but the Sabbath brings them all into the street to-gether—and then there is nothing but mischief from morning till night."

"Ah, that is a sad case indeed," said Mr. Raikes. "Can the blessed Sabbath itself bring no blessing to these poor children? This is the worst of all."

And then, again, he looked along the street, with pity and strong benevolence; for his whole heart was moved by what he saw. The longer he considered, the more terrible did it appear that those children should grow up in ignorance and sin, and that the germs of immortal goodness, which Heaven had implanted in their souls, should be for ever blighted by neglect. And the earnestness of his compassion quickened his mind to perceive what was to be done. As he stood gazing at the spectacle that had so saddened him, an expression of delightful hope broke forth upon his face, and made it look as if a bright gleam of sunshine fell across it. And, if moral sunshine could be discerned on physical objects, just such a brightness would have shone through the gloomy street, gladdening all the dusky windows, and causing the poor children to look beautiful and happy. Not only in that wretched street would the light of gladness have appeared; it might have spread from thence all round the earth; for there was now a thought on the mind of Mr. Raikes, that was destined, in no long time, to make the whole world brighter than it had been hitherto.

And what was that thought?

It must be considered that Mr. Raikes was not a very rich man. There were thousands of people in England, to whom Providence had assigned greater wealth than he possessed, and who, as one would suppose, might have done far more good to their fellow-creatures than it lay in his power to do. There was a king, too, and princes, lords and statesmen, who were set in lofty places, and entrusted with the making and administration of the laws. If the condition of the world was to be improved, were not these the men to accomplish it? But the true faculty of doing good consists not in wealth nor station, but in the energy and wisdom of a loving heart, that can sympathize with all mankind, and acknowledges a brother or a sister in every unfortunate man or woman, and an own child in each neglected orphan. Such a heart was that of Mr. Raikes; and God now rewarded him with a blessed opportunity of conferring more benefit on his race, than he, in his humility, had ever dreamed of. And it would not be too much to say, that the king and his nobles, and the wealthy gentlemen of England, with all their boundless means, had for many years, done nothing so worthy of grateful remembrance, as what was now to be effected by this humble individual.

And yet how simple was this great idea, and how small the means by which Mr. Raikes proceeded to put it in execution! It was merely, to hire respectable and intelligent women, at the rate of a shilling each, to come, every Sabbath, and keep little schools for the poor children whom he had seen at play. Perhaps the good woman with whom Mr. Raikes had spoken in the street, was one of his new school-mistresses. Be that as it might, the plan succeeded, and, attracting the notice of benevolent people, was soon adopted in many other dismal streets of London. And this was the origin of Sunday-schools. In course of time, similar schools were established all over that great city, and thence extended to the remotest parts of England, and across the ocean to America, and to countries at a world-wide distance, where the humble name of Robert Raikes had never been pronounced.

That good man has now long been dead. But still, on every Sabbath-morning, in the cities and country villages, and wheresoever the steeple of a church points upward to the sky, the children take their way to the Sunday-school. Thousands, and tens of thousands, have there received instruction, which has been more profitable to them than all the gold on earth. And we may be permitted to believe, that, in the celestial world, where the founder of the system now exists, he has often met with other happy spirits, who have blessed him as the earthly means by which they were rescued from hopeless ignorance and evil, and guided on the path to Heaven. Is not this a proof, that when the humblest person acts in the simplicity of a pure heart, and with no design but to do good, *God* may be expected to take the matter into His all-powerful hands, and adopt the action as His own?

The Intelligence Office

A GRAVE FIGURE, with a pair of mysterious spectacles on his nose and a pen behind his ear, was seated at a desk, in the corner of a metropolitan office. The apartment was fitted up with a counter, and furnished with an oaken cabinet and a chair or two, in simple and business-like style. Around the walls were stuck advertisements of articles lost, or articles wanted, or articles to be disposed of; in one or another of which classes were comprehended nearly all the conveniences, or otherwise, that the imagination of man has contrived. The interior of the room was thrown into shadow, partly by the tall edifices that rose on the opposite side of the street, and partly by the immense show-bills of blue and crimson paper, that were expanded over each of the three windows. Undisturbed by the tramp of feet, the rattle of wheels, the hum of voices, the shout of the city-crier, the scream of the newsboys, and other tokens of the multitudinous life that surged along in front of the office, the figure at the desk pored diligently over a folio volume, of leger-like size and aspect. He looked like the spirit of a record—the soul of his own great volume—made visible in mortal shape.

But scarcely an instant elapsed without the appearance at the door of some individual from the busy population whose vicinity was manifested by so much buzz, and clatter, and outcry. Now, it was a thriving mechanic, in quest of a tenement that should come within his moderate means of rent; now, a ruddy Irish girl from the banks of Killarney, wandering from kitchen to kitchen of our land, while her heart still hung in the peat-smoke of her native cottage; now, a single gentleman, looking out for economical board; and now—for this establishment offered an epitome of worldly pursuits—it was a faded beauty inquiring for her lost bloom; or Peter Schlemihl for his lost shadow; or an author, of ten years standing, for his vanished reputation; or a moody man for yesterday's sunshine.

At the next lifting of the latch there entered a person with his hat awry upon his head, his clothes perversely ill-suited to his form, his eyes staring in directions opposite to their intelligence, and a certain odd unsuitableness pervading his whole figure. Wherever he might chance to be, whether in palace or cottage, church or market, on land or sea, or even at his own fireside, he must have worn the characteristic expression of a man out of his right place.

"This," inquired he, putting his question in the form of an assertion, "this is the Central Intelligence Office?"

"Even so," answered the figure at the desk, turning another leaf of his volume; he then looked the applicant in the face, and said briefly—"Your business?"

"I want," said the latter, with tremulous earnestness, "a place!"

"A place!—and of what nature?" asked the Intelligencer. "There are many vacant, or soon to be so, some of which will probably suit, since they range from that of a footman up to a seat at the council-board, or in the cabinet, on a throne, or a presidential chair."

The stranger stood pondering before the desk, with an unquiet, dissatisfied air—a dull, vague pain of heart, expressed by a slight contortion of the brow—an earnestness of glance, that asked and expected, yet continually wavered, as if distrusting. In short, he evidently wanted, not in a physical or intellectual sense, but with an urgent moral necessity that is the hardest of all things to satisfy, since it knows not its own object.

"Ah, you mistake me!" said he at length, with a gesture of nervous impatience. "Either of the places you mention, indeed, might answer my purpose—or, more probably, none of them. I want my place!—my own place!—my true place in the world!—my proper sphere!—my thing to do, which nature intended me to perform when she fashioned me thus awry, and which I have vainly sought, all my lifetime! Whether it be a footman's duty, or a king's, is of little consequence, so it be naturally mine. Can you help me here?"

"I will enter your application," answered the Intelligencer, at the same time writing a few lines in his volume. "But to undertake such a business, I tell you frankly, is quite apart from the ground covered by my official duties. Ask for something specific, and it may doubtless be negotiated for you, on your compliance with the conditions. But were I to go further, I should have the whole population of the city upon my shoulders; since far the greater proportion of them are, more or less, in your predicament."

The applicant sank into a fit of despondency, and passed out of the door without again lifting his eyes; and, if he died of the disappointment, he was probably buried in the wrong tomb; inasmuch as the fatality of such people never deserts them, and, whether alive or dead, they are invariably out of place.

Almost immediately, another foot was heard on the threshold. A youth entered hastily, and threw a glance around the office to ascertain whether the Man of Intelligence was alone. He then approached close to the desk, blushed like a maiden, and seemed at a loss how to broach his business.

"You come upon an affair of the heart," said the official personage, looking into him through his mysterious spectacles. "State it in as few words as may be."

"You are right," replied the youth. "I have a heart to dispose of."

"You seek an exchange?" said the Intelligencer. "Foolish youth, why not be contented with your own?"

"Because," exclaimed the young man, losing his embarrassment in a passionate glow,—"because my heart burns me with an intolerable fire; it tortures me all day long with yearnings for I know not what, and feverish throbbings, and the pangs of a vague sorrow; and it awakens me in the night-time with a quake, when there is nothing to be feared! I cannot endure it any longer. It were wiser to throw away such a heart, even if it brings me nothing in return!"

"Oh, very well," said the man of office, making an entry in his volume. "Your affair will be easily transacted. This species of brokerage makes no inconsiderable part of my business; and there is always a large assortment of the article to select from. Here, if I mistake not, comes a pretty fair sample."

Even as he spoke, the door was gently and slowly thrust ajar, affording a glimpse of the slender figure of a young girl, who, as she timidly entered, seemed to bring the light and cheerfulness of the outer atmosphere into the somewhat gloomy apartment. We know not her errand there; nor can we reveal whether the young man gave up his heart into her custody. If so, the arrangement was neither better nor worse than in ninety-nine cases out of a hundred, where the parallel sensibilities of a similar age, importunate affections, and the easy satisfaction of characters not deeply conscious of themselves, supply the place of any profounder sympathy.

Not always, however, was the agency of the passions and affections an office of so little trouble. It happened—rarely, indeed, in proportion to the cases that came under an ordinary rule, but still it did happen—that a heart was occasionally brought hither, of such exquisite material, so delicately attempered, and so curiously wrought, that no other heart could be found to match it. It might almost be considered a misfortune, in a worldly point of view, to be the possessor of such a diamond of the purest water; since in any reasonable probability, it could only be exchanged for an ordinary pebble, or a bit of cunningly manufactured glass, or, at least, for a jewel of native richness, but ill-set, or with some fatal flaw, or an earthy vein running through its central lustre. To choose another figure, it is sad that hearts which have their well-spring in the infinite, and contain inexhaustible sympathies, should ever be doomed to pour themselves into shallow vessels, and thus lavish their rich affections on the ground. Strange, that the finer and deeper nature, whether in man or woman, while possessed of every other delicate instinct, should so often lack that most invaluable one, of preserving itself from contamination with what is of a baser kind! Sometimes, it is true, the spiritual fountain is kept pure by a wisdom within itself, and sparkles into the light of heaven, without a stain from the earthy strata through which it has gushed upward. And sometimes, even here on earth, the pure mingles with the pure, and the inexhaustible is recompensed with the infinite. But these miracles, though he should claim the credit of them, are far beyond the scope of such a superficial agent in human affairs, as the figure in the mysterious spectacles.

Again the door was opened, admitting the bustle of the city with a fresher reverberation into the Intelligence Office. Now entered a man of wo-begone and downcast look; it was such an aspect as if he had lost the very soul out of his body, and had traversed all the world over, searching in the dust of the highways, and along the shady footpaths, and beneath the leaves of the forest, and among the sands of the sea-shore, in hopes to recover it again. He had bent an anxious glance along the pavement of the street, as he came hitherward; he looked, also, in the angle of the door-step, and upon the floor of the room; and, finally, coming up to the Man of Intelligence, he gazed through the inscrutable spectacles which the latter wore, as if the lost treasure might be hidden within his eyes.

"I have lost—" he began; and then he paused.

"Yes," said the Intelligencer, "I see that you have lost—but what?"

"I have lost a precious jewel," replied the unfortunate person, "the like of which is not to be found among any prince's treasures. While I possessed it, the contemplation of it was my sole and sufficient happiness. No price should have purchased it of me; but it has fallen from my bosom, where I wore it, in my careless wanderings about the city."

After causing the stranger to describe the marks of his lost jewel, the Intelligencer opened a drawer of the oaken cabinet, which has been mentioned as forming a part of the furniture of the room. Here were deposited whatever articles had been picked up in the streets, until the right owners should claim them. It was a strange and heterogeneous collection. Not the least remarkable part of it, was a great number of wedding-rings, each one of which had been riveted upon the finger with holy vows, and all the mystic potency that the most solemn rites could attain, but had, nevertheless, proved too slippery for the wearer's vigilance. The gold of some was worn thin, betokening the attrition of years of wedlock; others, glittering from the jeweller's shop, must have been lost within the honey-moon. There were ivory tablets, the leaves scribbled over with sentiments that had been the deepest truths of the writer's earlier years, but which were now quite obliterated from his memory. So scrupulously were articles preserved in this depository, that not even withered flowers were rejected; white roses, and blush roses, and moss-roses, fit emblems of virgin purity and shamefacedness, which had been lost or flung away, and trampled into the pollution of the streets; locks of hair—the golden, and the glossy dark—the long tresses of woman and the crisp curls of man—signified that lovers were now and then so heedless of the faith entrusted to them, as to drop its symbol from the treasure-place of the bosom. Many of these things were imbued with perfumes; and perhaps a sweet scent had departed from the lives of their former possessors, ever since they had so wilfully or negligently lost them. Here were gold pencil-cases, little ruby hearts with golden arrows through them, bosom-pins, pieces of coin, and small articles of every description, comprising nearly all that have been lost, since a long time ago. Most of them, doubtless, had a history and a meaning, if there were time to search it out and room to tell it. Whoever has missed anything valuable, whether out of his heart, mind, or pocket, would do well to make inquiry at the Central Intelligence Office.

And, in the corner of one of the drawers of the oaken cabinet, after considerable research, was found a great pearl, looking like the soul of celestial purity, congealed and polished.

"There is my jewel! my very pearl!" cried the stranger, almost beside himself with rapture. "It is mine! Give it me—this moment!—or I shall perish!"

"I perceive," said the Man of Intelligence, examining it more closely, "that this is the Pearl of Great Price."

"The very same," answered the stranger. "Judge, then, of my misery at losing it out of my bosom! Restore it to me! I must not live without it an instant longer."

"Pardon me," rejoined the Intelligencer, calmly. "You ask what is beyond my duty. This pearl, as you well know, is held upon a peculiar tenure; and having once let it escape from your keeping, you have no greater claim to it—nay, not so great—as any other person. I cannot give it back."

Nor could the entreaties of the miserable man—who saw before his eyes the jewel of his life, without the power to reclaim it—soften the heart of this stern being, impassive to human sympathy, though exercising such an apparent influence over human fortunes. Finally, the loser of the inestimable pearl clutched his hands among his hair, and ran madly forth into the world, which was affrighted at his desperate looks. There passed him on the door-step a fashionable young gentleman, whose business was to inquire for a damask rose-bud, the gift of his lady-love, which he had lost out of his button-hole within an hour after receiving it. So various were the errands of those who visited this Central Office, where all human wishes seemed to be made known, and, so far as destiny would allow, negotiated to their fulfilment.

The next that entered was a man beyond the middle age, bearing the look of one who knew the world and his own course in it. He had just alighted from a handsome private carriage, which had orders to wait in the street while its owner transacted his business. This person came up to the desk with a quick, determined step, and looked the Intelligencer in the face with a resolute eye; though, at the same time, some secret trouble gleamed from it in red and dusky light.

"I have an estate to dispose of," said he, with a brevity that seemed characteristic.

"Describe it," said the Intelligencer.

The applicant proceeded to give the boundaries of his property, its nature, comprising tillage, pasture, woodland, and pleasure-grounds, in ample circuit; together with a man-sion-house, in the construction of which it had been his object to realize a castle in the air, hardening its shadowy walls into granite, and rendering its visionary splendor perceptible to the awakened eye. Judging from his description, it was beautiful enough to vanish like a dream, yet substantial enough to endure for centuries. He spoke, too, of the gor-geous furniture, the refinements of upholstery, and all the lux-urious artifices that combined to render this a residence where life might flow onward in a stream of golden days, undis-turbed by the ruggedness which fate loves to fling into it.

"I am a man of strong will," said he, in conclusion; "and at my first setting out in life, as a poor, unfriended youth, I resolved to make myself the possessor of such a mansion and estate as this, together with the abundant revenue necessary to uphold it. I have succeeded to the extent of my utmost wish. And this is the estate which I have now concluded to dispose of."

"And your terms?" asked the Intelligencer, after taking

down the particulars with which the stranger had supplied him.

"Easy—abundantly easy!" answered the successful man, smiling, but with a stern and almost frightful contraction of the brow, as if to quell an inward pang. "I have been engaged in various sorts of business—a distiller, a trader to Africa, an East India merchant, a speculator in the stocks—and, in the course of these affairs, have contracted an incumbrance of a certain nature. The purchaser of the estate shall merely be required to assume this burthen to himself."

"I understand you," said the Man of Intelligence, putting his pen behind his ear. "I fear that no bargain can be negotiated on these conditions. Very probably, the next possessor may acquire the estate with a similar incumbrance, but it will be of his own contracting, and will not lighten your burthen in the least."

"And am I to live on," fiercely exclaimed the stranger, "with the dirt of these accursed acres, and the granite of this infernal mansion, crushing down my soul? How, if I should turn the edifice into an almshouse or a hospital, or tear it down and build a church?"

"You can at least make the experiment," said the Intelligencer; "but the whole matter is one which you must settle for yourself."

The man of deplorable success withdrew, and got into his coach, which rattled off lightly over the wooden pavements, though laden with the weight of much land, a stately house, and ponderous heaps of gold, all compressed into an evil conscience.

There now appeared many applicants for places; among the most note-worthy of whom was a small, smoke-dried figure, who gave himself out to be one of the bad spirits that had waited upon Doctor Faustus in his laboratory. He pretended to show a certificate of character, which, he averred, had been given him by that famous necromancer, and countersigned by several masters whom he had subsequently served.

"I am afraid, my good friend," observed the Intelligencer, "that your chance of getting a service is but poor. Now-a-days, men act the evil spirit for themselves and their neighbors, and play the part more effectually than ninety-nine out of a hundred of your fraternity."

But, just as the poor fiend was assuming a vaporous consistency, being about to vanish through the floor in sad disappointment and chagrin, the editor of a political newspaper chanced to enter the office, in quest of a scribbler of party paragraphs. The former servant of Doctor Faustus, with some misgivings as to his sufficiency of venom, was allowed to try his hand in this capacity. Next appeared, likewise seeking a service, the mysterious Man in Red, who had aided Buonaparte in his ascent to imperial power. He was examined as to his qualifications by an aspiring politician, but finally rejected, as lacking familiarity with the cunning tactics of the present day.

People continued to succeed each other, with as much briskness as if everybody turned aside, out of the roar and tumult of the city, to record here some want, or superfluity, or desire. Some had goods or possessions, of which they wished to negotiate the sale. A China merchant had lost his health by a long residence in that wasting climate; he very liberally offered his disease, and his wealth along with it, to any physician who would rid him of both together. A soldier offered his wreath of laurels for as good a leg as that which it had cost him, on the battle-field. One poor weary wretch desired nothing but to be accommodated with any creditable method of laying down his life; for misfortune and pecuniary troubles had so subdued his spirits, that he could no longer conceive the possibility of happiness, nor had the heart to try for it. Nevertheless, happening to overhear some conversation in the Intelligence Office, respecting wealth to be rapidly accumulated by a certain mode of speculation, he resolved to live out this one other experiment of better fortune. Many persons desired to exchange their youthful vices for others better suited to the gravity of advancing age; a few, we are glad to say, made earnest efforts to exchange vice for virtue, and, hard as the bargain was, succeeded in effecting it. But it was remarkable, that what all were the least willing to give up, even on the most advantageous terms, were the habits, the oddities, the characteristic traits, the little ridiculous indulgences, somewhere between faults and follies, of which nobody but themselves could understand the fascination.

The great folio, in which the Man of Intelligence recorded all these freaks of idle hearts, and aspirations of deep hearts, and desperate longings of miserable hearts, and evil prayers of perverted hearts, would be curious reading, were it possible to obtain it for publication. Human character in its individual developments—human nature in the mass—may best be studied in its wishes; and this was the record of them all. There was an endless diversity of mode and circumstance, yet withal such a similarity in the real ground-work, that any one page of the volume—whether written in the days before the Flood, or the yesterday that is just gone by, or to be written on the morrow that is close at hand, or a thousand ages hence—might serve as a specimen of the whole. Not but that there were wild sallies of fantasy that could scarcely occur to more than one man's brain, whether reasonable or lunatic. The strangest wishes—yet most incident to men who had gone deep into scientific pursuits, and attained a high intellectual stage, though not the loftiest—were, to contend with Nature, and wrest from her some secret, or some power, which she had seen fit to withhold from mortal grasp. She loves to delude her aspiring students, and mock them with mysteries that seem but just beyond their utmost reach. To concoct new minerals—to produce new forms of vegetable life—to create an insect, if nothing higher in the living scale—is a sort of wish that has often revelled in the breast of a man of science. An astronomer, who lived far more among the distant worlds of space than in this lower sphere, recorded a wish to behold the opposite side of the moon, which, unless the system of the firmament be reversed, she can never turn towards the earth. On the same page of the volume, was written the wish of a little child, to have the stars for playthings.

The most ordinary wish, that was written down with wearisome recurrence, was, of course, for wealth, wealth, wealth, in sums from a few shillings up to unreckonable thousands. But, in reality, this often repeated expression covered as many different desires. Wealth is the golden essence of the outward world, embodying almost everything that exists beyond the limits of the soul; and therefore it is the natural yearning for the life in the midst of which we find ourselves, and of which gold is the condition of enjoyment, that men abridge into this general wish. Here and there, it is true, the volume testified to some heart so perverted as to desire gold for its own sake. Many wished for power; a strange desire, indeed, since it is but another form of slavery. Old people wished for the delights of youth; a fop, for a fashionable coat; an idle reader, for a new novel; a versifier, for a rhyme to some stubborn word; a painter, for Titian's secret of coloring; a prince, for a cottage; a republican, for a kingdom and a palace; a libertine, for his neighbor's wife; a man of palate, for green peas; and a poor man, for a crust of bread. The ambitious desires of public men, elsewhere so craftily concealed, were here expressed openly and boldly, side by side with the unselfish wishes of the philanthropist, for the welfare of the race, so beautiful, so comforting, in contrast with the egotism that continually weighed self against the world. Into the darker secrets of the Book of Wishes, we will not penetrate.

It would be an instructive employment for a student of mankind, perusing this volume carefully, and comparing its records with men's perfected designs, as expressed in their deeds and daily life, to ascertain how far the one accorded with the other. Undoubtedly, in most cases, the correspondence would be found remote. The holy and generous wish, that rises like incense from a pure heart towards heaven, often lavishes its sweet perfume on the blast of evil times. The foul, selfish, murderous wish, that steams forth from a corrupted heart, often passes into the spiritual atmosphere, without being concreted into an earthly deed. Yet this volume is probably truer, as a representation of the human heart, than is the living drama of action, as it evolves around us. There is more of good and more of evil in it; more redeeming points of the bad, and more errors of the virtuous; higher up-soarings, and baser degradation of the soul; in short, a more perplexing amalgamation of vice and virtue, than we witness in the outward world. Decency, and external conscience, often produce a far fairer outside, than is warranted by the stains within. And be it owned, on the other hand, that a man seldom repeats to his nearest friend, any more than he realizes in act, the purest wishes, which, at some blessed time or other, have arisen from the depths of his nature, and witnessed for him in this volume. Yet there is enough, on every leaf, to make the good man shudder for his own wild and idle wishes, as well as for the sinner, whose whole life is the incarnation of a wicked desire.

But again the door is opened; and we hear the tumultuous stir of the world—a deep and awful sound, expressing in another form, some portion of what is written in the volume that lies before the Man of Intelligence. A grandfatherly personage tottered hastily into the office, with such an earnestness in his infirm alacrity that his white hair floated backward, as he hurried up to the desk; while his dim eyes caught a momentary lustre from his vehemence of purpose. This venerable figure explained that he was in search of To-morrow.

"I have spent all my life in pursuit of it," added the sage old gentleman, "being assured that To-morrow has some vast benefit or other in store for me. But I am now getting a little in years, and must make haste; for unless I overtake To-morrow soon, I begin to be afraid it will finally escape me."

"This fugitive To-morrow, my venerable friend," said the Man of Intelligence, "is a stray child of Time, and is flying from his father into the region of the infinite. Continue your pursuit, and you will doubtless come up with him; but as to the earthly gifts which you expect, he has scattered them all among a throng of Yesterdays."

Obliged to content himself with this enigmatical response, the grandsire hastened forth, with a quick clatter of his staff upon the floor; and as he disappeared, a little boy scampered through the door in chase of a butterfly, which had got astray amid the barren sunshine of the city. Had the old gentleman been shrewder, he might have detected To-morrow under the semblance of that gaudy insect. The golden butterfly glistened through the shadowy apartment, and brushed its wings against the Book of Wishes, and fluttered forth again with the child still in pursuit.

A man now entered, in neglected attire, with the aspect of a thinker, but somewhat too rough-hewn and brawny for a scholar. His face was full of sturdy vigor, with some finer and keener attribute beneath; though harsh at first, it was tempered with the glow of a large, warm heart, which had force enough to heat his powerful intellect through and through. He advanced to the Intelligencer, and looked at him with a glance of such stern sincerity, that perhaps few secrets were beyond its scope.

"I seek for Truth," said he.

"It is precisely the most rare pursuit that has ever come under my cognizance," replied the Intelligencer, as he made the new inscription in his volume. "Most men seek to impose some cunning falsehood upon themselves for truth. But I can lend no help to your researches. You must achieve the miracle for yourself. At some fortunate moment, you may find Truth at your side—or, perhaps, she may be mistily discerned, far in advance—or, possibly, behind you."

"Not behind me," said the seeker, "for I have left nothing on my track without a thorough investigation. She flits before me, passing now through a naked solitude, and now mingling with the throng of a popular assembly, and now writing with the pen of a French philosopher, and now standing at the altar of an old cathedral, in the guise of a Catholic priest, performing the high mass. Oh weary search! But I must not falter; and surely my heart-deep quest of Truth shall avail at last."

He paused, and fixed his eyes upon the Intelligencer, with a depth of investigation that seemed to hold commerce with the inner nature of this being, wholly regardless of his external development.

"And what are you?" said he. "It will not satisfy me to point to this fantastic show of an Intelligence Office, and this mockery of business. Tell me what is beneath it, and what your real agency in life, and your influence upon mankind?"

"Yours is a mind," answered the Man of Intelligence, "before which the forms and fantasies that conceal the inner idea from the multitude, vanish at once, and leave the naked reality beneath. Know, then, the secret. My agency in worldly action—my connection with the press, and tumult, and intermingling, and development of human affairs—is merely delusive. The desire of man's heart does for him whatever I seem to do. I am no minister of action, but the Recording Spirit!"

What further secrets were then spoken, remains a mystery;
inasmuch as the roar of the city, the bustle of human business, the outcry of the jostling masses, the rush and tumult of
man's life, in its noisy and brief career, arose so high that it
drowned the words of these two talkers. And whether they
stood talking in the Moon, or in Vanity Fair, or in a city of
this actual world, is more than I can say.

Earth's Holocaust

O NCE upon a time—but whether in time past or time to come, is a matter of little or no moment—this wide world had become so overburthened with an accumulation of worn-out trumpery, that the inhabitants determined to rid themselves of it by a general bonfire. The site fixed upon, at the representation of the Insurance Companies, and as being as central a spot as any other on the globe, was one of the broadest prairies of the West, where no human habitation would be endangered by the flames, and where a vast assemblage of spectators might commodiously admire the show. Having a taste for sights of this kind, and imagining, likewise, that the illumination of the bonfire might reveal some profundity of moral truth, heretofore hidden in mist or darkness, I made it convenient to journey thither and be present. At my arrival, although the heap of condemned rubbish was as yet comparatively small, the torch had already been applied. Amid that boundless plain, in the dusk of evening, like a far-off star alone in the firmament, there was merely visible one tremulous gleam, whence none could have anticipated so fierce a blaze as was destined to ensue. With every moment, however, there came foot-travellers, women holding up their aprons, men on horseback, wheelbarrows, lumbering baggage-wagons, and other vehicles great and small, and from far and near, laden with articles that were judged fit for nothing but to be burnt.

"What materials have been used to kindle the flames?" inquired I of a bystander; for I was desirous of knowing the whole process of the affair, from beginning to end.

The person whom I addressed was a grave man, fifty years old or thereabout, who had evidently come thither as a looker-on; he struck me immediately as having weighed for himself the true value of life and its circumstances, and therefore as feeling little personal interest in whatever judgment the world might form of them. Before answering my question, he looked me in the face, by the kindling light of the fire.

"Oh, some very dry combustibles," replied he, "and extremely suitable to the purpose—no other, in fact, than yesterday's newspapers, last month's magazines, and last year's withered leaves. Here, now, comes some antiquated trash, that will take fire like a handfull of shavings."

As he spoke, some rough-looking men advanced to the verge of the bonfire, and threw in, as it appeared, all the rubbish of the Herald's Office; the blazonry of coat-armor; the crests and devices of illustrious families; pedigrees that extended back, like lines of light, into the mist of the dark ages; together with stars, garters, and embroidered collars; each of which, as paltry a bauble as it might appear to the uninstructed eye, had once possessed vast significance, and was still, in truth, reckoned among the most precious of moral or material facts, by the worshippers of the gorgeous past. Mingled with this confused heap, which was tossed into the flames by armsfull at once, were innumerable badges of knighthood; comprising those of all the European sovereignties, and Napoleon's decoration of the Legion of Honor, the ribands of which were entangled with those of the ancient order of St. Louis. There, too, were the medals of our own society of Cincinnati, by means of which, as history tells us, an order of hereditary knights came near being constituted out of the king-quellers of the Revolution. And, besides, there were the patents of nobility of German counts and barons, Spanish grandees, and English peers, from the worm-eaten instrument signed by William the Conqueror, down to the bran-new parchment of the latest lord, who has received his honors from the fair hand of Victoria.

At sight of the dense volumes of smoke, mingled with vivid jets of flame, that gushed and eddied forth from this immense pile of earthly distinctions, the multitude of plebeian spectators set up a joyous shout, and clapt their hands with an emphasis that made the welkin echo. That was their moment of triumph, achieved after long ages, over creatures of the same clay and same spiritual infirmities, who had dared to assume the privileges due only to Heaven's better workmanship. But now there rushed towards the blazing heap a gray-haired man, of stately presence, wearing a coat from the breast of which some star, or other badge of rank, seemed to have been forcibly wrenched away. He had not the tokens of intellectual power in his face; but still there was the demeanor—the habitual, and almost native dignity—of one who had been born to the idea of his own social superiority, and had never felt it questioned, till that moment.

"People," cried he, gazing at the ruin of what was dearest in his eyes, with grief and wonder, but, nevertheless, with a degree of stateliness—"people, what have you done! This fire is consuming all that marked your advance from barbarism, or that could have prevented your relapse thither. We—the men of the privileged orders—were those who kept alive, from age to age, the old chivalrous spirit; the gentle and generous thought; the higher, the purer, the more refined and delicate life! With the nobles, too, you cast off the poet, the painter, the sculptor—all the beautiful arts;—for we were their patrons, and created the atmosphere in which they flourish. In abolishing the majestic distinctions of rank, society loses not only its grace, but its steadfastness—"

More he would doubtless have spoken; but here there arose an outcry, sportive, contemptuous, and indignant, that altogether drowned the appeal of the fallen nobleman; insomuch that, casting one look of despair at his own half-burnt pedigree, he shrunk back into the crowd, glad to shelter himself under his new-found insignificance.

"Let him thank his stars that we have not flung him into the same fire!" shouted a rude figure, spurning the embers with his foot. "And, henceforth, let no man dare to show a piece of musty parchment, as his warrant for lording it over his fellows! If he have strength of arm, well and good; it is one species of superiority. If he have wit, wisdom, courage, force of character, let these attributes do for him what they may. But, from this day forward, no mortal must hope for place and consideration, by reckoning up the mouldy bones of his ancestors! That nonsense is done away."

"And in good time," remarked the grave observer by my side—in a low voice however—"if no worse nonsense come in its place. But at all events, this species of nonsense has fairly lived out its life."

There was little space to muse or moralize over the embers of this time-honored rubbish; for, before it was half burnt out, there came another multitude from beyond the sea, bearing the purple robes of royalty, and the crowns, globes, and sceptres of emperors and kings. All these had been condemned as useless baubles; playthings, at best, fit only for the infancy of the world, or rods to govern and chastise it in its nonage; but with which universal manhood, at its full-grown stature, could no longer brook to be insulted. Into such contempt had these regal insignia now fallen, that the gilded crown and tinselled robes of the player-king, from Drury Lane Theatre, had been thrown in among the rest, doubtless as a mockery of his brother-monarchs, on the great stage of the world. It was a strange sight, to discern the crown-jewels of England, glowing and flashing in the midst of the fire. Some of them had been delivered down from the times of the Saxon princes; others were purchased with vast revenues, or, perchance, ravished from the dead brows of the native potentates of Hindostan; and the whole now blazed with a dazzling lustre, as if a star had fallen in that spot, and been shattered into fragments. The splendor of the ruined monarchy had no reflection, save in those inestimable precious-stones. But, enough on this subject! It were but tedious to describe how the Emperor of Austria's mantle was converted to tinder, and how the posts and pillars of the French throne became a heap of coals, which it was impossible to distinguish from those of any other wood. Let me add, however, that I noticed one of the exiled Poles, stirring up the bonfire with the Czar of Russia's sceptre, which he afterwards flung into the flames.

"The smell of singed garments is quite intolerable here," observed my new acquaintance, as the breeze enveloped us in the smoke of a royal wardrobe. "Let us get to windward, and see what they are doing on the other side of the bonfire."

We accordingly passed round, and were just in time to witness the arrival of a vast procession of Washingtonians—as the votaries of temperance call themselves now-a-days—accompanied by thousands of the Irish disciples of Father Mathew, with that great apostle at their head. They brought a rich contribution to the bonfire; being nothing less than all the hogsheads and barrels of liquor in the world, which they rolled before them across the prairie.

"Now, my children," cried Father Mathew, when they

reached the verge of the fire—"one shove more, and the work is done! And now let us stand off, and see Satan deal with his own liquor!"

Accordingly, having placed their wooden vessels within reach of the flames, the procession stood off at a safe distance, and soon beheld them burst into a blaze that reached the clouds, and threatened to set the sky itself on fire. And well it might. For here was the whole world's stock of spirituous liquors, which, instead of kindling a frenzied light in the eyes of individual topers as of yore, soared upward with a bewildering gleam that startled all mankind. It was the aggregate of that fierce fire, which would otherwise have scorched the hearts of millions. Meantime, numberless bottles of precious wine were flung into the blaze; which lapped up the contents as if it loved them, and grew, like other drunkards, the merrier and fiercer for what it quaffed. Never again will the insatiable thirst of the fire-fiend be so pampered! Here were the treasures of famous bon-vivants—liquors that had been tossed on ocean, and mellowed in the sun, and hoarded long in the recesses of the earth—the pale, the gold, the ruddy juice of whatever vineyards were most delicate—the entire vintage of Tokay—all mingling in one stream with the vile fluids of the common pot-house, and contributing to heighten the self-same blaze. And while it rose in a gigantic spire, that seemed to wave against the arch of the firmament, and combine itself with the light of stars, the multitude gave a shout, as if the broad earth were exulting in its deliverance from the curse of ages.

But the joy was not universal. Many deemed that human life would be gloomier than ever, when that brief illumination should sink down. While the reformers were at work, I had overheard muttered expostulations from several respectable gentlemen with red noses, and wearing gouty shoes; and a ragged worthy, whose face looked like a hearth where the fire is burnt out, now expressed his discontent more openly and boldly.

"What is this world good for," said the Last Toper, "now that we can never be jolly any more? What is to comfort the poor man in sorrow and perplexity?—how is he to keep his heart warm against the cold winds of this cheerless earth?—

and what do you propose to give him, in exchange for the solace that you take away? How are old friends to sit together by the fireside, without a cheerful glass between them? A plague upon your reformation! It is a sad world, a cold world, a selfish world, a low world, not worth an honest fellow's living in, now that good-fellowship is gone forever!"

This harangue excited great mirth among the bystanders. But, preposterous as was the sentiment, I could not help commiserating the forlorn condition of the Last Toper, whose boon-companions had dwindled away from his side, leaving the poor fellow without a soul to countenance him in sipping his liquor, nor, indeed, any liquor to sip. Not that this was quite the true state of the case; for I had observed him, at a critical moment, filch a bottle of fourth-proof brandy that fell beside the bonfire, and hide it in his pocket.

The spirituous and fermented liquors being thus disposed of, the zeal of the reformers next induced them to replenish the fire with all the boxes of tea and bags of coffee in the world. And now came the planters of Virginia, bringing their crops of tobacco. These, being cast upon the heap of inutility, aggregated it to the size of a mountain, and incensed the atmosphere with such potent fragrance, that methought we should never draw pure breath again. The present sacrifice seemed to startle the lovers of the weed, more than any that they had hitherto witnessed.

"Well;—they've put my pipe out," said an old gentleman, flinging it into the flames in a pet. "What is this world coming to? Everything rich and racy—all the spice of life—is to be condemned as useless. Now that they have kindled the bonfire, if these nonsensical reformers would fling themselves into it, all would be well enough!"

"Be patient," responded a staunch conservative;—"it will come to that in the end. They will first fling us in, and finally themselves."

From the general and systematic measures of reform, I now turned to consider the individual contributions to this memorable bonfire. In many instances, these were of a very amusing character. One poor fellow threw in his empty purse, and another, a bundle of counterfeit or insolvable banknotes. Fashionable ladies threw in their last season's bonnets, to-

gether with heaps of ribbon, yellow lace, and much other
half-worn milliner's ware; all of which proved even more evanescent in the fire, than it had been in the fashion. A multitude of lovers, of both sexes—discarded maids or bachelors,
and couples, mutually weary of one another—tossed in bundles of perfumed letters and enamored sonnets. A hack-poli-
tician, being deprived of bread by the loss of office, threw in
his teeth, which happened to be false ones. The Rev. Sydney
Smith—having voyaged across the Atlantic for that sole purpose—came up to the bonfire, with a bitter grin, and threw
in certain repudiated bonds, fortified though they were with
the broad seal of a sovereign state. A little boy of five years
old, in the premature manliness of the present epoch, threw
in his playthings; a college-graduate, his diploma; an apothecary, ruined by the spread of homœopathy, his whole stock
of drugs and medicines; a physician, his library; a parson, his
old sermons; and a fine gentleman of the old school, his code
of manners, which he had formerly written down for the benefit of the next generation. A widow, resolving on a second
marriage, slily threw in her dead husband's miniature. A
young man, jilted by his mistress, would willingly have flung
his own desperate heart into the flames, but could find no
means to wrench it out of his bosom. An American author,
whose works were neglected by the public, threw his pen and
paper into the bonfire, and betook himself to some less discouraging occupation. It somewhat startled me to overhear a
number of ladies, highly respectable in appearance, proposing
to fling their gowns and petticoats into the flames, and assume the garb, together with the manners, duties, offices, and
responsibilities, of the opposite sex.

What favor was accorded to this scheme, I am unable to
say; my attention being suddenly drawn to a poor, deceived,
and half-delirious girl, who, exclaiming that she was the most
worthless thing alive or dead, attempted to cast herself into
the fire, amid all that wrecked and broken trumpery of the
world. A good man, however, ran to her rescue.

"Patience, my poor girl!" said he, as he drew her back from
the fierce embrace of the destroying angel. "Be patient, and
abide Heaven's will. So long as you possess a living soul, all
may be restored to its first freshness. These things of matter,

and creations of human fantasy, are fit for nothing but to be burnt, when once they have had their day. But your day is Eternity!"

"Yes," said the wretched girl, whose frenzy seemed now to have sunk down into deep despondency;—"yes; and the sunshine is blotted out of it!"

It was now rumored among the spectators, that all the weapons and munitions of war were to be thrown into the bonfire; with the exception of the world's stock of gunpowder, which, as the safest mode of disposing of it, had already been drowned in the sea. This intelligence seemed to awaken great diversity of opinion. The hopeful philanthropist esteemed it a token that the millenium was already come; while persons of another stamp, in whose view mankind was a breed of bull-dogs, prophesied that all the old stoutness, fervor, nobleness, generosity, and magnanimity of the race, would disappear; these qualities, as they affirmed, requiring blood for their nourishment. They comforted themselves, however, in the belief that the proposed abolition of war was impracticable, for any length of time together.

Be that as it might, numberless great guns, whose thunder had long been the voice of battle—the artillery of the Armada, the battering-trains of Marlborough, and the adverse cannon of Napoleon and Wellington—were trundled into the midst of the fire. By the continual addition of dry combustibles, it had now waxed so intense, that neither brass nor iron could withstand it. It was wonderful to behold, how those terrible instruments of slaughter melted away like playthings of wax. Then the armies of the earth wheeled around the mighty furnace, with their military music playing triumphant marches, and flung in their muskets and swords. The standard-bearers, likewise, cast one look upward at their banners, all tattered with shot-holes, and inscribed with the names of victorious fields; and giving them a last flourish on the breeze, they lowered them into the flame, which snatched them upward in its rush towards the clouds. This ceremony being over, the world was left without a single weapon in its hands, except, possibly, a few old King's arms and rusty swords, and other trophies of the Revolution, in some of our state-armories. And now the drums were beaten and the trumpets brayed all together, as a prelude to the proclamation of universal and eternal peace, and the announcement that glory was no longer to be won by blood; but that it would henceforth be the contention of the human race, to work out the greatest mutual good; and that beneficence, in the future annals of the earth, would claim the praise of valor. The blessed tidings were accordingly promulgated, and caused infinite rejoicings among those who had stood aghast at the horror and absurdity of war.

But I saw a grim smile pass over the scarred visage of a stately old commander—by his war-worn figure and rich military dress, he might have been one of Napoleon's famous marshals—who, with the rest of the world's soldiery, had just flung away the sword, that had been familiar to his right hand for half-a-century.

"Aye, aye!" grumbled he. "Let them proclaim what they please; but, in the end, we shall find that all this foolery has only made more work for the armorers and cannon-founderies."

"Why, Sir," exclaimed I, in astonishment, "do you imagine that the human race will ever so far return on the steps of its past madness, as to weld another sword, or cast another cannon?"

"There will be no need," observed, with a sneer, one who neither felt benevolence, nor had faith in it. "When Cain wished to slay his brother, he was at no loss for a weapon."

"We shall see," replied the veteran commander.—"If I am mistaken, so much the better; but, in my opinion—without pretending to philosophize about the matter—the necessity of war lies far deeper than these honest gentlemen suppose. What! Is there a field for all the petty disputes of individuals, and shall there be no great law-court for the settlement of national difficulties? The battle-field is the only court where such suits can be tried!"

"You forget, General," rejoined I, "that, in this advanced stage of civilization, Reason and Philanthropy combined will constitute just such a tribunal as is requisite."

"Ah, I had forgotten that, indeed!" said the old warrior, as he limped away.

The fire was now to be replenished with materials that had

hitherto been considered of even greater importance to the
well-being of society, than the warlike munitions which we
had already seen consumed. A body of reformers had travelled all over the earth, in quest of the machinery by which
the different nations were accustomed to inflict the punishment of death. A shudder passed through the multitude, as
these ghastly emblems were dragged forward. Even the flames
seemed at first to shrink away, displaying the shape and murderous contrivance of each in a full blaze of light, which, of
itself, was sufficient to convince mankind of the long and
deadly error of human law. Those old implements of cruelty—
those horrible monsters of mechanism—those inventions
which it seemed to demand something worse than man's natural heart to contrive, and which had lurked in the dusky
nooks of ancient prisons, the subject of terror-stricken legends—were now brought forth to view. Headsmen's axes,
with the rust of noble and royal blood upon them, and a vast
collection of halters that had choked the breath of plebeian
victims, were thrown in together. A shout greeted the arrival
of the guillotine, which was thrust forward on the same
wheels that had borne it from one to another of the blood-
stained streets of Paris. But the loudest roar of applause went
up, telling the distant sky of the triumph of the earth's re-
demption, when the gallows made its appearance. An ill-looking fellow, however, rushed forward, and putting himself in
the path of the reformers, bellowed hoarsely, and fought with
brute fury to stay their progress.

It was little matter of surprise, perhaps, that the executioner
should thus do his best to vindicate and uphold the machinery by which he himself had his livelihood, and worthier
individuals their death. But it deserved special note, that
men of a far different sphere—even of that consecrated class
in whose guardianship the world is apt to trust its benevolence—were found to take the hangman's view of the
question.

"Stay, my brethren!" cried one of them. "You are misled
by a false philanthropy!—you know not what you do. The
gallows is a heaven-oriented instrument! Bear it back, then,
reverently, and set it up in its old place; else the world will
fall to speedy ruin and desolation!"

"Onward, onward!" shouted a leader in the reform. "Into the flames with the accursed instrument of man's bloody policy! How can human law inculcate benevolence and love, while it persists in setting up the gallows as its chief symbol? One heave more, good friends; and the world will be redeemed from its greatest error!"

A thousand hands, that, nevertheless, loathed the touch, now lent their assistance, and thrust the ominous burthen far, far, into the centre of the raging furnace. There its fatal and abhorred image was beheld, first black, then a red coal, then ashes.

"That was well done!" exclaimed I.

"Yes; it was well done," replied—but with less enthusiasm than I expected—the thoughtful observer who was still at my side; "well done, if the world be good enough for the measure. Death, however, is an idea that cannot easily be dispensed with, in any condition between the primal innocence and that other purity and perfection, which, perchance, we are destined to attain, after travelling round the full circle. But, at all events, it is well that the experiment should now be tried."

"Too cold!—too cold!" impatiently exclaimed the young and ardent leader in this triumph. "Let the heart have its voice here, as well as the intellect. And as for ripeness—and as for progress—let mankind always do the highest, kindest, noblest thing, that, at any given period, it has attained to the perception of; and surely that thing cannot be wrong, nor wrongly timed!"

I know not whether it were the excitement of the scene, or whether the good people around the bonfire were really growing more enlightened, every instant; but they now proceeded to measures, in the full length of which I was hardly prepared to keep them company. For instance, some threw their marriage-certificates into the flames, and declared themselves candidates for a higher, holier, and more comprehensive union than that which had subsisted from the birth of time, under the form of the connubial tie. Others hastened to the vaults of banks, and to the coffers of the rich—all of which were open to the first-comer, on this fated occasion—and brought entire bales of paper-money to enliven the blaze,

and tons of coin to be melted down by its intensity. Henceforth, they said, universal benevolence, uncoined and exhaustless, was to be the golden currency of the world. At this
intelligence, the bankers, and speculators in the stocks,
grew pale; and a pick-pocket, who had reaped a rich harvest
among the crowd, fell down in a deadly fainting-fit. A few
men of business burnt their day-books and legers, the notes
and obligations of their creditors, and all other evidences
of debts due to themselves; while perhaps a somewhat larger
number satisfied their zeal for reform with the sacrifice of any
uncomfortable recollection of their own indebtment. There
was then a cry, that the period was arrived, when the title-
deeds of landed property should be given to the flames, and
the whole soil of the earth revert to the public, from whom it
had been wrongfully abstracted, and most unequally distributed
among individuals. Another party demanded, that all written
constitutions, set forms of government, legislative acts,
statute-books, and everything else on which human invention had endeavored to stamp its arbitrary laws, should at once
be destroyed, leaving the consummated world as free as the
man first created.

Whether any ultimate action was taken with regard to these
propositions, is beyond my knowledge; for, just then, some
matters were in progress that concerned my sympathies more
nearly.

"See!—see!—what heaps of books and pamphlets," cried
a fellow, who did not seem to be a lover of literature. "Now
we shall have a glorious blaze!"

"That's just the thing," said a modern philosopher. "Now
we shall get rid of the weight of dead men's thought, which
has hitherto pressed so heavily on the living intellect, that it
has been incompetent to any effectual self-exertion. Well
done, my lads! Into the fire with them! Now you are enlight-
ening the world, indeed!"

"But what is to become of the Trade?" cried a frantic bookseller.

"Oh, by all means, let them accompany their merchandise,"
coolly observed an author. "It will be a noble funeral-pile!"

The truth was, that the human race had now reached a
stage of progress, so far beyond what the wisest and wittiest

men of former ages had ever dreamed of, that it would have been a manifest absurdity to allow the earth to be any longer encumbered with their poor achievements in the literary line. Accordingly, a thorough and searching investigation had swept the booksellers' shops, hawkers' stands, public and private libraries, and even the little book-shelf by the country fireside, and had brought the world's entire mass of printed paper, bound or in sheets, to swell the already mountain-bulk of our illustrious bonfire. Thick, heavy folios, containing the labors of lexicographers, commentators, and encyclopediasts, were flung in, and, falling among the embers with a leaden thump, smouldered away to ashes, like rotten wood. The small, richly-gilt, French tomes, of the last age, with the hundred volumes of Voltaire among them, went off in a brilliant shower of sparkles, and little jets of flame; while the current literature of the same nation burnt red and blue, and threw an infernal light over the visages of the spectators, converting them all to the aspect of parti-colored fiends. A collection of German stories emitted a scent of brimstone. The English standard authors made excellent fuel, generally exhibiting the properties of sound oak logs. Milton's works, in particular, sent up a powerful blaze, gradually reddening into a coal, which promised to endure longer than almost any other material of the pile. From Shakspeare there gushed a flame of such marvellous splendor, that men shaded their eyes as against the sun's meridian glory; nor, even when the works of his own elucidators were flung upon him, did he cease to flash forth a dazzling radiance, from beneath the ponderous heap. It is my belief, that he is still blazing as fervidly as ever.

"Could a poet but light a lamp at that glorious flame," remarked I, "he might then consume the midnight oil to some good purpose."

"That is the very thing which modern poets have been too apt to do—or, at least, to attempt," answered a critic. "The chief benefit to be expected from this conflagration of past literature, undoubtedly is, that writers will henceforth be compelled to light their lamps at the sun or stars."

"If they can reach so high," said I. "But that task requires a giant, who may afterwards distribute the light among inferior men. It is not every one that can steal the fire from

Heaven, like Prometheus; but when once he had done the deed, a thousand hearths were kindled by it."

It amazed me much to observe, how indefinite was the proportion between the physical mass of any given author, and the property of brilliant and long-continued combustion. For instance, there was not a quarto volume of the last century—nor, indeed, of the present—that could compete, in that particular, with a child's little gilt-covered book, containing Mother Goose's Melodies. The Life and Death of Tom Thumb outlasted the biography of Marlborough. An epic—indeed, a dozen of them—was converted to white ashes, before the single sheet of an old ballad was half-consumed. In more than one case, too, when volumes of applauded verse proved incapable of anything better than a stifling smoke, an unregarded ditty of some nameless bard—perchance, in the corner of a newspaper—soared up among the stars, with a flame as brilliant as their own. Speaking of the properties of flame, methought Shelley's poetry emitted a purer light than almost any other productions of his day; contrasting beautifully with the fitful and lurid gleams, and gushes of black vapor, that flashed and eddied from the volumes of Lord Byron. As for Tom Moore, some of his songs diffused an odor like a burning pastille.

I felt particular interest in watching the combustion of American authors, and scrupulously noted, by my watch, the precise number of moments that changed most of them from shabbily-printed books to indistinguishable ashes. It would be invidious, however, if not perilous, to betray these awful secrets; so that I shall content myself with observing, that it was not invariably the writer most frequent in the public mouth, that made the most splendid appearance in the bonfire. I especially remember, that a great deal of excellent inflammability was exhibited in a thin volume of poems by Ellery Channing; although, to speak the truth, there were certain portions that hissed and spluttered in a very disagreeable fashion. A curious phenomenon occurred, in reference to several writers, native as well as foreign. Their books, though of highly respectable figure, instead of bursting into a blaze, or even smouldering out their substance in smoke, suddenly melted away, in a manner that proved them to be ice.

If it be no lack of modesty to mention my own works, it must here be confessed, that I looked for them with fatherly interest, but in vain. Too probably, they were changed to vapor by the first action of the heat; at best, I can only hope, that, in their quiet way, they contributed a glimmering spark or two to the splendor of the evening.

"Alas, and woe is me!" thus bemoaned himself a heavy-looking gentleman in green spectacles. "The world is utterly ruined, and there is nothing to live for any longer! The business of my life is snatched from me. Not a volume to be had for love or money!"

"This," remarked the sedate observer beside me, "is a book-worm—one of those men who are born to gnaw dead thoughts. His clothes, you see, are covered with the dust of libraries. He has no inward fountain of ideas; and, in good earnest, now that the old stock is abolished, I do not see what is to become of the poor fellow. Have you no word of comfort for him?"

"My dear Sir," said I to the desperate book-worm, "is not Nature better than a book?—is not the human heart deeper than any system of philosophy?—is not life replete with more instruction than past observers have found it possible to write down in maxims? Be of good cheer! The great book of Time is still spread wide open before us; and, if we read it aright, it will be to us a volume of eternal Truth."

"Oh, my books, my books, my precious, printed books!" reiterated the forlorn book-worm. "My only reality was a bound volume; and now they will not leave me even a shadowy pamphlet!"

In fact, the last remnant of the literature of all the ages was now descending upon the blazing heap, in the shape of a cloud of pamphlets from the press of the New World. These, likewise, were consumed in the twinkling of an eye, leaving the earth, for the first time since the days of Cadmus, free from the plague of letters—an enviable field for the authors of the next generation!

"Well!—and does anything remain to be done?" inquired I, somewhat anxiously. "Unless we set fire to the earth itself, and then leap boldly off into infinite space, I know not that we can carry reform to any further point."

"You are vastly mistaken, my good friend," said the observer. "Believe me, the fire will not be allowed to settle down, without the addition of fuel that will startle many persons, who have lent a willing hand thus far."

Nevertheless, there appeared to be a relaxation of effort, for a little time, during which, probably, the leaders of the movement were considering what should be done next. In the interval, a philosopher threw his theory into the flames; a sacrifice, which, by those who knew how to estimate it, was pronounced the most remarkable that had yet been made. The combustion, however, was by no means brilliant. Some indefatigable people, scorning to take a moment's ease, now employed themselves in collecting all the withered leaves and fallen boughs of the forest, and thereby recruited the bonfire to a greater height than ever. But this was mere by-play.

"Here comes the fresh fuel that I spoke of," said my companion.

To my astonishment, the persons who now advanced into the vacant space, around the mountain of fire, bore surplices and other priestly garments, mitres, crosiers, and a confusion of popish and protestant emblems, with which it seemed their purpose to consummate this great Act of Faith. Crosses, from the spires of old cathedrals, were cast upon the heap, with as little remorse as if the reverence of centuries, passing in long array beneath the lofty towers, had not looked up to them as the holiest of symbols. The font, in which infants were consecrated to God; the sacramental vessels, whence Piety had received the hallowed draught; were given to the same destruction. Perhaps it most nearly touched my heart, to see, among these devoted relics, fragments of the humble communion-tables and undecorated pulpits, which I recognized as having been torn from the meeting-houses of New-England. Those simple edifices might have been permitted to retain all of sacred embellishment that their Puritan founders had bestowed, even though the mighty structure of St. Peter's had sent its spoils to the fire of this terrible sacrifice. Yet I felt that these were but the externals of religion, and might most safely be relinquished by spirits that best knew their deep significance.

"All is well," said I, cheerfully. "The wood-paths shall be

the aisles of our cathedral—the firmament itself shall be its ceiling! What needs an earthly roof between the Deity and his worshipper? Our faith can well afford to lose all the drapery that even the holiest men have thrown around it, and be only the more sublime in its simplicity."

"True," said my companion. "But will they pause here?"

The doubt, implied in his question, was well-founded. In the general destruction of books, already described, a holy volume—that stood apart from the catalogue of human literature, and yet, in one sense, was at its head—had been spared. But the Titan of innovation—angel or fiend, double in his nature, and capable of deeds befitting both characters— at first shaking down only the old and rotten shapes of things, had now, as it appeared, laid his terrible hand upon the main pillars, which supported the whole edifice of our moral and spiritual state. The inhabitants of the earth had grown too enlightened to define their faith within a form of words, or to limit the spiritual by any analogy to our material existence. Truths, which the Heavens trembled at, were now but a fable of the world's infancy. Therefore, as the final sacrifice of human error, what else remained, to be thrown upon the embers of that awful pile, except the Book, which, though a celestial revelation to past ages, was but a voice from a lower sphere, as regarded the present race of man? It was done! Upon the blazing heap of falsehood and worn-out truth— things that the earth had never needed, or had ceased to need, or had grown childishly weary of—fell the ponderous church-Bible, the great old volume, that had lain so long on the cushions of the pulpit, and whence the pastor's solemn voice had given holy utterances, on so many a Sabbath-day. There, likewise, fell the family-Bible, which the long-buried patriarch had read to his children—in prosperity or sorrow, by the fireside, and in the summer-shade of trees—and had bequeathed downward, as the heirloom of generations. There fell the bosom-Bible, the little volume that had been the soul's friend of some sorely tried Child of Dust, who thence took courage, whether his trial were for life or death, steadfastly confronting both, in the strong assurance of Immortality.

All these were flung into the fierce and riotous blaze; and then a mighty wind came roaring across the plain, with a desolate howl, as if it were the angry lamentation of the Earth for the loss of Heaven's sunshine; and it shook the gigantic pyramid of flame, and scattered the cinders of half-consumed abominations around upon the spectators.

"This is terrible!" said I, feeling that my cheek grew pale, and seeing a like change in the visages about me.

"Be of good courage yet," answered the man with whom I had so often spoken. He continued to gaze steadily at the spectacle, with a singular calmness, as if it concerned him merely as an observer.—"Be of good courage—nor yet exult too much; for there is far less both of good and evil, in the effect of this bonfire, than the world might be willing to believe."

"How can that be?" exclaimed I, impatiently.—"Has it not consumed everything? Has it not swallowed up, or melted down, every human or divine appendage of our mortal state, that had substance enough to be acted on by fire? Will there be anything left us, tomorrow morning, better or worse than a heap of embers and ashes?"

"Assuredly there will," said my grave friend. "Come hither tomorrow morning—or whenever the combustible portion of the pile shall be quite burnt out—and you will find among the ashes everything really valuable that you have seen cast into the flames. Trust me; the world of tomorrow will again enrich itself with the gold and diamonds, which have been cast off by the world of to-day. Not a truth is destroyed—nor buried so deep among the ashes, but it will be raked up at last."

This was a strange assurance. Yet I felt inclined to credit it; the more especially as I beheld, among the wallowing flames, a copy of the Holy Scriptures, the pages of which, instead of being blackened into tinder, only assumed a more dazzling whiteness, as the finger-marks of human imperfection were purified away. Certain marginal notes and commentaries, it is true, yielded to the intensity of the fiery test, but without detriment to the smallest syllable that had flamed from the pen of inspiration.

"Yes;—there is the proof of what you say," answered I, turning to the observer. "But, if only what is evil can feel the action of the fire, then, surely, the conflagration has been of inestimable utility. Yet, if I understand aright, you intimate a doubt whether the world's expectation of benefit will be realized by it."

"Listen to the talk of these worthies," said he, pointing to a group in front of the blazing pile.—"Possibly, they may teach you something useful, without intending it."

The persons, whom he indicated, consisted of that brutal and most earthy figure, who had stood forth so furiously in defence of the gallows—the hangman, in short—together with the Last Thief and the Last Murderer; all three of whom were clustered about the Last Toper. The latter was liberally passing the brandy-bottle, which he had rescued from the general destruction of wines and spirits. This little convivial party seemed at the lowest pitch of despondency; as considering that the purified world must needs be utterly unlike, the sphere that they had hitherto known, and therefore but a strange and desolate abode for gentlemen of their kidney.

"The best counsel for all of us, is," remarked the hangman, "that—as soon as we have finished the last drop of liquor— I help you, my three friends, to a comfortable end upon the nearest tree, and then hang myself on the same bough. This is no world for us, any longer."

"Poh, poh, my good fellows!" said a dark-complexioned personage, who now joined the group—his complexion was indeed fearfully dark; and his eyes glowed with a redder light than that of the bonfire—"Be not so cast down, my dear friends; you shall see good days yet. There is one thing that these wiseacres have forgotten to throw into the fire, and without which all the rest of the conflagration is just nothing at all—yes; though they had burnt the earth itself to a cinder!"

"And what may that be?" eagerly demanded the Last Murderer.

"What, but the human heart itself!" said the dark-visaged stranger, with a portentous grin. "And, unless they hit upon some method of purifying that foul cavern, forth from it will re-issue all the shapes of wrong and misery—the same old shapes, or worse ones—which they have taken such a vast deal of trouble to consume to ashes. I have stood by, this livelong night, and laughed in my sleeve at the whole business. Oh, take my word for it, it will be the old world yet!"

This brief conversation supplied me with a theme for lengthened thought. How sad a truth—if true it were—that Man's age-long endeavor for perfection had served only to render him the mockery of the Evil Principle, from the fatal circumstance of an error at the very root of the matter! The Heart—the Heart—there was the little, yet boundless sphere, wherein existed the original wrong, of which the crime and misery of this outward world were merely types. Purify that inner sphere; and the many shapes of evil that haunt the outward, and which now seem almost our only realities, will turn to shadowy phantoms, and vanish of their own accord. But, if we go no deeper than the Intellect, and strive, with merely that feeble instrument, to discern and rectify what is wrong, our whole accomplishment will be a dream; so unsubstantial, that it matters little whether the bonfire, which I have so faithfully described, were what we choose to call a real event, and a flame that would scorch the finger—or only a phosphoric radiance, and a parable of my own brain!

The Artist of the Beautiful

AN elderly man, with his pretty daughter on his arm, was passing along the street, and emerged from the gloom of the cloudy evening into the light that fell across the pavement from the window of a small shop. It was a projecting window; and on the inside were suspended a variety of watches,—pinchbeck, silver, and one or two of gold,—all with their faces turned from the street, as if churlishly disinclined to inform the wayfarers what o'clock it was. Seated within the shop, sidelong to the window, with his pale face bent earnestly over some delicate piece of mechanism, on which was thrown the concentrated lustre of a shade-lamp, appeared a young man.

"What can Owen Warland be about?" muttered old Peter Hovenden,—himself a retired watchmaker, and the former master of this same young man, whose occupation he was now wondering at. "What can the fellow be about? These six months past, I have never come by his shop without seeing him just as steadily at work as now. It would be a flight beyond his usual foolery to seek for the Perpetual Motion. And yet I know enough of my old business to be certain, that what he is now so busy with is no part of the machinery of a watch."

"Perhaps, father," said Annie, without showing much interest in the question, "Owen is inventing a new kind of timekeeper. I am sure he has ingenuity enough."

"Poh, child! he has not the sort of ingenuity to invent anything better than a Dutch toy," answered her father, who had formerly been put to much vexation by Owen Warland's irregular genius. "A plague on such ingenuity! All the effect that ever I knew of it, was to spoil the accuracy of some of the best watches in my shop. He would turn the sun out of its orbit, and derange the whole course of time, if, as I said before, his ingenuity could grasp anything bigger than a child's toy!"

"Hush, father! he hears you," whispered Annie, pressing the old man's arm. "His ears are as delicate as his feelings, and you know how easily disturbed they are. Do let us move on."

So Peter Hovenden and his daughter Annie plodded on, without further conversation, until, in a by-street of the town, they found themselves passing the open door of a black-smith's shop. Within was seen the forge, now blazing up, and illuminating the high and dusky roof, and now confining its lustre to a narrow precinct of the coal-strewn floor, according as the breath of the bellows was puffed forth, or again inhaled into its vast leathern lungs. In the intervals of brightness, it was easy to distinguish objects in remote corners of the shop, and the horse-shoes that hung upon the wall; in the momentary gloom, the fire seemed to be glimmering amidst the vagueness of unenclosed space. Moving about in this red glare and alternate dusk, was the figure of the blacksmith, well worthy to be viewed in so picturesque an aspect of light and shade, where the bright blaze struggled with the black night, as if each would have snatched his comely strength from the other. Anon, he drew a white-hot bar of iron from the coals, laid it on the anvil, uplifted his arm of might, and was soon enveloped in the myriads of sparks which the strokes of his hammer scattered into the surrounding gloom.

"Now, that is a pleasant sight," said the old watchmaker. "I know what it is to work in gold, but give me the worker in iron, after all is said and done. He spends his labor upon a reality. What say you, daughter Annie?"

"Pray don't speak so loud, father," whispered Annie. "Robert Danforth will hear you."

"And what if he should hear me?" said Peter Hovenden; "I say again, it is a good and a wholesome thing to depend upon main strength and reality, and to earn one's bread with the bare and brawny arm of a blacksmith. A watchmaker gets his brain puzzled by his wheels within a wheel, or loses his health or the nicety of his eyesight, as was my case; and finds himself, at middle age, or a little after, past labor at his own trade, and fit for nothing else, yet too poor to live at his ease. So, I say once again, give me main strength for my money. And then, how it takes the nonsense out of a man! Did you ever hear of a blacksmith being such a fool as Owen Warland, yonder?"

"Well said, uncle Hovenden!" shouted Robert Danforth, from the forge, in a full, deep, merry voice, that made the roof re-echo. "And what says Miss Annie to that doctrine? She, I suppose, will think it a genteeler business to tinker up a lady's watch, than to forge a horse-shoe or make a grid-iron!"

Annie drew her father onward, without giving him time for reply.

But we must return to Owen Warland's shop, and spend more meditation upon his history and character than either Peter Hovenden, or probably his daughter Annie, or Owen's old schoolfellow, Robert Danforth, would have thought due to so slight a subject. From the time that his little fingers could grasp a pen-knife, Owen had been remarkable for a delicate ingenuity, which sometimes produced pretty shapes in wood, principally figures of flowers and birds, and sometimes seemed to aim at the hidden mysteries of mechanism. But it was always for purposes of grace, and never with any mockery of the useful. He did not, like the crowd of school-boy artizans, construct little windmills on the angle of a barn, or watermills across the neighboring brook. Those who discovered such peculiarity in the boy, as to think it worth their while to observe him closely, sometimes saw reason to suppose that he was attempting to imitate the beautiful movements of Nature, as exemplified in the flight of birds or the activity of little animals. It seemed, in fact, a new development of the love of the Beautiful, such as might have made him a poet, a painter, or a sculptor, and which was as completely refined from all utilitarian coarseness, as it could have been in either of the fine arts. He looked with singular distaste at the stiff and regular processes of ordinary machinery. Being once carried to see a steam-engine, in the expectation that his intuitive comprehension of mechanical principles would be gratified, he turned pale, and grew sick, as if something monstrous and unnatural had been presented to him. This horror was partly owing to the size and terrible energy of the Iron Laborer; for the character of Owen's mind was microscopic, and tended naturally to the minute, in accordance with his diminutive frame, and the marvellous smallness and delicate power of his fingers. Not that his sense of beauty was thereby diminished into a sense of prettiness. The Beautiful Idea has no relation to size, and may be as perfectly developed in a space too minute for any but microscopic investigation, as within the ample verge that is measured by the arc of the rainbow. But, at all events, this characteristic minuteness in his objects and accomplishments made the world even more incapable, than it might otherwise have been, of appreciating Owen Warland's genius. The boy's relatives saw nothing better to be done—as perhaps there was not—than to bind him apprentice to a watchmaker, hoping that his strange ingenuity might thus be regulated, and put to utilitarian purposes.

Peter Hovenden's opinion of his apprentice has already been expressed. He could make nothing of the lad. Owen's apprehension of the professional mysteries, it is true, was inconceivably quick. But he altogether forgot or despised the grand object of a watchmaker's business, and cared no more for the measurement of time than if it had been merged into eternity. So long, however, as he remained under his old master's care, Owen's lack of sturdiness made it possible, by strict injunctions and sharp oversight, to restrain his creative eccentricity within bounds. But when his apprenticeship was served out, and he had taken the little shop which Peter Hovenden's failing eyesight compelled him to relinquish, then did people recognize how unfit a person was Owen Warland to lead old blind Father Time along his daily course. One of his most rational projects was, to connect a musical operation with the machinery of his watches, so that all the harsh dissonances of life might be rendered tuneful, and each flitting moment fall into the abyss of the Past in golden drops of harmony. If a family-clock was entrusted to him for repair—one of those tall, ancient clocks that have grown nearly allied to human nature, by measuring out the lifetime of many generations—he would take upon himself to arrange a dance or funeral procession of figures, across its venerable face, representing twelve mirthful or melancholy hours. Several freaks of this kind quite destroyed the young watchmaker's credit with that steady and matter-of-fact class of people who hold the opinion that time is not to be trifled with, whether considered as the medium of advancement and prosperity in this world, or preparation for the next. His custom rapidly diminished—a misfortune, however, that was probably reckoned among his better accidents by Owen Warland, who was becoming more and more absorbed in a secret occupation, which drew all his science and manual dexterity into itself, and likewise gave full employment to the characteristic tendencies of his genius. This pursuit had already consumed many months.

After the old watchmaker and his pretty daughter had gazed at him, out of the obscurity of the street, Owen Warland was seized with a fluttering of the nerves, which made his hand tremble too violently to proceed with such delicate labor as he was now engaged upon.

"It was Annie herself!" murmured he. "I should have known it, by this throbbing of my heart, before I heard her father's voice. Ah, how it throbs! I shall scarcely be able to work again on this exquisite mechanism to-night. Annie— dearest Annie—thou shouldst give firmness to my heart and hand, and not shake them thus; for if I strive to put the very spirit of Beauty into form, and give it motion, it is for thy sake alone. Oh, throbbing heart, be quiet! If my labor be thus thwarted, there will come vague and unsatisfied dreams, which will leave me spiritless to-morrow."

As he was endeavoring to settle himself again to his task, the shop-door opened, and gave admittance to no other than the stalwart figure which Peter Hovenden had paused to admire, as seen amid the light and shadow of the blacksmith's shop. Robert Danforth had brought a little anvil of his own manufacture, and peculiarly constructed, which the young artist had recently bespoken. Owen examined the article, and pronounced it fashioned according to his wish.

"Why, yes," said Robert Danforth, his strong voice filling the shop as with the sound of a bass-viol, "I consider myself equal to anything in the way of my own trade; though I should have made but a poor figure at yours, with such a fist as this,"—added he, laughing, as he laid his vast hand beside the delicate one of Owen. "But what then? I put more main strength into one blow of my sledge-hammer, than all that you have expended since you were a 'prentice. Is not that the truth?"

"Very probably," answered the low and slender voice of Owen. "Strength is an earthly monster. I make no pretensions to it. My force, whatever there may be of it, is altogether spiritual."

"Well; but, Owen, what are you about!" asked his old schoolfellow, still in such a hearty volume of tone that it made the artist shrink; especially as the question related to a subject so sacred as the absorbing dream of his imagination. "Folks do say, that you are trying to discover the Perpetual Motion."

"The Perpetual Motion?—nonsense!" replied Owen Warland, with a movement of digust; for he was full of little petulances. "It can never be discovered! It is a dream that may delude men whose brains are mystified with matter, but not me. Besides, if such a discovery were possible, it would not be worth my while to make it, only to have the secret turned to such purposes as are now effected by steam and water-power. I am not ambitious to be honored with the paternity of a new kind of cotton-machine."

"That would be droll enough!" cried the blacksmith, breaking out into such an uproar of laughter, that Owen himself, and the bell-glasses on his work-board, quivered in unison. "No, no, Owen! No child of yours will have iron joints and sinews. Well, I won't hinder you any more. Good night, Owen, and success; and if you need any assistance, so far as a downright blow of hammer upon anvil will answer the purpose, I'm your man!"

And with another laugh, the man of main strength left the shop.

"How strange it is," whispered Owen Warland to himself, leaning his head upon his hand, "that all my musings, my purposes, my passion for the Beautiful, my consciousness of power to create it—a finer, more ethereal power, of which this earthly giant can have no conception—all, all, look so vain and idle, whenever my path is crossed by Robert Danforth! He would drive me mad, were I to meet him often. His hard, brute force darkens and confuses the spiritual element within me. But I, too, will be strong in my own way. I will not yield to him!"

He took from beneath a glass, a piece of minute machinery, which he set in the condensed light of his lamp, and, looking intently at it through a magnifying glass, proceeded to operate with a delicate instrument of steel. In an instant, however, he fell back in his chair, and clasped his hands, with a look of horror on his face, that made its small features as impressive as those of a giant would have been.

"Heaven! What have I done!" exclaimed he. "The vapor!—the influence of that brute force!—it has bewildered me, and obscured my perception. I have made the very stroke—the fatal stroke—that I have dreaded from the first! It is all over—the toil of months—the object of my life! I am ruined!"

And there he sat, in strange despair, until his lamp flickered in the socket, and left the Artist of the Beautiful in darkness.

Thus it is, that ideas which grow up within the imagination, and appear so lovely to it, and of a value beyond whatever men call valuable, are exposed to be shattered and annihilated by contact with the Practical. It is requisite for the ideal artist to possess a force of character that seems hardly compatible with its delicacy; he must keep his faith in himself, while the incredulous world assails him with its utter disbelief; he must stand up against mankind and be his own sole disciple, both as respects his genius, and the objects to which it is directed.

For a time, Owen Warland succumbed to this severe, but inevitable test. He spent a few sluggish weeks, with his head so continually resting in his hands, that the townspeople had scarcely an opportunity to see his countenance. When, at last, it was again uplifted to the light of day, a cold, dull, nameless change was perceptible upon it. In the opinion of Peter Hovenden, however, and that order of sagacious understandings who think that life should be regulated, like clock-work, with leaden weights, the alteration was entirely for the better. Owen now indeed, applied himself to business with dogged industry. It was marvellous to witness the obtuse gravity with which he would inspect the wheels of a great, old silver watch; thereby delighting the owner, in whose fob it had been worn till he deemed it a portion of his own life, and was accordingly jealous of its treatment. In consequence of the good report thus acquired, Owen Warland was invited by the proper authorities to regulate the clock in the church-steeple.

He succeeded so admirably in this matter of public interest, that the merchants gruffly acknowledged his merits on 'Change; the nurse whispered his praises, as she gave the potion in the sick-chamber; the lover blessed him at the hour of appointed interview; and the town in general thanked Owen for the punctuality of dinner-time. In a word, the heavy weight upon his spirits kept everything in order, not merely within his own system, but wheresoever the iron accents of the church-clock were audible. It was a circumstance, though minute, yet characteristic of his present state, that, when employed to engrave names or initials on silver spoons, he now wrote the requisite letters in the plainest possible style; omitting a variety of fanciful flourishes, that had heretofore distinguished his work in this kind.

One day, during the era of this happy transformation, old Peter Hovenden came to visit his former apprentice.

"Well, Owen," said he, "I am glad to hear such good accounts of you from all quarters; and especially from the town-clock yonder, which speaks in your commendation every hour of the twenty-four. Only get rid altogether of your nonsensical trash about the Beautiful—which I, nor nobody else, nor yourself to boot, could never understand—only free yourself of that, and your success in life is as sure as daylight. Why, if you go on in this way, I should even venture to let you doctor this precious old watch of mine; though, except my daughter Annie, I have nothing else so valuable in the world."

"I should hardly dare touch it, sir," replied Owen in a depressed tone; for he was weighed down by his old master's presence.

"In time," said the latter, "in time, you will be capable of it."

The old watchmaker, with the freedom naturally consequent on his former authority, went on inspecting the work which Owen had in hand at the moment, together with other matters that were in progress. The artist, meanwhile, could scarcely lift his head. There was nothing so antipodal to his nature as this man's cold, unimaginative sagacity, by contact with which everything was converted into a dream, except the densest matter of the physical world. Owen groaned in spirit, and prayed fervently to be delivered from him.

"But what is this?" cried Peter Hovenden abruptly, taking up a dusty bell-glass, beneath which appeared a mechanical something, as delicate and minute as the system of a butterfly's anatomy. "What have we here! Owen, Owen! there is witchcraft in these little chains, and wheels, and paddles! See! with one pinch of my finger and thumb, I am going to deliver you from all future peril."

"For Heaven's sake," screamed Owen Warland, springing up with wonderful energy, "as you would not drive me mad—do not touch it! The slightest pressure of your finger would ruin me for ever."

"Aha, young man! And is it so?" said the old watchmaker, looking at him with just enough of penetration to torture Owen's soul with the bitterness of worldly criticism. "Well; take your own course. But I warn you again, that in this small piece of mechanism lives your evil spirit. Shall I exorcise him?"

"You are my Evil Spirit," answered Owen, much excited— "you, and the hard, coarse world! The leaden thoughts and the despondency that you fling upon me are my clogs. Else, I should long ago have achieved the task that I was created for."

Peter Hovenden shook his head, with the mixture of contempt and indignation which mankind, of whom he was partly a representative, deem themselves entitled to feel towards all simpletons who seek other prizes than the dusty ones along the highway. He then took his leave with an uplifted finger, and a sneer upon his face, that haunted the artist's dreams for many a night afterwards. At the time of his old master's visit, Owen was probably on the point of taking up the relinquished task; but, by this sinister event, he was thrown back into the state whence he had been slowly emerging.

But the innate tendency of his soul had only been accumulating fresh vigor, during its apparent sluggishness. As the summer advanced, he almost totally relinquished his business, and permitted Father Time, so far as the old gentleman was represented by the clocks and watches under his control, to stray at random through human life, making infinite confusion among the train of bewildered hours. He wasted the sunshine, as people said, in wandering through the woods and fields, and along the banks of streams. There, like a child, he found amusement in chasing butterflies, or watching the motions of water-insects. There was something truly mysterious in the intentness with which he contemplated these living playthings, as they sported on the breeze; or examined the structure of an imperial insect whom he had imprisoned. The chase of butterflies was an apt emblem of the ideal pursuit in which he had spent so many golden hours. But, would the Beautiful Idea ever be yielded to his hand, like the butterfly that symbolized it? Sweet, doubtless, were these days, and congenial to the artist's soul. They were full of bright conceptions, which gleamed through his intellectual world, as the butterflies gleamed through the outward atmosphere, and were real to him for the instant, without the toil, and perplexity, and many disappointments, of attempting to make them visible to the sensual eye. Alas, that the artist, whether in poetry or whatever other material, may not content himself with the inward enjoyment of the Beautiful, but must chase the flitting mystery beyond the verge of his ethereal domain, and crush its frail being in seizing it with a material grasp! Owen Warland felt the impulse to give external reality to his ideas, as irresistibly as any of the poets or painters, who have arrayed the world in a dimmer and fainter beauty, imperfectly copied from the richness of their visions.

The night was now his time for the slow process of recreating the one Idea, to which all his intellectual activity referred itself. Always at the approach of dusk, he stole into the town, locked himself within his shop, and wrought with patient delicacy of touch, for many hours. Sometimes he was startled by the rap of the watchman, who, when all the world should be asleep, had caught the gleam of lamp-light through the crevices of Owen Warland's shutters. Daylight, to the morbid sensibility of his mind, seemed to have an intrusiveness that interfered with his pursuits. On cloudy and inclement days, therefore, he sat with his head upon his hands, muffling, as it were, his sensitive brain in a mist of indefinite musings; for it was a relief to escape from the sharp distinctness with which he was compelled to shape out his thoughts, during his nightly toil.

From one of these fits of torpor, he was aroused by the

entrance of Annie Hovenden, who came into the shop with the freedom of a customer, and also with something of the familiarity of a childish friend. She had worn a hole through her silver thimble, and wanted Owen to repair it.

"But I don't know whether you will condescend to such a task," said she, laughing, "now that you are so taken up with the notion of putting spirit into machinery."

"Where did you get that idea, Annie?" said Owen, starting in surprise.

"Oh, out of my own head," answered she, "and from something that I heard you say, long ago, when you were but a boy, and I a little child. But, come! will you mend this poor thimble of mine?"

"Anything for your sake, Annie," said Owen Warland—"anything; even were it to work at Robert Danforth's forge."

"And that would be a pretty sight!" retorted Annie, glancing with imperceptible slightness at the artist's small and slender frame. "Well; here is the thimble."

"But that is a strange idea of yours," said Owen, "about the spiritualization of matter!"

And then the thought stole into his mind, that this young girl possessed the gift to comprehend him, better than all the world beside. And what a help and strength would it be to him, in his lonely toil, if he could gain the sympathy of the only being whom he loved! To persons whose pursuits are insulated from the common business of life—who are either in advance of mankind, or apart from it—there often comes a sensation of moral cold, that makes the spirit shiver, as if it had reached the frozen solitudes around the pole. What the prophet, the poet, the reformer, the criminal, or any other man, with human yearnings, but separated from the multitude by a peculiar lot, might feel, poor Owen Warland felt.

"Annie," cried he, growing pale as death at the thought, "how gladly would I tell you the secret of my pursuit! You, methinks, would estimate it rightly. You, I know, would hear it with a reverence that I must not expect from the harsh, material world."

"Would I not? to be sure I would!" replied Annie Hovenden, lightly laughing. "Come; explain to me quickly what is the meaning of this little whirligig, so delicately wrought that it might be a plaything for Queen Mab. See; I will put it in motion."

"Hold," exclaimed Owen, "hold!"

Annie had but given the slightest possible touch, with the point of a needle, to the same minute portion of complicated machinery which has been more than once mentioned, when the artist seized her by the wrist with a force that made her scream aloud. She was affrighted at the convulsion of intense rage and anguish that writhed across his features. The next instant he let his head sink upon his hands.

"Go, Annie," murmured he, "I have deceived myself, and must suffer for it. I yearned for sympathy—and thought—and fancied—and dreamed—that you might give it me. But you lack the talisman, Annie, that should admit you into my secrets. That touch has undone the toil of months, and the thought of a lifetime! It was not your fault, Annie—but you have ruined me!"

Poor Owen Warland! He had indeed erred, yet pardonably; for if any human spirit could have sufficiently reverenced the processes so sacred in his eyes, it must have been a woman's. Even Annie Hovenden, possibly, might not have disappointed him, had she been enlightened by the deep intelligence of love.

The artist spent the ensuing winter in a way that satisfied any persons, who had hitherto retained a hopeful opinion of him, that he was, in truth, irrevocably doomed to inutility as regarded the world, and to an evil destiny on his own part. The decease of a relative had put him in possession of a small inheritance. Thus freed from the necessity of toil, and having lost the steadfast influence of a great purpose—great, at least to him—he abandoned himself to habits from which, it might have been supposed, the mere delicacy of his organization would have availed to secure him. But when the ethereal portion of a man of genius is obscured, the earthly part assumes an influence the more uncontrollable, because the character is now thrown off the balance to which Providence had so nicely adjusted it, and which, in coarser natures, is adjusted by some other method. Owen Warland made proof of whatever show of bliss may be found in riot. He looked at the world through the golden medium of wine, and contemplated the visions that bubble up so gaily around the brim of the glass, and that people the air with shapes of pleasant madness, which so soon grow ghostly and forlorn. Even when this dismal and inevitable change had taken place, the young man might still have continued to quaff the cup of enchantments, though its vapor did but shroud life in gloom, and fill the gloom with spectres that mocked at him. There was a certain irksomeness of spirit, which, being real, and the deepest sensation of which the artist was now conscious, was more intolerable than any fantastic miseries and horrors that the abuse of wine could summon up. In the latter case, he could remember, even out of the midst of his trouble, that all was but a delusion; in the former, the heavy anguish was his actual life.

From this perilous state, he was redeemed by an incident which more than one person witnessed, but of which the shrewdest could not explain nor conjecture the operation on Owen Warland's mind. It was very simple. On a warm afternoon of spring, as the artist sat among his riotous companions, with a glass of wine before him, a splendid butterfly flew in at the open window, and fluttered about his head.

"Ah!" exclaimed Owen, who had drank freely, "Are you alive again, child of the sun, and playmate of the summer breeze, after your dismal winter's nap! Then it is time for me to be at work!"

And leaving his unemptied glass upon the table, he departed, and was never known to sip another drop of wine.

And now, again, he resumed his wanderings in the woods and fields. It might be fancied that the bright butterfly, which had come so spiritlike into the window, as Owen sat with the rude revellers, was indeed a spirit, commissioned to recall him to the pure, ideal life that had so etherealized him among men. It might be fancied, that he went forth to seek this spirit, in its sunny haunts; for still, as in the summer-time gone by, he was seen to steal gently up, wherever a butterfly had alighted, and lose himself in contemplation of it. When it took flight, his eyes followed the winged vision, as if its airy track would show the path to heaven. But what could be the purpose of the unseasonable toil, which was again resumed, as the watchman knew by the lines of lamp-light through the crevices of Owen Warland's shutters? The towns-people had one comprehensive explanation of all these sin-gularities. Owen Warland had gone mad! How universally ef-ficacious—how satisfactory, too, and soothing to the injured sensibility of narrowness and dullness—is this easy method of accounting for whatever lies beyond the world's most or-dinary scope! From Saint Paul's days, down to our poor little Artist of the Beautiful, the same talisman has been applied to the elucidation of all mysteries in the words or deeds of men, who spoke or acted too wisely or too well. In Owen War-land's case, the judgment of his townspeople may have been correct. Perhaps he was mad. The lack of sympathy—that contrast between himself and his neighbors, which took away the restraint of example—was enough to make him so. Or, possibly, he had caught just so much of ethereal radiance as served to bewilder him, in an earthly sense, by its intermix-ture with the common daylight.

One evening, when the artist had returned from a custom-ary ramble, and had just thrown the lustre of his lamp on the delicate piece of work, so often interrupted, but still taken up again, as if his fate were embodied in its mechanism, he was surprised by the entrance of old Peter Hovenden. Owen never met this man without a shrinking of the heart. Of all the world, he was most terrible, by reason of a keen under-standing, which saw so distinctly what it did see, and disbe-lieved so uncompromisingly in what it could not see. On this occasion, the old watchmaker had merely a gracious word or two to say.

"Owen, my lad," said he, "we must see you at my house to-morrow night."

The artist began to mutter some excuse.

"Oh, but it must be so," quoth Peter Hovenden, "for the sake of the days when you were one of the household. What, my boy, don't you know that my daughter Annie is engaged to Robert Danforth? We are making an entertainment, in our humble way, to celebrate the event."

"Ah!" said Owen.

That little monosyllable was all he uttered; its tone seemed cold and unconcerned, to an ear like Peter Hovenden's; and yet there was in it the stifled outcry of the poor artist's heart, which he compressed within him like a man holding down an evil spirit. One slight outbreak, however, imperceptible to the old watchmaker, he allowed himself. Raising the instrument with which he was about to begin his work, he let it fall upon the little system of machinery that had, anew, cost him months of thought and toil. It was shattered by the stroke!

Owen Warland's story would have been no tolerable representation of the troubled life of those who strive to create the Beautiful, if, amid all other thwarting influences, love had not interposed to steal the cunning from his hand. Outwardly, he had been no ardent or enterprising lover; the career of his passion had confined its tumults and vicissitudes so entirely within the artist's imagination, that Annie herself had scarcely more than a woman's intuitive perception of it. But, in Owen's view, it covered the whole field of his life. Forgetful of the time when she had shown herself incapable of any deep response, he had persisted in connecting all his dreams of artistical success with Annie's image; she was the visible shape in which the spiritual power that he worshipped, and on whose altar he hoped to lay a not unworthy offering, was made manifest to him. Of course he had deceived himself; there were no such attributes in Annie Hovenden as his imagination had endowed her with. She, in the aspect which she wore to his inward vision, was as much a creation of his own, as the mysterious piece of mechanism would be were it ever realized. Had he become convinced of his mistake through the medium of successful love; had he won Annie to his bosom, and there beheld her fade from angel into ordinary woman, the disappointment might have driven him back, with concentrated energy, upon his sole remaining object. On the other hand, had he found Annie what he fancied, his lot would have been so rich in beauty, that, out of its mere redundancy, he might have wrought the Beautiful into many a worthier type than he had toiled for. But the guise in which his sorrow came to him, the sense that the angel of his life had been snatched away and given to a rude man of earth and iron, who could neither need nor appreciate her ministrations; this was the very perversity of fate, that makes human existence appear too absurd and contradictory to be the scene of one other hope or one other fear. There was nothing left for Owen Warland but to sit down like a man that had been stunned.

He went through a fit of illness. After his recovery, his small and slender frame assumed an obtuser garniture of flesh than it had ever before worn. His thin cheeks became round; his delicate little hand, so spiritually fashioned to achieve fairy task-work, grew plumper than the hand of a thriving infant. His aspect had a childishness, such as might have induced a stranger to pat him on the head—pausing, however, in the act, to wonder what manner of child was here. It was as if the spirit had gone out of him, leaving the body to flourish in a sort of vegetable existence. Not that Owen Warland was idiotic. He could talk, and not irrationally. Somewhat of a babbler, indeed, did people begin to think him; for he was apt to discourse at wearisome length, of marvels of mechanism that he had read about in books, but which he had learned to consider as absolutely fabulous. Among them he enumerated the Man of Brass, constructed by Albertus Magnus, and the Brazen Head of Friar Bacon; and, coming down to later times, the automata of a little coach and horses, which, it was pretended, had been manufactured for the Dauphin of France; together with an insect that buzzed about the ear like a living fly, and yet was but a contrivance of minute steel springs. There was a story, too, of a duck that waddled, and quacked, and ate; though, had any honest citizen purchased it for dinner, he would have found himself cheated with the mere mechanical apparition of a duck.

"But all these accounts," said Owen Warland, "I am now satisfied, are mere impositions."

Then, in a mysterious way, he would confess that he once thought differently. In his idle and dreamy days, he had considered it possible, in a certain sense, to spiritualize machinery; and to combine with the new species of life and motion, thus produced, a beauty that should attain to the ideal which Nature has proposed to herself, in all her creatures, but has never taken pains to realize. He seemed, however, to retain no very distinct perception either of the process of achieving this object, or of the design itself.

"I have thrown it all aside now," he would say. "It was a dream, such as young men are always mystifying themselves with. Now that I have acquired a little common sense, it makes me laugh to think of it."

Poor, poor, and fallen Owen Warland! These were the symptoms that he had ceased to be an inhabitant of the better sphere that lies unseen around us. He had lost his faith in the invisible, and now prided himself, as such unfortunates invariably do, in the wisdom which rejected much that even his eye could see, and trusted confidently in nothing but what his hand could touch. This is the calamity of men whose spiritual part dies out of them, and leaves the grosser understanding to assimilate them more and more to the things of which alone it can take cognizance. But, in Owen Warland, the spirit was not dead, nor past away; it only slept.

How it awoke again, is not recorded. Perhaps, the torpid slumber was broken by a convulsive pain. Perhaps, as in a former instance, the butterfly came and hovered about his head, and reinspired him—as, indeed, this creature of the sunshine had always a mysterious mission for the artist—reinspired him with the former purpose of his life. Whether it were pain or happiness that thrilled through his veins, his first impulse was to thank Heaven for rendering him again the being of thought, imagination, and keenest sensibility, that he had long ceased to be.

"Now for my task," said he. "Never did I feel such strength for it as now."

Yet, strong as he felt himself, he was incited to toil the more diligently, by an anxiety lest death should surprise him in the midst of his labors. This anxiety, perhaps, is common to all men who set their hearts upon anything so high, in their own view of it, that life becomes of importance only as conditional to its accomplishment. So long as we love life for itself, we seldom dread the losing it. When we desire life for the attainment of an object, we recognize the frailty of its texture. But, side by side with this sense of insecurity, there is a vital faith in our invulnerability to the shaft of death, while engaged in any task that seems assigned by Providence as our proper thing to do, and which the world would have cause to mourn for, should we leave it unaccomplished. Can the philosopher, big with the inspiration of an idea that is to reform mankind, believe that he is to be beckoned from this sensible existence, at the very instant when he is mustering his breath to speak the word of light? Should he perish so, the weary ages may pass away—the world's whole life-sand may fall, drop by drop—before another intellect is prepared to develop the truth that might have been uttered then. But history affords many an example, where the most precious spirit, at any particular epoch manifested in human shape, has gone hence untimely, without space allowed him, so far as mortal judgment could discern, to perform his mission on the earth. The prophet dies; and the man of torpid heart and sluggish brain lives on. The poet leaves his song half sung, or finishes it, beyond the scope of mortal ears, in a celestial choir. The painter—as Allston did—leaves half his conception on the canvass, to sadden us with its imperfect beauty, and goes to picture forth the whole, if it be no irreverence to say so, in the hues of Heaven. But, rather, such incomplete designs of this life will be perfected nowhere. This so frequent abortion of man's dearest projects must be taken as a proof, that the deeds of earth, however etherealized by piety or genius, are without value, except as exercises and manifestations of the spirit. In Heaven, all ordinary thought is higher and more melodious than Milton's song. Then, would he add another verse to any strain that he had left unfinished here?

But to return to Owen Warland. It was his fortune, good or ill, to achieve the purpose of his life. Pass we over a long space of intense thought, yearning effort, minute toil, and wasting anxiety, succeeded by an instant of solitary triumph; let all this be imagined; and then behold the artist, on a winter evening, seeking admittance to Robert Danforth's fireside circle. There he found the Man of Iron, with his massive substance thoroughly warmed and attempered by domestic influences. And there was Annie, too, now transformed into a matron, with much of her husband's plain and sturdy nature, but imbued, as Owen Warland still believed, with a finer grace, that might enable her to be the interpreter between Strength and Beauty. It happened, likewise, that old Peter Hovenden was a guest, this evening, at his daughter's fireside; and it was his well-remembered expression of keen, cold criticism, that first encountered the artist's glance.

"My old friend Owen!" cried Robert Danforth, starting up,

and compressing the artist's delicate fingers within a hand that was accustomed to gripe bars of iron. "This is kind and neighborly, to come to us at last! I was afraid your Perpetual Motion had bewitched you out of the remembrance of old times."

"We are glad to see you!" said Annie, while a blush reddened her matronly cheek. "It was not like a friend, to stay from us so long."

"Well, Owen," inquired the old watchmaker, as his first greeting, "how comes on the Beautiful? Have you created it at last?"

The artist did not immediately reply, being startled by the apparition of a young child of strength, that was tumbling about on the carpet; a little personage who had come mysteriously out of the infinite, but with something so sturdy and real in his composition that he seemed moulded out of the densest substance which earth could supply. This hopeful infant crawled towards the new-comer, and setting himself on end—as Robert Danforth expressed the posture—stared at Owen with a look of such sagacious observation, that the mother could not help exchanging a proud glance with her husband. But the artist was disturbed by the child's look, as imagining a resemblance between it and Peter Hovenden's habitual expression. He could have fancied that the old watchmaker was compressed into this baby-shape, and was looking out of those baby-eyes, and repeating—as he now did—the malicious question:

"The Beautiful, Owen! How comes on the Beautiful? Have you succeeded in creating the Beautiful?"

"I have succeeded," replied the artist, with a momentary light of triumph in his eyes, and a smile of sunshine, yet steeped in such depth of thought that it was almost sadness. "Yes, my friends, it is the truth. I have succeeded!"

"Indeed!" cried Annie, a look of maiden mirthfulness peeping out of her face again. "And it is lawful, now, to inquire what the secret is?"

"Surely; it is to disclose it, that I have come," answered Owen Warland. "You shall know, and see, and touch, and possess, the secret! For Annie—if by that name I may still address the friend of my boyish years—Annie, it is for your bridal gift that I have wrought this spiritualized mechanism, this harmony of motion, this Mystery of Beauty! It comes late, indeed; but it is as we go onward in life, when objects begin to lose their freshness of hue, and our souls their delicacy of perception, that the spirit of Beauty is most needed. If—forgive me, Annie—if you know how to value this gift, it can never come too late!"

He produced, as he spoke, what seemed a jewel-box. It was carved richly out of ebony by his own hand, and inlaid with a fanciful tracery of pearl, representing a boy in pursuit of a butterfly, which, elsewhere, had become a winged spirit, and was flying heavenward; while the boy, or youth, had found such efficacy in his strong desire, that he ascended from earth to cloud, and from cloud to celestial atmosphere, to win the Beautiful. This case of ebony the artist opened, and bade Annie place her finger on its edge. She did so, but almost screamed, as a butterfly fluttered forth, and alighting on her finger's tip, sat waving the ample magnificence of its purple and gold-speckled wings, as if in prelude to a flight. It is impossible to express by words the glory, the splendor, the delicate gorgeousness, which were softened into the beauty of this object. Nature's ideal butterfly was here realized in all its perfection; not in the pattern of such faded insects as flit among earthly flowers, but of those which hover across the meads of Paradise, for child-angels and the spirits of departed infants to disport themselves with. The rich down was visible upon its wings; the lustre of its eyes seemed instinct with spirit. The firelight glimmered around this wonder—the candles gleamed upon it—but it glistened apparently by its own radiance, and illuminated the finger and outstretched hand on which it rested, with a white gleam like that of precious stones. In its perfect beauty, the consideration of size was entirely lost. Had its wings overarched the firmament, the mind could not have been more filled or satisfied.

"Beautiful! Beautiful!" exclaimed Annie. "Is it alive? Is it alive?"

"Alive? To be sure it is," answered her husband. "Do you suppose any mortal has skill enough to make a butterfly,—or would put himself to the trouble of making one, when any child may catch a score of them in a summer's afternoon?

Alive? Certainly! But this pretty box is undoubtedly of our friend Owen's manufacture; and really it does him credit."

At this moment, the butterfly waved its wings anew, with a motion so absolutely lifelike that Annie was startled, and even awe-stricken; for, in spite of her husband's opinion, she could not satisfy herself whether it was indeed a living creature, or a piece of wondrous mechanism.

"Is it alive?" she repeated, more earnestly than before.

"Judge for yourself," said Owen Warland, who stood gazing in her face with fixed attention.

The butterfly now flung itself upon the air, fluttered round Annie's head, and soared into a distant region of the parlor, still making itself perceptible to sight by the starry gleam in which the motion of its wings enveloped it. The infant on the floor, followed its course with his sagacious little eyes. After flying about the room, it returned, in a spiral curve, and settled again on Annie's finger.

"But is it alive?" exclaimed she again; and the finger, on which the gorgeous mystery had alighted, was so tremulous that the butterfly was forced to balance himself with his wings. "Tell me if it be alive, or whether you created it?"

"Wherefore ask who created it, so it be beautiful?" replied Owen Warland. "Alive? Yes, Annie; it may well be said to possess life, for it absorbed my own being into itself; and in the secret of that butterfly, and in its beauty—which is not merely outward, but deep as its whole system—is represented the intellect, the imagination, the sensibility, the soul, of an Artist of the Beautiful! Yes, I created it. But"—and here his countenance somewhat changed—"this butterfly is not now to me what it was when I beheld it afar off, in the day-dreams of my youth."

"Be it what it may, it is a pretty plaything," said the blacksmith, grinning with childlike delight. "I wonder whether it would condescend to alight on such a great clumsy finger as mine? Hold it hither, Annie!"

By the artist's direction, Annie touched her finger's tip to that of her husband; and, after a momentary delay, the butterfly fluttered from one to the other. It preluded a second flight by a similar, yet not precisely the same waving of wings, as in the first experiment; then, ascending from the blacksmith's stalwart finger, it rose in a gradually enlarging curve to the ceiling, made one wide sweep around the room, and returned with an undulating movement to the point whence it had started.

"Well, that does beat all nature!" cried Robert Danforth, bestowing the heartiest praise that he could find expression for; and, indeed, had he paused there, a man of finer words and nicer perception, could not easily have said more. "That goes beyond me, I confess! But what then? There is more real use in one downright blow of my sledge-hammer, than in the whole five years' labor that our friend Owen has wasted on this butterfly!"

Here the child clapped his hands, and made a great babble of indistinct utterance, apparently demanding that the butterfly should be given him for a plaything.

Owen Warland, meanwhile, glanced sidelong at Annie, to discover whether she sympathized in her husband's estimate of the comparative value of the Beautiful and the Practical. There was, amid all her kindness towards himself, amid all the wonder and admiration with which she contemplated the marvelous work of his hands, and incarnation of his idea, a secret scorn; too secret, perhaps, for her own consciousness, and perceptible only to such intuitive discernment as that of the artist. But Owen, in the latter stages of his pursuit, had risen out of the region in which such a discovery might have been torture. He knew that the world, and Annie as the representative of the world, whatever praise might be bestowed, could never say the fitting word, nor feel the fitting sentiment which should be the perfect recompense of an artist who, symbolizing a lofty moral by a material trifle—converting what was earthly, to spiritual gold—had won the Beautiful into his handiwork. Not at this latest moment, was he to learn that the reward of all high performance must be sought within itself, or sought in vain. There was, however, a view of the matter, which Annie, and her husband, and even Peter Hovenden, might fully have understood, and which would have satisfied them that the toil of years had here been worthily bestowed. Owen Warland might have told them, that this butterfly, this plaything, this bridal-gift of a poor watchmaker to a blacksmith's wife, was, in truth, a gem of art that a monarch would have purchased with honors and abundant wealth, and have treasured it among the jewels of his kingdom, as the most unique and wondrous of them all! But the artist smiled, and kept the secret to himself.

"Father," said Annie, thinking that a word of praise from the old watchmaker might gratify his former apprentice, "do come and admire this pretty butterfly!"

"Let us see," said Peter Hovenden, rising from his chair, with the sneer upon his face that always made people doubt, as he himself did, in everything but a material existence. "Here is my finger for it to alight upon. I shall understand it better when once I have touched it."

But, to the increased astonishment of Annie, when the tip of her father's finger was pressed against that of her husband, on which the butterfly still rested, the insect drooped its wings, and seemed on the point of falling to the floor. Even the bright spots of gold upon its wings and body, unless her eyes deceived her, grew dim, and the glowing purple took a dusky hue, and the starry lustre that gleamed around the blacksmith's hand, became faint, and vanished.

"It is dying! it is dying!" cried Annie, in alarm.

"It has been delicately wrought," said the artist calmly. "As I told you, it has imbibed a spiritual essence—call it magnetism, or what you will. In an atmosphere of doubt and mockery, its exquisite susceptibility suffers torture, as does the soul of him who instilled his own life into it. It has already lost its beauty; in a few moments more, its mechanism would be irreparably injured."

"Take away your hand, father!" entreated Annie, turning pale. "Here is my child; let it rest on his innocent hand. There, perhaps, its life will revive, and its colors grow brighter than ever."

Her father, with an acrid smile, withdrew his finger. The butterfly then appeared to recover the power of voluntary motion; while its hues assumed much of their original lustre, and the gleam of starlight, which was its most ethereal attribute, again formed a halo round about it. At first, when transferred from Robert Danforth's hand to the small finger of the child, this radiance grew so powerful that it positively threw the little fellow's shadow back against the wall. He, meanwhile, extended his plump hand as he had seen his father and mother do, and watched the waving of the insect's wings, with infantine delight. Nevertheless, there was a certain odd expression of sagacity, that made Owen Warland feel as if here were old Peter Hovenden, partially, and but partially, redeemed from his hard scepticism into childish faith.

"How wise the little monkey looks!" whispered Robert Danforth to his wife.

"I never saw such a look on a child's face," answered Annie, admiring her own infant, and with good reason, far more than the artistic butterfly. "The darling knows more of the mystery than we do."

As if the butterfly, like the artist, were conscious of something not entirely congenial in the child's nature, it alternately sparkled and grew dim. At length, it arose from the small hand of the infant with an airy motion, that seemed to bear it upward without an effort; as if the ethereal instincts, with which its master's spirit had endowed it, impelled this fair vision involuntarily to a higher sphere. Had there been no obstruction, it might have soared into the sky, and grown immortal. But its lustre gleamed upon the ceiling; the exquisite texture of its wings brushed against that earthly medium; and a sparkle or two, as of star-dust, floated downward and lay glimmering on the carpet. Then the butterfly came fluttering down, and instead of returning to the infant, was apparently attracted towards the artist's hand.

"Not so, not so!" murmured Owen Warland, as if his handiwork could have understood him. "Thou hast gone forth out of thy master's heart. There is no return for thee!"

With a wavering movement, and emitting a tremulous radiance, the butterfly struggled, as it were, towards the infant, and was about to alight upon his finger. But, while it still hovered in the air, the little Child of Strength, with his grandsire's sharp and shrewd expression in his face, made a snatch at the marvellous insect, and compressed it in his hand. Annie screamed! Old Peter Hovendon burst into a cold and scornful laugh. The blacksmith, by main force, unclosed the infant's hand, and found within the palm a small heap of glittering fragments, whence the Mystery of Beauty had fled for ever. And as for Owen Warland, he looked placidly at what seemed the ruin of his life's labor, and which was yet no ruin. He had caught a far other butterfly than this. When the artist rose high enough to achieve the Beautiful, the symbol by which he made it perceptible to mortal senses became of little value in his eyes, while his spirit possessed itself in the enjoyment of the Reality.

Drowne's Wooden Image

O NE sunshiny morning, in the good old times of the town of Boston, a young carver in wood, well known by the name of Drowne, stood contemplating a large oaken log, which it was his purpose to convert into the figure-head of a vessel. And while he discussed within his own mind what sort of shape or similitude it were well to bestow upon this excellent piece of timber, there came into Drowne's workshop a certain Captain Hunnewell, owner and commander of the good brig called the Cynosure, which had just returned from her first voyage to Fayal.

"Ah! that will do, Drowne, that will do!" cried the jolly captain, tapping the log with his rattan. "I bespeak this very piece of oak for the figure-head of the Cynosure. She has shown herself the sweetest craft that ever floated, and I mean to decorate her prow with the handsomest image that the skill of man can cut out of timber. And, Drowne, you are the fellow to execute it."

"You give me more credit than I deserve, Captain Hunnewell," said the carver, modestly, yet as one conscious of eminence in his art. "But, for the sake of the good brig, I stand ready to do my best. And which of these designs would you prefer? Here—" pointing to a staring, half length figure, in a white wig and scarlet coat—"here is an excellent model, the likeness of our gracious king. Here is the valiant Admiral Vernon. Or, if you prefer a female figure, what say you to Britannia with the trident?"

"All very fine, Drowne; all very fine," answered the mariner. "But as nothing like the brig ever swam the ocean, so I am determined she shall have such a figure-head as old Neptune never saw in his life. And what is more, as there is a secret in the matter, you must pledge your credit not to betray it."

"Certainly," said Drowne, marvelling, however, what possible mystery there could be in reference to an affair so open, of necessity, to the inspection of all the world, as the figure-head of a vessel. "You may depend, captain, on my being as secret as the nature of the case will permit."

Captain Hunnewell then took Drowne by the button, and communicated his wishes in so low a tone, that it would be unmannerly to repeat what was evidently intended for the carver's private ear. We shall, therefore, take the opportunity to give the reader a few desirable particulars about Drowne himself.

He was the first American who is known to have attempted,—in a very humble line, it is true,—that art in which we can now reckon so many names already distinguished, or rising to distinction. From his earliest boyhood, he had exhibited a knack—for it would be too proud a word to call it genius—a knack, therefore, for the imitation of the human figure, in whatever material came most readily to hand. The snows of a New England winter had often supplied him with a species of marble as dazzling white, at least, as the Parian or the Carrara, and if less durable, yet sufficiently so to correspond with any claims to permanent existence possessed by the boy's frozen statues. Yet they won admiration from maturer judges than his schoolfellows, and were, indeed, remarkably clever, though destitute of the native warmth that might have made the snow melt beneath his hand. As he advanced in life, the young man adopted pine and oak as eligible materials for the display of his skill, which now began to bring him a return of solid silver, as well as the empty praise that had been an apt reward enough for his productions of evanescent snow. He became noted for carving ornamental pump-heads, and wooden urns for gate-posts, and decorations, more grotesque than fanciful, for mantelpieces. No apothecary would have deemed himself in the way of obtaining custom, without setting up a gilded mortar, if not a head of Galen or Hippocrates, from the skilful hand of Drowne. But the great scope of his business lay in the manufacture of figure-heads for vessels. Whether it were the monarch himself, or some famous British admiral or general, or the governor of the province, or perchance the favourite daughter of the ship-owner, there the image stood above the prow, decked out in gorgeous colours, magnificently gilded, and staring the whole world out of countenance, as if from an innate consciousness of its own superiority. These specimens of native sculpture had crossed the sea in all directions,

and been not ignobly noticed among the crowded shipping
of the Thames, and wherever else the hardy mariners of New
England had pushed their adventures. It must be confessed,
that a family likeness pervaded these respectable progeny of
Drowne's skill—that the benign countenance of the king resembled those of his subjects, and that Miss Peggy Hobart,
the merchant's daughter, bore a remarkable similitude to Britannia, Victory, and other ladies of the allegoric sisterhood;
and, finally, that they had all had a kind of wooden aspect,
which proved an intimate relationship with the unshaped
blocks of timber in the carver's workshop. But, at least, there
was no inconsiderable skill of hand, nor a deficiency of any
attribute to render them really works of art, except that deep
quality, be it of soul or intellect, which bestows life upon the
lifeless, and warmth upon the cold, and which, had it been
present, would have made Drowne's wooden image instinct
with spirit.

The captain of the Cynosure had now finished his instructions.

"And Drowne," said he, impressively, "you must lay aside
all other business, and set about this forthwith. And as to the
price, only do the job in first rate style, and you shall settle
that point yourself."

"Very well, captain," answered the carver, who looked
grave and somewhat perplexed, yet had a sort of smile upon
his visage. "Depend upon it, I'll do my utmost to satisfy you."

From that morning, the men of taste about Long Wharf
and the Town Dock, who were wont to show their love for
the arts by frequent visits to Drowne's workshop, and admiration of his wooden images, began to be sensible of a mystery in the carver's conduct. Often he was absent in the day-
time. Sometimes, as might be judged by gleams of light from
the shop windows, he was at work until a late hour of the
evening; although neither knock nor voice, on such occasions,
could gain admittance for a visitor, or elicit any word of response. Nothing remarkable, however, was observed in the
shop at those hours when it was thrown open. A fine piece
of timber, indeed, which Drowne was known to have reserved for some work of especial dignity, was seen to be gradually assuming shape. What shape it was destined ultimately

to take, was a problem to his friends, and a point on which the carver preserved a rigid silence. But day after day, though Drowne was seldom noticed in the act of working upon it, this rude form began to be developed, until it became evident to all observers, that a female figure was growing into mimic life. At each new visit they beheld a larger pile of wooden chips, and a nearer approximation to something beautiful. It seemed as if the hamadryad of the oak had sheltered herself from the unimaginative world within the heart of her native tree, and that it was only necessary to remove the strange shapelessness that had incrusted her, and reveal the grace and loveliness of a divinity. Imperfect as the design, the attitude, the costume, and especially the face of the image, still remained, there was already an effect that drew the eye from the wooden cleverness of Drowne's earlier productions, and fixed it upon the tantalizing mystery of this new project.

Copley, the celebrated painter, than a young man, and a resident of Boston, came one day to visit Drowne; for he had recognized so much of moderate ability in the carver, as to induce him, in the dearth of any professional sympathy, to cultivate his acquaintance. On entering the shop, the artist glanced at the inflexible images of king, commander, dame, and allegory, that stood around; on the best of which might have been bestowed the questionable praise, that it looked as if a living man had here been changed to wood, and that not only the physical, but the intellectual and spiritual part, partook of the stolid transformation. But in not a single instance did it seem as if the wood were imbibing the ethereal essence of humanity. What a wide distinction is here, and how far would the slightest portion of the latter merit have outvalued the utmost degree of the former!

"My friend Drowne," said Copley, smiling to himself, but alluding to the mechanical and wooden cleverness that so invariably distinguished the images, "you are really a remarkable person! I have seldom met with a man, in your line of business, that could do so much; for one other touch might make this figure of General Wolfe, for instance, a breathing and intelligent human creature."

"You would have me think that you are praising me highly, Mr. Copley," answered Drowne, turning his back upon

Wolfe's image in apparent disgust. "But there has come a light into my mind. I know, what you know as well, that the one touch, which you speak of as deficient, is the only one that would be truly valuable, and that, without it, these works of mine are no better than worthless abortions. There is the same difference between them and the works of an inspired artist, as between a sign post daub and one of your best pictures."

"This is strange!" cried Copley, looking him in the face, which now, as the painter fancied, had a singular depth of intelligence, though, hitherto, it had not given him greatly the advantage over his own family of wooden images. "What has come over you? How is it that, possessing the idea which you have now uttered, you should produce only such works as these?"

The carver smiled, but made no reply. Copley turned again to the images, conceiving that the sense of deficiency which Drowne had just expressed, and which is so rare in a merely mechanical character, must surely imply a genius, the tokens of which had heretofore been overlooked. But no; there was not a trace of it. He was about to withdraw, when his eyes chanced to fall upon a half-developed figure which lay in a corner of the workshop, surrounded by scattered chips of oak. It arrested him at once.

"What is here? Who has done this?" he broke out, after contemplating it in speechless astonishment for an instant. "Here is the divine, the life-giving touch! What inspired hand is beckoning this wood to arise and live? Whose work is this?"

"No man's work," replied Drowne. "The figure lies within that block of oak, and it is my business to find it."

"Drowne," said the true artist, grasping the carver fervently by the hand, "you are a man of genius!"

As Copley departed, happening to glance backward from the threshold, he beheld Drowne bending over the half created shape, and stretching forth his arms as if he would have embraced and drawn it to his heart; while, had such a miracle been possible, his countenance expressed passion enough to communicate warmth and sensibility to the lifeless oak.

"Strange enough!" said the artist to himself. "Who would

have looked for a modern Pygmalion in the person of a Yankee mechanic!"

As yet, the image was but vague in its outward present-
ment; so that, as in the cloud-shapes around the western sun,
the observer rather felt, or was led to imagine, than really saw
what was intended by it. Day by day, however, the work assumed greater precision, and settled its irregular and misty
outline into distincter grace and beauty. The general design
was now obvious to the common eye. It was a female figure,
in what appeared to be a foreign dress; the gown being laced
over the bosom, and opening in front, so as to disclose a skirt
or petticoat, the folds and inequalities of which were admirably represented in the oaken substance. She wore a hat of
singular gracefulness, and abundantly laden with flowers,
such as never grew in the rude soil of New England, but
which, with all their fanciful luxuriance, had a natural truth
that it seemed impossible for the most fertile imagination to
have attained without copying from real prototypes. There
were several little appendages to this dress, such as a fan, a
pair of ear-rings, a chain about the neck, a watch in the bosom, and a ring upon the finger, all of which would have
been deemed beneath the dignity of sculpture. They were put
on, however, with as much taste as a lovely woman might
have shown in her attire, and could therefore have shocked
none but a judgment spoiled by artistic rules.

The face was still imperfect; but, gradually, by a magic
touch, intelligence and sensibility brightened through the features, with all the effect of light gleaming forth from within
the solid oak. The face became alive. It was a beautiful,
though not precisely regular, and somewhat haughty aspect,
but with a certain piquancy about the eyes and mouth which,
of all expressions, would have seemed the most impossible to
throw over a wooden countenance. And now, so far as carving went, this wonderful production was complete.

"Drowne," said Copley, who had hardly missed a single
day in his visits to the carver's workshop, "if this work were
in marble, it would make you famous at once; nay, I would
almost affirm that it would make an era in the art. It is as
ideal as an antique statue, and yet as real as any lovely woman
whom one meets at a fireside or in the street. But I trust you

do not mean to desecrate this exquisite creature with paint, like those staring kings and admirals yonder?"

"Not paint her?" exclaimed Captain Hunnewell, who stood by;—"not paint the figure-head of the Cynosure! And what sort of a figure should I cut in a foreign port, with such an unpainted oaken stick as this over my prow? She must, and she shall, be painted to the life, from the topmost flower in her hat down to the silver spangles on her slippers."

"Mr. Copley," said Drowne, quietly, "I know nothing of marble statuary, and nothing of a sculptor's rules of art. But of this wooden image—this work of my hands—this creature of my heart—" and here his voice faltered and choked, in a very singular manner—"of this—of her—I may say that I know something. A well-spring of inward wisdom gushed within me, as I wrought upon the oak with my whole strength, and soul, and faith! Let others do what they may with marble, and adopt what rules they choose. If I can produce my desired effect by painted wood, those rules are not for me, and I have a right to disregard them."

"The very spirit of genius!" muttered Copley to himself. "How otherwise should this carver feel himself entitled to transcend all rules, and make me ashamed of quoting them."

He looked earnestly at Drowne, and again saw that expression of human love which, in a spiritual sense, as the artist could not help imagining, was the secret of the life that had been breathed into this block of wood.

The carver, still in the same secrecy that marked all his operations upon this mysterious image, proceeded to paint the habiliments in their proper colours, and the countenance with nature's red and white. When all was finished, he threw open his workshop, and admitted the townspeople to behold what he had done. Most persons, at their first entrance, felt impelled to remove their hats, and pay such reverence as was due to the richly dressed and beautiful young lady, who seemed to stand in a corner of the room, with oaken chips and shavings scattered at her feet. Then came a sensation of fear; as if, not being actually human, yet so like humanity, she must therefore be something preternatural. There was, in truth, an indefinable air and expression that might reasonably induce the query—who and from what sphere this daughter of the oak should be. The strange rich flowers of Eden on her head; the complexion, so much deeper and more brilliant than those of our native beauties; the foreign, as it seemed, and fantastic garb, yet not too fantastic to be worn decorously in the street; the delicately wrought embroidery of the skirt; the broad gold chain about her neck; the curious ring upon her finger; the fan, so exquisitely sculptured in open work, and painted to resemble pearl and ebony;—where could Drowne, in his sober walk of life, have beheld the vision here so matchlessly embodied! And then her face! In the dark eyes, and around the voluptuous mouth, there played a look made up of pride, coquetry, and a gleam of mirthfulness, which impressed Copley with the idea that the image was secretly enjoying the perplexed admiration of himself and all other beholders.

"And will you," said he to the carver, "permit this master-piece to become the figure-head of a vessel? Give the honest captain yonder figure of Britannia—it will answer his purpose far better,—and send this fairy queen to England, where, for aught I know, it may bring you a thousand pounds."

"I have not wrought it for money," said Drowne.

"What sort of a fellow is this!" thought Copley. "A Yankee, and throw away the chance of making his fortune! He has gone mad; and thence has come this gleam of genius."

There was still further proof of Drowne's lunacy, if credit were due to the rumour that he had been seen kneeling at the feet of the oaken lady, and gazing with a lover's passionate ardour into the face that his own hands had created. The bigots of the day hinted that it would be no matter of surprise if an evil spirit were allowed to enter this beautiful form, and seduce the carver to destruction.

The fame of the image spread far and wide. The inhabitants visited it so universally, that, after a few days of exhibition, there was hardly an old man or a child who had not become minutely familiar with its aspect. Even had the story of Drowne's wooden image ended here, its celebrity might have been prolonged for many years, by the reminiscences of those who looked upon it in their childhood, and saw nothing else so beautiful in after life. But the town was now astounded by an event, the narrative of which has formed itself into one of the most singular legends that are yet to be met with in the traditionary chimney-corners of the New England metropolis, where old men and women sit dreaming of the past, and wag their heads at the dreamers of the present and the future.

One fine morning, just before the departure of the Cynosure on her second voyage to Fayal, the commander of that gallant vessel was seen to issue from his residence in Hanover street. He was stylishly dressed in a blue broadcloth coat, with gold lace at the seams and button-holes, an embroidered scarlet waistcoat, a triangular hat, with a loop and broad binding of gold, and wore a silver-hilted hanger at his side. But the good captain might have been arrayed in the robes of a prince or the rags of a beggar, without in either case attracting notice, while obscured by such a companion as now leaned on his arm. The people in the street started, rubbed their eyes, and either leaped aside from their path, or stood as if transfixed to wood or marble in astonishment.

"Do you see it?—do you see it?" cried one, with tremulous eagerness. "It is the very same!"

"The same?" answered another, who had arrived in town only the night before. "What do you mean? I see only a sea-captain in his shore-going clothes, and a young lady in a foreign habit, with a bunch of beautiful flowers in her hat. On my word, she is as fair and bright a damsel as my eyes have looked on this many a day!"

"Yes; the same!—the very same!" repeated the other. "Drowne's wooden image has come to life!"

Here was a miracle indeed! Yet, illuminated by the sunshine, or darkened by the alternate shade of the houses, and with its garments fluttering lightly in the morning breeze, there passed the image along the street. It was exactly and minutely the shape, the garb, and the face, which the townspeople had so recently thronged to see and admire. Not a rich flower upon her head, not a single leaf, but had had its prototype in Drowne's wooden workmanship, although now their fragile grace had become flexible, and was shaken by every footstep that the wearer made. The broad gold chain upon the neck was identical with the one represented on the image, and glistened with the motion imparted by the rise and fall of the bosom which it decorated. A real diamond sparkled on her finger. In her right hand she bore a pearl and ebony fan, which she flourished with a fantastic and bewitching coquetry, that was likewise expressed in all her movements, as well as in the style of her beauty and the attire that so well harmonized with it. The face, with its brilliant depth of complexion, had the same piquancy of mirthful mischief that was fixed upon the countenance of the image, but which was here varied and continually shifting, yet always essentially the same, like the sunny gleam upon a bubbling fountain. On the whole, there was something so airy and yet so real in the figure, and withal so perfectly did it represent Drowne's image, that people knew not whether to suppose the magic wood etherealized into a spirit, or warmed and softened into an actual woman.

"One thing is certain," muttered a Puritan of the old stamp. "Drowne has sold himself to the devil; and doubtless this gay Captain Hunnewell is a party to the bargain."

"And I," said a young man who overheard him, "would almost consent to be the third victim, for the liberty of saluting those lovely lips."

"And so would I," said Copley, the painter, "for the privilege of taking her picture."

The image, or the apparition, whichever it might be, still escorted by the bold captain, proceeded from Hanover street through some of the cross-lanes that make this portion of the town so intricate, to Ann street, thence into Dock-square, and so downward to Drowne's shop, which stood just on the water's edge. The crowd still followed, gathering volume as it rolled along. Never had a modern miracle occurred in such broad daylight, nor in the presence of such a multitude of witnesses. The airy image, as if conscious that she was the object of the murmurs and disturbance that swelled behind her, appeared slightly vexed and flustered, yet still in a manner consistent with the light vivacity and sportive mischief that were written in her countenance. She was observed to flutter her fan with such vehement rapidity, that the elaborate delicacy of its workmanship gave way, and it remained broken in her hand.

Arriving at Drowne's door, while the captain threw it

open, the marvellous apparition paused an instant on the threshold, assuming the very attitude of the image, and casting over the crowd that glance of sunny coquetry which all remembered on the face of the oaken lady. She and her cavalier then disappeared.

"Ah!" murmured the crowd, drawing a deep breath, as with one vast pair of lungs.

"The world looks darker, now that she has vanished," said some of the young men.

But the aged, whose recollections dated as far back as witch-times, shook their heads, and hinted that our forefathers would have thought it a pious deed to burn the daughter of the oak with fire.

"If she be other than a bubble of the elements," exclaimed Copley, "I must look upon her face again!"

He accordingly entered the shop; and there, in her usual corner, stood the image, gazing at him, as it might seem, with the very same expression of mirthful mischief that had been the farewell look of the apparition when, but a moment before, she turned her face towards the crowd. The carver stood beside his creation, mending the beautiful fan, which by some accident was broken in her hand. But there was no longer any motion in the life-like image, nor any real woman in the workshop, nor even the witchcraft of a sunny shadow, that might have deluded people's eyes as it flitted along the street. Captain Hunnewell, too, had vanished. His hoarse, seabreezy tones, however, were audible on the other side of a door that opened upon the water.

"Sit down in the stern sheets, my lady," said the gallant captain. "Come, bear a hand, you lubbers, and set us on board in the turning of a minute-glass."

And then was heard the stroke of oars.

"Drowne," said Copely, with a smile of intelligence, "you have been a truly fortunate man. What painter or statuary ever had such a subject! No wonder that she inspired a genius into you, and first created the artist who afterwards created her image."

Drowne looked at him with a visage that bore the traces of tears, but from which the light of imagination and sensibility, so recently illuminating it, had departed. He was again the mechanical carver that he had been known to be all his life-time.

"I hardly understand what you mean, Mr. Copley," said he, putting his hand to his brow. "This image! Can it have been my work? Well—I have wrought it in a kind of dream; and now that I am broad awake, I must set about finishing yonder figure of Admiral Vernon."

And forthwith he employed himself on the stolid countenance of one of his wooden progeny, and completed it in his own mechanical style, from which he was never known afterwards to deviate. He followed his business industriously for many years, acquired a competence, and, in the latter part of his life, attained to a dignified station in the church, being remembered in records and traditions as Deacon Drowne, the carver. One of his productions, an Indian chief, gilded all over, stood during the better part of a century on the cupola of the Province House, bedazzling the eyes of those who looked upward, like an angel of the sun. Another work of the good deacon's hand—a reduced likeness of his friend Captain Hunnewell, holding a telescope and quadrant—may be seen, to this day, at the corner of Broad and State streets, serving in the useful capacity of sign to the shop of a nautical instrument maker. We know not how to account for the inferiority of this quaint old figure, as compared with the recorded excellence of the Oaken Lady, unless on the supposition, that in every human spirit there is imagination, sensibility, creative power, genius, which, according to circumstances, may either be developed in this world, or shrouded in a mask of dulness until another state of being. To our friend Drowne, there came a brief season of excitement, kindled by love. It rendered him a genius for that one occasion, but, quenched in disappointment, left him again the mechanical carver in wood, without the power even of appreciating the work that his own hands had wrought. Yet who can doubt, that the very highest state to which a human spirit can attain, in its loftiest aspirations, is its truest and most natural state, and that Drowne was more consistent with himself when he wrought the admirable figure of the mysterious lady, than when he perpetrated a whole progeny of blockheads?

There was a rumor in Boston, about this period, that a

young Portuguese lady of rank, on some occasion of political
or domestic disquietude, had fled from her home in Fayal,
and put herself under the protection of Captain Hunnewell,
on board of whose vessel, and at whose residence, she was
sheltered until a change of affairs. This fair stranger must have
been the original of Drowne's Wooden Image.

A Select Party

A MAN of Fancy made an entertainment at one of of his castles in the air, and invited a select number of distinguished personages to favor him with their presence. The mansion, though less splendid than many that have been situated in the same region, was, nevertheless, of a magnificence such as is seldom witnessed by those acquainted only with terrestrial architecture. Its strong foundations and massive walls were quarried out of a ledge of heavy and sombre clouds, which had hung brooding over the earth, apparently as dense and ponderous as its own granite, throughout a whole autumnal day. Perceiving that the general effect was gloomy—so that the airy castle looked like a feudal fortress, or a monastery of the middle ages, or a state-prison of our own times, rather than the home of pleasure and repose which he intended it to be—the owner, regardless of expense, resolved to gild the exterior from top to bottom. Fortunately, there was just then a flood of evening sunshine in the air. This being gathered up and poured abundantly upon the roof and walls, imbued them with a kind of solemn cheerfulness; while the cupolas and pinnacles were made to glitter with the purest gold, and all the hundred windows gleamed with a glad light, as if the edifice itself were rejoicing in its heart. And now, if the people of the lower world chanced to be looking upward, out of the turmoil of their petty perplexities, they probably mistook the castle in the air for a heap of sunset clouds, to which the magic of light and shade had imparted the aspect of a fantastically constructed mansion. To such beholders it was unreal, because they lacked the imaginative faith. Had they been worthy to pass within its portal, they would have recognized the truth, that the dominions which the spirit conquers for itself among unrealities, become a thousand times more real than the earth whereon they stamp their feet, saying, "This is solid and substantial!—this may be called a fact!"

At the appointed hour, the host stood in his great saloon to receive the company. It was a vast and noble room, the vaulted ceiling of which was supported by double rows of gigantic pillars, that had been hewn entire out of masses of variegated clouds. So brilliantly were they polished, and so exquisitely wrought by the sculptor's skill, as to resemble the finest specimens of emerald, porphyry, opal, and chrysolite, thus producing a delicate richness of effect, which their immense size rendered not incompatible with grandeur. To each of these pillars a meteor was suspended. Thousands of these ethereal lustres are continually wandering about the firmament, burning out to waste, yet capable of imparting a useful radiance to any person who has the art of converting them to domestic purposes. As managed in the saloon, they are far more economical than ordinary lamp-light. Such, however, was the intensity of their blaze, that it had been found expedient to cover each meteor with a globe of evening mist, thereby muffling the too potent glow, and soothing it into a mild and comfortable splendor. It was like the brilliancy of a powerful, yet chastened, imagination; a light which seemed to hide whatever was unworthy to be noticed, and give effect to every beautiful and noble attribute. The guests, therefore, as they advanced up the centre of the saloon, appeared to better advantage than ever before in their lives.

The first that entered, with old-fashioned punctuality, was a venerable figure in the costume of by-gone days, with his white hair flowing down over his shoulders, and a reverend beard upon his breast. He leaned upon a staff, the tremulous stroke of which, as he set it carefully upon the floor, re-echoed through the saloon at every footstep. Recognizing at once this celebrated personage, whom it had cost him a vast deal of trouble and research to discover, the host advanced nearly three-fourths of the distance, down between the pillars, to meet and welcome him.

"Venerable sir," said the Man of Fancy, bending to the floor, "the honor of this visit would never be forgotten, were my term of existence to be as happily prolonged as your own."

The old gentleman received the compliment with gracious condescension; he then thrust up his spectacles over his forehead, and appeared to take a critical survey of the saloon.

"Never, within my recollection," observed he, "have I entered a more spacious and noble hall. But are you sure that it is built of solid materials, and that the structure will be permanent?"

"Oh, never fear, my venerable friend," replied the host. "In reference to a lifetime like your own, it is true, my castle may well be called a temporary edifice. But it will endure long enough to answer all the purposes for which it was erected."

But we forget that the reader has not yet been made acquainted with the guest. It was no other than that universally accredited character, so constantly referred to in all seasons of intense cold or heat—he that remembers the hot Sunday and the cold Friday—the witness of a past age, whose negative reminiscences find their way into every newspaper, yet whose antiquated and dusky abode is so overshadowed by accumulated years, and crowded back by modern edifices, that none but the Man of Fancy could have discovered it—it was, in short, that twin-brother of Time, and great-grandsire of mankind, and hand-and-glove associate of all forgotten men and things, the Oldest Inhabitant! The host would willingly have drawn him into conversation, but succeeded only in eliciting a few remarks as to the oppressive atmosphere of this present summer evening, compared with one which the guest had experienced, about four-score years ago. The old gentleman, in fact, was a good deal overcome by his journey among the clouds, which, to a frame so earth-incrusted by long continuance in a lower region, was unavoidably more fatiguing than to younger spirits. He was therefore conducted to an easy-chair, well cushioned, and stuffed with vaporous softness, and left to take a little repose.

The Man of Fancy now discerned another guest, who stood so quietly in the shadow of one of the pillars, that he might easily have been overlooked.

"My dear sir," exclaimed the host, grasping him warmly by the hand, "allow me to greet you as the hero of the evening. Pray do not take it as an empty compliment; for if there were not another guest in my castle, it would be entirely pervaded with your presence!"

"I thank you," answered the unpretending stranger, "but, though you happened to overlook me, I have not just arrived.

I came very early, and, with your permission, shall remain after the rest of the company have retired."

And who does the reader imagine was this unobtrusive guest? It was the famous performer of acknowledged impossibilities; a character of superhuman capacity and virtue, and, if his enemies are to be credited, of no less remarkable weaknesses and defects. With a generosity of which he alone sets us the example, we will glance merely at his nobler attributes. He it is, then, who prefers the interests of others to his own, and a humble station to an exalted one. Careless of fashion, custom, the opinions of men, and the influence of the press, he assimilates his life to the standard of ideal rectitude, and thus proves himself the one independent citizen of our free country. In point of ability, many people declare him to be the only mathematician capable of squaring the circle; the only mechanic acquainted with the principle of perpetual motion; the only scientific philosopher who can compel water to run up hill; the only writer of the age whose genius is equal to the production of an epic poem; and, finally—so various are his accomplishments—the only professor of gymnastics who has succeeded in jumping down his own throat. With all these talents, however, he is so far from being considered a member of good society, that it is the severest censure of any fashionable assemblage, to affirm that this remarkable individual was present. Public orators, lecturers, and theatrical performers, particularly eschew his company. For especial reasons, we are not at liberty to disclose his name, and shall mention only one other trait—a most singular phenomenon in natural philosophy—that when he happens to cast his eyes upon a looking-glass, he beholds Nobody reflected there!

Several other guests now made their appearance, and among them, chattering with immense volubility, a brisk little gentleman of universal vogue in private society, and not unknown in the public journals, under the title of Monsieur On-Dit. The name would seem to indicate a Frenchman; but, whatever be his country, he is thoroughly versed in all the languages of the day, and can express himself quite as much to the purpose in English as in any other tongue. No sooner were the ceremonies of salutation over, than this talkative little person put his mouth to the host's ear, and whispered three secrets of state, an important piece of commercial intelligence, and a rich item of fashionable scandal. He then assured the Man of Fancy that he would not fail to circulate in the society of the lower world a minute description of this magnificent castle in the air, and of the festivities at which he had the honor to be a guest. So saying, Monsieur On-Dit made his bow and hurried from one to another of the company, with all of whom he seemed to be acquainted, and to possess some topic of interest or amusement for every individual. Coming at last to the Oldest Inhabitant, who was slumbering comfortably in the easy-chair, he applied his mouth to that venerable ear.

"What do you say?" cried the old gentleman, starting from his nap, and putting up his hand to serve the purpose of an ear-trumpet.

Monsieur On-Dit bent forward again, and repeated his communication.

"Never, within my memory," exclaimed the Oldest Inhabitant, lifting his hands in astonishment, "has so remarkable an incident been heard of!"

Now came in the Clerk of the Weather, who had been invited out of deference to his official station, although the host was well aware that his conversation was likely to contribute but little to the general enjoyment. He soon, indeed, got into a corner with his acquaintance of long ago, the Oldest Inhabitant, and began to compare notes with him in reference to the great storms, gales of wind, and other atmospherical facts that had occurred during a century past. It rejoiced the Man of Fancy, that his venerable and much respected guest had met with so congenial an associate. Entreating them both to make themselves perfectly at home, he now turned to receive the Wandering Jew. This personage, however, had latterly grown so common, by mingling in all sorts of society, and appearing at the beck of every entertainer, that he could hardly be deemed a proper guest in a very exclusive circle. Besides, being covered with dust from his continual wanderings along the highways of the world, he really looked out of place in a dress party, so that the host felt relieved of an incommodity, when the restless individual in question, after a brief stay, took his departure on a ramble towards Oregon.

The portal was now thronged by a crowd of shadowy people, with whom the Man of Fancy had been acquainted in his
visionary youth. He had invited them hither for the sake of
observing how they would compare, whether advantageously
or otherwise, with the real characters to whom his maturer
life had introduced him. They were beings of crude imagination, such as glide before a young man's eye, and pretend to
be actual inhabitants of the earth; the wise and witty, with
whom he would hereafter hold intercourse; the generous and
heroic friends, whose devotion would be requited with his
own; the beautiful dream-woman, who would become the
help-mate of his human toils and sorrows, and at once the
source and partaker of his happiness. Alas! it is not good for
the full grown man to look too closely at these old acquaintances, but rather to reverence them at a distance, through the
medium of years that have gathered duskily between. There
was something laughably untrue in their pompous stride and
exaggerated sentiment; they were neither human, nor tolerable likenesses of humanity, but fantastic masquers, rendering
heroism and nature alike ridiculous by the grave absurdity of
their pretensions to such attributes. And as for the peerless
dream-lady, behold! there advanced up the saloon, with a
movement like a jointed-doll, a sort of wax figure of an angel—a creature as cold as moonshine—an artifice in petticoats, with an intellect of pretty phrases, and only the semblance of a heart—yet, in all these particulars, the true type
of a young man's imaginary mistress. Hardly could the host's
punctilious courtesy restrain a smile, as he paid his respects to
this unreality, and met the sentimental glance with which the
Dream sought to remind him of their former love-passages.

"No, no, fair lady," murmured he, betwixt sighing and
smiling; "my taste is changed! I have learned to love what
Nature makes, better than my own creations in the guise of
womanhood."

"Ah, false one!" shrieked the dream-lady, pretending to
faint, but dissolving into thin air, out of which came the deplorable murmur of her voice—"your inconstancy has annihilated me!"

"So be it," said the cruel Man of Fancy to himself—"and
a good riddance, too!"

Together with these shadows, and from the same region, there came an uninvited multitude of shapes, which, at any time during his life, had tormented the Man of Fancy in his moods of morbid melancholy, or had haunted him in the delirium of fever. The walls of his castle in the air were not dense enough to keep them out; nor would the strongest of earthly architecture have availed to their exclusion. Here were those forms of dim terror, which had beset him at the entrance of life, waging warfare with his hopes. Here were strange uglinesses of earlier date, such as haunt children in the night time. He was particularly startled by the vision of a deformed old black woman, whom he imagined as lurking in the garret of his native home, and who, when he was an infant, had once come to his bedside and grinned at him, in the crisis of a scarlet fever. This same black shadow, with others almost as hideous, now glided among the pillars of the magnificent saloon, grinning recognition, until the man shuddered anew at the forgotten terrors of his childhood. It amused him, however, to observe the black woman, with the mischievous caprice peculiar to such beings, steal up to the chair of the Oldest Inhabitant, and peep into his half-dreamy mind.

"Never within my memory," muttered that venerable personage, aghast, "did I see such a face!"

Almost immediately after the unrealities just described, arrived a number of guests, whom incredulous readers may be inclined to rank equally among creatures of imagination. The most noteworthy were an incorruptible Patriot; a Scholar without pedantry; a Priest without worldly ambition, and a Beautiful Woman without pride or coquetry; a Married Pair, whose life had never been disturbed by incongruity of feeling; a Reformer, untrammelled by his theory; and a Poet, who felt no jealousy towards other votaries of the lyre. In truth, however, the host was not one of the cynics who consider these patterns of excellence, without the fatal flaw, such rarities in the world; and he had invited them to his select party chiefly out of humble deference to the judgment of society, which pronounces them almost impossible to be met with.

"In my younger days," observed the Oldest Inhabitant, "such characters might be seen at the corner of every street."

Be that as it might, these specimens of perfection proved to be not half so entertaining companions as people with the ordinary allowance of faults.

But now appeared a stranger, whom the host had no sooner recognized, than, with an abundance of courtesy unlavished on any other, he hastened down the whole length of the saloon, in order to pay him emphatic honor. Yet he was a young man in poor attire, with no insignia of rank or acknowledged eminence, nor anything to distinguish him among the crowd except a high, white forehead, beneath which a pair of deep-set eyes were glowing with warm light. It was such a light as never illuminates the earth, save when a great heart burns as the household fire of a grand intellect. And who was he? Who, but the Master Genius, for whom our country is looking anxiously into the mist of time, as destined to fulfil the great mission of creating an American literature, hewing it, as it were, out of the unwrought granite of our intellectual quarries. From him, whether moulded in the form of an epic poem, or assuming a guise altogether new, as the spirit itself may determine, we are to receive our first great original work, which shall do all that remains to be achieved for our glory among the nations. How this child of a mighty destiny had been discovered by the Man of Fancy, it is of little consequence to mention. Suffice it, that he dwells as yet unhonored among men, unrecognized by those who have known him from his cradle;—the noble countenance, which should be distinguished by a halo diffused around it, passes daily amid the throng of people, toiling and troubling themselves about the trifles of a moment—and none pay reverence to the worker of immortality. Nor does it matter much to him, in his triumph over all the ages, though a generation or two of his own times shall do themselves the wrong to disregard him.

By this time, Monsieur On-Dit had caught up the stranger's name and destiny, and was busily whispering the intelligence among the other guests.

"Pshaw!" said one, "there can never be an American Genius."

"Pish!" cried another, "we have already as good poets as any in the world. For my part, I desire to see no better."

And the Oldest Inhabitant, when it was proposed to introduce him to the Master Genius, begged to be excused, observing, that a man who had been honored with the acquaintance of Dwight, and Freneau, and Joel Barlow, might be allowed a little austerity of taste.

The saloon was now fast filling up, by the arrival of other remarkable characters; among whom were noticed Davy Jones, the distinguished nautical personage, and a rude, carelessly dressed, harum-scarum sort of elderly fellow, known by the nickname of Old Harry. The latter, however, after being shown to a dressing room, re-appeared with his grey hair nicely combed, his clothes brushed, a clean dicky on his neck, and altogether so changed in aspect as to merit the more respectful appellation of Venerable Henry. John Doe and Richard Roe came arm-in-arm, accompanied by a Man of Straw, a fictitious endorser, and several persons who had no existence except as voters in closely contested elections. The celebrated Seatsfield, who now entered, was at first supposed to belong to the same brotherhood, until he made it apparent that he was a real man of flesh and blood, and had his earthly domicile in Germany. Among the latest comers, as might reasonably be expected, arrived a guest from the far future.

"Do you know him?—do you know him?" whispered Monsieur On-Dit, who seemed to be acquainted with everybody. "He is the representative of Posterity—the man of an age to come!"

"And how came he here?" asked a figure who was evidently the prototype of the fashion-plate in a magazine, and might be taken to represent the vanities of the passing moment. "The fellow infringes upon our rights by coming before his time."

"But you forget where we are," answered the Man of Fancy, who overheard the remark; "the lower earth, it is true, will be forbidden ground to him for many long years hence; but a castle in the air is a sort of no-man's land, where Posterity may make acquaintance with us on equal terms."

No sooner was his identity known, than a throng of guests gathered about Posterity, all expressing the most generous interest in his welfare, and many boasting of the sacrifices which they had made, or were willing to make, in his behalf. Some, with as much secresy as possible, desired his judgment upon certain copies of verses, or great manuscript rolls of prose; others accosted him with the familiarity of old friends, taking it for granted that he was perfectly cognizant of their names and characters. At length, finding himself thus beset, Posterity was put quite beside his patience.

"Gentlemen, my good friends," cried he, breaking loose from a misty poet, who strove to hold him by the button, "I pray you to attend to your own business, and leave me to take care of mine! I expect to owe you nothing, unless it be certain national debts, and other incumbrances and impediments, physical and moral, which I shall find it troublesome enough to remove from my path. As to your verses, pray read them to your contemporaries. Your names are as strange to me as your faces; and even were it otherwise—let me whisper you a secret—the cold, icy memory which one generation may retain of another, is but a poor recompense to barter life for. Yet, if your heart is set on being known to me, the surest, the only method, is, to live truly and wisely for your own age, whereby, if the native force be in you, you may likewise live for posterity!"

"It is nonsense," murmured the Oldest Inhabitant, who, as a man of the past, felt jealous that all notice should be withdrawn from himself, to be lavished on the future,—"sheer nonsense, to waste so much thought on what only is to be!"

To divert the minds of his guests, who were considerably abashed by this little incident, the Man of Fancy led them through several apartments of the castle, receiving their compliments upon the taste and varied magnificence that were displayed in each. One of these rooms was filled with moonlight, which did not enter through the window, but was the aggregate of all the moon-shine that is scattered around the earth on a summer night, while no eyes are awake to enjoy its beauty. Airy spirits had gathered it up, wherever they found it gleaming on the broad bosom of a lake, or silvering the meanders of a stream, or glimmering among the wind-stirred boughs of a wood, and had garnered it in this one spacious hall. Along the walls, illuminated by the mild intensity of the moon-shine, stood a multitude of ideal statues, the original conceptions of the great works of ancient or modern art, which the sculptors did but imperfectly succeed in putting into marble. For it is not to be supposed that the pure idea of an immortal creation ceases to exist; it is only necessary to know where they are deposited, in order to obtain possession of them. In the alcoves of another vast apartment was arranged a splendid library, the volumes of which were inestimable, because they consisted not of actual performances, but of the works which the authors only planned, without ever finding the happy season to achieve them. To take familiar instances, here were the untold tales of Chaucer's Canterbury Pilgrims; the unwritten Cantos of the Fairy Queen; the conclusion of Coleridge's Christabel; and the whole of Dryden's projected Epic on the subject of King Arthur. The shelves were crowded; for it would not be too much to affirm that every author has imagined, and shaped out in his thought, more and far better works than those which actually proceeded from his pen. And here, likewise, were the unrealized conceptions of youthful poets, who died of the very strength of their own genius, before the world had caught one inspired murmur from their lips.

When the peculiarities of the library and statue-gallery were explained to the Oldest Inhabitant, he appeared infinitely perplexed, and exclaimed, with more energy than usual, that he had never heard of such a thing within his memory, and, moreover, did not at all understand how it could be.

"But my brain, I think," said the good old gentleman, "is getting not so clear as it used to be. You young folks, I suppose, can see your way through these strange matters. For my part, I give it up."

"And so do I," muttered the Old Harry. "It is enough to puzzle the——ahem!"

Making as little reply as possible to these observations, the Man of Fancy preceded the company to another noble saloon, the pillars of which were solid golden sunbeams, taken out of the sky in the first hour in the morning. Thus, as they retained all their living lustre, the room was filled with the most cheerful radiance imaginable, yet not too dazzling to be borne with comfort and delight. The windows were beautifully adorned with curtains, made of the many-colored clouds of sunrise, all imbued with virgin light, and hanging in magnif-

icent festoons from the ceiling to the floor. Moreover, there
were fragments of rainbows scattered through the room; so
that the guests, astonished at one another, reciprocally saw
their heads made glorious by the seven primary hues; or, if
they chose—as who would not?—they could grasp a rainbow in the air, and convert it to their own apparel and adornment. But the morning light and scattered rainbows were
only a type and symbol of the real wonders of the apartment.
By an influence akin to magic, yet perfectly natural, whatever
means and opportunities of joy are neglected in the lower
world, had been carefully gathered up, and deposited in the
saloon of morning sunshine. As may well be conceived, therefore, there was material enough to supply not merely a joyous
evening, but also a happy lifetime, to more than as many people
as that spacious apartment could contain. The company seemed
to renew their youth; while that pattern and proverbial standard
of innocence, the Child Unborn, frolicked to and fro among
them, communicating his own unwrinkled gaiety to all who
had the good fortune to witness his gambols.

"My honored friends," said the Man of Fancy, after they
had enjoyed themselves awhile, "I am now to request your
presence in the banqueting-hall, where a slight collation is
awaiting you."

"Ah, well said!" ejaculated a cadaverous figure, who had
been invited for no other reason than that he was pretty constantly in the habit of dining with Duke Humphrey. "I was
beginning to wonder whether a castle in the air were provided with a kitchen."

It was curious, in truth, to see how instantaneously the
guests were diverted from the high moral enjoyments which
they had been tasting with so much apparent zest, by a suggestion of the more solid as well as liquid delights of the festive board. They thronged eagerly in the rear of the host, who
now ushered them into a lofty and extensive hall, from end to
end of which was arranged a table, glittering all over with
innumerable dishes and drinking-vessels of gold. It is an uncertain point, whether these rich articles of plate were made
for the occasion, out of molten sunbeams, or recovered from
the wrecks of Spanish galleons, that had lain for ages at the
bottom of the sea. The upper end of the table was overshad-

owed by a canopy, beneath which was placed a chair of elaborate magnificence, which the host himself declined to occupy, and besought his guests to assign it to the worthiest among them. As a suitable homage to his incalculable antiquity and eminent distinction, the post of honor was at first tendered to the Oldest Inhabitant. He, however, eschewed it, and requested the favor of a bowl of gruel at a side-table, where he could refresh himself with a quiet nap. There was some little hesitation as to the next candidate, until Posterity took the Master Genius of our country by the hand, and led him to the chair of state, beneath the princely canopy. When once they beheld him in his true place, the company acknowledged the justice of the selection by a long thunder-roll of vehement applause.

Then was served up a banquet, combining, if not all the delicacies of the season, yet all the rarities which careful purveyors had met with in the flesh, fish, and vegetable markets of the land of Nowhere. The bill of fare being unfortunately lost, we can only mention a Phœnix, roasted in its own flames, cold potted birds of Paradise, ice-creams from the Milky Way, and whip-syllabubs and flummery from the Paradise of Fools, whereof there was a very great consumption. As for drinkables, the temperance-people contented themselves with water, as usual, but it was the water of the Fountain of Youth; the ladies sipped Nepenthe; the love-lorn, the care-worn, and the sorrow-stricken, were supplied with brimming goblets of Lethe; and it was shrewdly conjectured that a certain golden vase, from which only the more distinguished guests were invited to partake, contained nectar that had been mellowing ever since the days of classical mythology. The cloth being removed, the company, as usual, grew eloquent over their liquor, and delivered themselves of a succession of brilliant speeches; the task of reporting which we resign to the more adequate ability of Counsellor Gill, whose indispensable co-operation the Man of Fancy had taken the precaution to secure.

When the festivity of the banquet was at its most ethereal point, the Clerk of the Weather was observed to steal from the table, and thrust his head between the purple and golden curtains of one of the windows.

"My fellow-guests," he remarked aloud, after carefully noting the signs of the night, "I advise such of you as live at a distance, to be going as soon as possible; for a thunder-storm is certainly at hand."

"Mercy on me!" cried Mother Carey, who had left her brood of chickens, and come hither in gossamer drapery, with pink silk stockings, "How shall I ever get home?"

All now was confusion and hasty departure, with but little superfluous leave-taking. The Oldest Inhabitant, however, true to the rule of those long-past days in which his courtesy had been studied, paused on the threshold of the meteor-lighted hall, to express his vast satisfaction at the entertainment.

"Never, within my memory," observed the gracious old gentleman, "has it been my good fortune to spend a pleasanter evening, or in more select society."

The wind here took his breath away, whirled his three-cornered hat into infinite space, and drowned what further compliments it had been his purpose to bestow. Many of the company had bespoken Will o' the Whisps to convoy them home; and the host, in his general beneficence, had engaged the Man in the Moon, with an immense horn lantern, to be the guide of such desolate spinsters as could do no better for themselves. But a blast of the rising tempest blew out all their lights in the twinkling of an eye. How, in the darkness that ensued, the guests contrived to get back to earth, or whether the greater part of them contrived to get back at all, or are still wandering among clouds, mists, and puffs of tempestuous wind, bruised by the beams and rafters of the overthrown castle in the air, and deluded by all sorts of unrealities, are points that concern themselves, much more than the writer or the public. People should think of these matters, before they trust themselves on a pleasure-party into the realm of Nowhere.

A Book of Autographs

W E have before us a volume of autograph letters, chiefly of soldiers and statesmen of the Revolution, and addressed to a good and brave man, General Palmer, who himself drew his sword in the cause. They are profitable reading in a quiet afternoon, and in a mood withdrawn from too intimate relation with the present time; so that we can glide backward some three-quarters of a century, and surround ourselves with the ominous sublimity of circumstance that then frowned upon the writers. To give them their full effect, we should imagine that these letters have this moment been brought to town by the splashed and way-worn post-rider, or perhaps by an orderly dragoon, who has ridden in a perilous hurry to deliver his despatches. They are magic scrolls, if read in the right spirit. The roll of the drum and the fanfare of the trumpet is latent in some of them; and in others, an echo of the oratory that resounded in the old halls of the Continental Congress, at Philadelphia; or the words may come to us as with the living utterance of one of those illustrious men, speaking face to face, in friendly communion. Strange, that the mere identity of paper and ink should be so powerful. The same thoughts might look cold and ineffectual, in a printed book. Human nature craves a certain materialism, and clings pertinaciously to what is tangible, as if that were of more importance than the spirit accidentally involved in it. And, in truth, the original manuscript has always something which print itself must inevitably lose. An erasure, even a blot, a casual irregularity of hand, and all such little imperfections of mechanical execution, bring us close to the writer, and perhaps convey some of those subtle intimations for which language has no shape.

There are several letters from John Adams, written in a small, hasty, ungraceful hand, but earnest, and with no unnecessary flourish. The earliest is dated at Philadelphia, Sept. 26, 1774, about twenty days after the first opening of the Continental Congress. We look at this old yellow document, scribbled on half a sheet of foolscap, and ask of it many ques-

tions for which the words have no response. We would fain
know what were their mutual impressions, when all those
venerable faces, that have since been traced on steel or chiselled out of marble, and thus made familiar to posterity, first
met one another's gaze! Did one spirit harmonize them, in
spite of the dissimilitude of manners between the North and
the South, which were now for the first time brought into
political relations? Could the Virginian descendant of the
Cavaliers, and the New-Englander with his hereditary Puritanism—the aristocratic Southern planter, and the self-made
man from Massachusetts or Connecticut—at once feel that
they were countrymen and brothers? What did John Adams
think of Jefferson?—and Samuel Adams of Patrick Henry?
Did not North and South combine in their deference for the
sage Franklin—so long the defender of the Colonies in England, and whose scientific renown was already world-wide?
And was there yet any whispered prophecy, any vague conjecture, circulating among the delegates, as to the destiny which
might be in reserve for one stately man, who sat, for the most
part silent, among them?—what station he was to assume in
the world's history?—and how many statues would repeat his
form and countenance, and successively crumble beneath his
immortality?

The letter before us does not answer these inquiries. Its
main feature is the strong expression of the uncertainty and
awe that pervaded even the firm hearts of the Old Congress,
while anticipating the struggle which was to ensue:—

"The commencement of hostilities," it says, "is exceedingly dreaded here. It is thought that an attack upon the
troops, even should it prove successful, would certainly involve the whole continent in a war. It is generally thought
that the Ministry would rejoice at a rupture in Boston, because it would furnish an excuse to the people *at home;*"—
[this was the last time, we suspect, that John Adams spoke
of England thus affectionately]—"and unite them in an
opinion of the necessity of pushing hostilities against us."

His next letter bears on the superscription—'Favored by
General Washington.' The date is June 20, 1775, three days
after the battle of Bunker Hill, the news of which could not

yet have arrived at Philadelphia. But the war, so much dreaded, had begun, on the quiet banks of Concord river; an army of twenty thousand men was beleaguering Boston; and here was Washington journeying northward, to take the command. It seems to place us in a nearer relation with the hero, to find him performing the little courtesy of bearing a letter between friend and friend, and to hold in our hands the very document entrusted to such a messenger. John Adams says simply—'We send you Generals Washington and Lee for your comfort'—but adds nothing in regard to the character of the commander-in-chief. This letter displays much of the writer's ardent temperament; if he had been anywhere but in the hall of Congress, it would have been in the entrenchment before Boston.

"I hope," he writes, "a good account will be given of Gage, Haldiman, Burgoyne, Clinton, and Howe, before winter. Such a wretch as Howe, with a statue in honor of his family in Westminster Abbey, erected by the Massachusetts, to come over with the design to cut the throats of the Massachusetts people, is too much. I most sincerely, coolly, and devoutly wish, that a lucky ball or bayonet may make a signal example of him, in warning to all such unprincipled, unsentimental miscreants for the future!"

He goes on in a strain that smacks somewhat of aristocratic feeling:—"Our camp will be an illustrious school of military virtue, and will be resorted to and frequented, as such, by gentlemen in great numbers from the other colonies." The term "gentleman" has seldom been used in this sense subsequently to the Revolution. Another letter introduces us to two of these gentlemen, Messrs. Aquilla Hall and Josias Carvill, volunteers, who are recommended as "of the first families in Maryland, and possessing independent fortunes."

After the British had been driven out of Boston, Adams cries out,—"Fortify, fortify; and never let them get in again!" It is agreeable enough to perceive the filial affection with which John Adams, and the other delegates from the North, regard New England, and especially the good old capital of the Puritans. Their love of country was hardly yet so diluted as to extend over the whole thirteen colonies, which were rather looked upon as allies than as composing one nation. In truth, the patriotism of a citizen of the United States is a sentiment by itself, of a peculiar nature, and requiring a lifetime, or at least the custom of many years, to naturalize it among the other possessions of the heart.

The collection is enriched by a letter—dated "Cambridge, August 26, 1775"—from Washington himself. He wrote it in that house—now so venerable with his memory—in that very room, where his bust now stands upon a poet's table. Down this sheet of paper passed the hand that held the leading-staff! Nothing can be more perfectly in keeping with all other manifestations of Washington, than the whole visible aspect and embodiment of this letter. The manuscript is as clear as daylight; the punctuation exact, to a comma. There is a calm accuracy throughout, which seems the production of a species of intelligence that cannot err, and which, if we may so speak, would affect us with a more human warmth, if we could conceive it capable of some slight human error. The chirography is characterized by a plain and easy grace, which, in the signature, is somewhat elaborated, and becomes a type of the personal manner of a gentleman of the old school, but without detriment to the truth and clearness that distinguish the rest of the manuscript. The lines are as straight and equidistant as if ruled; and from beginning to end, there is no physical symptom—as how should there be?—of varying mood, of jets of emotion, or any of those fluctuating feelings that pass from the hearts into the fingers of common men. The paper itself (like most of those Revolutionary letters, which are written on fabrics fit to endure the burthen of ponderous and earnest thought) is stout, and of excellent quality, and bears the water-mark of Britannia, surmounted by the crown.

The subject of the letter is a statement of reasons for not taking possession of Point Alderton; a position commanding the entrance of Boston harbor. After explaining the difficulties of the case, arising from his want of men and munitions for the adequate defence of the lines which he already occupies, Washington proceeds:—

"To you, sir, who are a well-wisher to the cause, and can

reason upon the effects of such conduct, I may open myself with freedom, because no improper disclosures will be made of our situation. But I cannot expose my weakness to the enemy (though I believe they are pretty well informed of everything that passes), by telling this and that man, who are daily pointing out this, and that, and t'other place, of all the motives that govern my actions; notwithstanding I know what will be the consequence of not doing it—namely, that I shall be accused of inattention to the public service, and perhaps of want of spirit to prosecute it. But this shall have no effect upon my conduct. I will steadily (as far as my judgment will assist me) pursue such measures as I think conducive to the interest of the cause, and rest satisfied under any obloquy that shall be thrown, conscious of having discharged my duty to the best of my abilities."

The above passage, like every other passage that could be quoted from his pen, is characteristic of Washington, and entirely in keeping with the calm elevation of his soul. Yet how imperfect a glimpse do we obtain of him, through the medium of this, or any of his letters! We imagine him writing calmly, with a hand that never falters; his majestic face neither darkens nor gleams with any momentary ebullition of feeling, or irregularity of thought; and thus flows forth an expression precisely to the extent of his purpose, no more, no less. Thus much we may conceive. But still we have not grasped the man; we have caught no glimpse of his interior; we have not detected his personality. It is the same with all the recorded traits of his daily life. The collection of them, by different observers, seems sufficiently abundant, and strictly harmonizes with itself, yet never brings us into intimate relationship with the hero, nor makes us feel the warmth and the human throb of his heart. What can be the reason? Is it, that his great nature was adapted to stand in relation to his country, as man stands towards man, but could not individualize itself in brotherhood to an individual?

There are two letters from Franklin, the earliest dated, "London, August 8, 1767," and addressed to "Mrs. Franklin, at Philadelphia." He was then in England, as agent for the Colonies in their resistance to the oppressive policy of Mr.

Grenville's administration. The letter, however, makes no reference to political, or other business. It contains only ten or twelve lines, beginning—"My dear child"—and conveying an impression of long and venerable matrimony, which has lost all its romance, but retained a familiar and quiet tenderness. He speaks of making a little excursion into the country for his health; mentions a longer letter, despatched by another vessel; alludes with homely affiability to "Mrs. Stevenson," "Sally," and "our dear Polly," desires to be remembered to "all inquiring friends;" and signs himself—"Your ever loving husband." In this conjugal epistle, brief and unimportant as it is, there are the elements that summon up the past, and enable us to create anew the man, his connexions, and circumstances. We can see the sage in his London lodgings—with his wig cast aside, and replaced by a velvet cap—penning this very letter; and then can step across the Atlantic, and behold its reception by the elderly, but still comely Madam Franklin, who breaks the seal and begins to read, first remembering to put on her spectacles. The seal, by the way, is a pompous one of armorial bearings, rather symbolical of the dignity of the Colonial Agent, and Postmaster General of America, than of the humble origin of the New England printer. The writing is in the free, quick style of a man with great practice of the pen, and is particularly agreeable to the reader.

Another letter, from the same famous hand, is addressed to General Palmer, and dated "Passy, October 27, 1779." By an endorsement on the outside it appears to have been transmitted to the United States through the medium of La Fayette. Franklin was now the ambassador of his country at the court of Versailles, enjoying an immense celebrity, caressed by the French ladies, and idolized alike by the fashionable and the learned, who saw something sublime and philosophic even in his blue yarn stockings. Still, as before, he writes with the homeliness and simplicity that cause a human face to look forth from the old, yellow sheet of paper, and in words that make our ears re-echo, as with the sound of his long extinct utterance. Yet this brief epistle, like the former, has so little of tangible matter that we are ashamed to copy it.

Next, we come to the fragment of a letter by Samuel

Adams; an autograph more utterly devoid of ornament or
flourish than any other in the collection. It would not have
been characteristic, had his pen traced so much as one hair-
line in tribute to grace, beauty, or the elaborateness of manner; for this earnest-hearted man had been produced out of
the past elements of his native land, a real Puritan, with the
religion of his forefathers, and likewise with their principles
of government, taking the aspect of Revolutionary politics.
At heart, Samuel Adams was never so much a citizen of the
United States, as he was a New-Englander, and a son of the
Old Bay Province. The following passage has much of the
man in it:—

> "I heartily congratulate you," he writes from Philadel-
> phia, after the British have left Boston, "upon the sudden
> and important change in our affairs, in the removal of the
> barbarians from the capital. We owe our grateful acknowl-
> edgments to Him who is, as he is frequently styled in sa-
> cred Writ, 'The Lord of Hosts.' We have not yet been in-
> formed with certainty what course the enemy have steered.
> I hope we shall be on our guard against future attempts.
> Will not care be taken to fortify the harbor, and thereby
> prevent the entrance of ships of war hereafter?"

From Hancock, we have only the envelope of a document
"on public service," directed to "The Hon. the Assembly, or
the Council of Safety of New-Hampshire," and with the autograph affixed, that stands out so prominently in the Declaration of Independence. As seen in the engraving of that instrument, the signature looks precisely what we should expect
and desire in the handwriting of a princely merchant, whose
penmanship had been practised in the ledger which he is represented as holding, in Copley's brilliant picture, but to
whom his native ability, and the circumstances and customs
of his country had given a place among its rulers. But, on the
coarse and dingy paper before us, the effect is very much inferior; the direction, all except the signature, is a scrawl, large
and heavy, but not forcible; and even the name itself, while
almost identical in its strokes with that of the Declaration, has
a strangely different and more vulgar aspect. Perhaps it is all
right, and typical of the truth. If we may trust tradition, and

unpublished letters, and a few witnesses in print, there was quite as much difference between the actual man and his historical aspect, as between the manuscript signature and the engraved one. One of his associates, both in political life and permanent renown, is said to have characterized him as a "man without a head or heart." We, of an after generation, should hardly be entitled, on whatever evidence, to assume such ungracious liberty with a name that has occupied a lofty position until it has grown almost sacred, and which is associated with memories more sacred than itself, and has thus become a valuable reality to our countrymen, by the aged reverence that clusters round about it. Nevertheless it may be no impiety to regard Hancock not precisely as a real personage, but as a majestic figure, useful and necessary in its way, but producing its effect far more by an ornamental outside than by any intrinsic force or virtue. The page of history would be half unpeopled, if all such characters were banished from it.

From General Warren we have a letter dated January 14, 1775, only a few months before he attested the sincerity of his patriotism, in his own blood, on Bunker Hill. His handwriting has many ungraceful flourishes. All the small *d*'s spout upward in parabolic curves, and descend at a considerable distance. His pen seems to have had nothing but hair-lines in it; and the whole letter, though perfectly legible, has a look of thin and unpleasant irregularity. The subject is a plan for securing to the Colonial party, the services of Colonel Gridley, the engineer, by an appeal to his private interests. Though writing to General Palmer, an intimate friend, Warren signs himself, most ceremoniously, "Your obedient servant." Indeed, these stately formulas in winding up a letter, were scarcely laid aside, whatever might be the familiarity of intercourse: husband and wife were occasionally, on paper at least, the "obedient servants" of one another; and not improbably, among well-bred people, there was a corresponding ceremonial of bows and courtesies, even in the deepest interior of domestic life. With all the reality that filled men's hearts, and which has stamped its impress on so many of these letters, it was a far more formal age than the present.

It may be remarked, that Warren was almost the only man

eminently distinguished in the intellectual phase of the Revolution, previous to the breaking out of the war, who actually
uplifted his arm to do battle. The legislative patriots were a
distinct class from the patriots of the camp, and never laid
aside the gown for the sword. It was very different in the
great civil war of England, where the leading minds of the
age, when argument had done its office, or left it undone, put
on their steel breast-plates and appeared as leaders in the field.
Educated young men, members of the old colonial families—
gentlemen, as John Adams terms them—seem not to have
sought employment in the Revolutionary army, in such numbers as might have been expected. Respectable as the officers
generally were, and great as were the abilities sometimes elicited, the intellect and cultivation of the country was inade-
quately represented in them, as a body.

Turning another page, we find the frank of a letter from
Henry Laurens, President of Congress,—him whose destiny
it was, like so many noblemen of old, to pass beneath the
Traitor's Gate of the Tower of London,—him whose chivalrous son sacrificed as brilliant a future as any young American
could have looked forward to, in an obscure skirmish. Likewise, we have the address of a letter to Messrs. Leroy and
Bayard, in the handwriting of Jefferson; too slender a material to serve as a talisman for summoning up the writer; a
most unsatisfactory fragment, affecting us like a glimpse of
the retreating form of the sage of Monticello, turning the distant corner of a street. There is a scrap from Robert Morris,
the financier; a letter or two from Judge Jay; and one from
General Lincoln, written, apparently, on the gallop, but without any of those characteristic sparks that sometimes fly out
in a hurry, when all the leisure in the world would fail to
elicit them. Lincoln was the type of a New England soldier;
a man of fair abilities, not especially of a warlike cast, without
much chivalry, but faithful and bold, and carrying a kind of
decency and restraint into the wild and ruthless business of
arms.

From good old Baron Steuben, we find—not a manuscript
essay on the method of arraying a battle—but a commercial
draft, in a small, neat hand, as plain as print, elegant without
flourish, except a very complicated one beneath the signature.

On the whole, the specimen is sufficiently characteristic, as well of the Baron's soldierlike and German simplicity, as of the polish of the Great Frederick's aide-de-camp, a man of courts and of the world. How singular and picturesque an effect is produced, in the array of our Revolutionary army, by the intermingling of these titled personages from the continent of Europe, with feudal associations clinging about them—Steuben, De Kalb, Pulaski, La Fayette!—the German veteran, who had ridden from the smoke of one famous battle-field to another for thirty years; and the young French noble, who had come hither, though yet unconscious of his high office, to light the torch that should set fire to the antiquated trumpery of his native institutions! Among these autographs, there is one from La Fayette, written long after our Revolution, but while that of his own country was in full progress. The note is merely as follows:—

"Enclosed you will find, my dear Sir, two tickets for the sitting of this day. One part of the debate will be on the Honors of the Pantheon, agreeably to what has been decreed by the Constitutional Assembly."

It is a pleasant and comfortable thought, that we have no such classic folly as is here indicated, to lay to the charge of our Revolutionary fathers. Both in their acts, and in the drapery of those acts, they were true to their severe and simple selves, and thus left nothing behind them for a fastidious taste to sneer at. But it must be considered that our Revolution did not, like that of France, go so deep as to disturb the common sense of the country.

General Schuyler writes a letter, under date of February 22, 1780, relating not to military affairs, from which the prejudices of his countrymen had almost disconnected him, but to the salt springs of Onondaga. The expression is peculiarly direct, and the hand that of a man of business, free and flowing. The uncertainty, the vague, hearsay evidence respecting these springs, then gushing into dim daylight beneath the shadows of a remote wilderness, is such as might now be quoted in reference to the quality of the water that supplies the fountains of the Nile. The following sentence shows us an Indian woman and her son, practising their simple processes in the manufacture of salt, at a fire of wind-strewn boughs, the flame of which gleams duskily through the arches of the forest:—"From a variety of information, I find the smallest quantity made by a squaw, with the assistance of one boy, with a kettle of about ten gallons capacity, is half a bushel per day; the greatest, with the same kettle, about two bushels." It is particularly interesting to find out anything as to the embryo, yet stationary arts of life among the red people, their manufactures, their agriculture, their domestic labors. It is partly the lack of this knowledge—the possession of which would establish a ground of sympathy on the part of civilized men—that makes the Indian race so shadowlike and unreal to our conception.

We could not select a greater contrast to the upright and unselfish patriot whom we have just spoken of, than the traitor Arnold, from whom there is a brief note, dated, "Crown-Point, January 19, 1775," addressed to an officer under his command. The three lines, of which it consists, can prove bad spelling, erroneous grammar, and misplaced and superfluous punctuation; but, with all this complication of iniquity, the ruffian General contrives to express his meaning as briefly and clearly as if the rules of correct composition had been ever so scrupulously observed. This autograph, impressed with the foulest name in our history, has somewhat of the interest that would attach to a document on which a fiend-devoted wretch had signed away his salvation. But there was not substance enough in the man—a mere cross between the bull-dog and the fox—to justify much feeling of any sort about him personally. The interest, such as it is, attaches but little to the man, and far more to the circumstances amid which he acted, rendering the villainy almost sublime, which, exercised in petty affairs, would only have been vulgar.

We turn another leaf, and find a memorial of Hamilton. It is but a letter of introduction, addressed to Governor Jay in favor of Mr. Davies, of Kentucky; but it gives an impression of high breeding and courtesy, as little to be mistaken as if we could see the writer's manner and hear his cultivated accents, while personally making one gentleman known to another. There is likewise a rare vigor of expression and pregnancy of meaning, such as only a man of habitual energy of thought could have conveyed into so common-place a thing as an introductory letter. This autograph is a graceful one, with an easy and picturesque flourish beneath the signature, symbolical of a courteous bow at the conclusion of the social ceremony so admirably performed. Hamilton might well be the leader and idol of the Federalists; for he was pre-eminent in all the high qualities that characterized the great men of that party, and which should make even a democrat feel proud that his country had produced such a noble old band of aristocrats; and he shared all the distrust of the people, which so inevitably and so righteously brought about their ruin. With his autograph we associate that of another Federalist, his friend in life; a man far narrower than Hamilton, but endowed with a native vigor, that caused many partisans to grapple to him for support; upright, sternly inflexible, and of a simplicty of manner that might have befitted the sturdiest republican among us. In our boyhood we used to see a thin, severe figure of an ancient man, time-worn, but apparently indestructible, moving with a step of vigorous decay along the street, and knew him as "Old Tim Pickering."

Side by side, too, with the autograph of Hamilton, we would place one from the hand that shed his blood. It is a few lines of Aaron Burr, written in 1823; when all his ambitious schemes, whatever they once were, had been so long shattered that even the fragments had crumbled away, leaving him to exert his withered energies on petty law cases, to one of which the present note refers. The hand is a little tremulous with age, yet small and fastidiously elegant, as became a man who was in the habit of writing billet-doux on scented note-paper, as well as documents of war and state. This is to us a deeply interesting autograph. Remembering what has been said of the power of Burr's personal influence, his art to tempt men, his might to subdue them, and the fascination that enabled him, though cold at heart, to win the love of woman, we gaze at this production of his pen as into his own inscrutable eyes, seeking for the mystery of his nature. How singular that a character, imperfect, ruined, blasted, as this man's was, excites a stronger interest than if it had reached the highest earthly perfection of which its original elements would admit! It is by the diabolical part of Burr's character, that he produces his effect on the imagination. Had he been a better man, we doubt, after all, whether the present age would not already have suffered him to wax dusty and fade out of sight, among the more respectable mediocrities of his own epoch. But, certainly, he was a strange, wild off-shoot to have sprung from the united stock of those two singular Christians, President Burr, of Princeton College, and Jonathan Edwards!

Omitting many, we have come almost to the end of these memorials of historical men. We observe one other autograph of a distinguished soldier of the Revolution, Henry Knox, but written in 1791, when he was Secretary of War. In its physical aspect, it is well worthy to be a soldier's letter. The hand is large, round, and legible at a glance; the lines far apart, and accurately equi-distant; and the whole affair looks not unlike a company of regular troops in marching order. The signature has a print-like firmness and simplicity. It is a curious observation, sustained by these autographs, though we know not how generally correct, that Southern gentlemen are more addicted to a flourish of the pen beneath their names, than those of the North.

And now we come to the men of a later generation, whose active life reaches almost within the verge of present affairs; people of great dignity, no doubt, but whose characters have not acquired, either from time or circumstances, the interest that can make their autographs valuable to any but the collector. Those whom we have hitherto noticed were the men of an heroic age. They are departed, and now so utterly departed, as not even to touch upon the passing generation through the medium of persons still in life, who can claim to have known them familiarly. Their letters, therefore, come to us like material things out of the hands of mighty shadows, long historical and traditionary, and fit companions for the sages and warriors of a thousand years ago. In spite of the proverb, it is not in a single day, or in a very few years, that a man can be reckoned "as dead as Julius Cæsar." We feel little interest in scraps from the pens of old gentlemen, ambassadors, governors, senators, heads of departments, even presidents though they were, who lived lives of praiseworthy respectability, and whose powdered heads and black knee-breeches have but just vanished out of the drawing-room. Still less do we value the blotted paper of those whose reputations are dusty, not with oblivious time, but with present political turmoil and newspaper vogue. Really great men, however, seem, as to their effect on the imagination, to take their place amongst past worthies, even while walking in the very sunshine that illuminates the autumnal day in which we write. We look, not without curiosity, at the small, neat hand of Henry Clay, who, as he remarks with his habitual deference to the wishes of the fair, responds to a young lady's request for his seal; and we dwell longer over the torn-off conclusion of a note from Mr. Calhoun, whose words are strangely dashed off without letters, and whose name, were it less illustrious, would be unrecognizable in his own autograph. But of all hands that can still grasp a pen, we know not the one, belonging to a soldier or a statesman, which could interest us more than the hand that wrote the following:—

"Sir:

"Your note of the 6th inst. is received. I hasten to answer that there was no man 'in the station of colonel, by the name of J. T. Smith,' under my command, at the battle of New Orleans; and am, respectfully,

Yours,
"Andrew Jackson.
"Octr. 19th, 1833."

The old general, we suspect, has been ensnared by a pardonable little stratagem on the part of the autograph collector. The battle of New Orleans would hardly have been won, without better aid than that of this problematical Colonel J. T. Smith!

Intermixed with and appended to these historical autographs, there are a few literary ones. Timothy Dwight—the "old Timotheus" who sang the Conquest of Canaan, instead of choosing a more popular subject, in the British conquest of Canada—is of eldest date. Colonel Trumbull, whose hand, at various epochs of his life, was familiar with sword, pen, and pencil, contributes two letters, which lack the picturesqueness of execution that should distinguish the chirography of an artist. The value of Trumbull's pictures is of the same nature with that of daguerreotypes, depending not upon the ideal but the actual. The beautiful signature of Washington Irving appears as the endorsement of a draft, dated in 1814, when, if we may take this document as evidence, his individuality seems to have been merged into the firm of "P. E. Irving & Co." Never was anything less mercantile than this autograph, though as legible as the writing of a bank-clerk. Without apparently aiming at artistic beauty, it has all the Sketch Book in it. We find the signature and seal of Pierpont, the latter stamped with the poet's almost living countenance. What a pleasant device for a seal is one's own face, which he may thus multiply at pleasure, and send letters to his friends,—the Head without, and the Heart within! There are a few lines in the school-girl hand of Margaret Davidson, at nine years old; and a scrap of a letter from Washington Allston, a gentle and delicate autograph, in which we catch a glimpse of thanks to his correspondent for the loan of a volume of poetry. Nothing remains, save a letter from Noah Webster, whose early toils were manifested in a spelling book, and those of his latter age in a ponderous dictionary. Under date of February 10, 1843, he writes in a sturdy, awkward hand, very fit for a lexicographer—an epistle of old man's reminiscences, from which we extract the following anecdote of Washington, presenting the patriot in a festive light:

"When I was travelling to the South, in the year 1785, I called on General Washington at Mount Vernon. At dinner, the last course of dishes was a species of pancakes, which were handed round to each guest, accompanied with a bowl of sugar and another of molasses for seasoning them, that each guest might suit himself. When the dish came to me, I pushed by me the bowl of molasses, observing to the gentlemen present, that I had enough of *that* in my own country. The General burst out with a *loud laugh*, a thing very unusual with him. 'Ah,' said he, 'there is nothing in that story about your eating molasses in New England.' There was a gentleman from Maryland at the table; and the General immediately told a story, stating that, during the Revolution, a hogshead of molasses was stove in

West-Chester by the oversetting of a wagon; and a body of
Maryland troops being near, the soldiers ran hastily,
and saved all they could by filling their hats or caps with
molasses."

There are said to be temperaments endowed with sympathies so exquisite, that, by merely handling an autograph,
they can detect the writer's character with unerring accuracy,
and read his inmost heart as easily as a less gifted eye would
peruse the written page. Our faith in this power, be it a spiritual one, or only a refinement of the physical nature, is not
unlimited, in spite of evidence. God has imparted to the human soul a marvellous strength in guarding its secrets, and
He keeps at least the deepest and most inward record for His
own perusal. But if there be such sympathies as we have alluded to, in how many instances would History be put to the
blush by a volume of autograph letters, like this which we
now close!

Rappaccini's Daughter

FROM THE WRITINGS OF AUBÉPINE

WE do not remember to have seen any translated specimens of the productions of M. de l'Aubépine; a fact the less to be wondered at, as his very name is unknown to many of his own countrymen, as well as to the student of foreign literature. As a writer, he seems to occupy an unfortunate position between the Transcendentalists (who, under one name or another, have their share in all the current literature of the world), and the great body of pen-and-ink men who address the intellect and sympathies of the multitude. If not too refined, at all events too remote, too shadowy and unsubstantial in his modes of development, to suit the taste of the latter class, and yet too popular to satisfy the spiritual or metaphysical requisitions of the former, he must necessarily find himself without an audience; except here and there an individual, or possibly an isolated clique. His writings, to do them justice, are not altogether destitute of fancy and originality; they might have won him greater reputation but for an inveterate love of allegory, which is apt to invest his plots and characters with the aspect of scenery and people in the clouds, and to steal away the human warmth out of his conceptions. His fictions are sometimes historical, sometimes of the present day, and sometimes, so far as can be discovered, have little or no reference either to time or space. In any case, he generally contents himself with a very slight embroidery of outward manners,—the faintest possible counterfeit of real life,—and endeavors to create an interest by some less obvious peculiarity of the subject. Occasionally, a breath of nature, a rain-drop of pathos and tenderness, or a gleam of humor, will find its way into the midst of his fantastic imagery, and make us feel as if, after all, we were yet within the limits of our native earth. We will only add to this very cursory notice, that M. de l'Aubépine's productions, if the reader chance to take them in precisely the proper point of view, may amuse a leisure hour as well as those of a brighter man; if otherwise, they can hardly fail to look excessively like nonsense.

Our author is voluminous; he continues to write and publish with as much praiseworthy and indefatigable prolixity, as
if his efforts were crowned with the brilliant success that so
justly attends those of Eugene Sue. His first appearance was
by a collection of stories, in a long series of volumes, entitled
"Contes deux fois racontées." The titles of some of his more
recent works (we quote from memory) are as follows:—*"Le
Voyage Céleste à Chemin de Fer,"* 3 tom. 1838. *"Le nouveau Père
Adam et la nouvelle Mère Eve,"* 2 tom. 1839. *"Roderic; ou le
Serpent à l'estomac,"* 2 tom. 1840. *"Le Culte du Feu,"* a folio
volume of ponderous research into the religion and ritual of
the old Persian Ghebers, published in 1841. *"La Soirée du Chateau en Espagne,"* 1 tom. 8vo. 1842; and *"L'Artiste du Beau; ou
le Papillon Mécanique,"* 5 tom. 4to. 1843. Our somewhat wearisome perusal of this startling catalogue of volumes has left
behind it a certain personal affection and sympathy, though
by no means admiration, for M. de l'Aubépine; and we would
fain do the little in our power towards introducing him favorably to the American public. The ensuing tale is a translation of his *"Beatrice; ou la Belle Empoisonneuse,"* recently published in *"La Revue Anti-Aristocratique."* This journal, edited
by the Comte de Bearhaven, has, for some years past, led the
defence of liberal principles and popular rights, with a faith-
fulness and ability worthy of all praise.

A YOUNG man, named Giovanni Guasconti, came, very long
ago, from the more southern region of Italy, to pursue his
studies at the University of Padua. Giovanni, who had but a
scanty supply of gold ducats in his pocket, took lodgings in
a high and gloomy chamber of an old edifice, which looked
not unworthy to have been the palace of a Paduan noble, and
which, in fact, exhibited over its entrance the armorial bearings of a family long since extinct. The young stranger, who
was not unstudied in the great poem of his country, recollected that one of the ancestors of this family, and perhaps an
occupant of this very mansion, had been pictured by Dante
as a partaker of the immortal agonies of his Inferno. These
reminiscences and associations, together with the tendency to
heart-break natural to a young man for the first time out of

his native sphere, caused Giovanni to sigh heavily, as he looked around the desolate and ill-furnished apartment.

"Holy Virgin, Signor," cried old dame Lisabetta, who, won by the youth's remarkable beauty of person, was kindly endeavoring to give the chamber a habitable air, "what a sigh was that to come out of a young man's heart! Do you find this old mansion gloomy? For the love of heaven, then, put your head out of the window, and you will see as bright sunshine as you have left in Naples."

Guasconti mechanically did as the old woman advised, but could not quite agree with her that the Paduan sunshine was as cheerful as that of southern Italy. Such as it was, however, it fell upon a garden beneath the window, and expended its fostering influences on a variety of plants, which seemed to have been cultivated with exceeding care.

"Does this garden belong to the house?" asked Giovanni.

"Heaven forbid, Signor!—unless it were fruitful of better pot-herbs than any that grow there now," answered old Lisabetta. "No; that garden is cultivated by the own hands of Signor Giacomo Rappaccini, the famous Doctor, who, I warrant him, has been heard of as far as Naples. It is said that he distils these plants into medicines that are as potent as a charm. Oftentimes you may see the Signor Doctor at work, and perchance the Signora his daughter, too, gathering the strange flowers that grow in the garden."

The old woman had now done what she could for the aspect of the chamber, and, commending the young man to the protection of the saints, took her departure.

Giovanni still found no better occupation than to look down into the garden beneath his window. From its appearance, he judged it to be one of those botanic gardens, which were of earlier date in Padua than elsewhere in Italy, or in the world. Or, not improbably, it might once have been the pleasure-place of an opulent family; for there was the ruin of a marble fountain in the centre, sculptured with rare art, but so wofully shattered that it was impossible to trace the original design from the chaos of remaining fragments. The water, however, continued to gush and sparkle into the sunbeams as cheerfully as ever. A little gurgling sound ascended to the young man's window, and made him feel as if the fountain

were an immortal spirit, that sung its song unceasingly, and
without heeding the vicissitudes around it; while one century
embodied it in marble, and another scattered the perishable
garniture on the soil. All about the pool into which the water
subsided, grew various plants, that seemed to require a plentiful supply of moisture for the nourishment of gigantic
leaves, and, in some instances, flowers gorgeously magnificent. There was one shrub in particular, set in a marble vase
in the midst of the pool, that bore a profusion of purple blossoms, each of which had the lustre and richness of a gem; and
the whole together made a show so resplendent that it
seemed enough to illuminate the garden, even had there been
no sunshine. Every portion of the soil was peopled with
plants and herbs, which, if less beautiful, still bore tokens of
assiduous care; as if all had their individual virtues, known to
the scientific mind that fostered them. Some were placed in
urns, rich with old carving, and others in common garden-
pots; some crept serpent-like along the ground, or climbed
on high, using whatever means of ascent was offered them.
One plant had wreathed itself round a statue of Vertumnus,
which was thus quite veiled and shrouded in a drapery of
hanging foliage, so happily arranged that it might have served
a sculptor for a study.

While Giovanni stood at the window, he heard a rustling
behind a screen of leaves, and became aware that a person
was at work in the garden. His figure soon emerged into
view, and showed itself to be that of no common laborer, but
a tall, emaciated, sallow, and sickly-looking man, dressed in a
scholar's garb of black. He was beyond the middle term of
life, with grey hair, a thin grey beard, and a face singularly
marked with intellect and cultivation, but which could never,
even in his more youthful days, have expressed much warmth
of heart.

Nothing could exceed the intentness with which this scientific gardener examined every shrub which grew in his path;
it seemed as if he was looking into their inmost nature, making observations in regard to their creative essence, and discovering why one leaf grew in this shape, and another in that,
and wherefore such and such flowers differed among themselves in hue and perfume. Nevertheless, in spite of this deep

intelligence on his part, there was no approach to intimacy between himself and these vegetable existences. On the contrary, he avoided their actual touch, or the direct inhaling of their odors, with a caution that impressed Giovanni most disagreeably; for the man's demeanor was that of one walking among malignant influences, such as savage beasts, or deadly snakes, or evil spirits, which, should he allow them one moment of license, would wreak upon him some terrible fatality. It was strangely frightful to the young man's imagination, to see this air of insecurity in a person cultivating a garden, that most simple and innocent of human toils, and which had been alike the joy and labor of the unfallen parents of the race. Was this garden, then, the Eden of the present world?— and this man, with such a perception of harm in what his own hands caused to grow, was he the Adam?

The distrustful gardener, while plucking away the dead leaves or pruning the too luxuriant growth of the shrubs, defended his hands with a pair of thick gloves. Nor were these his only armor. When, in his walk through the garden, he came to the magnificent plant that hung its purple gems beside the marble fountain, he placed a kind of mask over his mouth and nostrils, as if all this beauty did but conceal a deadlier malice. But finding his task still too dangerous, he drew back, removed the mask, and called loudly, but in the infirm voice of a person affected with inward disease:

"Beatrice!—Beatrice!"

"Here am I, my father! What would you?" cried a rich and youthful voice from the window of the opposite house; a voice as rich as a tropical sunset, and which made Giovanni, though he knew not why, think of deep hues of purple or crimson, and of perfumes heavily delectable.—"Are you in the garden?"

"Yes, Beatrice," answered the gardener, "and I need your help."

Soon there emerged from under a sculptured portal the figure of a young girl, arrayed with as much richness of taste as the most splendid of the flowers, beautiful as the day, and with a bloom so deep and vivid that one shade more would have been too much. She looked redundant with life, health, and energy; all of which attributes were bound down and

compressed, as it were, and girdled tensely, in their luxuriance, by her virgin zone. Yet Giovanni's fancy must have
grown morbid, while he looked down into the garden; for
the impression which the fair stranger made upon him was as
if here were another flower, the human sister of those vegetable ones, as beautiful as they—more beautiful than the richest of them—but still to be touched only with a glove, nor
to be approached without a mask. As Beatrice came down the
garden path, it was observable that she handled and inhaled
the odor of several of the plants, which her father had most
sedulously avoided.

"Here, Beatrice," said the latter,—"see how many needful
offices require to be done to our chief treasure. Yet, shattered
as I am, my life might pay the penalty of approaching it so
closely as circumstances demand. Henceforth, I fear, this
plant must be consigned to your sole charge."

"And gladly will I undertake it," cried again the rich tones
of the young lady, as she bent towards the magnificent plant,
and opened her arms as if to embrace it. "Yes, my sister, my
splendor, it shall be Beatrice's task to nurse and serve thee;
and thou shalt reward her with thy kisses and perfumed
breath, which to her is as the breath of life!"

Then, with all the tenderness in her manner that was so
strikingly expressed in her words, she busied herself with such
attentions as the plant seemed to require; and Giovanni, at
his lofty window, rubbed his eyes, and almost doubted
whether it were a girl tending her favorite flower, or one sister performing the duties of affection to another. The scene
soon terminated. Whether Doctor Rappaccini had finished
his labors in the garden, or that his watchful eye had caught
the stranger's face, he now took his daughter's arm and retired. Night was already closing in; oppressive exhalations
seemed to proceed from the plants, and steal upward past the
open window; and Giovanni, closing the lattice, went to his
couch, and dreamed of a rich flower and beautiful girl.
Flower and maiden were different and yet the same, and
fraught with some strange peril in either shape.

But there is an influence in the light of morning that tends
to rectify whatever errors of fancy, or even of judgment, we
may have incurred during the sun's decline, or among the

shadows of the night, or in the less wholesome glow of moonshine. Giovanni's first movement on starting from sleep, was to throw open the window, and gaze down into the garden which his dreams had made so fertile of mysteries. He was surprised, and a little ashamed, to find how real and matter-of-fact an affair it proved to be, in the first rays of the sun, which gilded the dew-drops that hung upon leaf and blossom, and, while giving a brighter beauty to each rare flower, brought everything within the limits of ordinary experience. The young man rejoiced, that, in the heart of the barren city, he had the privilege of overlooking this spot of lovely and luxuriant vegetation. It would serve, he said to himself, as a symbolic language, to keep him in communion with Nature. Neither the sickly and thought-worn Doctor Giacomo Rappaccini, it is true, nor his brilliant daughter, were now visible; so that Giovanni could not determine how much of the singularity which he attributed to both, was due to their own qualities, and how much to his wonder-working fancy. But he was inclined to take a most rational view of the whole matter.

In the course of the day, he paid his respects to Signor Pietro Baglioni, professor of medicine in the University, a physician of eminent repute, to whom Giovanni had brought a letter of introduction. The Professor was an elderly personage, apparently of genial nature, and habits that might almost be called jovial; he kept the young man to dinner, and made himself very agreeable by the freedom and liveliness of his conversation, especially when warmed by a flask or two of Tuscan wine. Giovanni, conceiving that men of science, inhabitants of the same city, must needs be on familiar terms with one another, took an opportunity to mention the name of Doctor Rappaccini. But the Professor did not respond with so much cordiality as he had anticipated.

"Ill would it become a teacher of the divine art of medicine," said Professor Pietro Baglioni, in answer to a question of Giovanni, "to withhold due and well-considered praise of a physician so eminently skilled as Rappaccini. But, on the other hand, I should answer it but scantily to my conscience, were I to permit a worthy youth like yourself, Signor Giovanni, the son of an ancient friend, to imbibe erroneous ideas respecting a man who might hereafter chance to hold your life and death in his hands. The truth is, our worshipful Doctor Rappaccini has as much science as any member of the faculty—with perhaps one single exception—in Padua, or all Italy. But there are certain grave objections to his professional character."

"And what are they?" asked the young man.

"Has my friend Giovanni any disease of body or heart, that he is so inquisitive about physicians?" said the Professor, with a smile. "But as for Rappaccini, it is said of him—and I, who know the man well, can answer for its truth—that he cares infinitely more for science than for mankind. His patients are interesting to him only as subjects for some new experiment. He would sacrifice human life, his own among the rest, or whatever else was dearest to him, for the sake of adding so much as a grain of mustard-seed to the great heap of his accumulated knowledge."

"Methinks he is an awful man, indeed," remarked Guasconti, mentally recalling the cold and purely intellectual aspect of Rappaccini. "And yet, worshipful Professor, is it not a noble spirit? Are there many men capable of so spiritual a love of science?"

"God forbid," answered the Professor, somewhat testily—"at least, unless they take sounder views of the healing art than those adopted by Rappaccini. It is his theory, that all medicinal virtues are comprised within those substances which we term vegetable poisons. These he cultivates with his own hands, and is said even to have produced new varieties of poison, more horribly deleterious than Nature, without the assistance of this learned person, would ever have plagued the world withal. That the Signor Doctor does less mischief than might be expected, with such dangerous substances, is undeniable. Now and then, it must be owned, he has effected—or seemed to effect—a marvellous cure. But, to tell you my private mind, Signor Giovanni, he should receive little credit for such instances of success—they being probably the work of chance—but should be held strictly accountable for his failures, which may justly be considered his own work."

The youth might have taken Baglioni's opinions with many grains of allowance, had he known that there was a professional warfare of long continuance between him and Doctor Rappaccini, in which the latter was generally thought to have gained the advantage. If the reader be inclined to judge for himself, we refer him to certain black-letter tracts on both sides, preserved in the medical department of the University of Padua.

"I know not, most learned Professor," returned Giovanni, after musing on what had been said of Rappaccini's exclusive zeal for science—"I know not how dearly this physician may love his art; but surely there is one object more dear to him. He has a daughter."

"Aha!" cried the Professor with a laugh. "So now our friend Giovanni's secret is out. You have heard of this daughter, whom all the young men in Padua are wild about, though not half a dozen have ever had the good hap to see her face. I know little of the Signora Beatrice, save that Rappaccini is said to have instructed her deeply in his science, and that, young and beautiful as fame reports her, she is already qualified to fill a professor's chair. Perchance her father destines her for mine! Other absurd rumors there be, not worth talking about, or listening to. So now, Signor Giovanni, drink off your glass of Lacryma."

Guasconti returned to his lodgings somewhat heated with the wine he had quaffed, and which caused his brain to swim with strange fantasies in reference to Doctor Rappaccini and the beautiful Beatrice. On his way, happening to pass by a florist's, he bought a fresh bouquet of flowers.

Ascending to his chamber, he seated himself near the window, but within the shadow thrown by the depth of the wall, so that he could look down into the garden with little risk of being discovered. All beneath his eye was a solitude. The strange plants were basking in the sunshine, and now and then nodding gently to one another, as if in acknowledgment of sympathy and kindred. In the midst, by the shattered fountain, grew the magnificent shrub, with its purple gems clustering all over it; they glowed in the air, and gleamed back again out of the depths of the pool, which thus seemed to overflow with colored radiance from the rich reflection that was steeped in it. At first, as we have said, the garden was a solitude. Soon, however,—as Giovanni had half-hoped, half-feared, would be the case,—a figure appeared beneath the antique sculptured portal, and came down between the rows of plants, inhaling their various perfumes, as if she were one of those beings of old classic fable, that lived upon sweet odors. On again beholding Beatrice, the young man was even startled to perceive how much her beauty exceeded his recollection of it; so brilliant, so vivid was its character, that she glowed amid the sunlight, and, as Giovanni whispered to himself, positively illuminated the more shadowy intervals of the garden path. Her face being now more revealed than on the former occasion, he was struck by its expression of simplicity and sweetness; qualities that had not entered into his idea of her character, and which made him ask anew, what manner of mortal she might be. Nor did he fail again to observe, or imagine, an analogy between the beautiful girl and the gorgeous shrub that hung its gem-like flowers over the fountain; a resemblance which Beatrice seemed to have indulged a fantastic humor in heightening, both by the arrangement of her dress and the selection of its hues.

Approaching the shrub, she threw open her arms, as with a passionate ardor, and drew its branches into an intimate embrace; so intimate, that her features were hidden in its leafy bosom, and her glistening ringlets all intermingled with the flowers.

"Give me thy breath, my sister," exclaimed Beatrice; "for I am faint with common air! And give me this flower of thine, which I separate with gentlest fingers from the stem, and place it close beside my heart."

With these words, the beautiful daughter of Rappaccini plucked one of the richest blossoms of the shrub, and was about to fasten it in her bosom. But now, unless Giovanni's draughts of wine had bewildered his senses, a singular incident occurred. A small orange-colored reptile, of the lizard or chameleon species, chanced to be creeping along the path, just at the feet of Beatrice. It appeared to Giovanni—but, at the distance from which he gazed, he could scarcely have seen anything so minute—it appeared to him, however, that a drop or two of moisture from the broken stem of the flower descended upon the lizard's head. For an instant, the reptile contorted itself violently, and then lay motionless in the sunshine. Beatrice observed this remarkable phenomenon, and crossed herself, sadly, but without surprise; nor did she therefore hesitate to arrange the fatal flower in her bosom. There it blushed, and almost glimmered with the dazzling effect of a precious stone, adding to her dress and aspect the one appropriate charm, which nothing else in the world could have supplied. But Giovanni, out of the shadow of his window, bent forward and shrank back, and murmured and trembled.

"Am I awake? Have I my senses?" said he to himself. "What is this being?—beautiful, shall I call her?—or inexpressibly terrible?"

Beatrice now strayed carelessly through the garden, approaching closer beneath Giovanni's window, so that he was compelled to thrust his head quite out of its concealment in order to gratify the intense and painful curiosity which she excited. At this moment, there came a beautiful insect over the garden wall; it had perhaps wandered through the city and found no flowers nor verdure among those antique haunts of men, until the heavy perfumes of Doctor Rappaccini's shrubs had lured it from afar. Without alighting on the flowers, this winged brightness seemed to be attracted by Beatrice, and lingered in the air and fluttered about her head. Now, here it could not be but that Giovanni Guasconti's eyes deceived him. Be that as it might, he fancied that while Beatrice was gazing at the insect with childish delight, it grew faint and fell at her feet;—its bright wings shivered; it was dead—from no cause that he could discern, unless it were the atmosphere of her breath. Again Beatrice crossed herself and sighed heavily, as she bent over the dead insect.

An impulsive movement of Giovanni drew her eyes to the window. There she beheld the beautiful head of the young man—rather a Grecian than an Italian head, with fair, regular features, and a glistening of gold among his ringlets—gazing down upon her like a being that hovered in midair. Scarcely knowing what he did, Giovanni threw down the bouquet which he had hitherto held in his hand.

"Signora," said he, "there are pure and healthful flowers. Wear them for the sake of Giovanni Guasconti!"

"Thanks, Signor," replied Beatrice, with her rich voice, that came forth as it were like a gush of music; and with a mirthful expression half childish and half woman-like. "I accept your gift, and would fain recompense it with this precious purple flower; but if I toss it into the air, it will not reach you. So Signor Guasconti must even content himself with my thanks."

She lifted the bouquet from the ground, and then as if inwardly ashamed at having stepped aside from her maidenly reserve to respond to a stranger's greeting, passed swiftly homeward through the garden. But, few as the moments were, it seemed to Giovanni when she was on the point of vanishing beneath the sculptured portal, that his beautiful bouquet was already beginning to wither in her grasp. It was an idle thought; there could be no possibility of distinguishing a faded flower from a fresh one at so great a distance.

For many days after this incident, the young man avoided the window that looked into Doctor Rappaccini's garden, as if something ugly and monstrous would have blasted his eyesight, had he been betrayed into a glance. He felt conscious of having put himself, to a certain extent, within the influence of an unintelligible power, by the communication which he had opened with Beatrice. The wisest course would have been, if his heart were in any real danger, to quit his lodgings and Padua itself, at once; the next wiser, to have accustomed himself, as far as possible, to the familiar and day-light view of Beatrice; thus bringing her rigidly and systematically within the limits of ordinary experience. Least of all, while avoiding her sight, ought Giovanni to have remained so near this extraordinary being, that the proximity and possibility even of intercourse, should give a kind of substance and reality to the wild vagaries which his imagination ran riot continually in producing. Guasconti had not a deep heart—or at all events, its depths were not sounded now—but he had a quick fancy, and an ardent southern temperament, which rose every instant to a higher fever-pitch. Whether or no Beatrice possessed those terrible attributes—that fatal breath—the affinity with those so beautiful and deadly flowers—which were indicated by what Giovanni had witnessed, she had at least instilled a fierce and subtle poison into his system. It was not love, although her rich beauty was a madness to him; nor horror, even while he fancied her spirit to be imbued with the same baneful essence that seemed to pervade her physical frame; but a wild offspring of both love and horror that had each parent in it, and burned like one and shivered like the other. Giovanni knew not what to dread; still less did he know what to hope; yet hope and dread kept a continual warfare in his breast, alternately vanquishing one another and starting up afresh to renew the contest. Blessed are all simple emotions, be they dark or bright! It is the lurid intermixture of the two that produces the illuminating blaze of the infernal regions.

Sometimes he endeavored to assuage the fever of his spirit by a rapid walk through the streets of Padua, or beyond its gates; his footsteps kept time with the throbbings of his brain, so that the walk was apt to accelerate itself to a race. One day, he found himself arrested; his arm was seized by a portly personage who had turned back on recognizing the young man, and expended much breath in overtaking him.

"Signor Giovanni!—stay, my young friend!" cried he. "Have you forgotten me? That might well be the case, if I were as much altered as yourself."

It was Baglioni, whom Giovanni had avoided, ever since their first meeting, from a doubt that the Professor's sagacity would look too deeply into his secrets. Endeavoring to recover himself, he stared forth wildly from his inner world into the outer one, and spoke like a man in a dream:

"Yes; I am Giovanni Guasconti. You are Professor Pietro Baglioni. Now let me pass!"

"Not yet—not yet, Signor Giovanni Guasconti," said the Professor, smiling, but at the same time scrutinizing the youth with an earnest glance.—"What; did I grow up side by side with your father, and shall his son pass me like a stranger, in these old streets of Padua? Stand still, Signor Giovanni; for we must have a word or two, before we part."

"Speedily, then, most worshipful Professor, speedily!" said Giovanni, with feverish impatience. "Does not your worship see that I am in haste?"

Now, while he was speaking, there came a man in black along the street, stooping and moving feebly, like a person in inferior health. His face was all overspread with a most sickly and sallow hue, but yet so pervaded with an expression of piercing and active intellect, that an observer might easily have overlooked the merely physical attributes, and have seen only this wonderful energy. As he passed, this person exchanged a cold and distant salutation with Baglioni, but fixed his eyes upon Giovanni with an intentness that seemed to bring out whatever was within him worthy of notice. Nevertheless, there was a peculiar quietness in the look, as if taking merely a speculative, not a human, interest in the young man.

"It is Doctor Rappaccini!" whispered the Professor, when the stranger had passed.—"Has he ever seen your face before?"

"Not that I know," answered Giovanni, starting at the name.

"He *has* seen you!—he must have seen you!" said Baglioni, hastily. "For some purpose or other, this man of science is making a study of you. I know that look of his! It is the same that coldly illuminates his face, as he bends over a bird, a mouse, or a butterfly, which, in pursuance of some experiment, he has killed by the perfume of a flower;—a look as deep as Nature itself, but without Nature's warmth of love. Signor Giovanni, I will stake my life upon it, you are the subject of one of Rappaccini's experiments!"

"Will you make a fool of me?" cried Giovanni, passionately. "*That*, Signor Professor, were an untoward experiment."

"Patience, patience!" replied the imperturbable Professor. —"I tell thee, my poor Giovanni, that Rappaccini has a scientific interest in thee. Thou hast fallen into fearful hands! And the Signora Beatrice? What part does she act in this mystery?"

But Guasconti, finding Baglioni's pertinacity intolerable, here broke away, and was gone before the Professor could again seize his arm. He looked after the young man intently, and shook his head.

"This must not be," said Baglioni to himself. "The youth is the son of my old friend, and shall not come to any harm from which the arcana of medical science can preserve him. Besides, it is too insufferable an impertinence in Rappaccini, thus to snatch the lad out of my own hands, as I may say, and make use of him for his infernal experiments. This daughter of his! It shall be looked to. Perchance, most learned Rappaccini, I may foil you where you little dream of it!"

Meanwhile, Giovanni had pursued a circuitous route, and at length found himself at the door of his lodgings. As he crossed the threshold, he was met by old Lisabetta, who smirked and smiled, and was evidently desirous to attract his attention; vainly, however, as the ebullition of his feelings had momentarily subsided into a cold and dull vacuity. He turned his eyes full upon the withered face that was puckering itself into a smile, but seemed to behold it not. The old dame, therefore, laid her grasp upon his cloak.

"Signor!—Signor!" whispered she, still with a smile over the whole breadth of her visage, so that it looked not unlike a grotesque carving in wood, darkened by centuries—"Listen, Signor! There is a private entrance into the garden!"

"What do you say?" exclaimed Giovanni, turning quickly about, as if an inanimate thing should start into feverish life.—"A private entrance into Doctor Rappaccini's garden!"

"Hush! hush!—not so loud!" whispered Lisabetta, putting her hand over his mouth. "Yes; into the worshipful Doctor's garden, where you may see all his fine shrubbery. Many a young man in Padua would give gold to be admitted among those flowers."

Giovanni put a piece of gold into her hand.

"Show me the way," said he.

A surmise, probably excited by his conversation with Baglioni, crossed his mind, that this interposition of old Lisabetta might perchance be connected with the intrigue, whatever were its nature, in which the Professor seemed to suppose that Doctor Rappaccini was involving him. But such a suspicion, though it disturbed Giovanni, was inadequate to restrain him. The instant that he was aware of the possibility of approaching Beatrice, it seemed an absolute necessity of his existence to do so. It mattered not whether she were angel or demon; he was irrevocably within her sphere, and must obey the law that whirled him onward, in ever lessening circles, towards a result which he did not attempt to foreshadow. And yet, strange to say, there came across him a sudden doubt, whether this intense interest on his part were not delusory—whether it were really of so deep and positive a nature as to justify him in now thrusting himself into an incalculable position—whether it were not merely the fantasy of a young man's brain, only slightly, or not at all, connected with his heart!

He paused—hesitated—turned half about—but again went on. His withered guide led him along several obscure passages, and finally undid a door, through which, as it was opened, there came the sight and sound of rustling leaves, with the broken sunshine glimmering among them. Giovanni stepped forth, and forcing himself through the entanglement of a shrub that wreathed its tendrils over the hidden entrance, he stood beneath his own window, in the open area of Doctor Rappaccini's garden.

How often is it the case, that, when impossibilities have come to pass, and dreams have condensed their misty substance into tangible realities, we find ourselves calm, and even coldly self-possessed, amid circumstances which it would have been a delirium of joy or agony to anticipate! Fate delights to thwart us thus. Passion will choose his own time to rush upon the scene, and lingers sluggishly behind, when an appropriate adjustment of events would seem to summon his appearance. So was it now with Giovanni. Day after day, his pulses had throbbed with feverish blood, at the improbable idea of an interview with Beatrice, and of standing with her, face to face, in this very garden, basking in the Oriental sunshine of her beauty, and snatching from her full gaze the mystery which he deemed the riddle of his own existence. But now there was a singular and untimely equanimity within his breast. He threw a glance around the garden to discover if Beatrice or her father were present, and perceiving that he was alone, began a critical observation of the plants.

The aspect of one and all of them dissatisfied him; their gorgeousness seemed fierce, passionate, and even unnatural. There was hardly an individual shrub which a wanderer, straying by himself through a forest, would not have been startled to find growing wild, as if an unearthly face had glared at him out of the thicket. Several, also, would have shocked a delicate instinct by an appearance of artificialness, indicating that there had been such commixture, and, as it were, adultery of various vegetable species, that the production was no longer of God's making, but the monstrous off-spring of man's depraved fancy, glowing with only an evil mockery of beauty. They were probably the result of experiment, which, in one or two cases, had succeeded in mingling plants individually lovely into a compound possessing the questionable and ominous character that distinguished the whole growth of the garden. In fine, Giovanni recognized but two or three plants in the collection, and those of a kind that he well knew to be poisonous. While busy with these contemplations, he heard the rustling of a silken garment, and turning, beheld Beatrice emerging from beneath the sculptured portal.

Giovanni had not considered with himself what should be his deportment; whether he should apologize for his intrusion into the garden, or assume that he was there with the privity, at least, if not by the desire, of Doctor Rappaccini or his daughter. But Beatrice's manner placed him at his ease, though leaving him still in doubt by what agency he had gained admittance. She came lightly along the path, and met him near the broken fountain. There was surprise in her face, but brightened by a simple and kind expression of pleasure.

"You are a connoisseur in flowers, Signor," said Beatrice with a smile, alluding to the bouquet which he had flung her from the window. "It is no marvel, therefore, if the sight of my father's rare collection has tempted you to take a nearer view. If he were here, he could tell you many strange and interesting facts as to the nature and habits of these shrubs, for he has spent a life-time in such studies, and this garden is his world."

"And yourself, lady"—observed Giovanni—"if fame says true—you, likewise, are deeply skilled in the virtues indicated by these rich blossoms, and these spicy perfumes. Would you deign to be my instructress, I should prove an apter scholar than if taught by Signor Rappaccini himself."

"Are there such idle rumors?" asked Beatrice, with the music of a pleasant laugh. "Do people say that I am skilled in my father's science of plants? What a jest is there! No; though I have grown up among these flowers, I know no more of them than their hues and perfume; and sometimes, methinks I would fain rid myself of even that small knowledge. There are many flowers here, and those not the least brilliant, that shock and offend me, when they meet my eye. But, pray, Signor, do not believe these stories about my science. Believe nothing of me save what you see with your own eyes."

"And must I believe all that I have seen with my own eyes?" asked Giovanni pointedly, while the recollection of former scenes made him shrink. "No, Signora, you demand too little of me. Bid me believe nothing, save what comes from your own lips."

It would appear that Beatrice understood him. There came a deep flush to her cheek; but she looked full into Giovanni's eyes, and responded to his gaze of uneasy suspicion with a queen-like haughtiness.

"I do so bid you, Signor!" she replied. "Forget whatever you may have fancied in regard to me. If true to the outward senses, still it may be false in its essence. But the words of Beatrice Rappaccini's lips are true from the depths of the heart outward. Those you may believe!"

A fervor glowed in her whole aspect, and beamed upon Giovanni's consciousness like the light of truth itself. But while she spoke, there was a fragrance in the atmosphere around her, rich and delightful, though evanescent, yet which the young man, from an indefinable reluctance, scarcely dared to draw into his lungs. It might be the odor of the flowers. Could it be Beatrice's breath, which thus embalmed her words with a strange richness, as if by steeping them in her heart? A faintness passed like a shadow over Giovanni, and flitted away; he seemed to gaze through the beautiful girl's eyes into her transparent soul, and felt no more doubt or fear.

The tinge of passion that had colored Beatrice's manner vanished; she became gay, and appeared to derive a pure delight from her communion with the youth, not unlike what the maiden of a lonely island might have felt, conversing with a voyager from the civilized world. Evidently her experience of life had been confined within the limits of that garden. She talked now about matters as simple as the day-light or summer-clouds, and now asked questions in reference to the city, or Giovanni's distant home, his friends, his mother, and his sisters; questions indicating such seclusion, and such lack of familiarity with modes and forms, that Giovanni responded as if to an infant. Her spirit gushed out before him like a fresh rill, that was just catching its first glimpse of the sunlight, and wondering at the reflections of earth and sky which were flung into its bosom. There came thoughts, too, from a deep source, and fantasies of a gem-like brilliancy, as if diamonds and rubies sparkled upward among the bubbles of the fountain. Ever and anon, there gleamed across the young man's mind a sense of wonder, that he should be walking side by side with the being who had so wrought upon his imagination—whom he had idealized in such hues of terror—in whom he had positively witnessed such manifestations of dreadful attributes—that he should be conversing with Beatrice like a brother, and should find her so human and so maiden-like. But such reflections were only momentary; the effect of her character was too real, not to make itself familiar at once.

In this free intercourse, they had strayed through the garden, and now, after many turns among its avenues, were come to the shattered fountain, beside which grew the magnificent shrub with its treasury of glowing blossoms. A fragrance was diffused from it, which Giovanni recognized as identical with that which he had attributed to Beatrice's breath, but incomparably more powerful. As her eyes fell upon it, Giovanni beheld her press her hand to her bosom, as if her heart were throbbing suddenly and painfully.

"For the first time in my life," murmured she, addressing the shrub, "I had forgotten thee!"

"I remember, Signora," said Giovanni, "that you once promised to reward me with one of these living gems for the bouquet, which I had the happy boldness to fling to your feet. Permit me now to pluck it as a memorial of this interview."

He made a step towards the shrub, with extended hand. But Beatrice darted forward, uttering a shriek that went through his heart like a dagger. She caught his hand, and drew it back with the whole force of her slender figure. Giovanni felt her touch thrilling through his fibres.

"Touch it not!" exclaimed she, in a voice of agony. "Not for thy life! It is fatal!"

Then, hiding her face, she fled from him, and vanished beneath the sculptured portal. As Giovanni followed her with his eyes, he beheld the emaciated figure and pale intelligence of Doctor Rappaccini, who had been watching the scene, he knew not how long, within the shadow of the entrance.

No sooner was Guasconti alone in his chamber, than the image of Beatrice came back to his passionate musings, invested with all the witchery that had been gathering around it ever since his first glimpse of her, and now likewise imbued with a tender warmth of girlish womanhood. She was human: her nature was endowed with all gentle and feminine qualities; she was worthiest to be worshipped; she was capable, surely, on her part, of the height and heroism of love. Those tokens, which he had hitherto considered as proofs of a frightful peculiarity in her physical and moral system, were now either forgotten, or, by the subtle sophistry of passion, transmuted into a golden crown of enchantment, rendering Beatrice the more admirable, by so much as she was the more unique. Whatever had looked ugly, was now beautiful; or, if incapable of such a change, it stole away and hid itself among those shapeless half-ideas, which throng the dim region beyond the daylight of our perfect consciousness. Thus did he spend the night, nor fell asleep, until the dawn had begun to awake the slumbering flowers in Doctor Rappaccini's garden, whither Giovanni's dreams doubtless led him. Up rose the sun in his due season, and flinging his beams upon the young man's eyelids, awoke him to a sense of pain. When thoroughly aroused, he became sensible of a burning and tingling agony in his hand—in his right hand—the very hand which Beatrice had grasped in her own, when he was on the point of plucking one of the gem-like flowers. On the back of that hand there was now a purple print, like that of four small fingers, and the likeness of a slender thumb upon his wrist.

Oh, how stubbornly does love—or even that cunning semblance of love which flourishes in the imagination, but strikes no depth of root into the heart—how stubbornly does it hold its faith, until the moment come, when it is doomed to vanish into thin mist! Giovanni wrapt a handkerchief about his hand, and wondered what evil thing had stung him, and soon forgot his pain in a reverie of Beatrice.

After the first interview, a second was in the inevitable

course of what we call fate. A third; a fourth; and a meeting
with Beatrice in the garden was no longer an incident in
Giovanni's daily life, but the whole space in which he might
be said to live; for the anticipation and memory of that ecstatic hour made up the remainder. Nor was it otherwise with
the daughter of Rappaccini. She watched for the youth's appearance, and flew to his side with confidence as unreserved
as if they had been playmates from early infancy—as if they
were such playmates still. If, by any unwonted chance, he
failed to come at the appointed moment, she stood beneath
the window, and sent up the rich sweetness of her tones to
float around him in his chamber, and echo and reverberate
throughout his heart—"Giovanni! Giovanni! Why tarriest
thou? Come down!"—And down he hastened into that Eden
of poisonous flowers.

But, with all this intimate familiarity, there was still a reserve in Beatrice's demeanor, so rigidly and invariably sustained, that the idea of infringing it scarcely occurred to his
imagination. By all appreciable signs, they loved; they had
looked love, with eyes that conveyed the holy secret from the
depths of one soul into the depths of the other, as if it were
too sacred to be whispered by the way; they had even spoken
love, in those gushes of passion when their spirits darted
forth in articulated breath, like tongues of long-hidden flame;
and yet there had been no seal of lips, no clasp of hands, nor
any slightest caress, such as love claims and hallows. He had
never touched one of the gleaming ringlets of her hair; her
garment—so marked was the physical barrier between
them—had never been waved against him by a breeze. On
the few occasions when Giovanni had seemed tempted to
overstep the limit, Beatrice grew so sad, so stern, and withal
wore such a look of desolate separation, shuddering at itself,
that not a spoken word was requisite to repel him. At such
times, he was startled at the horrible suspicions that rose,
monster-like, out of the caverns of his heart, and stared him
in the face; his love grew thin and faint as the morning-mist;
his doubts alone had substance. But when Beatrice's face
brightened again, after the momentary shadow, she was transformed at once from the mysterious, questionable being,
whom he had watched with so much awe and horror;

she was now the beautiful and unsophisticated girl, whom he felt that his spirit knew with a certainty beyond all other knowledge.

A considerable time had now passed since Giovanni's last meeting with Baglioni. One morning, however, he was disagreeably surprised by a visit from the Professor, whom he had scarcely thought of for whole weeks, and would willingly have forgotten still longer. Given up, as he had long been, to a pervading excitement, he could tolerate no companions, except upon condition of their perfect sympathy with his present state of feeling. Such sympathy was not to be expected from Professor Baglioni.

The visitor chatted carelessly, for a few moments, about the gossip of the city and the University, and then took up another topic.

"I have been reading an old classic author lately," said he, "and met with a story that strangely interested me. Possibly you may remember it. It is of an Indian prince, who sent a beautiful woman as a present to Alexander the Great. She was as lovely as the dawn, and gorgeous as the sunset; but what especially distinguished her was a certain rich perfume in her breath—richer than a garden of Persian roses. Alexander, as was natural to a youthful conqueror, fell in love at first sight with this magnificent stranger. But a certain sage physician, happening to be present, discovered a terrible secret in regard to her."

"And what was that?" asked Giovanni, turning his eyes downward to avoid those of the Professor.

"That this lovely woman," continued Baglioni, with emphasis, "had been nourished with poisons from her birth upward, until her whole nature was so imbued with them, that she herself had become the deadliest poison in existence. Poison was her element of life. With that rich perfume of her breath, she blasted the very air. Her love would have been poison!—her embrace death! Is not this a marvelous tale?"

"A childish fable," answered Giovanni, nervously starting from his chair. "I marvel how your worship finds time to read such nonsense, among your graver studies."

"By the bye," said the Professor, looking uneasily about him, "what singular fragrance is this in your apartment? Is it the perfume of your gloves? It is faint, but delicious, and yet, after all, by no means agreeable. Were I to breathe it long, methinks it would make me ill. It is like the breath of a flower—but I see no flowers in the chamber."

"Nor are there any," replied Giovanni, who had turned pale as the Professor spoke; "nor, I think, is there any fragrance, except in your worship's imagination. Odors, being a sort of element combined of the sensual and the spiritual, are apt to deceive us in this manner. The recollection of a perfume— the bare idea of it—may easily be mistaken for a present reality."

"Aye; but my sober imagination does not often play such tricks," said Baglioni; "and were I to fancy any kind of odor, it would be that of some vile apothecary drug, wherewith my fingers are likely enough to be imbued. Our worshipful friend Rappaccini, as I have heard, tinctures his medicaments with odors richer than those of Araby. Doubtless, likewise, the fair and learned Signora Beatrice would minister to her patients with draughts as sweet as a maiden's breath. But wo to him that sips them!"

Giovanni's face evinced many contending emotions. The tone in which the Professor alluded to the pure and lovely daughter of Rappaccini was a torture to his soul; and yet, the intimation of a view of her character, opposite to his own, gave instantaneous distinctness to a thousand dim suspicions, which now grinned at him like so many demons. But he strove hard to quell them, and to respond to Baglioni with a true lover's perfect faith.

"Signor Professor," said he, "you were my father's friend— perchance, too, it is your purpose to act a friendly part towards his son. I would fain feel nothing towards you, save respect and deference. But I pray you to observe, Signor, that there is one subject on which we must not speak. You know not the Signora Beatrice. You cannot, therefore, estimate the wrong—the blasphemy, I may even say—that is offered to her character by a light or injurious word."

"Giovanni!—my poor Giovanni!" answered the Professor, with a calm expression of pity, "I know this wretched girl far better than yourself. You shall hear the truth in respect to the poisoner Rappaccini, and his poisonous daughter. Yes; poisonous as she is beautiful! Listen; for even should you do violence to my grey hairs, it shall not silence me. That old fable of the Indian woman has become a truth, by the deep and deadly science of Rappaccini, and in the person of the lovely Beatrice!"

Giovanni groaned and hid his face.

"Her father," continued Baglioni, "was not restrained by natural affection from offering up his child, in this horrible manner, as the victim of his insane zeal for science. For—let us do him justice—he is as true a man of science as ever distilled his own heart in an alembic. What, then, will be your fate? Beyond a doubt, you are selected as the material of some new experiment. Perhaps the result is to be death—perhaps a fate more awful still! Rappaccini, with what he calls the interest of science before his eyes, will hesitate at nothing."

"It is a dream!" muttered Giovanni to himself, "surely it is a dream!"

"But," resumed the Professor, "be of good cheer, son of my friend! It is not yet too late for the rescue. Possibly, we may even succeed in bringing back this miserable child within the limits of ordinary nature, from which her father's madness has estranged her. Behold this little silver vase! It was wrought by the hands of the renowned Benvenuto Cellini, and is well worthy to be a love-gift to the fairest dame in Italy. But its contents are invaluable. One little sip of this antidote would have rendered the most virulent poisons of the Borgias innocuous. Doubt not that it will be as efficacious against those of Rappaccini. Bestow the vase, and the precious liquid within it, on your Beatrice, and hopefully await the result."

Baglioni laid a small, exquisitely wrought silver phial on the table, and withdrew, leaving what he had said to produce its effect upon the young man's mind.

"We will thwart Rappaccini yet!" thought he, chuckling to himself, as he descended the stairs. "But, let us confess the truth of him, he is a wonderful man!—a wonderful man indeed! A vile empiric, however, in his practice, and therefore not to be tolerated by those who respect the good old rules of the medical profession!"

Throughout Giovanni's whole acquaintance with Beatrice,

he had occasionally, as we have said, been haunted by dark surmises as to her character. Yet, so thoroughly had she made herself felt by him as a simple, natural, most affectionate and guileless creature, that the image now held up by Professor Baglioni, looked as strange and incredible, as if it were not in accordance with his own original conception. True, there were ugly recollections connected with his first glimpses of the beautiful girl; he could not quite forget the bouquet that withered in her grasp, and the insect that perished amid the sunny air, by no ostensible agency, save the fragrance of her breath. These incidents, however, dissolving in the pure light of her character, had no longer the efficacy of facts, but were acknowledged as mistaken fantasies, by whatever testimony of the senses they might appear to be substantiated. There is something truer and more real, than what we can see with the eyes, and touch with the finger. On such better evidence, had Giovanni founded his confidence in Beatrice, though rather by the necessary force of her high attributes, than by any deep and generous faith, on his part. But, now, his spirit was incapable of sustaining itself at the height to which the early enthusiasm of passion had exalted it; it fell down, grovelling among earthly doubts, and defiled therewith the pure whiteness of Beatrice's image. Not that he gave her up; he did but distrust. He resolved to institute some decisive test that should satisfy him, once for all, whether there were those dreadful peculiarities in her physical nature, which could not be supposed to exist without some corresponding monstrosity of soul. His eyes, gazing down afar, might have deceived him as to the lizard, the insect, and the flowers. But if he could witness, at the distance of a few paces, the sudden blight of one fresh and healthful flower in Beatrice's hand, there would be room for no further question. With this idea, he hastened to the florist's, and purchased a bouquet that was still gemmed with the morning dew-drops.

It was now the customary hour of his daily interview with Beatrice. Before descending into the garden, Giovanni failed not to look at his figure in the mirror; a vanity to be expected in a beautiful young man, yet, as displaying itself at that troubled and feverish moment, the token of a certain shallowness of feeling and insincerity of character. He did gaze, however,

and said to himself, that his features had never before possessed so rich a grace, nor his eyes such vivacity, nor his
cheeks so warm a hue of superabundant life.

"At least," thought he, "her poison has not yet insinuated
itself into my system. I am no flower to perish in her grasp!"

With that thought, he turned his eyes on the bouquet,
which he had never once laid aside from his hand. A thrill of
indefinable horror shot through his frame, on perceiving that
those dewy flowers were already beginning to droop; they
wore the aspect of things that had been fresh and lovely, yesterday. Giovanni grew white as marble, and stood motionless
before the mirror, staring at his own reflection there, as at the
likeness of something frightful. He remembered Baglioni's remark about the fragrance that seemed to pervade the chamber. It must have been the poison in his breath! Then he
shuddered—shuddered at himself! Recovering from his stupor, he began to watch, with curious eye, a spider that was
busily at work, hanging its web from the antique cornice of
the apartment, crossing and re-crossing the artful system of
interwoven lines, as vigorous and active a spider as ever dangled from an old ceiling. Giovanni bent towards the insect,
and emitted a deep, long breath. The spider suddenly ceased
its toil; the web vibrated with a tremor originating in the
body of the small artizan. Again Giovanni sent forth a breath,
deeper, longer, and imbued with a venomous feeling out of
his heart; he knew not whether he were wicked or only desperate. The spider made a convulsive gripe with his limbs,
and hung dead across the window.

"Accursed! Accursed!" muttered Giovanni, addressing himself. "Hast thou grown so poisonous, that this deadly insect
perishes by thy breath?"

At that moment, a rich, sweet voice came floating up from
the garden:—

"Giovanni! Giovanni! It is past the hour! Why tarriest
thou! Come down!"

"Yes," muttered Giovanni again. "She is the only being
whom my breath may not slay! Would that it might!"

He rushed down, and in an instant, was standing before
the bright and loving eyes of Beatrice. A moment ago, his
wrath and despair had been so fierce that he could have de-

sired nothing so much as to wither her by a glance. But, with her actual presence, there came influences which had too real an existence to be at once shaken off; recollections of the delicate and benign power of her feminine nature, which had so often enveloped him in a religious calm; recollections of many a holy and passionate outgush of her heart, when the pure fountain had been unsealed from its depths, and made visible in its transparency to his mental eye; recollections which, had Giovanni known how to estimate them, would have assured him that all this ugly mystery was but an earthly illusion, and that, whatever mist of evil might seem to have gathered over her, the real Beatrice was a heavenly angel. Incapable as he was of such high faith, still her presence had not utterly lost its magic. Giovanni's rage was quelled into an aspect of sullen insensibility. Beatrice, with a quick spiritual sense, immediately felt that there was a gulf of blackness between them, which neither he nor she could pass. They walked on together, sad and silent, and came thus to the marble fountain, and to its pool of water on the ground, in the midst of which grew the shrub that bore gem-like blossoms. Giovanni was affrighted at the eager enjoyment—the appetite, as it were—with which he found himself inhaling the fragrance of the flowers.

"Beatrice," asked he abruptly, "whence came this shrub?"

"My father created it," answered she, with simplicity.

"Created it! created it!" repeated Giovanni. "What mean you, Beatrice?"

"He is a man fearfully acquainted with the secrets of nature," replied Beatrice; "and, at the hour when I first drew breath, this plant sprang from the soil, the offspring of his science, of his intellect, while I was but his earthly child. Approach it not!" continued she, observing with terror that Giovanni was drawing nearer to the shrub. "It has qualities that you little dream of. But I, dearest Giovanni,—I grew up and blossomed with the plant, and was nourished with its breath. It was my sister, and I loved it with a human affection: for—alas! hast thou not suspected it? there was an awful doom."

Here Giovanni frowned so darkly upon her that Beatrice paused and trembled. But her faith in his tenderness reassured her, and made her blush that she had doubted for an instant.

"There was an awful doom," she continued,—"the effect of my father's fatal love of science—which estranged me from all society of my kind. Until Heaven sent thee, dearest Giovanni, Oh! how lonely was thy poor Beatrice!"

"Was it a hard doom?" asked Giovanni, fixing his eyes upon her.

"Only of late have I known how hard it was," answered she tenderly. "Oh, yes; but my heart was torpid, and therefore quiet."

Giovanni's rage broke forth from his sullen gloom like a lightning-flash out of a dark cloud.

"Accursed one!" cried he, with venomous scorn and anger. "And finding thy solitude wearisome, thou hast severed me, likewise, from all the warmth of life, and enticed me into thy region of unspeakable horror!"

"Giovanni!" exclaimed Beatrice, turning her large bright eyes upon his face. The force of his words had not found its way into her mind; she was merely thunder-struck.

"Yes, poisonous thing!" repeated Giovanni, beside himself with passion. "Thou hast done it! Thou hast blasted me! Thou hast filled my veins with poison! Thou hast made me as hateful, as ugly, as loathsome and deadly a creature as thyself,—a world's wonder of hideous monstrosity! Now—if our breath be happily as fatal to ourselves as to all others— let us join our lips in one kiss of unutterable hatred, and so die!"

"What has befallen me?" murmured Beatrice, with a low moan out of her heart. "Holy Virgin pity me, a poor heart-broken child!"

"Thou! Dost thou pray?" cried Giovanni, still with the same fiendish scorn. "Thy very prayers, as they come from thy lips, taint the atmosphere with death. Yes, yes; let us pray! Let us to church, and dip our fingers in the holy water at the portal! They that come after us will perish as by a pestilence. Let us sign crosses in the air! It will be scattering curses abroad in the likeness of holy symbols!"

"Giovanni," said Beatrice calmly, for her grief was beyond passion, "why dost thou join thyself with me thus in those terrible words? I, it is true, am the horrible thing thou namest me. But thou!—what hast thou to do, save with one other shudder at my hideous misery, to go forth out of the garden and mingle with thy race, and forget that there ever crawled on earth such a monster as poor Beatrice?"

"Dost thou pretend ignorance?" asked Giovanni, scowling upon her. "Behold! This power have I gained from the pure daughter of Rappaccini!"

There was a swarm of summer-insects flitting through the air, in search of the food promised by the flower-odors of the fatal garden. They circled round Giovanni's head, and were evidently attracted towards him by the same influence which had drawn them, for an instant, within the sphere of several of the shrubs. He sent forth a breath among them, and smiled bitterly at Beatrice, as at least a score of the insects fell dead upon the ground.

"I see it! I see it!" shrieked Beatrice. "It is my father's fatal science! No, no, Giovanni; it was not I! Never, never! I dreamed only to love thee, and be with thee a little time, and so to let thee pass away, leaving but thine image in mine heart. For, Giovanni—believe it—though my body be nourished with poison, my spirit is God's creature, and craves love as its daily food. But my father!—he has united us in this fearful sympathy. Yes; spurn me!—tread upon me!—kill me! Oh, what is death, after such words as thine? But it was not I! Not for a world of bliss would I have done it!"

Giovanni's passion had exhausted itself in its outburst from his lips. There now came across him a sense, mournful, and not without tenderness, of the intimate and peculiar relationship between Beatrice and himself. They stood, as it were, in an utter solitude, which would be made none the less solitary by the densest throng of human life. Ought not, then, the desert of humanity around them to press this insulated pair closer together? If they should be cruel to one another, who was there to be kind to them? Besides, thought Giovanni, might there not still be a hope of his returning within the limits of ordinary nature, and leading Beatrice—the redeemed Beatrice—by the hand? Oh, weak, and selfish, and unworthy spirit, that could dream of an earthly union and earthly happiness as possible, after such deep love had been so bitterly wronged as was Beatrice's love by Giovanni's blighting words! No, no; there could be no such hope. She must pass heavily, with that broken heart, across the borders of Time—she must bathe her hurts in some fount of Paradise, and forget her grief in the light of immortality—and *there* be well!

But Giovanni did not know it.

"Dear Beatrice," said he, approaching her, while she shrank away, as always at his approach, but now with a different impulse—"dearest Beatrice, our fate is not yet so desperate. Behold! There is a medicine, potent, as a wise physician has assured me, and almost divine in its efficacy. It is composed of ingredients the most opposite to those by which thy awful father has brought this calamity upon thee and me. It is distilled of blessed herbs. Shall we not quaff it together, and thus be purified from evil?"

"Give it me!" said Beatrice, extending her hand to receive the little silver phial which Giovanni took from his bosom. She added, with a peculiar emphasis: "I will drink—but do thou await the result."

She put Baglioni's antidote to her lips; and, at the same moment, the figure of Rappaccini emerged from the portal, and came slowly towards the marble fountain. As he drew near, the pale man of science seemed to gaze with a triumphant expression at the beautiful youth and maiden, as might an artist who should spend his life in achieving a picture or a group of statuary, and finally be satisfied with his success. He paused—his bent form grew erect with conscious power, he spread out his hands over them, in the attitude of a father imploring a blessing upon his children. But those were the same hands that had thrown poison into the stream of their lives! Giovanni trembled. Beatrice shuddered nervously, and pressed her hand upon her heart.

"My daughter," said Rappaccini, "thou art no longer lonely in the world! Pluck one of those precious gems from thy sister shrub, and bid thy bridegroom wear it in his bosom. It will not harm him now! My science, and the sympathy between thee and him, have so wrought within his system, that he now stands apart from common men, as thou dost, daughter of my pride and triumph, from ordinary women. Pass on, then, through the world, most dear to one another, and dreadful to all besides!"

"My father," said Beatrice, feebly—and still, as she spoke, she kept her hand upon her heart—"wherefore didst thou inflict this miserable doom upon thy child?"

"Miserable!" exclaimed Rappaccini. "What mean you, foolish girl? Dost thou deem it misery to be endowed with marvellous gifts, against which no power nor strength could avail an enemy? Misery, to be able to quell the mightiest with a breath? Misery, to be as terrible as thou art beautiful? Wouldst thou, then, have preferred the condition of a weak woman, exposed to all evil, and capable of none?"

"I would fain have been loved, not feared," murmured Beatrice, sinking down upon the ground.—"But now it matters not; I am going, father, where the evil, which thou hast striven to mingle with my being, will pass away like a dream—like the fragrance of these poisonous flowers, which will no longer taint my breath among the flowers of Eden. Farewell, Giovanni! Thy words of hatred are like lead within my heart—but they, too, will fall away as I ascend. Oh, was there not, from the first, more poison in thy nature than in mine?"

To Beatrice—so radically had her earthly part been wrought upon by Rappaccini's skill—as poison had been life, so the powerful antidote was death. And thus the poor victim of man's ingenuity and of thwarted nature, and of the fatality that attends all such efforts of perverted wisdom, perished there, at the feet of her father and Giovanni. Just at that moment, Professor Pietro Baglioni looked forth from the window, and called loudly, in a tone of triumph mixed with horror, to the thunder-stricken man of science:

"Rappaccini! Rappaccini! And is *this* the upshot of your experiment?"

P.'s Correspondence

M Y unfortunate friend P. has lost the thread of his life,
by the interposition of long intervals of partially disordered reason. The past and present are jumbled together in
his mind, in a manner often productive of curious results; and
which will be better understood after a perusal of the following letter, than from any description that I could give. The
poor fellow, without once stirring from the little white-
washed, iron-grated room, to which he alludes in his first paragraph, is nevertheless a great traveller, and meets, in his wanderings, a variety of personages who have long ceased to be
visible to any eye save his own. In my opinion, all this is not
so much a delusion, as a partly wilful and partly involuntary
sport of the imagination, to which his disease has imparted
such morbid energy that he beholds these spectral scenes and
characters with no less distinctness than a play upon the stage,
and with somewhat more of illusive credence. Many of his
letters are in my possession, some based upon the same vagary as the present one, and others upon hypotheses not a
whit short of it in absurdity. The whole form a series of correspondence, which, should fate seasonably remove my poor
friend from what is to him a world of moonshine, I promise
myself a pious pleasure in editing for the public eye. P. had
always a hankering after literary reputation, and has made
more than one unsuccessful effort to achieve it. It would not
be a little odd, if, after missing his object while seeking it by
the light of reason, he should prove to have stumbled upon it
in his misty excursions beyond the limits of sanity.

LONDON, February 29, 1845.

MY DEAR FRIEND:

Old associations cling to the mind with astonishing tenac-
ity. Daily custom grows up about us like a stone-wall, and
consolidates itself into almost as material an entity as mankind's strongest architecture. It is sometimes a serious question with me, whether ideas be not really visible and tangible,
and endowed with all the other qualities of matter. Sitting as
I do, at this moment, in my hired apartment, writing beside

the hearth, over which hangs a print of Queen Victoria—listening to the muffled roar of the world's metropolis, and with a window at but five paces distant, through which, whenever I please, I can gaze out on actual London—with all this positive certainty, as to my whereabouts, what kind of notion, do you think, is just now perplexing my brain? Why—would you believe it?—that, all this time, I am still an inhabitant of that wearisome little chamber,—that white-washed little chamber—that little chamber with its one small window, across which, from some inscrutable reason of taste or convenience, my landlord had placed a row of iron bars—that same little chamber, in short, whither your kindness has so often brought you to visit me! Will no length of time, or breadth of space, enfranchise me from that unlovely abode? I travel, but it seems to be like the snail, with my house upon my head. Ah, well! I am verging, I suppose, on that period of life when present scenes and events make but feeble impressions, in comparison with those of yore; so that I must reconcile myself to be more and more the prisoner of Memory, who merely lets me hop about a little, with her chain around my leg.

My letters of introduction have been of the utmost service, enabling me to make the acquaintance of several distinguished characters, who, until now, have seemed as remote from the sphere of my personal intercourse as the wits of Queen Anne's time, or Ben Jonson's compotators at the Mermaid. One of the first of which I availed myself, was the letter to Lord Byron. I found his lordship looking much older than I had anticipated; although—considering his former irregularities of life, and the various wear and tear of his constitution—not older than a man on the verge of sixty reasonably may look. But I had invested his earthly frame, in my imagination, with the poet's spiritual immortality. He wears a brown wig, very luxuriantly curled, and extending down over his forehead. The expression of his eyes is concealed by spectacles. His early tendency to obesity having increased, Lord Byron is now enormously fat; so fat as to give the impression of a person quite overladen with his own flesh, and without sufficient vigor to diffuse his personal life through the great mass of corporeal substance, which weighs upon him so cruelly. You gaze at the mortal heap; and, while it fills your eye with what purports to be Byron, you murmur within yourself—"For Heaven's sake, where is he?" Were I disposed to be caustic, I might consider this mass of earthly matter as the symbol, in a material shape, of those evil habits and carnal vices which unspiritualize man's nature, and clog up his avenues of communication with the better life. But this would be too harsh; and besides, Lord Byron's morals have been improving, while his outward man has swollen to such unconscionable circumference. Would that he were leaner; for, though he did me the honor to present his hand, yet it was so puffed out with alien substance, that I could not feel as if I had touched the hand that wrote Childe Harold.

On my entrance, his lordship apologized for not rising to receive me, on the sufficient plea that the gout, for several years past, had taken up its constant residence in his right foot; which, accordingly, was swathed in many rolls of flannel, and deposited upon a cushion. The other foot was hidden in the drapery of his chair. Do you recollect whether Byron's right or left foot was the deformed one?

The noble poet's reconciliation with Lady Byron is now, as you are aware, of ten years' standing; nor does it exhibit, I am assured, any symptom of breach or fracture. They are said to be, if not a happy, at least a contented, or, at all events, a quiet couple, descending the slope of life with that tolerable degree of mutual support, which will enable them to come easily and comfortably to the bottom. It is pleasant to reflect how entirely the poet has redeemed his youthful errors, in this particular. Her ladyship's influence, it rejoices me to add, has been productive of the happiest results upon Lord Byron in a religious point of view. He now combines the most rigid tenets of Methodism with the ultra-doctrines of the Puseyites: the former being perhaps due to the convictions wrought upon his mind by his noble consort; while the latter are the embroidery and picturesque illumination, demanded by his imaginative character. Much of whatever expenditure his increasing habits of thrift continue to allow him, is bestowed in the reparation or beautifying of places of worship; and this nobleman, whose name was one considered a synonym of the foul fiend, is now all but canonized as a saint, in many pulpits of the metropolis and elsewhere. In politics, Lord Byron is an uncompromising conservative, and loses no opportunity, whether in the House of Lords or in private circles, of denouncing and repudiating the mischievous and anarchical notions of his earlier day. Nor does he fail to visit similar sins, in other people, with the severest vengeance which his somewhat blunted pen is capable of inflicting. Southey and he are on the most intimate terms. You are aware that some little time before the death of Moore, Byron caused that brilliant but reprehensible man to be ejected from his house. Moore took the insult so much to heart, that it is said to have been one great cause of the fit of illness which brought him to the grave. Others pretend that the Lyrist died in a very happy state of mind, singing one of his own sacred melodies, and expressing his belief that it would be heard within the gate of paradise, and gain him instant and honorable admittance. I wish he may have found it so.

I failed not, as you may suppose, in the course of conversation with Lord Byron, to pay the meed of homage due to a mighty poet, by allusions to passages in Childe Harold, and Manfred, and Don Juan, which have made so large a portion of the music of my life. My words, whether apt or otherwise, were at least warm with the enthusiasm of one worthy to discourse of immortal poesy. It was evident, however, that they did not go precisely to the right spot. I could perceive that there was some mistake or other, and was not a little angry with myself, and ashamed of my abortive attempt to throw back, from my own heart to the gifted author's ear, the echo of those strains that have resounded throughout the world. But, by and by, the secret peeped quietly out. Byron— I have the information from his own lips, so that you need not hesitate to repeat it in literary circles—Byron is preparing a new edition of his complete works, carefully corrected, expurgated and amended, in accordance with his present creed of taste, morals, politics and religion. It so happened, that the very passages of highest inspiration, to which I had alluded, were among the condemned and rejected rubbish, which it is his purpose to cast into the gulf of oblivion. To whisper you the truth, it appears to me that his passions having burnt out, the extinction of their vivid and riotous flame has deprived

Lord Byron of the illumination by which he not merely wrote, but was enabled to feel and comprehend what he had written. Positively, he no longer understands his own poetry.

This became very apparent on his favoring me so far as to read a few specimens of Don Juan in the moralized version. Whatever is licentious—whatever disrespectful to the sacred mysteries of our faith—whatever morbidly melancholic, or splenetically sportive—whatever assails settled constitutions of government, or systems of society—whatever could wound the sensibility of any mortal, except a pagan, a republican, or a dissenter—has been unrelentingly blotted out, and its place supplied by unexceptionable verses, in his lordship's later style. You may judge how much of the poem remains as hitherto published. The result is not so good as might be wished; in plain terms, it is a very sad affair indeed; for though the torches kindled in Tophet have been extinguished, they leave an abominably ill odor, and are succeeded by no glimpses of hallowed fire. It is to be hoped, nevertheless, that this attempt, on Lord Byron's part, to atone for his youthful errors, will at length induce the Dean of Westminster, or whatever churchman is concerned, to allow Thorwaldsen's statue of the poet its due niche in the grand old Abbey. His bones, you know, when brought from Greece, were denied sepulture among those of his tuneful brethren there.

What a vile slip of the pen was that! How absurd in me to talk about burying the bones of Byron, whom I have just seen alive, and encased in a big, round bulk of flesh! But, to say the truth, a prodigiously fat man always impresses me as a kind of hobgoblin; in the very extravagance of his mortal system, I find something akin to the immateriality of a ghost. And then that ridiculous old story darted into my mind, how that Byron died of fever at Missolonghi, above twenty years ago. More and more I recognize that we dwell in a world of shadows; and, for my part, I hold it hardly worth the trouble to attempt a distinction between shadows in the mind, and shadows out of it. If there be any difference, the former are rather the more substantial.

Only think of my good fortune! The venerable Robert Burns—now, if I mistake not, in his eighty-seventh year—

happens to be making a visit to London, as if on purpose to afford me an opportunity of grasping him by the hand. For upwards of twenty years past he has hardly left his quiet cottage in Ayrshire for a single night, and has only been drawn hither now by the irresistible persuasions of all the distinguished men in England. They wish to celebrate the patriarch's birthday by a festival. It will be the greatest literary triumph on record. Pray Heaven the little spark of life within the aged bard's bosom may not be extinguished in the lustre of that hour! I have already had the honor of an introduction to him, at the British Museum, where he was examining a collection of his own unpublished letters, interspersed with songs, which have escaped the notice of all his biographers.

Poh! Nonsense! What am I thinking of! How should Burns have been embalmed in biography, when he is still a hearty old man!

The figure of the bard is tall, and in the highest degree reverend; nor the less so, that it is much bent by the burthen of time. His white hair floats like a snow-drift around his face, in which are seen the furrows of intellect and passion, like the channels of headlong torrents that have foamed themselves away. The old gentleman is in excellent preservation, considering his time of life. He has that cricketty sort of liveliness—I mean the cricket's humor of chirping for any cause or none—which is perhaps the most favorable mood that can befall extreme old age. Our pride forbids us to desire it for ourselves, although we perceive it to be a beneficence of nature in the case of others. I was surprised to find it in Burns. It seems as if his ardent heart and brilliant imagination had both burnt down to the last embers, leaving only a little flickering flame in one corner, which keeps dancing upward and laughing all by itself. He is no longer capable of pathos. At the request of Allan Cunningham, he attempted to sing his own song to Mary in Heaven; but it was evident that the feeling of those verses, so profoundly true, and so simply expressed, was entirely beyond the scope of his present sensibilities; and when a touch of it did partially awaken him, the tears immediately gushed into his eyes, and his voice broke into a tremulous cackle. And yet he but indistinctly knew

wherefore he was weeping. Ah! he must not think again of
Mary in Heaven, until he shake off the dull impediment of
time, and ascend to meet her there.

Burns then began to repeat Tam O'Shanter, but was so
tickled with its wit and humor—of which, however, I suspect
he had but a traditionary sense—that he soon burst into a fit
of chirruping laughter, succeeded by a cough, which brought
this not very agreeable exhibition to a close. On the whole, I
would rather not have witnessed it. It is a satisfactory idea,
however, that the last forty years of the peasant-poet's life
have been passed in competence and perfect comfort. Having
been cured of his bardic improvidence for many a day past,
and grown as attentive to the main chance as a canny Scots-
man should be, he is now considered to be quite well off, as
to pecuniary circumstances. This, I suppose, is worth having
lived so long for.

I took occasion to inquire of some of the countrymen of
Burns in regard to the health of Sir Walter Scott. His condition, I am sorry to say, remains the same as for ten years past;
it is that of a hopeless paralytic, palsied not more in body
than in those nobler attributes of which the body is the instrument. And thus he vegetates from day to day, and from
year to year, at that splendid fantasy of Abbotsford, which
grew out of his brain, and became a symbol of the great romancer's tastes, feelings, studies, prejudices, and modes of intellect. Whether in verse, prose, or architecture, he could
achieve but one thing, although that one in infinite variety.
There he reclines, on a couch in his library, and is said to
spend whole hours of every day in dictating tales to an amanuensis. To an imaginary amanuensis; for it is not deemed
worth any one's trouble now to take down what flows from
that once brilliant fancy, every image of which was formerly
worth gold, and capable of being coined. Yet, Cunningham,
who has lately seen him, assures me that there is now and
then a touch of the genius; a striking combination of incident, or a picturesque trait of character, such as no other man
alive could have hit off; a glimmer from that ruined mind, as
if the sun had suddenly flashed on a half-rusted helmet in the
gloom of an ancient hall. But the plots of these romances
become inextricably confused; the characters melt into one

another; and the tale loses itself like the course of a stream flowing through muddy and marshy ground.

For my part, I can hardly regret that Sir Walter Scott had lost his consciousness of outward things, before his works went out of vogue. It was good that he should forget his fame, rather than that fame should first have forgotten him. Were he still a writer, and as brilliant a one as ever, he could no longer maintain anything like the same position in literature. The world, now-a-days, requires a more earnest purpose, a deeper moral, and a closer and homelier truth, than he was qualified to supply it with. Yet who can be, to the present generation, even what Scott has been to the past? I had expectations from a young man—one Dickens—who published a few magazine articles, very rich in humor, and not without symptoms of genuine pathos; but the poor fellow died, shortly after commencing an odd series of sketches, entitled, I think, the Pickwick Papers. Not impossibly, the world has lost more than it dreams of, by the untimely death of this Mr. Dickens.

Whom do you think I met in Pall Mall, the other day? You would not hit it in ten guesses. Why, no less a man than Napoleon Bonaparte!—or all that is now left of him—that is to say, the skin, bones, and corporeal substance, little cocked hat, green coat, white breeches and small sword, which are still known by his redoubtable name. He was attended only by two policemen, who walked quietly behind the phantasm of the old ex-Emperor, appearing to have no duty in regard to him, except to see that none of the light-fingered gentry should possess themselves of his star of the Legion of Honor. Nobody, save myself, so much as turned to look after him; nor, it grieves me to confess, could even I contrive to muster up any tolerable interest, even by reminiscences of all that the warlike spirit, formerly manifested within that now decrepit shape, had wrought upon our globe. There is no surer method of annihilating the magic influence of a great renown, than by exhibiting the possessor of it in the decline, the overthrow, the utter degradation of his powers—buried beneath his own mortality—and lacking even the qualities of sense, that enable the most ordinary men to bear themselves decently in the eye of the world. This is the state to which disease, aggravated by long endurance of a tropical climate, and assisted by old age—for he is now above seventy—has reduced Bonaparte. The British government has acted shrewdly, in re-transporting him from St. Helena to England. They should now restore him to Paris, and there let him once again review the relics of his armies. His eye is dull and rheumy; his nether lip hung down upon his chin. While I was observing him, there chanced to be a little extra bustle in the street; and he, the brother of Cæsar and Hannibal—the Great Captain, who had veiled the world in battle smoke, and tracked it round with bloody footsteps—was seized with a nervous trembling, and claimed the protection of the two policemen by a cracked and dolorous cry. The fellows winked at one another, laughed aside, and patting Napoleon on the back, took each an arm and led him away.

Death and fury! Ha, villain, how came you hither? Avaunt!—or I fling my inkstand at your head. Tush, tush; it is all a mistake. Pray, my dear friend, pardon this little outbreak. The fact is, the mention of those two policemen, and their custody of Bonaparte, had called up the idea of that odious wretch—you remember him well—who was pleased to take such gratuitous and impertinent care of my person, before I quitted New England. Forthwith, up rose before my mind's eye that same little white-washed room, with the iron-grated window—strange, that it should have been iron-grated—where, in too easy compliance with the absurd wishes of my relatives, I have wasted several good years of my life. Positively, it seemed to me that I was still sitting there, and that the keeper—not that he ever was my keeper neither, but only a kind of intrusive devil of a body-servant—had just peeped in at the door. The rascal! I owe him an old grudge, and will find a time to pay it yet! Fie, fie! The mere thought of him has exceedingly discomposed me. Even now, that hateful chamber—the iron-grated window, which blasted the blessed sunshine as it fell through the dusty panes, and made it poison to my soul—looks more distinct to my view than does this, my comfortable apartment in the heart of London. The reality—that which I know to be such—hangs like remnants of tattered scenery over the intolerably prominent illusion. Let us think of it no more.

You will be anxious to hear of Shelley. I need not say, what is known to all the world, that this celebrated poet has, for many years past, been reconciled to the Church of England. In his more recent works, he has applied his fine powers to the vindication of the Christian faith, with an especial view to that particular development. Latterly—as you may not have heard—he has taken orders, and been inducted to a small country living, in the gift of the Lord Chancellor. Just now, luckily for me, he has come to the metropolis to superintend the publication of a volume of discourses, treating of the poetico-philosophical proofs of Christianity, on the basis of the Thirty-nine Articles. On my first introduction, I felt no little embarrassment as to the manner of combining what I had to say to the author of Queen Mab, the Revolt of Islam, and Prometheus Unbound, with such acknowledgments as might be acceptable to a Christian minister, and zealous upholder of the Established Church. But Shelley soon placed me at my ease. Standing where he now does, and reviewing all his successive productions from a higher point, he assures me that there is a harmony, an order, a regular procession, which enables him to lay his hand upon any one of the earlier poems, and say, "This is my work!" with precisely the same complacency of conscience, wherewithal he contemplates the volume of discourses above-mentioned. They are like the successive steps of a staircase, the lowest of which, in the depth of chaos, is as essential to the support of the whole, as the highest and final one, resting upon the threshold of the heavens. I felt half inclined to ask him, what would have been his fate, had he perished on the lower steps of his staircase, instead of building his way aloft into the celestial brightness.

How all this may be, I neither pretend to understand nor greatly care, so long as Shelley has really climbed, as it seems he has, from a lower region to a loftier one. Without touching upon their religious merits, I consider the productions of his maturity superior, as poems, to those of his youth. They are warmer with human love, which has served as an interpreter between his mind and the multitude. The author has learned to dip his pen oftener into his heart, and has thereby avoided the faults into which a too exclusive use of fancy and intellect was wont to betray him. Formerly, his page was often little other than a concrete arrangement of crystallizations, or even of icicles, as cold as they were brilliant. Now, you take it to your heart, and are conscious of a heart-warmth responsive to your own. In his private character, Shelley can hardly have grown more gentle, kind and affectionate, than his friends always represented him to be, up to that disastrous night when he was drowned in the Mediterranean. Nonsense, again!—sheer nonsense! What am I babbling about? I was thinking of that old figment of his being lost in the Bay of Spezia, and washed ashore near Via Reggio, and burned to ashes on a funeral pyre, with wine and spices and frankincense; while Byron stood on the beach, and beheld a flame of marvellous beauty rise heavenward from the dead poet's heart; and that his fire-purified relics were finally buried near his child, in Roman earth. If all this happened three-and-twenty years ago, how could I have met the drowned, and burned, and buried man, here in London, only yesterday?

Before quitting the subject, I may mention that Dr. Reginald Heber, heretofore Bishop of Calcutta, but recently translated to a see in England, called on Shelley while I was with him. They appeared to be on terms of very cordial intimacy, and are said to have a joint poem in contemplation. What a strange, incongruous dream is the life of man!

Coleridge has at last finished his poem of Christabel; it will be issued entire, by old John Murray, in the course of the present publishing season. The poet, I hear, is visited with a troublesome affection of the tongue, which has put a period, or some lesser stop, to the life-long discourse that has hitherto been flowing from his lips. He will not survive it above a month, unless his accumulation of ideas be sluiced off in some other way. Wordsworth died only a week or two ago. Heaven rest his soul, and grant that he may not have completed the Excursion! Methinks I am sick of everything he wrote, except his Laodamia. It is very sad—this inconstancy of the mind to the poets whom it once worshipped. Southey is as hale as ever, and writes with his usual diligence. Old Gifford is still alive, in the extremity of age, and with most pitiable decay of what little sharp and narrow intellect the devil had gifted him withal. One hates to allow such a man the privilege of growing old and infirm. It takes away our speculative license of kicking him.

Keats? No; I have not seen him, except across a crowded street, with coaches, drays, horsemen, cabs, omnibuses, foot-passengers, and divers other sensual obstructions, intervening betwixt his small and slender figure and my eager glance. I would fain have met him on the sea-shore—or beneath a natural arch of forest trees—or the Gothic arch of an old cathedral—or among Grecian ruins—or at a glimmering fireside on the verge of evening—or at the twilight entrance of a cave, into the dreamy depths of which he would have led me by the hand; anywhere, in short, save at Temple Bar, where his presence was blotted out by the porter-swollen bulks of these gross Englishmen. I stood and watched him, fading away, fading away, along the pavement, and could hardly tell whether he were an actual man, or a thought that had slipped out of my mind, and clothed itself in human form and habiliments, merely to beguile me. At one moment he put his handkerchief to his lips, and withdrew it, I am almost certain, stained with blood. You never saw anything so fragile as his person. The truth is, Keats has all his life felt the effects of that terrible bleeding at the lungs, caused by the article on his Endymion, in the Quarterly Review, and which so nearly brought him to the grave. Ever since, he has glided about the world like a ghost, sighing a melancholy tone in the ear of here and there a friend, but never sending forth his voice to greet the multitude. I can hardly think him a great poet. The burthen of a mighty genius would never have been imposed upon shoulders so physically frail, and a spirit so infirmly sensitive. Great poets should have iron sinews.

Yet Keats, though for so many years he has given nothing to the world, is understood to have devoted himself to the composition of an epic poem. Some passages of it have been communicated to the inner circle of his admirers, and impressed them as the loftiest strains that have been audible on earth since Milton's days. If I can obtain copies of these specimens, I will ask you to present them to James Russell Lowell, who seems to be one of the poet's most fervent and worthiest worshippers. The information took me by surprise. I had supposed that all Keats's poetic incense, without being embodied in human language, floated up to heaven, and mingled with the songs of the immortal choristers, who perhaps were conscious of an unknown voice among them, and thought their melody the sweeter for it. But it is not so; he has positively written a poem on the subject of Paradise Regained, though in another sense than that which presented itself to the mind of Milton. In compliance, it may be imagined, with the dogma of those who pretend that all epic possibilities, in the past history of the world, are exhausted, Keats has thrown his poem forward into an indefinitely remote futurity. He pictures mankind amid the closing circumstances of the time-long warfare between Good and Evil. Our race is on the eve of its final triumph. Man is within the last stride of perfection; Woman, redeemed from the thraldom against which our Sybil uplifts so powerful and so sad a remonstrance, stands equal by his side, or communes for herself with angels; the Earth, sympathizing with her children's happier state, has clothed herself in such luxuriant and loving beauty as no eye ever witnessed since our first parents saw the sunrise over dewy Eden. Nor then, indeed; for this is the fulfilment of what was then but a golden promise. But the picture has its shadows. There remains to mankind another peril; a last encounter with the Evil Principle. Should the battle go against us, we sink back into the slime and misery of ages. If we triumph!—but it demands a poet's eye to contemplate the splendor of such a consummation, and not to be dazzled.

To this great work Keats is said to have brought so deep and tender a spirit of humanity, that the poem has all the sweet and warm interest of a village tale, no less than the grandeur which befits so high a theme. Such, at least, is the perhaps partial representation of his friends; for I have not read or heard even a single line of the performance in question. Keats, I am told, withholds it from the press, under an idea that the age has not enough of spiritual insight to receive it worthily. I do not like this distrust; it makes me distrust the poet. The Universe is waiting to respond to the highest word that the best child of time and immortality can utter. If it refuse to listen, it is because he mumbles and stammers, or discourses things unseasonable and foreign to the purpose.

I visited the House of Lords, the other day, to hear Canning, who, you know, is now a peer, with I forget what title. He disappointed me. Time blunts both point and edge, and does great mischief to men of his order of intellect. Then I stept into the Lower House, and listened to a few words from Cobbett, who looked as earthy as a real clodhopper, or, rather, as if he had lain a dozen years beneath the clods. The men, whom I meet now-a-days, often impress me thus; probably because my spirits are not very good, and lead me to think much about graves, with the long grass upon them, and weather-worn epitaphs, and dry bones of people who made noise enough in their day, but now can only clatter, clatter, clatter, when the sexton's spade disturbs them. Were it only possible to find out who are alive, and who dead, it would contribute infinitely to my peace of mind. Every day of my life, somebody comes and stares me in the face, whom I had quietly blotted out of the tablet of living men, and trusted never more to be pestered with the sight or sound of him. For instance, going to Drury Lane Theatre, a few evenings since, up rose before me, in the ghost of Hamlet's father, the bodily presence of the elder Kean, who did die, or ought to have died, in some drunken fit or other, so long ago that his fame is scarcely traditionary now. His powers are quite gone; he was rather the ghost of himself than the ghost of the Danish king.

In the stage-box sat several elderly and decrepit people, and among them a stately ruin of a woman, on a very large scale, with a profile—for I did not see her front face—that stamped itself into my brain, as a seal impresses hot wax. By the tragic gesture with which she took a pinch of snuff, I was sure it must be Mrs. Siddons. Her brother, John Kemble, sat behind, a broken-down figure, but still with a kingly majesty about him. In lieu of all former achievements, nature enables him to look the part of Lear far better than in the meridian of his genius. Charles Matthews was likewise there; but a paralytic affection has distorted his once mobile countenance into a most disagreeable one-sidedness, from which he could no more wrench it into proper form than he could re-arrange the face of the great globe itself. It looks as if, for the joke's sake, the poor man had twisted his features into an expression at once the most ludicrous and horrible that he could contrive; and, at that very moment, as a judgment for making himself so hideous, an avenging Providence had seen fit to petrify him. Since it is out of his own power, I would gladly assist him to change countenance; for his ugly visage haunts me both at noontide and night-time. Some other players of the past generation were present, but none that greatly interested me. It behoves actors, more than all other men of publicity, to vanish from the scene betimes. Being, at best, but painted shadows flickering on the wall, and empty sounds that echo another's thought, it is a sad disenchantment when the colors begin to fade, and the voices to croak with age.

What is there new, in the literary way, on your side of the water? Nothing of the kind has come under my inspection, except a volume of poems, published above a year ago, by Dr. Channing. I did not before know that this eminent writer is a poet; nor does the volume alluded to exhibit any of the characteristics of the author's mind, as displayed in his prose works; although some of the poems have a richness that is not merely of the surface, but glows still the brighter, the deeper and more faithfully you look into them. They seem carelessly wrought, however, like those rings and ornaments of the very purest gold, but of rude, native manufacture, which are found among the gold dust from Africa. I doubt whether the American public will accept them; it looks less to the assay of metal than to the neat and cunning manufacture. How slowly our literature grows up! Most of our writers of promise have come to untimely ends. There was that wild fellow, John Neal, who almost turned my boyish brain with his romances; he surely has long been dead, else he never could keep himself so quiet. Bryant has gone to his last sleep, with the Thanatopsis gleaming over him, like a sculptured marble sepulchre by moonlight. Halleck, who used to write queer verses in the newspapers, and published a Don Juanic poem called Fanny, is defunct as a poet, though averred to be exemplifying the metempsychosis as a man of business. Somewhat later there was Whittier, a fiery Quaker youth, to whom the muse had perversely assigned a battle-trumpet, and who got himself lynched, ten years agone, in South Carolina. I remember, too, a lad just from college, Longfellow by name, who scattered some delicate verses to the winds, and went to

Germany, and perished, I think, of intense application, at the University of Gottingen. Willis—what a pity!—was lost, if I recollect rightly, in 1833, on his voyage to Europe, whither he was going, to give us sketches of the world's sunny face. If these had lived, they might, one or all of them, have grown to be famous men.

And yet there is no telling—it may be as well that they have died. I was myself a young man of promise. Oh, shattered brain!—oh, broken spirit!—where is the fulfilment of that promise? The sad truth is, that when fate would gently disappoint the world, it takes away the hopefullest mortals in their youth;—when it would laugh the world's hopes to scorn, it lets them live. Let me die upon this apophthegm, for I shall never make a truer one!

What a strange substance is the human brain! Or rather—for there is no need of generalizing the remark—what an odd brain is mine! Would you believe it? Daily and nightly there come scraps of poetry humming in my intellectual ear—some as airy as bird-notes, and some as delicately neat as parlor-music, and a few as grand as organ-peals—that seem just such verses as those departed poets would have written, had not an inexorable destiny snatched them from their inkstands. They visit me in spirit, perhaps desiring to engage my services as the amanuensis of their posthumous productions, and thus secure the endless renown that they have forfeited by going hence too early. But I have my own business to attend to; and, besides, a medical gentleman, who interests himself in some little ailments of mine, advises me not to make too free use of pen and ink. There are clerks enough out of employment who would be glad of such a job.

Good bye! Are you alive or dead? And what are you about? Still scribbling for the Democratic? And do those infernal compositors and proof-readers misprint your unfortunate productions, as vilely as ever? It is too bad. Let every man manufacture his own nonsense, say I! Expect me home soon, and—to whisper you a secret—in company with the poet Campbell, who purposes to visit Wyoming, and enjoy the shadow of the laurels that he planted there. Campbell is now an old man. He calls himself well, better than ever in his life, but looks strangely pale, and so shadow-like, that one might almost poke a finger through his densest material. I tell him, by way of joke, that he is as dim and forlorn as Memory, though as unsubstantial as Hope.

Your true friend, P.

P.S. Pray present my most respectful regards to our venerable and revered friend, Mr. Brockden Brown. It gratifies me to learn that a complete edition of his works, in a double-columned octavo volume, is shortly to issue from the press, at Philadelphia. Tell him that no American writer enjoys a more classic reputation on this side of the water. *Is* old Joel Barlow yet alive? Unconscionable man! Why, he must have nearly fulfilled his century! And *does* he meditate an epic on the war between Mexico and Texas, with machinery contrived on the principle of the steam-engine, as being the nearest to celestial agency that our epoch can boast? How can he expect ever to rise again, if, while just sinking into his grave, he persists in burthening himself with such a ponderosity of leaden verses?

Main-street

A RESPECTABLE-LOOKING individual makes his bow, and addresses the public. In my daily walks along the principal street of my native town, it has often occurred to me, that, if its growth from infancy upward, and the vicissitude of characteristic scenes that have passed along this thoroughfare, during the more than two centuries of its existence, could be presented to the eye in a shifting panorama, it would be an exceedingly effective method of illustrating the march of time. Acting on this idea, I have contrived a certain pictorial exhibition, somewhat in the nature of a puppet-show, by means of which I propose to call up the multiform and many-colored Past before the spectator, and show him the ghosts of his forefathers, amid a succession of historic incidents, with no greater trouble than the turning of a crank. Be pleased, therefore, my indulgent patrons, to walk into the show-room, and take your seats before yonder mysterious curtain. The little wheels and springs of my machinery have been well oiled; a multitude of puppets are dressed in character, representing all varieties of fashion, from the Puritan cloak and jerkin to the latest Oak Hall coat; the lamps are trimmed, and shall brighten into noontide sunshine, or fade away in moonlight, or muffle their brilliancy in a November cloud, as the nature of the scene may require; and, in short, the exhibition is just ready to commence. Unless something should go wrong,—as, for instance, the misplacing of a picture, whereby the people and events of one century might be thrust into the middle of another; or the breaking of a wire, which would bring the course of time to a sudden period,— barring, I say, the casualties to which such a complicated piece of mechanism is liable, I flatter myself, ladies and gentlemen, that the performance will elicit your generous approbation.

Ting-a-ting-ting! goes the bell; the curtain rises; and we behold—not, indeed, the Main-street—but the tract of leaf-strewn forest-land, over which its dusty pavement is hereafter to extend.

You perceive, at a glance, that this is the ancient and primitive wood,—the ever-youthful and venerably old,—verdant with new twigs, yet hoary, as it were, with the snowfall of innumerable years, that have accumulated upon its intermingled branches. The white man's axe has never smitten a single tree; his footstep has never crumpled a single one of the withered leaves, which all the autumns since the flood have been harvesting beneath. Yet, see! along through the vista of impending boughs, there is already a faintly-traced path, running nearly east and west, as if a prophecy or foreboding of the future street had stolen into the heart of the solemn old wood. Onward goes this hardly perceptible track, now ascending over a natural swell of land, now subsiding gently into a hollow; traversed here by a little streamlet, which glitters like a snake through the gleam of sunshine, and quickly hides itself among the underbrush, in its quest for the neighboring cove; and impeded there by the massy corpse of a giant of the forest, which had lived out its incalculable term of life, and been overthrown by mere old age, and lies buried in the new vegetation that is born of its decay. What footsteps can have worn this half-seen path? Hark! Do we not hear them now rustling softly over the leaves? We discern an Indian woman—a majestic and queenly woman, or else her spectral image does not represent her truly—for this is the great Squaw Sachem, whose rule, with that of her sons, extends from Mystic to Agawam. That red chief, who stalks by her side, is Wappacowet, her second husband, the priest and magician, whose incantations shall hereafter affright the pale-faced settlers with grisly phantoms, dancing and shrieking in the woods, at midnight. But greater would be the affright of the Indian necromancer, if, mirrored in the pool of water at his feet, he could catch a prophetic glimpse of the noon-day marvels which the white man is destined to achieve; if he could see, as in a dream, the stone-front of the stately hall, which will cast its shadow over this very spot; if he could be aware that the future edifice will contain a noble Museum, where, among countless curiosities of earth and sea, a few Indian arrow-heads shall be treasured up as memorials of a vanished race!

No such forebodings disturb the Squaw Sachem and Wappacowet. They pass on, beneath the tangled shade, holding high talk on matters of state and religion, and imagine, doubtless, that their own system of affairs will endure for ever. Meanwhile, how full of its own proper life is the scene that lies around them! The gray squirrel runs up the trees, and rustles among the upper branches. Was not that the leap of a deer? And there is the whirr of a partridge! Methinks, too, I catch the cruel and stealthy eye of a wolf, as he draws back into yonder impervious density of underbrush. So, there, amid the murmur of boughs, go the Indian queen and the Indian priest; while the gloom of the broad wilderness impends over them, and its sombre mystery invests them as with something preternatural; and only momentary streaks of quivering sunlight, once in a great while, find their way down, and glimmer among the feathers in their dusky hair. Can it be that the thronged street of a city will ever pass into this twilight solitude,—over those soft heaps of the decaying tree-trunks,—and through the swampy places, green with water-moss,—and penetrate that hopeless entanglement of great trees, which have been uprooted and tossed together by a whirlwind! It has been a wilderness from the creation. Must it not be a wilderness for ever?

Here an acidulous-looking gentleman in blue glasses, with bows of Berlin steel, who has taken a seat at the extremity of the front row, begins, at this early stage of the exhibition, to criticise.

"The whole affair is a manifest catch-penny," observes he, scarcely under his breath. "The trees look more like weeds in a garden, than a primitive forest; the Squaw Sachem and Wappacowet are stiff in their pasteboard joints; and the squirrels, the deer, and the wolf, move with all the grace of a child's wooden monkey, sliding up and down a stick."

"I am obliged to you, sir, for the candor of your remarks," replies the showman, with a bow. "Perhaps they are just. Human art has its limits, and we must now and then ask a little aid from the spectator's imagination."

"You will get no such aid from mine," responds the critic. "I make it a point to see things precisely as they are. But come! go ahead!—the stage is waiting!"

The showman proceeds.

Casting our eyes again over the scene, we perceive that strangers have found their way into the solitary place. In more than one spot, among the trees, an upheaved axe is glittering in the sunshine. Roger Conant, the first settler in Naumkeag, has built his dwelling, months ago, on the border of the forest-path; and at this moment he comes eastward through the vista of woods, with his gun over his shoulder, bringing home the choice portions of a deer. His stalwart figure, clad in a leathern jerkin and breeches of the same, strides sturdily onward, with such an air of physical force and energy, that we might almost expect the very trees to stand aside, and give him room to pass. And so, indeed, they must; for, humble as is his name in history, Roger Conant still is of that class of men who do not merely find, but make, their place in the system of human affairs: a man of thoughtful strength, he has planted the germ of a city. There stands his habitation, showing in its rough architecture some features of the Indian wigwam, and some of the log-cabin, and somewhat, too, of the straw-thatched cottage in Old England, where this good yeoman had his birth and breeding. The dwelling is surrounded by a cleared space of a few acres, where Indian corn grows thrivingly among the stumps of the trees; while the dark forest hems it in, and seems to gaze silently and solemnly, as if wondering at the breadth of sunshine which the white man spreads around him. An Indian, half hidden in the dusky shade, is gazing and wondering too.

Within the door of the cottage, you discern the wife, with her ruddy English cheek. She is singing, doubtless, a psalm-tune, at her household work; or perhaps she sighs at the remembrance of the cheerful gossip, and all the merry social life, of her native village beyond the vast and melancholy sea. Yet the next moment she laughs, with sympathetic glee, at the sports of her little tribe of children, and soon turns round, with the home-look in her face, as her husband's foot is heard approaching the rough-hewn threshold. How sweet must it be for those who have an Eden in their hearts, like Roger Conant and his wife, to find a new world to project it into, as they have; instead of dwelling among old haunts of men, where so many household fires have been kindled and burnt out, that the very glow of happiness has something dreary in it! Not that this pair are alone in their wild Eden; for here comes Goodwife Massey, the young spouse of Jeffrey Massey, from her home hard by, with an infant at her breast. Dame Conant has another of like age; and it shall hereafter be one of the disputed points of history, which of these two babies was the first town-born child.

But see! Roger Conant has other neighbors within view. Peter Palfrey likewise has built himself a house, and so has Balch and Norman and Woodbury. Their dwellings, indeed, —such is the ingenious contrivance of this piece of pictorial mechanism,—seem to have arisen, at various points of the scene, even while we have been looking at it. The forest-track, trodden more and more by the hob-nailed shoes of these sturdy and ponderous Englishmen, has now a distinctness which it never could have acquired from the light tread of a hundred times as many Indian moccasins. It will be a street, anon. As we observe it now, it goes onward from one clearing to another, here plunging into a shadowy strip of woods, there open to the sunshine, but everywhere showing a decided line, along which human interests have begun to hold their career. Over yonder swampy spot, two trees have been felled, and laid side by side, to make a causeway. In another place, the axe has cleared away a confused intricacy of fallen trees and clustered boughs, which had been tossed together by a hurricane. So, now, the little children, just beginning to run alone, may trip along the path, and not often stumble over an impediment, unless they stray from it to gather wood-berries beneath the trees. And, besides the feet of grown people and children, there are the cloven hoofs of a small herd of cows, who seek their subsistence from the native grasses, and help to deepen the track of the future thoroughfare. Goats also browse along it, and nibble at the twigs that thrust themselves across the way. Not seldom, in its more secluded portions, where the black shadow of the forest strives to hide the trace of human footsteps, stalks a gaunt wolf, on the watch for a kid or a young calf; or fixes his hungry gaze on the group of children gathering berries, and can hardly forbear to rush upon them. And the Indians, coming from their distant wigwams to view the white man's settlement, marvel at the deep track which he makes, and perhaps are saddened by a flitting presentiment, that this heavy tread will find its way over all the land; and that the wild woods, the wild wolf, and the wild Indian, will alike be trampled beneath it. Even so shall it be. The pavements of the Main-street must be laid over the red man's grave.

Behold! here is a spectacle which should be ushered in by the peal of trumpets, if Naumkeag had ever yet heard that cheery music, and by the roar of cannon, echoing among the woods. A procession—for, by its dignity, as marking an epoch in the history of the street, it deserves that name—a procession advances along the pathway. The good ship Abigail has arrived from England, bringing wares and merchandise, for the comfort of the inhabitants, and traffic with the Indians; bringing passengers too, and, more important than all, a Governor for the new settlement. Roger Conant and Peter Palfrey, with their companions, have been to the shore to welcome him; and now, with such honor and triumph as their rude way of life permits, are escorting the sea-flushed voyagers to their habitations. At the point where Endicott enters upon the scene, two venerable trees unite their branches high above his head; thus forming a triumphal arch of living verdure, beneath which he pauses, with his wife leaning on his arm, to catch the first impression of their new-found home. The old settlers gaze not less earnestly at him, than he at the hoary woods and the rough surface of the clearings. They like his bearded face, under the shadow of the broad-brimmed and steeple-crowned Puritan hat;—a visage, resolute, grave, and thoughtful, yet apt to kindle with that glow of a cheerful spirit, by which men of strong character are enabled to go joyfully on their proper tasks. His form, too, as you see it, in a doublet and hose of sad-colored cloth, is of a manly make, fit for toil and hardship, and fit to wield the heavy sword that hangs from his leathern belt. His aspect is a better warrant for the ruler's office, than the parchment commission which he bears, however fortified it may be with the broad seal of the London council. Peter Palfrey nods to Roger Conant. "The worshipful Court of Assistants have done wisely," say they between themselves. "They have chosen for our governor a man out of a thousand." Then they toss up their hats,—they, and all the uncouth figures of their company, most of whom are clad in skins, inasmuch as their old kersey and linsey-woolsey garments have been torn and tattered by many a long month's wear,—they all toss up their hats, and salute their new governor and captain with a hearty English shout of welcome. We seem to hear it with our own ears; so perfectly is the action represented in this life-like, this almost magic picture!

But have you observed the lady who leans upon the arm of Endicott?— a rose of beauty from an English garden, now to be transplanted to a fresher soil. It may be, that, long years— centuries, indeed—after this fair flower shall have decayed, other flowers of the same race will appear in the same soil, and gladden other generations with hereditary beauty. Does not the vision haunt us yet? Has not Nature kept the mould unbroken, deeming it a pity that the idea should vanish from mortal sight for ever, after only once assuming earthly substance? Do we not recognize, in that fair woman's face, the model of features which still beam, at happy moments, on what was then the woodland pathway, but has long since grown into a busy street?

"This is too ridiculous!—positively insufferable!" mutters the same critic who had before expressed his disapprobation. "Here is a pasteboard figure, such as a child would cut out of a card, with a pair of very dull scissors; and the fellow modestly requests us to see in it the prototype of hereditary beauty!"

"But, sir, you have not the proper point of view," remarks the showman. "You sit altogether too near to get the best effect of my pictorial exhibition. Pray, oblige me by removing to this other bench; and, I venture to assure you, the proper light and shadow will transform the spectacle into quite another thing."

"Pshaw!" replies the critic: "I want no other light and shade. I have already told you, that it is my business to see things just as they are."

"I would suggest to the author of this ingenious exhibition," observes a gentlemanly person, who has shown signs of being much interested,—"I would suggest, that Anna Gower, the first wife of Governor Endicott, and who came with him from England, left no posterity; and that, consequently, we cannot be indebted to that honorable lady for any specimens of feminine loveliness, now extant among us."

Having nothing to allege against this genealogical objection, the showman points again to the scene.

During this little interruption, you perceive that the Anglo-Saxon energy—as the phrase now goes—has been at work in the spectacle before us. So many chimneys now send up their smoke, that it begins to have the aspect of a village street; although every thing is so inartificial and inceptive, that it seems as if one returning wave of the wild nature might overwhelm it all. But the one edifice, which gives the pledge of permanence to this bold enterprise, is seen at the central point of the picture. There stands the meeting-house, a small structure, low-roofed, without a spire, and built of rough timber, newly hewn, with the sap still in the logs, and here and there a strip of bark adhering to them. A meaner temple was never consecrated to the worship of the Deity. With the alternative of kneeling beneath the awful vault of the firmament, it is strange that men should creep into this pent-up nook, and expect God's presence there. Such, at least, one would imagine, might be the feeling of these forest-settlers, accustomed, as they had been, to stand under the dim arches of vast cathedrals, and to offer up their hereditary worship in the old, ivy-covered churches of rural England, around which lay the bones of many generations of their forefathers. How could they dispense with the carved altar-work?—how, with the pictured windows, where the light of common day was hallowed by being transmitted through the glorified figures of saints?—how, with the lofty roof, imbued, as it must have been, with the prayers that had gone upward for centuries?—how, with the rich peal of the solemn organ, rolling along the aisles, pervading the whole church, and sweeping the soul away on a flood of audible religion? They needed nothing of all this. Their house of worship, like their ceremonial, was naked, simple, and severe. But the zeal of a recovered faith burned like a lamp within their hearts, enriching every thing around them with its radiance; making of these new walls, and this narrow compass, its own cathedral; and being, in itself, that spiritual mystery and experience, of which sacred architecture, pictured windows, and the organ's grand so-

lemnity, are remote and imperfect symbols. All was well, so
long as their lamps were freshly kindled at the heavenly flame.
After a while, however, whether in their time or their children's, these lamps began to burn more dimly, or with a less
genuine lustre; and then it might be seen, how hard, cold,
and confined, was their system,—how like an iron cage was
that which they called Liberty!

Too much of this. Look again at the picture, and observe
how the aforesaid Anglo-Saxon energy is now trampling
along the street, and raising a positive cloud of dust beneath
its sturdy footsteps. For there the carpenters are building a
new house, the frame of which was hewn and fitted in England, of English oak, and sent hither on shipboard; and here
a blacksmith makes huge clang and clatter on his anvil, shaping out tools and weapons; and yonder a wheelwright, who
boasts himself a London workman, regularly bred to his
handicraft, is fashioning a set of wagon-wheels, the track of
which shall soon be visible. The wild forest is shrinking back;
the street has lost the aromatic odor of the pine-trees, and of
the sweet fern that grew beneath them. The tender and modest wild-flowers, those gentle children of savage nature that
grew pale beneath the ever-brooding shade, have shrunk away
and disappeared, like stars that vanish in the breadth of light.
Gardens are fenced in, and display pumpkin-beds and rows of
cabbages and beans; and, though the governor and the minister both view them with a disapproving eye, plants of
broad-leaved tobacco, which the cultivators are enjoined to
use privily, or not at all. No wolf, for a year past, has been
heard to bark, or known to range among the dwellings, except that single one whose grisly head, with a plash of blood
beneath it, is now affixed to the portal of the meeting-house.
The partridge has ceased to run across the too-frequented
path. Of all the wild life that used to throng here, only the
Indians still come into the settlement, bringing the skins of
beaver and otter, bear and elk, which they sell to Endicott for
the wares of England. And there is little John Massey, the son
of Jeffrey Massey and first-born of Naumkeag, playing beside
his father's threshold, a child of six or seven years old. Which
is the better-grown infant,—the town or the boy?

The red men have become aware, that the street is no

longer free to them, save by the sufferance and permission of the settlers. Often, to impress them with an awe of English power, there is a muster and training of the town-forces, and a stately march of the mail-clad band, like this which we now see advancing up the street. There they come, fifty of them, or more; all with their iron breastplates and steel-caps well burnished, and glimmering bravely against the sun; their ponderous muskets on their shoulders, their bandaliers about their waists, their lighted matches in their hands, and the drum and fife playing cheerily before them. See! do they not step like martial men? Do they not manœuvre like soldiers who have seen stricken fields? And well they may; for this band is composed of precisely such materials as those with which Cromwell is preparing to beat down the strength of a kingdom; and his famous regiment of Ironsides might be recruited from just such men. In every thing, at this period, New England was the essential spirit and flower of that which was about to become uppermost in the mother-country. Many a bold and wise man lost the fame which would have accrued to him in English history, by crossing the Atlantic with our forefathers. Many a valiant captain, who might have been foremost at Marston Moor or Naseby, exhausted his martial ardor in the command of a log-built fortress, like that which you observe on the gently rising ground at the right of the pathway,—its banner fluttering in the breeze, and the culverins and sakers showing their deadly muzzles over the rampart.

A multitude of people were now thronging to New England; some, because the ancient and ponderous frame-work of Church and State threatened to crumble down upon their heads; others, because they despaired of such a downfall. Among those who came to Naumkeag were men of history and legend, whose feet leave a track of brightness along any pathway which they have trodden. You shall behold their life-like images,—their spectres, if you choose so to call them,— passing, encountering with a familiar nod, stopping to converse together, praying, bearing weapons, laboring or resting from their labors, in the Main-street. Here, now, comes Hugh Peters, an earnest, restless man, walking swiftly, as being impelled by that fiery activity of nature which shall hereafter thrust him into the conflict of dangerous affairs, make him the chaplain and counsellor of Cromwell, and finally bring him to a bloody end. He pauses, by the meeting-house, to exchange a greeting with Roger Williams, whose face indicates, methinks, a gentler spirit, kinder and more expansive, than that of Peters; yet not less active for what he discerns to be the will of God, or the welfare of mankind. And look! here is a guest for Endicott, coming forth out of the forest, through which he has been journeying from Boston, and which, with its rude branches, has caught hold of his attire, and has wet his feet with its swamps and streams. Still there is something in his mild and venerable, though not aged presence,—a propriety, an equilibrium in Governor Winthrop's nature,—that causes the disarray of his costume to be unnoticed, and gives us the same impression as if he were clad in such grave and rich attire as we may suppose him to have worn in the Council Chamber of the colony. Is not this characteristic wonderfully perceptible in our spectral representative of his person? But what dignitary is this crossing from the other side to greet the governor? A stately personage, in a dark velvet cloak, with a hoary beard, and a gold chain across his breast; he has the authoritative port of one who has filled the highest civic station in the first of cities. Of all men in the world, we should least expect to meet the Lord Mayor of London—as Sir Richard Saltonstall has been, once and again—in a forest-bordered settlement of the western wilderness.

Farther down the street, we see Emanuel Downing, a grave and worthy citizen, with his son George, a stripling who has a career before him; his shrewd and quick capacity and pliant conscience shall not only exalt him high, but secure him from a downfall. Here is another figure, on whose characteristic make and expressive action I will stake the credit of my pictorial puppet-show. Have you not already detected a quaint, sly humor in that face,—an eccentricity in the manner,—a certain indescribable waywardness,—all the marks, in short, of an original man, unmistakeably impressed, yet kept down by a sense of clerical restraint? That is Nathaniel Ward, the minister of Ipswich, but better remembered as the simple cobbler of Agawam. He hammered his sole so faithfully, and

stitched his upper-leather so well, that the shoe is hardly yet
worn out, though thrown aside for some two centuries past.
And next, among these Puritans and Roundheads, we observe
the very model of a Cavalier, with the curling lovelock, the
fantastically trimmed beard, the embroidery, the ornamented
rapier, the gilded dagger, and all other foppishnesses that distinguished the wild gallants who rode headlong to their overthrow in the cause of King Charles. This is Morton of Merry
Mount, who has come hither to hold a council with Endicott,
but will shortly be his prisoner. Yonder pale, decaying figure
of a white-robed woman who glides slowly along the street,
is the Lady Arabella, looking for her own grave in the virgin
soil. That other female form, who seems to be talking—we
might almost say preaching or expounding—in the centre of
a group of profoundly attentive auditors, is Ann Hutchinson.
And here comes Vane.——

"But, my dear sir," interrupts the same gentleman who before questioned the showman's genealogical accuracy, "allow
me to observe, that these historical personages could not possibly have met together in the Main-street. They might, and
probably did, all visit our old town, at one time or another,
but not simultaneously; and you have fallen into anachro-
nisms that I positively shudder to think of!"

"The fellow," adds the scarcely civil critic, "has learned a
bead-roll of historic names, whom he lugs into his pictorial
puppet-show, as he calls it, helter-skelter, without caring
whether they were contemporaries or not,—and sets them all
by the ears together. But was there ever such a fund of im-
pudence! To hear his running commentary, you would suppose that these miserable slips of painted pasteboard, with
hardly the remotest outlines of the human figure, had all the
character and expression of Michael Angelo's pictures.
Well!—go on, sir!"

"Sir, you break the illusion of the scene," mildly remon-
strates the showman.

"Illusion! What illusion?" rejoins the critic, with a contemptuous snort. "On the word of a gentleman, I see nothing
illusive in the wretchedly bedaubed sheet of canvass that
forms your back-ground, or in these pasteboard slips that
hitch and jerk along the front. The only illusion, permit me

to say, is in the puppet-showman's tongue,—and that but a wretched one, into the bargain!"

"We public men," replies the showman, meekly, "must lay our account, sometimes, to meet an uncandid severity of criticism. But—merely for your own pleasure, sir—let me entreat you to take another point of view. Sit further back, by that young lady, in whose face I have watched the reflection of every changing scene; only oblige me by sitting there; and, take my word for it, the slips of pasteboard shall assume spiritual life, and the bedaubed canvass become an airy and changeable reflex of what it purports to represent."

"I know better," retorts the critic, settling himself in his seat, with sullen, but self-complacent immovableness. "And, as for my own pleasure, I shall best consult it by remaining precisely where I am."

The showman bows, and waves his hand; and, at the signal, as if time and vicissitude had been awaiting his permission to move onward, the mimic street becomes alive again.

Years have rolled over our scene, and converted the forest-track into a dusty thoroughfare, which, being intersected with lanes and cross-paths, may fairly be designated as the Main-street. On the ground-sites of many of the log-built sheds, into which the first settlers crept for shelter, houses of quaint architecture have now risen. These later edifices are built, as you see, in one generally accordant style, though with such subordinate variety as keeps the beholder's curiosity excited, and causes each structure, like its owner's character, to produce its own peculiar impression. Most of them have one huge chimney in the centre, with flues so vast that it must have been easy for the witches to fly out of them, as they were wont to do, when bound on an aerial visit to the Black Man in the forest. Around this great chimney the wooden house clusters itself, in a whole community of gable-ends, each ascending into its own separate peak; the second story, with its lattice-windows, projecting over the first; and the door, which is perhaps arched, provided on the outside with an iron hammer, wherewith the visitor's hand may give a thundering rat-a-tat. The timber frame-work of these houses, as compared with those of recent date, is like the skeleton of an old giant, beside the frail bones of a modern man of fash-

ion. Many of them, by the vast strength and soundness of
their oaken substance, have been preserved through a length
of time which would have tried the stability of brick and
stone; so that, in all the progressive decay and continual re-
construction of the street, down to our own days, we shall
still behold these old edifices occupying their long-accus-
tomed sites. For instance, on the upper corner of that green
lane which shall hereafter be North-street, we see the Curwen
House, newly built, with the carpenters still at work on the
roof, nailing down the last sheaf of shingles. On the lower
corner stands another dwelling,—destined, at some period of
its existence, to be the abode of an unsuccessful alchymist,—
which shall likewise survive to our own generation, and perhaps long outlive it. Thus, through the medium of these patriarchal edifices, we have now established a sort of kindred
and hereditary acquaintance with the Main-street.

Great as is the transformation produced by a short term of
years, each single day creeps through the Puritan settlement
sluggishly enough. It shall pass before your eyes, condensed
into the space of a few moments. The gray light of early
morning is slowly diffusing itself over the scene; and the bellman, whose office it is to cry the hour at the street-corners,
rings the last peal upon his hand-bell, and goes wearily home-
wards, with the owls, the bats, and other creatures of the
night. Lattices are thrust back on their hinges, as if the town
were opening its eyes, in the summer morning. Forth stum-
bles the still drowsy cow-herd, with his horn; putting which
to his lips, it emits a bellowing bray, impossible to be represented in the picture, but which reaches the pricked-up ears
of every cow in the settlement, and tells her that the dewy
pasture-hour is come. House after house awakes, and sends
the smoke up curling from its chimney, like frosty breath
from living nostrils; and as those white wreaths of smoke,
though impregnated with earthy admixtures, climb skyward,
so, from each dwelling, does the morning worship—its spiritual essence bearing up its human imperfection—find its way
to the heavenly Father's throne.

The breakfast-hour being past, the inhabitants do not, as
usual, go to their fields or workshops, but remain within
doors; or perhaps walk the street, with a grave sobriety, yet

a disengaged and unburthened aspect, that belongs neither
to a holiday nor a Sabbath. And, indeed, this passing day is
neither, nor is it a common week-day, although partaking of
all the three. It is the Thursday Lecture; an institution which
New England has long ago relinquished, and almost forgotten, yet which it would have been better to retain, as bearing
relations to both the spiritual and ordinary life, and bringing
each acquainted with the other. The tokens of its observance,
however, which here meet our eyes, are of rather a questionable cast. It is, in one sense, a day of public shame; the day
on which transgressors, who have made themselves liable to
the minor severities of the Puritan law, receive their reward
of ignominy. At this very moment, the constable has bound
an idle fellow to the whipping-post, and is giving him his
deserts with a cat-o'-nine-tails. Ever since sunrise, Daniel Fair-
field has been standing on the steps of the meeting-house,
with a halter about his neck, which he is condemned to wear
visibly throughout his lifetime; Dorothy Talby is chained to
a post at the corner of Prison Lane, with the hot sun blazing
on her matronly face, and all for no other offence than lifting
her hand against her husband; while, through the bars of
that great wooden cage, in the centre of the scene, we discern
either a human being or a wild beast, or both in one, whom
this public infamy causes to roar, and gnash his teeth, and
shake the strong oaken bars, as if he would break forth, and
tear in pieces the little children who have been peeping at
him. Such are the profitable sights that serve the good people
to while away the earlier part of lecture-day. Betimes in the
forenoon, a traveller—the first traveller that has come hitherward this morning—rides slowly into the street, on his patient steed. He seems a clergyman; and, as he draws near, we
recognize the minister of Lynn, who was pre-engaged to lecture here, and has been revolving his discourse, as he rode
through the hoary wilderness. Behold, now, the whole town
thronging into the meeting-house, mostly with such sombre
visages, that the sunshine becomes little better than a shadow,
when it falls upon them. There go the Thirteen Men, grim
rulers of a grim community! There goes John Massey, the
first town-born child, now a youth of twenty, whose eye wanders with peculiar interest towards that buxom damsel who

comes up the steps at the same instant. There hobbles Goody Foster, a sour and bitter old beldam, looking as if she went to curse, and not to pray, and whom many of her neighbors suspect of taking an occasional airing on a broomstick. There, too, slinking shamefacedly in, you observe that same poor do-nothing and good-for-nothing, whom we saw castigated just now at the whipping-post. Last of all, there goes the tithing-man, lugging in a couple of small boys, whom he has caught at play beneath God's blessed sunshine, in a back lane. What native of Naumkeag, whose recollections go back more than thirty years, does not still shudder at that dark ogre of his infancy, who perhaps had long ceased to have an actual existence, but still lived in his childish belief, in a horrible idea, and in the nurse's threat, as the Tidy Man!

It will be hardly worth our while to wait two, or it may be three, turnings of the hour-glass, for the conclusion of the lecture. Therefore, by my control over light and darkness, I cause the dusk, and then the starless night, to brood over the street; and summon forth again the bellman, with his lantern casting a gleam about his footsteps, to pace wearily from corner to corner, and shout drowsily the hour to drowsy or dreaming ears. Happy are we, if for nothing else, yet because we did not live in those days. In truth, when the first novelty and stir of spirit had subsided,—when the new settlement, between the forest-border and the sea, had become actually a little town,—its daily life must have trudged onward with hardly any thing to diversify and enliven it, while also its rigidity could not fail to cause miserable distortions of the moral nature. Such a life was sinister to the intellect, and sinister to the heart; especially when one generation had bequeathed its religious gloom, and the counterfeit of its religious ardor, to the next; for these characteristics, as was inevitable, assumed the form both of hypocrisy and exaggeration, by being inherited from the example and precept of other human beings, and not from an original and spiritual source. The sons and grandchildren of the first settlers were a race of lower and narrower souls than their progenitors had been. The latter were stern, severe, intolerant, but not superstitious, not even fanatical; and endowed, if any men of that age were, with a far-seeing worldly sagacity. But it was im-

possible for the succeeding race to grow up, in Heaven's freedom, beneath the discipline which their gloomy energy of
character had established; nor, it may be, have we even yet
thrown off all the unfavorable influences which, among many
good ones, were bequeathed to us by our Puritan forefathers.
Let us thank God for having given us such ancestors; and let
each successive generation thank him, not less fervently, for
being one step further from them in the march of ages.

"What is all this?" cries the critic. "A sermon? If so, it is
not in the bill."

"Very true," replies the showman; "and I ask pardon of the
audience."

Look now at the street, and observe a strange people entering it. Their garments are torn and disordered, their faces
haggard, their figures emaciated; for they have made their
way hither through pathless deserts, suffering hunger and
hardship, with no other shelter than a hollow tree, the lair of
a wild beast, or an Indian wigwam. Nor, in the most inhospitable and dangerous of such lodging-places, was there half
the peril that awaits them in this thoroughfare of Christian
men, with those secure dwellings and warm hearths on either
side of it, and yonder meeting-house as the central object of
the scene. These wanderers have received from Heaven a gift
that, in all epochs of the world, has brought with it the penalties of mortal suffering and persecution, scorn, enmity, and
death itself;—a gift that, thus terrible to its possessors, has
ever been most hateful to all other men, since its very existence seems to threaten the overthrow of whatever else the
toilsome ages have built up;—the gift of a new idea. You can
discern it in them, illuminating their faces—their whole persons, indeed, however earthly and cloddish—with a light that
inevitably shines through, and makes the startled community
aware that these men are not as they themselves are; not
brethren nor neighbors of their thought. Forthwith, it is as if
an earthquake rumbled through the town, making its vibrations felt at every hearthstone, and especially causing the spire
of the meeting-house to totter. The Quakers have come! We
are in peril! See! they trample upon our wise and well-established laws in the person of our chief magistrate; for Governor Endicott is passing, now an aged man, and dignified with

long habits of authority,—and not one of the irreverent vagabonds has moved his hat! Did you note the ominous frown
of the white-bearded Puritan governor, as he turned himself
about, and, in his anger, half uplifted the staff that has become a needful support to his old age? Here comes old Mr.
Norris, our venerable minister. Will they doff their hats, and
pay reverence to him? No: their hats stick fast to their ungracious heads, as if they grew there; and—impious varlets that
they are, and worse than the heathen Indians!—they eye our
reverend pastor with a peculiar scorn, distrust, unbelief, and
utter denial of his sanctified pretensions, of which he himself
immediately becomes conscious; the more bitterly conscious,
as he never knew nor dreamed of the like before.

But look yonder! Can we believe our eyes? A Quaker
woman, clad in sackcloth, and with ashes on her head, has
mounted the steps of the meeting-house. She addresses the
people in a wild, shrill voice,—wild and shrill it must be, to
suit such a figure,—which makes them tremble and turn pale,
although they crowd open-mouthed to hear her. She is bold
against established authority; she denounces the priest and his
steeple-house. Many of her hearers are appalled; some weep;
and others listen with a rapt attention, as if a living truth had
now, for the first time, forced its way through the crust of
habit, reached their hearts, and awakened them to life. This
matter must be looked to; else we have brought our faith
across the seas with us in vain; and it had been better that the
old forest were still standing here, waving its tangled boughs,
and murmuring to the sky out of its desolate recesses, instead
of this goodly street, if such blasphemies be spoken in it.

So thought the old Puritans. What was their mode of action may be partly judged from the spectacles which now pass
before your eyes. Joshua Buffum is standing in the pillory.
Cassandra Southwick is led to prison. And there a woman,—
it is Ann Coleman,—naked from the waist upward, and
bound to the tail of a cart, is dragged through the Main-street
at the pace of a brisk walk, while the constable follows with
a whip of knotted cords. A strong-armed fellow is that constable; and each time that he flourishes his lash in the air, you
see a frown wrinkling and twisting his brow, and, at the same
instant, a smile upon his lips. He loves his business, faithful

officer that he is, and puts his soul into every stroke, zealous to fulfil the injunction of Major Hawthorne's warrant, in the spirit and to the letter. There came down a stroke that has drawn blood! Ten such stripes are to be given in Salem, ten in Boston, and ten in Dedham; and, with those thirty stripes of blood upon her, she is to be driven into the forest. The crimson trail goes wavering along the Main-street; but Heaven grant, that, as the rain of so many years has wept upon it, time after time, and washed it all away, so there may have been a dew of mercy, to cleanse this cruel blood-stain out of the record of the persecutor's life!

Pass on, thou spectral constable, and betake thee to thine own place of torment! Meanwhile, by the silent operation of the mechanism behind the scenes, a considerable space of time would seem to have lapsed over the street. The older dwellings now begin to look weather-beaten, through the effect of the many eastern storms that have moistened their unpainted shingles and clapboards, for not less than forty years. Such is the age we would assign to the town, judging by the aspect of John Massey, the first town-born child, whom his neighbors now call Goodman Massey, and whom we see yonder, a grave, almost autumnal-looking man, with children of his own about him. To the patriarchs of the settlement, no doubt, the Main-street is still but an affair of yesterday, hardly more antique, even if destined to be more permanent, than a path shovelled through the snow. But to the middle-aged and elderly men who came hither in childhood or early youth, it presents the aspect of a long and well-established work, on which they have expended the strength and ardor of their life. And the younger people, native to the street, whose earliest recollections are of creeping over the paternal threshold, and rolling on the grassy margin of the track, look at it as one of the perdurable things of our mortal state,—as old as the hills of the great pasture, or the headland at the harbor's mouth. Their fathers and grandsires tell them, how, within a few years past, the forest stood here with but a lonely track beneath its tangled shade. Vain legend! They cannot make it true and real to their conceptions. With them, moreover, the Main-street is a street indeed, worthy to hold its way with the thronged and stately avenues of cities beyond the sea. The old

Puritans tell them of the crowds that hurry along Cheapside and Fleet-street and the Strand, and of the rush of tumultuous life at Temple Bar. They describe London Bridge, itself a street, with a row of houses on each side. They speak of the vast structure of the Tower, and the solemn grandeur of Westminster Abbey. The children listen, and still inquire if the streets of London are longer and broader than the one before their father's door; if the Tower is bigger than the jail in Prison Lane; if the old Abbey will hold a larger congregation than our meeting-house. Nothing impresses them, except their own experience.

It seems all a fable, too, that wolves have ever prowled here; and not less so, that the Squaw Sachem, and the Sagamore her son, once ruled over this region, and treated as sovereign potentates with the English settlers, then so few and storm-beaten, now so powerful. There stand some schoolboys, you observe, in a little group around a drunken Indian, himself a prince of the Squaw Sachem's lineage. He brought hither some beaver-skins for sale, and has already swallowed the larger portion of their price, in deadly draughts of firewater. Is there not a touch of pathos in that picture? and does it not go far towards telling the whole story of the vast growth and prosperity of one race, and the fated decay of another?—the children of the stranger making game of the great Squaw Sachem's grandson!

But the whole race of red men have not vanished with that wild princess and her posterity. This march of soldiers along the street betokens the breaking out of King Philip's war; and these young men, the flower of Essex, are on their way to defend the villages on the Connecticut; where, at Bloody Brook, a terrible blow shall be smitten, and hardly one of that gallant band be left alive. And there, at that stately mansion, with its three peaks in front, and its two little peaked towers, one on either side of the door, we see brave Captain Gardner issuing forth, clad in his embroidered buff-coat, and his plumed cap upon his head. His trusty sword, in its steel scabbard, strikes clanking on the door-step. See how the people throng to their doors and windows, as the cavalier rides past, reining his mettled steed so gallantly, and looking so like the very soul and emblem of martial achievement,—destined,

too, to meet a warrior's fate, at the desperate assault on the
fortress of the Narragansetts!

"The mettled steed looks like a pig," interrupts the critic,
"and Captain Gardner himself like the devil, though a very
tame one, and on a most diminutive scale."

"Sir, sir!" cries the persecuted showman, losing all patience,—for, indeed, he had particularly prided himself on
these figures of Captain Gardner and his horse,—"I see that
there is no hope of pleasing you. Pray, sir, do me the favor
to take back your money, and withdraw!"

"Not I!" answers the unconscionable critic. "I am just beginning to get interested in the matter. Come! turn your
crank, and grind out a few more of these fooleries!"

The showman rubs his brow impulsively, whisks the little
rod with which he points out the notabilities of the scene,—
but, finally, with the inevitable acquiescence of all public servants, resumes his composure, and goes on.

Pass onward, onward, Time! Build up new houses here,
and tear down thy works of yesterday, that have already the
rusty moss upon them! Summon forth the minister to the
abode of the young maiden, and bid him unite her to the
joyful bridegroom! Let the youthful parents carry their first-
born to the meeting-house, to receive the baptismal rite!
Knock at the door, whence the sable line of the funeral is next
to issue! Provide other successive generations of men, to
trade, talk, quarrel, or walk in friendly intercourse along the
street, as their fathers did before them! Do all thy daily and
accustomed business, Father Time, in this thoroughfare,
which thy footsteps, for so many years, have now made
dusty! But here, at last, thou leadest along a procession
which, once witnessed, shall appear no more, and be remembered only as a hideous dream of thine, or a frenzy of thy old
brain.

"Turn your crank, I say," bellows the remorseless critic,
"and grind it out, whatever it be, without further preface!"

The showman deems it best to comply.

Then, here comes the worshipful Captain Curwen, Sheriff
of Essex, on horseback, at the head of an armed guard, escorting a company of condemned prisoners from the jail to
their place of execution on Gallows Hill. The witches! There

is no mistaking them! The witches! As they approach up Prison Lane, and turn into the Main-street, let us watch their faces, as if we made a part of the pale crowd that presses so eagerly about them, yet shrinks back with such shuddering dread, leaving an open passage betwixt a dense throng on either side. Listen to what the people say.

There is old George Jacobs, known hereabouts, these sixty years, as a man whom we thought upright in all his way of life, quiet, blameless, a good husband before his pious wife was summoned from the evil to come, and a good father to the children whom she left him. Ah! but when that blessed woman went to heaven, George Jacobs' heart was empty, his hearth lonely, his life broken up; his children were married, and betook themselves to habitations of their own; and Satan, in his wanderings up and down, beheld this forlorn old man, to whom life was a sameness and a weariness, and found the way to tempt him. So the miserable sinner was prevailed with to mount into the air, and career among the clouds; and he is proved to have been present at a witch-meeting as far off as Falmouth, on the very same night that his next neighbors saw him, with his rheumatic stoop, going in at his own door. There is John Willard too; an honest man we thought him, and so shrewd and active in his business, so practical, so intent on every-day affairs, so constant at his little place of trade, where he bartered English goods for Indian corn and all kinds of country produce! How could such a man find time, or what could put it into his mind, to leave his proper calling, and become a wizard? It is a mystery, unless the Black Man tempted him with great heaps of gold. See that aged couple,—a sad sight truly,—John Proctor, and his wife Elizabeth. If there were two old people in all the County of Essex who seemed to have led a true Christian life, and to be treading hopefully the little remnant of their earthly path, it was this very pair. Yet have we heard it sworn, to the satisfaction of the worshipful Chief Justice Sewall, and all the Court and Jury, that Proctor and his wife have shown their withered faces at children's bedsides, mocking, making mouths, and affrighting the poor little innocents in the night-time. They, or their spectral appearances, have stuck pins into the Afflicted Ones, and thrown them into deadly fainting-fits with a touch,

or but a look. And, while we supposed the old man to be
reading the Bible to his old wife,—she meanwhile knitting in
the chimney-corner,—the pair of hoary reprobates have
whisked up the chimney, both on one broomstick, and flown
away to a witch-communion, far into the depths of the chill,
dark forest. How foolish! Were it only for fear of rheumatic
pains in their old bones, they had better have stayed at home.
But away they went; and the laughter of their decayed, cackling voices has been heard at midnight, aloft in the air. Now,
in the sunny noontide, as they go tottering to the gallows, it
is the devil's turn to laugh.

Behind these two,—who help one another along, and seem
to be comforting and encouraging each other, in a manner
truly pitiful, if it were not a sin to pity the old witch and
wizard,—behind them comes a woman, with a dark, proud
face that has been beautiful, and a figure that is still majestic.
Do you know her? It is Martha Carrier, whom the devil
found in a humble cottage, and looked into her discontented
heart, and saw pride there, and tempted her with his promise
that she should be Queen of Hell. And now, with that lofty
demeanor, she is passing to her kingdom, and, by her un-
quenchable pride, transforms this escort of shame into a
triumphal procession, that shall attend her to the gates of her
infernal palace, and seat her upon the fiery throne. Within
this hour, she shall assume her royal dignity.

Last of the miserable train comes a man clad in black, of
small stature and a dark complexion, with a clerical band
about his neck. Many a time, in the years gone by, that face
has been uplifted heavenward from the pulpit of the East
Meeting-house, when the Reverend Mr. Burroughs seemed
to worship God. What!—he? The holy man!—the learned!
—the wise! How has the devil tempted him? His fellow-
criminals, for the most part, are obtuse, uncultivated creatures, some of them scarcely half-witted by nature, and
others greatly decayed in their intellects through age. They were
an easy prey for the destroyer. Not so with this George
Burroughs, as we judge by the inward light which glows
through his dark countenance, and, we might almost say, glo-
rifies his figure, in spite of the soil and haggardness of long
imprisonment,—in spite of the heavy shadow that must fall

on him, while Death is walking by his side. What bribe could
Satan offer, rich enough to tempt and overcome this man?
Alas! it may have been in the very strength of his high and
searching intellect, that the Tempter found the weakness
which betrayed him. He yearned for knowledge; he went
groping onward into a world of mystery; at first, as the witnesses have sworn, he summoned up the ghosts of his two
dead wives, and talked with them of matters beyond the
grave; and, when their responses failed to satisfy the intense
and sinful craving of his spirit, he called on Satan, and was
heard. Yet—to look at him—who, that had not known the
proof, could believe him guilty? Who would not say, while
we see him offering comfort to the weak and aged partners of
his horrible crime,—while we hear his ejaculations of prayer,
that seem to bubble up out of the depths of his heart, and fly
heavenward, unawares,—while we behold a radiance brightening on his features as from the other world, which is but a
few steps off,—who would not say, that, over the dusty track
of the Main-street, a Christian saint is now going to a martyr's death? May not the Arch Fiend have been too subtle for
the court and jury, and betrayed them—laughing in his sleeve
the while—into the awful error of pouring out sanctified
blood as an acceptable sacrifice upon God's altar? Ah! no; for
listen to wise Cotton Mather, who, as he sits there on his
horse, speaks comfortably to the perplexed multitude, and
tells them that all has been religiously and justly done, and
that Satan's power shall this day receive its death-blow in
New England.

Heaven grant it be so!—the great scholar must be right!
so, lead the poor creatures to their death! Do you see that
group of children and half-grown girls, and, among them, an
old, hag-like Indian woman, Tituba by name? Those are the
Afflicted Ones. Behold, at this very instant, a proof of Satan's
power and malice! Mercy Parris, the minister's daughter, has
been smitten by a flash of Martha Carrier's eye, and falls
down in the street, writhing with horrible spasms and foaming at the mouth, like the possessed ones spoken of in Scripture. Hurry on the accursed witches to the gallows, ere they
do more mischief!—ere they fling out their withered arms,
and scatter pestilence by handfuls among the crowd!—ere, as

their parting legacy, they cast a blight over the land, so that henceforth it may bear no fruit nor blade of grass, and be fit for nothing but a sepulchre for their unhallowed carcasses! So, on they go; and old George Jacobs has stumbled by reason of his infirmity; but Goodman Proctor and his wife lean on one another, and walk at a reasonably steady pace, considering their age. Mr. Burroughs seems to administer counsel to Martha Carrier, whose face and mien, methinks, are milder and humbler than they were. Among the multitude, meanwhile, there is horror, fear, and distrust; and friend looks askance at friend, and the husband at his wife, and the wife at him, and even the mother at her little child; as if, in every creature that God has made, they suspected a witch, or dreaded an accuser. Never, never again, whether in this or any other shape, may Universal Madness riot in the Main-street!

I perceive in your eyes, my indulgent spectators, the criticism which you are too kind to utter. These scenes, you think, are all too sombre. So, indeed, they are; but the blame must rest on the sombre spirit of our forefathers, who wove their web of life with hardly a single thread of rose-color or gold, and not on me, who have a tropic love of sunshine, and would gladly gild all the world with it, if I knew where to find so much. That you may believe me, I will exhibit one of the only class of scenes, so far as my investigation has taught me, in which our ancestors were wont to steep their tough old hearts in wine and strong drink, and indulge an outbreak of grisly jollity.

Here it comes, out of the same house whence we saw brave Captain Gardner go forth to the wars. What! A coffin, borne on men's shoulders, and six aged gentlemen as pall-bearers, and a long train of mourners, with black gloves and black hat-bands, and every thing black, save a white handkerchief in each mourner's hand, to wipe away his tears withal. Now, my kind patrons, you are angry with me. You were bidden to a bridal-dance, and find yourselves walking in a funeral procession. Even so; but look back through all the social customs of New England, in the first century of her existence, and read all her traits of character; and if you find one occasion, other than a funeral-feast, where jollity was sanctioned by universal practice, I will set fire to my puppet-show without another word. These are the obsequies of old Governor Bradstreet, the patriarch and survivor of the first settlers, who, having intermarried with the Widow Gardner, is now resting from his labors, at the great age of ninety-four. The white-bearded corpse, which was his spirit's earthly garniture, now lies beneath yonder coffin-lid. Many a cask of ale and cider is on tap, and many a draught of spiced wine and aquavitæ has been quaffed. Else why should the bearers stagger, as they tremulously uphold the coffin?—and the aged pall-bearers, too, as they strive to walk solemnly beside it?—and wherefore do the mourners tread on one another's heels?—and why, if we may ask without offence, should the nose of the Reverend Mr. Noyes, through which he has just been delivering the funeral discourse, glow like a ruddy coal of fire? Well, well, old friends! Pass on, with your burthen of mortality, and lay it in the tomb with jolly hearts. People should be permitted to enjoy themselves in their own fashion; every man to his taste; but New England must have been a dismal abode for the man of pleasure, when the only boon-companion was Death!

Under cover of a mist that has settled over the scene, a few years flit by, and escape our notice. As the atmosphere becomes transparent, we perceive a decrepit grandsire, hobbling along the street. Do you recognize him? We saw him, first as the baby in Goodwife Massey's arms, when the primeval trees were flinging their shadow over Roger Conant's cabin; we have seen him, as the boy, the youth, the man, bearing his humble part in all the successive scenes, and forming the index-figure whereby to note the age of his coeval town. And here he is, old Goodman Massey, taking his last walk,—often pausing,—often leaning over his staff,—and calling to mind whose dwelling stood at such and such a spot, and whose field or garden occupied the site of those more recent houses. He can render a reason for all the bends and deviations of the thoroughfare, which, in its flexible and plastic infancy, was made to swerve aside from a straight line, in order to visit every settler's door. The Main-street is still youthful; the coeval Man is in his latest age. Soon he will be gone, a patriarch of fourscore, yet shall retain a sort of infantine life in our local history, as the first town-born child.

Behold here a change, wrought in the twinkling of an eye, like an incident in a tale of magic, even while your observation has been fixed upon the scene. The Main-street has vanished out of sight. In its stead appears a wintry waste of snow, with the sun just peeping over it, cold and bright, and tinging the white expanse with the faintest and most ethereal rose-color. This is the Great Snow of 1717, famous for the mountain-drifts in which it buried the whole country. It would seem as if the street, the growth of which we have noted so attentively,—following it from its first phase, as an Indian track, until it reached the dignity of side-walks,—were all at once obliterated, and resolved into a drearier pathlessness than when the forest covered it. The gigantic swells and billows of the snow have swept over each man's metes and bounds, and annihilated all the visible distinctions of human property. So that now, the traces of former times and hitherto accomplished deeds being done away, mankind should be at liberty to enter on new paths, and guide themselves by other laws than heretofore; if, indeed, the race be not extinct, and it be worth our while to go on with the march of life, over the cold and desolate expanse that lies before us. It may be, however, that matters are not so desperate as they appear. That vast icicle, glittering so cheerlessly in the sunshine, must be the spire of the meeting-house, incrusted with frozen sleet. Those great heaps, too, which we mistook for drifts, are houses, buried up to their eaves, and with their peaked roofs rounded by the depth of snow upon them. There, now, comes a gush of smoke from what I judge to be the chimney of the Ship Tavern—and another—another—and another— from the chimneys of other dwellings, where fireside comfort, domestic peace, the sports of children, and the quietude of age, are living yet, in spite of the frozen crust above them.

But it is time to change the scene. Its dreary monotony shall not test your fortitude like one of our actual New England winters, which leave so large a blank—so melancholy a death-spot—in lives so brief that they ought to be all summer-time. Here, at least, I may claim to be ruler of the sea-

sons. One turn of the crank shall melt away the snow from
the Main-street, and show the trees in their full foliage, the
rose-bushes in bloom, and a border of green grass along the
side-walk. There! But what! How! The scene will not move.
A wire is broken. The street continues buried beneath the
snow, and the fate of Herculaneum and Pompeii has its parallel in this catastrophe.

Alas! my kind and gentle audience, you know not the extent of your misfortune. The scenes to come were far better
than the past. The street itself would have been more worthy
of pictorial exhibition; the deeds of its inhabitants, not less
so. And how would your interest have deepened, as, passing
out of the cold shadow of antiquity, in my long and weary
course, I should arrive within the limits of man's memory,
and, leading you at last into the sunshine of the present,
should give a reflex of the very life that is flitting past us!
Your own beauty, my fair townswomen, would have beamed
upon you, out of my scene. Not a gentleman that walks the
street but should have beheld his own face and figure, his
gait, the peculiar swing of his arm, and the coat that he put
on yesterday. Then, too,—and it is what I chiefly regret,—I
had expended a vast deal of light and brilliancy on a representation of the street in its whole length, from Buffum's Corner
downward, on the night of the grand illumination for General Taylor's triumph. Lastly, I should have given the crank
one other turn, and have brought out the future, showing
you who shall walk the Main-street tomorrow, and, perchance, whose funeral shall pass through it!

But these, like most other human purposes, lie unaccomplished; and I have only further to say, that any lady or
gentleman, who may feel dissatisfied with the evening's entertainment, shall receive back the admission fee at the door.

"Then give me mine," cries the critic, stretching out his
palm. "I said that your exhibition would prove a humbug,
and so it has turned out. So hand over my quarter!"

Ethan Brand

A Chapter from an Abortive Romance

BARTRAM, the lime-burner, a rough, heavy-looking man, begrimed with charcoal, sat watching his kiln, at nightfall, while his little son played at building houses with the scattered fragments of marble; when, on the hill-side below them, they heard a roar of laughter, not mirthful, but slow, and even solemn, like a wind shaking the boughs of the forest.

"Father, what is that?" asked the little boy, leaving his play, and pressing betwixt his father's knees.

"Oh, some drunken man, I suppose," answered the lime-burner;—"some merry fellow from the bar-room in the village, who dared not laugh loud enough within doors, lest he should blow the roof of the house off. So here he is, shaking his jolly sides, at the foot of Graylock."

"But, father," said the child, more sensitive than the obtuse, middle-aged clown, "he does not laugh like a man that is glad. So the noise frightens me!"

"Don't be a fool, child!" cried his father, gruffly. "You will never make a man, I do believe; there is too much of your mother in you. I have known the rustling of a leaf startle you. Hark! Here comes the merry fellow now. You shall see that there is no harm in him."

Bartram and his little son, while they were talking thus, sat watching the same lime-kiln that had been the scene of Ethan Brand's solitary and meditative life, before he began his search for the Unpardonable Sin. Many years, as we have seen, had now elapsed, since that portentous night when the IDEA was first developed. The kiln, however, on the mountain-side, stood unimpaired, and was in nothing changed, since he had thrown his dark thoughts into the intense glow of its furnace, and melted them, as it were, into the one thought that took possession of his life. It was a rude, round, tower-like structure, about twenty feet high, heavily built of rough stones, and with a hillock of earth heaped about the larger part of its circumference; so that blocks and fragments of marble might be drawn by cart-loads, and thrown in at the top. There was an opening at the bottom of the tower, like an oven-mouth, but large enough to admit a man in a stooping posture, and provided with a massive iron door. With the smoke and jets of flame issuing from the chinks and crevices of this door, which seemed to give admittance into the hill-side, it resembled nothing so much as the private entrance to the infernal regions, which the shepherds of the Delectable Mountains were accustomed to show to pilgrims.

There are many such lime-kilns in that tract of country, for the purpose of burning the white marble which composes a large part of the substance of the hills. Some of them, built years ago, and long deserted, with weeds growing in the vacant round of the interior, which is open to the sky, and grass and wild flowers rooting themselves into the chinks of the stones, look already like relics of antiquity, and may yet be overspread with the lichens of centuries to come. Others, where the lime-burner still feeds his daily and night-long fire, afford points of interest to the wanderer among the hills, who seats himself on a log of wood or a fragment of marble, to hold chat with the solitary man. It is a lonesome, and, when the character is inclined to thought, may be an intensely thoughtful occupation; as it proved in the case of Ethan Brand, who had mused to such strange purpose, in days gone by, while the fire in this very kiln was burning.

The man, who now watched the fire, was of a different order, and troubled himself with no thoughts save the very few that were requisite to his business. At frequent intervals he flung back the clashing weight of the iron door, and, turning his face from the insufferable glare, thrust in huge logs of oak, or stirred the immense brands with a long pole. Within the furnace, was seen the curling and riotous flames, and the burning marble, almost molten with the intensity of heat; while, without, the reflection of the fire quivered on the dark intricacy of the surrounding forest, and showed, in the foreground, a bright and ruddy little picture of the hut, the spring beside its door, the athletic and coal-begrimed figure of the lime-burner, and the half-frightened child, shrinking into the protection of his father's shadow. And when, again, the iron door was closed, then re-appeared the tender light of the half-full moon, which vainly strove to trace out the indistinct shapes of the neighboring mountains; and, in the upper sky, there was a flitting congregation of clouds, still faintly tinged with the rosy sunset, though, thus far down into the valley, the sunshine had vanished long and long ago.

The little boy now crept still closer to his father, as footsteps were heard ascending the hill-side, and a human form thrust aside the bushes that clustered beneath the trees.

"Halloo! who is it?" cried the lime-burner, vexed at his son's timidity, yet half-infected by it. "Come forward, and show yourself, like a man; or I'll fling this chunk of marble at your head!"

"You offer me a rough welcome," said a gloomy voice, as the unknown man drew nigh. "Yet I neither claim nor desire a kinder one, even at my own fireside."

To obtain a distincter view, Bartram threw open the iron door of the kiln, whence immediately issued a gush of fierce light, that smote full upon the stranger's face and figure. To a careless eye, there appeared nothing very remarkable in his aspect, which was that of a man in a coarse, brown, country-made suit of clothes, tall and thin, with the staff and heavy shoes of a wayfarer. As he advanced, he fixed his eyes, which were very bright, intently upon the brightness of the furnace, as if he beheld, or expected to behold, some object worthy of note within it.

"Good evening, stranger," said the lime-burner, "whence come you, so late in the day?"

"I come from my search," answered the wayfarer; "for, at last, it is finished."

"Drunk, or crazy!" muttered Bartram to himself. "I shall have trouble with the fellow. The sooner I drive him away, the better."

The little boy, all in a tremble, whispered to his father, and begged him to shut the door of the kiln, so that there might not be so much light; for that there was something in the man's face which he was afraid to look at, yet could not look away from. And, indeed, even the lime-burner's dull and torpid sense began to be impressed by an indescribable something in that thin, rugged, thoughtful visage, with the grizzled hair hanging wildly about it, and those deeply sunken eyes, which gleamed like fires within the entrance of a mysterious cavern. But, as he closed the door, the stranger turned towards him, and spoke in a quiet, familiar way, that made Bartram feel as if he were a sane and sensible man, after all.

"Your task draws to an end, I see," said he. "This marble has already been burning three days. A few hours more will convert the stone to lime."

"Why, who are you?" exclaimed the lime-burner. "You seem as well acquainted with my business as I myself."

"And well I may be," said the stranger, "for I followed the same craft, many a long year; and here, too, on this very spot. But you are a new comer in these parts. Did you never hear of Ethan Brand?"

"The man that went in search of the Unpardonable Sin?" asked Bartram, with a laugh.

"The same," answered the stranger. "He has found what he sought, and therefore he comes back again."

"What! then you are Ethan Brand, himself?" cried the lime-burner in amazement. "I am a new comer here, as you say; and they call it eighteen years since you left the foot of Graylock. But, I can tell you, the good folks still talk about Ethan Brand, in the village yonder, and what a strange errand took him away from his lime-kiln. Well, and so you have found the Unpardonable Sin?"

"Even so!" said the stranger, calmly.

"If the question is a fair one," proceeded Bartram, "where might it be?"

Ethan Brand laid his finger on his own heart. "Here!" replied he.

And then, without mirth in his countenance, but as if moved by an involuntary recognition of the infinite absurdity of seeking throughout the world for what was the closest of all things to himself, and looking into every heart, save his own, for what was hidden in no other breast, he broke into a laugh of scorn. It was the same slow, heavy laugh, that had almost appalled the lime-burner, when it heralded the wayfarer's approach.

The solitary mountain-side was made dismal by it. Laughter, when out of place, mistimed, or bursting forth from a disordered state of feeling, may be the most terrible modulation of the human voice. The laughter of one asleep, even if it be a little child—the madman's laugh—the wild, screaming laugh of a born idiot, are sounds that we sometimes tremble to hear, and would always willingly forget. Poets have imagined no utterance of fiends or hobgoblins so fearfully appropriate as a laugh. And even the obtuse lime-burner felt his nerves shaken, as this strange man looked inward at his own heart, and burst into laughter that rolled away into the night, and was indistinctly reverberated among the hills.

"Joe," said he to his little son, "scamper down to the tavern in the village, and tell the jolly fellows there that Ethan Brand has come back, and that he has found the Unpardonable Sin!"

The boy darted away on his errand, to which Ethan Brand made no objection, nor seemed hardly to notice it. He sat on a log of wood, looking steadfastly at the iron door of the kiln. When the child was out of sight, and his swift and light footsteps ceased to be heard, treading first on the fallen leaves, and then on the rocky mountain-path, the lime-burner began to regret his departure. He felt that the little fellow's presence had been a barrier between his guest and himself, and that he must now deal, heart to heart, with a man who, on his own confession, had committed the only crime for which Heaven could afford no mercy. That crime, in its indistinct blackness, seemed to overshadow him. The lime-burner's own sins rose up within him, and made his memory riotous with a throng of evil shapes that asserted their kindred with the Master Sin, whatever it might be, which it was within the scope of man's corrupted nature to conceive and cherish. They were all of one family; they went to and fro between his breast and Ethan Brand's, and carried dark greetings from one to the other.

Then Bartram remembered the stories which had grown traditionary in reference to this strange man, who had come upon him like a shadow of the night, and was making himself at home in his old place, after so long absence that the dead people, dead and buried for years, would have had more right to be at home, in any familiar spot, than he. Ethan Brand, it was said, had conversed with Satan himself, in the lurid blaze of this very kiln. The legend had been matter of mirth heretofore, but looked grisly now. According to this tale, before Ethan Brand departed on his search, he had been accustomed to evoke a fiend from the hot furnace of the lime-kiln, night after night, in order to confer with him about the Unpardonable Sin; the Man and the Fiend each laboring to frame the image of some mode of guilt, which could neither be atoned for, nor forgiven. And, with the first gleam of light upon the mountain-top, the fiend crept in at the iron door, there to abide in the intensest element of fire, until again summoned forth to share in the dreadful task of extending man's possible guilt beyond the scope of Heaven's else infinite mercy.

While the lime-burner was struggling with the horror of these thoughts, Ethan Brand rose from the log and flung open the door of the kiln. The action was in such accordance with the idea in Bartram's mind, that he almost expected to see the Evil One issue forth, red-hot from the raging furnace.

"Hold, hold!" cried he, with a tremulous attempt to laugh; for he was ashamed of his fears, although they overmastered him. "Don't, for mercy's sake, bring out your devil now!"

"Man!" sternly replied Ethan Brand, "what need have I of the devil? I have left him behind me on my track. It is with such half-way sinners as you that he busies himself. Fear not, because I open the door. I do but act by old custom, and am going to trim your fire, like a lime-burner, as I was once."

He stirred the vast coals, thrust in more wood, and bent forward to gaze into the hollow prison-house of the fire, regardless of the fierce glow that reddened upon his face. The lime-burner sat watching him, and half suspected his strange guest of a purpose, if not to evoke a fiend, at least to plunge bodily into the flames, and thus vanish from the sight of man. Ethan Brand, however, drew quietly back, and closed the door of the kiln.

"I have looked," said he, "into many a human heart that was seven times hotter with sinful passions than yonder furnace is with fire. But I found not there what I sought. No; not the Unpardonable Sin!"

"What is the Unpardonable Sin?" asked the lime-burner; and then he shrank farther from his companion, trembling lest his question should be answered.

"It is a sin that grew within my own breast," replied Ethan

Brand, standing erect, with the pride that distinguishes all enthusiasts of his stamp. "A sin that grew nowhere else! The sin of an intellect that triumphed over the sense of brotherhood with man, and reverence for God, and sacrificed everything to its own mighty claims! The only sin that deserves a recompense of immortal agony! Freely, were it to do again, would I incur the guilt. Unshrinkingly, I accept the retribution!"

"The man's head is turned," muttered the lime-burner to himself. "He may be a sinner, like the rest of us—nothing more likely—but I'll be sworn, he is a madman, too."

Nevertheless, he felt uncomfortable at his situation, alone with Ethan Brand on the wild mountain-side, and was right glad to hear the rough murmur of tongues, and the footsteps of what seemed a pretty numerous party, stumbling over the stones, and rustling through the underbrush. Soon appeared the whole lazy regiment that was wont to infest the village tavern, comprehending three or four individuals who had drunk flip beside the bar-room fire, through all the winters, and smoked their pipes beneath the stoop, through all the summers since Ethan Brand's departure. Laughing boisterously, and mingling all their voices together in unceremonious talk, they now burst into the moonshine and narrow streaks of fire-light that illuminated the open space before the lime-kiln. Bartram set the door ajar again, flooding the spot with light, that the whole company might get a fair view of Ethan Brand, and he of them.

There, among other old acquaintances, was a once ubiquitous man, now almost extinct, but whom we were formerly sure to encounter at the hotel of every thriving village throughout the country. It was the stage-agent. The present specimen of the genus was a wilted and smoke-dried man, wrinkled and red-nosed, in a smartly cut, brown, bob-tailed coat, with brass buttons, who, for a length of time unknown, had kept his desk and corner in the bar-room, and was still puffing what seemed to be the same cigar that he had lighted twenty years before. He had great fame as a dry joker, though, perhaps, less on account of any intrinsic humor, than from a certain flavor of brandy-toddy and tobacco-smoke, which impregnated all his ideas and expressions, as well as his person. Another well-remembered, though strangely-altered face was that of Lawyer Giles, as people still called him in courtesy; an elderly ragamuffin, in his soiled shirt-sleeves and tow-cloth trowsers. This poor fellow had been an attorney, in what he called his better days, a sharp practitioner, and in great vogue among the village litigants; but flip, and sling, and toddy, and cocktails, imbibed at all hours, morning, noon, and night, had caused him to slide from intellectual, to various kinds and degrees of bodily labor, till, at last, to adopt his own phrase, he slid into a soap-vat. In other words, Giles was now a soap-boiler, in a small way. He had come to be but the fragment of a human being, a part of one foot having been chopped off by an axe, and an entire hand torn away by the devilish gripe of a steam-engine. Yet, though the corporeal hand was gone, a spiritual member remained; for, stretching forth the stump, Giles steadfastly averred, that he felt an invisible thumb and fingers, with as vivid a sensation as before the real ones were amputated. A maimed and miserable wretch he was; but one, nevertheless, whom the world could not trample on, and had no right to scorn, either in this or any previous stage of his misfortunes, since he had still kept up the courage and spirit of a man, asked nothing in charity, and, with his one hand—and that the left one—fought a stern battle against want and hostile circumstances.

Among the throng, too, came another personage, who, with certain points of similarity to Lawyer Giles, had more of difference. It was the village Doctor, a man of some fifty years, whom, at an earlier period of his life, we should have introduced as paying a professional visit to Ethan Brand, during the latter's supposed insanity. He was now a purple-visaged, rude, and brutal, yet half-gentlemanly figure, with something wild, ruined, and desperate in his talk, and in all the details of his gesture and manners. Brandy possessed this man like an evil spirit, and made him as surly and savage as a wild beast, and as miserable as a lost soul; but there was supposed to be in him such wonderful skill, such native gifts of healing, beyond any which medical science could impart, that society caught hold of him, and would not let him sink out of its reach. So, swaying to and fro upon his horse, and grumbling thick accents at the bedside, he visited all the sick chambers for miles about among the mountain towns; and some-times raised a dying man, as it were, by miracle, or, quite as often, no doubt, sent his patient to a grave that was dug many a year too soon. The Doctor had an everlasting pipe in his mouth, and, as somebody said, in allusion to his habit of swearing, it was always alight with hell-fire.

These three worthies pressed forward, and greeted Ethan Brand, each after his own fashion, earnestly inviting him to partake of the contents of a certain black bottle; in which, as they averred, he would find something far better worth seeking for, than the Unpardonable Sin. No mind, which has wrought itself, by intense and solitary meditation, into a high state of enthusiasm, can endure the kind of contact with low and vulgar modes of thought and feeling, to which Ethan Brand was now subjected. It made him doubt—and, strange to say, it was a painful doubt—whether he had indeed found the Unpardonable Sin, and found it within himself. The whole question on which he had exhausted life, and more than life, looked like a delusion.

"Leave me," he said bitterly, "ye brute beasts, that have made yourselves so, shrivelling up your souls with fiery li-quors! I have done with you. Years and years ago, I groped into your hearts and found nothing there for my purpose. Get ye gone!"

"Why, you uncivil scoundrel," cried the fierce Doctor, "is that the way you respond to the kindness of your best friends? Then let me tell you the truth. You have no more found the Unpardonable Sin than yonder boy Joe has. You are but a crazy fellow—I told you so, twenty years ago—neither better nor worse than a crazy fellow, and the fit com-panion of old Humphrey, here!"

He pointed to an old man, shabbily dressed, with long white hair, thin visage, and unsteady eyes. For some years past, this aged person had been wandering about among the hills, inquiring of all travellers whom he met, for his daugh-ter. The girl, it seemed, had gone off with a company of cir-cus-performers; and, occasionally, tidings of her came to the village, and fine stories were told of her glittering appearance, as she rode on horseback in the ring, or performed marvellous feats on the tight-rope.

The white-haired father now approached Ethan Brand, and gazed unsteadily into his face.

"They tell me you have been all over the earth," said he, wringing his hands with earnestness. "You must have seen my daughter; for she makes a grand figure in the world, and everybody goes to see her. Did she send any word to her old father, or say when she is coming back?"

Ethan Brand's eye quailed beneath the old man's. That daughter, from whom he so earnestly desired a word of greeting, was the Esther of our tale; the very girl whom, with such cold and remorseless purpose, Ethan Brand had made the subject of a psychological experiment, and wasted, absorbed, and perhaps annihilated her soul, in the process.

"Yes," murmured he, turning away from the hoary wanderer; "it is no delusion. There is an Unpardonable Sin!"

While these things were passing, a merry scene was going forward in the area of cheerful light, besides the spring and before the door of the hut. A number of the youth of the village, young men and girls, had hurried up the hill-side, impelled by curiosity to see Ethan Brand, the hero of so many a legend familiar to their childhood. Finding nothing, however, very remarkable in his aspect—nothing but a sun-burnt wayfarer, in plain garb and dusty shoes, who sat looking into the fire, as if he fancied pictures among the coals—these young people speedily grew tired of observing him. As it happened, there was other amusement at hand. An old German Jew, travelling with a diorama on his back, was passing down the mountain-road towards the village, just as the party turned aside from it; and, in hopes of eking out the profits of the day, the showman had kept them company to the lime-kiln.

"Come, old Dutchman," cried one of the young men, "let us see your pictures, if you can swear they are worth looking at!"

"Oh, yes, Captain," answered the Jew—whether as a matter of courtesy or craft, he styled everybody Captain—"I shall show you, indeed, some very superb pictures!"

So, placing his box in a proper position, he invited the young men and girls to look through the glass orifices of the machine, and proceeded to exhibit a series of the most outrageous scratchings and daubings, as specimens of the fine arts, that ever an itinerant showman had the face to impose upon his circle of spectators. The pictures were worn out, moreover, tattered, full of cracks and wrinkles, dingy with tobacco-smoke, and otherwise in a most pitiable condition. Some purported to be cities, public edifices, and ruined castles, in Europe; others represented Napoleon's battles, and Nelson's sea-fights; and in the midst of these would be seen a gigantic, brown, hairy hand—which might have been mistaken for the Hand of Destiny, though, in truth, it was only the showman's—pointing its forefinger to various scenes of the conflict, while its owner gave historical illustrations. When, with much merriment at its abominable deficiency of merit, the exhibition was concluded, the German bade little Joe put his head into the box. Viewed through the magnifying glasses, the boy's round, rosy visage assumed the strangest imaginable aspect of an immense, Titanic child, the mouth grinning broadly, and the eyes, and every other feature, overflowing with fun at the joke. Suddenly, however, that merry face turned pale, and its expression changed to horror; for this easily impressed and excitable child had become sensible that the eye of Ethan Brand was fixed upon him through the glass.

"You make the little man to be afraid, Captain," said the German Jew, turning up the dark and strong outline of his visage, from his stooping posture. "But, look again; and, by chance, I shall cause you to see somewhat that is very fine, upon my word!"

Ethan Brand gazed into the box for an instant, and then starting back, looked fixedly at the German. What had he seen? Nothing, apparently; for a curious youth, who had peeped in, almost at the same moment, beheld only a vacant space of canvass.

"I remember you now," muttered Ethan Brand to the showman.

"Ah, Captain," whispered the Jew of Nuremberg, with a dark smile, "I find it to be a heavy matter in my show-box— this Unpardonable Sin! By my faith, Captain, it has wearied my shoulders, this long day, to carry it over the mountain."

"Peace!" answered Ethan Brand, sternly, "or get thee into the furnace yonder!"

The Jew's exhibition had scarcely concluded, when a great, elderly dog—who seemed to be his own master, as no person in the company laid claim to him—saw fit to render himself the object of public notice. Hitherto, he had shown himself a very quiet, well-disposed old dog, going round from one to another, and, by way of being sociable, offering his rough head to be patted by any kindly hand that would take so much trouble. But, now, all of a sudden, this grave and venerable quadruped, of his own mere notion, and without the slightest suggestion from anybody else, began to run round after his tail, which, to heighten the absurdity of the proceeding, was a great deal shorter than it should have been. Never was seen such headlong eagerness in pursuit of an object that could not possibly be attained; never was heard such a tremendous outbreak of growling, snarling, barking, and snapping—as if one end of the ridiculous brute's body were at deadly and most unforgivable enmity with the other. Faster and faster, roundabout went the cur; and faster and still faster fled the unapproachable brevity of his tail; and louder and fiercer grew his yells of rage and animosity; until, utterly exhausted, and as far from the goal as ever, the foolish old dog ceased his performance as suddenly as he had begun it. The next moment, he was as mild, quiet, sensible, and respectable in his deportment, as when he first scraped acquaintance with the company.

As may be supposed, the exhibition was greeted with universal laughter, clapping of hands, and shouts of encore; to which the canine performer responded by wagging all that there was to wag of his tail, but appeared totally unable to repeat his very successful effort to amuse the spectators.

Meanwhile, Ethan Brand had resumed his seat upon the log; and, moved, it might be, by a perception of some remote analogy between his own case and that of this self-pursuing cur, he broke into the awful laugh, which, more than any other token, expressed the condition of his inward being. From that moment, the merriment of the party was at an end; they stood aghast, dreading lest the inauspicious sound should be reverberated around the horizon, and that mountain would thunder it to mountain, and so the horror be prolonged upon their ears. Then, whispering one to another, that it was late—that the moon was almost down—that the August night was growing chill—they hurried homeward, leaving the lime-burner and little Joe to deal as they might with their unwelcome guest. Save for these three human beings, the open space on the hill-side was a solitude, set in a vast gloom of forest. Beyond that darksome verge, the fire-light glimmered on the stately trunks and almost black foliage of pines, intermixed with the lighter verdure of sapling oaks, maples, and poplars, while, here and there, lay the gigantic corpses of dead trees, decaying on the leaf-strewn soil. And it seemed to little Joe—a timorous and imaginative child—that the silent forest was holding its breath, until some fearful thing should happen.

Ethan Brand thrust more wood into the fire, and closed the door of the kiln; then looking over his shoulder at the lime-burner and his son, he bade, rather than advised, them to retire to rest.

"For myself I cannot sleep," said he. "I have matters that it concerns me to meditate upon. I will watch the fire, as I used to do in the old time."

"And call the devil out of the furnace to keep you company, I suppose," muttered Bartram, who had been making intimate acquaintance with the black bottle above-mentioned. "But watch, if you like, and call as many devils as you like! For my part, I shall be all the better for a snooze. Come, Joe!"

As the boy followed his father into the hut, he looked back to the wayfarer, and the tears came into his eyes; for his tender spirit had an intuition of the bleak and terrible loneliness in which this man had enveloped himself.

When they had gone, Ethan Brand sat listening to the crackling of the kindled wood, and looking at the little spirts of fire that issued through the chinks of the door. These trifles, however, once so familiar, had but the slightest hold of his attention; while deep within his mind, he was reviewing the gradual, but marvellous change, that had been wrought upon him by the search to which he had devoted himself. He remembered how the night-dew had fallen upon him—how the dark forest had whispered to him—how the stars had gleamed upon him—a simple and loving man, watching his fire in the years gone by, and ever musing as it burned. He remembered with what tenderness, with what love and sympathy for mankind, and what pity for human guilt and wo, he had first begun to contemplate those ideas which afterwards became the inspiration of his life; with what reverence he had then looked into the heart of man, viewing it as a temple originally divine, and however desecrated, still to be held sacred by a brother; with what awful fear he had deprecated the success of his pursuit, and prayed that the Unpardonable Sin might never be revealed to him. Then ensued that vast intellectual development, which, in its progress, disturbed the counterpoise between his mind and heart. The Idea that possessed his life had operated as a means of education; it had gone on cultivating his powers to the highest point of which they were susceptible; it had raised him from the level of an unlettered laborer, to stand on a star-light eminence, whither the philosophers of the earth, laden with the lore of universities, might vainly strive to clamber after him. So much for the intellect! But where was the heart? That, indeed, had withered—had contracted—had hardened—had perished! It had ceased to partake of the universal throb. He had lost his hold of the magnetic chain of humanity. He was no longer a brother-man, opening the chambers or the dungeons of our common nature by the key of holy sympathy, which gave him a right to share in all its secrets; he was now a cold observer, looking on mankind as the subject of his experiment, and, at length, converting man and woman to be his puppets, and pulling the wires that moved them to such degrees of crime as were demanded for his study.

Thus Ethan Brand became a fiend. He began to be so from the moment that his moral nature had ceased to keep the pace of improvement with his intellect. And now, as his highest effort and inevitable development—as the bright and gorgeous flower, and rich, delicious fruit of his life's labor—he had produced the Unpardonable Sin!

"What more have I to seek? What more to achieve?" said Ethan Brand to himself. "My task is done, and well done!"

Starting from the log with a certain alacrity in his gait, and ascending the hillock of earth that was raised against the stone circumference of the lime-kiln, he thus reached the top of the structure. It was a space of perhaps ten feet across, from edge to edge, presenting a view of the upper surface of the immense mass of broken marble with which the kiln was heaped. All these innumerable blocks and fragments of marble were red-hot, and vividly on fire, sending up great spouts of blue flame, which quivered aloft and danced madly, as within a magic circle, and sank and rose again, with continual and multitudinous activity. As the lonely man bent forward over this terrible body of fire, the blasting heat smote up against his person with a breath that, it might be supposed, would have scorched and shrivelled him up in a moment.

Ethan Brand stood erect and raised his arms on high. The blue flames played upon his face, and imparted the wild and ghastly light which alone could have suited its expression; it was that of a fiend on the verge of plunging into his gulf of intensest torment.

"Oh, Mother Earth," cried he, "who art no more my Mother, and into whose bosom this frame shall never be resolved! Oh, mankind, whose brotherhood I have cast off, and trampled thy great heart beneath my feet! Oh, stars of Heaven, that shone on me of old, as if to light me onward and upward!—farewell all, and forever! Come, deadly element of Fire—henceforth my familiar friend! Embrace me as I do thee!"

That night the sound of a fearful peal of laughter rolled heavily through the sleep of the lime-burner and his little son; dim shapes of horror and anguish haunted their dreams, and seemed still present in the rude hovel when they opened their eyes to the daylight.

"Up, boy, up!" cried the lime-burner, staring about him. "Thank Heaven, the night is gone at last; and rather than pass such another, I would watch my lime-kiln, wide awake, for a twelvemonth. This Ethan Brand, with his humbug of an Unpardonable Sin, has done me no such mighty favor in taking my place!"

He issued from the hut, followed by little Joe, who kept fast hold of his father's hand. The early sunshine was already pouring its gold upon the mountain-tops, and though the valleys were still in shadow, they smiled cheerfully in the promise of the bright day that was hastening onward. The village, completely shut in by hills, which swelled away gently about it, looked as if it had rested peacefully in the hollow of the great hand of Providence. Every dwelling was distinctly visible; the little spires of the two churches pointed upward, and caught a fore-glimmering of brightness from the sun-gilt skies upon their gilded weathercocks. The tavern was astir, and the figure of the old, smoke-dried stage-agent, cigar in mouth, was seen beneath the stoop. Old Graylock was glorified with a golden cloud upon his head. Scattered, likewise, over the breasts of the surrounding mountains, there were heaps of hoary mist, in fantastic shapes, some of them far down into the valley, others high up towards the summits, and still others, of the same family of mist or cloud, hovering in the gold radiance of the upper atmosphere. Stepping from one to another of the clouds that rested on the hills, and thence to the loftier brotherhood that sailed in air, it seemed almost as if a mortal man might thus ascend into the heavenly regions. Earth was so mingled with sky that it was a daydream to look at it.

To supply that charm of the familiar and homely, which Nature so readily adopts into a scene like this, the stage-coach was rattling down the mountain-road, and the driver sounded his horn; while echo caught up the notes and intertwined them into a rich, and varied, and elaborate harmony, of which the original performer could lay claim to little share. The great hills played a concert among themselves, each contributing a strain of airy sweetness.

Little Joe's face brightened at once.

"Dear father," cried he, skipping cheerily to and fro, "that strange man is gone, and the sky and the mountains all seem glad of it!"

"Yes," growled the lime-burner with an oath, "but he has let the fire go down, and no thanks to him, if five hundred bushels of lime are not spoilt. If I catch the fellow hereabouts again I shall feel like tossing him into the furnace!"

With his long pole in his hand he ascended to the top of the kiln. After a moment's pause he called to his son.

"Come up here, Joe!" said he.

So little Joe ran up the hillock and stood by his father's side. The marble was all burnt into perfect, snow-white lime.

But on its surface, in the midst of the circle—snow-white too, and thoroughly converted into lime—lay a human skeleton, in the attitude of a person who, after long toil, lies down to long repose. Within the ribs—strange to say—was the shape of a human heart.

"Was the fellow's heart made of marble?" cried Bartram, in some perplexity at this phenomenon. "At any rate, it is burnt into what looks like special good lime; and, taking all the bones together, my kiln is half a bushel the richer for him."

So saying, the rude lime-burner lifted his pole, and letting it fall upon the skeleton, the relics of Ethan Brand were crumbled into fragments.

The Great Stone Face

ONE AFTERNOON, when the sun was going down, a mother and her little boy sat at the door of their cottage, talking about the Great Stone Face. They had but to lift their eyes, and there it was plainly to be seen, though miles away, with the sunshine brightening all its features.

And what was the Great Stone Face?

Embosomed amongst a family of lofty mountains, there was a valley so spacious that it contained many thousand inhabitants. Some of these good people dwelt in log huts, with the black forest all around them, on the steep and difficult hill-sides. Others had their homes in comfortable farm-houses, and cultivated the rich soil on the gentle slopes or level surfaces of the valley. Others, again, were congregated into populous villages, where some wild, highland rivulet, tumbling down from its birth-place in the upper mountain region, had been caught and tamed by human cunning, and compelled to turn the machinery of cotton factories. The inhabitants of this valley, in short, were numerous, and of many modes of life. But all of them, grown people and children, had a kind of familiarity with the Great Stone Face, although some possessed the gift of distinguishing this grand natural phenomenon more perfectly than many of their neighbors.

The Great Stone Face, then, was a work of Nature in her mood of majestic playfulness, formed on the perpendicular side of a mountain by some immense rocks, which had been thrown together in such a position, as, when viewed at a proper distance, precisely to resemble the features of the human countenance. It seemed as if an enormous giant, or a Titan, had sculptured his own likeness on the precipice. There was the broad arch of the forehead, a hundred feet in height, the nose, with its long bridge, and the vast lips, which, if they could have spoken, would have rolled their thunder accents from one end of the valley to the other. True it is, that if the spectator approached too near, he lost the outline of the gigantic visage, and could discern only a heap of ponderous and gigantic rocks, piled in chaotic ruin one upon another. Retracing his steps, however, the wondrous features would again be seen, and the farther he withdrew from them, the more like a human face, with all its original divinity intact, did they appear; until, as it grew dim in the distance, with the clouds and glorified vapor of the mountains clustering about it, the Great Stone Face seemed positively to be alive.

It was a happy lot for children to grow up to manhood or womanhood, with the Great Stone Face before their eyes, for all the features were noble, and the expression was at once grand and sweet, as if it were the glow of a vast, warm heart, that embraced all mankind in its affections, and had room for more. It was an education only to look at it. According to the belief of many people, the valley owed much of its fertility to this benign aspect that was continually beaming over it, illuminating the clouds, and infusing its tenderness into the sunshine.

As we began with saying, a mother and her little boy sat at their cottage door, gazing at the Great Stone Face, and talking about it. The child's name was Ernest.

"Mother," said he, while the Titanic visage smiled on him, "I wish that it could speak, for it looks so very kindly that its voice must needs be pleasant. If I were to see a man with such a face, I should love him dearly."

"If an old prophecy should come to pass," answered his mother, "we may see a man, some time or other, with exactly such a face as that."

"What prophecy do you mean, dear mother?" eagerly inquired Ernest. "Pray tell me all about it!"

So his mother told him a story that her own mother had told to her, when she herself was younger than little Ernest; a story, not of things that were past, but of what was yet to come; a story, nevertheless, so very old, that even the Indians, who formerly inhabited this valley, had heard it from their forefathers, to whom, as they affirmed, it had been murmured by the mountain streams, and whispered by the wind among the tree-tops. The purport was, that, at some future day, a child should be born hereabouts, who was destined to become the greatest and noblest personage of his time, and whose countenance, in manhood, should bear an exact resemblance to the Great Stone Face. Not a few old-fashioned people, and young ones likewise, in the ardor of their hopes, still cherished an enduring faith in this old prophecy. But others—who had seen more of the world, had watched and waited till they were weary, and had beheld no man with such a face, nor any man that proved to be much greater or nobler than his neighbors—concluded it to be nothing but an idle tale. At all events, the great man of the prophecy had not yet appeared.

"Oh, mother, dear mother," cried Ernest, clapping his hands above his head, "I do hope that I shall live to see him!"

His mother was an affectionate and thoughtful woman, and felt that it was wisest not to discourage the generous hopes of her little boy. So she only said to him—"Perhaps you may!"

And Ernest never forgot the story that his mother told him. It was always in his mind whenever he looked upon the Great Stone Face. He spent his childhood in the log-cottage where he was born, and was dutiful to his mother, and helpful to her in many things, assisting her much with his little hands, and more with his loving heart. In this manner, from a happy yet often pensive child, he grew up to be a mild, quiet, unobtrusive boy, and sun-browned with labor in the fields, but with more intelligence brightening his aspect than is seen in many lads who have been taught at famous schools. Yet Ernest had had no teacher, save only that the Great Stone Face became one to him. When the toil of the day was over, he would gaze at it for hours, until he began to imagine that those vast features recognized him, and gave him a smile of kindness and encouragement, responsive to his own look of veneration. We must not take upon us to affirm that this was a mistake, although the Face may have looked no more kindly at Ernest than at all the world besides. But the secret was, that the boy's tender and confiding simplicity discerned what other people could not see; and thus the love, which was meant for all, became his peculiar portion.

About this time, there went a rumor throughout the valley, that the great man, foretold from ages long ago, who was to bear a resemblance to the Great Stone Face, had appeared at last. It seems that, many years before, a young man had migrated from the valley and settled at a distant seaport, where, after getting together a little money, he had set up as a shop-keeper. His name—but I could never learn whether it was his real one, or a nickname that had grown out of his habits and success in life—was Gathergold. Being shrewd and active, and endowed by Providence with that inscrutable faculty which develops itself in what the world calls luck, he became an exceedingly rich merchant, and owner of a whole fleet of bulky-bottomed ships. All the countries of the globe appeared to join hands for the mere purpose of adding heap after heap to the mountainous accumulation of this one man's wealth. The cold regions of the north, almost within the gloom and shadow of the Arctic Circle, sent him their tribute in the shape of furs; hot Africa sifted for him the golden sands of her rivers, and gathered up the ivory tusks of her great ele-phants out of the forests; the East came bringing him the rich shawls, and spices, and teas, and the effulgence of diamonds, and the gleaming purity of large pearls. The ocean, not to be behindhand with the earth, yielded up her mighty whales, that Mr. Gathergold might sell their oil, and make a profit on it. Be the original commodity what it might, it was gold within his grasp. It might be said of him, as of Midas in the fable, that whatever he touched with his finger immediately glistened, and grew yellow, and was changed at once into sterling metal, or, which suited him still better, into piles of coin. And, when Mr. Gathergold had become so very rich that it would have taken him a hundred years only to count his wealth, he bethought himself of his native valley, and re-solved to go back thither, and end his days where he was born. With this purpose in view, he sent a skilful architect to build him such a palace as should be fit for a man of his vast wealth to live in.

As I have said above, it had already been rumored in the valley that Mr. Gathergold had turned out to be the prophetic personage, so long and vainly looked for, and that his visage was the perfect and undeniable similitude of the Great Stone Face. People were the more ready to believe that this must needs be the fact, when they beheld the splendid edifice that rose, as if by enchantment, on the site of his father's old weather-beaten farm-house. The exterior was of marble, so dazzlingly white that it seemed as though the whole structure might melt away in the sunshine, like those humbler ones which Mr. Gathergold, in his young play-days, before his fingers were gifted with the touch of transmutation, had been accustomed to build of snow. It had a richly ornamented portico, supported by tall pillars, beneath which was a lofty door, studded with silver knobs, and made of a kind of variegated wood that had been brought from beyond the sea. The windows, from the floor to the ceiling of each stately apartment, were composed, respectively, of but one enormous pane of glass, so transparently pure that it was said to be a finer medium than even the vacant atmosphere. Hardly anybody had been permitted to see the interior of this palace; but it was reported, and with good semblance of truth, to be far more gorgeous than the outside, insomuch that, whatever was iron or brass in other houses, was silver or gold in this; and Mr. Gathergold's bed-chamber, especially, made such a glittering appearance that no ordinary man would have been able to close his eyes there. But, on the other hand, Mr. Gathergold was now so inured to wealth, that perhaps he could not have closed his eyes, unless where the gleam of it was certain to find its way beneath his eyelids.

In due time, the mansion was finished; next came the upholsterers, with magnificent furniture; then, a whole troop of black and white servants, the harbingers of Mr. Gathergold, who, in his own majestic person, was expected to arrive at sunset. Our friend Ernest, meanwhile, had been deeply stirred by the idea that the great man, the noble man, the Man of Prophecy, after so many ages of delay, was at length to be made manifest to his native valley. He knew, boy as he was, that there were a thousand ways in which Mr. Gathergold, with his vast wealth, might transform himself into an angel of beneficence, and assume a control over human affairs as wide and benignant as the smile of the Great Stone Face. Full of faith and hope, Ernest doubted not that what the people said was true, and that now he was to behold the living likeness of those wondrous features on the mountainside. While the boy was still gazing up the valley, and fancying, as he always did, that the Great Stone Face returned his gaze and looked kindly at him, the rumbling of wheels was heard, approaching swiftly along the winding road.

"Here he comes!" cried a group of people who were assembled to witness the arrival—"Here comes the great Mr. Gathergold!"

A carriage, drawn by four horses, dashed round the turn of the road. Within it, thrust partly out of the window, appeared the physiognomy of a little old man, with a skin as yellow as if his own Midas-hand had transmuted it. He had a low forehead, small, sharp eyes, puckered about with innumerable wrinkles, and very thin lips, which he made still thinner by pressing them forcibly together.

"The very image of the Great Stone Face!" shouted the people. "Sure enough, the old prophecy is true; and here we have the great man, come at last!"

And, what greatly perplexed Ernest, they seemed actually to believe that here was the likeness which they spoke of. By the road-side there chanced to be an old beggar-woman and two little beggar-children, stragglers from some far-off region, who, as the carriage rolled onward, held out their hands and lifted up their doleful voices, most piteously beseeching charity. A yellow claw—the very same that had clawed together so much wealth—poked itself out of the coach-window, and dropt some copper coins upon the ground; so that, though the great man's name seems to have been Gathergold, he might just as suitably have been nicknamed Scattercopper! Still, nevertheless, with an earnest shout, and evidently with as much good faith as ever, the people bellowed—

"He is the very image of the Great Stone Face!"

But Ernest turned sadly from the wrinkled shrewdness of that sordid visage, and gazed up the valley, where, amid a gathering mist, gilded by the last sunbeams, he could still distinguish those glorious features which had impressed themselves into his soul. Their aspect cheered him. What did the benign lips seem to say?

"He will come! Fear not, Ernest—the man will come!"

The years went on, and Ernest ceased to be a boy. He had grown to be a young man now. He attracted little notice from the other inhabitants of the valley; for they saw nothing remarkable in his way of life, save that when the labor of the day was over, he still loved to go apart and gaze and meditate upon the Great Stone Face. According to their idea of the matter, it was a folly, indeed, but pardonable, inasmuch as Ernest was industrious, kind, and neighborly, and neglected no duty for the sake of indulging this idle habit. They knew not that the Great Stone Face had become a teacher to him, and that the sentiment, which was expressed in it, would enlarge the young man's heart, and fill it with wider and deeper sympathies than other hearts. They knew not that thence would come a better wisdom than could be learned from books, and a better life than could be moulded on the defaced example of other human lives. Neither did Ernest know that the thoughts and affections which came to him so naturally, in the fields and at the fireside, and wherever he communed with himself, were of a higher tone than those which all men shared with him. A simple soul—simple as when his mother first taught him the old prophecy—he beheld the marvellous features beaming adown the valley, and still wondered that their human counterpart was so long in making his appearance.

By this time poor Mr. Gathergold was dead and buried; and the oddest part of the matter was, that his wealth, which was the body and spirit of his existence, had disappeared before his death, leaving nothing of him but a living skeleton, covered over with a wrinkled yellow skin. Since the melting away of his gold, it had been very generally conceded that there was no such striking resemblance, after all, betwixt the ignoble features of the ruined merchant and that majestic face upon the mountain-side. So the people ceased to honor him during his lifetime, and quietly consigned him to forgetfulness after his decease. Once in a while, it is true, his memory was brought up in connection with the magnificent palace which he had built, and which had long ago been turned into a hotel for the accommodation of strangers, multitudes of whom came, every summer, to visit that famous natural curiosity—the Great Stone Face. Thus, Mr. Gathergold being discredited and thrown into the shade, the Man of Prophecy was yet to come.

It so happened that a native-born son of the valley, many years before, had enlisted as a soldier, and, after a great deal of hard fighting, had now become an illustrious commander. Whatever he may be called in history, he was known in camps

and on the battle-field, under the nickname of Old Blood-
and-Thunder. This war-worn veteran, being now infirm with
age and wounds, and weary of the turmoil of a military life,
and of the roll of the drum and the clangor of the trumpet,
that had so long been ringing in his ears, had lately signified
a purpose of returning to his native valley, hoping to find
repose where he remembered to have left it. The inhabitants,
his old neighbors and their grown-up children, were resolved
to welcome the renowned warrior with a salute of cannon
and a public dinner; and all the more enthusiastically, it being
affirmed that now, at last, the likeness of the Great Stone Face
had actually appeared. An aid-de-camp of old Blood-and-
Thunder, travelling through the valley, was said to have been
struck with the resemblance. Moreover, the schoolmates and
early acquaintances of the General were ready to testify on
oath that, to the best of their recollection, the aforesaid General had been exceedingly like the majestic image, even when
a boy, only that the idea had never occurred to them at that
period. Great, therefore, was the excitement throughout the
valley; and many people, who had never once thought of
glancing at the Great Stone Face for years before, now spent
their time in gazing at it, for the sake of knowing exactly how
General Blood-and-Thunder looked.

On the day of the grand festival, Ernest, with all the other
people of the valley, left their work, and proceeded to the
spot where the sylvan banquet was prepared. As he approached, the loud voice of the Reverend Doctor Battleblast
was heard, beseeching a blessing on the good things set before them, and on the distinguished Friend of Peace, in
whose honor they were assembled. The tables were arranged
in a cleared space of the woods, shut in by the surrounding
trees, except where a vista opened eastward, and afforded a
distant view of the Great Stone Face. Over the General's
chair, which was a relic from the home of Washington, there
was an arch of verdant boughs, with the laurel profusely intermixed, and surmounted by his country's banner, beneath
which he had won his victories. Our friend Ernest raised himself on his tip-toes, in hopes to get a glimpse of the celebrated
guest; but there was a mighty crowd about the tables, anxious
to hear the toasts and speeches, and to catch any word that

might fall from the General in reply; and a volunteer company, doing duty as a guard, pricked ruthlessly with their bayonets at any particularly quiet person among the throng. So Ernest, being of an unobtrusive character, was thrust quite into the background, where he could see no more of Old Blood-and-Thunder's physiognomy than if it had been still blazing on the battle-field. To console himself, he turned towards the Great Stone Face, which, like a faithful and long-remembered friend, looked back and smiled upon him through the vista of the forest. Meantime, however, he could overhear the remarks of various individuals, who were comparing the features of the hero with the face on the distant mountain-side.

"'Tis the same face, to a hair!" cried one man, cutting a caper for joy.

"Wonderfully like, that's a fact!" responded another.

"Like!—why, I call it Old Blood-and-Thunder himself, in a monstrous looking-glass!" cried a third. "And why not? He's the greatest man of this or any other age, beyond a doubt."

And then, all three of the speakers gave a great shout, which communicated electricity to the crowd, and called forth a roar from a thousand voices, that went reverberating for miles among the mountains, until you might have supposed that the Great Stone Face had poured its thunder-breath into the cry. All these comments, and this vast enthusiasm, served the more to interest our friend; nor did he think of questioning that now, at length, the mountain-visage had found its human counterpart. It is true, Ernest had imagined that this long-looked-for personage would appear in the character of a Man of Peace, uttering wisdom, and doing good, and making people happy. But, taking a habitual breadth of view, with all his simplicity, he contended that Providence should choose its own method of blessing mankind, and could conceive that this great end might be effected even by a warrior and a bloody sword, should Inscrutable Wisdom see fit to order matters so.

"The General! the General!" was now the cry. "Hush! silence! Old Blood-and-Thunder's going to make a speech."

Even so; for, the cloth being removed, the General's health

had been drunk amid shouts of applause, and he now stood upon his feet to thank the company. Ernest saw him! There he was, over the shoulders of the crowd, from the two glittering epaulets and embroidered collar upward, beneath the arch of green boughs with intertwined laurel, and the banner drooping as if to shade his brow! And there, too, visible in the same glance, through the vista of the forest, appeared the Great Stone Face! And was there, indeed, such a resemblance as the crowd had testified? Alas, Ernest could not recognize it! He beheld a war-worn and weather-beaten countenance, full of energy, and expressive of an iron will; but the gentle wisdom, the deep, broad, tender sympathies, were altogether wanting in Old Blood-and-Thunder's visage; and even if the Great Stone Face had assumed his look of stern command, the milder traits would still have tempered it.

"This is not the Man of Prophecy," sighed Ernest to himself, as he made his way out of the throng. "And must the world wait longer yet?"

The mists had congregated about the distant mountainside, and there were seen the grand and awful features of the Great Stone Face, awful but benignant, as if a mighty angel were sitting among the hills, and enrobing himself in a cloud-vesture of gold and purple. As he looked, Ernest could hardly believe but that a smile beamed over the whole visage, with a radiance still brightening, although without motion of the lips. It was probably the effect of the western sunshine, melting through the thinly diffused vapors that had swept between him and the object that he gazed at. But—as it always did—the aspect of his marvellous friend made Ernest as hopeful as if he had never hoped in vain.

"Fear not, Ernest," said his heart, even as if the Great Face were whispering him, "fear not, Ernest, he will come."

More years sped swiftly and tranquilly away. Ernest still dwelt in his native valley, and was now a man of middle age. By imperceptible degrees, he had become known among the people. Now, as heretofore, he labored for his bread, and was the same simple-hearted man that he had always been. But he had thought and felt so much—he had given so many of the best hours of his life to unworldly hopes for some great good to mankind, that it seemed as though he had been talking with the angels, and had imbibed a portion of their wisdom unawares. It was visible in the calm and well-considered beneficence of his daily life, the quiet stream of which had made a wide green margin all along its course. Not a day passed by, that the world was not the better because this man, humble as he was, had lived. He never stepped aside from his own path, yet would always reach a blessing to his neighbor. Almost involuntarily, too, he had become a preacher. The pure and high simplicity of his thought, which, as one of its manifestations, took shape in the good deeds that dropped silently from his hand, flowed also forth in speech. He uttered truths that wrought upon and moulded the lives of those who heard him. His auditors, it may be, never suspected that Ernest, their own neighbor and familiar friend, was more than an ordinary man; least of all, did Ernest himself suspect it; but, inevitably as the murmur of a rivulet, came thoughts out of his mouth that no other human lips had spoken.

When the people's minds had had a little time to cool, they were ready enough to acknowledge their mistake in imagining a similarity between General Blood-and-Thunder's truculent physiognomy and the benign visage on the mountainside. But now, again, there were reports and many paragraphs in the newspapers, affirming that the likeness of the Great Stone Face had appeared upon the broad shoulders of a certain eminent statesman. He, like Mr. Gathergold and Old Blood-and-Thunder, was a native of the valley, but had left it in his early days, and taken up the trades of law and politics. Instead of the rich man's wealth and the warrior's sword, he had but a tongue, and it was mightier than both together. So wonderfully eloquent was he, that whatever he might choose to say, his auditors had no choice but to believe him; wrong looked like right, and right like wrong; for when it pleased him, he could make a kind of illuminated fog with his mere breath, and obscure the natural daylight with it. His tongue, indeed, was a magic instrument; sometimes it rumbled like the thunder; sometimes it warbled like the sweetest music. It was the blast of war—the song of peace; and it seemed to have a heart in it, when there was no such matter. In good truth, he was a wondrous man; and when his tongue had acquired him all other imaginable success—when it had been

heard in halls of state, and in the courts of princes and potentates—after it had made him known all over the world, even
as a voice crying from shore to shore—it finally persuaded
his countrymen to select him as a candidate for the Presidency. Before this time—indeed, as soon as he began to grow
celebrated—his admirers had found out the resemblance between him and the Great Stone Face; and so much were they
struck by it, that throughout the country this distinguished
gentleman was known by the name of Old Stony Phiz. The
phrase was considered as giving a highly favorable aspect to
his political prospects; for as is likewise the case with the
Popedom, nobody ever becomes President without taking a
name other than his own.

While his friends were doing their best to make him President, Old Stony Phiz, as he was called, set out on a visit to
the valley where he was born. Of course, he had no other
object than to shake hands with his fellow-citizens, and neither thought nor cared about any effect which his progress
through the country might have upon the election. Magnificent preparations were made to receive the illustrious statesman; a cavalcade of horsemen set forth to meet him at the
boundary line of the State; and all the people left their business and gathered along the wayside to see him pass. Among
these was Ernest. Though more than once disappointed, as
we have seen, he had such a hopeful and confiding nature,
that he was always ready to believe in whatever seemed beautiful and good. He kept his heart continually open, and thus
was sure to catch the blessing from on high, when it should
come. So now again, as buoyantly as ever, he went forth to
behold the likeness of the Great Stone Face.

The cavalcade came prancing along the road, with a great
clattering of hoofs and a mighty cloud of dust, which rose up
so dense and high that the visage of the mountain-side was
completely hidden from Ernest's eyes. All the great men of
the neighborhood were there on horseback; militia officers,
in uniform; the member of Congress; the sheriff of the
county; the editors of newspapers; and many a farmer, too,
had mounted his patient steed, with his Sunday coat upon his
back. It really was a very brilliant spectacle, especially as there
were numerous banners flaunting over the cavalcade, on some

of which were gorgeous portraits of the illustrious statesman
and the Great Stone Face, smiling familiarly at one another,
like two brothers. If the pictures were to be trusted, the mutual resemblance, it must be confessed, was marvellous. We
must not forget to mention, that there was a band of music,
which made the echoes of the mountains ring and reverberate
with the loud triumph of its strains; so that airy and soul-
thrilling melodies broke out among all the heights and hollows, as if every nook of his native valley had found a voice,
to welcome the distinguished guest. But the grandest effect
was when the far-off mountain precipice flung back the music; for then the Great Stone Face itself seemed to be swelling
the triumphant chorus, in acknowledgment that, at length,
the Man of Prophecy was come.

All this while the people were throwing up their hats and
shouting, with enthusiasm so contagious that the heart of
Ernest kindled up, and he likewise threw up his hat, and
shouted, as loudly as the loudest—"Huzza for the great man!
Huzza for Old Stony Phiz!" But as yet he had not seen him.

"Here he is now!" cried those who stood near Ernest.
"There! There! Look at Old Stony Phiz and then at the Old
Man of the Mountain, and see if they are not as like as two
twin-brothers!"

In the midst of all this gallant array, came an open barouche, drawn by four white horses; and in the barouche,
with his massive head uncovered, sat the illustrious statesman,
Old Stony Phiz himself.

"Confess it," said one of Ernest's neighbors to him, "the
Great Stone Face has met its match at last!"

Now, it must be owned that, at his first glimpse of the
countenance which was bowing and smiling from the barouche, Ernest did fancy that there was a resemblance between
it and the old familiar face upon the mountain-side. The
brow, with its massive depth and loftiness, and all the other
features, indeed, were boldly and strongly hewn, as if in em-
ulation of a more than heoric, of a Titanic model. But the
sublimity and stateliness, the grand expression of a divine
sympathy, that illuminated the mountain visage, and etherealized its ponderous granite substance into spirit, might here
be sought in vain. Something had been originally left out, or

had departed. And therefore the marvellously gifted statesman had always a weary gloom in the deep caverns of his eyes, as of a child that has outgrown its playthings, or a man of mighty faculties and little aims, whose life, with all its high performances, was vague and empty, because no high purpose had endowed it with reality.

Still, Ernest's neighbor was thrusting his elbow into his side, and pressing him for an answer—

"Confess! Confess! Is not he the very picture of your Old Man of the Mountain?"

"No!" said Ernest, bluntly, "I see little or no likeness."

"Then so much the worse for the Great Stone Face!" answered his neighbor; and again he set up a shout for Old Stony Phiz.

But Ernest turned away, melancholy, and almost despondent; for this was the saddest of his disappointments, to behold a man who might have fulfilled the prophecy, and had not willed to do so. Meantime, the cavalcade, the banners, the music, and the barouches swept past him, with the vociferous crowd in the rear, leaving the dust to settle down, and the Great Stone Face to be revealed again, with the grandeur that it had worn for untold centuries.

"Lo, here I am, Ernest!" the benign lips seemed to say. "I have waited longer than thou, and am not yet weary. Fear not; the man will come."

The years hurried onward, treading in their haste on one another's heels. And now they began to bring white hairs, and scatter them over the head of Ernest; they made reverend wrinkles across his forehead, and furrows in his cheeks. He was an aged man. But not in vain had he grown old; more than the white hairs on his head were the sage thoughts in his mind; his wrinkles and furrows were inscriptions that Time had graved, and in which he had written legends of wisdom that had been tested by the tenor of a life. And Ernest had ceased to be obscure. Unsought for, undesired, had come the fame which so many seek, and made him known in the great world, beyond the limits of the valley in which he had dwelt so quietly. College professors, and even the active men of cities, came from far to see and converse with Ernest; for the report had gone abroad that this simple husbandman had ideas unlike those of other men, not gained from books, but of a higher tone—a tranquil and familiar majesty, as if he had been talking with the angels as his daily friends. Whether it were sage, statesman, or philanthropist, Ernest received these visiters with the gentle sincerity that had characterized him from boyhood, and spoke freely with them of whatever came uppermost, or lay deepest in his heart or their own. While they talked together, his face would kindle, unawares, and shine upon them, as with a mild evening light. Pensive with the fulness of such discourse, his guests took leave and went their way; and, passing up the valley, paused to look at the Great Stone Face, imagining that they had seen its likeness in a human countenance, but could not remember where.

While Ernest had been growing up and growing old, a bountiful Providence had granted a new poet to this earth. He, likewise, was a native of the valley, but had spent the greater part of his life at a distance from that romantic region, pouring out his sweet music amid the bustle and din of cities. Often, however, did the mountains which had been familiar to him in his childhood, lift their snowy peaks into the clear atmosphere of his poetry. Neither was the Great Stone Face forgotten, for the poet had celebrated it in an ode, which was grand enough to have been uttered by its own majestic lips. This man of genius, we may say, had come down from heaven with wonderful endowments. If he sang of a mountain, the eyes of all mankind beheld a mightier grandeur reposing on its breast or soaring to its summit, than had before been seen there. If his theme were a lovely lake, a celestial smile had now been thrown over it, to gleam forever on its surface. If it were the vast, old sea, even the deep immensity of its dread bosom seemed to swell the higher, as if moved by the emotions of the song. Thus the world assumed another and a better aspect from the hour that the poet blessed it with his happy eyes. The Creator had bestowed him, as the last, best touch to his own handiwork. Creation was not finished till the poet came to interpret, and so complete it.

The effect was no less high and beautiful, when his human brethren were the subject of his verse. The man or woman, sordid with the common dust of life, who crossed his daily path, and the little child who played in it, were glorified if he beheld them in his mood of poetic faith. He showed the golden links of the great chain that intertwined them with an angelic kindred; he brought out the hidden traits of a celestial birth that made them worthy of such kin. Some, indeed, there were, who thought to show the soundness of their judgment by affirming that all the beauty and dignity of the natural world existed only in the poet's fancy. Let such men speak for themselves, who undoubtedly appear to have been spawned forth by Nature with a contemptuous bitterness; she having plastered them up out of her refuse stuff, after all the swine were made. As respects all things else, the poet's ideal was the truest truth.

The songs of this poet found their way to Ernest. He read them, after his customary toil, seated on the bench before his cottage door, where, for such a length of time, he had filled his repose with thought, by gazing at the Great Stone Face. And now, as he read stanzas that caused the soul to thrill within him, he lifted his eyes to the vast countenance beaming on him so benignantly.

"Oh, majestic friend," he murmured, addressing the Great Stone Face, "is not this man worthy to resemble thee?"

The Face seemed to smile, but answered not a word.

Now it happened that the poet, though he dwelt so far away, had not only heard of Ernest, but had meditated much upon his character, until he deemed nothing so desirable as to meet this man, whose untaught wisdom walked hand in hand with the noble simplicity of his life. One summer morning, therefore, he took passage by the railroad, and, in the decline of the afternoon, alighted from the cars at no great distance from Ernest's cottage. The great hotel, which had formerly been the palace of Mr. Gathergold, was close at hand, but the poet, with his carpet-bag on his arm, inquired at once where Ernest dwelt, and was resolved to be accepted as his guest.

Approaching the door, he there found the good old man, holding a volume in his hand, which alternately he read, and then, with a finger between the leaves, looked lovingly at the Great Stone Face.

"Good evening," said the poet. "Can you give a traveller a night's lodging?"

"Willingly," answered Ernest; and then he added, smiling, "methinks I never saw the Great Stone Face look so hospitably at a stranger."

The poet sat down on the bench beside him, and he and Ernest talked together. Often had the poet held intercourse with the wittiest and the wisest, but never before with a man like Ernest, whose thoughts and feelings gushed up with such a natural freedom, and who made great truths so familiar by his simple utterance of them. Angels, as had been so often said, seemed to have wrought with him at his labor in the fields; angels seemed to have sat with him by the fireside; and, dwelling with angels as friend with friends, he had imbibed the sublimity of their ideas, and imbued it with the sweet and lowly charm of household words. So thought the poet. And Ernest, on the other hand, was moved and agitated by the living images which the poet flung out of his mind, and which peopled all the air about the cottage door with shapes of beauty, both gay and pensive. The sympathies of these two men instructed them with a profounder sense than either could have attained alone. Their minds accorded into one strain, and made delightful music which neither of them could have claimed as all his own, nor distinguished his own share from the other's. They led one another, as it were, into a high pavilion of their thoughts, so remote, and hitherto so dim that they had never entered it before, and so beautiful, that they desired to be there always.

As Ernest listened to the poet, he imagined that the Great Stone Face was bending forward to listen too. He gazed earnestly into the poet's glowing eyes.

"Who are you, my strangely gifted guest?" he said.

The poet laid his finger on the volume that Ernest had been reading.

"You have read these poems," said he. "You know me, then—for I wrote them!"

Again, and still more earnestly than before, Ernest examined the poet's features; then turned towards the Great Stone Face; then back, with an uncertain aspect, to his guest. But his countenance fell; he shook his head, and sighed.

"Wherefore are you sad?" inquired the poet.

"Because," replied Ernest, "all through life, I have awaited the fulfilment of a prophecy; and, when I read these poems, I hoped that it might be fulfilled in you."

"You hoped," answered the poet, faintly smiling, "to find in me the likeness of the Great Stone Face! And you are disappointed, as formerly with Mr. Gathergold, and Old Blood-and-Thunder, and Old Stony Phiz! Yes, Ernest, it is my doom. You must add my name to those of the illustrious Three, and record another failure of your hopes. For—in shame and sadness do I speak it, Ernest—I am not worthy to be typified by yonder benign and majestic image!"

"And why?" asked Ernest; he pointed to the volume. "Are not those thoughts divine?"

"They have a strain of the Divinity," replied the poet. "You can hear in them the far-off echo of a heavenly song. But my life, dear Ernest, has not corresponded with my thought. I have had grand dreams, but they have been only dreams, because I have lived—and that, too, by my own choice—among poor and mean realities. Sometimes even—shall I dare to say it?—I lack faith in the grandeur, the beauty, and the goodness, which my own works are said to have made more evident in nature and in human life. Why, then, pure Seeker of the Good and True, should'st thou hope to find me, in yonder image of the Divine!"

The poet spoke sadly, and his eyes were dim with tears. So, likewise, were those of Ernest.

At the hour of sunset, as had long been his frequent custom, Ernest was to discourse to an assemblage of the neighboring inhabitants, in the open air. He and the poet, arm in arm, still talking together as they went along, proceeded to the spot. It was a small nook among the hills, with a gray precipice behind, the stern front of which was relieved by the pleasant foliage of many creeping plants, that made a tapestry for the naked rock, by hanging their festoons from all its rugged angles. At a small elevation above the ground, set in a rich frame-work of verdure, there appeared a niche, spacious enough to admit a human figure, with freedom for such gestures as spontaneously accompany earnest thought and genuine emotion. Into this natural pulpit Ernest ascended, and threw a look of familiar kindness around upon his audience. They stood, or sat, or reclined upon the grass, as seemed good to each, with the departing sunshine falling obliquely over them, and mingling its subdued cheerfulness with the solemnity of a grove of ancient trees, beneath and amid the boughs of which the golden rays were constrained to pass. In another direction was seen the Great Stone Face, with the same cheer, combined with the same solemnity, in its benignant aspect.

Ernest began to speak, giving to the people of what was in his heart and mind. His words had power, because they accorded with his thoughts, and his thoughts had reality and depth, because they harmonized with the life which he had always lived. It was not mere breath that this preacher uttered; they were the words of life, because a life of good deeds and holy love was melted into them. Pearls, pure and rich, had been dissolved into this precious draught. The poet, as he listened, felt that the being and character of Ernest were a nobler strain of poetry than he had ever written. His eyes glistening with tears, he gazed reverentially at the venerable man, and said within himself, that never was there an aspect so worthy of a prophet and a sage as that mild, sweet, thoughtful countenance, with the glory of white hair diffused about it. At a distance, but distinctly to be seen, high up in the golden light of the setting sun, appeared the Great Stone Face, with hoary mists around it, like the white hairs around the brow of Ernest. Its look of grand beneficence seemed to embrace the world.

At that moment, in sympathy with a thought which he was about to utter, the face of Ernest assumed a grandeur of expression, so imbued with benevolence, that the poet, by an irresistible impulse, threw his arms aloft, and shouted—

"Behold! Behold! Ernest is himself the likeness of the Great Stone Face!"

Then all the people looked, and saw that what the deep-sighted poet said was true. The prophecy was fulfilled. But Ernest, having finished what he had to say, took the poet's arm, and walked slowly homeward, still hoping that some wiser and better man than himself would by-and-by appear, bearing a resemblance to the GREAT STONE FACE.

The Snow-Image

A CHILDISH MIRACLE

ONE afternoon of a cold winter's day, when the sun shone forth with chilly brightness, after a long storm, two children asked leave of their mother to run out and play in the new-fallen snow. The elder child was a little girl, whom, because she was of a tender and modest disposition, and was thought to be very beautiful, her parents, and other people that were familiar with her, used to call Violet. But her brother was known by the style and title of Peony, on account of the ruddiness of his broad and round little phiz, which made everybody think of sunshine and great scarlet flowers. The father of these two children, a certain Mr. Lindsey, it is important to say, was an excellent, but exceedingly matter-of-fact sort of man, a dealer in hardware, and was sturdily accustomed to take what is called the common-sense view of all matters that came under his consideration. With a heart about as tender as other people's, he had a head as hard and impenetrable, and therefore perhaps as empty, as one of the iron-pots which it was a part of his business to sell. The mother's character, on the other hand, had a strain of poetry in it, a trait of unworldly beauty, a delicate and dewy flower, as it were, that had survived out of her imaginative youth, and still kept itself alive amid the dusty realities of matrimony and motherhood.

So, Violet and Peony, as I began with saying, besought their mother to let them run out and play in the new snow; for, though it had looked so dreary and dismal, drifting downward out of the grey sky, it had a very cheerful aspect, now that the sun was shining on it. The children dwelt in a city, and had no wider play-place than a little garden before the house, divided by a white fence from the street, and with a pear-tree and two or three plum-trees overshadowing it, and some rose-bushes just in front of the parlor-windows. The trees and shrubs, however, were now leafless, and their twigs were enveloped in the light snow, which thus made a kind of wintry foliage, with here-and-there a pendant icicle for the fruit.

"Yes, Violet—yes, my little Peony," said their kind mother, "you may go out and play in the new snow."

Accordingly, the good lady bundled up her darlings in woollen jackets and wadded sacks, and put comforters round their necks, and a pair of striped gaiters on each little pair of legs, and worsted mittens on their hands, and gave them a kiss apiece, by way of a spell to keep away Jack Frost. Forth sallied the two children with a hop-skip-and-jump, that carried them at once into the very heart of a huge snow-drift, whence Violet emerged like a snow-bunting, while little Peony floundered out with his round face in full bloom. Then what a merry time had they! To look at them, frolicking in the wintry garden, you would have thought that the dark and pitiless storm had been sent for no other purpose but to provide a new plaything for Violet and Peony; and that they themselves had been created, as the snow-birds were, to take delight only in the tempest, and in the white mantle which it spread over the earth.

At last, when they had frosted one another all over with handfulls of snow, Violet, after laughing heartily at little Peony's figure, was struck with a new thought.

"You look exactly like a snow-image, Peony," said she, "if your cheeks were not so red. And that puts me in mind! Let us make an image out of snow—an image of a little girl—and it shall be our sister, and shall run about and play with us, all winter long. Won't it be nice?"

"Oh, yes!" cried Peony, as plainly as he could speak, for he was but a little boy. "That will be nice! And mamma shall see it!"

"Yes," answered Violet, "mamma shall see the new little girl. But she must not make her come into the warm parlor; for, you know, our little snow-sister will not love the warmth."

And, forthwith, the children began this great business of making a snow-image that should run about; while their mother, who was sitting at the window and overheard some of their talk, could not help smiling at the gravity with which they set about it. They really seemed to imagine that there would be no difficulty whatever in creating a live little girl out of the snow. And, to say the truth, if miracles are ever to be wrought, it will be by putting our hands to the work, in precisely such a simple and undoubting frame of mind as that in which Violet and Peony now undertook to perform one, without so much as knowing that it was a miracle. So thought the mother, and thought, likewise, that the new snow, just fallen from heaven, would be excellent material to make new beings of, if it were not so very cold. She gazed at the children, a moment longer, delighting to watch their little figures—the girl, tall for her age, graceful and agile, and so delicately colored that she looked like a cheerful Thought, more than a physical reality—while Peony expanded in breadth rather than height, and rolled along on his short and sturdy legs, as substantial as an elephant, though not quite so big. Then the mother resumed her work; what it was I forget; but she was either trimming a silken bonnet for Violet, or darning a pair of stockings for little Peony's short legs. Again, however, and again, and yet other agains, she could not help turning her head to the window, to see how the children got on with their snow-image.

Indeed, it was an exceedingly pleasant sight, those bright little souls at their tasks! Moreover, it was really wonderful to observe how knowingly and skilfully they managed the matter. Violet assumed the chief direction, and told Peony what to do, while, with her own delicate fingers, she shaped out all the nicer parts of the snow-figure. It seemed, in fact, not so much to be made by the children, as to grow up under their hands, while they were playing and prattling about it. Their mother was quite surprised at this; and the longer she looked, the more and more surprised she grew.

"What remarkable children mine are!" thought she, smiling with a mother's pride, and smiling at herself, too, for being so proud of them. What other children could have made anything so like a little girl's figure out of snow, at the first trial? Well;—but now I must finish Peony's new frock; for his grandfather is coming tomorrow, and I want the little fellow to look as handsome as possible."

So she took up the frock, and was soon as busily at work again with her needle, as the two children with their snow-image. But still, as the needle travelled hither and thither through the seams of the dress, the mother·made her toil light and happy by listening to the airy voices of Violet and Peony. They kept talking to one another all the time, their tongues being quite as active as their feet and hands. Except at intervals, she could not distinctly hear what was said, but had merely a sweet impression that they were in a most loving mood, and were enjoying themselves highly, and that the business of making the snow-image went prosperously on. Now and then, however, when Violet and Peony happened to raise their voices, the words were as audible as if they had been spoken in the very parlor, where the mother sat. Oh, how delightfully those words echoed in her heart, even though they meant nothing so very wise or wonderful, after all!

But, you must know, a mother listens with her heart, much more than with her ears; and thus she is often delighted with the trills of celestial music, when other people can hear nothing of the kind.

"Peony, Peony!" cried Violet to her brother, who had gone to another part of the garden. "Bring me some of that fresh snow, Peony, from the very furthest corner, where we have not been trampling. I want it to shape our little snow-sister's bosom with. You know that part must be quite pure, just as it came out of the sky!"

"Here it is, Violet!" answered Peony, in his bluff tone— but a very sweet tone too—as he came floundering through the half-trodden drifts. "Here is the snow for her 'ittle bosom. Oh, Violet, how beau-ti-ful she begins to look!"

"Yes," said Violet, thoughtfully and quietly, "our snow-sister does look very lovely. I did not quite know, Peony, that we could make such a sweet little girl as this."

The mother, as she listened, thought how fit and delightful an incident it would be, if fairies, or, still better, if angel-children were to come from Paradise, and play invisibly with her own darlings, and help them to make their snow-image, giving it the features of celestial babyhood! Violet and Peony would not be aware of their immortal playmates; only they would see that the image grew very beautiful, while they worked at it, and would think that they themselves had done it all.

"My little girl and boy deserve such playmates, if mortal children ever did!" said the mother to herself; and then she smiled again at her own motherly pride.

Nevertheless, the idea seized upon her imagination; and, ever and anon, she took a glimpse out of the window, half-dreaming that she might see the golden-haired children of Paradise, sporting with her own golden-haired Violet and bright-cheeked Peony.

Now, for a few moments, there was a busy and earnest, but indistinct hum of the two children's voices, as Violet and Peony wrought together with one happy consent. Violet still seemed to be the guiding spirit; while Peony acted rather as a laborer, and brought her the snow from far and near. And yet the little urchin evidently had a proper understanding of the matter, too!

"Peony, Peony!" cried Violet; for her brother was again at the other side of the garden. "Bring me those light wreaths of snow that have rested on the lower branches of the pear-tree. You can clamber on the snow-drift, Peony, and reach them easily. I must have them to make some ringlets for our snow-sister's head!"

"Here they are, Violet!" answered the little boy. "Take care you do not break them. Well done! Well done! How pretty!"

"Does she not look sweetly?" said Violet, with a very satisfied tone. "And now we must have some little shining bits of ice, to make the brightness of her eyes. She is not finished yet. Mamma will see how very beautiful she is; but papa will say, 'Tush!—nonsense!—come in out of the cold!' "

"Let us call mamma to look out," said Peony; and then he shouted lustily, "Mamma! Mamma!! Mamma!!! Look out, and see what a nice 'ittle girl we are making!"

The mother put down her work, for an instant, and looked out of the window. But it so happened that the sun—for this was one of the shortest days of the whole year—had sunken so nearly to the edge of the world, that his setting shine came obliquely into the lady's eyes. So she was dazzled, you must understand, and could not very distinctly observe what was in the garden. Still, however, through all that bright, blinding dazzle of the sun and the new snow, she beheld a small white figure in the garden, that seemed to have a wonderful deal of human likeness about it. And she saw Violet and Peony—indeed, she looked more at them than at the image—she saw the two children still at work; Peony bringing fresh snow, and Violet applying it to the figure, as scientifically as a sculptor adds clay to his model. Indistinctly as she discerned the snow-child, the mother thought to herself, that never before was there a snow-figure so cunningly made, nor ever such a dear little girl and boy to make it.

"They do everything better than other children," said she, very complacently. "Then no wonder they make better snow-images!"

She sate down again to her work, and made as much haste with it as possible; because twilight would soon come, and Peony's frock was not yet finished, and grandfather was expected, by railroad, pretty early in the morning. Faster and faster, therefore, went her flying fingers. The children, likewise, kept busily at work in the garden, and still the mother listened, whenever she could catch a word. She was amused to observe how their little imaginations had got mixed up with what they were doing, and were carried away by it.—They seemed positively to think that the snow-child would run about and play with them.

"What a nice playmate she will be for us, all winter long!" said Violet. "I hope papa will not be afraid of her giving us a cold! Shan't you love her dearly, Peony?"

"Oh, yes!" cried Peony. "And I will hug her, and she shall sit down close by me, and drink some of my warm milk!"

"Oh, no, Peony!" answered Violet, with grave wisdom. "That will not do at all. Warm milk will not be wholesome for our little snow-sister. Little snow-people, like her, eat nothing but icicles. No, no, Peony;—we must not give her anything warm to drink!"

There was a minute or two of silence; for Peony, whose short legs were never weary, had gone on pilgrimage again to the other side of the garden. All of a sudden, Violet cried out, loudly and joyfully:—

"Look here, Peony! Come quickly! A light has been shining on her cheek out of that rose-colored cloud!—and the color does not go away! Is not that beautiful?"

"Yes; it is beau-ti-ful," answered Peony, pronouncing the three syllables with deliberate accuracy. "Oh, Violet, only look at her hair! It is all like gold!"

"Oh, certainly," said Violet, with tranquillity, as if it were very much a matter of course. "That color, you know, comes from the golden clouds, that we see up there in the sky. She is almost finished now. But her lips must be made very red— redder than her cheeks. Perhaps, Peony, it will make them red, if we both kiss them!"

Accordingly, the mother heard two smart little smacks, as if both her children were kissing the snow-image on its frozen mouth. But, as this did not seem to make the lips quite red enough, Violet next proposed that the snow-child should be invited to kiss Peony's scarlet cheek.

"Come, 'ittle snow-sister, kiss me!" cried Peony.

"There! She has kissed you," added Violet, "and now her lips are very red. And she blushed a little, too!"

"Oh, what a cold kiss!" cried Peony.

Just then, there came a breeze of the pure west-wind, sweeping through the garden and rattling the parlor-windows. It sounded so wintry cold, that the mother was about to tap on the window-pane with her thimbled finger, to summon the two children in; when they both cried out to her with one voice. The tone was not a tone of surprise, although they were evidently a good deal excited; it appeared rather as if they were very much rejoiced at some event that had now happened, but which they had been looking for, and had reckoned upon all along.

"Mamma! Mamma! We have finished our little snow-sister, and she is running about the garden with us!"

"What imaginative little beings my children are!" thought the mother, putting the last few stitches into Peony's frock. "And it is strange, too, that they make me almost as much a child as they themselves are! I can hardly help believing, now, that the snow-image has really come to life!"

"Dear mamma," cried Violet, "pray look out, and see what a sweet playmate we have!"

The mother, being thus entreated, could no longer delay to

look forth from the window. The sun was now gone out of the sky, leaving, however, a rich inheritance of his brightness among those purple and golden clouds which make the sunsets of winter so magnificent. But there was not the slightest gleam or dazzle, either on the window or on the snow; so that the good lady could look all over the garden, and see everything and everybody in it. And what do you think she saw there? Violet and Peony, of course, her own two darling children. Ah, but whom or what did she see besides? Why, if you will believe me, there was a small figure of a girl, dressed all in white, with rose-tinged cheeks and ringlets of golden hair, playing about the garden with the two children. A stranger though she was, the child seemed to be on as familiar terms with Violet and Peony, and they with her, as if all the three had been playmates during the whole of their little lives. The mother thought to herself, that it must certainly be the daughter of one of the neighbors, and that, seeing Violet and Peony in the garden, the child had run across the street to play with them. So this kind lady went to the door, intending to invite the little runaway into her comfortable parlor; for, now that the sunshine was withdrawn, the atmosphere, out of doors, was already growing very cold.

But, after opening the house-door, she stood an instant on the threshold, hesitating whether she ought to ask the child to come in, or whether she should even speak to her. Indeed, she almost doubted whether it were a real child, after all, or only a light wreath of the new-fallen snow, blown hither and thither about the garden by the intensely cold west-wind. There was certainly something very singular in the aspect of the little stranger. Among all the children of the neighborhood, the lady could remember no such face, with its pure white, and delicate rose-color, and the golden ringlets tossing about the forehead and cheeks. And as for her dress, which was entirely of white, and fluttering in the breeze, it was such as no reasonable woman would put upon a little girl, when sending her out to play, in the depth of winter. It made this kind and careful mother shiver only to look at those small feet, with nothing in the world on them, except a very thin pair of white slippers. Nevertheless, airily as she was clad, the child seemed to feel not the slightest inconvenience from the cold, but danced so lightly over the snow that the tips of her toes left hardly a print in its surface; while Violet could but just keep pace with her, and Peony's short legs compelled him to lag behind.

Once, in the course of their play, the strange child placed herself between Violet and Peony, and taking a hand of each, skipt merrily forward, and they along with her. Almost immediately, however, Peony pulled away his little fist, and began to rub it as if the fingers were tingling with cold; while Violet also released herself, though with less abruptness, gravely remarking that it was better not to take hold of hands. The white-robed damsel said not a word, but danced about, just as merrily as before. If Violet and Peony did not choose to play with her, she could make just as good a playmate of the brisk and cold west-wind, which kept blowing her all about the garden, and took such liberties with her that they seemed to have been friends for a long time. All this while, the mother stood on the threshold, wondering how a little girl could look so much like a flying snow-drift, or how a snow-drift could look so very like a little girl.

She called Violet, and whispered to her.

"Violet, my darling, what is this child's name?" asked she. "Does she live near us?"

"Why, dearest mamma," answered Violet, laughing to think that her mother did not comprehend so very plain an affair, "this is our little snow-sister, whom we have just been making!"

"Yes, dear mamma," cried Peony, running to his mother and looking up simply into her face. "This is our snow-image! Is it not a nice 'ittle child?"

At this instant, a flock of snow-birds came flitting through the air. As was very natural, they avoided Violet and Peony. But—and this looked strange—they flew at once to the white-robed child, fluttered eagerly about her head, alighted on her shoulders, and seemed to claim her as an old acquaintance. She, on her part, was evidently as glad to see these little birds, old Winter's grandchildren, as they were to see her, and welcomed them by holding out both her hands. Hereupon, they each and all tried to alight on her two palms and ten small fingers and thumbs, crowding one another off, with an immense fluttering of their tiny wings. One dear little bird nestled tenderly in her bosom; another put its bill to her lips. They were as joyous, all the while, and seemed as much in their element, as you may have seen them when sporting with a snow-storm.

Violet and Peony stood laughing at this pretty sight; for they enjoyed the merry time which their new playmate was having with these small winged visitants, almost as much as if they themselves took part in it.

"Violet," said her mother, greatly perplexed, "tell me the truth, without any jest. Who is this little girl?"

"My darling mamma," answered Violet, looking seriously into her mother's face, and apparently surprised that she should need any further explanation, "I have told you truly who she is. It is our little snow-image, which Peony and I have been making. Peony will tell you so, as well as I."

"Yes, mamma!" asseverated Peony, with much gravity in his crimson little phiz. "This is 'ittle snow-child. Is not she a nice one. But, mamma, her hand is, oh, so very cold!"

While mamma still hesitated what to think and what to do, the street-gate was thrown open, and the father of Violet and Peony appeared, wrapt in a pilot-cloth sack, with a fur-cap drawn down over his ears, and the thickest of gloves upon his hands. Mr. Lindsey was a middle-aged man, with a weary, and yet a happy look in his wind-flushed and frost-pinched face, as if he had been busy all day long, and was glad to get back to his quiet home. His eyes brightened at sight of his wife and children, although he could not help uttering a word or two of surprise, at finding the whole family in the open air, on so bleak a day, and after sunset too. He soon perceived the little white stranger, sporting to-and-fro in the garden, like a dancing snow-wreath, and the flock of snow-birds fluttering about her head.

"Pray what little girl may that be?" inquired this very sensible man. "Surely her mother must be crazy, to let her go out in such bitter weather as it has been to-day, with only that flimsy white gown, and those thin slippers!"

"My dear husband," said his wife, "I know no more about the little thing than you do. Some neighbor's child, I suppose. Our Violet and Peony," she added, laughing at herself for repeating so absurd a story, "insist that she is nothing but a snow-image, which they have been busy about in the garden, almost all the afternoon."

As she said this, the mother glanced her eyes towards the spot where the children's snow-image had been made. What was her surprise, on perceiving that there was not the slightest trace of so much labor!—no image at all!—no piled-up heap of snow!—nothing whatever, save the prints of little footsteps around a vacant space.

"This is very strange!" said she.

"What is strange, dear mother?" asked Violet. "Dear father, do not you see how it is? This is our snow-image, which Peony and I have made, because we wanted another playmate. Did not we, Peony?"

"Yes, papa," said crimson Peony. "This be our 'ittle snow-sister. Is not she beau-ti-ful? But she gave me such a cold kiss!"

"Poh, nonsense, children!" cried their good, honest father, who, as we have already intimated, had an exceedingly common-sensible way of looking at matters. "Do not tell me of making live figures out of snow! Come, wife; this little stranger must not stay out in the bleak air a moment longer. We will bring her into the parlor; and you shall give her a supper of warm bread and milk, and make her as comfortable as you can. Meanwhile, I will inquire among the neighbors; or, if necessary, send the city-crier about the streets, to give notice of a lost child."

So saying, this honest and very kind-hearted man was going towards the little white damsel, with the best intentions in the world. But Violet and Peony, each seizing their father by a hand, earnestly besought him not to make her come in.

"Dear father," cried Violet, putting herself before him, "it is true, what I have been telling you! This is our little snow-girl, and she cannot live any longer than while she breathes the cold west-wind. Do not make her come into the hot room!"

"Yes, father!" shouted Peony, stamping his little foot, so mightily was he in earnest.—"This be nothing but our 'ittle snow-child! She will not love the hot fire!"

"Nonsense, children, nonsense, nonsense!" cried the father,

half-vexed, half-laughing at what he considered their foolish obstinacy. "Run into the house, this moment! It is too late to play any longer, now. I must take care of this little girl immediately, or she will catch her death-a-cold!"

"Husband!—dear husband!" said his wife, in a low voice; for she had been looking narrowly at the snow-child, and was more perplexed than ever.—"There is something very singular in all this. You will think me foolish—but—but—may it not be that some invisible angel has been attracted by the simplicity and good faith with which our children set about their undertaking? May he not have spent an hour of his immortality in playing with those dear little souls?—and so the result is what we call a miracle. No, no! Do not laugh at me. I see what a foolish thought it is!"

"My dear wife," replied the husband, laughing heartily, "you are as much a child as Violet and Peony."

And, in one sense, so she was; for, all through life, she had kept her heart full of childlike simplicity, and faith, which was as pure and clear as crystal; and, looking at all matters through this transparent medium, she sometimes saw truths so profound, that other people laughed at them as nonsense and absurdity.

But, now, kind Mr. Lindsey had entered the garden, breaking away from his two children, who still sent their shrill voices after him, beseeching him to let the snow-child stay and enjoy herself in the cold west-wind. As he approached, the snow-birds took to flight. The little white damsel, also, fled backward, shaking her head as if to say—'Pray do not touch me!'—and roguishly, as it appeared, leading him through the deepest of the snow. Once, the good man stumbled, and floundered down upon his face; so that, gathering himself up again, with the snow sticking to his rough pilot-cloth sack, he looked as white and wintry as a snow-image of the largest size. Some of the neighbors, meanwhile, seeing him from their windows, wondered what could possess poor Mr. Lindsey to be running about his garden in pursuit of a snow-drift, which the west-wind was driving hither and thither! At length, after a vast deal of trouble, he chased the little stranger into a corner, where she could not possibly escape him. His wife had been looking on, and, it being now nearly twilight, was wonder-struck to observe how the snow-child gleamed and sparkled, and how she seemed to shed a glow all roundabout her, and how, when driven into the corner, she positively glistened like a star! It was a frosty kind of brightness, too, like that of an icicle in the moonlight. The wife thought it strange, that good Mr. Lindsey should see nothing remarkable in the snow-child's appearance.

"Come, you odd little thing!" cried the honest man, seizing her by the hand. "I have caught you at last, and will make you comfortable in spite of yourself. We will put a nice warm pair of worsted stockings on your frozen little feet; and you shall have a good thick shawl to wrap yourself in. Your poor, white nose, I am afraid, is actually frost-bitten. But we will make it all right. Come along in!"

And so, with a most benevolent smile on his sagacious visage, all purple as it was with the cold, this very well-meaning gentleman took the snow-child by the hand and led her towards the house. She followed him, droopingly and reluctant; for all the glow and sparkle was gone out of her figure; and, whereas, just before, she had resembled a bright, frosty, star-gemmed evening, with a crimson gleam on the cold horizon, she now looked as dull and languid as a thaw. As kind Mr. Lindsey led her up the steps of the door, Violet and Peony looked into his face—their eyes full of tears, which froze before they could run down their cheeks—and again entreated him not to bring their snow-image into the house.

"Not bring her in!" exclaimed the kind-hearted man. "Why, you are crazy, my little Violet!—quite crazy, my small Peony! She is so cold, already, that her hand has almost frozen mine, in spite of my thick gloves. Would you have her freeze to death?"

His wife, as he came up the steps, had been taking another long, earnest, almost awe-stricken gaze at the little white stranger. She hardly knew whether it were a dream or no; but she could not help fancying that she saw the delicate print of Violet's fingers on the child's neck. It looked just as if, while Violet was shaping out the image, she had given it a gentle pat with her hand, and had neglected to smooth the impression quite away.

"After all, husband," said the mother, recurring to her idea, that the angels would be as much delighted to play with Violet and Peony, as she herself was, "after all, she does look strangely like a snow-image! I do believe she is made of snow!"

A puff of the west-wind blew against the snow-child; and again she sparkled like a star.

"Snow!" repeated good Mr. Lindsey, drawing the reluctant guest over his hospitable threshold. "No wonder she looks like snow. She is half-frozen, poor little thing! But a good fire will put everything to rights."

Without further talk, and always with the very best intentions, this highly benevolent and common-sensible individual led the little white damsel—drooping, drooping, drooping, more and more—out of the frosty air, and into his comfortable parlor. A Heidenberg stove, filled to the brim with intensely burning anthracite, was sending a bright gleam through the isinglass of its iron-door, and causing the vase of water on its top to fume and bubble with excitement. A warm, sultry smell was diffused throughout the room. A thermometer, on the wall farthest from the stove, stood at eighty degrees. The parlor was hung with red curtains, and covered with a red carpet, and looked just as warm as it felt. The difference betwixt the atmosphere here, and the cold, wintry twilight, out of doors, was like stepping at once from Nova Zembla to the hottest part of India, or from the North-pole into an oven. Oh, this was a fine place for the little white stranger!

The common-sensible man placed the snow-child on the hearth-rug, right in front of the hissing and fuming stove.

"Now she will be comfortable!" cried kind Mr. Lindsey, rubbing his hands and looking about him, with the pleasantest smile you ever saw. "Make yourself at home, my child!"

Sad, sad, and drooping, looked the little white maiden, as she stood on the hearth-rug, with the hot blast of the stove striking through her like a pestilence. Once, she threw a glance wistfully towards the window, and caught a glimpse, through its red curtains, of the snow-covered roofs, and the stars glimmering frostily, and all the delicious intensity of the cold night. The bleak wind rattled the window-panes, as if it were summoning her to come forth. But there stood the snow-child, drooping, before the hot stove!

But the common-sensible man saw nothing amiss.

"Come, wife," said he, "let her have a pair of thick stockings and a woollen shawl or blanket directly; and tell Dora to give her some warm supper as soon as the milk boils. You, Violet and Peony, amuse your little friend. She is out of spirits, you see, at finding herself in a strange place. For my part, I will go round among the neighbors, and find out where she belongs."

The mother, meanwhile, had gone in search of the shawl and stockings; for her own view of the matter, however subtle and delicate, had given way, as it always did, to the stubborn materialism of her husband. Without heeding the remonstrances of his two children, who still kept murmuring that their little snow-sister did not love the warmth, good Mr. Lindsey took his departure, shutting the parlor-door carefully behind him. Turning up the collar of his sack over his ears, he emerged from the house, and had barely reached the street-gate, when he was recalled by the screams of Violet and Peony, and the rapping of a thimbled finger against the parlor-window.

"Husband! Husband!" cried his wife, showing her horror-stricken face through the window-panes. "There is no need of going for the child's parents!"

"We told you so, father!" screamed Violet and Peony, as he re-entered the parlor. "You would bring her in; and now our poor—dear—beau-ti-ful little snow-sister is thawed!"

And their own sweet little faces were already dissolved in tears; so that their father, seeing what strange things occasionally happen in this every-day world, felt not a little anxious lest his children might be going to thaw too! In the utmost perplexity, he demanded an explanation of his wife. She could only reply, that, being summoned to the parlor by the cries of Violet and Peony, she found no trace of the little white maiden, unless it were the remains of a heap of snow, which, while she was gazing at it, melted quite away upon the hearth-rug.

"And there you see all that is left of it!" added she, pointing to a pool of water, in front of the stove.

"Yes, father," said Violet, looking reproachfully at him, through her tears, "there is all that is left of our dear little snow-sister!"

"Naughty father!" cried Peony, stamping his foot, and—I shudder to say—shaking his little fist at the common-sensible man. "We told you how it would be! What for did you bring her in?"

And the Heidenberg stove, through the isinglass of its door, seemed to glare at good Mr. Lindsey, like a red-eyed demon, triumphing in the mischief which it had done!

This, you will observe, was one of those rare cases, which yet will occasionally happen, where common-sense finds itself at fault. The remarkable story of the snow-image, though, to that sagacious class of people to whom good Mr. Lindsey belongs, it may seem but a childish affair, is nevertheless capable of being moralized in various methods, greatly for their edification. One of its lessons, for instance, might be, that it behoves men, and especially men of benevolence, to consider well what they are about, and, before acting on their philanthropic purposes, to be quite sure that they comprehend the nature and all the relations of the business in hand. What has been established as an element of good to one being, may prove absolute mischief to another; even as the warmth of the parlor was proper enough for children of flesh and blood, like Violet and Peony—though by no means very wholesome, even for them—but involved nothing short of annihilation to the unfortunate snow-image.

But, after all, there is no teaching anything to wise men of good Mr. Lindsey's stamp. They know everything—Oh, to be sure!—everything that has been, and everything that is, and everything that, by any future possibility, can be. And, should some phenomenon of Nature or Providence transcend their system, they will not recognize it, even if it come to pass under their very noses.

"Wife," said Mr. Lindsey, after a fit of silence, "see what a quantity of snow the children have brought in on their feet! It has made quite a puddle here before the stove. Pray tell Dora to bring some towels and sop it up!"

Feathertop

A Moralized Legend

"DICKON," cried Mother Rigby, "a coal for my pipe!"
The pipe was in the old dame's mouth, when she
said these words. She had thrust it there after filling it with
tobacco, but without stooping to light it at the hearth; where,
indeed, there was no appearance of a fire having been kindled,
that morning. Forthwith, however, as soon as the order was
given, there was an intense red glow out of the bowl of
the pipe, and a whiff of smoke from Mother Rigby's lips.
Whence the coal came, and how brought thither by an invisible hand, I have never been able to discover.

"Good!" quoth Mother Rigby, with a nod of her head.
"Thank ye, Dickon! And now for making this scarecrow. Be
within call, Dickon, in case I need you again."

The good woman had risen thus early, (for, as yet, it was
scarcely sunrise,) in order to set about making a scarecrow,
which she intended to put in the middle of her corn-patch. It
was now the latter week of May, and the crows and blackbirds had already discovered the little, green, rolled-up leaf of
the Indian corn, just peeping out of the soil. She was determined, therefore, to contrive as lifelike a scarecrow as ever
was seen, and to finish it immediately, from top to toe, so
that it should begin its sentinel's duty that very morning.
Now, Mother Rigby (as everybody must have heard) was one
of the most cunning and potent witches in New England, and
might, with very little trouble, have made a scarecrow ugly
enough to frighten the minister himself. But, on this occasion, as she had awakened in an uncommonly pleasant humor, and was further dulcified by her pipe of tobacco, she
resolved to produce something fine, beautiful, and splendid,
rather than hideous and horrible.

"I don't want to set up a hobgoblin in my own corn-patch
and almost at my own door-step," said Mother Rigby to herself, puffing out a whiff of smoke. "I could do it if I pleased;
but I'm tired of doing marvellous things, and so I'll keep

within the bounds of every-day business, just for variety's sake. Besides, there's no use in scaring the little children, for a mile roundabout, though 'tis true I'm a witch!"

It was settled, therefore, in her own mind, that the scarecrow should represent a fine gentleman of the period, so far as the materials at hand would allow. Perhaps it may be as well to enumerate the chief of the articles that went to the composition of this figure.

The most important item of all, probably, although it made so little show, was a certain broomstick, on which Mother Rigby had taken many an airy gallop at midnight, and which now served the scarecrow by way of a spinal column, or, as the unlearned phrase it, a backbone. One of its arms was a disabled flail, which used to be wielded by Goodman Rigby, before his spouse worried him out of this troublesome world; the other, if I mistake not, was composed of the pudding-stick and a broken rung of a chair, tied loosely together at the elbow. As for its legs, the right was a hoe-handle, and the left, an undistinguished and miscellaneous stick from the wood-pile. Its lungs, stomach, and other affairs of that kind, were nothing better than a meal-bag stuffed with straw. Thus, we have made out the skeleton and entire corporosity of the scarecrow, with the exception of its head; and this was admirably supplied by a somewhat withered and shrivelled pumpkin in which Mother Rigby cut two holes for the eyes and a slit for the mouth, leaving a bluish-colored knob, in the middle, to pass for a nose. It was really quite a respectable face.

"I've seen worse ones on human shoulders, at any rate," said Mother Rigby. "And many a fine gentleman has a pumpkin-head, as well as my scarecrow!"

But the clothes, in this case, were to be the making of the man. So the good old woman took down from a peg an ancient plum-colored coat, of London make, and with relics of embroidery on its seams, cuffs, pocket-flaps, and button-holes, but lamentably worn and faded, patched at the elbows, tattered at the skirts, and threadbare all over. On the left breast was a round hole, whence either a star of nobility had been rent away, or else the hot heart of some former wearer had scorched it through and through. The neighbors said, that this rich garment belonged to the Black Man's wardrobe,

and that he kept it at Mother Rigby's cottage for the convenience of slipping it on, whenever he wished to make a grand
appearance at the governor's table. To match the coat, there
was a velvet waistcoat of very ample size, and formerly embroidered with foliage, that had been as brightly golden as
the maple-leaves in October, but which had now quite vanished out of the substance of the velvet. Next came a pair of
scarlet breeches, once worn by the French governor of Louisbourg, and the knees of which had touched the lower step of
the throne of Louis le Grand. The Frenchman had given these
small-clothes to an Indian powwow, who parted with them
to the old witch for a gill of strong-waters, at one of their
dances in the forest. Furthermore, Mother Rigby produced a
pair of silk stockings and put them on the figure's legs, where
they showed as unsubstantial as a dream, with the wooden
reality of the two sticks making itself miserably apparent
through the holes. Lastly, she put her dead husband's wig on
the bare scalp of the pumpkin, and surmounted the whole
with a rusty three-cornered hat, in which was stuck the longest tail-feather of a rooster.

Then the old dame stood the figure up in a corner of her
cottage, and chuckled to behold its yellow semblance of a visage, with its knobby little nose thrust into the air. It had a
strangely self-satisfied aspect, and seemed to say—"Come
look at me!"

"And you are well worth looking at—that's a fact!" quoth
Mother Rigby, in admiration at her own handiwork. "I've
made many a puppet, since I've been a witch; but methinks
this is the finest of them all. 'Tis almost too good for a scarecrow. And, by the by, I'll just fill a fresh pipe of tobacco, and
then take him out to the corn-patch."

While filling her pipe, the old woman continued to gaze
with almost motherly affection at the figure in the corner. To
say the truth—whether it were chance, or skill, or downright
witchcraft—there was something wonderfully human in this
ridiculous shape, bedizened with its tattered finery; and as for
the countenance, it appeared to shrivel its yellow surface into
a grin—a funny kind of expression, betwixt scorn and merriment, as if it understood itself to be a jest at mankind. The
more Mother Rigby looked, the better she was pleased.

"Dickon," cried she, sharply, "another coal for my pipe!"

Hardly had she spoken, than, just as before, there was a red glowing coal on the top of the tobacco. She drew in a long whiff, and puffed it forth again into the bar of morning sunshine, which struggled through the one dusty pane of her cottage window. Mother Rigby always liked to flavor her pipe with a coal of fire from the particular chimney-corner, whence this had been brought. But where that chimney-corner might be, or who brought the coal from it—further than that the invisible messenger seemed to respond to the name of Dickon—I cannot tell.

"That puppet yonder," thought Mother Rigby, still with her eyes fixed on the scarecrow, "is too good a piece of work to stand all summer in a corn-patch, frightening away the crows and blackbirds. He's capable of better things. Why, I've danced with a worse one, when partners happened to be scarce, at our witch meetings in the forest! What if I should let him take his chance among the other men of straw and empty fellows, who go bustling about the world?"

The old witch took three or four more whiffs of her pipe, and smiled.

"He'll meet plenty of his brethren, at every street-corner!" continued she. "Well; I didn't mean to dabble in witchcraft to-day, further than the lighting of my pipe; but a witch I am, and a witch I'm likely to be, and there's no use trying to shirk it. I'll make a man of my scarecrow, were it only for the joke's sake!"

While muttering these words, Mother Rigby took the pipe from her own mouth, and thrust it into the crevice which represented the same feature in the pumpkin-visage of the scarecrow.

"Puff, darling, puff!" said she. "Puff away, my fine fellow! Your life depends on it!"

This was a strange exhortation, undoubtedly, to be addressed to a mere thing of sticks, straw, and old clothes, with nothing better than a shrivelled pumpkin for a head; as we know to have been the scarecrow's case. Nevertheless, as we must carefully hold in remembrance, Mother Rigby was a witch of singular power and dexterity; and, keeping this fact duly before our minds, we shall see nothing beyond credibil-

ity in the remarkable incidents of our story. Indeed, the great
difficulty will be at once got over, if we can only bring ourselves to believe, that, as soon as the old dame bade him puff,
there came a whiff of smoke from the scarecrow's mouth. It
was the very feeblest of whiffs, to be sure; but it was followed
by another and another, each more decided than the preceding one.

"Puff away, my pet! Puff away, pretty one!" Mother Rigby
kept repeating, with her pleasantest smile. "It is the breath of
life to ye; and that you may take my word for!"

Beyond all question, the pipe was bewitched. There must
have been a spell, either in the tobacco, or in the fiercely
glowing coal that so mysteriously burned on top of it, or in
the pungently aromatic smoke, which exhaled from the kindled weed. The figure, after a few doubtful attempts, at
length blew forth a volley of smoke, extending all the way
from the obscure corner into the bar of sunshine. There it
eddied and melted away among the motes of dust. It seemed
a convulsive effort; for the two or three next whiffs were fainter, although the coal still glowed, and threw a gleam over
the scarecrow's visage. The old witch clapt her skinny palms
together, and smiled encouragingly upon her handiwork. She
saw that the charm worked well. The shrivelled, yellow face,
which heretofore had been no face at all, had already a thin,
fantastic haze, as it were, of human likeness, shifting to-and-
fro across it; sometimes vanishing entirely, but growing more
perceptible than ever, with the next whiff from the pipe. The
whole figure, in like manner, assumed a show of life, such as
we impart to ill-defined shapes among the clouds, and half-
deceive ourselves with the pastime of our own fancy.

If we must needs pry closely into the matter, it may be
doubted whether there was any real change, after all, in the
sordid, worn-out, worthless, and ill-joined substance of the
scarecrow; but merely a spectral illusion, and a cunning effect
of light and shade, so colored and contrived as to delude the
eyes of most men. The miracles of witchcraft seem always to
have had a very shallow subtlety; and, at least, if the above
explanation do not hit the truth of the process, I can suggest
no better.

"Well puffed, my pretty lad!" still cried old Mother Rigby.

"Come; another good, stout whiff; and let it be with might and main! Puff for thy life, I tell thee! Puff out of the very bottom of thy heart; if any heart thou hast, or any bottom to it! Well done, again! Thou didst suck in that mouthfull, as if for the pure love of it."

And then the witch beckoned to the scarecrow, throwing so much magnetic potency into her gesture, that it seemed as if it must inevitably be obeyed, like the mystic call of the load-stone, when it summons the iron.

"Why lurkest thou in the corner, lazy one?" said she. "Step forth! Thou hast the world before thee!"

Upon my word, if the legend were not one which I heard on my grandmother's knee, and which had established its place among things credible before my childish judgment could analyze its probability, I question whether I should have the face to tell it now!

In obedience to Mother Rigby's word, and extending its arm as if to reach her outstretched hand, the figure made a step forward—a kind of hitch and jerk, however, rather than a step—then tottered, and almost lost its balance. What could the witch expect? It was nothing, after all, but a scarecrow, stuck upon two sticks. But the strong-willed old beldam scowled, and beckoned, and flung the energy of her pur-pose so forcibly at this poor combination of rotten wood, and musty straw, and ragged garments, that it was com-pelled to show itself a man, in spite of the reality of things. So it stept into the bar of sunshine. There it stood—poor devil of a contrivance that it was!—with only the thinnest vesture of human similitude about it, through which was evident the stiff, ricketty, incongruous, faded, tattered, good-for-nothing patchwork of its substance, ready to sink in a heap upon the floor, as conscious of its own unworthi-ness to be erect. Shall I confess the truth? At its present point of vivification, the scarecrow reminds me of some of the lukewarm and abortive characters, composed of hetero-geneous materials, used for the thousandth time, and never worth using, with which romance-writers (and myself, no doubt, among the rest) have so over-peopled the world of fiction.

But the fierce old hag began to get angry and show a

glimpse of her diabolic nature, (like a snake's head peeping with a hiss out of her bosom,) at this pusillanimous behavior of the thing, which she had taken the trouble to put together.

"Puff away, wretch!" cried she wrathfully. "Puff, puff, puff, thou thing of straw and emptiness!—thou rag or two!—thou meal bag!—thou pumpkin-head!—thou nothing!—where shall I find a name vile enough to call thee by! Puff, I say, and suck in thy fantastic life along with the smoke; else I snatch the pipe from thy mouth, and hurl thee where that red coal came from!"

Thus threatened, the unhappy scarecrow had nothing for it, but to puff away for dear life. As need was, therefore, it applied itself lustily to the pipe, and sent forth such abundant vollies of tobacco-smoke that the small cottage-kitchen became all vaporous. The one sunbeam struggled mistily through, and could but imperfectly define the image of the cracked and dusty window-pane on the opposite wall. Mother Rigby, meanwhile, with one brown arm akimbo and the other stretched towards the figure, loomed grimly amid the obscurity, with such port and expression as when she was wont to heave a ponderous nightmare on her victims, and stand at the bedside to enjoy their agony. In fear and trembling did this poor scarecrow puff. But its efforts, it must be acknowledged, served an excellent purpose; for, with each successive whiff, the figure lost more and more of its dizzy and perplexing tenuity, and seemed to take denser substance. Its very garments, moreover, partook of the magical change, and shone with the gloss of novelty, and glistened with the skilfully embroidered gold that had long ago been rent away. And, half-revealed among the smoke, a yellow visage bent its lustreless eyes on Mother Rigby.

At last, the old witch clenched her fist, and shook it at the figure. Not that she was positively angry, but merely acting on the principle—perhaps untrue, or not the only truth, though as high a one as Mother Rigby could be expected to attain—that feeble and torpid natures, being incapable of better inspiration, must be stirred up by fear. But, here was the crisis. Should she fail in what she now sought to effect, it was her ruthless purpose to scatter the miserable simulacre into its original elements.

"Thou hast a man's aspect," said she sternly. "Have also the echo and mockery of a voice! I bid thee speak!"

The scarecrow gasped, struggled, and at length emitted a murmur, which was so incorporated with its smoky breath that you could scarcely tell whether it were indeed a voice, or only a whiff of tobacco. Some narrators of this legend hold the opinion, that Mother Rigby's conjurations, and the fierceness of her will, had compelled a familiar spirit into the figure, and that the voice was his.

"Mother," mumbled the poor, stifled voice, "be not so awful with me! I would fain speak; but being without wits, what can I say?"

"Thou canst speak, darling, canst thou?" cried Mother Rigby, relaxing her grim countenance into a smile. "And what shalt thou say, quoth-a! Say, indeed! Art thou of the brotherhood of the empty skull, and demandest of me what thou shalt say? Thou shalt say a thousand things, and saying them a thousand times over, thou shalt still have said nothing! Be not afraid, I tell thee! When thou comest into the world, (whither I purpose sending thee, forthwith,) thou shalt not lack the wherewithal to talk. Talk! Why, thou shalt babble like a mill-stream, if thou wilt. Thou hast brains enough for that, I trow!"

"At your service, mother," responded the figure.

"And that was well said, my pretty one!" answered Mother Rigby. "Then thou spakest like thyself, and meant nothing. Thou shalt have a hundred such set phrases, and five hundred to the boot of them. And now, darling, I have taken so much pains with thee, and thou art so beautiful, that, by my troth, I love thee better than any witch's puppet in the world; and I've made them of all sorts—clay, wax, straw, sticks, night-fog, morning-mist, sea-foam, and chimney-smoke! But thou art the very best. So give heed to what I say!"

"Yes, kind mother," said the figure, "with all my heart!"

"With all thy heart!" cried the old witch, setting her hands to her sides, and laughing loudly. "Thou hast such a pretty way of speaking! With all thy heart! And thou didst put thy hand to the left side of thy waistcoat, as if thou really hadst one!"

So now, in high good-humor with this fantastic contriv-

ance of hers, Mother Rigby told the scarecrow that it must
go and play its part in the great world, where not one man in
a hundred, she affirmed, was gifted with more real substance
than itself. And, that he might hold up his head with the best
of them, she endowed him, on the spot, with an unreckonable amount of wealth. It consisted partly of a gold mine in
Eldorado, and of ten thousand shares in a broken bubble, and
of half a million acres of vineyard at the North pole, and of a
castle in the air and a chateau in Spain, together with all the
rents and income therefrom accruing. She further made over
to him the cargo of a certain ship, laden with salt of Cadiz,
which she herself, by her necromantic arts, had caused to
founder, ten years before, in the deepest of mid-ocean. If the
salt were not dissolved, and could be brought to market, it
would fetch a pretty penny among the fishermen. That he
might not lack ready money, she gave him a copper farthing,
of Birmingham manufacture, being all the coin she had about
her, and likewise a great deal of brass, which she applied to
his forehead, thus making it yellower than ever.

"With that brass alone," quoth Mother Rigby, "thou canst
pay thy way all over the earth. Kiss me, pretty darling! I have
done my best for thee."

Furthermore, that the adventurer might lack no possible
advantage towards a fair start in life, this excellent old dame
gave him a token, by which he was to introduce himself to a
certain magistrate, member of the council, merchant, and
elder of the church, (the four capacities constituting but one
man,) who stood at the head of society in the neighboring
metropolis. The token was neither more nor less than a single
word, which Mother Rigby whispered to the scarecrow, and
which the scarecrow was to whisper to the merchant.

"Gouty as the old fellow is, he'll run thy errands for thee,
when once thou hast given him that word in his ear," said the
old witch. "Mother Rigby knows the worshipful Justice
Gookin, and the worshipful justice knows Mother Rigby!"

Here the witch thrust her wrinkled face close to the puppet's, chuckling irrepressibly, and fidgetting all through her
system, with delight at the idea which she meant to communicate.

"The worshipful Master Gookin," whispered she, "hath a

comely maiden to his daughter! And hark ye, my pet! Thou
hast a fair outside, and a pretty wit enough of thine own.
Yea; a pretty wit enough! Thou wilt think better of it, when
thou hast seen more of other people's wits. Now, with thy
outside and thy inside, thou art the very man to win a young
girl's heart. Never doubt it! I tell thee it shall be so. Put but
a bold face on the matter, sigh, smile, flourish thy hat, thrust
forth thy leg like a dancing-master, put thy right hand to the
left side of thy waistcoat—and pretty Polly Gookin is thine
own!"

All this while, the new creature had been sucking in and
exhaling the vapory fragrance of his pipe, and seemed now to
continue this occupation as much for the enjoyment which it
afforded, as because it was an essential condition of his existence. It was wonderful to see how exceedingly like a human
being it behaved. Its eyes (for it appeared to possess a pair)
were bent on Mother Rigby, and at suitable junctures, it nodded or shook its head. Neither did it lack words proper for
the occasion—'Really! Indeed! Pray tell me! Is it possible!
Upon my word! By no means! Oh! Ah! Hem!'—and other
such weighty utterances as imply attention, inquiry, acquiescence, or dissent, on the part of the auditor. Even had you
stood by, and seen the scarecrow made, you could scarcely
have resisted the conviction that it perfectly understood the
cunning counsels, which the old witch poured into its counterfeit of an ear. The more earnestly it applied its lips to the
pipe, the more distinctly was its human likeness stamped
among visible realities; the more sagacious grew its expression; the more lifelike its gestures and movements, and the
more intelligibly audible its voice. Its garments, too, glistened
so much the brighter with an illusory magnificence. The very
pipe, in which burned the spell of all this wonderwork, ceased
to appear as a smoke-blackened earthen stump, and became a
meerschaum, with painted bowl and amber mouth-piece.

It might be apprehended, however, that, as the life of the
illusion seemed identical with the vapor of the pipe, it would
terminate simultaneously with the reduction of the tobacco to
ashes. But the beldam foresaw the difficulty.

"Hold thou the pipe, my precious one," said she, "while I
fill it for thee again."

It was sorrowful to behold how the fine gentleman began to fade back into a scarecrow, while Mother Rigby shook the ashes out of the pipe, and proceeded to replenish it from her tobacco-box.

"Dickon," cried she, in her high, sharp tone, "another coal for this pipe!"

No sooner said than the intensely red speck of fire was glowing within the pipe-bowl; and the scarecrow, without waiting for the witch's bidding, applied the tube to its lips, and drew in a few short, convulsive whiffs, which soon, however, became regular and equable.

"Now, mine own heart's darling," quoth Mother Rigby, "whatever may happen to thee, thou must stick to thy pipe. Thy life is in it; and that, at least, thou knowest well, if thou knowest naught besides. Stick to thy pipe, I say! Smoke, puff, blow thy cloud; and tell the people, if any question be made, that it is for thy health, and that so the physician orders thee to do. And, sweet one, when thou shalt find thy pipe getting low, go apart into some corner, and (first filling thyself with smoke) cry sharply—'Dickon, a fresh pipe of tobacco!' and—'Dickon, another coal for my pipe!'—and have it into thy pretty mouth, as speedily as may be. Else, instead of a gallant gentleman in a gold-laced coat, thou wilt be but a jumble of sticks, and tattered clothes, and a bag of straw, and a withered pumpkin! Now depart, my treasure, and good luck go with thee!"

"Never fear, mother!" said the figure, in a stout voice, and sending forth a courageous whiff of smoke. "I will thrive, if an honest man and a gentleman may!"

"Oh, thou wilt be the death of me!" cried the old witch, convulsed with laughter. "That was well said! If an honest man and a gentleman may! Thou playest thy part to perfection. Get along with thee for a smart fellow; and I will wager on thy head, as a man of pith and substance, with a brain, and what they call a heart, and all else that a man should have, against any other thing on two legs. I hold myself a better witch than yesterday, for thy sake. Did not I make thee? And I defy any witch in New England to make such another! Here; take my staff along with thee!"

The staff, though it was but a plain oaken stick, immediately took the aspect of a gold-headed cane.

"That gold-head has as much sense in it as thine own," said Mother Rigby, "and it will guide thee straight to worshipful Master Gookin's door. Get thee gone, my pretty pet, my darling, my precious one, my treasure; and if any ask thy name, it is Feathertop. For thou hast a feather in thy hat, and I have thrust a handfull of feathers into the hollow of thy head, and thy wig, too, is of the fashion they call Feathertop—so be Feathertop thy name!"

And, issuing from the cottage, Feathertop strode manfully towards town. Mother Rigby stood at the threshold, well pleased to see how the sunbeams glistened on him, as if all his magnificence were real, and how diligently and lovingly he smoked his pipe, and how handsomely he walked, in spite of a little stiffness of his legs. She watched him, until out of sight, and threw a witch-benediction after her darling, when a turn of the road snatched him from her view.

Betimes in the forenoon, when the principal street of the neighboring town was just at its acme of life and bustle, a stranger of very distinguished figure was seen on the sidewalk. His port, as well as his garments, betokened nothing short of nobility. He wore a richly embroidered plum-colored coat, a waistcoat of costly velvet, magnificently adorned with golden foliage, a pair of splendid scarlet breeches, and the finest and glossiest of white silk stockings. His head was covered with a peruque, so daintily powdered and adjusted that it would have been sacrilege to disorder it with a hat; which, therefore, (and it was a gold-laced hat, set off with a snowy feather,) he carried beneath his arm. On the breast of his coat glistened a star. He managed his gold-headed cane with an airy grace, peculiar to the fine gentleman of the period; and, to give the highest possible finish to his equipment, he had lace ruffles at his wrists, of a most ethereal delicacy, sufficiently avouching how idle and aristocratic must be the hands which they half concealed.

It was a remarkable point in the accoutrement of this brilliant personage, that he held in his left hand a fantastic kind of a pipe, with an exquisitely painted bowl, and an amber mouth-piece. This he applied to his lips, as often as every five or six paces, and inhaled a deep whiff of smoke, which, after being retained a moment in his lungs, might be seen to eddy gracefully from his mouth and nostrils.

As may well be supposed, the street was all a-stir to find out the stranger's name.

"It is some great nobleman, beyond question," said one of the townspeople. "Do you see the star at his breast?"

"Nay; it is too bright to be seen," said another. "Yes; he must needs be a nobleman, as you say. But, by what convey- ance, think you, can his lordship have voyaged or travelled hither? There has been no vessel from the old country for a month past; and if he have arrived overland from the south- ward, pray where are his attendants and equipage?"

"He needs no equipage to set off his rank," remarked a third. "If he came among us in rags, nobility would shine through a hole in his elbow. I never saw such dignity of as- pect. He has the old Norman blood in his veins, I warrant him!"

"I rather take him to be a Dutchman, or one of your High Germans," said another citizen. "The men of those countries have always the pipe at their mouths."

"And so has a Turk," answered his companion. "But, in my judgment, this stranger hath been bred at the French court, and hath there learned politeness and grace of manner, which none understand so well as the nobility of France. That gait, now! A vulgar spectator might deem it stiff—he might call it a hitch and jerk—but, to my eye, it hath an unspeakable maj- esty, and must have been acquired by constant observation of the deportment of the Grand Monarque. The stranger's char- acter and office are evident enough. He is a French ambas- sador, come to treat with our rulers about the cession of Canada."

"More probably a Spaniard," said another, "and hence his yellow complexion. Or, most likely, he is from the Havana, or from some port on the Spanish Main, and comes to make investigation about the piracies which our Governor is thought to connive at. Those settlers in Peru and Mexico have skins as yellow as the gold which they dig out of their mines."

"Yellow or not," cried a lady, "he is a beautiful man!—so tall—so slender!—such a fine, noble face, with so well-shaped a nose, and all that delicacy of expression about the mouth! And, bless me, how bright his star is! It positively shoots out flames!"

"So do your eyes, fair lady!" said the stranger, with a bow, and a flourish of his pipe; for he was just passing at the instant. "Upon my honor, they have quite dazzled me!"

"Was ever so original and exquisite a compliment?" murmured the lady, in an ecstasy of delight.

Amid the general admiration, excited by the stranger's appearance, there were only two dissenting voices. One was that of an impertinent cur, which, after snuffing at the heels of the glistening figure, put its tail between its legs and skulked into its master's back-yard, vociferating an execrable howl. The other dissentient was a young child, who squalled at the fullest stretch of his lungs, and babbled some unintelligible nonsense about a pumpkin.

Feathertop, meanwhile, pursued his way along the street. Except for the few complimentary words to the lady, and, now and then, a slight inclination of the head, in requital of the profound reverences of the by-standers, he seemed wholly absorbed in his pipe. There needed no other proof of his rank and consequence, than the perfect equanimity with which he comported himself, while the curiosity and admiration of the town swelled almost into clamor around him. With a crowd still gathering behind his footsteps, he finally reached the mansion-house of the worshipful Justice Gookin, entered the gate, ascended the steps of the front-door, and knocked. In the interim, before his summons was answered, the stranger was observed to shake the ashes out of his pipe.

"What did he say, in that sharp voice?" inquired one of the spectators.

"Nay, I know not," answered his friend. "But the sun dazzles my eyes strangely! How dim and faded his lordship looks, all of a sudden! Bless my wits, what is the matter with me!"

"The wonder is," said the other, "that his pipe, (which was out only an instant ago,) should be all a-light again, and with the reddest coal I ever saw! There is something mysterious about this stranger. What a whiff of smoke was that! Dim and faded, do you call him? Why, as he turns about, the star on his breast is all a-blaze."

"It is, indeed," said his companion; "and it will go near to dazzle pretty Polly Gookin, whom I see peeping at it out of the chamber-window."

The door being now opened, Feathertop turned to the crowd, made a stately bend of his body, like a great man acknowledging the reverence of the meaner sort, and vanished into the house. There was a mysterious kind of a smile, if it might not better be called a grin or grimace, upon his visage; but of all the throng that beheld him, not an individual appears to have possessed insight enough to detect the illusive character of the stranger, except a little child and a cur-dog.

Our legend here loses somewhat of its continuity, and, passing over the preliminary explanation between Feathertop and the merchant, goes in quest of the pretty Polly Gookin. She was a damsel of a soft, round figure, with light hair and blue eyes, and a fair rosy face, which seemed neither very shrewd nor very simple. This young lady had caught a glimpse of the glistening stranger, while standing at the threshold, and had forthwith put on a laced cap, a string of beads, her finest kerchief, and her stiffest damask petticoat, in preparation for the interview. Hurrying from her chamber to the parlor, she had ever since been viewing herself in the large looking-glass, and practising pretty airs—now a smile, now a ceremonious dignity of aspect, and now a softer smile than the former—kissing her hand, likewise, tossing her head, and managing her fan; while, within the mirror, an unsubstantial little maid repeated every gesture, and did all the foolish things that Polly did, but without making her ashamed of them. In short, it was the fault of pretty Polly's ability, rather than her will, if she failed to be as complete an artifice as the illustrious Feathertop himself; and when she thus tampered with her own simplicity, the witch's phantom might well hope to win her.

No sooner did Polly hear her father's gouty footsteps approaching the parlor-door, accompanied with the stiff clatter of Feathertop's high-heeled shoes, than she seated herself bolt upright, and innocently began warbling a song.

"Polly! Daughter Polly!" cried the old merchant. "Come hither, child!"

Master Gookin's aspect, as he opened the door, was doubtful and troubled.

"This gentleman," continued he, presenting the stranger, "is the Chevalier Feathertop—nay, I beg his pardon, my Lord Feathertop!—who hath brought me a token of remembrance from an ancient friend of mine. Pay your duty to his lordship, child, and honor him as his quality deserves."

After these few words of introduction, the worshipful magistrate immediately quitted the room. But, even in that brief moment, (had the fair Polly glanced aside at her father, instead of devoting herself wholly to the brilliant guest,) she might have taken warning of some mischief nigh at hand. The old man was nervous, fidgetty, and very pale. Purposing a smile of courtesy, he had deformed his face with a sort of galvanic grin, which, when Feathertop's back was turned, he exchanged for a scowl; at the same time shaking his fist, and stamping his gouty foot—an incivility which brought its retribution along with it. The truth appears to have been, that Mother Rigby's word of introduction, whatever it might be, had operated far more on the rich merchant's fears, than on his good-will. Moreover, being a man of wonderfully acute observation, he had noticed that the painted figures, on the bowl of Feathertop's pipe, were in motion. Looking more closely, he became convinced, that these figures were a party of little demons, each duly provided with horns and a tail, and dancing hand in hand, with gestures of diabolical merriment, round the circumference of the pipe-bowl. As if to confirm his suspicions, while Master Gookin ushered his guest along a dusky passage, from his private room to the parlor, the star on Feathertop's breast had scintillated actual flames, and threw a flickering gleam upon the wall, the ceiling, and the floor.

With such sinister prognostics manifesting themselves on all hands, it is not to be marvelled at that the merchant should have felt that he was committing his daughter to a very questionable acquaintance. He cursed, in his secret soul, the insinuating elegance of Feathertop's manners, as this brilliant personage bowed, smiled, put his hand on his heart, inhaled a long whiff from his pipe, and enriched the atmosphere with the smoky vapor of a fragrant and visible sigh. Gladly would poor Master Gookin have thrust his dangerous guest into the street. But there was a constraint and terror within him. This respectable old gentleman, we fear, at an earlier period of life, had given some pledge or other to the Evil Principle, and perhaps was now to redeem it by the sacrifice of his daughter.

It so happened that the parlor-door was partly of glass, shaded by a silken curtain, the folds of which hung a little awry. So strong was the merchant's interest in witnessing what was to ensue between the fair Polly and the gallant Feathertop, that, after quitting the room, he could by no means refrain from peeping through the crevice of the curtain.

But there was nothing very miraculous to be seen; nothing—except the trifles previously noticed—to confirm the idea of a supernatural peril, environing the pretty Polly. The stranger, it is true, was evidently a thorough and practised man of the world, systematic and self-possessed, and therefore the sort of person to whom a parent ought not to confide a simple young girl, without due watchfulness for the result. The worthy magistrate, who had been conversant with all degrees and qualities of mankind, could not but perceive that every motion and gesture of the distinguished Feathertop came in its proper place; nothing had been left rude or native in him; a well-digested conventionalism had incorporated itself thoroughly with his substance, and transformed him into a work of art. Perhaps it was this peculiarity that invested him with a species of ghastliness and awe. It is the effect of anything completely and consummately artificial, in human shape, that the person impresses us as an unreality, and as having hardly pith enough to cast a shadow upon the floor. As regarded Feathertop, all this resulted in a wild, extravagant, and fantastical impression, as if his life and being were akin to the smoke that curled upward from his pipe.

But pretty Polly Gookin felt not thus. The pair were now promenading the room; Feathertop with his dainty stride, and no less dainty grimace; the girl with a native maidenly grace, just touched, not spoiled, by a slightly affected manner, which seemed caught from the perfect artifice of her companion. The longer the interview continued, the more charmed was pretty Polly, until, within the first quarter of an hour, (as the old magistrate noted by his watch,) she was evidently beginning to be in love. Nor need it have been witchcraft that subdued her in such a hurry; the poor child's heart, it may be, was so very fervent, that it melted her with its own warmth, as reflected from the hollow semblance of a lover. No matter what Feathertop said, his words found depth and reverberation in her ear; no matter what he did, his action was heroic to her eye. And, by this time, it is to be supposed, there was a blush on Polly's cheek, a tender smile about her mouth, and a liquid softness in her glance; while the star kept coruscating on Feathertop's breast, and the little demons careered, with more frantic merriment than ever, about the circumference of his pipe-bowl. Oh, pretty Polly Gookin, why should these imps rejoice so madly that a silly maiden's heart was about to be given to a shadow! Is it so unusual a misfortune?—so rare a triumph?

By and by, Feathertop paused, and throwing himself into an imposing attitude, seemed to summon the fair girl to survey his figure, and resist him longer, if she could. His star, his embroidery, his buckles, glowed, at that instant, with unutterable splendor; the picturesque hues of his attire took a richer depth of coloring; there was a gleam and polish over his whole presence, betokening the perfect witchery of well-ordered manners. The maiden raised her eyes, and suffered them to linger upon her companion with a bashful and admiring gaze. Then, as if desirous of judging what value her own simple comeliness might have, side by side with so much brilliancy, she cast a glance towards the full-length looking-glass, in front of which they happened to be standing. It was one of the truest plates in the world, and incapable of flattery. No sooner did the images, therein reflected, meet Polly's eye, than she shrieked, shrank from the stranger's side, gazed at him, for a moment, in the wildest dismay, and sank insensible upon the floor. Feathertop, likewise, had looked towards the mirror, and there beheld, not the glittering mockery of his outside show, but a picture of the sordid patchwork of his real composition, stript of all witchcraft.

The wretched simulacrum! We almost pity him. He threw

up his arms, with an expression of despair, that went farther than any of his previous manifestations, towards vindicating his claims to be reckoned human. For perchance the only time, since this so often empty and deceptive life of mortals began its course, an Illusion had seen and fully recognized itself.

Mother Rigby was seated by her kitchen-hearth, in the twilight of this eventful day, and had just shaken the ashes out of a new pipe, when she heard a hurried tramp along the road. Yet it did not seem so much the tramp of human foot-steps, as the clatter of sticks or the rattling of dry bones.

"Ha!" thought the old witch. "What step is that? Whose skeleton is out of its grave now, I wonder!"

A figure burst headlong into the cottage-door. It was Feathertop! His pipe was still a-light; the star still flamed upon his breast; the embroidery still glowed upon his garments; nor had he lost, in any degree or manner that could be estimated, the aspect that assimilated him with our mortal-brotherhood. But yet, in some indescribable way, (as is the case with all that has deluded us, when once found out,) the poor reality was felt beneath the cunning artifice.

"What has gone wrong?" demanded the witch. "Did yonder snuffling hypocrite thrust my darling from his door? The villain! I'll set twenty fiends to torment him, till he offer thee his daughter on his bended knees!"

"No, mother," said Feathertop despondingly, "it was not that!"

"Did the girl scorn my precious one?" asked Mother Rigby, her fierce eyes glowing like two coals of Tophet. "I'll cover her face with pimples! Her nose shall be as red as the coal in thy pipe! Her front teeth shall drop out! In a week hence, she shall not be worth thy having!"

"Let her alone, mother!" answered poor Feathertop. "The girl was half-won; and methinks a kiss from her sweet lips might have made me altogether human! But," he added, after a brief pause, and then a howl of self-contempt, "I've seen myself, mother!—I've seen myself for the wretched, ragged, empty thing I am! I'll exist no longer!"

Snatching the pipe from his mouth, he flung it with all his might against the chimney, and, at the same instant, sank upon the floor, a medley of straw and tattered garments, with some sticks protruding from the heap; and a shrivelled pumpkin in the midst. The eye-holes were now lustreless; but the rudely-carved gap, that just before had been a mouth, still seemed to twist itself into a despairing grin, and was so far human.

"Poor fellow!" quoth Mother Rigby, with a rueful glance at the relics of her ill-fated contrivance. "My poor, dear, pretty Feathertop! There are thousands upon thousands of coxcombs and charlatans in the world, made up of just such a jumble of worn-out, forgotten, and good-for-nothing trash, as he was! Yet they live in fair repute, and never see themselves for what they are! And why should my poor puppet be the only one to know himself, and perish for it?"

While thus muttering, the witch had filled a fresh pipe of tobacco, and held the stem between her fingers, as doubtful whether to thrust it into her own mouth or Feathertop's.

"Poor Feathertop!" she continued. "I could easily give him another chance, and send him forth again to-morrow. But, no! his feelings are too tender; his sensibilities too deep. He seems to have too much heart to bustle for his own advantage, in such an empty and heartless world. Well, well! I'll make a scarecrow of him, after all. 'Tis an innocent and a useful vocation, and will suit my darling well; and if each of his human brethren had as fit a one, 'twould be the better for mankind; and as for this pipe of tobacco, I need it more than he!"

So saying, Mother Rigby put the stem between her lips. "Dickon!" cried she, in her high, sharp tone, "another coal for my pipe!"

Preface to Mosses from an Old Manse

THE OLD MANSE

THE AUTHOR MAKES THE READER ACQUAINTED
WITH HIS ABODE

Between two tall gate-posts of rough-hewn stone, (the gate itself having fallen from its hinges, at some unknown epoch,) we beheld the gray front of the old parsonage, terminating the vista of an avenue of black-ash trees. It was now a twelvemonth since the funeral procession of the venerable clergyman, its last inhabitant, had turned from that gate-way towards the village burying-ground. The wheel-track, leading to the door, as well as the whole breadth of the avenue, was almost overgrown with grass, affording dainty mouthfuls to two or three vagrant cows, and an old white horse, who had his own living to pick up along the roadside. The glimmering shadows, that lay half-asleep between the door of the house and the public highway, were a kind of spiritual medium, seen through which, the edifice had not quite the aspect of belonging to the material world. Certainly it had little in common with those ordinary abodes, which stand so imminent upon the road that every passer-by can thrust his head, as it were, into the domestic circle. From these quiet windows, the figures of passing travellers looked too remote and dim to disturb the sense of privacy. In its near retirement, and accessible seclusion, it was the very spot for the residence of a clergyman; a man not estranged from human life, yet enveloped, in the midst of it, with a veil woven of intermingled gloom and brightness. It was worthy to have been one of the time-honored parsonages of England, in which, through many generations, a succession of holy occupants pass from youth to age, and bequeath each an inheritance of sanctity to pervade the house and hover over it, as with an atmosphere.

Nor, in truth, had the old Manse ever been prophaned by a lay occupant, until that memorable summer-afternoon when I entered it as my home. A priest had built it; a priest had succeeded to it; other priestly men, from time to time, had dwelt in it; and children, born in its chambers, had grown up to assume the priestly character. It was awful to reflect how many sermons must have been written there. The latest inhabitant alone—he, by whose translation to Paradise the dwelling was left vacant—had penned nearly three thousand discourses, besides the better, if not the greater number, that gushed living from his lips. How often, no doubt, had he paced to-and-fro along the avenue, attuning his meditations, to the sighs and gentle murmurs, and deep and solemn peals of the wind, among the lofty tops of the trees! In that variety of natural utterances, he could find something accordant with every passage of his sermon, were it of tenderness or reverential fear. The boughs over my head seemed shadowy with solemn thoughts, as well as with rustling leaves. I took shame to myself for having been so long a writer of idle stories, and ventured to hope that wisdom would descend upon me with the falling leaves of the avenue; and that I should light upon an intellectual treasure in the old Manse, well worth those hoards of long-hidden gold, which people seek for in moss-grown houses. Profound treatises of morality;—a layman's unprofessional, and therefore unprejudiced views of religion; —histories, (such as Bancroft might have written, had he taken up his abode here, as he once purposed,) bright with picture, gleaming over a depth of philosophic thought;— these were the works that might fitly have flowed from such a retirement. In the humblest event, I resolved at least to achieve a novel, that should evolve some deep lesson, and should possess physical substance enough to stand alone.

In furtherance of my design, and as if to leave me no pretext for not fulfilling it, there was, in the rear of the house, the most delightful little nook of a study that ever afforded its snug seclusion to a scholar. It was here that Emerson wrote 'Nature'; for he was then an inhabitant of the Manse, and used to watch the Assyrian dawn and the Paphian sunset and moonrise, from the summit of our eastern hill. When I first saw the room, its walls were blackened with the smoke of unnumbered years, and made still blacker by the grim prints of Puritan ministers that hung around. These worthies looked strangely like bad angels, or, at least, like men who had wrestled so continually and so sternly with the devil, that somewhat of his sooty fierceness had been imparted to their own visages. They had all vanished now. A cheerful coat of paint, and golden-tinted paper-hangings, lighted up the small apartment; while the shadow of a willow-tree, that swept against the overhanging eaves, attempered the cheery western sunshine. In place of the grim prints, there was the sweet and lovely head of one of Raphael's Madonnas, and two pleasant little pictures of the Lake of Como. The only other decorations were a purple vase of flowers, always fresh, and a bronze one containing graceful ferns. My books (few, and by no means choice; for they were chiefly such waifs as chance had thrown in my way) stood in order about the room, seldom to be disturbed.

The study had three windows, set with little, old-fashioned panes of glass, each with a crack across it. The two on the western side looked, or rather peeped, between the willow-branches, down into the orchard, with glimpses of the river through the trees. The third, facing northward, commanded a broader view of the river, at a spot where its hitherto obscure waters gleam forth into the light of history. It was at this window that the clergyman, who then dwelt in the Manse, stood watching the outbreak of a long and deadly struggle between two nations; he saw the irregular array of his parishioners on the farther side of the river, and the glittering line of the British, on the hither bank. He awaited, in an agony of suspense, the rattle of the musketry. It came—and there needed but a gentle wind to sweep the battle-smoke around this quiet house.

Perhaps the reader—whom I cannot help considering as my guest in the old Manse, and entitled to all courtesy in the way of sight-showing—perhaps he will choose to take a nearer view of the memorable spot. We stand now on the river's brink. It may well be called the Concord—the river of peace and quietness—for it is certainly the most unexcitable and sluggish stream that ever loitered, imperceptibly, towards its eternity, the sea. Positively, I had lived three weeks beside it, before it grew quite clear to my perception which way the current flowed. It never has a vivacious aspect, except when a north-western breeze is vexing its surface, on a sunshiny day. From the incurable indolence of its nature, the stream is happily incapable of becoming the slave of human ingenuity, as is the fate of so many a wild, free mountain-torrent. While all things else are compelled to subserve some useful purpose, it idles its sluggish life away, in lazy liberty, without turning a solitary spindle, or affording even water-power enough to grind the corn that grows upon its banks. The torpor of its movement allows it nowhere a bright pebbly shore, nor so much as a narrow strip of glistening sand, in any part of its course. It slumbers between broad prairies, kissing the long meadow-grass, and bathes the overhanging boughs of elder-bushes and willows, or the roots of elms and ash-trees, and clumps of maples. Flags and rushes grow along its plashy shore; the yellow water-lily spreads its broad, flat leaves on the margin; and the fragrant white pond-lily abounds, gener-ally selecting a position just so far from the river's brink, that it cannot be grasped, save at the hazard of plunging in.

It is a marvel whence this perfect flower derives its loveli-ness and perfume, springing, as it does, from the black mud over which the river sleeps, and where lurk the slimy eel, and speckled frog, and the mud turtle, whom continual washing cannot cleanse. It is the very same black mud out of which the yellow lily sucks its obscene life and noisome odor. Thus we see, too, in the world, that some persons assimilate only what is ugly and evil from the same moral circumstances which supply good and beautiful results—the fragrance of ce-lestial flowers—to the daily life of others.

The reader must not, from any testimony of mine, contract a dislike towards our slumberous stream. In the light of a calm and golden sunset, it becomes lovely beyond expression; the more lovely for the quietude that so well accords with the hour, when even the wind, after blustering all day long, usu-ally hushes itself to rest. Each tree and rock, and every blade of grass, is distinctly imaged, and, however unsightly in real-ity, assumes ideal beauty in the reflection. The minutest things of earth, and the broad aspect of the firmament, are pictured equally without effort, and with the same felicity of success. All the sky glows downward at our feet; the rich clouds float through the unruffled bosom of the stream, like heavenly thoughts through a peaceful heart. We will not,

then, malign our river as gross and impure, while it can glorify itself with so adequate a picture of the heaven that broods
above it; or, if we remember its tawny hue and the muddiness
of its bed, let it be a symbol that the earthliest human soul
has an infinite spiritual capacity, and may contain the better
world within its depths. But, indeed, the same lesson might
be drawn out of any mud-puddle in the streets of a city—
and, being taught us everywhere, it must be true.

Come; we have pursued a somewhat devious track, in our
walk to the battle-ground. Here we are, at the point where
the river was crossed by the old bridge, the possession of
which was the immediate object of the contest. On the hither
side, grow two or three elms, throwing a wide circumference
of shade, but which must have been planted at some period
within the threescore years and ten, that have passed since the
battle-day. On the farther shore, overhung by a clump of
elder-bushes, we discern the stone abutment of the bridge.
Looking down into the river, I once discovered some heavy
fragments of the timbers, all green with half-a-century's
growth of water-moss; for, during that length of time, the
tramp of horses and human footsteps have ceased, along this
ancient highway. The stream has here about the breadth of
twenty strokes of a swimmer's arm; a space not too wide,
when the bullets were whistling across. Old people, who
dwell hereabouts, will point out the very spots, on the western bank, where our countrymen fell down and died; and, on
this side of the river, an obelisk of granite has grown up from
the soil that was fertilized with British blood. The monument, not more than twenty feet in height, is such as it befitted the inhabitants of a village to erect, in illustration of a
matter of local interest, rather than what was suitable to commemorate an epoch of national history. Still, by the fathers of
the village this famous deed was done; and their descendants
might rightfully claim the privilege of building a memorial.

A humbler token of the fight, yet a more interesting one
than the granite obelisk, may be seen close under the stone-
wall, which separates the battle-ground from the precincts of
the parsonage. It is the grave—marked by a small, moss-
grown fragment of stone at the head, and another at the
foot—the grave of two British soldiers, who were slain in the

skirmish, and have ever since slept peacefully where Zechariah
Brown and Thomas Davis buried them. Soon was their warfare ended;—a weary night-march from Boston—a rattling
volley of musketry across the river;—and then these many
years of rest! In the long procession of slain invaders, who
passed into eternity from the battle-fields of the Revolution,
these two nameless soldiers led the way.

Lowell, the poet, as we were once standing over this grave,
told me a tradition in reference to one of the inhabitants below. The story has something deeply impressive, though its
circumstances cannot altogether be reconciled with probability. A youth, in the service of the clergyman, happened to be
chopping wood, that April morning, at the back door of the
Manse; and when the noise of battle rang from side to side
of the bridge, he hastened across the intervening field, to see
what might be going forward. It is rather strange, by the way,
that this lad should have been so diligently at work, when the
whole population of town and county were startled out of
their customary business, by the advance of the British
troops. Be that as it might, the tradition says that the lad now
left his task, and hurried to the battle-field, with the axe still
in his hand. The British had by this time retreated—the
Americans were in pursuit—and the late scene of strife was
thus deserted by both parties. Two soldiers lay on the
ground; one was a corpse; but, as the young New-Englander
drew nigh, the other Briton raised himself painfully upon his
hands and knees, and gave a ghastly stare into his face. The
boy—it must have been a nervous impulse, without purpose,
without thought, and betokening a sensitive and impressible
nature, rather than a hardened one—the boy uplifted his axe,
and dealt the wounded soldier a fierce and fatal blow upon
the head.

I could wish that the grave might be opened; for I would
fain know whether either of the skeleton soldiers have the
mark of an axe in his skull. The story comes home to me like
truth. Oftentimes, as an intellectual and moral exercise, I have
sought to follow that poor youth through his subsequent career, and observe how his soul was tortured by the blood-
stain, contracted, as it had been, before the long custom of
war had robbed human life of its sanctity, and while it still

seemed murderous to slay a brother man. This one circumstance has borne more fruit for me, than all that history tells
us of the fight.

Many strangers come, in the summer-time, to view the battle-ground. For my own part, I have never found my imagination much excited by this, or any other scene of historic
celebrity; nor would the placid margin of the river have lost
any of its charm for me, had men never fought and died
there. There is a wilder interest in the tract of land—perhaps
a hundred yards in breadth—which extends between the battle-field and the northern face of our old Manse, with its contiguous avenue and orchard. Here, in some unknown age,
before the white man came, stood an Indian village, convenient to the river, whence its inhabitants must have drawn so
large a part of their subsistence. The site is identified by the
spear and arrow-heads, the chisels, and other implements of
war, labor, and the chase, which the plough turns up from
the soil. You see a splinter of stone, half hidden beneath a
sod; it looks like nothing worthy of note; but, if you have
faith enough to pick it up—behold a relic! Thoreau, who has
a strange faculty of finding what the Indians have left behind
them, first set me on the search; and I afterwards enriched
myself with some very perfect specimens, so rudely wrought
that it seemed almost as if chance had fashioned them. Their
great charm consists in this rudeness, and in the individuality
of each article, so different from the productions of civilized
machinery, which shapes everything on one pattern. There is
an exquisite delight, too, in picking up, for one's self, an ar-
row-head that was dropt centuries ago, and has never been
handled since, and which we thus receive directly from the
hand of the red hunter, who purposed to shoot it at his game,
or at an enemy. Such an incident builds up again the Indian
village, amid its encircling forest, and recalls to life the
painted chiefs and warriors, the squaws at their household
toil, and the children sporting among the wigwams; while the
little wind-rocked papoose swings from the branch of a tree.
It can hardly be told whether it is a joy or a pain, after such
a momentary vision, to gaze around in the broad daylight of
reality, and see stone-fences, white houses, potatoe-fields, and
men doggedly hoeing, in their shirt-sleeves and homespun

pantaloons. But this is nonsense. The old Manse is better than a thousand wigwams.

The old Manse! We had almost forgotten it, but will return thither through the orchard. This was set out by the last clergyman, in the decline of his life, when the neighbors laughed at the hoary-headed man for planting trees, from which he could have no prospect of gathering fruit. Even had that been the case, there was only so much the better motive for planting them, in the pure and unselfish hope of benefitting his successors—an end so seldom achieved by more ambitious efforts. But the old minister, before reaching his patriarchal age of ninety, ate the apples from this orchard during many years, and added silver and gold to his annual stipend, by disposing of the superfluity. It is pleasant to think of him, walking among the trees in the quiet afternoons of early autumn, and picking up here and there a windfall; while he observes how heavily the branches are weighed down, and computes the number of empty flour-barrels that will be filled by their burthen. He loved each tree, doubtless, as if it had been his own child. An orchard has a relation to mankind, and readily connects itself with matters of the heart. The trees possess a domestic character; they have lost the wild nature of their forest-kindred, and have grown humanized by receiving the care of man, as well as by contributing to his wants. There is so much individuality of character, too, among apple-trees, that it gives them an additional claim to be the objects of human interest. One is harsh and crabbed in its manifestations; another gives us fruit as mild as charity. One is churlish and illiberal, evidently grudging the few apples that it bears; another exhausts itself in free-hearted benevolence. The variety of grotesque shapes, into which apple-trees contort themselves, has its effect on those who get acquainted with them; they stretch out their crooked branches, and take such hold of the imagination that we remember them as humorists and odd fellows. And what is more melancholy than the old apple-trees, that linger about the spot where once stood a homestead, but where there is now only a ruined chimney, rising out of a grassy and weed-grown cellar? They offer their fruit to every wayfarer—apples that are bittersweet with the moral of time's vicissitude.

I have met with no other such pleasant trouble in the world, as that of finding myself, with only the two or three mouths which it was my privilege to feed, the sole inheritor of the old clergyman's wealth of fruits. Throughout the summer, there were cherries and currants; and then came Autumn, with this immense burthen of apples, dropping them continually from his over-laden shoulders, as he trudged along. In the stillest afternoon, if I listened, the thump of a great apple was audible, falling without a breath of wind, from the mere necessity of perfect ripeness. And, besides, there were pear-trees, that flung down bushels upon bushels of heavy pears, and peach-trees, which, in a good year, tormented me with peaches, neither to be eaten nor kept, nor, without labor and perplexity, to be given away. The idea of an infinite generosity and exhaustless bounty, on the part of our Mother Nature, was well worth obtaining through such cares as these. That feeling can be enjoyed in perfection only by the natives of the summer islands, where the bread-fruit, the cocoa, the palm, and the orange, grow spontaneously, and hold forth the ever-ready meal; but, likewise, almost as well, by a man long habituated to city-life, who plunges into such a solitude as that of the old Manse, where he plucks the fruit of trees that he did not plant, and which therefore, to my heterodox taste, bear the closest resemblance to those that grew in Eden. It has been an apophthegm, these five thousand years, that toil sweetens the bread it earns. For my part, (speaking from hard experience, acquired while belaboring the rugged furrows of Brook Farm,) I relish best the free gifts of Providence.

Not that it can be disputed, that the light toil, requisite to cultivate a moderately sized garden, imparts such zest to kitchen-vegetables as is never found in those of the market-gardener. Childless men, if they would know something of the bliss of paternity, should plant a seed—be it squash, bean, Indian corn, or perhaps a mere flower, or worthless weed—should plant it with their own hands, and nurse it from infancy to maturity, altogether by their own care. If there be not too many of them, each individual plant becomes an object of separate interest. My garden, that skirted the avenue of the Manse, was of precisely the right extent. An hour or two of morning labor was all that it required. But I used to visit and re-visit it, a dozen times a day, and stand in deep contemplation over my vegetable progeny, with a love that nobody could share nor conceive of, who had never taken part in the process of creation. It was one of the most bewitching sights in the world, to observe a hill of beans thrusting aside the soil, or a row of early peas, just peeping forth sufficiently to trace a line of delicate green. Later in the season, the humming-birds were attracted by the blossoms of a peculiar variety of bean; and they were a joy to me, those little spiritual visitants, for deigning to sip airy food out of my nectar-cups. Multitudes of bees used to bury themselves in the yellow blossoms of the summer-squashes. This, too, was a deep satisfaction; although, when they had laden themselves with sweets, they flew away to some unknown hive, which would give back nothing in requital of what my garden had contributed. But I was glad thus to fling a benefaction upon the passing breeze, with the certainty that somebody must profit by it, and that there would be a little more honey in the world, to allay the sourness and bitterness which mankind is always complaining of. Yes, indeed; my life was the sweeter for that honey.

Speaking of summer-squashes, I must say a word of their beautiful and varied forms. They presented an endless diversity of urns and vases, shallow or deep, scalloped or plain, moulded in patterns which a sculptor would do well to copy, since Art has never invented anything more graceful. A hundred squashes in the garden were worthy—in my eyes, at least—of being rendered indestructible in marble. If ever Providence (but I know it never will) should assign me a superfluity of gold, part of it shall be expended for a service of plate, or most delicate porcelain, to be wrought into the shapes of summer-squashes, gathered from vines which I will plant with my own hands. As dishes for containing vegetables, they would be peculiarly appropriate.

But, not merely the squeamish love of the Beautiful was gratified by my toil in the kitchen-garden. There was a hearty enjoyment, likewise, in observing the growth of the crook-necked winter squashes, from the first little bulb, with the withered blossom adhering to it, until they lay strewn upon the soil, big, round fellows, hiding their heads beneath the leaves, but turning up their great yellow rotundities to the noontide sun. Gazing at them, I felt that, by my agency, something worth living for had been done. A new substance was borne into the world. They were real and tangible existences, which the mind could seize hold of and rejoice in. A cabbage, too,—especially the early Dutch cabbage, which swells to a monstrous circumference, until its ambitious heart often bursts asunder,—is a matter to be proud of, when we can claim a share with the earth and sky in producing it. But, after all, the hugest pleasure is reserved, until these vegetable children of ours are smoking on the table, and we, like Saturn, make a meal of them.

What with the river, the battle-field, the orchard, and the garden, the reader begins to despair of finding his way back into the old Manse. But, in agreeable weather, it is the truest hospitality to keep him out of doors. I never grew quite acquainted with my habitation, till a long spell of sulky rain had confined me beneath its roof. There could not be a more sombre aspect of external Nature, than as then seen from the windows of my study. The great willow-tree had caught, and retained among its leaves, a whole cataract of water, to be shaken down, at intervals, by the frequent gusts of wind. All day long, and for a week together, the rain was drip-drip-dripping and splash-splash-splashing from the eaves, and bubbling and foaming into the tubs beneath the spouts. The old, unpainted shingles of the house and outbuildings were black with moisture; and the mosses, of ancient growth upon the walls, looked green and fresh, as if they were the newest things and after-thought of Time. The usually mirrored surface of the river was blurred by an infinity of rain-drops; the whole landscape had a completely water-soaked appearance, conveying the impression that the earth was wet through, like a sponge; while the summit of a wooded hill, about a mile distant, was enveloped in a dense mist, where the demon of the tempest seemed to have his abiding-place, and to be plotting still direr inclemencies.

Nature has no kindness—no hospitality—during a rain. In the fiercest heat of sunny days, she retains a secret mercy, and welcomes the wayfarer to shady nooks of the woods, whither the sun cannot penetrate; but she provides no shelter against her storms. It makes us shiver to think of those deep, umbrageous recesses—those overshadowing banks—where we found such enjoyment during the sultry afternoons. Not a twig of foliage there, but would dash a little shower into our faces. Looking reproachfully towards the impenetrable sky— if sky there be, above that dismal uniformity of cloud—we are apt to murmur against the whole system of the universe, since it involves the extinction of so many summer days, in so short a life, by the hissing and spluttering rain. In such spells of weather—and, it is to be supposed, such weather came— Eve's bower in Paradise must have been but a cheerless and aguish kind of shelter, nowise comparable to the old parsonage, which had resources of its own, to beguile the week's imprisonment. The idea of sleeping on a couch of wet roses!

Happy the man who, in a rainy day, can betake himself to a huge garret, stored, like that of the Manse, with lumber that each generation has left behind it, from a period before the Revolution. Our garret was an arched hall, dimly illuminated through small and dusty windows; it was but a twilight at the best; and there were nooks, or rather caverns of deep obscurity, the secrets of which I never learned, being too reverent of their dust and cobwebs. The beams and rafters, roughly hewn, and with strips of bark still on them, and the rude masonry of the chimneys, made the garret look wild and uncivilized; an aspect unlike what was seen elsewhere, in the quiet and decorous old house. But, on one side, there was a little white-washed apartment, which bore the traditionary title of the Saints' Chamber, because holy men, in their youth, had slept, and studied, and prayed there. With its elevated retirement, its one window, its small fireplace, and its closet, convenient for an oratory, it was the very spot where a young man might inspire himself with solemn enthusiasm, and cherish saintly dreams. The occupants, at various epochs, had left brief records and ejaculations, inscribed upon the walls. There, too, hung a tattered and shrivelled roll of canvass, which, on inspection, proved to be the forcibly wrought picture of a clergyman, in wig, band, and gown, holding a Bible in his hand. As I turned his face towards the light, he eyed me with an air of authority such as men of his profession seldom assume, in our days. The original had been pastor of the parish, more than a century ago, a friend of Whitefield, and almost his equal in fervid eloquence. I bowed before the effigy of the dignified divine, and felt as if I had now met face to face with the ghost, by whom, as there was reason to apprehend, the Manse was haunted.

Houses of any antiquity, in New England, are so invariably possessed with spirits, that the matter seems hardly worth alluding to. Our ghost used to heave deep sighs in a particular corner of the parlor; and sometimes rustled paper, as if he were turning over a sermon, in the long upper entry;— where, nevertheless, he was invisible, in spite of the bright moonshine that fell through the eastern window. Not improbably, he wished me to edit and publish a selection from a chest full of manuscript discourses, that stood in the garret. Once, while Hillard and other friends sat talking with us in the twilight, there came a rustling noise, as of a minister's silk gown, sweeping through the very midst of the company, so closely as almost to brush against the chairs. Still, there was nothing visible. A yet stranger business was that of a ghostly servant-maid, who used to be heard in the kitchen, at deepest midnight, grinding coffee, cooking, ironing—performing, in short, all kinds of domestic labor—although no traces of anything accomplished could be detected, the next morning. Some neglected duty of her servitude—some ill-starched ministerial band—disturbed the poor damsel in her grave, and kept her at work without any wages.

But, to return from this digression. A part of my predecessor's library was stored in the garret; no unfit receptacle, indeed, for such dreary trash as comprised the greater number of volumes. The old books would have been worth nothing at an auction. In this venerable garret, however, they possessed an interest quite apart from their literary value, as heirlooms, many of which had been transmitted down through a series of consecrated hands, from the days of the mighty Puritan divines. Autographs of famous names were to be seen, in faded ink, on some of their fly-leaves; and there were marginal observations, or interpolated pages closely covered with manuscript, in illegible short-hand, perhaps concealing matter of profound truth and wisdom. The world will never be the better for it. A few of the books were Latin folios, written by Catholic authors; others demolished Papistry as with a sledge-hammer, in plain English. A dissertation on the book of Job—which only Job himself could have had patience to read—filled at least a score of small, thickset quartos, at the rate of two or three volumes to a chapter. Then there was a vast folio Body of Divinity; too corpulent a body, it might be feared, to comprehend the spiritual element of religion. Volumes of this form dated back two hundred years, or more, and were generally bound in black leather, exhibiting precisely such an appearance as we should attribute to books of enchantment. Others, equally antique, were of a size proper to be carried in the large waistcoat-pockets of old times; diminutive, but as black as their bulkier brethren, and abundantly interfused with Greek and Latin quotations. These little old volumes impressed me as if they had been intended for very large ones, but had been unfortunately blighted, at an early stage of their growth.

The rain pattered upon the roof, and the sky gloomed through the dusty garret-windows; while I burrowed among these venerable books, in search of any living thought, which should burn like a coal of fire, or glow like an inextinguishable gem, beneath the dead trumpery that had long hidden it. But I found no such treasure; all was dead alike; and I could not but muse deeply and wonderingly upon the humiliating fact, that the works of man's intellect decay like those of his hands. Thought grows mouldy. What was good and nourishing food for the spirits of one generation, affords no sustenance for the next. Books of religion, however, cannot be considered a fair test of the enduring and vivacious properties of human thought; because such books so seldom really touch upon their ostensible subject, and have therefore so little business to be written at all. So long as an unlettered soul can attain to saving grace, there would seem to be no deadly error in holding theological libraries to be accumulations of, for the most part, stupendous impertinence.

Many of the books had accrued in the latter years of the last clergyman's lifetime. These threatened to be of even less interest than the elder works, a century hence, to any curious inquirer who should then rummage among them, as I was doing now. Volumes of the Liberal Preacher and Christian Examiner, occasional sermons, controversial pamphlets, tracts, and other productions of a like fugitive nature, took the place of the thick and heavy volumes of past time. In a physical point of view, there was much the same difference as between a feather and a lump of lead; but, intellectually regarded, the specific gravity of old and new was about upon a par. Both, also, were alike frigid. The elder books, nevertheless, seemed to have been earnestly written, and might be conceived to have possessed warmth, at some former period; although, with the lapse of time, the heated masses had cooled down even to the freezing point. The frigidity of the modern productions, on the other hand, was characteristic and inherent, and evidently had little to do with the writer's qualities of mind and heart. In fine, of this whole dusty heap of literature, I tossed aside all the sacred part, and felt myself none the less a Christian for eschewing it. There appeared no hope of either mounting to the better world on a Gothic staircase of ancient folios, or of flying thither on the wings of a modern tract.

Nothing, strange to say, retained any sap, except what had been written for the passing day and year, without the remotest pretension or idea of permanence. There were a few old newspapers, and still older almanacs, which reproduced, to my mental eye, the epochs when they had issued from the press, with a distinctness that was altogether unaccountable. It was as if I had found bits of magic looking-glass among the books, with the images of a vanished century in them. I turned my eyes towards the tattered picture, abovementioned, and asked of the austere divine, wherefore it was that he and his brethren, after the most painful rummaging and groping into their minds, had been able to produce nothing half so real, as these newspaper scribblers and almanacmakers had thrown off, in the effervescence of a moment. The portrait responded not; so I sought an answer for myself. It is the Age itself that writes newspapers and almanacs, which therefore have a distinct purpose and meaning, at the time, and a kind of intelligible truth for all times; whereas, most other works—being written by men who, in the very act, set themselves apart from their age—are likely to possess little significance when new, and none at all, when old. Genius, indeed, melts many ages into one, and thus effects something permanent, yet still with a similarity of office to that of the more ephemeral writer. A work of genius is but the newspaper of a century, or perchance of a hundred centuries.

Lightly as I have spoken of these old books, there yet lingers with me a superstitious reverence for literature of all kinds. A bound volume has a charm in my eyes, similar to what scraps of manuscript possess, for the good Mussulman. He imagines, that those wind-wafted records are perhaps hallowed by some sacred verse; and I, that every new book, or antique one, may contain the 'Open Sesame'—the spell to disclose treasures, hidden in some unsuspected cave of Truth. Thus, it was not without sadness, that I turned away from the library of the old Manse.

Blessed was the sunshine when it came again, at the close of another stormy day, beaming from the edge of the western horizon; while the massive firmament of clouds threw down all the gloom it could, but served only to kindle the golden light into a more brilliant glow, by the strongly contrasted shadows. Heaven smiled at the earth, so long unseen, from beneath its heavy eyelid. Tomorrow for the hill-tops and the wood-paths!

Or it might be that Ellery Channing came up the avenue, to join me in a fishing-excursion on the river. Strange and happy times were those, when we cast aside all irksome forms and straight-laced habitudes, and delivered ourselves up to the free air, to live like the Indians or any less conventional race, during one bright semi-circle of the sun. Rowing our boat against the current, between wide meadows, we turned aside into the Assabeth. A more lovely stream than this, for a mile above its junction with the Concord, has never flowed on earth—nowhere, indeed, except to lave the interior regions of a poet's imagination. It is sheltered from the breeze by woods and a hill-side; so that elsewhere there might be a hurricane, and here scarcely a ripple across the shaded water. The current lingers along so gently, that the mere force of the boatman's will seems sufficient to propel his craft against it. It comes flowing softly through the midmost privacy and deepest heart of a wood, which whispers it to be quiet, while the stream whispers back again from its sedgy borders, as if river and wood were hushing one another to sleep. Yes; the river sleeps along its course, and dreams of the sky, and of the clustering foliage, amid which fall showers of broken sunlight, imparting specks of vivid cheerfulness, in contrast with the quiet depth of the prevailing tint. Of all this scene, the slumbering river has a dream-picture in its bosom. Which, after all, was the most real—the picture, or the original?— the objects palpable to our grosser senses, or their apotheosis in the stream beneath? Surely, the disembodied images stand in closer relation to the soul. But, both the original and the reflection had here an ideal charm; and, had it been a thought more wild, I could have fancied that this river had strayed forth out of the rich scenery of my companion's inner world;—only the vegetation along its banks should then have had an Oriental character.

Gentle and unobtrusive as the river is, yet the tranquil woods seem hardly satisfied to allow it passage. The trees are rooted on the very verge of the water, and dip their pendent branches into it. At one spot, there is a lofty bank, on the slope of which grow some hemlocks, declining across the stream, with outstretched arms, as if resolute to take the plunge. In other places, the banks are almost on a level with the water; so that the quiet congregation of trees set their feet in the flood, and are fringed with foliage down to the surface. Cardinal-flowers kindle their spiral flames, and illuminate the dark nooks among the shrubbery. The pond-lily grows abundantly along the margin; that delicious flower which, as Thoreau tells me, opens its virgin bosom to the first sunlight, and perfects its being through the magic of that genial kiss. He has beheld beds of them unfolding in due succession, as the sunrise stole gradually from flower to flower; a sight not to be hoped for, unless when a poet adjusts his inward eye to a proper focus with the outward organ. Grape-vines, here and there, twine themselves around shrub and tree, and hang their clusters over the water, within reach of the boatman's hand. Oftentimes, they unite two trees of alien race in an inextricable twine, marrying the hemlock and the maple against their will, and enriching them with a purple offspring, of which neither is the parent. One of these ambitious parasites has climbed into the upper branches of a tall white-pine, and is still ascending from bough to bough, unsatisfied, till it shall crown the tree's airy summit with a wreath of its broad foliage and a cluster of its grapes.

The winding course of the stream continually shut out the scene behind us, and revealed as calm and lovely a one before. We glided from depth to depth, and breathed new seclusion at every turn. The shy kingfisher flew from the withered branch, close at hand, to another at a distance, uttering a shrill cry of anger or alarm. Ducks—that had been floating there, since the preceding eve—were startled at our approach, and skimmed along the glassy river, breaking its dark surface with a bright streak. The pickerel leaped from among the lily-pads. The turtle, sunning itself upon a rock, or at the root of a tree, slid suddenly into the water with a plunge. The painted Indian, who paddled his canoe along the Assabeth, three hundred years ago, could hardly have seen a wilder gentleness, displayed upon its banks and reflected in its bosom, than we did. Nor could the same Indian have prepared his noontide meal with more simplicity. We drew up our skiff at some point where the overarching shade formed a natural bower, and there kindled a fire with the pine-cones and decayed branches that lay strewn plentifully around. Soon, the smoke ascended among the trees, impregnated with a savory incense, not heavy, dull, and surfeiting, like the steam of cookery within doors, but sprightly and piquant. The smell of our feast was akin to the woodland odors with which it mingled; there was no sacrilege committed by our intrusion there; the sacred solitude was hospitable, and granted us free leave to cook and eat, in the recess that was at once our kitchen and banquetting-hall. It is strange what humble offices may be performed, in a beautiful scene, without destroying its poetry. Our fire, red-gleaming among the trees, and we beside it, busied with culinary rites and spreading out our meal on a moss-grown log, all seemed in unison with the river gliding by, and the foliage rustling over us. And, what was strangest, neither did our mirth seem to disturb the propriety of the solemn woods; although the hobgoblins of the old wilderness, and the will-of-the-whisps that glimmered in the marshy places, might have come trooping to share our table-talk, and have added their shrill laughter to our merriment. It was the very spot in which to utter the extremest nonsense, or the profoundest wisdom—or that ethereal product of the mind which partakes of both, and may become one or the other, in correspondence with the faith and insight of the auditor.

So, amid sunshine and shadow, rustling leaves, and sighing waters, up-gushed our talk, like the babble of a fountain. The evanescent spray was Ellery's; and his, too, the lumps of golden thought, that lay glimmering in the fountain's bed, and brightened both our faces by the reflection. Could he have drawn out that virgin gold, and stamped it with the mint-mark that alone gives currency, the world might have had the profit, and he the fame. My mind was the richer, merely by the knowledge that it was there. But the chief profit of those wild days, to him and me, lay—not in any definite idea—not in any angular or rounded truth, which we dug out of the shapeless mass of problematical stuff—but in the freedom which we thereby won from all custom and conventionalism, and fettering influences of man on man. We were so free to-day, that it was impossible to be slaves again tomorrow. When we crossed the threshold of a house, or trod the thronged pavements of a city, still the leaves of the trees, that overhung the Assabeth, were whispering to us—'Be free! Be free!' Therefore, along that shady river-bank, there are spots, marked with a heap of ashes and half-consumed brands, only less sacred in my remembrance than the hearth of a household-fire.

And yet how sweet—as we floated homeward adown the golden river, at sunset—how sweet was it to return within the system of human society, not as to a dungeon and a chain, but as to a stately edifice, whence we could go forth at will into statelier simplicity! How gently, too, did the sight of the old Manse—best seen from the river, overshadowed with its willow, and all environed about with the foliage of its orchard and avenue—how gently did its gray, homely aspect rebuke the speculative extravagances of the day! It had grown sacred, in connection with the artificial life against which we inveighed; it had been a home, for many years, in spite of all;

it was my home, too;—and, with these thoughts, it seemed to me that all the artifice and conventionalism of life was but an impalpable thinness upon its surface, and that the depth below was none the worse for it. Once, as we turned our boat to the bank, there was a cloud in the shape of an immensely gigantic figure of a hound, couched above the house, as if keeping guard over it. Gazing at this symbol, I prayed that the upper influences might long protect the institutions that had grown out of the heart of mankind.

If ever my readers should decide to give up civilized life, cities, houses; and whatever moral or material enormities, in addition to these, the perverted ingenuity of our race has contrived,—let it be in the early autumn. Then, Nature will love him better than at any other season, and will take him to her bosom with a more motherly tenderness. I could scarcely endure the roof of the old house above me, in those first autumnal days. How early in the summer, too, the prophecy of autumn comes!—earlier in some years than in others,—sometimes, even in the first weeks of July. There is no other feeling like what is caused by this faint, doubtful, yet real perception, if it be not rather a foreboding, of the year's decay—so blessedly sweet and sad, in the same breath.

Did I say that there was no feeling like it? Ah, but there is a half-acknowledged melancholy, like to this, when we stand in the perfected vigor of our life, and feel that Time has now given us all his flowers, and that the next work of his never idle fingers must be—to steal them, one by one, away!

I have forgotten whether the song of the cricket be not as early a token of autumn's approach, as any other;—that song, which may be called an audible stillness; for, though very loud and heard afar, yet the mind does not take note of it as a sound; so completely is its individual existence merged among the accompanying characteristics of the season. Alas, for the pleasant summer-time! In August, the grass is still verdant on the hills and in the vallies; the foliage of the trees is as dense as ever, and as green; the flowers gleam forth in richer abundance along the margin of the river, and by the stone-walls, and deep among the woods; the days, too, are as fervid now as they were a month ago;—and yet, in every breath of wind, and in every beam of sunshine, we hear the whispered farewell, and behold the parting smile, of a dear friend. There is a coolness amid all the heat; a mildness in the blazing noon. Not a breeze can stir, but it thrills us with the breath of autumn. A pensive glory is seen in the far, golden gleams, among the shadows of the trees. The flowers—even the brightest of them, and they are the most gorgeous of the year—have this gentle sadness wedded to their pomp, and typify the character of the delicious time, each within itself. The brilliant cardinal-flower has never seemed gay to me.

Still later in the season, Nature's tenderness waxes stronger. It is impossible not to be fond of our Mother now; for she is so fond of us! At other periods, she does not make this impression on me, or only at rare intervals; but, in these genial days of autumn, when she has perfected her harvests, and accomplished every needful thing that was given her to do, then she overflows with a blessed superfluity of love. She has leisure to caress her children now.

It is good to be alive, at such times. Thank heaven for breath!—yes, for mere breath!—when it is made up of a heavenly breeze like this! It comes with a real kiss upon our cheeks; it would linger fondly around us, if it might; but, since it must be gone, it embraces us with its whole kindly heart, and passes onward, to embrace likewise the next thing that it meets. A blessing is flung abroad, and scattered far and wide over the earth, to be gathered up by all who choose. I recline upon the still unwithered grass, and whisper to myself:—'Oh, perfect day!—Oh, beautiful world!—Oh, beneficent God!' And it is the promise of a blissful Eternity; for our Creator would never have made such lovely days, and have given us the deep hearts to enjoy them, above and beyond all thought, unless we were meant to be immortal. This sunshine is the golden pledge thereof. It beams through the gates of Paradise, and shows us glimpses far inward.

By-and-by—in a little time—the outward world puts on a drear austerity. On some October morning, there is a heavy hoar-frost on the grass, and along the tops of the fences; and, at sunrise, the leaves fall from the trees of our avenue without a breath of wind, quietly descending by their own weight. All summer long, they have murmured like the noise of waters; they have roared loudly, while the branches were wrestling with the thunder-gust; they have made music, both glad and solemn; they have attuned my thoughts by their quiet sound, as I paced to-and-fro beneath the arch of intermingling boughs. Now, they can only rustle under my feet. Henceforth, the gray parsonage begins to assume a larger importance, and draws to its fireside—for the abomination of the air-tight stove is reserved till wintry weather—draws closer and closer to its fireside the vagrant impulses, that had gone wandering about, through the summer.

When summer was dead and buried, the old Manse became as lonely as a hermitage. Not that ever—in my time, at least —it had been thronged with company; but, at no rare intervals, we welcomed some friend out of the dusty glare and tumult of the world, and rejoiced to share with him the transparent obscurity that was flung over us. In one respect, our precincts were like the Enchanted Ground, through which the pilgrim travelled on his way to the Celestial City. The guests, each and all, felt a slumberous influence upon them; they fell asleep in chairs, or took a more deliberate siesta on the sofa, or were seen stretched among the shadows of the orchard, looking up dreamily through the boughs. They could not have paid a more acceptable compliment to my abode, nor to my own qualities as a host. I held it as a proof, that they left their cares behind them, as they passed between the stone gate-posts, at the entrance of our avenue; and that the so powerful opiate was the abundance of peace and quiet, within and all around us. Others could give them pleasure and amusement; or instruction—these could be picked up anywhere—but it was for me to give them rest—rest, in a life of trouble. What better could be done for those weary and world-worn spirits?—for him, whose career of perpetual action was impeded and harassed by the rarest of his powers, and the richest of his acquirements?—for another, who had thrown his ardent heart, from earliest youth, into the strife of politics, and now, perchance, began to suspect that one lifetime is too brief for the accomplishment of any lofty aim?— for her, on whose feminine nature had been imposed the heavy gift of intellectual power, such as a strong man might have staggered under, and with it the necessity to act upon the world?—in a word, not to multiply instances, what better could be done for anybody, who came within our magic circle, than to throw the spell of a tranquil spirit over him? And when it had wrought its full effect, then we dismissed him, with but misty reminiscences, as if he had been dreaming of us.

Were I to adopt a pet idea, as so many people do, and fondle it in my embraces to the exclusion of all others, it would be, that the great want which mankind labors under, at this present period, is—sleep! The world should recline its vast head on the first convenient pillow, and take an age-long nap. It has gone distracted, through a morbid activity, and, while preternaturally wide-awake, is nevertheless tormented by visions, that seem real to it now, but would assume their true aspect and character, were all things once set right by an interval of sound repose. This is the only method of getting rid of old delusions, and avoiding new ones—of regenerating our race, so that it might in due time awake, as an infant out of dewy slumber—of restoring to us the simple perception of what is right, and the single-hearted desire to achieve it; both of which have long been lost, in consequence of this weary activity of brain, and torpor or passion of the heart, that now afflicts the universe. Stimulants, the only mode of treatment hitherto attempted, cannot quell the disease; they do but heighten the delirium.

Let not the above paragraph ever be quoted against the author; for, though tinctured with its modicum of truth, it is the result and expression of what he knew, while he was writing, to be but a distorted survey of the state and prospects of mankind. There were circumstances around me, which made it difficult to view the world precisely as it exists; for, serene and sober as was the old Manse, it was necessary to go but a little way beyond its threshold, before meeting with stranger moral shapes of men than might have been encountered elsewhere, in a circuit of a thousand miles.

These hobgoblins of flesh and blood were attracted thither by the wide-spreading influence of a great original Thinker, who had his earthly abode at the opposite extremity of our village. His mind acted upon other minds, of a certain constitution, with wonderful magnetism, and drew many men upon long pilgrimages, to speak with him face to face. Young visionaries—to whom just so much of insight had been imparted, as to make life all a labyrinth around them—came to seek the clue that should guide them out of their self-involved bewilderment. Gray-headed theorists—whose systems, at first air, had finally imprisoned them in an iron frame-work—travelled painfully to his door, not to ask deliverance, but to invite this free spirit into their own thraldom. People that had lighted on a new thought, or a thought that they fancied new, came to Emerson, as the finder of a glittering gem hastens to a lapidary, to ascertain its quality and value. Uncertain, troubled, earnest wanderers, through the midnight of the moral world, beheld his intellectual fire, as a beacon burning on a hill-top, and, climbing the difficult ascent, looked forth into the surrounding obscurity, more hopefully than hitherto. The light revealed objects unseen before—mountains, gleaming lakes, glimpses of a creation among the chaos—but also, as was unavoidable, it attracted bats and owls, and the whole host of night-birds, which flapped their dusky wings against the gazer's eyes, and sometimes were mistaken for fowls of angelic feather. Such delusions always hover nigh, whenever a beacon-fire of truth is kindled.

For myself, there had been epochs of my life, when I, too, might have asked of this prophet the master-word, that should solve me the riddle of the universe; but now, being happy, I felt as if there were no question to be put, and therefore admired Emerson as a poet of deep beauty and austere tenderness, but sought nothing from him as a philosopher. It was good, nevertheless, to meet him in the wood-paths, or sometimes in our avenue, with that pure, intellectual gleam diffused about his presence, like the garment of a shining-one; and he so quiet, so simple, so without pretension, encountering each man alive as if expecting to receive more than he could impart. And, in truth, the heart of many an ordinary man had, perchance, inscriptions which he could not read. But it was impossible to dwell in his vicinity, without inhaling, more or less, the mountain-atmosphere of his lofty thought, which, in the brains of some people, wrought a singular giddiness—new truth being as heady as new wine. Never was a poor little country village infested with such a variety of queer, strangely dressed, oddly behaved mortals, most of whom took upon themselves to be important agents of the world's destiny, yet were simply bores of a very intense water. Such, I imagine, is the invariable character of persons who crowd so closely about an original thinker, as to draw in his unuttered breath, and thus become imbued with a false originality. This triteness of novelty is enough to make any man, of common sense, blaspheme at all ideas of less than a century's standing; and pray that the world may be petrified and rendered immovable, in precisely the worst moral and physical state that it ever yet arrived at, rather than be benefitted by such schemes of such philosophers.

And now, I begin to feel—and perhaps should have sooner felt—that we have talked enough of the old Manse. Mine honored reader, it may be, will vilify the poor author as an egotist, for babbling through so many pages about a moss-grown country parsonage, and his life within its walls, and on the river, and in the woods,—and the influences that wrought upon him, from all these sources. My conscience, however, does not reproach me with betraying anything too sacredly individual to be revealed by a human spirit, to its brother or sister spirit. How narrow—how shallow and scanty too—is the stream of thought that has been flowing from my pen, compared with the broad tide of dim emotions, ideas, and associations, which swell around me from that portion of my existence! How little have I told!—and, of that little, how almost nothing is even tinctured with any quality that makes it exclusively my own! Has the reader gone wandering, hand in hand with me, through the inner passages of my being, and have we groped together into all its chambers, and examined their treasures or their rubbish? Not so. We have been standing on the green sward, but just within the cavern's mouth, where the common sunshine is free to penetrate, and where every footstep is therefore free to come. I have appealed to no sentiment or sensibilities, save such as are diffused among us all. So far as I am a man of really individual attributes, I veil my face; nor am I, nor have ever been, one of those supremely hospitable people, who serve up their own hearts delicately fried, with brain-sauce, as a tidbit for their beloved public.

Glancing back over what I have written, it seems but the

scattered reminiscences of a single summer. In fairy-land, there is no measurement of time; and, in a spot so sheltered from the turmoil of life's ocean, three years hastened away with a noiseless flight, as the breezy sunshine chases the cloud-shadows across the depths of a still valley. Now came hints, growing more and more distinct, that the owner of the old house was pining for his native air. Carpenters next appeared, making a tremendous racket among the outbuildings, strewing the green grass with pine-shavings and chips of chestnut joists, and vexing the whole antiquity of the place with their discordant renovations. Soon, moreover, they divested our abode of the veil of woodbine, which had crept over a large portion of its southern face. All the aged mosses were cleaned unsparingly away; and there were horrible whispers about brushing up the external walls with a coat of paint—a purpose as little to my taste, as might be that of rouging the venerable cheeks of one's grandmother. But the hand that renovates is always more sacrilegious than that which destroys. In fine, we gathered up our household goods, drank a farewell cup of tea in our pleasant little breakfast-room—delicately fragrant tea, an unpurchaseable luxury, one of the many angel-gifts that had fallen like dew upon us—and passed forth between the tall stone gate-posts, as uncertain as the wandering Arabs where our tent might next be pitched. Providence took me by the hand, and—an oddity of dispensation which, I trust, there is no irreverence in smiling at—has led me, as the newspapers announce while I am writing, from the Old Manse into a Custom-House! As a storyteller, I have often contrived strange vicissitudes for my imaginary personages, but none like this.

The treasure of intellectual gold, which I hoped to find in our secluded dwelling, had never come to light. No profound treatise of ethics—no philosophic history—no novel, even, that could stand, unsupported, on its edges. All that I had to show, as a man of letters, were these few tales and essays, which had blossomed out like flowers in the calm summer of my heart and mind. Save editing (an easy task) the journal of my friend of many years, the African Cruiser, I had done nothing else. With these idle weeds and withering blossoms, I have intermixed some that were produced long ago—old, faded things, reminding me of flowers pressed between the leaves of a book—and now offer the bouquet, such as it is, to any whom it may please. These fitful sketches, with so little of external life about them, yet claiming no profundity of purpose,—so reserved, even while they sometimes seem so frank,—often but half in earnest, and never, even when most so, expressing satisfactorily the thoughts which they profess to image—such trifles, I truly feel, afford no solid basis for a literary reputation. Nevertheless, the public—if my limited number of readers, whom I venture to regard rather as a circle of friends, may be termed a public—will receive them the more kindly, as the last offering, the last collection of this nature, which it is my purpose ever to put forth. Unless I could do better, I have done enough in this kind. For myself, the book will always retain one charm, as reminding me of the river, with its delightful solitudes, and of the avenue, the garden, and the orchard, and especially the dear old Manse, with the little study on its western side, and the sunshine glimmering through the willow-branches while I wrote.

Let the reader, if he will do me so much honor, imagine himself my guest, and that, having seen whatever may be worthy of notice, within and about the old Manse, he has finally been ushered into my study. There, after seating him in an antique elbow-chair, an heirloom of the house, I take forth a roll of manuscript, and intreat his attention to the following tales:—an act of personal inhospitality, however, which I never was guilty of, nor ever will be, even to my worst enemy.

Preface to Twice-told Tales

THE author of *Twice-told Tales* has a claim to one distinction, which, as none of his literary brethren will care about disputing it with him, he need not be afraid to mention. He was, for a good many years, the obscurest man of letters in America.

These stories were published in Magazines and Annuals, extending over a period of ten or twelve years, and comprising the whole of the writer's young manhood, without making (so far as he has ever been aware) the slightest impression on the Public. One or two among them—THE RILL FROM THE TOWN-PUMP in perhaps a greater degree than any other —had a pretty wide newspaper-circulation; as for the rest, he has no grounds for supposing, that, on their first appearance, they met with the good or evil fortune to be read by anybody. Throughout the time above-specified, he had no incitement to literary effort in a reasonable prospect of reputation or profit; nothing but the pleasure itself of composition—an enjoyment not at all amiss in its way, and perhaps essential to the merit of the work in hand, but which, in the long run, will hardly keep the chill out of a writer's heart, or the numbness out of his fingers. To this total lack of sympathy, at the age when his mind would naturally have been most effervescent, the Public owe it, (and it is certainly an effect not to be regretted, on either part,) that the Author can show nothing for the thought and industry of that portion of his life, save the forty sketches, or thereabouts, included in these volumes.

Much more, indeed, he wrote; and some very small part of it might yet be rummaged out (but it would not be worth the trouble) among the dingy pages of fifteen-or-twenty-year-old periodicals, or within the shabby morocco-covers of faded Souvenirs. The remainder of the works, alluded to, had a very brief existence, but, on the score of brilliancy, enjoyed a fate vastly superior to that of their brotherhood, which succeeded in getting through the press. In a word, the Author burned them without mercy or remorse, (and, moreover, without any subsequent regret,) and had more than one occasion to marvel that such very dull stuff, as he knew his condemned manuscripts to be, should yet have possessed inflammability enough to set the chimney on fire!

After a long while, the first collected volume of the Tales was published. By this time, if the Author had ever been greatly tormented by literary ambition, (which he does not remember or believe to have been the case,) it must have perished, beyond resuscitation, in the dearth of nutriment. This was fortunate; for the success of the volume was not such as would have gratified a craving desire for notoriety. A moderate edition was "got rid of" (to use the Publisher's very significant phrase) within a reasonable time, but apparently without rendering the writer or his productions much more generally known than before. The great bulk of the reading Public probably ignored the book altogether. A few persons read it, and liked it better than it deserved. At an interval of three or four years, the second volume was published, and encountered much the same sort of kindly, but calm, and very limited reception. The circulation of the two volumes was chiefly confined to New England; nor was it until long after this period, if it even yet be the case, that the Author could regard himself as addressing the American Public, or, indeed, any Public at all. He was merely writing to his known or unknown friends.

As he glances over these long-forgotten pages, and considers his way of life, while composing them, the Author can very clearly discern why all this was so. After so many sober years, he would have reason to be ashamed if he could not criticise his own work as fairly as another man's; and—though it is little his business, and perhaps still less his interest—he can hardly resist a temptation to achieve something of the sort. If writers were allowed to do so, and would perform the task with perfect sincerity and unreserve, their opinions of their own productions would often be more valuable and instructive than the works themselves.

At all events, there can be no harm in the Author's remarking, that he rather wonders how the TWICE-TOLD TALES should have gained what vogue they did, than that it was so little and so gradual. They have the pale tint of flowers that blossomed in too retired a shade—the coolness of a meditative habit, which diffuses itself through the feeling and observation of every sketch. Instead of passion, there is sentiment; and, even in what purport to be pictures of actual life, we have allegory, not always so warmly dressed in its habiliments of flesh and blood, as to be taken into the reader's mind without a shiver. Whether from lack of power, or an unconquerable reserve, the Author's touches have often an effect of tameness; the merriest man can hardly contrive to laugh at his broadest humor; the tenderest woman, one would suppose, will hardly shed warm tears at his deepest pathos. The book, if you would see anything in it, requires to be read in the clear, brown, twilight atmosphere in which it was written; if opened in the sunshine, it is apt to look exceedingly like a volume of blank pages.

With the foregoing characteristics, proper to the productions of a person in retirement, (which happened to be the Author's category, at the time,) the book is devoid of others that we should quite as naturally look for. The sketches are not, it is hardly necessary to say, profound; but it is rather more remarkable that they so seldom, if ever, show any design on the writer's part to make them so. They have none of the abstruseness of idea, or obscurity of expression, which mark the written communications of a solitary mind with itself. They never need translation. It is, in fact, the style of a man of society. Every sentence, so far as it embodies thought or sensibility, may be understood and felt by anybody, who will give himself the trouble to read it, and will take up the book in a proper mood.

This statement of apparently opposite peculiarities leads us to a perception of what the sketches truly are. They are not the talk of a secluded man with his own mind and heart, (had it been so, they could hardly have failed to be more deeply and permanently valuable,) but his attempts, and very imperfectly successful ones, to open an intercourse with the world.

The Author would regret to be understood as speaking sourly or querulously of the slight mark, made by his earlier literary efforts, on the Public at large. It is so far the contrary, that he has been moved to write this preface, chiefly as affording him an opportunity to express how much enjoyment he has owed to these volumes, both before and since their publication. They are the memorials of very tranquil and not un-happy years. They failed, it is true—nor could it have been otherwise—in winning an extensive popularity. Occasionally, however, when he deemed them entirely forgotten, a para-graph or an article, from a native or foreign critic, would gratify his instincts of authorship with unexpected praise;—too generous praise, indeed, and too little alloyed with cen-sure, which, therefore, he learned the better to inflict upon himself. And, by-the-by, it is a very suspicious symptom of a deficiency of the popular element in a book, when it calls forth no harsh criticism. This has been particularly the fortune of the TWICE-TOLD TALES. They made no enemies, and were so little known and talked about, that those who read, and chanced to like them, were apt to conceive the sort of kind-ness for the book, which a person naturally feels for a discov-ery of his own.

This kindly feeling, (in some cases, at least,) extended to the Author, who, on the internal evidence of his sketches, came to be regarded as a mild, shy, gentle, melancholic, ex-ceedingly sensitive, and not very forcible man, hiding his blushes under an assumed name, the quaintness of which was supposed, somehow or other, to symbolize his personal and literary traits. He is by no means certain, that some of his subsequent productions have not been influenced and modi-fied by a natural desire to fill up so amiable an outline, and to act in consonance with the character assigned to him; nor, even now, could he forfeit it without a few tears of tender sensibility. To conclude, however;—these volumes have opened the way to most agreeable associations, and to the formation of imperishable friendships; and there are many golden threads, interwoven with his present happiness, which he can follow up more or less directly, until he finds their commencement here; so that his pleasant pathway among realities seems to proceed out of the Dream-Land of his youth, and to be bordered with just enough of its shadowy foliage to shelter him from the heat of the day. He is there-fore satisfied with what the TWICE-TOLD TALES have done for him, and feels it to be far better than fame.

LENOX, January 11, 1851.

Preface to The Snow-Image

TO HORATIO BRIDGE, ESQ., U. S. N.

M Y DEAR BRIDGE:
Some of the more crabbed of my critics, I understand, have pronounced your friend egotistical, indiscreet,
and even impertinent, on account of the Prefaces and Introductions with which, on several occasions, he has seen fit to
pave the reader's way into the interior edifice of a book. In
the justice of this censure I do not exactly concur, for the
reasons, on the one hand, that the public generally has nega-
tived the idea of undue freedom on the author's part, by evincing, it seems to me, rather more interest in these aforesaid
Introductions than in the stories which followed,—and that,
on the other hand, with whatever appearance of confidential
intimacy, I have been especially careful to make no disclosures
respecting myself which the most indifferent observer might
not have been acquainted with, and which I was not perfectly
willing that my worst enemy should know. I might further
justify myself, on the plea that, ever since my youth, I have
been addressing a very limited circle of friendly readers, without much danger of being overheard by the public at large;
and that the habits thus acquired might pardonably continue,
although strangers may have begun to mingle with my audience.

But the charge, I am bold to say, is not a reasonable one,
in any view which we can fairly take of it. There is no harm,
but, on the contrary, good, in arraying some of the ordinary
facts of life in a slightly idealized and artistic guise. I have
taken facts which relate to myself, because they chance to be
nearest at hand, and likewise are my own property. And, as
for egotism, a person, who has been burrowing, to his utmost
ability, into the depths of our common nature, for the purposes of psychological romance,—and who pursues his researches in that dusky region, as he needs must, as well by the
tact of sympathy as by the light of observation,—will smile
at incurring such an imputation in virtue of a little preliminary talk about his external habits, his abode, his casual asso-

ciates, and other matters entirely upon the surface. These things hide the man, instead of displaying him. You must make quite another kind of inquest, and look through the whole range of his fictitious characters, good and evil, in order to detect any of his essential traits.

Be all this as it may, there can be no question as to the propriety of my inscribing this volume of earlier and later sketches to you, and pausing here, a few moments, to speak of them, as friend speaks to friend; still being cautious, however, that the public and the critics shall overhear nothing which we care about concealing. On you, if on no other person, I am entitled to rely, to sustain the position of my Dedicatee. If anybody is responsible for my being at this day an author, it is yourself. I know not whence your faith came; but, while we were lads together at a country college,—gathering blue-berries, in study-hours, under those tall academic pines; or watching the great logs, as they tumbled along the current of the Androscoggin; or shooting pigeons and gray squirrels in the woods; or bat-fowling in the summer twilight; or catching trouts in that shadowy little stream which, I suppose, is still wandering riverward through the forest,—though you and I will never cast a line in it again,—two idle lads, in short (as we need not fear to acknowledge now), doing a hundred things that the Faculty never heard of, or else it had been the worse for us,—still it was your prognostic of your friend's destiny, that he was to be a writer of fiction.

And a fiction-monger, in due season, he became. But, was there ever such a weary delay in obtaining the slightest recognition from the public, as in my case? I sat down by the wayside of life, like a man under enchantment, and a shrubbery sprung up around me, and the bushes grew to be saplings, and the saplings became trees, until no exit appeared possible, through the entangling depths of my obscurity. And there, perhaps, I should be sitting at this moment, with the moss on the imprisoning tree-trunks, and the yellow leaves of more than a score of autumns piled above me, if it had not been for you. For it was through your interposition,—and that, moreover, unknown to himself,—that your early friend was brought before the public, somewhat more prominently than theretofore, in the first volume of Twice-told Tales. Not a publisher in America, I presume, would have thought well enough of my forgotten or never noticed stories, to risk the expense of print and paper; nor do I say this with any purpose of casting odium on the respectable fraternity of booksellers, for their blindness to my wonderful merit. To confess the truth, I doubted of the public recognition quite as much as they could do. So much the more generous was your confidence; and knowing, as I do, that it was founded on old friendship rather than cold criticism, I value it only the more for that.

So, now, when I turn back upon my path, lighted by a transitory gleam of public favor, to pick up a few articles which were left out of my former collections, I take pleasure in making them the memorial of our very long and unbroken connection. Some of these sketches were among the earliest that I wrote, and, after lying for years in manuscript, they at last skulked into the Annuals or Magazines, and have hidden themselves there ever since. Others were the productions of a later period; others, again, were written recently. The comparison of these various trifles—the indices of intellectual condition at far separated epochs—affects me with a singular complexity of regrets. I am disposed to quarrel with the earlier sketches, both because a mature judgment discerns so many faults, and still more because they come so nearly up to the standard of the best that I can achieve now. The ripened autumnal fruit tastes but little better than the early windfalls. It would, indeed, be mortifying to believe that the summertime of life has passed away, without any greater progress and improvement than is indicated here. But,—at least, so I would fain hope,—these things are scarcely to be depended upon, as measures of the intellectual and moral man. In youth, men are apt to write more wisely than they really know or feel; and the remainder of life may be not idly spent in realizing and convincing themselves of the wisdom which they uttered long ago. The truth that was only in the fancy then may have since become a substance in the mind and heart.

I have nothing further, I think, to say; unless it be that the public need not dread my again trespassing on its kindness, with any more of these musty and mouse-nibbled leaves of old periodicals, transformed, by the magic arts of my friendly publishers, into a new book. These are the last. Or, if a few still remain, they are either such as no paternal partiality could induce the author to think worth preserving, or else they have got into some very dark and dusty hiding-place, quite out of my own remembrance and whence no researches can avail to unearth them. So there let them rest.

Very sincerely yours,

N. H.

LENOX, NOVEMBER 1st, 1851.

A WONDER BOOK

FOR GIRLS AND BOYS

(1852)

Contents

Preface

THE author has long been of opinion, that many of the classical myths were capable of being rendered into very capital reading for children. In the little volume here offered to the Public, he has worked up half-a-dozen of them, with this end in view. A great freedom of treatment was necessary to his plan; but it will be observed by every one, who attempts to render these legends malleable in his intellectual furnace, that they are marvellously independent of all temporary modes and circumstances. They remain essentially the same, after changes that would affect the identity of almost anything else.

He does not, therefore, plead guilty to a sacrilege, in having sometimes shaped anew, as his fancy dictated, the forms that have been hallowed by an antiquity of two or three thousand years. No epoch of time can claim a copyright in these immortal fables. They seem never to have been made; and certainly, so long as man exists, they can never perish; but, by their indestructibility itself, they are legitimate subjects for every age to clothe with its own garniture of manners and sentiment, and to imbue with its own morality. In the present version, they may have lost much of their classical aspect, (or, at all events, the Author has not been careful to preserve it,) and have perhaps assumed a Gothic or romantic guise.

In performing this pleasant task—for it has been really a task fit for hot weather, and one of the most agreeable, of a literary kind, which he ever undertook—the Author has not always thought it necessary to write downward, in order to meet the comprehension of children. He has generally suffered the theme to soar, whenever such was its tendency, and when he himself was buoyant enough to follow without an effort. Children possess an unestimated sensibility to whatever is deep or high, in imagination or feeling, so long as it is simple, likewise. It is only the artificial and the complex that bewilders them.

LENOX, July 15th, 1851.

Tanglewood Porch

BENEATH the porch of the country-seat called Tanglewood, one fine autumnal morning, was assembled a
merry party of little folks, with a tall youth in the midst of
them. They had planned a nutting expedition, and were impatiently waiting for the mists to roll up the hill-slopes, and
for the sun to pour the warmth of the Indian Summer over
the fields and pastures, and into the nooks of the many-
colored woods. There was the prospect of as fine a day as
ever gladdened the aspect of this beautiful and comfortable
world. As yet, however, the morning mist filled up the whole
length and breadth of the valley, above which, on a gently
sloping eminence, the mansion stood.

This body of white vapor extended to within less than a
hundred yards of the house. It completely hid everything beyond that distance, except a few ruddy or yellow tree-tops,
which here and there emerged, and were glorified by the early
sunshine, as was likewise the broad surface of the mist. Four
or five miles off, to the southward, rose the summit of Monument Mountain, and seemed to be floating on a cloud. Some
fifteen miles farther away, in the same direction, appeared the
loftier Dome of Taconic, looking blue and indistinct, and
hardly so substantial as the vapory sea that almost rolled over
it. The nearer hills, which bordered the valley, were half sub-
merged, and were specked with little cloud-wreaths all the
way to their tops. On the whole, there was so much cloud,
and so little solid earth, that it had the effect of a vision.

The children above-mentioned, being as full of life as they
could hold, kept overflowing from the porch of Tanglewood,
and scampering along the gravel-walk, or rushing across the
dewy herbage of the lawn. I can hardly tell how many of
these small people there were; not less than nine or ten, however, nor more than a dozen, of all sorts, sizes, and ages,
whether girls or boys. They were brothers, sisters, and cousins, together with a few of their young acquaintances, who

had been invited by Mr. and Mrs. Pringle to spend some of this delightful weather with their own children, at Tanglewood. I am afraid to tell you their names, or even to give them any names which other children have ever been called by; because, to my certain knowledge, authors sometimes get themselves into great trouble by accidentally giving the names of real persons to the characters in their books. For this reason, I mean to call them Primrose, Periwinkle, Sweet Fern, Dandelion, Blue Eye, Clover, Huckleberry, Cowslip, Squash Blossom, Milkweed, Plantain, and Butter-cup; although, to be sure, such titles might better suit a group of fairies than a company of earthly children.

It is not to be supposed that these little folks were to be permitted by their careful fathers and mothers, uncles, aunts, or grandparents, to stray abroad into the woods and fields, without the guardianship of some particularly grave and elderly person. Oh, no, indeed! In the first sentence of my book, you will recollect that I spoke of a tall youth, standing in the midst of the children. His name—(and I shall let you know his real name, because he considers it a great honor to have told the stories that are here to be printed)—his name was Eustace Bright. He was a student at Williams College, and had reached, I think, at this period, the venerable age of eighteen years; so that he felt quite like a grandfather towards Periwinkle, Dandelion, Huckleberry, Squash Blossom, Milkweed, and the rest, who were only half or a third as venerable as he. A trouble in his eyesight (such as many students think it necessary to have, now-a-days, in order to prove their diligence at their books) had kept him from college a week or two after the beginning of the term. But, for my part, I have seldom met with a pair of eyes that looked as if they could see farther or better, than those of Eustace Bright.

This learned student was slender, and rather pale, as all Yankee students are, but yet of a healthy aspect, and as light and active as if he had wings to his shoes. By-the-by, being much addicted to wading through streamlets and across meadows, he had put on cow-hide boots for the expedition. He wore a linen blouse, a cloth cap, and a pair of green spectacles, which he had assumed, probably, less for the preservation of his eyes, than for the dignity that they imparted to his countenance. In either case, however, he might as well have let them alone; for Huckleberry, a mischievous little elf, crept behind Eustace as he sat on the steps of the porch; snatched the spectacles from his nose, and clapt them on her own; and, as the student forgot to take them back, they fell off into the grass, and lay there till the next spring.

Now, Eustace Bright, you must know, had won great fame among the children as a narrator of wonderful stories; and though he sometimes pretended to be annoyed, when they teazed him for more, and more, and always for more, yet I really doubt whether he liked anything quite so well as to tell them. You might have seen his eyes twinkle, therefore, when Clover, Sweet Fern, Cowslip, Butter-cup, and most of their playmates, besought him to relate one of his stories, while they were waiting for the mist to clear up.

"Yes, Cousin Eustace," said Primrose, who was a bright girl of twelve, with laughing eyes, and a nose that turned up a little, "the morning is certainly the best time for the stories, with which you so often tire out our patience. We shall be in less danger of hurting your feelings by falling asleep at the most interesting points—as little Cowslip and I did, last night!"

"Naughty Primrose," cried Cowslip, a child of six years old, "I did not fall asleep, and I only shut my eyes, so as to see a picture of what Cousin Eustace was telling about. His stories are good to hear at night, because we can dream about them, asleep;—and good in the morning, too, because then we can dream about them, awake. So I hope he will tell us one, this very minute!"

"Thank you, my little Cowslip," said Eustace. "Certainly, you shall have the best story I can think of, if it were only for defending me so well from that naughty Primrose. But, children, I have already told you so many fairy tales, that I doubt whether there is a single one which you have not heard at least twice over. I am afraid you will fall asleep, in reality, if I repeat any of them again."

"No, no, no!" cried Blue Eye, Periwinkle, Plantain, and half-a-dozen others. "We like a story all the better for having heard it two or three times before."

And it is a truth, as regards children, that a story seems

often to deepen its mark in their interest, not merely by two or three, but by numberless repetitions. But Eustace Bright, in the exuberance of his resources, scorned to avail himself of an advantage, which an older story-teller would have been glad to grasp at.

"It would be a great pity," said he, "if a man of my learning (to say nothing of original fancy) could not find a new story, every day, year in and year out, for children such as you. I will tell you one of the nursery-tales that were made for the amusement of our great, old grandmother, the Earth, when she was a child in frock and pin-a-fore. There are a hundred such; and it is a wonder to me, that they have not long ago been put into picture-books for little girls and boys. But, instead of that, old gray-bearded grandsires pore over them, in musty volumes of Greek, and puzzle themselves with trying to find out when, and how, and for what, they were made."

"Well, well, well, well, Cousin Eustace!" cried all the children at once. "Talk no more about your stories, but begin!"

"Sit down, then, every soul of you," said Eustace Bright, "and be all as still as so many mice. At the slightest interruption, whether from great, naughty Primrose, little Dandelion, or any other, I shall bite the story short off between my teeth, and swallow the untold part. But, in the first place, do any of you know what a Gorgon is?"

"I do," said Primrose.

"Then hold your tongue!" rejoined Eustace, who had rather she would have known nothing about the matter. "Hold all your tongues; and I shall tell you a sweet-pretty story of a Gorgon's Head."

And so he did, as you may begin to read on the next page. Working up his sophomorical erudition, with a good deal of tact, and incurring great obligations to Professor Anthon, he, nevertheless, disregarded all classical authorities, whenever the vagrant audacity of his imagination impelled him to do so.

The Gorgon's Head

PERSEUS was the son of Danaë, who was the daughter of a king. And when Perseus was a very little boy, some wicked people put his mother and himself into a chest, and set them afloat upon the sea. The wind blew freshly, and drove the chest away from the shore, and the uneasy billows tossed it up and down; while Danaë clasped her child closely to her bosom, and dreaded that some big wave would dash its foamy crest over them both. The chest sailed on, however, and neither sank nor was upset; until, when night was coming, it floated so near an island that it got entangled in a fisherman's nets, and was drawn out high and dry upon the sand. The island was called Seriphus, and it was reigned over by King Polydectes, who happened to be the fisherman's brother.

This fisherman, I am glad to tell you, was an exceedingly humane and upright man. He showed great kindness to Danaë and her little boy, and continued to befriend them, until Perseus had grown to be a handsome youth, very strong and active, and skilful in the use of arms. Long before this time, King Polydectes had seen the two strangers—the mother and her child—who had come to his dominions in a floating chest. As he was not good and kind, like his brother the fisherman, but extremely wicked, he resolved to send Perseus on a dangerous enterprise, in which he would probably be killed, and then to do some great mischief to Danaë herself. So this bad-hearted king spent a long while in considering what was the most dangerous thing that a young man could possibly undertake to perform. At last, having hit upon an enterprise that promised to turn out as fatally as he desired, he sent for the youthful Perseus.

The young man came to the palace, and found the king sitting upon his throne.

"Perseus," said King Polydectes, smiling craftily upon him, "you are grown up a fine young man. You and your good mother have received a great deal of kindness from myself, as well as from my worthy brother, the fisherman, and I suppose you would not be sorry to repay some of it!"

"Please your majesty," answered Perseus, "I would willingly risk my life to do so."

"Well, then," continued the king, still with a cunning smile on his lips, "I have a little adventure to propose to you; and, as you are a brave and enterprising youth, you will doubtless look upon it as a great piece of good luck to have so rare an opportunity of distinguishing yourself. You must know, my good Perseus, I think of getting married to the beautiful Princess Hippodamia; and it is customary, on these occasions, to make the bride a present of some far-fetched and elegant curiosity. I have been a little perplexed, I must honestly confess, where to obtain anything likely to please a princess of her exquisite taste. But, this morning, I flatter myself, I have thought of precisely the article."

"And can I assist your majesty in obtaining it?" cried Perseus eagerly.

"You can, if you are as brave a youth as I believe you to be," replied King Polydectes, with the utmost graciousness of manner. "The bridal gift, which I have set my heart on presenting to the beautiful Hippodamia, is the head of the Gorgon Medusa, with the snaky locks; and I depend on you, my dear Perseus, to bring it to me. So, as I am anxious to settle affairs with the princess, the sooner you go in quest of the Gorgon, the better I shall be pleased."

"I will set out tomorrow morning," answered Perseus.

"Pray do so, my gallant youth!" rejoined the king. "And, Perseus, in cutting off the Gorgon's head, be careful to make a clean stroke, so as not to injure its appearance. You must bring it home in the very best condition, in order to suit the exquisite taste of the beautiful Princess Hippodamia."

Perseus left the palace, but was scarcely out of hearing before Polydectes burst into a laugh; being greatly amused, wicked king that he was, to find how readily the young man fell into the snare. The news quickly spread abroad, that Perseus had undertaken to cut off the head of Medusa with the snaky locks. Everybody was rejoiced; for most of the inhabitants of the island were as wicked as the king himself, and would have liked nothing better than to see some enormous mischief happen to Danaë and her son. The only good man, in this unfortunate island of Seriphus, appears to have been the fisherman. As Perseus walked along, therefore, the people pointed after him, and made mouths, and winked to one another, and ridiculed him as loudly as they dared.

"Ho, ho!" cried they. "Medusa's snakes will sting him soundly!"

Now, there were three Gorgons alive, at that period; and they were the most strange and terrible monsters that had ever been seen, since the world was made, or that have been seen in after days, or that are likely to be seen, in all time to come. I hardly know what sort of creature or hobgoblin to call them. They were three sisters, and seem to have borne some distant resemblance to women, but were really a very frightful and mischievous species of dragon. It is indeed difficult to imagine what hideous beings these three sisters were. Why, instead of locks of hair, if you can believe me, they had each of them a hundred enormous snakes growing on their heads, all alive, twisting, wriggling, curling, and thrusting out their venomous tongues, with forked stings at the end! The teeth of the Gorgons were terribly long tusks; their hands were made of brass; and their bodies were all over scales, which, if not iron, were something as hard and impenetrable. They had wings, too, and exceedingly splendid ones, I can assure you; for every feather in them was pure, bright, glittering, burnished gold, and they looked very dazzlingly, no doubt, when the Gorgons were flying about in the sunshine.

But, when people happened to catch a glimpse of their glittering brightness, aloft in the air, they seldom stopt to gaze, but ran and hid themselves as speedily as they could. You will think, perhaps, that they were afraid of being stung by the serpents that served the Gorgons instead of hair—or of having their heads bitten off by their ugly tusks—or of being torn all to pieces by their brazen claws. Well, to be sure, these were some of the dangers, but by no means the greatest, nor the most difficult to avoid. For the worst thing about these abominable Gorgons was, that, if once a poor mortal fixed his eyes full upon one of their faces, he was certain, that very instant, to be changed from warm flesh and blood into cold and lifeless stone!

Thus, as you will easily perceive, it was a very dangerous adventure that the wicked King Polydectes had contrived for this innocent young man. Perseus himself, when he had thought over the matter, could not help seeing that he had very little chance of coming safely through it, and that he was far more likely to become a stone image, than to bring back the head of Medusa with the snaky locks. For, not to speak of other difficulties, there was one which it would have puzzled an older man than Perseus to get over. Not only must he fight with and slay this golden-winged, iron-scaled, long-tusked, brazen-clawed, snaky-haired monster, but he must do it with his eyes shut, or, at least, without so much as a glance at the enemy with whom he was contending. Else, while his arm was lifted to strike, he would stiffen into stone, and stand with that uplifted arm for centuries, until time, and the wind and weather, should crumble him quite away. This would be a very sad thing to befal a young man, who wanted to perform a great many brave deeds, and to enjoy a great deal of happiness, in this bright and beautiful world.

So disconsolate did these thoughts make him, that Perseus could not bear to tell his mother what he had undertaken to do. He therefore took his shield, girded on his sword, and crossed over from the island to the mainland, where he sat down in a solitary place, and hardly refrained from shedding tears.

But while he was in this sorrowful mood, he heard a voice close beside him.

"Perseus," said the voice, "why are you sad?"

He lifted his head from his hands, in which he had hidden it; and, behold! all alone as Perseus had supposed himself to be, there was a stranger in the solitary place. It was a brisk, intelligent, and remarkably shrewd-looking young man, with a cloak over his shoulders, an odd sort of cap on his head, a strangely twisted staff in his hand, and a short and very crooked sword hanging by his side. He was exceedingly light and active in his figure, like a person much accustomed to gymnastic exercises, and well able to leap or run. Above all, the stranger had such a cheerful, knowing, and helpful aspect, (though it was certainly a little mischievous, into the bargain,) that Perseus could not help feeling his spirits grow livelier, as he gazed at him. Besides, being really a courageous youth, he felt greatly ashamed that anybody should have found him with tears in his eyes, like a timid little school-boy, when, after all, there might be no occasion for despair. So Perseus wiped his eyes, and answered the stranger pretty briskly, putting on as brave a look as he could.

"I am not so very sad," said he—"only thoughtful about an adventure that I have undertaken."

"Oho!" answered the stranger. "Well, tell me all about it, and possibly I may be of service to you. I have helped a good many young men through adventures that looked difficult enough beforehand. Perhaps you may have heard of me. I have more names than one; but the name of Quicksilver suits me as well as any other. Tell me what your trouble is; and we will talk the matter over, and see what can be done."

The stranger's words and manner put Perseus into quite a different mood from his former one. He resolved to tell Quicksilver all his difficulties; since he could not easily be worse off than he already was, and, very possibly, his new friend might give him some advice that would turn out well in the end. So he let the stranger know, in few words, precisely what the case was;—how that King Polydectes wanted the head of Medusa with the snaky locks, as a bridal gift for the beautiful Princess Hippodamia, and how that he had undertaken to get it for him, but was afraid of being turned into stone.

"And that would be a great pity," said Quicksilver, with his mischievous smile. "You would make a very handsome marble statue, it is true; and it would be a considerable number of centuries before you crumbled away. But, on the whole, one would rather be a young man for a few years, than a stone image for a great many."

"Oh, far rather!" exclaimed Perseus, with the tears again standing in his eyes. "And, besides, what would my dear mother do, if her beloved son were turned into a stone!"

"Well, well, let us hope that the affair will not turn out so very badly," replied Quicksilver, in an encouraging tone. "I am the very person to help you, if anybody can. My sister and myself will do our utmost to bring you safe through the adventure, ugly as it now looks."

"Your sister?" repeated Perseus.

"Yes; my sister," said the stranger. "She is very wise, I promise you; and as for myself, I generally have all my wits about me, such as they are. If you show yourself bold and cautious, and follow our advice, you need not fear being a stone image yet awhile. But, first of all, you must polish your shield till you can see your face in it as distinctly as in a mirror."

This seemed to Perseus rather an odd beginning of the adventure; for he thought it of far more consequence that the shield should be strong enough to defend him from the Gorgon's brazen claws, than that it should be bright enough to show him the reflection of his face. However, concluding that Quicksilver knew better than himself, he immediately set to work, and scrubbed the shield with so much diligence and good-will, that it very quickly shone like the moon at harvest-time. Quicksilver looked at it with a smile, and nodded his approbation. Then, taking off his own short and crooked sword, he girded it about Perseus, instead of the one which he had before worn.

"No sword but mine will answer your purpose," observed he. "The blade has a most excellent temper, and will cut through iron and brass as easily as through the slenderest twig. And now we will set out. The next thing is to find the Three Gray Women, who will tell us where to find the Nymphs."

"The Three Gray Women!" cried Perseus, to whom this seemed only a new difficulty in the path of his adventure. "Pray, who may the Three Gray Women be? I never heard of them before."

"They are three very strange old ladies," said Quicksilver, laughing. "They have but one eye among them, and only one tooth! Moreover, you must find them out by starlight, or in the dusk of the evening; for they never show themselves by the light either of the sun or moon."

"But," said Perseus, "why should I waste my time with these Three Gray Women? Would it not be better to set out at once in search of the terrible Gorgons?"

"No, no," answered his friend. "There are other things to be done, before you can find your way to the Gorgons. There is nothing for it, but to hunt up these old ladies; and when we meet with them, you may be sure that the Gorgons are not a great way off. Come; let us be stirring!"

Perseus, by this time, felt so much confidence in his companion's sagacity, that he made no more objections, and professed himself ready to begin the adventure immediately. They accordingly set out, and walked at a pretty brisk pace; so brisk, indeed, that Perseus found it rather difficult to keep up with his nimble friend Quicksilver. To say the truth, he had a singular idea that Quicksilver was furnished with a pair of winged shoes, which, of course, helped him along marvellously. And then, too, when Perseus looked sideways at him, out of the corner of his eye, he seemed to see wings on the side of his head; although, if he turned a full gaze, there were no such things to be perceived, but only an odd kind of cap. But, at all events, the twisted staff was evidently a great convenience to Quicksilver, and enabled him to proceed so fast, that Perseus, though a remarkably active young man, began to be out of breath.

"Here!" cried Quicksilver, at last—for he knew well enough, rogue that he was, how hard Perseus found it to keep pace with him—"Take you the staff, for you need it a great deal more than I. Are there no better walkers than yourself, in the island of Seriphus?"

"I could walk pretty well," said Perseus, glancing slily at his companion's feet, "if I had only a pair of winged shoes."

"We must see about getting you a pair," answered Quicksilver.

But the staff helped Perseus along so bravely, that he no longer felt the slightest weariness. In fact, the stick seemed to be alive in his hand, and to lend some of its life to Perseus. He and Quicksilver now walked onward, at their ease, talking very sociably together; and Quicksilver told so many pleasant stories about his former adventures, and how well his wits had served him on various occasions, that Perseus began to think him a very wonderful person. He evidently knew the world; and nobody is so charming to a young man, as a friend who has that kind of knowledge. Perseus listened the more eagerly, in the hope of brightening his own wits by what he heard.

At last, he happened to recollect that Quicksilver had spoken of a sister, who was to lend her assistance in the adventure which they were now bound upon.

"Where is she?" he inquired. "Shall we not meet her soon?"

"All at the proper time," said his companion. "But this sister of mine, you must understand, is quite a different sort of character from myself. She is very grave and prudent, seldom smiles, never laughs, and makes it a rule not to utter a word, unless she has something particularly profound to say. Neither will she listen to any but the wisest conversation."

"Dear me!" ejaculated Perseus. "I shall be afraid to say a syllable."

"She is a very accomplished person, I assure you," continued Quicksilver, "and has all the arts and sciences at her fingers' ends. In short, she is so immoderately wise, that many people call her Wisdom personified. But, to tell you the truth, she has hardly vivacity enough for my taste; and I think you would scarcely find her so pleasant a travelling companion as myself. She has her good points, nevertheless, and you will find the benefit of them in your encounter with the Gorgons."

By this time, it had grown quite dusk. They were now come to a very wild and desert place, overgrown with shaggy bushes, and so silent and solitary that nobody seemed ever to have dwelt or journeyed there. All was waste and desolate, in the gray twilight, which grew every moment more obscure. Perseus looked about him, rather disconsolately, and asked Quicksilver whether they had a great deal farther to go.

"Hist! Hist!" whispered his companion. "Make no noise! This is just the time and place to meet the Three Gray Women. Be careful that they do not see you before you see them; for though they have but a single eye among the three, it is as sharp-sighted as half-a-dozen common eyes."

"But what must I do," asked Perseus, "when we meet them?"

Quicksilver explained to Perseus how the Three Gray Women managed with their one eye. They were in the habit, it seems, of changing it from one to another, as if it had been a pair of spectacles, or—which would have suited them better—a quizzing-glass. When one of the three had kept the eye a certain time, she took it out of the socket and passed it to one of her sisters, whose turn it might happen to be, and who immediately clapt it into her own head, and enjoyed a peep at the visible world. Thus it will easily be understood, that only one of the Three Gray Women could see, while the other two were in utter darkness; and, moreover, at the instant when the eye was passing from hand to hand, neither of the poor old ladies was able to see a wink. I have heard of a great many strange things, in my day, and have witnessed not a few, but none, it seems to me, that can compare with the oddity of these Three Gray Women, all peeping through a single eye.

So thought Perseus, likewise, and was so astonished that he almost fancied his companion was joking with him, and that there were no such old women in the world.

"You will soon find whether I tell the truth or no," observed Quicksilver. "Hark! Hush! Hist! Hist! There they come, now!"

Perseus looked earnestly through the dusk of the evening, and there, sure enough, at no great distance off, he descried the Three Gray Women. The light being so faint, he could not well make out what sort of figures they were; only he discerned that they had long gray hair; and, as they came nearer, he saw that two of them had but the empty socket of an eye, in the middle of their foreheads. But, in the middle of the third sister's forehead, there was a very large, bright, and piercing eye, which sparkled like a great diamond in a ring; and so penetrating did it seem to be, that Perseus could not help thinking it must possess the gift of seeing in the darkest midnight, just as perfectly as at noon-day. The sight of three persons' eyes was melted and collected into that single one.

Thus the three old dames got along about as comfortably, upon the whole, as if they could all see at once. She, who chanced to have the eye in her forehead, led the other two by the hands, peeping sharply about her, all the while; insomuch that Perseus dreaded lest she should see right through the thick clump of bushes, behind which he and Quicksilver had hidden themselves. My stars! It was positively terrible to be within reach of so very sharp an eye!

But, before they reached the clump of bushes, one of the Three Gray Women spoke.

"Sister! Sister Scarecrow!" cried she. "You have had the eye long enough. It is my turn now!"

"Let me keep it a moment longer, Sister Nightmare," answered Scarecrow. "I thought I had a glimpse of something behind that thick bush."

"Well; and what of that?" retorted Nightmare, peevishly. "Can't I see into a thick bush as easily as yourself? The eye is mine as well as yours; and I know the use of it as well as you, or may be a little better. I insist upon taking a peep immediately!"

But here the third sister, whose name was Shake-joint, began to complain, and said that it was her turn to have the eye, and that Scarecrow and Nightmare wanted to keep it all to themselves. To end the dispute, old Dame Scarecrow took the eye out of her forehead, and held it forth in her hand.

"Take it, one of you," cried she, "and quit this foolish quarrelling. For my part, I shall be glad of a little thick darkness. Take it quickly, however; or I must clap it into my own head again!"

Accordingly, both Nightmare and Shake-joint stretched out their hands, groping eagerly to snatch the eye out of the hand of Scarecrow. But, being both alike blind, they could not easily find where Scarecrow's hand was; and Scarecrow, being now just as much in the dark as Shake-joint and Nightmare, could not at once meet either of their hands, in order to put the eye into it. Thus, (as you will see with half an eye, my wise little auditors,) these good old dames had fallen into a strange perplexity. For, though the eye shone and glistened like a star, as Scarecrow held it out, yet the Gray Women caught not the least glimpse of its light, and were all three in utter darkness, from too impatient a desire to see.

Quicksilver was so much tickled at beholding Shake-joint and Nightmare both groping for the eye, and each finding fault with Scarecrow and one another, that he could scarcely help laughing aloud.

"Now is your time!" he whispered to Perseus. "Quick, quick; before they can clap the eye into either of their heads! Rush out upon the old ladies, and snatch it from Scarecrow's hand!"

In an instant, while the Three Gray Women were still scolding each other, Perseus leaped from behind the clump of bushes, and made himself master of the prize. The marvellous eye, as he held it in his hand, shone very brightly, and seemed to look up into his face with a knowing air, and an expression as if it would have winked, had it been provided with a pair of eyelids for that purpose. But the Gray Women knew nothing of what had happened, and, each supposing that one of her sisters was in possession of the eye, they began their quarrel anew. At last, as Perseus did not wish to put these respectable dames to greater inconvenience than was really necessary, he thought it right to explain the matter.

"My good ladies," said he, "pray do not be angry with one another! If anybody is in fault, it is myself; for I have the honor to hold your very brilliant and excellent eye in my own hand!"

"You! You have our eye! And who are you?" screamed the Three Gray Women, all in a breath; for they were terribly frightened, of course, at hearing a strange voice, and discovering that their eyesight had got into the hands of they could not guess whom. "Oh, what shall we do, sisters, what shall we do! We are all in the dark! Give us our eye! Give us our one, precious, solitary eye! You have two of your own! Give us our eye!"

"Tell them," whispered Quicksilver to Perseus, "that they shall have back the eye, as soon as they direct you where to find the Nymphs, who have the flying slippers, the magic wallet, and the helmet of darkness."

"My dear, good, admirable old ladies," said Perseus, addressing the Gray Women, "there is no occasion for putting yourselves into such a fright. I am by no means a bad young man. You shall have back your eye, safe and sound, and as bright as ever, the moment you tell me where to find the Nymphs!"

"The Nymphs! Goodness me, sisters, what Nymphs does he mean?" screamed Scarecrow. "There are a great many Nymphs, people say:—some that go a-hunting in the woods, and some that live inside of trees, and some that have a comfortable home in fountains of water. We know nothing at all about them. We are three unfortunate old souls that go wandering about in the dusk, and never had but one eye amongst us, and that one you have stolen away. Oh, give it back, good stranger!—whoever you are—give it back!"

All this while, the Three Gray Women were groping with their outstretched hands, and trying their utmost to get hold of Perseus. But he took good care to keep out of their reach.

"My respectable dames," said he—for his mother had taught him always to use the greatest civility—"I hold your eye fast in my hand, and shall keep it safely for you, until you please to tell me where to find these Nymphs. The Nymphs, I mean, who keep the enchanted wallet, the flying slippers, and the—what is it?—the helmet of invisibility!"

"Mercy on us, sisters, what is the young man talking about?" exclaimed Scarecrow, Nightmare, and Shake-joint, one to another, with great appearance of astonishment. "A pair of flying slippers, quoth he! His heels would quickly fly higher than his head, if he were silly enough to put them on! And a helmet of invisibility! How could a helmet make him invisible, unless it were big enough for him to hide under it? And an enchanted wallet! What sort of a contrivance may that be, I wonder? No, no, good stranger! We can tell you nothing of these marvellous things. You have two eyes of your own, and we but a single one amongst us three. You can find out such wonders better than three blind old creatures, like us!"

Perseus, hearing them talk in this way, began really to think that the Gray Women knew nothing of the matter; and, as it grieved him to have put them to so much trouble, he was just on the point of restoring their eye, and asking pardon for his rudeness in snatching it away. But Quicksilver caught his hand.

"Don't let them make a fool of you!" said he. "These Three Gray Women are the only persons in the world, that can tell you where to find the Nymphs; and, unless you get that information, you will never succeed in cutting off the head of Medusa with the snaky locks. Keep fast hold of the eye, and all will go well!"

As it turned out, Quicksilver was in the right. There are but few things that people prize so much as they do their eyesight; and the Gray Women valued their single eye as highly as if it had been half-a-dozen, which was the number they ought to have had. Finding that there was no other way of recovering it, they at last told Perseus what he wanted to know. No sooner had they done so, than he immediately, and with the utmost respect, clapt the eye into the vacant socket in one of their foreheads, thanked them for their kindness, and bade them farewell. Before the young man was out of hearing, however, they had got into a new dispute; because he happened to have given the eye to Scarecrow, who had already taken her turn of it, when their trouble with Perseus commenced.

It is greatly to be feared, that the Three Gray Women were very much in the habit of disturbing their mutual harmony by bickerings of this sort; which was the more pity, as they could not conveniently do without one another, and were evidently intended to be inseparable companions. As a general rule, I would advise all people, whether sisters or brothers, old or young, who chance to have but one eye amongst them, to cultivate forbearance, and not all insist upon peeping through it at once.

Quicksilver and Perseus, in the mean time, were making the best of their way in quest of the Nymphs. The old dames had given them such particular directions, that they were not long in finding them out. They proved to be very different persons from Nightmare, Shake-joint and Scarecrow; for instead of being old, they were young and beautiful; and instead of one eye amongst the sisterhood, each Nymph had two exceedingly bright eyes of her own, with which she looked very kindly at Perseus. They seemed to be acquainted with Quicksilver; and when he told them the adventure which Perseus had undertaken, they made no difficulty about giving him the valuable articles that were in their custody. In the first place, they brought out what appeared to be a small purse, made of deer-skin, and curiously embroidered, and bade him be sure and keep it safe. This was the magic wallet. The Nymphs next produced a pair of shoes, or slippers, or sandals, with a nice little pair of wings at the heel of each.

"Put them on, Perseus," said Quicksilver. "You will find yourself as light-heeled as you can desire, for the remainder of our journey."

So Perseus proceeded to put one of the slippers on, while he laid the other on the ground by his side. Unexpectedly, however, this other slipper spread its wings, fluttered up off the ground, and would probably have flown away, if Quicksilver had not made a leap, and luckily caught it in the air.

"Be more careful," said he, as he gave it back to Perseus. "It would frighten the birds, up aloft, if they should see a flying slipper amongst them!"

When Perseus had got on both of these wonderful slippers, he was altogether too buoyant to tread on earth. Making a step or two, lo and behold! upward he popt into the air, high above the heads of Quicksilver and the Nymphs, and found it very difficult to clamber down again. Winged slippers, and all such high-flying contrivances, are seldom quite easy to manage, until one grows a little accustomed to them. Quicksilver laughed at his companion's involuntary activity, and told him that he must not be in so desperate a hurry, but must wait for the invisible helmet.

The good-natured Nymphs had the helmet, with its dark tuft of waving plumes, all in readiness to put upon his head. And now there happened about as wonderful an incident as anything that I have yet told you. The instant before the helmet was put on, there stood Perseus, a beautiful young man, with golden ringlets and rosy cheeks, the crooked sword by his side, and the brightly polished shield upon his arm; a figure that seemed all made up of courage, sprightliness, and glorious light. But, when the helmet had descended over his white brow, there was no longer any Perseus to be seen! Nothing but empty air! Even the helmet, that covered him with its invisibility, had vanished!

"Where are you, Perseus?" asked Quicksilver.

"Why, here, to be sure!" answered Perseus, very quietly, although his voice seemed to come out of the transparent atmosphere. "Just where I was a moment ago. Don't you see me?"

"No indeed!" answered his friend. "You are hidden under the helmet. But if I cannot see you, neither can the Gorgons. Follow me, therefore, and we will try your dexterity in using the winged slippers."

With these words, Quicksilver's cap spread its wings, as if his head were about to fly away from his shoulders; but his whole figure rose lightly into the air, and Perseus followed. By the time they had ascended a few hundred feet, the young man began to feel what a delightful thing it was to leave the dull earth so far beneath him, and to be able to flit about like a bird.

It was now deep night. Perseus looked upward, and saw the round, bright, silvery moon, and thought that he should desire nothing better than to soar up thither, and spend his life there. Then he looked downward again, and saw the earth, with its seas, and lakes, and the silver courses of its rivers, and its snowy mountain-peaks, and the breadth of its fields, and the dark cluster of its woods, and its cities of white marble; and, with the moonshine sleeping over the whole scene, it was as beautiful as the moon or any star could be. And, among other objects, he saw the island of Seriphus, where his dear mother was. Sometimes, he and Quicksilver approached a cloud, that, at a distance, looked as if it were made of fleecy silver; although, when they plunged into it, they found themselves chilled and moistened with gray mist. So swift was their flight, however, that, in an instant, they emerged from the cloud into the moonlight again. Once, a high-soaring eagle flew right against the invisible Perseus. The bravest sights were the meteors, that gleamed suddenly out, as if a bonfire had been kindled in the sky, and made the moonshine pale for as much as a hundred miles around them.

As the two companions flew onward, Perseus fancied that he could hear the rustle of a garment close by his side; and it was on the side opposite to the one where he beheld Quicksilver. Yet only Quicksilver was visible.

"Whose garment is this," inquired Perseus, "that keeps rustling close beside me, in the breeze?"

"Oh, it is my sister's!" answered Quicksilver. "She is coming along with us, as I told you she would. We could do nothing without the help of my sister. You have no idea how wise she is. She has such eyes, too! Why, she can see you at this moment, just as distinctly as if you were not invisible; and I'll venture to say, she will be the first to discover the Gorgons."

By this time, in their swift voyage through the air, they had come within sight of the great ocean, and were soon flying over it. Far beneath them, the waves tossed themselves tumultuously, in mid-sea, or rolled a white surf-line upon the long beaches, or foamed against the rocky cliffs, with a roar that was thunderous, in the lower world; although it became a gentle murmur, like the voice of a baby half-asleep, before it reached the ears of Perseus. Just then, a voice spoke in the air, close by him. It seemed to be a woman's voice, and was melodious, though not exactly what might be called sweet, but grave and mild.

"Perseus," said the voice, "there are the Gorgons."

"Where?" exclaimed Perseus. "I cannot see them!"

"On the shore of that island, beneath you," replied the voice. "A pebble, dropt from your hand, would strike in the midst of them."

"I told you she would be the first to discover them," said Quicksilver to Perseus. "And there they are!"

Straight downward, two or three thousand feet below him, Perseus perceived a small island, with the sea breaking into white foam all round its rocky shore, except on one side, where there was a beach of snowy sand. He descended towards it, and looking earnestly at a cluster or heap of brightness, at the foot of a precipice of black rocks, behold! there were the terrible Gorgons. They lay fast asleep, soothed by the thunder of the sea; for it required a tumult that would have deafened everybody else, to lull such fierce creatures into slumber. The moonlight glistened on their steely scales, and on their golden wings, which drooped idly over the sand. Their brazen claws, horrible to look at, were thrust out, and clutched the wave-beaten fragments of rock, while the sleeping Gorgons dreamed of tearing some poor mortal all to pieces. The snakes, that served them instead of hair, seemed likewise to be asleep; although, now and then, one would writhe, and lift its head, and thrust out its forked tongue, emitting a drowsy hiss, and then let itself subside among its sister snakes.

The Gorgons were more like an awful, gigantic kind of insect—immense, golden-winged beetles, or dragon-flies, or things of that sort—at once ugly and beautiful—than like anything else; only that they were a thousand and a million times as big. And with all this, there was something partly human about them, too. Luckily for Perseus, their faces were completely hidden from him by the posture in which they lay; for, had he but looked one instant at them, he would have fallen heavily out of the air, an image of senseless stone.

"Now," whispered Quicksilver, as he hovered by the side of Perseus, "now is your time to do the deed! Be quick; for if one of the Gorgons should awake, you are too late!"

"Which shall I strike at?" asked Perseus, drawing his sword and descending a little lower. "They all three look alike! All three have snaky locks! Which of the three is Medusa?"

It must be understood, that Medusa was the only one of these dragon-monsters, whose head Perseus could possibly cut off. As for the other two, let him have the sharpest sword that ever was forged, and he might have hacked away by the hour together, without doing them the least harm.

"Be cautious!" said the calm voice which had before spoken to him. "One of the Gorgons is stirring in her sleep, and is just about to turn over. That is Medusa. Do not look at her! The sight would turn you to stone! Look at the reflection of her face and figure, in the bright mirror of your shield."

Perseus now understood Quicksilver's motive for so earnestly exhorting him to polish his shield. In its surface, he could safely look at the reflection of the Gorgon's face. And there it was—that terrible countenance—mirrored in the brightness of the shield, with the moonlight falling over it, and displaying all its horror. The snakes, whose venomous natures could not altogether sleep, kept twisting themselves over the forehead. It was the fiercest and most horrible face that ever was seen or imagined, and yet with a strange, fearful, and savage kind of beauty in it. The eyes were closed, and the Gorgon was still in a deep slumber; but there was an unquiet expression disturbing her features, as if the monster were troubled with an ugly dream. She gnashed her white tusks, and dug into the sand with her brazen claws.

The snakes, too, seemed to feel Medusa's dream, and to be made more restless by it. They twined themselves into tumultuous knots, writhed fiercely, and uplifted a hundred hissing heads, without opening their eyes.

"Now, now!" whispered Quicksilver, who was growing impatient. "Make a dash at the monster!"

"But be calm!" said the grave, melodious voice, at the

young man's side. "Look in your shield, as you fly downward, and take care that you do not miss your first stroke!"

Perseus flew cautiously downward, still keeping his eyes on Medusa's face, as reflected in his shield. The nearer he came, the more terrible did the snaky visage and metallic body of the monster grow. At last, when he found himself hovering over her within arm's length, Perseus uplifted his sword; while, at the same instant, each separate snake upon the Gorgon's head stretched threateningly upward, and Medusa unclosed her eyes. But she awoke too late. The sword was sharp; the stroke fell like a lightning-flash; and the head of the wicked Medusa tumbled from her body!

"Admirably done!" cried Quicksilver. "Make haste, and clap the head into your magic wallet!"

To the astonishment of Perseus, the small, embroidered wallet, which he had hung about his neck, and which had hitherto been no bigger than a purse, grew all at once large enough to contain Medusa's head. As quick as thought, he snatched it up, with the snakes still writhing upon it, and thrust it in.

"Your task is done," said the calm voice. "Now, fly; for the other Gorgons will do their utmost to take vengeance for Medusa's death."

It was indeed necessary to take flight; for Perseus had not done the deed so quietly, but that the clash of his sword, and the hissing of the snakes, and the thump of Medusa's head as it tumbled upon the sea-beaten sand, awoke the other two monsters. There they sat, for an instant, sleepily rubbing their eyes with their brazen-fingers, while all the snakes on their heads reared themselves on end with surprise, and with venomous malice against they knew not what. But when the Gorgons saw the scaly carcass of Medusa, headless, and her golden wings all ruffled, and half spread out on the sand, it was really awful to hear what yells and screeches they set up. And then the snakes! They sent forth a hundred-fold hiss, with one consent, and Medusa's snakes answered them, out of the magic wallet.

No sooner were the Gorgons broad awake, than they hurtled upward into the air, brandishing their brass talons, gnashing their horrible tusks, and flapping their huge wings so wildly that some of the golden feathers were shaken out, and floated down upon the shore. And there, perhaps, those very feathers lie scattered, till this day. Uprose the Gorgons, as I tell you, staring horribly about, in hopes of turning somebody to stone. Had Perseus looked them in the face, or had he fallen into their clutches, his poor mother would never have kissed her boy again! But he took good care to turn his eyes another way; and, as he wore the helmet of invisibility, the Gorgons knew not in what direction to follow him; nor did he fail to make the best use of the winged slippers, by soaring upward a perpendicular mile or so. At that height, when the screams of those abominable creatures sounded faintly beneath him, he made a straight course for the island of Seriphus, in order to carry Medusa's head to King Polydectes.

I have no time to tell you of several marvellous things that befel Perseus, on his way homeward; such as his killing a hideous sea-monster, just as it was on the point of devouring a beautiful maiden; nor how he changed an enormous giant into a mountain of stone, merely by showing him the head of the Gorgon. If you doubt this latter story, you may make a voyage to Africa, some day or other, and see the very mountain, which is still known by the ancient giant's name.

Finally, our brave Perseus arrived at the island, where he expected to see his dear mother. But, during his absence, the wicked king had treated Danaë so very ill, that she was compelled to make her escape, and had taken refuge in a temple, where some good old priests were extremely kind to her. These praiseworthy priests—and the kind-hearted fisherman, who had first shown hospitality to Danaë and little Perseus, when he found them afloat in the chest—seem to have been the only persons in the island who cared about doing right. All the rest of the people, as well as King Polydectes himself, were remarkably ill-behaved, and deserved no better destiny than that which was now to happen.

Not finding his mother at home, Perseus went straight to the palace, and was immediately ushered into the presence of the king. Polydectes was by no means rejoiced to see him; for he had felt almost certain, in his own evil mind, that the Gorgons would have torn the poor young man to pieces, and have eaten him up, out of the way. However, seeing him safely returned, he put the best face he could upon the matter, and asked Perseus how he had succeeded.

"Have you performed your promise?" inquired he. "Have you brought me the head of Medusa with the snaky locks? If not, young man, it will cost you dear; for I must have a bridal present for the beautiful Princess Hippodamia, and there is nothing else that she would admire so much!"

"Yes; please your majesty," answered Perseus, in a quiet way, as if it were no very wonderful deed for such a young man as he to perform. "I have brought you the Gorgon's head, snaky locks and all!"

"Indeed! Pray let me see it!" quoth King Polydectes. "It must be a very curious spectacle, if all that travellers tell about it be true!"

"Your majesty is in the right," replied Perseus. "It is really an object that will be pretty certain to fix the regards of all who look at it. And, if your majesty think fit, I would suggest that a holiday be proclaimed, and that all your majesty's subjects be summoned to behold this wonderful curiosity. Few of them, I imagine, have seen a Gorgon's head before, and perhaps never may again!"

The king well knew that his subjects were an idle set of reprobates, and very fond of sight-seeing, as idle persons usually are. So he took the young man's advice, and sent out heralds and messengers, in all directions, to blow the trumpet at the street-corners, and in the market-places, and wherever two roads met, and summon everybody to court. Thither, accordingly, came a great multitude of good-for-nothing vagabonds, all of whom, out of pure love of mischief, would have been glad if Perseus had met with some ill-hap, in his encounter with the Gorgons. If there were any better people in the island, (as I really hope there may have been, although the story tells nothing about any such,) they staid quietly at home, minding their own business, and taking care of their little children. Most of the inhabitants, at all events, ran as fast as they could to the palace, and shoved, and pushed, and elbowed one another, in their eagerness to get near a balcony, on which Perseus showed himself, holding the embroidered wallet in his hand.

On a platform, within full view of the balcony, sat the mighty King Polydectes, amid his evil-counsellors, and with his flattering courtiers in a semi-circle round about him. Monarch, counsellors, courtiers, and subjects, all gazed eagerly towards Perseus.

"Show us the head! Show us the head!" shouted the people; and there was a fierceness in their cry, as if they would tear Perseus to pieces, unless he should satisfy them with what he had to show. "Show us the head of Medusa with the snaky locks!"

A feeling of sorrow and pity came over the youthful Perseus.

"Oh, King Polydectes," cried he, "and ye many people, I am very loth to show you the Gorgon's head!"

"Ah, the villain and coward!" yelled the people, more fiercely than before. "He is making game of us! He has no Gorgon's head! Show us the head, if you have it, or we will take your own head for a foot-ball!"

The evil-counsellors whispered bad advice in the king's ear; the courtiers murmured, with one consent, that Perseus had shown disrespect to their royal lord and master; and the great King Polydectes himself waved his hand, and ordered him, with the stern, deep voice of authority, on his peril to produce the head.

"Show me the Gorgon's head; or I will cut off your own!"

And Perseus sighed.

"This instant," repeated Polydectes; "or you die!"

"Behold it, then!" cried Perseus, in a voice like the blast of a trumpet.

And suddenly holding up the head, not an eyelid had time to wink before the wicked King Polydectes, his evil-counsellors, and all his fierce subjects, were no longer anything but the mere images of a monarch and his people. They were all fixed, forever, in the look and attitude of that moment. At the first glimpse of the terrible head of Medusa, they whitened into marble! And Perseus thrust the head back into his wallet, and went to tell his dear mother that she need no longer be afraid of the wicked King Polydectes.

Tanglewood Porch

AFTER THE STORY

W AS NOT that a very fine story?" asked Eustace.
"Oh, yes, yes!" cried Cowslip, clapping her hands.
"And those funny old women with only one eye amongst
them! I never heard of anything so strange."

"As to their one tooth, which they shifted about," observed
Primrose, "there was nothing so very wonderful in that. I
suppose it was a false tooth! But think of your turning Mer-
cury into Quicksilver, and talking about his sister! You are
too ridiculous!"

"And was she not his sister?" asked Eustace Bright. "If I
had thought of it sooner, I would have described her as a
maiden lady, who kept a pet-owl!"

"Well, at any rate," said Primrose, "your story seems to
have driven away the mist."

And, indeed, while the tale was going forward, the vapors
had been quite exhaled from the landscape. A scene was now
disclosed, which the spectators might almost fancy as having
been created, since they had last looked in the direction where
it lay. About half a mile distant, in the lap of the valley, now
appeared a beautiful lake, which reflected a perfect image of
its own wooded banks, and of the summits of the more distant hills. It gleamed in perfect tranquillity, without the trace
of a winged breeze on any part of its bosom. Beyond its farther shore was Monument Mountain, in a recumbent position, stretching almost across the valley. Eustace Bright compared it to a huge, headless Sphinx, wrapped in a Persian
shawl; and, indeed, so rich and diversified was the autumnal
foliage of its woods, that the simile of the shawl was by no
means too high-colored for the reality. In the lower ground
between Tanglewood and the lake, the clumps of trees and
borders of woodland were chiefly golden-leaved, or dusky
brown, as having suffered more from frost than the foliage
on the hill-sides.

Over all this scene there was a genial sunshine, intermingled with a slight haze, which made it unspeakably soft and

tender. Oh, what a day of Indian Summer was it going to be! The children snatched their baskets and set forth, with hop, skip, and jump, and all sorts of frisks and gambols; while Cousin Eustace proved his fitness to preside over the party by outdoing all their antics, and performing several new capers, which none of them could ever hope to imitate. Behind went a good old dog, whose name was Ben. He was one of the most respectable and kind-hearted of quadrupeds, and probably felt it to be his duty not to trust the children away from their parents, without some better guardian than this feather-brained Eustace Bright.

Shadow Brook

AT NOON, our juvenile party assembled in a dell, through the depths of which ran a little brook. The dell was narrow, and its steep sides, from the margin of the stream, upward, were thickly set with trees, chiefly walnuts and chestnuts, among which grew a few oaks and maples. In the summer-time, the shade of so many clustering branches, meeting and intermingling across the rivulet, was deep enough to produce a noontide twilight. Hence came the name of Shadow Brook. But now, ever since Autumn had crept into this secluded place, all the dark verdure was changed to gold; so that it really kindled up the dell, instead of shading it. The bright yellow leaves, even had it been a cloudy day, would have seemed to keep the sunlight among them; and enough of them had fallen, to strew all the bed and margin of the brook with sunlight, too. Thus the shady nook, where Summer had cooled herself, was now the sunniest spot anywhere to be found.

The little brook ran along over its pathway of gold, here pausing to form a pool, in which minnows were darting to-and-fro; and then it hurried onward at a swifter pace, as if in haste to reach the lake; and forgetting to look whither it went, it tumbled over the root of a tree, which stretched quite across its current. You would have laughed to hear how noisily it babbled about this accident. And even after it had run onward, the brook still kept talking to itself, as if it were in a maze. It was wonder-smitten, I suppose, at finding its dark dell so illuminated, and at hearing the prattle and merriment of so many children. So it stole away as quickly as it could, and hid itself in the lake.

In the dell of Shadow Brook, Eustace Bright and his little friends had eaten their dinner. They had brought plenty of good things from Tanglewood, in their baskets, and had spread them out on the stumps of trees, and on mossy trunks, and had feasted merrily, and made a very nice dinner indeed. After it was over, nobody felt like stirring.

"We will rest ourselves here," said several of the children, "while Cousin Eustace tells us another of his pretty stories."

Cousin Eustace had a good right to be tired, as well as the children; for he had performed great feats, on that memorable forenoon. Dandelion, Clover, Cowslip, and Butter-cup, were almost persuaded that he had winged slippers, like those which the Nymphs gave Perseus; so often had the student shown himself at the tip-top of a nut-tree, when only a moment before, he had been standing on the ground. And then what showers of walnuts had he sent rattling down upon their heads, for their busy little hands to gather into the baskets! In short, he had been as active as a squirrel or a monkey, and now, flinging himself down on the yellow leaves, seemed inclined to take a little rest.

But children have no mercy nor consideration for anybody's weariness; and if you had but a single breath left, they would ask you to spend it in telling them a story.

"Cousin Eustace," said Cowslip, "that was a very nice story of the Gorgon's Head. Do you think you could tell us another as good?"

"Yes, child," said Eustace, pulling the brim of his cap over his eyes, as if preparing for a nap. "I can tell you a dozen, as good or better, if I choose."

"Oh, Primrose and Periwinkle, do you hear what he says?" cried Cowslip, dancing with delight. "Cousin Eustace is going to tell us a dozen better stories than that about the Gorgon's Head!"

"I did not promise you even one, you foolish little Cowslip!" said Eustace, half-pettishly. "However, I suppose you must have it. This is the consequence of having earned a reputation! I wish I were a great deal duller than I am, or that I had never shown half the bright qualities with which Nature has endowed me; and then I might have had my nap out, in peace and comfort!"

But Cousin Eustace, as I think I have hinted before, was as fond of telling his stories, as the children of hearing them. His mind was in a free and happy state, and took delight in its own activity, and scarcely required any external impulse to set it at work. How different is this spontaneous play of the intellect, from the trained diligence of maturer years, when toil has perhaps grown easy by long habit, and the day's work may have become essential to the day's comfort, although the zest of the matter has bubbled away! This remark, however, is not meant for the children to hear.

Without further solicitation, Eustace Bright proceeded to tell the following really splendid story. It had come into his mind, as he lay looking upward into the depths of a tree, and observing how the touch of Autumn had transmuted every one of its green leaves into what resembled the purest gold. And this change, which we have all of us witnessed, is as wonderful as anything that Eustace told about, in the story of Midas.

The Golden Touch

ONCE upon a time, there lived a very rich man, and a king besides, whose name was Midas; and he had a little daughter, whom nobody but myself ever heard of, and whose name I either never knew, or have entirely forgotten. So, because I love odd names for little girls, I choose to call her Marygold.

This King Midas was fonder of gold than of any thing else in the world. He valued his royal crown chiefly because it was composed of that precious metal. If he loved anything better, or half so well, it was the one little maiden who played so merrily around her father's footstool. But, the more Midas loved his daughter, the more did he desire and seek for wealth. He thought, foolish man! that the best thing he could possibly do for this dear child, would be, to bequeath her the immensest pile of yellow, glistening coin, that had ever been heaped together since the world was made. Thus, he gave all his thoughts and all his time to this one purpose. If ever he happened to gaze, for an instant, at the gold-tinted clouds of sunset, he wished that they were real gold, and that they could be squeezed safely into his strong-box. When little Marygold ran to meet him, with a bunch of butter-cups and dandelions, he used to say—"Poh, poh, child! If these flowers were as golden as they look, they would be worth the plucking!"

And yet, in his earlier days, before he was so entirely possessed with this insane desire for riches, King Midas had shown a great taste for flowers. He had planted a garden, in which grew the biggest, and beautifullest, and sweetest roses, that any mortal ever saw or smelt. These roses were still growing in the garden, as large, as lovely, and as fragrant, as when Midas used to pass whole hours in gazing at them, and inhaling their perfume. But now, if he looked at them at all, it was only to calculate how much the garden would be worth, if each of the innumerable rose-petals were a thin plate of gold! And though he once was fond of music, (in spite of an idle story about his ears, which were said to resemble those of an ass,) the only music for poor Midas, now, was the chink of one coin against another.

At length, (as people always grow more and more foolish, unless they take care to grow wiser and wiser,) Midas had got to be so exceedingly unreasonable, that he could scarcely bear to see or touch any object that was not gold. He made it his custom, therefore, to pass a large portion of every day in a dark and dreary apartment, under ground, at the basement of his palace. It was here that he kept his wealth. To this dismal hole—for it was little better than a dungeon—Midas betook himself, whenever he wanted to be particularly happy. Here, after carefully locking the door, he would take a bag of gold coin, or a gold cup, as big as a wash-bowl, or a heavy golden bar, or a peck-measure of gold dust, and bring them from the obscurer corners of the room into the one bright and narrow sunbeam, that fell from the dungeon-like window. He valued the sunbeam, for no other reason but that his treasure would not shine without its help. And then would he reckon over the coins in the bag—toss up the bar, and catch it as it came down—sift the gold dust through his fingers—look at the funny image of his own face, as reflected in the burnished circumference of the cup—and whisper to himself, "Oh Midas, rich King Midas, what a happy man art thou!" But it was laughable to see how the image of his face kept grinning at him, out of the polished surface of the cup. It seemed to be aware of his foolish behavior, and to have a naughty inclination to make fun of him.

Midas called himself a happy man, but felt that he was not yet quite so happy as he might be. The very tip-top of enjoyment would never be reached, unless the whole world were to become his treasure-room, and be filled with yellow metal which should be all his own.

Now, I need hardly remind such wise little people as you are, that in the old, old times, when King Midas was alive, a great many things came to pass, which we should consider wonderful, if they were to happen in our own day and country. And, on the other hand, a great many things take place now-a-days, which seem not very wonderful to us, but at which the people of old times would have stared their eyes out. On the whole, I regard our own times as the strangest of the two; but, however that may be, I must go on with my story.

Midas was enjoying himself in his treasure-room, one day, as usual, when he perceived a shadow fall over the heaps of gold; and looking suddenly up, what should he behold but the figure of a stranger, standing in the bright and narrow sunbeam! It was a young man, with a cheerful and ruddy face. Whether it was that the imagination of King Midas threw a yellow tinge over everything, or whatever the cause might be, he could not help fancying that the smile, with which the stranger regarded him, had a kind of golden radiance in it. Certainly, although his figure intercepted the sunshine, there was now a brighter gleam upon all the piled-up treasures, than before. Even the remotest corners had their share of it, and were lighted up, when the stranger smiled, as with tips of flame and sparkles of fire.

As Midas knew that he had carefully turned the key in the lock, and that no mortal strength could possibly break into his treasure-room, he of course concluded that his visiter must be something more than mortal. It is no matter about telling you who he was. In those days, when the earth was comparatively a new affair, it was supposed to be often the resort of beings, endowed with supernatural powers, and who used to interest themselves in the joys and sorrows of men, women, and children, half playfully, and half seriously. Midas had met such beings, before now, and was not sorry to meet one of them again. The stranger's aspect, indeed, was so good-humored and kindly, if not beneficent, that it would have been unreasonable to suspect him of intending any mischief. It was far more probable that he came to do Midas a favor. And what could that favor be, unless to multiply his heaps of treasure?

The stranger gazed about the room; and when his lustrous smile had glistened upon all the golden objects that were there, he turned again to Midas.

"You are a wealthy man, friend Midas!" he observed. "I doubt whether any other four walls, on earth, contain so much gold as you have contrived to pile up in this room."

"I have done pretty well—pretty well," answered Midas, in a discontented tone. "But, after all, it is but a trifle, when you

consider that it has taken me my whole life to get it together.
If one could live a thousand years, he might have time to
grow rich!"

"What!" exclaimed the stranger. "Then you are not satisfied?"

Midas shook his head.

"And pray what would satisfy you?" asked the stranger.
"Merely for the curiosity of the thing, I should be glad to
know."

Midas paused and meditated. He felt a presentiment that
this stranger, with such a golden lustre in his good-humored
smile, had come thither with both the power and the purpose
of gratifying his utmost wishes. Now, therefore, was the fortunate moment, when he had but to speak, and obtain whatever possible, or seemingly impossible thing it might come
into his head to ask. So he thought, and thought, and
thought, and heaped up one golden mountain upon another,
in his imagination, without being able to imagine them big
enough. At last, a bright idea occurred to King Midas. It
seemed really as bright as the glistening metal which he loved
so much.

Raising his head, he looked the lustrous stranger in the
face.

"Well, Midas," observed his visiter, "I see that you have at
length hit upon something that will satisfy you. Tell me your
wish!"

"It is only this!" replied Midas. "I am weary of collecting
my treasures with so much trouble, and beholding the heap
so diminutive, after I have done my best. I wish everything
that I touch to be changed to gold!"

The stranger's smile grew so very broad, that it seemed to
fill the room like an outburst of the sun, gleaming into a
shadowy dell, where the yellow autumnal leaves—for so
looked the lumps and particles of gold—lie strewn in the
glow of light.

"The Golden Touch!" exclaimed he. "You certainly deserve
credit, friend Midas, for striking out so brilliant a conception.
But are you quite sure that this will satisfy you?"

"How could it fail?" said Midas.

"And will you never regret the possession of it?"

"What could induce me?" asked Midas. "I ask nothing else, to render me perfectly happy!"

"Be it as you wish, then," replied the stranger, waving his hand in token of farewell. "Tomorrow, at sunrise, you will find yourself gifted with the Golden Touch!"

The figure of the stranger then became exceedingly bright, and Midas involuntarily closed his eyes. On opening them again, he beheld only one yellow sunbeam in the room, and, all around him, the glistening of the precious metal which he had spent his life in hoarding up.

Whether Midas slept as usual, that night, the story does not say. Asleep or awake, however, his mind was probably in the state of a child's, to whom a beautiful new plaything has been promised, in the morning. At any rate, day had hardly peeped over the hills, when King Midas was broad awake, and stretching his arms out of bed, began to touch the objects that were within reach. He was anxious to prove whether the Golden Touch had really come, according to the stranger's promise. So he laid his finger on a chair by the bedside, and on various other things, but was grievously disappointed to perceive that they remained of exactly the same substance as before. Indeed, he felt very much afraid that he had only dreamed about the lustrous stranger, or else that the latter had been making game of him. And what a miserable affair would it be, if, after all his hopes, Midas must content himself with what little gold he could scrape together by ordinary means, instead of creating it by a touch!

All this while, it was only the gray of the morning, with but a streak of brightness along the edge of the sky, where Midas could not see it. He lay in a very disconsolate mood, regretting the downfal of his hopes, and kept growing sadder and sadder, until the earliest sunbeam shone through the window, and gilded the ceiling over his head. It seemed to Midas, that this bright yellow sunbeam was reflected, in rather a singular way, on the white covering of the bed. Looking more closely, what was his astonishment and delight, when he found that this linen fabric had been transmuted to what seemed a woven texture of the purest and brightest gold! The Golden Touch had come to him, with the first sunbeam!

Midas started up, in a kind of joyful frenzy, and ran about

the room, grasping at everything that happened to be in his way. He seized one of the bed-posts, and it became immediately a fluted golden pillar. He pulled aside a window-curtain, in order to admit a clear spectacle of the wonders which he was performing; and the tassel grew heavy in his hand, a mass of gold. He took up a book from the table. At his first touch, it assumed the appearance of such a splendidly bound and gilt-edged volume, as one often meets with, now-a-days; but, on running his fingers through the leaves, behold! it was a bundle of thin golden plates, in which all the wisdom of the book had grown illegible. He hurriedly put on his clothes, and was enraptured to see himself in a magnificent suit of gold cloth, which retained its flexibility and softness, although it burthened him a little with its weight. He drew out his handkerchief, which little Marygold had hemmed for him. That was likewise gold, with the dear child's neat and pretty stitches running all along the border, in gold thread!

Somehow or other, this last transformation did not quite please King Midas. He would rather that his little daughter's handiwork should have remained just the same as when she climbed his knee, and put it into his hand.

But it was not worth while to vex himself about a trifle. Midas now took his spectacles from his pocket, and put them on his nose, in order that he might see more distinctly what he was about. In those days, spectacles for common people had not been invented, but were already worn by kings; else how could Midas have had any? To his great perplexity, however, excellent as the glasses were, he discovered that he could not possibly see through them. But this was the most natural thing in the world; for, on taking them off, the transparent crystals turned out to be plates of yellow metal, and, of course, were worthless, as spectacles, though valuable as gold. It struck Midas as rather inconvenient, that, with all his wealth, he could never again be rich enough to own a pair of serviceable spectacles!

"It is no great matter, nevertheless," said he to himself, very philosophically. "We cannot expect any great good, without its being accompanied with some small inconvenience. The Golden Touch is worth the sacrifice of a pair of spectacles, at least, if not of one's very eyesight. My own eyes will serve for ordinary purposes; and little Marygold will soon be old enough to read to me."

Wise King Midas was so exalted by his good fortune, that the palace seemed not sufficiently spacious to contain him. He therefore went down stairs, and smiled, on observing that the balustrade of the staircase became a bar of burnished gold, as his hand passed over it, in his descent. He lifted the door-latch, (it was brass, only a moment ago, but golden, when his fingers quitted it,) and emerged into the garden. Here, as it happened, he found a great number of beautiful roses in full bloom, and others in all the stages of lovely bud and blossom. Very delicious was their fragrance in the morning breeze! Their delicate blush was one of the fairest sights in the world; so gentle, so modest, and so full of sweet tranquillity, did these roses seem to be.

But Midas knew a way to make them far more precious, according to his way of thinking, than roses had ever been before. So he took great pains in going from bush to bush, and exercised his magic touch most indefatigably; until every individual flower and bud, and even the worms at the heart of some of them, were changed to gold. By the time this good work was completed, King Midas was summoned to breakfast; and, as the morning air had given him an excellent appetite, he made haste back to the palace.

What was usually a king's breakfast, in the days of Midas, I really do not know, and cannot stop now to investigate. To the best of my belief, however, on this particular morning, the breakfast consisted of hot cakes, some nice little brook-trout, roasted potatoes, fresh boiled eggs, and coffee, for King Midas himself, and a bowl of bread and milk for his daughter Marygold. At all events, this is a breakfast fit to set before a king; and, whether he had it or no, King Midas could not have had a better.

Little Marygold had not yet made her appearance. Her father ordered her to be called, and, seating himself at table, awaited the child's coming, in order to begin his own break-fast. To do Midas justice, he really loved his daughter, and loved her so much the more, this morning, on account of the good fortune which had befallen him. It was not a great while before he heard her coming along the passage-way, crying bitterly. This circumstance surprised him, because Marygold was one of the cheerfullest little people whom you would see in a summer's day, and hardly shed a thimble-full of tears in a twelvemonth. When Midas heard her sobs, he determined to put little Marygold into better spirits by an agreeable surprise; so, leaning across the table, he touched his daughter's bowl, (which was a china one, with pretty figures all around it,) and transmuted it to gleaming gold.

Meanwhile, Marygold slowly and disconsolately opened the door, and showed herself with her apron at her eyes, still sobbing as if her heart would break.

"How now, my little lady!" cried Midas. "Pray what is the matter with you, this bright morning?"

Marygold, without taking the apron from her eyes, held out her hand, in which was one of the roses which Midas had so recently transmuted.

"Beautiful!" exclaimed her father. "And what is there in this magnificent golden rose, to make you cry?"

"Ah, dear father," answered the child, as well as her sobs would let her, "it is not beautiful, but the ugliest flower that ever grew! As soon as I was dressed, I ran into the garden to gather some roses for you; because I know you like them, and like them the better when gathered by your little daughter. But, Oh, dear, dear me! What do you think has happened? Such a misfortune! All the beautiful roses, that smelled so sweetly, and had so many lovely blushes, are blighted and spoilt! They are grown quite yellow, as you see this one, and have no longer any fragrance! What can have been the matter with them?"

"Poh, my dear little girl, pray don't cry about it!" said Midas, who was ashamed to confess that he himself had wrought the change, which so greatly afflicted her. "Sit down and eat your bread and milk! You will find it easy enough to exchange a golden rose like that (which will last hundreds of years) for an ordinary one, which would wither in a day."

"I don't care for such roses as this," cried Marygold, tossing it contemptuously away. "It has no smell, and the hard petals prick my nose!"

The child now sat down to table, but was so occupied with her grief for the blighted roses, that she did not even notice the wonderful transmutation of her china bowl. Perhaps this was all the better; for Marygold was accustomed to take pleasure in looking at the queer figures, and strange trees and houses, that were painted on the circumference of the bowl; and these ornaments were now entirely lost in the yellow hue of the metal.

Midas, meanwhile, had poured out a cup of coffee; and, as a matter of course, the coffee-pot, whatever metal it may have been when he took it up, was gold when he set it down. He thought to himself, that it was rather an extravagant style of splendor, in a king of his simple habits, to breakfast off a service of gold, and began to be puzzled with the difficulty of keeping his treasures safe. The cupboard and the kitchen would no longer be a secure place of deposit for articles so valuable as golden bowls and coffee-pots.

Amid these thoughts, he lifted a spoonfull of coffee to his lips, and sipping it, was astonished to perceive that, the instant his lips touched the liquid, it became molten gold, and, the next moment, hardened into a lump!

"Ha!" exclaimed Midas, rather aghast.

"What is the matter, father?" asked little Marygold, gazing at him with the tears still standing in her eyes.

"Nothing, child, nothing!" said Midas. "Eat your milk, before it gets quite cold."

He took one of the nice little trouts on his plate, and, by way of experiment, touched its tail with his finger. To his horror, it was immediately transmuted from an admirably fried brook-trout into a gold fish, though not one of those gold-fishes which people often keep in glass globes, as ornaments for the parlor. No; but it was really a metallic fish, and looked as if it had been very cunningly made by the nicest goldsmith in the world. Its little bones were now golden wires; its fins and tail were thin plates of gold; and there were the marks of the fork in it, and all the delicate, frothy appearance of a nicely fried fish, exactly imitated in metal. A very pretty piece of work, as you may suppose; only King Midas, just at that moment, would much rather have had a real trout in his dish, than this elaborate and valuable imitation of one!

"I don't quite see," thought he to himself, "how I am to get any breakfast!"

He took one of the smoking hot cakes, and had scarcely broken it, when, to his cruel mortification—though, a moment before, it had been of the whitest wheat—it assumed the yellow hue of Indian meal. To say the truth, if it had really been a hot Indian cake, Midas would have prized it a good deal more than he now did, when its solidity and increased weight made him too bitterly sensible that it was gold. Almost in despair, he helped himself to a boiled egg, which immediately underwent a change similar to those of the trout and the cake. The egg, indeed, might have been mistaken for one of those which the famous goose, in the story-book, was in the habit of laying; but King Midas was the only goose that had had any thing to do with the matter!

"Well; this is a quandary!" thought he, leaning back in his chair, and looking quite enviously at little Marygold, who was now eating her bread and milk, with great satisfaction. "Such a costly breakfast before me, and nothing that can be eaten!"

Hoping that, by dint of great dispatch, he might avoid what he now felt to be a considerable inconvenience, King Midas next snatched a hot potatoe, and attempted to cram it into his mouth and swallow it in a hurry. But the Golden Touch was too nimble for him. He found his mouth full, not of mealy potatoe, but of solid metal, which so burnt his tongue that he roared aloud, and jumping up from the table began to dance and stamp about the room, both with pain and affright.

"Father, dear father," cried little Marygold, who was a very affectionate child, "pray what is the matter? Have you burnt your mouth?"

"Ah, dear child," groaned Midas, dolefully, "I don't know what is to become of your poor father!"

And, truly, my dear little folks, did you ever hear of such a pitiable case in all your lives? Here was literally the richest breakfast that could be set before a king; and its very richness made it absolutely good for nothing. The poorest laborer, sitting down to his crust of bread and cup of water, was far better off than King Midas, whose delicate food was really worth its weight in gold. And what was to be done? Already, at breakfast, Midas was excessively hungry. Would he be less so, by dinner-time? And how ravenous would be his appetite for supper, which must undoubtedly consist of the same sort of indigestible dishes as those now before him? How many days, think you, could he survive a continuance of this rich fare?

These reflections so troubled wise King Midas, that he began to doubt whether, after all, riches are the one desirable thing in the world, or even the most desirable. But this was only a passing thought. So fascinated was Midas with the glitter of the yellow metal, that he would still have refused to give up the Golden Touch for so paltry a consideration as a breakfast. Just imagine what a price for one meal's victuals! It would have been the same as paying millions and millions of money, (and as many millions more as would take forever to reckon up,) for some fried trout, an egg, a potatoe, a hot cake, and a cup of coffee!

"It would be quite too dear!" thought Midas.

Nevertheless, so great was his hunger and the perplexity of his situation, that he again groaned aloud, and very grievously too. Our pretty Marygold could endure it no longer. She sat, a moment, gazing at her father, and trying with all the might of her little wits to find out what was the matter with him. Then, with a sweet and sorrowful impulse to comfort him, she started from her chair, and running to Midas, threw her arms affectionately about his knees. He bent down and kissed her. He felt that his little daughter's love was worth a thousand times more than he had gained by the Golden Touch.

"My precious, precious Marygold," cried he.

But Marygold made no answer.

Alas, what had he done! How fatal was the gift which the stranger had bestowed! The moment the lips of Midas touched Marygold's forehead, a change had taken place. Her sweet, rosy face, so full of affection as it had been, assumed a glittering yellow color, with yellow tear-drops congealing on her cheeks. Her beautiful brown ringlets took the same tint. Her soft and tender little form grew hard and inflexible within her father's encircling arms. Oh, terrible misfortune! The victim of his insatiable desire for wealth, little Marygold was a human child no longer, but a golden statue!

Yes; there she was, with the questioning look of love, grief, and pity, hardened into her face. It was the prettiest and most woeful sight that ever mortal saw. All the features and tokens of Marygold were there; even the beloved little dimple remained in her golden chin. But, the more perfect was the resemblance, the greater was the father's agony at beholding this golden image, which was all that was left him of a daughter. It had been a favorite phrase of Midas, whenever he felt particularly fond of the child, to say that she was worth her weight in gold. And now the phrase had become literally true. And now, at last, when it was too late, he felt how infinitely a warm and tender heart, that loved him, exceeded in value all the wealth that could be piled up betwixt the earth and sky!

It would be too sad a story, if I were to tell you how Midas, in the fullness of all his gratified desires, began to wring his hands and bemoan himself; and how he could neither bear to look at Marygold, nor yet to look away from her. Except when his eyes were fixed on the image, he could not possibly believe that she was changed to gold. But, stealing another glance, there was the precious little figure, with a yellow teardrop on its yellow cheek, and a look so piteous and tender, that it seemed as if that very expression must needs soften the gold, and make it flesh again. This, however, could not be. So Midas had only to wring his hands, and to wish that he were the poorest man in the wide world, if the loss of all his wealth might bring back the faintest rose-color to his dear child's face.

While he was in this tumult of despair, he suddenly beheld a stranger, standing near the door. Midas bent down his head, without speaking; for he recognized the same figure which had appeared to him, the day before, in the treasure-room, and had bestowed on him this disastrous faculty of the Golden Touch. The stranger's countenance still wore a smile, which seemed to shed a yellow lustre all about the room, and gleamed on little Marygold's image, and on the other objects that had been transmuted by the touch of Midas.

"Well, friend Midas," said the stranger, "pray how do you succeed with the Golden Touch?"

Midas shook his head.

"I am very miserable!" said he.

"Very miserable, indeed?" exclaimed the stranger. "And

how happens that? Have I not faithfully kept my promise with you? Have you not everything that your heart desired?"

"Gold is not everything," answered Midas. "And I have lost all that my heart really cared for!"

"Ah! So you have made a discovery, since yesterday!" observed the stranger. "Let us see, then! Which of these two things do you think is really worth the most—the gift of the Golden Touch, or one cup of clear, cold water?"

"Oh, blessed water!" exclaimed Midas. "It will never moisten my parched throat again!"

"The Golden Touch," continued the stranger, "or a crust of bread?"

"A piece of bread," answered Midas, "is worth all the gold on earth!"

"The Golden Touch," asked the stranger, "or your own little Marygold, warm, soft, and loving, as she was an hour ago?"

"Oh, my child, my dear child!" cried poor Midas, wringing his hands. "I would not have given that one small dimple in her chin, for the power of changing this whole big earth into a solid lump of gold!"

"You are wiser than you were, King Midas!" said the stranger, looking seriously at him. "Your own heart, I perceive, has not been entirely changed from flesh to gold. Were it so, your case would indeed be desperate. But you appear to be still capable of understanding that the commonest things, such as lie within everybody's grasp, are more valuable than the riches which so many mortals sigh and struggle after. Tell me, now! Do you sincerely desire to rid yourself of this Golden Touch?"

"It is hateful to me!" replied Midas.

A fly settled on his nose, but immediately fell to the floor; for it, too, had become gold. Midas shuddered.

"Go, then," said the stranger, "and plunge into the river that glides past the bottom of your garden. Take likewise a vase of the same water, and sprinkle it over any object, that you may desire to change back again from gold into its former substance. If you do this in earnestness and sincerity, it may possibly repair the mischief which your avarice has occasioned!"

King Midas bowed low; and when he lifted his head, the lustrous stranger had vanished.

You will easily believe, that Midas lost no time in snatching up a great earthen pitcher (but, alas me! it was no longer earthen after he touched it) and hastening to the river-side. As he scampered along, and forced his way through the shrubbery, it was positively marvellous to see how the foliage turned yellow behind him, as if the Autumn had been there, and nowhere else. On reaching the river's brink, he plunged headlong in, without waiting so much as to pull off his shoes.

"Poof! poof! poof!" snorted King Midas, as his head emerged out of the water. "Well; this is really a refreshing bath, and I think it must have quite washed away the Golden Touch. And now for filling my pitcher!"

As he dipt the pitcher into the water, it gladdened his very heart to see it change from gold into the same good, honest earthen vessel which it had been, before he touched it. He was conscious, also, of a change within himself. A cold, hard, and heavy weight seemed to have gone out of his bosom. No doubt, his heart had been gradually losing its human substance, and transmuting itself into insensible metal, but had now softened back again into flesh. Perceiving a violet, that grew on the bank of the river, Midas touched it with his finger, and was overjoyed to find that the delicate flower retained its purple hue, instead of undergoing a yellow blight. The curse of the Golden Touch had therefore really been removed from him.

King Midas hastened back to the palace; and, I suppose, the servants knew not what to make of it, when they saw their royal master so carefully bringing home an earthen pitcher of water. But that water, which was to undo all the mischief that his folly had wrought, was more precious to Midas than an ocean of molten gold would have been. The first thing he did, as you need hardly be told, was to sprinkle it by handfulls over the golden figure of little Marygold.

No sooner did it fall on her, than you would have laughed to see how the rosy color came back to the dear child's cheek!—and how she began to sneeze and sputter!—and how astonished she was to find herself dripping wet, and her father still throwing more water over her!

"Pray do not, dear father!" cried she. "See how you have wet my nice frock, which I put on only this morning!"

For Marygold did not know that she had been a little golden statue; nor could she remember anything that had happened, since the moment when she ran, with outstretched arms, to comfort poor King Midas.

Her father did not think it necessary to tell his beloved child how very foolish he had been, but contented himself with showing how much wiser he had now grown. For this purpose, he led little Marygold into the garden, where he sprinkled all the remainder of the water over the rose-bushes, and with such good effect that above five thousand roses recovered their beautiful bloom. There were two circumstances, however, which, as long as he lived, used to put King Midas in mind of the Golden Touch. One was, that the sands of the river sparkled like gold; the other, that little Marygold's hair had now a golden tinge, which he had never observed in it, before she had been transmuted by the effect of his kiss. This change of hue was really an improvement, and made Marygold's hair richer than in her babyhood.

When King Midas had grown quite an old man, and used to trot Marygold's children on his knee, he was fond of telling them this marvellous story, pretty much as I have now told it to you. And then would he stroke their glossy ringlets, and tell them that their hair, likewise, had a rich shade of gold, which they had inherited from their mother.

"And, to tell you the truth, my precious little folks," quoth King Midas, diligently trotting the children all the while, "ever since that morning, I have hated the very sight of all other gold, save this!"

Shadow Brook

AFTER THE STORY

WELL, children," inquired Eustace, who was very fond of eliciting a definite opinion from his auditors, "did you ever, in all your lives, listen to a better story than this of 'The Golden Touch'?"

"Why, as to the story of King Midas," said saucy Primrose, "it was a famous one, thousands of years before Mr. Eustace Bright came into the world, and will continue to be so, as long after he quits it. But some people have what we may call 'The Leaden Touch,' and make everything dull and heavy that they lay their fingers upon!"

"You are a smart child, Primrose, to be not yet in your teens," said Eustace, taken rather aback by the piquancy of her criticism. "But you well know, in your naughty little heart, that I have burnished the old gold of Midas all over anew, and have made it shine as it never shone before. And then that figure of Marygold! Do you perceive no nice workmanship in that? And how finely I have brought out and deepened the moral! What say you, Sweet Fern, Dandelion, Clover, Periwinkle? Would any of you, after hearing this story, be so foolish as to desire the faculty of changing things to gold?"

"I should like," said Periwinkle, a girl of ten, "to have the power of turning everything to gold with my right forefinger; but, with my left forefinger, I should want the power of changing it back again, if the first change did not please me. And I know what I would do, this very afternoon!"

"Pray tell me," said Eustace.

"Why," answered Periwinkle, "I would touch every one of these golden leaves on the trees, with my left forefinger, and make them all green again; so that we might have the summer back at once, with no ugly winter in the mean time."

"Oh, Periwinkle," cried Eustace Bright, "there you are wrong, and would do a great deal of mischief. Were I Midas, I would make nothing else but just such golden days as these, over and over again, all the year throughout. My best thoughts always come a little too late. Why did not I tell you how old King Midas came to America, and changed the dusky autumn, such as it is in other countries, into the burnished beauty which it here puts on? He gilded the leaves of the great volume of Nature."

"Cousin Eustace," said Sweet Fern, a good little boy, who was always making particular inquiries about the precise height of giants and the littleness of fairies, "how big was Marygold, and how much did she weigh, after she was turned to gold?"

"She was about as tall as you are," replied Eustace, "and, as gold is very heavy, she weighed at least two thousand pounds, and might have been coined into thirty or forty thousand gold dollars. I wish Primrose were worth half as much. Come, little people, let us clamber out of the dell, and look about us."

They did so. The sun was now an hour or two beyond its noontide mark, and filled the great hollow of the valley with its western radiance; so that it seemed to be brimming with mellow light, and to spill it over the surrounding hill-sides, like golden wine out of a bowl. It was such a day, that you could not help saying of it—"There never was such a day before!"—although yesterday was just such a day, and to-morrow will be just such another. Ah, but there are very few of them in a twelvemonth's circle! It is a remarkable peculiarity of these October days, that each of them seems to occupy a great deal of space; although the sun rises rather tardily, at that season of the year, and goes to bed, as little children ought, at sober six o'clock, or even earlier. We cannot, therefore, call the days long; but they appear, somehow or other, to make up for their shortness by their breadth; and when the cool night comes, we are conscious of having enjoyed a big armfull of life, since morning.

"Come, children, come!" cried Eustace Bright. "More nuts, more nuts, more nuts! Fill all your baskets; and, at Christmas-time, I will crack them for you, and tell you beautiful stories!"

So away they went; all of them in excellent spirits, except little Dandelion, who, I am sorry to tell you, had been sitting on a chestnut-burr, and was stuck as full as a pincushion of its prickles. Dear me, how uncomfortably he must have felt!

Tanglewood Play-Room

THE golden days of October passed away, as so many other Octobers have, and brown November likewise, and the greater part of chill December, too. At last came merry Christmas, and Eustace Bright along with it, making it all the merrier by his presence. And, the day after his arrival from college, there came a mighty snow-storm. Up to this time, the winter had held back, and had given us a good many mild days, which were like smiles upon its wrinkled visage. The grass had kept itself green, in sheltered places, such as the nooks of southern hill-slopes, and along the lee of the stone-fences. It was but a week or two ago, and since the beginning of the month, that the children had found a dandelion in bloom, on the margin of Shadow Brook, where it glides out of the dell.

But no more green grass and dandelions, now! This was such a snow-storm! Twenty miles of it might have been visible at once, between the windows of Tanglewood and the Dome of Taconic, had it been possible to see so far, among the eddying drifts that whitened all the atmosphere. It seemed as if the hills were giants, and were flinging monstrous handfulls of snow at one another, in their enormous sport. So thick were the fluttering snow-flakes, that even the trees, mid-way down the valley, were hidden by them, the greater part of the time. Sometimes, it is true, the little prisoners of Tanglewood could discern a dim outline of Monument Mountain, and the smooth whiteness of the frozen lake at its base, and the black or gray tracts of woodland, in the nearer landscape. But these were merely peeps through the tempest.

Nevertheless, the children rejoiced greatly in the snowstorm. They had already made acquaintance with it, by tumbling heels over head into its highest drifts, and flinging snow at one another, as we have just fancied the Berkshire mountains to be doing. And now they had come back to their spacious play-room, which was as big as the great drawing-room, and was lumbered with all sorts of playthings, large and small. The biggest was a rocking-horse, that looked like a real pony; and there was a whole family of wooden, waxen, plaster and china-dolls, besides rag-babies; and blocks enough to build Bunker-hill monument, and nine-pins, and balls, and humming-tops, and battledoors, and grace-sticks, and skipping-ropes, and more of such valuable property than I could tell of, in a printed page. But the children liked the snow-storm better than them all. It suggested so many brisk enjoyments for tomorrow, and all the remainder of the winter! The sleigh-ride; the slides down-hill into the valley; the snow-images that were to be shaped out; the snow-fortresses that were to be built, and the snow-balling to be carried on!

So the little folks blessed the snow-storm, and were glad to see it come thicker and thicker, and watched hopefully the long drift that was piling itself up in the avenue, and was already higher than any of their heads.

"Why, we shall be blocked up till spring!" cried they, with the hugest delight. "What a pity, that the house is too high to be quite covered up! The little red house, down yonder, will be buried up to its eaves."

"You silly children, what do you want of more snow?" asked Eustace, who, tired of some novel that he was skimming through, had strolled into the play-room. "It has done mischief enough already, by spoiling the only skating that I could hope for, through the winter. We shall see nothing more of the lake, till April; and this was to have been my first day upon it! Don't you pity me, Primrose?"

"Oh, to be sure!" answered Primrose, laughing. "But, for your comfort, we will listen to another of your old stories, such as you told us under the porch, and down in the hollow, by Shadow Brook. Perhaps I shall like them better now, when there is nothing to do, than while there were nuts to be gathered, and beautiful weather to enjoy."

Hereupon, Periwinkle, Clover, Sweet Fern, and as many others of the little fraternity and cousinhood as were still at Tanglewood, gathered about Eustace, and earnestly besought him for a story. The student yawned, stretched himself, and then, to the vast admiration of the small people, skipped three times back and forth over the top of a chair, in order, as he explained to them, to set his wits in motion.

"Well, well, children," said he, after these preliminaries, "since you insist, and Primrose has set her heart upon it, I will see what can be done for you. And, that you may know what happy days there were, before snow-storms came into fashion, I will tell you a story of the oldest of all old times, when the world was as new as Sweet Fern's bran-new humming-top. There was then but one season in the year, and that was the delightful summer; and but one age for mortals—and that was childhood."

"I never heard of that before," said Primrose.

"Of course, you never did," answered Eustace. "It shall be a story of what nobody but myself ever dreamed of—a Paradise of Children—and how, by the naughtiness of just such a little imp as Primrose here, it all came to nothing."

So Eustace Bright sat down in the chair which he had just been skipping over, took Cowslip upon his knee, ordered silence throughout the auditory, and began a story about a sad naughty child, whose name was Pandora, and about her playfellow Epimetheus. You may read it, word for word, in the pages that come next.

The Paradise of Children

L ONG, long ago, when this old world was in its tender infancy, there was a child, named Epimetheus, who never
had either father or mother; and that he might not be lonely,
another child, fatherless and motherless like himself, was sent
from a far country, to live with him, and be his playfellow
and helpmate. Her name was Pandora.

The first thing that Pandora saw, when she entered the cottage where Epimetheus dwelt, was a great box. And almost
the first question which she put to him, after crossing the
threshold, was this:—

"Epimetheus, what have you in that box?"

"My dear little Pandora," answered Epimetheus, "that is a
secret; and you must be kind enough not to ask any questions
about it. The box was left here to be kept safely, and I do not
myself know what it contains."

"But who gave it to you?" asked Pandora. "And where did
it come from?"

"That is a secret too," replied Epimetheus.

"How provoking!" exclaimed Pandora, pouting her lip. "I
wish the great ugly box were out of the way!"

"Oh, come, don't think of it any more!" cried Epimetheus.
"Let us run out of doors, and have some nice play with the
other children!"

It is thousands of years since Epimetheus and Pandora were
alive; and the world, now-a-days, is a very different sort of
thing from what it was in their time. Then, everybody was a
child. There needed no fathers and mothers, to take care of
the children; because there was no danger, nor trouble of any
kind, and no clothes to be mended, and there was always
plenty to eat and drink. Whenever a child wanted his dinner,
he found it growing on a tree; and, if he looked at the tree in
the morning, he could see the expanding blossom of that
night's supper; or, at eventide, he saw the tender bud of to-
morrow's breakfast. It was a very pleasant life indeed. No
labor to be done, no tasks to be studied; nothing but sports
and dances, and sweet voices of children talking, or carolling

like birds, or gushing out in merry laughter, throughout the
live-long day.

What was most wonderful of all, the children never quar-
relled among themselves; neither had they any crying-fits;
nor, since time first began, had a single one of these little
mortals ever gone apart into a corner, and sulked! Oh, what
a good time was that, to be alive in! The truth is, those ugly
little winged monsters, called Troubles, which are now almost
as numerous as musquitoes, had never yet been seen on the
earth. It is probable that the very greatest disquietude, which
a child had ever experienced, was Pandora's vexation at not
being able to discover the secret of the mysterious box.

This was at first only the faint shadow of a Trouble; but,
every day, it grew more and more substantial; until, before a
great while, the cottage of Epimetheus and Pandora was less
sunshiny than those of the other children.

"Whence can the box have come!" Pandora continually
kept saying to herself and to Epimetheus. "And what in the
world can be inside of it!"

"Always talking about this box!" said Epimetheus, at last;
for he had grown extremely tired of the subject. "I wish, dear
Pandora, you would try to talk of something else. Come; let
us go and gather some ripe figs, and eat them under the trees,
for our supper! And I know a vine that has the sweetest and
juiciest grapes you ever tasted!"

"Always talking about grapes and figs!" cried Pandora, pet-
tishly.

"Well then," said Epimetheus, who was a very good-
tempered child, like a multitude of children, in those days,
"let us run out and have a merry time with our playmates!"

"I am tired of merry times, and don't care if I never have
any more," answered our pettish little Pandora. "And, besides, I never do have any! This ugly box! I am so taken up
with thinking about it, all the time! I insist upon your telling
me what is inside of it."

"As I have already said, fifty times over, I do not know!"
replied Epimetheus, getting a little vexed. "How, then, can I
tell you what is inside?"

"You might open it," said Pandora, looking sideways at
Epimetheus, "and then we could see for ourselves."

"Pandora, what are you thinking of!" exclaimed Epimetheus.

And his face expressed so much horror at the idea of looking into a box, which had been confided to him on the condition of his never opening it, that Pandora thought it best not to suggest it any more. Still, however, she could not help thinking and talking about the box.

"At least," said she, "you can tell me how it came here."

"It was left at the door," replied Epimetheus, "just before you came, by a person who looked very smiling and intelligent, and who could hardly forbear laughing, as he put it down. He was dressed in an odd kind of a cloak, and had on a cap that seemed to be made partly of feathers, so that it looked almost as if it had wings."

"What sort of a staff had he?" asked Pandora.

"Oh, the most curious staff you ever saw!" cried Epimetheus. "It was like two serpents twisting around a stick, and was carved so naturally, that I at first thought the serpents were alive."

"I know him," said Pandora, thoughtfully. "Nobody else has such a staff. It was Quicksilver; and he brought me hither, as well as the box. No doubt, he intended it for me; and, most probably, it contains pretty dresses for me to wear, or toys for you and me to play with, or something very nice for us both to eat!"

"Perhaps so," answered Epimetheus, turning away. "But, until Quicksilver comes back and tells us so, we have neither of us any right to lift the lid of the box!"

"What a dull boy he is!" muttered Pandora, as Epimetheus left the cottage. "I do wish he had a little more enterprise!"

For the first time since her arrival, Epimetheus had gone out, without asking Pandora to accompany him. He went to gather figs and grapes by himself, or to seek whatever amusement he could find, in other society than his little playfellow's. He was tired to death of hearing about the box, and heartily wished that Quicksilver, or whatever was the messenger's name, had left it at some other child's door, where Pandora would never have set eyes on it. So perseveringly as she did babble about this one thing! The box; the box; and nothing but the box! It seemed as if the box were bewitched, and as if the cottage were not big enough to hold it, without Pandora's continually stumbling over it, and making Epimetheus stumble over it likewise, and bruising all four of their shins.

Well; it was really hard that poor Epimetheus should have a box in his ears, from morning till night; especially as the little people of the earth were so unaccustomed to vexations, in those happy days, that they knew not how to deal with them. Thus, a small vexation made as much disturbance, then, as a far bigger one would, in our own times.

After Epimetheus was gone, Pandora stood gazing at the box. She had called it ugly, above a hundred times; but, in spite of all that she had said against it, it was positively a very handsome article of furniture, and would have been quite an ornament to any room in which it should be placed. It was made of a beautiful kind of wood, with dark and rich veins spreading over its surface, which was so highly polished that little Pandora could see her face in it. As the child had no other looking-glass, it is odd that she did not value the box, merely on this account.

The edges and corners of the box were carved with most wonderful skill. Around the margin there were figures of graceful men and women, and the prettiest children ever seen, reclining or sporting amid a profusion of flowers and foliage; and these various objects were so exquisitely represented, and were wrought together in such harmony, that flowers, foliage and human beings, seemed to combine into a wreath of mingled beauty. But, here and there, peeping forth from behind the carved foliage, Pandora once or twice fancied that she saw a face not so lovely, or something or other that was disagreeable, and which stole the beauty out of all the rest. Nevertheless, on looking more closely, and touching the spot with her finger, she could discover nothing of the kind. Some face, that was really beautiful, had been made to look ugly by her catching a sideway glimpse at it.

The most beautiful face of all was done, in what is called high relief, in the centre of the lid. There was nothing else, save the dark, smooth richness of the polished wood, and this one face, in the centre, with a garland of flowers about its brow. Pandora had looked at this face, a great many times, and imagined that the mouth could smile if it liked, or be graver, when it chose, the same as any living mouth. The features, indeed, all wore a very lively and rather mischievous expression, which looked almost as if it needs must burst out of the carved lips, and utter itself in words.

Had the mouth spoken, it would probably have been something like this:—

"Do not be afraid, Pandora! What harm can there be in opening the box? Never mind that poor, simple Epimetheus! You are wiser than he, and have ten times as much spirit. Open the box, and see if you do not find something very pretty!"

The box, I had almost forgotten to say, was fastened; not by a lock, nor by any other such contrivance, but by a very intricate knot of gold cord. There appeared to be no end to this knot, and no beginning. Never was a knot so cunningly twisted, nor with so many ins and outs, which roguishly defied the skilfullest fingers to disentangle them. And yet, by the very difficulty that there was in it, Pandora was the more tempted to examine the knot, and just see how it was made. Two or three times, already, she had stooped over the box, and taken the knot between her thumb and forefinger, but without positively trying to undo it.

"I really believe," said she to herself, "that I begin to see how it was done. Nay, perhaps I could tie it up again, after undoing it. There would be no harm in that, surely! Even Epimetheus would not blame me for that. I need not open the box, and should not, of course, without the foolish boy's consent, even if the knot were untied!"

It might have been better for Pandora if she had had a little work to do, or anything to employ her mind upon, so as not to be so constantly thinking of this one subject. But children led so easy a life, before any Troubles came into the world, that they had really a great deal too much leisure. They could not be forever playing at hide-and-seek among the flower-shrubs, or at blindman's buff with garlands over their eyes, or at whatever other games had been found out, while Mother Earth was in her babyhood. When life is all sport, toil is the real play. There was absolutely nothing to do. A little sweeping and dusting about the cottage, I suppose, and the gath-

ering of fresh flowers, (which were only too abundant, everywhere,) and arranging them in vases;—and poor little
Pandora's day's work was over! And then, for the rest of the
day, there was the box!

After all, I am not quite so sure that the box was not a
blessing to her, in its way. It supplied her with such a variety
of ideas to think of, and to talk about, whenever she had
anybody to listen! When she was in good humor, she could
admire the bright polish of its sides, and the rich border of
beautiful faces and foliage that ran all around it. Or, if she
chanced to be ill-tempered, she could give it a push, or kick
it with her naughty little foot. And many a kick did the box—
(but it was a mischievous box, as we shall see, and deserved
all it got)—many a kick did it receive! But, certain it is, if it
had not been for the box, our active-minded little Pandora
would not have known half so well how to spend her time,
as she now did.

For it was really an endless employment to guess what was
inside. What could it be, indeed? Just imagine, my little hearers, how busy your wits would be, if there were a great box
in the house, which, as you might have reason to suppose,
contained something new and pretty for your Christmas or
New Year's gifts! Do you think that you should be less curious than Pandora? If you were left alone with the box, might
you not feel a little tempted to lift the lid? But you would not
do it! Oh, fie! No, no! Only, if you thought there were toys
in it, it would be so very hard to let slip an opportunity of
taking just one peep! I know not whether Pandora expected
any toys; for none had yet begun to be made, probably, in
those days, when the world itself was one great plaything for
the children that dwelt upon it. But Pandora was convinced
that there was something very beautiful and valuable in the
box; and therefore she felt just as anxious to take a peep, as
any of these little girls, here around me, would have felt. And,
possibly, a little more so;—but of that, I am not quite so
certain.

On this particular day, however, which we have so long
been talking about, her curiosity grew so much greater than
it usually was, that, at last, she approached the box. She was

more than half determined to open it, if she could. Ah, naughty Pandora!

First, however, she tried to lift it. It was heavy; quite too heavy for the slender strength of a child, like Pandora. She raised one end of the box a few inches from the floor, and let it fall again, with a pretty loud thump. A moment afterwards, she almost fancied that she heard something stir, inside of the box. She applied her ear as closely as possible, and listened. Positively, there did seem to be a kind of stifled murmur, within! Or was it merely the singing in Pandora's ears? Or could it be the beating of her heart? The child could not quite satisfy herself whether she had heard anything or no. But, at all events, her curiosity was stronger than ever.

As she drew back her head, her eyes fell upon the knot of gold cord.

"It must have been a very ingenious person who tied this knot," said Pandora to herself. "But I think I could untie it, nevertheless! I am resolved, at least, to find the two ends of the cord."

So she took the golden knot in her fingers, and pryed into its intricacies as sharply as she could. Almost without intending it, or quite knowing what she was about, she was soon busily engaged in attempting to undo it. Meanwhile, the bright sunshine came through the open window; as did likewise the merry voices of the children, playing at a distance, and perhaps the voice of Epimetheus among them. Pandora stopt to listen. What a beautiful day it was! Would it not be wiser, if she were to let the troublesome knot alone, and think no more about the box, but run and join her little playfellows, and be happy?

All this time, however, her fingers were half unconsciously busy with the knot; and happening to glance at the flower-wreathed face, on the lid of the enchanted box, she seemed to perceive it slily grinning at her.

"That face looks very mischievous," thought Pandora. "I wonder whether it smiles because I am doing wrong! I have the greatest mind in the world to run away!"

But, just then, by the merest accident, she gave the knot a kind of a twist, which produced a wonderful result. The gold cord untwined itself, as if by magic, and left the box without a fastening.

"This is the strangest thing I ever knew!" said Pandora. "What will Epimetheus say? And how can I possibly tie it up again?"

She made one or two attempts to restore the knot, but soon found it quite beyond her skill. It had disentangled itself so suddenly, that she could not in the least remember how the strings had been doubled into one another; and when she tried to recollect the shape and appearance of the knot, it seemed to have gone entirely out of her mind. Nothing was to be done, therefore, but to let the box remain as it was, until Epimetheus should come in.

"But," said Pandora, "when he finds the knot untied, he will know that I have done it. How shall I make him believe that I have not looked into the box?"

And then the thought came into her naughty little heart, that, since she would be suspected of having looked into the box, she might just as well do so, at once. Oh, very naughty, and very foolish Pandora! You should have thought only of doing what was right, and of leaving undone what was wrong, and not of what your playfellow Epimetheus would have said or believed. And so perhaps she might, if the enchanted face, on the lid of the box, had not looked so bewitchingly persuasive at her, and if she had not seemed to hear, more distinctly than before, the murmur of small voices within. She could not tell whether it was fancy or no; but there was quite a little tumult of whispers in her ear—or else it was her curiosity that whispered,

"Let us out, dear Pandora, pray let us out! We will be such nice pretty playfellows for you! Only let us out!"

"What can it be?" thought Pandora. "Is there something alive in the box? Well!—yes!—I am resolved to take just one peep! Only one peep; and then the lid shall be shut down as safely as ever! There cannot possibly be any harm in just one little peep!"

But it is now time for us to see what Epimetheus was doing.

This was the first time, since his little playmate had come to dwell with him, that he had attempted to enjoy any plea-

sure in which she did not partake. But nothing went right;
nor was he nearly so happy as on other days. He could not
find a sweet grape or a ripe fig, (if Epimetheus had a fault, it
was a little too much fondness for figs,) or, if ripe at all, they
were over-ripe, and so sweet as to be cloying. There was no
mirth in his heart, such as usually made his voice gush out, of
its own accord, and swell the merriment of his companions.
In short, he grew so uneasy and discontented, that the other
children could not imagine what was the matter with Epimetheus. Neither did he himself know what ailed him, any
better than they did. For you must recollect, that, at the time
we are speaking of, it was everybody's nature, and constant
habit, to be happy. The world had not yet learned to be otherwise. Not a single soul or body, since these children were
first sent to enjoy themselves on the beautiful earth, had ever
been sick or out of sorts.

At length, discovering that, somehow or other, he put a
stop to all the play, Epimetheus judged it best to go back to
Pandora, who was in a humor better suited to his own. But,
with a hope of giving her pleasure, he gathered some flowers
and made them into a wreath, which he meant to put upon
her head. The flowers were very lovely—roses, and lilies, and
orange-blossoms, and a great many more, which left a trail of
fragrance behind, as Epimetheus carried them along;—and
the wreath was put together with as much skill as could reasonably be expected of a boy. The fingers of little girls, it has
always appeared to me, are the fittest to twine flower-wreaths;
but boys could do it, in those days, rather better than they
can now.

And here I must mention, that a great black cloud had been
gathering in the sky, for some time past, although it had not
yet overspread the sun. But, just as Epimetheus reached the
cottage-door, this cloud began to intercept the sunshine, and
thus to make a sudden and sad obscurity.

He entered softly; for he meant, if possible, to steal behind
Pandora, and fling the wreath of flowers over her head, before she should be aware of his approach. But, as it happened,
there was no need of his treading so very lightly. He might
have trod as heavily as he pleased—as heavily as a grown
man—as heavily, I was going to say, as an elephant—with-

out much probability of Pandora's hearing his footsteps. She was too intent upon her purpose. At the moment of his entering the cottage, the naughty child had put her hand to the lid, and was on the point of opening the mysterious box. Epimetheus beheld her. If he had cried out, Pandora would probably have withdrawn her hand, and the fatal mystery of the box might never have been known.

But Epimetheus himself, although he said very little about it, had his own share of curiosity to know what was inside. Perceiving that Pandora was resolved to find out the secret, he determined that his playfellow should not be the only wise person in the cottage. And if there were anything pretty or valuable in the box, he meant to take half of it to himself. Thus, after all his sage speeches to Pandora about restraining her curiosity, Epimetheus turned out to be quite as foolish, and nearly as much in fault, as she. So, whenever we blame Pandora for what happened, we must not forget to shake our heads at Epimetheus likewise.

As Pandora raised the lid, the cottage grew very dark and dismal; for the black cloud had now swept quite over the sun, and seemed to have buried it alive. There had, for a little while past, been a low growling and muttering, which all at once broke into a heavy peal of thunder. But Pandora, heeding nothing of all this, lifted the lid nearly upright, and looked inside. It seemed as if a sudden swarm of winged creatures brushed past her, taking flight out of the box; while, at the same instant, she heard the voice of Epimetheus, with a lamentable tone, as if he were in pain.

"Oh, I am stung!" cried he. "I am stung! Naughty Pandora! Why have you opened this wicked box?"

Pandora let fall the lid, and starting up, looked about her, to see what had befallen Epimetheus. The thunder-cloud had so darkened the room, that she could not very clearly discern what was in it. But she heard a disagreeable buzzing, as if a great many huge flies, or gigantic musquitoes, or those insects which we call dor-bugs and pinching-dogs, were darting about. And, as her eyes grew more accustomed to the imperfect light, she saw a crowd of ugly little shapes, with bats' wings, looking abominably spiteful, and armed with terribly long stings in their tails. It was one of these that had stung

Epimetheus. Nor was it a great while, before Pandora herself began to scream, in no less pain and affright than her playfellow, and making a vast deal more hubbub about it. An odious little monster had settled on her forehead, and would have stung her I know not how deeply, if Epimetheus had not run and brushed it away.

Now, if you wish to know what these ugly things might be, which had made their escape out of the box, I must tell you that they were the whole family of earthly Troubles. There were evil Passions; there were a great many species of Cares; there were more than a hundred and fifty Sorrows; there were Diseases, in a vast number of miserable and painful shapes; there were more kinds of Naughtiness, than it would be of any use to talk about. In short, everything, that has since afflicted the souls and bodies of mankind, had been shut up in the mysterious box, and given to Epimetheus and Pandora to be kept safely, in order that the happy children of the world might never be molested by them. Had they been faithful to their trust, all would have gone well. No grown person would ever have been sad, nor any child have had cause to shed a single tear, from that hour until this moment.

But—and you may see by this how a wrong act of any one mortal is a calamity to the whole world—by Pandora's lifting the lid of that miserable box, and by the fault of Epimetheus, too, in not preventing her, these Troubles have obtained a foothold among us, and do not seem very likely to be driven away in a hurry. For it was impossible, as you will easily guess, that the two children should keep the ugly swarm in their own little cottage. On the contrary, the first thing that they did was to fling open the doors and windows, in hopes of getting rid of them; and sure enough, away flew the winged Troubles all abroad, and so pestered and tormented the small people, everywhere about, that none of them so much as smiled for many days afterwards. And what was very singular, all the flowers and dewy blossoms on earth, not one of which had hitherto faded, now began to droop and shed their leaves, after a day or two. The children, moreover, who before seemed immortal in their childhood, now grew older, day by day, and came soon to be youths and maidens, and men and women by-and-by, and aged people, before they dreamed of such a thing.

Meanwhile, the naughty Pandora, and hardly less naughty Epimetheus, remained in their cottage. Both of them had been grievously stung, and were in a good deal of pain, which seemed the more intolerable to them, because it was the very first pain that had ever been felt since the world began. Of course, they were entirely unaccustomed to it, and could have no idea what it meant. Besides all this, they were in exceedingly bad humor, both with themselves and with one another. In order to indulge it to the utmost, Epimetheus sat down sullenly in a corner, with his back towards Pandora; while Pandora flung herself upon the floor, and rested her head on the fatal and abominable box. She was crying bitterly, and sobbing as if her heart would break.

Suddenly, there was a gentle little tap, on the inside of the lid.

"What can that be?" cried Pandora, lifting her head.

But either Epimetheus had not heard the tap, or was too much out of humor to notice it. At any rate, he made no answer.

"You are very unkind," said Pandora, sobbing anew, "not to speak to me!"

Again, the tap! It sounded like the tiny knuckles of a fairy's hand, knocking lightly and playfully on the inside of the box.

"Who are you?" asked Pandora, with a little of her former curiosity. "Who are you, inside of this naughty box?"

A sweet little voice spoke from within,

"Only lift the lid, and you shall see!"

"No, no," answered Pandora, again beginning to sob, "I have had enough of lifting the lid! You are inside of the box, naughty creature, and there you shall stay! There are plenty of your ugly brothers and sisters, already flying about the world. You need never think that I shall be so foolish as to let you out!"

She looked towards Epimetheus, as she spoke, perhaps expecting that he would commend her for her wisdom. But the sullen boy only muttered, that she was wise a little too late.

"Ah," said the sweet little voice again, "you had much better let me out! I am not like those naughty creatures that have stings in their tails. They are no brothers and sisters of mine, as you would see at once, if you were only to get a glimpse of me. Come, come, my pretty Pandora! I am sure you will let me out!"

And, indeed, there was a kind of cheerful witchery in the tone, that made it almost impossible to refuse anything which this little voice asked. Pandora's heart had insensibly grown lighter, at every word that came from within the box. Epimetheus, too, though still in the corner, had turned half round, and seemed to be in rather better spirits than before.

"My dear Epimetheus," cried Pandora, "have you heard this little voice?"

"Yes; to be sure I have!" answered he, but in no very good humor, as yet. "And what of it?"

"Shall I lift the lid again?" asked Pandora.

"Just as you please!" said Epimetheus. "You have done so much mischief already, that perhaps you may as well do a little more. One other Trouble, in such a swarm as you have set adrift about the world, can make no very great difference!"

"You might speak a little more kindly!" murmured Pandora, wiping her eyes.

"Ah, naughty boy!" cried the little voice within the box, in an arch and laughing tone. "He knows he is longing to see me! Come, my dear Pandora, lift up the lid! I am in a great hurry to comfort you. Only let me have some fresh air, and you shall soon see that matters are not quite so dismal as you think them!"

"Epimetheus," exclaimed Pandora, "come what may, I am resolved to open the box!"

"And, as the lid seems very heavy," cried Epimetheus, running across the room, "I will help you!"

So, with one consent, the two children again lifted the lid. Out flew a sunny and smiling little personage, and hovered about the room, throwing a light wherever she went. Have you never made the sunshine dance into dark corners, by reflecting it from a bit of looking-glass? Well; so looked the winged cheerfulness of this fairylike stranger, amid the gloom of the cottage. She flew to Epimetheus, and laid the least touch of her finger on the inflamed spot where the Trouble had stung him; and immediately the anguish of it was gone.

Then, she kissed Pandora on the forehead; and her hurt was cured likewise.

After performing these good offices, the bright stranger fluttered sportively over the children's heads, and looked so sweetly at them, that they both began to think it not so very much amiss to have opened the box; since, otherwise, their cheery guest must have been kept a prisoner, among those naughty imps with stings in their tails.

"Pray, who are you, beautiful creature?" inquired Pandora.

"I am to be called Hope!" answered the sunshiny figure. "And because I am such a cheery little body, I was packed into the box, to make amends to the human race for that swarm of ugly Troubles, which was destined to be let loose among them. Never fear! we shall do pretty well, in spite of them all."

"Your wings are colored like the rainbow!" exclaimed Pandora. "How very beautiful!"

"Yes; they are like the rainbow," said Hope, "because, glad as my nature is, I am partly made of tears as well as smiles!"

"And will you stay with us," asked Epimetheus, "forever and ever?"

"As long as you need me," said Hope, with her pleasant smile—"and that will be as long as you live in the world—I promise never to desert you! There may come times and seasons, now and then, when you will think that I have utterly vanished. But again, and again, and again, when perhaps you least dream of it, you shall see the glimmer of my wings on the ceiling of your cottage. Yes, my dear children; and I know something very good and beautiful that is to be given you, hereafter!"

"Oh, tell us," they exclaimed, "tell us what it is!"

"Do not ask me," replied Hope, putting her finger on her rosy mouth. "But do not despair, even if it should never happen while you live on this earth. Trust in my promise; for it is true!"

"We do trust you!" cried Epimetheus and Pandora, both in one breath.

And so they did; and not only they, but so has everybody trusted Hope, that has since been alive. And, to tell you the truth, I cannot help being glad—(though, to be sure, it was an uncommonly naughty thing for her to do)—but I cannot help being glad that our foolish Pandora peeped into the box. No doubt—no doubt—the Troubles are still flying about the world, and have increased in multitude, rather than lessened, and are a very ugly set of imps, and carry most venomous stings in their tails. I have felt them already, and expect to feel them more, as I grow older. But then that lovely and lightsome little figure of Hope! What in the world could we do without her? Hope spiritualizes the earth; Hope makes it always new; and, even in the earth's best and brightest aspect, Hope shows it to be only the shadow of an infinite bliss, hereafter!

Tanglewood Play-Room

"PRIMROSE," asked Eustace, pinching her ear, "how do you like my little Pandora? Don't you think her the exact picture of yourself? But you would not have hesitated half so long about opening the box."

"Then I should have been well punished for my naughtiness," retorted Primrose smartly; "for the first thing to pop out, after the lid was lifted, would have been Mr. Eustace Bright, in the shape of a Trouble!"

"Cousin Eustace," said Sweet Fern, "did the box hold all the trouble that has ever come into the world?"

"Every mite of it!" answered Eustace. "This very snow-storm, which has spoilt my skating, was packed up there."

"And how big was the box?" asked Sweet Fern.

"Why, perhaps three feet long," said Eustace, "two feet wide, and two feet and a half high."

"Ah," said the child, "you are making fun of me, Cousin Eustace! I know there is not trouble enough in the world to fill such a great box as that. As for the snow-storm, it is no trouble at all, but a pleasure; so it could not have been in the box."

"Hear the child!" cried Primrose, with an air of superiority. "How little he knows about the troubles of this world! Poor fellow! He will be wiser when he has seen as much of life as I have."

So saying, she began to skip the rope.

Meantime, the day was drawing towards its close. Out of doors the scene certainly looked dreary. There was a gray drift, far and wide, through the gathering twilight;—the earth was as pathless as the air;—and the bank of snow, over the steps of the porch, proved that nobody had entered or gone out, for a good many hours past. Had there been only one child at the window of Tanglewood, gazing at this wintry prospect, it would perhaps have made him sad. But half-a-dozen children together, though they cannot quite turn the world into a paradise, may defy old Winter and all his storms to put them out of spirits. Eustace Bright, moreover, on the spur of the moment, invented several new kinds of play, which kept them all in a roar of merriment till bedtime, and served for the next stormy day besides.

Tanglewood Fireside

THE snow-storm lasted another day; but what became of it afterwards, I cannot possibly imagine. At any rate, it entirely cleared away, during the night; and when the sun arose, the next morning, it shone brightly down on as bleak a tract of hill-country, here in Berkshire, as could be seen anywhere in the world. The frost-work had so covered the window-panes, that it was hardly possible to get a glimpse at the scenery outside. But, while waiting for breakfast, the small populace of Tanglewood had scratched peep-holes with their finger-nails, and saw with vast delight, that—unless it were one or two bare patches on a precipitous hill-side, or the gray effect of the snow, intermingled with the black pine-forest— all nature was as white as a sheet. How exceedingly pleasant! And, to make it all the better, it was cold enough to nip one's nose short off! If people have but life enough in them to bear it, there is nothing that so raises the spirits, and makes the blood ripple and dance so nimbly, like a brook down the slope of a hill, as a bright, hard frost.

No sooner was breakfast over, than the whole party, well muffled in furs and woollens, floundered forth into the midst of the snow. Well, what a day of frosty sport was this! They slid down-hill into the valley, a hundred times, nobody knows how far, and, to make it all the merrier, upsetting their sledges and tumbling head over heels, quite as often as they came safely to the bottom. And, once, Eustace Bright took Periwinkle, Sweet Fern, and Squash Blossom on the sledge with him, by way of ensuring a safe passage; and down they went, full speed. But, behold! half way down, the sledge hit against a hidden stump, and flung all four of its passengers into a heap, and, on gathering themselves up, there was no little Squash Blossom to be found. Why, what could have become of the child? And while they were wondering and staring about, up-started Squash Blossom out of a snow-bank, with the reddest face you ever saw, and looking as if a large scarlet flower had suddenly sprouted up in mid-winter. Then there was a great laugh.

When they had grown tired of sliding down-hill, Eustace set the children to digging a cave in the biggest snow-drift that they could find. Unluckily, just as it was completed, and the party had squeezed themselves into the hollow, down came the roof upon their heads, and buried every soul of them alive! The next moment, up popped all their little heads out of the ruins, and the tall student's head in the midst of them, looking hoary and venerable with the snow-dust that had got amongst his brown curls. And then, to punish Cousin Eustace for advising them to dig such a tumble-down cavern, the children attacked him in a body, and so be-pelted him with snow-balls that he was fain to take to his heels.

So he ran away, and went into the woods, and thence to the margin of Shadow Brook, where he could hear the streamlet grumbling along, under great, overhanging banks of snow and ice, which would scarcely let it see the light of day. There were adamantine icicles, glittering around all its little cascades. Thence he strolled to the shore of the lake, and beheld a white, untrodden plain before him, stretching from his own feet to the foot of Monument Mountain. And, it being now almost sunset, Eustace thought that he had never beheld anything so fresh and beautiful as the scene. He was glad that the children were not with him; for their lively spirits and tumble-about activity would quite have chased away his higher and graver mood; so that he would merely have been merry, (as he had already been, the whole day long,) and would not have known the loveliness of the winter-sunset among the hills.

When the sun was fairly down, our friend Eustace went home to eat his supper. After the meal was over, he betook himself to the study, with a purpose, I rather imagine, to write an ode, or two or three sonnets, or verses of some kind or other, in praise of the purple and golden clouds, which he had seen around the setting sun. But, before he had hammered out the very first rhyme, the door opened, and Primrose and Periwinkle made their appearance.

"Go away, children! I can't be troubled with you now!" cried the student, looking over his shoulder, with the pen between his fingers. "What in the world do you want here? I thought you were all in bed!"

"Hear him, Periwinkle, trying to talk like a grown man!" said Primrose. "And he seems to forget that I am now thirteen years old, and may sit up almost as late as I please. But, Cousin Eustace, you must put off your airs, and come with us to the drawing-room. The children have talked so much about your stories, that my father wishes to hear one of them, in order to judge whether they are likely to do any mischief."

"Poh, poh, Primrose!" exclaimed the student, rather vexed. "I don't believe I can tell one of my stories in the presence of grown people. Besides, your father is a classical scholar; not that I am much afraid of his scholarship, neither, for I doubt not it is as rusty as an old case-knife, by this time. But then he will be sure to quarrel with the admirable nonsense that I put into these stories, out of my own head, and which makes the great charm of the matter for children, like yourself. No man of fifty, who has read the classical myths in his youth, can possibly understand my merit as a re-inventor and improver of them."

"All this may be very true," said Primrose; "but come you must! My father will not open his book, nor will mamma open the piano, till you have given us some of your nonsense, as you very correctly call it. So be a good boy, and come along."

Whatever he might pretend, the student was rather glad than otherwise, on second thoughts, to catch at the opportunity of proving to Mr. Pringle what an excellent faculty he had in modernizing the myths of ancient times. Until twenty years of age, a young man may indeed be rather bashful about showing his poetry and his prose; but, for all that, he is pretty apt to think that these very productions would place him at the tip-top of literature, if once they could be known. Accordingly, without much more resistance, Eustace suffered Primrose and Periwinkle to drag him into the drawing-room.

It was a large and handsome apartment, with a semi-circular window at one end, in the recess of which stood a marble copy of Greenough's Angel and Child. On one side of the fire-place, there were many shelves of books, gravely, but richly bound. The white light of the astral-lamp, and the red glow of the bright coal-fire, made the room brilliant and cheerful; and before the fire, in a deep arm-chair, sat Mr. Pringle, looking just fit to be seated in such a chair, and in such a room. He was a tall and quite a handsome gentleman, with a bald brow, and was always so nicely dressed, that even Eustace Bright never liked to enter his presence, without at least pausing at the threshold to settle his shirt-collar. But now, as Primrose had hold of one of his hands, and Periwinkle of the other, he was forced to make his appearance with a rough-and-tumble sort of look, as if he had been rolling all day in a snow-bank. And so he had.

Mr. Pringle turned towards the student, benignly enough, but in a way that made him feel how uncombed and unbrushed he was, and how uncombed and unbrushed, likewise, were his mind and thoughts.

"Eustace," said Mr. Pringle, with a smile, "I find that you are producing a great sensation among the little public of Tanglewood, by the exercise of your gifts of narrative. Primrose here, as the little folks choose to call her, and the rest of the children, have been so loud in praise of your stories, that Mrs. Pringle and myself are really curious to hear a specimen. It would be so much the more gratifying to myself, as the stories appear to be an attempt to render the fables of classical antiquity into the idiom of modern fancy and feeling. At least, so I judge from a few of the incidents, which have come to me at second hand."

"You are not exactly the auditor that I should have chosen, Sir," observed the student, "for fantasies of this nature."

"Possibly not," replied Mr. Pringle. "I suspect, however, that a young author's most useful critic is precisely the one whom he would be least apt to choose. Pray oblige me, therefore."

"Sympathy, methinks, should have some little share in the critic's qualifications," murmured Eustace Bright. "However, Sir, if you will find patience, I will find stories. But be kind enough to remember, that I am addressing myself to the imagination and sympathies of the children, not to your own."

Accordingly, the student snatched hold of the first theme which presented itself. It was suggested by a plate of apples that he happened to espy on the mantel-piece.

The Three Golden Apples

D ID you ever hear of the golden apples, that grew in the garden of the Hesperides? Ah, those were such apples as would bring a great price, by the bushel, if any of them could be found growing in the orchards of now-a-days. But there is not, I suppose, a graft of that wonderful fruit, on a single tree in the wide world. Not so much as a seed of those apples exists any longer.

And even in the old, old, half-forgotten times, before the garden of the Hesperides was over-run with weeds, a great many people doubted whether there could be real trees, that bore apples of solid gold upon their branches. All had heard of them, but nobody remembered to have seen any. Children, nevertheless, used to listen, open-mouthed, to stories of the golden apple-tree, and resolved to discover it, when they should be big enough. Adventurous young men, who desired to do a braver thing than any of their fellows, set out in quest of this fruit. Many of them returned no more; none of them brought back the apples. No wonder that they found it impossible to gather them! It is said that there was a dragon beneath the tree, with a hundred terrible heads, fifty of which were always on the watch, while the other fifty slept.

In my opinion, it was hardly worth running so much risk for the sake of a solid golden apple. Had the apples been sweet, mellow, and juicy, indeed, that would be another matter. There might then have been some sense in trying to get at them, in spite of the hundred-headed dragon!

But, as I have already told you, it was quite a common thing with young persons, when tired of too much peace and rest, to go in search of the garden of the Hesperides. And, once, the adventure was undertaken by a hero, who had enjoyed very little peace or rest, since he came into the world. At the time of which I am going to speak, he was wandering through the pleasant land of Italy, with a mighty club in his hand, and a bow and quiver slung across his shoulders. He was wrapt in the skin of the biggest and fiercest lion that ever had been seen, and which he himself had killed; and though, on the whole, he was kind, and generous, and noble, there was a good deal of the lion's fierceness in his heart. As he went on his way, he continually inquired whether that were the right road to the famous garden. But none of the country people knew anything about the matter, and many looked as if they would have laughed at the question, if the stranger had not carried so very big a club.

So he journeyed on and on, still making the same inquiry; until, at last, he came to the brink of a river, where some beautiful young women sat twining wreaths of flowers.

"Can you tell me, pretty maidens," asked the stranger, "whether this is the right way to the garden of the Hesperides?"

The young women had been having a fine time together, weaving the flowers into wreaths, and crowning one another's heads. And there seemed to be a kind of magic in the touch of their fingers, that made the flowers more fresh and dewy, and of brighter hues, and sweeter fragrance, while they played with them, than even when they had been growing on their native stems. But, on hearing the stranger's question, they dropt all their flowers on the grass, and gazed at him with astonishment.

"The garden of the Hesperides!" cried one. "We thought mortals had been weary of seeking it, after so many disappointments. And, pray, adventurous traveller, what do you want there?"

"A certain king, who is my cousin," replied he, "has ordered me to get him three of the golden apples."

"Most of the young men, who go in quest of these apples," observed another of the damsels, "desire to obtain them for themselves, or to present them to some fair maiden whom they love. Do you then love this king, your cousin, so very much?"

"Perhaps not," replied the stranger, sighing. "He has often been severe and cruel to me. But it is my destiny to obey him!"

"And do you know," asked the damsel who had first spoken, "that a terrible dragon, with a hundred heads, keeps watch under the golden apple-tree?"

"I know it well," answered the stranger, calmly. "But from

my cradle upwards, it has been my business, and almost my pastime, to deal with serpents and dragons."

The young women looked at his massive club, and at the shaggy lion's skin which he wore, and likewise at his heroic limbs and figure; and they whispered to each other, that the stranger appeared to be one, who might reasonably expect to perform deeds far beyond the might of other men. But, then, the dragon with a hundred heads! What mortal, even if he possessed a hundred lives, could hope to escape the fangs of such a monster? So kind-hearted were the maidens, that they could not bear to see this brave and handsome traveller attempt what was so very dangerous, and devote himself, most probably, to become a meal for the dragon's hundred ravenous mouths.

"Go back," cried they all, "go back to your own home! Your mother, beholding you safe and sound, will shed tears of joy; and what can she do more, should you win ever so great a victory? No matter for the golden apples! No matter for the king, your cruel cousin! We do not wish the dragon with the hundred heads to eat you up!"

The stranger seemed to grow impatient at these remonstrances. He carelessly lifted his mighty club, and let it fall upon a rock that lay half-buried in the earth, near by. With the force of that idle blow, the great rock was shattered all to pieces. It cost the stranger no more effort to achieve this feat of a giant's strength, than for one of the young maidens to touch her sister's rosy cheek with a flower.

"Do you not believe," said he, looking at the damsels with a smile, "that such a blow would have crushed one of the dragon's hundred heads?"

Then he sat down on the grass, and told them the story of his life, or as much of it as he could remember, from the day when he was first cradled in a warrior's brazen shield. While he lay there, two immense serpents came gliding over the floor, and opened their hideous jaws to devour him; and he, a baby of a few months old, had griped one of the fierce snakes in each of his little fists, and strangled them to death. When he was but a stripling he had killed a huge lion, almost as big as the one whose vast and shaggy hide he now wore upon his shoulders. The next thing that he had done, was to fight a battle with an ugly sort of monster, called a hydra, which had no less than nine heads, and exceedingly sharp teeth in every one of them.

"But the dragon of the Hesperides, you know," observed one of the damsels, "has a hundred heads!"

"Nevertheless," replied the stranger, "I would rather fight two such dragons than a single hydra. For, as fast as I cut off a head, two others grew in its place; and, besides, there was one of the heads that could not possibly be killed, but kept biting as fiercely as ever, long after it was cut off. So I was forced to bury it under a stone, where it is doubtless alive, to this very day. But the hydra's body, and its eight other heads, will never do any further mischief."

The damsels, judging that the story was likely to last a good while, had been preparing a repast of bread and grapes, that the stranger might refresh himself in the intervals of his talk. They took pleasure in helping him to this simple food; and, now and then, one of them would put a sweet grape between her rosy lips, lest it should make him bashful, to eat alone.

The traveller proceeded to tell how he had chased a very swift stag, for a twelvemonth together, without ever stopping to take breath, and had at last caught it by the antlers, and carried it home alive. And he had fought with a very odd race of people, half horses and half men, and had put them all to death, from a sense of duty, in order that their ugly figures might never be seen any more. Besides all this, he took to himself great credit for having cleaned out a stable.

"Do you call that a wonderful exploit?" asked one of the young maidens, with a smile. "Any clown in the country has done as much!"

"Had it been an ordinary stable," replied the stranger, "I should not have mentioned it. But this was so gigantic a task that it would have taken me all my life to perform it, if I had not luckily thought of turning the channel of a river through the stable-door. That did the business, in a very short time!"

Seeing how earnestly his fair auditors listened, he next told them how he had shot some monstrous birds, and had caught a wild bull alive, and let him go again, and had tamed a num-

ber of very wild horses, and had conquered Hippolyta, the
warlike queen of the Amazons. He mentioned, likewise, that
he had taken off Hippolyta's enchanted girdle, and had given
it to the daughter of his cousin, the king.

"Was it the girdle of Venus," inquired the prettiest of the
damsels, "which makes women beautiful?"

"No," answered the stranger. "It had formerly been the
sword-belt of Mars; and it can only make the wearer valiant
and courageous."

"An old sword-belt!" cried the damsel, tossing her head.
"Then I should not care about having it!"

"You are right," said the stranger.

Going on with his wonderful narrative, he informed the
maidens that as strange an adventure, as ever happened, was
when he fought with Geryon, the six-legged man. This was a
very odd and frightful sort of figure, as you may well believe.
Any person, looking at his tracks in the sand or snow, would
suppose that three sociable companions had been walking
along together. Or, hearing his footsteps at a little distance, it
was no more than reasonable to judge that several people
must be coming. But it was only the strange man, Geryon,
clattering onward, with his six legs!

Six legs and one gigantic body! Certainly, he must have
been a very queer monster to look at; and, my stars, what a
waste of shoe-leather!

When the stranger had finished the story of his adventures,
he looked around at the attentive faces of the maidens.

"Perhaps you may have heard of me before," said he, modestly. "My name is Hercules!"

"We had already guessed it," replied the maidens; "for your
wonderful deeds are known all over the world. We do not
think it strange, any longer, that you should set out in quest
of the golden apples of the Hesperides. Come, sisters, let us
crown the hero with flowers!"

Then they flung beautiful wreaths over his stately head and
mighty shoulders, so that the lion's skin was almost entirely
covered with roses. They took possession of his ponderous
club, and so entwined it about with the brightest, softest, and
most fragrant blossoms, that not a finger's breadth of its
oaken substance could be seen. It looked all like a huge bunch

of flowers. Lastly, they joined hands, and danced around him, chanting words which became poetry of their own accord, and grew into a choral song, in honor of the illustrious Hercules.

And Hercules was rejoiced, as any other hero would have been, to know that these fair young girls had heard of the valiant deeds, which it had cost him so much toil and danger to achieve. But, still, he was not satisfied. He could not think that what he had already done was worthy of so much honor, while there remained any bold or difficult adventure to be undertaken.

"Dear maidens," said he, when they paused to take breath, "now that you know my name, will you not tell me how I am to reach the garden of the Hesperides?"

"Ah, must you go so soon?" they exclaimed. "You—that have performed so many wonders, and spent such a toilsome life—cannot you content yourself to repose, a little while, on the margin of this peaceful river?"

Hercules shook his head.

"I must depart now!" said he.

"We will then give you the best directions we can," replied the damsels. "You must go to the sea-shore, and find out the Old One, and compel him to inform you where the golden apples are to be found."

"The Old One!" repeated Hercules, laughing at this odd name. "And, pray, who may the Old One be?"

"Why, the Old Man of the Sea, to be sure!" answered one of the damsels. "He has fifty daughters, whom some people call very beautiful; but we do not think it proper to be acquainted with them, because they have sea-green hair, and taper away like fishes. You must talk with this Old Man of the Sea. He is a sea-faring person, and knows all about the garden of the Hesperides; for it is situated in an island, which he is often in the habit of visiting."

Hercules then asked whereabouts the Old One was most likely to be met with. When the damsels had informed him, he thanked them for all their kindness—for the bread and grapes, with which they had fed him, the lovely flowers with which they had crowned him, and the songs and dances wherewith they had done him honor—and he thanked them, most of all, for telling him the right way, and immediately set forth upon his journey.

But, before he was out of hearing, one of the maidens called after him.

"Keep fast hold of the Old One, when you catch him!" cried she, smiling, and lifting her finger to make the caution more impressive. "Do not be astonished at anything that may happen. Only hold him fast, and he will tell you what you wish to know."

Hercules again thanked her, and pursued his way, while the maidens resumed their pleasant labor of making flower-wreaths. They talked about the hero, long after he was gone.

"We will crown him with the loveliest of our garlands," said they, "when he returns hither with the three golden apples, after slaying the dragon with a hundred heads!"

Meanwhile, Hercules travelled constantly onward, over hill and dale, and through the solitary woods. Sometimes he swung his club aloft, and splintered a mighty oak with a downright blow. His mind was so full of the giants and monsters, with whom it was the business of his life to fight, that perhaps he mistook the great tree for a giant or a monster. And so eager was Hercules to achieve what he had undertaken, that he almost regretted to have spent so much time with the damsels, wasting idle breath upon the story of his adventures. But thus it always is with persons who are destined to perform great things. What they have already done, seems less than nothing. What they have taken in hand to do, seems worth toil, danger, and life itself.

Persons, who happened to be passing through the forest, must have been affrighted to see him smite the trees with his great club. With but a single blow, the trunk was riven as by the stroke of lightning, and the broad boughs came rustling and crashing down.

Hastening forward, without ever pausing or looking behind, he by-and-by heard the sea roaring at a distance. At this sound, he increased his speed, and soon came to a beach, where the great surf-waves tumbled themselves upon the hard sand, in a long line of snowy foam. At one end of the beach, however, there was a pleasant spot, where some green shrubbery clambered up a cliff, making its rocky face look soft and beautiful. A carpet of verdant grass, largely intermixed with sweet-smelling clover, covered the narrow space between the bottom of the cliff and the sea. And what should Hercules espy there, but an old man, fast asleep!

But was it really and truly an old man? Certainly, at first sight, it looked very like one; but, on closer inspection, it rather seemed to be some kind of a creature that lived in the sea. For, on his legs and arms, there were scales, such as fishes have; he was web-footed and web-fingered, after the fashion of a duck; and his long beard, being of a greenish tinge, had more the appearance of a tuft of sea-weed than of an ordinary beard. Have you never seen a stick of timber, that has been long tossed about by the waves, and has got all overgrown with barnacles, and, at last drifting ashore, seems to have been thrown up from the very deepest bottom of the sea? Well; the old man would have put you in mind of just such a wave-tost spar! But, Hercules, the instant he set eyes on this strange figure, was convinced that it could be no other than the Old One, who was to direct him on his way.

Yes; it was the self-same Old Man of the Sea, whom the hospitable maidens had talked to him about. Thanking his stars for the lucky accident of finding the old fellow asleep, Hercules stole on tiptoe towards him, and caught him by the arm and leg.

"Tell me," cried he, before the Old One was well awake, "which is the way to the garden of the Hesperides?"

As you may easily imagine, the Old Man of the Sea awoke in a fright. But his astonishment could hardly have been greater than was that of Hercules, the next moment. For, all of a sudden, the Old One seemed to disappear out of his grasp, and he found himself holding a stag by the fore and hind-leg! But still he kept fast hold. Then the stag disappeared, and in its stead there was a sea-bird, fluttering and screaming, while Hercules clutched it by the wing and claw. But the bird could not get away. Immediately afterwards, there was an ugly three-headed dog, which growled and barked at Hercules, and snapt fiercely at the hands by which he held him. But Hercules would not let him go. In another minute, instead of the three-headed dog, what should appear but Geryon, the six-legged man-monster, kicking at Hercules

with five of his legs, in order to get the remaining one at
liberty! But Hercules held on. By-and-by, no Geryon was
there, but a huge snake, like one of those which Hercules had
strangled in his babyhood, only a hundred times as big; and
it twisted and twined about the hero's neck and body, and
threw its tail high into the air, and opened its deadly jaws
as if to devour him outright; so that it was really a very terrible spectacle. But Hercules was no whit disheartened, and
squeezed the great snake so tightly that he soon began to hiss
with pain.

You must understand that the Old Man of the Sea, though
he generally looked so much like the wave-beaten figure-head
of a vessel, had the power of assuming any shape he pleased.
When he found himself so roughly seized by Hercules, he had
been in hopes of putting him into such surprise and terror,
by these magical transformations, that the hero would be glad
to let him go. If Hercules had relaxed his grasp, the Old One
would certainly have plunged down to the very bottom of the
sea, whence he would not soon have given himself the trouble
of coming up, in order to answer any impertinent questions.
Ninety-nine people out of a hundred, I suppose, would have
been frightened out of their wits by the very first of his ugly
shapes, and would have taken to their heels at once. For, one
of the hardest things in this world is, to see the difference
between real dangers and imaginary ones.

But, as Hercules held on so stubbornly, and only squeezed
the Old One so much the tighter at every change of shape,
and really put him to no small torture, he finally thought it
best to re-appear in his own figure. So there he was again, a
fishy, scaly, web-footed sort of personage, with something
like a tuft of sea-weed at his chin.

"Pray what do you want with me?" cried the Old One, as
soon as he could take breath; for it is quite a tiresome affair
to go through so many false shapes. "Why do you squeeze
me so hard? Let me go, this moment; or I shall begin to
consider you an extremely uncivil person!"

"My name is Hercules!" roared the mighty stranger. "And
you will never get out of my clutch, until you tell me the
nearest way to the garden of the Hesperides!"

When the old fellow heard who it was that had caught him,

he saw, with half an eye, that it would be necessary to tell him everything that he wanted to know. The Old One was an inhabitant of the sea, you must recollect, and roamed about everywhere, like other sea-faring people. Of course, he had often heard of the fame of Hercules, and of the wonderful things that he was constantly performing, in various parts of the earth, and how determined he always was to accomplish whatever he undertook. He therefore made no more attempts to escape, but told the hero how to find the garden of the Hesperides, and likewise warned him of many difficulties which must be overcome, before he could arrive thither.

"You must go on, thus and thus," said the Old Man of the Sea, after taking the points of the compass, "till you come in sight of a very tall giant, who holds the sky on his shoulders. And the giant, if he happens to be in the humor, will tell you exactly where the garden of the Hesperides lies."

"And if the giant happens not to be in the humor," remarked Hercules, balancing his club on the tip of his finger, "perhaps I shall find means to persuade him!"

Thanking the Old Man of the Sea, and begging his pardon for having squeezed him so roughly, the hero resumed his journey. He met with a great many strange adventures, which would be well worth your hearing, if I had leisure to narrate them as minutely as they deserve.

It was in this journey, if I mistake not, that he encountered a prodigious giant, who was so wonderfully contrived by nature, that, every time he touched the earth, he became ten times as strong as ever he had been before. His name was Antæus. You may see, plainly enough, that it was a very difficult business to fight with such a fellow; for, as often as he got a knock-down blow, up he started again, stronger, fiercer, and abler to use his weapons, than if his enemy had let him alone. Thus, the harder Hercules pounded the giant with his club, the farther he seemed from winning the victory. I have sometimes argued with such people, but never fought with one. The only way in which Hercules found it possible to finish the battle, was by lifting Antæus off his feet into the air, and squeezing, and squeezing, and squeezing him, until, finally, the strength was quite squeezed out of his enormous body.

When this affair was finished, Hercules continued his travels, and went to the land of Egypt, where he was taken prisoner and would have been put to death, if he had not slain the king of the country, and made his escape. Passing through the deserts of Africa, and going as fast as he could, he arrived at last on the shore of the great ocean. And here, unless he could walk on the crests of the billows, it seemed as if his journey must needs be at an end.

Nothing was before him, save the foaming, dashing, measureless ocean. But, suddenly, as he looked towards the horizon, he saw something, a great way off, which he had not seen, the moment before. It gleamed very brightly, almost as you may have beheld the round, golden disk of the sun, when it rises or sets over the edge of the world. It evidently drew nearer; for, at every instant, this wonderful object became larger and more lustrous. At length, it had come so nigh that Hercules discovered it to be an immense cup or bowl, made either of gold or burnished brass. How it had got afloat upon the sea, is more than I can tell you. There it was, at all events, rolling on the tumultuous billows, which tossed it up and down, and heaved their foamy tops against its sides, but without ever throwing their spray over the brim.

"I have seen many giants, in my time," thought Hercules; "but never one that would need to drink his wine out of a cup like this!"

And, true enough, what a cup it must have been! It was as large—as large—but, in short, I am afraid to say how immeasurably large it was. To speak within bounds, it was ten times larger than a great mill-wheel; and, all of metal as it was, it floated over the heaving surges more lightly than an acorn-cup a-down the brook. The waves tumbled it onward, until it grazed against the shore, within a short distance of the spot where Hercules was standing.

As soon as this happened, he knew what was to be done; for he had not gone through so many remarkable adventures without learning pretty well how to conduct himself, whenever anything came to pass, a little out of the common rule. It was just as clear as daylight, that this marvellous cup had been set adrift by some unseen power, and guided hitherward, in order to carry Hercules across the sea on his way to

the garden of the Hesperides. Accordingly, without a moment's delay, he clambered over the brim, and slid down on
the inside, where, spreading out his lion's skin, he proceeded
to take a little repose. He had scarcely rested, until now, since
he bade farewell to the damsels on the margin of the river.
The waves dashed, with a pleasant and ringing sound, against
the circumference of the hollow cup; it rocked lightly to-and-
fro; and the motion was so soothing, that it speedily rocked
Hercules into an agreeable slumber.

His nap had probably lasted a good while, when the cup
chanced to graze against a rock, and, in consequence, immediately resounded and reverberated through its golden or brazen substance, a hundred times as loudly as ever you heard a
church-bell. The noise awoke Hercules, who instantly started
up and gazed around him, wondering whereabouts he was.
He was not long in discovering that the cup had floated
across a great part of the sea, and was approaching the shore
of what seemed to be an island. And, on that island, what do
you think he saw?

No;—you will never guess it; not if you were to try fifty-
thousand times! It positively appears to me, that this was the
most marvellous spectacle that had ever been seen by Hercules, in the whole course of his wonderful travels and adventures. It was a greater marvel than the hydra with nine heads,
which kept growing twice as fast as they were cut off; greater
than the six-legged man-monster; greater than Antæus;
greater than anything that was ever beheld by anybody,
before or since the days of Hercules, or than anything that
remains to be beheld, by travellers in all time to come. It
was a giant!

But, such an intolerably big giant! A giant, as tall as a
mountain; so vast a giant, that the clouds rested about his
midst, like a girdle, and hung like a hoary beard from his
chin, and flitted before his huge eyes, so that he could neither
see Hercules nor the golden cup in which he was voyaging.
And, most wonderful of all, the giant held up his great hands
and appeared to support the sky, which, so far as Hercules
could discern through the clouds, was resting upon his head!
This does really seem almost too much to believe.

Meanwhile, the bright cup continued to float onward, and

finally touched the strand. Just then, a breeze wafted away the clouds from before the giant's visage, and Hercules beheld it, with all its enormous features;—eyes, each of them as big as yonder lake, a nose a mile long, and a mouth of the same width. It was a countenance terrible from its enormity of size, but disconsolate and weary, even as you may see the faces of many people, now-a-days, who are compelled to sustain burthens above their strength. What the sky was to the giant, such are the cares of earth to those who let themselves be weighed down by them. And whenever men undertake what is beyond the just measure of their abilities, they encounter precisely such a doom as had befallen this poor giant.

Poor fellow! He had evidently stood there a long while. An ancient forest had been growing and decaying around his feet; and oak-trees, of six or seven centuries old, had sprung from the acorn and forced themselves between his toes.

The giant now looked down from the far height of his great eyes, and perceiving Hercules, roared out in a voice that resembled thunder, proceeding out of the cloud that had just flitted away from his face.

"Who are you, down at my feet there? And whence do you come, in that little cup?"

"I am Hercules!" thundered back the hero, in a voice pretty nearly or quite as loud as the giant's own. "And I am seeking for the garden of the Hesperides!"

"Ho! Ho! Ho!" roared the giant, in a fit of immense laughter. "That is a wise adventure, truly!"

"And why not?" cried Hercules, getting a little angry at the giant's mirth. "Do you think I am afraid of the dragon with a hundred heads?"

Just at this time, while they were talking together, some black clouds gathered about the giant's middle, and burst into a tremendous storm of thunder and lightning, causing such a pother that Hercules found it impossible to distinguish a word. Only the giant's immeasurable legs were to be seen, standing up into the obscurity of the tempest and, now-and-then, a momentary glimpse of his whole figure, mantled in a volume of mist. He seemed to be speaking, most of the time; but his big, deep, rough voice chimed in with the reverberations of the thunder-claps, and rolled away over the hills, like them. Thus, by talking out of season, the foolish giant expended an incalculable quantity of breath, to no purpose; for the thunder spoke quite as intelligibly as he.

At last, the storm swept over, as suddenly as it had come. And there again was the clear sky, and the weary giant holding it up, and the pleasant sunshine beaming over his vast height, and illuminating it against the background of the sullen thunder-clouds. So far above the shower had been his head, that not a hair of it was moistened by the rain-drops.

When the giant could see Hercules, still standing on the sea-shore, he roared out to him anew.

"I am Atlas, the mightiest giant in the world! And I hold the sky upon my head!"

"So I see!" answered Hercules. "But, can you show me the way to the garden of the Hesperides?"

"What do you want there?" asked the giant.

"I want three of the Golden Apples," shouted Hercules, "for my cousin, the king!"

"There is nobody but myself," quoth the giant, "that can go to the garden of the Hesperides, and gather the golden apples. If it were not for this little business of holding up the sky, I would make half-a-dozen steps across the sea, and get them for you."

"You are very kind," replied Hercules. "And cannot you rest the sky upon a mountain?"

"None of them are quite high enough," said Atlas, shaking his head. "But, if you were to take your stand on the summit of that nearest one, your head would be pretty nearly on a level with mine. You seem to be a fellow of some strength. What if you should take my burthen on your shoulders, while I do your errand for you?"

Hercules, as you must be careful to remember, was a remarkably strong man; and though it certainly requires a great deal of muscular power to uphold the sky, yet, if any mortal could be supposed capable of such an exploit, he was the one. Nevertheless, it seemed so difficult an undertaking, that, for the first time in his life, he hesitated.

"Is the sky very heavy?" he inquired.

"Why, not particularly so, at first," answered the giant,

shrugging his shoulders. "But it gets to be a little burthensome, after a thousand years!"

"And how long a time," asked the hero, "will it take you to get the golden apples?"

"Oh, that will be done in a few moments," cried Atlas. "I shall take ten or fifteen miles at a stride, and be at the garden and back again, before your shoulders begin to ache."

"Well then," answered Hercules, "I will climb the mountain, behind you there, and relieve you of your burthen!"

The truth is, Hercules had a kind heart of his own, and considered that he should be doing the giant a favor, by allowing him this opportunity for a ramble. And, besides, he thought that it would be still more for his own glory, if he could boast of upholding the sky, than merely to do so ordinary a thing as to conquer a dragon with a hundred heads. Accordingly, without more words, the sky was shifted from the shoulders of Atlas, and placed upon those of Hercules.

When this was safely accomplished, the first thing that the giant did was to stretch himself; and you may imagine what a prodigious spectacle he was then! Next, he slowly lifted one of his feet out of the forest that had grown up around it; then, the other. Then, all at once, he began to caper, and leap, and dance, for joy at his freedom; flinging himself nobody knows how high into the air, and floundering down again with a shock that made the earth tremble. Then he laughed— Ho! Ho! Ho!—with a thunderous roar that was echoed from the mountains, far and near, as if they and the giant had been so many rejoicing brothers. When his joy had a little subsided, he stept into the sea; ten miles at the first stride, which brought him mid-leg deep; and ten miles at the second, when the water came just above his knees; and ten miles more at the third, by which he was immersed nearly to his waist. This was the greatest depth of the sea.

Hercules watched the giant, as he still went onward; for it was really a wonderful sight—this immense human form, more than thirty miles off, half-hidden in the ocean, but with his upper half as tall, and misty, and blue, as a distant mountain! At last, the gigantic shape faded entirely out of view. And now Hercules began to consider what he should do, in case Atlas should be drowned in the sea, or if he were to be stung to death by the dragon with the hundred heads, which guarded the golden apples of the Hesperides. If any such misfortune were to happen, how could he ever get rid of the sky? And, by-the-by, its weight began already to be a little irksome to his head and shoulders.

"I really pity the poor giant," thought Hercules. "If it wearies me so much, in ten minutes, how must it have wearied him, in a thousand years!"

Oh, my sweet little people, you have no idea what a weight there was in that same blue sky, which looks so soft and aerial above our heads! And there, too, was the bluster of the wind, and the chill and watery clouds, and the blazing sun, all taking their turns to make Hercules uncomfortable! He began to be afraid that the giant would never come back. He gazed wistfully at the world beneath him, and acknowledged to himself, that it was a far happier kind of life to be a shepherd at the foot of a mountain, than to stand on its dizzy summit, and bear up the firmament with his might and main! For, of course, as you will easily understand, Hercules had an immense responsibility on his mind, as well as a weight on his head and shoulders. Why, if he did not stand perfectly still, and keep the sky immoveable, the sun would perhaps be put ajar! Or, after nightfall, a great many of the stars might be loosened from their places, and shower down like fiery rain upon the people's heads! And how ashamed would the hero be, if, owing to his unsteadiness beneath its weight, the sky should crack, and show a great fissure quite across it!

I know not how long it was, before, to his unspeakable joy, he beheld the huge shape of the giant, like a cloud on the far-off edge of the sea. At his nearer approach, Atlas held up his hand, in which Hercules could perceive three magnificent golden apples, as big as pumpkins, all hanging from one branch.

"I am glad to see you again!" shouted Hercules, when the giant was within hearing. "So, you have got the golden apples!"

"Certainly, certainly," answered Atlas; "and very fair apples they are. I took the finest that grew on the tree, I assure you. Ah, it is a beautiful spot, that garden of the Hesperides! Yes; and the dragon with a hundred heads is a sight worth any man's seeing. After all, you had better have gone for the apples yourself!"

"No matter!" replied Hercules. "You have had a pleasant ramble, and have done the business as well as I could. I heartily thank you for your trouble. And now, as I have a long way to go, and am rather in haste—and as the king, my cousin, is anxious to receive the golden apples—will you be kind enough to take the sky off my shoulders again?"

"Why, as to that," said the giant, chucking the golden apples into the air, twenty miles high, or thereabouts, and catching them as they came down—"as to that, my good friend, I consider you a little unreasonable! Cannot I carry the golden apples to the king, your cousin, much quicker than you could? As his majesty is in such a hurry to get them, I promise you to take my longest strides. And, besides, I have no fancy for burthening myself with the sky, just now!"

Here Hercules grew impatient, and gave a great shrug of his shoulders. It being now twilight, you might have seen two or three stars tumble out of their places. Everybody on earth looked upward in affright, thinking that the sky might be going to fall next.

"Oh, that will never do!" cried Giant Atlas, with a great roar of laughter. "I have not let fall so many stars, within the last five centuries. By the time you have stood there as long as I did, you will begin to learn patience!"

"What!" shouted Hercules, very wrathfully. "Do you intend to make me bear this burthen forever?"

"We will see about that, one of these days," answered the giant. "At all events, you ought not to complain, if you have to bear it the next hundred years, or perhaps the next thousand. I bore it a good while longer, in spite of the backache. Well, then, after a thousand years, if I happen to feel in the mood, we may possibly shift about again. You are certainly a very strong man, and can never have a better opportunity to prove it. Posterity will talk of you, I warrant it!"

"Pish! A fig for its talk!" cried Hercules, with another hitch of his shoulders. "Just take the sky upon your head, one instant, will you? I want to make a cushion of my lion's skin, for the weight to rest upon. It really chafes me, and will cause unnecessary inconvenience in so many centuries as I am to stand here!"

"That's no more than fair, and I'll do it!" quoth the giant; for he had no unkind feeling towards Hercules, and was merely acting with a too selfish consideration of his own ease. "For just five minutes, then, I'll take back the sky. Only for five minutes, recollect! I have no idea of spending another thousand years, as I spent the last. Variety is the spice of life, say I!"

Ah, the thick-witted old rogue of a giant! He threw down the golden apples, and received back the sky, from the head and shoulders of Hercules, upon his own, where it rightly belonged. And Hercules picked up the three golden apples, that were as big or bigger than pumpkins, and straightway set out on his journey homeward, without paying the slightest heed to the thundering tones of the giant, who bellowed after him to come back. Another forest sprang up around his feet, and grew ancient there; and again might be seen oaktrees, of six or seven centuries old, that had waxed thus aged betwixt his enormous toes.

And there stands the giant, to this day; or, at any rate, there stands a mountain as tall as he, and which bears his name; and when the thunder rumbles about its summit, we may imagine it to be the voice of Giant Atlas, bellowing after Hercules!

Tanglewood Fireside

After the Story

"COUSIN EUSTACE," demanded Sweet Fern, who had been sitting at the story-teller's feet, with his mouth wide open, "exactly how tall was this giant?"

"Oh, Sweet Fern, Sweet Fern," cried the student, "do you think I was there, to measure him with a yard-stick? Well, if you must know to a hair's breadth, I suppose he might be from three to fifteen miles straight upward, and that he might have seated himself on Taconic, and had Monument Mountain for a footstool!"

"Dear me," ejaculated the good little boy, with a contented sort of a grunt, "that was a giant, sure enough! And how long was his little finger?"

"As long as from Tanglewood to the lake," said Eustace.

"Sure enough, that was a giant!" repeated Sweet Fern, in an ecstasy at the precision of these measurements. "And how broad, I wonder, were the shoulders of Hercules?"

"That is what I have never been able to find out," answered the student. "But I think they must have been a great deal broader than mine, or than your father's, or than almost any shoulders which one sees, now-a-days."

"I wish," whispered Sweet Fern, with his mouth close to the student's ear, "that you would tell me how big were some of the oak-trees, that grew between the giant's toes!"

"They were bigger," said Eustace, "than the great chestnut-tree, which stands beyond Captain Smith's house."

"Eustace," remarked Mr. Pringle, after some deliberation, "I find it impossible to express such an opinion of this story as will be likely to gratify, in the smallest degree, your pride of authorship. Pray let me advise you never more to meddle with a classical myth. Your imagination is altogether Gothic, and will inevitably gothicise everything that you touch. The effect is like bedaubing a marble statue with paint. This giant, now! How can you have ventured to thrust his huge, dispro-portioned mass among the seemly outlines of Grecian fable, the tendency of which is to reduce even the extravagant within limits, by its pervading elegance?"

"I described the giant as he appeared to me," replied the student, rather piqued. "And, Sir, if you would only bring your mind into such a relation with these fables, as is necessary, in order to re-model them, you would see at once that an old Greek had no more exclusive right to them, than a modern Yankee has. They are the common property of the world, and of all time. The ancient poets re-modelled them at pleasure, and held them plastic in their hands; and why should they not be plastic in my hands as well?"

Mr. Pringle could not forbear a smile.

"And besides," continued Eustace, "the moment you put any warmth of heart, any passion or affection, any human or divine morality, into a classic mould, you make it quite another thing from what it was before. My own opinion is, that the Greeks, by taking possession of these legends, (which were the immemorial birthright of mankind,) and putting them into shapes of indestructible beauty, indeed, but cold and heartless, have done all subsequent ages an incalculable injury."

"Which you, doubtless, were born to remedy," said Mr. Pringle, laughing outright. "Well, well, go on; but take my advice, and never put any of your travesties on paper. And, as your next effort, what if you should try your hand on some one of the legends of Apollo?"

"Ah, Sir, you propose it as an impossibility," observed the student, after a moment's meditation; "and, to be sure, at first thought, the idea of a Gothic Apollo strikes one rather ludicrously. But I will turn over your suggestion in my mind, and do not quite despair of success."

During the above discussion, the children (who understood not a word of it) had grown very sleepy, and were now sent off to bed. Their drowsy babble was heard, ascending the staircase, while a north-west wind roared loudly among the tree-tops of Tanglewood, and played an anthem around the house. Eustace Bright went back to the study, and again endeavored to hammer out some verses, but fell asleep between two of the rhymes.

The Hill-Side

AND when, and where, do you think we find the children, next? No longer in the winter-time, but in the merry month of May. No longer in Tanglewood play-room, or at Tanglewood fireside, but more than half-way up a monstrous hill, or a mountain, as perhaps it would be better pleased to have us call it. They had set out from home with the mighty purpose of climbing this high hill, even to the very tip-top of its bald head. To be sure it was not quite so high as Chimborazo, or Mount Blanc, and was even a good deal lower than old Graylock. But, at any rate, it was higher than a thousand ant-hillocks, or a million of mole-hills, and, when measured by the short strides of little children, might be reckoned a very respectable mountain.

And was Cousin Eustace with the party? Of that you may be certain; else how could the book go on a step farther? He was now in the middle of the Spring vacation, and looked pretty much as we saw him, four or five months ago, except that, if you gazed quite closely at his upper lip, you could discern the funniest little bit of a moustache upon it. Setting aside this mark of mature manhood, you might have considered Cousin Eustace just as much a boy, as when you first became acquainted with him. He was as merry, as playful, as good-humored, as light of foot and of spirits, and equally a favorite with the little folks, as he had always been. This expedition up the mountain was entirely of his contrivance. All the way up the steep ascent, he had encouraged the elder children with his cheerful voice, and when Dandelion, Cowslip, and Squash Blossom grew weary, he had lugged them along, alternately, on his back. In this manner, they had passed through the orchards and pastures, on the lower part of the hill, and had reached the wood, which extends thence towards its bare summit.

The month of May, thus far, had been more amiable than it often is; and this was as sweet and genial a day, as the heart of man or child could wish. In their progress up the hill, the small people had found enough of violets, blue and white, and some that were as golden as if they had the touch of Midas on them. That sociablest of flowers, the little Houstonia, was very abundant. It is a flower that never lives alone, but which loves its own kind and is always fond of dwelling with a great many friends and relatives around it. Sometimes you see a family of them, covering a space no bigger than the palm of your hand, and sometimes a large community, whitening a whole tract of pasture, and all keeping one another in cheerful heart and life.

Within the verge of the wood, there were columbines, looking more pale than red, because they were so modest, and had thought proper to seclude themselves too anxiously from the sun. There were wild geraniums, too, and a thousand white blossoms of the strawberry. The trailing arbutus was not yet quite out of bloom; but it hid its precious flowers under the last year's withered forest-leaves, as carefully as a mother-bird hides its little young ones. It knew, I suppose, how beautiful and sweet-scented they were. So cunning was their concealment, that the children sometimes smelt the delicate richness of their perfume, before they knew whence it proceeded.

Amid so much new life, it was strange and truly pitiful to behold, here and there, in the fields and pastures, the hoary periwigs of dandelions that had already gone to seed. They had done with summer, before the summer came. Within those small globes of winged seeds, it was autumn now!

Well; but we must not waste our valuable pages with any more talk about the spring-time and wild flowers. There is something, we hope, more interesting to be talked about. If you look at the group of children, you may see them all gathered around Eustace Bright, who, sitting on the stump of a tree, seems to be just beginning a story. The fact is, the younger part of the troop have found out that it takes rather too many of their short strides, to measure the long ascent of the hill. Cousin Eustace, therefore, has decided to leave Sweet Fern, Cowslip, Squash Blossom, and Dandelion, at this point, mid-way up, until the return of the rest of the party from the summit. And because they complain a little, and do not quite like to stay behind, he gives them some apples out of his pocket, and proposes to tell them a very pretty story. Here-upon, they brighten up, and change their grieved looks into the broadest kind of smiles.

As for the story, I was there to hear it, hidden behind a bush, and shall tell it over to you in the pages that come next.

The Miraculous Pitcher

ONE EVENING, in times long ago, old Philemon and his old wife Baucis sat at their cottage-door, enjoying the calm and beautiful sunset. They had already eaten their frugal supper, and intended now to spend a quiet hour or two, before bedtime. So they talked together about their garden, and their cow, and their bees, and their grape-vine, which clambered over the cottage-wall, and on which the grapes were beginning to turn purple. But the rude shouts of children and the fierce barking of dogs, in the village near at hand, grew louder and louder; until, at last, it was hardly possible for Baucis and Philemon to hear each other speak.

"Ah, wife," cried Philemon, "I fear some poor traveller is seeking hospitality among our neighbors yonder; and instead of giving him food and lodging they have set their dogs at him, as their custom is!"

"Well-a-day!" answered old Baucis, "I do wish our neighbors felt a little more kindness for their fellow-creatures! And only think of bringing up their children in this naughty way, and patting them on the head when they fling stones at strangers!"

"Those children will never come to any good," said Philemon, shaking his white head. "To tell you the truth, wife, I should not wonder if some terrible thing were to happen to all the people in the village, unless they mend their manners. But as for you and me, so long as Providence affords us a crust of bread, let us be ready to give half to any poor, homeless stranger, that may come along and need it!"

"That's right, husband!" said Baucis. "So we will!"

These old folks, you must know, were quite poor, and had to work pretty hard for a living. Old Philemon toiled diligently in his garden, while Baucis was always busy with her distaff, or making a little butter and cheese with their cow's milk, or doing one thing and another about the cottage. Their food was seldom anything but bread, milk, and vegetables, with sometimes a portion of honey from their beehive, and now and then a bunch of grapes, that had ripened against the cottage-wall. But they were two of the kindest old people in the world, and would cheerfully have gone without their dinners, any day, rather than refuse a slice of their brown loaf, a cup of new milk, and a spoonfull of honey, to the weary traveller who might pause before their door. They felt as if such guests had a sort of holiness, and that they ought therefore to treat them better and more bountifully than their own selves.

Their cottage stood on a rising ground, at some short distance from a village, which lay in a hollow valley that was about half a mile in breadth. This valley, in past ages, when the world was new, had probably been the bed of a lake. There, fishes had glided to-and-fro, in the depths, and water-weeds had grown along the margin, and trees and hills had seen their reflected images in the broad and peaceful mirror. But, as the waters subsided, men had cultivated the soil and built houses on it; so that it was now a fertile spot, and bore no traces of the ancient lake, except a very small brook, which meandered through the midst of the village, and supplied the inhabitants with water. The valley had been dry land so long, that oaks had sprung up, and grown great and high, and perished with old age, and been succeeded by others, as tall and stately as the first. Never was there a prettier or more fruitful valley. The very sight of the plenty around them should have made the inhabitants kind and gentle, and ready to show their gratitude to Providence by doing good to their fellow-creatures.

But, we are sorry to say, the people of this lovely village were not worthy to dwell in a spot on which heaven had smiled so beneficently. They were a very selfish and hard-hearted people, and had no pity for the poor, nor sympathy with the homeless. They would only have laughed, had anybody told them that human beings owe a debt of love to one another, because there is no other method of paying the debt of love and care, which all of us owe to Providence. You will hardly believe what I am going to tell you. These naughty people taught their children to be no better than themselves, and used to clap their hands, by way of encouragement, when they saw the little boys and girls run after some poor stranger, shouting at his heels, and pelting him with stones. They kept large and fierce dogs; and whenever a traveller ventured to show himself in the village-street, this pack of disagreeable curs scampered to meet him, barking, snarling, and showing their teeth. Then they would seize him by his leg, or by his clothes, just as it happened; and if he were ragged when he came, he was generally a pitiable object before he had time to run away. This was a very terrible thing to poor travellers, as you may suppose, especially when they chanced to be sick, or feeble, or lame, or old. Such persons (if they once knew how badly these unkind people, and their unkind children and curs, were in the habit of behaving) would go miles and miles out of their way, rather than try to pass through the village again.

What made the matter seem worse, if possible, was, that when rich persons came in their chariots, or riding on beautiful horses, with their servants in rich liveries attending on them, nobody could be more civil and obsequious than the inhabitants of the village. They would take off their hats, and make the humblest bows you ever saw. If the children were rude, they were pretty certain to get their ears boxed; and as for the dogs, if a single cur in the pack presumed to yelp, his master instantly beat him with a club, and tied him up without any supper. This would have been all very well; only it proved that the villagers cared much about the money that a stranger had in his pocket, and nothing whatever for the human soul, which lives equally in the beggar and the prince.

So now you can understand why old Philemon spoke so sorrowfully, when he heard the shouts of the children and the barking of the dogs, at the farther extremity of the village-street. There was a confused din, which lasted a good while, and seemed to pass quite through the breadth of the valley.

"I never heard the dogs so loud!" observed the good old man.

"Nor the children so rude!" answered his good old wife.

They sat shaking their heads, one to another, while the noise came nearer and nearer; until, at the foot of the little eminence on which their cottage stood, they saw two travellers approaching on foot. Close behind them came the fierce dogs, snarling at their very heels. A little farther off, ran a crowd of children, who sent up shrill cries, and flung stones at the two strangers, with all their might. Once or twice, the younger of the two men (he was a slender and very active figure) turned about, and drove back the dogs with a staff which he carried in his hand. His companion, who was a very tall person, walked calmly along, as if disdaining to notice either the naughty children, or the pack of curs, whose manners the children seemed to imitate.

Both of the travellers were very humbly clad, and looked as if they might not have money enough in their pockets to pay for a night's lodging. And this, I am afraid, was the reason why the villagers had allowed their children and dogs to treat them so rudely.

"Come, wife," said Philemon to Baucis, "let us go and meet these poor people! No doubt, they feel almost too heavy-hearted to climb the hill."

"Go you and meet them," answered Baucis, "while I make haste within doors, and see whether we can get them anything for supper. A comfortable bowl of bread and milk would do wonders towards raising their spirits."

Accordingly, she hastened into the cottage. Philemon, on his part, went forward, and extended his hand with so hospitable an aspect that there was no need of saying, what nevertheless he did say, in the heartiest tone imaginable:—

"Welcome, strangers, welcome!"

"Thank you!" replied the younger of the two, in a lively kind of way, notwithstanding his weariness and trouble. "This is quite another greeting than we have met with yonder, in the village. Pray, why do you live in such a bad neighborhood?"

"Ah," observed old Philemon, with a quiet and benign smile, "Providence put me here, I hope, among other reasons, in order that I may make you what amends I can for the inhospitality of my neighbors!"

"Well said, old father!" cried the traveller, laughing; "and, if the truth must be told, my companion and myself need some amends. Those children (the little rascals!) have bespattered us finely with their mud-balls; and one of the curs has torn my cloak, which was ragged enough already. But I took him across the muzzle with my staff; and I think you may have heard him yelp, even thus far off!"

Philemon was glad to see him in such good spirits; nor, indeed, would you have fancied, by the traveller's look and manner, that he was weary with a long day's journey, besides being disheartened by rough treatment at the end of it. He was dressed in rather an odd way, with a sort of cap on his head, the brim of which stuck out over both ears. Though it was a summer evening, he wore a cloak, which he kept wrapt closely about him, perhaps because his under garments were shabby. Philemon perceived, too, that he had on a singular pair of shoes; but, as it was now growing dusk, and as the old man's eyesight was none of the sharpest, he could not precisely tell in what the strangeness consisted. One thing, certainly, seemed queer. The traveller was so wonderfully light and active, that it appeared as if his feet sometimes rose from the ground of their own accord, or could only be kept down by an effort.

"I used to be light-footed in my youth," said Philemon to the traveller. "But I always found my feet grow heavier, towards nightfall."

"There is nothing like a good staff to help one along," answered the stranger; "and I happen to have an excellent one, as you see!"

This staff, in fact, was the oddest-looking staff, that Philemon had ever beheld. It was made of olive-wood, and had something like a little pair of wings near the top. Two snakes, carved in the wood, were represented as twining themselves about the staff, and were so very skilfully executed, that old Philemon (whose eyes, you know, were getting rather dim) almost thought them alive, and that he could see them wriggling and twisting.

"A curious piece of work, sure enough!" said he. "A staff with wings! It would be an excellent kind of stick for a little boy to ride astride of!"

By this time, Philemon and his two guests had reached the cottage-door.

"Friends," said the old man, "sit down and rest yourselves here on this bench. My good wife Baucis has gone to see what you can have for supper. We are poor folks; but you shall be welcome to whatever we have in the cupboard."

The younger stranger threw himself carelessly on the

bench, letting his staff fall as he did so. And here happened something rather marvellous, though trifling enough, too. The staff seemed to get up from the ground of its own ac- cord, and, spreading its little pair of wings, it half hopt, half flew, and leaned itself against the wall of the cottage. There it stood quite still, except that the snakes continued to wriggle. But, in my private opinion, old Philemon's eyesight had been playing him tricks again.

Before he could ask any questions, the elder stranger drew his attention from the wonderful staff, by speaking to him.

"Was there not," asked the stranger, in a remarkably deep tone of voice, "a lake, in very ancient times, covering the spot where now stands yonder village?"

"Not in my day, friend," answered Philemon; "and yet I am an old man, as you see. There were always the fields and meadows, just as they are now, and the old trees, and the little stream murmuring through the midst of the valley. My father, nor his father before him, ever saw it otherwise, so far as I know; and doubtless it will still be the same, when old Philemon shall be gone and forgotten!"

"That is more than can be safely foretold," observed the stranger; and there was something very stern in his deep voice. He shook his head, too, so that his dark and heavy curls were shaken with the movement. "Since the inhabitants of yonder village have forgotten the affections and sympathies of their nature, it were better that the lake should be rippling over their dwellings again!"

The traveller looked so stern, that Philemon was really al- most frightened; the more so, that, at his frown, the twilight seemed suddenly to grow darker, and that, when he shook his head, there was a roll as of thunder in the air.

But, in a moment afterwards, the stranger's face became so kindly and mild, that the old man quite forgot his terror. Nevertheless, he could not help feeling that this elder traveller must be no ordinary personage, although he happened now to be attired so humbly, and to be journeying on foot. Not that Philemon fancied him a prince in disguise, or any char- acter of that sort, but rather some exceedingly wise man, who went about the world in this poor garb, despising wealth and all worldly objects, and seeking everywhere to add a mite to his wisdom. This idea appeared the more probable, because, when Philemon raised his eyes to the stranger's face, he seemed to see more thought there, in one look, than he could have studied out, in a lifetime.

While Baucis was getting the supper, the travellers both began to talk very sociably with Philemon. The younger, indeed, was extremely loquacious, and made such shrewd and witty remarks, that the good old man continually burst out a-laughing, and pronounced him the merriest fellow whom he had seen for many a day.

"Pray, my young friend," said he, as they grew familiar together, "what may I call your name?"

"Why, I am very nimble, as you see," answered the traveller. "So, if you call me Quicksilver, the name will fit tolerably well!"

"Quicksilver? Quicksilver!" repeated Philemon, looking in the traveller's face to see if he were making fun of him. "It is a very odd name! And your companion there? Has he as strange a one?"

"You must ask the thunder to tell it you!" replied Quicksilver, putting on a mysterious look. "No other voice is loud enough!"

This remark, whether it were serious, or in jest, might have caused Philemon to conceive a very great awe of the elder stranger, if, on venturing to gaze at him, he had not beheld so much beneficence in his visage. But, undoubtedly, here was the grandest figure that ever sate so humbly beside a cottage-door. When the stranger conversed, it was with gravity, and in such a way that Philemon felt irresistibly moved to tell him everything which he had most at heart. This is always the feeling that people have, when they meet with any one wise enough to comprehend all their good and evil, and to despise not a tittle of it.

But Philemon, simple and kind-hearted old man that he was! had not many secrets to disclose. He talked, however, quite garrulously, about the events of his past life, in the whole course of which, he had never been a score of miles from this very spot. His wife Baucis and himself had dwelt in the cottage, from their youth upward, earning their bread by honest labor, always poor, but still contented. He told what excellent butter and cheese Baucis made, and how nice were the vegetables which he raised in his garden. He said, too, that, because they loved one another so very much, it was the wish of both that Death might not separate them, but that they should die, as they had lived, together.

As the stranger listened, a smile beamed over his countenance, and made its expression as sweet as it was grand.

"You are a good old man," said he to Philemon, "and you have a good old wife to be your help-meet. It is fit that your wish be granted!"

And it seemed to Philemon, just then, as if the sunset clouds threw up a bright flush from the west, and kindled a sudden light in the sky.

Baucis had now got supper ready, and coming to the door, began to make apologies for the poor fare which she was forced to set before her guests.

"Had we known you were coming," said she, "my good man and myself would have gone without a morsel, rather than you should lack a better supper. But I took the most part of to-day's milk to make cheese; and our last loaf is already half-eaten. Ah, me! I never feel the sorrow of being poor, save when a poor traveller knocks at our door!"

"All will be very well!—do not trouble yourself, my good dame," replied the elder stranger, kindly. "An honest, hearty welcome to a guest works miracles with the fare, and is capable of turning the coarsest food to nectar and ambrosia."

"A welcome you shall have," cried Baucis; "and likewise a little honey that we happen to have left, and a bunch of purple grapes besides!"

"Why, Mother Baucis, it is a feast," exclaimed Quicksilver laughing, "an absolute feast; and you shall see how bravely I will play my part at it! I think I never felt hungrier in my life."

"Mercy on us!" whispered Baucis to her husband. "If the young man has such a terrible appetite, I am afraid there will not be half enough supper!"

They all went into the cottage.

And now, my little auditors, shall I tell you something that will make you open your eyes very wide? It is really one of the oddest circumstances in the whole story. Quicksilver's staff, you recollect, had set itself up against the wall of the cottage. Well; when its master entered the door, leaving this wonderful staff behind, what should it do, but immediately spread its little wings, and go hopping and fluttering up the door-steps! Tap, tap, went the staff, on the kitchen-floor; nor did it rest, until it had stood itself on end, with the greatest gravity and decorum, beside Quicksilver's chair. Old Philemon, however, as well as his wife, was so taken up in attending to their guests, that no notice was given to what the staff had been about.

As Baucis had said, there was but a scanty supper for two hungry travellers. In the middle of the table was the remnant of a brown loaf, with a piece of cheese on one side of it, and a dish of honeycomb on the other. There was a pretty good bunch of grapes for each of the guests. A moderately sized earthen pitcher, nearly full of milk, stood at a corner of the board; and when Baucis had filled two bowls, and set them before the strangers, only a little milk remained in the bottom of the pitcher. Alas! it is a very sad business, when a bountiful heart finds itself pinched and squeezed among narrow circumstances. Poor Baucis kept wishing that she might starve, for a week to come, if it were possible, by so doing, to provide these hungry folks a more plentiful supper.

And since the supper was so exceedingly small, she could not help wishing that their appetites had not been quite so large. Why, at their very first sitting down, the travellers both drank off all the milk in their two bowls, at a draught!

"A little more milk, kind Mother Baucis, if you please!" said Quicksilver. "The day has been hot, and I am very much athirst."

"Now, my dear people," answered Baucis, in great confusion, "I am so sorry and ashamed! But the truth is, there is hardly a drop more milk in the pitcher. Oh, husband, husband, why didn't we go without our supper!"

"Why, it appears to me," cried Quicksilver, starting up from table and taking the pitcher by the handle, "it really appears to me that matters are not quite so bad as you represent them. Here is certainly more milk in the pitcher!"

So saying, and to the vast astonishment of Baucis, he proceeded to fill not only his own bowl, but his companion's likewise, from the pitcher that was supposed to be almost empty. The good woman could scarcely believe her eyes. She had certainly poured out nearly all the milk, and had peeped in, afterwards, and seen the bottom of the pitcher, as she set it down upon the table.

"But I am old," thought Baucis to herself, "and apt to be forgetful. I suppose I must have made a mistake. At all events, the pitcher cannot help being empty, now, after filling the bowls twice over!"

"What excellent milk!" observed Quicksilver, after quaffing the contents of the second bowl. "Excuse me, my kind hostess, but I must really ask you for a little more!"

Now Baucis had seen, as plainly as she could see anything, that Quicksilver had turned the pitcher upside down, and consequently had poured out every drop of milk, in filling the last bowl. Of course, there could not possibly be any left. However, in order to let him know precisely how the case was, she lifted the pitcher, and made a gesture as if pouring milk into Quicksilver's bowl, but without the remotest idea that any milk would stream forth. What was her surprise, therefore, when such an abundant cascade fell bubbling into the bowl, that it was immediately filled to the brim, and overflowed upon the table! The two snakes that were twisted about Quicksilver's staff (but neither Baucis nor Philemon happened to observe this circumstance) stretched out their heads and began to lap up the spilt milk.

And then what a delicious fragrance the milk had! It seemed as if Philemon's only cow must have pastured, that day, on the richest herbage that could be found anywhere in the world. I only wish that each of you, my beloved little souls, could have a bowl of such nice milk, at supper-time!

"And now a slice of your brown loaf, Mother Baucis," said Quicksilver; "and a little of that honey!"

Baucis cut him a slice, accordingly; and though the loaf, when she and her husband ate of it, had been rather too dry and crusty to be palatable, it was now as light and moist as if but a few hours out of the oven. Tasting a crumb, which had fallen on the table, she found it more delicious than bread ever was before, and could hardly believe that it was a loaf of her own kneading and baking. Yet, what other loaf could it possibly be?

But, oh, the honey! I may just as well let it alone, without trying to describe how exquisitely it smelt and looked. Its color was that of the purest and most transparent gold; and it had the odor of a thousand flowers, but of such flowers as never grew in an earthly garden, and, to seek which, the bees must have flown high above the clouds. The wonder is, that, after alighting on a flower-bed of so delicious fragrance and immortal bloom, they should have been content to fly down again to their hive in Philemon's garden. Never was such honey tasted, seen, or smelt. The perfume floated around the kitchen, and made it so delightful, that, had you closed your eyes, you would instantly have forgotten the low ceiling and smoky walls, and have fancied yourself in an arbor, with celestial honeysuckles creeping over it.

Although good Mother Baucis was a simple old dame, she could not but think that there was something rather out of the common way, in all that had been going on. So, after helping the guests to bread and honey, and laying a bunch of grapes by each of their plates, she sat down by Philemon, and told him what she had seen, in a whisper.

"Did you ever hear the like?" asked she.

"No; I never did," answered Philemon with a smile. "And I rather think, my dear old wife, you have been walking about in a sort of a dream! If I had poured out the milk, I should have seen through the business, at once. There happened to be a little more in the pitcher than you thought—that is all!"

"Ah, husband," said Baucis, "say what you will, these are very uncommon people!"

"Well, well," replied Philemon, still smiling, "perhaps they are. They certainly do look as if they had seen better days; and I am heartily glad to see them making so comfortable a supper."

Each of the guests had now taken his bunch of grapes upon his plate. Baucis (who rubbed her eyes, in order to see the more clearly) was of opinion that the clusters had grown larger and richer, and that each separate grape seemed to be on the point of bursting with ripe juice. It was entirely a mystery to her, how such grapes could ever have been produced from the old, stunted vine that clambered against the cottage-wall.

"Very admirable grapes these!" observed Quicksilver, as he swallowed one after another, without apparently diminishing his cluster. "Pray, my good host, whence did you gather them?"

"From my own vine," answered Philemon. "You may see one of its branches twisting across the window, yonder. But, wife and I have never thought the grapes very fine ones."

"I never tasted better," said the guest. "Another cup of this delicious milk, if you please; and I shall then have supt better than a prince!"

This time, old Philemon bestirred himself and took up the pitcher; for he was curious to discover whether there was any reality in the marvels which Baucis had whispered to him. He knew that his good old wife was incapable of falsehood, and that she was seldom mistaken in what she supposed to be true; but this was so very singular a case, that he wanted to see into it with his own eyes. On taking up the pitcher, therefore, he slily peeped into it, and was fully satisfied that it contained not so much as a single drop. All at once, however, he beheld a little white fountain, which gushed up from the bottom of the pitcher, and speedily filled it to the brim with foaming and deliciously fragrant milk. It was lucky that Philemon, in his surprise, did not drop the miraculous pitcher from his hand.

"Who are ye, wonder-working strangers?" cried he, even more bewildered than his wife had been.

"Your guests, my good Philemon, and your friends!" replied the elder traveller, in his mild, deep voice, that had something at once sweet and awe-inspiring in it. "Give me likewise a cup of the milk; and may your pitcher never be empty for kind Baucis and yourself, any more than for the needy wayfarer!"

The supper being now over, the strangers requested to be shown to their place of repose. The old people would gladly have talked with them a little longer, and have expressed the wonder which they felt, and their delight at finding the poor and meagre supper prove so much better and more abundant

than they hoped. But the elder traveller had inspired them
with such reverence, that they dared not ask him any questions. And when Philemon drew Quicksilver aside, and inquired how, under the sun, a fountain of milk could have got
into an old earthen pitcher, this latter personage pointed to
his staff.

"There is the whole mystery of the affair," quoth Quicksilver; "and if you can make it out, I'll thank you to let me
know! I can't tell what to make of my staff. It is always playing such odd tricks as this;—sometimes getting me a supper,
and, quite as often, stealing it away. If I had any faith in such
nonsense, I should say the stick was bewitched!"

He said no more, but looked so slily in their faces, that
they rather fancied he was laughing at them. The magic staff
went hopping at his heels, as Quicksilver quitted the room.
When left alone, the good old couple spent some little time
in conversation about the events of the evening, and then lay
down on the floor, and fell fast asleep. They had given up
their sleeping-room to the guests, and had no other bed for
themselves, save these planks, which I wish had been as soft
as their own hearts.

The old man and his wife were stirring, betimes, in the
morning, and the strangers likewise arose with the sun, and
made their preparations to depart. Philemon hospitably entreated them to remain a little longer, until Baucis could milk
the cow, and bake a cake upon the hearth, and perhaps find
them a few fresh eggs, for breakfast. The guests, however,
seemed to think it better to accomplish a good part of their
journey, before the heat of the day should come on. They
therefore persisted in setting out immediately, but asked Philemon and Baucis to walk forth with them, a short distance,
and show them the road which they were to take.

So they all four issued from the cottage, chatting together
like old friends. It was very remarkable, indeed, how familiar
the old couple insensibly grew with the elder traveller, and
how their good and simple spirits melted into his, even as
two drops of water would melt into the illimitable ocean.
And as for Quicksilver, with his keen, quick, laughing wits,
he appeared to discover every little thought that but peeped
into their minds, before they suspected it themselves. They

sometimes wished, it is true, that he had not been quite so quick-witted, and also that he would fling away his staff, which looked so mysteriously mischievous, with the snakes always writing about it. But then, again, Quicksilver showed himself so very good-humored, that they would have been rejoiced to keep him in their cottage, staff, snakes, and all, every day, and the whole day long.

"Ah me! Well-a-day!" exclaimed Philemon, when they had walked a little way from their door. "If our neighbors only knew what a blessed thing it is to show hospitality to strangers, they would tie up all their dogs, and never allow their children to fling another stone!"

"It is a sin and shame for them to behave so!—that it is!" cried good old Baucis, vehemently. "And I mean to go, this very day, and tell some of them what naughty people they are!"

"I fear," remarked Quicksilver, slily smiling, "that you will find none of them at home!"

The elder traveller's brow, just then, assumed such a grave, stern, and awful grandeur, yet serene withal, that neither Baucis nor Philemon dared to speak a word. They gazed reverently into his face, as if they had been gazing at the sky.

"When men do not feel towards the humblest stranger as if he were a brother," said the traveller, in tones so deep that they sounded like those of an organ, "they are unworthy to exist on earth, which was created as the abode of a great human brotherhood!"

"And, by-the-by, my dear old people," cried Quicksilver, with the liveliest look of fun and mischief in his eyes, "where is this same village that you talk about? On which side of us does it lie? Methinks I do not see it, hereabouts!"

Philemon and his wife turned towards the valley, where, at sunset, only the day before, they had seen the meadows, the houses, the gardens, the clumps of trees, the wide, green-margined street, with children playing in it, and all the tokens of business, enjoyment, and prosperity. But what was their astonishment! There was no longer any appearance of a village! Even the fertile vale, in the hollow of which it lay, had ceased to have existence. In its stead, they beheld the broad, blue surface of a lake, which filled the great basin of the valley, from brim to brim, and reflected the surrounding hills in its bosom; with as tranquil an image as if it had been there ever since the creation of the world. For an instant, the lake remained perfectly smooth. Then, a little breeze sprang up, and caused the water to dance, glitter, and sparkle in the early sunbeams, and to dash, with a pleasant rippling murmur, against the hither shore.

The lake seemed so strangely familiar, that the old couple were greatly perplexed, and felt as if they could only have been dreaming about a village having lain there. But, the next moment, they remembered the vanished dwellings, and the faces and characters of the inhabitants, far too distinctly for a dream. The village had been there, yesterday, and now was gone!

"Alas," cried these kind-hearted old people, "what has become of our poor neighbors!"

"They exist no longer as men and women," said the elder traveller, in his grand and deep voice, while a roll of thunder seemed to echo it, at a distance. "There was neither use nor beauty in such a life as theirs; for they never softened or sweetened the hard lot of mortality by the exercise of kindly affections, between man and man. They retained no image of the better life, in their bosoms. Therefore, the lake, that was of old, has spread itself forth again, to reflect the sky!"

"And as for those foolish people," said Quicksilver, with his mischievous smile, "they are all transformed to fishes. There needed but little change; for they were already a scaly set of rascals, and the coldest-blooded beings in existence. So, kind Mother Baucis, whenever you or your husband have an appetite for a dish of broiled trout, he can throw in a line, and pull out half-a-dozen of your old neighbors!"

"Ah," cried Baucis, shuddering, "I would not, for the world, put one of them on the gridiron!"

"No," added Philemon, making a wry face, "we could never relish them!"

"As for you, good Philemon," continued the elder traveller,—"and you, kind Baucis—you, with your scanty means, have mingled so much heart-felt hospitality with your entertainment of the homeless stranger, that the milk became an inexhaustible fount of nectar, and the brown loaf and the

honey were ambrosia. Thus, the divinities have feasted at
your board, off the same viands that supply their banquets,
on Olympus. You have done well, my dear old friends! Wherefore, request whatever favor you have most at heart, and it is
granted!"

Philemon and Baucis looked at one another; and then—I
know not which of the two it was, who spoke—but that one
uttered the desire of both their hearts.

"Let us live together, while we live, and leave the world at
the same instant, when we die! For we have always loved one
another!"

"Be it so!" replied the stranger, with majestic kindness.
"Now, look towards your cottage!"

They did so. But what was their surprise, on beholding a
tall edifice of white marble, with a wide-open portal, occupying the spot where their humble residence had so lately stood!

"There is your home!" said the stranger, beneficently smiling on them both. "Exercise your hospitality in yonder palace,
as freely as in the poor hovel to which you welcomed us, last
evening!"

The old folks fell on their knees, to thank him: but, behold!
neither he nor Quicksilver was there.

So Philemon and Baucis took up their residence in the marble palace, and spent their time, with vast satisfaction to
themselves, in making everybody jolly and comfortable, who
happened to pass that way. The milk-pitcher, I must not forget to say, retained its marvellous quality of being never
empty, when it was desirable to have it full. Whenever an
honest, good-humored, and free-hearted guest took a draught
from this pitcher, he invariably found it the sweetest and
most invigorating fluid, that ever ran down his throat. But if
a cross and disagreeable curmudgeon happened to sip, he was
pretty certain to twist his visage into a hard knot, and pronounce it a pitcher of sour milk!

Thus, the old couple lived in their palace, a great, great
while, and grew older, and older, and very old indeed. At
length, however, there came a summer-morning, when Philemon and Baucis failed to make their appearance, as on other
mornings, with one hospitable smile over-spreading both
their pleasant faces, to invite the guests of over-night to

breakfast. The guests searched everywhere, from top to bottom of the spacious palace, and all to no purpose. But, after a great deal of perplexity, they espied, in front of the portal, two venerable trees, which nobody could remember to have seen there, the day before. Yet there they stood, with their roots fastened deep into the soil, and a huge breadth of foliage over-shadowing the whole front of the edifice. One was an oak, and the other a linden-tree. Their boughs—it was strange and beautiful to see—were intertwined together, and embraced one another, so that each tree seemed to live in the other tree's bosom, much more than in its own.

While the guests were marvelling how these trees, that must have required at least a century to grow, could have come to be so tall and venerable in a single night, a breeze sprang up and set their intermingled boughs a-stir. And then there was a deep, broad murmur in the air, as if the two mysterious trees were speaking.

"I am old Philemon!" murmured the oak.

"I am old Baucis!" murmured the linden-tree.

But, as the breeze grew stronger, the trees both spoke at once—"Philemon! Baucis! Baucis! Philemon!"—as if one were both, and both were one, and talking together in the depths of their mutual heart. It was plain enough to perceive, that the good old couple had renewed their age; and were now to spend a quiet and delightful hundred years or so, Philemon as an oak, and Baucis as a linden-tree. And, Oh, what a hospitable shade did they fling around them! Whenever a wayfarer paused beneath it, he heard a pleasant whisper of the leaves above his head, and wondered how the sound should so much resemble words like these:—

"Welcome, welcome, dear traveller, welcome!"

And some kind soul, that knew what would have pleased old Baucis and old Philemon best, built a circular seat around both their trunks, where, for a great while afterwards, the weary, and the hungry, and the thirsty, used to repose themselves, and quaff milk abundantly out of the miraculous pitcher.

And I wish, for all our sakes, that we had the pitcher here, now!

The Hill-Side

"How much did the pitcher hold?" asked Sweet Fern.

"It did not hold quite a quart," answered the student; "but you might keep pouring milk out of it, till you should fill a hogshead, if you pleased. The truth is, it would run on forever, and not be dry even at mid-summer—which is more than can be said of yonder rill, that goes babbling down the hill-side."

"And what has become of the pitcher now?" inquired the little boy.

"It was broken, I am sorry to say, about twenty-five thousand years ago," replied Cousin Eustace. "The people mended it, as well as they could; but, though it would hold milk pretty well, it was never afterwards known to fill itself of its own accord. So, you see, it was no better than any other cracked earthen pitcher."

"What a pity!" cried all the children at once.

The respectable dog Ben had accompanied the party, as did likewise a half-grown Newfoundland puppy, who went by the name of Bruin, because he was just as black as a bear. Ben, being elderly, and of very circumspect habits, was respectfully requested by Cousin Eustace to stay behind, with the four little children, in order to keep them out of mischief. As for black Bruin, who was himself nothing but a child, the student thought it best to take him along, lest, in his rude play with the other children, he should trip them up, and send them rolling and tumbling down the hill. Advising Cowslip, Sweet Fern, Dandelion, and Squash Blossom, to sit pretty still, in the spot where he left them, the student, with Primrose and the elder children, began to ascend, and were soon out of sight among the trees.

Bald Summit

INTRODUCTORY TO "THE CHIMÆRA"

UPWARD, along the steep and wooded hill-side, went Eustace Bright and his companions. The trees were not yet in full leaf, but had budded forth sufficiently to throw an airy shadow, while the sunshine filled them with green light. There were moss-grown rocks, half-hidden among the old, brown, fallen leaves; there were rotten tree-trunks, lying at full length where they had long ago fallen; there were decayed boughs, that had been shaken down by the wintry gales, and were scattered everywhere about. But still, though these things looked so aged, the aspect of the wood was that of the newest life; for, whichever way you turned your eyes, something fresh and green was springing forth, so as to be ready for the summer.

At last, the young people reached the upper verge of the wood, and found themselves almost at the summit of the hill. It was not a peak, nor a great round ball, but a pretty wide plain, or table-land, with a house and barn upon it, at some distance. That house was the home of a solitary family; and oftentimes the clouds, whence fell the rain, and whence the snow-storm drifted down into the valley, hung lower than this bleak and lonely dwelling-place.

On the highest point of the hill was a heap of stones, in the centre of which was stuck a long pole, with a little flag fluttering at the end of it. Eustace led the children thither, and bade them look around, and see how large a tract of our beautiful world they could take in at a glance. And their eyes grew wider as they looked.

Monument Mountain, to the southward, was still in the centre of the scene, but seemed to have sunk and subsided; so that it was now but an undistinguished member of a large family of hills. Beyond it, the Taconic range looked higher and bulkier than before. Our pretty lake was seen, with all its little bays and inlets; and not that alone, but two or three new lakes were opening their blue eyes to the sun. Several white villages, each with its steeple, were scattered about in the distance. There were so many farm-houses, with their acres of woodland, pasture, mowing-fields, and tillage, that the children could hardly make room in their minds to receive all these different objects. There, too, was Tanglewood, which they had hitherto thought such an important apex of the world. It now occupied so small a space, that they gazed far beyond it, and on either side, and searched a good while with all their eyes, before discovering whereabout it stood.

White fleecy clouds were hanging in the air, and threw the dark spots of their shadow here and there over the landscape. But, by-and-by, the sunshine was where the shadow had been, and the shadow was somewhere else.

Far to the westward was a range of blue mountains, which Eustace Bright told the children were the Catskills. Among those misty hills, he said, was a spot where some old Dutchmen were playing an everlasting game of nine-pins, and where an idle fellow, whose name was Rip Van Winkle, had fallen asleep, and slept twenty years at a stretch. The children eagerly besought Eustace to tell them all about this wonderful affair. But the student replied, that the story had been told once already, and better than it ever could be told again, and that nobody would have a right to alter a word of it, until it should have grown as old as "The Gorgon's Head," and "The Three Golden Apples," and the rest of those miraculous legends.

"At least," said Periwinkle, "while we rest ourselves here, and are looking about us, you can tell us another of your own stories."

"Yes, Cousin Eustace," cried Primrose, "I advise you to tell us a story here. Take some lofty subject or other, and see if your imagination will not come up to it. Perhaps the mountain air may make you poetical, for once. And no matter how strange and wonderful the story may be. Now that we are up among the clouds, we can believe anything!"

"Can you believe," asked Eustace, "that there was once a winged horse?"

"Yes," said saucy Primrose; "but I am afraid you will never be able to catch him!"

"For that matter, Primrose," rejoined the student, "I might possibly catch Pegasus, and get upon his back, too, as well as a dozen other fellows that I know of. At any rate, here is a story about him; and, of all places in the world, it ought certainly to be told upon a mountain-top!"

So, sitting on the pile of stones, while the children clustered themselves at its base, Eustace fixed his eyes on a white cloud that was sailing by, and began as follows.

The Chimæra

O NCE, in the old, old times (for all the strange things, which I tell you about, happened long before anybody can remember) a fountain gushed out of a hill-side, in the marvellous land of Greece. And, for aught I know, after so many thousand years, it is still gushing out of the very self-same spot. At any rate, there was the pleasant fountain, well-ing freshly forth and sparkling adown the hill-side, in the golden sunset, when a handsome young man, named Beller-ophon, drew near its margin. In his hand he held a bridle, studded with brilliant gems, and adorned with a golden bit. Seeing an old man, and another of middle age, and a little boy, near the fountain, and likewise a maiden, who was dip-ping up some of the water in a pitcher, he paused, and begged that he might refresh himself with a draught.

"This is very delicious water," he said to the maiden, as he rinsed and filled her pitcher, after drinking out of it. "Will you be kind enough to tell me whether the fountain has any name?"

"Yes; it is called the Fountain of Pirene," answered the maiden; and then she added, "My grandmother has told me that this clear fountain was once a beautiful woman; and when her son was killed by the arrows of the huntress Diana, she melted all away into tears. And so the water, which you find so cool and sweet, is the sorrow of that poor mother's heart!"

"I should not have dreamed," observed the young stranger, "that so clear a well-spring, with its gush and gurgle, and its cheery dance out of the shade into the sunlight, had so much as one tear-drop in its bosom! And this, then, is Pirene! I thank you, pretty maiden, for telling me its name. I have come from a far-away country to find this very spot."

A middle-aged country fellow (he had driven his cow to drink out of the spring) stared hard at young Bellerophon, and at the handsome bridle which he carried in his hand.

"The water-courses must be getting low, friend, in your part of the world," remarked he, "if you come so far only to find the Fountain of Pirene. But, pray, have you lost a horse? I see you carry the bridle in your hand; and a very pretty one it is, with that double row of bright stones upon it! If the horse was as fine as the bridle, you are much to be pitied for losing him."

"I have lost no horse," said Bellerophon, with a smile. "But I happen to be seeking a very famous one, which, as wise people have informed me, must be found hereabouts, if anywhere. Do you know whether the winged horse Pegasus still haunts the Fountain of Pirene, as he used to do, in your forefather's days?"

But then the country fellow laughed.

Some of you, my little friends, have probably heard, that this Pegasus was a snow-white steed, with beautiful silvery wings, who spent most of his time on the summit of Mount Helicon. He was as wild, and as swift, and as buoyant, in his flight through the air, as any eagle that ever soared into the clouds. There was nothing else like him in the world. He had no mate; he had never been backed or bridled by a master; and, for many a long year, he led a solitary and a happy life.

Oh, how fine a thing it is to be a winged horse! Sleeping at night, as he did, on a lofty mountain-top, and passing the greater part of the day in the air, Pegasus seemed hardly to be a creature of the earth. Whenever he was seen, up very high above people's heads, with the sunshine on his silvery wings, you would have thought that he belonged to the sky, and that, skimming a little too low, he had got astray among our mists and vapors, and was seeking his way back again. It was very pretty to behold him plunge into the fleecy bosom of a bright cloud, and be lost in it, for a moment or two, and then break forth from the other side. Or, in a sullen rain-storm, when there was a gray pavement of clouds over the whole sky, it would sometimes happen that the winged horse descended right through it, and the glad light of the upper region would gleam after him. In another instant, it is true, both Pegasus and the pleasant light would be gone away together. But any one, that was fortunate enough to see this wondrous spectacle, felt cheerful the whole day afterwards, and as much longer as the storm lasted.

In the summer-time, and in the beautifullest of weather,

Pegasus often alighted on the solid earth, and, closing his silvery wings, would gallop over hill and dale for pastime, as fleetly as the wind. Oftener than in any other place, he had been seen near the Fountain of Pirene, drinking the delicious water, or rolling himself upon the soft grass of the margin. Sometimes, too, (but Pegasus was very dainty in his food,) he would crop a few of the clover-blossoms that happened to be sweetest.

To the Fountain of Pirene, therefore, people's great-grandfathers had been in the habit of going (as long as they were youthful, and retained their faith in winged horses) in hopes of getting a glimpse at the beautiful Pegasus. But, of late years, he had been very seldom seen. Indeed, there were many of the country folks, dwelling within half an hour's walk of the fountain, who had never beheld Pegasus, and did not believe that there was any such creature in existence. The country fellow, to whom Bellerophon was speaking, chanced to be one of those incredulous persons.

And that was the reason why he laughed.

"Pegasus, indeed!" cried he, turning up his nose, as high as such a flat nose could be turned up. "Pegasus, indeed! A winged horse, truly! Why, friend, are you in your senses? Of what use would wings be to a horse? Could he drag the plough so well, think you? To be sure, there might be a little saving in the expense of shoes; but then how would a man like to see his horse flying out of the stable-window?—yes; or whisking him up above the clouds, when he only wanted to ride to mill? No, no! I don't believe in Pegasus. There never was such a ridiculous kind of a horse-fowl made!"

"I have some reason to think otherwise," said Bellerophon, quietly.

And then he turned to an old, gray man, who was leaning on a staff and listening very attentively, with his head stretched forward and one hand at his ear, because, for the last twenty years, he had been getting rather deaf.

"And what say you, venerable Sir?" inquired he. "In your younger days, I should imagine, you must frequently have seen the winged steed!"

"Ah, young stranger, my memory is very poor!" said the aged man. "When I was a lad, if I remember rightly, I used to believe there was such a horse, and so did everybody else. But, now-a-days, I hardly know what to think, and very seldom think about the winged horse at all. If I ever saw the creature, it was a long, long while ago; and, to tell you the truth, I doubt whether I ever did see him. One day, to be sure, when I was quite a youth, I remember seeing some hoof-tramps roundabout the brink of the fountain. Pegasus might have made those hoof-marks; and so might some other horse!"

"And have you never seen him, my fair maiden?" asked Bellerophon of the girl, who stood with the pitcher on her head, while this talk went on. "You certainly could see Pegasus, if anybody can, for your eyes are very bright!"

"Once I thought I saw him," replied the maiden, with a smile and a blush. "It was either Pegasus, or a large white bird, a very great way up in the air. And one other time, as I was coming to the fountain with my pitcher, I heard a neigh. Oh, such a brisk and melodious neigh as that was! My very heart leaped with delight at the sound! But it startled me, nevertheless; so that I ran home without filling my pitcher."

"That was truly a pity!" said Bellerophon.

And he turned to the child, whom I mentioned at the beginning of the story, and who was gazing at him, as children are apt to gaze at strangers, with his rosy mouth wide open.

"Well, my little fellow," cried Bellerophon, playfully pulling one of his curls, "I suppose you have often seen the winged horse!"

"That I have!" answered the child, very readily. "I saw him yesterday, and many times before!"

"You are a fine little man!" said Bellerophon, drawing the child closer to him. "Come; tell me all about it!"

"Why," replied the child, "I often come here to sail little boats in the fountain, and to gather pretty pebbles out of its basin. And sometimes, when I look down into the water, I see the image of the winged horse, in the picture of the sky that is there. I wish he would come down, and take me on his back, and let me ride him up to the moon! But, if I so much as stir to look at him, he flies far away out of sight!"

And Bellerophon put his faith in the child, who had seen the image of Pegasus in the water, and in the maiden, who had heard him neigh so melodiously, rather than in the middle-aged clown who believed only in cart-horses, or in the old man, who had forgotten the beautiful things of his youth.

Therefore, he haunted about the Fountain of Pirene, for a great many days afterwards. He kept continually on the watch, looking upward at the sky, or else down into the water, hoping forever that he should see either the reflected image of the winged horse, or the marvellous reality. He held the bridle, with its bright gems and golden bit, always ready in his hand. The rustic people, who dwelt in the neighborhood, and drove their cattle to the fountain to drink, would often laugh at poor Bellerophon, and sometimes take him pretty severely to task. They told him that an able-bodied young man, like himself, ought to have better business than to be wasting his time in such an idle pursuit. They offered to sell him a horse, if he wanted one; and when Bellerophon declined the purchase, they tried to drive a bargain with him for his fine bridle.

Even the country boys thought him so very foolish, that they used to have a great deal of sport about him, and were rude enough not to care a fig, although Bellerophon saw and heard it. One little urchin, for example, would play Pegasus, and cut the oddest imaginable capers, by way of flying; while one of his schoolfellows would scamper after him, holding forth a twist of bulrushes, which was intended to represent Bellerophon's ornamented bridle. But the gentle child, who had seen the picture of Pegasus in the water, comforted the young stranger more than all the naughty boys could torment him. The dear little fellow, in his play-hours, often sat down beside him, and, without speaking a word, would look down into the fountain and up towards the sky, with so innocent a faith that Bellerophon could not help feeling encouraged.

Now, you will perhaps wish to be told why it was, that Bellerophon had undertaken to catch the winged horse. And we shall find no better opportunity to speak about this matter, than while he is waiting for Pegasus to appear.

If I were to relate the whole of Bellerophon's previous adventures, they might easily grow into a very long story. It will be quite enough to say, that, in a certain country of Asia, a terrible monster called a Chimæra had made its appearance, and was doing more mischief than could be talked about between now and sunset. According to the best accounts which I have been able to obtain, this Chimæra was nearly, if not quite, the ugliest and most poisonous creature, and the strangest and unaccountablest, and the hardest to fight with, and the most difficult to run away from, that ever came out of the earth's inside. It had a tail like a boa-constrictor; its body was like I do not care what; and it had three separate heads, one of which was a lion's, the second a goat's, and the third an abominably great snake's. And a hot blast of fire came flaming out of each of its three mouths! Being an earthly monster, I doubt whether it had any wings; but, wings or no, it ran like a goat and a lion, and wriggled along like a serpent, and thus contrived to make about as much speed as all the three together.

Oh, the mischief, and mischief, and mischief, that this naughty creature did! With its flaming breath, it could set a forest on fire, or burn up a field of grain, or, for that matter, a village with all its fences and houses. It laid waste the whole country roundabout, and used to eat up people and animals alive, and cook them afterwards in the burning oven of its stomach. Mercy on us, little children, I hope neither you nor I will ever happen to meet a Chimæra!

While the hateful beast (if a beast we can anywise call it) was doing all these horrible things, it so chanced that Bellerophon came to that part of the world, on a visit to the king. The king's name was Iobates, and Lycia was the country which he ruled over. Bellerophon was one of the bravest youths in the world, and desired nothing so much as to do some valiant and beneficent deed, such as would make all mankind admire and love him. In those days, the only way for a young man to distinguish himself was by fighting battles, either with the enemies of his country, or with wicked giants, or with troublesome dragons, or with wild beasts, when he could find nothing more dangerous to encounter. King Iobates, perceiving the courage of his youthful visiter, proposed to him to go and fight the Chimæra, which everybody else was afraid of, and which, unless it should be soon killed, was likely to convert Lycia into a desert. Bellerophon hesitated not a moment, but assured the king that he would either slay this dreaded Chimæra, or perish in the attempt.

But in the first place, as the monster was so prodigiously swift, he bethought himself that he should never win the victory by fighting on foot. The wisest thing he could do, therefore, was to get the very best and fleetest horse, that could anywhere be found. And what other horse, in all the world, was half so fleet as the marvellous horse Pegasus, who had wings as well as legs, and was even more active in the air than on the earth! To be sure, a great many people denied that there was any such horse with wings, and said that the stories about him were all poetry and nonsense. But, wonderful as it appeared, Bellerophon believed that Pegasus was a real steed, and hoped that he himself might be fortunate enough to find him; and, once fairly mounted on his back, he would be able to fight the Chimæra at better advantage.

And this was the purpose with which he had travelled from Lycia to Greece, and had brought the beautifully ornamented bridle in his hand. It was an enchanted bridle. If he could only succeed in putting the golden bit into the mouth of Pegasus, the winged horse would be submissive, and would own Bellerophon for his master, and fly whithersoever he might choose to turn the rein.

But, indeed, it was a weary and anxious time, while Bellerophon waited and waited for Pegasus, in hopes that he would come and drink at the Fountain of Pirene. He was afraid lest King Iobates should imagine that he had fled from the Chimæra. It pained him, too, to think how much mischief the monster was doing, while he himself, instead of fighting with it, was compelled to sit idly poring over the bright waters of Pirene, as they gushed out of the sparkling sand. And as Pegasus came thither so seldom, in these latter years, and scarcely alighted there more than once in a lifetime, Bellerophon feared that he might grow an old man, and have no strength left in his arms nor courage in his heart, before the winged horse would appear. Oh, how heavily passes the time, while an adventurous youth is yearning to do his part in life, and to gather in the harvest of his renown! How hard a lesson it is, to wait! Our life is brief; and how much of it is spent in teaching us only this!

Well was it for Bellerophon, that the gentle child had grown so fond of him, and was never weary of keeping him company. Every morning, the child gave him a new hope to put in his bosom, instead of yesterday's withered one.

"Dear Bellerophon," he would cry, looking up hopefully into his face, "I think we shall see Pegasus to-day!"

And, at length, if it had not been for the little boy's unwavering faith, Bellerophon would have given up all hope, and would have gone back to Lycia, and have done his best to slay the Chimæra without the help of the winged horse. And in that case, poor Bellerophon would at least have been terribly scorched by the creature's breath, and would most probably have been killed and devoured. Nobody should ever try to fight an earth-born Chimæra, unless he can first get upon the back of an aerial steed!

One morning, the child spoke to Bellerophon even more hopefully than usual.

"Dear, dear Bellerophon," cried he, "I know not why it is; but I feel as if we should certainly see Pegasus to-day!"

And all that day, he would not stir a step from Bellerophon's side; so they ate a crust of bread together, and drank some of the water of the fountain. In the afternoon, there they sat; and Bellerophon had thrown his arm around the child, who likewise had put one of his little hands into Bellerophon's. The latter was lost in his own thoughts, and was fixing his eyes vacantly on the trunks of the trees that overshadowed the fountain, and on the grape-vines that clambered up among their branches. But the gentle child was gazing down into the water; he was grieved, for Bellerophon's sake, that the hope of another day should be deceived, like so many before it; and two or three quiet tear-drops fell from his eyes, and mingled with what were said to be the many tears of Pirene, when she wept for her slain children.

But, when he least thought of it, Bellerophon felt the pressure of the child's little hand, and heard a soft, almost breathless whisper.

"See there, dear Bellerophon! There is an image in the water!"

The young man looked down into the dimpling mirror of the fountain, and saw what he took to be the reflection of a bird, which seemed to be flying at a great height in the air, with a gleam of sunshine on its snowy or silvery wings.

"What a splendid bird it must be!" said he. "And how very large it looks, though it must really be flying higher than the clouds!"

"It makes me tremble!" whispered the child. "I am afraid to look up into the air! It is very beautiful; and yet I dare only look at its image in the water. Dear Bellerophon, do you not see that it is no bird? It is the winged horse Pegasus!"

Bellerophon's heart began to throb! He gazed keenly upward, but could not see the winged creature, whether bird or horse; because, just then, it had plunged into the fleecy depths of a summer-cloud. It was but a moment, however, before the object re-appeared, sinking lightly down out of the cloud, although still at a vast distance from the earth. Bellerophon caught the child in his arms, and shrank back with him, so that they were both hidden among the thick shrubbery which grew all around the fountain. Not that he was afraid of any harm; but he dreaded lest, if Pegasus caught a glimpse of them, he would fly far away, and alight on some inaccessible mountain-top. For it was really the winged horse! After they had expected him so long, he was coming to quench his thirst with the water of Pirene!

Nearer and nearer came the aerial wonder, flying in great circles, as you may have seen a dove when about to alight. Downward came Pegasus, in those wide, sweeping circles, which grew narrower, and narrower still, as he gradually approached the earth. The nigher the view of him, the more beautiful he was, and the more marvellous the sweep of his silvery wings. At last, with so light a pressure as hardly to bend the grass about the fountain, or imprint a hoof-tramp in the sand of its margin, he alighted, and, stooping his wild head, began to drink. He drew in the water, with long and pleasant sighs, and tranquil pauses of enjoyment, and then another draught, and another, and another. For, nowhere in the world, or up among the clouds, did Pegasus love any water as he loved this of Pirene! And when his thirst was slaked, he cropt a few of the honey-blossoms of the clover, delicately tasting them, but not caring to make a hearty meal; because the herbage, just beneath the clouds, on the lofty sides of

Mount Helicon, suited his palate better than this ordinary grass.

After thus drinking to his heart's content, and, in his dainty fashion, condescending to take a little food, the winged horse began to caper to-and-fro, and dance, as it were, out of mere idleness and sport. There never was a more playful creature made, than this very Pegasus. So there he frisked, in a way that it delights me to think about, fluttering his great wings as lightly as ever did a linnet, and running little races, half on earth and half in air, and which I know not whether to call a flight or a gallop. When a creature is perfectly able to fly, he sometimes chooses to run, just for the pastime of the thing; and so did Pegasus, although it cost him some little trouble to keep his hoofs so near the ground. Bellerophon, meanwhile, holding the child's hand, peeped forth from the shrubbery, and thought that never was any sight so beautiful as this, nor ever a horse's eyes so wild and spirited as those of Pegasus. It seemed a sin to think of bridling him and riding on his back.

Once or twice, Pegasus stopt, and snuffed the air, pricking up his ears, tossing his head, and turning it on all sides, as if he partly suspected some mischief or other. Seeing nothing, however, and hearing no sound, he soon began his antics again.

At length—not that he was weary, but only idle and luxurious—Pegasus folded his wings, and lay down on the soft green turf. But, being too full of aerial life to remain quiet for many moments together, he soon rolled over on his back, with his four slender legs in the air. It was beautiful to see him, this one solitary creature, whose mate had never been created, but who needed no companion, and, living a great many hundred years, was as happy as the centuries were long! The more he did such things as mortal horses are accustomed to do, the less earthly and the more wonderful he seemed. Bellerophon and the child almost held their breath, partly from a delightful awe, but still more because they dreaded lest the slightest stir or murmur should send him up, with the speed of an arrow-flight, into the farthest blue of the sky.

Finally, when he had had enough of rolling over and over, Pegasus turned himself about, and, indolently, like any other horse, put out his fore-legs, in order to rise from the ground; and Bellerophon, who had guessed that he would do so, darted suddenly from the thicket, and leaped astride of his back.

Yes; there he sat, on the back of the winged horse!

But what a bound did Pegasus make, when, for the first time, he felt the weight of a mortal man upon his loins! A bound, indeed! Before he had time to draw a breath, Bellerophon found himself five hundred feet aloft, and still shooting upward; while the winged horse snorted and trembled with terror and anger. Upward he went, up, up, up, until he plunged into the cold, misty bosom of a cloud, at which, only a little while before, Bellerophon had been gazing, and fancying it a very pleasant spot. Then again, out of the heart of the cloud, Pegasus shot down like a thunder-bolt, as if he meant to dash both himself and his rider headlong against a rock. Then he went through about a thousand of the wildest caprioles that had ever been performed either by a bird or a horse.

I cannot tell you half that he did. He skimmed straightforward, and sideways, and backward. He reared himself erect, with his fore-legs on a wreath of mist, and his hind-legs on nothing at all. He flung out his heels behind, and put down his head between his legs, with his wings pointing right upward. At about two miles' height above the earth, he turned a somerset, so that Bellerophon's heels were where his head should have been, and he seemed to look down into the sky, instead of up. He twisted his head about, and looking Bellerophon in the face, with fire flashing from his eyes, made a terrible attempt to bite him. He fluttered his pinions so wildly that one of the silver feathers was shaken out, and floating earthward, was picked up by the child, who kept it as long as he lived, in memory of Pegasus and Bellerophon.

But the latter (who, as you may judge, was as good a horseman as ever galloped) had been watching his opportunity, and at last clapt the golden bit of the enchanted bridle between the winged steed's jaws. No sooner was this done, than Pegasus became as manageable as if he had taken food, all his life, out of Bellerophon's hand. To speak what I really feel, it was almost a sadness, to see so wild a creature grow suddenly so tame. And Pegasus seemed to feel it so, likewise. He looked round to Bellerophon, with the tears in his beautiful eyes, instead of the fire that so recently flashed from them. But when Bellerophon patted his head, and spoke a few authoritative, yet kind and soothing words, another look came into the eyes of Pegasus; for he was glad at heart, after so many lonely centuries, to have found a companion and a master.

Thus it always is with winged horses, and with all such wild and solitary creatures. If you can catch and overcome them, it is the surest way to win their love.

While Pegasus had been doing his utmost to shake Bellerophon off his back, he had flown a very long distance; and they had come within sight of a lofty mountain, by the time the bit was in his mouth. Bellerophon had seen this mountain before, and knew it to be Helicon, on the summit of which was the winged horse's abode. Thither (after looking gently into his rider's face, as if to ask leave) Pegasus now flew, and alighting, waited patiently until Bellerophon should please to dismount. The young man, accordingly, leaped from his steed's back, but still held him fast by the bridle. Meeting his eyes, however, he was so affected by the gentleness of his aspect, and by his beauty, and by the thought of the free life which Pegasus had heretofore lived, that he could not bear to keep him a prisoner, if he really desired his liberty.

Obeying this generous impulse, he slipt the enchanted bridle off the head of Pegasus, and took the bit from his mouth.

"Leave me, Pegasus!" said he. "Either leave me, or love me!"

In an instant, the winged horse shot almost out of sight, soaring straight upward from the summit of Mount Helicon. Being long after sunset, it was now twilight on the mountain-top, and dusky evening over all the country roundabout. But Pegasus flew so high, that he overtook the departed day, and was bathed in the upper radiance of the sun. Ascending higher and higher, he looked like a bright speck, and, at last, could no longer be seen in the hollow waste of the sky. And Bellerophon was afraid that he should never behold him more. But, while he was lamenting his own folly, the bright speck re-appeared, and drew nearer and nearer, until it de-

scended lower than the sunshine; and behold, Pegasus had
come back! After this trial, there was no more fear of the
winged horse's making his escape. He and Bellerophon were
friends, and put loving faith in one another.

That night, they lay down and slept together, with Bellerophon's arm about the neck of Pegasus, not as a caution, but
for kindness. And they awoke at peep of day, and bade one
another good morning, each in his own language.

In this manner, Bellerophon and the wondrous steed spent
several days, and grew better acquainted and fonder of each
other, all the time. They went on long aerial journeys, and
sometimes ascended so high that the earth looked hardly bigger than the moon. They visited distant countries, and
amazed the inhabitants, who thought that the beautiful
young man, on the back of the winged horse, must have
come down out of the sky. A thousand miles a day was no
more than an easy space for the fleet Pegasus to pass over.
Bellerophon was delighted with this kind of life, and would
have liked nothing better than to live always in the same way,
aloft in the clear atmosphere; for it was always sunny weather,
up there, however cheerless and rainy it might be in the lower
region. But he could not forget the horrible Chimæra, which
he had promised King Iobates to slay. So, at last, when he
had become well accustomed to feats of horsemanship in the
air, and could manage Pegasus with the least motion of his
hand, and had taught him to obey his voice, he determined
to attempt the performance of this perilous adventure.

At daybreak, therefore, as soon as he unclosed his eyes, he
gently pinched the winged horse's ear, in order to arouse him.
Pegasus immediately started from the ground, and pranced
about a quarter of a mile aloft, and made a grand sweep
around the mountain-top, by way of showing that he was
wide-awake and ready for any kind of an excursion. During
the whole of this little flight, he uttered a loud, brisk, and
melodious neigh, and finally came down at Bellerophon's
side, as lightly as ever you saw a sparrow hop upon a twig.

"Well done, dear Pegasus! Well done, my sky-skimmer!"
cried Bellerophon, fondly stroking the horse's neck. "And
now, my fleet and beautiful friend, we must break our fast.
To-day, we are to fight the terrible Chimæra!"

As soon as they had eaten their morning-meal, and drank some sparkling water from a spring called Hippocrene, Pegasus held out his head, of his own accord, so that his master might put on the bridle. Then, with a great many playful leaps and airy caperings, he showed his impatience to be gone; while Bellerophon was girding on his sword, and hanging his shield about his neck, and preparing himself for battle. When everything was ready, the rider mounted, and (as was his custom, when going a long distance) ascended five miles perpendicularly, so as the better to see whither he was directing his course. He then turned the head of Pegasus towards the east, and set out for Lycia. In their flight, they overtook an eagle, and came so nigh him, before he could get out of their way, that Bellerophon might easily have caught him by the leg. Hastening onward at this rate, it was still early in the forenoon when they beheld the lofty mountains of Lycia, with their deep and shaggy vallies. If Bellerophon had been told truly, it was in one of those dismal vallies that the hideous Chimæra had taken up its abode.

Being now so near their journey's end, the winged horse gradually descended with his rider; and they took advantage of some clouds, that were floating over the mountain-tops, in order to conceal themselves. Hovering on the upper surface of a cloud, and peeping over its edge, Bellerophon had a pretty distinct view of the mountainous part of Lycia, and could look into all its shadowy vales at once. At first, there appeared to be nothing remarkable. It was a wild, savage, and rocky tract of high and precipitous hills. In the more level part of the country, there were the ruins of houses that had been burnt, and, here and there, the carcasses of dead cattle, strewn about the pastures where they had been feeding.

"The Chimæra must have done this mischief," thought Bellerophon. "But where can the monster be?"

As I have already said, there was nothing remarkable to be detected, at first sight, in any of the vallies and dells that lay among the precipitous heights of the mountains. Nothing at all; unless, indeed, it were three spires of black smoke, which issued from what seemed to be the mouth of a cavern, and clambered sullenly into the atmosphere. Before reaching the mountain-top, these three black smoke-wreaths mingled themselves into one. The cavern was almost directly beneath the winged horse and his rider, at the distance of about a thousand feet. The smoke, as it crept heavily upward, had an ugly, sulphurous, stifling scent, which caused Pegasus to snort and Bellerophon to sneeze. So disagreeable was it to the marvellous steed (who was accustomed to breathe only the purest air) that he waved his wings, and shot half a mile out of the range of this offensive vapor.

But, on looking behind him, Bellerophon saw something that induced him first to draw the bridle, and then to turn Pegasus about. He made a sign, which the winged horse understood, and sank slowly through the air, until his hoofs were scarcely more than a man's height above the rocky bottom of the valley. In front, as far off as you could throw a stone, was the cavern's mouth, with the three smoke-wreaths oozing out of it. And what else did Bellerophon behold there?

There seemed to be a heap of strange and terrible creatures, curled up within the cavern. Their bodies lay so close together, that Bellerophon could not distinguish them apart; but, judging by their heads, one of these creatures was a huge snake, the second, a fierce lion, and the third, an ugly goat. The lion and the goat were asleep; the snake was broad awake, and kept staring around him with a great pair of fiery eyes. But—and this was the most wonderful part of the matter—the three spires of smoke evidently issued from the nostrils of these three heads! So strange was the spectacle, that, though Bellerophon had been all along expecting it, the truth did not immediately occur to him, that here was the terrible, three-headed Chimæra. He had found out the Chimæra's cavern. The snake, the lion, and the goat, as he supposed them to be, were not three separate creatures, but one monster!

The wicked, hateful thing! Slumbering as two-thirds of it were, it still held, in its abominable claws, the remnant of an unfortunate lamb—or possibly (but I hate to think so) it was a dear little boy—which its three mouths had been gnawing, before two of them fell asleep!

All at once, Bellerophon started as from a dream, and knew it to be the Chimæra. Pegasus seemed to know it, at the same instant, and sent forth a neigh, that sounded like the call of a trumpet to battle. At this sound, the three heads reared themselves erect, and belched out great flashes of flame. Before Bellerophon had time to consider what to do next, the monster flung itself out of the cavern and sprang straight towards him, with its immense claws extended, and its snaky tail twisting itself venomously behind. If Pegasus had not been as nimble as a bird, both he and his rider would have been overthrown by the Chimæra's headlong rush, and thus the battle have been ended before it was well begun. But the winged horse was not to be caught so! In the twinkling of an eye, he was up aloft, half-way to the clouds, snorting with anger. He shuddered, too, not with affright, but with utter disgust at the loathsomeness of this poisonous thing with three heads.

The Chimæra, on the other hand, raised itself up so as to stand absolutely on the tip-end of its tail, with its talons pawing fiercely in the air, and its three heads spluttering fire at Pegasus and his rider. My stars, how it roared, and hissed, and bellowed! Bellerophon, meanwhile, was fitting his shield on his arm, and drawing his sword.

"Now, my beloved Pegasus," he whispered in the winged horse's ear, "thou must help me to slay this insufferable monster; or else thou shalt fly back to thy solitary mountain-peak, without thy friend Bellerophon! For either the Chimæra dies, or its three mouths shall gnaw this head of mine, which has slumbered upon thy neck!"

Pegasus whinnied, and turning back his head, rubbed his nose tenderly against his rider's cheek. It was his way of telling him, that, though he had wings and was an immortal horse, yet he would perish, if it were possible for immortality to perish, rather than leave Bellerophon behind.

"I thank you, Pegasus!" answered Bellerophon. "Now, then, let us make a dash at the monster!"

Uttering these words, he shook the bridle; and Pegasus darted down aslant, as swift as the flight of an arrow, right towards the Chimæra's three-fold head, which, all this time, was poking itself as high as it could into the air. As he came within arm's length, Bellerophon made a cut at the monster, but was carried onward by his steed, before he could see whether the blow had been successful. Pegasus continued his course, but soon wheeled round, at about the same distance from the Chimæra as before. Bellerophon then perceived that he had cut the goat's head of the monster almost off, so that it dangled downward by the skin, and seemed quite dead.

But, to make amends, the snake's head and the lion's head had taken all the fierceness of the dead one into themselves, and spit flame, and hissed, and roared, with a vast deal more fury than before.

"Never mind, my brave Pegasus!" cried Bellerophon. "With another stroke like that, we will stop either its hissing or its roaring."

And again he shook the bridle. Dashing aslantwise, as before, the winged horse made another arrow-flight towards the Chimæra, and Bellerophon aimed another downright stroke at one of the two remaining heads, as he shot by. But, this time, neither he nor Pegasus escaped so well as at first. With one of its claws, the Chimæra had given the young man a deep scratch in his shoulder, and had slightly damaged the left wing of the flying steed, with the other. On his part, Bellerophon had mortally wounded the lion's head of the monster; insomuch that it now hung downward, with its fire almost extinguished, and sending out gasps of thick black smoke. The snake's head, however, (which was the only one now left,) was twice as fierce and venomous as ever before. It belched forth shoots of fire, five hundred yards long, and emitted hisses so loud, so harsh, and so ear-piercing, that King Iobates heard them, fifty miles off, and trembled till the throne shook under him.

"Well-a-day!" thought the poor king. "The Chimæra is certainly coming to devour me!"

Meanwhile, Pegasus had again paused in the air, and neighed angrily, while sparkles of a pure, crystal flame darted out of his eyes. How unlike the lurid fire of the Chimæra! The aerial steed's spirit was all aroused, and so was that of Bellerophon.

"Dost thou bleed, my immortal horse?" cried the young man, caring less for his own hurt than for the anguish of this glorious creature, that ought never to have tasted pain. "The execrable Chimæra shall pay for this mischief, with his last head!"

Then he shook the bridle, shouted loudly, and guided Pegasus, not aslantwise as before, but straight at the monster's hideous front. So rapid was the onset, that it seemed but a dazzle and a flash, before Bellerophon was at close gripes with his enemy.

The Chimæra, by this time, after losing its second head, had got into a red-hot passion of pain and rampant rage. It so flounced about, half on earth and partly in the air, that it was impossible to say which element it rested upon. It opened its snake-jaws to such an abominable width, that Pegasus might almost, I was going to say, have flown right down its throat, wings outspread, rider and all! At their approach, it shot out a tremendous blast of its fiery breath, and enveloped Bellerophon and his steed in a perfect atmosphere of flame; singeing the wings of Pegasus, scorching off one whole side of the young man's golden ringlets, and making them both far hotter than was comfortable, from head to foot.

But this was nothing to what followed.

When the airy rush of the winged horse had brought him within the distance of a hundred yards, the Chimæra gave a spring, and flung its huge, aukward, venomous, and utterly detestable carcass right upon poor Pegasus, clung round him with might and main, and tied up its snaky tail into a knot! Up flew the aerial steed, higher, higher, higher, above the mountain-peaks, above the clouds, and almost out of sight of the solid earth. But still the earth-born monster kept its hold, and was borne upward along with the creature of light and air. Bellerophon, meanwhile, turning about, found himself face to face with the ugly grimness of the Chimæra's visage, and could only avoid being scorched to death, or bitten right in twain, by holding up his shield. Over the upper edge of the shield, he looked sternly into the savage eyes of the monster.

But the Chimæra was so mad and wild with pain, that it did not guard itself so well as might else have been the case. Perhaps, after all, the best way to fight a Chimæra is by getting as close to it as you can. In its efforts to stick its horrible iron claws into its enemy, the creature left its own breast quite exposed; and perceiving this, Bellerophon thrust his sword up to the hilt into its cruel heart. Immediately, the snaky tail untied its knot. The monster let go its hold of Pegasus, and fell from that vast height, downward; while the fire within its bosom, instead of being put out, burned fiercer than ever, and quickly began to consume the dead carcass. Thus it fell out of the sky, all a-flame, and (it being nightfall before it reached the earth) was mistaken for a shooting star or a comet. But, at early sunrise, some cottagers were going to their day's labor, and saw, to their astonishment, that several acres of ground were strewn with black ashes. In the middle of a field, there was a heap of whitened bones, a great deal higher than a haystack. Nothing else was ever seen of the dreadful Chimæra!

And when Bellerophon had won the victory, he bent forward and kissed Pegasus, while the tears stood in his eyes.

"Back now, my beloved steed!" said he. "Back to the Fountain of Pirene!"

Pegasus skimmed through the air, quicker than ever he did before, and reached the fountain in a very short time. And there he found the old man, leaning on his staff, and the country fellow, watering his cow, and the pretty maiden, filling her pitcher.

"I remember now," quoth the old man, "I saw this winged horse once before, when I was quite a lad. But he was ten times handsomer, in those days!"

"I own a cart-horse, worth three of him!" said the country fellow. "If this pony were mine, the first thing I should do, would be to clip his wings!"

But the poor maiden said nothing; for she had always the luck to be afraid at the wrong time. So she ran away, and let her pitcher tumble down, and broke it.

"Where is the gentle child," asked Bellerophon, "who used to keep me company, and never lost his faith, and never was weary of gazing into the fountain!"

"Here am I, dear Bellerophon!" said the child, softly.

For the little boy had spent day after day, on the margin of Pirene, waiting for his friend to come back; but when he perceived Bellerophon descending through the clouds, mounted on the winged horse, he had shrunk back into the shrubbery. He was a delicate and tender child, and dreaded lest the old man and the country fellow should see the tears gushing from his eyes.

"Thou hast won the victory," said he, joyfully, running to the knee of Bellerophon, who still sat on the back of Pegasus. "I knew thou wouldst!"

"Yes; dear child!" replied Bellerophon, alighting from the winged horse. "But, if thy faith had not helped me, I should never have waited for Pegasus, and never have gone up above the clouds, and never have conquered the terrible Chimæra! Thou, my beloved little friend, hast done it all! And now let us give Pegasus his liberty."

So he slipt off the enchanted bridle from the head of the marvellous steed.

"Be free, forever more, my Pegasus!" cried he, with a shade of sadness in his tone. "Be as free as thou art fleet!"

But Pegasus rested his head on Bellerophon's shoulder, and would not be persuaded to take flight.

"Well, then," said Bellerophon, caressing the airy horse, "thou shalt be with me, as long as thou wilt; and we will go together, forthwith, and tell King Iobates that the Chimæra is destroyed!"

Then Bellerophon embraced the gentle child, and promised to come to him again, and departed. But, in after years, that child took higher flights upon the aerial steed, than ever did Bellerophon, and achieved more honorable deeds than his friend's victory over the Chimæra. For, gentle and tender as he was, he grew to be a mighty Poet!

Bald Summit

AFTER THE STORY

EUSTACE BRIGHT told the legend of Bellerophon with as much fervor and animation as if he had really been taking a gallop on the winged horse. At the conclusion, he was gratified to discern, by the glowing countenances of his auditors, how greatly they had been interested. All their eyes were dancing in their heads, except those of Primrose. In her eyes, there were positively tears; for she was conscious of something in the legend, which the rest of them were not yet old enough to feel. Child's story as it was, the student had contrived to breathe through it the ardor, the generous hope, and the imaginative enterprise of youth.

"I forgive you now, Primrose," said he, "for all your ridicule of myself and my stories. One tear pays for a great deal of laughter."

"Well, Mr. Bright," answered Primrose, wiping her eyes, and giving him another of her mischievous smiles, "it certainly does elevate your ideas, to get your head above the clouds. I advise you never to tell another story, unless it be, as at present, from the top of a mountain!"

"Or from the back of Pegasus," replied Eustace, laughing. "Don't you think that I succeeded pretty well in catching that wonderful pony?"

"It was so like one of your mad-cap pranks!" cried Primrose, clapping her hands. "I think I see you now on his back, two miles high, and with your head downward! It is well that you have not really an opportunity of trying your horsemanship on any wilder steed than our sober Davy, or Old Hundred."

"For my part, I wish I had Pegasus here, at this moment," said the student. "I would mount him, forthwith, and gallop about the country, within a circumference of a few miles, making literary calls on my brother-authors. Dr. Dewey would be within my reach, at the foot of Taconic. In Stockbridge, yonder, is Mr. James, conspicuous to all the world on his mountain-pile of history and romance. Longfellow, I believe, is not yet at the Ox-bow; else the winged horse would neigh at the sight of him. But, here in Lenox, I should find our most truthful novelist, who has made the scenery and life of Berkshire all her own. On the hither side of Pittsfield sits Herman Melville, shaping out the gigantic conception of his 'White Whale,' while the gigantic shape of Graylock looms upon him from his study-window. Another bound of my flying steed would bring me to the door of Holmes, whom I mention last, because Pegasus would certainly unseat me, the next minute, and claim the poet as his rider."

"Have we not an author for our next neighbor?" asked Primrose. "That silent man, who lives in the old red house, near Tanglewood avenue, and whom we sometimes meet, with two children at his side, in the woods or at the lake. I think I have heard of his having written a poem, or a romance, or an arithmetic, or a school-history, or some other kind of a book."

"Hush, Primrose, hush!" exclaimed Eustace, in a thrilling whisper, and putting his finger on his lip. "Not a word about that man, even on a hill-top! If our babble were to reach his ears, and happen not to please him, he has but to fling a quire or two of paper into the stove; and you, Primrose, and I, and Periwinkle, Sweet Fern, Squash Blossom, Blue Eye, Huckleberry, Clover, Cowslip, Plantain, Milkweed, Dandelion, and Butter-cup—yes, and wise Mr. Pringle with his unfavorable criticisms on my legends, and poor Mrs. Pringle, too—would all turn to smoke, and go whisking up the funnel! Our neighbor in the red house is a harmless sort of person enough, for aught I know, as concerns the rest of the world; but something whispers me that he has a terrible power over ourselves, extending to nothing short of annihilation."

"And would Tanglewood turn to smoke, as well as we?" asked Periwinkle, quite appalled at the threatened destruction. "And what would become of Ben and Bruin?"

"Tanglewood would remain," replied the student, "looking just as it does now, but occupied by an entirely different family. And Ben and Bruin would be still alive, and would make themselves very comfortable with the bones from the dinner-table, without ever thinking of the good times which they and we have had together!"

"What nonsense you are talking!" exclaimed Primrose.

With idle chat of this kind, the party had already begun to descend the hill, and were now within the shadow of the woods. Primrose gathered some mountain-laurel, the leaf of which, though of last year's growth, was still as verdant and elastic as if the frost and thaw had not alternately tried their force upon its texture. Of these twigs of laurel she twined a wreath, and took off the student's cap, in order to place it on his brow.

"Nobody else is likely to crown you for your stories," observed saucy Primrose. "So take this from me!"

"Do not be too sure," answered Eustace, looking really like a youthful poet, with the laurel among his glossy curls, "that I shall not win other wreaths by these wonderful and admirable stories. I mean to spend all my leisure, during the rest of the vacation, and throughout the summer-term at college, in writing them out for the press. Mr. J. T. Fields (with whom I became acquainted when he was in Berkshire, last summer, and who is a poet, as well as a publisher) will see their uncommon merit, at a glance. He will get them illustrated, I hope, by Billings, and will bring them before the world under the very best of auspices, through the eminent house of TICKNOR & CO. In about five months from this moment, I make no doubt of being reckoned among the lights of the age!"

"Poor boy!" said Primrose, half aside. "What a disappointment awaits him!"

Descending a little lower, Bruin began to bark, and was answered by the graver bow-wow of the respectable Ben. They soon saw the good old dog, keeping careful watch over Dandelion, Sweet Fern, Cowslip, and Squash Blossom. These little people, quite recovered from their fatigue, had set about gathering checkerberries, and now came clambering to meet their playfellows. Thus re-united, the whole party went down through Luther Butler's orchard, and made the best of their way home to Tanglewood.

THE END

TANGLEWOOD TALES

FOR GIRLS AND BOYS

BEING A SECOND WONDER BOOK

(1853)

Contents

The Wayside

INTRODUCTORY

A SHORT TIME AGO, I was favored with a flying visit from my young friend, Eustace Bright, whom I had not before met with, since quitting the breezy mountains of Berkshire. It being the winter-vacation at his college, Eustace was allowing himself a little relaxation, in the hope, he told me, of repairing the inroads which severe application to study had made upon his health; and I was happy to conclude, from the excellent physical condition in which I saw him, that the remedy had already been attended with very desirable success. He had now run up from Boston by the noon-train, partly impelled by the friendly regard with which he is pleased to honor me, and partly, as I soon found, on a matter of literary business.

It delighted me to receive Mr. Bright, for the first time, under a roof, though a very humble one, which I could really call my own. Nor did I fail (as is the custom of landed proprietors, all about the world) to parade the poor fellow up and down over my half-a-dozen acres; secretly rejoicing, nevertheless, that the disarray of the inclement season, and particularly the six inches of snow, then upon the ground, prevented him from observing the ragged neglect of soil and shrubbery, into which the place has lapsed. It was idle, however, to imagine that an airy guest from Monument Mountain, Bald Summit, and old Graylock, shaggy with primeval forests, could see anything to admire in my poor little hillside, with its growth of frail and insect-eaten locust-trees. Eustace very frankly called the view from my hill-top, tame; and so, no doubt, it was, after rough, broken, rugged, headlong Berkshire, and especially the northern parts of the county, with which his college-residence had made him familiar. But, to me, there is a peculiar, quiet charm in these broad meadows and gentle eminences. They are better than mountains, because they do not stamp and stereotype themselves into the brain, and thus grow wearisome with the same strong impression, repeated day after day. A few summer weeks among mountains; a lifetime among green meadows and placid slopes, with outlines forever new, because continually fading out of the memory. Such would be my sober choice.

I doubt whether Eustace did not internally pronounce the whole thing a bore, until I led him to my predecessor's little ruined, rustic summer-house, mid-way on the hill-side. It is a mere skeleton of slender, decaying, tree-trunks, with neither walls nor a roof; nothing but a tracery of branches and twigs, which the next wintry blast will be very likely to scatter in fragments along the terrace. It looks, and is, as evanescent as a dream; and yet, in its rustic net-work of boughs, it has somehow inclosed a hint of spiritual beauty, and has become a true emblem of the subtile and ethereal mind that planned it. I made Eustace Bright sit down on a snow-bank, which had heaped itself over the mossy seat, and gazing through the arched-window, opposite, he acknowledged that the scene at once grew picturesque.

"Simple as it looks," said he, "this little edifice seems to be the work of magic. It is full of suggestiveness, and, in its way, is as good as a cathedral. Ah, it would be just the spot for one to sit in, of a summer-afternoon, and tell the children some more of those wild stories from the classic myths!"

"It would, indeed," answered I. "The summer-house itself, so airy and so broken, is like one of those old tales, imperfectly remembered; and these living branches of the Baldwin apple-tree, thrusting themselves so rudely in, are like your unwarrantable interpolations. But, by-the-by, have you added any more legends to the series, since the publication of the Wonder Book?"

"Many more;" said Eustace. "Primrose, Periwinkle, and the rest of them, allow me no comfort of my life, unless I tell them a story, every day or two. I have run away from home, partly to escape the importunity of those little wretches! But I have written out six of the new stories, and have brought them for you to look over."

"Are they as good as the first?" I enquired.

"Better chosen, and better handled," replied Eustace Bright. "You will say so, when you read them."

"Possibly not," I remarked. "I know, from my own experience, that an author's last work is always his best one, in his
own estimate, until it quite loses the red-heat of composition.
After that, it falls into its true place, quietly enough. But let
us adjourn to my study, and examine these new stories. It
would hardly be doing yourself justice, were you to bring me
acquainted with them, sitting here on this snow-bank!"

So we descended the hill to my small, old cottage, and shut
ourselves up in the south-eastern room, where the sunshine
comes in, warmly and brightly, through the better half of a
winter's day. Eustace put his bundle of manuscript into my
hands; and I skimmed through it pretty rapidly, trying to find
out its merits and demerits by the touch of my fingers, as a
veteran story-teller ought to know how to do.

It will be remembered, that Mr. Bright condescended to
avail himself of my literary experience by constituting me editor of the Wonder Book. As he had no reason to complain
of the reception of that erudite work, by the public, he was
now disposed to retain me in a similar position, with respect
to the present volume, which he entitled "TANGLEWOOD
TALES." Not, as Eustace hinted, that there was any real necessity for my services as introductor, inasmuch as his own name
had become established, in some good degree of favor, with
the literary world. But the connection with myself, he was
kind enough to say, had been highly agreeable; nor was he
by any means desirous, as most people are, of kicking away
the ladder that had perhaps helped him to reach his present
elevation. My young friend was willing, in short, that the
fresh verdure of his growing reputation should spread over
my straggling, and half-naked boughs; even as I have sometimes thought of training a vine, with its broad leafiness and
purple fruitage, over the worm-eaten posts and rafters of the
rustic summer-house. I was not insensible to the advantages
of his proposal, and gladly assured him of my acceptance.

Merely from the titles of the stories, I saw at once that the
subjects were not less rich than those of the former volume;
nor did I at all doubt that Mr. Bright's audacity (so far as
that endowment might avail) had enabled him to take full
advantage of whatever capabilities they offered. Yet, in spite
of my experience of his free way of handling them, I did not

quite see, I confess, how he could have obviated all the difficulties in the way of rendering them presentable to children.
These old legends, so brimming over with everything that is
most abhorrent to our Christianized moral-sense—some of
them so hideous—others so melancholy and miserable, amid
which the Greek Tragedians sought their themes, and
moulded them into the sternest forms of grief that ever the
world saw;—was such material the stuff that children's playthings should be made of! How were they to be purified?
How was the blessed sunshine to be thrown into them?

But Eustace told me that these myths were the most singular things in the world, and that he was invariably astonished, whenever he began to relate one, by the readiness with
which it adapted itself to the childish purity of his auditors.
The objectionable characteristics seem to be a parasitical
growth, having no essential connection with the original fable. They fall away, and are thought of no more, the instant
he puts his imagination in sympathy with the innocent little
circle, whose wide-open eyes are fixed so eagerly upon him.
Thus the stories (not by any strained effort of the narrator's,
but in harmony with their inherent germ) transform themselves, and re-assume the shapes which they might be supposed to possess in the pure childhood of the world. When
the first poet or romancer told these marvellous legends (such
is Eustace Bright's opinion) it was still the Golden Age. Evil
had never yet existed; and sorrow, misfortune, crime, were
mere shadows which the mind fancifully created for itself, as
a shelter against too sunny realities—or, at most, but prophetic dreams, to which the dreamer himself did not yield a
waking credence. Children are now the only representatives
of the men and women of that happy era; and therefore it is
that we must raise the intellect and fancy to the level of childhood, in order to re-create the original myths.

I let the youthful author talk, as much and as extravagantly
as he pleased, and was glad to see him commencing life with
such confidence in himself and his performances. A few years
will do all that is necessary towards showing him the truth, in
both respects. Meanwhile, it is but right to say, he does really
appear to have overcome the moral objections against these
fables; although at the expence of such liberties with their

structure, as must be left to plead their own excuse, without any help from me. Indeed, except that there was a necessity for it—and that the inner life of the legends cannot be come at, save by making them entirely one's own property—there is no defence to be made.

Eustace informed me that he had told his stories to the children in various situations,—in the woods, on the shore of the lake, in the dell of Shadow Brook, in the play-room, at Tanglewood fireside, and in a magnificent palace of snow, with ice-windows, which he helped his little friends to build. His auditors were even more delighted with the contents of the present volume, than with the specimens which have already been given to the world. The classically learned Mr. Pringle, too, had listened to two or three of the tales, and censured them even more bitterly than he did THE THREE GOLDEN APPLES; so that, what with praise, and what with criticism, Eustace Bright thinks that there is good hope of at least as much success with the public, as in the case of the Wonder Book.

I made all sorts of inquiries about the children, not doubting that there would be great eagerness to hear of their welfare, among some good little folks who have written to me, to ask for another volume of myths. They are all, I am happy to say, (unless we except Clover,) in excellent health and spirits. Primrose is now almost a young lady, and, Eustace tells me, is just as saucy as ever. She pretends to consider herself quite beyond the age to be interested by such idle stories as these; but, for all that, whenever a story is to be told, Primrose never fails to be one of the listeners, and to make fun of it, when finished. Periwinkle is very much grown, and is expected to shut up her baby-house and throw away her doll, in a month or two more. Sweet Fern has learned to read and write, and has put on a jacket and pair of pantaloons—all of which improvements I am sorry for. Squash Blossom, Blue Eye, Plantain, and Butter-cup, have had the scarlet-fever, but came easily through it. Huckleberry, Milkweed, and Dandelion, were attacked with the hooping-cough, but bore it bravely, and kept out-of-doors, whenever the sun shone. Cowslip, during the autumn, had either the measles or some eruption that looked very much like it, but was hardly sick a day. Poor Clover has been a good deal troubled with her second teeth, which have made her meagre in aspect and rather fractious in temper; nor, even when she smiles, is the matter much mended, since it discloses a gap, just within her lips, almost as wide as the barn-door. But all this will pass over; and it is predicted that she will turn out a very pretty girl.

As for Mr. Bright himself, he is now in his senior year at Williams College, and has a prospect of graduating with some degree of honorable distinction, at the next Commencement. In his oration for the bachelor's degree, he gives me to understand, he will treat of the Classical Myths, viewed in the aspect of baby-stories, and has a great mind to discuss the expediency of using up the whole of ancient history, for the same purpose. I do not know what he means to do with himself, after leaving college, but trust that, by dabbling so early with the dangerous and seductive business of authorship, he will not be tempted to become an author by profession. If so, I shall be very sorry for the little that I have had to do with the matter, in encouraging these first beginnings.

I wish there were any likelihood of my soon seeing Primrose, Periwinkle, Dandelion, Sweet Fern, Clover, Plantain, Huckleberry, Milkweed, Cowslip, Butter-cup, Blue Eye, and Squash Blossom, again. But as I do not know when I shall re-visit Tanglewood, and as Eustace Bright probably will not ask me to edit a third Wonder Book, the public of little folks must not expect to hear any more about those dear children, from me. Heaven bless them, and everybody else, whether grown people or children!

THE WAYSIDE, CONCORD, (MASS.)
March 13, 1853.

The Minotaur

In the old city of Trœzene, at the foot of a lofty mountain, there lived, a very long time ago, a little boy named Theseus. His grandfather, King Pittheus, was the sovereign of that country, and was reckoned a very wise man; so that Theseus, being brought up in the royal palace, and being naturally a bright lad, could hardly fail of profiting by the old king's instructions. His mother's name was Æthra. As for his father, the boy had never seen him. But, from his earliest remembrance, Æthra used to go with little Theseus into a wood, and sit down upon a moss-grown rock, which was deeply sunken into the earth. Here she often talked with her son about his father, and said that he was called Ægeus, and that he was a great king, and ruled over Attica, and dwelt at Athens, which was as famous a city as any in the world. Theseus was very fond of hearing about King Ægeus, and often asked his good mother Æthra why he did not come and live with them, at Trœzene.

"Ah, my dear son," answered Æthra, with a sigh, "a monarch has his people to take care of. The men and women, over whom he rules, are in the place of children to him; and he can seldom spare time to love his own children, as other parents do. Your father will never be able to leave his kingdom, for the sake of seeing his little boy."

"Well, but, dear mother," asked the boy, "why cannot I go to this famous city of Athens, and tell King Ægeus that I am his son?"

"That may happen, by-and-by," said Æthra. "Be patient, and we shall see. You are not yet big and strong enough to set out on such an errand."

"And how soon shall I be strong enough?" Theseus persisted in inquiring.

"You are but a tiny boy as yet," replied his mother. "See if you can lift this rock on which we are sitting!"

The little fellow had a great opinion of his own strength. So, grasping the rough protuberances of the rock, he tugged and toiled amain, and got himself quite out of breath, without being able to stir the heavy stone. It seemed to be rooted into the ground. No wonder he could not move it; for it would have taken all the force of a very strong man to lift it out of its earthy bed.

His mother stood looking on, with a sad kind of a smile on her lips and in her eyes, to see the zealous, and yet puny efforts of her little boy. She could not help being sorrowful, at finding him already so impatient to begin his adventures in the world.

"You see how it is, my dear Theseus," said she. "You must possess far more strength than now, before I can trust you to go to Athens, and tell King Ægeus that you are his son. But when you can lift this rock, and show me what is hidden beneath it, I promise you my permission to depart!"

Often and often, after this, did Theseus ask his mother whether it was yet time for him to go to Athens; and still his mother pointed to the rock, and told him that, for years to come, he would not be strong enough to move it. And again, and again, the rosy-cheeked and curly-headed boy would tug and strain at the huge mass of stone, striving, child as he was, to do what a giant could hardly have done, without taking both of his great hands to the task. Meanwhile, the rock seemed to be sinking farther and farther into the ground. The moss grew over it, thicker and thicker; until at last it looked almost like a soft green seat, with only a few gray knobs of granite peeping out. The overhanging trees, also, shed their brown leaves upon it, as often as the autumn came; and at its base grew ferns and wild flowers, some of which crept quite over its surface. To all appearance, the rock was as firmly fastened as any other portion of the earth's substance.

But, difficult as the matter looked, Theseus was now growing up to be such a vigorous youth, that, in his own opinion, the time would quickly come, when he might hope to get the upper hand of this ponderous lump of stone.

"Mother, I do believe it has started!" cried he, after one of his attempts. "The earth around it is certainly a little cracked!"

"No, no, child!" his mother hastily answered. "It is not possible you can have moved it, such a boy as you still are!"

Nor would she be convinced, although Theseus showed

her the place, where he fancied that the stem of a flower had been partly uprooted by the movement of the rock. But Æthra sighed, and looked disquieted; for, no doubt, she began to be conscious that her son was no longer a child, and that, in a little while hence, she must send him forth among the perils and troubles of the world.

It was not more than a year afterwards, when they were again sitting on the moss-covered stone. Æthra had once more told him the oft-repeated story of his father, and how gladly he would receive Theseus at his stately palace, and how he would present him to his courtiers and the people, and tell them that here was the heir of his dominions. The eyes of Theseus glowed with enthusiasm, and he could hardly sit still to hear his mother speak.

"Dear mother Æthra," he exclaimed, "I never felt half so strong as now! I am no longer a child, nor a boy, nor a mere youth! I feel myself a man! It is now time to make one earnest trial to remove the stone."

"Ah, my dearest Theseus," replied his mother, "not yet!— not yet!"

"Yes, mother," said he resolutely,—"the time has come!"

Then Theseus bent himself in good earnest to the task, and strained every sinew, with manly strength and resolution. He put his whole brave heart into the effort. He wrestled with the big and sluggish stone, as if it had been a living enemy. He heaved; he lifted; he resolved now to succeed, or else to perish there, and let the rock be his monument forever! Æthra stood gazing at him, and clasped her hands, partly with a mother's pride, and partly with a mother's sorrow. The great rock stirred! Yes; it was raised slowly from the bedded moss and earth, uprooting the shrubs and flowers along with it, and was turned upon its side. Theseus had conquered!

While taking breath, he looked joyfully at his mother; and she smiled upon him through her tears.

"Yes, Theseus," she said, "the time has come; and you must stay no longer at my side! See what King Ægeus, your royal father, left for you, beneath the stone, when he lifted it in his mighty arms, and laid it on the spot whence you have now removed it."

Theseus looked, and saw that the rock had been placed over another slab of stone, containing a cavity within it; so that it somewhat resembled a roughly-made chest or coffer, of which the upper mass had served as the lid. Within the cavity lay a sword, with a golden hilt, and a pair of sandals.

"That was your father's sword," said Æthra, "and those were his sandals. When he went to be King of Athens, he bade me treat you as a child, until you should prove yourself a man by lifting this heavy stone. That task being accomplished, you are to put on his sandals, in order to follow in your father's footsteps, and to gird on his sword, so that you may fight giants and dragons, as King Ægeus did in his youth."

"I will set out for Athens, this very day!" cried Theseus.

But his mother persuaded him to stay a day or two longer, while she got ready some necessary articles for his journey. When his grandfather, the wise King Pittheus, heard that Theseus intended to present himself at his father's palace, he earnestly advised him to get on board of a vessel, and go by sea; because he might thus arrive within fifteen miles of Athens, without either fatigue or danger.

"The roads are very bad, by land," quoth the venerable king; "and they are terribly infested with robbers and monsters. A mere lad, like Theseus, is not fit to be trusted on such a perilous journey, all by himself. No, no; let him go by sea!"

But when Theseus heard of robbers and monsters, he pricked up his ears, and was so much the more eager to take the road along which they were to be met with. On the third day, therefore, he bade a respectful farewell to his grandfather, thanking him for all his kindness; and after affectionately embracing his mother, he set forth, with a good many of her tears glistening on his cheeks, and some, if the truth must be told, that had gushed out of his own eyes. But he let the sun and wind dry them, and walked stoutly on, playing with the golden hilt of his sword, and taking very manly strides in his father's sandals.

I cannot stop to tell you hardly any of the adventures that befel Theseus, on the road to Athens. It is enough to say, that he quite cleared that part of the country of the robbers, about whom King Pittheus had been so much alarmed. One of these bad people was named Procrustes; and he was indeed a terrible fellow, and had an ugly way of making fun of the poor travellers who happened to fall into his clutches. In his cavern, he had a bed, on which, with great pretence of hospitality, he invited his guests to lie down; but, if they happened to be shorter than the bed, this wicked villain stretched them out, by main force; or, if they were too tall, he lopt off their heads or feet, and laughed at what he had done, as an excellent joke. Thus, however weary a man might be, he never liked to lie in the bed of Procrustes. Another of these robbers, named Scinis, must likewise have been a very great scoundrel. He was in the habit of flinging his victims off a high cliff into the sea; and, in order to give him exactly his deserts, Theseus tossed him off the very same place. But, if you will believe me, the sea would not pollute itself by receiving such a bad person into its bosom; neither would the earth, having once got rid of him, consent to take him back; so that, between the cliff and the sea, Scinis stuck fast in the air, which was forced to bear the burthen of his naughtiness.

After these memorable deeds, Theseus heard of an enormous sow, which ran wild, and was the terror of all the farmers roundabout; and, as he did not consider himself above doing any good thing that came in his way, he killed this monstrous creature, and gave the carcass to the poor people for bacon. The great sow had been an awful beast, while ramping about the woods and fields, but was a pleasant object enough, when cut up into joints, and smoking on I know not how many dinner-tables.

Thus, by the time he reached his journey's end, Theseus had done many valiant feats with his father's golden-hilted sword, and had gained the renown of being one of the bravest young men of the day. His fame travelled faster than he did, and reached Athens before him. As he entered the city, he heard the inhabitants talking at the street-corners, and saying that Hercules was brave, and Jason too, and Castor and Pollux likewise, but that Theseus, the son of their own king, would turn out as great a hero as the best of them. Theseus took longer strides, on hearing this, and fancied himself sure of a magnificent reception at his father's court; since he came thither with Fame to blow her trumpet before him, and cry to King Ægeus—"Behold your son!"

He little suspected, innocent youth that he was, that here, in this very Athens, where his father reigned, a greater danger awaited him than any which he had encountered on the road. Yet this was the truth. You must understand that the father of Theseus, though not very old in years, was almost worn out with the cares of government, and had thus grown aged before his time. His nephews, not expecting him to live a very great while, intended to get all the power of the kingdom into their own hands. But when they heard that Theseus had arrived in Athens, and learnt what a gallant young man he was, they saw that he would not be at all the kind of person to let them steal away his father's crown and sceptre, which ought to be his own by right of inheritance. Thus, these bad-hearted nephews of King Ægeus, who were the own cousins of Theseus, at once became his enemies. A still more danger-ous enemy was Medea, the wicked enchantress; for she was now the king's wife, and wanted to give the kingdom to her son Medus, instead of letting it be given to the son of Æthra, whom she hated.

It so happened that the king's nephews met Theseus, and found out who he was, just as he reached the entrance of the royal palace. With all their evil designs against him, they pre-tended to be their cousin's best friends, and expressed great joy at making his acquaintance. They proposed to him that he should come into the king's presence as a stranger, in or-der to try whether Ægeus would discover in the young man's features any likeness either to himself or his mother Æthra, and thus recognize him for a son. Theseus consented; for he fancied that his father would know him in a moment, by the love that was in his heart. But, while he waited at the door, the nephews ran and told King Ægeus, that a young man had arrived in Athens, who, to their certain knowledge, intended to put him to death, and get possession of his royal crown.

"And he is now waiting for admission to your majesty's presence!" added they.

"Aha!" cried the old king, on hearing this. "Why, he must be a very wicked young fellow, indeed! Pray what would you advise me to do with him?"

In reply to this question, the wicked Medea put in her word. As I have already told you, she was a famous enchantress. According to some stories, she was in the habit of boiling old people in a large cauldron, under pretence of making them young again; but King Ægeus, I suppose, did not fancy such an uncomfortable way of growing young, or perhaps was contented to be old, and therefore would never let himself be popt into the cauldron. If there were time to spare from more important matters, I should be glad to tell you of Medea's fiery chariot, drawn by winged dragons, in which the enchantress used often to take an airing among the clouds. This chariot, in fact, was the vehicle that first brought her to Athens, where she had done nothing but mischief, ever since her arrival. But these, and many other wonders, must be left untold; and it is enough to say, that Medea, amongst a thousand other bad things, knew how to prepare a poison, that was instantly fatal to whomsoever might so much as touch it with his lips.

So, when the king asked what he should do with Theseus, this naughty woman had an answer ready at her tongue's end.

"Leave that to me, please your majesty!" she replied. "Only admit this evil-minded young man to your presence, treat him civilly, and invite him to drink a goblet of wine. Your majesty is well aware that I sometimes amuse myself with distilling very powerful medicines. Here is one of them, in this small phial. As to what it is made of, that is one of my secrets of state. Do but let me put a single drop into the goblet, and, let the young man taste it; and, I will answer for it, he shall quite lay aside the bad designs with which he comes hither!"

As she said this, Medea smiled; but, for all her smiling face, she meant nothing less than to poison the poor innocent Theseus, before his father's eyes. And King Ægeus, like most other kings, thought any punishment mild enough for a person who was accused of plotting against his life. He therefore made little or no objection to Medea's scheme, and, as soon as the poisonous wine was ready, gave orders that the young stranger should be admitted into his presence. The goblet was set on a table beside the king's throne; and a fly, meaning just to sip a little from the brim, immediately tumbled into it, dead. Observing this, Medea looked round at the nephews, and smiled again.

When Theseus was ushered into the royal apartment, the only object, that he seemed to behold, was the white-bearded old king. There he sat on his magnificent throne, a dazzling crown on his head, and a sceptre in his hand. His aspect was stately and majestic, although his years and infirmities weighed heavily upon him; as if each year were a lump of lead, and each infirmity a ponderous stone, and all were bundled up together, and laid upon his weary shoulders. The tears, both of joy and sorrow, sprang into the young man's eyes; for he thought how sad it was to see his dear father so infirm, and how sweet it would be to support him with his own youthful strength, and to cheer him up with the alacrity of his loving spirit. When a son takes his father into his warm heart, it renews the old man's youth in a better way than by the heat of Medea's magic cauldron. And this was what Theseus resolved to do. He could scarcely wait to see whether King Ægeus would recognize him, so eager was he to throw himself into his arms.

Advancing to the foot of the throne, he attempted to make a little speech, which he had been thinking about, as he came up the stairs. But he was almost choked by a great many tender feelings that gushed out of his heart and swelled into his throat, all struggling to find utterance together. And, therefore, unless he could have laid his full, over-brimming heart into the king's hand, poor Theseus knew not what to do or say. The cunning Medea observed what was passing in the young man's mind. She was more wicked, at that moment, than ever she had been before; for (and it makes me tremble to tell you of it) she did her worst to turn all this unspeakable love, with which Theseus was agitated, to his own ruin and destruction.

"Does your majesty see his confusion?" she whispered in the king's ear. "He is so conscious of guilt, that he trembles and cannot speak. The wretch lives too long! Quick!—offer him the wine!"

Now King Ægeus had been gazing earnestly at the young stranger, as he drew near the throne. There was something, he knew not what, either in his white brow, or in the fine expression of his mouth, or in his beautiful and tender eyes, that made him indistinctly feel as if he had seen this youth before; as if, indeed, he had trotted him on his knee when a baby, and had beheld him growing to be a stalwart man, while he himself grew old. But Medea guessed how the king felt, and would not suffer him to yield to these natural sensibilities; although they were the voice of his deepest heart, telling him, as plainly as it could speak, that here was our dear son, and Æthra's son, coming to claim him for a father. The enchantress again whispered in the king's ear, and compelled him, by her witchcraft, to see everything under a false aspect.

He made up his mind, therefore, to let Theseus drink off the poisoned wine.

"Young man," said he, "you are welcome! I am proud to show hospitality to so heroic a youth. Do me the favor to drink the contents of this goblet. It is brimming over, as you see, with delicious wine, such as I bestow only on those who are worthy of it! None is more worthy to quaff it, than yourself."

So saying, King Ægeus took the golden goblet from the table, and was about to offer it to Theseus. But, partly through his infirmities, and partly because it seemed so sad a thing to take away this young man's life, however wicked he might be—and partly, no doubt, because his heart was wiser than his head, and quaked within him at the thought of what he was going to do—for all these reasons, the king's hand trembled so much that a great deal of the wine slopped over. In order to strengthen his purpose, and fearing lest the whole of the precious poison should be wasted, one of his nephews now whispered to him:—

"Has your majesty any doubt of this stranger's guilt? There is the very sword with which he meant to slay you. How sharp, and bright, and terrible it is! Quick!—let him taste the wine; or perhaps he may do the deed even yet!"

At these words, Ægeus drove every thought and feeling out of his breast, except the one idea of how justly the young man deserved to be put to death. He sat erect on his throne, and held out the goblet of wine with a steady hand, and bent on Theseus a frown of kingly severity; for, after all, he had too noble a spirit to murder even a treacherous enemy with a deceitful smile upon his face.

"Drink!" said he, in the stern tone with which he was wont to condemn a criminal to be beheaded. "You have well deserved of me such wine as this!"

Theseus held out his hand to take the wine. But, before he touched it, King Ægeus trembled again. His eyes had fallen on the gold-hilted sword that hung at the young man's side. He drew back the goblet.

"That sword!" he exclaimed. "How came you by it?"

"It was my father's sword!" replied Theseus, with a tremulous voice. "These were his sandals! My dear mother (her name is Æthra) told me his story, while I was yet a little child. But it is only a month since I grew strong enough to lift the heavy stone, and take the sword and sandals from beneath it, and come to Athens to seek my father!"

"My son! my son!" cried King Ægeus, flinging away the fatal goblet, and tottering down from the throne to fall into the arms of Theseus. "Yes; these are Æthra's eyes! It is my son!"

I have quite forgotten what became of the king's nephews. But when the wicked Medea saw this new turn of affairs, she hurried out of the room, and going to her private chamber, lost no time in setting her enchantments at work. In a few moments, she heard a great noise of hissing snakes, outside of the chamber window; and, behold! there was her fiery chariot, and four huge winged serpents, wriggling and twisting in the air, flourishing their tails higher than the top of the palace, and all ready to set off on an aerial journey. Medea staid only long enough to take her son with her, and to steal the crown-jewels, together with the king's best robes, and whatever other valuable things she could lay hands on; and getting into the chariot, she whipped up the snakes, and ascended high over the city.

The king, hearing the hiss of the serpents, scrambled as fast as he could to the window, and bawled out to the abominable enchantress never to come back. The whole people of Athens, too, who had run out of doors to see this wonderful spectacle, set up a shout of joy at the prospect of getting rid of her. Medea, almost bursting with rage, uttered precisely such a hiss as one of her own snakes, only ten times more venomous and spiteful; and, glaring fiercely out of the blaze of the chariot, she shook her hands over the multitude below, as if she were scattering a million of curses among them. In so doing, however, she unintentionally let fall about five hundred diamonds of the first water, together with a thousand great pearls, and two thousand emeralds, rubies, sapphires, opals, and topazes, to which she had helped herself out of the king's strong-box. All these came pelting down, like a shower of many-colored hail-stones, upon the heads of grown people and children, who forthwith gathered them up, and carried them back to the palace. But King Ægeus told them that they were welcome to the whole, and to twice as many more, if he had them, for the sake of his delight at finding his son, and losing the wicked Medea. And, indeed, if you had seen how hateful was her last look, as the flaming chariot flew upward, you would not have wondered that both king and people should think her departure a good riddance.

And now Prince Theseus was taken into great favor by his royal father. The old king was never weary of having him sit beside him on his throne, (which was quite wide enough for two,) and of hearing him tell about his dear mother, and his childhood, and his many boyish efforts to lift the ponderous stone. Theseus, however, was much too brave and active a young man to be willing to spend all his time in relating things which had already happened. His ambition was, to perform other and more heroic deeds, which should be better worth telling in prose and verse. Nor had he been long in Athens, before he caught and chained a terrible mad bull, and made a public show of him, greatly to the wonder and admiration of good King Ægeus and his subjects. But, pretty soon, he undertook an affair that made all his foregone adventures seem like mere boy's play. The occasion of it was as follows.

One morning, when Prince Theseus awoke, he fancied that he must have had a very sorrowful dream, and that it was still running in his mind, even now that his eyes were open. For it appeared as if the air was full of a melancholy wail; and when he listened more attentively, he could hear sobs, and groans, and screams of woe, mingled with deep, quiet sighs, which came from the king's palace, and from the streets, and from the temples, and from every habitation in the city. And all these mournful noises, issuing out of thousands of separate hearts, united themselves into the one great sound of affliction, which had startled Theseus from slumber. He put on his clothes as quickly as he could, (not forgetting his sandals and gold-hilted sword,) and hastening to the king, inquired what it all meant.

"Alas, my son," quoth King Ægeus, heaving a long sigh, "here is a very lamentable matter in hand! This is the woefullest anniversary in the whole year. It is the day when we annually draw lots, to see which of the youths and maidens of Athens shall go to be devoured by the horrible Minotaur!"

"The Minotaur!" exclaimed Prince Theseus; and like a brave young prince as he was, he put his hand to the hilt of his sword. "What kind of a monster may that be? Is it not possible, at the risk of one's life, to slay him?"

But King Ægeus shook his venerable head, and, to convince Theseus that it was quite a hopeless case, he gave him an explanation of the whole affair. It seems, that, in the island of Crete, there lived a certain dreadful monster, called a Minotaur, which was shaped partly like a man and partly like a bull, and was altogether such a hideous sort of a creature, that it is really disagreeable to think of him. If he were suffered to exist at all, it should have been on some desert island, or in the duskiness of some deep cavern, where nobody would ever be tormented by his abominable aspect. But King Minos, who reigned over Crete, laid out a vast deal of money in building a habitation for the Minotaur, and took great care of his health and comfort, merely for mischief's sake. A few years before this time, there had been a war between the city of Athens and the island of Crete, in which the Athenians were beaten, and compelled to beg for peace. No peace could they obtain, however, except on condition that they should send seven young men and seven maidens, every year, to be devoured by the pet-monster of the cruel King Minos. For three years past, this grievous calamity had been borne. And the sobs, and groans, and shrieks, with which the city was now filled, were caused by the people's woe, because the fatal day had come again, when the fourteen victims were to be chosen by lot; and the old people feared lest their sons or daughters might be taken, and the youths and damsels dreaded lest they themselves might be destined to glut the ravenous maw of that detestable man-brute.

But when Theseus heard the story, he straightened himself up, so that he seemed taller than ever before; and as for his face, it was indignant, despiteful, bold, tender, and compassionate, all in one look.

"Let the people of Athens, this year, draw lots for only six young men, instead of seven!" said he. "I will myself be the seventh; and let the Minotaur devour me, if he can!"

"Oh, my dear son," cried King Ægeus, "why should you expose yourself to this horrible fate? You are a royal prince, and have a right to hold yourself above the destinies of common men."

"It is because I am a prince, your son, and the rightful heir of your kingdom, that I freely take upon me the calamity of your subjects!" answered Theseus. "And you, my father, being king over this people, and answerable to heaven for their welfare, are bound to sacrifice what is dearest to you, rather than that the son or daughter of the poorest citizen should come to any harm!"

The old king shed tears, and besought Theseus not to leave him desolate in his old age, more especially as he had but just begun to know the happiness of possessing a good and valiant son. Theseus, however, felt that he was in the right, and therefore would not give up his resolution. But he assured his father that he did not intend to be eaten up, unresistingly, like a sheep, and that, if the Minotaur devoured him, it should not be without a battle for his dinner. And finally, since he could not help it, King Ægeus consented to let him go. So a vessel was got ready, and rigged with black sails; and Theseus, with six other young men, and seven tender and beautiful damsels, came down to the harbor to embark. A sorrowful multitude accompanied them to the shore. There was the poor old king, too, leaning on his son's arm, and looking as if his single heart held all the grief of Athens.

Just as Prince Theseus was going on board, his father bethought himself of one last word to say.

"My beloved son," said he, grasping the prince's hand,

"you observe that the sails of this vessel are black; as indeed they ought to be, since it goes upon a voyage of sorrow and despair. Now, being weighed down with infirmities, I know not whether I can survive till the vessel shall return. But, as long as I do live, I shall creep daily to the top of yonder cliff, to watch if there be a sail upon the sea. And, dearest Theseus, if, by some happy chance, you should escape the jaws of the Minotaur, then tear down those dismal sails, and hoist others that shall be bright as the sunshine! Beholding them on the horizon, myself and all the people will know that you are coming back victorious, and will welcome you with such a festal uproar as Athens never heard before!"

Theseus promised that he would do so. Then going on board, the mariners trimmed the vessel's black sails to the wind, which blew faintly off the shore, being pretty much made up of the sighs that everybody kept pouring forth, on this melancholy occasion. But, by-and-by, when they had got fairly out to sea, there came a stiff breeze from the north-west, and drove them along as merrily over the white-capt waves, as if they had been going on the most delightful errand imaginable. And, though it was a sad business enough, I rather question whether fourteen young people, without any old persons to keep them in order, could contrive to spend the whole time of the voyage in being miserable. There had been some few dances upon the undulating deck, I suspect, and some hearty bursts of laughter, and other such unseasonable merriment among the victims, before the high, blue mountains of Crete began to show themselves among the far-off clouds. That sight, to be sure, made them all very grave again.

Theseus stood among the sailors, gazing eagerly towards the land; although, as yet, it seemed hardly more substantial than the clouds, amidst which the mountains were looming up. Once or twice, he fancied that he saw a glare of some bright object, a long way off, flinging a gleam across the waves.

"Did you see that flash of light?" he inquired of the master of the vessel.

"No, prince; but I have seen it before," answered the master. "It came from Talus, I suppose."

As the breeze came fresher, just then, the master was busy with trimming his sails, and had no more time to answer questions. But, while the vessel flew faster and faster towards Crete, Theseus was astonished to behold a human figure, gigantic in size, which appeared to be striding, with a measured movement, along the margin of the island. It stept from cliff to cliff, and sometimes from one headland to another; while the sea foamed and thundered on the shore beneath, and dashed its jets of spray over the giant's feet. What was still more remarkable, whenever the sun shone on this huge figure, it flickered and glimmered; its vast countenance, too, had a metallic lustre, and threw great flashes of splendor through the air. The folds of its garments, moreover, instead of waving in the wind, fell heavily over its limbs, as if woven of some kind of metal.

The nigher the vessel came, the more Theseus wondered what this immense giant could be, and whether it actually had life or no. For, though it walked, and made other lifelike motions, there yet was a kind of jerk in its gait, which, together with its brazen aspect, caused the young prince to suspect that it was no true giant, but only a wonderful piece of machinery. The figure looked all the more terrible, because it carried an enormous brass club on its shoulder.

"What is this wonder?" Theseus asked of the master of the vessel, who was now at leisure to answer him.

"It is Talus, the Man of Brass," said the master.

"And is he a live giant, or a brazen image?" asked Theseus.

"That, truly," replied the master, "is the point which has always perplexed me. Some say, indeed, that this Talus was hammered out for King Minos by Vulcan himself, the skilfullest of all workers in metal. But who ever saw a brazen image that had sense enough to walk round an island, three times a day, as this giant walks round the island of Crete, challenging every vessel that comes nigh the shore? And, on the other hand, what living thing, unless his sinews were made of brass, would not be weary of marching eighteen hundred miles in the twenty-four hours, as Talus does, without ever sitting down to rest? He is a puzzler, take him how you will!"

Still, the vessel went bounding onward; and now Theseus could hear the brazen clangor of the giant's footsteps, as he trode heavily upon the sea-beaten rocks, some of which were seen to crack and crumble into the foamy waves, beneath his weight. As they approached the entrance of the port, the giant straddled clear across it, with a foot firmly planted on each headland; and uplifting his club to such a height that its but-end was hidden in a cloud, he stood in that formidable posture, with the sun gleaming all over his metallic surface. There seemed nothing else to be expected, but that, the next moment, he would fetch his great club down, slam-bang, and smash the vessel into a thousand pieces, without heeding how many innocent people he might destroy; for there is seldom any mercy in a giant, you know, and quite as little in a piece of brass clockwork. But, just when Theseus and his companions thought the blow was coming, the brazen lips unclosed themselves, and the figure spoke.

"Whence come you, strangers?"

And when the ringing voice ceased, there was just such a reverberation as you may have heard within a great church-bell, for a moment or two after the stroke of the hammer.

"From Athens!" shouted the master in reply.

"On what errand?" thundered the Man of Brass.

And he whirled his club aloft more threateningly than ever, as if he were about to smite them with a thunder-stroke, right amidships, because Athens, so little while ago, had been at war with Crete.

"We bring the seven youths and the seven maidens," answered the master, "to be devoured by the Minotaur!"

"Pass!" cried the brazen giant.

That one loud word rolled all about the sky, while again there was a booming reverberation within the figure's breast. The vessel glided between the headlands of the port, and the giant resumed his march. In a few moments, this wondrous centinel was far away, flashing in the distant sunshine, and revolving with immense strides around the island of Crete, as it was his never-ceasing task to do.

No sooner had they entered the harbor, than a party of the guards of King Minos came down to the water-side, and took charge of the fourteen young men and damsels. Surrounded by these armed warriors, Prince Theseus and his companions were led to the king's palace, and ushered into his presence.

Now, Minos was a stern and pitiless king. If the figure, that guarded Crete, was made of brass, then the monarch, who ruled over it, might be thought to have a still harder metal in his breast, and might have been called a man of iron. He bent his shaggy brows upon the poor Athenian victims. Any other mortal, beholding their fresh and tender beauty, and their innocent looks, would have felt himself sitting on thorns until he had made every soul of them happy, by bidding them go free as the summer-wind. But this immitigable Minos cared only to examine whether they were plump enough to satisfy the Minotaur's appetite. For my part, I wish he himself had been the only victim; and the monster would have found him a pretty tough one!

One after another, King Minos called these pale, frightened youths and sobbing maidens to his footstool, gave them each a poke in the ribs with his sceptre (to try whether they were in good flesh, or no) and dismissed them with a nod to his guards. But when his eyes rested on Theseus, the king looked at him more attentively, because his face was calm and brave.

"Young man," asked he, with his stern voice, "are you not appalled at the certainty of being devoured by this terrible Minotaur?"

"I have offered my life in a good cause," answered Theseus; "and therefore I give it freely and gladly. But thou, King Minos, art thou not thyself appalled, who, year after year, hast perpetrated this dreadful wrong, by giving seven innocent youths and as many maidens to be devoured by a monster? Dost thou not tremble, wicked king, to turn thine eyes inward on thine own heart? Sitting there on thy golden throne, and in thy robes of majesty, I tell thee to thy face, King Minos, thou art a more hideous monster than the Minotaur himself!"

"Aha, do you think me so?" cried the king, laughing in his cruel way. "Tomorrow, at breakfast-time, you shall have an opportunity of judging which is the greater monster, the Minotaur or the king! Take them away, guards; and let this free-spoken youth be the Minotaur's first morsel!"

Near the king's throne (though I had no time to tell you so, before) stood his daughter Ariadne. She was a beautiful and tender-hearted maiden, and looked at these poor doomed captives with very different feelings from those of the iron-breasted King Minos. She really wept, indeed, at the idea of how much human happiness would be needlessly thrown away, by giving so many young people, in the first bloom and rose-blossom of their lives, to be eaten up by a creature who, no doubt, would have preferred a fat ox, or even a large pig, to the plumpest of them. And when she beheld the brave, spirited figure of Prince Theseus, bearing himself so calmly in his terrible peril, she grew a hundred times more pitiful than before. As the guards were taking him away, she flung herself at the king's feet, and besought him to set all the captives free; and especially this one young man.

"Peace, foolish girl!" answered King Minos. "What hast thou to do with an affair like this? It is a matter of state-policy, and therefore quite beyond thy weak comprehension. Go water thy flowers, and think no more of these Athenian caitiffs, whom the Minotaur shall as certainly eat up for breakfast, as I will eat a partridge for my supper!"

So saying, the king looked cruel enough to devour Theseus and all the rest of the captives, himself, had there been no Minotaur to save him the trouble. As he would hear not another word in their favor, the prisoners were now led away and clapt into a dungeon, where the jailer advised them to go to sleep as soon as possible, because the Minotaur was in the habit of calling for breakfast early. The seven maidens, and six of the young men, soon sobbed themselves to slumber. But Theseus was not like them. He felt conscious that he was wiser, and braver, and stronger than his companions, and that therefore he had the responsibility of all their lives upon him, and must consider whether there was no way to save them, even in this last extremity. So he kept himself awake, and paced to-and-fro across the gloomy dungeon in which they were shut up.

Just before midnight, the door was softly unbarred, and the gentle Ariadne showed herself, with a torch in her hand.

"Are you awake, Prince Theseus?" she whispered.

"Yes!" answered Theseus. "With so little time to live, I do not choose to waste any of it in sleep."

"Then follow me," said Ariadne, "and tread softly."

What had become of the jailer and the guards, Theseus

never knew. But, however that might be, Ariadne opened all the doors, and led him forth from the darksome prison into the pleasant moonlight.

"Theseus," said the maiden, "you can now get on board your vessel, and sail away for Athens."

"No!" answered the young man. "I will never leave Crete, unless I can first slay the Minotaur, and save my poor companions, and deliver Athens from this cruel tribute!"

"I knew that this would be your resolution," said Ariadne. "Come then with me, brave Theseus! Here is your own sword, which the guards deprived you of. You will need it; and pray Heaven you may use it well!"

Then she led Theseus along, by the hand, until they came to a dark, shadowy grove, where the moonlight wasted itself on the tops of the trees, without shedding hardly so much as a glimmering beam upon their pathway. After going a good way through this obscurity, they reached a high, marble wall, which was overgrown with creeping-plants that made it shaggy with their verdure. The wall seemed to have no door, nor any windows, but rose up, lofty, and massive, and mysterious, and was neither to be clambered over, nor, so far as Theseus could perceive, to be passed through. Nevertheless, Ariadne did but press one of her soft little fingers against a particular block of marble, and though it looked as solid as any other part of the wall, it yielded to her touch, disclosing an entrance just wide enough to admit them. They crept through; and the marble-stone swung back into its place.

"We are now," said Ariadne, "in the famous labyrinth which Dædalus built, before he made himself a pair of wings, and flew away from our island like a bird. That Dædalus was a very cunning workman; but of all his artful contrivances, this labyrinth is the most wondrous. Were we to take but a few steps from the doorway, we might wander about, all our lifetime, and never find it again. Yet, in the very centre of this labyrinth is the Minotaur; and, Theseus, you must go thither to seek him!"

"But how shall I ever find him," asked Theseus, "if the labyrinth so bewilders me as you say it will?"

Just as he spoke, they heard a rough and very disagreeable roar, which greatly resembled the lowing of a fierce bull, but

yet had some sort of sound like the human voice. Theseus
even fancied a rude articulation in it, as if the creature, that
uttered it, were trying to shape his hoarse breath into words.
It was at some distance, however; and he really could not tell
whether it sounded most like a bull's roar or a man's harsh
voice.

"That is the Minotaur's noise," whispered Ariadne, closely
grasping the hand of Theseus, and pressing one of her own
hands to her heart, which was all in a tremble. "You must
follow that sound through the windings of the labyrinth, and,
by-and-by, you will find him. Stay! Take the end of this silken
string. I will hold the other end; and then, if you win the
victory, it will lead you again to this spot. Farewell, brave
Theseus!"

So the young man took the end of the silken string in his
left hand, and his gold-hilted sword, ready drawn from its
scabbard, in the other, and trod boldly into the inscrutable
labyrinth. How this labyrinth was built, is more than I can
tell you. But so cunningly contrived a mizmaze was never
seen in the world, before nor since. There can be nothing else
so intricate, unless it were the brain of a man like Dædalus,
who planned it, or the heart of any ordinary man; which last,
to be sure, is ten times as great a mystery as the labyrinth of
Crete. Theseus had not taken five steps, before he lost sight
of Ariadne; and, in five more, his head was growing dizzy.
But still he went on, now creeping through a low arch, now
ascending a flight of steps, now in one crooked passage, and
now in another, with here a door opening before him, and
there one banging behind; until it really seemed as if the walls
spun round, and whirled him round along with them. And,
all the while, through these hollow avenues, now nearer, now
farther off again, resounded the cry of the Minotaur; and the
sound was so fierce, so cruel, so ugly—so like a bull's roar,
and withal so like a human voice, and yet like neither of
them—that the brave heart of Theseus grew sterner and an-
grier at every step. For he felt it an insult to the moon and
sky, and to our affectionate and simple Mother Earth, that
such a monster should have the audacity to exist.

As he pressed onward, the clouds gathered over the moon,
and the labyrinth grew so dusky that Theseus could no longer

discern the bewilderment through which he was passing. He would have felt quite lost, and utterly hopeless of ever again walking in a straight path, if, every little while, he had not been conscious of a gentle twitch at the silken cord. Then he knew that the tender-hearted Ariadne was still holding the other end, and that she was fearing for him, and hoping for him, and giving him just as much of her sympathy as if she were close by his side. Oh, indeed, I can assure you, there was a vast deal of human sympathy running along that slender thread of silk! But still he followed the dreadful roar of the Minotaur, which now grew louder and louder, and finally so very loud, that Theseus fully expected to come close upon him, at every new zig-zag and wriggle of the path. And, at last, in an open space, at the very centre of the labyrinth, he did discern the hideous creature!

Sure enough, what an ugly monster it was! Only his horned head belonged to a bull; and yet, somehow or other, he looked like a bull all over, preposterously waddling on his hind-legs; or, if you happened to view him in another way, he seemed wholly a man, and all the more monstrous for being so. And there he was, the wretched thing, with no society, no companion, no kind of a mate, living only to do mischief, and incapable of knowing what affection means! Theseus hated him, and shuddered at him, and yet could not but be sensible of some sort of pity, and all the more, the uglier and more detestable the creature was. For he kept striding to-and-fro, in a solitary frenzy of rage, continually emitting a hoarse roar, which was oddly mixed up with half-shaped words; and, after listening a while, Theseus understood that the Minotaur was saying to himself how miserable he was, and how hungry, and how he hated everybody, and how he longed to eat up the human race alive!

Ah, the bull-headed villain! And, Oh, my good little people, you will perhaps see, one of these days, as I do now, that every human being, who suffers anything evil to get into his nature, or to remain there, is a kind of Minotaur, an enemy of his fellow-creatures, and separated from all good companionship, as this poor monster was!

Was Theseus afraid? By no means, my dear auditors. What! A hero like Theseus afraid! Not had the Minotaur had twenty bull-heads instead of one. Bold as he was, however, I rather fancy that it strengthened his valiant heart, just at this crisis, to feel a tremulous twitch at the silken cord, which he was still holding in his left hand. It was as if Ariadne were giving him all her might and courage; and, much as he already had, and little as she had to give, it made his own seem twice as much. And, to confess the honest truth, he needed the whole; for now the Minotaur, turning suddenly about, caught sight of Theseus, and instantly lowered his horribly sharp horns, exactly as a mad bull does when he means to rush against an enemy. At the same time, he belched forth a tremendous roar, in which there was something like the words of human language, but all disjointed and shaken to pieces by passing through the gullet of a miserably enraged brute.

Theseus could only guess what the creature intended to say, and that rather by his gestures than his words; for the Minotaur's horns were sharper than his wits, and of a great deal more service to him than his tongue. But probably this was the sense of what he uttered: —

"Ah, wretch of a human being! I'll stick my horns through you, and toss you fifty feet high, and eat you up the moment you come down!"

"Come on, then, and try it!" was all that Theseus deigned to reply; for he was far too magnanimous to assault his enemy with insolent language.

Without more words on either side, there ensued the most awful fight between Theseus and the Minotaur, that ever happened beneath the sun or moon. I really know not how it might have turned out, if the monster, in his first headlong rush against Theseus, had not missed him, by a hair's breadth, and broken one of his horns short off against the stone-wall. On this mishap, he bellowed so intolerably that a part of the labyrinth tumbled down, and all the inhabitants of Crete mistook the noise for an uncommonly heavy thunderstorm. Smarting with the pain, he galloped around the open space in so ridiculous a way that Theseus laughed at it, long afterwards, though not precisely at the moment. After this, the two antagonists stood valiantly up to one another, and fought, sword to horn, for a long while. At last, the Minotaur made a run at Theseus, grazed his left side with his horn, and flung him down; and thinking that he had stabbed him to the heart, he cut a great caper in the air, opened his bull-mouth from ear to ear, and prepared to snap his head off. But Theseus, by this time, had leaped up, and caught the monster off his guard. Fetching a sword-stroke at him, with all his force, he hit him fair upon the neck, and made his bull-head skip six yards from his human body, which fell down flat upon the ground.

So now the battle was ended! Immediately, the moon shone out as brightly as if all the troubles of the world, and all the wickedness and the ugliness that infest human life, were past and gone forever. And Theseus, as he leaned on his sword, taking breath, felt another twitch of the silken cord; for, all through the terrible encounter, he had held it fast in his left hand. Eager to let Ariadne know of his success, he followed the guidance of the thread, and soon found himself at the entrance of the labyrinth.

"Thou hast slain the monster!" cried Ariadne, clasping her hands.

"Thanks to thee, dear Ariadne," answered Theseus, "I return victorious."

"Then," said Ariadne, "we must quickly summon thy friends, and get them and thyself on board the vessel, before dawn. If morning finds thee here, my father will avenge the Minotaur!"

To make my story short, the poor captives were awakened, and, hardly knowing whether it was not a joyful dream, were told of what Theseus had done, and that they must set sail for Athens before daybreak. Hastening down to the vessel, they all clambered on board, except Prince Theseus, who lingered behind them, on the strand, holding Ariadne's hand clasped in his own.

"Dear maiden," said he, "thou wilt surely go with us! Thou art too gentle and sweet a child for such an iron-hearted father as King Minos. He cares no more for thee, than a granite-rock cares for the little flower that grows in one of its crevices! But my father, King Ægeus, and my dear mother Æthra, and all the fathers and mothers in Athens, and all the sons and daughters too, will love and honor thee as their benefactress. Come with us, then; for

King Minos will be very angry, when he knows what thou hast done!"

Now, some low-minded people, who pretend to tell the story of Theseus and Ariadne, have the face to say that this royal and honorable maiden did really flee away, under cover of the night, with the young stranger whose life she had preserved. They say, too, that Prince Theseus (who would have died, sooner than wrong the meanest creature in the world) ungratefully deserted Ariadne, on a solitary island, where the vessel touched on its voyage to Athens. But, had the noble Theseus heard these falsehoods, he would have served their slanderous authors as he served the Minotaur! Here is what Ariadne answered, when the brave Prince of Athens besought her to accompany him.

"No, Theseus!" the maiden said, pressing his hand, and then drawing back a step or two. "I cannot go with you. My father is old, and has nobody but myself to love him. Hard as you think his heart is, it would break to lose me. At first, King Minos will be angry; but he will soon forgive his only child; and, by-and-by, he will rejoice, I know, that no more youths and maidens must come from Athens, to be devoured by the Minotaur! I have saved you, Theseus, as much for my father's sake as for your own. Farewell! Heaven bless you!"

All this was so true, and so maidenlike, and was spoken with so sweet a dignity, that Theseus would have blushed to urge her any longer. Nothing remained for him, therefore, but to bid Ariadne an affectionate farewell, and to go on board the vessel, and set sail.

In a few moments, the white foam was boiling up before their prow, as Prince Theseus and his companions sailed out of the harbor, with a whistling breeze behind them. Talus, the brazen giant, on his never-ceasing centinel's march, happened to be approaching that part of the coast; and they saw him, by the glimmering of the moonbeams on his polished surface, while he was yet a great way off. As the figure moved like clockwork, however, and could neither hasten his enormous strides nor retard them, he arrived at the port when they were just beyond the reach of his club. Nevertheless, straddling from headland to headland, as his custom was, Talus attempted to strike a blow at the vessel, and, overreaching himself, tumbled at full length into the sea, which splashed high over his gigantic shape, as when an iceberg turns a somerset. There he lies yet; and whoever desires to enrich himself by means of brass, had better go thither with a diving-bell, and fish up Talus!

On the homeward voyage, the fourteen youths and damsels were in excellent spirits, as you will easily suppose. They spent most of their time in dancing, unless when the sidelong breeze made the deck slope too much. In due season, they came within sight of the coast of Attica, which was their native country. But here, I am grieved to tell you, happened a sad misfortune.

You will remember (what Theseus unfortunately forgot) that his father, King Ægeus, had enjoined it upon him to hoist sunshiny sails, instead of black ones, in case he should overcome the Minotaur, and return victorious. In the joy of their success, however, and amidst the sports, dancing, and other merriment, with which these young folks wore away the time, they never once thought whether their sails were black, white, or rainbow-colored, and, indeed, left it entirely to the mariners whether they had any sails at all. Thus, the vessel returned, like a raven, with the same sable wings that had wafted her away. But poor King Ægeus, day after day, infirm as he was, had clambered to the summit of a cliff that overhung the sea, and there sat watching for Prince Theseus, homeward bound; and no sooner did he behold the fatal blackness of the sails, than he concluded that his dear son, whom he loved so much, and felt so proud of, had been eaten by the Minotaur. He could not bear the thought of living any longer; so, first flinging his crown and sceptre into the sea, (useless baubles that they were to him, now!) King Ægeus merely stooped forward, and fell headlong over the cliff, and was drowned, poor soul, in the waves that foamed at its base!

This was melancholy news for Prince Theseus, who, when he stept ashore, found himself king of all the country, whether he would or no; and such a turn of fortune was enough to make any young man feel very much out of spirits. However, he sent for his dear mother to Athens, and, by taking her advice in matters of state, became a very excellent monarch, and was greatly beloved by his people.

The Pygmies

A GREAT while ago, when the world was full of wonders, there lived an earth-born giant, named Antæus, and a million or more of curious little earth-born people, who were called Pygmies. This giant and these Pygmies, being children of the same mother, (that is to say, our good old Grandmother Earth,) were all brethren, and dwelt together in a very friendly and affectionate manner, far, far off, in the middle of hot Africa. The Pygmies were so small, and there were so many sandy deserts and such high mountains between them and the rest of mankind, that nobody could get a peep at them oftener than once in a hundred years. As for the giant, being of a very lofty stature, it was easy enough to see him, but safest to keep out of his sight.

Among the Pygmies, I suppose, if one of them grew to the height of six or eight inches, he was reckoned a prodigiously tall man. It must have been very pretty to behold their little cities, with streets two or three feet wide, paved with the smallest pebbles, and bordered by habitations about as big as a squirrel's cage. The king's palace attained to the stupendous magnitude of Periwinkle's baby-house, and stood in the centre of a spacious square, which could hardly have been covered by our hearth-rug. Their principal temple, or cathedral, was as lofty as yonder bureau, and was looked upon as a wonderfully sublime and magnificent edifice. All these structures were built neither of stone nor wood. They were neatly plastered together by the Pygmy-workmen, pretty much like birds' nests, out of straw, feathers, egg-shells, and other small bits of stuff, with stiff clay instead of mortar; and when the hot sun had dried them, they were just as snug and comfortable as a Pygmy could desire.

The country roundabout was conveniently laid out in fields, the largest of which was nearly of the same extent as one of Sweet Fern's flower-beds. Here the Pygmies used to plant wheat and other kinds of grain, which, when it grew up and ripened, overshadowed these tiny people, as the pines, and the oaks, and the walnut and chestnut-trees, overshadow

you and me, when we walk in our own tracts of woodland.
At harvest-time, they were forced to go with their little axes
and cut down the grain, exactly as a wood-cutter makes a
clearing in the forest; and when a stalk of wheat, with its
over-burthened top, chanced to come crashing down upon an
unfortunate Pygmy, it was apt to be a very sad affair. If it did
not smash him all to pieces, at least, I am sure, it must have
made the poor little fellow's head ache! And, Oh, my stars!
If the fathers and mothers were so small, what must the children and babies have been? A whole family of them might
have been put to bed in a shoe, or have crept into an old
glove, and played at hide-and-seek in its thumb and fingers!
You might have hidden a year-old baby under a thimble!

Now these funny Pygmies, as I told you before, had a giant
for their neighbor and brother, who was bigger, if possible,
than they were little. He was so very tall that he carried a
pine-tree, which was eight feet through the but, for a walking-stick. It took a far-sighted Pygmy, I can assure you, to
discern his summit without the help of a telescope; and sometimes, in misty weather, they could not see his upper half, but
only his long legs, which seemed to be striding about by
themselves. But at noon-day, in a clear atmosphere, when the
sun shone brightly over him, the giant Antæus presented a
very grand spectacle. There he used to stand, a perfect mountain of a man, with his great countenance smiling down upon
his little brothers, and his one vast eye (which was as big as
a cart-wheel, and placed right in the centre of his forehead)
giving a friendly wink to the whole nation at once.

The Pygmies loved to talk with Antæus; and fifty times a
day, one or another of them would turn up his head, and
shout through the hollow of his fists—"Halloo, brother
Antæus! How are you, my good fellow?"—And when the
small, distant squeak of their voices reached his ear, the giant
would make answer—"Pretty well, brother Pygmy, I thank
you!"—in a thunderous roar that would have shaken down
the walls of their strongest temple, only that it came from so
far aloft.

It was a happy circumstance that Antæus was the Pygmy
people's friend; for there was more strength in his little finger, than in ten million of such bodies as theirs. If he had

been as ill-natured to them as he was to everybody else, he might have beaten down their biggest city at one kick, and hardly have known that he did it. With the tornado of his breath, he could have stript the roofs from a hundred dwellings, and sent thousands of the inhabitants whirling through the air. He might have set his immense foot upon a multitude; and when he took it up again, there would have been a pitiful sight, to be sure! But, being the son of Mother Earth, as they likewise were, the giant gave them his brotherly kindness, and loved them with as big a love, as it was possible to feel for creatures so very small. And, on their parts, the Pygmies loved Antæus with as much affection as their tiny hearts could hold. He was always ready to do them any good offices that lay in his power; as, for example, when they wanted a breeze to turn their wind-mills, the giant would set all the sails a-going with the mere natural respiration of his lungs. When the sun was too hot, he often sat himself down and let his shadow fall over the kingdom, from one frontier to the other; and as for matters in general, he was wise enough to let them alone, and leave the Pygmies to manage their own affairs—which, after all, is about the best thing that great people can do for little ones.

In short, as I said before, Antæus loved the Pygmies, and the Pygmies loved Antæus. The giant's life being as long as his body was large, while the lifetime of a Pygmy was but a span, this friendly intercourse had been going on for innumerable generations and ages. It was written about, in the Pygmy histories, and talked about, in their ancient traditions. The most venerable and white-bearded Pygmy had never heard of a time, even in his greatest of grandfather's days, when the giant was not their enormous friend. Once, to be sure, (as was recorded on an obelisk, three feet high, erected on the place of the catastrophe,) Antæus sat down upon about five thousand Pygmies, who were assembled at a military review. But this was one of those unlucky accidents for which nobody is to blame; so that the small folks never took it to heart, and only requested the giant to be careful, forever afterwards, to examine the acre of ground where he intended to squat himself.

It is a very pleasant picture to imagine Antæus standing

among the Pygmies, like the spire of the tallest cathedral that
ever was built, while they ran about like pismires at his feet;
and to think that, in spite of their difference in size, there was
affection and sympathy between them and him! Indeed, it has
always seemed to me that the giant needed the little people,
more than the Pygmies needed the giant. For, unless they had
been his neighbors and well-wishers, and, as we may say, his
playfellows, Antæus would not have had a single friend in the
world. No other being, like himself, had ever been created.
No creature of his own size had ever talked with him, in
thunder-like accents, face to face. When he stood with his
head among the clouds, he was quite alone, and had been so,
for hundreds of years, and would be so, forever! Even if he
had met another giant, Antæus would have fancied the world
not big enough for two such vast personages, and, instead of
being friends with him, would have fought him till one of the
two was killed. But, with the Pygmies, he was the most sportive, and humorous, and merry-hearted, and sweet-tempered
old giant, that ever washed his face in a wet cloud!

His little friends, like all other small people, had a great
opinion of their own importance, and used to assume quite a
patronizing air towards the giant.

"Poor creature!" they said one to another. "He has a very
dull time of it, all by himself; and we ought not to grudge
wasting a little of our precious time to amuse him. He is not
half so bright as we are, to be sure; and, for that reason, he
needs us to look after his comfort and happiness. Let us be
kind to the old fellow! Why, if Mother Earth had not been
very kind to ourselves, we might all have been giants too!"

On all their holidays, the Pygmies had excellent sport with
Antæus. He often stretched himself out at full length on the
ground, where he looked like the long ridge of a hill; and it
was a good hour's walk, no doubt, for a short-legged Pygmy
to journey from head to foot of the giant. He would lay
down his great hand flat on the grass, and challenge the tallest
of them to clamber upon it, and straddle from finger to finger. So fearless were they, that they made nothing of creeping
in among the folds of his garments. When his head lay sideways on the earth, they would march boldly up and peep into
the great cavern of his mouth, and take it all as a joke (as,

indeed, it was meant) when Antæus gave a sudden snap with his jaws, as if he were going to swallow fifty of them at once. You would have laughed to see the children dodging in and out among his hair, or swinging from his beard. It is impossible to tell half of the funny tricks that they played with their huge comrade; but I do not know that anything was more curious, than when a party of boys were seen running races on his forehead, to try which of them could get first round the circle of his one, great eye. It was another favorite feat with them, to march along the bridge of his nose, and jump down upon his upper lip!

If the truth must be told, they were sometimes as troublesome to the giant as a swarm of ants or musquitoes; especially as they had a fondness for mischief, and liked to prick his skin with their little swords and lances, to see how thick and tough it was. But Antæus took it all kindly enough; although, once in a while, when he happened to be sleepy, he would grumble out a peevish word or two, like the muttering of a tempest, and ask them to have done with their nonsense. A great deal oftener, however, he watched their merriment and gambols, until his huge, heavy, clumsy wits were completely stirred up by them; and then would he roar out such a tremendous volume of immeasurable laughter, that the whole nation of Pygmies had to put their hands to their ears—else it would certainly have deafened them.

"Ho! Ho! Ho!" quoth the giant, shaking his mountainous sides. "What a funny thing it is to be little! If I were not Antæus, I should like to be a Pygmy, just for the joke's sake!"

The Pygmies had but one thing to trouble them in the world. They were constantly at war with the cranes, and had always been so, ever since the long-lived giant could remember. From time to time, very terrible battles had been fought, in which sometimes the little men won the victory, and sometimes the cranes. According to some historians, the Pygmies used to go to the battle, mounted on the backs of goats and rams; but such animals as these must have been far too big for Pygmies to ride upon; so that, I rather suppose, they rode on squirrel-back, or rabbit-back, or rat-back, or, perhaps, got upon hedge-hogs, whose prickly quills would be very terrible to the enemy. However this might be, and whatever creatures the Pygmies rode upon, I do not doubt that they made a formidable appearance, armed with sword and spear, and bow and arrow, blowing their tiny trumpet, and shouting their little war-cry. They never failed to exhort one another to fight bravely, and recollect that the world had its eyes upon them; although, in simple truth, the only spectator was the giant Antæus, with his one, great, stupid eye, in the middle of his forehead.

When the two armies joined battle, the cranes would rush forward, flapping their wings and stretching out their necks, and would perhaps snatch up some of the Pygmies crosswise in their beaks. Whenever this happened, it was truly an awful spectacle to see those little men of might kicking and sprawl-ing in the air, and at last disappearing down the crane's long, crooked throat, swallowed up alive! A hero, you know, must hold himself in readiness for any kind of fate; and, doubtless, the glory of the thing was a consolation to him, even in the crane's gizzard. If Antæus observed that the battle was going hard against his little allies, he generally stopped laughing, and ran with mile-long strides to their assistance, flourishing his club aloft and shouting at the cranes, who quacked and croaked, and retreated as fast as they could. Then the Pygmy army would march homeward in triumph, attributing the vic-tory entirely to their own valor, and to the warlike skill and strategy of whomsoever happened to be captain-general; and, for a tedious while afterwards, nothing would be heard of but grand processions, and public banquets, and brilliant illumi-nations, and shows of wax-work, with likenesses of the distin-guished officers, as small as life!

In the above-described warfare, if a Pygmy chanced to pluck out a crane's tail-feather, it proved a very great feather in his cap. Once or twice, if you will believe me, a little man was made chief-ruler of the nation, for no other merit in the world than bringing home such a feather!

But I have now said enough to let you see what a gallant little people these were, and how happily they and their fore-fathers, for nobody knows how many generations, had lived with the immeasurable giant Antæus. In the remaining part of the story, I shall tell you of a far more astonishing battle than any that was fought between the Pygmies and the cranes.

One day, the mighty Antæus was lolling at full length among his little friends. His pine-tree walking-stick lay on the ground, close by his side. His head was in one part of the kingdom, and his feet extended across the boundaries of another part; and he was taking whatever comfort he could get, while the Pygmies scrambled over him, and peeped into his cavernous mouth, and played among his hair. Sometimes, for a minute or two, the giant dropped asleep, and snored like the rush of a whirlwind. During one of these little bits of slumber, a Pygmy chanced to climb upon his shoulder, and took a view around the horizon, as from the summit of a hill; and he beheld something, a long way off, which made him rub the bright specks of his eyes, and look sharper than before. At first, he mistook it for a mountain, and wondered how it had grown up so suddenly out of the earth. But, soon, he saw the mountain move. As it came nearer and nearer, what should it turn out to be, but a human shape, not so big as Antæus, it is true, although a very enormous figure, in comparison with Pygmies, and a vast deal bigger than the men whom we see, now-a-days!

When the Pygmy was quite satisfied that his eyes had not deceived him, he scampered, as fast as his legs would carry him, to the giant's ear, and stooping over its cavity, shouted lustily into it.

"Halloo, brother Antæus! Get up, this minute, and take your pine-tree walking-stick in your hand. Here comes another giant to have a tustle with you!"

"Poh, poh!" grumbled Antæus, only half awake. "None of your nonsense, my little fellow! Don't you see I'm sleepy. There is not a giant on earth for whom I would take the trouble to get up!"

But the Pygmy looked again, and now perceived that the stranger was coming directly towards the prostrate form of Antæus. With every step, he looked less like a blue mountain, and more like an immensely large man. He was soon so nigh, that there could be no possible mistake about the matter. There he was, with the sun flaming on his golden helmet, and flashing from his polished breastplate; he had a sword by his side, and a lion's skin over his back, and on his right shoulder he carried a club, which looked bulkier and heavier than the pine-tree walking-stick of Antæus.

By this time, the whole nation of Pygmies had seen the new wonder, and a million of them set up a shout, all together; so that it really made quite an audible squeak.

"Get up, Antæus! Bestir yourself, you lazy old giant! Here comes another giant, as strong as you are, to fight with you!"

"Nonsense, nonsense!" growled the sleepy giant. "I'll have my nap out, come who may!"

Still, the stranger drew nearer; and now the Pygmies could plainly discern, that, if his stature were less lofty than the giant's, yet his shoulders were even broader. And, in truth, what a pair of shoulders they must have been! As I told you, a long while ago, they once upheld the sky! The Pygmies, being ten times as vivacious as their great numskull of a brother, could not abide the giant's slow movements, and were determined to have him on his feet. So they kept shouting to him, and even went so far as to prick him with their swords.

"Get up, get up, get up!" they cried. "Up with you, lazybones! The strange giant's club is bigger than your own, his shoulders are the broadest, and we think him the stronger of the two!"

Antæus could not endure to have it said, that any mortal was half so mighty as himself. This latter remark of the Pygmies pricked him deeper than their swords; and sitting up, in rather a sulky humor, he gave a gape of several yards wide, rubbed his eyes, and finally turned his stupid head in the direction whither his little friends were eagerly pointing.

No sooner did he set eyes on the stranger, than, leaping on his feet and seizing his walking-stick, he strode a mile or two to meet him; all the while, brandishing the sturdy pine-tree, so that it whistled through the air.

"Who are you?" thundered the giant. "And what do you want in my dominions?"

There was one strange thing about Antæus, of which I have not yet told you; lest, hearing of so many wonders all in a lump, you might not believe much more than half of them.

You are to know, then, that, whenever this redoubtable giant touched the ground, either with his hand, his foot, or any other part of his body, he grew stronger than ever he had been before. The Earth, you remember, was his mother, and was very fond of him, as being almost the biggest of her children; and so she took this method of keeping him always in full vigor. Some persons affirm, that he grew ten times stronger, at every touch; others say, that it was only twice as strong. But, only think of it! Whenever Antæus took a walk, supposing it were but ten miles, and that he stepped a hundred yards at a stride, you may try to cypher out how much mightier he was, on sitting down again, than when he first started. And whenever he flung himself on the earth, to take a little repose, even if he got up the very next instant, he would be as strong as exactly ten just such giants as his former self! It was well for the world that Antæus happened to be of a sluggish disposition, and liked ease better than exercise; for, if he had frisked about like the Pygmies, and touched the earth as often as they did, he would long ago have been strong enough to pull down the sky about people's ears! But these great lubberly fellows resemble mountains, not only in bulk, but in their disinclination to move.

Any other mortal man, except the very one whom Antæus had now encountered, would have been half frightened to death by the giant's ferocious aspect and terrible voice. But the stranger did not seem at all disturbed. He carelessly lifted his club and balanced it in his hand, measuring Antæus with his eye, from head to foot, not as if wonder-smitten at his stature, but as if he had seen a great many giants before, and this was by no means the biggest of them. In fact, if the giant had been no bigger than the Pygmies, (who stood pricking up their ears, and looking and listening to what was going forward,) the stranger could not have been less afraid of him.

"Who are you, I say?" roared Antæus again. "What's your name? Why do you come hither? Speak, you vagabond; or I'll try the thickness of your skull, with my walking-stick!"

"You are a very discourteous giant," answered the stranger, quietly; "and I shall probably have to teach you a little civility, before we part. As for my name, it is Hercules. I have come hither, because this is my most convenient road to the garden of the Hesperides, whither I am going to get three of the golden apples for King Eurystheus."

"Caitiff, you shall go no farther!" bellowed Antæus, putting on a grimmer look than before; for he had heard of the mighty Hercules, and hated him because he was said to be so strong. "Neither shall you go back whence you came!"

"How will you prevent me," asked Hercules, "from going whither I please?"

"By hitting you a rap with this pine-tree here!" shouted Antæus, scowling so, that he made himself the ugliest monster in Africa. "I am fifty times stronger than you; and, now that I stamp my foot upon the ground, I am five hundred times stronger! I am ashamed to kill such a puny little dwarf as you seem to be. I will make a slave of you; and you shall likewise be the slave of my brethren, here, the Pygmies. So throw down your club and your other weapons; and as for that lion's skin, I intend to have a pair of gloves made of it!"

"Come and take it off my shoulders, then!" answered Hercules, lifting his club.

Then the giant, grinning with rage, strode tower-like towards the stranger, (ten times strengthened at every step,) and fetched a monstrous blow at him with his pine-tree, which Hercules caught upon his club; and being more skilful than Antæus, he paid him back such a rap upon the sconce, that down tumbled the great lumbering man-mountain, flat upon the ground. The poor little Pygmies (who really never dreamed that anybody in the world was half so strong as their brother Antæus) were a good deal dismayed at this. But no sooner was the giant down, than up he bounced again, with tenfold might, and such a furious visage as was horrible to behold. He aimed another blow at Hercules, but struck awry, being blinded with wrath, and only hit his poor innocent Mother Earth, who groaned and trembled at the stroke. His pine-tree went so deep into the ground, and stuck there so fast, that, before Antæus could get it out, Hercules brought down his club across his shoulders with a mighty thwack, which made the giant roar, as if all sorts of intolerable noises had come screeching and rumbling out of his immeasurable lungs, in that one cry! Away it went, over mountains and vallies, and, for aught I know, was heard on the other side of the African deserts.

As for the Pygmies, their capital city was laid in ruins by the concussion and vibration of the air; and, though there was uproar enough without their help, they all set up a shriek out of three million of little throats, fancying, no doubt, that they swelled the giant's bellow by at least ten times as much. Meanwhile, Antæus had scrambled upon his feet again, and pulled his pine-tree out of the earth; and, all a-flame with fury, and more outrageously strong than ever, he ran at Hercules and brought down another blow.

"This time, rascal," shouted he, "you shall not escape me!"

But, once more, Hercules warded off the stroke with his club; and the giant's pine-tree was shattered into a thousand splinters, most of which flew among the Pygmies, and did them more mischief than I like to think about. Before Antæus could get out of the way, Hercules let drive again and gave him another knock-down blow, which sent him heels over head, but served only to increase his already enormous and insufferable strength. As for his rage, there is no telling what a fiery furnace it had now got to be. His one eye was nothing but a circle of red flame. Having now no weapons but his fists, he doubled them up, (each bigger than a hogshead,) smote one against the other, and danced up and down with absolute frenzy, flourishing his immense arms about, as if he meant not merely to kill Hercules, but to smash the whole world to pieces!

"Come on!" roared this thundering giant. "Let me hit you but one box on the ear, and you'll never have the headache again!"

Now Hercules (though strong enough, as you already know, to hold the sky up) began to be sensible that he should never win the victory, if he kept on knocking Antæus down. For, by-and-by, if he hit him such hard blows, the giant would inevitably, by the help of his Mother Earth, become stronger than the mighty Hercules himself. So, throwing down his club, with which he had fought so many dreadful battles, the hero stood ready to receive his antagonist with naked arms.

"Step forward!" cried he. "Since I've broken your pine-tree, we'll try which is the better man at a wrestling-match!"

"Aha, then, I'll soon satisfy you!" shouted the giant; for, if there was one thing on which he prided himself more than another, it was his skill in wrestling. "Villain, I'll fling you where you can never pick yourself up again!"

On came Antæus, hopping and capering with the scorching heat of his rage, and getting new vigor wherewith to wreak his passion, every time he hopped. But Hercules, you must understand, was wiser than this numskull of a giant, and had thought of a way to fight him—huge, earth-born monster that he was!—and to conquer him, too, in spite of all that his Mother Earth could do for him. Watching his opportunity, as the mad giant made a rush at him, Hercules caught him round the middle with both hands, lifted him high into the air, and held him aloft overhead.

Just imagine it, my dear little friends! What a spectacle it must have been, to see this monstrous fellow sprawling in the air, face downward, kicking out his long legs and wriggling his whole vast body, like a baby when its father holds it at arm's length towards the ceiling!

But the most wonderful thing was, that, as soon as Antæus was fairly off the earth, he began to lose the vigor which he had gained by touching it. Hercules very soon perceived that his troublesome enemy was growing weaker, both because he struggled and kicked with less violence, and because the thunder of his big voice subsided into a grumble. The truth was, that, unless the giant touched Mother Earth as often as once in five minutes, not only his overgrown strength, but the very breath of his life, would depart from him. Hercules had guessed this secret; and it may be well for us all to remember it, in case we should ever have to fight a battle with a fellow like Antæus. For these earth-born creatures are only difficult to conquer on their own ground, but may easily be managed, if we can contrive to lift them into a loftier and purer region. So it proved with the poor giant, whom I am really a little sorry for, notwithstanding his uncivil way of treating strangers who came to visit him.

When his strength and breath were quite gone, Hercules gave his huge body a toss, and flung it about a mile off, where it fell heavily, and lay with no more motion than a sand-hill. It was too late for the giant's Mother Earth to help him now; and I should not wonder if his ponderous bones were lying on the same spot, to this very day, and were mistaken for those of an uncommonly large elephant.

But, alas me! what a wailing did the poor little Pygmies set up, when they saw their enormous brother treated in this terrible manner! If Hercules heard their shrieks, however, he took no notice, and perhaps fancied them only the shrill, plaintive twittering of small birds, that had been frightened from their nests by the uproar of the battle between himself and Antæus. Indeed, his thoughts had been so much taken up with the giant, that he had never once looked at the Pygmies, nor even knew that there was such a funny little nation in the world. And now, as he had travelled a good way, and was also rather weary with his exertions in the fight, he spread out his lion's skin on the ground, and reclining himself upon it, fell fast asleep.

As soon as the Pygmies saw Hercules preparing for a nap, they nodded their little heads at one another, and winked with their little eyes. And, when his deep, regular breathing gave them notice that he was asleep, they assembled together in an immense crowd, spreading over a space of about twenty-seven feet square. One of their most eloquent orators (and a valiant warrior enough, besides, though hardly so good at any other weapon as he was with his tongue) climbed upon a toad-stool, and, from that elevated position, addressed the multitude. His sentiments were pretty much as follows; or, at all events, something like this was probably the upshot of his speech.

"Tall Pygmies and mighty little-men! You and all of us have seen what a public calamity has been brought to pass, and what an insult has here been offered to the majesty of our nation. Yonder lies Antæus, our great friend and brother, slain, within our territory, by a miscreant who took him at disadvantage, and fought him (if fighting it can be called) in a way that neither man, nor giant, nor Pygmy, ever dreamed of fighting, until this hour. And, adding a grievous contumely to the wrong already done us, the miscreant has now fallen asleep, as quietly as if nothing were to be dreaded from our wrath! It behooves you, fellow-countrymen, to consider in what aspect we shall stand before the world, and what will be the verdict of impartial history, should we suffer these accumulated outrages to go unavenged.

"Antæus was our brother, born of that same beloved parent to whom we owe the thews and sinews, as well as the courageous hearts, which made him proud of our relationship. He was our faithful ally, and fell fighting as much for our national rights and immunities, as for his own personal ones. We and our forefathers have dwelt in friendship with him, and held affectionate intercourse, as man to man, through immemorial generations. You remember how often our entire people have reposed in his great shadow, and how our little ones have played at hide-and-seek in the tangles of his hair, and how his mighty footsteps have familiarly gone to-and-fro among us, and never trodden upon any of our toes. And there lies this dear brother—this sweet and amiable friend— this brave and faithful ally—this virtuous giant—this blameless and excellent Antæus—dead! Dead! Silent! Powerless! A mere mountain of clay! Forgive my tears! Nay; I behold your own! Were we to drown the world with them, could the world blame us?

"But, to resume! Shall we, my countrymen, suffer this wicked stranger to depart, unharmed, and triumph in his treacherous victory, among distant communities of the earth? Shall we not, rather, compel him to leave his bones here on our soil, by the side of our slain brother's bones?—so that, while one skeleton shall remain as the everlasting monument of our sorrow, the other shall endure as long, exhibiting to the whole human race a terrible example of Pygmy vengeance! Such is the question! I put it to you in full confidence of a response that shall be worthy of our national character, and calculated to increase, rather than diminish, the glory which our ancestors have transmitted to us, and which we ourselves have proudly vindicated in our warfare with the cranes."

The orator was here interrupted by a burst of irrepressible enthusiasm; every individual Pygmy crying out that the national honor must be preserved, at all hazards. He bowed, and making a gesture for silence, wound up his harangue in the following admirable manner.

"It only remains for us, then, to decide whether we shall carry on the war in our national capacity, one united people against a common enemy—or whether some champion, famous in former fights, shall be selected to defy the slayer of our brother Antæus to single combat. In the latter case, though not unconscious that there may be taller men among you, I hereby offer myself for that enviable duty. And believe me, dear countrymen, whether I live or die, the honor of this great country, and the fame bequeathed us by our heroic progenitors, shall suffer no diminution in my hands! Never, while I can wield this sword, of which I now fling away the scabbard! Never, never, never, even if the crimson hand, that slew the great Antæus, shall lay me prostrate, like him, on the soil which I give my life to defend!"

So saying, this valiant Pygmy drew out his weapon, (which was terrible to behold, being as long as the blade of a penknife,) and sent the scabbard whirling over the heads of the multitude. His speech was followed by an uproar of applause, as its patriotism and self-devotion unquestionably deserved; and the shouts and clapping of hands would have been greatly prolonged, had they not been rendered quite inaudible by a deep respiration, vulgarly called a snore, from the sleeping Hercules.

It was finally decided, that the whole nation of Pygmies should set to work to destroy Hercules; not, be it understood, from any doubt that a single champion would be capable of putting him to the sword, but because he was a public enemy, and all were desirous of sharing in the glory of his defeat. There was a debate whether the national honor did not demand, that a herald should be sent with a trumpet, to stand over the ear of Hercules, and, after blowing a blast right into it, to defy him to the combat by formal proclamation. But two or three venerable and sagacious Pygmies, well versed in state-affairs, gave it as their opinion that war already existed, and that it was their rightful privilege to take the enemy by surprise. Moreover, if awakened, and allowed to get upon his feet, Hercules might happen to do them a mischief, before he could be beaten down again. For, as these sage counsellors remarked, the stranger's club was really very big, and had rattled like a thunderbolt against the skull of Antæus.

So the Pygmies resolved to set aside all foolish punctilios, and assail their antagonist at once.

Accordingly, all the fighting men of the nation took their weapons, and went boldly up to Hercules, who still lay fast asleep, little dreaming of the harm which the Pygmies meant to do him. A body of twenty thousand archers marched in front, with their little bows all ready, and the arrows on the string. The same number were ordered to clamber upon Hercules, some with spades, to dig his eyes out, and others with bundles of hay, and all manner of rubbish, with which they intended to plug up his mouth and nostrils, so that he might perish for lack of breath. These last, however, could by no means perform their appointed duty; inasmuch as the enemy's breath rushed out of his nose in an obstreperous hurricane and whirlwind, which blew the Pygmies away as fast as they came nigh. It was found necessary, therefore, to hit upon some other method of carrying on the war.

After holding a council, the captains ordered their troops to collect sticks, straws, dry weeds, and whatever combustible stuff they could find, and make a pile of it, heaping it high around the head of Hercules. As a great many thousand Pygmies were employed in this task, they soon brought together several bushels of inflammatory matter, and raised so tall a heap, that, mounting on its summit, they were quite upon a level with the sleeper's face. The archers, meanwhile, were stationed within bow-shot, with orders to let fly at Hercules, the instant that he stirred. Everything being in readiness, a torch was applied to the pile, which immediately burst into flames, and soon waxed hot enough to roast the enemy, had he but chosen to lie still. A Pygmy, you know, though so very small, might set the world on fire, just as easily as a giant could; so that this was certainly the very best way of dealing with their foe, provided they could have kept him quiet while the conflagration was going forward.

But no sooner did Hercules begin to be scorched, than up he started, with his hair in a red blaze.

"What's all this?" he cried, bewildered with sleep, and staring about him, as if he expected to see another giant.

At that moment, the twenty thousand archers twanged their bowstrings, and the arrows came whizzing, like so many winged musquitoes, right into the face of Hercules. But I doubt whether more than half-a-dozen of them punctured the skin, which was remarkably tough; as, you know, the skin of a hero has good need to be.

"Villain!" shouted all the Pygmies at once. "You have killed the giant Antæus, our great brother, and the ally of our nation. We declare bloody war against you, and will slay you on the spot!"

Surprised at the shrill piping of so many little voices, Hercules, after putting out the conflagration of his hair, gazed all roundabout, but could see nothing. At last, however, looking narrowly on the ground, he espied the innumerable assemblage of Pygmies at his feet. He stooped down, and taking up the nearest one between his thumb and finger, set him on the palm of his left hand, and held him at a proper distance for examination. It chanced to be the very identical Pygmy, who had spoken from the top of the toad-stool, and had offered himself as a champion to meet Hercules in single combat.

"What in the world, my little fellow," ejaculated Hercules, "may you be?"

"I am your enemy!" answered the valiant Pygmy, in his mightiest squeak. "You have slain the enormous Antæus, our brother by the mother's side, and, for ages, the faithful ally of our illustrious nation. We are determined to put you to death; and, for my own part, I challenge you to instant battle, on equal ground!"

Hercules was so tickled with the Pygmy's big words and warlike gestures, that he burst into a great explosion of laughter, and almost dropped the poor little mite of a creature off the palm of his hand, through the ecstasy and convulsion of his merriment.

"Upon my word," cried he, "I thought I had seen wonders before to-day;—hydras with nine heads, stags with golden horns, six-legged men, three-headed dogs, giants with furnaces in their stomachs, and nobody knows what besides! But here, on the palm of my hand, stands a wonder that outdoes them all! Your body, my little friend, is about the size of an ordinary man's finger. Pray how big may your soul be?"

"As big as your own!" said the Pygmy.

Hercules was touched with the little man's dauntless courage, and could not help acknowledging such a brotherhood with him, as one hero feels for another.

"My good little people," said he, making a low obeisance to the grand nation, "not for all the world, would I do an intentional injury to such brave fellows as you! Your hearts seem to me so exceedingly great, that, upon my honor, I marvel how your small bodies can contain them. I sue for peace, and, as a condition of it, will take five strides, and be out of your kingdom at the sixth. Good bye! I shall pick my steps carefully, for fear of treading upon some fifty of you, without knowing it. Ha, Ha, Ha! Ho, Ho, Ho! For once, Hercules acknowledges himself vanquished!"

Some writers say, that Hercules gathered up the whole race of Pygmies in his lion's skin, and carried them home to Greece, for the children of King Eurystheus to play with. But this is a mistake. He left them, one and all, within their own territory, where, for aught I can tell, their descendants are alive, to the present day, building their little houses, cultivating their little fields, spanking their little children, waging their little warfare with the cranes, doing their little business, whatever it may be, and reading their little histories of ancient times. In those histories, perhaps, it stands recorded, that, a great many centuries ago, the valiant Pygmies avenged the death of the giant Antæus, by scaring away the mighty Hercules!

The Dragon's Teeth

CADMUS, Phœnix, and Cilix, the three sons of King Agenor, and their little sister Europa, (who was a very beautiful child,) were at play together, near the sea-shore, in their father's kingdom of Phœnicia. They had rambled to some distance from the palace where their parents dwelt, and were now in a verdant meadow, on one side of which lay the sea, all sparkling and dimpling in the sunshine, and murmuring gently against the beach. The three boys were very happy gathering flowers, and twining them into garlands, with which they adorned the little Europa. Seated on the grass, the child was almost hidden under an abundance of buds and blossoms, whence her rosy face peeped merrily out, and, as Cadmus said, was the prettiest of all the flowers.

Just then, there came a splendid butterfly, fluttering along the meadow; and Cadmus, Phœnix, and Cilix, set off in pursuit of it, crying out that it was a flower with wings. Europa, who was a little wearied with playing, all day long, did not chase the butterfly with her brothers, but sat still where they had left her, and closed her eyes. For a while, she listened to the pleasant murmur of the sea, which was like a voice saying "Hush!" and bidding her go to sleep. But the pretty child, if she slept at all, could not have slept more than a moment, when she heard something trample on the grass, not far from her, and peeping out from the heap of flowers, beheld a snow-white bull.

And whence could this bull have come? Europa and her brothers had been a long time playing in the meadow, and had seen no cattle nor other living thing, either there, or on the neighboring hills.

"Brother Cadmus!" cried Europa, starting up out of the midst of the roses and lilies. "Phœnix! Cilix! Where are you all? Help! Help! Come and drive away this bull!"

But her brothers were too far off to hear; especially as the fright took away Europa's voice, and hindered her from calling very loudly. So there she stood, with her pretty mouth wide open, as pale as the white lilies that were twisted among the other flowers in her garlands.

Nevertheless, it was the suddenness with which she had perceived the bull, rather than anything frightful in his appearance, that caused Europa so much alarm. On looking at him more attentively, she began to see that he was a beautiful animal, and even fancied a particularly amiable expression in his face. As for his breath, (the breath of cattle, you know, is always sweet,) it was as fragrant as if he had been grazing on no other food than rosebuds, or, at least, the most delicate of clover-blossoms. Never before did a bull have such bright and tender eyes, and such smooth horns of ivory, as this one. And the bull ran little races, and capered sportively around the child; so that she quite forgot how big and strong he was, and, from the gentleness and playfulness of his actions, soon came to consider him as innocent a creature as a pet-lamb.

Thus, frightened as she at first was, you might by-and-by have seen Europa stroking the bull's forehead with her small white hand, and taking the garlands off her own head to hang them on his neck and ivory horns. Then she pulled up some blades of grass, and he ate them out of her hand, not as if he were hungry, but because he wanted to be friends with the child, and took pleasure in eating what she had touched. Well, my stars! Was there ever such a gentle, sweet, pretty, and amiable creature, as this bull, and ever such a nice play-mate for a little girl?

When the animal saw, (for the bull had so much intelligence that it is really wonderful to think of,) when he saw that Europa was no longer afraid of him, he grew overjoyed, and could hardly contain himself for delight. He frisked about the meadow, now here, now there, making sprightly leaps, with as little effort as a bird expends in hopping from twig to twig. Indeed, his motion was as light as if he were flying through the air, and his hoofs seemed hardly to leave their print in the grassy soil over which he trod. With his spotless hue, he resembled a snow-drift, wafted along by the wind. Once, he galloped so far away that Europa feared lest she might never see him again; so, setting up her childish voice, she called him back.

"Come back, pretty creature!" she cried. "Here is a nice clover-blossom!"

And then it was delightful to witness the gratitude of this

amiable bull, and how he was so full of joy and thankfulness that he capered higher than ever! He came running, and bowed his head before Europa, as if he knew her to be a king's daughter, or else recognized the important truth, that a little girl is everybody's queen. And not only did the bull bend his neck. He absolutely knelt down at her feet, and made such intelligent nods, and other inviting gestures, that Europa understood what he meant, just as well as if he had put it in so many words.

"Come, dear child!"—was what he wanted to say—"Let me give you a ride on my back!"

At the first thought of such a thing, Europa drew back. But then she considered, in her wise little head, that there could be no possible harm in taking just one gallop on the back of this docile and friendly animal, who would certainly set her down, the very instant she desired it. And how it would surprise her brothers, to see her riding across the green meadow! And what merry times they might have, either taking turns for a gallop, or clambering on the gentle creature, all four children together, and careering round the field, with shouts of laughter that would be heard as far off as King Agenor's palace!

"I think I will do it!" said the child to herself.

And, indeed, why not? She cast a glance around, and caught a glimpse of Cadmus, Phœnix, and Cilix, who were still in pursuit of the butterfly, almost at the other end of the meadow. It would be the quickest way of rejoining them, to get upon the white bull's back. She came a step nearer to him, therefore; and—sociable creature that he was!—he showed so much joy at this mark of her confidence, that the child could not find in her heart to hesitate any longer. Making one bound, (for this little princess was active as a squirrel,) there sat Europa on the beautiful bull, holding an ivory horn in each hand, lest she should fall off.

"Softly, pretty bull, softly!" she said, rather frightened at what she had done. "Do not gallop too fast!"

Having got the child on his back, the animal gave a leap into the air, and came down so like a feather that Europa did not know when his hoofs touched the ground. He then began a race to that part of the flowery plain where her three broth-

ers were, and where they had just caught their splendid butterfly. Europa screamed with delight; and Phœnix, Cilix, and
Cadmus, stood gaping at the spectacle of their sister mounted
on a white bull, not knowing whether to be frightened, or to
wish the same good luck for themselves. The gentle and innocent creature (for who could possibly doubt that he was
so?) pranced round among the children as sportively as a kit-
ten. Europa, all the while, looked down upon her brothers,
nodding and laughing, but yet with a sort of stateliness in her
rosy little face. As the bull wheeled about, to take another
gallop across the meadow, the child waved her hand and said
"Good bye!"—playfully pretending that she was now bound
on a distant journey, and might not see her brothers again for
nobody could tell how long.

"Good bye!" shouted Cadmus, Phœnix, and Cilix, all in
one breath.

But, together with her enjoyment of the sport, there was
still a little remnant of fear in the child's heart; so that her last
look at the three boys was a troubled one, and made them
feel as if their dear sister were really leaving them forever.
And what do you think the snowy bull did next? Why, he set
off, as swift as the wind, straight down to the sea-shore,
scampered across the sand, took an airy leap, and plunged
right in among the foaming billows! The white spray rose in
a shower over him and little Europa, and fell spattering down
upon the water.

Then what a scream of terror did the poor child send forth!
The three brothers screamed manfully, likewise, and ran to
the shore as fast as their legs would carry them, with Cadmus
at their head. But it was too late! When they reached the margin
of the sand, the treacherous animal was already far away in the
wide blue sea, with only his snowy head and tail emerging, and
poor little Europa between them, stretching out one hand towards her dear brothers, while she grasped the bull's ivory horn
with the other. And there stood Cadmus, Phœnix, and Cilix,
gazing at this sad spectacle, through their tears; until they could
no longer distinguish the bull's snowy head from the white-capt
billows that seemed to boil up out of the sea's depths, around
him. Nothing more was ever seen of the white bull; nothing
more of the beautiful child!

This was a mournful story, as you may well think, for the three boys to carry home to their parents. King Agenor, their father, was the ruler of the whole country; but he loved his little daughter Europa better than his kingdom, or than all his other children, or than anything else in the world. Therefore, when Cadmus and his two brothers came crying home, and told him how that a white bull had carried off their sister, and swum with her over the sea, the king was quite beside himself with grief and rage. Although it was now twilight, and fast growing dark, he bade them set out instantly in search of her.

"Never shall you see my face again," he cried, "unless you bring me back my little Europa, to gladden me with her smiles and her pretty ways. Begone, and enter my presence no more, till you come leading her by the hand!"

As King Agenor said this, his eyes flashed fire, (for he was a very passionate king,) and he looked so terribly angry that the poor boys did not even venture to ask for their suppers, but slunk away out of the palace, and only paused on the steps, a moment, to consult whither they should go first. While they were standing there, all in dismay, their mother, Queen Telephassa, (who happened not to be by, when they told the story to the king,) came hurrying after them, and said that she, too, would go in quest of her daughter.

"Oh no, mother!" cried the boys. "The night is dark; and there is no knowing what troubles and perils we may meet with!"

"Alas, my dear children," answered poor Queen Telephassa, weeping bitterly, "that is only another reason why I should go with you! If I should lose you, too, as well as my little Europa, what would become of me!"

"And let me go, likewise!" said their playfellow Thasus, who came running to join them.

Thasus was the son of a sea-faring person, in the neighborhood; he had been brought up with the young princes, and was their intimate friend, and loved Europa very much; so they consented that he should accompany them. The whole party, therefore, set forth together. Cadmus, Phœnix, Cilix, and Thasus, clustered round Queen Telephassa, grasping her

skirts, and begging her to lean upon their shoulders, whenever she felt weary. In this manner, they went down the palace-steps, and began a journey, which turned out to be a great
deal longer than they dreamed of. The last that they saw of
King Agenor, he came to the door, with a servant holding a
torch beside him, and called after them into the gathering
darkness:—

"Remember! Never ascend these steps again, without the
child!"

"Never!" sobbed Queen Telephassa; and the three brothers
and Thasus answered, "Never! Never! Never! Never!"

And they kept their word! Year after year, King Agenor sat
in the solitude of his beautiful palace, listening in vain for
their returning footsteps, hoping to hear the familiar voice of
the queen, and the cheerful talk of his sons and their playfellow Thasus, entering the door together, and the sweet, childish accents of little Europa in the midst of them. But so long
a time went by, that, at last, if they had really come, the king
would not have known that this was the voice of Telephassa,
and these the younger voices that used to make such joyful
echoes, when the children were playing about the palace. We
must now leave King Agenor to sit on his throne, and must
go along with Queen Telephassa and her four youthful companions.

They went on and on, and travelled a long way, and passed
over mountains and rivers, and sailed over seas. Here, and
there, and everywhere, they made continual inquiry if any
person could tell them what had become of Europa. The rustic people, of whom they asked this question, paused a little
while from their labors in the field, and looked very much
surprised. They thought it strange to behold a woman in the
garb of a queen, (for Telephassa, in her haste, had forgotten
to take off her crown and her royal robes,) roaming about the
country, with four lads around her, on such an errand as this
seemed to be. But nobody could give them any tidings of
Europa; nobody had seen a little girl dressed like a princess,
and mounted on a snow-white bull, which galloped as swiftly
as the wind.

I cannot tell you how long Queen Telephassa, and Cad-

mus, Phœnix, and Cilix, her three sons, and Thasus, their
playfellow, went wandering along the highways and by-paths,
or through the pathless wildernesses of the earth, in this manner. But, certain it is, that, before they reached any place of
rest, their splendid garments were quite worn out. They all
looked very much travel-stained, and would have had the dust
of many countries on their shoes, if the streams, through
which they waded, had not washed it all away. When they
had been gone a year, Telephassa threw away her crown, because it chafed her forehead.

"It has given me many a head-ache," said the poor queen;
"and it cannot cure my heart-ache!"

As fast as their princely robes got torn and tattered, they
exchanged them for such mean attire as ordinary people wore.
By-and-by, they came to have a wild and homeless aspect; so
that you would much sooner have taken them for a gipsey
family, than a queen, and three princes, and a young nobleman, who had once a palace for their home, and a train of
servants to do their bidding. The four boys grew up to be tall
young men, with sun-burned faces. Each of them girded on
a sword, to defend themselves against the perils of the way.
When the husbandmen, at whose farm-houses they sought
hospitality, needed their assistance in the harvest-field, they
gave it willingly; and Queen Telephassa (who had done no
work, in her palace, save to braid silk threads with golden
ones) came behind them to bind the sheaves. If payment was
offered, they shook their heads, and only asked for tiding of
Europa.

"There are bulls enough in my pasture," the old farmers
would reply; "but I never heard of one like this you tell me
of! A snow-white bull with a little princess on his back! Ho!
Ho! I ask your pardon, good folks; but there never was such
a sight seen hereabouts!"

At last, when his upper lip began to have the down on it,
Phœnix grew weary of rambling hither and thither, to no
purpose. So, one day, when they happened to be passing
through a pleasant and solitary tract of country, he sat himself
down on a heap of moss.

"I can go no farther!" said Phœnix. "It is a mere foolish
waste of life to spend it, as we do, in always wandering up

and down, and never coming to any home at nightfall. Our sister is lost, and never will be found. She probably perished in the sea; or, to whatever shore the white bull may have carried her, it is now so many years ago, that there would be neither love nor acquaintance between us, should we meet again. My father has forbidden us to return to his palace; so I shall build me a hut of branches, and dwell here!"

"Well, son Phœnix," replied Telephassa, sorrowfully, "you have grown to be a man, and must do as you judge best. But, for my part, I will still go in quest of my poor child!"

"And we three will go along with you!" cried Cadmus and Cilix, and their faithful friend Thasus.

But, before setting out, they all helped Phœnix to build a habitation. When completed, it was a sweet, rural bower, roofed overhead with an arch of living boughs. Inside, there were two pleasant rooms, one of which had a soft heap of moss, for a bed, while the other was furnished with a rustic seat or two, curiously fashioned out of the crooked roots of trees. So comfortable and home-like did it seem, that Telephassa and her three companions could not help sighing, to think that they must still roam about the world, instead of spending the remainder of their lives in some such cheerful abode as they had here built for Phœnix. But, when they bade him farewell, Phœnix shed tears, and probably regretted that he was no longer to keep them company.

However, he had fixed upon an admirable place to dwell in. And, by-and-by, there came other people, who chanced to have no homes; and seeing how pleasant a spot it was, they built themselves huts in the neighborhood of Phœnix's habitation. Thus, before many years went by, a city had grown up there, in the centre of which was seen a stately palace of marble, wherein dwelt Phœnix, clothed in a purple robe, and wearing a golden crown upon his head. For the inhabitants of the new city, finding that he had royal blood in his veins, had chosen him to be their king. The very first decree of state, which King Phœnix issued, was, that, if a maiden happened to arrive in the kingdom, mounted on a snow-white bull, and calling herself Europa, his subjects should treat her with the greatest kindness and respect, and immediately bring her to the palace. You may see, by this, that Phœnix's conscience never quite ceased to trouble him, for giving up the quest of his dear sister, and sitting himself down to be comfortable, while his mother and her companions went onward.

But, often and often, at the close of a weary day's journey, did Telephassa, and Cadmus, Cilix, and Thasus, remember the pleasant spot in which they had left Phœnix. It was a sorrowful prospect for these wanderers, that, on the morrow, they must again set forth, and that, after many nightfalls, they would perhaps be no nearer the close of their toilsome pilgrimage, than now. These thoughts made them all melancholy, at times, but appeared to torment Cilix more than the rest of the party. At length, one morning, when they were taking their staffs in hand, to set out, he thus addressed them: —

"My dear mother, and you, good brother Cadmus, and my friend Thasus, methinks we are like people in a dream! There is no substance in the life which we are leading. It is such a dreary length of time since the white bull carried off my sister Europa, that I have quite forgotten how she looked, and the tones of her voice, and, indeed, almost doubt whether such a little girl ever lived in the world! And whether she once lived or no, I am convinced that she no longer survives, and that therefore it is the merest folly to waste our own lives and happiness in seeking her. Were we to find her, she would now be a woman grown, and would look upon us all as strangers. So, to tell you the truth, I have resolved to take up my abode here; and I entreat you, mother, and brother, and friend, to follow my example!"

"Not I, for one!" said Telephassa; although the poor queen, firmly as she spoke, was so travel-worn that she could hardly put her foot to the ground. "Not I, for one! In the depths of my heart, little Europa is still the rosy child, who ran to gather flowers, so many years ago. She has not grown to womanhood, nor forgotten me. At noon, at night, journeying onward, sitting down to rest, her childish voice is always in my ears, calling 'Mother! Mother!' Stop here who may, there is no repose for me!"

"Nor for me," said Cadmus, "while my dear mother pleases to go onward!"

And the faithful Thasus, too, was resolved to bear them

company. They remained with Cilix a few days, however, and helped him to build a rustic bower, closely resembling the one which they had formerly built for Phœnix.

When they were bidding him farewell, Cilix burst into tears, and told his mother that it seemed just as melancholy a dream, to stay there, in solitude, as to go onward. If she really believed that they would ever find Europa, he was willing to continue the search with them, even now. But Telephassa bade him remain there, and be happy, if his own heart would let him. So the pilgrims took their leave of him, and departed, and were hardly out of sight, before some other wandering people came along that way, and saw Cilix's habitation, and were greatly delighted with the appearance of the place. There being abundance of unoccupied ground, in the neighbor-hood, these strangers built huts for themselves, and were soon joined by a multitude of new settlers, who quickly formed a city. In the middle of it, was seen a magnificent palace of colored marble, on the balcony of which, every noontide, appeared Cilix, in a long purple robe, and with a jewelled crown upon his head; for the inhabitants, when they found out that he was a king's son, had considered him the fittest of all men to be a king, himself.

One of the first acts of King Cilix's government was to send out an expedition, consisting of a grave ambassador and an escort of bold and hardy young men, with orders to visit the principal kingdoms of the earth, and inquire whether a young maiden had passed through those regions, galloping swiftly on a white bull. It is therefore plain to my mind, that Cilix secretly blamed himself for giving up the search for Europa, as long as he was able to put one foot before the other.

As for Telephassa, and Cadmus, and the good Thasus, it grieves me to think of them, still keeping up that weary pil-grimage! The two young men did their best for the poor queen, helping her over the rough places, often carrying her across rivulets in their faithful arms, and seeking to shelter her at nightfall, even when they themselves lay on the ground. Sad, sad it was to hear them asking of every-passer-by, if he had seen Europa, so long after the white bull had carried her away! But, though the gray years thrust themselves between, and made the child's figure dim in their remembrance, neither of these true-hearted three ever dreamed of giving up the search.

One morning, however, poor Thasus found that he had sprained his ancle, and could not possibly go a step farther.

"After a few days, to be sure," said he, mournfully, "I might make shift to hobble along with a stick. But that would only delay you, and perhaps hinder you from finding dear little Europa, after all your pains and trouble! Do you go forward, therefore, my beloved companions, and leave me to follow as I may."

"Thou hast been a true friend, dear Thasus!" said Queen Telephassa, kissing his forehead. "Being neither my son, nor the brother of our lost Europa, thou hast shown thyself truer to me and her, than Phœnix and Cilix did, whom we have left behind us. Without thy loving help, and that of my son Cadmus, my limbs could not have borne me half so far as this. Now, take thy rest, and be at peace! For—and it is the first time I have owned it to myself—I begin to question whether we shall ever find my beloved daughter, in this world!"

Saying this, the poor queen shed tears, because it was a grievous trial to the mother's heart, to confess that her hopes were growing faint. From that day forward, Cadmus noticed that she never travelled with the same alacrity of spirit that had heretofore supported her. Her weight was heavier upon his arm.

Before setting out, Cadmus helped Thasus build a bower; while Telephassa, being too infirm to give any great assistance, advised them how to fit it up and furnish it, so that it might be as comfortable as a hut of branches could. Thasus, however, did not spend all his days in this green bower. For it happened to him, as to Phœnix and Cilix, that other homeless people visited the spot, and liked it, and built themselves habitations in the neighborhood. So here, in the course of a few years, was another thriving city, with a red freestone palace in the centre of it, where Thasus sat upon a throne, doing justice to the people, with a purple robe over his shoulders, a sceptre in his hand, and a crown upon his head. The inhabitants had made him king, not for the sake of any royal blood, (for none was in his veins,) but because Thasus was an upright, true-hearted, and courageous man, and therefore fit to rule.

But, when the affairs of his kingdom were all settled, King Thasus laid aside his purple robe, and crown and sceptre, and bade his worthiest subject distribute justice to the people, in his stead. Then, grasping the pilgrim's staff that had supported him so long, he set forth again, hoping still to discover some hoof-mark of the snow-white bull; some trace of the vanished child! He returned, after a lengthened absence, and sat down wearily upon his throne. To his latest hour, nevertheless, King Thasus showed his true-hearted remembrance of Europa, by ordering that a fire should always be kept burning in his palace, and a bath steaming-hot, and food ready to be served up, and a bed with snow-white sheets, in case the maiden should arrive, and require immediate refreshment. And though Europa never came, the good Thasus had the blessings of many a poor traveller, who profited by the food and lodging which were meant for the little playmate of the king's boyhood.

Telephassa and Cadmus were now pursuing their weary way, with no companion but each other. The queen leaned heavily upon her son's arm, and could walk only a few miles a day. But, for all her weakness and weariness, she would not be persuaded to give up the search. It was enough to bring tears into the eyes of bearded men, to hear the melancholy tone with which she inquired of every stranger, whether he could tell her any news of the lost child.

"Have you seen a little girl—no, no, I mean a young maiden of full growth!—passing by this way, mounted on a snow-white bull, which gallops as swiftly as the wind?"

"We have seen no such wondrous sight!" the people would reply; and very often, taking Cadmus aside, they whispered to him, "Is this stately and sad-looking woman your mother? Surely, she is not in her right mind; and you ought to take her home, and make her comfortable, and do your best to get this dream out of her fancy!"

"It is no dream!" said Cadmus. "Everything else is a dream, save that!"

But, one day, Telephassa seemed feebler than usual, and leaned almost her whole weight on the arm of Cadmus, and walked more slowly than ever before. At last, they reached a solitary spot, where she told her son that she must needs lie down, and take a good, long rest.

"A good, long rest!" she repeated, looking Cadmus tenderly in the face. "A good, long rest, thou dearest one!"

"As long as you please, dear mother," answered Cadmus.

Telephassa bade him sit down on the turf beside her, and then she took his hand.

"My son," said she, fixing her dim eyes most lovingly upon him, "this rest, that I speak of, will be very long indeed! You must not wait till it is finished. Dear Cadmus, you do not comprehend me! You must make a grave here, and lay your mother's weary frame into it. My pilgrimage is over!"

Cadmus burst into tears, and, for a long time, refused to believe that his dear mother was now to be taken from him. But Telephassa reasoned with him, and kissed him, and, at length, made him discern that it was better for her spirit to pass away, out of the toil, the weariness, the grief, and disappointment, which had burdened her, on earth, ever since the child was lost. He therefore repressed his sorrow, and listened to her last words.

"Dearest Cadmus," said she, "thou hast been the truest son that ever mother had, and faithful, to the very last! Who else would have borne with my infirmities, as thou hast! It is owing to thy care, thou tenderest child, that my grave was not dug, long years ago, in some valley or on some hill-side, that lies far, far behind us. It is enough! Thou shalt wander no more on this hopeless search. But, when thou hast laid thy mother in the earth, then go, my son, to Delphi, and inquire of the oracle what thou shalt do next."

"Oh, mother, mother," cried Cadmus, "couldst thou but have seen my sister, before this hour!"

"It matters little, now!" answered Telephassa; and there was a smile upon her face. "I go now to the better world, and, sooner or later, shall find my daughter there!"

I will not sadden you, my little hearers, with telling how Telephassa died and was buried, but will only say, that her dying smile grew brighter, instead of vanishing from her dead face; so that Cadmus felt convinced, that, at her very first step into the better world, she had caught Europa in her arms. He

planted some flowers on his mother's grave, and left them to
grow there and make the place beautiful, when he should be
far away.

After performing this last sorrowful duty, he set forth
alone, and took the road towards the famous oracle of Delphi, as Telephassa had advised him. On his way thither, he
still inquired of most people whom he met, whether they had
seen Europa; for, to say the truth, Cadmus had grown so
accustomed to ask the question, that it came to his lips as
readily as a remark about the weather. He received various
answers. Some told him one thing, and some another.
Among the rest, a mariner affirmed, that, many years before,
in a distant country, he had heard a rumor about a white bull,
which came swimming across the sea with a child on his back,
dressed up in flowers that were blighted by the sea-water. He
did not know what had become of the child or the bull; and
Cadmus suspected, indeed, by a queer twinkle in the mariner's eyes, that he was putting a joke upon him, and had
never really heard anything about the matter.

Poor Cadmus found it more wearisome to travel alone,
than to bear all his dear mother's weight, while she had kept
him company. His heart, you will understand, was now so
heavy, that it seemed impossible, sometimes, to carry it any
farther. But his limbs were strong and active, and well accustomed to exercise. He walked swiftly along, thinking of King
Agenor, and Queen Telephassa, and his brothers, and the
friendly Thasus, all of whom he had left behind him, at one
point of his pilgrimage or another, and never expected to see
them any more. Full of these remembrances, he came within
sight of a lofty mountain, which, the people thereabouts told
him, was called Parnassus. On the slope of Mount Parnassus
was the famous Delphi, whither Cadmus was going.

This Delphi was supposed to be the very midmost spot of
the whole world. The place of the oracle was a certain cavity
in the mountain-side, over which, when Cadmus came
thither, he found a rude bower of branches. It reminded him
of those which he had helped to build for Phœnix and Cilix,
and afterwards for Thasus. In later times, when multitudes of
people came, from great distances, to put questions to the
oracle, a spacious temple of marble was erected over the spot.

But, in the days of Cadmus, as I have told you, there was only this rustic bower, with its abundance of green foliage, and a tuft of shrubbery, that ran wild over the mysterious hole in the hill-side.

When Cadmus had thrust a passage through the tangled boughs, and made his way into the bower, he did not at first discern the half-hidden cavity. But, soon, he felt a cold stream of air rushing out of it, with so much force that it shook the ringlets on his cheek. Pulling away the shrubbery, which clustered over the hole, he bent forward, and spoke in a distinct, but reverential tone, as if addressing some unseen personage, inside of the mountain.

"Sacred Oracle of Delphi," said he, "whither shall I go next, in quest of my dear sister Europa?"

There was at first a deep silence, and then a rushing sound, or a noise like a long sigh, proceeding out of the interior of the earth. This cavity, you must know, was looked upon as a sort of fountain of truth, which sometimes gushed out in audible words; although, for the most part, these words were such a riddle that they might just as well have staid at the bottom of the hole. But Cadmus was more fortunate than many others, who went to Delphi in search of truth. By-and-by, the rushing noise began to sound like articulate language. It repeated, over and over again, the following sentence, which, after all, was so like the vague whistle of a blast of air, that Cadmus really did not quite know whether it meant anything, or not: —

"Seek her no more! Seek her no more! Seek her no more!"

"What, then, shall I do?" asked Cadmus.

For, ever since he was a child you know, it had been the great object of his life to find his sister. From the very hour that he left following the butterfly, in the meadow, near his father's palace, he had done his best to follow Europa, over land and sea. And, now, if he must give up the search, he seemed to have no more business in the world.

But, again, the sighing gust of air grew into something like a hoarse voice.

"Follow the cow!" it said. "Follow the cow! Follow the cow!"

And when these words had been repeated until Cadmus

was tired of hearing them, (especially as he could not imagine what cow it was, or why he was to follow her,) the gusty hole gave vent to another sentence.

"Where the stray cow lies down, there is your home!"

These words were pronounced but a single time, and died away into a whisper before Cadmus was fully satisfied that he had caught the meaning. He put other questions, but received no answer; only the gust of wind sighed continually out of the cavity, and blew the withered leaves rustling along the ground, before it.

"Did there really come any words out of the hole?" thought Cadmus. "Or have I been dreaming, all this while?"

He turned away from the oracle, and thought himself no wiser than when he came thither. Caring little what might happen to him, he took the first path that offered itself, and went along at a sluggish pace; for, having no object in view, nor any reason to go one way more than another, it would certainly have been foolish to make haste. Whenever he met anybody, the old question was at his tongue's end:—

"Have you seen a beautiful maiden, dressed like a king's daughter, and mounted on a snow-white bull, that gallops as swiftly as the wind?"

But, remembering what the oracle had said, he only half uttered the words, and then mumbled the rest indistinctly; and, from his confusion, people must have imagined that this handsome young man had lost his wits.

I know not how far Cadmus had gone, nor could he himself have told you, when, at no great distance before him, he beheld a brindled cow. She was lying down by the wayside, and quietly chewing her cud; nor did she take any notice of the young man, until he had approached pretty nigh. Then getting leisurely upon her feet, and giving her head a gentle toss, she began to move along at a moderate pace, often pausing, just long enough to crop a mouthful of grass. Cadmus loitered behind, whistling idly to himself, and scarcely noticing the cow; until the thought occurred to him, whether this could possibly be the animal, which, according to the oracle's response, was to serve him for a guide. But he smiled at himself for fancying such a thing! He could not seriously think that this was the cow, because she went along so quietly, behaving just like any other cow. Evidently, she neither knew nor cared so much as a wisp of hay about Cadmus, and was only thinking how to get her living along the wayside, where the herbage was green and fresh. Perhaps she was going home to be milked.

"Cow, cow, cow!" cried Cadmus. "Hey, Brindle, hey! Stop, my good cow!"

He wanted to come up with the cow, so as to examine her, and see if she would appear to know him, or whether there were any peculiarities to distinguish her from a thousand other cows, whose only business is to fill the milk-pail, and sometimes kick it over. But still the brindled cow trudged on, whisking her tail to keep the flies away, and taking as little notice of Cadmus as she well could. If he walked slowly, so did the cow, and seized the opportunity to graze. If he quickened his pace, the cow went just so much the faster; and once, when Cadmus tried to catch her by running, she threw out her heels, stuck her tail straight on end, and set off at a gallop, looking as queerly as cows generally do, while putting themselves to their speed.

When Cadmus saw that it was impossible to come up with her, he walked on moderately, as before. The cow, too, went leisurely on, without looking behind. Wherever the grass was greenest, there she nibbled a mouthful or two. Where a brook glistened brightly across the path, there the cow drank, and breathed a comfortable sigh, and drank again, and trudged onward, at the pace that best suited herself and Cadmus.

"I do believe," thought Cadmus, "that this may be the cow that was foretold me! If it be the one, I suppose she will lie down, somewhere hereabouts."

Whether it were the oracular cow, or some other one, it did not seem reasonable that she should travel a great way farther. So, whenever they reached a particularly pleasant spot, on a breezy hill-side, or in a sheltered vale of flowery meadow, on the shore of a calm lake, or along the bank of a clear stream, Cadmus looked eagerly around, to see if the situation would suit him for a home. But still, whether he liked the place or no, the brindled cow never offered to lie down. On she went, at the quiet pace of a cow going homeward to the barn-yard; and, every moment, Cadmus expected to see a milkmaid approaching with a pail, or a herdsman running to head the stray animal, and turn her back towards the pasture. But no milkmaid came; no herdsman drove her back; and Cadmus followed the stray brindle, till he was almost ready to drop down with fatigue.

"Oh, brindled cow," cried he, in a tone of despair, "do you never mean to stop!"

He had now grown too intent on following her, to think of lagging behind, however long the way, and whatever might be his fatigue. Indeed, it seemed as if there were something about the animal, that bewitched people. Several persons, who happened to see the brindled cow, and Cadmus following behind, began to trudge after her, precisely as he did. Cadmus was glad of somebody to converse with, and therefore talked very freely to these good people. He told them all his adventures, and how he had left King Agenor in his palace, and Phœnix at one place, and Cilix at another, and Thasus at a third, and his dear mother, Queen Telephassa, under a flowery sod; so that now he was quite alone, both friendless and homeless. He mentioned, likewise, that the oracle had bidden him be guided by a cow, and inquired of the strangers, whether they supposed that this brindled animal could be the one.

"Why, 'tis a very wonderful affair!" answered one of his new companions. "I am pretty well acquainted with the ways of cattle; and I never knew a cow, of her own accord, to go so far without stopping. If my legs will let me, I'll never leave following the beast, till she lies down!"

"Nor I!" said a second.

"Nor I!" cried a third. "If she goes a hundred miles farther, I'm determined to see the end of it!"

The secret of it was, you must know, that the cow was an enchanted cow, and that, without their being conscious of it, she threw some of her enchantment over everybody that took so much as half-a-dozen steps behind her. They could not possibly help following her, though, all the time, they fancied themselves doing it of their own accord. The cow was by no means very nice in choosing her path; so that sometimes they had to scramble over rocks, or wade through mud and mire, and were all in a terribly be-draggled condition, and tired to

death, and very hungry, into the bargain. What a weary business it was!

But still they kept trudging stoutly forward, and talking as
they went. The strangers grew very fond of Cadmus, and resolved never to leave him, but to help him build a city, wherever the cow might lie down. In the centre of it, there should
be a noble palace, in which Cadmus might dwell, and be their
king, with a throne, a crown and sceptre, a purple robe, and
everything else that a king ought to have; for, in him, there
was the royal blood and the royal heart, and the head that
knew how to rule.

While they were talking of these schemes, and beguiling
the tediousness of the way with laying out the plan of the
new city, one of the company happened to look at the cow.

"Joy! Joy!" cried he, clapping his hands. "Brindle is going
to lie down!"

They all looked; and, sure enough, the cow had stopt, and
was staring leisurely about her, as other cows do, when on
the point of lying down. And slowly, slowly, did she recline
herself on the soft grass, first bending her fore-legs, and then
crouching her hind ones. When Cadmus and his companions
came up with her, there was the brindled cow taking her ease,
chewing her cud, and looking them quietly in the face; as if
this was just the spot she had been seeking for, and as if it
were all a matter of course!

"This, then," said Cadmus, gazing around him, "this is to
be my home!"

It was a fertile and lovely plain, with great trees flinging
their sun-speckled shadows over it, and hills fencing it in from
the rough weather. At no great distance, they beheld a river
gleaming in the sunshine. A home-feeling stole into the heart
of poor Cadmus. He was very glad to know, that here he
might awake in the morning, without the necessity of putting
on his dusty sandals to travel farther and farther. The days
and the years would pass over him, and find him still in this
pleasant spot. If he could have had his brothers with him, and
his friend Thasus, and could have seen his dear mother under
a roof of his own, he might here have been happy, after all
their disappointments. Some day or other, too, his sister Europa might have come quietly to the door of his home, and

smiled round upon the familiar faces! But, indeed, since there
was no hope of regaining the friends of his boyhood, or ever
seeing his dear sister again, Cadmus resolved to make himself
happy with these new companions, who had grown so fond
of him while following the cow.

"Yes, my friends!" said he to them. "This is to be our
home. Here we will build our habitations. The brindled cow,
which has led us hither, will supply us with milk. We will
cultivate the neighboring soil, and lead an innocent and
happy life."

His companions joyfully assented to this plan; and, in the
first place, being very hungry and thirsty, they looked about
them for the means of providing a comfortable meal. Not far
off, they saw a tuft of trees, which appeared as if there might
be a spring of water beneath them. They went thither to fetch
some, leaving Cadmus stretched on the ground, along with
the brindled cow; for, now that he had found a place of rest,
it seemed as if all the weariness of his pilgrimage, ever since
he left King Agenor's palace, had fallen upon him at once.
But his new friends had not long been gone, when he was
suddenly startled by cries, shouts, and screams, and the noise
of a terrible struggle, and, in the midst of it all, a most awful
hissing, which went right through his ears like a rough saw!

Running towards the tuft of trees, he beheld the head and
fiery eyes of an immense serpent or dragon, with the widest
jaws that ever a dragon had, and a vast many rows of horribly
sharp teeth. Before Cadmus could reach the spot, this pitiless
reptile had killed his poor companions, and was busily devouring them, making but a mouthful of each man.

It appears that the fountain of water was enchanted, and
that the dragon had been set to guard it, so that no mortal
might ever quench his thirst there. As the neighboring inhabitants carefully avoided the spot, it was now a long time (not
less than a hundred years, or thereabouts) since the monster
had broken his fast; and, as was natural enough, his appetite
had grown to be enormous, and was not half satisfied by the
poor people whom he had just eaten up. When he caught
sight of Cadmus, therefore, he set up another abominable
hiss, and flung back his immense jaws, until his mouth looked
like a great red cavern, at the farther end of which were seen

the legs of his last victim, whom he had hardly had time to swallow.

But Cadmus was so enraged at the destruction of his friends, that he cared neither for the size of the dragon's jaws, nor for his hundreds of sharp teeth. Drawing his sword, he rushed at the monster, and flung himself right into his cavernous mouth. This bold method of attacking him took the dragon by surprise; for, in fact, Cadmus had leaped so far down into his throat, that the rows of terrible teeth could not close upon him, nor do him the least harm in the world. Thus, though the struggle was a tremendous one, and though the dragon shattered the tuft of trees into small splinters by the lashing of his tail, yet, as Cadmus was all the while slashing and stabbing at his very vitals, it was not long before the scaly wretch bethought himself of slipping away. He had not gone his length, however, when the brave Cadmus gave him a sword-thrust that finished the battle; and, creeping out of the gateway of the creature's jaws, there he beheld him, still wriggling his vast bulk, although there was no longer life enough in him to harm a little child.

But do not you suppose that it made Cadmus sorrowful, to think of the melancholy fate which had befallen those poor, friendly people, who had followed the cow along with him? It seemed as if he were doomed to lose everybody whom he loved, or to see them perish, in one way or another. And here he was, after all his toils and troubles, in a solitary place, with not a single human being to help him build a hut.

"What shall I do!" cried he aloud. "It were better for me to have been devoured by the dragon, as my poor companions were!"

"Cadmus!" said a voice—but whether it came from above or below him, or whether it spoke within his own breast, the young man could not tell—"Cadmus, pluck out the dragon's teeth, and plant them in the earth!"

This was a strange thing to do; nor was it very easy, I should imagine, to dig out all those deep-rooted fangs from the dead dragon's jaws. But Cadmus toiled and tugged, and after pounding the monstrous head almost to pieces with a great stone, he at last collected as many teeth as might have filled a bushel or two. The next thing was to plant them. This, likewise, was a tedious piece of work, especially as Cadmus was already exhausted with killing the dragon and knocking his head to pieces, and had nothing to dig the earth with, that I know of, unless it were his sword-blade. Finally, however, a sufficiently large tract of ground was turned up, and sown with this new kind of seed; although half of the dragon's teeth still remained, to be planted some other day.

Cadmus, quite out of breath, stood leaning upon his sword, and wondering what was to happen next. He had waited but a few moments, when he began to see a sight, which was as great a marvel as the most marvellous thing I ever told you about.

The sun was shining aslantwise over the field, and showed all the moist, dark soil, just like any other newly planted piece of ground. All at once, Cadmus fancied he saw something glisten very brightly, first at one spot, then at another, and then at a hundred and a thousand spots together. Soon, he perceived them to be the steel-heads of spears, sprouting up everywhere, like so many stalks of grain, and continually growing taller and taller. Next appeared a vast number of bright sword-blades, thrusting themselves up in the same way. A moment afterwards, the whole surface of the ground was broken by a multitude of polished brass helmets, coming up like a crop of enormous beans! So rapidly did they grow, that Cadmus now discerned the fierce countenance of a man, beneath every one. In short, before he had time to think what a wonderful affair it was, he beheld an abundant harvest of what looked like human beings, armed with helmets and breastplates, shields, swords, and spears; and, before they were well out of the earth, they brandished their weapons and clashed them one against another, seeming to think, little while as they had yet lived, that they had wasted too much of life without a battle. Every tooth of the dragon had produced one of these sons of deadly mischief!

Up-sprouted, also, a great many trumpeters; and, with the first breath that they drew, they put their brazen trumpets to their lips, and sounded a tremendous and ear-shattering blast; so that the whole space, just now so quiet and solitary, reverberated with the clash and clang of arms, the bray of warlike music, and the shouts of angry men. So enraged did they all look, that

Cadmus fully expected them to put the whole world to the sword. How fortunate would it be for a great conqueror, if he could get a bushel of the dragon's teeth to sow!

"Cadmus!" said the same voice which he had before heard. "Throw a stone into the midst of the armed men!"

So Cadmus seized a large stone, and flinging it into the middle of the earth-army, saw it strike the breastplate of a gigantic and fierce-looking warrior. Immediately on feeling the blow, he seemed to take it for granted that somebody had struck him; and uplifting his weapon, he smote his next neighbor a blow that cleft his helmet asunder, and stretched him on the ground. In an instant, those nearest the fallen warrior began to strike at one another with their swords, and stab with their spears. The confusion spread wider and wider. Each man smote down his brother, and was himself smitten down, before he had time to exult in his victory. The trumpeters, all the while, blew their blasts shriller and shriller; each soldier shouted a battle-cry, and often fell with it on his lips. It was the strangest spectacle of causeless wrath, and of mischief for no good end, that had ever been witnessed; but, after all, it was neither more foolish nor more wicked than a thousand battles that have since been fought, in which men have slain their brothers with just as little reason as these children of the dragon's teeth. It ought to be considered, too, that the dragon-people were made for nothing else; whereas, other mortals were born to love and help one another.

Well; this memorable battle continued to rage, until the ground was strewn with helmeted heads that had been cut off. Of all the thousands that began the fight, there were only five left standing. These now rushed from different parts of the field, and, meeting in the middle of it, clashed their swords, and struck at each other's hearts as fiercely as ever.

"Cadmus!" said the voice again. "Bid those five warriors sheathe their swords. They will help you to build the city."

Without hesitating an instant, Cadmus stepped forward, with the aspect of a king and a leader, and extending his drawn sword amongst them, spoke to the warriors in a stern and commanding voice.

"Sheathe your weapons!" said he.

And forthwith, feeling themselves bound to obey him, the

five remaining sons of the dragon's teeth made him a military salute with their swords, returned them to the scabbards, and stood before Cadmus in a rank, eyeing him as soldiers eye their captain, while awaiting the word of command.

These five men had probably sprung from the biggest of the dragon's teeth, and were the boldest and strongest of the whole army. They were almost giants, indeed, and had good need to be so; else they never could have lived through so terrible a fight. They still had a very furious look, and, if Cadmus happened to glance aside, would glare at one another, with fire flashing out of their eyes. It was strange, too, to observe how the earth, out of which they had so lately grown, was incrusted, here-and-there, on their bright breastplates, and even begrimed their faces; just as you may have seen it clinging to beets and carrots, when pulled out of their native soil. Cadmus hardly knew whether to consider them as men, or some odd kind of vegetable; although, on the whole, he concluded that there was human nature in them, because they were so fond of trumpets and weapons, and so ready to shed blood.

They looked him earnestly in the face, waiting for his next order, and evidently desiring no other employment than to follow him from one battle-field to another, all over the wide world. But Cadmus was wiser than these earth-born creatures, with the dragon's fierceness in them, and knew better how to use their strength and hardihood.

"Come!" said he. "You are sturdy fellows. Make yourselves useful! Quarry some stones with those great swords of yours, and help me to build a city!"

The five soldiers grumbled a little, and muttered that it was their business to overthrow cities, not to build them up. But Cadmus looked at them with a stern eye, and spoke to them in a tone of authority; so that they knew him for their master, and never again thought of disobeying his commands. They set to work in good earnest, and toiled so diligently, that, in a very short time, a city began to make its appearance. At first, to be sure, the workmen showed a quarrelsome disposition. Like savage beasts, they would doubtless have done one another a mischief, if Cadmus had not kept watch over them, and quelled the fierce old serpent that lurked in their hearts, when he saw it gleaming out of their wild eyes. But, in course of time, they got accustomed to honest labor, and had sense enough to feel that there was more true enjoyment in living at peace, and doing good to one's neighbor, than in striking at him with a two-edged sword. It may not be too much to hope, that the rest of mankind will by-and-by grow as wise and peaceable, as these five earth-begrimed warriors, who sprang from the dragon's teeth!

And now the city was built, and there was a home in it for each of the workmen. But the palace of Cadmus was not yet erected, because they had left it till the last, meaning to introduce all the new improvements of architecture, and make it very commodious, as well as stately and beautiful. After finishing the rest of their labors, they all went to bed betimes, in order to rise in the gray of the morning, and get at least the foundation of the edifice laid, before nightfall. But, when Cadmus arose, and took his way towards the site where the palace was to be built, followed by his five sturdy workmen, marching all in a row—what do you think he saw?

What should it be, but the most magnificent palace that had ever been seen in the world. It was built of marble, and other beautiful kinds of stone, and rose high into the air, with a splendid dome, and a portico along the front, and carved pillars, and everything else that befitted the habitation of a mighty king. It had grown up out of the earth, in almost as short a time as it had taken the armed host to spring from the dragon's teeth; and what made the matter more strange, no seed of this stately edifice had ever been planted!

When the five workmen beheld the dome, with the morning sunshine making it look golden and glorious, they gave a great shout.

"Long live King Cadmus," they cried, "in his beautiful palace!"

And the new king, with his five faithful followers at his heels, shouldering their pickaxes and marching in a rank, (for they still had a soldierlike sort of behavior, as their nature was,) ascended the palace-steps. Halting at the entrance, they gazed through a long vista of lofty pillars, that were ranged from end to end of a great hall. At the farther extremity of this hall, approaching slowly towards him, Cadmus beheld a female figure, wonderfully beautiful, and adorned with a royal

robe, and a crown of diamonds over her golden ringlets, and
the richest necklace that ever a queen wore. His heart thrilled
with delight. He fancied it his long-lost sister Europa, now
grown to womanhood, coming to make him happy, and to
repay him, with her sweet sisterly affection, for all those
weary wanderings in quest of her, since he left King Agenor's
palace!—for the tears that he had shed, on parting with
Phœnix, and Cilix, and Thasus!—for the heart-break that had
made the whole world seem dismal to him, over his dear
mother's grave!

But, as Cadmus advanced to meet the beautiful stranger, he
saw that her features were unknown to him, although, in the
little time that it required to tread along the hall, he had already felt a sympathy betwixt himself and her.

"No, Cadmus!" said the same voice that had spoken to him
in the field of the armed men. "This is not that dear sister
Europa, whom you have sought so faithfully, all over the
wide world. This is Harmonia, a daughter of the sky, who is
given you instead of sister, and brothers, and friend, and
mother. You will find all those dear ones in her alone!"

So King Cadmus dwelt in the palace, with his new friend
Harmonia, and found a great deal of comfort in his magnificent abode, but would doubtless have found as much, if not
more, in the humblest cottage by the wayside. Before many
years went by, there was a group of rosy little children (but
how they came thither, has always been a mystery to me)
sporting in the great hall, and on the marble steps of the palace, and running joyfully to meet King Cadmus, when affairs
of state left him at leisure to play with them. They called him
father, and Queen Harmonia, mother. The five old soldiers of
the dragon's teeth grew very fond of these small urchins, and
were never weary of showing them how to shoulder sticks,
flourish wooden swords, and march in military order, blowing a penny-trumpet, or beating an abominable rub-a-dub
upon a little drum.

But King Cadmus, lest there should be too much of the
dragon's tooth in his children's disposition, used to find time
from his kingly duties to teach them their A.B.C.;—which he
invented for their benefit, and for which many little people, I
am afraid, are not half so grateful to him as they ought to be!

Circe's Palace

Some of you have heard, no doubt, of the wise King Ulysses, and how he went to the siege of Troy, and how, after that famous city was taken and burnt, he spent ten long years in trying to get back again to his own little kingdom of Ithaca. At one time, in the course of this weary voyage, he arrived at an island that looked very green and pleasant, but the name of which was unknown to him. For, only a little while before he came thither, he had met with a terrible hurricane, or, rather, a great many hurricanes at once, which drove his fleet of vessels into a strange part of the sea, where neither himself nor any of his mariners had ever sailed. This misfortune was entirely owing to the foolish curiosity of his shipmates, who, while Ulysses lay asleep, had untied some very bulky leathern bags, in which they supposed a valuable treasure to be concealed. But, in each of these stout bags, King Æolus, the ruler of the winds, had tied up a tempest, and had given it to Ulysses to keep, in order that he might be sure of a favorable passage homeward to Ithaca; and when the strings were loosened, forth rushed the whistling blasts, like air out of a blown bladder, whitening the sea with foam, and scattering the vessels nobody could tell whither!

Immediately after escaping from this peril, a still greater one had befallen him. Scudding before the hurricane, he reached a place which, as he afterwards found, was called Læstrygonia, where some monstrous giants had eaten up many of his companions, and had sunk every one of his vessels, except that in which he himself sailed, by flinging great masses of rock at them, from the cliffs along the shore. After going through such troubles as these, you cannot wonder that King Ulysses was glad to moor his tempest-beaten bark in a quiet cove of the green island, which I began with telling you about. But he had encountered so many dangers from giants, and one-eyed Cyclopes, and monsters of the sea and land, that he could not help dreading some mischief, even in this pleasant and seemingly solitary spot. For two days, therefore, the poor weather-worn voyagers kept quiet, and either staid on board of their vessel, or merely crept along under the cliffs that bordered the shore; and, to keep themselves alive, they dug shell-fish out of the sand, and sought for any little rill of fresh water that might be running towards the sea.

Before the two days were spent, they grew very weary of this kind of life; for the followers of King Ulysses, as you will find it important to remember, were terrible gormandizers, and pretty sure to grumble if they missed their regular meals, and their irregular ones, besides. Their stock of provisions was quite exhausted, and even the shell-fish began to get scarce; so that they had now to choose between starving to death, or venturing into the interior of the island, where perhaps some huge three-headed dragon or other horrible monster had his den. Such mis-shapen creatures were very numerous, in those days; and nobody ever expected to make a voyage, or take a journey, without running more or less risk of being devoured by them.

But King Ulysses was a bold man, as well as a prudent one; and, on the third morning, he determined to discover what sort of a place the island was, and whether it were possible to obtain a supply of food for the hungry mouths of his companions. So, taking a spear in his hand, he clambered to the summit of a cliff, and gazed roundabout him. At a distance, towards the centre of the island, he beheld the stately towers of what seemed to be a palace, built of snow-white marble, and rising in the midst of a grove of lofty trees. The thick branches of these trees stretched across the front of the edifice, and more than half concealed it; although, from the portion which he saw, Ulysses judged it to be spacious and exceedingly beautiful, and probably the residence of some great nobleman or prince. A blue smoke went curling up from the chimney, and was almost the pleasantest part of the spectacle to Ulysses. For, from the abundance of this smoke, it was reasonable to conclude that there was a good fire in the kitchen, and that, at dinner time, a plentiful banquet would be served up to the inhabitants of the palace, and to whatever guests might happen to drop in.

With so agreeable a prospect before him, Ulysses fancied that he could not do better than to go straight to the palace-gate, and tell the master of it that there was a crew of poor shipwrecked mariners, not far off, who had eaten nothing, for a day or two, save a few clams and oysters, and would therefore be thankful for a little food. And the prince or nobleman must be a very stingy curmudgeon, to be sure, if, at least, when his own dinner was over, he would not bid them welcome to the broken victuals from the table!

Pleasing himself with this idea, King Ulysses had made a few steps in the direction of the palace, when there was a great twittering and chirping from the branch of a neighboring tree. A moment afterwards, a bird came flying towards him, and hovered in the air, so as almost to brush his face with its wings. It was a very pretty little bird, with purple wings and body, and yellow legs, and a circle of golden feathers round its neck, and on its head a golden tuft, which looked like a king's crown in miniature. Ulysses tried to catch the bird. But it fluttered nimbly out of his reach, still chirping in a piteous tone, as if it could have told a lamentable story, had it only been gifted with human language. And when he attempted to drive it away, the bird flew no farther than the bough of the next tree, and again came fluttering about his head, with its doleful chirp, as soon as he showed a purpose of going forward.

"Have you any thing to tell me, little bird?" asked Ulysses.

And he was ready to listen attentively to whatever the bird might communicate; for, at the siege of Troy, and elsewhere, he had known such odd things to happen, that he would not have considered it much out of the common run, had this little feathered creature talked as plainly as himself.

"Peep!" said the bird. "Peep, peep, pe—weep!"

And nothing else would it say, but only 'peep, peep, pe—weep!' in a melancholy cadence, and over and over, and over again. As often as Ulysses moved forward, however, the bird showed the greatest alarm, and did its best to drive him back, with the anxious flutter of its purple wings. Its unaccountable behavior made him conclude, at last, that the bird knew of some danger that awaited him, and which must needs be very terrible, beyond all question, since it moved even a little fowl to feel compassion for a human being. So he resolved, for the present, to return to the vessel, and tell his companions what he had seen.

This appeared to satisfy the bird. As soon as Ulysses turned back, it ran up the trunk of a tree, and began to pick insects out of the bark with its long, sharp bill; for it was a kind of woodpecker, you must know, and had to get its living in the same manner as other birds of that species. But, every little while, as it pecked at the bark of the tree, the purple bird bethought itself of some secret sorrow, and repeated its plaintive note of 'peep, peep, pe—weep!'

On his way to the shore, Ulysses had the good luck to kill a large stag by thrusting his spear into its back. Taking it on his shoulders, (for he was a remarkably strong man,) he lugged it along with him, and flung it down before his hungry companions. I have already hinted to you what gormandizers some of the comrades of King Ulysses were. From what is related of them, I reckon that their favorite diet was pork, and that they had lived upon it until a good part of their physical substance was swine's flesh, and their tempers and dispositions were very much akin to the hog. A dish of venison, however, was no unacceptable meal to them, especially after feeding so long on oysters and clams. So, beholding the dead stag, they felt of its ribs, in a knowing way, and lost no time in kindling a fire of drift-wood, to cook it. The rest of the day was spent in feasting; and if these enormous eaters got up from table, at sunset, it was only because they could not scrape another morsel off the poor animal's bones.

The next morning, their appetites were as sharp as ever. They looked at Ulysses, as if they expected him to clamber up the cliff again, and come back with another fat deer upon his shoulders. Instead of setting out, however, he summoned the whole crew together, and told them it was in vain to hope that he could kill a stag every day, for their dinner, and therefore it was advisable to think of some other mode of satisfying their hunger.

"Now," said he, "when I was on the cliff, yesterday, I discovered that this island is inhabited. At a considerable distance from the shore, stood a marble palace, which appeared to be very spacious, and had a great deal of smoke curling out of one of its chimneys."

"Aha!" muttered some of his companions, smacking their lips. "That smoke must have come from the kitchen-fire.

There was a good dinner on the spit; and, no doubt, there will be as good a one, to-day!"

"But," continued the wise Ulysses, "you must remember, my good friends, our mis-adventure in the cavern of one-eyed Polyphemus, the Cyclops! Instead of his ordinary milk-diet, did he not eat up two of our comrades for his supper, and a couple more for breakfast, and two at his supper again? Methinks I see him yet, the hideous monster, scanning us with that great red eye, in the middle of his forehead, to single out the fattest! And then, again, only a few days ago, did we not fall into the hands of the king of the Læstrygons, and those other horrible giants, his subjects, who devoured a great many more of us than are now left? To tell you the truth, if we go to yonder palace, there can be no question that we shall make our appearance at the dinner-table; but whether seated as guests, or served up as food, is a point to be seriously considered."

"Either way," murmured some of the hungriest of the crew, "it will be better than starvation; particularly if one could be sure of being well fattened beforehand, and daintily cooked afterwards!"

"That is a matter of taste," said King Ulysses, "and, for my own part, neither the most careful fattening nor the daintiest of cookery would reconcile me to being dished at last. My proposal is, therefore, that we divide ourselves into two equal parties, and ascertain, by drawing lots, which of the two shall go to the palace, and beg for food and assistance. If these can be obtained, all is well. If not, and if the inhabitants prove as inhospitable as Polyphemus or the Læstrygons, then there will but half of us perish, and the remainder may set sail and escape."

As nobody objected to this scheme, Ulysses proceeded to count the whole band, and found that there were forty-six men, including himself. He then numbered off twenty-two of them, and put Eurylochus (who was one of his chief-officers, and second only to himself in sagacity) at their head. Ulysses took command of the remaining twenty-two men, in person. Then, taking off his helmet, he put two shells into it, on one of which was written, 'Go,' and on the other, 'Stay.' Another person now held the helmet, while Ulysses and Eurylochus

drew out each a shell; and the word 'Go' was found written
on that which Eurylochus had drawn. In this matter, it was
decided that Ulysses and his twenty-two men were to remain
at the sea-side, until the other party should have found out
what sort of treatment they might expect, at the mysterious
palace. As there was no help for it, Eurylochus immediately
set forth, at the head of his twenty-two followers, who went
off in a very melancholy state of mind, leaving their friends in
hardly better spirits than themselves.

No sooner had they clambered up the cliff, than they discerned the tall marble towers of the palace, ascending, as
white as snow, out of the lovely green shadow of the trees
which surrounded it. A gush of smoke came from a chimney
in the rear of the edifice. This vapor rose high in the air, and,
meeting with a breeze, was wafted seaward, and made to pass
over the heads of the hungry mariners. When people's appetites are keen, they have a very quick scent for anything savory
in the wind.

"That smoke comes from the kitchen!" cried one of them,
turning up his nose as high as he could, and snuffing eagerly.
"And, as sure as I'm a half-starved vagabond, I smell roast-
meat in it!"

"Pig! Roast pig!" said another. "Ah, the dainty little pork-
er! My mouth waters for him!"

"Let us make haste," cried the others, "or we shall be too
late for the good cheer!"

But scarcely had they made half-a-dozen steps from the
edge of the cliff, when a bird came fluttering to meet them.
It was the same pretty little bird, with the purple wings and
body, the yellow legs, the golden collar round its neck, and
the crown-like tuft upon its head, whose behavior had so
much surprised Ulysses. It hovered about Eurylochus, and almost brushed his face with its wings.

"Peep, peep, pe—weep!" chirped the bird.

So plaintively intelligent was the sound, that it seemed as if
the little creature were going to break its heart, with some
mighty secret that it had to tell, and only this one poor note
to tell it with.

"My pretty bird," said Eurylochus, for he was a wary person, and let no token of harm escape his notice, "my pretty

bird, who sent you hither? And what is the message which you bring?"

"Peep, peep, pe—weep!" replied the bird, very sorrowfully.

Then it flew towards the edge of the cliff, and looked round at them, as if exceedingly anxious that they should return whence they came. Eurylochus and a few of the others were inclined to turn back. They could not help suspecting that the purple bird must be aware of something mischievous that would befal them, at the palace, and the knowledge of which affected its airy spirit with a human sympathy and sorrow. But the rest of the voyagers, snuffing up the smoke from the palace-kitchen, ridiculed the idea of returning to the vessel. One of them (more brutal than his fellows, and the most notorious gormandizer in the whole crew) said such a cruel and wicked thing, that I wonder the mere thought did not turn him into a wild beast, in shape, as he already was in his nature.

"This troublesome and impertinent little fowl," said he, "would make a delicate tit-bit to begin dinner with! Just one plump morsel, melting away between the teeth! If he comes within my reach, I'll catch him, and give him to the palace-cook to be roasted on a skewer!"

The words were hardly out of his mouth, before the purple bird flew away, crying 'Peep, peep, pe—weep,' more dolorously than ever.

"That bird," remarked Eurylochus, "knows more than we do about what awaits us at the palace!"

"Come on, then," cried his comrades; "and we'll soon know as much as he does!"

The party, accordingly, went onward through the green and pleasant wood. Every little while, they caught new glimpses of the marble palace, which looked more and more beautiful, the nearer they approached it. They soon entered a broad pathway, which seemed to be very neatly kept, and which went winding along, with streaks of sunshine falling across it, and specks of light quivering among the deepest shadows that fell from the lofty trees. It was bordered, too, with a great many sweet-smelling flowers, such as the mariners had never seen before. So rich and beautiful they were, that, if the shrubs grew wild here, and were native in the soil, then this island was surely the flower-garden of the whole earth; or, if transplanted from some other clime, it must have been from the Happy Islands that lay towards the golden sunset.

"There has been a great deal of pains foolishly wasted on these flowers!" observed one of the company; and I tell you what he said, that you may keep in mind what gormandizers they were. "For my part, if I were the owner of the palace, I would bid my gardener cultivate nothing but savory potherbs, to make a stuffing for roast-meat, or to flavor a stew with."

"Well said!" cried the others. "But, I'll warrant you, there's a kitchen garden in the rear of the palace."

At one place, they came to a crystal spring, and paused to drink at it, for want of liquor which they liked better. Looking into its bosom, they beheld their own faces dimly reflected, but so extravagantly distorted by the gush and motion of the water, that each one of them appeared to be laughing at himself and all his companions. So ridiculous were these images of themselves, indeed, that they did really laugh aloud, and could hardly be grave again as soon as they wished. And after they had drunk, they grew still merrier than before.

"It has a twang of the wine-cask in it!" said one, smacking his lips.

"Make haste!" cried his fellows. "We'll find the wine-cask itself at the palace; and that will be better than a hundred crystal fountains!"

Then they quickened their pace, and capered for joy at the thought of the savory banquet at which they hoped to be guests. But Eurylochus told them, that he felt as if he were walking in a dream.

"If I am really awake," continued he, "then, in my opinion, we are on the point of meeting with some stranger adventure than any that befel us in the cave of Polyphemus, or among the gigantic man-eating Læstrygons, or in the windy palace of King Æolus, which stands on a brazen-walled island. This kind of dreamy feeling always comes over me, before any wonderful occurrence. If you take my advice, you will turn back."

"No, no!" answered his comrades, snuffing the air, in

which the scent from the palace-kitchen was now very perceptible. "We would not turn back, though we were certain that
the king of the Læstrygons, as big as a mountain, would sit
at the head of the table, and huge Polyphemus, the one-eyed
Cyclops, at its foot!"

At length, they came within full sight of the palace, which
proved to be very large and lofty, with a great number of airy
pinnacles upon its roof. Though it was now mid-day, and the
sun shone brightly over the marble front, yet its snowy whiteness, and its fantastic style of architecture, made it look unreal, like the frost-work on a window-pane, or like the shapes
of castles which one sees among the clouds, by moonlight.
But, just then, a puff of wind brought down the smoke of the
kitchen-chimney among them, and caused each man to smell
the odor of the dish that he liked best; and, after scenting it,
they thought everything else moonshine, and nothing real
save this palace, and save the banquet that was evidently ready
to be served up in it.

So they hastened their steps towards the portal, but had
not got half-way across the wide lawn, when a pack of lions,
tigers, and wolves, came bounding to meet them. The terrified mariners started back, expecting no better fate than to be
torn to pieces and devoured. To their surprise and joy, however, these wild beasts merely capered around them, wagging
their tails, offering their heads to be stroked and patted, and
behaving just like so many well-bred house-dogs, when they
wish to express their delight at meeting their master, or their
master's friends. The biggest lion licked the feet of Eurylochus; and every other lion, and every wolf and tiger, singled
out one of his two-and-twenty followers, whom the beast
fondled as if he loved him better than a beef-bone.

But, for all that, Eurylochus imagined that he saw something fierce and savage in their eyes; nor would he have been
surprised, at any moment, to feel the big lion's terrible claws,
or to see each of the tigers make a deadly spring, or each wolf
leap at the throat of the man whom he had fondled. Their
mildness seemed unreal, and a mere freak; but their savage
nature was as true as their teeth and claws.

Nevertheless, the men went safely across the lawn, with the
wild beasts frisking about them, and doing no manner of

harm; although, as they mounted the steps of the palace, you might possibly have heard a low growl, particularly from the wolves; as if they thought it a pity, after all, to let the strangers pass without so much as tasting what they were made of.

Eurylochus and his followers now passed under a lofty portal, and looked through the open doorway into the interior of the palace. The first thing that they saw was a spacious hall, and a fountain in the middle of it, gushing up towards the ceiling out of a marble basin, and falling back into it with a continual plash. The water of this fountain, as it spouted upward, was constantly taking new shapes, not very distinctly, but plainly enough for a nimble fancy to recognize what they were. Now it was the shape of a man in a long robe, the fleecy whiteness of which was made out of the fountain's spray; now it was a lion, or a tiger, or a wolf, or an ass, or, as often as anything else, a hog, wallowing in the marble basin as if it were his sty. It was either magic or some very curious machinery that caused the gushing water-spout to assume all these forms. But, before the strangers had time to look closely at this wonderful sight, their attention was drawn off by a very sweet and agreeable sound. A woman's voice was singing melodiously in another room of the palace; and with her voice was mingled the noise of a loom, at which she was probably seated, weaving a rich texture of cloth, and intertwining the high and low sweetness of her voice into a rich tissue of harmony.

By-and-by, the song came to an end; and then, all at once, there were several feminine voices, talking airily and cheerfully, with now-and-then a merry burst of laughter, such as you may always hear, when three or four young women sit at work together.

"What a sweet song that was!" exclaimed one of the voyagers.

"Too sweet, indeed!" answered Eurylochus, shaking his head. "Yet it was not so sweet as the song of the Sirens, those bird-like damsels, who wanted to tempt us on the rocks, so that our vessel might be wrecked and our bones left whitening along the shore!"

"But just listen to the pleasant voices of those maidens, and that buzz of the loom, as the shuttle passes to-and-fro!" said another comrade. "What a domestic, household, home-like sound it is! Ah, before that weary siege of Troy, I used to hear the buzzing loom and the women's voices, under my own roof! Shall I never hear them again?—nor taste those nice, little savory dishes, which my dearest wife knew how to serve up?"

"Tush! we shall fare better here," said another. "But how innocently those women are babbling together, without guessing that we overhear them! And mark that richest voice of all, so pleasant and familiar, but which yet seems to have the authority of a mistress among them! Let us show ourselves, at once. What harm can the lady of the palace and her maidens do to mariners and warriors, like us?"

"Remember," said Eurylochus, "that it was a young maiden who beguiled three of our friends into the palace of the king of the Læstrygons, who ate up one of them in the twinkling of an eye!"

No warning or persuasion, however, had any effect on his companions. They went up to a pair of folding-doors, at the farther end of the hall, and throwing them wide open, passed into the next room. Eurylochus, meanwhile, had stept behind a pillar. In the short moment, while the folding-doors opened and closed again, he caught a glimpse of a very beautiful woman rising from the loom, and coming to meet the poor weather-beaten wanderers, with a hospitable smile, and her hand stretched out in welcome. There were four other young women, who joined their hands and danced merrily forward, making gestures of obeisance to the strangers. They were only less beautiful than the lady who seemed to be their mistress. Yet Eurylochus fancied that one of them had sea-green hair, and that the close-fitting boddice of a second looked like the bark of a tree, and that both the others had something odd in their aspect; although he could not quite determine what it was, in the little while that he had to examine them.

The folding-doors swung quickly back, and left him standing behind the pillar, in the solitude of the outer hall. There Eurylochus waited until he was quite weary, and listened eagerly to every sound, but without hearing anything that could help him to guess what had become of his friends. Footsteps, it is true, seemed to be passing and re-passing, in other parts of the palace. Then there was a clatter of silver dishes, or golden ones, which made him imagine a rich feast in a splendid banquetting-hall. But, by-and-by, he heard a tremendous grunting and squealing, and then a sudden scampering, like that of small, hard hoofs over a marble floor; while the voices of the mistress and her four handmaidens were screaming all together, in tones of anger and derision. Eurylochus could not conceive what had happened, unless a drove of swine had broken into the palace, attracted by the smell of the feast. Chancing to cast his eyes at the fountain, he saw that it did not shift its shape, as formerly, nor looked either like a long-robed man, or a lion, a tiger, a wolf, or an ass. It looked like nothing but a hog, which lay wallowing in the marble basin, and filled it from brim to brim.

But we must leave the prudent Eurylochus waiting in the outer hall, and follow his friends into the inner secrecy of the palace. As soon as the beautiful woman saw them, she arose from the loom, as I have told you, and came forward, smiling, and stretching out her hand. She took the hand of the foremost among them, and bade him and the whole party welcome.

"You have been long expected, my good friends!" said she. "I and my maidens are well acquainted with you, although you do not appear to recognize us. Look at this piece of tapestry, and judge if your faces must not have been familiar to us!"

So the voyagers examined the web of cloth, which the beautiful woman had been weaving in her loom; and, to their vast astonishment, they saw their own figures perfectly represented in different-colored threads. It was a life-like picture of their recent adventures, showing them in the cave of Polyphemus, and how they had put out his one, great, moony eye; while, in another part of the tapestry, they were untying the leathern bags, puffed out with contrary winds; and, further on, they beheld themselves scampering away from the gigantic king of the Læstrygons, who had caught one of them by the leg. Lastly, there they were, sitting on the desolate shore of this very island, hungry and downcast, and looking ruefully at the bare bones of the stag which they devoured yesterday. This was as far as the work had yet proceeded; but when the beautiful woman should again sit down at her loom, she would probably make a picture of what had since happened to the strangers, and of what was now going to happen.

"You see," she said, "that I know all about your troubles; and you cannot doubt that I desire to make you happy, for as long a time as you may remain with me. For this purpose, my honored guests, I have ordered a banquet to be prepared. Fish, fowl, and flesh, roasted, and in luscious stews, and seasoned, I trust, to all your tastes, are ready to be served up. If your appetites tell you it is dinner-time, then come with me to the festal saloon!"

At this kind invitation, the hungry mariners were quite overjoyed; and one of them, taking upon himself to be spokesman, assured their hospitable hostess that any hour of the day was dinner-time with them, whenever they could get flesh to put in the pot, and fire to boil it with. So the beautiful woman led the way; and the four maidens (one of them had sea-green hair, another a boddice of oak bark, a third sprinkled a shower of water-drops from her fingers' ends, and the fourth had some other oddity, which I have forgotten)—all these followed behind, and hurried the guests along, until they entered a magnificent saloon. It was built in a perfect oval, and lighted from a crystal dome above. Around the walls were ranged two-and-twenty thrones, overhung by canopies of crimson and gold, and provided with the softest of cushions, which were tasselled and fringed with gold cord. Each of the strangers was invited to sit down; and there they were, two-and-twenty storm-beaten mariners, in worn and tattered garb, sitting on two-and-twenty cushioned and canopied thrones, so rich and gorgeous that the proudest monarch had nothing more splendid, in his stateliest hall.

Then you might have seen the guests nodding, winking with one eye, and leaning from one throne to another, to communicate their satisfaction in hoarse whispers.

"Our good hostess has made kings of us all!" said one. "Ha! Do you smell the feast? I'll engage, it will be fit to set before two-and-twenty kings!"

"I hope," said another, "it will be, mainly, good, substantial joints, sirloins, spare-ribs, and hinder quarters, without too many kick-shaws! If I thought the good lady would not take it amiss, I should call for a fat slice of fried bacon, to begin with!"

Ah, the gluttons and gormandizers! You see how it was with them. In the loftiest seats of dignity, on royal thrones, they could think of nothing but their greedy appetite, which was the portion of their nature that they shared with wolves and swine; so that they resembled those vilest of animals far more than they did kings—if, indeed, kings were what they ought to be!

But the beautiful woman now clapt her hands; and immediately there entered a train of two-and-twenty serving-men, bringing dishes of the richest food, all hot from the kitchen-fire, and sending up such a steam that it hung like a cloud below the crystal dome of the saloon. An equal number of attendants brought great flagons of wine, of various kinds, some of which sparkled as it was poured out, and went bubbling down the throat; while, of other sorts, the purple liquor was so clear that you could see the wrought figures at the bottom of the goblet. While the servants supplied the two-and-twenty guests with food and drink, the hostess and her four maidens went from one throne to another, exhorting them to eat their fill, and to quaff wine abundantly, and thus to recompense themselves, at this one banquet, for the many days when they had gone without a dinner. But, whenever the mariners were not looking at them, (which was pretty often, as they looked chiefly into the basins and platters,) the beautiful woman and her damsels turned aside, and laughed. Even the servants, as they knelt down to present the dishes, might be seen to grin and sneer, while the guests were helping themselves to the offered dainties.

And, once in a while, the strangers seemed to taste something that they did not like.

"Here is an odd kind of a spice in this dish!" said one. "I can't say it quite suits my palate. Down it goes, however!"

"Send a good draught of wine down your throat!" said his comrade on the next throne. "That is the stuff to make this sort of cookery relish well. Though, I must needs say, the wine has a queer taste too! But the more I drink of it, the better I like the flavor."

Whatever little fault they might find with the dishes, they sat at dinner a prodigiously long while; and it would really have made you ashamed, to see how they swilled down the liquor and gobbled up the food. They sat on golden thrones, to be sure; but they behaved like pigs in a sty; and, if they had had their wits about them, they might have guessed that this was the opinion of their beautiful hostess and her maidens. It brings a blush into my face, to reckon up, in my own mind, what mountains of meat and pudding, and what gallons of wine, these two-and-twenty guzzlers and gormandizers ate and drank. They forgot all about their homes, and their wives and children, and all about Ulysses, and everything else, except this banquet, at which they wanted to keep feasting forever! But at length they began to give over, from mere incapacity to hold any more.

"That last bit of fat is too much for me!" said one.

"And I have not room for another morsel!" said his next neighbor, heaving a sigh. "What a pity. My appetite is as sharp as ever!"

In short, they all left off eating, and leaned back on their thrones, with such a stupid and helpless aspect as made them ridiculous to behold. When their hostess saw this, she laughed aloud; so did her four damsels; so did the two-and-twenty serving-men that bore the dishes, and their two-and-twenty fellows that poured out the wine. And the louder they all laughed, the more stupid and helpless did the two-and-twenty gormandizers look. Then the beautiful woman took her stand in the middle of the saloon, and stretching out a slender rod, (it had been all the while in her hand, although they never noticed it till this moment,) she turned it from one guest to another, until each had felt it pointed at himself. Beautiful as her face was, and though there was a smile on it, it looked just as wicked and mischievous as the ugliest serpent that ever was seen; and, fat-witted as the voyagers had made themselves, they began to suspect that they had fallen into the power of an evil-minded enchantress.

"Wretches," cried she, "you have abused a lady's hospitality; and, in this princely saloon, your behavior has been suited to a hog-pen! You are already swine in everything but the human form, which you disgrace, and which I myself should be ashamed to keep a moment longer, were you to share it with me. But it will require only the slightest exercise of magic, to make the exterior conform to the hoggish disposition. Assume your proper shapes, gormandizers, and begone to the sty!"

Uttering these last words, she waved her wand; and stamping her foot imperiously, each of the guests was struck aghast at beholding, instead of his comrades in human shape, one-and-twenty hogs sitting on the same number of golden thrones! Each man (as he still supposed himself to be) essayed to give a cry of surprise, but found that he could merely grunt, and that, in a word, he was just such another beast as his companions. It looked so intolerably absurd to see hogs on cushioned thrones, that they made haste to wallow down upon all-fours, like other swine. They tried to groan and beg for mercy, but forthwith emitted the most awful grunting and squealing, that ever came out of swinish throats. They would have wrung their hands in despair, but, attempting to do so, grew all the more desperate for seeing themselves squatted on their hams, and pawing the air with their fore-trotters! Dear me, what pendulous ears they had; what little red eyes, half-buried in fat; and what long snouts, instead of Grecian noses!

But, brutes as they certainly were, they yet had enough of human nature in them to be shocked at their own hideousness; and, still intending to groan, they uttered a viler grunt and squeal than before. So harsh and ear-piercing it was, that you would have fancied a butcher sticking his knife into each of their throats, or, at the very least, that somebody was pulling every hog by his funny little twist of a tail!

"Begone to your sty!" cried the enchantress, giving them some smart strokes with her wand; and then she turned to the serving-men. "Drive out these swine, and throw down some acorns for them to eat!"

The door of the saloon being flung open, the drove of hogs ran in all directions save the right one, in accordance with their hoggish perversity, but were finally driven into the back-yard of the palace. It was a sight to bring tears into one's eyes, (and I hope none of you will be cruel enough to laugh at it,) to see the poor creatures go snuffing along, picking up here a cabbage-leaf, and there a turnip-top, and rooting their noses in the earth for whatever they could find. In their sty, moreover, they behaved more piggishly than the pigs that had been born so; for they bit and snorted at one another, put their feet in the trough, and gobbled up their victuals in a ridiculous hurry; and, when there was nothing more to be had, they made a great pile of themselves among some unclean straw, and fell fast asleep. If they had any human reason left, it was just enough to keep them wondering when they should be slaughtered, and what quality of bacon they should make!

Meantime, as I told you before, Eurylochus had waited, and waited, and waited, in the entrance-hall of the palace, without being able to comprehend what had befallen his friends. At last, when the swinish uproar resounded through the palace, and when he saw the image of a hog in the marble basin, he thought it best to hasten back to the vessel, and inform the wise Ulysses of these marvellous occurrences. So he ran as fast as he could down the steps, and never stopped to draw breath till he reached the shore.

"Why do you come alone?" asked King Ulysses, as soon as he saw him. "Where are your two-and-twenty comrades?"

At these questions, Eurylochus burst into tears.

"Alas!" cried he, "I greatly fear that we shall never see one of their faces again!"

Then he told Ulysses all that had happened, as far as he knew it, and added that he suspected the beautiful woman to be a vile enchantress, and the marble palace, magnificent as it looked, to be only a dismal cavern in reality. As for his companions, he could not imagine what had become of them, unless they had been given to the swine, to be devoured alive. At this intelligence, all the voyagers were greatly affrighted. But Ulysses lost no time in girding on his sword, and hanging his bow and quiver over his shoulders, and taking a spear in his right hand. When his followers saw their wise leader making these preparations, they inquired whither he was going, and earnestly besought him not to leave them.

"You are our king," cried they; "and what is more, you are the wisest man in the whole world; and nothing but your wisdom and courage can get us out of this danger. If you desert us, and go to the enchanted palace, you will suffer the same fate as our poor companions; and not a soul of us will ever see our dear Ithaca again!"

"As I am your king," answered Ulysses, "and wiser than any of you, it is therefore the more my duty to see what has befallen our comrades, and whether anything can yet be done to rescue them. Wait for me here, until tomorrow. If I do not then return, you must hoist sail, and endeavor to find your way to our native land. For my part, I am answerable for the fate of these poor mariners, who have stood by my side in battle, and been so often drenched to the skin, along with me, by the same tempestuous surges. I will either bring them back with me, or perish!"

Had his followers dared, they would have detained him by force. But King Ulysses frowned sternly on them, and shook his spear, and bade them stop him at their peril. Seeing him so determined, they let him go, and sat down on the sand, as disconsolate a set of people as could be, waiting and praying for his return.

It happened to Ulysses, just as before, that, when he had gone a few steps from the edge of the cliff, the purple bird came fluttering towards him, crying, "Peep, peep, pe—weep!" and using all the art it could, to persuade him to go no farther.

"What mean you, little bird?" cried Ulysses. "You are arrayed like a king, in purple and gold, and wear a golden crown upon your head. Is it because I too am a king, that you desire so earnestly to speak with me? If you can talk in human language, say what you would have me do!"

"Peep!" answered the purple bird, very dolorously. "Peep, peep, pe—wee—ep!"

Certainly, there lay some heavy anguish at the little bird's heart; and it was a sorrowful predicament, that he could not, at least, have the consolation of telling what it was. But Ulysses had no time to waste in trying to get at the mystery. He therefore quickened his pace, and had gone a good way along the pleasant wood-path, when there met him a young man of very brisk and intelligent aspect, and clad in a rather singular garb. He wore a short cloak, and a sort of cap that seemed to be furnished with a pair of wings; and, from the lightness of his step, you would have supposed that there might likewise be wings on his feet. To enable him to walk still better, (for he was always on one journey or another,) he carried a winged staff, around which two serpents were wriggling and twisting. In short, I have said enough to make you guess that it was Quicksilver; and Ulysses (who knew him of old, and had learned a great deal of his wisdom from him) recognized him in a moment.

"Whither are you going in such a hurry, wise Ulysses?" asked Quicksilver. "Do you not know that this island is enchanted? The wicked enchantress (whose name is Circe, the sister of King Æetes) dwells in the marble palace, which you see yonder among the trees. By her magic arts, she changes every human being into the brute beast or fowl, whom he happens most to resemble."

"That little bird, which met me at the edge of the cliff!" exclaimed Ulysses. "Was he a human being once?"

"Yes!" answered Quicksilver. "He was once a king, named Picus, and a pretty good sort of a king too, only rather too proud of his purple robe, and his crown, and the golden chain about his neck; so he was forced to take the shape of a gaudy-feathered bird. The lions, and wolves, and tigers, who will come running to meet you, in front of the palace, were formerly fierce and cruel men, resembling in their dispositions the wild beasts, whose forms they now rightfully wear."

"And my poor companions!" said Ulysses. "Have they undergone a similar change, through the arts of this wicked Circe?"

"You well know what gormandizers they were," replied Quicksilver; and, rogue that he was, he could not help laughing at the joke. "So you will not be surprised to hear that they have all taken the shapes of swine! If Circe had never done anything worse, I really should not think her so very much to blame."

"But can I do nothing to help them?" inquired Ulysses.

"It will require all your wisdom," said Quicksilver, "and a little of my own, into the bargain, to keep your royal and sagacious self from being transformed into a fox! But, do as I bid you; and the matter may end better than it has begun."

While he was speaking, Quicksilver seemed to be in search

of something; he went stooping along the ground, and soon laid his hand on a little plant with a snow-white flower, which he plucked and smelt of. Ulysses had been looking at that very spot, only just before; and it appeared to him that the plant had burst into full flower, the instant when Quicksilver touched it with his fingers.

"Take this flower, King Ulysses!" said he. "Guard it as you do your eyesight; for, I can assure you, it is exceedingly rare and precious, and you might seek the whole earth over, without ever finding another like it. Keep it in your hand, and smell of it frequently after you enter the palace, and while you are talking with the enchantress. Especially when she offers you food, or a draught of wine out of her goblet, be careful to fill your nostrils with the flower's fragrance! Follow these directions, and you may defy her magic arts to change you into a fox!"

Quicksilver then gave him some further advice how to behave, and, bidding him be bold and prudent, again assured him, that, powerful as Circe was, he would have a fair prospect of coming safely out of her enchanted palace. After listening attentively, Ulysses thanked his good friend, and resumed his way. But he had taken only a few steps, when, recollecting some other questions which he wished to ask, he turned round again, and beheld nobody on the spot where Quicksilver had stood; for that winged cap of his, and those winged shoes, with the help of the winged staff, had carried him quickly out of sight.

When Ulysses reached the lawn, in front of the palace, the lions and other savage animals came bounding to meet him, and would have fawned upon him and licked his feet. But the wise king struck at them with his long spear, and sternly bade them begone out of his path; for he knew that they had once been blood-thirsty men, and would now tear him limb from limb, instead of fawning upon him, could they do the mischief that was in their hearts. The wild beasts yelped and glared at him, and stood at a distance, while he ascended the palace steps.

On entering the hall, Ulysses saw the magic fountain in the centre of it. The up-gushing water had now again taken the shape of a man in a long, white, fleecy robe, who appeared to be making gestures of welcome. The king likewise heard the noise of the shuttle in the loom, and the sweet melody of the beautiful woman's song, and then the pleasant voices of herself and the four maidens talking together, with peals of merry laughter intermixed. But Ulysses did not waste much time in listening to the laughter or the song. He leaned his spear against one of the pillars of the hall, and then, after loosening his sword in the scabbard, stepped boldly forward, and threw the folding-doors wide open. The moment she beheld his stately figure, standing in the door-way, the beautiful woman rose from the loom and ran to meet him, with a glad smile throwing its sunshine over her face, and both her hands extended.

"Welcome, brave stranger!" cried she. "We were expecting you!"

And the nymph with the sea-green hair made a courtesy down to the ground, and likewise bade him welcome; so did her sister, with the boddice of oaken bark, and she that sprinkled dew-drops from her fingers' ends, and the fourth one, with some oddity which I cannot remember. And Circe, as the beautiful enchantress was called, (who had deluded so many persons, that she did not doubt of being able to delude Ulysses, not imagining how wise he was,) again addressed him.

"Your companions," said she, "have already been received into my palace, and have enjoyed the hospitable treatment to which the propriety of their behavior so well entitles them. If such be your pleasure, you shall first take some refreshment, and then join them in the elegant apartment which they now occupy. See! I and my maidens have been weaving their figures into this piece of tapestry."

She pointed to the web of beautifully woven cloth, in the loom. Circe and the four nymphs must have been very diligently at work, since the arrival of the mariners; for a great many yards of tapestry had now been wrought, in addition to what I before described. In this new part, Ulysses saw his two-and-twenty friends represented as sitting on cushioned and canopied thrones, greedily devouring dainties, and quaffing deep draughts of wine. The work had not yet gone any further. Oh no, indeed! The enchantress was far too cunning to let Ulysses see the mischief which her magic arts had since brought upon the gormandizers.

"As for yourself, valiant Sir," said Circe, "judging by the dignity of your aspect, I take you to be nothing less than a king. Deign to follow me, and you shall be treated as befits your rank."

So Ulysses followed her into the oval saloon, where his two-and-twenty comrades had devoured the banquet, which ended so disastrously for themselves. But, all this while, he had held the snow-white flower in his hand, and had constantly smelt of it while Circe was speaking; and as he crossed the threshold of the saloon, he took good care to inhale several long and deep snuffs of its fragrance. Instead of two-and-twenty thrones, which had before been ranged around the wall, there was now only a single throne, in the centre of the apartment. But this was surely the most magnificent seat that ever a king or an emperor reposed himself upon, all made of chased gold, studded with precious stones, with a cushion that looked like a soft heap of living roses, and overhung by a canopy of sunlight, which Circe knew how to weave into drapery. The enchantress took Ulysses by the hand, and made him sit down upon this dazzling throne. Then, clapping her hands, she summoned the chief-butler.

"Bring hither," said she, "the goblet that is set apart for kings to drink out of! And fill it with the same delicious wine which my royal brother, King Æetes, praised so highly, when he last visited me with his fair daughter Medea. That good and amiable child! Were she now here, it would delight her to see me offering this wine to my honored guest!"

But Ulysses, while the butler was gone for the wine, held the snow-white flower to his nose.

"Is it a wholesome wine?" he asked.

At this, the four maidens tittered; whereupon, the enchantress looked round at them, with an aspect of severity.

"It is the wholesomest juice that ever was squeezed out of the grape," said she; "for, instead of disguising a man, as other liquor is apt to do, it brings him to his true self, and shows him as he ought to be!"

The chief-butler liked nothing better than to see people

turned into swine, or making any kind of a beast of themselves; so he made haste to bring the royal goblet, filled with
a liquid as bright as gold, and which kept sparkling upward
and throwing a sunny spray over the brim. But, delightfully
as the wine looked, it was mingled with the most potent enchantments that Circe knew how to concoct. For every drop
of the pure grape-juice, there were two drops of the pure
mischief; and the danger of the thing was, that the mischief
made it taste all the better. The mere smell of the bubbles,
which effervesced at the brim, was enough to turn a man's
beard into pig's bristles, or make a lion's claws grow out of
his fingers, or a fox's brush behind him!

"Drink, my noble guest!" said Circe, smiling as she presented him with the goblet. "You will find in this draught a
solace for all your troubles!"

King Ulysses took the goblet with his right hand, while,
with his left, he held the snow-white flower to his nostrils,
and drew in so long a breath that his lungs were quite filled
with its pure and simple fragrance. Then, drinking off all the
wine, he looked the enchantress calmly in the face.

"Wretch," cried Circe, giving him a smart stroke with her
wand, "how dare you keep your human shape a moment
longer? Take the form of the brute whom you most resemble!
If a hog, go join your fellow-swine in the sty; if a lion, a wolf,
a tiger, go howl with the wild beasts on the lawn; if a fox, go
exercise your craft in stealing poultry! Thou hast quaffed off
my wine, and canst be man no longer!"

But, such was the virtue of the snow-white flower, instead
of wallowing down from his throne in swinish shape, or taking any other brutal form, Ulysses looked even more manly
and kinglike than before. He gave the magic goblet a toss,
and sent it clashing over the marble floor, to the farthest end
of the saloon. Then drawing his sword, he seized the enchantress by her beautiful ringlets, and made a gesture as if he
meant to strike off her head at one blow.

"Wicked Circe," cried he, in a terrible voice, "this sword
shall put an end to thy enchantments! Thou shalt die, vile
witch, and do no more mischief in the world, by tempting
human beings into the vices which make beasts of them!"

The tone and countenance of Ulysses were so awful, and

his sword gleamed so brightly, and seemed to have so intolerably keen an edge, that Circe was almost killed by the mere fright, without waiting for a blow. The chief-butler scrambled out of the saloon, picking up the golden goblet as he went; and the enchantress and the four maidens fell on their knees, wringing their hands and screaming for mercy.

"Spare me!" cried Circe. "Spare me, royal and wise Ulysses! For now I know that thou art he of whom Quicksilver forewarned me, the most prudent of mortals, against whom no enchantments can prevail. Thou only couldst have conquered Circe! Spare me, wisest of men! I will show thee true hospitality, and even give myself to be thy slave, and this magnificent palace to be henceforth thy home!"

The four nymphs, meanwhile, were making a most piteous ado; and especially the ocean-nymph, with the sea-green hair, wept a great deal of salt-water, and the fountain-nymph, besides scattering dew-drops from her fingers' ends, nearly melted away into tears. But Ulysses would not be pacified, until Circe had taken a solemn oath to change back his companions, and as many others as he should direct, from their present forms of beast or bird, into their former shapes of men.

"On these conditions," said he, "I consent to spare your life. Otherwise, you must die upon the spot!"

With a drawn sword hanging over her, the enchantress would readily have consented to do as much good as she had hitherto done mischief, however little she might like such employment. She therefore led Ulysses out of the back-entrance of the palace, and showed him the swine in their sty. There were about fifty of these unclean beasts, in the whole herd; and though the greater part were hogs by birth and education, there was wonderfully little difference to be seen betwixt them and their new brethren, who had so recently worn the human shape. To speak critically, indeed, the latter rather carried the thing to excess, and seemed to make it a point to wallow in the miriest part of the sty, and otherwise to outdo the original swine in their own natural vocation. When men once turn to brutes, the trifle of man's wit, that remains in them, adds tenfold to their brutality.

The comrades of Ulysses, however, had not quite lost the

remembrance of having formerly stood erect. When he approached the sty, two-and-twenty enormous swine separated themselves from the herd, and scampered towards him, with such a chorus of horrible squealing as made him clap both hands to his ears. And yet they did not seem to know what they wanted, nor whether they were merely hungry, or miserable from some other cause. It was curious, in the midst of their distress, to observe them thrusting their noses into the mire, in quest of something to eat. The nymph with the boddice of oaken bark (she was the hamadryad of an oak) threw a handful of acorns among them; and the two-and-twenty hogs scrambled and fought for the prize, as if they had tasted not so much as a noggin of sour milk for a twelvemonth.

"These must certainly be my comrades," said Ulysses. "I recognize their dispositions. They are hardly worth the trouble of changing them into the human form again. Nevertheless, we will have it done, lest their bad example should corrupt the other hogs! Let them take their original shapes, therefore, Dame Circe, if your skill is equal to the task. It will require greater magic, I trow, than it did to make swine of them!"

So Circe waved her wand again, and repeated a few magic words, at the sound of which the two-and-twenty hogs pricked up their pendulous ears. It was a wonder to behold how their snouts grew shorter and shorter, and their mouths (which they seemed to be sorry for, because they could not gobble so expeditiously) smaller and smaller, and how one and another began to stand upon his hind-legs, and scratch his nose with his fore-trotters! At first, the spectators hardly knew whether to call them hogs or men, but, by-and-by, came to the conclusion that they rather resembled the latter. Finally, there stood the twenty-two comrades of Ulysses, looking pretty much the same as when they left the vessel.

You must not imagine, however, that the swinish quality had entirely gone out of them. When once it fastens itself into a person's character, it is very difficult getting rid of it. This was proved by the hamadryad, who, being exceedingly fond of mischief, threw another handful of acorns before the twenty-two newly restored people; whereupon, down they wallowed, in a moment, and gobbled them up in a very shameful way. Then, recollecting themselves, they scrambled to their feet, and looked more than commonly foolish.

"Thanks, noble Ulysses!" they cried. "From brute beasts, you have restored us to the condition of men again!"

"Do not put yourselves to the trouble of thanking me," said the wise king. "I fear I have done but little for you!"

To say the truth, there was a suspicious kind of a grunt in their voices, and, for a long time afterwards, they spoke gruffly, and were apt to set up a squeal.

"It must depend on your own future behavior," added Ulysses, "whether you do not find your way back to the sty!"

At this moment, the note of a bird sounded from the branch of a neighboring tree.

"Peep, peep, pe—wee—ep!"

It was the purple bird, who, all this while, had been sitting over their heads, watching what was going forward, and hoping that Ulysses would remember how he had done his utmost to keep him and his followers out of harm's way. Ulysses ordered Circe instantly to make a king of this good little fowl, and leave him exactly as she found him. Hardly were the words spoken, and before the bird had time to utter another 'pe—weep,' King Picus leaped down from the bough of the tree, as majestic a sovereign as any in the world, dressed in a long purple robe and gorgeous yellow stockings, with a splendidly wrought collar about his neck, and a golden crown upon his head. He and King Ulysses exchanged with one another the courtesies which belong to their elevated rank. But, from that time forth, King Picus was no longer proud of his crown and his trappings of royalty, nor of the fact of his being a king; he felt himself merely the upper servant of his people, and that it must be his life-long labor to make them better and happier.

As for the lions, tigers, and wolves, (though Circe would have restored them to their former shapes, at his slightest word,) Ulysses thought it advisable that they should remain as they now were, and thus give warning of their cruel dispositions; instead of going about under the guise of men, and pretending to human sympathies, while their hearts had the blood-thirstiness of wild beasts. So he let them howl as much as they liked, but never troubled his head about them. And, when everything was settled according to his pleasure, he sent to summon the remainder of his comrades, whom he had left at the sea-shore. These being arrived, with the prudent Eurylochus at their head, they all made themselves comfortable in Circe's enchanted palace, until quite rested and refreshed from the toils and hardships of their voyage.

The Pomegranate-Seeds

MOTHER CERES was exceedingly fond of her daughter Proserpina, and seldom let her go alone into the fields. But, just at the time when my story begins, the good lady was very busy, because she had the care of the wheat, and the Indian corn, and the rye and barley, and, in short, of the crops of every kind, all over the earth; and as the season had thus far been uncommonly backward, it was necessary to make the harvest ripen more speedily than usual. So she put on her turban, made of poppies, (a kind of flower which she was always noted for wearing,) and got into her car, drawn by a pair of winged dragons, and was just ready to set off.

"Dear mother," said Proserpina, "I shall be very lonely, while you are away. May I not run down to the shore, and ask some of the sea-nymphs to come up out of the waves and play with me?"

"Yes, child," answered Mother Ceres. "The sea-nymphs are good creatures, and will never lead you into any harm. But you must take care not to stray away from them, nor go wandering about the fields by yourself. Young girls, without their mothers to take care of them, are very apt to get into mischief."

The child promised to be as prudent as if she were a grown-up woman; and, by the time the winged dragons had whirled the car out of sight, she was already on the shore, calling to the sea-nymphs to come and play with her. They knew Proserpina's voice, and were not long in showing their glistening faces and sea-green hair above the water, at the bottom of which was their home. They brought along with them a great many beautiful shells; and sitting down on the moist sand, where the surf-wave broke over them, they busied themselves in making a necklace, which they hung round Proserpina's neck. By way of showing her gratitude, the child besought them to go with her a little way into the fields, so that they might gather abundance of flowers, with which she would make each of her kind playmates a wreath.

"Oh no, dear Proserpina," cried the sea-nymphs, "we dare

not go with you upon the dry land. We are apt to grow faint, unless, at every breath, we can snuff up the salt breeze of the ocean. And don't you see how careful we are to let the surf-wave break over us, every moment or two, so as to keep ourselves comfortably moist. If it were not for that, we should soon look like bunches of uprooted sea-weed, dried in the sun!"

"It is a great pity!" said Proserpina. "But do you wait for me here, and I will run and gather my apronful of flowers, and be back again before the surf-wave has broken ten times over you. I long to make you some wreaths that shall be as lovely as this necklace of many-colored shells."

"We will wait, then," answered the sea-nymphs. "But, while you are gone, we may as well lie down on a bank of soft sponge, under the water. The air to-day is a little too dry for our comfort. But we will pop up our heads, every few minutes, to see if you are coming."

The young Proserpina ran quickly to a spot, where, only the day before, she had seen a great many flowers. These, however, were now a little past their bloom; and, wishing to give her friends the freshest and loveliest blossoms, she strayed farther into the fields, and found some that made her scream with delight. Never had she met with such exquisite flowers before—violets so large and fragrant—roses, with so rich and delicate a blush—such superb hyacinths and such aromatic pinks—and many others, some of which seemed to be of new shapes and colors. Two or three times, moreover, she could not help thinking that a tuft of most splendid flowers had suddenly sprouted out of the earth, before her very eyes, as if on purpose to tempt her a few steps farther. Proserpina's apron was soon filled and brimming over with delightful blossoms. She was on the point of turning back, in order to rejoin the sea-nymphs and sit with them on the moist sands, all twining wreaths together. But, a little farther on, what should she behold? It was a large shrub, completely covered with the most magnificent flowers in the world!

"The darlings!" cried Proserpina; and then she thought to herself, "I was looking at that spot, only a moment ago. How strange it is that I did not see the flowers!"

The nearer she approached the shrub, the more attractive it

looked, until she came quite close to it; and then, although its beauty was richer than words can tell, she hardly knew whether to like it or not. It bore above a hundred flowers, of the most brilliant hues, and each different from the others, but all having a kind of resemblance among themselves, which showed them to be sister-blossoms. But there was a deep, glossy lustre on the leaves of the shrub, and on the petals of the flowers, that made Proserpina doubt whether they might not be poisonous. To tell you the truth, foolish as it may seem, she was half-inclined to turn round and run away.

"What a silly child I am!" thought she, taking courage. "It is really the most beautiful shrub that ever sprang out of the earth. I will pull it up by the roots, and carry it home, and plant it in my mother's garden."

Holding up her apronful of flowers with her left hand, Proserpina seized the large shrub with the other, and pulled, and pulled, but was hardly able to loosen the soil about its roots. What a deep-rooted plant it was! Again the girl pulled, with all her might, and observed that the earth began to stir and crack, to some distance around the stem. She gave another pull, but relaxed her hold, fancying that there was a rumbling sound right beneath her feet. Did the roots extend down into some enchanted cavern? Then, laughing at herself for so childish a notion, she made another effort—up came the shrub!—and Proserpina staggered back, holding the stem triumphantly in her hand, and gazing at the deep hole which its roots had left in the soil.

Much to her astonishment, this hole kept spreading wider and wider, and growing deeper and deeper, until it really seemed to have no bottom; and, all the while, there came a rumbling noise out of its depths, louder and louder, and nearer and nearer, and sounding like the tramp of horses' hoofs and the rattling of wheels. Too much frightened to run away, she stood straining her eyes into this wonderful cavity, and soon saw a team of four sable horses, snorting smoke out of their nostrils and tearing their way out of the earth, with a splendid golden chariot whirling at their heels. They leaped out of the bottomless hole, chariot and all; and there they were, tossing their black manes, flourishing their black tails,

and curvetting with every one of their hoofs off the ground
at once, close by the spot where Proserpina stood. In the
chariot sat the figure of a man, richly dressed, with a crown
on his head, all flaming with diamonds. He was of a noble
aspect, and rather handsome, but looked sullen and discontented; and he kept rubbing his eyes and shading them with
his hand, as if he did not live enough in the sunshine to be
very fond of its light.

As soon as this personage saw the affrighted Proserpina, he
beckoned her to come a little nearer.

"Do not be afraid!" said he, with as cheerful a smile as he
knew how to put on. "Come! Will not you like to ride a little
way with me, in my beautiful chariot?"

But Proserpina was so alarmed, that she wished for nothing
but to get out of his reach. And no wonder! The stranger did
not look remarkably good-natured, in spite of his smile; and
as for his voice, its tones were deep and stern, and sounded
as much like the rumbling of an earthquake, under ground,
as anything else. As is always the case with children in trouble, Proserpina's first thought was to call for her mother.

"Mother! Mother Ceres!" cried she, all in a tremble. "Come
quickly and save me!"

But her voice was too faint for her mother to hear. Indeed,
it is most probable that Ceres was then a thousand miles off,
making the corn grow, in some far distant country. Nor could
it have availed her poor daughter, even had she been within
hearing; for no sooner did Proserpina begin to cry out, than
the stranger leaped to the ground, caught the child in his
arms, and again mounting the chariot, shook the reins, and
shouted to the four black horses to set off. They immediately
broke into so swift a gallop, that it seemed rather like flying
through the air than running along the earth. In a moment,
Proserpina lost sight of the pleasant vale of Enna, in which
she had always dwelt. Another instant; and even the summit
of Mount Ætna, had become so blue in the distance, that she
could scarcely distinguish it from the smoke that gushed out
of its crater. But still the poor child screamed, and scattered
her apronful of flowers along the way, and left a long cry
trailing behind the chariot; and many mothers, to whose ears
it came, ran quickly to see if any mischief had befallen their

children. But Mother Ceres was a great way off, and could not hear the cry.

As they rode on, the stranger did his best to soothe her.

"Why should you be so frightened, my pretty child?" said he, trying to soften his rough voice. "I promise not to do you any harm. What! You have been gathering flowers? Wait till we come to my palace, and I will give you a garden full of prettier flowers than those, all made of pearls, and diamonds, and rubies. Can you guess who I am? They call my name Pluto; and I am the king of diamonds and all other precious stones. Every atom of the gold and silver, that lies under the earth, belongs to me, to say nothing of the copper and iron, and of the coal-mines, which supply me with abundance of fuel. Do you see this splendid crown upon my head? You may have it for a plaything! Oh, we shall be very good friends, and you will find me more agreeable than you expect, when once we get out of this troublesome sunshine!"

"Let me go home!" cried Proserpina. "Let me go home!"

"My home is better than your mother's," answered King Pluto. "It is a palace, all made of gold, with crystal windows; and because there is little or no sunshine thereabouts, the apartments are illuminated with diamond lamps. You never saw anything half so magnificent as my throne. If you like, you may sit down on it, and be my little queen, and I will sit on the footstool."

"I don't care for golden palaces and thrones," sobbed Proserpina. "Oh, my mother, my mother! Carry me back to my mother!"

But King Pluto, as he called himself, only shouted to his steeds to go faster.

"Pray do not be foolish, Proserpina," said he, in rather a sullen tone. "I offer you my palace, and my crown, and all the riches that are under the earth; and you treat me as if I were doing you an injury! The one thing which my palace needs is a merry little maid, to run up stairs and down, and cheer up the rooms with her smile. And this is what you must do for King Pluto!"

"Never!" answered Proserpina, looking as miserable as she could. "I shall never smile again, till you set me down at my mother's door."

But she might just as well have talked to the wind that whistled past them; for Pluto urged on his horses, and went faster than ever. Proserpina continued to cry out, and screamed so long and so loudly, that her poor little voice was almost screamed away; and when it was nothing but a whisper, she happened to cast her eyes over a great, broad field of waving grain—and whom do you think she saw? Who, but Mother Ceres, making the corn grow, and too busy to notice the golden chariot as it went rattling along! The child mustered all her strength, and gave one more scream, but was out of sight before Ceres had time to turn her head.

King Pluto had taken a road which now began to grow excessively gloomy. It was bordered on each side with rocks and precipices, between which the rumbling of the chariot-wheels was reverberated, with a noise like rolling thunder. The trees and bushes, that grew in the crevices of the rocks, had very dismal foliage; and, by-and-by, although it was hardly noon, the air became obscured with a gray twilight. The black horses had rushed along so swiftly, that they were already beyond the limits of the sunshine. But the duskier it grew, the more did Pluto's visage assume an air of satisfaction. After all, he was not an ill-looking person, especially when he left off twisting his features into a smile that did not belong to them. Proserpina peeped at his face, through the gathering dusk, and hoped that he might not be so very wicked as she at first thought him.

"Ah, this twilight is truly refreshing," said King Pluto, "after being so tormented with that ugly and impertinent glare of the sun! How much more agreeable is lamplight or torchlight, more particularly when reflected from diamonds! It will be a magnificent sight, when we get to my palace."

"Is it much farther?" asked Proserpina. "And will you carry me back, when I have seen it?"

"We will talk of that, by-and-by," answered Pluto. "We are just entering my dominions. Do you see that tall gateway before us? When we pass those gates, we are at home. And there lies my faithful mastiff at the threshold. Cerberus! Cerberus! Come hither, my good dog!"

So saying, Pluto pulled at the reins, and stopt the chariot right between the tall, massive pillars of the gateway. The mastiff, of which he had spoken, got up from the threshold, and stood on his hinder legs, so as to put his fore-paws on the chariot-wheel. But, my stars, what a strange dog it was! Why, he was a big, rough, ugly-looking monster, with three separate heads, and each of them fiercer than the two others; but, fierce as they were, King Pluto patted them all. He seemed as fond of his three-headed dog, as if it had been a sweet little spaniel, with silken ears and curly hair. Cerberus, on the other hand, was evidently rejoiced to see his master, and expressed his attachment, as other dogs do, by wagging his tail at a great rate. Proserpina's eyes being drawn to it by its brisk motion, she saw that this tail was neither more nor less than a live dragon, with fiery eyes, and fangs that had a very poisonous aspect. And, while the three-headed Cerberus was fawning so lovingly on King Pluto, there was the dragon-tail wagging against its will, and looking as cross and ill-natured as you can imagine, on its own separate account!

"Will the dog bite me?" asked Proserpina, shrinking closer to Pluto. "What an ugly creature he is!"

"Oh, never fear!" answered her companion. "He never harms people, unless they try to enter my dominions without being sent for, or to get away when I wish to keep them here. Down, Cerberus! Now, my pretty Proserpina, we will drive on."

On went the chariot; and King Pluto seemed greatly pleased to find himself once more in his own kingdom. He drew Proserpina's attention to the rich veins of gold that were to be seen among the rocks, and pointed to several places, where one stroke of a pickaxe would loosen a bushel of diamonds. All along the road, indeed, there were sparkling gems, which would have been of inestimable value, above ground, but which here were reckoned of the meaner sort, and hardly worth a beggar's stooping for.

Not far from the gateway, they came to a bridge, which seemed to be built of iron. Pluto stopt the chariot, and bade Proserpina look at the stream which was gliding so lazily beneath it. Never in her life had she beheld so torpid, so black, so muddy-looking a stream; its waters reflected no images of anything that was on the banks; and it moved as sluggishly as if it had quite forgotten which way it ought to flow, and had rather stagnate than flow either one way or the other.

"This is the river Lethe," observed King Pluto. "Is it not a very pleasant stream?"

"I think it a very dismal one," said Proserpina.

"It suits my taste, however," answered Pluto, who was apt to be sullen when anybody disagreed with him. "At all events, its water has one very excellent quality; for a single draught of it makes people forget every care and sorrow that has hitherto tormented them. Only sip a little of it, my dear Proserpina; and you will instantly cease to grieve for your mother, and will have nothing in your memory that can prevent your being perfectly happy in my palace. I will send for some, in a golden goblet, the moment we arrive."

"Oh, no, no, no!" cried Proserpina, weeping afresh. "I had a thousand times rather be miserable with remembering my mother, than be happy in forgetting her. That dear, dear mother! I never, never will forget her!"

"We shall see," said King Pluto. "You do not know what fine times we will have in my palace. Here we are just at the portal. These pillars are solid gold, I assure you!"

He alighted from the chariot, and taking Proserpina in his arms, carried her up a lofty flight of steps into the great hall of the palace. It was splendidly illuminated by means of large precious stones, of various hues, which seemed to burn like so many lamps, and glowed with a hundred-fold radiance all through the vast apartment. And yet there was a kind of gloom in the midst of this enchanted light; nor was there a single object in the hall that was really agreeable to behold, except the little Proserpina herself, a lovely child, with one earthly flower which she had not let fall from her hand. It is my opinion that even King Pluto had never been happy in his palace, and that this was the true reason why he had stolen away Proserpina, in order that he might have something to love, instead of cheating his heart any longer with this tiresome magnificence. And, though he pretended to dislike the sunshine of the upper world, yet the effect of the child's presence, bedimmed as she was by her tears, was as if a faint and watery sunbeam had somehow or other found its way into the enchanted hall.

Pluto now summoned his domestics, and bade them lose no time in preparing a most sumptuous banquet, and, above all things, not to fail of setting a golden beaker of the water of Lethe by Proserpina's plate.

"I will neither drink that, nor anything else," said Proserpina. "Nor will I taste a morsel of food, even if you keep me forever in your palace!"

"I should be sorry for that," replied King Pluto, patting her cheek; for he really wished to be kind, if he had only known how. "You are a spoilt child, I perceive, my little Proserpina; but when you see the nice things which my cook will make for you, your appetite will quickly come again!"

Then, sending for the head-cook, he gave strict orders that all sorts of delicacies, such as young people are usually fond of, should be set before Proserpina. He had a secret motive in this; for, you are to understand, it is a fixed law, that, when persons are carried off to the land of magic, if they once taste any food there, they can never get back to their friends. Now, if King Pluto had been cunning enough to offer Proserpina some fruit, or bread and milk, (which was the simple fare to which the child had always been accustomed,) it is very probable that she would soon have been tempted to eat it. But he left the matter entirely to his cook, who, like all other cooks, considered nothing fit to eat unless it were rich pastry, or highly seasoned meat, or spiced sweet-cakes—things which Proserpina's mother had never given her, and the smell of which quite took away her appetite, instead of sharpening it.

But my story must now clamber out of King Pluto's dominions, and see what Mother Ceres has been about, since she was bereft of her daughter. We had a glimpse of her, as you remember, half-hidden among the waving grain, while the four black steeds were swiftly whirling along the chariot, in which her beloved Proserpina was so unwillingly borne away. You recollect, too, the loud scream which Proserpina gave, just when the chariot was out of sight.

Of all the child's outcries, this last shriek was the only one that reached the ears of Mother Ceres. She had mistaken the rumbling of the chariot-wheels for a peal of thunder, and imagined that a shower was coming up, and that it would assist her in making the corn grow. But, at the sound of Proserpina's shriek, she started, and looked about in every direction, not knowing whence it came, but feeling almost certain that it was her daughter's voice. It seemed so unaccountable, however, that the girl should have strayed over so many lands and seas, (which she herself could not have traversed without the aid of her winged dragons,) that the good Ceres tried to believe that it must be the child of some other parent, and not her own darling Proserpina, who had uttered this lamentable cry. Nevertheless, it troubled her with a vast many tender fears, such as are ready to bestir themselves in every mother's heart, when she finds it necessary to go away from her dear children without leaving them under the care of some maiden-aunt, or other such faithful guardian. So she quickly left the field in which she had been so busy; and, as her work was not half done, the grain looked, next day, as if it needed both sun and rain, and as if it were blighted in the ear and had something the matter with its roots.

The pair of dragons must have had very nimble wings; for, in less than an hour, Mother Ceres had alighted at the door of her home, and found it empty! Knowing, however, that the child was fond of sporting on the sea-shore, she hastened thither as fast as she could, and there beheld the wet faces of the poor sea-nymphs peeping over a wave. All this while, the good creatures had been waiting on the bank of sponge, and, once every half-minute or so, had popt up their four heads above water, to see if their playmate were yet coming back. When they saw Mother Ceres, they sat down on the crest of the surf-wave, and let it toss them ashore at her feet.

"Where is Proserpina?" cried Ceres. "Where is my child? Tell me, you naughty sea-nymphs, have you enticed her under the sea?"

"Oh no, good Mother Ceres!" said the innocent sea-nymphs, tossing back their green ringlets and looking her in the face. "We never should dream of such a thing. Proserpina has been at play with us, it is true; but she left us a long while ago, meaning only to run a little way upon the dry land, and gather some flowers for a wreath. This was early in the day, and we have seen nothing of her since!"

Ceres scarcely waited to hear what the nymphs had to say, before she hurried off to make inquiries all through the neighborhood. But nobody told her anything that could enable the poor mother to guess what had become of Proserpina. A fisherman, it is true, had noticed her little footprints in the sand, as he went homeward along the beach with a basket of fish; a rustic had seen the child stooping to gather flowers; several persons had heard either the rattling of chariot-wheels, or the rumbling of distant thunder; and one old woman, while plucking vervain and catnip, had heard a scream, but supposed it to be some childish nonsense, and therefore did not take the trouble to look up. The stupid people! It took them such a tedious while to tell the nothing that they knew, that it was dark night before Mother Ceres found out that she must seek her daughter elsewhere. So she lighted a torch and set forth, resolving never to come back until Proserpina was discovered.

In her haste and trouble of mind, she quite forgot her car and the winged dragons; or, it may be, she thought that she could follow up the search more thoroughly, on foot. At all events, this was the way in which she began her sorrowful journey, holding her torch before her, and looking carefully at every object along the path. And, as it happened, she had not gone far, before she found one of the magnificent flowers which grew on the shrub, that Proserpina had pulled up.

"Ha!" thought Mother Ceres, examining it by torchlight. "Here is mischief in this flower! The earth did not produce it by any help of mine, nor of its own accord. It is the work of enchantment, and is therefore poisonous; and perhaps it has poisoned my poor child!"

But she put the poisonous flower in her bosom, not knowing whether she might ever find any other memorial of Proserpina.

All night long, at the door of every cottage and farm-house, Ceres knocked, and called up the weary laborers to inquire if they had seen her child; and they stood, gaping and half-asleep, at the threshold, and answered her pityingly, and besought her to come in and rest. At the portal of every palace, too, she made so loud a summons that the menials hurried to throw open the gate, thinking that it must be some great king or queen, who would demand a banquet for supper, and a stately chamber to repose in. And when they saw only a sad and anxious woman, with a torch in her hand and a wreath of withered poppies on her head, they spoke rudely, and sometimes threatened to set the dogs upon her. But nobody had seen Proserpina, nor could give Mother Ceres the least hint which way to seek her. Thus passed the night; and still she continued her search, without sitting down to rest, or stopping to take food, or even remembering to put out the torch; although first the rosy dawn, and then the glad light of the morning sun, made its red flame look thin and pale. But I wonder what sort of stuff this torch was made of; for it burned dimly through the day, and, at night, was as bright as ever, and never was extinguished by the rain or wind, in all the weary days and nights while Ceres was seeking for Proserpina.

It was not merely of human beings that she asked tidings of her daughter. In the woods and by the streams, she met creatures of another nature, who used, in those old times, to haunt the pleasant and solitary places, and were very sociable with persons who understood their language and customs, as Mother Ceres did. Sometimes, for instance, she tapped with her finger against the knotted trunk of a majestic oak; and immediately its rude bark would cleave asunder, and forth would step a beautiful maiden who was the hamadryad of the oak, dwelling inside of it, and sharing its long life, and rejoicing when its green leaves sported with the breeze. But not one of these leafy damsels had seen Proserpina. Then, going a little farther, Ceres would perhaps come to a fountain, gushing out of a pebbly hollow in the earth, and would dabble with her hand in the water. Behold, up through its sandy and pebbly bed, along with the fountain's gush, a young woman with dripping hair would arise, and stand gazing at Mother Ceres, half out of the water, and undulating up and down with its ever-restless motion! But when the mother asked whether her poor, lost child had stopt to drink out of the fountain, the naiad, with weeping eyes, (for these water-nymphs had tears to spare for everybody's grief,) would answer 'No!'—in a murmuring voice, which was just like the murmur of the stream.

Often, likewise, she encountered fauns, who looked like sun-burnt country people, except that they had hairy ears, and little horns upon their foreheads, and the hinder legs of goats, on which they gambolled merrily about the woods and fields. They were a frolicksome kind of creature, but grew as sad as their cheerful dispositions would allow, when Ceres inquired for her daughter, and they had no good news to tell. But, sometimes, she came suddenly upon a rude gang of satyrs, who had faces like monkeys, and horses' tails behind them, and who were generally dancing in a very boisterous manner, with shouts of noisy laughter. When she stopt to question them, they would only laugh the louder, and make new merriment out of the lone woman's distress. How unkind of those ugly satyrs! And once, while crossing a solitary sheep-pasture, she saw a personage named Pan, seated at the foot of a tall rock, and making music on a shepherd's flute. He, too, had horns, and hairy ears, and goat's feet; but, being acquainted with Mother Ceres, he answered her question as civilly as he knew how, and invited her to taste some milk and honey out of a wooden bowl. But neither could Pan tell her what had become of Proserpina, any better than the rest of these wild people.

And thus Mother Ceres went wandering about, for nine long days and nights, finding no trace of Proserpina, unless it were now-and-then a withered flower; and these she picked up and put in her bosom, because she fancied that they might have fallen from her poor child's hand. All day, she travelled onward through the hot sun; and at night, again, the flame of the torch would redden and gleam along the pathway, and she continued her search by its light, without ever sitting down to rest.

On the tenth day, she chanced to espy the mouth of a cavern, within which (though it was bright noon, everywhere else) there would have been only a dusky twilight; but it so happened that a torch was burning there. It flickered, and struggled with the duskiness, but could not half light up the gloomy cavern, with all its melancholy glimmer. Ceres was resolved to leave no spot without a search; so she peeped into the entrance of the cave, and lighted it up a little more, by holding her own torch before her. In so doing, she caught a glimpse of what seemed to be a woman, sitting on the brown leaves of the last autumn, a great heap of which had been swept into the cave by the wind. This woman (if woman it were) was by no means so beautiful as many of her sex; for her head, they tell me, was shaped very much like a dog's, and, by way of ornament, she wore a wreath of snakes around it. But Mother Ceres, the moment she saw her, knew that this was an odd kind of a person, who put all her enjoyment in being miserable, and never would have a word to say to other people, unless they were as melancholy and wretched as she herself delighted to be.

"I am wretched enough now," thought poor Ceres, "to talk with this melancholy Hecate, were she ten times sadder than ever she was yet!"

So she stept into the cave, and sat down on the withered leaves by the dog-headed woman's side. In all the world, since her daughter's loss, she had found no other companion.

"Oh, Hecate," said she, "if ever you lose a daughter, you will know what sorrow is! Tell me, for pity's sake, have you seen my poor child Proserpina pass by the mouth of your cavern?"

"No," answered Hecate, in a cracked voice, and sighing betwixt every word or two; "no, Mother Ceres, I have seen nothing of your daughter. But my ears, you must know, are made in such a way that all cries of distress and affright, all over the world, are pretty sure to find their way to them; and nine days ago, as I sat in my cave, making myself very miserable, I heard the voice of a young girl, shrieking as if in great distress. Something terrible has happened to the child, you may rest assured. As well as I could judge, a dragon or some other cruel monster was carrying her away."

"You kill me by saying so!" cried Ceres, almost ready to faint. "Where was the sound, and which way did it seem to go?"

"It passed very swiftly along," said Hecate, "and, at the same time, there was a heavy rumbling of wheels towards the eastward. I can tell you nothing more, except that, in my honest opinion, you will never see your daughter again. The best advice I can give you is, to take up your abode in this cavern, where we will be the two most wretched women in the world."

"Not yet, dark Hecate!" replied Ceres. "But do you first

come with your torch, and help me to seek for my lost child. And when there shall be no more hope of finding her, (if that black day is ordained to come,) then, if you will give me room to fling myself down, either on these withered leaves or on the naked rock, I will show you what it is to be miserable! But, until I know that she has perished from the face of the earth, I will not allow myself space even to grieve!"

The dismal Hecate did not much like the idea of going abroad into the sunny world. But then she reflected that the sorrow of the disconsolate Ceres would be like a gloomy twilight roundabout them both, let the sun shine ever so brightly, and that therefore she might enjoy her bad spirits quite as well, as if she were to stay in the cave. So she finally consented to go, and they set out together, both carrying torches, although it was broad daylight and clear sunshine. The torchlight seemed to make a gloom; so that the people whom they met, along the road, could not very distinctly see their figures; and, indeed, if they once caught a glimpse of Hecate, with the wreath of snakes round her forehead, they generally thought it prudent to run away, without waiting for a second glance.

As the pair travelled along, in this woe-begone manner, a thought struck Ceres.

"There is one person," she exclaimed, "who must have seen my poor child, and can doubtless tell what has become of her! Why did not I think of him before? It is Phœbus."

"What," said Hecate, "the young man that always sits in the sunshine? Oh, pray do not think of going near him! He is a gay, light, frivolous young fellow, and will only smile in your face. And besides, there is such a glare of the sun about him that he will quite blind my poor eyes, which I have almost wept away, already."

"You have promised to be my companion," answered Ceres. "Come; let us make haste, or the sunshine will be gone, and Phœbus along with it."

Accordingly, they went along in quest of Phœbus, both of them sighing grievously, and Hecate, to say the truth, making a great deal worse lamentation than Ceres; for all the pleasure she had, you know, lay in being miserable, and therefore she made the most of it. By-and-by, after a pretty long journey,

they arrived at the sunniest spot in the whole world. There
they beheld a beautiful young man with long, curling ringlets,
which seemed to be made of golden sunbeams; his garments
were like light summer clouds; and the expression of his face
was so exceedingly vivid, that Hecate held her hands before
her eyes, muttering that he ought to wear a black veil.
Phœbus (for this was the very person whom they were seeking) had a lyre in his hands, and was making its chords tremble with sweet music; at the same time singing a most exquisite song, which he had recently composed. For, besides a
great many other accomplishments, this young man was renowned for his admirable poetry.

As Ceres and her dismal companion approached him,
Phœbus smiled on them so cheerfully that Hecate's wreath of
snakes gave a spiteful hiss, and Hecate heartily wished herself
back in her cave. But as for Ceres, she was too earnest in her
grief either to know or care whether Phœbus smiled or
frowned.

"Phœbus!" exclaimed she, "I am in great trouble, and have
come to you for assistance. Can you tell me what has become
of my dear child Proserpina?"

"Proserpina! Proserpina, did you call her name?" answered
Phœbus, endeavoring to recollect; for there was such a continual flow of pleasant ideas in his mind, that he was apt to
forget what had happened no longer ago than yesterday. "Ah,
yes, I remember her now! A very lovely child, indeed! I am
happy to tell you, my dear madam, that I did see the little
Proserpina, not many days ago. You may make yourself perfectly easy about her. She is safe, and in excellent hands!"

"Oh, where is my dear child?" cried Ceres, clasping her
hands and flinging herself at his feet.

"Why," said Phœbus—and as he spoke, he kept touching
his lyre so as to make a thread of music run in and out among
his words—"as the little damsel was gathering flowers, (and
she has really a very exquisite taste for flowers,) she was suddenly snatched up by King Pluto, and carried off to his dominions. I have never been in that part of the universe; but
the royal palace, I am told, is built in a very noble style of
architecture, and of the most splendid and costly materials.
Gold, diamonds, pearls, and all manner of precious stones,

will be your daughter's ordinary playthings. I recommend to you, my dear lady, to give yourself no uneasiness. Proserpina's sense of beauty will be duly gratified, and, even in spite of the lack of sunshine, she will lead a very enviable life."

"Hush! Say not such a word!" answered Ceres indignantly. "What is there to gratify her heart! What are all the splendors you speak of, without affection! I must have her back again! Will you go with me, Phœbus, to demand my daughter of this wicked Pluto?"

"Pray excuse me," replied Phœbus, with an elegant obeisance. "I certainly wish you success, and regret that my own affairs are so immediately pressing, that I cannot have the pleasure of attending you. Besides, I am not upon the best of terms with King Pluto. To tell you the truth, his three-headed mastiff would never let me pass the gateway; for I should be compelled to take a sheaf of sunbeams along with me, and those, you know, are forbidden things in Pluto's kingdom."

"Ah, Phœbus," said Ceres, with bitter meaning in her words, "you have a harp instead of a heart! Farewell."

"Will not you stay a moment," asked Phœbus, "and hear me turn the pretty and touching story of Proserpina into extemporary verses?"

But Ceres shook her head, and hastened away, along with Hecate. Phœbus (who, as I have told you, was an exquisite poet) forthwith began to make an ode about the poor mother's grief; and, if we were to judge of his sensibility by this beautiful production, he must have been endowed with a very tender heart. But when a poet gets into the habit of using his heart-strings to make chords for his lyre, he may thrum upon them as much as he will, without any great pain to himself. Accordingly, though Phœbus sang a very sad song, he was as merry, all the while, as were the sunbeams amid which he dwelt.

Poor Mother Ceres had now found out what had become of her daughter, but was not a whit happier than before. Her case, on the contrary, looked more desperate than ever. As long as Proserpina was above ground, there might have been hopes of regaining her. But, now that the poor child was shut up within the iron gates of the King of the Mines, at the threshold of which lay the three-headed Cerberus, there seemed no possibility of her ever making her escape. The dismal Hecate, who loved to take the darkest view of things, told Ceres that she had better come with her to the cavern, and spend the rest of her life in being miserable. Ceres answered, that Hecate was welcome to go back thither herself, but that, for her part, she would wander about the earth in quest of the entrance to King Pluto's dominions. And Hecate took her at her word, and hurried back to her beloved cave, frightening a great many little children with a glimpse of her dog's face, as she went.

Poor Mother Ceres! It is melancholy to think of her, pursuing her toilsome way, all alone, and holding up that never-dying torch, the flame of which seemed an emblem of the grief and hope that burned together in her heart. So much did she suffer, that, though her aspect had been quite youthful when her troubles began, she grew to look like an elderly person, in a very brief time. She cared not how she was dressed, nor had she ever thought of flinging away the wreath of withered poppies, which she put on the very morning of Proserpina's disappearance. She roamed about in so wild a way, and with her hair so dishevelled, that people took her for some distracted creature, and never dreamed that this was Mother Ceres, who had the oversight of every seed which the husbandman planted. Now-a-days, however, she gave herself no trouble about seed-time nor harvest, but left the farmers to take care of their own affairs, and the crops to fade or flourish, as the case might be. There was nothing, now, in which Ceres seemed to feel an interest, unless when she saw children at play, or gathering flowers along the wayside. Then, indeed, she would stand and gaze at them with tears in her eyes. The children, too, appeared to have a sympathy with her grief, and would cluster themselves in a little group about her knees, and look up wistfully in her face; and Ceres, after giving them a kiss all round, would lead them to their homes, and advise their mothers never to let them stray out of sight.

"For, if they do," said she, "it may happen to you, as it has to me, that the iron-hearted King Pluto will take a liking to your darlings, and snatch them up in his chariot, and carry them away!"

One day, during her pilgrimage in quest of the entrance to

Pluto's kingdom, she came to the palace of King Celeus, who reigned at Eleusis. Ascending a lofty flight of steps, she entered the portal, and found the royal household in very great alarm about the queen's baby. The infant, it seems, was sickly, (being troubled with its teeth, I suppose,) and would take no food, and was all the time moaning with pain. The queen— her name was Metanira—was desirous of finding a nurse; and when she beheld a woman of matronly aspect coming up the palace-steps, she thought, in her own mind, that here was the very person whom she needed. So Queen Metanira ran to the door, with the poor wailing baby in her arms, and besought Ceres to take charge of it, or, at least, to tell her what would do it good.

"Will you trust the child entirely to me?" asked Ceres.

"Yes; and gladly too," answered the queen, "if you will devote all your time to him. For I can see that you have been a mother."

"You are right," said Ceres. "I once had a child of my own. Well; I will be the nurse of this poor, sickly boy. But beware, I warn you, that you do not interfere with any kind of treatment which I may judge proper for him. If you do so, the poor infant must suffer for his mother's folly."

Then she kissed the child, and it seemed to do him good; for he smiled, and nestled closely into her bosom.

So Mother Ceres set her torch in a corner, (where it kept burning, all the while,) and took up her abode in the palace of King Celeus, as nurse to the little Prince Demophoön. She treated him as if he were her own child, and allowed neither the king nor the queen to say whether he should be bathed in warm or cold water, or what he should eat, or how often he should take the air, or when he should be put to bed. You would hardly believe me, if I were to tell how quickly the baby-prince got rid of his ailments, and grew fat, and rosy, and strong, and how he had two rows of ivory teeth in less time than any other little fellow, before or since. Instead of the palest, and wretchedest, and puniest imp in the world, (as his own mother confessed him to be, when Ceres first took him in charge,) he was now a strapping baby, crowing, laughing, kicking up his heels, and rolling from one end of the room to the other. All the good women of the neighborhood crowded to the palace, and held up their hands, in unutter-able amazement, at the beauty and wholesomeness of this dar-ling little prince. Their wonder was the greater, because he was never seen to taste any food; not even so much as a cup of milk.

"Pray, nurse," the queen kept saying, "how is it that you make the child thrive so?"

"I was a mother once," Ceres always replied; "and having nursed my own child, I know what other children need."

But Queen Metanira, as was very natural, had a great curi-osity to know precisely what the nurse did to her child. One night, therefore, she hid herself in the chamber where Ceres and the little prince were accustomed to sleep. There was a fire in the chimney, and it had now crumbled into great coals and embers, which lay glowing on the hearth, with a blaze flickering up, now-and-then, and flinging a warm and ruddy light upon the walls. Ceres sat before the hearth, with the child in her lap, and the firelight making her shadow dance upon the ceiling overhead. She undressed the little prince, and bathed him all over with some fragrant liquid out of a vase. The next thing she did was to rake back the red embers, and make a hollow place among them, just where the back-log had been. At last, while the baby was crowing, and clap-ping its fat little hands, and laughing in the nurse's face, (just as you may have seen your little brother or sister do, before going into its warm bath,) Ceres suddenly laid him, all naked as he was, in the hollow among the red-hot embers. She then raked the ashes over him, and turned quietly away.

You may imagine, if you can, how Queen Metanira shrieked, thinking nothing less than that her dear child would be burnt to a cinder. She burst forth from her hiding-place, and, running to the hearth, raked open the fire, and snatched up poor little Prince Demophoön out of his bed of live coals, one of which he was griping in each of his fists. He immedi-ately set up a grievous cry, as babies are apt to do, when rudely startled out of a sound sleep. To the queen's astonish-ment and joy, she could perceive no token of the child's being injured by the hot fire in which he had lain. She now turned to Mother Ceres, and asked her to explain the mystery.

"Foolish woman," answered Ceres, "did you not promise

to entrust this poor infant entirely to me? You little know the mischief you have done him. Had you left him to my care, he would have grown up like a child of celestial birth, endowed with superhuman strength and intelligence, and would have lived forever. Do you imagine that earthly children are to become immortal, without being tempered to it in the fiercest heat of the fire? But you have ruined your own son! For, (though he will be a strong man and a hero in his day,) yet, on account of your folly, he will grow old, and finally die, like the sons of other women. The weak tenderness of his mother has cost the poor boy an immortality! Farewell!"

Saying these words, she kissed the little Prince Demophoön, and sighed to think what he had lost, and took her departure, without heeding Queen Metanira, who intreated her to remain, and cover up the child among the hot embers as often as she pleased. Poor baby! He never slept so warmly again.

While she dwelt in the king's palace, Mother Ceres had been so continually occupied with taking care of the young prince, that her heart was a little lightened of its grief for Proserpina. But now, having nothing else to busy herself about, she became just as wretched as before. At length, in her despair, she came to the dreadful resolution that not a stalk of grain, nor a blade of grass, not a potatoe nor a turnip, nor any other vegetable that was good for man or beast to eat, should be suffered to grow, until her daughter were restored. She even forbade the flowers to bloom, lest somebody's heart should be cheered by their beauty.

Now, as not so much as a head of asparagus ever presumed to poke itself out of the ground, without the especial permission of Ceres, you may conceive what a terrible calamity had here fallen upon the earth! The husbandmen ploughed and planted, as usual; but there lay the rich, black furrows all as barren as a desert of sand. The pastures looked as brown, in the sweet month of June, as ever they did in chill November. The rich man's broad acres and the cottager's small garden patch were equally blighted. Every little girl's flower-bed showed nothing but dry stalks. The old people shook their white heads, and said that the earth had grown aged, like themselves, and was no longer capable of wearing the warm smile of summer on its face. It was really piteous to see the poor starving cattle and sheep, how they followed behind Ceres, lowing and bleating, as if their instinct taught them to expect help from her; and everybody, that was acquainted with her power, besought her to have mercy on the human race, and, at all events, to let the grass grow. But Mother Ceres, though naturally of an affectionate disposition, was now inexorable.

"Never!" said she. "If the earth is ever again to see any verdure, it must first grow along the path which my daughter will tread, in coming back to me!"

Finally, as there seemed to be no other remedy, our old friend Quicksilver was sent post-haste to King Pluto, in hopes that he might be persuaded to undo the mischief he had done, and to set everything right again, by giving up Proserpina. Quicksilver, accordingly, made the best of his way to the great gate, took a flying leap right over the three-headed mastiff, and stood at the door of the palace in an inconceivably short time. The servants knew him both by his face and garb; for his short cloak, and his winged cap and shoes, and his snaky staff, had often been seen thereabouts, in times gone by. He requested to be shown immediately into the king's presence; and Pluto, who heard his voice from the top of the stairs, and who loved to recreate himself with Quicksilver's merry talk, called out to him to come up. And while they settle their business together, we must inquire what Proserpina has been doing, ever since we saw her last.

The child had declared, as you may remember, that she would not taste a mouthful of food, as long as she should be compelled to remain in King Pluto's palace. How she contrived to maintain her resolution, and, at the same time, to keep herself tolerably plump and rosy, is more than I can explain; but some young ladies, I am given to understand, possess the faculty of living on air, and Proserpina seems to have possessed it, too. At any rate, it was now six months since she left the outside of the earth; and not a morsel, so far as the attendants were able to testify, had yet passed between her teeth. This was the more creditable to Proserpina; inasmuch as King Pluto had caused her to be tempted, day after day, with all manner of sweetmeats, and richly preserved fruits, and delicacies of every sort, such as young people are generally most fond of. But her good mother had often told her of the hurtfulness of these things; and for that reason alone, if there had been no other, she would have resolutely refused to taste them.

All this time, being of a cheerful and active disposition, the little damsel was not quite so unhappy as you may have supposed. The immense palace had a thousand rooms, and was full of beautiful and wonderful objects. There was a never-ceasing gloom, it is true, which half-hid itself among the innumerable pillars, gliding before the child as she wandered among them, and treading stealthily behind her in the echo of her footsteps. Neither was all the dazzle of the precious stones, which flamed with their own light, worth one gleam of natural sunshine; nor could the most brilliant of the many-colored gems, which Proserpina had for playthings, vie with the simple beauty of the flowers she used to gather. But still, wherever the girl went, among those gilded halls and chambers, it seemed as if she carried nature and sunshine along with her, and as if she scattered dewy blossoms on her right hand and on her left. After Proserpina came, the palace was no longer the same abode of stately artifice and dismal magnificence, that it had before been. The inhabitants all felt this, and King Pluto more than any of them.

"My own little Proserpina," he used to say, "I wish you could like me a little better! We gloomy and cloudy-natured persons have often as warm hearts, at bottom, as those of a more cheerful character. If you would only stay with me of your own accord, it would make me happier than the possession of a hundred such palaces as this."

"Ah," said Proserpina, "you should have tried to make me like you before carrying me off! And the best thing you can now do, is to let me go again. Then I might remember you, sometimes, and think that you were as kind as you knew how to be. Perhaps, too, one day or other, I might come back and pay you a visit."

"No, no," answered Pluto, with his gloomy smile, "I will not trust you for that! You are too fond of living in the broad daylight and gathering flowers. What an idle and childish taste that is! Are not these gems, which I have ordered to be

dug for you, and which are richer than any in my crown—
are they not prettier than a violet?"

"Not half so pretty!" said Proserpina, snatching the gems
from Pluto's hand and flinging them to the other end of the
hall. "Oh, my sweet violets, shall I never see you again!"

And then she burst into tears. But young people's tears
have very little saltness or acidity in them, and do not inflame
the eyes so much as those of grown persons; so that it is not
to be wondered at, if, a few moments afterwards, Proserpina
was sporting through the hall, almost as merrily as she and
the four sea-nymphs had sported along the edge of the surf-
wave. King Pluto gazed after her, and wished that he too was
a child. And little Proserpina, when she turned about, and
beheld this great king standing in his splendid hall, and looking so grand, and so melancholy, and so lonesome, was smitten with a kind of pity. She ran back to him, and, for the first
time in all her life, put her small, soft hand in his.

"I love you a little!" whispered she, looking up in his face.

"Do you indeed, my dear child?" cried Pluto, bending his
dark face down to kiss her; but Proserpina shrank away from
the kiss, for, though his features were noble, they were very
dusky and grim. "Well! I have not deserved it of you, after
keeping you a prisoner for so many months, and starving you,
besides. Are you not terrible hungry? Is there nothing which
I can get you to eat?"

In asking this question, the King of the Mines had a very
cunning purpose; for, you will recollect, if Proserpina tasted
a morsel of food in his dominions, she would never afterwards be at liberty to quit them.

"No, indeed," said Proserpina. "Your head-cook is always
baking, and stewing, and roasting, and rolling out paste, and
contriving one dish or another, which he imagines may be to
my liking. But he might just as well save himself the trouble,
poor fat little man that he is! I have no appetite for anything
in the world, unless it were a slice of bread, of my mother's
own baking, or a little fruit out of her garden."

When Pluto heard this, he began to see that he had mistaken the best method of tempting Proserpina to eat. The
cook's made-dishes and artificial dainties were not half so delicious, in the good child's opinion, as the simple fare to

which Mother Ceres had accustomed her. Wondering that he had never thought of it before, the king now sent one of his trusty attendants, with a large basket, to get some of the finest and juiciest pears, peaches, and plums, which could anywhere be found in the upper world. Unfortunately, however, this was during the time when Ceres had forbidden any fruits or vegetables to grow; and, after seeking all over the earth, King Pluto's servant found only a single pomegranate, and that so dried up as to be not worth eating. Nevertheless, since there was no better to be had, he brought this dry, old, withered pomegranate home to the palace, put it on a magnificent golden salver, and carried it up to Proserpina. Now it happened, curiously enough, that, just as the servant was bringing the pomegranate into the back-door of the palace, our friend Quicksilver had gone up the front-steps, on his errand to get Proserpina away from King Pluto.

As soon as Proserpina saw the pomegranate, on the golden salver, she told the servant he had better take it away again.

"I shall not touch it, I assure you!" said she. "If I were ever so hungry, I should never think of eating such a miserable dry pomegranate as that!"

"It is the only one in the world!" said the servant.

He set down the golden salver, with the wizened pomegranate upon it, and left the room. When he was gone, Proserpina could not help coming close to the table, and looking at this poor specimen of dried fruit with a great deal of eagerness; for, to say the truth, on seeing something that suited her taste, she felt all the six months' appetite taking possession of her at once. To be sure, it was a very wretched-looking pomegranate, and seemed to have no more juice in it than an oyster-shell. But there was no choice of such things in King Pluto's palace. This was the first fruit she had seen there, and the last she was ever likely to see; and unless she ate it up immediately, it would grow drier than it already was, and be wholly unfit to eat.

"At least, I may smell it," thought Proserpina.

So she took up the pomegranate, and applied it to her nose; and, somehow or other, being in such close neighborhood to her mouth, the fruit found its way into that little red cave. Dear me, what an everlasting pity! Before Proserpina knew what she was about, her teeth had actually bitten it, of their own accord! Just as this fatal deed was done, the door of the apartment opened, and in came King Pluto, followed by Quicksilver, who had been urging him to let his little prisoner go. At the first noise of their entrance, Proserpina withdrew the pomegranate from her mouth. But Quicksilver (whose eyes were very keen, and his wits the sharpest that ever anybody had) perceived that the child was a little confused; and seeing the empty salver, he suspected that she had been taking a sly nibble of something or other. As for honest Pluto, he never guessed at the secret.

"My little Proserpina," said the king, sitting down, and affectionately drawing her between his knees, "here is Quicksilver, who tells me that a great many misfortunes have befallen innocent people, on account of my detaining you in my dominions. To confess the truth, I myself had already reflected that it was an unjustifiable act, to take you away from your good mother. But, then, you must consider, my dear child, that this vast palace is apt to be gloomy, (although the precious stones certainly shine very bright,) and that I am not of the most cheerful disposition, and that therefore it was a natural thing enough, to seek for the society of some merrier creature than myself. I hoped you would take my crown for a plaything, and me—ah, you laugh, naughty Proserpina!—me, grim as I am, for a playmate. It was a silly expectation."

"Not so extremely silly," whispered Proserpina. "You have really amused me very much, sometimes."

"Thank you!" said King Pluto, rather dryly. "But I can see, plainly enough, that you think my palace a dusky prison, and me the iron-hearted keeper of it. And an iron heart I should surely have, if I could detain you here any longer, my poor child, when it is now six months since you tasted food. I give you your liberty! Go with Quicksilver! Hasten home to your dear mother!"

Now, although you may not have supposed it, Proserpina found it impossible to take leave of poor King Pluto, without some regrets, and a good deal of compunction for not telling him about the pomegranate. She even shed a tear or two, thinking how lonely and cheerless the great palace would seem to him, with all its ugly glare of artificial light, after she herself— his one little ray of natural sunshine, whom he had stolen, to be sure, but only because he valued her so much— after she should have departed. I know not how many kind things she might have said to the disconsolate King of the Mines, had not Quicksilver hurried her away.

"Come along quickly," whispered he in her ear, "or his Majesty may change his royal mind. And take care, above all things, that you say nothing of what was brought you on the golden salver!"

In a very short time, they had passed the great gateway, (leaving the three-headed Cerberus, barking, and yelping, and growling, with threefold din, behind them,) and emerged upon the surface of the earth. It was delightful to behold, as Proserpina hastened along, how the path grew verdant, be-hind, and on either side of her. Wherever she set her blessed foot, there was at once a dewy flower. The violets gushed up, along the wayside. The grass and the grain began to sprout, with tenfold vigor and luxuriance, to make up for the dreary months that had been wasted in barrenness. The starved cattle immediately set to work grazing, after their long fast, and ate enormously, all day, and got up at midnight to eat more. But, I can assure you, it was a busy time of year with the farmers, when they found the summer coming upon them with such a rush. Nor must I forget to say, that all the birds in the whole world hopt about upon the newly blossoming trees, and sang together, in a prodigious ecstasy of joy.

Mother Ceres had returned to her deserted home, and was sitting disconsolately on the door-step, with her torch burn-ing in her hand. She had been idly watching the flame, for some moments past, when, all at once, it flickered and went out.

"What does this mean?" thought she. "It was an enchanted torch, and should have kept burning till my child came back!"

Lifting her eyes, she was surprised to see a sudden verdure flashing over the brown and barren fields, exactly as you may have observed a golden hue gleaming far and wide across the landscape, from the just-risen sun.

"Does the earth disobey me?" exclaimed Mother Ceres, in-dignantly. "Does it presume to be green, when I have bidden it be barren, until my daughter shall be restored to my arms?"

"Then open your arms, dear mother," cried a well-known voice, "and take your little daughter into them!"

And Proserpina came running, and flung herself upon her mother's bosom. Their mutual transport is not to be described. The grief of their separation had caused both of them to shed a great many tears; and now they shed a great many more, because their joy could not so well express itself in any other way.

When their hearts had grown a little more quiet, Mother Ceres looked anxiously at Proserpina.

"My child," said she, "did you taste any food, while you were in King Pluto's palace?"

"Dearest mother," answered Proserpina, "I will tell you the whole truth. Until this very morning, not a morsel of food had passed my lips. But, to-day, they brought me a pomegranate, (a very dry one it was, and all shrivelled up, till there was little left of it, but seeds and skin,) and having seen no fruit for so long a time, and being faint with hunger, I was tempted just to bite it. The instant I tasted it, King Pluto and Quicksilver came into the room. I had not swallowed a morsel; but—dear mother, I hope it was no harm—but, six of the pomegranate-seeds, I am afraid, remained in my mouth!"

"Ah, unfortunate child, and miserable me!" exclaimed Ceres. "For each of those six pomegranate-seeds you must spend one month of every year in King Pluto's palace. You are but half restored to your mother. Only six months with me, and six with that good-for-nothing King of Darkness!"

"Do not speak so harshly of poor King Pluto," said Proserpina, kissing her mother. "He has some very good qualities; and I really think I can bear to spend six months in his palace, if he will only let me spend the other six with you. He certainly did very wrong to carry me off; but then, as he says, it was but a dismal sort of life for him, to live in that great, gloomy place, all alone; and it has made a wonderful change in his spirits, to have a little girl to run up stairs and down. There is some comfort in making him so happy; and so, upon the whole, dearest mother, let us be thankful that he is not to keep me the whole year round!"

The Golden Fleece

WHEN Jason, the son of the dethroned King of Iolcos, was a little boy, he was sent away from his parents, and placed under the queerest schoolmaster that ever you heard of. This learned person was one of the people, or quadrupeds, called Centaurs. He lived in a cavern, and had the body and legs of a white horse with the head and shoulders of a man. His name was Chiron; and, in spite of his odd appearance, he was a very excellent teacher, and had several scholars who afterwards did him credit, by making a great figure in the world. The famous Hercules was one, and so was Achilles, and Philoctetes, likewise, and Esculapius, who acquired immense repute as a doctor. The good Chiron taught his pupils how to play upon the harp, and how to cure diseases, and how to use the sword and shield, together with various other branches of education, in which the lads of those days used to be instructed, instead of writing and arithmetic.

I have sometimes suspected that Master Chiron was not really very different from other people, but that, being a kind-hearted and merry old fellow, he was in the habit of making-believe that he was a horse, and scrambling about the school-room on all-fours, and letting the little boys ride upon his back. And so, when his scholars had grown up, and grown old, and were trotting their grandchildren on their knees, they told them about the sports of their school-days; and these young folks took the idea that their grandfathers had been taught their letters by a Centaur, half-man and half-horse. Little children, not quite understanding what is said to them, often get such absurd notions into their heads, you know!

Be that as it may, it has always been told for a fact, (and always will be told, as long as the world lasts,) that Chiron, with the head of a schoolmaster, had the body and legs of a horse. Just imagine the grave old gentleman clattering and stamping into the schoolroom on his four hoofs, perhaps treading on some little fellow's toes, flourishing his switch-tail instead of a rod, and, now-and-then, trotting out of doors to eat a mouthful of grass! I wonder what the blacksmith charged him for a set of iron shoes!

So Jason dwelt in the cave, with this four-footed Chiron, from the time that he was an infant, only a few months old, until he had grown to the full height of a man. He became a very good harper, I suppose, and skilful in the use of weapons, and tolerably acquainted with herbs and other doctor's stuff, and, above all, an admirable horseman; for, in teaching young people to ride, the good Chiron must have been without a rival among schoolmasters. At length, being now a tall and athletic youth, Jason resolved to seek his fortune in the world, without asking Chiron's advice, or telling him anything about the matter. This was very unwise, to be sure; and I hope none of you, my little hearers, will ever follow Jason's example. But, you are to understand, he had heard how that he himself was a prince royal, and how his father, King Æson, had been deprived of the kingdom of Iolcos by a certain Pelias, who would also have killed Jason, had he not been hidden in the Centaur's cave. And, being come to the strength of a man, Jason determined to set all this business to rights, and to punish the wicked Pelias for wronging his dear father, and to cast him down from the throne, and seat himself there instead.

With this intention, he took a spear in each hand, and threw a leopard's skin over his shoulders, to keep off the rain, and set forth on his travels, with his long yellow ringlets waving in the wind. The part of his dress, on which he most prided himself, was a pair of sandals that had been his father's. They were handsomely embroidered, and were tied upon his feet with strings of gold. But his whole attire was such as people did not very often see; and as he passed along, the women and children ran to the doors and windows, wondering whither this beautiful youth was journeying, with his leopard's skin and his golden-tied sandals, and what heroic deeds he meant to perform, with a spear in his right hand and another in his left!

I know not how far Jason had travelled, when he came to a turbulent river, which rushed right across his pathway, with specks of white foam among its black eddies, hurrying tumultuously onward, and roaring angrily as it went. Though not a very broad river, in the dry seasons of the year, it was now swollen by heavy rains, and by the melting of the snow on the sides of Mount Olympus; and it thundered so loudly, and looked so wild and dangerous, that Jason, bold as he was, thought it prudent to pause upon the brink. The bed of the stream seemed to be strewn with sharp and rugged rocks, some of which thrust themselves above the water. By-and-by, an uprooted tree, with shattered branches, came drifting along the current, and got entangled among the rocks. Now-and-then, a drowned sheep, and once, the carcass of a cow, floated past.

In short, the swollen river had already done a great deal of mischief. It was evidently too deep for Jason to wade, and too boisterous for him to swim; he could see no bridge; and as for a boat, had there been any, the rocks would have broken it to pieces in an instant.

"See the poor lad!" said a cracked voice close to his side. "He must have had but a poor education, since he does not know how to cross a little stream like this! Or is he afraid of wetting his fine golden-stringed sandals? It is a pity his four-footed schoolmaster is not here, to carry him safely across on his back!"

Jason looked round, greatly surprised, for he did not know that anybody was near. But beside him stood an old woman with a ragged mantle over her head, leaning on a staff, the top of which was carved into the shape of a cuckoo. She looked very aged, and wrinkled, and infirm; and yet her eyes, which were as brown as those of an ox, were so extremely large and beautiful, that, when they were fixed on Jason's eyes, he could see nothing else but them. The old woman had a pomegranate in her hand, although the fruit was then quite out of season.

"Whither are you going, Jason?" she now asked.

She seemed to know his name, you will observe; and, in-deed, those great brown eyes looked as if they had a knowl-edge of everything, whether past or to come. While Jason was gazing at her, a peacock strutted forward, and took his stand at the old woman's side.

"I am going to Iolcos," answered the young man, "to bid

the wicked King Pelias come down from my father's throne, and let me reign in his stead."

"Ah, well then," said the old woman, still with the same cracked voice, "if that is all your business, you need not be in a very great hurry! Just take me on your back, there's a good youth, and carry me across the river! I and my peacock have something to do on the other side, as well as yourself."

"Good mother," replied Jason, "your business can hardly be so important as the pulling down a king from his throne! Besides, as you may see for yourself, the river is very boisterous; and if I should chance to stumble, it would sweep both of us away, more easily than it has carried off yonder uprooted tree. I would gladly help you if I could; but I doubt whether I am strong enough to carry you across."

"Then," said she, very scornfully, "neither are you strong enough to pull King Pelias off his throne! And, Jason, unless you will help an old woman at her need, you ought not to be a king. What are kings made for, save to succor the feeble and distressed? But do as you please! Either take me on your back, or, with my poor old limbs, I shall try my best to struggle across the stream."

Saying this, the old woman poked with her staff in the river, as if to find the safest place in its rocky bed, where she might make the first step. But Jason, by this time, had grown ashamed of his reluctance to help her. He felt that he could never forgive himself, if this poor, feeble creature should come to any harm in attempting to wrestle against the headlong current. The good Chiron, whether half-horse or no, had taught him that the noblest use of his strength was, to assist the weak; and also that he must treat every young woman as if she were his sister, and every old one like a mother. Remembering these maxims, the vigorous and beautiful young man knelt down, and requested the good dame to mount upon his back.

"The passage seems to me not very safe," he remarked. "But, as your business is so urgent, I will try to carry you across. If the river sweeps you away, it shall take me too!"

"That, no doubt, will be a great comfort to both of us!" quoth the old woman. "But never fear! We shall get safely across."

So she threw her arms around Jason's neck; and lifting her from the ground, he stepped boldly into the raging and foamy current, and began to stagger away from the shore. As for the peacock, it alighted on the old dame's shoulder. Jason's two spears, one in each hand, kept him from stumbling, and enabled him to feel his way among the hidden rocks; although, every instant, he expected that his companion and himself would go down the stream, together with the driftwood of shattered trees, and the carcasses of the sheep and cow. Down came the cold, snowy torrent from the steep side of Olympus, raging and thundering as if it had a real spite against Jason, or, at all events, were determined to snatch off his living burthen from his shoulders. When he was half-way across, the uprooted tree (which I have already told you about) broke loose from among the rocks, and bore down upon him, with all its splintered branches sticking out like the hundred arms of the giant Briareus. It rushed past, however, without touching him. But, the next moment, his foot was caught in a crevice between two rocks, and stuck there so fast, that, in the effort to get free, he lost one of his golden-stringed sandals.

At this accident, Jason could not help uttering a cry of vexation.

"What is the matter, Jason?" asked the old woman.

"Matter enough!" said the young man. "I have lost a sandal here among the rocks. And what sort of a figure shall I cut, at the court of King Pelias, with a golden-stringed sandal on one foot, and the other foot bare?"

"Do not take it to heart," answered his companion, cheerily. "You never met with better fortune than in losing that sandal. It satisfies me that you are the very person whom the Speaking Oak has been talking about!"

There was no time, just then, to inquire what the Speaking Oak had said. But the briskness of her tone encouraged the young man; and, besides, he had never in his life felt so vigorous and mighty, as since taking this old woman on his back. Instead of being exhausted, he gathered strength as he went on; and struggling up against the torrent, he at last gained the opposite shore, clambered up the bank, and set down the old dame and her peacock, safely on the grass. As

soon as this was done, however, he could not help looking
rather despondently at his bare foot, with only a remnant of
the golden string of the sandal, clinging round his ancle.

"You will get a handsomer pair of sandals, by-and-by," said
the old woman, with a kindly look out of her beautiful brown
eyes. "Only let King Pelias get a glimpse of that bare foot,
and you shall see him turn as pale as ashes, I promise you!
There is your path. Go along, my good Jason, and my blessing go with you! And when you sit on your throne, remember the old woman whom you helped over the river!"

With these words she hobbled away, giving him a smile
over her shoulder, as she departed. Whether the light of her
beautiful brown eyes threw a glory roundabout her, or whatever the cause might be, Jason fancied that there was something very noble and majestic in her figure, after all, and that,
though her gait seemed to be a rheumatic hobble, yet she
moved with as much grace and dignity as any queen on earth.
Her peacock, which had now fluttered down from her shoulder, strutted behind her in prodigious pomp, and spread out
its magnificent tail on purpose for Jason to admire it.

When the old dame and her peacock were out of sight,
Jason set forward on his journey. After travelling a pretty
long distance, he came to a town, situated at the foot of a
mountain, and not a great way from the shore of the sea. On
the outside of the town, there was an immense crowd of people, not only men and women, but children too, all in their
best clothes, and evidently enjoying a holiday. The crowd was
thickest towards the sea-shore; and in that direction, over the
people's heads, Jason saw a wreath of smoke curling upward
to the blue sky. He inquired of one of the multitude, what
town it was, near by, and why so many persons were here
assembled together.

"This is the kingdom of Iolcos," answered the man; "and
we are the subjects of King Pelias. Our monarch has summoned us together, that we may see him sacrifice a black bull
to Neptune, who, they say, is his majesty's father. Yonder is
the king, where you see the smoke going up from the altar."

While the man spoke, he eyed Jason with great curiosity;
for his garb was quite unlike that of the Iolchians, and it
looked very odd to see a youth with a leopard's skin over his

shoulders, and each hand grasping a spear. Jason perceived, too, that the man stared particularly at his feet, one of which, you remember, was bare, while the other was decorated with his father's golden-stringed sandal.

"Look at him!—only look at him!" said the man to his next neighbor. "Do you see? He wears but one sandal!"

Upon this, first one person, and then another, began to stare at Jason, and everybody seemed to be greatly struck with something in his aspect; though they turned their eyes much oftener towards his feet, than to any other part of his figure. Besides, he could hear them whispering to one another.

"One sandal! One sandal!"—they kept saying.—"The man with one sandal! Here he is, at last! Whence has he come? What does he mean to do? What will the king say to the one-sandalled man?"

Poor Jason was greatly abashed, and made up his mind that the people of Iolcos were exceedingly ill-bred, to take such public notice of an accidental deficiency in his dress. Meanwhile, whether it were that they hustled him forward, or that Jason, of his own accord, thrust a passage through the crowd, it so happened that he soon found himself close to the smoking altar, where King Pelias was sacrificing the black bull. The murmur and hum of the multitude, in their surprise at the spectacle of Jason with his one bare foot, grew so loud that it disturbed the ceremonies; and the king, holding the great knife with which he was just going to cut the bull's throat, turned angrily about, and fixed his eyes on Jason. The people had now withdrawn from around him, so that the youth stood in an open space, near the smoking altar, front to front with the angry King Pelias.

"Who are you?" cried the king, with a terrible frown. "And how dare you make this disturbance, while I am sacrificing a black bull to my father Neptune?"

"It is no fault of mine!" answered Jason. "Your majesty must blame the rudeness of your subjects, who have raised all this tumult because one of my feet happens to be bare."

When Jason said this, the king gave a quick, startled glance down at his feet.

"Ha!" muttered he, "Here is the one-sandalled fellow, sure enough! What can I do with him?"

And he clutched more closely the great knife in his hand, as if he were half a mind to slay Jason, instead of the black bull. The people roundabout caught up the king's words, indistinctly as they were uttered; and first there was a murmur among them, and then a loud shout.

"The one-sandalled man has come! The prophecy must be fulfilled!"

For you are to know, that, many years before, King Pelias had been told by the Speaking Oak of Dodona, that a man with one sandal should cast him down from his throne. On this account, he had given strict orders that nobody should ever come into his presence, unless both sandals were securely tied upon his feet; and he kept an officer in his palace, whose sole business it was to examine people's sandals, and to supply them with a new pair, at the expense of the royal treasury, as soon as the old ones began to wear out. In the whole course of the king's reign, he had never been thrown into such a fright and agitation as by the spectacle of poor Jason's bare foot. But, as he was naturally a bold and hard-hearted man, he soon took courage, and began to consider in what way he might rid himself of this terrible one-sandalled stranger.

"My good young man," said King Pelias, taking the softest tone imaginable, in order to throw Jason off his guard, "you are excessively welcome to my kingdom! Judging by your dress, you must have travelled a long distance; for it is not the fashion to wear leopard-skins, in this part of the world. Pray what may I call your name?—and where did you receive your education?"

"My name is Jason," answered the young stranger. "Ever since my infancy, I have dwelt in the cave of Chiron the Centaur. He was my instructor, and taught me music, and horsemanship, and how to cure wounds, and likewise how to inflict wounds with my weapons!"

"I have heard of Chiron the schoolmaster," replied King Pelias, "and how that there is an immense deal of learning and wisdom in his head, although it happens to be set on a horse's body. It gives me great delight to see one of his scholars at my court. But, to test how much you have profited under so excellent a teacher, will you allow me to ask you a single question?"

"I do not pretend to be very wise," said Jason. "But ask me what you please, and I will answer to the best of my ability."

Now King Pelias meant cunningly to entrap the young man, and to make him say something that should be the cause of mischief and destruction to himself. So, with a crafty and evil smile upon his face, he spoke as follows.

"What would you do, brave Jason," asked he, "if there were a man in the world, by whom, as you had reason to believe, you were doomed to be ruined and slain—what would you do, I say, if that man stood before you, and in your power?"

When Jason saw the malice and wickedness, which King Pelias could not prevent from gleaming out of his eyes, he probably guessed that the king had discovered what he came for, and that he intended to turn his own words against himself. Still, he scorned to tell a falsehood. Like an upright and honorable prince, as he was, he determined to speak out the real truth. Since the king had chosen to ask him the question, and since Jason had promised him an answer, there was no right way, save to tell him precisely what would be the most prudent thing to do, if he had his worst enemy in his power.

Therefore, after a moment's consideration, he spoke up, with a firm and manly voice.

"I would send such a man," said he, "in quest of the Golden Fleece!"

This enterprise, you will understand, was, of all others, the most difficult and dangerous in the world. In the first place, it would be necessary to make a long voyage through unknown seas. There was hardly a hope, or a possibility, that any young man, who should undertake this voyage, would either succeed in obtaining the Golden Fleece, or would survive to return home, and tell of the perils he had run. The eyes of King Pelias sparkled with joy, therefore, when he heard Jason's reply.

"Well said, wise Man with the one Sandal!" cried he. "Go, then, and, at the peril of your life, bring me back the Golden Fleece!"

"I go!" answered Jason, composedly. "If I fail, you need not fear that I will ever come back to trouble you again. But, if I return to Iolcos with the prize, then, King Pelias, you must hasten down from your lofty throne, and give me your crown and sceptre!"

"That I will!" said the king, with a sneer. "Meantime, I will keep them very safely for you!"

The first thing that Jason thought of doing, after he left the king's presence, was to go to Dodona, and inquire of the Talking Oak what course it was best to pursue. This wonderful tree stood in the centre of an ancient wood. Its stately trunk rose up a hundred feet into the air, and threw a broad and dense shadow over more than an acre of ground. Standing beneath it, Jason looked up among the knotted branches and green leaves, and into the mysterious heart of the old tree, and spoke aloud, as if he were addressing some person who was hidden in the depths of the foliage.

"What shall I do," said he, "in order to win the Golden Fleece?"

At first, there was a deep silence, not only within the shadow of the Talking Oak, but all through the solitary wood. In a moment or two, however, the leaves of the oak began to stir and rustle, as if a gentle breeze were wandering amongst them, although the other trees of the wood were perfectly still. The sound grew louder, and became like the roar of a high wind. By-and-by, Jason imagined that he could distinguish words, but very confusedly, because each separate leaf of the tree seemed to be a tongue, and the whole myriad of tongues were babbling at once. But the noise waxed broader and deeper, until it resembled a tornado sweeping through the oak, and making one great utterance out of the thousand and thousand of little murmurs, which each leafy tongue had caused by its rustling. And now, though it still had the tone of a mighty wind roaring among the branches, it was also like a deep, bass voice, speaking, as distinctly as a tree could be expected to speak, the following words: —

"Go to Argus, the ship-builder, and bid him build a galley with fifty oars!"

Then the voice melted again into the indistinct murmur of the rustling leaves, and died gradually away. When it was quite gone, Jason felt inclined to doubt whether he had actually heard the words, or whether his fancy had not shaped them out of the ordinary sound made by a breeze, while passing through the thick foliage of the tree.

But, on inquiry among the people of Iolcos, he found that there was really a man in the city, by the name of Argus, who was a very skilful builder of vessels. This showed some intelligence in the oak; else how should it have known that any such person existed? At Jason's request, Argus readily consented to build him a galley, so big that it should require fifty strong men to row it; although no vessel of such a size and burden had heretofore been seen in the world. So the head-carpenter, and all his journeymen and apprentices, began their work; and, for a good while afterwards, there they were, busily employed, hewing out the timbers, and making a great clatter with their hammers; until the new ship, which was called the Argo, seemed to be quite ready for sea. And, as the Talking Oak had already given him such good advice, Jason thought that it would not be amiss to ask for a little more. He visited it again, therefore, and standing beside its huge, rough trunk, inquired what he should do next.

This time, there was no such universal quivering of the leaves, throughout the whole tree, as there had been before. But, after a while, Jason observed that the foliage of a great branch, which stretched above his head, had begun to rustle, as if the wind were stirring that one bough, while all the other boughs of the oak were at rest.

"Cut me off!" said the branch, as soon as it could speak distinctly. "Cut me off! Cut me off! And carve me into a figure-head for your galley!"

Accordingly, Jason took the branch at its word, and lopped it off the tree. A carver in the neighborhood engaged to make the figure-head. He was a tolerably good workman, and had already carved several figure-heads, in what he intended for feminine shapes, and looking pretty much like those which we see now-a-days, stuck up under a vessel's bowsprit, with great staring eyes that never wink at the dash of the spray. But (what was very strange) the carver found that his hand was guided by some unseen power, and by a skill beyond his own, and that his tools shaped out an image which he had never dreamed of. When the work was finished, it turned out to be the figure of a beautiful woman, with a helmet on her head, from beneath which the long ringlets fell down upon her shoulders. On the left arm was a shield, and in its centre appeared a lifelike representation of the head of Medusa with the snaky locks. The right arm was extended, as if pointing onward. The face of this wonderful statue, though not angry or forbidding, was so grave and majestic, that perhaps you might call it severe; and as for the mouth, it seemed just ready to unclose its lips, and utter words of the deepest wisdom.

Jason was delighted with the oaken image, and gave the carver no rest until it was completed, and set up where a figure-head has always stood, from that time to this, in the vessel's prow.

"And now," cried he, as he stood gazing at the calm, majestic face of the statue, "I must go to the Talking Oak, and inquire what next to do?"

"There is no need of that, Jason," said a voice which, though it was far lower, reminded him of the mighty tones of the great oak. "When you desire good advice, you can seek it of me!"

Jason had been looking straight into the face of the image, when these words were spoken. But he could hardly believe either his ears or his eyes. The truth was, however, that the oaken lips had moved, and, to all appearance, the voice had proceeded from the statue's mouth. Recovering a little from his surprise, Jason bethought himself that the image had been carved out of the wood of the Talking Oak, and that therefore it was really no great wonder, but, on the contrary, the most natural thing in the world, that it should possess the faculty of speech. It would have been very odd, indeed, if it had not! But, certainly, it was a great piece of good fortune that he should be able to carry so wise a block of wood along with him, in his perilous voyage.

"Tell me, wondrous image," exclaimed Jason—"(Since you inherit the wisdom of the Speaking Oak of Dodona, whose daughter you are)—tell me, where shall I find fifty bold youths, who will take each of them an oar of my galley? They must have sturdy arms to row, and brave hearts to encounter perils; or we shall never win the Golden Fleece!"

"Go!" replied the oaken image. "Go summon all the heroes of Greece!"

And, in fact, considering what a great deed was to be done, could any advice be wiser than this, which Jason received from the figure-head of his vessel? He lost no time in sending messengers to all the cities, and making known to the whole people of Greece, that Prince Jason, the son of King Æson, was going in quest of the Fleece of Gold, and that he desired the help of forty-nine of the bravest and strongest young men alive, to row his vessel and share his dangers. And Jason himself would be the fiftieth.

At this news, the adventurous youths, all over the country, began to bestir themselves. Some of them had already fought with giants and slain dragons; and the younger ones, who had not yet met with such good fortune, thought it a shame to have lived so long without getting astride of a flying serpent, or sticking their spears into a Chimæra, or, at least, thrusting their right arms down a monstrous lion's throat. There was a fair prospect that they would meet with plenty of such adventures, before finding the Golden Fleece. As soon as they could furbish up their helmets and shields, therefore, and gird on their trusty swords, they came thronging to Iolcos, and clambered on board the new galley. Shaking hands with Jason, they assured him that they did not care a pin for their lives, but would help row the vessel to the remotest edge of the world, and as much farther as he might think it best to go.

Many of these brave fellows had been educated by Chiron, the four-footed pedagogue, and were therefore old school-mates of Jason, and knew him to be a lad of spirit. The mighty Hercules, whose shoulders afterwards held up the sky, was one of them. And there were Castor and Pollux, the twin-brothers, who were never accused of being chicken-hearted, although they had been hatched out of an egg; and Theseus, who was so renowned for killing the Minotaur; and Lynceus, with his wonderfully sharp eyes, which could see through a mill-stone, or look right down into the depths of the earth, and discover the treasures that were there; and Orpheus, the very best of harpers, who sang and played upon his lyre so sweetly, that the brute-beasts stood upon their hind-legs, and capered merrily to the music. Yes; and, at some of his more moving tunes, the rocks bestirred their moss-grown bulk out of the ground, and a grove of forest-trees uprooted themselves, and, nodding their tops to one another, performed a country-dance!

One of the rowers was a beautiful young woman, named Atalanta, who had been nursed among the mountains by a bear. So light of foot was this fair damsel, that she could step from one foamy crest of a wave to the foamy crest of another, without wetting more than the sole of her sandal. She had grown up in a very wild way, and talked much about the rights of women, and loved hunting and war far better than her needle. But, in my opinion, the most remarkable of this famous company were two sons of the North Wind, (airy youngsters, and of rather a blustering disposition,) who had wings on their shoulders, and, in case of a calm, could puff out their cheeks and blow almost as fresh a breeze as their father. I ought not to forget the prophets and conjurers, of whom there were several in the crew, and who could foretell what would happen tomorrow, or the next day, or a hundred years hence, but were generally quite unconscious of what was passing at the moment.

Jason appointed Tiphys to be helmsman, because he was a star-gazer and knew the points of the compass. Lynceus, on account of his sharp sight, was stationed as a look-out in the prow, where he saw a whole day's sail ahead, but was rather apt to overlook things that lay directly under his nose. If the sea only happened to be deep enough, however, Lynceus could tell you exactly what kind of rocks or sands were at the bottom of it; and he often cried out to his companions, that they were sailing over heaps of sunken treasure, which yet he was none the richer for beholding. To confess the truth, few people believed him when he said it.

Well! But when the Argonauts, as these fifty brave adventurers were called, had prepared everything for the voyage, an unforeseen difficulty threatened to end it before it was begun. The vessel, you must understand, was so long, and broad, and ponderous, that the united force of all the fifty was insufficient to shove her into the water. Hercules, I suppose, had not grown to his full strength; else he might have set her afloat, as easily as a little boy launches his boat upon a puddle. But here were these fifty heroes, pushing and straining, and growing red in the face, without making the Argo start an inch! At last, quite wearied out, they sat themselves down on the shore, exceedingly disconsolate, and thinking that the vessel must be left to rot and fall in pieces, and that they must either swim across the sea, or lose the Golden Fleece.

All at once, Jason bethought himself of the galley's miraculous figure-head.

"Oh, Daughter of the Talking Oak," cried he, "how shall we set to work to get our vessel into the water?"

"Seat yourselves," answered the image, (for it had known what ought to be done, from the very first, and was only waiting for the question to be put,)—"Seat yourselves, and handle your oars, and let Orpheus play upon his harp!"

Immediately, the fifty heroes got on board, and seizing their oars, held them perpendicularly in the air, while Orpheus (who liked such a task far better than rowing) swept his fingers across the harp. At the first ringing note of the music, they felt the vessel stir. Orpheus thrummed away briskly, and the galley slid at once into the sea, dipping her prow so deeply that the figure-head drank the wave with its marvelous lips, and rising again as buoyant as a swan. The rowers plied their fifty oars; the white foam boiled up before the prow; the water gurgled and bubbled in their wake; while Orpheus continued to play so lively a strain of music, that the vessel seemed to dance over the billows by way of keeping time to it. Thus triumphantly did the Argo sail out of the harbor, amidst the huzzas and good wishes of everybody, except the wicked old Pelias, who stood on a promontory, scowling at her, and wishing that he could blow out of his lungs the tempest of wrath that was in his heart, and so sink the galley with all on board! When they had sailed above fifty miles over the sea, Lynceus happened to cast his sharp eyes behind, and said that there was this bad-hearted king, still perched upon the promontory, and scowling so gloomily that it looked like a black thunder-cloud, in that quarter of the horizon.

In order to make the time pass away more pleasantly, during the voyage, the heroes talked about the Golden Fleece. It originally belonged, it appears, to a Bœotian ram, who had taken on his back two children, when in danger of their lives, and fled with them over land and sea, as far as Colchis. One of the children, whose name was Helle, fell into the sea and was drowned. But the other, (a little boy, named Phrixus) was brought safe ashore by the faithful ram, who, however, was so exhausted that he immediately lay down and died. In memory of this good deed, and as a token of his true heart, the fleece of the poor, dead ram was miraculously changed to gold, and became one of the most beautiful objects ever seen on earth. It was hung upon a tree, in a sacred grove, where it had now been kept I know not how many years, and was the envy of mighty kings, who had nothing so magnificent in any of their palaces.

If I were to tell you all the adventures of the Argonauts, it would take me till nightfall, and perhaps a great deal longer. There was no lack of wonderful events, as you may judge from what you have already heard. At a certain island, they were hospitably received by King Cyzicus, its sovereign, who made a feast for them, and treated them like brothers. But the Argonauts saw that this good king looked downcast and very much troubled, and they therefore inquired of him what was the matter. King Cyzicus hereupon informed them, that he and his subjects were greatly abused and incommoded by the inhabitants of a neighboring mountain, who made war upon them, and killed many people, and ravaged the country. And while they were talking about it, Cyzicus pointed to the mountain, and asked Jason and his companions what they saw there.

"I see some very tall objects," answered Jason; "but they are at such a distance that I cannot distinctly make out what they are. To tell your majesty the truth, they look so very strangely that I am inclined to think them clouds, which have chanced to take something like human shapes."

"I see them very plainly," remarked Lynceus, whose eyes, you know, were as far-sighted as a telescope. "They are a band of enormous giants, all of whom have six arms a-piece, and a club, a sword, or some other weapon, in each of their hands!"

"You have excellent eyes!" said King Cyzicus. "Yes; they are six-armed giants, as you say; and these are the enemies whom I and my subjects have to contend with."

The next day, when the Argonauts were about setting sail, down came these terrible giants, stepping a hundred yards at a stride, brandishing their six arms a-piece, and looking very formidable, so far aloft in the air. Each of these monsters was able to carry on a whole war by himself; for, with one of his arms, he could fling immense stones, and wield a club with another, and a sword with a third, while the fourth was poking a long spear at the enemy, and the fifth and sixth were shooting him with a bow and arrow. But, luckily, though the giants were so huge, and had so many arms, they had each but one heart, and that no bigger nor braver than the heart of an ordinary man. Besides, if they had been like the hundred-armed Briareus, the brave Argonauts would have given them their handsful of fight. Jason and his friends went boldly to meet them, slew a great many, and made the rest take to their heels, so that, if the giants had had six legs a-piece, instead of six arms, it would have served them better to run away with!

Another strange adventure happened when the voyagers came to Thrace, where they found a poor blind king, named Phineus, deserted by his subjects, and living in a very sorrowful way, all by himself. On Jason's inquiring whether they could do him any service, the king answered that he was terribly tormented by three great winged creatures, called Harpies, which had the faces of women, and the wings, bodies, and claws of vultures. These ugly wretches were in the habit of snatching away his dinner, and allowed him no peace of his life. Upon hearing this, the Argonauts spread a plentiful feast on the sea-shore, well knowing, from what the blind king said of their greediness, that the Harpies would snuff up the scent of the victuals, and quickly come to steal them away. And so it turned out; for, hardly was the table set, before the three hideous vulture-women came flapping their wings, seized the food in their talons, and flew off as fast as they could. But the two sons of the North Wind drew their swords, spread their pinions, and set off through the air in pursuit of the thieves, whom they at last overtook among some islands, after a chase of hundreds of miles. The two winged youths blustered terribly at the Harpies, (for they had the rough temper of their father,) and so frightened them with their drawn swords, that they solemnly promised never to trouble King Phineus again.

Then the Argonauts sailed onward, and met with many other marvellous incidents, any one of which would make a story by itself. At one time, they landed on an island, and were reposing on the grass, when they suddenly found themselves assailed by what seemed a shower of steel-headed arrows. Some of them stuck in the ground, while others hit against their shields, and several penetrated their flesh. The fifty heroes started up, and looked about them for the hidden enemy, but could find none, nor see any spot, on the whole island, where even a single archer could lie concealed. Still, however, the steel-headed arrows came whizzing among them; and, at last, happening to look upward, they beheld a large flock of birds, hovering and wheeling aloft, and shooting their feathers down upon the Argonauts. These feathers were the steel-headed arrows that had so tormented them. There was no possibility of making any resistance; and the fifty heroic Argonauts might all have been killed or wounded by a flock of troublesome birds, without ever setting eyes on the Golden Fleece, if Jason had not thought of asking the advice of the oaken image.

So he ran to the galley, as fast as his legs would carry him.

"Oh, Daughter of the Speaking Oak," cried he, all out of breath, "we need your wisdom more than ever before! We are in great peril from a flock of birds, who are shooting us with their steel-pointed feathers! What can we do, to drive them away?"

"Make a clatter on your shields!" said the image.

On receiving this excellent counsel, Jason hurried back to his companions, (who were far more dismayed than when they fought with the six-armed giants,) and bade them strike with their swords upon their brazen shields. Forthwith, the fifty heroes set heartily to work, banging with might and main, and raised such a terrible clatter, that the birds made what haste they could to get away; and, though they had shot half the feathers out of their wings, they were soon seen skimming among the clouds, a long distance off, and looking like a flock of wild geese. Orpheus celebrated this victory by playing a triumphant anthem on his harp, and sang so melodi-

ously that Jason begged him to desist; lest, as the steel-feath-
ered birds had been driven away by an ugly sound, they
might be enticed back again by a sweet one.

While the Argonauts remained on this island, they saw a
small vessel approaching the shore, in which were two
young men of princely demeanor, and exceedingly handsome, as young princes generally were, in those days. Now,
who do you imagine these two voyagers turned out to be?
Why, if you will believe me, they were the sons of that
very Phrixus, who, in his childhood, had been carried to
Colchis on the back of the golden-fleeced ram! Since that
time, Phrixus had married the king's daughter; and the two
young princes had been born and brought up at Colchis,
and had spent their play days in the outskirts of the grove,
in the centre of which the Golden Fleece was hanging
upon a tree. They were now on their way to Greece, in
hopes of getting back a kingdom that had been wrongfully
taken from their father.

When the princes understood whither the Argonauts were
going, they offered to turn back and guide them to Colchis.
At the same time, however, they spoke as if it were very
doubtful whether Jason would succeed in getting the Golden
Fleece. According to their account, the tree, on which it
hung, was guarded by a terrible dragon, who never failed to
devour, at one mouthful, every person who might venture
within his reach.

"There are other difficulties in the way," continued the
young princes. "But is not this enough? Ah, brave Jason, turn
back before it is too late! It would grieve us to the heart, if
you and your nine-and-forty brave companions should be eat-
en up, at fifty mouthfulls, by this execrable dragon!"

"My young friends," quietly replied Jason, "I do not wonder that you think the dragon very terrible. You have grown
up from infancy in the fear of this monster, and therefore still
regard him with the awe that children feel for the bugbears
and hobgoblins, which their nurses have talked to them
about. But, in my view of the matter, the dragon is merely a
pretty large serpent, who is not half so likely to snap me up
at one mouthful, as I am to cut off his ugly head, and strip
the skin from his body. At all events, turn back who may, I

will never see Greece again, unless I carry with me the Golden Fleece!"

"We will none of us turn back!" cried his nine-and-forty brave comrades. "Let us get on board the galley, this instant; and if the dragon is to make a breakfast of us, much good may it do him!"

And Orpheus (whose custom it was to set everything to music) began to harp and sing most gloriously, and made every mother's son of them feel as if nothing in this world were so delectable as to fight dragons, and nothing so truly honorable as to be eaten up at one mouthful, in case of the worst.

After this, (being now under this guidance of the two princes, who were well acquainted with the way,) they quickly sailed to Colchis. When the king of the country, whose name was Æetes, heard of their arrival, he instantly summoned Jason to court. The king was a stern and cruel-looking potentate; and though he put on as polite and hospitable an expression as he could, Jason did not like his face a whit better than that of the wicked King Pelias, who dethroned his father.

"You are welcome, brave Jason!" said King Æetes. "Pray are you on a pleasure-voyage?—or do you meditate the discovery of unknown islands?—or what other cause has procured me the happiness of seeing you at my court?"

"Great Sir," replied Jason, with an obeisance—for Chiron had taught him how to behave with propriety, whether to kings or beggars—"I have come hither with a purpose which I now beg your majesty's permission to execute. King Pelias, who sits on my father's throne, (to which he has no more right, than to the one on which your excellent majesty is now seated,) has engaged to come down from it, and to give me his crown and sceptre, provided I bring him the Golden Fleece. This, as your majesty is aware, is now hanging on a tree here at Colchis; and I humbly solicit your gracious leave to take it away!"

In spite of himself, the king's face twisted itself into an angry frown; for, above all things else in the world, he prized the Golden Fleece, and was even suspected of having done a very wicked act, in order to get it into his own possession. It put him into the worst possible humor, therefore, to hear that the gallant Prince Jason, and forty-nine of the bravest young warriors of Greece, had come to Colchis with the sole purpose of taking away his chief treasure.

"Do you know," asked King Æetes, eyeing Jason very sternly, "what are the conditions which you must fulfil, before getting possession of the Golden Fleece?"

"I have heard," rejoined the youth, "that a dragon lies beneath the tree on which the prize hangs, and that whoever approaches him runs the risk of being devoured at a mouthful."

"True!" said the king, with a smile that did not look particularly good-natured. "Very true, young man! But there are other things as hard, or perhaps a little harder, to be done, before you can even have the privilege of being devoured by the dragon. For example, you must first tame my two brazen-footed and brazen-lunged bulls, which Vulcan, the wonderful blacksmith, made for me. There is a furnace in each of their stomachs; and they breathe such hot fire out of their mouths and nostrils, that nobody has hitherto gone nigh them without being instantly burnt to a small, black cinder! What do you think of this, my brave Jason?"

"I must encounter the peril," answered Jason composedly, "since it stands in the way of my purpose."

"After taming the fiery bulls," continued King Æetes, who was determined to scare Jason if possible, "you must yoke them to a plough, and must plough the sacred earth in the grove of Mars, and sow some of the same dragon's teeth from which Cadmus raised a crop of armed men. They are an unruly set of reprobates, those sons of the dragon's teeth; and unless you treat them suitably, they will fall upon you, sword in hand! You and your nine-and-forty Argonauts, my bold Jason, are hardly numerous or strong enough to fight with such a host as will spring up!"

"My master Chiron," replied Jason, "taught me, long ago, the story of Cadmus. Perhaps I can manage the quarrelsome sons of the dragon's teeth, as well as Cadmus did!"

"I wish the dragon had him," muttered King Æetes to himself, "and the four-footed pedant, his schoolmaster, into the bargain! Why, what a fool-hardy, self-conceited coxcomb he is! We'll see what my fire-breathing bulls will do for him! Well, Prince Jason," he continued, aloud, and as complaisantly as he could, "make yourself comfortable for to-day; and tomorrow morning, since you insist upon it, you shall try your skill at the plough."

While the king talked with Jason, a beautiful young woman was standing behind the throne. She fixed her eyes earnestly upon the youthful stranger, and listened attentively to every word that was spoken; and when Jason withdrew from the king's presence, this young woman followed him out of the room.

"I am the king's daughter," she said to him; "and my name is Medea. I know a great deal, of which other young princesses are ignorant, and can do many things, which they would be afraid so much as to dream of! If you will trust to me, I can instruct you how to tame the fiery bulls, and sow the dragon's teeth, and get the Golden Fleece!"

"Indeed, beautiful princess," answered Jason, "if you will do me this service, I promise to be grateful to you, my whole life long!"

Gazing at Medea, he beheld a wonderful intelligence in her face. She was one of those persons whose eyes are full of mystery; so that, while looking into them, you seem to see a very great way, as into a deep well, yet can never be certain whether you see into the farthest depths, or whether there be not something else hidden at the bottom. If Jason had been capable of fearing anything, he would have been afraid of making this young princess his enemy; for, beautiful as she now looked, she might, the very next instant, become as terrible as the dragon that kept watch over the Golden Fleece.

"Princess," he exclaimed, "you seem indeed very wise, and very powerful! But, how can you help me to do the things of which you speak? Are you an enchantress?"

"Yes, Prince Jason," answered Medea, with a smile, "you have hit upon the truth. I am an enchantress! Circe, my father's sister, taught me to be one. And I could tell you, if I pleased, who was the old woman, with the peacock, the pomegranate, and the cuckoo-staff, whom you carried over the river; and, likewise, who it is that speaks through the lips of the oaken image, that stands in the prow of your galley. I am acquainted with some of your secrets, you perceive! It is well for you, that I am favorably inclined; for, otherwise, you would hardly escape being snapt up by the dragon."

"I should not so much care for the dragon," replied Jason, "if I only knew to manage the brazen-footed and fiery-lunged bulls."

"If you are as brave as I think you, and as you have need to be," said Medea, "your own bold heart will teach you that there is but one way of dealing with a mad bull. What it is, I leave you to find out in the moment of peril. As for the fiery breath of these animals, I have a charmed ointment here, which will prevent you from being burned up, and cure you if you chance to be a little scorched."

So she put a golden box into his hand, and directed him how to apply the perfumed unguent which it contained, and where to meet her, at midnight.

"Only be brave," added she; "and, before daybreak, the brazen bulls shall be tamed!"

The young man assured her that his heart would not fail him. He then rejoined his comrades, and told them what had passed between the princess and himself, and warned them to be in readiness, in case there might be need of their help.

At the appointed hour, he met the beautiful Medea on the marble steps of the king's palace. She gave him a basket, in which were the dragon's teeth, just as they had been pulled out of the monster's jaws by Cadmus, long ago. Medea then led Jason down the palace-steps, and through the silent streets of the city, and into the royal pasture-ground, where the two brazen-footed bulls were kept. It was a starry night, with a bright gleam along the eastern edge of the sky, where the moon was soon going to show herself. After entering the pasture, the princess paused, and looked around.

"There they are," said she, "reposing themselves and chewing their fiery cuds, in that farthest corner of the field. It will be excellent sport, I assure you, when they catch a glimpse of your figure! My father and all his court delight in nothing so much as to see a stranger trying to yoke them, in order to come at the Golden Fleece. It makes a holiday in Colchis, whenever such a thing happens. For my part, I enjoy it immensely. You cannot imagine in what a mere twinkling of an eye, their hot breath shrivels a young man into a black cinder!"

"Are you sure, beautiful Medea," asked Jason, "quite sure, that the unguent in the gold box will prove a remedy against those terrible burns?"

"If you doubt—if you are in the least afraid—" said the princess, looking him in the face, by the dim starlight—"you had better never have been born, than go a step nigher to the bulls!"

But Jason had set his heart steadfastly on getting the Golden Fleece; and I positively doubt whether he would have gone back without it, even had he been certain of finding himself turned into a red-hot cinder, or a handful of white ashes, the instant he made a step farther. He therefore let go Medea's hand, and walked boldly forward in the direction whither she had pointed. At some distance before him, he perceived four streams of fiery vapor, regularly appearing, and again vanishing, after dimly lighting up the surrounding obscurity. These, you will understand, were caused by the breath of the brazen bulls, which was quietly stealing out of their four nostrils, as they lay chewing their cuds.

At the first two or three steps, which Jason made, the four fiery streams appeared to gush out somewhat more plentifully; for the two brazen bulls had heard his foot-tramp, and were lifting up their hot noses to snuff the air. He went a little farther; and by the way in which the red vapor now spouted forth, he judged that the creatures had got upon their feet. Now, he could see glowing sparks, and vivid jets of flame. At the next step, each of the bulls made the pasture echo with a terrible roar, while the burning breath, which they thus belched forth, lit up the whole field with a momentary flash. One other stride did bold Jason make; and, suddenly as a streak of lightning, on came these fiery animals, roaring like thunder, and sending out sheets of white flame, which so kindled up the scene that the young man could discern every object more distinctly than by daylight. Most distinctly of all, he saw the two horrible creatures, galloping right down upon him, their brazen hoofs rattling and ringing over the ground, and their tails sticking up stiffly into the air, as has always been the fashion with angry bulls. Their breath scorched the herbage before them. So intensely hot it was, indeed, that it caught a dry tree, under which Jason was now standing, and set it all in a light blaze. But as for Jason himself, (thanks to Medea's enchanted ointment,) the white flame curled around his body, without injuring him a jot more than if he had been made of asbestos!

Greatly encouraged at finding himself not yet turned into a cinder, the young man awaited the attack of the bulls. Just as the brazen brutes fancied themselves sure of tossing him into the air, he caught one of them by the horn, and the other by his screwed-up tail, and held them in a gripe like that of an iron vice, one with his right hand, the other with his left. Well; he must have been wonderfully strong in his arms, to be sure! But the secret of the matter was, that the brazen bulls were enchanted creatures, and that Jason had broken the spell of their fiery fierceness by his bold way of handling them. And, ever since that time, it has been the favorite method of brave men, when danger assails them, to do what they call 'taking the bull by the horns'—and to gripe him by the tail is pretty much the same thing—that is, to throw aside fear, and overcome the peril by despising it.

It was now easy to yoke the bulls, and to harness them to the plough, which had lain rusting on the ground for a great many years gone by; so long was it, before anybody could be found capable of ploughing that piece of land! Jason, I suppose, had been taught how to draw a furrow by the good old Chiron, who, perhaps, used to allow himself to be harnessed to the plough. At any rate, our hero succeeded perfectly well in breaking up the green sward; and, by the time that the moon was a quarter of her journey up the sky, the ploughed field lay before him, a large tract of black earth, ready to be sown with the dragon's teeth. So Jason scattered them broadcast, and harrowed them into the soil with a brush-harrow, and took his stand on the edge of the field, anxious to see what would happen next.

"Must we wait long for harvest-time?" he inquired of Medea, who was now standing by his side.

"Whether sooner or later, it will be sure to come," answered the princess. "A crop of armed men never fails to spring up, when the dragon's teeth have been sown."

The moon was now high aloft in the heavens, and threw its bright beams over the ploughed field, where as yet there was nothing to be seen. Any farmer, on viewing it, would have said that Jason must wait weeks before the green blades would peep from among the clods, and whole months, before the yellow grain would be ripened for the sickle. But, by-and-by, all over the field, there was something that glistened in the moonbeams, like sparkling drops of dew. These bright objects sprouted higher, and proved to be the steel-heads of spears. Then there was a dazzling gleam from a vast number of polished brass helmets, beneath which, as they grew farther out of the soil, appeared the dark and bearded visages of warriors, struggling to free themselves from the imprisoning earth. The first look that they gave at the upper world, was a glare of wrath and defiance. Next were seen their bright breastplates; in every right hand there was a sword or a spear, and on each left arm a shield; and when this strange crop of warriors had but half grown out of the earth, they struggled, such was their impatience of restraint, and, as it were, tore themselves up by the roots. Wherever a dragon's tooth had fallen, there stood a man armed for battle. They made a clangor with their swords against their shields, and eyed one another fiercely; for they had come into this beautiful world, and into the peaceful moonlight, full of rage and stormy passions, and ready to take the life of every human brother, in recompense of the boon of their own existence.

There have been many other armies in the world, that seemed to possess the same fierce nature with the one which had now sprouted from the dragon's teeth; but these, in the moonlit field, were the more excusable, because they never had women for their mothers. And how it would have rejoiced any great captain, who was bent on conquering the world, like Alexander or Napoleon, to raise a crop of armed soldiers as easily as Jason did!

For a while, the warriors stood flourishing their weapons, clashing their swords against their shields, and boiling over with the red-hot thirst for battle. Then they began to shout— 'Show us the enemy!'—'Lead us to the charge!'—'Death or victory!'—'Come on, brave comrades!'—'Conquer or die!'—

and a hundred other outcries, such as men always bellow forth, on a battle-field, and which these dragon-people seemed to have at their tongues-ends. At last, the front-rank caught sight of Jason, who, beholding the flash of so many weapons in the moonlight, had thought it best to draw his sword. In a moment, all the sons of the dragon's teeth appeared to take Jason for an enemy; and crying with one voice—'Guard the Golden Fleece!'—they ran at him with uplifted swords and protruded spears. Jason knew that it would be impossible to withstand this blood-thirsty battalion with his single arm, but determined, since there was nothing better to be done, to die as valiantly as if he himself had sprung from a dragon's tooth.

Medea, however, bade him snatch up a stone from the ground.

"Throw it among them quickly!" cried she. "It is the only way to save yourself!"

The armed men were now so nigh that Jason could discern the fire flashing out of their enraged eyes; when he let fly the stone, and saw it strike the helmet of a tall warrior, who was rushing upon him with his blade aloft. The stone glanced from this man's helmet to the shield of his nearest comrade, and thence flew right into the angry face of another, hitting him smartly between the eyes. Each of the three, who had been struck by the stone, took it for granted that his next neighbor had given him a blow; and, instead of running any farther towards Jason, they began a fight among themselves. The confusion spread through the host; so that it seemed scarcely a moment before they were all hacking, hewing, and stabbing at one another, lopping off arms, heads, and legs, and doing such memorable deeds that Jason was filled with immense admiration; although, at the same time, he could not help laughing to behold these mighty men punishing each other for an offence which he himself had committed. In an incredibly short space of time, (almost as short, indeed, as it had taken them to grow up,) all but one of the heroes of the dragon's teeth were stretched lifeless on the field. The last survivor, the bravest and strongest of the whole, had just force enough to wave his crimson sword over his head, and give a shout of exultation, crying—'Victory! Victory! Immortal fame!'—when he himself fell down, and lay quietly among his slain brethren.

And there was the end of the army that had sprouted from the dragon's teeth! That fierce and feverish fight was the only enjoyment which they had tasted, on this beautiful earth!

"Let them sleep in the bed of honor!" said the Princess Medea, with a sly smile at Jason. "The world will always have simpletons enough, just like them, fighting and dying for they know not what, and fancying that Posterity will take the trouble to put laurel wreaths on their rusty and battered helmets! Could you help smiling, Prince Jason, to see the self-conceit of that last fellow, just as he tumbled down?"

"It made me very sad," answered Jason, gravely. "And, to tell you the truth, Princess, the Golden Fleece does not appear so well worth the winning, after what I have here beheld."

"You will think differently, in the morning," said Medea. "True; the Golden Fleece may not be so valuable as you have thought it; but then there is nothing better in the world—and one must needs have an object, you know! Come! Your night's work has been well performed; and, tomorrow, you can inform King Æetes that the first part of your allotted task is fulfilled."

Agreeably to Medea's advice, Jason went, betimes in the morning, to the palace of King Æetes. Entering the presence-chamber, he stood at the foot of the throne, and made a low obeisance.

"Your eyes look heavy, Prince Jason!" observed the king. "You appear to have spent a sleepless night. I hope you have been considering the matter a little more wisely, and have concluded not to get yourself scorched to a cinder, in attempting to tame my brazen-lunged bulls!"

"That is already accomplished, may it please your majesty," replied Jason. "The bulls have been tamed and yoked; the field has been ploughed; the dragon's teeth have been sown broadcast, and harrowed into the soil; the crop of armed warriors have sprung up—and they have slain one another, to the last man! And, now, I solicit your majesty's permission to encounter the dragon, that I may take down the Golden

Fleece from the tree, and depart, with my nine-and-forty comrades!"

King Æetes scowled, and looked very angry and excessively disturbed; for he knew that, in accordance with his kingly promise, he ought now to permit Jason to win the fleece, if his courage and skill should enable him to do so. But, since the young man had met with such good luck in the matter of the brazen bulls and the dragon's teeth, the king feared that he would be equally successful in slaying the dragon. And, therefore, though he would gladly have seen Jason snapt up at a mouthful, he was resolved (and it was a very wrong thing of this wicked potentate) not to run any further risk of losing his beloved fleece.

"You never would have succeeded in this business, young man," said he, "if my undutiful daughter Medea had not helped you with her enchantments. Had you acted fairly, you would have been, at this instant, a black cinder, or a handful of white ashes! I forbid you, on pain of death, to make any more attempts to get the Golden Fleece! To speak my mind plainly, you shall never set eyes on so much as one of its glistening locks!"

Jason left the king's presence in great sorrow and anger. He could think of nothing better to be done, than to summon together his forty-nine brave Argonauts, march at once to the Grove of Mars, slay the dragon, take possession of the Golden Fleece, get on board the Argo, and spread all sail for Iolcos. The success of this scheme depended, it is true, on the doubtful point whether all the fifty heroes might not be snapt up, at so many mouthfuls, by the dragon. But, as Jason was hastening down the palace-steps, the Princess Medea called after him, and beckoned him to return. Her black eyes shone upon him with such a keen intelligence, that he felt as if there were a serpent peeping out of them; and, although she had done him so much service, only the night before, he was by no means very certain that she would not do him an equally great mischief, before sunset. These enchantresses, you must know, are never to be depended upon.

"What says King Æetes, my royal and upright father?" inquired Medea, slightly smiling. "Will he give you the Golden Fleece, without any further risk or trouble?"

"On the contrary," answered Jason, "he is very angry with me for taming the brazen bulls, and sowing the dragon's teeth. And he forbids me to make any more attempts, and positively refuses to give up the Golden Fleece, whether I slay the dragon or no!"

"Yes, Jason," said the princess; "and I can tell you more. Unless you set sail from Colchis before tomorrow's sunrise, the king means to burn your fifty-oared galley, and put yourself and your forty-nine brave comrades to the sword! But be of good courage! The Golden Fleece you shall have, if it lies within the power of my enchantments to get it for you. Wait for me here, an hour before midnight!"

At the appointed hour, you might again have seen Prince Jason and the Princess Medea, side by side, stealing through the streets of Colchis, on their way to the sacred grove, in the centre of which the Golden Fleece was suspended to a tree. While they were crossing the pasture-ground, the brazen bulls came towards Jason, lowing, nodding their heads, and thrusting forth their snouts, which, as other cattle do, they loved to have rubbed and caressed by a friendly hand. Their fierce nature was thoroughly tamed; and, with their fierceness, the two furnaces in their stomachs had likewise been extinguished, insomuch that they probably enjoyed far more comfort, in grazing and chewing their cuds, than ever before. Indeed, it had heretofore been a great inconvenience to these poor animals, that, whenever they wished to eat a mouthful of grass, the fire out of their nostrils had shrivelled it up, before they could manage to crop it. How they contrived to keep themselves alive, is more than I can imagine. But, now, instead of emitting jets of flame and streams of sulphurous vapor, they breathed the very sweetest of cow-breath!

After kindly patting the bulls, Jason followed Medea's guidance into the Grove of Mars, where the great oak-trees, that had been growing for centuries, threw so thick a shade that the moonbeams struggled vainly to find their way through it. Only, here and there, a glimmer fell upon the leaf-strewn earth; or, now-and-then, a breeze stirred the boughs aside, and gave Jason a glimpse of the sky, lest, in that deep obscurity, he might forget that there was one, overhead. At length, when they had gone farther and farther into the heart of the duskiness, Medea squeezed Jason's hand.

"Look yonder!" she whispered. "Do you see it?"

Gleaming among the venerable oaks, there was a radiance, not like the moonbeams, but rather resembling the golden glory of the setting sun. It proceeded from an object, which appeared to be suspended at about a man's height from the ground, a little farther within the wood.

"What is it?" asked Jason.

"Have you come so far to seek it," exclaimed Medea, "and do you not recognize the meed of all your toils and perils, when it glitters before your eyes? It is the Golden Fleece!"

Jason went onward a few steps farther, and then stopt to gaze. Oh, how beautiful it looked, shining with a marvellous light of its own, that inestimable prize, which so many heroes had longed to behold, but had perished in the quest of it, either by the perils of their voyage, or by the fiery breath of the brazen-lunged bulls!

"How gloriously it shines!" cried Jason, in a rapture. "It has surely been dipt in the richest gold of sunset! Let me hasten onward, and take it to my bosom!"

"Stay!" said Medea, holding him back. "Have you forgotten what guards it?"

To say the truth, in the joy of beholding the object of his desires, the terrible dragon had quite slipt out of Jason's memory. Soon, however, something came to pass, that reminded him what perils were still to be encountered. An antelope, that probably mistook the yellow radiance for sunrise, came bounding fleetly through the grove. He was rushing straight towards the Golden Fleece, when suddenly there was a frightful hiss, and the immense head and half the scaly body of the dragon was thrust forth, (for he was twisted round the trunk of the tree, on which the fleece hung,) and seizing the poor antelope, swallowed him with one snap of his jaws!

After this feat, the dragon seemed sensible that some other living creature was within reach, on which he felt inclined to finish his meal. In various directions, he kept poking his ugly snout among the trees, stretching out his neck a terrible long way, now here, now there, and now close to the spot where

Jason and the princess were hiding behind an oak. Upon my word, as the head came waving and undulating through the air, and reaching almost within arm's length of Prince Jason, it was a very hideous and uncomfortable sight! The gape of his enormous jaws was nearly as wide as the gateway of the king's palace.

"Well, Jason," whispered Medea, (for she was ill-natured, as all enchantresses are, and wanted to make the bold youth tremble,) "what do you think now of your prospect of winning the Golden Fleece?"

Jason answered only by drawing his sword, and making a step forward.

"Stay, foolish youth!" said Medea, grasping his arm. "Do not you see you are lost, without me as your good angel? In this gold box I have a magic potion, which will do the dragon's business far more effectually than your sword!"

The dragon had probably heard the voices; for swift as lightning, his black head and forked tongue came hissing among the trees again, darting full forty feet at a stretch. As it approached, Medea tossed the contents of the gold box right down the monster's wide-open throat. Immediately, with an outrageous hiss and a tremendous wriggle—flinging his tail up to the tip-top of the tallest tree, and shattering all its branches as it crashed heavily down again—the dragon fell at full length upon the ground, and lay quite motionless.

"It is only a sleeping-potion," said the enchantress to Prince Jason. "One always finds a use for these mischievous creatures, sooner or later; so I did not wish to kill him outright. Quick! Snatch the prize, and let us begone! You have won the Golden Fleece!"

Jason caught the fleece from the tree, and hurried through the grove, the deep shadows of which were illuminated, as he passed, by the golden glory of the precious object that he bore along. A little way before him, he beheld the old woman whom he had helped over the stream, with her peacock beside her. She clapped her hands for joy, and beckoning him to make haste, disappeared among the duskiness of the trees. Espying the two winged sons of the North Wind, (who were disporting themselves in the moonlight, a few hundred feet aloft), Jason bade them tell the rest of the Argonauts to embark as speedily as possible. But Lynceus, with his sharp eyes, had already caught a glimpse of him, bringing the Golden Fleece, although several stone-walls, a hill, and the black shadows of the Grove of Mars, intervened between. By his advice, the heroes had seated themselves on the benches of the galley, with their oars held perpendicularly, ready to let fall into the water.

As Jason drew near, he heard the Talking Image, calling to him with more than ordinary eagerness in its grave, sweet voice:—

"Make haste, Prince Jason! For your life, make haste!"

With one bound, he leaped aboard. At sight of the glorious radiance of the Golden Fleece, the nine-and-forty heroes gave a mighty shout; and Orpheus, striking his harp, sang a song of triumph, to the cadence of which the galley flew over the water, homeward bound, as if careering along with wings!

Chronology

1804   Born July 4, in Salem, Massachusetts, second of three children of Nathaniel and Elizabeth Manning Hathorne. (Hawthorne added a *w* to the family name sometime after 1830.)

1808   Death of father (b. 1775), a ship's captain, from yellow fever in Surinam (Dutch Guiana). Mrs. Hawthorne and her children move into her parents' home and are henceforth dependent upon their Manning relatives.

1813   Injury to foot incurred playing ball causes lameness which prevents regular school attendance for two years and four months. Is taught at home by Joseph Emerson Worcester, who is later a well-known lexicographer.

1818   Hawthornes move to family property in Raymond, Maine, and Nathaniel sent to school in Portland. During nine months in Raymond he "ran quite wild," he later remembered, skating, fishing, and hunting in the woods, reading Shakespeare and Bunyan on rainy days. There, by his account, he acquired his "cursed habits of solitude."

1819–21   Living with Manning relatives, attends school in Salem, 1819–20. Prepares for college under tutelage of a Salem lawyer, Benjamin Lynde Oliver. Is separated from his mother, who remains in Raymond, for two years.

1821–25   At Bowdoin College. Classmates include Henry W. Longfellow and lifelong friends Franklin Pierce, Horatio Bridge, and Jonathan Cilley. Of his college years he will write: "I was an idle student, negligent of college rules and the Procrustean details of academic life, rather choosing to nurse my own fancies than to dig into Greek roots and be numbered among the learned Thebans." Begins writing fiction, working on *Fanshawe* (with its Bowdoin-like setting) and, perhaps, a series of stories titled "Seven Tales of My Native Land." Graduates eighteenth in a class of thirty-five.

1825–35   Returns to Salem to live in the Manning house with his mother and sisters and tries to establish himself as a professional writer. "In this dismal and squalid chamber FAME was won," he will write in 1836, referring to his room "under the eaves." Discouraged by initially poor reception from publishers, he burns manuscript of "Seven Tales of My Native Land." Around 1829 he plans another collection, "Provincial Tales," and in 1834, a third, "The Story Teller." Portions of the last two groups were published in periodicals as separate tales and sketches. Though his mother and sisters live quite reclusively, often taking their meals apart, he is not as much a melancholic recluse as he later described himself. He takes trips from time to time by stagecoach and on foot into the New England countryside and begins the habit of keeping a notebook record of his encounters, impressions, and literary ideas.

1828   *Fanshawe* published in Boston at his own expense ($100, according to his sister Elizabeth, but in the context of contemporary publishing costs, more likely $200). Ashamed of this first effort, he destroys his own copy and refuses to discuss the book in later years. His wife is never told of its existence. It was not republished until 1876.

1830–32   First publications. "The Hollow of the Three Hills" and "An Old Woman's Tale" (perhaps versions of stories in the destroyed "Seven Tales of My Native Land") and three biographical sketches from New England history appear in the *Salem Gazette*, 1830. Sometime in 1831 the unsold copies of *Fanshawe* are destroyed in a Boston bookstore fire. Publisher Samuel Goodrich's annual *The Token and Atlantic Souvenir* (for 1831) contains "Sights from a Steeple." "The Gentle Boy," "The Wives of the Dead," "My Kinsman, Major Molineux," and "Roger Malvin's Burial" (meant for "Provincial Tales") in *The Token* for 1832. More sketches and stories in *The Token* for 1833.

1832   Takes extended trip alone, June to September, in New Hampshire and Vermont, and conceives of an itinerant narrator whose experiences would provide the frame for "The Story Teller."

1834   Goodrich rejects "The Story Teller." Portions will appear in *The Token* and another annual, *Youth's Keepsake*, and in *New-England Magazine*, *American Monthly Magazine*, and

American Magazine of Useful and Entertaining Knowledge from 1834 to 1837.

1835   Publishes stories and sketches, among them "The Minister's Black Veil" and "The May-Pole of Merry Mount" in *The Token* for 1836, and "Young Goodman Brown" in *New-England Magazine*.

1836   In January appointed editor of the *American Magazine of Useful and Entertaining Knowledge*, his first regular employment, and moves to Boston to assume duties. By June the publisher is bankrupt and Hawthorne receives only $20 of promised $500 annual salary. With sister Elizabeth edits *Peter Parley's Universal History, on the Basis of Geography* for a fee of $100.

1837   *Twice-told Tales*. This collection of eighteen of the stories that had appeared in periodicals is underwritten by Horatio Bridge without Hawthorne's knowledge. Receives laudatory review by Longfellow in the *North American Review*. Visits Peabody sisters in Salem and meets Sophia, his future wife. Elizabeth Peabody, friend of Emerson and, later, publisher of the *Dial*, begins her efforts to champion his reputation and assist his fortunes.

1838   Becomes active contributor to the *Democratic Review* (twenty-four tales and sketches in the next seven years) and friend of editor John O'Sullivan after initial misunderstanding over Salem coquette Mary Silsbee. Is deeply moved by the death of Jonathan Cilley, killed in a duel over a political dispute by a fellow congressman, and writes memorial essay.

1839   With the help of Elizabeth Peabody, is appointed Weigher and Gauger at Boston Custom House by historian George Bancroft, Collector of the Port. Becomes engaged to Sophia Peabody.

1840–41   Publishes three children's books: *Grandfather's Chair, Famous Old People, Liberty Tree*.

1841   Resigns from Custom House. Joins utopian community of Brook Farm in West Roxbury, Massachusetts, but leaves after eight months, convinced that he "can best attain the higher ends of [his] life by retaining the ordinary relation to society."

1842   Marries Sophia on July 9. Rents Old Manse in Concord, ancestral property of the Emerson family, where he lives for next three and a half years. New edition of *Twice-told Tales* with seventeen previously uncollected stories.

1842–45 During "Old Manse" period becomes acquainted with transcendentalist circle—Emerson, Thoreau, Ellery Channing, Bronson Alcott, Margaret Fuller. Publishes twenty sketches and stories including "The Birth-mark," "The Artist of the Beautiful," "Rappaccini's Daughter," "Egotism; or, The Bosom-Serpent," "Drowne's Wooden Image," "The Celestial Rail-road," and "Earth's Holocaust." May have contemplated once more a collection of linked stories to be called "Allegories of the Heart."

1844   Daughter, Una, born.

1845   Edits and writes introduction for Bridge's *Journal of an African Cruiser*. When their tenancy of the Old Manse is ended because the owners need the house, the Hawthornes move in with his mother and sisters in Salem.

1846   The political influence of Bridge and Pierce and other friends in the Democratic party secures him appointment as Surveyor in the Salem Custom House, where he works mornings. Son, Julian, born. *Mosses from an Old Manse* contains twenty-one previously uncollected stories and sketches and an introductory essay, "The Old Manse."

1847   Hawthornes rent a large house in Salem, where his mother and sisters live in a separate apartment.

1849   Hawthorne removed from his post following election of Whig President, Zachary Taylor. His dismissal becomes the subject of partisan controversy. Friends—among them Longfellow and Lowell—raise a subscription for his support. Is with his mother when she dies in late July ("the darkest hour I ever lived"). Begins *The Scarlet Letter*.

1850–51 *The Scarlet Letter*, 1850. Hawthorne "bids farewell forever to this abominable city [Salem]." Moves to Lenox in the Berkshire Mountains, center of an intellectual summer colony whose members include Lowell, Oliver Wendell Holmes, the novelist G. P. R. James, and the actress Fanny Kemble. Stays there for a year and a half. Meets Herman Melville, whose laudatory review, "Hawthorne and his Mosses," appears anonymously in the *Literary World*. Establishes a brief, though profound, mental communion with Melville, as indicated at least by Melville's letters to him (his own side of the correspondence not surviving). Melville writes, "I shall leave the world, I feel, with more satisfaction for having come to know you."

1851   *The House of the Seven Gables* and *A Wonder-Book for Girls and Boys* (both written in Lenox). New edition of *Twice-told Tales* with added preface reflecting on his early stories: "They have the pale tint of flowers that blossomed in too retired a shade." Third collection, *The Snow-Image, and Other Twice-told Tales*, contains seventeen previously uncollected stories, among them "Ethan Brand," "The Wives of the Dead," "My Kinsman, Major Molineux," and a dedicatory preface to Bridge, in which he writes of his early years: "I sat down by the wayside of life, like a man under enchantment, and a shrubbery sprung up around me, and the bushes grew to be saplings, and the saplings became trees, until no exit appeared possible, through the entangling depths of my obscurity." This is the first year that earnings from writings are enough to support his family. Birth of second daughter, Rose.

1852   *The Blithedale Romance*. Buys The Wayside, Alcott's former house, and returns to Concord after absence of seven years. Death of sister Louisa when boiler explodes in a Hudson River steamboat accident. His campaign biography of Pierce, Democratic candidate for President, resented by Hawthorne's antislavery friends, who deplore his tacit support for the Compromise of 1850.

1853   *Tanglewood Tales*, another children's book. Appointed American Consul at Liverpool by President Pierce.

1853–57 Carries on as Consul until October 1857 (having officially resigned the previous February). Conscientious in the execution of official responsibilities, tries to exert influence to effect reforms in the U. S. Merchant Marine. Saves $30,000 during this time. Writes little for publication but records his numerous impressions of English life in his notebooks. In spring 1857 visited by Herman Melville, en route to and returning from the Holy Land, for the last of their meetings.

1858–59   Hawthornes travel to France and then by sea to Italy. In Rome from January to May, where he writes a draft of an English romance. In Florence during summer; return to Rome in the fall. As in England, he keeps notebook record of observations of scenes and persons, particularly of the expatriate colony (sculptor William Wetmore Story, William Cullen Bryant, and Robert and Elizabeth Barrett Browning, among others) with whom he associated. Una seriously ill for six months. Begins *The Marble Faun*.

1859   Returns to England in June and remains there with his family until following year.

1860   *The Marble Faun* (in England the title is *The Transformation*) published in England and America in February and March.

1860–62   Depressed by the Civil War ("no nation ever came safe and sound through such a confounded difficulty as that of ours"). In Concord, at The Wayside, resumes work on his English romance but after two drafts abandons the project. Begins work on another romance about an elixir of life, also abandoned after two drafts.

1862   An essay on the Civil War, "Chiefly about War Matters," in July *Atlantic Monthly*. Publisher Fields omits portions of the essay, among them a description of "Uncle Abe" Lincoln that he thinks would "outrage the feelings of many Atlantic readers."

1863   *Our Old Home*, based on sketches published separately between 1857 and 1863 in the *Atlantic Monthly*, records publicly his English impressions. The dedication to Pierce in this war year arouses criticism because of Pierce's alleged pro-Southern sympathies.

1864   Gradual deterioration of health. Begins carriage trip with Pierce and dies in sleep, May 19, in Plymouth, New Hampshire. Portions of a work in progress, then being prepared for the press, published in July *Atlantic Monthly* as "Scenes from 'The Dolliver Romance.' "

Note on the Texts

Between 1830 and 1852, about one hundred tales and sketches by Nathaniel Hawthorne appeared (before 1837 anonymously or pseudonymously) in newspapers, magazines, and gift books—*Salem Gazette*, *The Token*, *New-England Magazine*, *United States Magazine and Democratic Review*, and *The Knickerbocker, or New-York Monthly Magazine*, among others.

In 1837 Hawthorne collected some of his previously published material in *Twice-told Tales* (Boston: American Stationers' Company) and added new tales to a subsequent edition in 1842 (Boston: James Munroe and Company). This enlarged *Twice-told Tales* was republished with a preface by the author in 1851 (Boston: Ticknor, Reed, and Fields) and was reissued in 1853. By then Hawthorne had published two other collections: *Mosses from an Old Manse* (New York: Wiley and Putnam, 1846)—soon to appear in an expanded version (Boston: Ticknor and Fields, 1854)—and *The Snow-Image, and Other Twice-told Tales* (Boston: Ticknor, Reed, and Fields, 1852), both with prefaces by the author.

The present volume gathers together all the tales and sketches collected by the author, as well as those which remained uncollected during his lifetime, and rearranges them in the order of their first appearance before the American public. The tables of contents from the original collections have been appended for reference, and the author's prefaces appear together at the end of the first section of this volume. The chronological arrangement has been twice adjusted slightly, so that "Old News," a series of connected sketches which appeared over the course of several months in *New-England Magazine* (1835), and "Legends of the Province-House," a set of framed tales first published separately in the *Democratic Review* (1838–39), may be read as integrated literary units, as Hawthorne intended, even though they do not follow the actual sequences of their initial printings. Otherwise, the order of the first printings has been strictly adhered to.

Because Hawthorne made various corrections and revisions in the collected versions of the tales and sketches, the texts of the periodical versions have not been adopted. The texts here printed are those established by the Centenary Edition of Hawthorne's *Works* (Columbus: Ohio State University Press): *Twice-told Tales* (IX, 1974, first printing); *Mosses from an Old Manse* (X, 1974, first printing); *The Snow-Image and Uncollected Tales* (XL, 1974, first printing); and portions of a forthcoming *Miscellany*. These are unmodernized, critical texts, constructed according to the principles accepted by the Center for Editions of American Authors of the Modern Language Association of America.

Wherever possible, the Centenary Edition uses as copy-text Hawthorne's manuscripts ("The Wedding-Knell," "Earth's Holocaust," "The Snow-Image," "Feathertop," the preface to *Twice-told Tales*, and "The Old Manse"). For the rest, copy-text derives from the first printings of tales and sketches. In most cases, the differences between periodical (or manuscript) and collected versions, though often important, are relatively uncomplicated. In several instances, however ("The Gentle Boy," "The Seven Vagabonds," "The Village Uncle," "Old News," "The Vision of the Fountain," "Sketches from Memory," "Old Ticonderoga," "Monsieur du Miroir," "The Toll-Gatherer's Day," "The Threefold Destiny," "The Sister Years," "The Hall of Fantasy," and "P.'s Correspondence"), Hawthorne made substantial deletions in preparing the collected versions, and these deletions are considered authoritative by the Centenary. In addition, Hawthorne occasionally altered the titles of his works for the collections, and the altered titles are also considered authoritative. Deleted passages and the original titles, recorded in the textual apparatus of the Centenary Edition, have been provided in the notes to the present volume. For more textual information, the interested reader should consult the copious editorial matter at the back of the appropriate Centenary volumes.

Omitted from the present collection are several sketches attributed to Hawthorne by the Centenary editors in volume IX ("The Battle Omen," "Graves and Goblins," and the uncollected parts of "Sketches from Memory"), because the evidence for Hawthorne's authorship of these three tales is not as strong as that for other attributed pieces. Added here to the tales and sketches are two volumes of mythological tales for children: *A Wonder-Book for Girls and Boys* (Boston: Ticknor, Reed, and Fields, 1851) and *Tanglewood Tales for Girls and Boys* (Boston: Ticknor, Reed, and Fields, 1853). The texts adopted here are again those established by the Centenary Edition (X, 1972, first printing), using the manuscripts as copy-texts.

The tales and sketches as Hawthorne collected them in book form are shown in the tables of contents below. The dates following each title are the year of first publication in a book or periodical, and the year of Hawthorne's final revision.

TWICE-TOLD TALES (1837, 1851)

Vol. I
Preface (1851)
The Gray Champion (1835, 1837)
Sunday at Home (1837, 1837)
The Wedding-Knell (1836, 1837)
The Minister's Black Veil (1836, 1837)
The May-Pole of Merry Mount (1836, 1837)
The Gentle Boy (1832, 1837)
Mr. Higginbotham's Catastrophe (1834, 1837)
Little Annie's Ramble (1835, 1837)
Wakefield (1835, 1837)
A Rill from the Town-Pump (1835, 1837)
The Great Carbuncle (1837, 1837)
The Prophetic Pictures (1837, 1837)
David Swan (1837, 1837)
Sights from a Steeple (1831, 1837)
The Hollow of the Three Hills (1830, 1837)
The Toll-Gatherer's Day (1837, 1842)
The Vision of the Fountain (1835, 1837)
Fancy's Show Box (1837, 1837)
Dr. Heidegger's Experiment (1837, 1837)

Vol. II
Legends of the Province House
I.   Howe's Masquerade (1838, 1842)
II. Edward Randolph's Portrait (1838, 1842)
III. Lady Eleanore's Mantle (1838, 1842)
IV. Old Esther Dudley (1839, 1842)

The Artist of the Beautiful (1844, 1846)
A Virtuoso's Collection (1842, 1846)

THE SNOW-IMAGE, AND OTHER TWICE-TOLD TALES (1852)

Preface (1852)
The Snow-Image (1850, 1852)
The Great Stone Face (1850, 1852)
Main-street (1849, 1852)
Ethan Brand (1850, 1852)
A Bell's Biography (1837, 1852)
Sylph Etherege (1838, 1852)
The Canterbury Pilgrims (1833, 1852)
Old News (1835, 1852)
The Man of Adamant (1837, 1852)
The Devil in Manuscript (1835, 1852)
John Inglefield's Thanksgiving (1840, 1852)
Old Ticonderoga (1836, 1852)
The Wives of the Dead (1832, 1852)
Little Daffydowndilly (1843, 1852)
My Kinsman, Major Molineux (1832, 1852)

The titles below appeared only in periodicals and were never collected by Hawthorne. The year given is the date of original publication.

Sir William Phips (1830)
Mrs. Hutchinson (1830)
An Old Woman's Tale (1830)
Dr. Bullivant (1831)
The Haunted Quack (1831)
Sir William Pepperell (1833)
Alice Doane's Appeal (1835)
My Visit to Niagara (1835)
A Visit to the Clerk of the Weather (1836)
Fragments from the Journal of a Solitary Man (1837)
Thomas Green Fessenden (1838)
Time's Portraiture (1838)
Jonathan Cilley (1838)
The Antique Ring (1843)
A Good Man's Miracle (1844)
A Book of Autographs (1844)

The standards for American English continue to fluctuate and in some ways were conspicuously different in earlier periods from what they are now. In nineteenth-century writings, for example, a word might be spelled in more than one way, even in the same work, and such variations might be carried into print. Commas were sometimes used expressively to suggest the movements of voice, and capitals were sometimes meant to give significances to a word beyond those it might have in its uncapitalized form. Since modernization would remove such effects, this volume has preserved the spelling, punctuation, capitalization, and wording of the Ohio Centenary Edition, which strives to be faithful to Hawthorne's usage.

The present volume is concerned only with representing the *texts* of the Centenary Edition; it does not attempt to reproduce the features of their typographical design. Obvious typographic errors have been corrected, and they are here listed: 39.8, hin; 70.22, "Let; 90.20, whenever; 111.17, here.";
136.19, me!"; 150.33, five more,; 304.39–40, dearier; 327.12, jealously; 335.11, in in; 363.35, then; 377.9, not; 399.18, thought; 401.12–13, a darksome dungeons; 426.29–30, Richard's Digby's; 441.14, castle hall."; 446.9, killed him,; 530.38, year; 538.15, Tabitha; 579.24, contined; 582.34–35, Cautic's; 612.21–22, countenence; 623.33–34, Cotton Mather . . . who; 722.28, poetry,; 737.22, that; 771.28, 33, Georgianna; 781.1, Egotism;* or; 801.12–13, proprietries; 811.25, me?; 811.34, enthusiasm,; 864.17, tht; 925.36, it?"; 937.20, neck; 949.34, entainer; 951.40, such; 964.23, writings; 970.23, Barr; 992.17, Rappacini; 1110.32, morning mist;; 1324.29, habitation or. Errors corrected third printing: 46.1, lighting; 380.16, us; 865.20, calamites; 922.12, soft; 955.26, is. Errors corrected sixth printing: 975.28, interst (*LOA*).

Notes

In the notes below, the reference numbers denote page and line of the present volume (the line count includes chapter headings). Notes printed at the foot of pages in the text are Hawthorne's own.

TALES AND SKETCHES

7.1   the Three Hills]   Boston was known as the Three Hills because of its terrain. Also mentioned at 661.39.

66.7   the first wife of Zadig.]   Doubting the fidelity of his wife, the hero of Voltaire's *Zadig* (1747) has the news of his death announced and sends a friend to woo her. She is altogether willing.

68.1   Molineux]   Hawthorne's contemporaries associated the name "Molineux" with that of William Molineux (d. 1774), a well-to-do radical Boston trader, an organizer and leader of anti-Loyalist mobs, member of the Boston Committee of Correspondence, one of those who are said to have been at the Boston Tea Party.

108.1   The Gentle Boy]   When Hawthorne collected this tale for the 1837 *Twice-told Tales*, he deleted numerous passages from the original 1832 *Token* version. These passages appear below, keyed to the word or phrase that immediately preceded it in the text.

109.5   crown of martyrdom.]   *That those who were active in, or consenting to, this measure, made themselves responsible for innocent blood, is not to be denied: yet the extenuating circumstances of their conduct are more numerous than can generally be pleaded by persecutors. The inhabitants of New England were a people, whose original bond of union was their peculiar religious principles. For the peaceful exercise of their own mode of worship, an object, the very reverse of universal liberty of conscience, they had hewn themselves a home in the wilderness; they had made vast sacrifices of whatever is dear to man; they had exposed themselves to the peril of death, and to a life which rendered the accomplishment of that peril almost a blessing. They had found no city of refuge prepared for them, but, with Heaven's assistance, they had created one; and it would be hard to say whether justice did not authorize their determination, to guard its gate against all who were destitute of the prescribed title to admittance. The principle of their foundation was such, that to destroy the unity of religion, might have been to subvert the government, and break up the colony, especially at a period when the state of affairs in England had stopped the tide of emigration, and drawn back many of the pilgrims to their native homes. The magistrates of Massachusetts Bay were, moreover, most imperfectly informed respecting the real tenets and character of the Quaker sect. They had heard of them, from various parts of the earth, as opposers of every known opinion, and enemies of all established governments; they had beheld extravagances which seemed to justify these accusations; and the idea suggested by their own wisdom may be gathered from the fact, that the persons of many individuals were searched, in the expectation of discovering witch-marks. But after all allowances, it is to be feared that the death of the Quakers was principally owing to the polemic fierceness, that distinct passion of human nature, which has so often produced frightful guilt in the most sincere and zealous advocates of virtue and religion.* This passage reinforces the retained subsequent reference (109.16–17) to "the historian of the sect"—i.e., William Sewel, in his *History of . . . the Christian People called Quakers* (1774).

113.27   departed from us.'] *The wife's eyes filled with tears; she inquired neither who little Ilbrahim was, nor whence he came, but kissed his cheek and led the way into the dwelling. The sitting-room, which was also the kitchen, was lighted by a cheerful fire upon the large stone-laid hearth, and a confused variety of objects shone out and disappeared in the unsteady blaze. There were the household articles, the many wooden trenchers, the one large pewter dish, and the copper kettle whose inner surface was glittering like gold. There were the lighter implements of husbandry, the spade, the sickle, and the scythe, all hanging by the door, and the axe before which a thousand trees had bowed themselves. On another part of the wall were the steel cap and iron breast-plate, the sword and the matchlock gun. There, in a corner, was a little chair, the memorial of a brood of children whose place by the fire-side was vacant forever. And there, on a table near the window, among all those tokens of labor, war, and mourning, was the Holy Bible, the book of life, an emblem of the blessed comforts which it offers, to those who can receive them, amidst the toil, the strife, and sorrow of this world. Dorothy hastened to bring the little chair from its corner; she placed it on the hearth, and, seating the poor orphan there, addressed him in words of tenderness, such as only a mother's experience could have taught her. At length, when he had timidly begun to taste his warm bread and milk, she drew her husband apart.*

114.4–5   and intentions.] *She drew near to Ilbrahim, who, having finished his repast, sat with the tears hanging upon his long eye-lashes, but with a singular and unchildlike composure on his little face.*

116.12   beat of a drum.] *in connexion with which peculiarity it may be mentioned, that an apartment of the meetinghouse served the purposes of a powder-magazine and armory.*

116.39   a certain age.] *On one side of the house sat the women, generally in sad-colored and most unfanciful apparel, although there were a few high head-dresses, on which the 'cobler of Agawam' would have lavished his empty wit of words. There was no veil to be seen among them all, and it must be allowed that the November sun, shining brightly through the windows, fell upon many a demure but pretty set of features, which no barbarity of art could spoil. The masculine department of the house presented somewhat more variety than that of the women. Most of the men, it is true, were clad in black or dark-grey broadcloth, and all coincided in the short, ungraceful, and ear-displaying cut of their hair. But those who were in martial authority, having arrayed themselves in their embroidered buff-coats, contrasted strikingly with the remainder of the congregation, and attracted many youthful thoughts, which should have been otherwise employed.*

118.6 depths.] *Into this discourse was worked much learning, both sacred and profane, which, however, came forth not digested into its original elements, but in short quotations, as if the preacher were unable to amalgamate his own mind with that of the author. His own language was generally plain, even to affectation, but there were frequent specimens of a dull man's efforts to be witty—little ripples fretting the surface of a stagnant pool.*

118.22 thundered.] *Having thus usurped a station to which her sex can plead no title,*

130.4 gibe.] *At length, when the change in his belief was fully accomplished, the contest grew very terrible between the love of the world, in its thousand shapes, and the power which moved him to sacrifice all for the one pure faith; to quote his own words, subsequently uttered at a meeting of Friends, it was as if 'Earth and Hell had garrisoned the fortress of his miserable soul, and Heaven came battering against it to storm the walls.'*

130.5—7 event . . . instrument.] *event enlisted with the besieging army, and decided the victory. There was a triumphant shout within him, and from that moment all was peace. Dorothy had not been the subject of a similar process, for her reason was as clear as her heart was tender.*

131.9 life.] *His features were strong and well connected, and seemed to express firmness of purpose and sober understanding, although his actions had frequently been at variance with this last attribute.*

138.31 grave.] *My heart is glad of this triumph of our better nature; it gives me a kindlier feeling for the fathers of my native land; and with it I will close the tale.*

144.38 born in it. This gay] Between these two sentences in the first publication of the tale (*The Token*, 1833), there occurs the following passage: *I hardly know how to hint, that, as the brevity of her gown displayed rather more than her ancles, I could not help wishing that I had stood at a little distance without, when she stept up the ladder into the wagon.*

174.1 Passages from a Relinquished Work] The "relinquished work" was "The Story Teller," projected as a set of framed tales. In the November and December 1834 issues of *New-England Magazine*, Hawthorne published the first two parts of the work as "The Story Teller No. I" and "The Story Teller No. II," the second of which included "Mr. Higginbotham's Catastrophe." When Hawthorne put together *Twice-told Tales* (1837), he lifted "Higginbotham" from its context. When he expanded *Mosses from an Old Manse* in 1854, he reprinted the remaining portions of "The Story Teller" (Nos. I and II) as "Passages."

217.1 The Village Uncle] Originally published in *The Token* (1835) as "The Mermaid; A Reverie."

222.19   naked Eve.]   Hawthorne deleted the following passage from the periodical version of the work (*The Token*, 1835): *Oh, Susan the sugar heart you gave me, and the old rhyme—'When this you see, remember me'—scratched on it with the point of your scissors! Inscriptions on marble have been sooner forgotten, than those words shall be on that frail heart.*

251.1   Old News]   In the *New-England Magazine* version of this series of sketches, Hawthorne included numerous footnotes, which he deleted when he republished the series in *The Snow-Image*. They are reprinted below, keyed to the appropriate words in the text.

254.9   wretches.]   *It might well have been the case, as there were no lightning-rods.*

254.16   land.]   *The printer intimates a doubt, whether any sound auguries could be drawn from these unaccountable noises. We have no patience with such a would-be sadducee, who, so long as general opinion countenances the belief, could struggle to be a sceptic, in regard to this most thrilling and sublime superstition.*

255.35   movement.]   *There was a dancing-school in Boston, for a short period, so long ago, we think, as in 1685.*

256.28   birth-day.]   *In some old pamphlet, we recollect a proposal to erect an equestrian statue of the 'glorious King William,' in front of the town-house, looking down King-street. It would have been pleasant to have had an historic monument, of any kind, in that street of historic recollections. Even the whig monarch, however, would hardly have kept his saddle through the Revolution, though himself a revolutionary king.*

257.20   bidder.]   Hawthorne deleted this passage from the *text* of "Old News": *Setting fine sentiment aside, slavery, as it existed in New-England, was precisely the state most favorable to the humble enjoyments of an alien race, generally incapable of self-direction, and whose claims to kindness will never be acknowledged by the whites, while they are asserted on the ground of equality.*

257.25   times.]   *Nevertheless, some time after this period, there is an advertisement of a run-away slave from Connecticut, who carried with him an iron collar rivetted round his neck, with a chain attached. This must have been rather galling. Undoubtedly, there had been a previous attempt at escape.*

260.9   peruke-makers.]   *There was a great competition among these artists. Two or three were French; of the Englishmen, one professed to have worked in the best shops about London, and another had studied the science in the chief cities of Europe. The price of white wigs and grizzels, made of picked human hair, was £20, old tenor; of light grizzels, £15, and of dark grizzels, £12 10s. These prices are not so formidable as they appear—money, in old tenor, being worth only about a fourth of its original value.*

264.9   month.]   *At one time, there was an impress for this ship, sanctioned by the provincial authorities. Throughout the war, the British frigates seized upon the crews of all vessels, without ceremony, to the great detriment of trade. But, some years before, a British admiral threw Boston into a memorable ferment, by recruiting, in the same arbitrary manner, from the wharves.*

268.8   Beacon-hill.]   *These bonfires were built on scaffolds, raised several stories above the ground.*

289.13   gloom.]   In the 1692 witchcraft trials, whose records Hawthorne knew well, "spectral evidence" was admitted—such evidence holding that Satan could assume the appearance of innocent persons. Goody Cloyse, Goody Cory, and Martha Carrier, all named above, were tried and sentenced in 1692 in part on the basis of such evidence.

314.1   The White Old Maid]   In the July 1835 issue of *New England Magazine*, this tale was entitled "The Old Maid in the Winding-Sheet."

324.2   At fifteen . . .]   In its original (1837) *New-England Magazine* appearance, the tale began with these two paragraphs: *Dear ladies, could I but look into your eyes, like a star-gazer, I might read secret intelligences. Will you read what I have written? You love music and the dance, and are passionate for flowers; you sometimes cherish singing-birds, and sometimes young kittens. You sigh by moonlight. Once or twice you have wept over a love-story in the annuals. Sleep falls upon you, like a lace veil, rich with gold-embroidered dreams, and is withdrawn as lightly, that you may see brighter dreams than them. Maiden pursuits, and gentle meditations, the sunshine of maiden glee, and the summer-cloud of maiden sadness—these make up the tale of your happy years. You are in your spring, fair reader—are you not? I am scarce in my summer-time. Yet, I have wandered through the world, till its weary dust has settled on me; and when I meet a bright, young girl, a girl of sixteen, with her untouched heart, so sweetly proud, so softly glorious, so fresh among faded things, I fancy that the gate of Paradise has been left ajar, and she has stolen out. Then I give a sigh to the memory of Rachel. ¶Oh, Rachel! How pleasant is the sound to me! thy sweet, old scriptural name. As I repeat it, thoughts and feelings grow vivid again, which I deemed long ago forgotten. There they are, yet in my heart, like the initials and devices engraved by virgin fingers in the wood of a young tree, remaining deep and permanent, though concealed by the furrowed bark of after years. The boy of fifteen was handsome; though you would shake your heads, could you glance at the altered features of the man. And the boy had lofty, sweet, and tender thoughts, and dim, but glorious visions; he was a child of poetry.*

338.1   Sketches from Memory]   Originally published in two installments in *New-England Magazine* (November and December 1835). It was then attributed to "a Pedestrian," and began with the following passage: *We are so fortunate as to have in our possession the portfolio of a friend, who traveled on foot in search of the picturesque over New-England and New-York. It contains many loose scraps and random sketches, which appear to have been thrown off at different intervals, as the scenes once observed were recalled to the mind of the writer by recent events or associations. He kept no journal nor set down any notes during his tour; but his recollection seems to have been faithful, and his powers of description as fresh and effective as if they had been tasked on the very spot which he describes. Some of his quiet delineations deserve rather to be called pictures than sketches, so lively are the colors shed over them. The first which we select, is a reminiscence of a day and night spent among the White Mountains, and will revive agreeable thoughts in the minds of those tourists who have but just returned from a visit to their sublime scenery.*

344.17   The Canal Boat]   The second installment of "Sketches from Memory" began here, preceded by the following passage: *We present to our readers a few more of the loose sketches from our friend's portfolio, which, we think, will, more clearly than those of the last month, shew the truth of our remark, that, like the careless drawings of a master-hand, they shadow forth a power and beauty, that might be visibly embodied into life-like forms on the canvass. 'The Afternoon Scene' and 'The Night Scene' will, we trust, suggest subjects to our landscape paint- ers. The former, which has the mellow richness of a Claude, might be exquisitely done by Doughty; and young Brown, whose promise is as great as the hopes of his friends, could employ his glowing pencil upon no subject better adapted to call forth all his genius, than the latter.* The installment also included several sketches whose attribution to Hawthorne has been questioned. They have been omit- ted here.

360.9   Strutt's Book]   Joseph Strutt's *The Sports and Pastimes of the People of England* (1801) was a standard antiquarian account of its subject.

367.38   The Rev. Mr. Blackstone]   William Blackstone (1595–1675), an Anglican who, having settled in the Boston area in 1623, left there in 1634 and ministered to the Indians.

376.23–25   If . . . wedding knell.]   Hawthorne is referring to his own sketch, "The Wedding-Knell," originally published in the same volume of *The Token* (1836) and also collected in the 1837 *Twice-told Tales.*

385.1   Old Ticonderoga]   In the *American Monthly Magazine* (February 1836), this sketch began with the following passage: *In returning once to New England, from a visit to Niagara, I found myself, one summer's day, before noon, at Orwell, about forty miles from the southern extremity of Lake Champlain, which has here the aspect of a river or a creek. We were on the Vermont shore, with a ferry, of less than a mile wide, between us and the town of Ti, in New-York. ¶On the bank of the lake, within ten yards of the water, stood a pretty white tavern, with a piazza along its front. A wharf and one or two stores were close at hand, and appeared to have a good run of trade, foreign as well as domestic; the latter with Vermont farmers, the former with vessels plying between Whitehall and the British dominions. Altogether, this was a pleasant and lively spot. I delighted in it, among other reasons, on account of the continual succession of travellers, who spent an idle quarter of an hour in waiting for the ferry-boat; affording me just time enough to make their acquaintance, penetrate their mysteries, and be rid of them without the risk of tediousness on either part.*

397.9   visage.]   In *The Token* for 1837, the sketch contained here this sentence: *If we chance to meet, when I am pale with midnight study, or haply flushed with a mere sip of silver-top champagne, the poor fellow is sure to exhibit an aspect of worn-out or over excited energy, graduated precisely to my own.*

397.34   counterfeit.]   The following paragraph was deleted from the collected version of the sketch (*Mosses*, 1846): *Intimate as, in some respects, we may be said to be, the reader will hardly conceive my ignorance in regard to many important points of M. du Miroir's mode of life. I never yet could discover, nor even guess, what is his business or pastime, in the long space which sometimes elapses without an interview between us. He seldom goes into society, except when introduced by me. Yet, occasionally, I have caught a dim glimpse of M. du Miroir's well-known countenance, gazing at me from the casement of some aristocratic mansion where I am not a guest; although, quite as often, I grieve to say, he has been imprudent enough to show himself within the dusty panes of the lowest pot-houses, or even more disreputable haunts. In such cases, meeting each other's eyes, we both look down abashed. It must not be concealed, however, that, while holding my course amid the week-day bustle which flows past a church, I have discerned my friend through the lofty windows, doubtless enjoying a private audience of Religion, who sits six days in her deserted fane, and sees all the world the seventh. With what sect he worships on the Sabbath, indispensable as the point is to a proper judgment of his moral character, I absolutely never knew. When the bells fling out their holy music, I generally see him, in his best black suit, of the same pattern as my own, and wearing a mild solemnity of aspect, that edifies me almost as much as the sound orthodoxy of my reverend pastor. But we meet no more, till the services are ended. Whether he goes to church with the Episcopalians, to chapel with the Methodists, or to the synagogue with the Jews—whether perverted to Roman Catholic idolatry, or to Universalist or Unitarian infidelity—is a matter which, being no controversialist, M. du Miroir keeps to himself. Of course, however exemplary in his worldly character, he cannot expect my full confidence, while there remains the slightest ambiguity on this head.*

470.1   Dr. Heidegger's Experiment]   In the periodical version of this tale (*Knickerbocker*, March 1837), it bore the title "The Fountain of Youth."

511.12–15   May . . . night!]   When Hawthorne collected this tale for the 1842 *Twice-told Tales*, he substituted this sentence for the following, which appeared in the *Democratic Review* (October 1837): *And when you shall have reached the close of that journey of life, on which you are thus brightly entering, hand grasped in hand, and heart folded to heart, may you lie down together to as sweet and happy a repose, as that queer parting smile on our good old friend's face seems to invoke for you, at the close of this day's travel, its first happy stage!*

605.18   within.]   The following lines of verse appeared in the *American Monthly Magazine* version of this tale (March 1838):

> Oh, Man can seek the downward glance,
> And each kind word—affection's spell—

Eye, voice, its value can enhance;
For eye may speak, and tongue can tell.

But Woman's love, it waits the while
To echo to another's tone,
To linger on another's smile
Ere dare to answer with its own.

679.38   pen.]   The original version of this sketch, published as a pamphlet by the *Salem Gazette* (January 1, 1839), contained here the following exchange: *'My whole history,' continued she, 'is here set down by a very able and faithful secretary of mine; and, now that I have no further use for his services, I would recommend you to employ him on the same footing!' ¶'What are his politics?' inquired the New Year, with an air of grave deliberation, and a dubious expression of countenance.—'Not Whig, I trust,' ¶'Whig—to the back bone,' answered her elder sister; 'and whatever your own opinions may be, his are not very likely to change. But, at any rate, his narratives of fact may pretty safely be depended on, and you may gain from this volume a compendious summary of my efforts and achievements, my good and evil fortune; and, in some degree, of my thoughts and feelings throughout my earthly career. Men will not look back to me as a very distinguished Year, in any part of the world.'*

734.1   The Hall of Fantasy]   Hawthorne deleted several passages from the periodical version of this sketch (*Pioneer*, 1843) when he collected it for the 1846 *Mosses*. They are listed below, keyed to the words that preceded them in the text.

736.31   them.]   *In the most vivacious of these, I recognised Holmes.*

736.39   heart.]   *Bryant had come hither from his editor's room, his face no longer wrinkled by political strife, but with such a look as if his soul were full of the Thanatopsis, or of those beautiful stanzas on the Future Life. Percival, whom to see is like catching a glimpse of some shy bird of the woods, had shrunk into the deepest shadow that he could find. Dana was also there; though, for a long time back, the public has been none the richer for his visits to the Hall of Fantasy; but, in his younger days, he descended to its gloomiest caverns, and brought thence a treasure of dark, distempered stories. Halleck, methought, had strayed into this purple atmosphere rather by way of amusement, than because the strong impulse of his nature compelled him hither; and Willis, though he had an indefeasible right of entrance, looked so much like a man of the world, that he seemed hardly to belong here. Sprague had stept across from the Globe Bank, with his pen behind his ear. Pierpont had come hither in the hope, I suppose, of allaying the angry glow of controversy; a fire unmeet for such an altar as a poet's kindly heart. ¶In the midst of these famous people, I beheld the figure of a friend, whom I fully believed to be thousands of leagues away. His glance was thrown upward to the lofty dome, as who should say,* EXCELSIOR. *¶"It is Longfellow!" I exclaimed. "When did he return from Germany?" ¶"His least essential part—that is to say, his physical man— is probably there at this moment, under a water-spout," replied my companion. "But wherever his body may be, his soul will find its way into the Hall of Fantasy.*

See; there is Washington Irving too, whom all the world supposes to be enacting the grave character of Ambassador to Spain." ¶And, indeed, there stood the renowned Geoffry Crayon, in the radiance of a window, which looked like the pictured symbol of his own delightful fancy. Mr. Cooper had chosen to show himself in a more sombre light, and was apparently meditating a speech in some libel case, rather than a scene of such tales as have made him a foremost man in this enchanted hall. But, woe is me! I tread upon slippery ground, among these poets and men of imagination, whom perhaps it is equally hazardous to notice, or to leave undistinguished in the throng. Would that I could emblazon all their names in star-dust! Let it suffice to mention indiscriminately such as my eye chanced to fall upon. There was Washington Allston, who possesses the freedom of the hall by the threefold claim of painter, novelist, and poet; and John Neal, whose rampant muse belches wild-fire, with huge volumes of smoke; and Lowell, the poet of the generation that now enters upon the stage. The young author of Dolon was here, involved in a deep mist of metaphysical fantasies. Epes Sargent and Mr. Tuckerman had come hither to engage contributors for their respective magazines. Hillard was an honorary member of the poetic band, as editor of Spenser, though he might well have preferred a claim on his own account. Mr. Poe had gained ready admittance for the sake of his imagination, but was threatened with ejectment, as belonging to the obnoxious class of critics. ¶There were a number of ladies among the tuneful and imaginative crowd. I know not whether their tickets of admission were signed with the authentic autograph of Apollo; but, at all events, they had an undoubted right of entrance by courtesy. Miss Sedgwick was an honored guest, although the atmosphere of the Hall of Fantasy is not precisely the light in which she appears to most advantage. Finally, I saw Mr. Rufus Griswold, with pencil and memorandum-book, busily noting down the names of all the poets and poetesses there, and likewise of some, whom nobody but himself had suspected of ever visiting the hall.

740.34   they.]   There was a dear friend of mine among them, who has striven with all his might to wash away the blood-stain from the statute-book; and whether he finally succeed or fail, no philanthropist need blush to stand on the same footing with O'Sullivan. ¶In the midst of these lights of the age, it gladdened me to greet my old friends of Brook Farm, with whom, though a recreant now, I had borne the heat of many a summer's day, while we labored together towards the perfect life. They seem so far advanced, however, in the realization of their idea, that their sun-burnt faces and toil-hardened frames may soon be denied admittance into the Hall of Fantasy. Mr. Emerson was likewise there, leaning against one of the pillars, and surrounded by an admiring crowd of writers and readers of the Dial, and all manner of Transcendentalists and disciples of the Newness, most of whom betrayed the power of his intellect by its modifying influence upon their own. He had come into the hall, in search, I suppose, either of a fact or a real man; both of which he was as likely to find there as elsewhere. No more earnest seeker after truth than he, and few more successful finders of it; although, sometimes, the truth assumes a mystic unreality and shadowyness in his grasp. In the same part of the hall, Jones Very stood alone, within a circle which no other of mortal race could enter, nor himself escape from. ¶Here, also was Mr. Alcott, with two or three *friends, whom his spirit had assimilated to itself and drawn to his New England home, though an ocean rolled between. There was no man in the enchanted hall, whose mere presence, the language of whose look and manner, wrought such an impression as that of this great mystic innovator. So calm and gentle was he, so holy in aspect, so quiet in the utterance of what his soul brooded upon, that one might readily conceive his Orphic Sayings to well upward from a fountain in his breast, which communicated with the infinite abyss of Thought. ¶"Here is a prophet," cried my friend, with enthusiasm—"a dreamer, a bodiless idea amid our actual existence. Another age may recognise him as a man; or perhaps his misty apparition will vanish into the sunshine. It matters little; for his influence will have impregnated the atmosphere, and be imbibed by generations that know not the original apostle of the ideas, which they shall shape into earthly business. Such a spirit cannot pass through human life, yet leave mankind entirely as he found them!" ¶"At all events, he may count you as a disciple," said I, smiling; "and doubtless there is the spirit of a system in him, but not the body of it. I love to contrast him with that acute and powerful Intellect, who stands not far off." ¶"Ah, you mean Mr. Brownson!" replied my companion. "Pray Heaven he do not stamp his foot or raise his voice; for if he should, the whole fabric of the Hall of Fantasy will dissolve like a smoke-wreath! I wonder how he came here?"*

746.12   Father Miller's interpretation]   William Miller (1782–1849), founder of the sect of Second Adventists, or Millerites, prophesied a second coming of Christ and consequent day of judgment between March 1843 and March 1844. "The New Adam and Eve" was originally published in the *Democratic Review* for February 1843.

765.39   the Eve of Powers]   The allusion is to a then renowned statue of Eve by Hiram Powers (1805–1873).

774.12–13   friar who created the prophetic Brazen Head]   Roger Bacon (1214?–1294?), the philosopher and scientist who was said to have constructed a head which would speak to him in response to questions about the progress of his projects. See also 922.19.

975.3–976.24   We do not . . . worthy of all praise.]   Hawthorne deleted these paragraphs, which refer to the *United States Magazine and Democratic Review* (as *La Revue Anti-Aristocratique*) and to its editor John L. O'Sullivan (as the Comte de Bearhaven), when it was collected in the 1846 edition of *Mosses*. The tale had first appeared in O'Sullivan's journal in 1844, but in 1846 Hawthorne was looking for a political appointment and may have judged it best to appear apolitical. He secured his custom house appointment, only to be dismissed from it in 1849 for his supposedly political activities. In 1854, with his friend Pierce in the presidency and with his Liverpool consular appointment, he reinserted these paragraphs in the edition of *Mosses* issued that year. *Aubépine* is French for "hawthorn," and the publications of Aubépine listed are French renderings of the titles of some of Hawthorne's writings.

1013.12   to the past?]   Hawthorne deleted the following passage from the *Democratic Review* (April 1845) version of the sketch: *Bulwer nauseates me; he is the very pimple of the age's humbug. There is no hope of the public, so long as he retains an admirer, a reader, or a publisher.*

1051.1   Ethan Brand]   Originally published in the *Boston Weekly Museum* (January 5, 1850) as "The Unpardonable Sin, From an Unpublished Work."

1168.32   Professor Anthon]   Charles Anthon (1797–1867), Jay Professor of Greek Language and Literature at Columbia College, was the author of *A Classical Dictionary: Containing an Account of the Principal Proper Names Mentioned in Ancient Authors* (1842)—Hawthorne's principal source for *A Wonder-Book* and *Tanglewood Tales*.

Library of Congress Cataloging in Publication Data

Hawthorne, Nathaniel, 1804–1864.
  Tales and sketches.

  (The Library of America)
  Contents: Twice-told tales—Mosses from an old manse—
The snow-image—A wonder book for girls and boys—Tanglewood
tales
  I. Pearce, Roy Harvey.   II. Title.   III. Series: Library of
America.
PS1853   1982   813'.3   81-20760
ISBN 0–940450–03–8   AACR2

This book is set in 10 point Linotron Galliard,
a face designed for photocomposition by Matthew Carter
and based on the sixteenth-century face Granjon. The paper
is acid-free Ecusta Nyalite and meets the requirements for perma-
nence of the American National Standards Institute. The binding
material is Brillianta, a 100% woven rayon cloth made by
Van Heek-Scholco Textielfabrieken, Holland. The com-
position is by Haddon Craftsmen, Inc., and The
Clarinda Company. Printing and binding
by R. R. Donnelley & Sons Company.
Designed by Bruce Campbell.